Discovering Computers 2008
Brief

Discovering Computers 2008

Brief

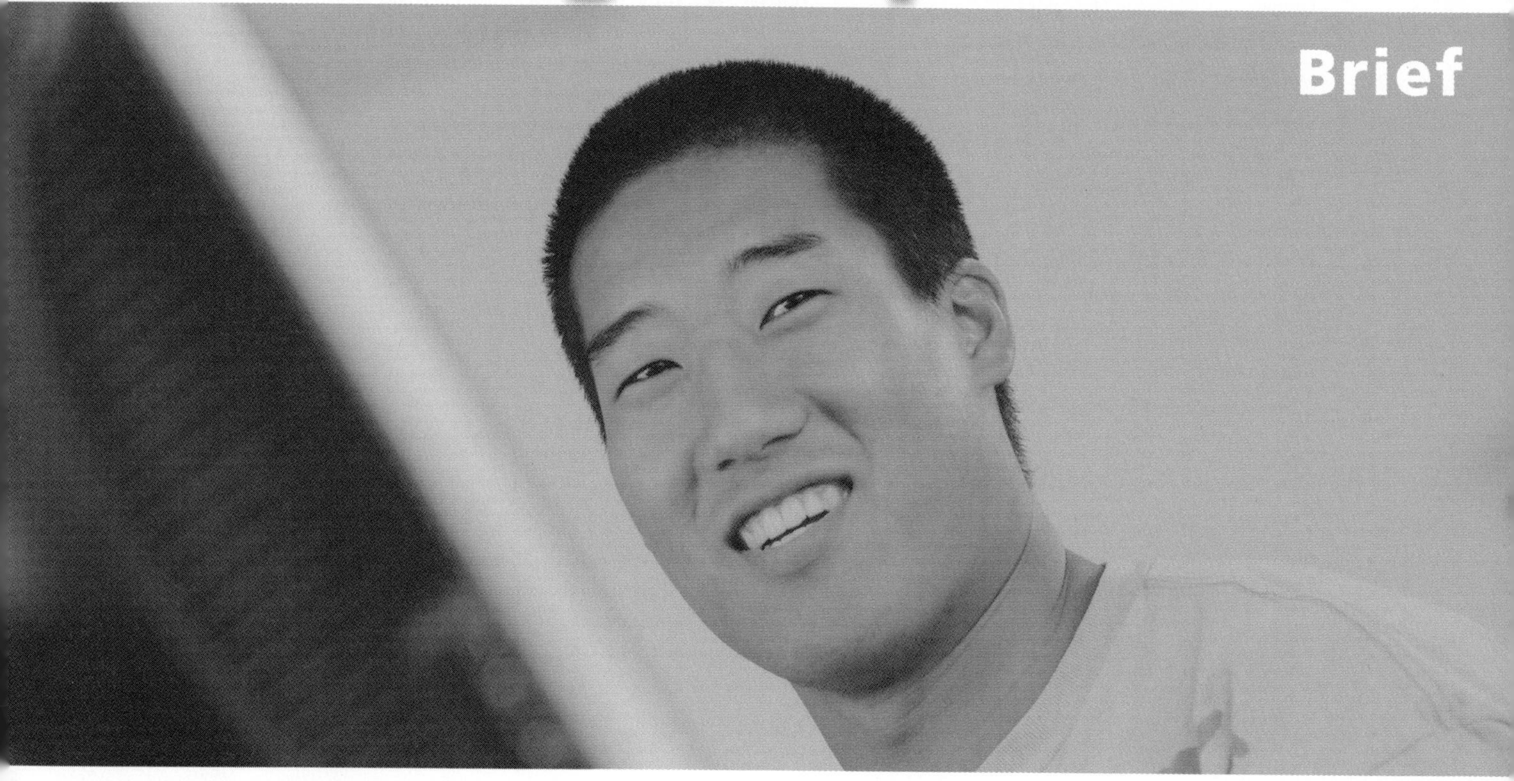

Gary B. Shelly
Thomas J. Cashman
Misty E. Vermaat

Contributing Authors
Steven M. Freund
Jeffrey J. Quasney
Susan L. Sebok
Jeffrey J. Webb

Australia • Brazil • Japan • Korea • Mexico • Singapore • Spain • United Kingdom • United States

Discovering Computers 2008: Brief
Gary B. Shelly, Thomas J. Cashman, Misty E. Vermaat

Executive Editor: Alexandra Arnold
Senior Product Manager: Reed Curry
Associate Product Manager: Klenda Martinez
Editorial Assistant: Jon Farnham
Senior Marketing Manager: Joy Stark-Vancs
Marketing Coordinator: Julie Schuster
Print Buyer: Julio Esperas
Course Technology Production Contact: Marissa Falco
Researcher: F. William Vermaat
Development Editor: Lyn Markowicz
Proofreader: Nancy Lamm
Final Reader: Kim Kosmatka
Management Services: Pre-Press Company, Inc.
Interior Designer: Pre-Press Company, Inc.
Art Director: Bruce Bond
Cover and text design: Joel Sadagursky
Cover photos: Jon Chomitz
Illustrator: Pre-Press Company, Inc.
Compositor: Pre-Press Company, Inc.

For product information and technology assistance, contact us at
Cengage Learning Customer & Sales Support, 1-800-354-9706
For permission to use material from this text or product,
submit all requests online at **cengage.com/permissions**
Further permissions questions can be emailed to
permissionrequest@cengage.com

ISBN-13: 978-1-4239-1203-3

ISBN-10: 1-4239-1203-9

Course Technology
25 Thomson Place
Boston, Massachusetts 02210
USA

Cengage Learning is a leading provider of customized learning solutions with office locations around the globe, including Singapore, the United Kingdom, Australia, Mexico, Brazil, and Japan. Locate your local office at: **international.cengage.com/region**

Cengage Learning products are represented in Canada by Nelson-Education, Ltd.

For your lifelong learning solutions, visit **course.cengage.com**

Visit our corporate website at **cengage.com**

Printed in the United States of America
3 4 5 6 7 11 10 09 08

Discovering Computers 2008
Brief

Contents

Discover Computers
and make concepts real with . . .

Online Companion

Use the Online Companion at scsite.com/dc2008 to bring unparalleled currency to the learning experience. Access additional information about important topics and make use of online learning games, practice tests, and additional reinforcement. Gain access to this dynamic site through CoursePort, Course Technology's login page.

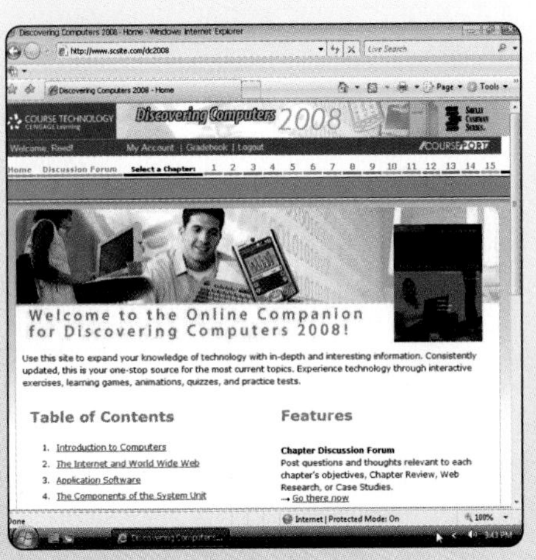

Learn How To

Apply the concepts presented in the chapter to everyday life with these hands-on activities. See the Learn How To activities in action with videos on the Online Companion.

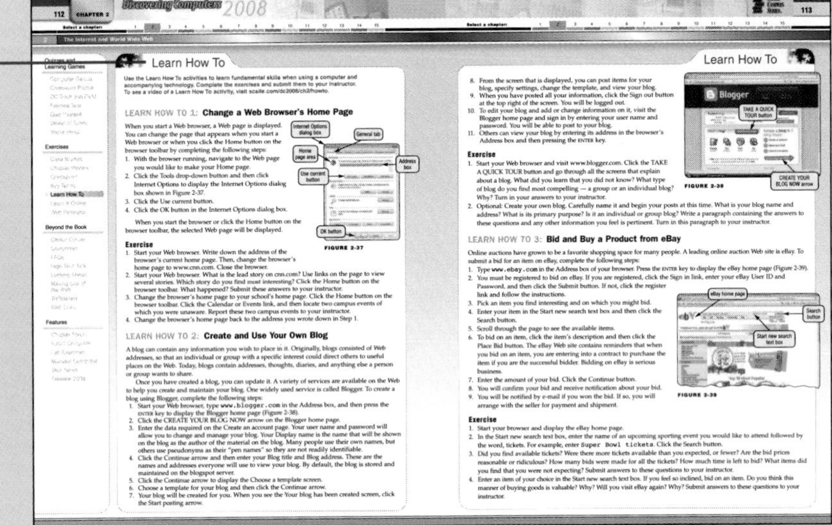

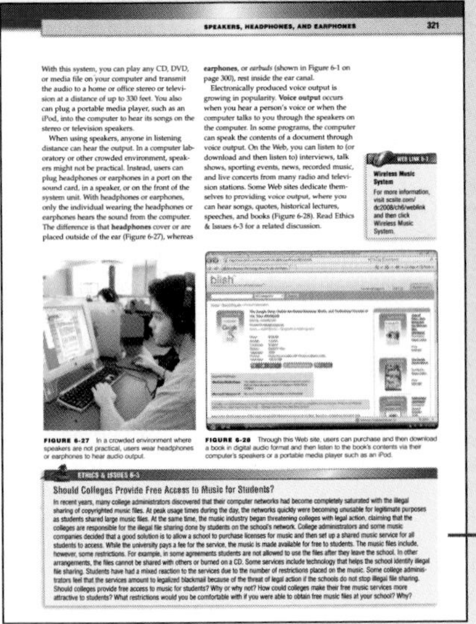

Ethics and Issues

Ethics and Issues boxes raise controversial, computer-related topics of the day, challenging readers to consider closely general concerns of computers in society.

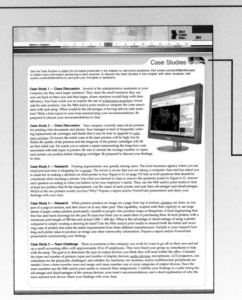

Case Studies

Exercise your mind and construct creative solutions to the thought-provoking case studies presented in each chapter. The Case Study exercises are constructed for class discussion, independent research, or examination in a team environment.

practical, hands-on elements.

High-Tech Talk

The High-Tech Talk article at the end of each chapter expands on a topic covered in the chapter and presents a more technical discussion.

430 CHAPTER 8 OPERATING SYSTEMS AND UTILITY PROGRAMS

High-Tech Talk

LOSSY VS. LOSSLESS DATA COMPRESSION: USING COMPRESSION ALGORITHMS TO REDUCE FILE SIZE

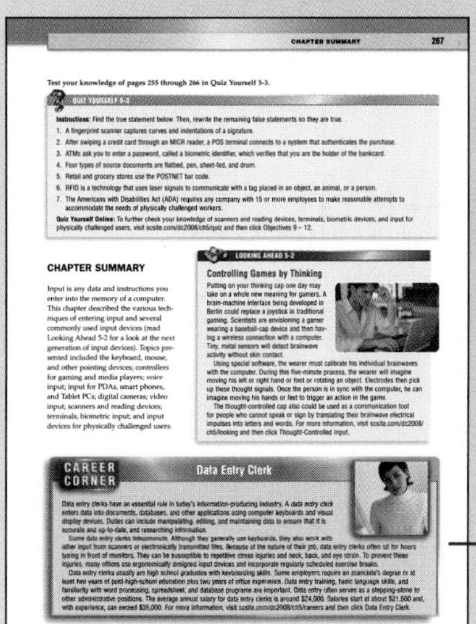
CHAPTER SUMMARY 267

Test your knowledge of pages 255 through 266 in Quiz Yourself 5-3.

CHAPTER SUMMARY

LOOKING AHEAD 5-2

Controlling Games by Thinking

CAREER CORNER

Data Entry Clerk

Career Corner

Each chapter ends with a Career Corner feature that introduces a computer career opportunity relating to a topic covered in the chapter.

Companies on the Cutting Edge

Everyone who interacts with computers should be aware of the key computer-related companies. Each chapter profiles two of these key companies.

Technology Trailblazers

The Technology Trailblazers section in each chapter offers a glimpse into the life and times of the more famous leaders of the computer industry.

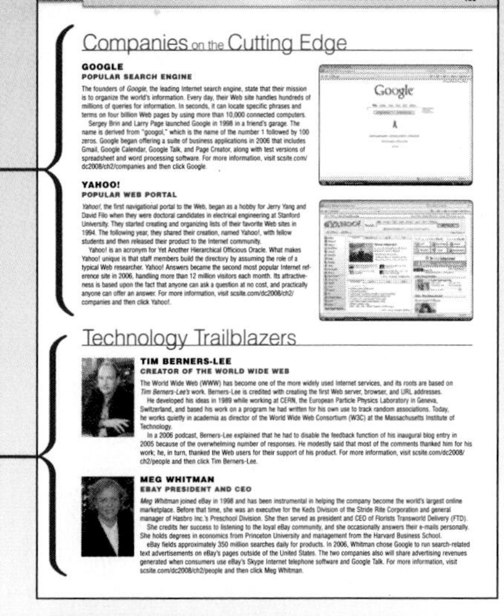
TECHNOLOGY TRAILBLAZERS 103

Companies on the Cutting Edge

GOOGLE

POPULAR SEARCH ENGINE

YAHOO!

POPULAR WEB PORTAL

Technology Trailblazers

TIM BERNERS-LEE

CREATOR OF THE WORLD WIDE WEB

MEG WHITMAN

EBAY PRESIDENT AND CEO

Discover Computers and make concepts real with . . .

Web Link

Obtain current information and a different perspective about key terms and concepts by visiting the Web addresses in the Web Links found in the margins throughout the book.

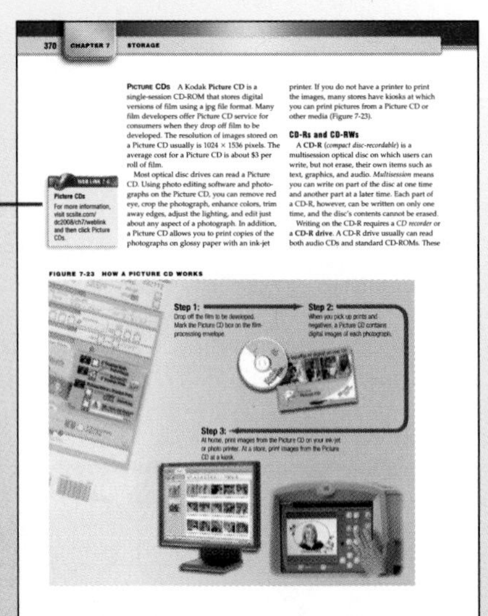

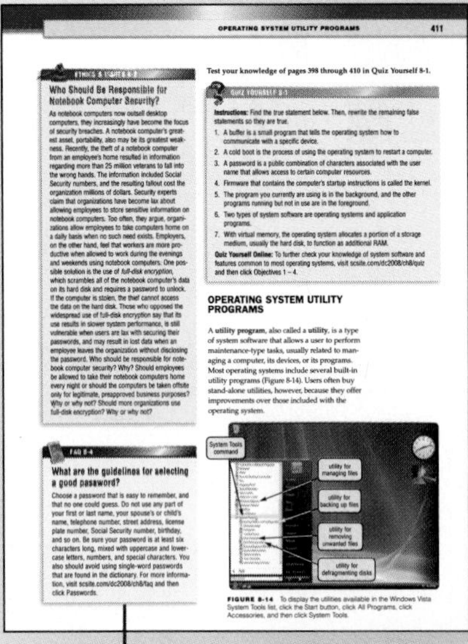

Looking Ahead

The Looking Ahead boxes offer a glimpse at the latest advances in computer technology that will be available, usually within five years.

FAQ

FAQ (frequently asked questions) boxes offer common questions and answers about subjects related to the topic at hand.

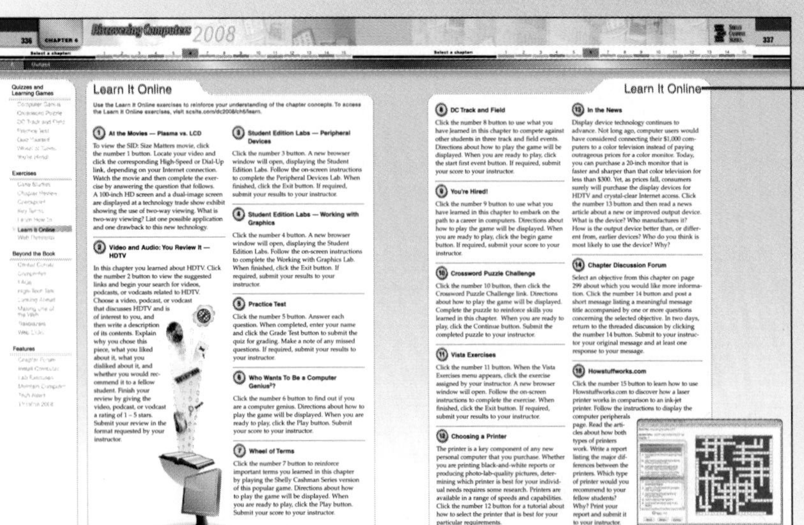

Learn It Online

The Learn It Online exercises, which include brand-new At the Movies online videos, practice tests, interactive labs, learning games, and Web-based activities offer a wealth of online reinforcement.

interactive Web elements.

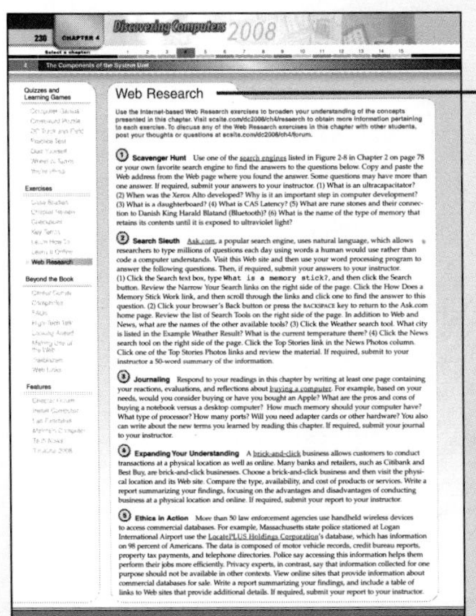

Web Research

Each Web Research exercise references an element in the book, requires follow-up research on the Web, and suggests writing a short article or presenting the findings of the research to the class.

Quiz Yourself

Three Quiz Yourself boxes per chapter help ensure retention by reinforcing sections of the chapter material, rather than waiting for the end of the chapter to test. Use Appendix B for a quick check of the answers, and access additional Quiz Yourself quizzes on the Online Companion for interactivity and easy use.

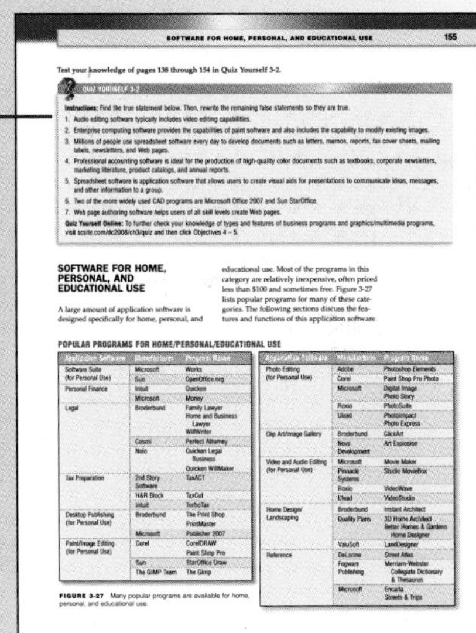

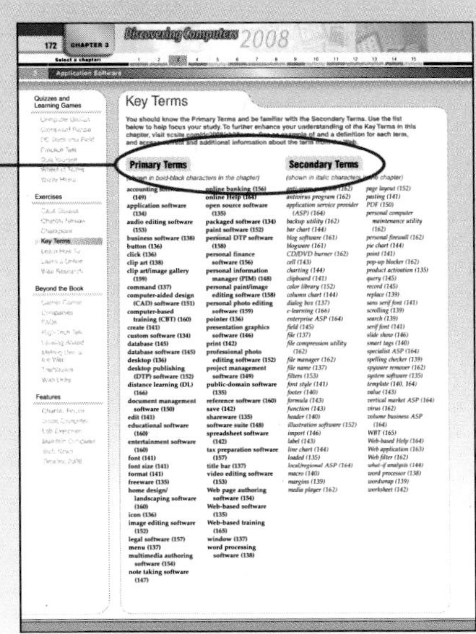

Primary and Secondary Key Terms

Before taking a test, use the Key Terms page as a checklist of terms to know. In the text, primary key terms appear in bold font and secondary key terms appear in italic font. Visit a Key Terms page on the Online Companion and click any term for additional information.

Discover Computers
and make concepts real with . . .

Picture Yourself
Picture yourself using the concepts presented in each chapter. This section at the beginning of each chapter bridges the gap between the chapter-specific material and everyday life using computers.

Chapter Objectives and Table of Contents
Before reading the chapter, carefully read through the Objectives and Contents to discover knowledge that will be gleaned from the chapter.

Step Figures
Each chapter includes numerous step figures that present the more complex computer concepts using a step-by-step pedagogy.

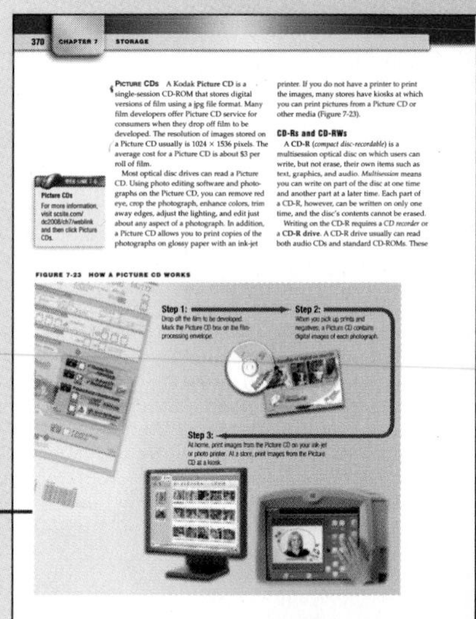

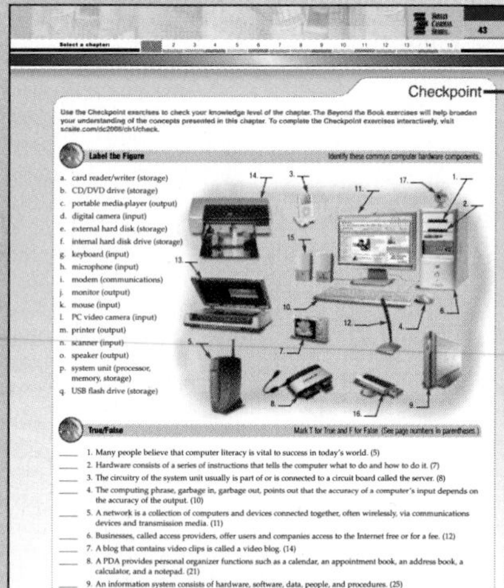

Checkpoint
Use these three pages of label-the-figure, multiple choice, true/false, matching, and short answer exercises to reinforce understanding of the topics presented in the chapter. Visit the Online Companion to complete an interactive version of the Checkpoint exercises.

Initial Chapter Figure
Carefully study the first figure in each chapter because it provides an easy-to-follow overview of the major purpose of the chapter.

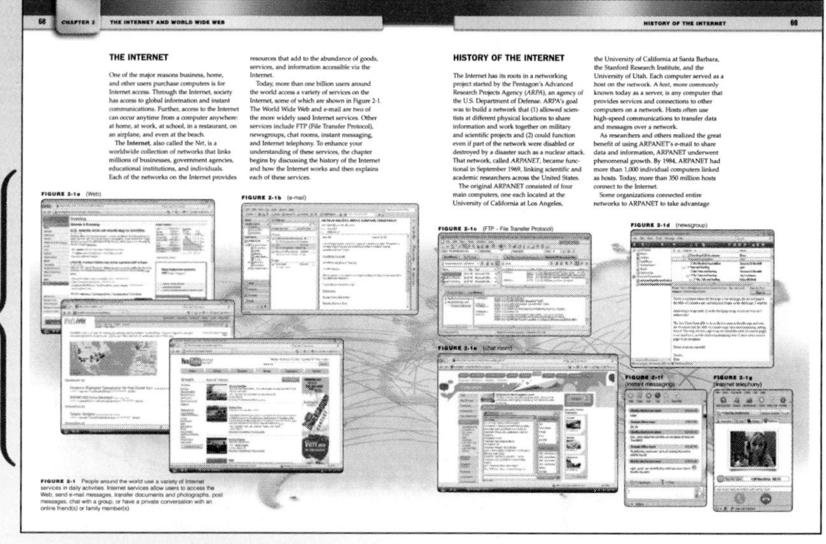

pedagogical elements.

Chapter Review

Use the two-page Chapter Review before taking an examination to ensure familiarity with the computer concepts presented. This section includes each objective, followed by a one- or two-paragraph summary. Visit a Chapter Review page on the Online Companion, and click the Audio button to listen to the Chapter Review.

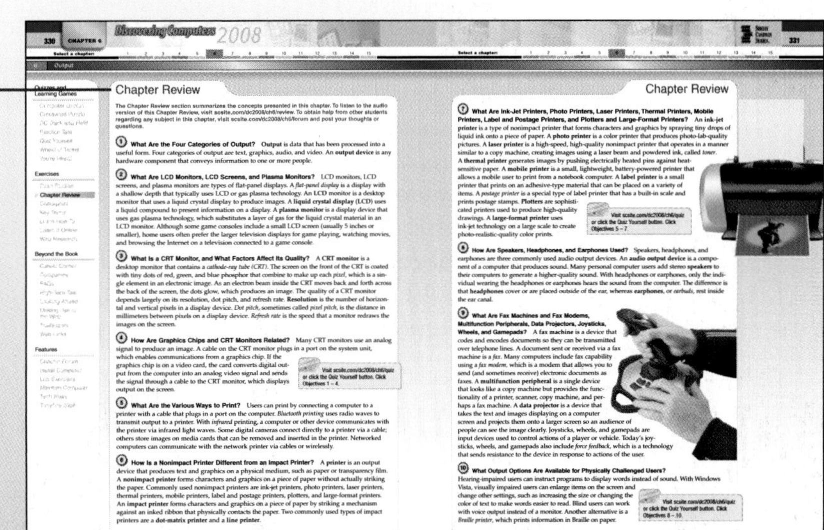

Special Features

Five special features following Chapters 1, 2, 5, 6, and 8 encompass topics from the history of computers, to what's hot on the Web, to a buyer's guide, to the latest in new technology.

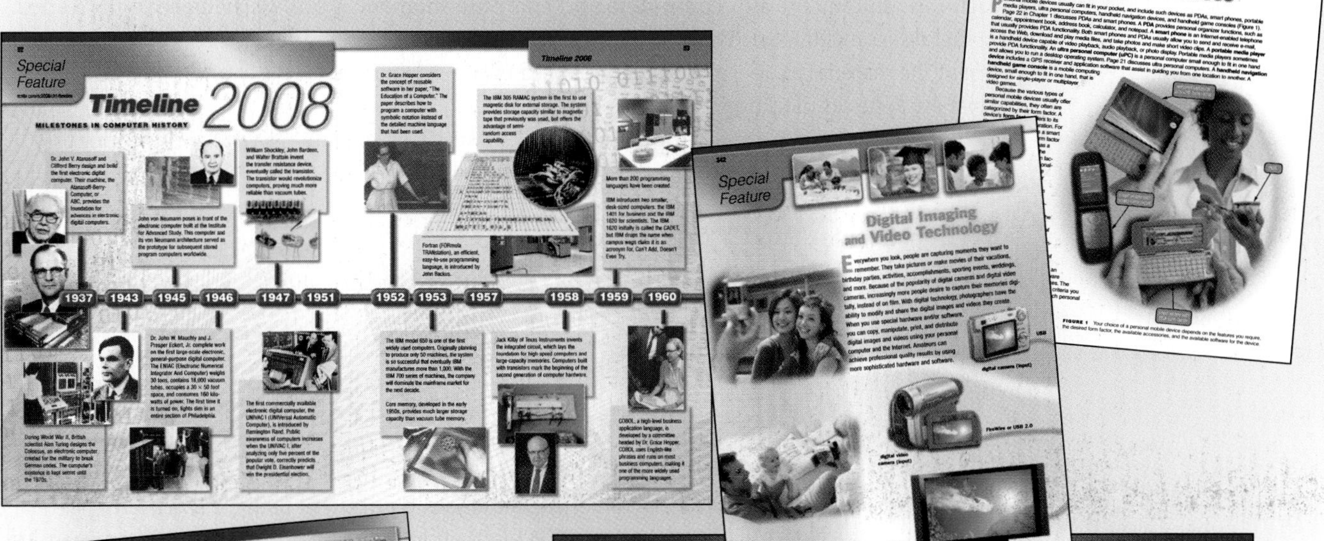

Preface

The Shelly Cashman Series® offers the finest textbooks in computer education. We are proud of the fact that the previous twelve editions of this textbook have been the most widely used in computer education. With each new edition of the book, we have implemented significant improvements based on current computer trends and comments made by instructors and students. *Discovering Computers 2008* continues with the innovation, quality, and reliability you have come to expect from the Shelly Cashman Series.

In *Discovering Computers 2008*, you will find an educationally sound, highly visual, and easy-to-follow pedagogy that presents an in-depth treatment of introductory computer subjects. Students will finish the course with a solid understanding of computers, how to use computers, and how to access information on the World Wide Web.

OBJECTIVES OF THIS TEXTBOOK

Discovering Computers 2008, Brief is intended for use as a stand-alone textbook or in combination with an applications, Internet, or programming textbook in a one-quarter or one-semester introductory computer course. No experience with computers is assumed. The objectives of this book are to:

- Present the most-up-to-date technology in an ever-changing discipline
- Give students an in-depth understanding of why computers are essential components in business and society
- Teach the fundamentals of computers and computer nomenclature, particularly with respect to personal computer hardware and software, and the World Wide Web
- Present the material in a visually appealing and exciting manner that motivates students to learn
- Assist students in planning a career
- Provide exercises and lab assignments that allow students to interact with a computer and learn by actually using the computer and the World Wide Web
- Present strategies for purchasing a desktop computer, a notebook computer, a Tablet PC, and a personal mobile device
- Provide alternative learning techniques and reinforcement via the Web
- Offer distance-education providers a textbook with a meaningful and exercise-rich Online Companion

DISTINGUISHING FEATURES

To date, more than six million students have learned about computers using a *Discovering Computers* textbook. With the additional World Wide Web integration and interactivity, streaming up-to-date audio and video, extraordinary step-by-step visual drawings and photographs, unparalleled currency, and the Shelly and Cashman touch, this book will make your computer concepts course exciting and dynamic. Distinguishing features of the Shelly Cashman Series *Discovering Computers* books include:

A Proven Pedagogy

Careful explanations of complex concepts, educationally-sound elements, and reinforcement highlight this proven method of presentation.

A Visually Appealing Book that Maintains Student Interest

The latest technology, pictures, drawings, and text are combined artfully to produce a visually appealing and easy-to-understand book. Many of the figures include a step-by-step presentation (see page 196), which simplifies the more complex computer concepts. Pictures and drawings reflect the latest trends in computer technology. This combination of pictures, step-by-step drawings, and easy-to-read text layout sets the standard for computer textbook design.

Latest Technologies and Terms

The technologies and terms your students see in this book are those they will encounter when they start using computers. Only the latest application software is shown throughout the book. New topics and terms include social networking Web site, video blog, vodcast, blogosphere, ccTLD, digital rights management (DRM), gTLD, hypermedia, hypertext, media sharing Web site, UMPC, online community, online social network, participatory Web, tabbed browsing, vlog, vlogger, vlogosphere, VoIP, Web 2.0, Wi-Fi, e-learning, media player, Web application, Web-based software, Centrino Duo, Core, eSATA port, ExpressCard, ExpressCard slot, external SATA, FireWire 800, form factor, front side bus (FSB), massively parallel processing, PCI Express bus, SETI@home, U3 smart drive, vPro technology, air mouse, dance pad, game controller, laser mouse, light gun, motion-sensing game controllers, Wii Remote, aspect ratio, PictBridge, UXGA, WQXGA, WSXGA, WUXGA, WXGA, BD-R, BD-RE, Blu-ray Disc-ROM (BD-ROM), HD DVD-R, HD DVD-ROM disc, HD DVD-RW, LightScribe technology, pocket hard drive, RAID, thumb drive, U3 smart drive, video CD (VCD), BlackBerry, Disk Cleanup, Explorers, Flip 3D, folder, index, Live CD, Live USB, media player, Music Explorer, Picture Explorer, Problem Reports and Solutions, search utility, Windows Aero, Windows Defender, Windows Photo Gallery, Windows Sidebar, Windows SideShow, Windows Vista Basic, Windows Vista Business, Windows Vista Enterprise, Windows Vista Home Basic, Windows Vista Home Premium, Windows Vista Ultimate.

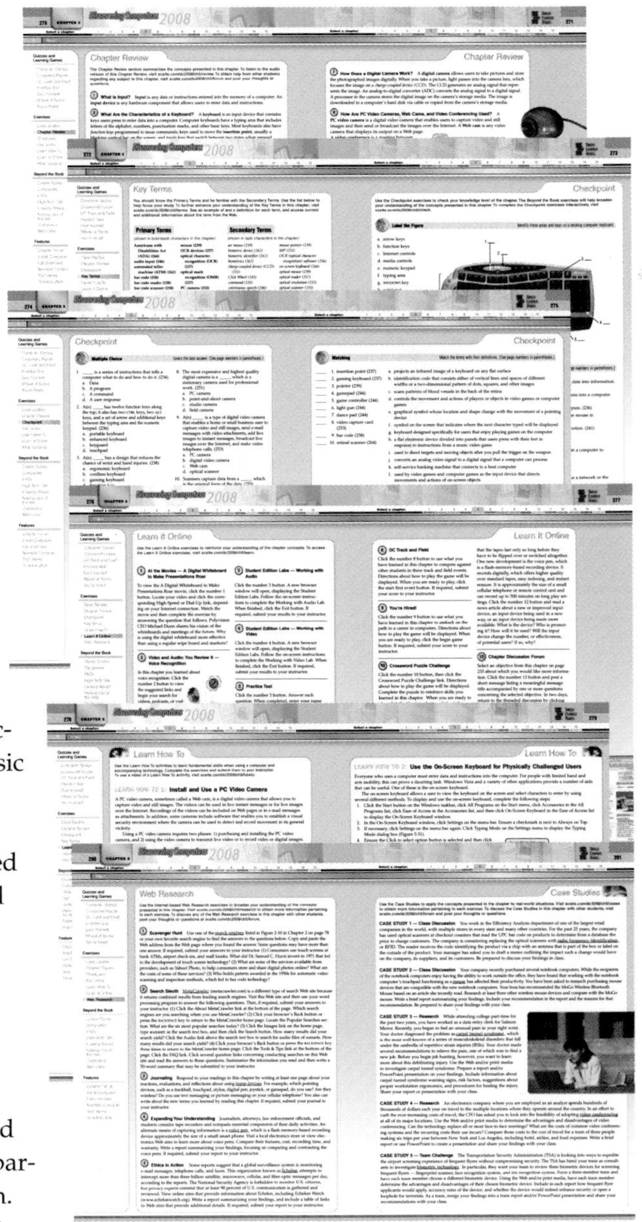

World Wide Web Enhanced

This book uses the World Wide Web as a major supplement. The purpose of integrating the World Wide Web into the book is to (1) offer students additional information and currency on important topics; (2) use its interactive capabilities to offer creative reinforcement and online quizzes; (3) make available alternative learning techniques with Web-based learning games, practice tests, and interactive labs; (4) underscore the relevance of the World Wide Web as a basic information tool that can be used in all facets of society; (5) introduce students to doing research on the Web; and (6) offer instructors the opportunity to organize and administer their traditional campus-based or distance-education-based courses on the Web using the Blackboard platform. This textbook, however, does not depend on Web access to be used successfully. The Web access adds to the already complete treatment of topics within the book.

Extensive End-of-Chapter Materials

A notable strength of the *Discovering Computers* textbooks is the extensive student activities at the end of each chapter. Well-structured student activities can make the difference between students merely participating in a class and students retaining the information they learn. The activities in the *Discovering Computers 2008* books include: Chapter Review, Key Terms, Checkpoint, Learn It Online, Learn How To, Web Research, and Case Studies.

ORGANIZATION OF THIS TEXTBOOK

Discovering Computers 2008, Brief provides a thorough introduction to computers. The material is divided into eight chapters, five special features, three appendices, and a glossary/index.

Chapter 1 – Introduction to Computers In Chapter 1, students are introduced to basic computer concepts, such as what a computer is, how it works, and what makes it a powerful tool.

Special Feature – Timeline 2008 Milestones in Computer History In this special feature, students learn about the major computer technology developments during the past 71 years.

Chapter 2 – The Internet and World Wide Web In Chapter 2, students learn about the Internet, World Wide Web, browsers, e-mail, FTP, and instant messaging.

Special Feature – Making Use of the Web In this special feature, more than 150 popular up-to-date Web sites are listed and described. Now includes a section on Online Social Networks and Media Sharing. Basic searching techniques also are introduced.

Chapter 3 – Application Software In Chapter 3, students are introduced to a variety of business software, graphics and multimedia software, home/personal/educational software, and communications software.

Chapter 4 – The Components of the System Unit In Chapter 4, students are introduced to the components of the system unit; how memory stores data, instructions, and information; and how the system unit executes an instruction.

Chapter 5 – Input Chapter 5 describes the various techniques of input and commonly used input devices.

Special Feature – Personal Mobile Devices In this special feature, students receive a detailed presentation of personal mobile device operating systems, built-in personal mobile device software, personal mobile device application software and services, and how to obtain and install personal mobile device software. Also included is a personal mobile device buyer's guide.

Chapter 6 – Output Chapter 6 describes the various methods of output and commonly used output devices.

Special Feature – Digital Imaging and Video Technology In this special feature, students are introduced to using a personal computer, digital camera, and digital video camera to manipulate and distribute photographs and video.

Chapter 7 – Storage In Chapter 7, students learn about various storage media and storage devices.

Chapter 8 – Operating Systems and Utility Programs In Chapter 8, students learn about a variety of stand-alone operating systems, network operating systems, and embedded operating systems.

Special Feature – Buyer's Guide 2008: How to Purchase a Personal Computer In this special feature, students are introduced to purchasing a desktop computer, notebook computer, and Tablet PC.

Appendix A – Coding Schemes and Number Systems Appendix A presents the ASCII, EBCDIC, and Unicode coding schemes.

Appendix B – Quiz Yourself Answers Appendix B provides the answers for the Quiz Yourself questions in the text.

Appendix C – Computer Acronyms Appendix C summarizes the computer acronyms discussed in the book.

Glossary/Index The Glossary/Index includes a definition and page references for every key term presented in the book.

SHELLY CASHMAN SERIES INSTRUCTOR RESOURCES

The Shelly Cashman Series is dedicated to providing you with all of the tools you need to make your class a success. The contents of the Instructor Resources and Course Presenter CD-ROMs (1-4239-1212-8) are described below. Information on all supplementary materials is available through your Course Technology representative or by calling one of the following telephone numbers: Colleges and Universities, 1-800-648-7450; High Schools, 1-800-824-5179; Private Career Colleges, 1-800-477-3692 ; Canada, 1-800-268-2222; Corporations with IT Training Centers, 1-800-477-3692; and Government Agencies, Health-Care Organizations, and Correctional Facilities, 1-800-477-3692.

Instructor Resources CD-ROM

The Instructor Resources CD-ROM includes both teaching and testing aids.

Instructor's Manual The Instructor's Manual is made up of Microsoft Word files, which include lecture notes that summarize the sections of the chapters, figures and boxed elements found in every chapter, teacher tips, classroom activities, lab activities, and quick quizzes.

Syllabus Sample syllabi, which can be customized easily to a course, are included. The syllabi cover policies, assignments, exams, and other course information.

Figure Files Illustrations for every figure in the textbook are available in electronic form. Use this ancillary to present a slide show in lecture or to print transparencies for use in lecture with an overhead projector. If you have a personal computer and LCD device, this ancillary can be an effective tool for presenting lectures.

Solutions to Exercises Solutions are included for end-of-chapter exercises.

Test Bank & Test Engine The ExamView test bank includes 220 questions for every chapter (80 multiple-choice, 50 true/false, and 40 completion) and features new objective-based question types (10 modified multiple-choice, 10 modified true/false, and 20 matching) and Critical Thinking questions (6 essays and 2 cases with 2 questions each). The test bank also includes page number references, and when appropriate, figure references. Each question also is identified by objective and type of term (primary or secondary). The test bank comes with a copy of the test engine, ExamView, the ultimate tool for your objective-based testing needs.

Printed Test Bank A Rich Text Format (.rtf) version of the test bank you can print also is included.

Test Out/Final Exam Use this objective-based exam to test students out of your course, or use it as a final examination. A master answer sheet is included.

Pretest/Posttest Use these carefully prepared tests at the beginning and the end of the semester to measure student progress. A master answer sheet is included.

Data Files for Students All the files that are required by students to complete the exercises are included. You can distribute the files on the Instructor Resources CD-ROM to your students over a network, or you can have them follow the instructions on the inside back cover of this book to obtain a copy of the files.

Course Presenter

Course Presenter is a one-click-per-slide presentation system on CD-ROM that provides PowerPoint slides for every subject in each chapter. Use this presentation system to give interesting, well-organized, and knowledge-based lectures. Several brand new computer-related video clips are available for optional presentation. Course Presenter provides consistent coverage for multiple lecturers.

Student Edition Labs

Our Web-based interactive labs will help your students master hundreds of computer concepts including input and output devices, file management and desktop applications, computer privacy, virus protection, and much more. Featuring up-to-the-minute content, eye-popping graphics, and rich animation, the highly interactive Student Edition Labs offer students an alternative way to learn through dynamic observation, step-by-step practice, and challenging review questions. Access the free Student Edition Labs from the *Discovering Computers 2008* Online Companion at scsite.com/dc2008 or see the Student Edition Lab exercises on the Learn It Online pages at the end of each chapter.

Online Content

Blackboard is the leading distance learning solution provider and class-management platform today. Course Technology has partnered with Blackboard to bring you premium online content. Content for use with *Discovering Computers 2008* is available in Blackboard Course Cartridge and includes topic reviews, case projects, review questions, test banks, practice tests, custom syllabus, and more.

SUPPLEMENTS

The following supplements can be used in combination with this textbook.

SAM Computer Concepts

Add more muscle and flexibility to your course with SAM Computer Concepts. SAM (Skills Assessment Manager) Computer Concepts helps you energize your training assignments by allowing students to learn and quiz on important computer skills in an active, hands-on environment. By adding SAM Computer Concepts to your curriculum, you can:

- Reinforce your students' knowledge of key computer concepts with hands-on application exercises.
- Allow your students to "learn by listening," with rich audio in their computer concepts labs.
- Build computer concepts exams from a test bank of more than 50,000 objective-based questions or even create your own custom questions.
- Schedule your students' computer concepts training and testing assignments with powerful administrative tools.
- Track student exam grades and training progress using more than one dozen student and classroom reports.

Study Guide

This highly popular *Study Guide* (ISBN 1-4239-1208-X) includes a variety of activities that help students recall, review, and master introductory computer concepts. The *Study Guide* complements the end-of-chapter material with a guided chapter outline; a self-test consisting of true/false, multiple-choice, short answer, fill-in, and matching questions; an entertaining puzzle; and other challenging exercises.

CourseCasts — Learning on the Go. Always available . . . always relevant.

Want to keep up with the latest technology trends relevant to you? Visit our site to find a library of podcasts, CourseCasts, featuring a "CourseCast of the Week", and download them to your mp3 player at http://coursecasts.course.com

Our fast-paced world is driven by technology. You know because you're an active participant — always on the go, always keeping up with technological trends, and always learning new ways to embrace technology to power your life.

Ken Baldauf, a faculty member of the Florida State University Computer Science Department, is responsible for teaching technology classes to thousands of FSU students each year. He knows what you know; he knows what you want to learn. He's also an expert in the latest technology and will sort through and aggregate the most pertinent news and information so you can spend your time enjoying technology, rather than trying to figure it out.

Visit us at http://coursecasts.course.com to learn on the go!

Learning styles of students have changed, but the Shelly Cashman Series' dedication to their success has remained steadfast for over 30 years. We are committed to continually updating our approach and content to reflect the way today's students learn and experience new technology. This focus on the user is reflected in our bold new cover design, which features photographs of real students using the Shelly Cashman Series in their courses. Each book features a different user, reflecting the many ages, experiences, and backgrounds of all of the students learning

Discovering Computers 2008

CHAPTER ONE

Introduction to Computers

Picture Yourself Taking a Computer Course

Before the lecture begins on the first day of your Introduction to Computers class, you hear several classmates announce they will be gathering in the student lounge after class to talk about homework and form study groups. A few of them confess they know little about computers and are looking forward to learning more. As they talk, you think about your experiences with computers. You had a beginning programming class in high school. You use the Internet and instant messaging regularly to communicate with friends. With your digital camera, you take pictures and e-mail them to family members. Most of your friends and family consider you to be rather computer savvy, so you are confident you will not need a study group.

During the lecture, the instructor reads several computer advertisements to the class. The ads use computer terms and acronyms you have never heard, like eSATA, Blu-ray, Vista, Core 2 Duo, VoIP, Web 2.0, router, Office 2007, U3, and earbud. As he reads, you quickly realize you know less than you thought. When he finishes reading, the instructor tells the class not to worry if some or most of the words in the ads are unfamiliar. "By the time this course is over," he says, "you will learn everything you need to know to buy a computer and will understand how computers are used in society." Excited by the prospect of gaining new knowledge, you decide to join the study group after all.

Read Chapter 1 to become familiar with some of the terms mentioned in the advertisement, discover practical uses of computers, and set a foundation for your further learning throughout this book.

OBJECTIVES

After completing this chapter, you will be able to:

1. Recognize the importance of computer literacy
2. Define the term, computer
3. Identify the components of a computer
4. Discuss the advantages and disadvantages of using computers
5. Recognize the purpose of a network
6. Discuss the uses of the Internet and World Wide Web
7. Distinguish between system software and application software
8. Describe the categories of computers
9. Identify the elements of an information system
10. Describe the various types of computer users
11. Discuss various computer applications in society

CONTENTS

A WORLD OF COMPUTERS

Computers are everywhere: at work, at school, and at home. Many daily activities either involve the use of or depend on information from a computer. As shown in Figure 1-1, people use all types and sizes of computers for a variety of reasons and in a range of places. Some computers sit on top of a desk or on the floor; others are small enough to carry.

Computers are a primary means of local and global communication for billions of people. Consumers use computers to correspond with businesses, employees with other employees and customers, students with classmates and teachers, and family members and military personnel with friends and other family members. In addition to sending text-based messages, people use computers to share pictures, drawings, journals, music, and videos.

Through computers, society has instant access to information from around the globe. Local and national news, weather reports, sports scores, airline schedules, telephone directories, maps and directions, job listings, credit reports, and countless forms of educational material always are accessible. From the computer, you can make a telephone call, meet new friends, share opinions or life stories, book flights, shop, fill prescriptions, file taxes, or take a course.

At home or while on the road, people use computers to manage schedules, balance checkbooks, pay bills, transfer funds, and buy or sell stocks. Banks place automated teller machines (ATMs) all over the world, making it easy for customers to deposit or withdraw funds at anytime. At the grocery store, a computer tracks

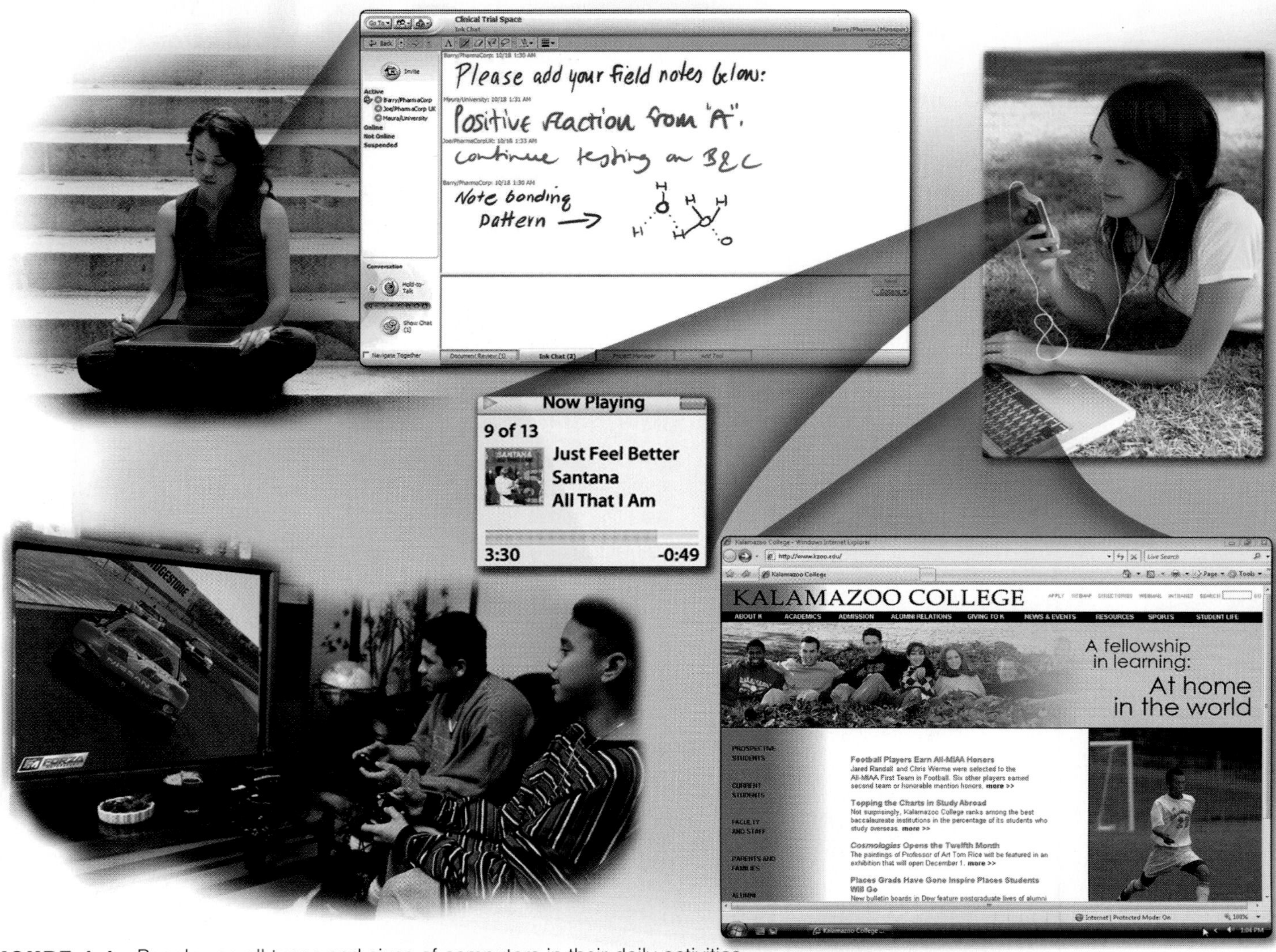

FIGURE 1-1 People use all types and sizes of computers in their daily activities.

purchases, calculates the amount of money due, and often generates coupons customized to buying patterns. Vehicles include onboard navigation systems that provide directions, call for emergency services, and track the vehicle if it is stolen.

In the workplace, employees use computers to create correspondence such as e-mail messages, memos, and letters; calculate payroll; track inventory; and generate invoices. Some applications such as automotive design and weather forecasting use computers to perform complex mathematical calculations. At school, teachers use computers to assist with classroom instruction. Students complete assignments and do research on computers in lab rooms, at home, or elsewhere.

People also spend hours of leisure time using a computer. They play games, listen to music or radio broadcasts, watch or compose videos and movies, read books and magazines, share stories, research genealogy, retouch photographs, and plan vacations.

As technology continues to advance, computers are becoming more a part of everyday life. Thus, many people believe that computer literacy is vital to success in today's world. **Computer literacy** involves having a knowledge and understanding of computers and their uses.

This book presents the knowledge you need to be computer literate. As you read this first chapter, keep in mind it is an overview. Many of the terms and concepts introduced in this chapter will be discussed in more depth later in the book.

WHAT IS A COMPUTER?

A **computer** is an electronic device, operating under the control of instructions stored in its own memory, that can accept data, process the data according to specified rules, produce results, and store the results for future use.

Data and Information

Computers process data into information. **Data** is a collection of unprocessed items, which can include text, numbers, images, audio, and video. **Information** conveys meaning and is useful to people.

As shown in Figure 1-2, for example, computers process several data items to print information in the form of a grade report.

> **FAQ 1-1**
>
> **Is data a singular or plural word?**
>
> The word data is plural for datum. With respect to computers, however, it is accepted and common practice to use the word data in both the singular and plural context. For more information, visit scsite.com/dc2008/ch1/faq and then click Data.
>
> A **FAQ** (frequently asked question) helps you find answers to commonly asked questions. Web sites often post an FAQ section, and each chapter in this book includes FAQ boxes related to topics in the text.

Information Processing Cycle

Computers process data (input) into information (output). A computer often holds data, information, and instructions in storage for future use. *Instructions* are the steps that tell the computer how to perform a particular task. Some people refer to the series of input, process, output, and storage activities as the *information processing cycle*.

Most computers today can communicate with other computers. As a result, communications also has become an essential element of the information processing cycle.

DATA

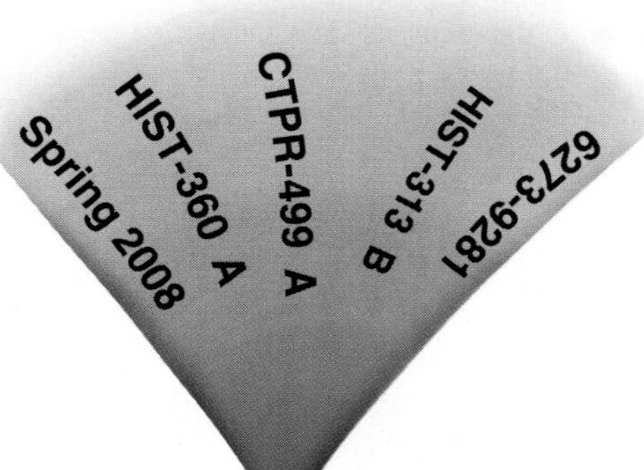

PROCESSES

- Computes each course's grade points by multiplying the credits earned by the grade value (i.e., 4.0 * 3.0 = 12.00)
- Organizes data
- Sums all credits attempted, credits earned, and grade points (10.00, 10.00, and 36.00)
- Divides total grade points by credits earned to compute term GPA (3.60)

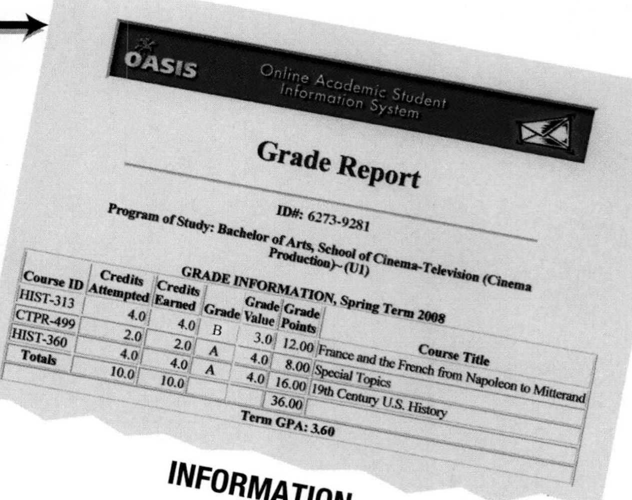

OASIS Online Academic Student Information System

Grade Report

ID#: 6273-9281

Program of Study: Bachelor of Arts, School of Cinema-Television (Cinema Production)~(U1)

GRADE INFORMATION, Spring Term 2008

Course ID	Credits Attempted	Credits Earned	Grade	Grade Value	Grade Points	Course Title
HIST-313	4.0	4.0	B	3.0	12.00	France and the French from Napoleon to Mitterand
CTPR-499	2.0	2.0	A	4.0	8.00	Special Topics
HIST-360	4.0	4.0	A	4.0	16.00	19th Century U.S. History
Totals	10.0	10.0			36.00	

Term GPA: 3.60

INFORMATION

FIGURE 1-2 A computer processes data into information. In this simplified example, the student identification number, semester, course codes, and course grades all represent data. The computer processes the data to produce the grade report (information).

THE COMPONENTS OF A COMPUTER

A computer contains many electric, electronic, and mechanical components known as **hardware**. These components include input devices, output devices, a system unit, storage devices, and communications devices. Figure 1-3 shows some common computer hardware components.

Input Devices

An **input device** is any hardware component that allows you to enter data and instructions into a computer. Six widely used input devices are the keyboard, mouse, microphone, scanner, digital camera, and PC video camera (Figure 1-3).

A computer keyboard contains keys you press to enter data into the computer. For security purposes, some keyboards have a built-in fingerprint scanner, which allows you to work with the computer only if your fingerprint is recognized.

A mouse is a small handheld device. With the mouse, you control movement of a small symbol on the screen, called the pointer, and you make selections from the screen.

A microphone allows you to speak into the computer. A scanner converts printed material (such as text and pictures) into a form the computer can use.

With a digital camera, you take pictures and then transfer them to the computer or printer instead of storing the images on traditional film. A PC video camera is a digital video camera that allows you to create movies or take still pictures electronically.

printer (output device)
portable media player (output device)
monitor (output device)
screen
PC video camera (input device)
CD/DVD drive (storage device)
speakers (output device)
hard disk drive (storage device)
system unit (processor, memory, and storage devices)
keyboard (input device)
mouse (input device)
scanner (input device)
digital camera (input device)
microphone (input device)
external hard disk (storage device)
card reader/writer (storage device)
USB flash drive (storage device)
modem (communications device)

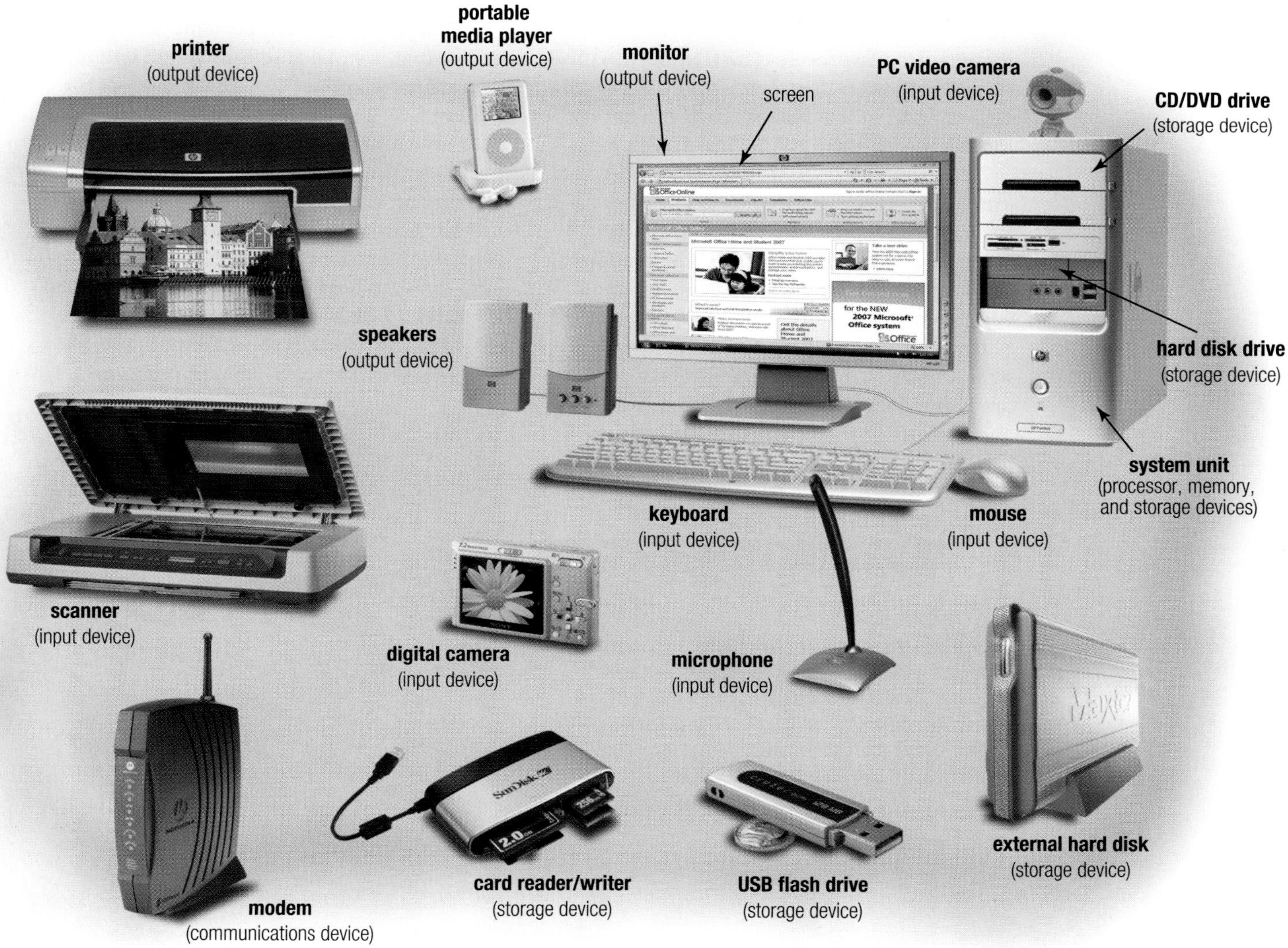

FIGURE 1-3 Common computer hardware components include a keyboard, mouse, microphone, scanner, digital camera, PC video camera, printer, monitor, speakers, portable media player, system unit, hard disk drive, external hard disk, USB flash drive, card reader/writer, and modem.

Output Devices

An **output device** is any hardware component that conveys information to one or more people. Four commonly used output devices are a printer, a monitor, speakers, and a portable media player (Figure 1-3 on the previous page).

A printer produces text and graphics on a physical medium such as paper. A monitor displays text, graphics, and videos on a screen. Speakers allow you to hear music, voice, and other audio (sounds). You can transfer audio, video, and digital images from your computer to a portable media player and then listen to the audio, watch the video, or view the images on the media player.

WEB LINK 1-2

Output Devices

For more information, visit scsite.com/dc2008/ch1/weblink and then click Output Devices.

System Unit

The **system unit** is a case that contains the electronic components of the computer that are used to process data (Figure 1-3). The circuitry of the system unit usually is part of or is connected to a circuit board called the motherboard.

Two main components on the motherboard are the processor and memory. The *processor* is the electronic component that interprets and carries out the basic instructions that operate the computer. *Memory* consists of electronic components that store instructions waiting to be executed and data needed by those instructions. Although some forms of memory are permanent, most memory keeps data and instructions temporarily, which means its contents are erased when the computer is shut off.

FAQ 1-2

What is a CPU?

The processor. Most people in the computer industry use the terms *CPU* (*central processing unit*) and processor to mean the same. A CPU is not the same as a computer; a computer contains a CPU. For more information, visit scsite.com/dc2008/ch1/faq and then click CPU.

Storage Devices

Storage holds data, instructions, and information for future use. For example, computers can store hundreds or millions of customer names and addresses. Storage holds these items permanently.

A computer keeps data, instructions, and information on **storage media**. Examples of storage media are USB flash drives, hard disks, CDs, DVDs, and memory cards. A **storage device** records (writes) and/or retrieves (reads) items to and from storage media. Drives and readers/writers, which are types of storage devices (Figure 1-3), accept a specific kind of storage media. For example, a DVD drive (storage device) accepts a DVD (storage media). Storage devices often function as a source of input because they transfer items from storage to memory.

A USB flash drive is a portable storage device that is small and lightweight enough to be transported on a keychain or in a pocket (Figure 1-3). The average USB flash drive can hold about 500 million characters. You plug a USB flash drive in a special, easily accessible opening on the computer.

A hard disk provides much greater storage capacity than a USB flash drive. The average hard disk can hold more than 250 billion characters. Hard disks are enclosed in an airtight, sealed case. Although some are portable, most are housed inside the system unit (Figure 1-4).

FIGURE 1-4 Hard disks are self-contained devices. The hard disk shown here must be installed in the system unit before it can be used.

Portable hard disks are either external or removable. An external hard disk is a separate, free-standing unit, whereas you insert and remove a removable hard disk from the computer or a device connected to the computer.

A compact disc is a flat, round, portable metal disc with a plastic coating. One type of compact disc is a CD-ROM, which can hold from 650 million to 1 billion characters. You can access a CD-ROM using most CD and DVD drives (Figure 1-5). Another type of compact disc is a DVD-ROM, some of which have enough storage capacity to store two full-length movies or 17 billion characters. To use a DVD-ROM, you need a DVD drive.

Some portable devices, such as digital cameras, use memory cards as the storage media. You then can transfer the stored items, such as digital photographs, from the memory card to a computer or printer using a card reader/writer (Figure 1-3 on page 7).

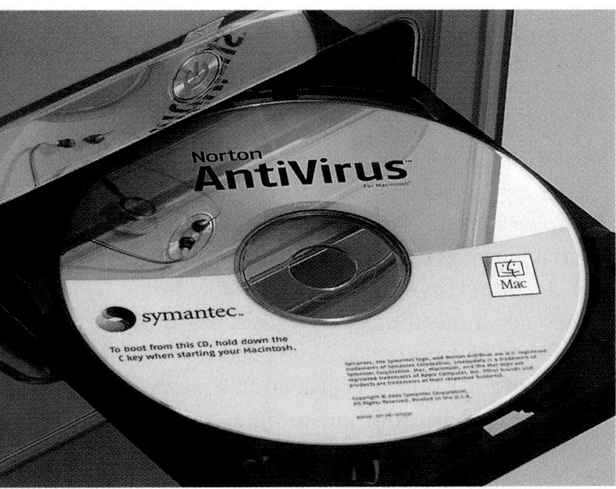

FIGURE 1-5 To use a CD or DVD, you need a CD or DVD drive.

Communications Devices

A **communications device** is a hardware component that enables a computer to send (transmit) and receive data, instructions, and information to and from one or more computers. A widely used communications device is a modem (Figure 1-3).

Communications occur over cables, telephone lines, cellular radio networks, satellites, and other transmission media. Some transmission media, such as satellites and cellular radio networks, are wireless, which means they have no physical lines or wires.

ADVANTAGES AND DISADVANTAGES OF USING COMPUTERS

Society has reaped many benefits from using computers. Both business and home users can make well-informed decisions because they have instant access to information from anywhere in the world. A **user** is anyone who communicates with a computer or utilizes the information it generates. Students, another type of user, have more tools to assist them in the learning process. Read Looking Ahead 1-1 for a look at the next generation of benefits from using computers.

LOOKING AHEAD 1-1

Medical Implants Can Enhance Lifestyles

Cellular phone manufacturers tout their small and powerful products, but the ultimate technology is the tiny cellular-phone-on-a-chip device. By implanting this processor directly into the brain and connecting electrodes to the brain's speech center, people would have the ability to communicate on any wireless network. While this technology might seem extreme, it illustrates the emergence of electronics inside the body to improve human life.

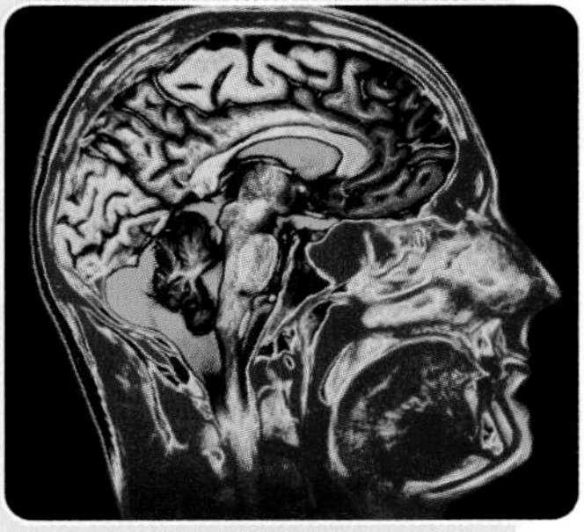

Other possible surgeries might implant a rechargeable electrical stimulator to treat pain or muscle dysfunction or to zap the stomach or nerves with electric current to boost metabolism. A brain computer interface may monitor and treat diseases, such as epilepsy and depression, that affect brain activity. A body-scanning machine might evaluate patients' pain when they cannot communicate.

In addition, a retinal prosthesis system with a light-sensing chip implanted in the eye might help patients with degenerative retinal diseases. For more information, visit scsite.com/dc2008/ch1/looking and then click Computer Implants.

Communications Devices

For more information, visit scsite.com/dc2008/ch1/weblink and then click Communications Devices.

Advantages of Using Computers Benefits of computers are possible because computers have the advantages of speed, reliability, consistency, storage, and communications.

- **Speed**: When data, instructions, and information flow along electronic circuits in a computer, they travel at incredibly fast speeds. Many computers process billions or trillions of operations in a single second. Processing involves computing (adding, subtracting, etc.), sorting (e.g., alphabetizing), organizing, displaying pictures, recording audio clips, playing music, and showing a movie or video. For a technical discussion about how computers process data, read the High-Tech Talk article on page 38.
- **Reliability**: The electronic components in modern computers are dependable and reliable because they rarely break or fail.
- **Consistency**: Given the same input and processes, a computer will produce the same results — consistently. A computing phrase — known as *garbage in, garbage out* — points out that the accuracy of a computer's output depends on the accuracy of the input. For example, if you do not use the flash on a digital camera when indoors, the resulting pictures that are displayed on the computer screen may be unusable because they are too dark.
- **Storage**: A computer can transfer data quickly from storage to memory, process it, and then store it again for future use. Many computers store enormous amounts of data and make this data available for processing anytime it is needed.
- **Communications**: Most computers today can communicate with other computers, often wirelessly. Computers with this capability can share any of the four information processing cycle operations — input, process, output, and storage — with another computer or a user.

Disadvantages of Using Computers Some disadvantages of computers relate to the violation of privacy, public safety, the impact on the labor force, health risks, and the impact on the environment.

- **Violation of Privacy**: Nearly every life event is stored in a computer somewhere…in medical records, credit reports, tax records, etc. In many instances, where personal and confidential records were not properly protected, individuals have found their privacy violated and identities stolen. Read Ethics & Issues 1-1 for a related discussion.
- **Public Safety**: Adults, teens, and children around the world are using computers to share publicly their photos, videos, journals, music, and other personal information. Some of these unsuspecting, innocent computer users have fallen victim to crimes committed by dangerous strangers. Protect yourself and your dependents from these criminals by being cautious. For example, do not share information that would allow others to identify or locate you.
- **Impact on Labor Force**: Although computers have improved productivity in many ways and created an entire industry with hundreds of thousands of new jobs, the skills of millions of employees have been replaced by computers. Thus, it is crucial that workers keep their education up-to-date. A separate impact on the labor force is that some companies are outsourcing jobs to foreign countries instead of keeping their homeland labor force employed.

ETHICS & ISSUES 1-1

What Should Be Done about Identity Theft?

Using e-mail and other techniques on the Internet, scam artists are employing a technique known as *phishing* to try to steal your personal information, such as credit card numbers, banking information, and passwords. For example, an e-mail message may appear to be a request from your credit card company to verify your Social Security number and online banking password. Instead, the information you submit ends up in the hands of the scammer, who then uses the information for a variety of unethical and illegal acts. Sadly, the result often is identity theft. You can help to deter identity theft in several ways: 1) shred your financial documents before discarding them, 2) do not click links in unsolicited e-mail messages, and 3) enroll in a credit monitoring service. Consumer advocates often blame credit card companies and credit bureaus for lax security standards. Meanwhile, the companies blame consumers for being too gullible and forthcoming with private information. Both sides blame the government for poor privacy laws and light punishments for identity thieves. But while the arguments go on, law enforcement agencies bear the brunt of the problem by spending hundreds of millions of dollars responding to complaints and finding and processing the criminals. Under current laws, who is responsible for Internet identity theft? Why? Should laws be changed to stop it, or should consumers change behavior? What is an appropriate punishment for identity thieves? Given the international nature of the Internet, how can foreign identity thieves be handled?

- **Health Risks**: Prolonged or improper computer use can lead to injuries or disorders of the hands, wrists, elbows, eyes, neck, and back. Computer users can protect themselves from these health risks through proper workplace design, good posture while at the computer, and appropriately spaced work breaks. Another health risk, called computer addiction, occurs when someone becomes obsessed with using the computer. Once recognized, computer addiction is a treatable disorder.
- **Impact on Environment**: Computer manufacturing processes and computer waste are depleting natural resources and polluting the environment. When computers are discarded in landfills, they release toxic materials and potentially dangerous levels of lead, mercury, and flame retardants. Strategies that can help protect the environment include recycling, regulating manufacturing processes, extending the life of computers, and immediately donating replaced computers. When you purchase a new computer, some retailers offer to dispose of your old computer properly.

Test your knowledge of pages 4 through 11 in Quiz Yourself 1-1.

QUIZ YOURSELF 1-1

Instructions: Find the true statement below. Then, rewrite the remaining false statements so they are true.

1. A computer is a motorized device that processes output into input.
2. A storage device records (reads) and/or retrieves (writes) items to and from storage media.
3. An output device is any hardware component that allows you to enter data and instructions into a computer.
4. Computer literacy involves having a knowledge and understanding of computers and their uses.
5. Computers have the disadvantages of fast speeds, high failure rates, producing consistent results, storing small amounts of data, and communicating with others.
6. Four commonly used input devices are a printer, a monitor, speakers, and a portable media player.

Quiz Yourself Online: To further check your knowledge of computer literacy, computers and their components, and the advantages and disadvantages of computers, visit scsite.com/dc2008/ch1/quiz and then click Objectives 1 – 4.

NETWORKS AND THE INTERNET

A **network** is a collection of computers and devices connected together, often wirelessly, via communications devices and transmission media. When a computer connects to a network, it is **online**.

Networks allow computers to share *resources*, such as hardware, software, data, and information. Sharing resources saves time and money. In many networks, one or more computers act as a server. The server controls access to the resources on a network. The other computers on the network, each called a client or workstation, request resources from the server (Figure 1-6). The major differences between the server and client computers are that the server ordinarily has more power, more storage space, and expanded communications capabilities.

Many homes and most businesses and schools network their computers and devices. Most allow users to connect their computers wirelessly to the network. Home networks usually are small, existing within a single structure. Business and school networks can be small, such as in a room or building, or widespread, connecting computers across a city, country, or the globe. The world's largest computer network is the Internet.

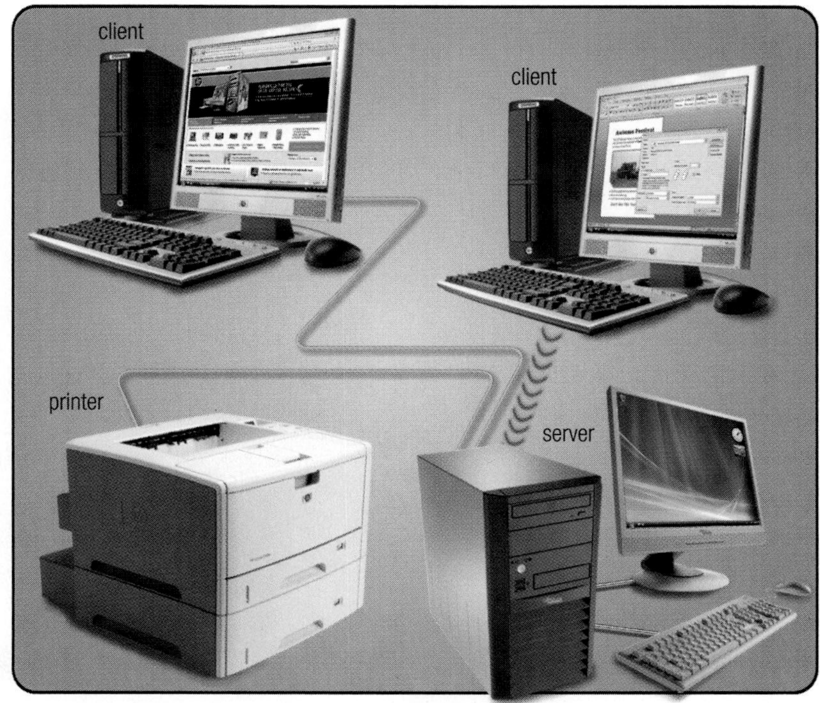

FIGURE 1-6 A server manages the resources on a network, and clients access the resources on the server. This network enables three separate computers to share the same printer, one wirelessly.

The Internet

The **Internet** is a worldwide collection of networks that connects millions of businesses, government agencies, educational institutions, and individuals (Figure 1-7).

More than one billion people around the world use the Internet daily for a variety of reasons, including the following:

- Communicate with and meet other people
- Access a wealth of information, news, and research findings
- Shop for goods and services
- Bank and invest
- Take a class
- Access sources of entertainment and leisure, such as online games, music, videos, books, and magazines
- Download music and video
- Share information

Figure 1-8 shows examples in each of these areas.

People connect to the Internet to exchange information with others around the world. E-mail allows you to send messages to other users. With instant messaging, you can have a live conversation with another connected user. In a chat room, you can communicate with multiple users at the same time — much like a group discussion. With Internet telephony, you can use the Internet to make a telephone call.

Businesses, called access providers, offer users and companies access to the Internet free or for a fee. By subscribing to an access provider, you can use your computer and a communications device, such as a modem, to connect to the many services of the Internet.

The Web, short for World Wide Web, is one of the more popular services on the Internet. Think of the Web as a global library of information available to anyone connected to the Internet. The **Web** contains billions of documents called Web pages. A **Web page** can contain text, graphics, audio, and video. The eight screens shown in Figure 1-8 are examples of Web pages. Web pages often have built-in connections, or links, to other documents, graphics, other Web pages, or Web sites. A Web site is a collection of related Web pages. Some Web sites allow users to access music and videos that can be downloaded, or transferred to storage media in a computer or portable media player, and then listen to the music through speakers, headphones, or earphones, or view the videos on a display device.

The Internet

For more information, visit scsite.com/dc2008/ch1/weblink and then click Internet.

FIGURE 1-7
The Internet is the largest computer network, connecting millions of computers around the world.

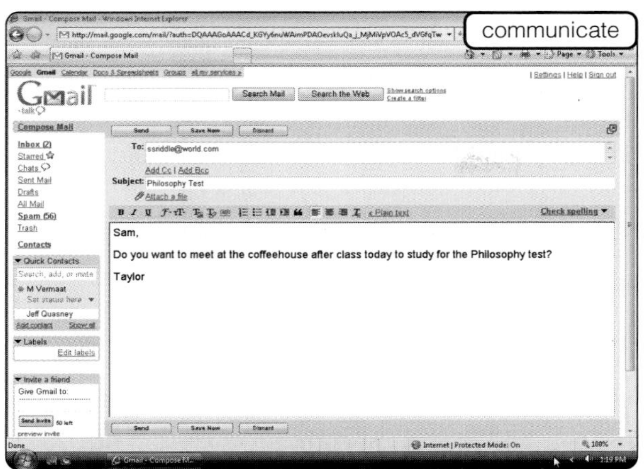

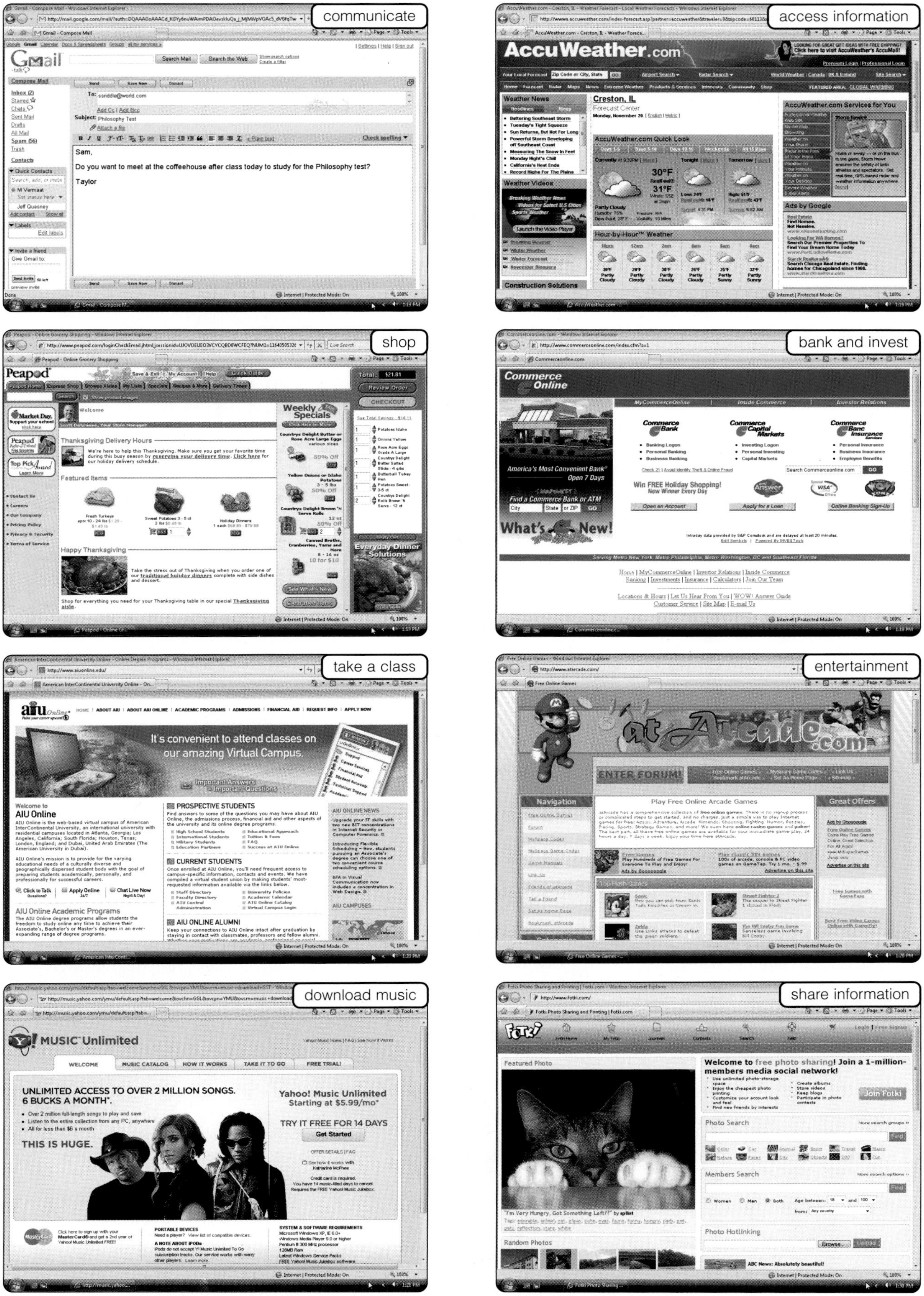

access information

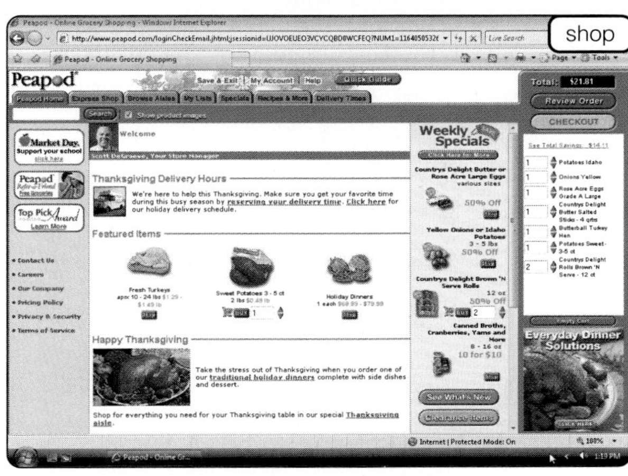

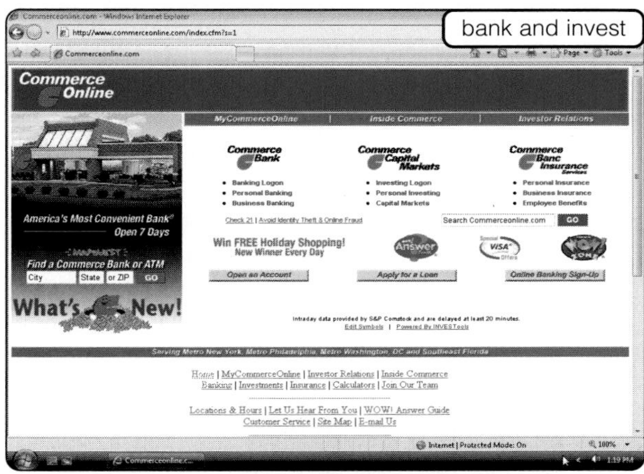

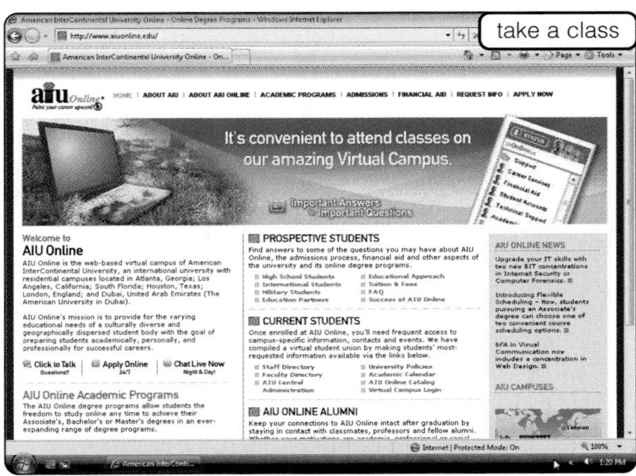

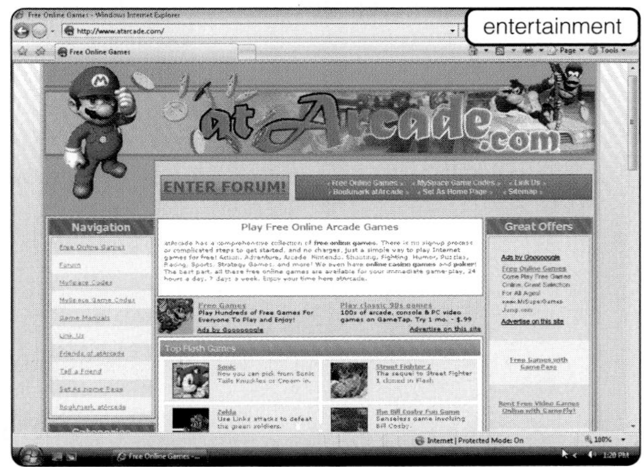

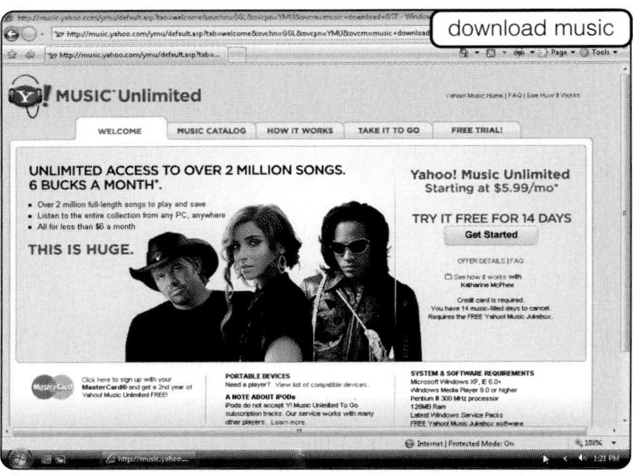

FIGURE 1-8 Users access the Internet for a variety of reasons.

In addition to accessing and using information on the Web, many people use the Web as a means to share personal information, photographs, videos, or artwork with the world. Anyone can create a Web page and then make it available, or *publish* it, on the Internet for others to see (read Ethics & Issues 1-2 for a related discussion). Millions of people worldwide join online communities, each called a **social networking Web site**, that encourage members to share their interests, ideas, stories, photos, music, and videos with other registered users (Figure 1-9). Some social networking Web sites are college oriented, some business oriented, others are more focused. A **photo sharing community**, for example, is a specific type of social networking Web site that allows users to create an online photo album and store their electronic photographs. Some Web sites provide publishing services free.

WEB LINK 1-5

Social Networking Web Sites

For more information, visit scsite.com/dc2008/ch1/weblink and then click Social Networking Web Sites.

Hundreds of thousands of people today also use blogs to publish their thoughts on the Web. A *blog* is an informal Web site consisting of time-stamped articles in a diary or journal format, usually listed in reverse chronological order. As others read the articles in a blog, they reply with their own thoughts. A blog that contains video clips is called a *video blog*.

Podcasts are a popular way people verbally share information on the Web. A *podcast* is recorded audio stored on a Web site that can be downloaded to a computer or a portable media player such as an iPod. A video podcast, or *vodcast*, is a podcast that contains video and usually audio. At a convenient time and location, the user listens to the downloaded podcast or watches the downloaded vodcast.

FIGURE 1-9 MySpace is a popular social networking Web site.

FAQ 1-3

What Web sites do users visit on the Internet?

A recent survey found that users visit various types of Web sites, as shown in the chart below. For more information, visit scsite.com/dc2008/ch1/faq and then click Web Sites.

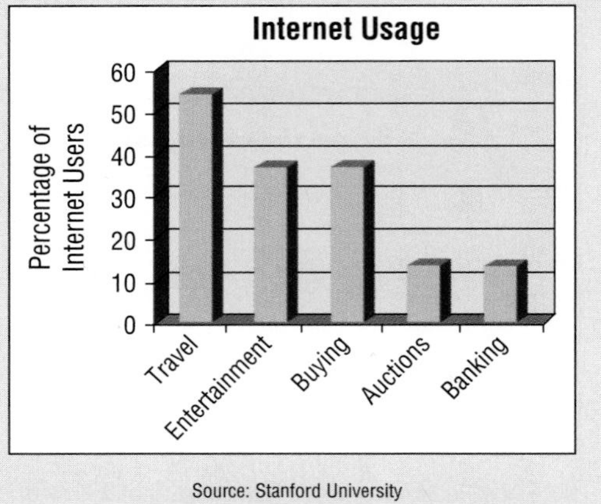

Source: Stanford University

ETHICS & ISSUES 1-2

Who Is Responsible for the Accuracy of Web Pages?

Since the dawn of the Web, some groups have used Web sites to try to convince people that the Holocaust in World War II did not occur. Using fake research papers and authoritative looking Web pages, these groups hope to revise history to their liking. In response, other groups have created Web sites to counter those claims and provide evidence of the truth. Many people think that anything in print is true, even what they read on the Web. Yet, authors with a wide range of expertise, authority, motives, and biases create Web pages. Web pages can be as accurate as the most scholarly journal, or no truer than the most disreputable supermarket tabloid. The Web makes it easy to obtain information, but Web page readers must make an extra effort to determine the quality of that information. In evaluating a Web page, experts suggest that you consider such factors as the purpose, scope, sponsor, timeliness, presentation, author, and permanence of the page. Ultimately, who is responsible for the accuracy of information on the Web? Why? What factors are most important in evaluating the accuracy of a Web page? Why? Should people be held accountable for what they publish on the Web? If so, by whom?

COMPUTER SOFTWARE

Software, also called a **program**, consists of a series of instructions that tells the computer what to do and how to do it.

You interact with a program through its user interface. The user interface controls how you enter data and instructions and how information is displayed on the screen. Software today often has a graphical user interface. With a **graphical user interface** (**GUI** pronounced gooey), you interact with the software using text, graphics, and visual images such as icons (Figure 1-10). An *icon* is a miniature image that represents a program, an instruction, or some other object. You can use the mouse to select icons that perform operations such as starting a program.

The two categories of software are system software and application software. The following sections describe these categories of software.

System Software

System software consists of the programs that control or maintain the operations of the computer and its devices. System software serves as the interface between the user, the application software, and the computer's hardware. Two types of system software are the operating system and utility programs.

OPERATING SYSTEM An *operating system* is a set of programs that coordinates all the activities among computer hardware devices. It provides a means for users to communicate with the computer and other software. Many of today's computers use Windows XP or Vista (Figure 1-10), which are two of Microsoft's operating systems, or Mac OS X, Apple's operating system.

When a user starts a computer, portions of the operating system load into memory from the computer's hard disk. It remains in memory while the computer is on.

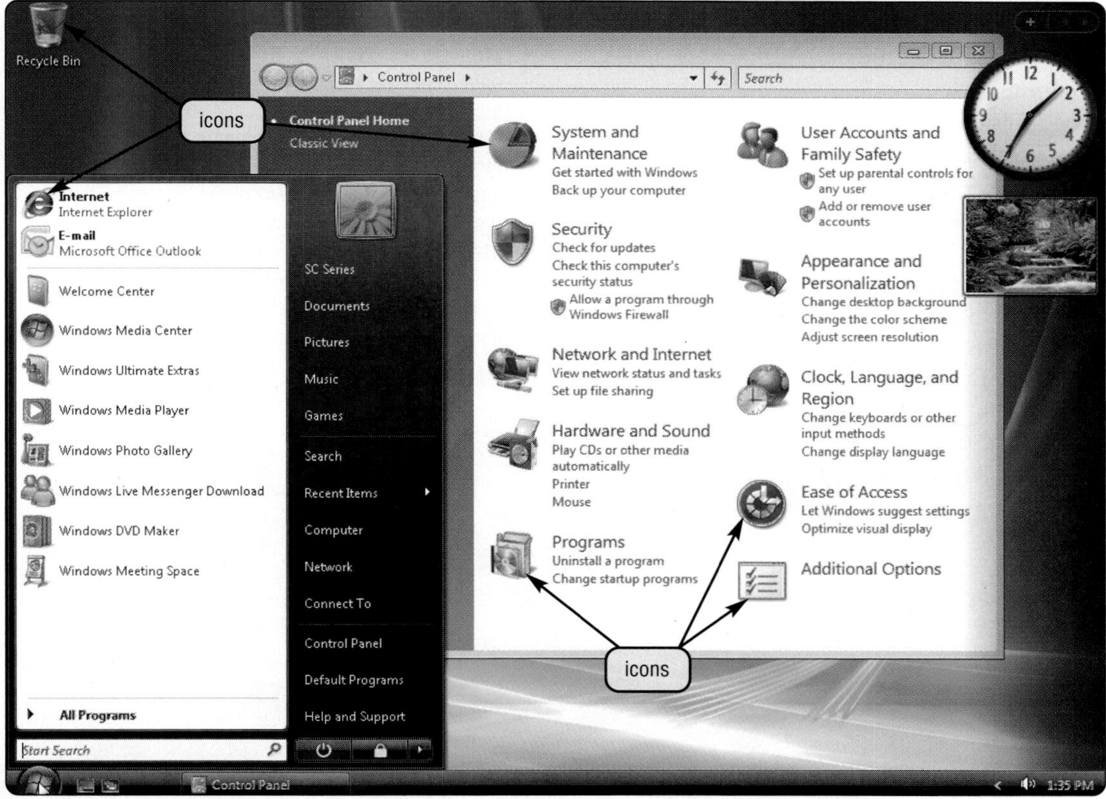

FIGURE 1-10 The graphical user interface of Windows Vista.

Utility Program A *utility program* allows a user to perform maintenance-type tasks usually related to managing a computer, its devices, or its programs. Most operating systems include several utility programs for managing disk drives, printers, and other devices and media. You also can buy utility programs that allow you to perform additional computer management functions.

Application Software

Application software consists of programs designed to make users more productive and/or assist them with personal tasks. A widely used type of application software related to communications is a Web browser, which allows users with an Internet connection to access and view Web pages. Other popular application software includes word processing software, spreadsheet software, database software, and presentation graphics software.

Many other types of application software exist that enable users to perform a variety of tasks. These include personal information management, note taking, project management, accounting, document management, computer-aided design, desktop publishing, paint/image editing, audio and video editing, multimedia authoring, Web page authoring, personal finance, legal, tax preparation, home design/landscaping, education, reference, and entertainment (e.g., games or simulations, etc.). As shown in Figure 1-11, you can purchase application software from a store that sells computer products. Read Ethics & Issues 1-3 for a related discussion.

ETHICS & ISSUES 1-3

Do Computer Games Do More Harm than Good?

Grand Theft Auto: San Andreas is one of today's most popular computer games. In the game, players advance through the mafia by conveying secret packages, following alleged snitches, and planting car bombs. Consumers have bought millions of copies of Grand Theft Auto. Purchasers praise the game's vivid graphics and wide range of allowable behaviors. After it was released, the game was found to contain hidden adult content accessible by using a special code. Despite investigations, the company was not fined or punished for the content. Some parents and politicians condemn the game's explicit violence and the rewards it gives players for participating in illegal acts. They fear that games like Grand Theft Auto eventually could lead to antisocial or criminal behavior. Even worse, critics fear that the game's popularity may influence future developers of computer games aimed at younger children. Despite the fears, research has shown that playing violent games has no impact on behavior or increased crime. In fact, in the time in which gaming has become popular, violent crime has decreased by 50 percent in America. Some researchers and parents note the positive aspects of gaming, such as increased dexterity for players, use of critical thinking skills to solve problems in games, meeting goals, and following rules. What impact, if any, do violent computer games or games that include unacceptable acts have on individual behavior? On balance, is computer gaming good or bad for people? Why? What other motivations might parents have who limit their children's computer gaming?

WEB LINK 1-6

Application Software

For more information, visit scsite.com/dc2008/ch1/weblink and then click Application Software.

FIGURE 1-11 Stores that sell computer products have shelves stocked with software for sale.

Installing and Running Programs

The instructions in a program are stored on storage media such as a hard disk or compact disc. When purchasing software from a computer store, you typically receive a box that includes a CD(s) or DVD(s) that contains the program. You also may receive a manual or printed instructions explaining how to install and use the software.

Installing is the process of setting up software to work with the computer, printer, and other hardware components. When you buy a computer, it usually has some software preinstalled on its hard disk. This enables you to use the computer the first time you turn it on. To begin installing additional software from a CD or DVD, insert the program disc in a CD or DVD drive. The computer then copies all or part of the program from the disc to the computer's hard disk.

Once software is installed, you can use, or **run**, it. When you instruct the computer to run an installed program, the computer *loads* it, which means the program is copied from storage to memory. Once in memory, the computer can carry out, or *execute*, the instructions in the program. Figure 1-12 illustrates the steps that occur when a user installs and runs a greeting card program.

FAQ 1-4

How do I know if computer software will run on my computer?

When you buy a computer, the box or the order summary will list the computer's specifications. Similarly, when you buy software, the software box lists specifications. Your computer's specifications should be the same as or greater than the software specifications. For more information, visit scsite.com/dc2008/ch1/faq and then click Computer Software.

FIGURE 1-12 INSTALLING AND RUNNING A COMPUTER PROGRAM

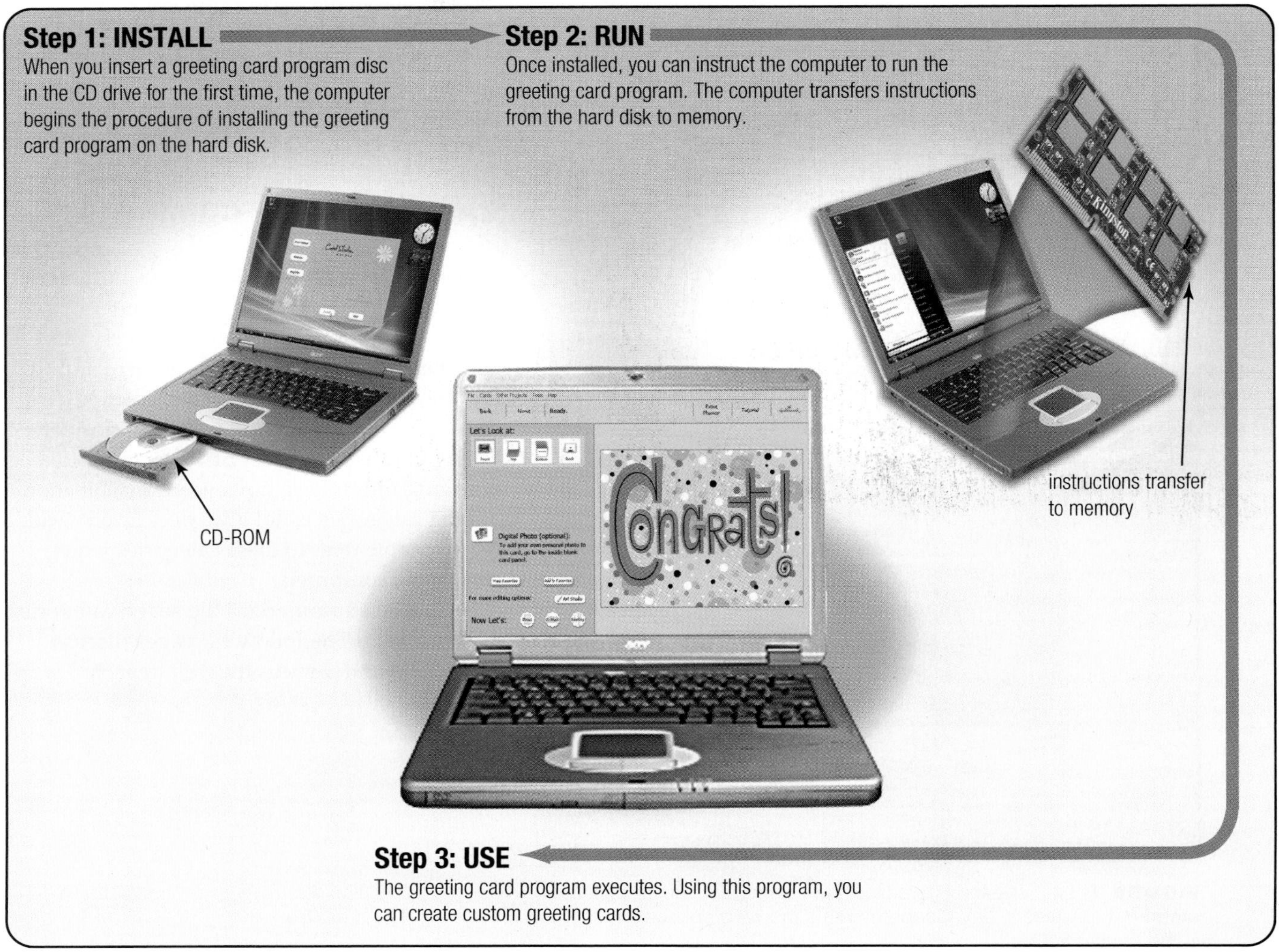

Step 1: INSTALL
When you insert a greeting card program disc in the CD drive for the first time, the computer begins the procedure of installing the greeting card program on the hard disk.

Step 2: RUN
Once installed, you can instruct the computer to run the greeting card program. The computer transfers instructions from the hard disk to memory.

CD-ROM

instructions transfer to memory

Step 3: USE
The greeting card program executes. Using this program, you can create custom greeting cards.

Software Development

A *programmer*, sometimes called a computer programmer or *developer*, is someone who develops software or writes the instructions that direct the computer to process data into information. When writing instructions, a programmer must be sure the program works properly so the computer generates the desired results. Complex programs can require thousands to millions of instructions.

Programmers use a programming language or program development tool to create computer programs. Popular programming languages include C++, Java, JavaScript, Visual C#, and Visual Basic. Figure 1-13 shows some of the instructions a programmer may write to create a Web application.

FIGURE 1-13 The top figure illustrates some of the instructions a programmer writes in JavaScript to create the Web application shown in the bottom figure.

Test your knowledge of pages 11 through 18 in Quiz Yourself 1-2.

QUIZ YOURSELF 1-2

Instructions: Find the true statement below. Then, rewrite the remaining false statements so they are true.

1. A resource is a collection of computers and devices connected together via communications devices and transmission media.
2. Installing is the process of setting up software to work with the computer, printer, and other hardware components.
3. Popular system software includes Web browsers, word processing software, spreadsheet software, database software, and presentation graphics software.
4. The Internet is one of the more popular services on the Web.
5. Two types of application software are the operating system and utility programs.

Quiz Yourself Online: To further check your knowledge of networks, the Internet and Web, and system software versus application software, visit scsite.com/dc2008/ch1/quiz and then click Objectives 5 – 7.

CATEGORIES OF COMPUTERS

Industry experts typically classify computers in seven categories: personal computers, mobile computers and mobile devices, game consoles, servers, mainframes, supercomputers, and embedded computers. A computer's size, speed, processing power, and price determine the category it best fits. Due to rapidly changing technology, however, the distinction among categories is not always clear-cut. Still, many people refer to these categories when discussing computers.

Figure 1-14 summarizes the seven categories of computers. The following pages discuss computers and devices that fall in each category.

CATEGORIES OF COMPUTERS

Category	Physical Size	Number of Simultaneously Connected Users	General Price Range
Personal computers (desktop)	Fits on a desk	Usually one (can be more if networked)	Several hundred to several thousand dollars
Mobile computers and mobile devices	Fits on your lap or in your hand	Usually one	Less than a hundred dollars to several thousand dollars
Game consoles	Small box or handheld device	One to several	Several hundred dollars or less
Servers	Small cabinet	Two to thousands	Several hundred to a million dollars
Mainframes	Partial room to a full room of equipment	Hundreds to thousands	$300,000 to several million dollars
Supercomputers	Full room of equipment	Hundreds to thousands	$500,000 to several billion dollars
Embedded computers	Miniature	Usually one	Embedded in the price of the product

FIGURE 1-14 This table summarizes some of the differences among the categories of computers. These should be considered general guidelines only because of rapid changes in technology.

PERSONAL COMPUTERS

A **personal computer** is a computer that can perform all of its input, processing, output, and storage activities by itself. A personal computer contains a processor, memory, and one or more input, output, and storage devices. They also often contain a communications device.

Two popular styles of personal computers are the PC (Figure 1-15) and the Apple (Figure 1-16). The term, *PC-compatible*, refers to any personal computer based on the original IBM personal computer design. Companies such as Dell, Gateway, Hewlett-Packard, and Toshiba sell PC-compatible computers. PC and PC-compatible computers use different operating systems. PC and PC-compatible computers usually use a Windows operating system. Apple computers usually use a Macintosh operating system (Mac OS X).

Two types of personal computers are desktop computers and notebook computers. The next section discusses desktop personal computers. Notebook computers are discussed in the mobile computers section.

WEB LINK 1-7

Personal Computers

For more information, visit scsite.com/dc2008/ch1/weblink and then click Personal Computers.

FIGURE 1-15 The PC and PC-compatible computers usually use a Windows operating system.

FIGURE 1-16 Apple computers, such as the iMac, usually use a Macintosh operating system.

Desktop Computers

A **desktop computer** is designed so the system unit, input devices, output devices, and any other devices fit entirely on or under a desk or table (Figures 1-15 and 1-16 on the previous page). In many models, the system unit is a tall and narrow *tower*, which can sit on the floor vertically — if desktop space is limited.

Some desktop computers function as a server on a network. Others, such as a gaming desktop computer and Media Center PC, target a specific audience. The *gaming desktop computer* offers high-quality audio, video, and graphics with optimal performance for sophisticated single-user and networked or Internet multiplayer games. A *Media Center PC* is a home entertainment desktop computer that provides a means of accessing television programs, radio broadcasts, photographs, and videos, as well as basic computing capabilities. These high-end computers cost much more than the basic desktop computer.

Another expensive, powerful desktop computer is the workstation, which is geared for work that requires intense calculations and graphics capabilities. An architect uses a workstation to design buildings and homes. A graphic artist uses a workstation to create computer-animated special effects for full-length motion pictures and video games.

FAQ 1-5

Does the term, workstation, have two meanings?

Yes. In the computer industry, a *workstation* can be a high-powered computer or a client computer on a network. For more information, visit scsite.com/dc2008/ch1/faq and then click Workstation.

MOBILE COMPUTERS AND MOBILE DEVICES

A **mobile computer** is a personal computer you can carry from place to place. Similarly, a **mobile device** is a computing device small enough to hold in your hand.

The most popular type of mobile computer is the notebook computer. The following sections discuss the notebook computer and widely used mobile devices.

Notebook Computers

A **notebook computer**, also called a **laptop computer**, is a portable, personal computer designed to fit on your lap. Notebook computers are thin and lightweight, yet they can be as powerful as the average desktop computer. Notebook computers usually are more expensive than desktop computers with equal capabilities.

On a typical notebook computer, the keyboard is on top of the system unit, and the monitor attaches to the system unit with hinges (Figure 1-17). These computers weigh on average between 2.5 and 9 pounds, which allows users easily to transport the computers from place to place. Most notebook computers can operate on batteries or a power supply or both.

FAQ 1-6

Are sales for notebook computers or desktop computers higher?

For the first time in history, notebook computer sales are consistently higher than desktop computer sales — a sure sign that we have entered an era of mobile computing. For more information, visit scsite.com/dc2008/ch1/faq and then click Computer Sales.

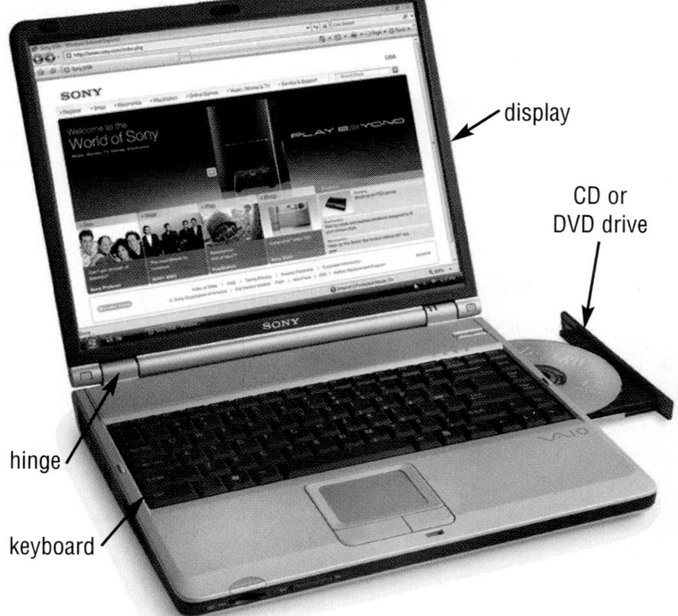

FIGURE 1-17 On a typical notebook computer, the keyboard is on top of the system unit, and the display attaches to the system unit with hinges.

TABLET PC Resembling a letter-sized slate, the **Tablet PC** is a special type of notebook computer that allows you to write or draw on the screen using a digital pen (Figure 1-18). With a *digital pen*, users write or draw by pressing the pen on the screen, and issue instructions to the Tablet PC by tapping on the screen. For users who prefer typing instead of handwriting, some Tablet PC designs have an attached keyboard; others allow you to connect a separate keyboard to the device. Tablet PCs also support voice input so users can enter text and issue instructions by speaking into the computer.

Tablet PCs are useful especially for taking notes in lectures, at meetings, conferences, and other forums where the standard notebook computer is not practical. With a cost of about $1,000 or more, some users may find Tablet PCs more appropriate for their needs than traditional notebook computers.

FIGURE 1-18 A Tablet PC combines the features of a traditional notebook computer with the simplicity of pencil and paper.

Mobile Devices

Mobile devices, which are small enough to carry in a pocket, usually do not have disk drives. Instead, these devices store programs and data permanently on special memory inside the system unit or on small storage media such as memory cards. You often can connect a mobile device to a personal computer to exchange information between the computer and the mobile device.

Some mobile devices are **Internet-enabled**, meaning they can connect to the Internet wirelessly. With an Internet-enabled device, users can chat, send e-mail and instant messages, and access the Web.

Three popular types of mobile devices are handheld computers, PDAs, and smart phones. Some combination mobile devices also are available, for example, a PDA/smart phone.

HANDHELD COMPUTER A **handheld computer**, sometimes referred to as an *ultra personal computer* (*uPC*), an *Ultra-Mobile PC* (*UMPC*), or a *handtop computer*, is a computer small enough to fit in one hand (Figure 1-19). Because of their reduced size, the screens on handheld computers are small. Many handheld computers communicate wirelessly with other devices or computers and also include a digital pen or stylus for input. Similar to a digital pen, a *stylus* is a small metal or plastic device that looks like a ballpoint pen but uses pressure instead of ink to write, draw, or make selections.

Some handheld computers have miniature or specialized keyboards. Many handheld computers are industry-specific and serve the needs of mobile employees, such as meter readers and parcel delivery people, whose jobs require them to move from place to place.

FIGURE 1-19 This handheld computer is a full PC that fits in your hand and weighs less than two pounds.

PDA A **PDA** (*personal digital assistant*) provides personal organizer functions such as a calendar, an appointment book, an address book, a calculator, and a notepad (Figure 1-20). Most PDAs also offer a variety of other application software such as word processing, spreadsheet, personal finance, and games.

The primary input device of a PDA is a stylus. Some PDAs have a built-in miniature keyboard. If you prefer to type on a PDA that does not have a keyboard, you can insert the PDA in a special separate keyboard. Some PDAs also support voice input and have built-in cameras.

FIGURE 1-20 PDAs provide personal information management functions as well as Internet access and telephone capabilities.

Many PDAs are Internet-enabled so users can check e-mail and access the Web. Some also provide telephone capabilities. Because of all the added features, increasingly more people are replacing their pocket-sized appointment books with PDAs or smart phones.

SMART PHONE Offering the convenience of one-handed operation, a **smart phone** is an Internet-enabled telephone that usually also provides PDA capabilities. In addition to basic telephone capabilities, a smart phone allows you to send and receive e-mail messages and access the Web. Most models have color screens and many play music and include built-in cameras so you can share photographs or videos with others as soon as you capture the image (Figure 1-21).

As smart phones and PDAs continue a trend of offering similar functions, it is becoming increasingly difficult to differentiate between the two devices. This trend, known as *convergence*, has led manufacturers to refer to PDAs and smart phones simply as *handhelds*. Some factors that affect a consumer's purchasing decision include the device's size, screen size, and capabilities of available software.

FIGURE 1-21 In addition to basic telephone functionality, smart phones allow you to check e-mail, access the Web, listen to music, and share photos and videos.

WEB LINK 1-8

Smart Phones

For more information, visit scsite.com/dc2008/ch1/weblink and then click Smart Phones.

CONSOLES

A **game console** is a mobile computing device designed for single-player or multiplayer video games (Figure 1-22). Standard game consoles use a handheld controller(s) as an input device(s); a television screen as an output device; and hard disks, CDs, DVDs, and/or memory cards for storage. Weighing on average between five and nine pounds, the compact size of game consoles makes them easy to use at home, in the car, in a hotel, or any location that has an electrical outlet. Three popular models are Microsoft's Xbox 360, Nintendo's Wii, and Sony's PlayStation 3.

A handheld game console is small enough to fit in one hand, making it more portable than the standard game console. With the handheld game console, the controls, screen, and speakers are built into the device. Because of their reduced size, the screens are small — three to four inches. Some models use cartridges to store games; others use a miniature type of CD or DVD. Many handheld game consoles can communicate wirelessly with other similar consoles for multiplayer gaming. Two popular models are Nintendo DS Lite and Sony's PlayStation Portable (PSP).

In addition to gaming, many console models allow users to listen to music, watch movies, and connect to the Internet. Game consoles can cost from a few hundred dollars to more than $500.

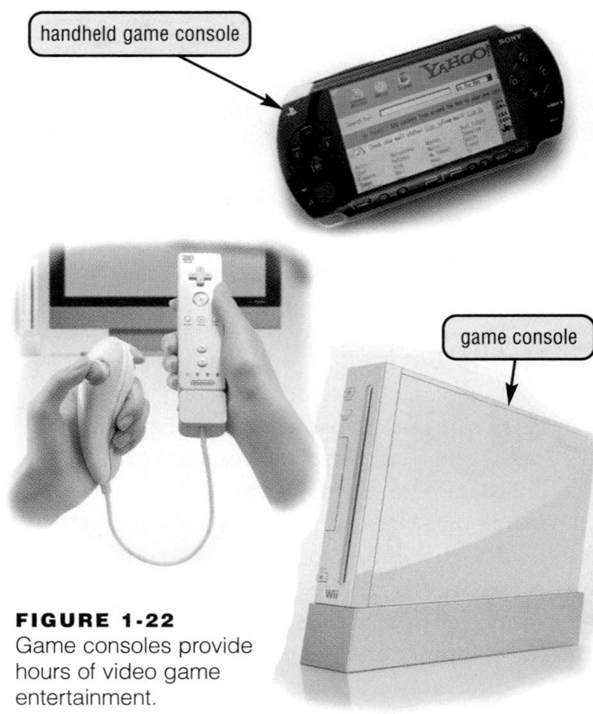

FIGURE 1-22 Game consoles provide hours of video game entertainment.

SERVERS

A **server** controls access to the hardware, software, and other resources on a network and provides a centralized storage area for programs, data, and information (Figure 1-23). Servers can support from two to several thousand connected computers at the same time.

In many cases, one server accesses data, information, and programs on another server. In other cases, people use personal computers or terminals to access data, information, and programs on a server. A terminal is a device with a monitor, keyboard, and memory.

FIGURE 1-23 A server controls access to resources on a network.

MAINFRAMES

A **mainframe** is a large, expensive, powerful computer that can handle hundreds or thousands of connected users simultaneously (Figure 1-24). Mainframes store tremendous amounts of data, instructions, and information. Most major corporations use mainframes for business activities. With mainframes, large businesses are able to bill millions of customers, prepare payroll for thousands of employees, and manage thousands of items in inventory. One study reported that mainframes process more than 83 percent of transactions around the world.

Mainframes also can act as servers in a network environment. Servers and other mainframes can access data and information from a mainframe. People also can access programs on the mainframe using terminals or personal computers.

FIGURE 1-24 Mainframe computers can handle thousands of connected computers and process millions of instructions per second.

SUPERCOMPUTERS

A **supercomputer** is the fastest, most powerful computer — and the most expensive (Figure 1-25). The fastest supercomputers are capable of processing more than 135 trillion instructions in a single second. With weights that exceed 100 tons, these computers can store more than 20,000 times the data and information of an average desktop computer.

Applications requiring complex, sophisticated mathematical calculations use supercomputers. Large-scale simulations and applications in medicine, aerospace, automotive design, online banking, weather forecasting, nuclear energy research, and petroleum exploration use a supercomputer.

FIGURE 1-25 This supercomputer simulates various environmental occurrences such as global climate changes, pollution, and earthquakes.

EMBEDDED COMPUTERS

An **embedded computer** is a special-purpose computer that functions as a component in a larger product. Embedded computers are everywhere — at home, in your car, and at work. The following list identifies a variety of everyday products that contain embedded computers.

- Consumer Electronics: mobile and digital telephones, digital televisions, cameras, video recorders, DVD players and recorders, answering machines
- Home Automation Devices: thermostats, sprinkling systems, security monitoring systems, appliances, lights
- Automobiles: antilock brakes, engine control modules, airbag controller, cruise control
- Process Controllers and Robotics: remote monitoring systems, power monitors, machine controllers, medical devices
- Computer Devices and Office Machines: keyboards, printers, faxes, copiers

Because embedded computers are components in larger products, they usually are small and have limited hardware. These computers perform various functions, depending on the requirements of the product in which they reside. Embedded computers in printers, for example, monitor the amount of paper in the tray, check the ink or toner level, signal if a paper jam has occurred, and so on. Figure 1-26 shows some of the many embedded computers in cars.

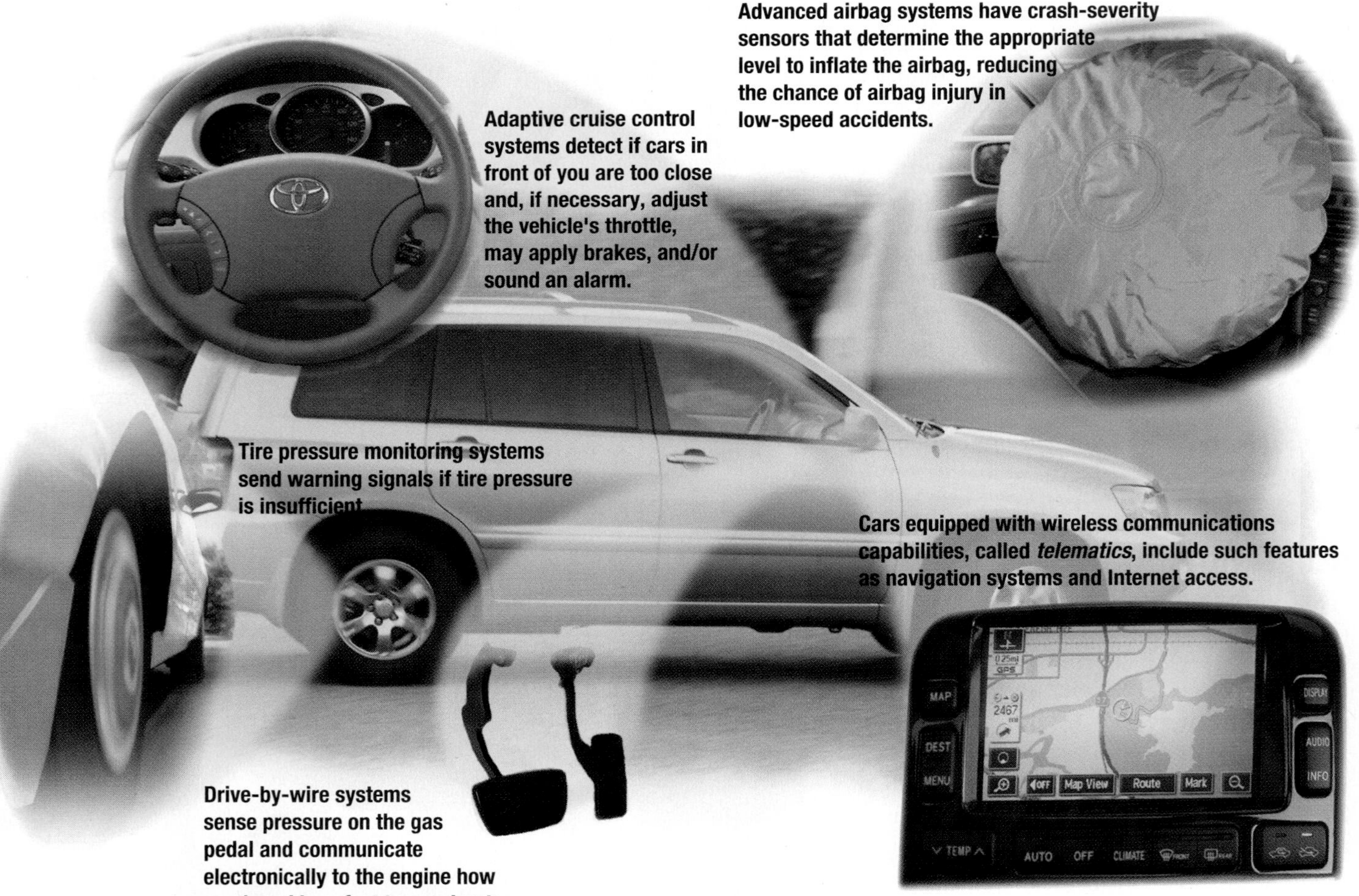

Advanced airbag systems have crash-severity sensors that determine the appropriate level to inflate the airbag, reducing the chance of airbag injury in low-speed accidents.
Adaptive cruise control systems detect if cars in front of you are too close and, if necessary, adjust the vehicle's throttle, may apply brakes, and/or sound an alarm.
Tire pressure monitoring systems send warning signals if tire pressure is insufficient.
Cars equipped with wireless communications capabilities, called *telematics*, include such features as navigation systems and Internet access.
Drive-by-wire systems sense pressure on the gas pedal and communicate electronically to the engine how much and how fast to accelerate.
MAP
DEST
MENU
Map View
Route
Mark
DISPLAY
AUDIO
INFO
AUTO
OFF
CLIMATE

FIGURE 1-26 Some of the embedded computers designed to improve your safety, security, and performance in today's automobiles.

ELEMENTS OF AN INFORMATION SYSTEM

To be valuable, information must be accurate, organized, timely, accessible, useful, and cost-effective to produce. Generating information from a computer requires the following five elements:

- Hardware
- Software
- Data
- People
- Procedures

Together, these elements (hardware, software, data, people, and procedures) comprise an *information system*. Figure 1-27 shows how each of the elements of an information system in a large business might interact.

The hardware must be reliable and capable of handling the expected workload. The software must be developed carefully and tested thoroughly. The data entered into the computer must be accurate.

Most companies with mid-sized and large computers have an IT (information technology) department. Staff in the IT department should be skilled and up-to-date on the latest technology. IT staff also should train users so they understand how to use the computer properly. Today's users also work closely with IT staff in the development of computer applications that relate to their areas of work.

Finally, all the IT applications should have readily available documented procedures that address operating the computer and using its applications.

FIGURE 1-27 HOW THE ELEMENTS OF AN INFORMATION SYSTEM IN A LARGE BUSINESS MIGHT INTERACT

Step 1:
IT staff (people) develop processes (procedures) for tabulating time cards (data).
Step 2:
Employees (people) in the payroll department use a program (software) to enter the time cards (data) in the computer.
Step 3:
The computer (hardware) performs calculations required to process the payroll and stores the results on storage media such as a hard disk (hardware).
Step 4:
Paychecks, the information, print on a corporate printer (hardware).

WEB LINK 1-9

Women in Technology

For more information, visit scsite.com/dc2008/ch1/weblink and then click Women in Technology.

WEB LINK 1-10

Minorities in Technology

For more information, visit scsite.com/dc2008/ch1/weblink and then click Minorities in Technology.

EXAMPLES OF COMPUTER USAGE

Every day, people around the world rely on different types of computers for a variety of applications. To illustrate the range of uses for computers, this section takes you on a visual and narrative tour of five categories of users:

- Home user
- Small office/home office (SOHO) user
- Mobile user
- Power user
- Large business user

The following pages discuss the types of hardware and software required by each category of user.

Home User

In an increasing number of homes, the computer no longer is a convenience. Instead, it is a basic necessity. Each family member, or **home user**, spends time on the computer for different reasons that include budgeting and personal financial management, Web access, communications, and entertainment (Figure 1-28).

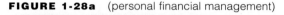

FIGURE 1-28a (personal financial management)

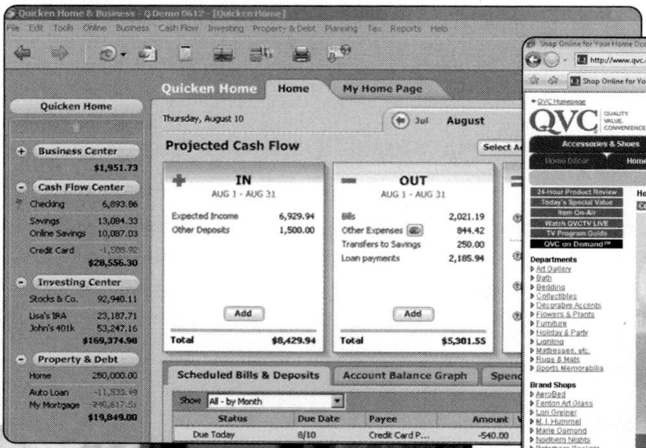

FIGURE 1-28b (Web access)

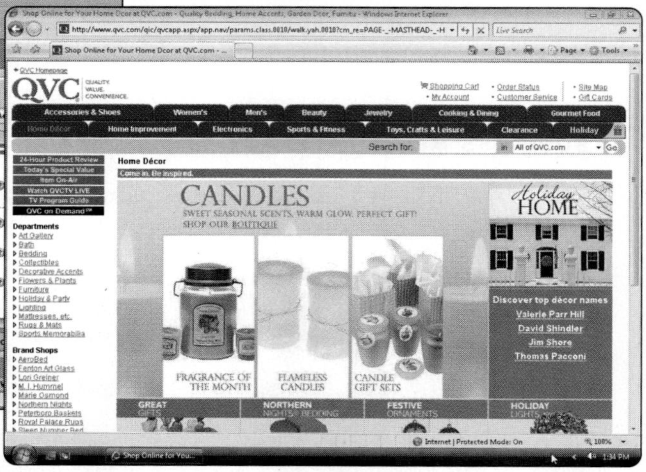

FIGURE 1-28c (communications)

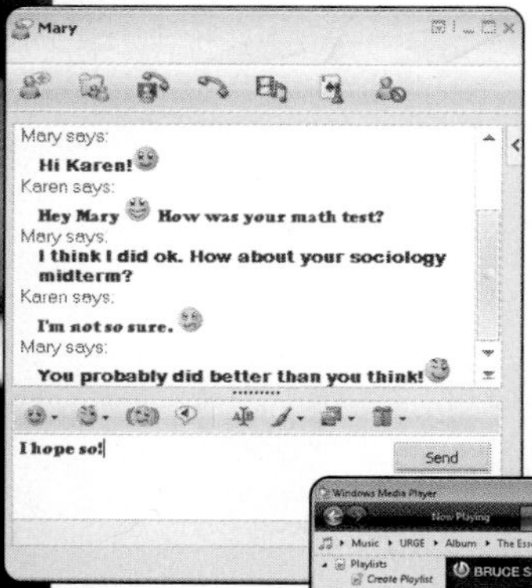

FIGURE 1-28d (entertainment)

FIGURE 1-28 The home user spends time on a computer for a variety of reasons.

On the Internet, home users access a huge amount of information, take college classes, pay bills, manage investments, shop, listen to the radio, watch movies, read books, play games, file taxes, book airline reservations, and make telephone calls. They also communicate with others around the world through e-mail, blogs, instant messaging, and chat rooms using personal computers, PDAs, and smart phones. Home users share ideas, interests, photos, music, and videos on social networking Web sites, or online social networks (read Ethics & Issues 1-4 for a related discussion). With a digital camera, home users take photographs and then send the electronic images to others (Figure 1-29). Using a PC video camera, which costs less than $100, home users easily have live video calls with friends, family members, and others.

Many home users have a portable media player, so they can download music or podcasts, and listen to the music and/or audio at a later time through earphones attached to the player. They also usually have one or more game consoles to play video games individually or with friends and family members.

Today's homes also typically have one or more desktop computers. Many home users network multiple desktop computers throughout the house, often wirelessly. These small networks allow family members to share an Internet connection and a printer.

To meet their needs, home users have a variety of software. They type letters, homework assignments, and other documents with word processing software. Personal finance software helps the home user with personal finances, investments, and family budgets. Other software assists with preparing taxes, keeping a household inventory, and setting up maintenance schedules.

Reference software, such as encyclopedias, medical dictionaries, or a road atlas, provides valuable information for everyone in the family. With entertainment software, the home user can play games, compose music, research genealogy, or create greeting cards. Educational software helps adults learn to speak a foreign language and youngsters to read, write, count, and spell.

FAQ 1-7

Can I watch a DVD on my computer?

Yes, in most cases. Simply insert the DVD in the computer's DVD drive. Within a few seconds, you should see the DVD begin to play on your computer's screen. If the DVD does not play, it is possible you need to run a program that starts the DVD. For more information, visit scsite.com/dc2008/ch1/faq and then click DVDs.

FIGURE 1-29 Home users take and view photographs on a digital camera.

ETHICS & ISSUES 1-4

Who Should Monitor Online Social Networks?

In recent years, online social networks such as MySpace exploded as a new means of communicating and socializing for teens and young adults. Not surprisingly, the problems associated with these online networks mirror some problems in society in general. Problems include bullying, smear campaigns against individuals, and inappropriate contact between adults and minors. Recently, a high-school-aged girl secretly left the country with the intent of marrying an adult in the foreign country whom she met on a social networking site. Fortunately, authorities in the foreign country intercepted her at the airport and sent her home. Some parents claim that the social networking sites should better monitor and report inappropriate behavior. While the sites have stepped up monitoring, they often claim that they are just providing a forum, and parents and authorities should be responsible for the inappropriate actions of its members. Many teens and young adults feel that the problems are simply a matter of personal responsibility and using care when online. Should providers of online social networks be required to monitor and stop inappropriate or socially unacceptable behavior? Why or why not? What role should parents play in overseeing a child's involvement in online social networks? Why? Should police or other government authorities be responsible for maintaining order in online social networks in the same way they are charged with maintaining order in society in general? Why or why not?

Small Office/Home Office User

Computers assist small business and home office users in managing their resources effectively. A **small office/home office** (*SOHO*) includes any company with fewer than 50 employees, as well as the self-employed who work from home. Small offices include local law practices, accounting firms, travel agencies, and florists. SOHO users typically have a desktop computer to perform some or all of their duties. Many also have PDAs or smart phones to manage appointments and contact information.

SOHO users access the Internet — often wirelessly — to look up information such as addresses, directions (Figure 1-30a), postal codes, flights, and package shipping rates or to make telephone calls. Nearly all SOHO users communicate with others through e-mail. Many are entering the *e-commerce* arena and conduct business on the Web. Their Web sites advertise products and services and may provide a means for taking orders. Small business Web sites sometimes use a *Web cam*, which is a video camera that displays its output on a Web page. A Web cam allows SOHO users to show the world a live view of some aspect of their business.

To save money on hardware and software, small offices often network their computers. For example, the small office connects one printer to a network for all employees to share.

SOHO users often have basic business software such as word processing and spreadsheet software to assist with document preparation and finances (Figure 1-30b). They are likely to use other industry-specific types of software. A candy shop, for example, will have software that allows for taking orders and payments, updating inventory, and paying vendors.

FIGURE 1-30a (Web access)

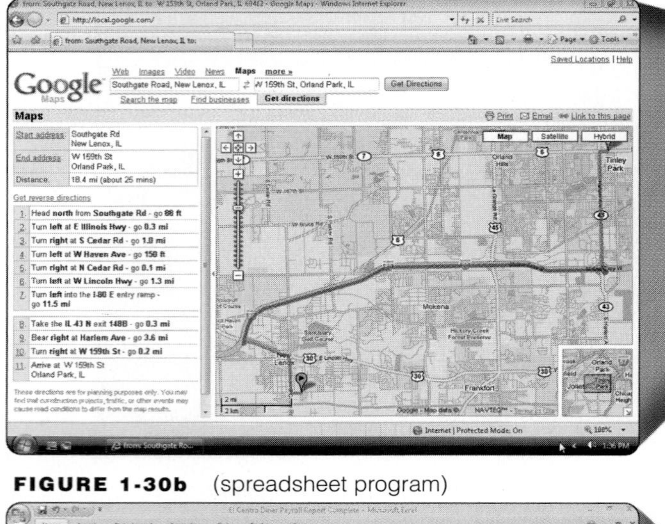

FIGURE 1-30b (spreadsheet program)

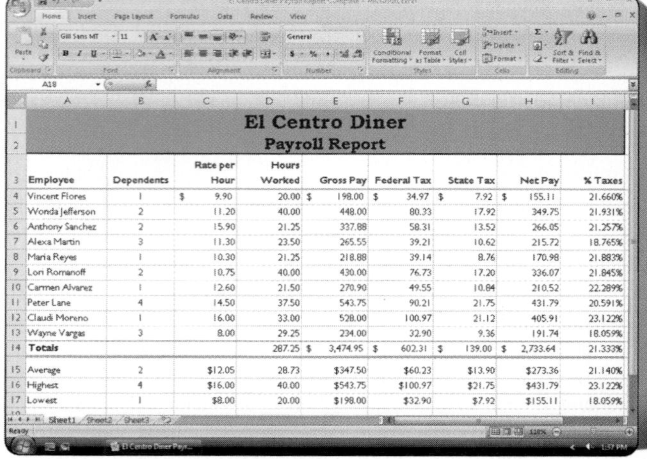

El Centro Diner
Payroll Report

Employee	Dependents	Rate per Hour	Hours Worked	Gross Pay	Federal Tax	State Tax	Net Pay	% Taxes
Vincent Flores	1	$ 9.90	20.00	$ 198.00	$ 34.97	$ 7.92	$ 155.11	21.660%
Wonda Jefferson	2	11.20	40.00	448.00	80.33	17.92	349.75	21.931%
Anthony Sanchez	2	15.90	21.25	337.88	58.31	13.52	266.05	21.257%
Alexa Martin	3	11.30	23.50	265.55	39.21	10.62	215.72	18.765%
Maria Reyes	1	10.30	21.25	218.88	39.14	8.76	170.98	21.883%
Lori Romanoff	2	10.75	40.00	430.00	76.73	17.20	336.07	21.845%
Carmen Alvarez	1	12.60	21.50	270.90	49.55	10.84	210.52	22.289%
Peter Lane	4	14.50	37.50	543.75	90.21	21.75	431.79	20.591%
Claudi Moreno	1	16.00	33.00	528.00	100.97	21.12	405.91	23.122%
Wayne Vargas	3	8.00	29.25	234.00	32.90	9.36	191.74	18.059%
Totals			287.25	$ 3,474.95	$ 602.31	$ 139.00	$ 2,733.64	21.333%
Average	2	$12.05	28.73	$347.50	$60.23	$13.90	$273.36	21.140%
Highest	4	$16.00	40.00	$543.75	$100.97	$21.75	$431.79	23.122%
Lowest	1	$8.00	20.00	$198.00	$32.90	$7.92	$155.11	18.059%

FIGURE 1-30 People with a home office and employees in small offices typically use a personal computer for some or all of their duties.

Mobile User

Today, businesses and schools are expanding to serve people across the country and around the world. Thus, increasingly more employees and students are **mobile users**, who work on a computer while away from a main office or school (Figure 1-31). Examples of mobile users are sales representatives, real estate agents, insurance agents, meter readers, package delivery people, journalists, consultants, and students.

Mobile users often have a notebook computer, Tablet PC, Internet-enabled PDA, or smart phone. With these computers and devices, the mobile user connects to other computers on a network or the Internet, often wirelessly accessing services such as e-mail and the Web. Mobile users can transfer information between their mobile device and another computer, such as one at the main office or school.

The mobile user works with basic business software such as word processing and spreadsheet software. With presentation graphics software, the mobile user can create and deliver presentations to a large audience by connecting a mobile computer or device to a video projector that displays the presentation on a full screen. Many scaled-down programs are available for mobile devices such as PDAs and smart phones.

FIGURE 1-31 Mobile users have notebook computers, Tablet PCs, PDAs, and smart phones so they can work, do homework, send messages, or connect to the Internet while away from a wired connection.

Power User

Another category of user, called a **power user**, requires the capabilities of a workstation or other type of powerful computer (Figure 1-32). Examples of power users include engineers, scientists, architects, desktop publishers, and graphic artists. Power users often work with *multimedia*, combining text, graphics, audio, and video into one application. These users need computers with extremely fast processors because of the nature of their work.

The power user's workstation contains industry-specific software. For example, engineers and architects use software to draft and design floor plans, mechanical assemblies, or vehicles. A desktop publisher uses software to prepare marketing literature such as newsletters, brochures, and annual reports. A geologist uses software to study the earth's surface. This software usually is expensive because of its specialized design.

Power users exist in all types of businesses. Some work at home. Their computers typically have network connections and Internet access.

FIGURE 1-32 This graphic artist uses a powerful computer to edit video.

Large Business User

A large business has hundreds or thousands of employees or customers that work in or do business with offices across a region, the country, or the world. Each employee or customer who uses a computer in the large business is a **large business user** (Figure 1-33).

Many large companies use the words, *enterprise computing*, to refer to the huge network of computers that meets their diverse computing needs. The network facilitates communications among employees at all locations. Users access the network of servers or mainframes through desktop computers, mobile computers, PDAs, and smart phones.

Large businesses use computers and the computer network to process high volumes of transactions in a single day. Although they may differ in size and in the products or services offered, all generally use computers for basic business activities. For example, they bill millions of customers, prepare payroll for thousands of employees, and manage thousands of items in inventory. Some large businesses use blogs to open communications among employees, customers, and/or vendors.

Large businesses typically have e-commerce Web sites, allowing customers and vendors to conduct business online. The Web site also showcases products, services, and other company information. Customers, vendors, and other interested parties can access this information on the Web. Once an order is placed, computers update inventory records to reflect goods sold and goods purchased.

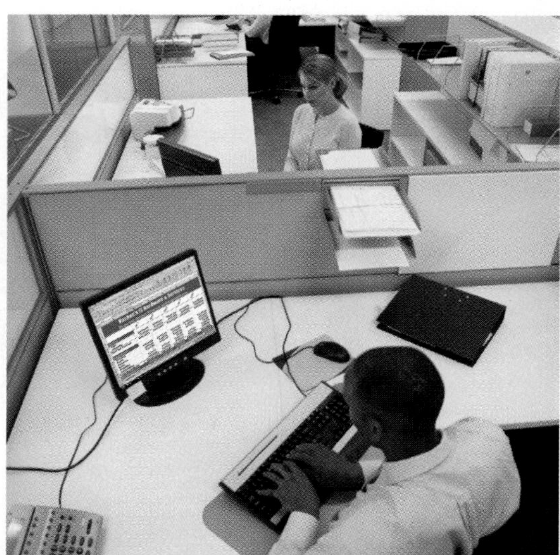

FIGURE 1-33 A large business can have hundreds or thousands of users in offices across a region, the country, or the world.

The marketing department in a large business uses desktop publishing software to prepare marketing literature. The accounting department uses software for accounts receivable, accounts payable, billing, general ledger, and payroll activities.

The employees in the *information technology (IT) department* keep the computers and the network running. They determine when the company requires new hardware or software.

Large business users work with word processing, spreadsheet, database, and presentation graphics software. They also may use calendar programs to post their schedules on the network. And, they might use PDAs or smart phones to maintain contact information. E-mail and Web browsers enable communications among employees, vendors, and customers.

Some large businesses place kiosks in public locations. A *kiosk* is a freestanding computer, usually with a touch screen (Figure 1-34). Some kiosks provide information such as maps, while others are interactive, allowing users to place orders, search records, print tickets, vote, and complete registrations.

Many employees of large businesses telecommute. **Telecommuting** is a work arrangement in which employees work away from a company's standard workplace and often communicate with the office through the computer. Employees who telecommute have flexible work schedules so they can combine work and personal responsibilities, such as child care.

FIGURE 1-34 Airline travelers check in using this self-service kiosk.

Putting It All Together

The previous pages discussed the hardware and software requirements for the home user, small office/home office user, mobile user, power user, and large business user. The table in Figure 1-35 summarizes these requirements.

CATEGORIES OF USERS

User	Hardware	Software
HOME 	• Desktop or notebook computer • PDA or smart phone • Game consoles	• Business (e.g., word processing) • Personal information manager • Personal finance, online banking, tax preparation • Web browser • E-mail, blogging, instant messaging, and chat rooms • Internet telephone calls • Photo editing • Reference (e.g., encyclopedias, medical dictionaries, road atlas) • Entertainment (e.g., games, music composition, greeting cards) • Educational (e.g., tutorials, children's math and reading software)
SMALL OFFICE/ HOME OFFICE 	• Desktop computer • PDA or smart phone • Shared network printer	• Business (e.g., word processing, spreadsheet, database) • Personal information manager • Company specific (e.g., accounting, legal reference) • Network management • Web browser • E-mail • Internet telephone calls
MOBILE 	• Notebook computer equipped with a wireless modem, or a Tablet PC • Video projector • PDA or smart phone	• Business (e.g., word processing, spreadsheet, note taking, presentation graphics) • Personal information manager • Web browser • E-mail
POWER 	• Workstation or other powerful computer with multimedia capabilities • PDA or smart phone	• Desktop publishing • Multimedia authoring • Computer-aided design • Photo, audio, and video editing • Personal information manager • Web browser • E-mail
LARGE BUSINESS	• Server or mainframe • Desktop or notebook computer • Industry-specific handheld computer • PDA or smart phone • Kiosk	• Business (e.g., word processing, spreadsheet, database, presentation graphics) • Personal information manager • Accounting • Network management • Web browser • E-mail • Blogging

FIGURE 1-35 Today, computers are used by millions of people for work tasks, school assignments, and leisure activities. Different computer users require different kinds of hardware and software to meet their needs effectively.

COMPUTER APPLICATIONS IN SOCIETY

The computer has changed society today as much as the industrial revolution changed society in the eighteenth and nineteenth centuries.

People interact directly with computers in fields such as education, finance, government, health care, science, publishing, travel, and manufacturing. In addition, they can reap the benefits from breakthroughs and advances in these fields. The following pages describe how computers have made a difference in people's interactions with these disciplines. Read Looking Ahead 1-2 for a look at the next generation of computer applications in society.

LOOKING AHEAD 1-2

Robots Perform Mundane, Dangerous Tasks

Playwright Karel Capek created the name, robot, for his humanoid machines that turned against their creators. Today, mobile, intelligent robots perform tasks typically reserved for humans in a $5 billion global market.

Tomorrow's practical and versatile robots will serve a variety of personal and industrial needs. By 2010, the expected $17 billion market should include products to care for senior citizens, transport people in major cities, and perform hundreds of thousands of mobile utility jobs, such as picking up and delivering items.

The Anna Konda is a snakelike robot built by Norway's Foundation for Industrial and Scientific Research that can maneuver over varied terrain. Engineers envision its possible uses include fighting fires, locating and bringing oxygen to earthquake victims buried under debris, and performing maintenance on underwater oil rigs. For more information, visit scsite.com/dc2008/ch1/looking and then click Robots.

Education

Education is the process of acquiring knowledge. In the traditional model, people learn from other people such as parents, teachers, and employers. Many forms of printed material such as books and manuals are used as learning tools. Today, educators also are turning to computers to assist with education (Figure 1-36).

Many schools and companies equip labs and classrooms with computers. Some schools require students to have a notebook computer or PDA to access the school's network or Internet wirelessly. To promote education by computer, many vendors offer substantial student discounts on software.

Sometimes, the delivery of education occurs at one place while the learning occurs at other locations. For example, students can take a class on the Web. Some classes are blended; that is, part of the learning occurs in a classroom and the other part occurs on the Web. More than 70 percent of colleges offer some type of distance learning classes. A few even offer entire degrees online.

FIGURE 1-36 In some schools, students have notebook computers on their desks during classroom lectures.

Finance

Many people and companies use computers to help manage their finances. Some use finance software to balance checkbooks, pay bills, track personal income and expenses, manage investments, and evaluate financial plans. This software usually includes a variety of online services. For example, computer users can track investments and do online banking. With **online banking**, users access account balances, pay bills, and copy monthly transactions from the bank's computer right into their personal computers.

Many financial institutions' Web sites also offer online banking (Figure 1-37). When using a Web site instead of finance software on your computer, all your account information is stored on the bank's computer. The advantage is you can access your financial records from anywhere in the world.

Investors often use **online investing** to buy and sell stocks and bonds — without using a broker. With online investing, the transaction fee for each trade usually is much less than when trading through a broker.

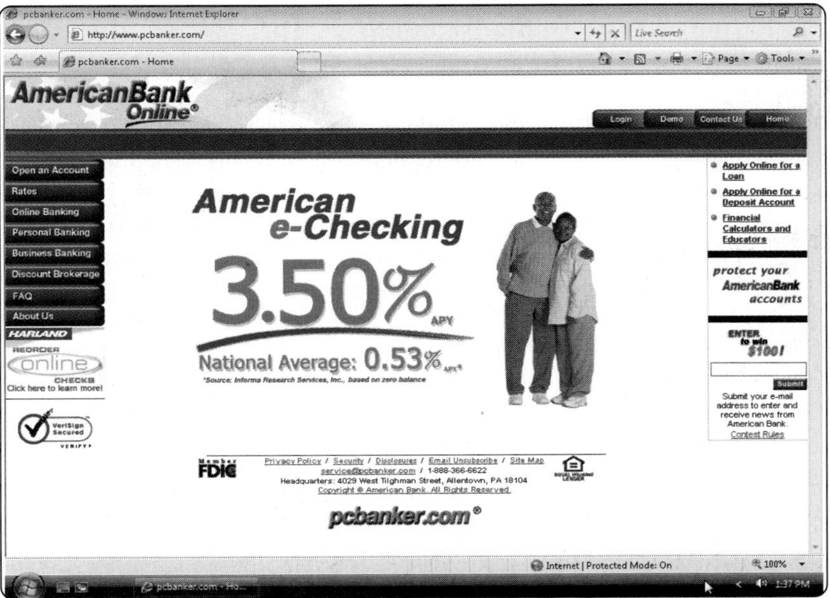

FIGURE 1-37 Many financial institutions' Web sites offer online banking.

Government

A government provides society with direction by making and administering policies. To provide citizens with up-to-date information, most government offices have Web sites. People in the United States access government Web sites to file taxes, apply for permits and licenses, pay parking tickets, buy stamps, report crimes, apply for financial aid, and renew vehicle registrations and driver's licenses.

Employees of government agencies use computers as part of their daily routine. North American 911 call centers use computers to dispatch calls for fire, police, and medical assistance. Military and other agency officials use the U.S. Department of Homeland Security's network of information about domestic security threats to help protect against terrorist attacks. Law enforcement officers have online access to the FBI's National Crime Information Center (NCIC) through in-vehicle notebook computers, fingerprint scanners, and PDAs (Figure 1-38). The NCIC contains more than 52 million missing persons and criminal records, including names, fingerprints, parole/probation records, mug shots, and other information. Read Ethics & Issues 1-5 for a related discussion.

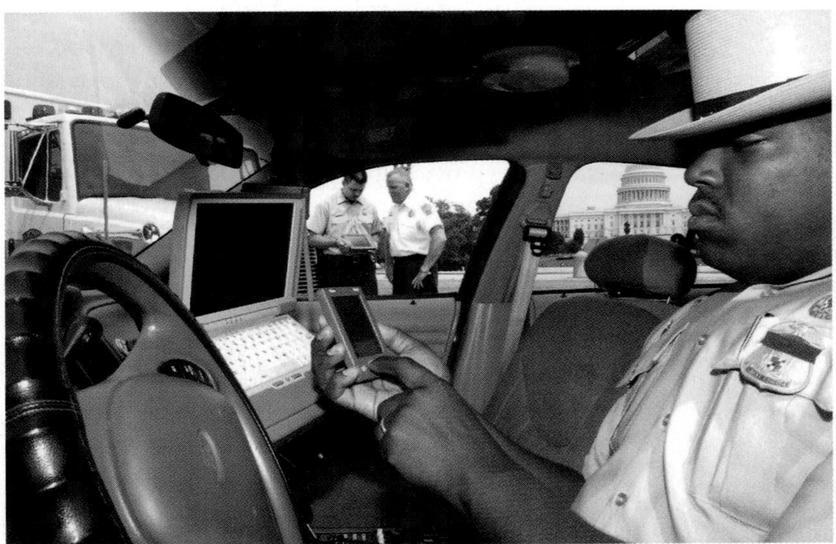

FIGURE 1-38 Law enforcement officials have in-vehicle computers and PDAs to access emergency, missing person, and criminal records in computer networks in local, state, and federal agencies.

ETHICS & ISSUES 1-5

Should the Government Be Able to Perform Surveillance on All Electronic Communications?

In the years following the terrorist attacks of September 11, 2001, the federal government began several electronic surveillance initiatives. Some activists say that the words snooping or eavesdropping better describe the programs. By law, government agencies are prohibited from spying on United States citizens. In special cases, agencies such as the CIA (Central Intelligence Agency) or NSA (National Security Agency) can obtain a warrant to monitor communications between a citizen and a foreigner. One controversial program called the Terrorist Surveillance Program allowed warrantless monitoring of electronic communications, such as phone calls and Internet communications. Another program involved the gathering of telephone records of tens of millions of Americans who were not suspects in any criminal acts. This program may have involved what some activists call fishing techniques, that is, gathering huge amounts of data and then sifting through it for patterns that may suggest illegal activity. Proponents of the programs say that they are necessary to protect the public and should be allowed in a time of war. Detractors of the programs claim that the programs are unconstitutional, are ineffective, and violate civil liberties. How much leeway should the government have when it comes to listening in on electronic communications? Why? Given the threat posed by terrorists, should the government be able to engage in warrantless searches of electronic communications? Why or why not? Who should oversee the government's behavior in these activities?

Health Care

Nearly every area of health care uses computers. Whether you are visiting a family doctor for a regular checkup, having lab work or an outpatient test, or being rushed in for emergency surgery, the medical staff around you will be using computers for various purposes:

- Hospitals and doctors use computers to maintain patient records.
- Computers monitor patients' vital signs in hospital rooms and at home.
- Computers and computerized devices assist doctors, nurses, and technicians with medical tests (Figure 1-39).
- Doctors use the Web and medical software to assist with researching and diagnosing health conditions.
- Doctors use e-mail to correspond with patients.
- Pharmacists use computers to file insurance claims.
- Surgeons implant computerized devices, such as pacemakers, that allow patients to live longer.
- Surgeons use computer-controlled devices to provide them with greater precision during operations, such as for laser eye surgery and robot-assisted heart surgery.

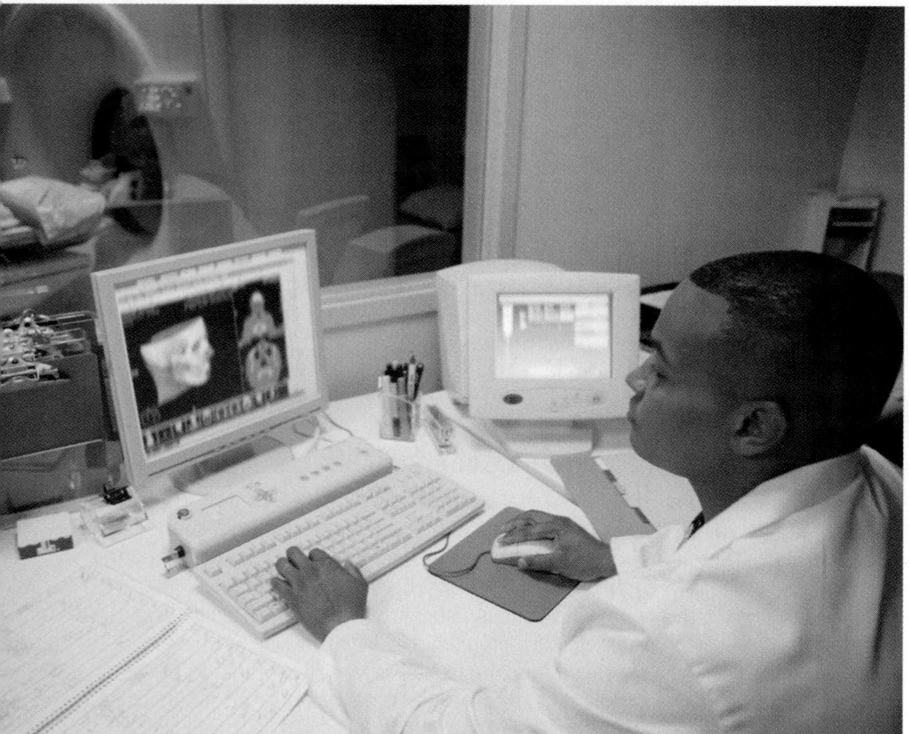

FIGURE 1-39 Doctors, nurses, technicians, and other medical staff use computers while performing tests on patients.

Many Web sites provide up-to-date medical, fitness, nutrition, or exercise information. These Web sites also maintain lists of doctors and dentists to help you find the one that suits your needs. They have chat rooms, so you can talk to others diagnosed with similar conditions. Some Web sites even allow you to order prescriptions online.

An exciting development in health care is telemedicine, which is a form of long-distance health care. Through *telemedicine*, health-care professionals in separate locations conduct live conferences on the computer. For example, a doctor at one location can have a conference with a doctor at another location to discuss a bone X-ray. Live images of each doctor, along with the X-ray, are displayed on each doctor's computer.

Science

All branches of science, from biology to astronomy to meteorology, use computers to assist them with collecting, analyzing, and modeling data. Scientists also use the Internet to communicate with colleagues around the world.

Breakthroughs in surgery, medicine, and treatments often result from scientists' use of computers. Tiny computers now imitate functions of the central nervous system, retina of the eye, and cochlea of the ear. A cochlear implant allows a deaf person to listen. Electrodes implanted in the brain stop tremors associated with Parkinson's disease. Cameras small enough to swallow — sometimes called a camera pill — take pictures inside your body to detect polyps, cancer, and other abnormalities (Figure 1-40).

A *neural network* is a system that attempts to imitate the behavior of the human brain. Scientists create neural networks by connecting thousands of processors together much like the neurons in the brain are connected. The capability of a personal computer to recognize spoken words is a direct result of scientific experimentation with neural networks.

FIGURE 1-40 HOW A CAMERA PILL WORKS

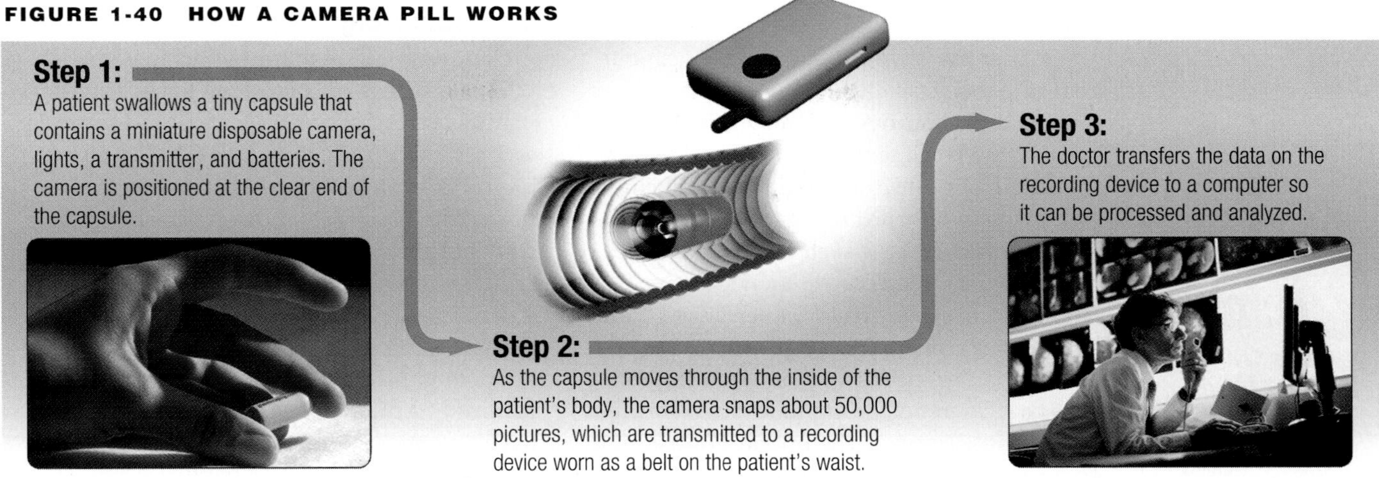

Step 1:
A patient swallows a tiny capsule that contains a miniature disposable camera, lights, a transmitter, and batteries. The camera is positioned at the clear end of the capsule.
Step 2:
As the capsule moves through the inside of the patient's body, the camera snaps about 50,000 pictures, which are transmitted to a recording device worn as a belt on the patient's waist.
Step 3:
The doctor transfers the data on the recording device to a computer so it can be processed and analyzed.

Publishing

Publishing is the process of making works available to the public. These works include books, magazines, newspapers, music, film, and video. Special software assists graphic designers in developing pages that include text, graphics, and photographs; artists in composing and enhancing songs; filmmakers in creating and editing film; and journalists and mobile users in capturing and modifying video clips.

Many publishers make their works available online (Figure 1-41). Some Web sites allow you to copy the work, such as a book or music, to your desktop computer, handheld computer, PDA, or smart phone.

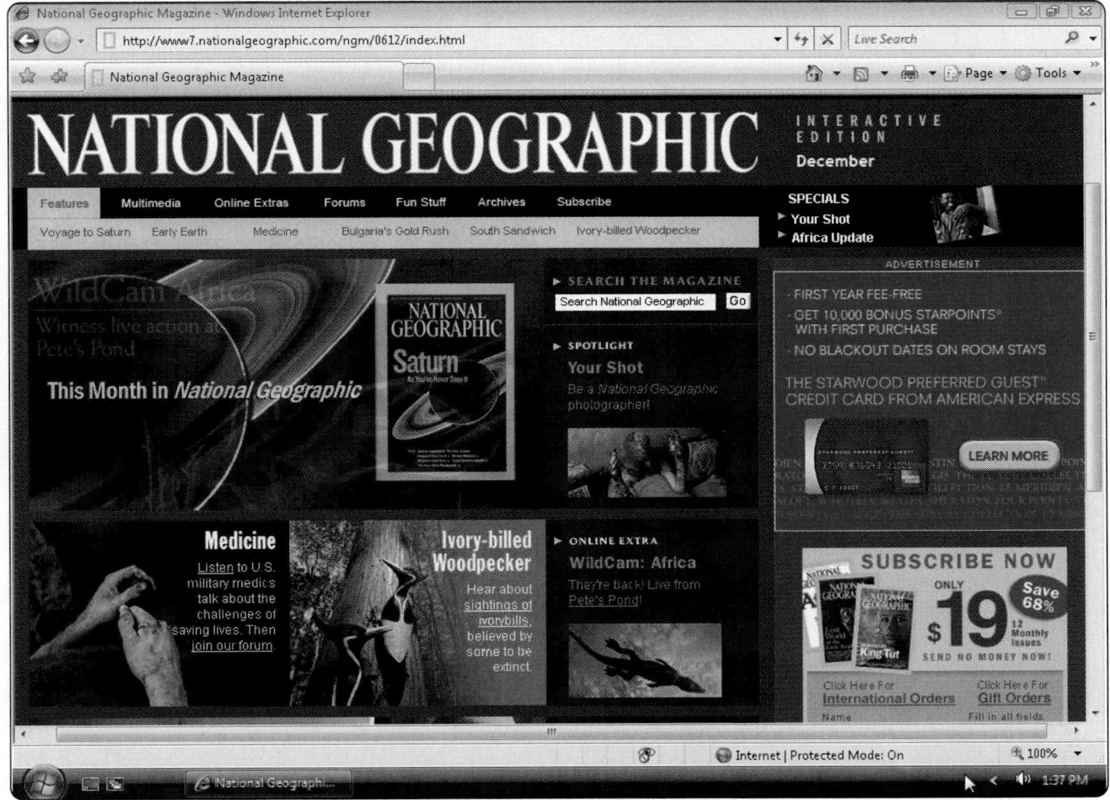

FIGURE 1-41 Many magazine and newspaper publishers make the content of their publications available online.

Travel

Whether traveling by car or airplane, your goal is to arrive safely at your destination. As you make the journey, you may interact with some of the latest technology.

Vehicles manufactured today often include some type of onboard navigation system. Many mobile devices such as PDAs and smart phones have built-in navigation systems. Some mobile users prefer to carry specialized handheld navigation devices (Figure 1-42).

In preparing for a trip, you may need to reserve a car, hotel, or flight. Many Web sites offer these services to the public. For example, you can order airline tickets on the Web. If you plan to drive somewhere and are unsure of the road to take to your destination, you can print directions and a map from the Web.

Handheld Navigation Devices

For more information, visit scsite.com/dc2008/ch1/weblink and then click Handheld Navigation Devices.

FAQ 1-8

Do home users book travel on the Web?

Yes, it is estimated that nearly 22 percent ($53 billion) of the travel industry's revenues stem from leisure travel bookings. As shown in the chart, computer users of all ages visit travel agency Web sites. For more information, visit scsite.com/dc2008/ch1/faq and then click Travel Bookings.

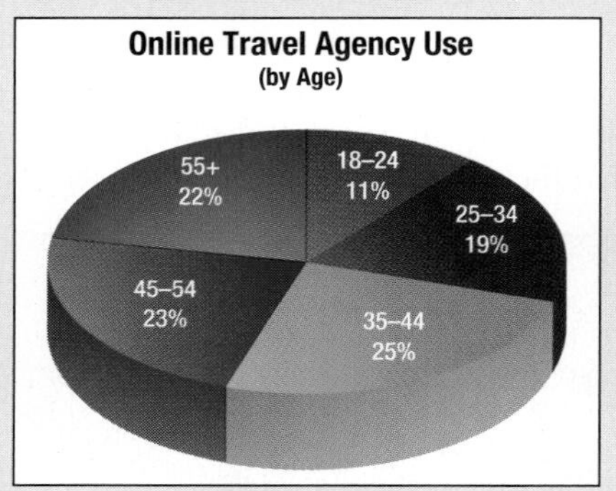

Source: The ClickZ Network

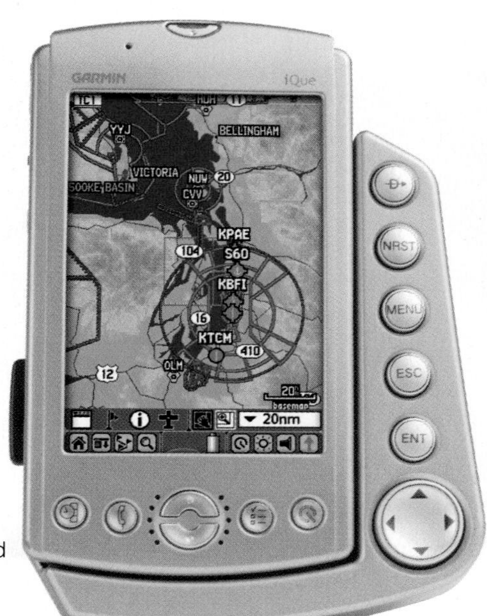

FIGURE 1-42 This handheld navigation device gives users turn-by-turn voice-prompted directions to a destination.

Manufacturing

Computer-aided manufacturing (*CAM*) refers to the use of computers to assist with manufacturing processes such as fabrication and assembly. Industries use CAM to reduce product development costs, shorten a product's time to market, and stay ahead of the competition.

Often, robots carry out processes in a CAM environment. CAM is used by a variety of industries, including oil drilling, power generation, food production, and automobile manufacturing. Automobile plants, for example, have an entire line of industrial robots that assemble a car (Figure 1-43).

Special computers on the shop floor record actual labor, material, machine, and computer time used to manufacture a particular product. The computers process this data and automatically update inventory, production, payroll, and accounting records on the company's network.

FIGURE 1-43 Automotive factories use industrial robots to weld car bodies.

Test your knowledge of pages 18 through 36 in Quiz Yourself 1-3.

QUIZ YOURSELF 1-3

Instructions: Find the true statement below. Then, rewrite the remaining false statements so they are true.

1. A desktop computer is a portable, personal computer designed to fit on your lap.
2. A personal computer contains a processor, memory, and one or more input, output, and storage devices.
3. Each large business user spends time on the computer for different reasons that include budgeting and personal financial management, Web access, communications, and entertainment.
4. A home user requires the capabilities of a workstation or other powerful computer.
5. Mainframes are the fastest, most powerful computers — and the most expensive.
6. The elements of an information system are hardware, e-mail, data, people, and the Internet.
7. With embedded computers, users access account balances, pay bills, and copy monthly transactions from the bank's computer right into their personal computers.

Quiz Yourself Online: To further check your knowledge of categories of computers, information system elements, computer users, and computer applications in society, visit scsite.com/dc2008/ch1/quiz and then click Objectives 8 – 11.

CHAPTER SUMMARY

Chapter 1 introduced you to basic computer concepts such as what a computer is, how it works, and its advantages and disadvantages. You learned about the components of a computer. Next, the chapter discussed networks, the Internet, and computer software. The many different categories of computers, computer users, and computer applications in society also were presented.

This chapter is an overview. Many of the terms and concepts introduced will be discussed further in later chapters. For a history of hardware and software developments, read the Timeline 2008 that follows this chapter.

CAREER CORNER

Personal Computer Salesperson

When you decide to buy or upgrade a personal computer, the most important person with whom you interact probably will be a personal computer salesperson. This individual will be a valuable resource to you in providing the information and expertise you need to select a computer that meets your requirements.

Computer manufacturers and retailers that sell several types of personal computers need competent salespeople. A *personal computer salesperson* must be computer literate and have a specific knowledge of the computers he or she sells. The salesperson also must have a working knowledge of computer peripherals (printers, scanners, cameras, etc.). In addition, a successful salesperson has a friendly, outgoing personality that helps customers feel comfortable. Through open-ended questions, the salesperson can determine a customer's needs and level of experience. With this information, the salesperson can choose the best computer for the customer and explain the features of the computer in language the customer will understand. Most computer salespeople also can recommend a qualified installer for your computer or qualified service technician.

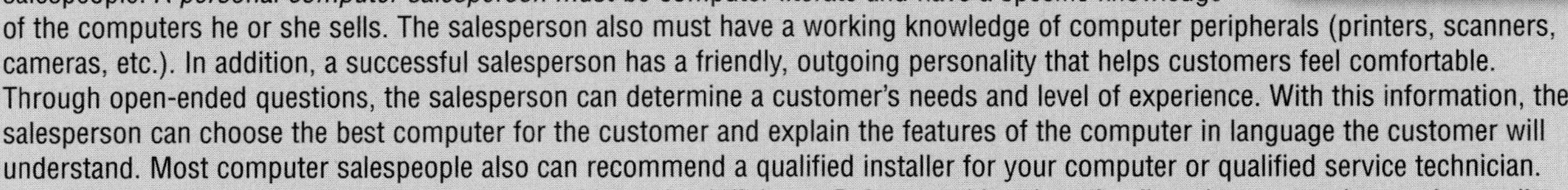

Computer salespeople typically have at least a high school diploma. Before reaching the sales floor, however, salespeople usually complete extensive company training programs. These programs often consist of self-directed, self-paced Web-training classes. Most salespeople also participate in training updates, often on a monthly basis.

Personal computer salespeople generally earn a guaranteed amount plus a commission for each sale. A computer salesperson can earn about $45,000 a year. Top salespeople can be among a company's more highly compensated employees, earning in excess of $90,000 including commissions. For more information, visit scsite.com/dc2008/ch1/careers and then click Personal Computer Salesperson.

High-Tech Talk

ANALOG VERSUS DIGITAL: MAKING THE CONVERSION

Data is processed in one of two ways: analog or digital. People generally process *analog* data — that is, continuous wave patterns. The sight and sound of a traveling subway car transmits to your eyes and ears as light and sound waves, or smooth up-and-down patterns (Figure 1-44a). A computer, by contrast, is *digital*, which means computers process data in two discrete states: positive (on, or 1) and non-positive (off, or 0) as shown in Figure 1-44b. The 1 and 0 represent the two digits used by the binary number system. While this system is at the heart of digital computing, binary digital impulses appear as long strings of 1s and 0s.

If sound and light waves are analog and a computer is digital, how does a computer record audio clips, play music, or show a movie? How can a digital computer use an analog telephone line to dial up to access the Internet?

The key lies in analog-to-digital and digital-to-analog conversions. For example, the computer allows you to record sounds and playback sounds. The computer performs these conversions to record a digital audio clip of your analog voice. The microphone, which is an analog input source, connects directly to the computer. The diaphragm in the microphone converts the analog sound waves into an analog electrical signal. This signal flows to the computer's *analog-to-digital converter (ADC)*, which converts the signal into digital data. The digital data flows to the *digital signal processor (DSP)*, compressing the data to save space. Finally, the compressed data is stored in an audio file format.

To play a recorded sound, the computer reverses the process. The processor retrieves and sends the digital data to the DSP to be decompressed. The DSP sends the decompressed digital data to the computer's *digital-to-analog converter (DAC)*, which converts the digital data back to an analog voltage for output via a speaker or headphones. In other words, a DAC takes that long binary number string of 1s and 0s and turns it into an electronic signal that the sound output devices can decode and use.

Similarly, a video card allows you to record a video or play a movie on a DVD. A camera and microphone capture and send the analog picture and sound signals to a video card. The video card's ADC converts the signals into digital data. The digital data is compressed and saved in a file format such as AVI (audio/video interleave) or MPEG (Moving Picture Experts Group). When playing a movie, the computer decompresses and separates the video and audio data. It then sends the signals to the video card's DAC. The DAC translates the digital data into analog signals and sends them to the monitor and speakers, where they are displayed as your movie.

The modem in a computer also links the analog and digital worlds. When using a dial-up modem, the computer does not transmit digital data directly across analog telephone lines. Instead, the modem converts the computer's digital signals to analog signals (called *modulation*) to be sent over telephone lines. When the analog signal reaches its destination, another modem recreates the original digital signal (*demodulation*). This allows the receiving computer to process the data. The next time you dial up using a modem, pick up the telephone. The loud, screeching noise you hear is the sound of digital data after being converted to analog sound waves. For more information, visit scsite.com/dc2008/ch1/tech and then click Analog versus Digital.

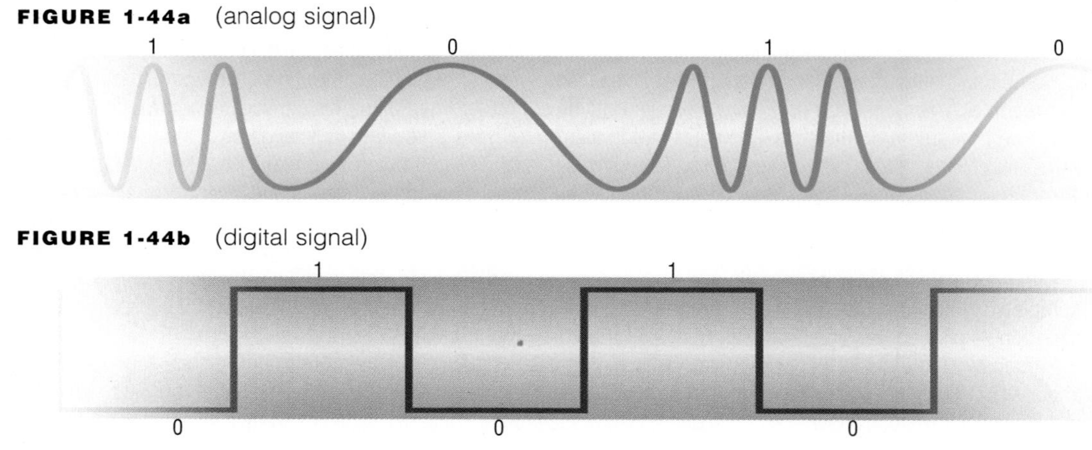

FIGURE 1-44 Analog versus digital signals.

Companies on the Cutting Edge

DELL

DIRECT BUSINESS COMPUTER MANUFACTURER

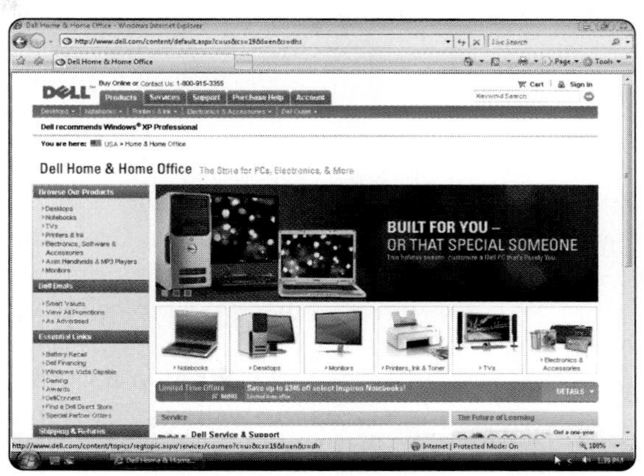

As a leading manufacturer of personal computers, *Dell* prides itself on its direct approach to computer sales. The company hosts one of the world's largest volume e-commerce Web sites where customers can configure and price computers and electronic components, order systems, and track their orders online.

Founded by Michael Dell in 1984, the company sells more computers globally than any computer company, placing it 25th on the FORTUNE 500.

The company set the industry standard for global recycling in 2006 when it provided free recycling of any Dell product for consumers throughout the world. Dell also has partnered with the National Cristina Foundation to distribute donated equipment to disabled and economically disadvantaged children and adults. For more information, visit scsite.com/dc2008/ch1/companies and then click Dell.

APPLE COMPUTER

INTRODUCING INNOVATIVE TECHNOLOGIES

Millions of computer users in more than 120 countries loyally use *Apple Computer*'s hardware and software with a passion usually reserved for sports teams and musical groups.

Steven Jobs and Stephen Wozniak founded Apple in 1976 when they marketed the Apple I, a circuit board they had developed in Jobs's garage. In 1977, Apple Computer incorporated and introduced the Apple II, the first mass-marketed personal computer. Apple introduced the Macintosh product line in 1984, which featured a graphical user interface.

Under Jobs's direction as CEO, Apple introduced award-winning desktop and notebook computers, the OS X operating system, iLife, and professional applications. The iPod is the world's most popular portable media player, and the iTunes Music Store is the number one online music store. More than 70 percent of 2007-model U.S. vehicles offer iPod integration. For more information, visit scsite.com/dc2008/ch1/companies and then click Apple Computer.

Technology Trailblazers

BILL GATES

MICROSOFT'S FOUNDER

Bill Gates, the founder of Microsoft Corporation, suggests that college students should learn how to learn by getting the best education they can. Because he is considered by many as the most powerful person in the computing industry, it might be wise to listen to him.

Gates learned to program computers when he was 13. Early in his career, he developed the BASIC programming language for the MITS Altair, one of the first microcomputers. He founded Microsoft in 1975 with Paul Allen, and five years later, they provided the first operating system, called MS-DOS, for the IBM PC. Today, Microsoft's Windows and Office products dominate the software market.

In July 2008, Gates plans to step out of his day-to-day role in the company. He will continue as chairman and advisor while devoting more time to his philanthropic efforts. For more information, visit scsite.com/dc2008/ch1/people and then click Bill Gates.

ANNE MULCAHY

XEROX CEO

Color printing and consulting services are the two areas where the Xerox Corporation can make a difference, according to *Anne Mulcahy*, the company's CEO and chairman of the board. She should know the nature of the business, having started her career with the Stamford, Connecticut-based corporation more than 30 years ago as a field sales representative.

One of Mulcahy's first decisions after landing the top job in 2001 was eliminating the corporation's tagline, "The Document Company." She believes the company's name, standing solo, speaks for itself in the printing, copying, and services worlds. Her ethical and values-based leadership decisions to revamp the company have revolved around Xerox's roots of innovation and customer care. She is a member of the boards of directors of Target Corporation, Citigroup, and Catalyst, a not-for-profit organization supporting women in business. For more information, visit scsite.com/dc2008/ch1/people and then click Anne Mulcahy.

Quizzes and Learning Games
Computer Genius
Crossword Puzzle
DC Track and Field
Practice Test
Quiz Yourself
Wheel of Terms
You're Hired!

Exercises
Case Studies
Chapter Review
Checkpoint
Key Terms
Learn How To
Learn It Online
Web Research

Beyond the Book
Career Corner
Companies
FAQs
High-Tech Talk
Looking Ahead
Making Use of the Web
Trailblazers
Web Links

Features
Chapter Forum
Install Computer
Lab Exercises
Maintain Computer
Tech News
Timeline 2008

Chapter Review

The Chapter Review section summarizes the concepts presented in this chapter. To listen to the audio version of this Chapter Review, visit scsite.com/dc2008/ch1/review. To obtain help from other students regarding any subject in this chapter, visit scsite.com/dc2008/ch1/forum and post your thoughts or questions.

1 **Why Is Computer Literacy Important?** **Computer literacy** involves having knowledge and understanding of computers and their uses. As computers become more a part of everyday life, many people believe that computer literacy is vital to success.

2 **What Is a Computer?** A **computer** is an electronic device, operating under the control of instructions stored in its own memory, that can accept data, process the data according to specified rules, produce results, and store the results for future use.

3 **What Are the Components of a Computer?** The electric, electronic, and mechanical components of a computer, or **hardware**, include input devices, output devices, a system unit, storage devices, and communications devices. An **input device** allows you to enter data or instructions into a computer. An **output device** conveys information to one or more people. The **system unit** is a case that contains the electronic components of a computer that are used to process data. A **storage device** records and/or retrieves items to and from **storage media**. A **communications device** enables a computer to send and receive data, instructions, and information to and from one or more computers.

4 **What Are the Advantages and Disadvantages of Using Computers?** Computers have the advantages of speed, reliability, consistency, storage, and communications. They perform operations at incredibly fast speeds, are dependable and reliable, consistently generate error-free results, can store enormous amounts of data, and can share processing with other computers. Disadvantages of computers relate to the violation of privacy, public safety, the impact on the labor force, health risks, and the impact on the environment.

connect
Visit scsite.com/dc2008/ch1/quiz or click the Quiz Yourself button. Click Objectives 1 – 4.

5 **What Is the Purpose of a Network?** A **network** is a collection of computers and devices connected together, often wirelessly, via communications devices and transmission media. Networks allow computers to share *resources*, such as hardware, software, data, and information.

6 **How Are the Internet and World Wide Web Used?** The **Internet** is a worldwide collection of networks that connects millions of businesses, government agencies, educational institutions, and individuals. People use the Internet to communicate with and meet other people, access news and information, shop for goods and services, bank and invest, take classes, for entertainment and leisure, download music and video, and share information. The **Web**, short for World Wide Web, is a global library of documents containing information that is available to anyone connected to the Internet.

7 **How Is System Software Different from Application Software?** **Software**, also called a **program**, is a series of instructions that tells the computer what to do and how to do it. **System software** consists of the programs that control or maintain the operations of a computer and its devices. Two types of system software are the *operating system*, which coordinates activities among computer hardware devices, and *utility programs*, which perform maintenance-type tasks usually related to managing a computer, its devices, or its programs.

Application software assists users with personal tasks. Popular application software includes Web browsers, word processing software, spreadsheet software, database software, and presentation graphics software.

connect
Visit scsite.com/dc2008/ch1/quiz or click the Quiz Yourself button. Click Objectives 5 – 7.

Chapter Review

(8) What Are the Categories of Computers? Industry experts typically classify computers in seven categories: personal computers, mobile computers and mobile devices, game consoles, servers, mainframes, supercomputers, and embedded computers. A **personal computer** is a computer that can perform all of its input, processing, output, and storage activities by itself. A **mobile computer** is a personal computer you can carry from place to place, and a **mobile device** is a computing device small enough to hold in your hand. A **game console** is a mobile computing device designed for single-player or multiplayer video games. A **server** controls access to the hardware, software, and other resources on a network and provides a centralized storage area for programs, data, and information. A **mainframe** is a large, expensive, powerful computer that can handle hundreds or thousands of connected users simultaneously and can store tremendous amounts of data, instructions, and information. A **supercomputer** is the fastest, most powerful, and most expensive computer and is used for applications requiring complex, sophisticated mathematical calculations. An **embedded computer** is a special-purpose computer that functions as a component in a larger product.

(9) What Are the Elements of an Information System? An *information system* combines hardware, software, data, people, and procedures to produce timely and useful information. People in an *information technology (IT) department* develop procedures for processing data. Following these procedures, people use hardware and software to enter the data into a computer. Software processes the data and directs the computer hardware to store changes on storage media and produce information in a desired form.

(10) What Are the Types of Computer Users? Computer users can be separated into five categories: home user, small office/home office user, mobile user, power user, and large business user. A **home user** is a family member who uses a computer for a variety of reasons, such as budgeting and personal financial management, Web access, communications, and entertainment. A **small office/home office** (*SOHO*) user is a small company or self-employed individual who works from home. SOHO users access the Internet to look up information and use basic business software and sometimes industry-specific software. **Mobile users** are employees and students who work on a computer while away from a main office or school. A **power user** uses a workstation or other powerful computer to work with industry-specific software. Power users exist in all types of businesses. A **large business user** works in a company with many employees and uses a computer and computer network to process high volumes of transactions.

(11) What Computer Applications Are Used in Society? People interact directly with computers in fields such as education, finance, government, health care, science, publishing, travel, and manufacturing. In education, students use computers and software to assist with learning or take distance learning classes. In finance, people use computers for **online banking** and **online investing**. Government offices have Web sites to provide citizens with up-to-date information, and government employees use computers as part of their daily routines. In health care, computers are used to maintain patient records, monitor patients, assist with medical tests and research, correspond with patients, file insurance claims, provide greater precision during operations, and as implants. All branches of science use computers to assist with collecting, analyzing, and modeling data and to communicate with colleagues around the world. Publishers use computers to assist in designing pages and make the content of their works available online. Many vehicles use some type of online navigation system to help people travel more quickly and safely. Manufacturers use **computer-aided manufacturing** (*CAM*) to assist with manufacturing processes.

connect
Visit scsite.com/dc2008/ch1/quiz or click the Quiz Yourself button. Click Objectives 8 – 11.

Quizzes and Learning Games
Computer Genius
Crossword Puzzle
DC Track and Field
Practice Test
Quiz Yourself
Wheel of Terms
You're Hired!

Exercises
Case Studies
Chapter Review
Checkpoint
Key Terms
Learn How To
Learn It Online
Web Research

Beyond the Book
Career Corner
Companies
FAQs
High-Tech Talk
Looking Ahead
Making Use of the Web
Trailblazers
Web Links

Features
Chapter Forum
Install Computer
Lab Exercises
Maintain Computer
Tech News
Timeline 2008

Key Terms

You should know the Primary Terms and be familiar with the Secondary Terms. Use the list below to help focus your study. To further enhance your understanding of the Key Terms in this chapter, visit scsite.com/dc2008/ch1/terms. See an example of and a definition for each term, and access current and additional information about the term from the Web.

Primary Terms

(shown in bold-black characters in the chapter)

Secondary Terms

(shown in italic characters in the chapter)

Checkpoint

Use the Checkpoint exercises to check your knowledge level of the chapter. The Beyond the Book exercises will help broaden your understanding of the concepts presented in this chapter. To complete the Checkpoint exercises interactively, visit scsite.com/dc2008/ch1/check.

Label the Figure

Identify these common computer hardware components.

a. card reader/writer (storage)
b. CD/DVD drive (storage)
c. portable media player (output)
d. digital camera (input)
e. external hard disk (storage)
f. internal hard disk drive (storage)
g. keyboard (input)
h. microphone (input)
i. modem (communications)
j. monitor (output)
k. mouse (input)
l. PC video camera (input)
m. printer (output)
n. scanner (input)
o. speaker (output)
p. system unit (processor, memory, storage)
q. USB flash drive (storage)

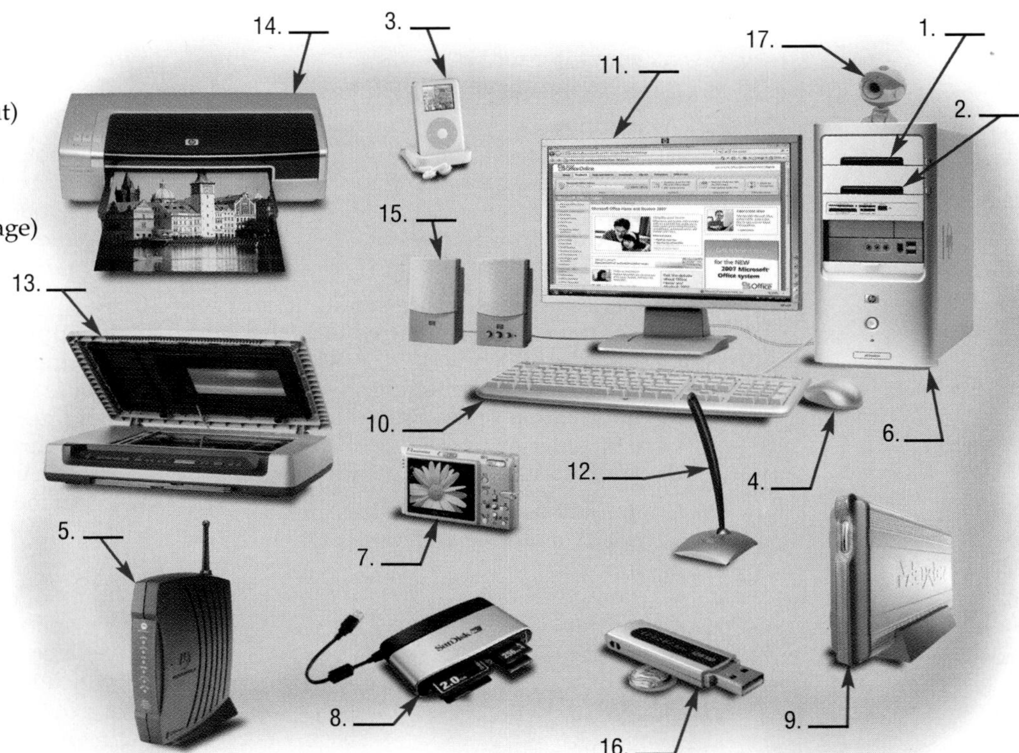

True/False

Mark T for True and F for False. (See page numbers in parentheses.)

_____ 1. Many people believe that computer literacy is vital to success in today's world. (5)

_____ 2. Hardware consists of a series of instructions that tells the computer what to do and how to do it. (7)

_____ 3. The circuitry of the system unit usually is part of or is connected to a circuit board called the server. (8)

_____ 4. The computing phrase, garbage in, garbage out, points out that the accuracy of a computer's input depends on the accuracy of the output. (10)

_____ 5. A network is a collection of computers and devices connected together, often wirelessly, via communications devices and transmission media. (11)

_____ 6. Businesses, called access providers, offer users and companies access to the Internet free or for a fee. (12)

_____ 7. A blog that contains video clips is called a video blog. (14)

_____ 8. A PDA provides personal organizer functions such as a calendar, an appointment book, an address book, a calculator, and a notepad. (21)

_____ 9. An information system consists of hardware, software, data, people, and procedures. (25)

_____ 10. Telecommuting is a work arrangement in which employees work away from a company's standard workplace and often communicate with the office through the computer. (30)

_____ 11. With online investing, the transaction fee for each trade usually is much more than when trading through a broker. (33)

Quizzes and Learning Games
Computer Genius
Crossword Puzzle
DC Track and Field
Practice Test
Quiz Yourself
Wheel of Terms
You're Hired!

Exercises
Case Studies
Chapter Review
Checkpoint
Key Terms
Learn How To
Learn It Online
Web Research

Beyond the Book
Career Corner
Companies
FAQs
High-Tech Talk
Looking Ahead
Making Use of the Web
Trailblazers
Web Links

Features
Chapter Forum
Install Computer
Lab Exercises
Maintain Computer
Tech News
Timeline 2008

Checkpoint

Multiple Choice

Select the best answer. (See page numbers in parentheses.)

1. Computer literacy involves having a knowledge and understanding of _____. (5)
   a. computer programming
   b. computers and their uses
   c. computer repair
   d. all of the above
2. A computer can _____. (6)
   a. accept data
   b. process data according to specified rules
   c. produce and store results
   d. all of the above
3. The series of input, process, output, and storage sometimes is referred to as the _____ cycle. (6)
   a. computer programming
   b. information processing
   c. data entering
   d. Web browsing
4. Commonly used _____ devices are a keyboard, a mouse, and a microphone. (7)
   a. input
   b. storage
   c. output
   d. mobile
5. A _____ controls access to the resources on a network. (11)
   a. server
   b. workstation
   c. client
   d. tower
6. Millions of people worldwide join online communities, each called a _____, that encourage members to share their interests, ideas, stories, photos, music, and videos with other registered users. (14)
   a. podcast
   b. social networking Web site
   c. vodcast
   d. blog
7. A _____ is a specific type of social networking Web site that allows users to create an online photo album and store their electronic photographs. (14)
   a. vodcast
   b. blog
   c. chat room
   d. photo sharing community
8. A _____ is recorded audio stored on a Web site that can be downloaded to a computer or portable media player. (14)
   a. podcast
   b. social networking Web site
   c. blog
   d. speaker
9. Two types of _____ are desktop computers and notebook computers. (19)
   a. embedded computers
   b. supercomputers
   c. servers
   d. personal computers
10. A _____ is a special type of notebook computer that is useful for taking notes in lectures, at meetings, and other forums where the standard notebook computer is not practical. (21)
    a. smart phone
    b. PDA
    c. game console
    d. Tablet PC
11. As smart phones and PDAs continue a trend of offering similar functions, it is becoming increasingly difficult to differentiate between the two devices, which is a trend known as _____. (22)
    a. installing
    b. mobile computing
    c. convergence
    d. telematics
12. Examples of the _____ category of computer users include engineers, scientists, architects, desktop publishers, and graphic artists. (29)
    a. power user
    b. large business user
    c. mobile user
    d. small office/home office user
13. When using _____, users access account balances, pay bills, and copy monthly transactions from a bank's computer right to their personal computers. (32)
    a. e-commerce
    b. personal finance software
    c. online banking
    d. accounting software
14. _____ is a system that attempts to imitate the behavior of the human brain. (34)
    a. Telemedicine
    b. A kiosk
    c. E-commerce
    d. A neural network

Checkpoint

Matching

Match the terms with their definitions. (See page numbers in parentheses.)

_____ 1. processor (8)
_____ 2. memory (8)
_____ 3. vodcast (14)
_____ 4. install (17)
_____ 5. execute (17)
_____ 6. stylus (21)
_____ 7. mainframe (23)
_____ 8. supercomputer (23)
_____ 9. multimedia (29)
_____ 10. kiosk (30)

a. interprets and carries out basic instructions that operate a computer
b. carry out the instructions in a computer program
c. combines text, graphics, audio, and video into one application
d. large, expensive, powerful computer that can handle hundreds or thousands of connected users simultaneously
e. fastest, most powerful computer — and the most expensive
f. collection of computers and devices connected together
g. mobile device that can connect to the Internet wirelessly
h. metal or plastic device that uses pressure to write, draw, or make selections
i. freestanding computer, usually with a touch screen
j. set up software to work with a computer and other hardware components
k. stores instructions waiting to be executed and the data needed
l. a podcast that contains video and also usually audio

Short Answer

Write a brief answer to each of the following questions.

1. How is data different from information? ____________ What is the information processing cycle? ____________
2. How can the use of computers lead to a violation of privacy? ____________ How can the use of computers cause a public safety problem? ____________
3. How is hardware different from software? ____________ What is a programmer? ____________
4. What are seven categories of computers? ____________ What determines how a computer is categorized? ____________
5. How do Web sites benefit individuals' health care? ____________ How can telemedicine benefit health care? ____________

Beyond the Book

Read the following book elements, learn more about each using the Web, and then write a brief report.

1. Ethics & Issues — What Should Be Done about Identity Theft? (10), Who Is Responsible for the Accuracy of Web Pages? (14), Do Computer Games Do More Harm than Good? (16), Who Should Monitor Online Social Networks? (27), Should the Government Be Able to Perform Surveillance on All Electronic Communications? (33)
2. Career Corner — Personal Computer Salesperson (37)
3. Companies on the Cutting Edge — Dell or Apple Computer (39)
4. FAQs (6, 8, 14, 17, 20, 27, 36)
5. High-Tech Talk — Analog versus Digital: Making the Conversion (38)
6. Looking Ahead — Medical Implants Can Enhance Lifestyles (9) or Robots Perform Mundane, Dangerous Tasks (32)
7. Making Use of the Web — Fun and Entertainment (117)
8. Picture Yourself Taking a Computer Course (2)
9. Technology Trailblazers — Bill Gates or Anne Mulcahy (39)
10. Timeline 2008 (52)
11. Web Links (7, 8, 9, 12, 14, 16, 19, 22, 26, 36)

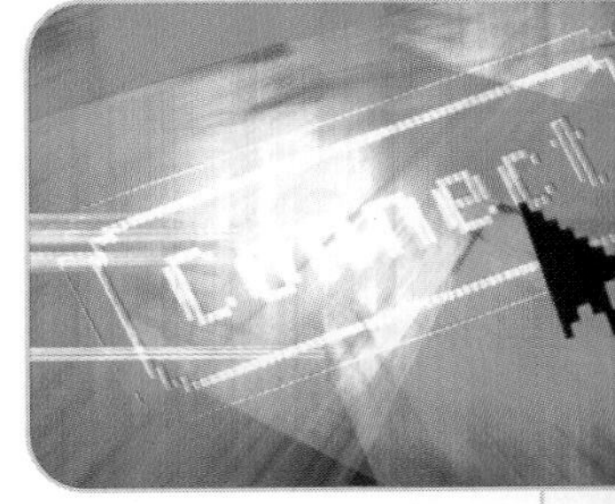

Quizzes and Learning Games
Computer Genius
Crossword Puzzle
DC Track and Field
Practice Test
Quiz Yourself
Wheel of Terms
You're Hired!

Exercises
Case Studies
Chapter Review
Checkpoint
Key Terms
Learn How To
Learn It Online
Web Research

Beyond the Book
Career Corner
Companies
FAQs
High-Tech Talk
Looking Ahead
Making Use of the Web
Trailblazers
Web Links

Features
Chapter Forum
Install Computer
Lab Exercises
Maintain Computer
Tech News
Timeline 2008

Learn It Online

Use the Learn It Online exercises to reinforce your understanding of the chapter concepts. To access the Learn It Online exercises, visit scsite.com/dc2008/ch1/learn.

1 At the Movies — Try a Free Operating System

To view the Try a Free Operating System movie, click the number 1 button. Locate your video and click the corresponding High-Speed or Dial-Up link, depending on your Internet connection. Watch the movie and then complete the exercise by answering the questions that follow. Learn how to try Ubuntu Linux operating system on your own computer without installing a thing. Explain the process by which you can try Linux's Ubuntu operating system on your computer without installing it. What is a downside to running your system from your CD-ROM?

2 Video and Audio: You Review It — Social Networking

In this chapter you learned about social networking. Click the number 2 button to view the suggested links and begin your search for videos, podcasts, or vodcasts related to social networking. Choose a video, podcast, or vodcast that discusses social networking and is of interest to you, and then write a description of its contents. Explain why you chose this piece, what you liked about it, what you disliked about it, and whether you would recommend it to a fellow student. Finish your review by giving the video, podcast, or vodcast a rating of 1-5 stars. Submit your review in the format requested by your instructor.

3 Student Edition Labs — Using Input Devices

Click the number 3 button. A new browser window will open, displaying the Student Edition Labs (screen shown in the figure below). Follow the on-screen instructions to complete the Using Input Devices Lab. When finished, click the Exit button. If required, submit your results to your instructor.

4 Student Edition Labs — Using Windows

Click the number 4 button. A new browser window will open, displaying the Student Edition Labs. Follow the on-screen instructions to complete the Using Windows Lab. When finished, click the Exit button. If required, submit your results to your instructor.

5 Practice Test

Click the number 5 button. Answer each question. When completed, enter your name and click the Grade Test button to submit the quiz for grading. Make a note of any missed questions. If required, submit your score to your instructor.

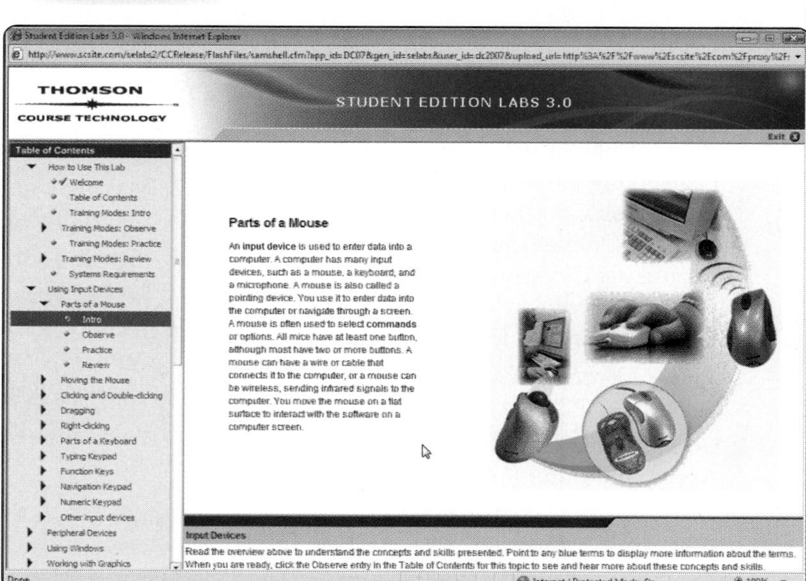

Learn It Online

6 Who Wants To Be a Computer Genius²?

Click the number 6 button to find out if you are a computer genius. Directions about how to play the game will be displayed. When you are ready to play, click the Play button. Submit your score to your instructor.

7 Wheel of Terms

Click the number 7 button to reinforce important terms you learned in this chapter by playing the Shelly Cashman Series version of this popular game. Directions about how to play the game will be displayed. When you are ready to play, click the Play button. Submit your score to your instructor.

8 DC Track and Field

Click the number 8 button to use what you have learned in this chapter to compete against other students in three track and field events. Directions about how to play the game will be displayed. When you are ready to play, click the start first event button. If required, submit your score to your instructor.

9 You're Hired!

Click the number 9 button to use what you have learned in this chapter to embark on the path to a career in computers. Directions about how to play the game will be displayed. When you are ready to play, click the begin game button. If required, submit your score to your instructor.

10 Crossword Puzzle Challenge

Click the number 10 button, and then click the Crossword Puzzle Challenge link. Directions about how to play the game will be displayed. Complete the puzzle to reinforce skills you learned in this chapter. When you are ready to play, click the Continue button. Submit the completed puzzle to your instructor.

11 Vista Exercises

Click the number 11 button. When the Vista Exercises menu appears, click the exercise assigned by your instructor. A new browser window will open. Follow the on-screen instructions to complete the exercise. When finished, click the Exit button. If required, submit your results to your instructor.

12 Learn the Web

No matter how much computer experience you have, navigating the Web for the first time can be intimidating. How do you get started? Click the number 12 button and click the links to discover how you can find out everything you want to know about the Internet.

13 Chapter Discussion Forum

Select an objective from this chapter on page 3 about which you would like more information. Click the number 13 button and post a short message listing a meaningful message title accompanied by one or more questions concerning the selected objective. In two days, return to the threaded discussion by clicking the number 13 button. Submit to your instructor your original message and at least one response to your message.

14 Google Maps

Click the number 14 button to learn how to locate businesses in your area, view a location's surroundings via satellite, and find directions from one location to another. Print a copy of the Google Maps page and then step through the exercise. If required, submit your results to your instructor.

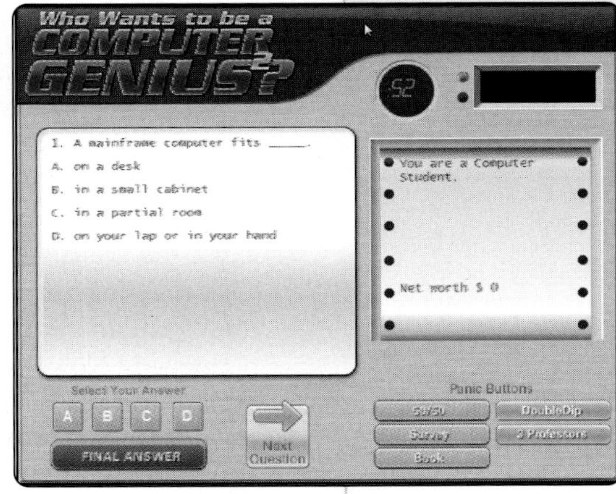

Quizzes and Learning Games
Computer Genius
Crossword Puzzle
DC Track and Field
Practice Test
Quiz Yourself
Wheel of Terms
You're Hired!

Exercises
Case Studies
Chapter Review
Checkpoint
Key Terms
Learn How To
Learn It Online
Web Research

Beyond the Book
Career Corner
Companies
FAQs
High-Tech Talk
Looking Ahead
Making Use of the Web
Trailblazers
Web Links

Features
Chapter Forum
Install Computer
Lab Exercises
Maintain Computer
Tech News
Timeline 2008

Learn How To

Use the Learn How To activities to learn fundamental skills when using a computer and accompanying technology. Complete the exercises and submit them to your instructor. To see a video of a Learn How To activity, visit scsite.com/dc2008/ch1/howto.

LEARN HOW TO 1: Start and Close an Application

An application accomplishes tasks on a computer. You can start any application by using the Start button.

Complete these steps to start the Web browser application called Internet Explorer:

1. Click the Start button ( ) at the left of the Windows taskbar on the bottom of the screen to display the Start menu.
2. Click All Programs on the Start menu to display the All Programs list (Figure 1-45).
3. Click the program name, Internet Explorer, in the All Programs list to open the Internet Explorer browser window (Figure 1-46).

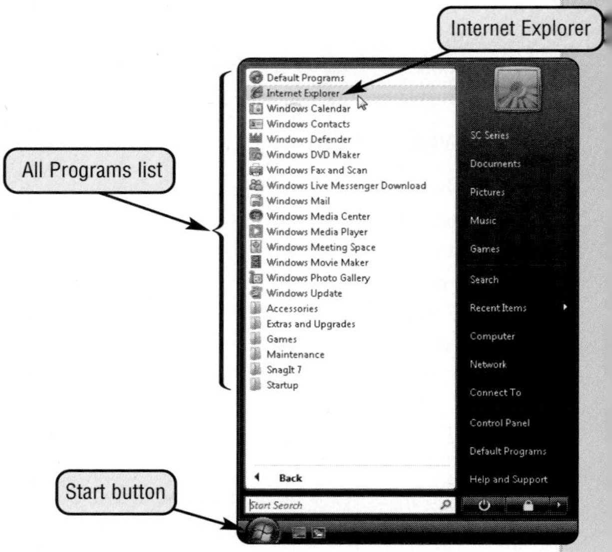

FIGURE 1-45

An item in the All Programs list might have an open folder icon next to it. When this occurs, click the item and another list will appear. Click the application name in this list to start the application. Some application names might appear on the Start menu itself. If so, click any of these names to start the corresponding application.

Below the line on the left side of the Start menu, Windows displays the names of the applications recently opened on the computer. You can start any of these applications by clicking the name of the application.

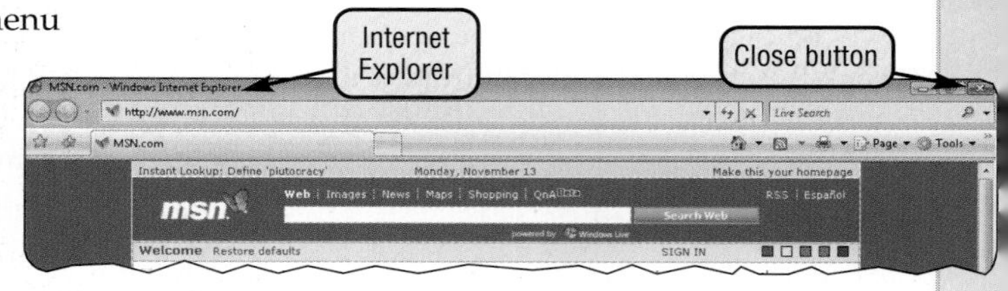

FIGURE 1-46

To close an application, click the Close button ( ) in the upper-right corner of the window. If you have created but not saved a document, Windows will ask if you want to save the document. If you do not want to save it, click the No button in the displayed dialog box. If you want to save it, refer to Learn How To number 1 in Chapter 3 on page 178.

Exercise

1. Using the Start button, start the application named WordPad found in the Accessories list of the All Programs list. WordPad is a word processing application. Type the following: `To start an application, click the application name in the All Programs list` and then type your name. Click the Print button ( ) on the toolbar. Submit the printout to your instructor.
2. Close the WordPad application. If you are asked if you want to save changes to the document, click the No button. Start the WordPad application again, type some new text, and then close the WordPad application. When the dialog box is displayed, click the Cancel button. What happened? Now, close the WordPad window without saving the document. Submit your answer to your instructor.
3. Using the Start button, start the e-mail program on the computer. What is the name of the e-mail program? In the program window, what menu names are displayed on the menu bar at the top of the window? Close the e-mail program. Submit your answers to your instructor.

As the popularity of YouTube has grown, so have video blogs, or vlogs. Vlogs allow users to video their message instead of entering text via a regular blog. The growth in the popularity of vlogs can be attributed to several factors, including the use of video portable media players. Podcasting also has increased in popularity for the same reasons. A podcast is distinguished from other digital audio formats by its capability to be downloaded automatically.

Intel introduces Clovertown, a four-core processor made for dual-processor servers. Multiplying the number of cores cuts down energy consumption for equivalent levels of performance. Intel projects that processors with tens of cores will be available by the end of the decade, and processors with hundreds of cores possible within 10 years.

CINEMANOW

CinemaNow, the leading Internet provider of premium videos, offers Burn to DVD service for movie downloads. The service allows users to legally download a complete DVD and burn one copy of the movie to a blank DVD. CinemaNow offers downloads for more than 4,000 feature-length films and television shows. TiVo introduces a new service for users of its set-top boxes to allow them to download videos from the Internet and watch them from their television sets.

Voice over Internet Protocol (VoIP) providers expand usage to include Wi-Fi telephones. The telephones enable high-quality service through a Wireless-G network and high-speed Internet connection.

Notebook computer sales continue to rise, overtaking desktop computers. Advances in technology, plus notebook computer prices reaching a low point have businesses as well as individuals rapidly replacing desktop computers with more mobile notebook computers.

2007

Microsoft releases the latest version of its flagship Office suite. New features include the most significant update to the user interface in more than a decade, including the introduction of the Ribbon, which replaces the toolbars in most of the programs, and the capability to save documents in XML and PDF formats.

Blu-ray and HD DVD increase in popularity. While a Blu-ray Disc (BD) can hold more data than an HD DVD disc, the HD DVD players are much less expensive and still have enough capacity to hold a high-definition movie. A Blu-ray disc can store about 9 hours of high-definition (HD) video on a 50 GB disc and about 23 hours of standard-definition (SD) video. HD DVD capacity is limited to a maximum of 45 GB.

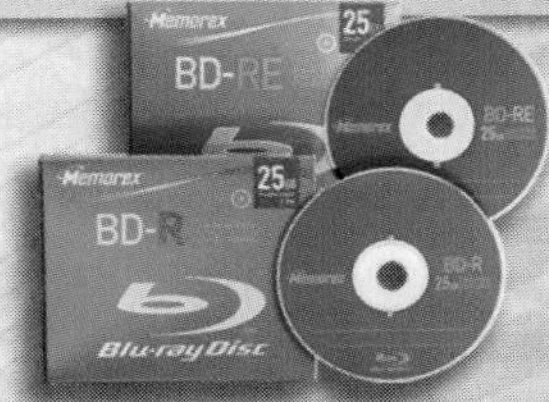

Microsoft ships the latest version of its widely used operating system, Windows Vista™. Windows Vista focuses on greatly improving security, deployment, manageability, and performance. Vista offers a Basic interface and the Aero interface, which offers several graphic features including translucent windows. Internet Explorer 7 is included with Windows Vista.

CHAPTER TWO

The Internet and World Wide Web

Picture Yourself in an Online Social Network

You have accepted a summer internship in a city about 300 miles from home. While thrilled with this opportunity, your feelings are mixed, because you will not see your friends all summer. At your going away party, everyone agrees to stay in touch over the summer via instant messaging, e-mail, and text messaging. Your friend, Derek, says, "We can do better than that on MySpace, a popular online social network." He will send an e-mail message explaining how to get started, along with some tips about using MySpace safely. Intrigued, you agree.

Once settled in your new city, you visit MySpace.com, create a profile, and designate your space as private, so that only friends and people you know can access it. You add a short video of you and your friends, digital pictures from your going away party, some music, and a personalized background. Referring to Derek's safety tips, you do not include any personal information that would make you easy to identify. When you sort MySpace members to see who lives nearby, you are excited to see Tina, an ex-classmate. You send her a request to be included in her friends on MySpace and she agrees. In her self-portrait, you see that she is in a band, which is playing in a concert this weekend. Tina alerts you to two of her friends with whom you might like to chat in a MySpace chat room and invites you to her concert. Suddenly, it seems the summer will not be long or lonely, after all.

To learn how technology enables you to communicate with people worldwide, read Chapter 2 and discover features of the Internet and World Wide Web.

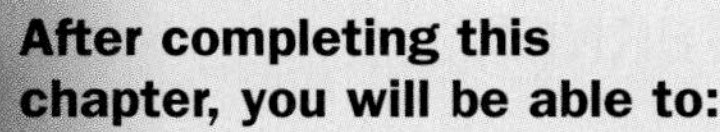

OBJECTIVES

After completing this chapter, you will be able to:

1. **Discuss the history of the Internet**
2. **Explain how to access and connect to the Internet**
3. **Analyze an IP address**
4. **Identify the components of a Web address**
5. **Explain the purpose of a Web browser**
6. **Search for information on the Web**
7. **Describe the types of Web sites**
8. **Recognize how Web pages use graphics, animation, audio, video, virtual reality, and plug-ins**
9. **Identify the steps required for Web publishing**
10. **Describe the types of e-commerce**
11. **Explain how e-mail, FTP, newsgroups and message boards, mailing lists, chat rooms, instant messaging, and Internet telephony work**
12. **Identify the rules of netiquette**

CONTENTS

THE INTERNET

One of the major reasons business, home, and other users purchase computers is for Internet access. Through the Internet, society has access to global information and instant communications. Further, access to the Internet can occur anytime from a computer anywhere: at home, at work, at school, in a restaurant, on an airplane, and even at the beach.

The **Internet**, also called the *Net*, is a worldwide collection of networks that links millions of businesses, government agencies, educational institutions, and individuals. Each of the networks on the Internet provides resources that add to the abundance of goods, services, and information accessible via the Internet.

Today, more than one billion users around the world access a variety of services on the Internet, some of which are shown in Figure 2-1. The World Wide Web and e-mail are two of the more widely used Internet services. Other services include FTP (File Transfer Protocol), newsgroups, chat rooms, instant messaging, and Internet telephony. To enhance your understanding of these services, the chapter begins by discussing the history of the Internet and how the Internet works and then explains each of these services.

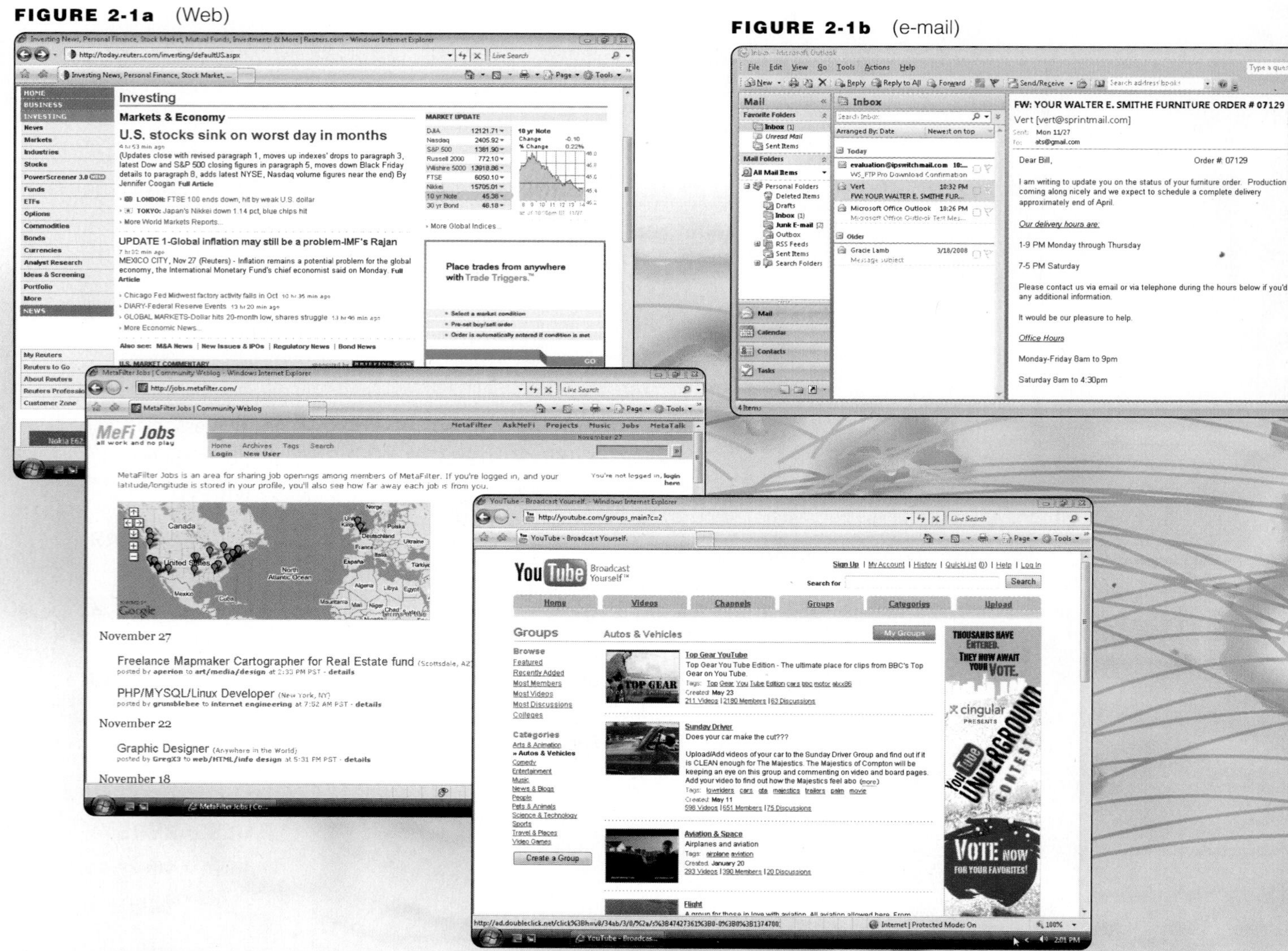

FIGURE 2-1 People around the world use a variety of Internet services in daily activities. Internet services allow users to access the Web, send e-mail messages, transfer documents and photographs, post messages, chat with a group, or have a private conversation with an online friend(s) or family member(s).

HISTORY OF THE INTERNET

The Internet has its roots in a networking project started by the Pentagon's Advanced Research Projects Agency (*ARPA*), an agency of the U.S. Department of Defense. ARPA's goal was to build a network that (1) allowed scientists at different physical locations to share information and work together on military and scientific projects and (2) could function even if part of the network were disabled or destroyed by a disaster such as a nuclear attack. That network, called *ARPANET*, became functional in September 1969, linking scientific and academic researchers across the United States.

The original ARPANET consisted of four main computers, one each located at the University of California at Los Angeles, the University of California at Santa Barbara, the Stanford Research Institute, and the University of Utah. Each computer served as a host on the network. A *host*, more commonly known today as a server, is any computer that provides services and connections to other computers on a network. Hosts often use high-speed communications to transfer data and messages over a network.

As researchers and others realized the great benefit of using ARPANET's e-mail to share data and information, ARPANET underwent phenomenal growth. By 1984, ARPANET had more than 1,000 individual computers linked as hosts. Today, more than 350 million hosts connect to the Internet.

Some organizations connected entire networks to ARPANET to take advantage

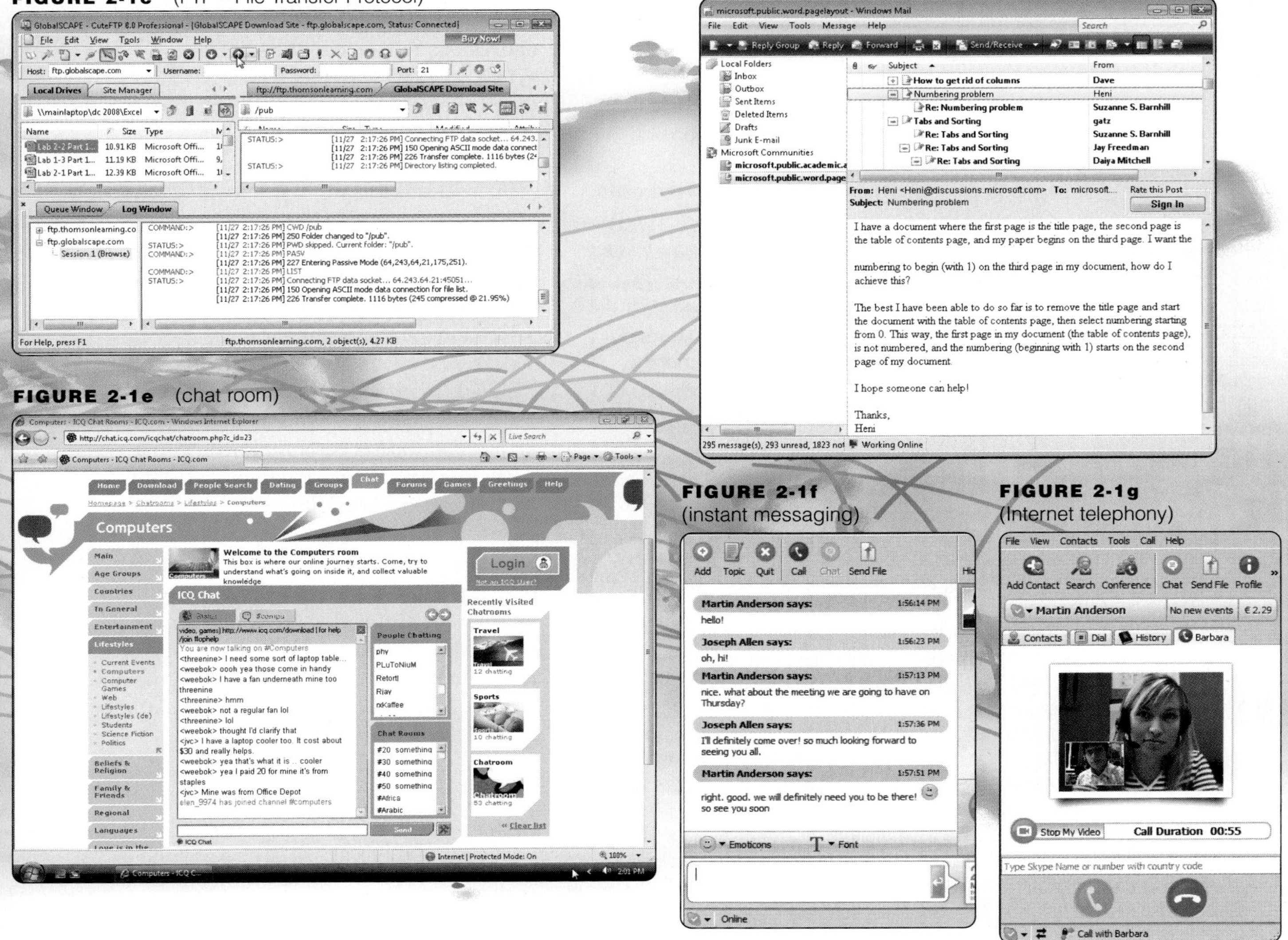

FIGURE 2-1c (FTP – File Transfer Protocol)

FIGURE 2-1d (newsgroup)

FIGURE 2-1e (chat room)

FIGURE 2-1f (instant messaging)

FIGURE 2-1g (Internet telephony)

of the high-speed communications it offered. In 1986, the National Science Foundation (NSF) connected its huge network of five supercomputer centers, called *NSFnet*, to ARPANET. This configuration of complex networks and hosts became known as the Internet.

Until 1995, NSFnet handled the bulk of the communications activity, or **traffic**, on the Internet. In 1995, NSFnet terminated its network on the Internet and resumed its status as a research network.

Today, the Internet consists of many local, regional, national, and international networks. Numerous corporations, commercial firms, and other companies such as IBM provide networks to handle the Internet traffic. Both public and private organizations own networks on the Internet. These networks, along with telephone companies such as Verizon and AT&T, cable and satellite companies, and the government, all contribute toward the internal structure of the Internet. Read Looking Ahead 2-1 for a look at the next generation of the Internet.

Even as the Internet grows, it remains a public, cooperative, and independent network. Each organization on the Internet is responsible only for maintaining its own network. No single person, company, institution, or government agency controls or owns the Internet. The *World Wide Web Consortium* (W3C), however, oversees research and sets standards and guidelines for many areas of the Internet. The mission of the W3C is to contribute to the growth of the Web. Nearly 400 organizations from around the world are members of the W3C. They advise, define standards, and address other issues.

WEB LINK 2-1

W3C

For more information, visit scsite.com/dc2008/ch2/weblink and then click W3C.

LOOKING AHEAD 2-1

Internet Speeds into the Future

The Internet of the future will be much larger and faster. According to some Internet experts, in the next 20 years, Web surfers will be able to browse more than 250 million Web sites.

This increase in volume will be based, in part, on *Internet2*. This not-for-profit project connects more than 206 educational and 60 research institutions via a high-speed private network. When used solely as a research tool, Internet2 applications process massive amounts of data, such as linking observatories atop Hawaii's tallest mountains and video conferences from 20 remote sites across the world.

Schools have used the Internet2 for interactive video conferences linking authors with readers, music composers with conductors, and operating room doctors with medical students. For more information, visit scsite.com/dc2008/ch2/looking and then click Internet2.

HOW THE INTERNET WORKS

Data sent over the Internet travels via many networks and communications media. The following sections present various ways to connect to these networks on the Internet.

Connecting to the Internet

Employees and students often connect to the Internet through a business or school network. In this case, the computers usually are part of a network that connects to an Internet access provider through a high-speed connection.

Some homes use dial-up access to connect to the Internet. **Dial-up access** takes place when the modem in your computer uses a standard telephone line to connect to the Internet. A dial-up connection, however, is slow-speed technology.

Many home and small business users are opting for higher-speed *broadband* Internet connections through DSL, cable television networks, radio signals, or satellite.

- **DSL** (digital subscriber line) is a technology that provides high-speed Internet connections using regular copper telephone lines.
- A **cable modem** allows access to high-speed Internet services through the cable television network.
- *Fixed wireless* high-speed Internet connections use a dish-shaped antenna on your house or business to communicate with a tower location via radio signals.
- A *Wi-Fi* (wireless fidelity) network uses radio signals to provide Internet connections to wireless computers and devices.
- A *satellite modem* communicates with a satellite dish to provide high-speed Internet connections via satellite.

In most cases, broadband Internet access is always on. That is, it is connected to the Internet the entire time the computer is running. With dial-up access, by contrast, you must establish the connection to the Internet. Usually a modem dials the telephone number to the Internet access provider.

Mobile users access the Internet using a variety of technologies. Most hotels and airports provide dial-up or broadband Internet connections. Wireless Internet access technologies, such as Wi-Fi networks, allow mobile users to connect easily to the Internet with notebook computers, Tablet PCs, PDAs, and smart phones while away from a telephone, cable, or other wired connection. Many public locations, such as airports, hotels, schools, shopping malls, and coffee shops, are *hot spots* that provide Wi-Fi Internet connections to users with mobile computers or devices. Some cities and counties provide free Wi-Fi Internet connections to all residents.

Access Providers

An **access provider** is a business that provides individuals and companies access to the Internet free or for a fee. For example, some Wi-Fi networks provide free access while others charge a per use fee. Other access providers often charge a fixed amount for an Internet connection, usually about $7 to $25 per month for dial-up, $13 to $40 for DSL, $20 to $45 for cable, $35 to $70 for fixed wireless, and $60 to $99 for satellite. To attract more customers, some access providers also offer Web publishing services. Web publishing is discussed later in the chapter.

Users access the Internet through regional or national ISPs, online service providers, and wireless Internet service providers (Figure 2-2).

FAQ 2-1

Is bandwidth important?

Yes. *Bandwidth* is a measure of how fast data and information travel over transmission media. Thus, higher-speed broadband Internet connections have a higher bandwidth than dial-up connections. For more information, visit scsite.com/dc2008/ch2/faq and then click Bandwidth.

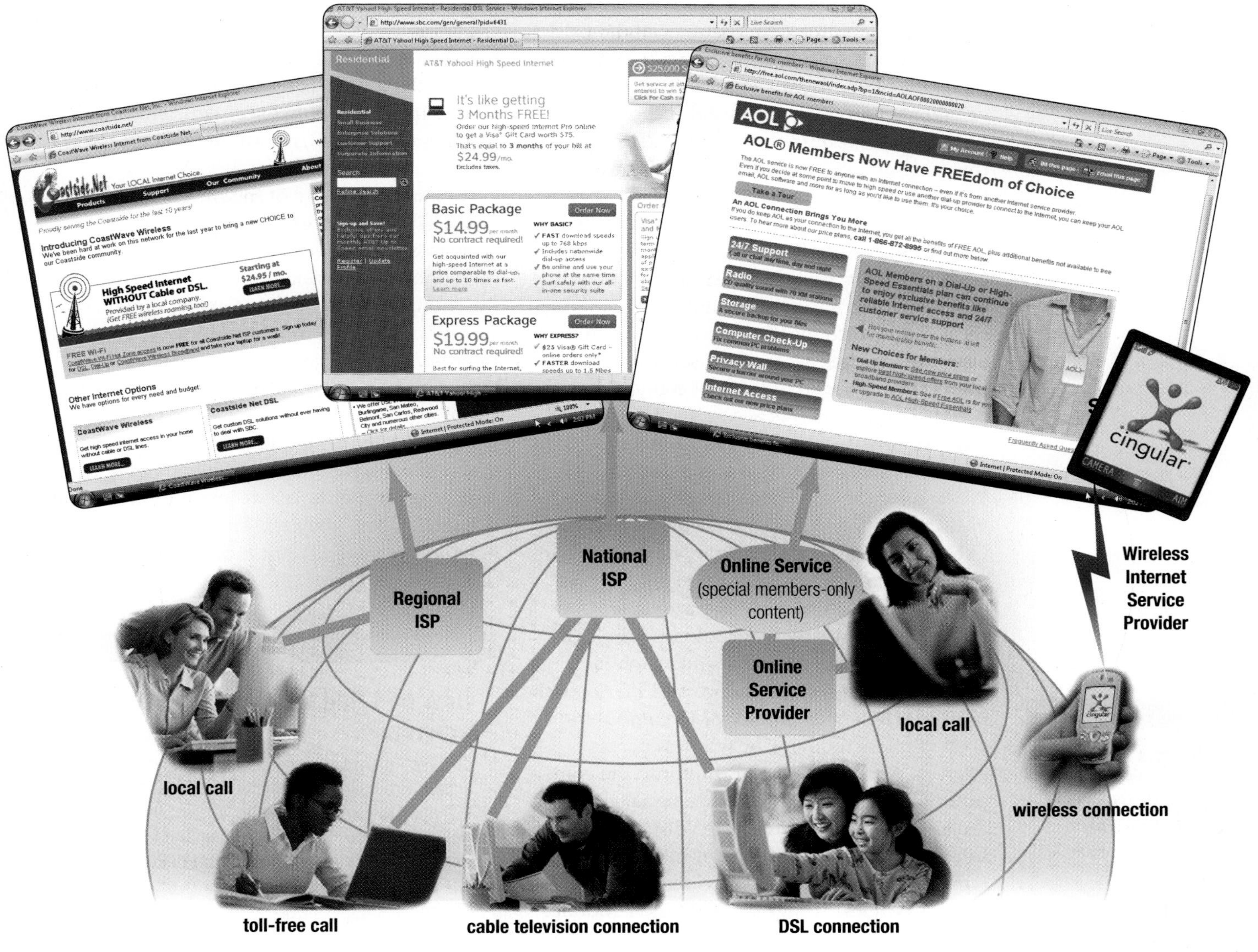

FIGURE 2-2 Common ways to access the Internet are through a regional or national Internet service provider, an online service provider, or a wireless Internet service provider.

An **ISP** (**Internet service provider**) is a regional or national access provider. A *regional ISP* usually provides Internet access to a specific geographic area. A *national ISP* is a business that provides Internet access in cities and towns nationwide. For dial-up access, some national ISPs provide both local and toll-free telephone numbers. Due to their larger size, national ISPs usually offer more services and have a larger technical support staff than regional ISPs. Examples of national ISPs are AT&T Worldnet Service and EarthLink.

In addition to providing Internet access, an **online service provider** (**OSP**) also has many members-only features. These features include special content and services such as news, weather, legal information, financial data, hardware and software guides, games, travel guides, e-mail, photo communities, online calendars, and instant messaging. Some even have their own built-in Web browser. The fees for using an OSP sometimes are slightly higher than fees for an ISP. The two more popular OSPs are AOL (America Online) and MSN (Microsoft Network). AOL differs from many OSPs in that it provides gateway functionality to the Internet, meaning it regulates the Internet services to which members have access. AOL also provides free access to its services to any user with a broadband Internet connection.

With dial-up Internet access, the telephone number you dial connects you to an access point on the Internet, called a *point of presence* (*POP*). When selecting an ISP or OSP, ensure it provides at least one local POP telephone number. Otherwise, long-distance telephone charges will apply for the time you connect to the Internet.

A **wireless Internet service provider** (*WISP*) is a company that provides wireless Internet access to computers and mobile devices, such as smart phones and PDAs, with built-in wireless capability or to computers with wireless modems or wireless access devices. An antenna on or built into the computer or device typically sends signals through the airwaves to communicate with a wireless Internet service provider. Some examples of wireless Internet service providers include Boingo Wireless, Cingular Wireless, T-Mobile, and Verizon Wireless.

WEB LINK 2-2

Wireless Internet Service Providers

For more information, visit scsite.com/dc2008/ch2/weblink and then click Wireless Internet Service Providers.

FAQ 2-2

Is free Internet access becoming more popular?

Free Internet access is growing in popularity. Internet access providers such as NetZero and AOL provide free Internet access and rely on revenue from advertisers to cover the costs associated with providing the free Internet service. For this reason, customers using a free Internet access provider may notice more advertisements. For more information, visit scsite.com/dc2008/ch2/faq and then click Free Internet Access.

How Data Travels the Internet

Computers connected to the Internet work together to transfer data and information around the world using servers and clients. On the Internet, your computer is a client that can access data, information, and services on a variety of servers.

The inner structure of the Internet works much like a transportation system. Just as interstate highways connect major cities and carry the bulk of the automotive traffic across the country, several main transmission media carry the heaviest amount of traffic on the Internet. These major carriers of network traffic are known collectively as the *Internet backbone.*

In the United States, the transmission media that make up the Internet backbone exchange data at several different major cities across the country. That is, they transfer data from one network to another until it reaches its final destination (Figure 2-3).

FAQ 2-3

How do I find the right access provider?

The Web provides many comprehensive lists of access providers. These lists often use the terms ISP and OSP interchangeably. One of the more popular lists on the Web is called The List. For more information, visit scsite.com/dc2008/ch2/faq and then click The List.

FIGURE 2-3 HOW A HOME USER'S DATA MIGHT TRAVEL THE INTERNET USING A CABLE MODEM CONNECTION

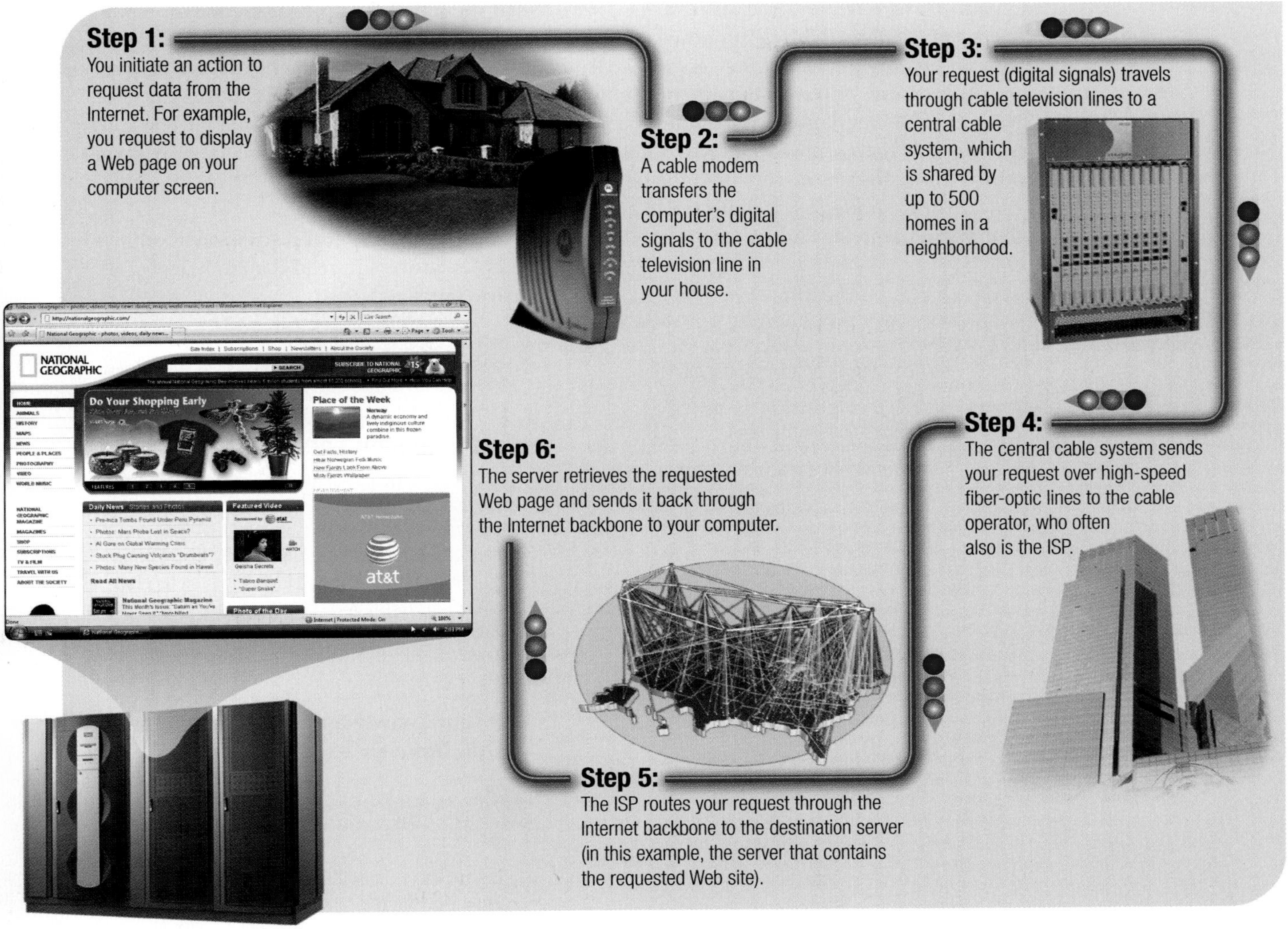

Step 1:
You initiate an action to request data from the Internet. For example, you request to display a Web page on your computer screen.
Step 2:
A cable modem transfers the computer's digital signals to the cable television line in your house.
Step 3:
Your request (digital signals) travels through cable television lines to a central cable system, which is shared by up to 500 homes in a neighborhood.
Step 4:
The central cable system sends your request over high-speed fiber-optic lines to the cable operator, who often also is the ISP.
Step 5:
The ISP routes your request through the Internet backbone to the destination server (in this example, the server that contains the requested Web site).
Step 6:
The server retrieves the requested Web page and sends it back through the Internet backbone to your computer.
NATIONAL GEOGRAPHIC

Internet Addresses

The Internet relies on an addressing system much like the postal service to send data to a computer at a specific destination. An **IP address**, short for *Internet Protocol address*, is a number that uniquely identifies each computer or device connected to the Internet. The IP address usually consists of four groups of numbers, each separated by a period. The number in each group is between 0 and 255. For example, the numbers 216.239.39.99 are an IP address. In general, the first portion of each IP address identifies the network and the last portion identifies the specific computer.

These all-numeric IP addresses are difficult to remember and use. Thus, the Internet supports the use of a text name that represents one or more IP addresses. A **domain name** is the text version of an IP address. Figure 2-4 shows an IP address and its associated domain name. As with an IP address, the components of a domain name are separated by periods.

In Figure 2-4, the com portion of the domain name is called the top-level domain. Every domain name contains a *top-level domain (TLD)*, which is the last section of the domain name. A generic TLD (*gTLD*), such as the one in Figure 2-4, identifies the type of organization associated with the domain. *Dot-com* is the term sometimes used to describe organizations with a TLD of com.

IP address → 216.239.39.99
Domain name → www.google.com
top-level domain

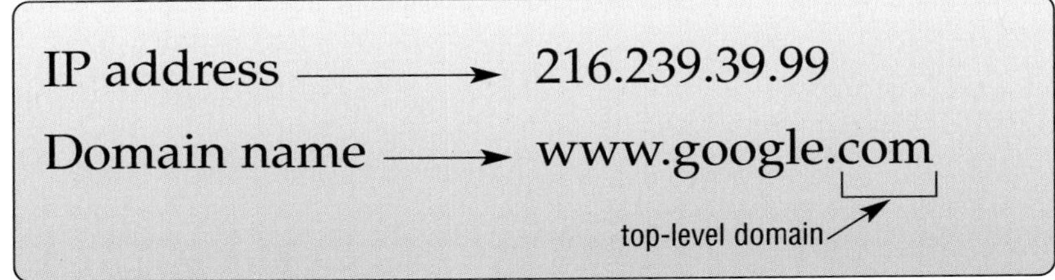

FIGURE 2-4 The IP address and domain name for the Google Web site.

The group that assigns and controls top-level domains is the *Internet Corporation for Assigned Names and Numbers (ICANN* pronounced EYE-can). Figure 2-5 lists some generic TLDs. For international Web sites outside the United States, the domain name also includes a country code TLD (*ccTLD*), which is a two-letter country code, such as au for Australia or fr for France. For example, www.philips.com.au is the domain name for Philips Australia.

The *domain name system (DNS)* is the method that the Internet uses to store domain names and their corresponding IP addresses. When you specify a domain name, a **DNS server** translates the domain name to its associated IP address so data can be routed to the correct computer. A DNS server is an Internet server that usually is associated with an Internet access provider.

For a more technical discussion about Internet addresses, read the High-Tech Talk article on page 102.

EXAMPLES OF GENERIC TOP-LEVEL DOMAINS

Original Generic TLD	Intended Purpose
com	Commercial organizations, businesses, and companies
edu	Educational institutions
gov	Government agencies
mil	Military organizations
net	Network providers and commercial companies
org	Nonprofit organizations
Newer Generic TLD	**Intended Purpose**
aero	Aviation community members
biz	Businesses of all sizes
cat	Catalan cultural community
coop	Business cooperatives such as credit unions and rural electric co-ops
info	Businesses, organizations, or individuals providing general information
jobs	Employment or human resource businesses
mobi	Delivery and management of mobile Internet services
museum	Accredited museums
name	Individuals or families
pro	Certified professionals such as doctors, lawyers, and accountants
tel	Internet communications
travel	Travel industry

FIGURE 2-5 In addition to the TLDs listed above, the Internet Corporation for Assigned Names and Numbers (ICANN) continually evaluates proposals for new TLDs.

FAQ 2-4

How does a person or company get a domain name?

For top-level domains such as biz, com, info, name, net, and org, you register for a domain name from a *registrar*, which is an organization that sells and manages domain names. In addition to determining prices and policies for domain name registration, a registrar may offer additional services such as Web site hosting. For more information, visit scsite.com/dc2008/ch2/faq and then click Registrar.

Test your knowledge of pages 68 through 74 in Quiz Yourself 2-1.

QUIZ YOURSELF 2-1

Instructions: Find the true statement below. Then, rewrite the remaining false statements so they are true.

1. An access provider is a business that provides individuals and companies access to the Internet free or for a fee.
2. A WISP is a number that uniquely identifies each computer or device connected to the Internet.
3. An IP address, such as www.google.com, is the text version of a domain name.
4. Dial-up access takes place when the modem in your computer uses the cable television network to connect to the Internet.
5. The World Wide Web Consortium (W3C) oversees research and owns the Internet.

Quiz Yourself Online: To further check your knowledge of Internet history, accessing and connecting to the Internet, and Internet addresses, visit scsite.com/dc2008/ch2/quiz and then click Objectives 1 – 3.

THE WORLD WIDE WEB

Although many people use the terms World Wide Web and Internet interchangeably, the World Wide Web actually is a service of the Internet. While the Internet was developed in the late 1960s, the World Wide Web emerged in the early 1990s. Since then, it has grown phenomenally to become one of the more widely used Internet services.

The **World Wide Web** (*WWW*), or **Web**, consists of a worldwide collection of electronic documents. Each electronic document on the Web is called a **Web page**, which can contain text, graphics, audio, and video. Additionally, Web pages usually have built-in connections to other documents.

Some Web pages are static (fixed); others are dynamic (changing). Visitors to a *static Web page* all see the same content. With a *dynamic Web page*, by contrast, visitors can customize some or all of the viewed content such as desired stock quotes, weather for a region, or ticket availability for flights.

A **Web site** is a collection of related Web pages and associated items, such as documents and pictures, stored on a Web server. A **Web server** is a computer that delivers requested Web pages to your computer. The same Web server can store multiple Web sites. Some industry experts use the terms **Web 2.0** and *participatory Web* to refer to Web sites that allow users to modify Web site content, provide a means for users to share personal information, and have application software built into the site for visitors to use.

The following pages discuss how to browse the Web, use a Web address, search for information on the Web, and recognize types of Web sites. Also discussed are multimedia on the Web and Web publishing.

Browsing the Web

A **Web browser**, or **browser**, is application software that allows users to access and view Web pages. To browse the Web, you need a computer that is connected to the Internet and has a Web browser. The more widely used Web browsers for personal computers are Internet Explorer, Netscape, Firefox, Opera, and Safari.

With an Internet connection established, you start a Web browser. The browser retrieves and displays a starting Web page, sometimes called the browser's home page. Figure 2-6 shows how a Web browser displays a home page. The initial home page that is displayed

FIGURE 2-6 HOW A WEB BROWSER DISPLAYS A HOME PAGE

Step 1:
Click the Web browser program name to start the Web browser software.

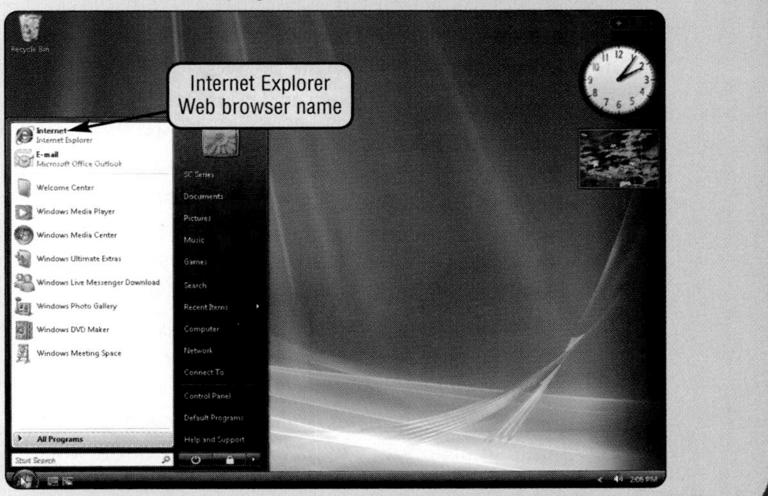

Step 2:
Behind the scenes, the Web browser looks up its home page setting. For illustration purposes only, the screen below shows the home page setting is msn.com.

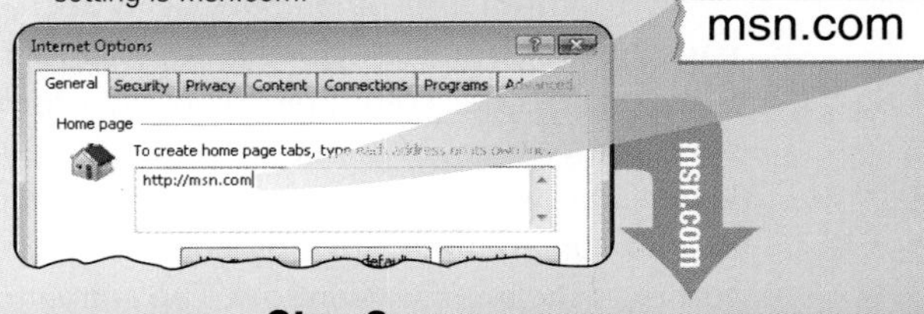

Step 3:
The Web browser communicates with a server maintained by your Internet access provider. The server translates the domain name of the home page to an IP address and then sends the IP address to your computer.

207.68.172.234

Step 4:
The Web browser uses the IP address to contact the Web server associated with the home page and then requests the home page from the server. The Web server sends the home page to the Web browser, which formats the page for display on your screen.

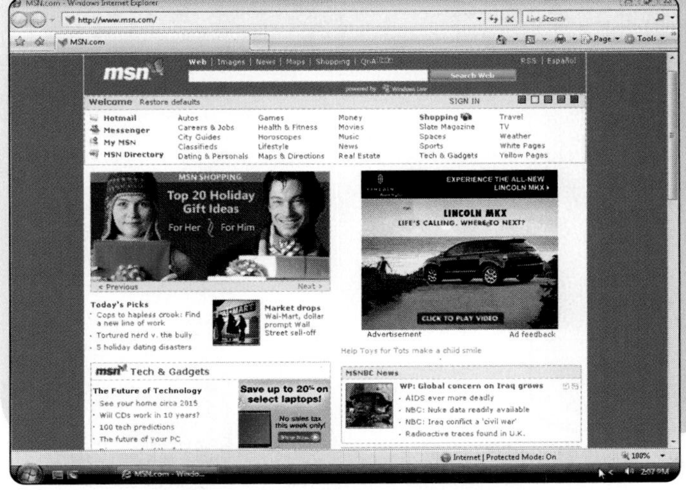

is one selected by your Web browser. You can change your browser's home page at anytime.

The more common usage of the term, **home page**, refers to the first page that a Web site displays. Similar to a book cover or a table of contents for a Web site, the home page provides information about the Web site's purpose and content. Often it provides connections to other documents, Web pages, or Web sites. Many Web sites allow you to personalize the home page so it contains areas of interest to you.

Many current Web browsers support *tabbed browsing*, where the top of the browser displays a tab (similar to a file folder tab) for each Web page you open. To move from one open Web page to another, you *click* the tab in the Web browser; that is, point to the tab and then press the left mouse button.

Internet-enabled mobile devices such as PDAs and smart phones use a special type of browser, called a *microbrowser*, which is designed for their small screens and limited computing power. Many Web sites design Web pages specifically for display on a microbrowser (Figure 2-7).

For a computer or mobile device to display a Web page, the page must be downloaded. **Downloading** is the process of a computer receiving information, such as a Web page, from a server on the Internet. While a browser downloads a Web page, it typically displays an animated logo or icon in the top-right corner of the browser window. The animation stops when the download is complete. Depending on the speed of your Internet connection and the amount of graphics involved, a Web page download can take from a few seconds to several minutes.

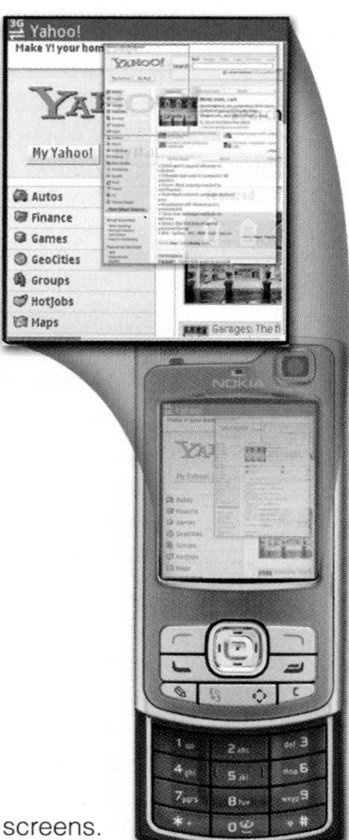

FIGURE 2-7 Sample microbrowser screens.

Web Addresses

A Web page has a unique address, called a **URL** (*Uniform Resource Locator*) or **Web address**. For example, the home page for the US National Parks Travel Guide Web site has http://www.us-parks.com as its Web address. A Web browser retrieves a Web page using its Web address.

If you know the Web address of a Web page, you can type it in the Address box at the top of the browser window. For example, if you type the Web address http://www.us-parks.com/grand_canyon/scenic_vistas.html in the Address box and then press the ENTER key, the browser downloads and displays the Web page shown in Figure 2-8.

A Web address consists of a protocol, domain name, and sometimes the path to a specific Web page or location on a Web page. Many Web page addresses begin with http://. The *http*, which stands for *Hypertext Transfer Protocol*, is a set of rules that defines how pages transfer on the Internet. The first portion of the domain name identifies the type of Internet server. For example, www indicates a Web server.

To help minimize errors, many browsers and Web sites do not require you enter the http:// portion of the Web address. For example, typing www.us-parks.com/grand_canyon/scenic_vistas.html, instead of the entire address, still accesses the Web site. If you enter an incorrect Web address, the browser may display a list of similar addresses from which you can select. Many Web sites also allow users to eliminate the www from the Web page name.

When you enter the Web address, http://www.us-parks.com/grand_canyon/scenic_vistas.html in the Web browser, it sends a request to the Web server that contains the us-parks.com Web site. The server then retrieves the Web page named scenic_vistas.html in the grand_canyon path and delivers it to your browser, which then displays the Web page on the screen.

When you enter a Web address in a browser, you request, or *pull*, information from a Web server. Some Web servers also can *push* content to your computer at regular intervals or whenever updates are made to the site. For example, some Web servers provide the capability of displaying current sporting event scores or weather reports on your computer screen.

For information about useful Web sites and their associated Web addresses, read the Making Use of the Web feature that follows this chapter.

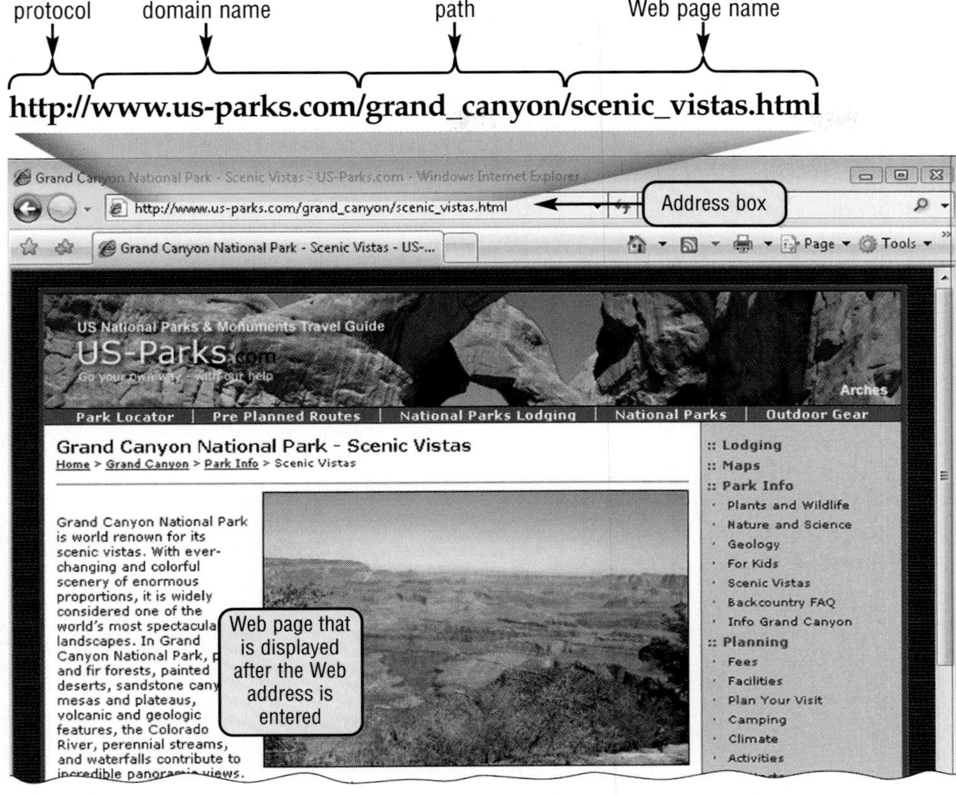

FIGURE 2-8 After entering the Web address http://www.us-parks.com/grand_canyon/scenic_vistas.html in the Address box, this Web page at the US National Parks Travel Guide Web site is displayed.

FAQ 2-5

Which Web browser currently has the highest market share?

Microsoft's Internet Explorer (IE) currently is the most popular browser, with approximately 76 percent of the market share. The chart below illustrates the market share of the more popular Web browsers. For more information, visit scsite.com/dc2008/ch2/faq and then click Browser Market Share.

IE
Firefox
Netscape
Other

Source: Janco Associates, Inc.

Navigating Web Pages

Most Web pages contain hypertext or hypermedia links. A **link**, short for *hyperlink*, is a built-in connection to another related Web page or part of a Web page. *Hypertext* refers to links in text-based documents, whereas *hypermedia* combines text-based links with graphic, audio, and video links. Links allow you to obtain information in a nonlinear way. That is, instead of accessing topics in a specified order, you move directly to a topic of interest. Branching from one related topic to another in a nonlinear fashion is what makes links so powerful. Some people use the phrase, **surfing the Web**, to refer to the activity of using links to explore the Web.

Text links may be underlined and/or displayed in a color different from other text on the Web page. Pointing to, or positioning the pointer on, a link on the screen typically changes the shape of the pointer to a small hand with a pointing index finger. The Web page shown in Figure 2-9 contains a variety of link types, with the pointer on one of the links.

Each link on a Web page corresponds to another Web address. To activate a link, you click it. Clicking a link causes the Web page associated with the link to be displayed on the screen. The linked object might be on the same Web page, a different Web page at the same Web site, or a separate Web page at a different Web site in another city or country. To remind you visually that you have clicked a link, a text link often changes color after you click it.

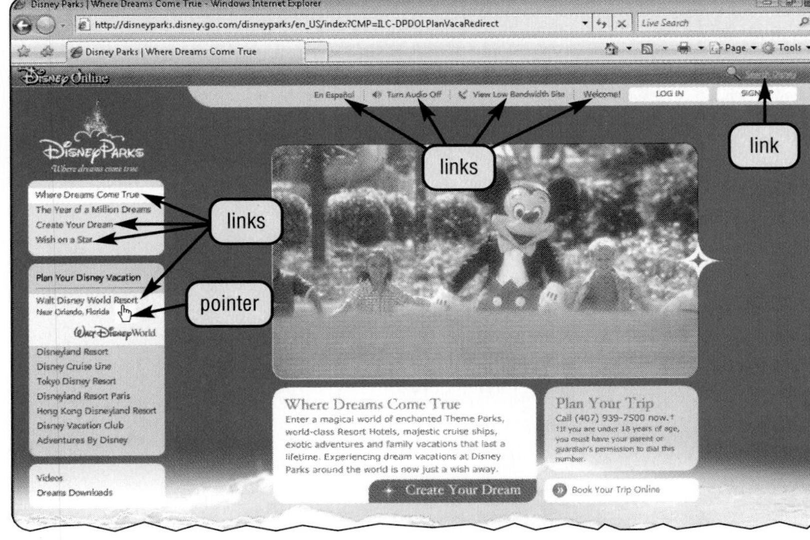

FIGURE 2-9 This Web page contains various types of links: text that is underlined, text in a different color, and images.

Searching for Information on the Web

The Web is a global resource of information. One primary use of the Web is to search for specific information, including text, graphics, audio, and video. The first step in successful searching is to identify the main idea or concept in the topic about which you are seeking information. Determine any synonyms, alternate spellings, or variant word forms for the topic. Then, use a search tool to locate the information.

The two most commonly used search tools are subject directories and search engines. A **subject directory** classifies Web pages in an organized set of categories, such as sports or shopping, and related subcategories. A **search engine** is a program that finds Web sites, Web pages, images, videos, news, and other information.

Some Web sites offer the functionality of both a subject directory and a search engine. Yahoo! and Google, for example, are widely used search engines that also provide a subject directory. To use Yahoo! or Google, you enter the Web address (yahoo.com or google.com) in the Address box in a browser window. The table in Figure 2-10 lists the Web addresses of several popular general-purpose subject directories and search engines.

WIDELY USED SEARCH TOOLS

Search Tool	Web Address	Subject Directory	Search Engine
A9.com	a9.com		X
AlltheWeb	alltheweb.com		X
AltaVista	altavista.com		X
AOL Search	search.aol.com	X	X
Ask.com	ask.com		X
Dogpile	dogpile.com		X
Excite	excite.com	X	X
Gigablast	gigablast.com	X	X
Google	google.com	X	X
Live Search	live.com		X
LookSmart	looksmart.com	X	X
Lycos	lycos.com		X
MSN	msn.com	X	X
Netscape Search	search.netscape.com		X
Open Directory Project	dmoz.org	X	X
Overture	overture.com		X
WebCrawler	webcrawler.com		X
Yahoo!	yahoo.com	X	X

FIGURE 2-10 Many subject directories and search engines allow searching about any topic on the Web.

SUBJECT DIRECTORIES A subject directory provides categorized lists of links arranged by subject. Figure 2-11 shows how to use Yahoo!'s

FIGURE 2-11 HOW TO USE A SUBJECT DIRECTORY

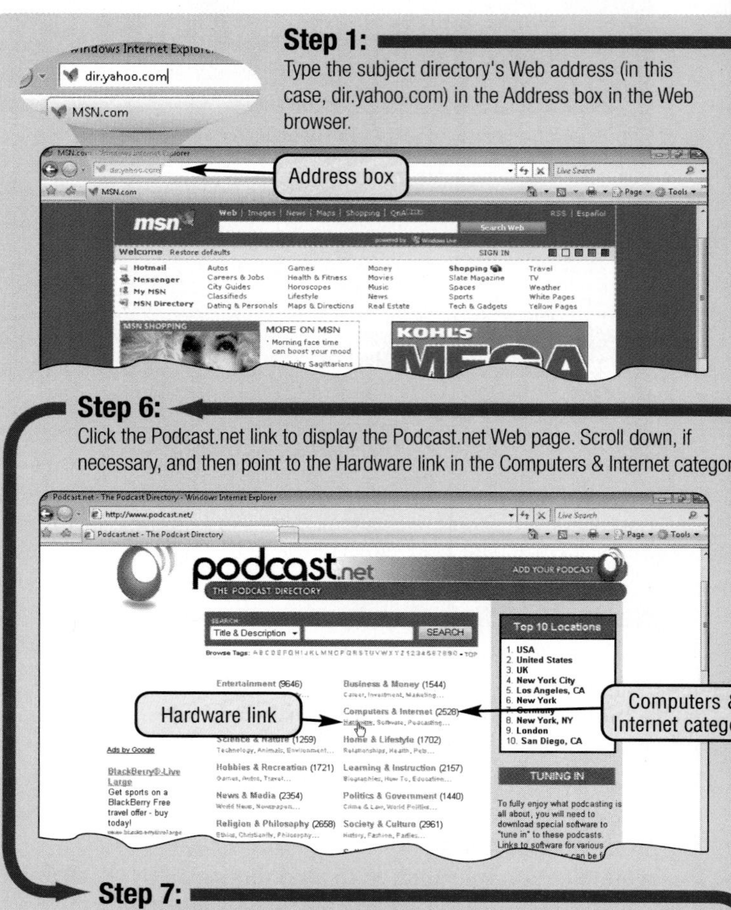
Step 1:
Type the subject directory's Web address (in this case, dir.yahoo.com) in the Address box in the Web browser.
dir.yahoo.com
Address box
Step 6:
Click the Podcast.net link to display the Podcast.net Web page. Scroll down, if necessary, and then point to the Hardware link in the Computers & Internet categor
Hardware link
Computers & Internet categ
Step 7:
Click the Hardware link to display a list of Hardware podcasts. Scroll through the list of podcasts, if necessary, and then point to the Mobile Media Developer link.

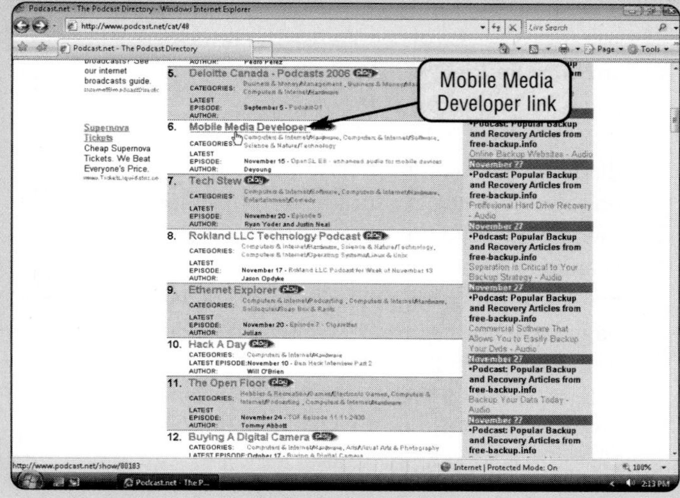
Mobile Media Developer link

subject directory to search for podcasts (audio broadcasts) that discuss mobile media. As shown in the figure, you locate a particular topic by clicking links through different levels, moving from the general to the specific. Each time you click a category link, the subject directory displays a list of subcategory links, from which you again choose. You continue in this fashion until the search tool displays a list of Web pages about the desired topic.

The major problem with a subject directory is deciding which categories to choose as you work through the menus of links presented.

Step 2:
Press the ENTER key. When the Yahoo! Directory Web page is displayed, point to the Blogs link in the Computer & Internet category.

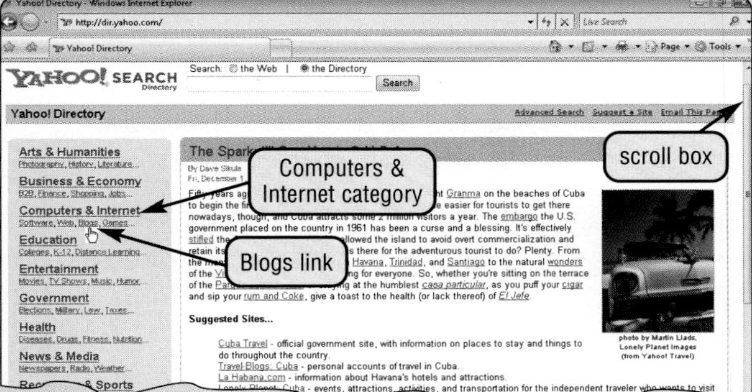

Step 3:
Click the Blogs link in the Computer & Internet category to display the Blogs page. Scroll down to the Additional Categories area, if necessary, and then point to the Podcasting and Audioblogging@ link.

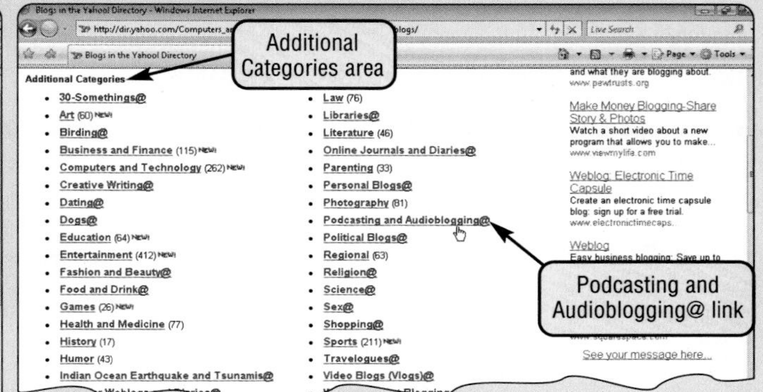

Step 4:
Click the Podcasting and Audioblogging@ link to display the Podcasting and Audioblogging page. Scroll down to the CATEGORIES area, if necessary, and then point to the Directories link.

Step 5:
Click the Directories link to display the Podcasting and Audioblogging Directories page. If necessary, scroll down to the SITE LISTINGS area and then point to the Podcast.net link.

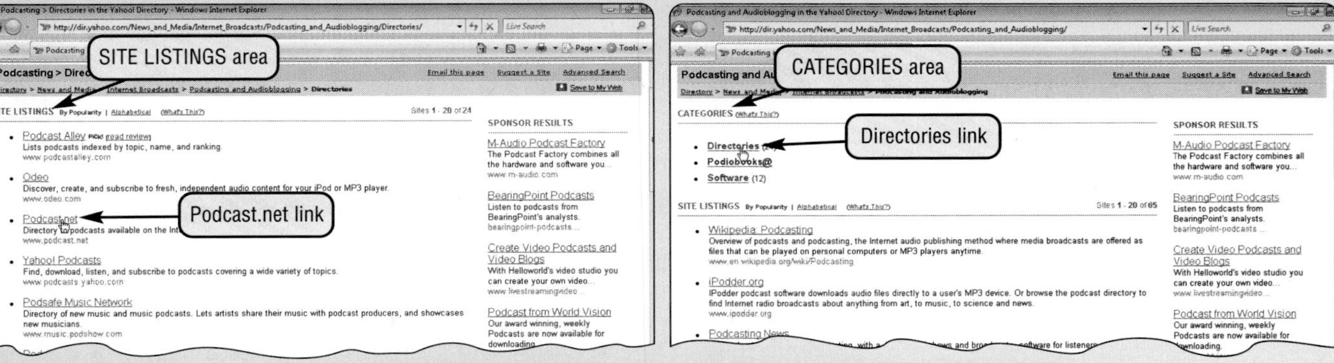

Step 8:
Click the Mobile Media Developer link to display the page, which contains a description of related podcasts and links to play the podcasts.

Search Engines A search engine is particularly helpful in locating Web pages about certain topics or in locating specific Web pages, images, videos, news, and other information for which you do not know the exact Web address. Thousands of search engines are available. Some are general and perform searches on any topic; others are restricted to certain subjects, such as finding people, job hunting, or locating real estate.

Instead of clicking through links, search engines require that you enter a word or phrase, called **search text** or *keywords*, that define the item about which you want information. Search engines often respond with results that include thousands of links to Web pages, many with little or no bearing on the information you are seeking. You can eliminate the superfluous pages by carefully crafting a keyword that limits the search.

Figure 2-12 shows how to use the Google search engine to search for the phrase, BBC news digital world podcast. The results of the search, called *hits*, shown in Step 3 include more than two million links to Web pages that reference BBC news digital world podcast. Each hit in the list has a link that, when clicked, displays an associated Web site or Web page.

FIGURE 2-12 HOW TO USE A SEARCH ENGINE

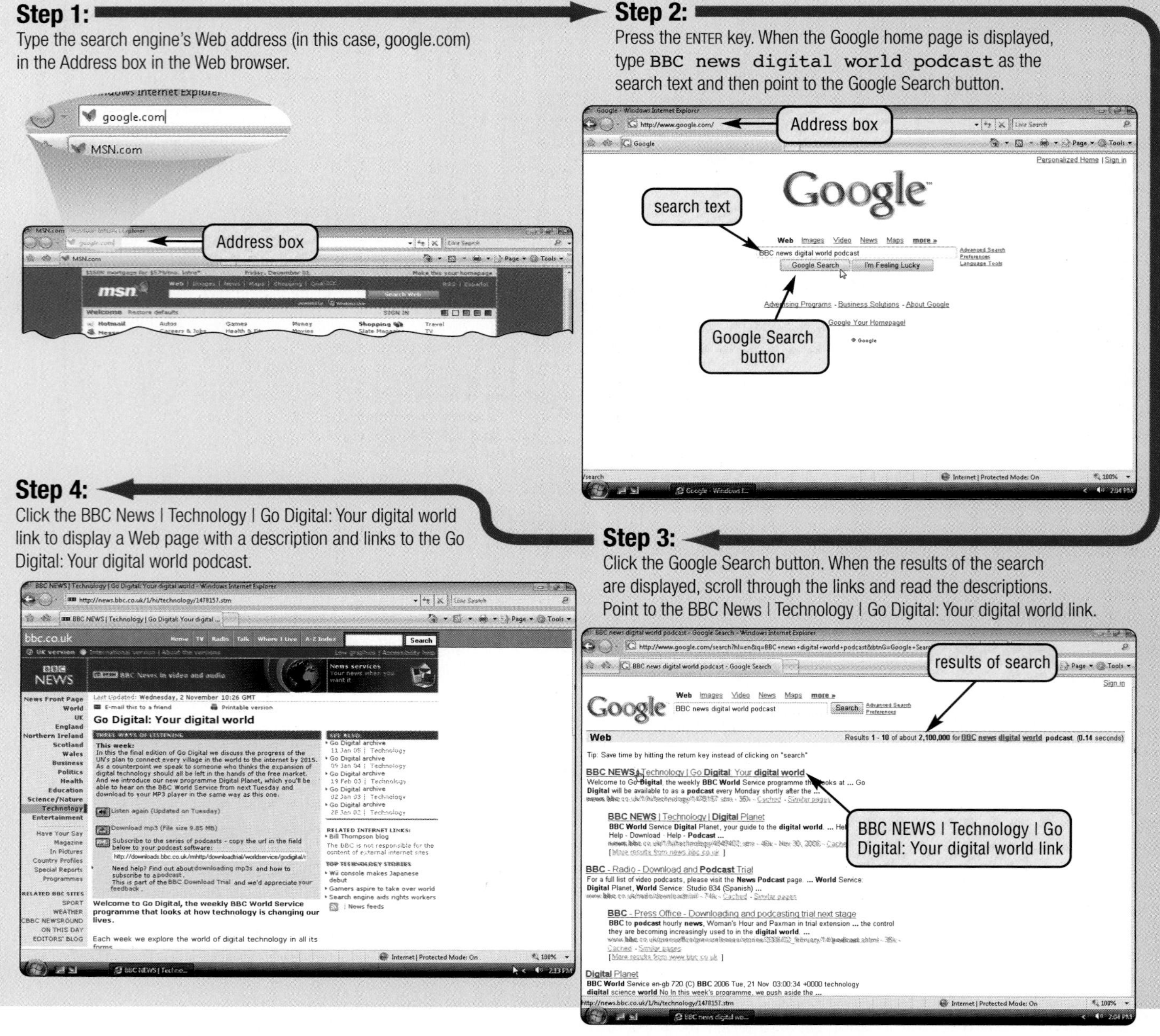
Step 1:
Type the search engine's Web address (in this case, google.com) in the Address box in the Web browser.
google.com
MSN.com
Address box
Step 2:
Press the ENTER key. When the Google home page is displayed, type BBC news digital world podcast as the search text and then point to the Google Search button.
Address box
search text
Google
Google Search button
Step 3:
Click the Google Search button. When the results of the search are displayed, scroll through the links and read the descriptions. Point to the BBC News | Technology | Go Digital: Your digital world link.
results of search
BBC NEWS | Technology | Go Digital: Your digital world link
Step 4:
Click the BBC News | Technology | Go Digital: Your digital world link to display a Web page with a description and links to the Go Digital: Your digital world podcast.
Go Digital: Your digital world

Most search engines sequence the hits based on how close the words in the search text are to one another in the Web page titles and their descriptions. Thus, the first few links probably contain more relevant information.

If you enter a phrase with spaces between the words in the search text, most search engines display results (hits) that include all of the words, except for common words (e.g., to, the, and). The table in Figure 2-13 lists some common operators you can include in your search text to refine your search. Other techniques you can use to improve your Web searches include the following:

- Use specific nouns and put the most important terms first in the search text.
- List all possible spellings, for example, email, e-mail.
- Before using a search engine, read its Help information.
- If the search is unsuccessful with one search engine, try another.

Many search engines use a program called a *spider* to build and maintain lists of words found on Web sites. When you enter search text, the search engine scans this prebuilt list for hits. The more sophisticated the search engine combined with precise search criteria, the more rapid the response and effective the search.

In addition to searching for Web pages, many search engines allow you to search for images, news articles, and local businesses. Read Looking Ahead 2-2 for a look at the next generation of searching techniques.

FAQ 2-6

How do Google and Yahoo! make money?

Google and Yahoo! are able to offer their services free to the public by charging a fee to companies that wish to advertise on their Web site. Advertisements can be very effective, because they often are related to your search results. For more information, visit scsite.com/dc2008/ch2/faq and then click Online Advertisements.

SEARCH ENGINE OPERATORS

Operator	Description	Examples	Explanation
Space or +	Use the space or plus operator (+) when you want search results to display hits that include specific words.	art + music art music	Results have both words art and music — in any order.
OR	Use the OR operator when you want search results to display hits that include only one word from a list.	dog OR puppy dog OR puppy OR canine	Results have either the word dog or puppy. Results have the word dog or puppy or canine.
-	Use the minus operator (-) when you want to exclude a word from your search results.	automobile -convertible	Results include automobile but do not include convertible.
" "	Use the quotation marks operator when you want to search for an exact phrase in a certain order.	"19th century literature"	Results include only hits that have the exact phrase, 19th century literature.
*	Use the asterisk operator (*) when you want search results to substitute characters in place of the asterisk.	writer*	Results include any word that begins with writer (e.g., writer, writers, writer's).

FIGURE 2-13 Use search engine operators to help refine a search.

LOOKING AHEAD 2-2

Facing Up to Search Technology

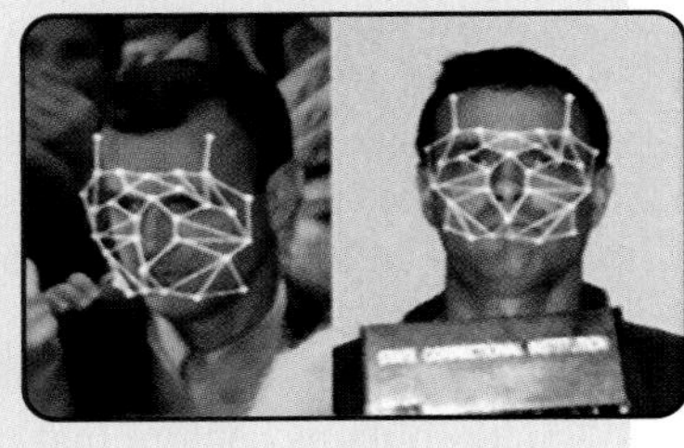

If you think a face looks familiar but you cannot recall the person's name, people-searching tools on the Internet may help solve the identity question. *Facial-recognition technology* being developed could identify pictures based on facial features, such as blue eyes or dimples. Once an individual is identified, the search engine then could search for other pictures of that person stored on a computer or on the Internet.

Other search engines being created are locating 3-D images for engineers and designers who use millions of inventoried parts at large industrial companies. When these employees need to locate a particular item based on a shape, not a part or model number, the search engines analyze shapes based on patterns and contours.

Researchers predict image searches will be common on the Internet in less than 15 years and will include a voice interface, a thesaurus, and customized results based on the researcher's background. For more information, visit scsite.com/dc2008/ch2/looking and then click Search Engines.

Types of Web Sites

Twelve types of Web sites are portal, news, informational, business/marketing, educational, entertainment, advocacy, blog, wiki, online social network, content aggregator, and personal (Figure 2-14). Many Web sites fall in more than one of these categories.

PORTAL A **portal** is a Web site that offers a variety of Internet services from a single, convenient location (Figure 2-14a). Most portals offer the following free services: search engine and/or subject directory; news; sports and weather; Web publishing; reference tools such as yellow pages, stock quotes, and maps; shopping; and e-mail and other forms of online communications.

Many portals have online communities. An **online community** is a Web site that joins a specific group of people with similar interests or relationships. These communities may offer online photo albums, chat rooms, and other services to facilitate communications among members.

Popular portals include AltaVista, AOL, Excite, GO.com, LookSmart, Lycos, MSN, NBCi, Netscape, and Yahoo!. A *wireless portal* is a portal designed for Internet-enabled mobile devices.

NEWS A news Web site contains newsworthy material including stories and articles relating to current events, life, money, sports, and the weather (Figure 2-14b). Many magazines and newspapers sponsor Web sites that provide summaries of printed articles, as well as articles not included in the printed versions. Newspapers and television and radio stations are some of the media that maintain news Web sites.

INFORMATIONAL An informational Web site contains factual information (Figure 2-14c). Many United States government agencies have informational Web sites providing information such as census data, tax codes, and the congressional budget. Other organizations provide information such as public transportation schedules and published research findings.

BUSINESS/MARKETING A business/marketing Web site contains content that promotes or sells products or services (Figure 2-14d). Nearly every business has a business/marketing Web site. Allstate Insurance Company, Dell Inc., General Motors Corporation, Kraft Foods Inc., and Walt Disney Company all have business/marketing Web sites. Many of these companies also allow you to purchase their products or services online.

EDUCATIONAL An educational Web site offers exciting, challenging avenues for formal and informal teaching and learning (Figure 2-14e). On the Web, you can learn how airplanes fly or how to cook a meal. For a more structured learning experience, companies provide online training to employees; and colleges offer online classes and degrees. Instructors often use the Web to enhance classroom teaching by publishing course materials, grades, and other pertinent class information.

ENTERTAINMENT An entertainment Web site offers an interactive and engaging environment (Figure 2-14f). Popular entertainment Web sites offer music, videos, sports, games, ongoing Web episodes, sweepstakes, chats, and more. Sophisticated entertainment Web sites often partner with other technologies. For example, you can cast your vote about a topic on a television show.

ADVOCACY An advocacy Web site contains content that describes a cause, opinion, or idea (Figure 2-14g). These Web sites usually present views of a particular group or association. Sponsors of advocacy Web sites include the Democratic National Committee, the Republican National Committee, the Society for the Prevention of Cruelty to Animals, and the Society to Protect Human Rights.

BLOG A **blog**, short for *Weblog*, is an informal Web site consisting of time-stamped articles, or posts, in a diary or journal format, usually listed in reverse chronological order (Figure 2-14h). A blog that contains video clips is called a video blog, or *vlog*. The term *blogosphere* refers to the worldwide collection of blogs, and the *vlogosphere* refers to all vlogs worldwide.

Blogs reflect the interests, opinions, and personalities of the author, called the *blogger* or *vlogger* (for vlog author), and sometimes site visitors.

Blogs have become an important means of worldwide communication. Businesses create blogs to communicate with employees, customers, and vendors. Teachers create blogs to collaborate with other teachers and students. Home users create blogs to share aspects of their personal life with family, friends, and others.

WIKI A **wiki** is a collaborative Web site that allows users to create, add to, modify, or delete the Web site content via their Web browser. Most wikis are open to modification by the general

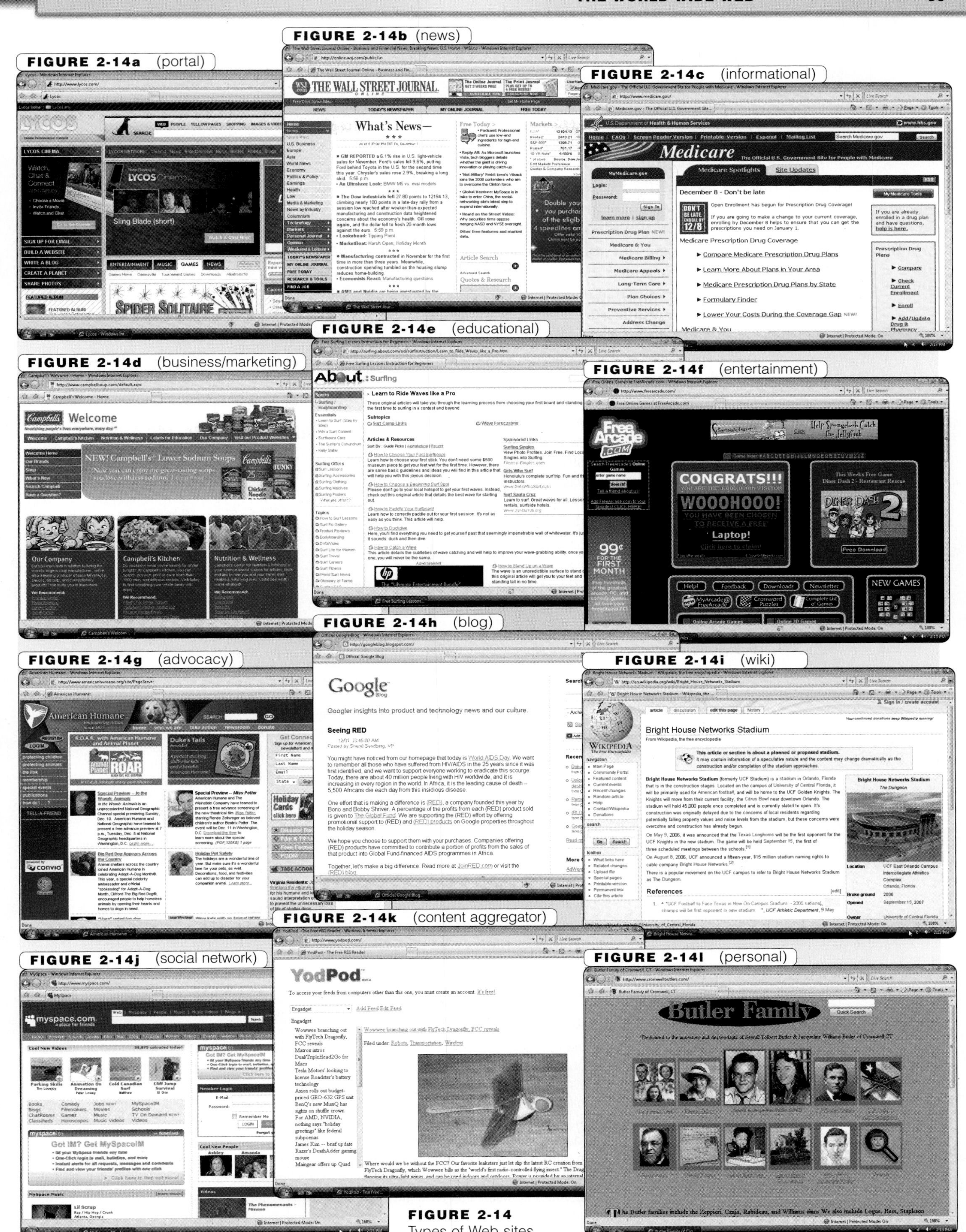

FIGURE 2-14a (portal)

FIGURE 2-14b (news)

FIGURE 2-14c (informational)

FIGURE 2-14d (business/marketing)

FIGURE 2-14e (educational)

FIGURE 2-14f (entertainment)

FIGURE 2-14g (advocacy)

FIGURE 2-14h (blog)

FIGURE 2-14i (wiki)

FIGURE 2-14j (social network)

FIGURE 2-14k (content aggregator)

FIGURE 2-14l (personal)

FIGURE 2-14
Types of Web sites.

public. Wikis usually collect recent edits on a Web page so someone can review them for accuracy. The difference between a wiki and a blog is that users cannot modify original posts made by the blogger. A popular wiki is Wikipedia, a free Web encyclopedia (Figure 2-14i on the previous page). Read Ethics & Issues 2-1 for a related discussion.

ONLINE SOCIAL NETWORKS An **online social network**, also called a **social networking Web site**, is a Web site that encourages members in its online community to share their interests, ideas, stories, photos, music, and videos with other registered users (Figure 2-14j). Most include chat rooms, newsgroups, and other communications services. Popular social networking Web sites include Facebook, Friendster, and MySpace, which alone has more than 12 million visitors each day. A **media sharing Web site** is a specific type of online social network that enables members to share media such as photos, music, and videos. Flickr, Fotki, and Webshots are popular photo sharing communities; Google Video and YouTube are popular video sharing communities.

MySpace

For more information, visit scsite.com/dc2008/ch2/weblink and then click MySpace.

CONTENT AGGREGATOR A *content aggregator* is a business that gathers and organizes Web content and then distributes, or feeds, the content to subscribers for free or a fee. Examples of distributed content include news, music, video, and pictures. Subscribers select content in which they are interested. Whenever this content changes, it is downloaded automatically (pushed) to the subscriber's computer or mobile device.

RSS 2.0, which stands for *Really Simple Syndication*, is a specification that content aggregators use to distribute content to subscribers (Figure 2-14k). *Atom* is another specification sometimes used by content aggregators to distribute content.

PERSONAL A private individual or family not usually associated with any organization may maintain a personal Web site or just a single Web page (Figure 2-14l). People publish personal Web pages for a variety of reasons. Some are job hunting. Others simply want to share life experiences with the world.

Evaluating a Web Site

Do not assume that information presented on the Web is correct or accurate. Any person, company, or organization can publish a Web page on the Internet. No one oversees the content of these Web pages. Figure 2-15 lists guidelines for assessing the value of a Web site or Web page before relying on its content.

GUIDELINES FOR EVALUATING THE VALUE OF A WEB SITE

Evaluation Criteria	Reliable Web Sites
Affiliation	A reputable institution should support the Web site without bias in the information.
Audience	The Web site should be written at an appropriate level.
Authority	The Web site should list the author and the appropriate credentials.
Content	The Web site should be well organized and the links should work.
Currency	The information on the Web page should be current.
Design	The pages at the Web site should download quickly and be visually pleasing and easy to navigate.
Objectivity	The Web site should contain little advertising and be free of preconceptions.

FIGURE 2-15 Criteria for evaluating a Web site's content.

ETHICS & ISSUES 2-1

Should You Trust a Wiki for Academic Research?

As wikis have grown in number, size, and popularity, some educators and librarians have shunned the sites as valid sources of research. While many wikis are tightly controlled with a limited number of contributors and expert editors, these usually focus on narrowly-defined, specialized topics. Large online wikis, such as Wikipedia, often involve thousands of editors, many of whom remain anonymous. Recently, an entry on Wikipedia was maliciously altered to suggest that a prominent journalist was involved in the assassination of John F. Kennedy. Editors corrected the information several months later after a friend of the journalist notified him of the errors. In other situations, rival political factions falsified or embellished wiki entries in an attempt to give their candidate an advantage. Some wiki supporters argue that most wikis provide adequate controls to quickly correct false or misleading content and to punish those who submit it. Some propose that wikis should be used as a starting point for researching a fact, but that the fact should be verified using traditional sources. Should wikis be allowed as valid sources for academic research? Why or why not? Would you submit a paper to your instructor that cites a wiki as a source? An encyclopedia? Why or why not? What policies could wikis enforce that could garner more confidence from the public?

Multimedia on the Web

Most Web pages include more than just formatted text and links. The more exciting Web pages use multimedia. **Multimedia** refers to any application that combines text with graphics, animation, audio, video, and/or virtual reality. Multimedia brings a Web page to life, increases the types of information available on the Web, expands the Web's potential uses, and makes the Internet a more entertaining place to explore. Multimedia Web pages often require proper hardware and software and take more time to download because they contain large graphics files and video or audio clips.

The sections that follow discuss how the Web uses graphics, animation, audio, video, and virtual reality.

FAQ 2-7

What is a file?

A *file* is a unit of storage. When you want the computer to store items (e.g., data, information, programs, graphics, audio clips, or video clips), it places them in files on storage media such as a hard disk. File sizes vary depending on items being stored. For example, graphics files usually consume more storage space than data files. For more information, visit scsite.com/dc2008/ch2/faq and then click Files.

GRAPHICS A **graphic**, or *graphical image*, is a digital representation of nontext information such as a drawing, chart, or photograph. Today, many Web pages use colorful graphical designs and images to convey messages (Figure 2-16).

The Web contains countless images about a variety of subjects. You can download many of these images at no cost and use them for noncommercial purposes. Recall that downloading is the process of transferring an object from the Web to your computer. For example, you can insert images into greeting cards, announcements, and other documents.

Of the graphics formats that exist on the Web (Figure 2-17), the two more common are JPEG and GIF formats. *JPEG* (pronounced JAY-peg) is a format that compresses graphics to reduce their file size, which means the file takes up less storage space. Smaller file sizes result in faster downloading of Web pages because small files transmit faster than large files. The more compressed the file, the smaller the image and the lower the quality. The goal with JPEG graphics is to reach a balance between image quality and file size. Digital photographs often use the JPEG format.

GIF (pronounced jiff) graphics also use compression techniques to reduce file sizes. The GIF format works best for images that have only a few distinct colors, such as company logos. The newer *PNG* (pronounced ping) graphics format improves upon the GIF format, and thus may eventually replace the GIF format.

The BMP and TIFF formats listed in Figure 2-17 may require special viewer software, and they have larger file sizes. Thus, these formats are not used on the Web as frequently as JPEG, GIF, and PNG formats.

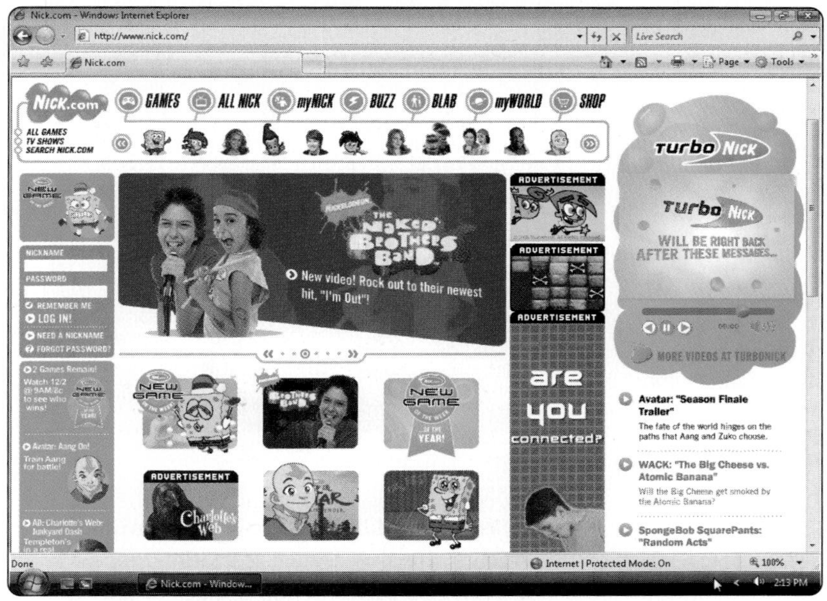

FIGURE 2-16 This Web page uses colorful graphical designs and images to convey its messages.

GRAPHICS FORMATS USED ON THE WEB

Abbreviation	Name	Uses
BMP	Bit Map	Desktop background, scanned images
GIF	Graphics Interchange Format	Simple diagrams, shapes, images with few colors
JPEG	Joint Photographic Experts Group	Digital camera photographs
PNG	Portable Network Graphics	Web graphics
TIFF	Tagged Image File Format	Photographs used by printing industry

FIGURE 2-17 The Web uses graphics file formats for images.

Some Web sites use thumbnails on their pages because graphics can be time-consuming to display. A *thumbnail* is a small version of a larger graphic. You usually can click a thumbnail to display a larger image (Figure 2-18).

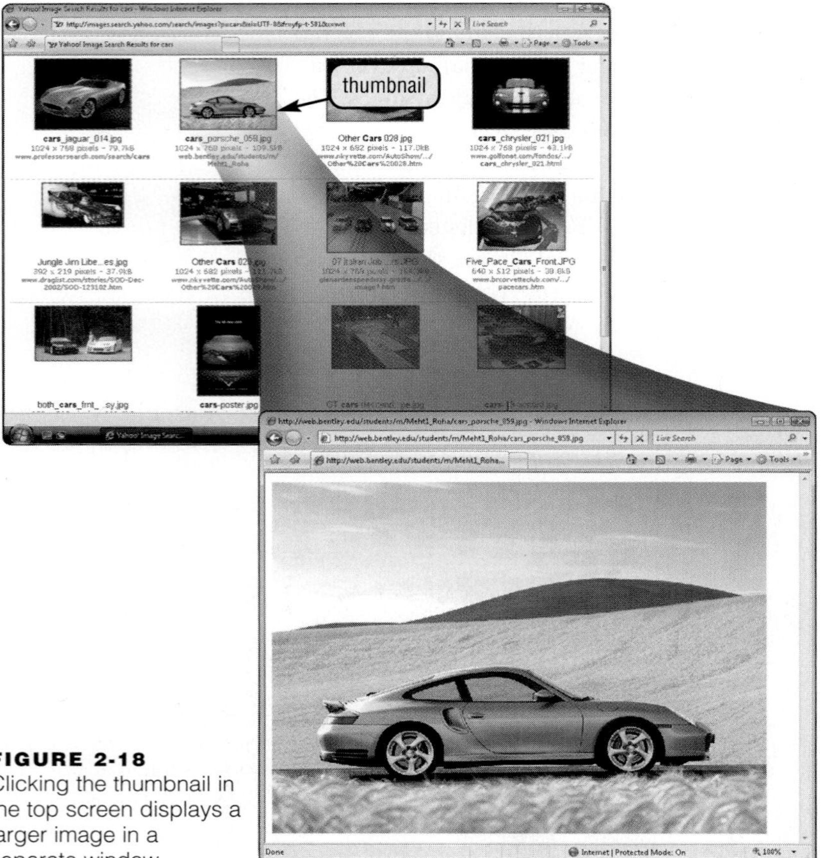

FIGURE 2-18 Clicking the thumbnail in the top screen displays a larger image in a separate window.

ANIMATION Many Web pages use **animation**, which is the appearance of motion created by displaying a series of still images in sequence. Animation can make Web pages more visually interesting or draw attention to important information or links. For example, text that animates by scrolling across the screen can serve as a ticker to display stock updates, news, sports scores, weather, or other information. Web-based games often use animation.

Web page developers add animation to Web pages using a variety of techniques. Web page authoring programs, such as Adobe Flash, enable Web site developers to combine animation and interactivity in Web pages. Developers unfamiliar with Web page authoring programs can create an *animated GIF*, which combines several GIF images in a single GIF file.

AUDIO On the Web, you can listen to audio clips and live audio. **Audio** includes music, speech, or any other sound. Simple applications consist of individual audio files available for download to a computer. Once downloaded, you can play (listen to) the contents of these files. Some common Web audio file formats are listed in Figure 2-19. Audio files are compressed to reduce their file sizes. For example, the **MP3** format reduces an audio file to about one-tenth its original size, while preserving much of the original quality of the sound.

Some music publishers have Web sites that allow users to download sample tracks free to persuade them to buy the entire CD. Other Web sites allow a user to purchase and download an entire CD (Figure 2-20). It is legal to download copyrighted music only if the song's copyright holder has granted permission for users to download and play the song. Copyright issues led to the development of *digital rights management (DRM)*, a strategy designed to prevent illegal distribution of music and other digital content. Read Ethics & Issues 2-2 for a related discussion.

To listen to an audio file on your computer, you need special software called a **player**. Most current operating systems contain a player. Popular players include iTunes, RealPlayer, and Windows Media Player. You can download the players free from the Web.

Some applications on the Web use streaming audio. **Streaming** is the process of transferring data in a continuous and even flow. Streaming allows users to access and use a file while it is transmitting. For example, *streaming audio* enables you to listen to music as it downloads to your computer. Many radio and television stations use streaming audio to broadcast music, interviews, talk shows, sporting events, music videos, news, live concerts, and other segments.

Podcasting is another popular method of distributing audio. A *podcast* is recorded audio, usually an MP3 file, stored on a Web site that can be downloaded to a computer or a portable media player such as an iPod. Examples of podcasts include music, radio shows, news stories, classroom lectures, political messages, and television commentaries. Podcasters register their podcasts with content aggregators. Subscribers select podcast feeds they want to be downloaded automatically whenever they connect. Some Web sites, such as podcast.net, specialize in podcast distribution. Others, such as National Public Radio, have incorporated a podcast component in their existing Web site.

AUDIO WEB FILE FORMATS

Format	Description	Format	Description
AAC	Advanced Audio Coding	WAV	Windows waveform
AIFF	Audio Interchange File Format	WMA	Windows Media Audio (part of Windows Media framework)
ASF	Advanced Streaming (or Systems) Format (part of Windows Media framework)	RA	RealAudio sound file (supported by RealPlayer)
MP3	Moving Pictures Experts Group Audio Layer 3 (MPEG-3)	QT	QuickTime audio, video, or 3-D animation

FIGURE 2-19 Popular Web audio file formats.

FIGURE 2-20 HOW TO PURCHASE AND DOWNLOAD MUSIC

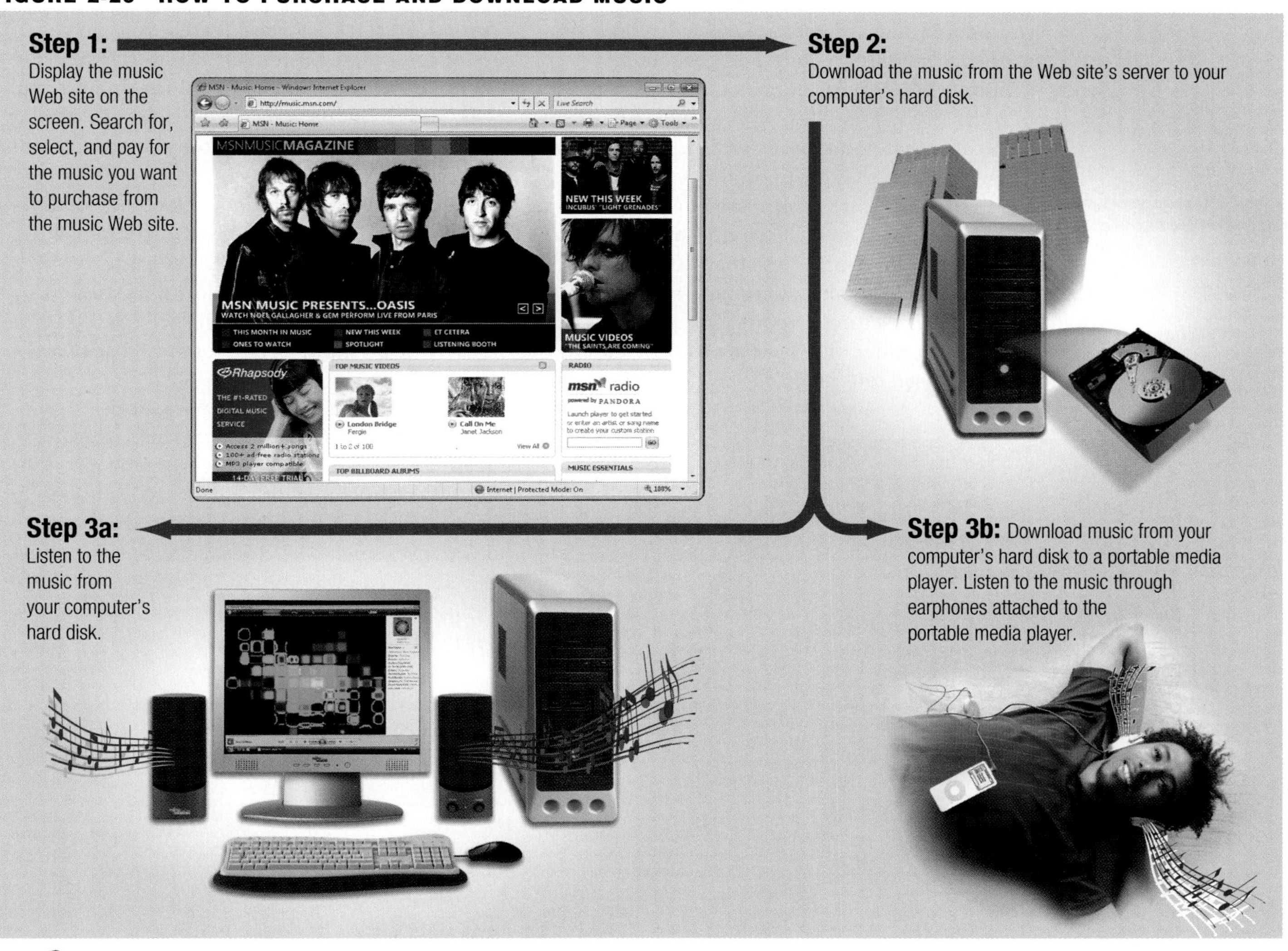

Step 1:
Display the music Web site on the screen. Search for, select, and pay for the music you want to purchase from the music Web site.
Step 2:
Download the music from the Web site's server to your computer's hard disk.
Step 3a:
Listen to the music from your computer's hard disk.
Step 3b: Download music from your computer's hard disk to a portable media player. Listen to the music through earphones attached to the portable media player.
MSNMUSICMAGAZINE
MSN MUSIC PRESENTS...OASIS
NEW THIS WEEK
MUSIC VIDEOS
Rhapsody
msn radio

ETHICS & ISSUES 2-2

Who Should Control the Content of Your CDs, DVDs, and Media Files?

When you purchase a CD, a DVD, or media files online, you are not purchasing the songs or movies they contain. You actually are purchasing a license to listen to or watch the digital content in a certain manner. The license limits what you can do with the CDs, DVDs, or media files. For example, you cannot play the music or movies in a public forum, nor can you copy and distribute the digital content. Some media companies now employ electronic means of digital rights management (DRM), which automatically restricts what you can do with digital content. Media companies claim that DRM helps them to stem the tide of piracy and the sharing of content. Consumers argue that DRM restrictions infringe on their rights of fair use, and that oftentimes DRM makes playing the content in certain devices impossible. In some cases, DRM prevents users from making backup copies of the content or copying the content to their computers or other devices. Some people have worked around DRM restrictions, but the *Digital Millennium Copyright Act* (DMCA) makes any attempt to circumvent DRM an illegal activity. Because you already own a license to the content, if you scratch or lose a CD or DVD, should you be able to obtain a free or low-cost replacement for the content? Why or why not? If you already purchased a license for music by purchasing a CD, is it fair that you should pay full price again if you also would like the music in MP3 format? Why? How can the rights of media companies and consumers best be balanced?

VIDEO On the Web, you can view video clips or watch live video. **Video** consists of full-motion images that are played back at various speeds. Most video also has accompanying audio. You can use the Internet to watch live and/or prerecorded coverage of your favorite television programs (Figure 2-21) or enjoy a live performance of your favorite vocalist. You can upload, share, or view video clips at a video sharing Web site such as YouTube. Educators, politicians, and businesses are using video blogs and video podcasts to engage students, voters, and consumers.

Simple video applications on the Web consist of individual video files, such as movie or television clips, that you must download completely before you can play them on the computer. Video files often are compressed because they are quite large in size. These clips also are quite short in length, usually less than 10 minutes, because they can take a long time to download. The Moving Pictures Experts Group *(MPEG)* defines a popular video compression standard, a widely used one called *MPEG-4* or *MP4*.

As with streaming audio, *streaming video* allows you to view longer or live video images as they download to your computer. Widely used standards supported by most Web browsers for transmitting streaming video data on the Internet are AVI (Audio Video Interleaved), QuickTime, Windows Media Format, and RealVideo. Like RealAudio, RealVideo is supported by RealPlayer.

VIRTUAL REALITY **Virtual reality** (**VR**) is the use of computers to simulate a real or imagined environment that appears as a three-dimensional (3-D) space. On the Web, VR involves the display of 3-D images that users explore and manipulate interactively (Figure 2-22).

Using special VR software, a Web developer creates an entire 3-D Web site that contains infinite space and depth, called a *VR world*. A VR world, for example, might show a room with furniture. Users walk through such a VR room by moving an input device forward, backward, or to the side.

Games often use VR. Many practical applications of VR also exist. Science educators create VR models of molecules, organisms, and other structures for students to examine. Companies use VR to showcase products or create advertisements. Architects create VR models of buildings and rooms so clients can see how a completed construction project will look before it is built.

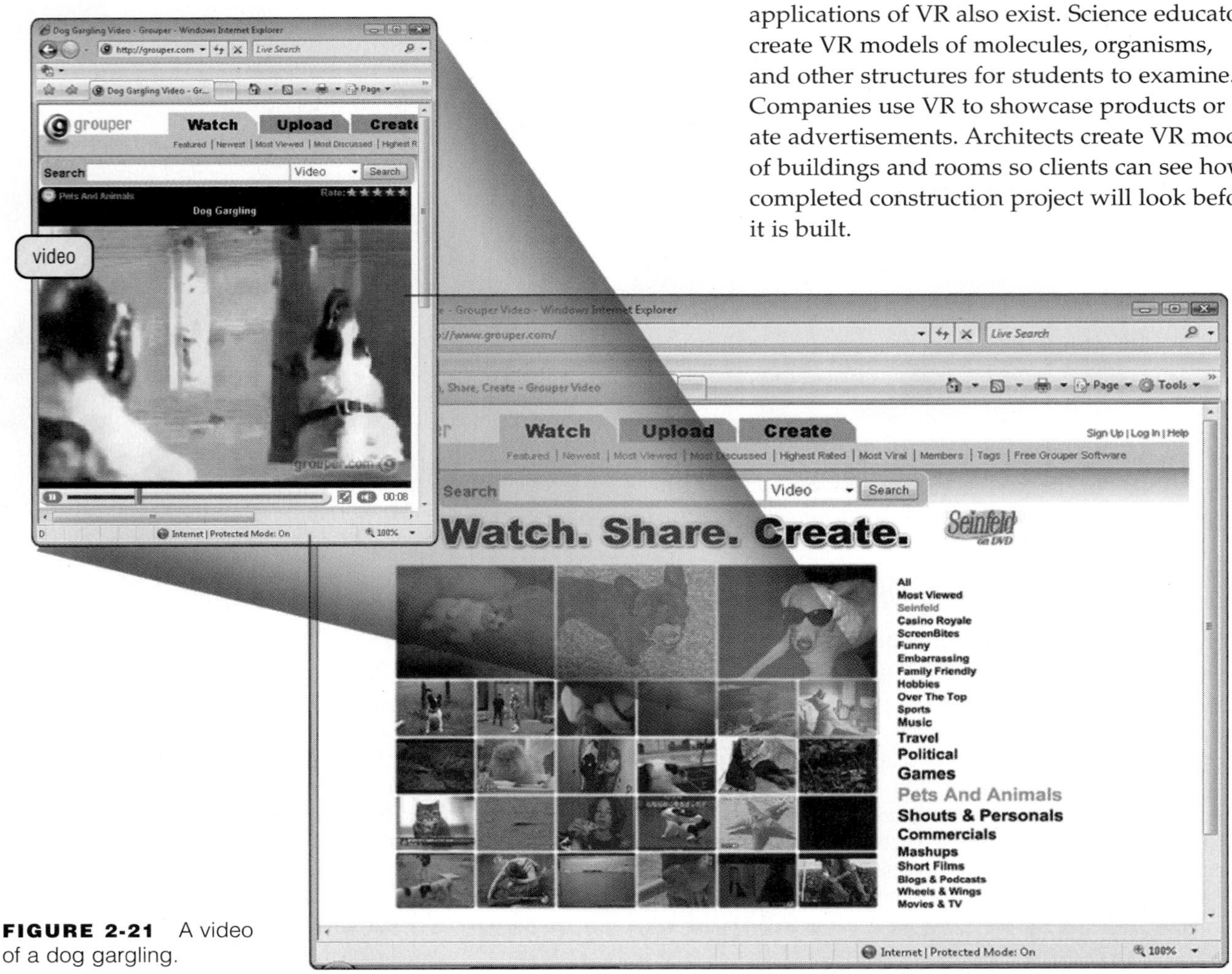

video

FIGURE 2-21 A video of a dog gargling.

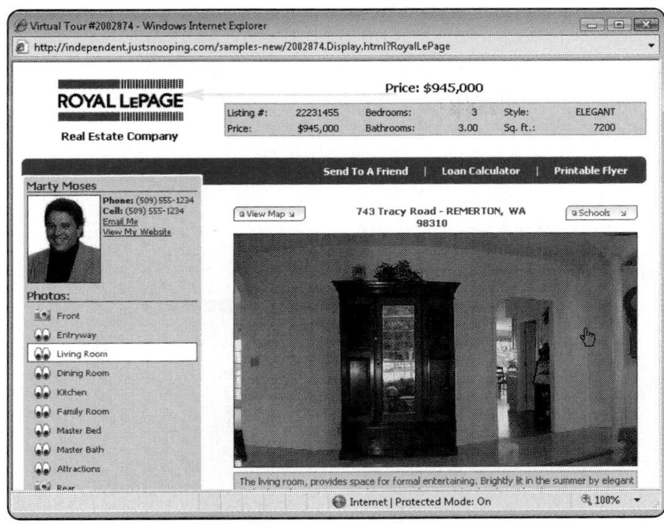

FIGURE 2-22 Web site visitors use VR to walk through the inside of this house for sale. The image automatically scrolls so you can see different views inside the house.

PLUG-INS Most Web browsers have the capability of displaying basic multimedia elements on a Web page. Sometimes, a browser might need an additional program, called a plug-in. A **plug-in** is a program that extends the capability of a browser. You can download many plug-ins at no cost from various Web sites (Figure 2-23). Some plug-ins run on all sizes of personal computers and mobile devices. Others have special versions for mobile devices.

Web Publishing

Before the World Wide Web, the means to share opinions and ideas with others easily and inexpensively was limited to the media, classroom, work, or social environments. Generating an advertisement or publication that could reach a massive audience required much expense. Today, businesses and individuals convey information to millions of people by creating their own Web pages. The content of the Web pages ranges from new stories to product information to blogs.

POPULAR PLUG-IN APPLICATIONS

Plug-In Application	Description	Web Address
Acrobat Reader	View, navigate, and print Portable Document Format (PDF) files — documents formatted to look just as they look in print	adobe.com
Flash Player	View dazzling graphics and animation, hear outstanding sound and music, display Web pages across an entire screen	adobe.com
QuickTime	View animation, music, audio, video, and VR panoramas and objects directly in a Web page	apple.com
RealPlayer	Listen to live and on-demand near-CD-quality audio and newscast-quality video; stream audio and video content for faster viewing; play MP3 files; create music CDs	real.com
Shockwave Player	Experience dynamic interactive multimedia, 3-D graphics, and streaming audio	adobe.com
Windows Media Player	Listen to live and on-demand audio, play or edit WMA and MP3 files, burn CDs, and watch DVD movies	microsoft.com

FIGURE 2-23 Most plug-ins can be downloaded free from the Web.

Web publishing is the development and maintenance of Web pages. To develop a Web page, you do not have to be a computer programmer. For the small business or home user, Web publishing is fairly easy as long as you have the proper tools. The five major steps to Web publishing are as follows: (1) plan a Web site, (2) analyze and design a Web site, (3) create a Web site, (4) deploy a Web site, and (5) maintain a Web site. Figure 2-24 illustrates these steps with respect to a personal Web site.

FIGURE 2-24 HOW TO PUBLISH YOUR RESUME ON THE WEB

Step 1:
Plan a Web site.
Think about issues that could affect the design of the Web site.

Step 2:
Analyze and design a Web site. Design the layout of the elements of the Web site.

Step 3:
Create a Web site. Use word processing software or Web page authoring software to create the Web site.

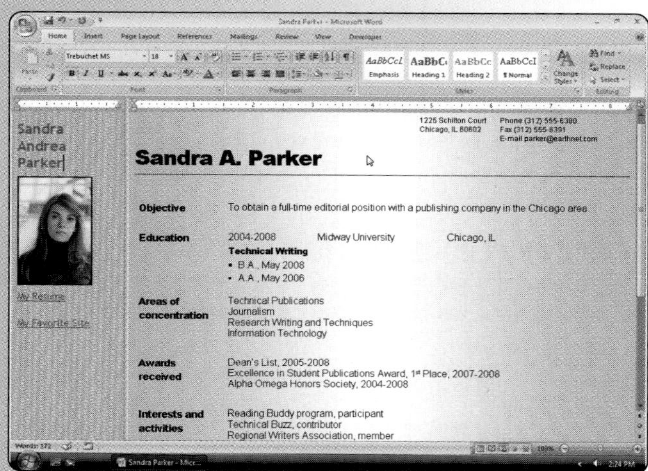

Step 4:
Deploy a Web site. Save the Web site on a Web server.

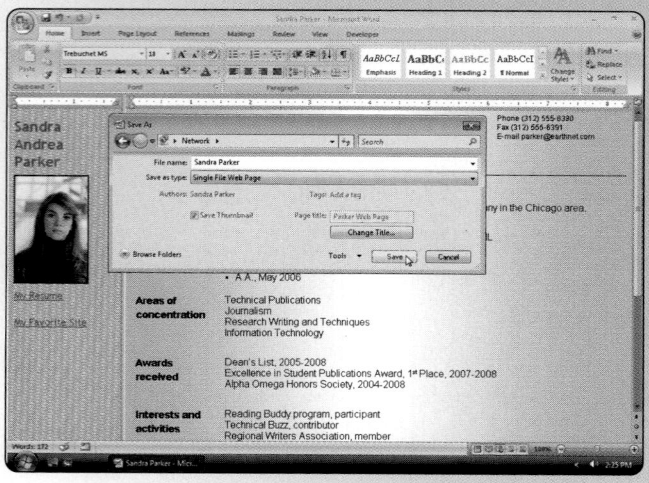

Step 5:
Maintain a Web site.
Visit your Web site regularly to be sure it is working and current.

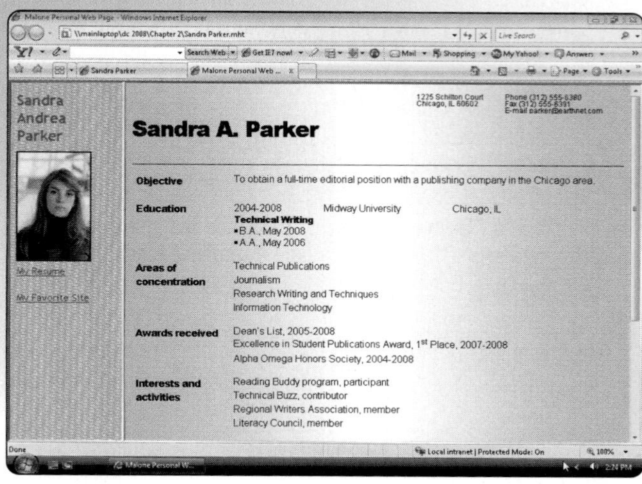

Test your knowledge of pages 75 through 90 in Quiz Yourself 2-2.

QUIZ YOURSELF 2-2

Instructions: Find the true statement below. Then, rewrite the remaining false statements so they are true.

1. A blog is a Web site that uses a regularly updated journal format to reflect the interests, opinions, and personalities of the author and sometimes site visitors.
2. A Web browser classifies Web pages in an organized set of categories, such as sports or shopping, and related subcategories.
3. Audio and video files are downloaded to reduce their file sizes.
4. Popular portals include iTunes, RealPlayer, and Windows Media Player.
5. The more widely used search engines for personal computers are Internet Explorer, Netscape, Firefox, Opera, and Safari.
6. To develop a Web page, you have to be a computer programmer.
7. To improve your Web searches, use general nouns and put the least important terms first in the search text.

Quiz Yourself Online: To further check your knowledge of Web addresses, Web browsers, searching, types of Web sites, elements of a Web page, and Web publishing, visit scsite.com/dc2008/ch2/quiz and then click Objectives 4 – 9.

E-COMMERCE

E-commerce, short for *electronic commerce*, is a business transaction that occurs over an electronic network such as the Internet. Anyone with access to a computer, an Internet connection, and a means to pay for purchased goods or services can participate in e-commerce (Figure 2-25).

In the past, e-commerce transactions were conducted primarily using desktop computers. Today, many mobile computers and devices, such as PDAs and smart phones, also access the Web wirelessly. Some people use the term *m-commerce* (mobile commerce) to identify e-commerce that takes place using mobile devices.

Popular uses of e-commerce by consumers include shopping, investing, and banking. Users can purchase just about any product or service on the Web. Some examples include flowers, books, computers, prescription drugs, music, movies, cars, airline tickets, and concert tickets. Through online investing, individuals buy and sell stocks or bonds without using a broker.

Three different types of e-commerce are business-to-consumer, consumer-to-consumer, and business-to-business. *Business-to-consumer (B2C) e-commerce* consists of the sale of goods

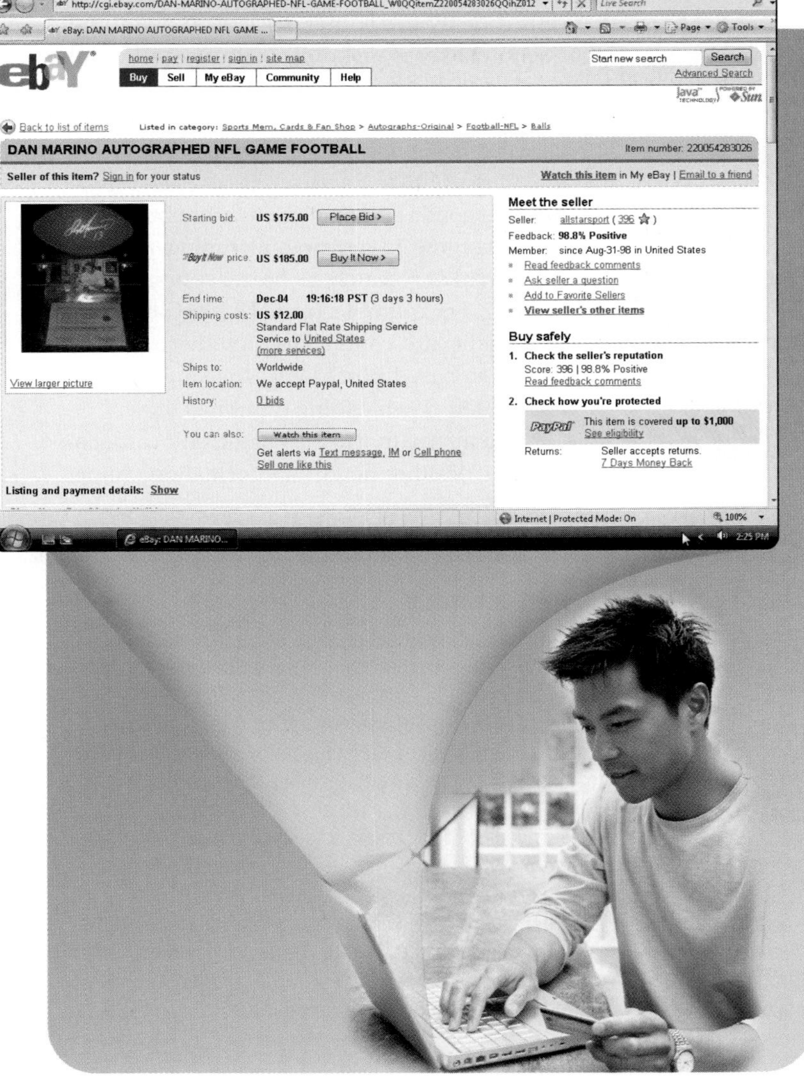

FIGURE 2-25 E-commerce activities include shopping for goods at an online auction, such as eBay.

and services to the general public. For example, Dell has a B2C Web site. Instead of visiting a computer store to purchase a computer, customers can order one that meets their specifications directly from the Dell Web site.

A customer (consumer) visits an online business through an **electronic storefront**, which contains product descriptions, graphics, and a shopping cart. The **shopping cart** allows the customer to collect purchases. When ready to complete the sale, the customer enters personal data and the method of payment, preferably through a secure Internet connection. Read Looking Ahead 2-3 for a look at the next generation of shopping carts.

Instead of purchasing from a business, consumers can purchase from each other. For example, with an **online auction**, users bid on an item being sold by someone else. The highest bidder at the end of the bidding period purchases the item. *Consumer-to-consumer (C2C) e-commerce* occurs when one consumer sells directly to another, such as in an online auction. eBay is one of the more popular online auction Web sites.

Most e-commerce, though, actually takes place between businesses, which is called *business-to-business (B2B) e-commerce*. Businesses often provide goods and services to other businesses, such as online advertising, recruiting, credit, sales, market research, technical support, and training. For example, some MasterCard and Visa credit card companies provide corporations with Web-based purchasing, tracking, and transaction downloading capabilities.

As an alternative to entering credit card, bank account, or other financial information online, some shopping and auction Web sites allow consumers to use an online payment service such as PayPal or Google Checkout. To use an online payment service, you create an account that is linked to your credit card or funds at a financial institution. When you make a purchase, you use your online payment service account, which transfers money for you without revealing your financial information.

WEB LINK 2-5

PayPal

For more information, visit scsite.com/dc2008/ch2/weblink and then click PayPal.

LOOKING AHEAD 2-3

Grocery Shopping with a Buddy

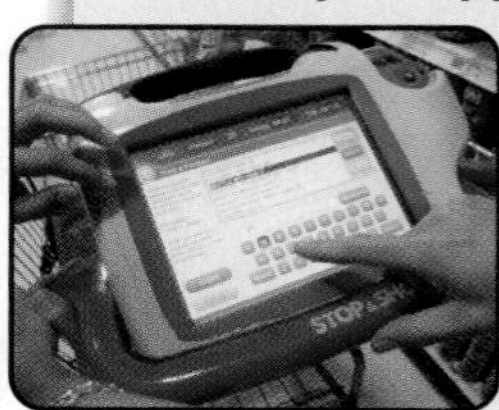

Finding items in the local grocery store may become quick and easy with the help of IBM's Shopping Buddy, a portable computer attached to a shopping cart.

Shoppers access the system by using their preferred customer card or a key. Once logged in, a miniature global positioning satellite system identifies their location in the store. As they roll down each aisle, the Shopping Buddy flashes an alert of sale items and favorite products. If they are looking for a particular item, they can type its name or select it from a list, and the computer will display a map showing the item's location.

Shoppers can scan each item's bar code with a detachable wand, and the Shopping Buddy will keep a running total. They also can order deli items without standing in line and bag their items as they shop. For more information, visit scsite.com/dc2008/ch2/looking and then click Shopping Buddy.

FAQ 2-8

Is it safe to shop online?

Not always. It always is best to conduct online transactions with well-established companies. If possible, research these companies and read about others' online shopping experiences before making a purchase. If you never have heard of a particular online business, do not entrust them with your credit card information. For more information, visit scsite.com/dc2008/ch2/faq and then click Online Shopping.

OTHER INTERNET SERVICES

The Web is only one of the many services on the Internet. The Web and other Internet services have changed the way we communicate. We can send e-mail messages to the president, have a discussion with experts about the stock market, chat with someone in another country about genealogy, and talk about homework assignments with classmates via instant messages. Many times, these communications take place completely in writing — without the parties ever meeting each other.

At home, work, and school, people use computers and Internet-enabled mobile devices so they always have instant access to e-mail, FTP (File Transfer Protocol), newsgroups and message boards, mailing lists, chat rooms, instant messaging, and Internet telephony. The following pages discuss each of these Internet services.

E-Mail

E-mail (short for *electronic mail*) is the transmission of messages and files via a computer network. E-mail was one of the original services on the Internet, enabling scientists and researchers working on government-sponsored projects to communicate with colleagues at other locations. Today, e-mail is a primary communications method for both personal and business use.

You use an **e-mail program** to create, send, receive, forward, store, print, and delete e-mail messages. Outlook and Outlook Express are two popular e-mail programs. The steps in Figure 2-26 illustrate how to send an e-mail message using Outlook. The message can be simple text or can include an attachment such as a word processing document, a graphic, an audio clip, or a video clip.

FIGURE 2-26 HOW TO SEND AN E-MAIL MESSAGE

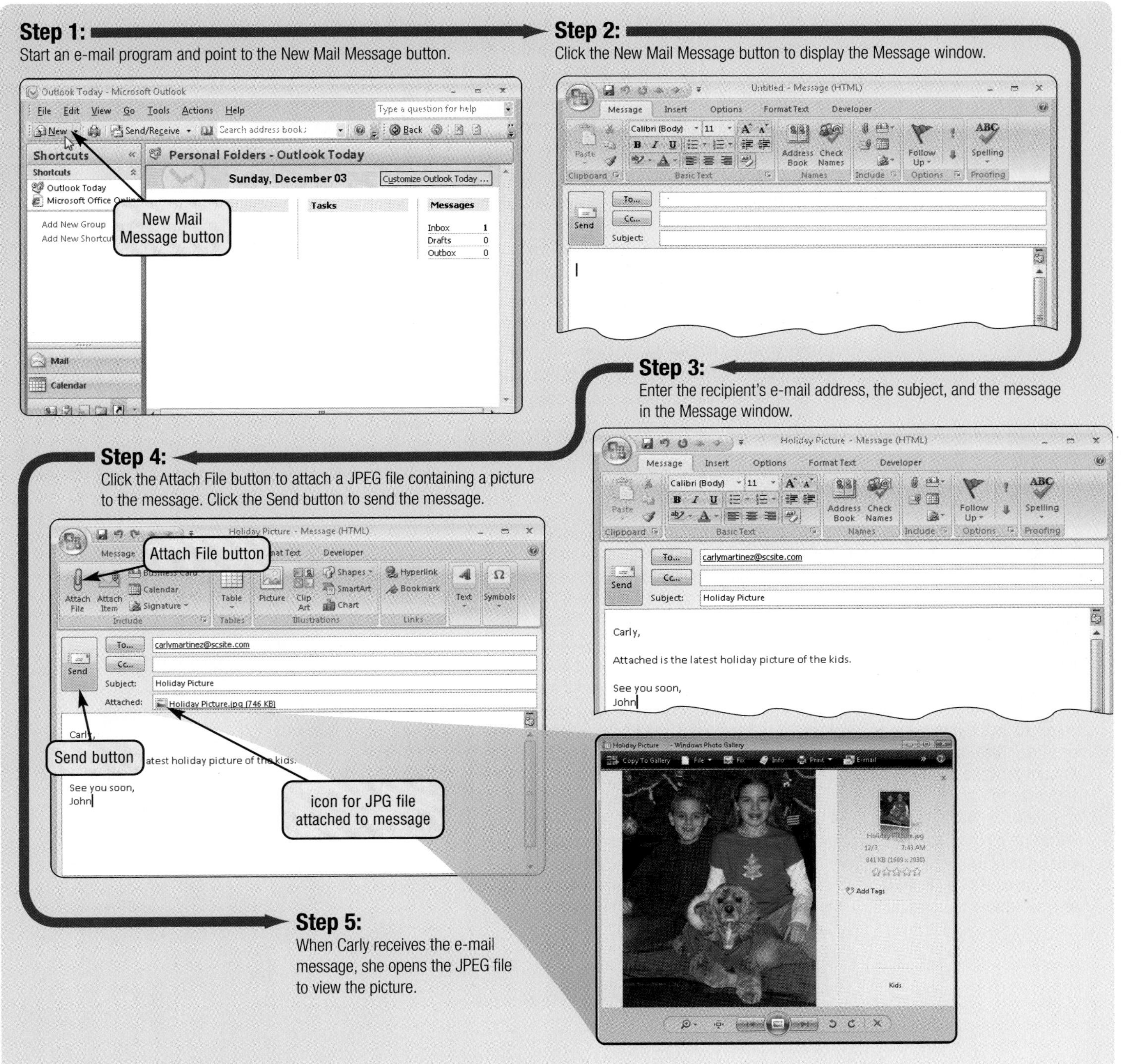

Step 1:
Start an e-mail program and point to the New Mail Message button.
New Mail Message button
Step 2:
Click the New Mail Message button to display the Message window.
Step 3:
Enter the recipient's e-mail address, the subject, and the message in the Message window.
Step 4:
Click the Attach File button to attach a JPEG file containing a picture to the message. Click the Send button to send the message.
Attach File button
Send button
icon for JPG file attached to message
Step 5:
When Carly receives the e-mail message, she opens the JPEG file to view the picture.

Internet access providers typically supply an e-mail program as a standard part of their Internet access services. Some Web sites, such as Google Gmail, MSN Hotmail, and Yahoo! Mail, provide free e-mail services. To use these Web-based e-mail programs, you connect to the Web site and set up an e-mail account, which typically includes an e-mail address and a password. Read Ethics & Issues 2-3 for a related discussion.

Just as you address a letter when using the postal system, you must address an e-mail message with the e-mail address of your intended recipient. Likewise, when someone sends you a message, they must have your e-mail address. An **e-mail address** is a combination of a user name and a domain name that identifies a user so he or she can receive Internet e-mail (Figure 2-27).

A **user name** is a unique combination of characters, such as letters of the alphabet and/or numbers, that identifies a specific user. Your user name must be different from the other user names in the same domain. For example, a user named Carly Martinez whose server has a domain name of scsite.com might want to select CMartinez as her user name. If scsite.com already has a CMartinez (for Carlos Martinez), Carly will have to select a different user name, such as carlymartinez or carly_martinez.

Sometimes, companies decide user names for employees. In many cases, however, users select their own user names, often selecting a nickname or any other combination of characters for their user name. Many users select a combination of their first and last names so others can remember it easily.

In an Internet e-mail address, an @ (pronounced at) symbol separates the user name from the domain name. Your service provider supplies the domain name. Using the example in Figure 2-27, a possible e-mail address for Carly Martinez would be carlymartinez@scsite.com, which would be read as follows: Carly Martinez at s c site dot com. Most e-mail programs allow you to create an **address book**, which contains a list of names and e-mail addresses.

When you send an e-mail message, an outgoing mail server that is operated by your Internet access provider determines how to route the message through the Internet and then sends the message. *SMTP* (simple mail transfer protocol) is a communications protocol used by some outgoing mail servers.

ETHICS & ISSUES 2-3

E-Mail: Irritant or Liberator?

E-mail is one of the more popular services on the Internet. Worldwide, approximately 1 billion people send and receive e-mail messages. E-mail makes business managers more productive by allowing them to share information, ideas, and opinions easily. But ironically, this easy sharing also can make managers less productive. Every day, managers wade through rivers of e-mail messages. Some of the messages are important, but many are copies of messages sent to others, notes on minor matters, or observations once shared in brief telephone calls or on walks to the water cooler. Most messages expect a quick reply, so hours can be spent dealing with e-mail. The constant flow of e-mail steals the time and interrupts the concentration needed for everyday work activities. Even worse, as managers become accustomed to the brief, rapid thinking demanded for e-mail, they can become unused to the creative, contemplative, persistent thought processes required for complex projects. Managers use a variety of measures to dam the flood of e-mail, including limiting the amount of time spent on messages, having colleagues telephone when they send important messages, and using filtering software to prioritize messages. What is the best way to deal with e-mail? Why? In terms of productivity, how can a company maximize the advantages of e-mail and minimize the disadvantages? Would you trust an automated tool to sort and organize your e-mail for you? Why or why not?

FIGURE 2-27 An e-mail address is a combination of a user name and a domain name.

As you receive e-mail messages, an incoming mail server — also operated by your Internet access provider — holds the messages in your mailbox until you use your e-mail program to retrieve them. *POP3*, the latest version of POP (*Post Office Protocol*), is a communications protocol used by some incoming mail servers. Most e-mail programs have a mail notification alert that informs you via a message and/or sound when you receive new mail. Figure 2-28 illustrates how an e-mail message may travel from a sender to a receiver.

E-Mail

For more information, visit scsite.com/dc2008/ch2/weblink and then click E-Mail.

FAQ 2-9

Can my computer get a virus through e-mail?

Yes. A *virus* is a computer program that can damage files and the operating system. One way that virus authors attempt to spread a virus is by sending virus-infected e-mail attachments. If you receive an e-mail attachment, you should use an antivirus program to verify that it is virus free.

For more information, read the High-Tech Talk article on page 168, the section about viruses and antivirus programs in Chapter 8, and visit scsite.com/dc2008/ch2/faq and then click Viruses.

FIGURE 2-28 HOW AN E-MAIL MESSAGE MAY TRAVEL FROM A SENDER TO A RECEIVER

Step 1: Using e-mail software, you create and send a message.

Internet service provider's outgoing mail server

outgoing mail server

Step 2: Your software contacts software on your service provider's outgoing mail server.

Step 3: Software on the outgoing mail server determines the best route for the data and sends the message, which travels along Internet routers to the recipient's incoming mail server.

Internet service provider's incoming mail server

INCOMING MAIL SERVER

Ann, Ed, Steve, Sally, Ted, Jean, Louie, Joe, Fred

Step 4: When the recipient uses e-mail software to check for e-mail messages, the message transfers from the incoming mail server to the recipient's computer.

Internet router

Internet router

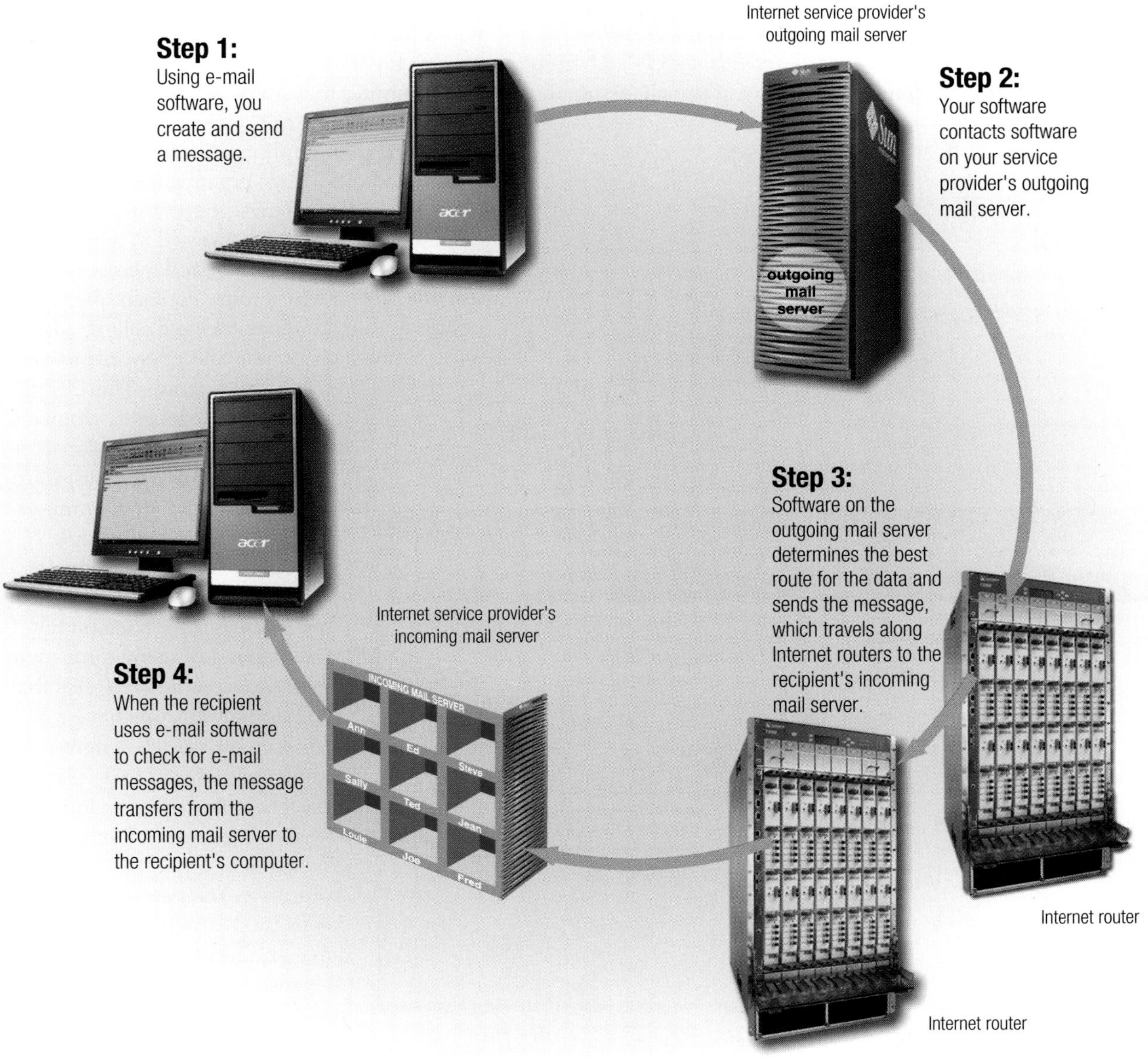

FTP

FTP (*File Transfer Protocol*) is an Internet standard that permits file uploading and downloading (transferring) with other computers on the Internet. Uploading is the opposite of downloading; that is, **uploading** is the process of transferring documents, graphics, and other objects from your computer to a server on the Internet. Web page authors, for example, often use FTP to upload their Web pages to a Web server.

Many operating systems include FTP capabilities (Figure 2-29). If yours does not, you can download FTP programs from the Web, usually for a small fee.

WEB LINK 2-7

FTP

For more information, visit scsite.com/dc2008/ch2/weblink and then click FTP.

An *FTP server* is a computer that allows users to upload and/or download files using FTP. An FTP site is a collection of files including text, graphics, audio clips, video clips, and program files that reside on an FTP server. Many FTP sites have *anonymous FTP*, whereby anyone can transfer some, if not all, available files. Some FTP sites restrict file transfers to those who have authorized accounts (user names and passwords) on the FTP server.

Large files on FTP sites often are compressed to reduce storage space and download time. Before you can use a compressed (zipped) file, you must uncompress (unzip) it. Chapter 8 discusses utilities that zip and unzip files.

FIGURE 2-29a (FTP site being added to My Network Places folder)

FIGURE 2-29b (FTP site link is displayed in My Network Places folder)

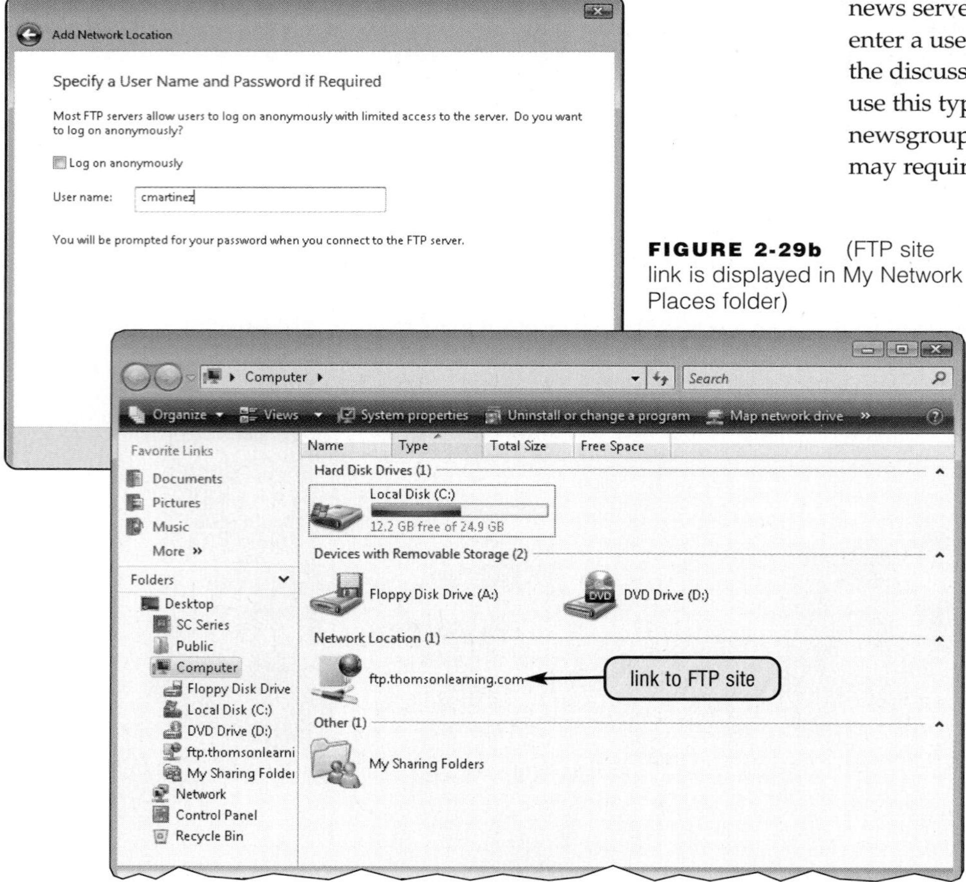

FIGURE 2-29 Many operating systems, such as Windows Vista, have built-in FTP capabilities.

Newsgroups and Message Boards

A **newsgroup** is an online area in which users have written discussions about a particular subject (Figure 2-30). To participate in a discussion, a user sends a message to the newsgroup, and other users in the newsgroup read and reply to the message. The entire collection of Internet newsgroups is called *Usenet*, which contains tens of thousands of newsgroups about a multitude of topics. Some major topic areas include news, recreation, society, business, science, and computers.

A computer that stores and distributes newsgroup messages is called a *news server*. Many universities, corporations, Internet access providers, and other large organizations have a news server. Some newsgroups require you to enter a user name and password to participate in the discussion. Only authorized members can use this type of newsgroup. For example, a newsgroup for students taking a college course may require a user name and password to access the newsgroup. This ensures that only students in the course participate in the discussion.

To participate in a newsgroup, typically you use a program called a *newsreader*. Outlook Express includes a newsreader. You also can download newsreaders free or for a fee on the Web. Instead of using your own newsreader, some Web sites that sponsor newsgroups have a built-in newsreader. A newsreader enables you to access a newsgroup to read previously entered messages, called *articles*. You can *post*, or add, articles of your own. The newsreader also keeps track of which articles you have and have not read.

Newsgroup members frequently post articles as a reply to another article — either to

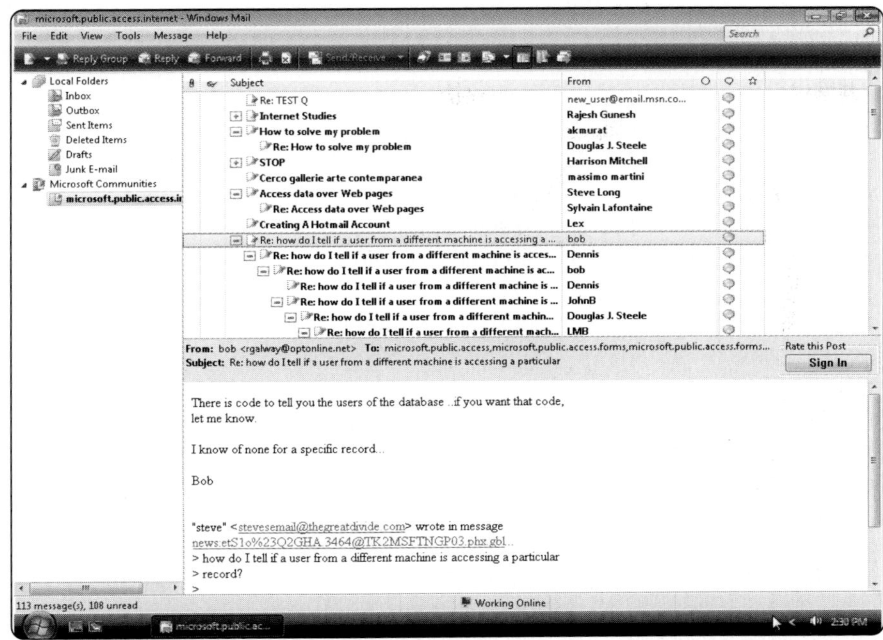

FIGURE 2-30 Users in a newsgroup read and reply to other users' messages.

answer a question or to comment on material in the original article. These replies may cause the author of the original article, or others, to post additional articles related to the original article. A *thread* or *threaded discussion* consists of the original article and all subsequent related replies. A thread can be short-lived or continue for some time, depending on the nature of the topic and the interest of the participants.

Using a newsreader, you can search for newsgroups discussing a particular subject such as a type of musical instrument, brand of sports equipment, or employment opportunities. If you like the discussion in a particular newsgroup, you can subscribe to it, which means its location is saved in your newsreader for easy future access.

In some newsgroups, posted articles are sent to a moderator instead of immediately displaying on the newsgroup. The *moderator* reviews the contents of the article and then posts it, if appropriate. With a *moderated newsgroup*, the moderator decides if the article is relevant to the discussion. The moderator may choose to edit or discard inappropriate articles. For this reason, the content of a moderated newsgroup is considered more valuable.

A popular Web-based type of discussion group that does not require a newsreader is a **message board**. Many Web sites use message boards instead of newsgroups because they are easier to use.

Mailing Lists

A **mailing list** is a group of e-mail names and addresses given a single name. When a message is sent to a mailing list, every person on the list receives a copy of the message in his or her mailbox. To add your e-mail name and address to a mailing list, you **subscribe** to it (Figure 2-31). To remove your name, you **unsubscribe** from the mailing list. Some mailing lists are called *LISTSERVs*, named after a popular mailing list program.

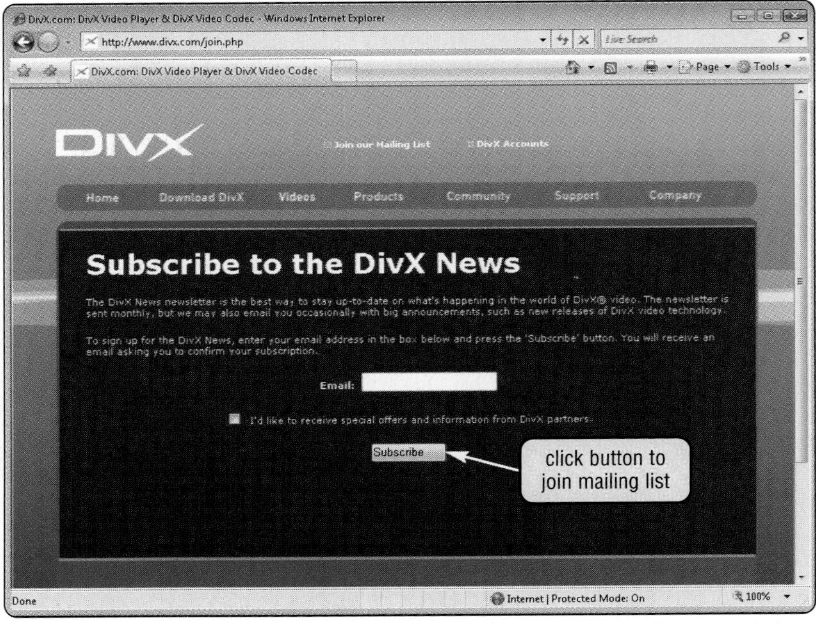

FIGURE 2-31 When you join a mailing list, you and all others on the mailing list receive e-mail messages from the Web site.

WEB LINK 2-9

Mailing Lists

For more information, visit scsite.com/dc2008/ch2/weblink and then click Mailing Lists.

Thousands of mailing lists exist about a variety of topics in areas of entertainment, business, computers, society, culture, health, recreation, and education. To locate a mailing list dealing with a particular topic, search for the keywords, mailing list or LISTSERV, in a search engine. Many vendors use mailing lists to communicate with their customer base.

Chat Rooms

A **chat** is a real-time typed conversation that takes place on a computer. **Real time** means that you and the people with whom you are conversing are online at the same time. A **chat room** is a location on an Internet server that permits users to chat with each other. Anyone in the chat room can participate in the conversation, which usually is specific to a particular topic.

WEB LINK 2-10

Chat Rooms

For more information, visit scsite.com/dc2008/ch2/weblink and then click Chat Rooms.

As you type on your keyboard, a line of characters and symbols is displayed on the computer screen. Others connected to the same chat room server also see what you have typed (Figure 2-32). Some chat rooms support voice chats and video chats, in which people hear or see each other as they chat.

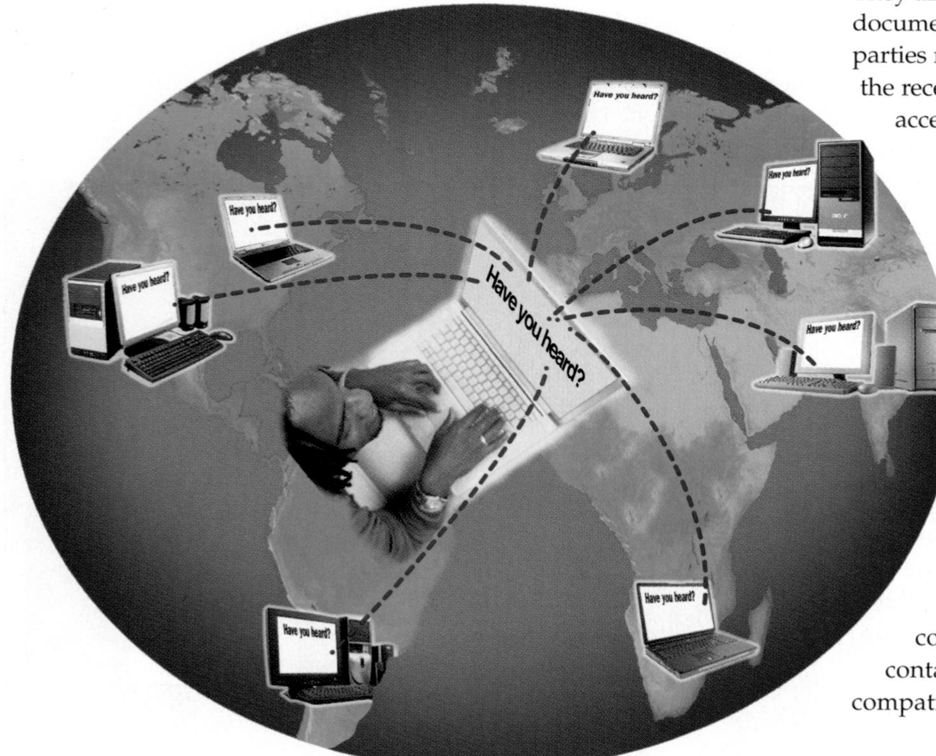

FIGURE 2-32 As you type, the words and symbols you enter are displayed on the computer screens of other people in the same chat room.

To start a chat session, you connect to a chat server through a program called a *chat client*. Today's browsers usually include a chat client. If yours does not, you can download a chat client from the Web. Some Web sites allow users to conduct chats without a chat client.

Once you have installed a chat client, you can create or join a conversation on the chat server to which you are connected. The chat room should indicate the discussion topic. The person who creates a chat room acts as the operator and has responsibility for monitoring the conversation and disconnecting anyone who becomes disruptive. Operator status can be shared or transferred to someone else.

Instant Messaging

Instant messaging (IM) is a real-time Internet communications service that notifies you when one or more people are online and then allows you to exchange messages or files or join a private chat room with them. Some IM services support voice and video conversations (Figure 2-33). Many IM services also can alert you to information such as calendar appointments, stock quotes, weather, or sports scores. They also allow you to send pictures or other documents to a recipient. For IM to work, both parties must be online at the same time. Also, the receiver of a message must be willing to accept messages.

People use IM on all types of computers, including desktop computers and mobile computers and devices, such as smart phones. To use IM, you may have to install *instant messenger* software on the computer or device you plan to use. Some operating systems, such as Windows Vista, include an instant messenger. Popular IM software includes AIM (AOL Instant Messenger), Google Talk, Windows Live Messenger, and Yahoo! Messenger. No standards currently exist for IM. To ensure successful communications, all individuals on the contact list need to use the same or a compatible instant messenger.

FIGURE 2-33 AN EXAMPLE OF INSTANT MESSAGING

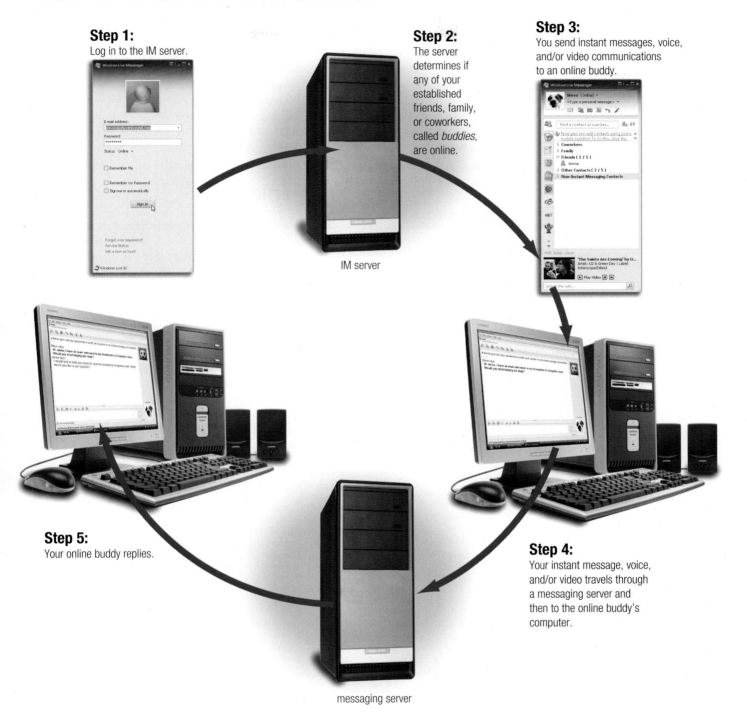

Step 1:
Log in to the IM server.

Step 2:
The server determines if any of your established friends, family, or coworkers, called *buddies*, are online.

IM server

Step 3:
You send instant messages, voice, and/or video communications to an online buddy.

Step 4:
Your instant message, voice, and/or video travels through a messaging server and then to the online buddy's computer.

messaging server

Step 5:
Your online buddy replies.

Internet Telephony

Internet telephony, also called *Voice over IP* (Internet Protocol) or *VoIP*, enables users to speak to other users over the Internet. That is, Internet telephony uses the Internet (instead of the public switched telephone network) to connect a calling party to one or more local or long-distance called parties.

To place an Internet telephone call, you need a high-speed Internet connection (e.g., via DSL or cable modem); Internet telephone service; a microphone or telephone, depending on the Internet telephone service; and Internet telephone software or a telephone adapter, depending on the Internet telephone service. Calls to other parties with the same Internet telephone service often are free, while calls that connect to the telephone network typically cost about $15 to $25 per month.

Internet Telephony
For more information, visit scsite.com/dc2008/ch2/weblink and then click Internet Telephony.

As you speak in a microphone connected to your computer or a telephone connected to the telephone adapter, the Internet telephone software and the computer's sound card or the telephone adapter convert your spoken words (analog signals) to digital signals and then transmit the digitized audio over the Internet to the called parties. Software and equipment at the receiving end reverse the process so the receiving parties can hear what you have said. Figure 2-34 illustrates a user's equipment configuration for Internet telephony.

FAQ 2-10

How popular is Internet telephony?

Vonage, a leader in Internet telephony service, recently indicated that it has more than 2 million subscriber lines. For more information, visit scsite.com/dc2008/ch2/faq and then click Internet Telephony.

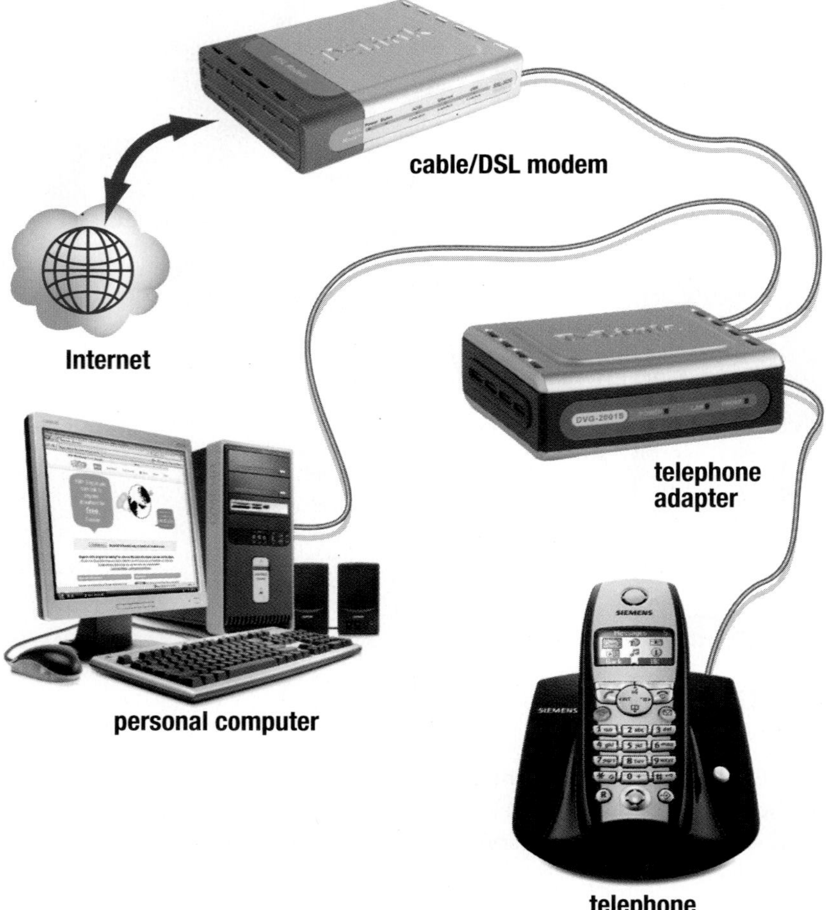

FIGURE 2-34 Equipment configuration for a user making a call via Internet telephony.

NETIQUETTE

Netiquette, which is short for Internet etiquette, is the code of acceptable behaviors users should follow while on the Internet; that is, it is the conduct expected of individuals while online. Netiquette includes rules for all aspects of the Internet, including the World Wide Web, e-mail, FTP, newsgroups and message boards, chat rooms, and instant messaging. Figure 2-35 outlines some of the rules of netiquette.

NETIQUETTE

Golden Rule: Treat others as you would like them to treat you.

1. In e-mail, newsgroups, and chat rooms:
   - Keep messages brief. Use proper grammar, spelling, and punctuation.
   - Be careful when using sarcasm and humor, as it might be misinterpreted.
   - Be polite. Avoid offensive language.
   - Read the message before you send it.
   - Use meaningful subject lines.
   - Avoid sending or posting *flames*, which are abusive or insulting messages. Do not participate in *flame wars*, which are exchanges of flames.
   - Avoid sending spam, which is the Internet's version of junk mail. *Spam* is an unsolicited e-mail message or newsgroup posting sent to many recipients or newsgroups at once.
   - Do not use all capital letters, which is the equivalent of SHOUTING!
   - Use **emoticons** to express emotion. Popular emoticons include

:)	Smile	:\	Undecided
:(	Frown	:o	Surprised
:I	Indifference		

   - Use abbreviations and acronyms for phrases:

BTW	by the way
FYI	for your information
FWIW	for what it's worth
IMHO	in my humble opinion
TTFN	ta ta for now
TYVM	thank you very much

   - Clearly identify a *spoiler*, which is a message that reveals a solution to a game or ending to a movie or program.
2. Read the *FAQ* (frequently asked questions), if one exists. Many newsgroups and Web pages have an FAQ.
3. Do not assume material is accurate or up-to-date. Be forgiving of other's mistakes.
4. Never read someone's private e-mail.

FIGURE 2-35 Some of the rules of netiquette.

Test your knowledge of pages 91 through 100 in Quiz Yourself 2-3.

QUIZ YOURSELF 2-3

Instructions: Find the true statement below. Then, rewrite the remaining false statements so they are true.

1. A chat room is a location on an Internet server that permits users to chat with each other.
2. An e-mail address is a combination of a user name and an e-mail program that identifies a user so he or she can receive Internet e-mail.
3. Business-to-consumer e-commerce occurs when one consumer sells directly to another, such as in an online auction.
4. FTP is an Internet standard that permits file reading and writing with other computers on the Internet.
5. Spam uses the Internet (instead of the public switched telephone network) to connect a calling party to one or more called parties.
6. Netiquette is the code of unacceptable behaviors while on the Internet.
7. On a newsgroup, a subscription consists of the original article and all subsequent related replies.

Quiz Yourself Online: To further check your knowledge of e-commerce, e-mail, FTP, newsgroups and message boards, mailing lists, chat rooms, instant messaging, Internet telephony, and netiquette, visit scsite.com/dc2008/ch2/quiz and then click Objectives 10 – 12.

CHAPTER SUMMARY

This chapter presented the history and structure of the Internet. It discussed the World Wide Web at length, including topics such as browsing, navigating, searching, Web publishing, and e-commerce (read Ethics & Issues 2-4 for a related discussion). It also introduced other services available on the Internet, such as e-mail, FTP, newsgroups and message boards, chat rooms, instant messaging, and Internet telephony. Finally, the chapter listed rules of netiquette.

ETHICS & ISSUES 2-4

Should Companies Be Able to Track Your Online Habits?

When you visit a Web site that includes an advertisement, someone probably is recording the fact that you visited that Web site and viewed the advertisement with your browser. Over time, companies that specialize in tracking who views which online advertisements can amass an enormous amount of information about your online Web surfing habits. This collection of information is considered to be part of your *online profile.* One company claims that through the use of advertisements on Web pages, it can track well over one billion Web page views per day. Through tracking the Web sites a user visits, the products they buy, and the articles they read, a company may attempt to profile the visitor's beliefs, associations, and habits. Although a user may think he or she is anonymous while navigating the Web, the company can attempt through various means to link the user's true identity with the user's online profile. The company can sell online profiles, with or without the user's true identity, to other advertisers or organizations. Should organizations be allowed to track your Web surfing habits? Why or why not? Should organizations be allowed to associate your real identity with your online identity and profit from the information? Should companies give you the option of not being tracked? What are the benefits and dangers of online tracking?

CAREER CORNER

Web Developer

If you are looking for a job working with the latest Internet technology, then Web developer could be the career for you. A *Web developer* analyzes, designs, develops, implements, and supports Web applications and functionality. Specialized programming skills required include HTML, JavaScript, Java, Perl, C++, and VBScript. Developers also need multimedia knowledge, including Photoshop, Flash, and Dreamweaver. Developers must be aware of emerging technologies and know how they can be used to enhance a Web presence.

A Web developer must be able to appreciate a client's needs, recognize the technologies involved to meet those needs, and explain those technologies to the client. For example, if the client is a large corporation seeking to set up an online store, a Web developer must understand e-commerce and be able to explain requirements, probable costs, and possible outcomes in a way the client can understand.

Educational requirements vary from company to company and can range from a high school education to a four-year degree. Many companies place heavy emphasis on certifications. Two of the more popular certifications are available through the International Webmasters Association (IWA) and the World Organization of Webmasters (WOW). A wide salary range exists — from \$40,000 to \$80,000 — depending on educational background and location. For more information, visit scsite.com/dc2008/ch2/careers and then click Web Developer.

High-Tech Talk

A COMPUTER'S INTERNET PROTOCOL (IP) ADDRESS

Every computer on the Internet has a unique address, called an IP address, that distinguishes it from other computers on the Internet. An IP address has two parts that identify a specific computer: one part to identify the network where that computer resides and a second part to pinpoint the specific computer or host within that network.

A typical IP address — such as 216.239.39.99 — has four groups of numbers that range from 0 through 255. This form of the IP address sometimes is called a *dotted decimal number* or *dotted quad*. The four groups of numbers in the dotted quad are called octets, because they each have 8 bits when viewed in binary form for a total of 32 bits in the IP address. For instance, the binary form of 216.239.39.99 is 11011000.11101111.00101001.01100011 (Figure 2-36). For more information about how the binary system works, see Appendix A.

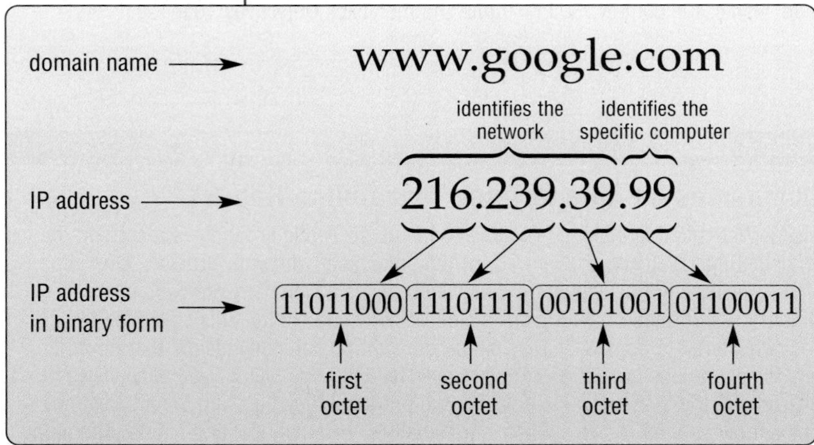

FIGURE 2-36 Components of an IP address.

Because each of the 8 bits can be 1 or 0, the total possible combinations per octet are 2^8, or 256. Combining the four octets of an IP address provides a possible 2^{32} or 4,294,967,296 unique values. The actual number of available addresses is about 3 billion, because some values are reserved for special use and are, therefore, off limits.

To request data such as a Web page from a computer on the Internet, you need only an IP address. For instance, if you type the Web address, http://216.239.39.99, your browser will display the home page on the machine hosting the Google Web site. Of course, remembering one IP address out of billions is a little overwhelming — so you probably would just type the domain name, www.google.com, in your browser. Your browser then contacts a domain name server (DNS) to resolve the human-readable domain name into a machine-readable IP address. Each domain name server houses a simple database that maps domain names to IP addresses. The DNS would resolve the human-readable domain name, www.google.com, into a machine-readable IP address, 216.239.39.99.

Domain names are helpful because they are easier for people to remember than IP addresses. You can learn more about a domain using the whois form at the Network Solutions Web site (www.netsol.com and then click the WHOIS link). If you type a domain name, such as google.com, the form displays the registration information for that domain, including its IP address.

Like all other computers, your computer must have an IP address to connect to the Internet or another computer that has an IP address. Servers generally have *static IP addresses*, because they usually are connected to the Internet and their IP addresses do not change often. When you connect to the Internet using your home computer, you most likely are using a temporary or *dynamic IP address*. Your access provider uses the *Dynamic Host Configuration Protocol (DHCP)* to assign your computer a temporary dynamic IP address from a pool of IP addresses. The dynamic IP address is unique only for that session. Once you disconnect, the DHCP server puts that IP address back in the IP address pool so it can assign it to the next requesting computer. Even if you immediately reconnect, the DHCP server might not assign you the same IP address. Using DHCP and dynamic IP addresses means an Internet service provider needs only one IP address for each modem it supports, rather than one for each of its millions of customers.

Billions of IP addresses sounds like a lot. But, because so many computers connected to the Internet need unique IP addresses, a growing shortage of IP addresses exists. A new IP addressing scheme, called *IPv6* or *IPng (IP Next Generation)* will lengthen IP addresses from 32 bits to 128 bits and increase the number of available IP addresses to a whopping 3.4×10^{38}, or 340,000,000,000,000,000,000,000,000,000,000,000,000.

Do you want to know the IP address currently assigned to your computer?

- With Windows Vista, click the Start button on the Windows taskbar and then click Control Panel. Click Network and Internet, and then click View Network Status and Tasks. Finally, click View status, and then click Details.
- With Windows 2000/XP, click the Start button on the taskbar and then click Run. Type `cmd` to open the MS-DOS window. Type `ipconfig` and then press the ENTER key.

If you are using an older version of AOL, the IP address might read 0.0.0.0 because AOL uses a proprietary method to assign IP addresses. For more information, visit scsite.com/dc2008/ch2/tech and then click IP Addresses.

Companies on the Cutting Edge

GOOGLE
POPULAR SEARCH ENGINE

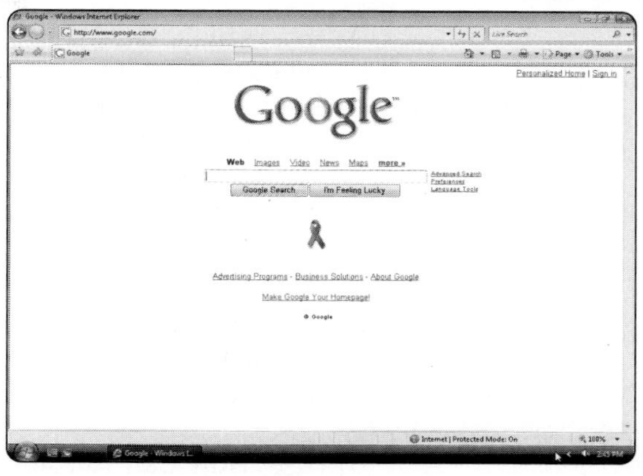

The founders of *Google*, the leading Internet search engine, state that their mission is to organize the world's information. Every day, their Web site handles hundreds of millions of queries for information. In seconds, it can locate specific phrases and terms on four billion Web pages by using more than 10,000 connected computers.

Sergey Brin and Larry Page launched Google in 1998 in a friend's garage. The name is derived from "googol," which is the name of the number 1 followed by 100 zeros. Google began offering a suite of business applications in 2006 that includes Gmail, Google Calendar, Google Talk, and Page Creator, along with test versions of spreadsheet and word processing software. For more information, visit scsite.com/dc2008/ch2/companies and then click Google.

YAHOO!
POPULAR WEB PORTAL

Yahoo!, the first navigational portal to the Web, began as a hobby for Jerry Yang and David Filo when they were doctoral candidates in electrical engineering at Stanford University. They started creating and organizing lists of their favorite Web sites in 1994. The following year, they shared their creation, named Yahoo!, with fellow students and then released their product to the Internet community.

Yahoo! is an acronym for Yet Another Hierarchical Officious Oracle. What makes Yahoo! unique is that staff members build the directory by assuming the role of a typical Web researcher. Yahoo! Answers became the second most popular Internet reference site in 2006, handling more than 12 million visitors each month. Its attractiveness is based upon the fact that anyone can ask a question at no cost, and practically anyone can offer an answer. For more information, visit scsite.com/dc2008/ch2/companies and then click Yahoo!.

Technology Trailblazers

TIM BERNERS-LEE
CREATOR OF THE WORLD WIDE WEB

The World Wide Web (WWW) has become one of the more widely used Internet services, and its roots are based on *Tim Berners-Lee's* work. Berners-Lee is credited with creating the first Web server, browser, and URL addresses.

He developed his ideas in 1989 while working at CERN, the European Particle Physics Laboratory in Geneva, Switzerland, and based his work on a program he had written for his own use to track random associations. Today, he works quietly in academia as director of the World Wide Web Consortium (W3C) at the Massachusetts Institute of Technology.

In a 2006 podcast, Berners-Lee explained that he had to disable the feedback function of his inaugural blog entry in 2005 because of the overwhelming number of responses. He modestly said that most of the comments thanked him for his work; he, in turn, thanked the Web users for their support of his product. For more information, visit scsite.com/dc2008/ch2/people and then click Tim Berners-Lee.

MEG WHITMAN
EBAY PRESIDENT AND CEO

Meg Whitman joined eBay in 1998 and has been instrumental in helping the company become the world's largest online marketplace. Before that time, she was an executive for the Keds Division of the Stride Rite Corporation and general manager of Hasbro Inc.'s Preschool Division. She then served as president and CEO of Florists Transworld Delivery (FTD).

She credits her success to listening to the loyal eBay community, and she occasionally answers their e-mails personally. She holds degrees in economics from Princeton University and management from the Harvard Business School.

eBay fields approximately 350 million searches daily for products. In 2006, Whitman chose Google to run search-related text advertisements on eBay's pages outside of the United States. The two companies also will share advertising revenues generated when consumers use eBay's Skype Internet telephone software and Google Talk. For more information, visit scsite.com/dc2008/ch2/people and then click Meg Whitman.

Quizzes and Learning Games
- Computer Genius
- Crossword Puzzle
- DC Track and Field
- Practice Test
- Quiz Yourself
- Wheel of Terms
- You're Hired!

Exercises
- Case Studies
- Chapter Review
- Checkpoint
- Key Terms
- Learn How To
- Learn It Online
- Web Research

Beyond the Book
- Career Corner
- Companies
- FAQs
- High-Tech Talk
- Looking Ahead
- Making Use of the Web
- Trailblazers
- Web Links

Features
- Chapter Forum
- Install Computer
- Lab Exercises
- Maintain Computer
- Tech News
- Timeline 2008

Chapter Review

The Chapter Review section summarizes the concepts presented in this chapter. To listen to the audio version of this Chapter Review, visit scsite.com/dc2008/ch2/review. To obtain help from other students regarding any subject in this chapter, visit scsite.com/dc2008/ch2/forum and post your thoughts or questions.

1 **What Is the History of the Internet?** The **Internet** is a worldwide collection of networks that links millions of businesses, government agencies, educational institutions, and individuals. The Internet has its roots in *ARPANET*, a network started in 1969 to link researchers across the United States. In 1986, the National Science Foundation connected its huge network, called *NSFnet*, to ARPANET, creating a configuration of complex networks and hosts that became known as the Internet.

2 **How Can You Access and Connect to the Internet?** Employees and students often connect to the Internet through a business or school network. The networks usually use a high-speed line. Some home and small businesses connect to the Internet with **dial-up access**, which uses a modem in the computer and a standard telephone line. Many home and small business users opt for higher-speed *broadband* connections, such as DSL, cable television networks, radio signals, or satellite. **DSL** provides Internet connections using regular copper telephone lines. A **cable modem** allows access to Internet services through the cable television network. *Fixed wireless* connections use a dish-shaped antenna to communicate via radio signals. A *Wi-Fi* network uses radio signals. A *satellite modem* communicates with a satellite dish. An **access provider** is a business that provides access to the Internet free or for a fee. An **ISP** (**Internet service provider**) is a regional or national access provider. An **online service provider** (**OSP**) provides Internet access in addition to members-only features. A **wireless Internet service provider** *(WISP)* provides wireless Internet access to computers and mobile devices with built-in wireless capabilities or access devices.

3 **What Is an IP Address?** An **IP address** (*Internet Protocol address*) is a number that uniquely identifies each computer or device connected to the Internet. The Internet relies on IP addresses to send data to computers at specific locations. A **domain name** is the text version of an IP address.

connect
Visit scsite.com/dc2008/ch2/quiz or click the Quiz Yourself button. Click Objectives 1 – 3.

4 **What Are the Components of a Web Address?** The **World Wide Web** (*WWW*), or **Web**, consists of a worldwide collection of electronic documents. Each electronic document is called a **Web page**. A **URL** (*Uniform Resource Locator*), or **Web address**, is a unique address for a Web page. A Web address consists of a protocol, a domain name, and sometimes the path to a specific Web page or location on a Web page.

5 **What Is the Purpose of a Web Browser?** A **Web browser**, or **browser**, is application software that allows users to access and view Web pages. When you type a Web address in the Address box of a browser window, a computer called a **Web server** delivers the requested Web page to your computer. Most Web pages contain links. A **link** is a built-in connection that, when clicked, displays a related Web page or part of a Web page.

6 **How Can You Search for Information on the Web?** Two commonly used search tools are subject directories and search engines. A **subject directory** classifies Web pages in an organized set of categories. By clicking links, you move through categories to display a list of Web pages about a desired topic. A **search engine** is a program that finds Web sites, Web pages, images, videos, news, and other information. To use a search engine, you enter a word or phrase, called **search text**, that defines the item about which you want information. The search engine displays a list of *hits*. When clicked, each hit displays an associated Web site or Web page.

Chapter Review

⑦ **What Are the Types of Web Sites?** A **portal** is a Web site that offers a variety of Internet services from a single location. A news Web site contains newsworthy material. An informational Web site contains factual information. A business/marketing Web site promotes or sells products or services. An educational Web site offers avenues for teaching and learning. An entertainment Web site provides an interactive and engaging environment. An advocacy Web site describes a cause, opinion, or idea. A **blog** is an informal Web site consisting of time-stamped articles, or posts, in a diary or journal format, usually listed in reverse chronological order. A **wiki** is a collaborative Web site that allows users to create, add to, modify, or delete the Web site content via their Web browser. An **online social network**, or **social networking Web site**, encourages members to share their interests, ideas, stories, photos, music, and videos with other registered users. A *content aggregator* is a business that gathers and organizes Web content and then distributes, or feeds, the content to subscribers for free or a fee. A personal Web site is maintained by a private individual or family.

⑧ **How Do Web Pages Use Graphics, Animation, Audio, Video, Virtual Reality, and Plug-Ins?** Some Web pages use **multimedia**, which combines text with graphics, animation, audio, video, and/or virtual reality. A **graphic** is a digital representation of nontext information such as a drawing or photograph. **Animation** is the appearance of motion created by displaying a series of still images. **Audio** includes music, speech, or any other sound. **Video** consists of full-motion images. **Virtual reality** (**VR**) is the use of computers to simulate an environment that appears as three-dimensional space. A **plug-in** is a program that extends a browser's capability to display multimedia elements.

⑨ **What Are the Steps Required for Web Publishing?** **Web publishing** is the development and maintenance of Web pages. The five major steps to Web publishing are: (1) plan a Web site, (2) analyze and design a Web site, (3) create a Web site, (4) deploy a Web site, and (5) maintain a Web site.

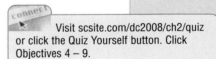

connect Visit scsite.com/dc2008/ch2/quiz or click the Quiz Yourself button. Click Objectives 4 – 9.

⑩ **What Are the Types of E-Commerce?** **E-commerce**, short for *electronic commerce*, is a business transaction that occurs over an electronic network such as the Internet. *Business-to-consumer (B2C) e-commerce* consists of the sale of goods and services to the general public. *Consumer-to-consumer (C2C) e-commerce* occurs when one consumer sells directly to another, such as an **online auction**. *Business-to-business (B2B) e-commerce* takes place between businesses that exchange goods and services.

⑪ **How Do E-Mail, FTP, Newsgroups and Message Boards, Mailing Lists, Chat Rooms, Instant Messaging, and Internet Telephony Work?** **E-mail** (short for *electronic mail*) is the transmission of messages and files via a computer network. **FTP** (*File Transfer Protocol*) is an Internet standard that permits file **uploading** and **downloading** with other computers. A **newsgroup** is an online area in which users have written discussions. A **message board** is a Web-based type of discussion group that is easier to use than a newsgroup. A **mailing list** is a group of e-mail names and addresses given a single name, so that everyone on the list receives a message sent to the list. A **chat room** is a location on an Internet server that permits users to conduct real-time typed conversations. **Instant messaging** (**IM**) is a real-time Internet communications service that notifies you when one or more people are online. **Internet telephony** enables users to speak to other users over the Internet.

⑫ **What Are the Rules of Netiquette?** **Netiquette**, which is short for Internet etiquette, is the code of acceptable behaviors users should follow while on the Internet. Netiquette rules include: keep messages short, be polite, avoid sending *flames* or *spam*, use **emoticons** and acronyms, read the *FAQ*, do not assume material is accurate or up-to-date, and never read someone's private e-mail.

connect Visit scsite.com/dc2008/ch2/quiz or click the Quiz Yourself button. Click Objectives 10 – 12.

Quizzes and Learning Games
Computer Genius
Crossword Puzzle
DC Track and Field
Practice Test
Quiz Yourself
Wheel of Terms
You're Hired!

Exercises
Case Studies
Chapter Review
Checkpoint
Key Terms
Learn How To
Learn It Online
Web Research

Beyond the Book
Career Corner
Companies
FAQs
High-Tech Talk
Looking Ahead
Making Use of the Web
Trailblazers
Web Links

Features
Chapter Forum
Install Computer
Lab Exercises
Maintain Computer
Tech News
Timeline 2008

Key Terms

You should know the Primary Terms and be familiar with the Secondary Terms. Use the list below to help focus your study. To further enhance your understanding of the Key Terms in this chapter, visit scsite.com/dc2008/ch2/terms. See an example of and a definition for each term, and access current and additional information about the term from the Web.

Primary Terms

(shown in bold-black characters in the chapter)

access provider (71)
address book (94)
animation (86)
audio (86)
blog (82)
browser (75)
cable modem (70)
chat (98)
chat room (98)
dial-up access (70)
DNS server (74)
domain name (73)
downloading (76)
DSL (70)
e-commerce (91)
electronic storefront (92)
e-mail (92)
e-mail address (94)
e-mail program (93)
emoticons (100)
FTP (96)
graphic (85)
home page (76)
instant messaging (IM) (98)
Internet (68)
Internet telephony (99)
IP address (73)
ISP (Internet service provider) (72)
link (77)
mailing list (97)
media sharing Web site (84)
message board (97)
MP3 (86)
multimedia (85)
netiquette (100)
newsgroup (96)
online auction (92)
online community (82)
online service provider (OSP) (72)
online social network (84)
player (86)
plug-in (89)
portal (82)
real time (98)
RSS 2.0 (84)
search engine (78)
search text (80)
shopping cart (92)
social networking Web site (84)
streaming (86)
subject directory (78)
subscribe (97)
surfing the Web (77)
traffic (70)
unsubscribe (97)
uploading (96)
URL (76)
user name (94)
video (88)
video blog (82)
virtual reality (VR) (88)
Web (75)
Web 2.0 (75)
Web address (76)
Web browser (75)
Web page (75)
Web publishing (90)
Web server (75)
Web site (75)
wiki (82)
wireless Internet service provider (72)
World Wide Web (75)

Secondary Terms

(shown in italic characters in the chapter)

ARPA (69)
animated GIF (86)
anonymous FTP (96)
ARPANET (69)
articles (96)
Atom (84)
blogger (82)
blogosphere (82)
broadband (70)
buddies (99)
business-to-business (B2B) e-commerce (92)
business-to-consumer (B2C) e-commerce (91)
ccTLD (74)
chat client (98)
click (76)
consumer-to-consumer (C2C) e-commerce (92)
content aggregator (84)
digital rights management (DRM) (86)
domain name system (DNS) (74)
dot-com (73)
dynamic Web page (75)
electronic commerce (91)
electronic mail (92)
FAQ (100)
File Transfer Protocol (96)
fixed wireless (70)
flame wars (100)
flames (100)
FTP server (96)
GIF (85)
graphical image (85)
gTLD (73)
hits (80)
host (69)
hot spots (71)
http (76)
hyperlink (77)
hypermedia (77)
hypertext (77)
Hypertext Transfer Protocol (76)
instant messenger (98)
Internet backbone (72)
Internet Corporation for Assigned Names and Numbers (ICANN) (74)
Internet Protocol address (73)
JPEG (85)
keywords (80)
LISTSERVs (97)
m-commerce (91)
microbrowser (76)
moderated newsgroup (97)
moderator (97)
MPEG (88)
MP4 (88)
MPEG-4 (88)
national ISP (72)
Net (68)
news server (96)
newsreader (96)
NSFnet (70)
participatory Web (75)
PNG (85)
podcast (86)
point of presence (POP) (72)
POP3 (95)
post (96)
Post Office Protocol (95)
pull (76)
push (76)
Really Simple Syndication (84)
regional ISP (72)
satellite modem (70)
SMTP (94)
spam (100)
spider (81)
spoiler (100)
static Web page (75)
streaming audio (86)
streaming video (88)
tabbed browsing (76)
thread (97)
threaded discussion (97)
thumbnail (86)
top-level domain (TLD) (73)
Uniform Resource Locator (76)
Usenet (96)
vlog (82)
vlogger (82)
vlogosphere (82)
Voice over IP (99)
VoIP (99)
VR world (88)
Weblog (82)
Wi-Fi (70)
wireless portal (82)
WISP (72)
World Wide Web Consortium (W3C) (70)
WWW (75)

Checkpoint

Use the Checkpoint exercises to check your knowledge level of the chapter. The Beyond the Book exercises will help broaden your understanding of the concepts presented in this chapter. To complete the Checkpoint exercises interactively, visit scsite.com/dc2008/ch2/check.

Label the Figure

Identify the types of Web sites.

a. advocacy
b. blog
c. business/marketing
d. content aggregator
e. educational
f. entertainment
g. informational
h. news
i. online social network
j. personal
k. portal
l. wiki

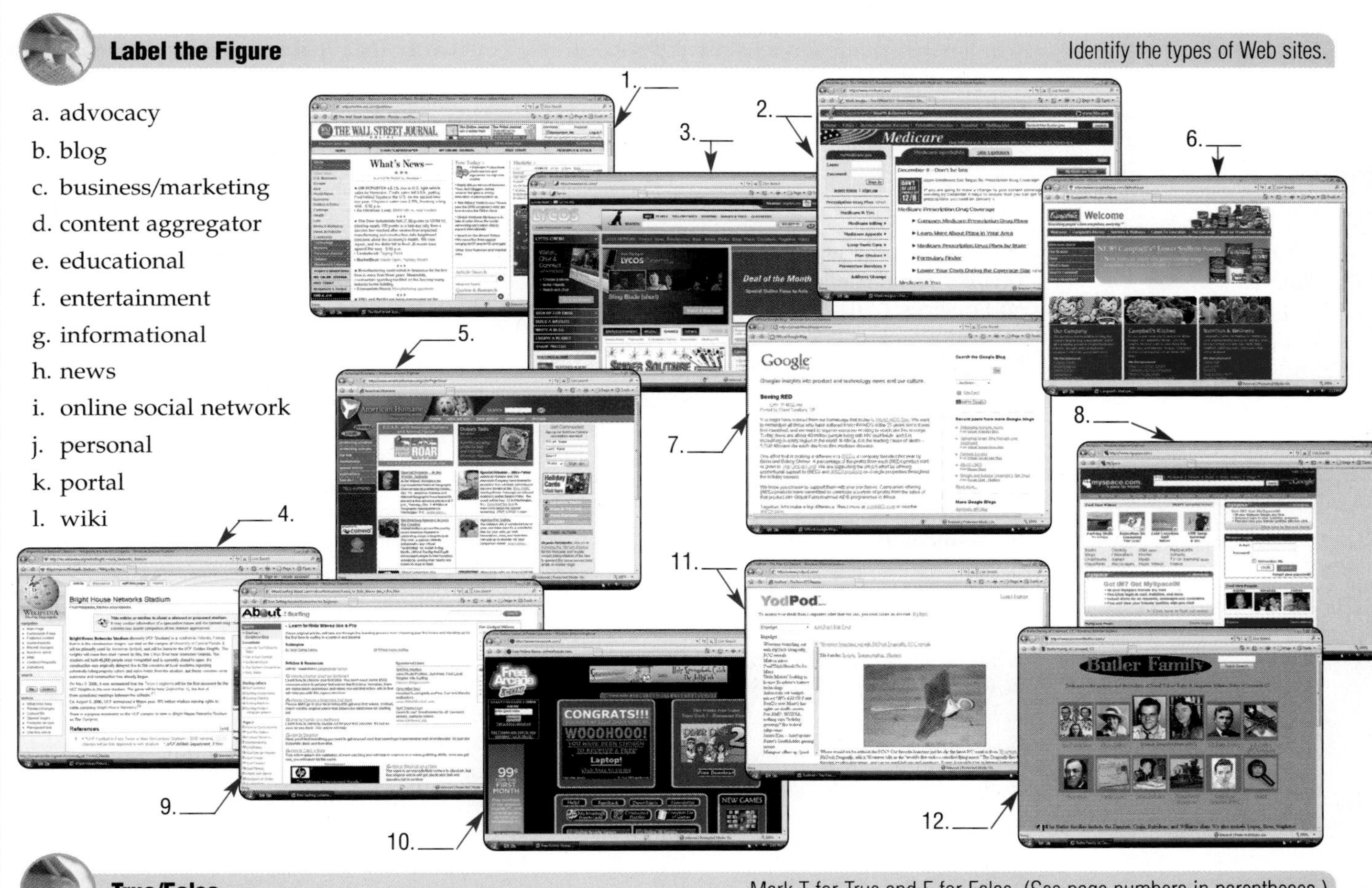

True/False

Mark T for True and F for False. (See page numbers in parentheses.)

_____ 1. A single government agency owns and controls the Internet. (70)

_____ 2. DSL is a technology that provides high-speed Internet connections over the cable television network. (70)

_____ 3. In general, the first portion of each IP address identifies the specific computer and the last portion identifies the network. (73)

_____ 4. A Web 2.0 Web site may include application software built into the site for visitors to use. (75)

_____ 5. Tabbed browsing refers to the practice of Web sites keeping tabs on their visitors. (76)

_____ 6. Hypertext combines text-based links with graphic, audio, and video links. (77)

_____ 7. A major problem with a subject directory is deciding which categories to choose as you work through the menus of links presented. (79)

_____ 8. Most social networking Web sites include chat rooms, newsgroups, and other communications services. (84)

_____ 9. A podcast is a collaborative Web site that allows users to add to, modify, or delete the Web site content via their Web browser. (86)

_____ 10. To develop a Web page, you do not have to be a computer programmer. (90)

_____ 11. An online auction is an example of business-to-consumer (B2C) e-commerce. (92)

_____ 12. A flame is an unsolicited e-mail message or newsgroup posting sent to many recipients or newsgroups at once. (100)

Checkpoint

Multiple Choice

Select the best answer. (See page numbers in parentheses.)

1. The Internet has its roots in _____, which was a networking project started by an agency of the U.S. Department of Defense. (69)
   a. ICANN
   b. NSFnet
   c. WISP
   d. ARPANET
2. A Wi-Fi network uses _____ to provide Internet connections to wireless computers and devices. (70)
   a. copper telephone lines
   b the cable television network
   c. radio signals
   d. a dish-shaped antenna
3. As with an IP address, the components of a domain name are separated by _____. (73)
   a. commas
   b. semicolons
   c. colons
   d. periods
4. Many Web page addresses begin with _____, which stands for a set of rules that defines how pages transfer on the Internet. (76)
   a. W3C
   b. http
   c. hits
   d. pop
5. _____ combines text-based links with graphic, audio, and video links. (77)
   a. Hypertext
   b. Multi-linking
   c. Hypermedia
   d. Tabbed Browsing
6. All of the following techniques can be used to improve Web searches except _____. (81)
   a. list all possible spellings
   b. read a search engine's Help information
   c. use general nouns and put the most important terms last
   d. if a search is unsuccessful, try another search engine
7. _____ may offer online photo albums, chat rooms, and other services to facilitate communications among members. (82)
   a. Online communities
   b. Informational Web sites
   c. Advocacy Web sites
   d. Wikis
8. A _____ is a specific type of online social network that enables members to share photos, music, and videos. (84)
   a. blog
   b. wiki
   c. podcast
   d. media sharing Web site
9. A(n) _____ is a business that gathers and organizes Web content and then distributes, or feeds, the content to subscribers for free or a fee. (84)
   a. WISP
   b. ISP
   c. content aggregator
   d. blogger
10. A _____ is recorded audio stored on a Web site that can be downloaded to a computer or a portable media player. (86)
    a. blog
    b. wiki
    c. portal
    d. podcast
11. _____ is a strategy designed to prevent illegal distribution of music and other digital content. (86)
    a. A threaded discussion
    b. Internet telephony
    c. Digital rights management
    d. Podcasting
12. _____ is the process of transferring data in a continuous and even flow, allowing users to access and use a file while it is transmitting. (86)
    a. Linking
    b. Streaming
    c. Surfing
    d. Clicking
13. At a consumer-to-consumer (C2C) Web site, a(n) _____ allows users to purchase from other consumers. (92)
    a. news server
    b. online auction
    c. wireless portal
    d. shopping cart
14. Use _____, such as :) for smile and :(for frown, to express emotions in e-mail, newsgroups, and chat rooms. (100)
    a. emoticons
    b. spam
    c. spoilers
    d. flames

Checkpoint

Matching

Match the terms with their definitions. (See page numbers in parentheses.)

_____ 1. gTLD (73)
_____ 2. ccTLD (74)
_____ 3. home page (76)
_____ 4. link (77)
_____ 5. spider (81)
_____ 6. MP3 (86)
_____ 7. player (86)
_____ 8. plug-in (89)
_____ 9. address book (94)
_____ 10. VoIP (99)

a. browser designed for the small screens and limited power of PDAs and smart phones
b. program that extends the capability of a browser
c. enables users to speak to other users over the Internet
d. software used to listen to an audio file on a computer
e. a two-letter country code for international Web sites outside the United States
f. built-in connection to a related Web page or part of a Web page
g. first page that a Web site displays
h. identifies the type of organization associated with a domain
i. copy a program from storage to memory
j. contains a list of names and e-mail addresses
k. format that reduces an audio file to about one-tenth its original size
l. program used to build and maintain lists of words found on Web sites

Short Answer

Write a brief answer to each of the following questions.

1. How is a regional ISP different from a national ISP? ____________ How is an ISP different from a WISP? ____________
2. How is a static Web page different from a dynamic Web page? ____________ What is a Web site? ____________
3. What are two types of specifications used by content aggregators to distribute content? ____________ How might you evaluate the accuracy of a Web site? ____________
4. What three graphics formats are used frequently on the Web? ____________ How are they different? ____________
5. When might you use an online payment system? ____________ How does the service work? ____________

Beyond the Book

Read the following book elements, learn more about each using the Web, and then write a brief report.

1. Ethics & Issues — Should You Trust a Wiki for Academic Research? (84), Who Should Control the Content of Your CDs, DVDs, and Media Files? (87), E-Mail: Irritant or Liberator? (94), or Should Companies Be Able to Track Your Online Habits? (101)
2. Career Corner — Web Developer (101)
3. Companies on the Cutting Edge — Google or Yahoo! (103)
4. FAQs (71, 72, 74, 77, 81, 85, 92, 95, 100)
5. High-Tech Talk — A Computer's Internet Protocol (IP) Address (102)
6. Looking Ahead — Internet Speeds into the Future (70), Facing Up to Search Technology (81), or Grocery Shopping with a Buddy (92)
7. Making Use of the Web — Travel (118)
8. Picture Yourself in an Online Social Network (66)
9. Technology Trailblazers — Tim Berners-Lee or Meg Whitman (103)
10. Web Links (70, 72, 84, 88, 92, 95, 96, 97, 98, 99)

Learn It Online

Use the Learn It Online exercises to reinforce your understanding of the chapter concepts. To access the Learn It Online exercises, visit scsite.com/dc2008/ch2/learn.

1 At the Movies — Tell Your Stories Via Vlog

To view the Tell Your Stories Via Vlog movie, click the number 1 button. Locate your video and click the corresponding High-Speed or Dial-Up link, depending on your Internet connection. Watch the movie and then complete the exercise by answering the question that follows. If jotting down your diary in text is not appealing, try a simple and free video blog. Explain briefly how to create a vlog.

2 Video and Audio: You Review It — Internet Telephony

In this chapter you learned about Internet telephony. Click the number 2 button to view the suggested links and begin your search for videos, podcasts, or vodcasts related to Internet telephony. Choose a video, podcast, or vodcast that discusses Internet telephony and is of interest to you, and then write a description of its contents. Explain why you chose this piece, what you liked about it, what you disliked about it, and whether you would recommend it to a fellow student. Finish your review by giving the video, podcast, or vodcast a rating of 1 – 5 stars. Submit your review in the format requested by your instructor.

3 Student Edition Labs — Connecting to the Internet

Click the number 3 button. A new browser window will open, displaying the Student Edition Labs. Follow the on-screen instructions to complete the Connecting to the Internet Lab. When finished, click the Exit button. If required, submit your results to your instructor.

4 Student Edition Labs — Getting the Most out of the Internet

Click the number 4 button. A new browser window will open, displaying the Student Edition Labs. Follow the on-screen instructions to complete the Getting the Most out of the Internet Lab. When finished, click the Exit button. If required, submit your results to your instructor.

5 Student Edition Labs — E-mail

Click the number 5 button. A new browser window will open, displaying the Student Edition Labs. Follow the on-screen instructions to complete the E-mail Lab. When finished, click the Exit button. If required, submit your results to your instructor.

6 Practice Test

Click the number 6 button. Answer each question. When completed, enter your name and click the Grade Test button to submit the quiz for grading. Make a note of any missed questions. If required, submit your score to your instructor.

7 Who Wants To Be a Computer Genius^2?

Click the number 7 button to find out if you are a computer genius. Directions about how to play the game will be displayed. When you are ready to play, click the Play button. Submit your score to your instructor.

Learn It Online

8 Wheel of Terms

Click the number 8 button to reinforce important terms you learned in this chapter by playing the Shelly Cashman Series version of this popular game. Directions about how to play the game will be displayed. When you are ready to play, click the Play button. Submit your score to your instructor.

9 DC Track and Field

Click the number 9 button to use what you have learned in this chapter to compete against other students in three track and field events. Directions about how to play the game will be displayed. When you are ready to play, click the start first event button. If required, submit your score to your instructor.

10 You're Hired!

Click the number 10 button to use what you have learned in this chapter to embark on the path to a career in computers. Directions about how to play the game will be displayed. When you are ready to play, click the begin game button. If required, submit your score to your instructor.

11 Crossword Puzzle Challenge

Click the number 11 button, then click the Crossword Puzzle Challenge link. Directions about how to play the game will be displayed. Complete the puzzle to reinforce skills you learned in this chapter. When you are ready to play, click the Continue button. Submit the completed puzzle to your instructor.

12 Vista Exercises

Click the number 12 button. When the Vista Exercises menu appears, click the exercise assigned by your instructor. A new browser window will open. Follow the on-screen instructions to complete the exercise. When finished, click the Exit button. If required, submit your results to your instructor.

13 In the News

In her book, *Caught in the Net*, Kimberly S. Young contends that the Internet can be addictive. Young's methodology and conclusions have been questioned by several critics, but Young remains resolute. She points out that at one time, no one admitted to the existence of alcoholism. Click the number 13 button and read a news article about the impact of Internet use on human behavior. What effect did the Internet have? Why? In your opinion, is the Internet's influence positive or negative? Why?

14 Chapter Discussion Forum

Select an objective from this chapter on page 67 about which you would like more information. Click the number 14 button and post a short message listing a meaningful message title accompanied by one or more questions concerning the selected objective. In two days, return to the threaded discussion by clicking the number 14 button. Submit to your instructor your original message and at least one response to your message.

15 Google Earth

Click the number 15 button to download Google Earth. Once you have downloaded Google Earth, use it to fly to your home, school, Grand Canyon, Baghdad, Paris, and Moscow. At each location, use the buttons to change the view. Print a copy of the map showing your school, handwrite on the map the school's elevation, and submit the map to your instructor.

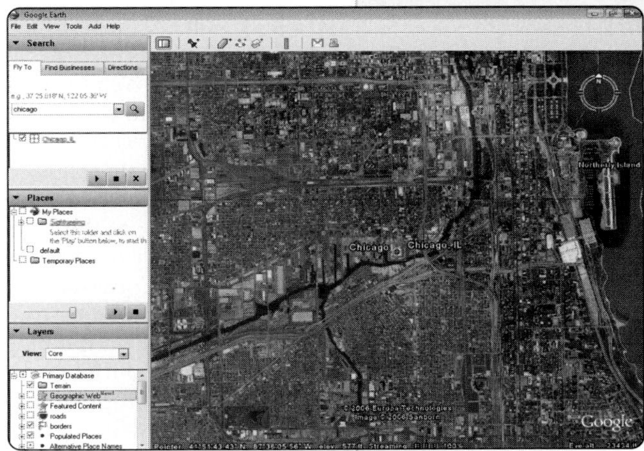

Learn How To

Use the Learn How To activities to learn fundamental skills when using a computer and accompanying technology. Complete the exercises and submit them to your instructor. To see a video of a Learn How To activity, visit scsite.com/dc2008/ch2/howto.

LEARN HOW TO 1: Change a Web Browser's Home Page

When you start a Web browser, a Web page is displayed. You can change the page that appears when you start a Web browser or when you click the Home button on the browser toolbar by completing the following steps:

1. With the browser running, navigate to the Web page you would like to make your Home page.
2. Click the Tools drop-down button and then click Internet Options to display the Internet Options dialog box shown in Figure 2-37.
3. Click the Use current button.
4. Click the OK button in the Internet Options dialog box.

When you start the browser or click the Home button on the browser toolbar, the selected Web page will be displayed.

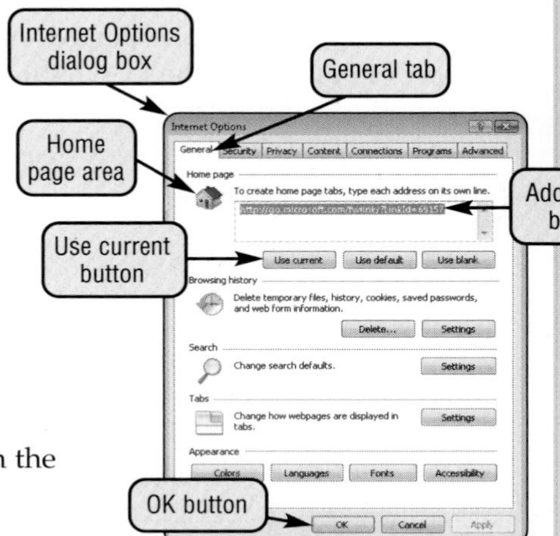

FIGURE 2-37

Exercise

1. Start your Web browser. Write down the address of the browser's current home page. Then, change the browser's home page to www.cnn.com. Close the browser.
2. Start your Web browser. What is the lead story on cnn.com? Use links on the page to view several stories. Which story do you find most interesting? Click the Home button on the browser toolbar. What happened? Submit these answers to your instructor.
3. Change the browser's home page to your school's home page. Click the Home button on the browser toolbar. Click the Calendar or Events link, and then locate two campus events of which you were unaware. Report these two campus events to your instructor.
4. Change the browser's home page back to the address you wrote down in Step 1.

LEARN HOW TO 2: Create and Use Your Own Blog

A blog can contain any information you wish to place in it. Originally, blogs consisted of Web addresses, so that an individual or group with a specific interest could direct others to useful places on the Web. Today, blogs contain addresses, thoughts, diaries, and anything else a person or group wants to share.

Once you have created a blog, you can update it. A variety of services are available on the Web to help you create and maintain your blog. One widely used service is called Blogger. To create a blog using Blogger, complete the following steps:

1. Start your Web browser, type `www.blogger.com` in the Address box, and then press the ENTER key to display the Blogger home page (Figure 2-38).
2. Click the CREATE YOUR BLOG NOW arrow on the Blogger home page.
3. Enter the data required on the Create an account page. Your user name and password will allow you to change and manage your blog. Your Display name is the name that will be shown on the blog as the author of the material on the blog. Many people use their own names, but others use pseudonyms as their "pen names" so they are not readily identifiable.
4. Click the Continue arrow and then enter your Blog title and Blog address. These are the names and addresses everyone will use to view your blog. By default, the blog is stored and maintained on the blogspot server.
5. Click the Continue arrow to display the Choose a template screen.
6. Choose a template for your blog and then click the Continue arrow.
7. Your blog will be created for you. When you see the Your blog has been created screen, click the Start posting arrow.

Learn How To

8. From the screen that is displayed, you can post items for your blog, specify settings, change the template, and view your blog.
9. When you have posted all your information, click the Sign out button at the top right of the screen. You will be logged out.
10. To edit your blog and add or change information on it, visit the Blogger home page and sign in by entering your user name and password. You will be able to post to your blog.
11. Others can view your blog by entering its address in the browser's Address box and then pressing the ENTER key.

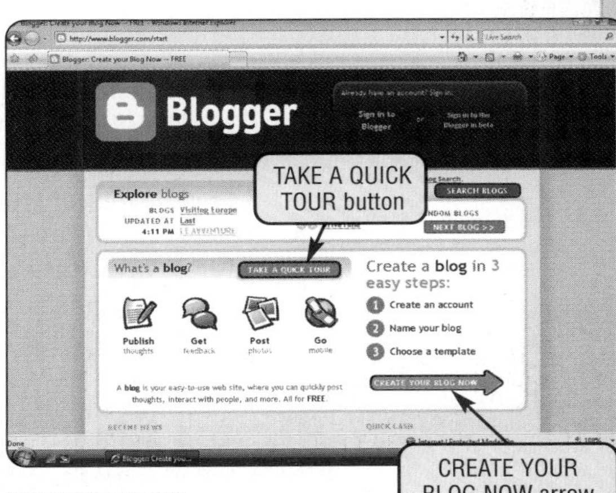

FIGURE 2-38

Exercise

1. Start your Web browser and visit www.blogger.com. Click the TAKE A QUICK TOUR button and go through all the screens that explain about a blog. What did you learn that you did not know? What type of blog do you find most compelling — a group or an individual blog? Why? Turn in your answers to your instructor.
2. Optional: Create your own blog. Carefully name it and begin your posts at this time. What is your blog name and address? What is its primary purpose? Is it an individual or group blog? Write a paragraph containing the answers to these questions and any other information you feel is pertinent. Turn in this paragraph to your instructor.

LEARN HOW TO 3: Bid and Buy a Product from eBay

Online auctions have grown to be a favorite shopping space for many people. A leading online auction Web site is eBay. To submit a bid for an item on eBay, complete the following steps:

1. Type `www.ebay.com` in the Address box of your browser. Press the ENTER key to display the eBay home page (Figure 2-39).
2. You must be registered to bid on eBay. If you are registered, click the Sign in link, enter your eBay User ID and Password, and then click the Submit button. If not, click the register link and follow the instructions.
3. Pick an item you find interesting and on which you might bid.
4. Enter your item in the Start new search text box and then click the Search button.
5. Scroll through the page to see the available items.
6. To bid on an item, click the item's description and then click the Place Bid button. The eBay Web site contains reminders that when you bid on an item, you are entering into a contract to purchase the item if you are the successful bidder. Bidding on eBay is serious business.
7. Enter the amount of your bid. Click the Continue button.
8. You will confirm your bid and receive notification about your bid.
9. You will be notified by e-mail if you won the bid. If so, you will arrange with the seller for payment and shipment.

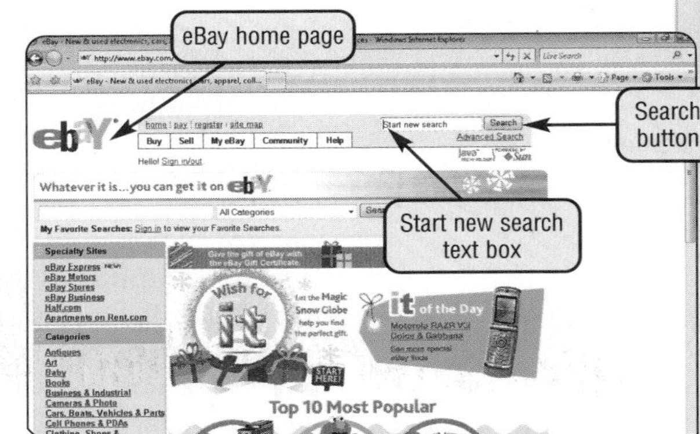

FIGURE 2-39

Exercise

1. Start your browser and display the eBay home page.
2. In the Start new search text box, enter the name of an upcoming sporting event you would like to attend followed by the word, tickets. For example, enter `Super Bowl tickets`. Click the Search button.
3. Did you find available tickets? Were there more tickets available than you expected, or fewer? Are the bid prices reasonable or ridiculous? How many bids were made for all the tickets? How much time is left to bid? What items did you find that you were not expecting? Submit answers to these questions to your instructor.
4. Enter an item of your choice in the Start new search text box. If you feel so inclined, bid on an item. Do you think this manner of buying goods is valuable? Why? Will you visit eBay again? Why? Submit answers to these questions to your instructor.

Quizzes and Learning Games
Computer Genius
Crossword Puzzle
DC Track and Field
Practice Test
Quiz Yourself
Wheel of Terms
You're Hired!

Exercises
Case Studies
Chapter Review
Checkpoint
Key Terms
Learn How To
Learn It Online
Web Research

Beyond the Book
Career Corner
Companies
FAQs
High-Tech Talk
Looking Ahead
Making Use of the Web
Trailblazers
Web Links

Features
Chapter Forum
Install Computer
Lab Exercises
Maintain Computer
Tech News
Timeline 2008

Web Research

Use the Internet-based Web Research exercises to broaden your understanding of the concepts presented in this chapter. Visit scsite.com/dc2008/ch2/research to obtain more information pertaining to each exercise. To discuss any of the Web Research exercises in this chapter with other students, post your thoughts or questions at scsite.com/dc2008/ch2/forum.

1 **Scavenger Hunt** Use one of the search engines listed in Figure 2-10 in Chapter 2 on page 78 or your own favorite search engine to find the answers to the questions below. Copy and paste the Web address from the Web page where you found the answer. Some questions may have more than one answer. If required, submit your answers to your instructor. (1) The World Wide Web Consortium (W3C) sets Internet standards. Who is the current CEO of the W3C? (2) What cable company was established in 1858 to carry instantaneous communications across the ocean that eventually would be used for Internet communications? (3) What American president in 1957 created both the interstate highway system and the Advanced Research Projects Agency (ARPA)? (4) What was eBay's original name, and what was the first item offered for auction? (5) How many Web pages is Google currently searching?

2 **Search Sleuth** The Internet has provided the opportunity to access encyclopedias online. One of the more comprehensive encyclopedia research sites is Encyclopedia.com. Visit this Web site and then use your word processing program to answer the following questions. Then, if required, submit your answers to your instructor. (1) On the site's home page you can search or browse encyclopedia articles alphabetically. Click the letter, W. Click the Wom-Wz link. Scroll down to the World Wide Web entry and then click this link. What is the definition of the World Wide Web according to the first sentence of this article? Who is the American computer consultant who promoted the idea of linking documents via hypertext during the 1960s? What words are hyperlinks within this article? (2) Type `"Web browser"` as the keyword in the Search text box and then press the ENTER key or click the Research button. How many articles discussing Web browsers are found on the Encyclopedia.com Web site? (3) In the search results list, click the link to find newspaper and magazine articles related to this term. How many articles are listed? (4) Type `multimedia` as the keyword in the Search text box and then press the ENTER key or click the Research button. In the search results list, click the multimedia link. What hardware typically is required to work with multimedia according to this article? What are some optional hardware devices? (5) Type `"personal computer"` as the keyword in the Search text box and then press the ENTER key or click the Research button. Click one of the personal computer links, review the material, and, if required, submit to your instructor a 50-word summary of the information you read.

3 **Newsgroups** One of the more popular topics for newsgroups is netiquette. Read the information Borland Software Corporation (info.borland.com/newsgroups/netiquette.html) provides on general newsgroup conduct. Then find three newsgroups, such as those listed in CyberFiber (cyberfiber.com/internet.htm) or Google Groups, that discuss this topic. Read the information and then summarize the advice provided.

4 **Journaling** Respond to your readings in this chapter by writing at least one page about your reactions, evaluations, and reflections about using the Internet. For example, do you prefer to use e-mail or instant messaging (IM) when communicating with friends? Have you downloaded music files or shopped online? Which Web sites do you visit frequently? Do you have a blog? You also can write about the new terms you learned by reading this chapter. If required, submit your journal to your instructor.

5 **Ethics in Action** Web cams are video cameras that display their output on a Web page. The feasibility of installing Web cams in 47,000 locations susceptible to terrorist threats, such as nuclear and chemical plants, national airports, and gas storage facilities, is being explored. Citizens would monitor the cameras and report suspicious activity. Critics of this proposal state that the constant surveillance is an invasion of privacy. Visit the USHomeGuard Web site (ushomeguard.org) and then write a summary of the citizen corps' roles in this project. Then locate other Web sites that oppose this plan and summarize their views. If required, submit your summary to your instructor.

Case Studies

Use the Case Studies to apply the concepts presented in the chapter to real-world situations. Visit scsite.com/dc2008/ch2/cases to obtain more information pertaining to each exercise. To discuss the Case Studies in this chapter with other students, visit scsite.com/dc2008/ch2/forum and post your thoughts or questions.

CASE STUDY 1 — Class Discussion Although Internet Explorer may be the most widely used Web browser, it is not the only Web browser program in use. Use the Internet or print media to compare reviews of other Web browsers such as Netscape, Opera, or Firefox with Internet Explorer. Prepare a brief report explaining any major differences between the browsers you researched and Internet Explorer. Include in your report which browser you would recommend and the reasons for your recommendation. Be prepared to discuss your findings.

CASE STUDY 2 — Class Discussion Many retailers, such as Sports Authority, Barnes and Noble, and Toys R Us, are brick-and-click businesses. That is, they allow customers to conduct complete transactions at a physical location as well as online at a Web site. Choose a local brick-and-click business in which you have shopped at the physical location and visit the Web site of the business. Compare the type, availability, and cost (include tax and shipping) of products or services available. Prepare a report that summarizes the advantages and disadvantages of dealing with the physical location versus the Web site of a brick-and-click business. Would you rather shop at the physical location or at the Web site? Why? Does the answer depend on the business, the product, or some other factor? Be prepared to share your findings in class.

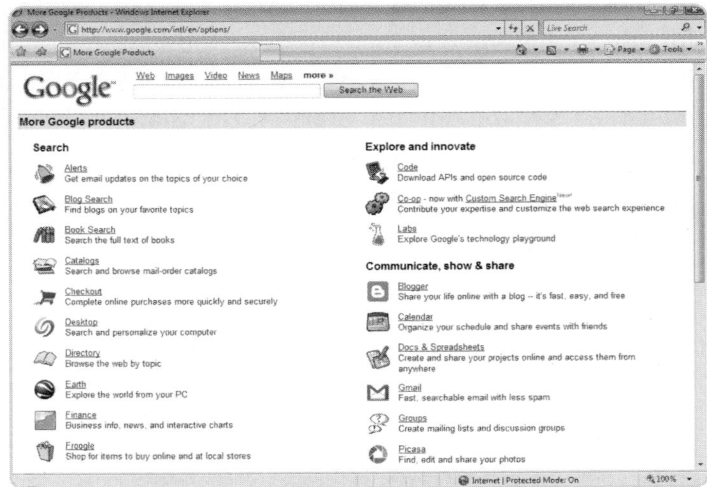

CASE STUDY 3 — Research Web search engines use different techniques for searching Web resources. If you were designing a search engine, what would you have the engine look for when determining whether a Web page successfully matches the keywords? Visit the Help page of Google, Ask.com, MSN Search, and Yahoo! to get an idea of what criteria they use. Compile a list containing the criteria you would have your search engine use to determine whether a Web page is a successful match for keywords. Include a short explanation for each criterion. Write a brief report or use PowerPoint to create a presentation and share your ideas with your class.

CASE STUDY 4 — Research The Internet has had a tremendous impact on business. For some businesses, that influence has not been positive. For example, surveys suggest that as a growing number of people order products online, traditional brick-and-mortar businesses are seeing fewer customers. Use the Web and/or print media to learn more about businesses that have been affected negatively by the Internet. What effect has the Internet had? How can the business compete with the Internet? How has the Internet changed business in positive ways? Write a brief report or use PowerPoint to create a presentation and share your findings with your class.

CASE STUDY 5 — Team Challenge Mr. Steve Sandberg is vice president of operations for a major luxury hotel chain. He and three of his associates want to start a new chain of discount hotels called Sleepy Hollow. They have made a plan that includes opening hotels initially in Chicago, St. Louis, Denver, and Houston. They plan to offer comfortable rooms, high-speed Internet access, and continental breakfast. Besides offering reservations over the telephone, they want to develop a Web site that will allow customers to negotiate a nightly rate as their check-in time approaches. Form a three-member team and assist Mr. Sandberg in evaluating existing major hotel Web sites by listing the advantages and disadvantages of each. Assign each member the task of evaluating three of the following hotel chains: Marriot, Hilton, Holiday Inn, Ramada, Super 8, Motel 6, Days Inn, Fairfield Inn, and Radisson. Make sure every hotel chain listed is assigned to at least one team member. Have each member print the home page of the hotel chain he or she is assigned. In evaluating the Web sites, each member should pay particular attention to the following areas: (1) design of Web site, (2) ease of use, (3) reservations, (4) awards programs, (5) specials, (6) online Help, (7) about the hotel, and (8) contact the hotel. Meet with your team to share each member's findings and then write a final report or create a PowerPoint presentation that summarizes the team's conclusions and ranks the sites in terms of their effectiveness.

Making Use of the Web

A wealth of information is available on the World Wide Web. The riches are yours if you know where to find this material. Locating useful Web sites may be profitable for your educational and professional careers, as the resources may help you research class assignments and make your life more fulfilling and manageable.

Because the World Wide Web does not have an organizational structure to assist you in locating reliable material, you need additional resources to guide you in searching. To help you find useful Web sites, this Special Feature describes specific information about a variety of Web pages, and it includes tables of Web addresses, so you can get started. The material is organized in several areas of interest.

AREAS OF INTEREST	
Fun and Entertainment	Learning
Travel	Science
Finance	Environment
Online Social Networks and Media Sharing	Health
Blogs	Research and Resources
Government	Careers
Shopping and Auctions	Arts and Literature
Weather, Sports, and News	

Web Exercises at the end of each category will reinforce the material and help you discover Web sites that may add a treasure trove of knowledge to your life.

Fun and Entertainment

THAT'S ENTERTAINMENT

Rock 'n' Roll on the Web

Consumers place great significance on buying entertainment products for fun and recreation. Nearly 10 percent of the United States's economy is spent on attending concerts and buying DVDs, CDs, reading materials, sporting goods, and toys.

Many Web sites supplement our cravings for fun and entertainment. For example, you can see and hear the musicians inducted into the Rock and Roll Hall of Fame and Museum (Figure 1). If you need an update on your favorite reality-based television program or a preview of an upcoming movie, E! Online and Entertainment Tonight provide the latest features on television and movie stars. The Internet Movie Database contains credits and reviews of more than 849,000 titles.

Watch the surfers riding the waves in Washington and romp with pandas at the San Diego Zoo. Web cams, which are video cameras that display their output on Web pages, take armchair travelers across the world for views of natural attractions, historical monuments, colleges, and cities. Many Web sites featuring Web cams are listed in the table in Figure 2.

FIGURE 1 Visitors exploring the Rock and Roll Hall of Fame and Museum Web site will find history, exhibitions, programs, and the names and particulars of the latest inductees.

FUN AND ENTERTAINMENT WEB SITES

Web Cams	Web Address
AfriCam Virtual Game Reserve	africam.com
CamVista.com	camvista.com
Discovery Kids — Live Cams	kids.discovery.com/cams/cams.html
EarthCam — Webcam Network	earthcam.com
Iowa State Insect Zoo Live Camera	zoocam.ent.iastate.edu
NOAA ESRL Global Monitoring Division — South Pole Live Camera	www.cmdl.noaa.gov/obop/spo/livecamera.html
Panda Cam San Diego Zoo	sandiegozoo.org/zoo/ex_panda_station.html
Westport, Washington Surfcam	westportlodging.com/westport_web_cams.html
Wild Birds Unlimited Bird FeederCam	wbu.com/feedercam_home.htm
WorldLIVE	worldlive.cz/en/webcams
Entertainment	**Web Address**
AMG All Music Guide	allmusic.com
E! Online	eonline.com
Entertainment Weekly's EW.com	ew.com/ew
The Internet Movie Database (IMDb)	imdb.com
MSN Entertainment	entertainment.msn.com
Old Time Radio (OTR) — Radio Days: A Soundbite History	otr.com
Rock and Roll Hall of Fame and Museum	rockhall.com
World Radio Network (WRN)	wrn.org
Yahoo! Entertainment	et.tv.yahoo.com
For more information about fun and entertainment Web sites, visit scsite.com/dc2008/ch2/web.	

FIGURE 2 When you visit Web sites offering fun and entertainment resources, you can be both amused and informed.

FUN AND ENTERTAINMENT WEB EXERCISES

1 Visit the WorldLIVE site listed in Figure 2. View two of the Web cams closest to your hometown, and describe the scenes. Then, visit the Discovery Kids — Live Cams Web site and view one of the animal cams in the Live Cams. What do you observe? Visit another Web site listed in Figure 2 and describe the view. What are the benefits of having Web cams at these locations throughout the world?

2 What are your favorite movies? Use The Internet Movie Database Web site listed in Figure 2 to search for information about two of these films, and write a brief description of the biographies of the major stars and director for each movie. Then, visit one of the entertainment Web sites and describe three of the featured stories. At the Rock and Roll Hall of Fame and Museum Web site, view the information about Elvis and one of your favorite musicians. Write a paragraph describing the information available about these rock stars.

Travel

GET PACKING!

Explore the World without Leaving Home

When you are ready to arrange your next travel adventure or just want to explore destination possibilities, the Internet provides ample resources to set your plans in motion.

To discover exactly where your destination is on this planet, cartography Web sites, including MapQuest and Maps.com, allow you to pinpoint your destination. View your exact destination using satellite imagery with Google Maps (Figure 3) and Windows Live Local.

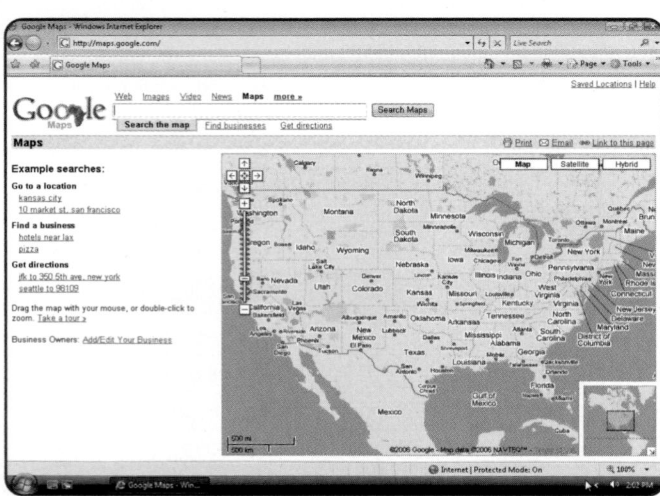

FIGURE 3 Google Maps provides location information and satellite imagery for many regions on this planet.

Some good starting places are general travel Web sites such as Expedia Travel, Cheap Tickets, and Travelocity, which is owned by the electronic booking service travel agents use. These all-encompassing Web sites, including those in Figure 4, have tools to help you find the lowest prices and details on flights, car rentals, cruises, and hotels.

TRAVEL WEB SITES

General Travel	Web Address
Cheap Tickets	cheaptickets.com
Expedia Travel	expedia.com
Orbitz	orbitz.com
PlanetRider Travel Directory	planetrider.com
Travelocity	travelocity.com
Cartography	**Web Address**
Google Maps	maps.google.com
MapQuest	mapquest.com
Maps.com	maps.com
Windows Live Local	local.live.com
Travel and City Guides	**Web Address**
Frommers	frommers.com
Greatest Cities	greatestcities.com
U.S.-Parks US National Parks Adventure Travel Guide	us-parks.com
VirtualTourist.com	virtualtourist.com
For more information about travel Web sites, visit scsite.com/dc2008/ch2/web.	

FIGURE 4 These travel resources Web sites offer travel information to exciting destinations throughout the world.

TRAVEL WEB EXERCISES

1. Visit one of the cartography Web sites listed in Figure 4 and obtain the directions from your campus to one of these destinations: the White House in Washington, D.C.; Elvis's home in Memphis, Tennessee; Walt Disney World in Orlando, Florida; or the Grand Old Opry in Nashville, Tennessee. How many miles is it to your destination? What is the estimated driving time? Then, visit one of the general travel Web sites listed in the table and plan a flight from the nearest major airport to one of the four destinations for the week after finals and a return trip one week later. What is the lowest economy coach fare for this round-trip flight? What airline, flight numbers, and departure and arrival times did you select?

2. Visit one of the travel and city guides Web sites listed in Figure 4, and choose a destination for a getaway this coming weekend. Write a one-page paper giving details about this location, such as popular hotels and lodging, expected weather, population, local colleges and universities, parks and recreation, ancient and modern history, and tours. Include a map or satellite photograph of this place. Why did you select this destination? How would you travel there and back? What is the breakdown of expected costs for this weekend, including travel expenditures, meals, lodging, and tickets to events and activities? What Web addresses did you use to complete this exercise?

Finance

MONEY MATTERS

Cashing In on Financial Advice

You can manage your money with advice from financial Web sites that offer online banking, tax help, personal finance, and small business and commercial services.

If you do not have a personal banker or a financial planner, consider a Web adviser to guide your investment decisions. The Yahoo! Finance Web site (Figure 5) provides financial news and investment information.

If you are ready to ride the ups and downs of the NASDAQ and the Dow, an abundance of Web sites listed in Figure 6, including Reuters and Morningstar.com, can help you pick companies that fit your interests and financial needs.

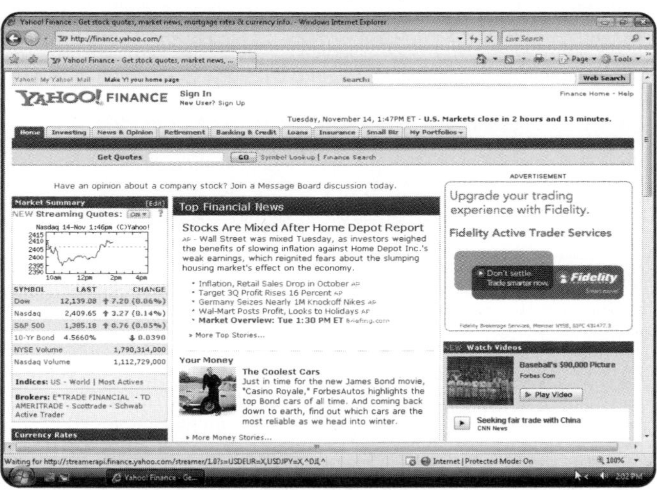

FIGURE 5 Yahoo! Finance Web site contains charting features that graphically depict information related to financing and investing.

Claiming to be the fastest, easiest tax publication on the planet, the Internal Revenue Service Web site contains procedures for filing tax appeals and contains IRS forms, publications, and legal regulations.

FINANCE WEB SITES

Advice and Education	Web Address
Bankrate.com	bankrate.com
LendingTree	lendingtree.com
Loan.com	loan.com
The Motley Fool	fool.com
MSN Money	moneycentral.msn.com
Wells Fargo	wellsfargo.com
Yahoo! Finance	finance.yahoo.com
Stock Market	**Web Address**
AIG VALIC	valic.com
E*TRADE Financial	us.etrade.com
Financial Engines	financialengines.com
Merrill Lynch Direct	mldirect.ml.com
Morningstar.com	morningstar.com
Reuters	investor.reuters.com
Vanguard	vanguard.com
Taxes	**Web Address**
H&R Block	hrblock.com
Internal Revenue Service	irs.gov
Jackson Hewitt	jacksonhewitt.com
Liberty Tax Service	libertytax.com
For more information about finance Web sites, visit scsite.com/dc2008/ch2/web.	

FIGURE 6 Financial resources Web sites offer general information, stock market analyses, and tax advice, as well as guidance and money-saving tips.

FINANCE WEB EXERCISES

1 Visit three advice and education Web sites listed in Figure 6 and read their top business world reports. Write a paragraph about each, summarizing these stories. Which stocks or mutual funds do these Web sites predict as being sound investments today? What are the current market indexes for the DJIA (Dow Jones Industrial Average), S&P 500, and NASDAQ, and how do these figures compare with the previous day's numbers?

2 Using two of the stock market Web sites listed in Figure 6, search for information about Microsoft, Adobe Systems, and one other software vendor. Write a paragraph about each of these stocks describing the revenues, net incomes, total assets for the previous year, current stock price per share, highest and lowest prices of each stock during the past year, and other relevant investment information.

Online Social Networks and Media Sharing

CHECK OUT MY NEW PHOTOS

Online Social Networks and Media Sharing Web Sites More Popular than Ever

Do you ever wonder what your friends are doing? What about your friends' friends? Over the past two years, the popularity of online social networks has increased dramatically. Online social networks such as MySpace and AIM Pages allow you to create a personalized profile that others are able to view online. These profiles may include information about you such as your hometown, your age, your hobbies, and pictures. You also may create links to your friends' pages, post messages for individual friends, or bulletins for all of your friends to see. Online social networks are great places not only to keep in touch with your friends, but to reconnect with old friends and meet new friends!

FIGURE 7 The Phanfare Web site allows subscribers to share their photos and videos with others.

If you would like to post pictures and videos and do not require the full functionality of an online social network, you might consider a media sharing Web site, which is a type of online social network. Media sharing Web sites such as YouTube and Phanfare (Figure 7) allow you to post media, including photos and videos, for others to view, print, and/or download. Media sharing Web sites, which may be free or charge a fee, provide a quick, efficient way to share photos of your last vacation or videos of your brother's high school graduation.

ONLINE SOCIAL NETWORKS AND MEDIA SHARING

Online Social Networks	Web Address
AIM Pages Social Network	aimpages.com
Facebook	facebook.com
Friendster	friendster.com
MySpace — a place for friends	myspace.com
Media Sharing	**Web Address**
flickr	flickr.com
iFeeder Media Sharing Portal	ifeeder.com
Phanfare	phanfare.com
Picasa Web Albums	picasa.com
Shutterfly * Shutterfly Studio	shutterfly.com
Twango	twango.com
Yahoo! Video	video.yahoo.com
YouTube	youtube.com

For more information about online social networks and media sharing Web sites, visit scsite.com/dc2008/ch2/web.

FIGURE 8 Online social networks and media sharing Web sites are popular ways to keep in touch with friends, meet new people, and share media.

ONLINE SOCIAL NETWORKS AND MEDIA SHARING WEB EXERCISES

1. Many individuals now use online social networks. Visit two online social networks listed in Figure 8. If you are attempting to access an online social network from your classroom and are unable to do so, your school may have restricted use of social networking Web sites. Compare and contrast these two sites by performing the following actions and recording your findings. First, create a profile on each of these sites. If you find a Web site that charges a fee to sign up, choose another Web site. How easy is the sign-up process? Does either Web site ask for any personal information you are uncomfortable sharing? If so, what information? Once you sign up, make a list of five of your closest friends, and search for their profiles on each of these two sites. What site contains more of your friends? Browse each site and make a list of its features. In your opinion, what site is better? Explain why.

2. Media sharing Web sites make it extremely easy to share photos and videos with friends, family, and colleagues. Before choosing an online media sharing Web site to use, you should do some research. Visit two media sharing Web sites in Figure 8. Is there a fee to post media to these Web sites? If so, how much? Are these Web sites supported by advertisements? Locate the instructions for posting media to these Web sites. Are the instructions straightforward? Do these Web sites impose a limit on the number and/or size of media files you can post? Summarize your responses to these questions in two or three paragraphs.

Blogs

EXPRESS YOURSELF

Blogosphere Growing Swiftly

Internet users are feeling the need to publish their views, and they are finding Weblogs, or blogs for short, the ideal vehicle. The blogosphere began as an easy way for individuals to express their opinions on the Web. Today, this communication vehicle has become a powerful tool, for individuals, groups, and corporations are using blogs to promote their ideas and advertise their products. It is not necessary to have a background in Web design to be able to post to a blog.

Bloggers generally update their Web sites frequently to reflect their views. Their posts range from a paragraph to an entire essay and often contain links to other Web sites. The more popular blogs discuss politics, lifestyles, and technology.

Individuals easily may set up a blog free or for a fee, using Web sites such as Blogger, Cooeey (Figure 9), and TypePad. In addition, online social networks may have a built-in blogging feature. Be cautious of the information you post on your blog, especially if it is accessible to everyone online.

Corporate blogs, such as The GM FastLane Blog, discuss all aspects of the company's products, whereas all-encompassing blogs, such as the Metafilter Community Weblog and others in Figure 10, are designed to keep general readers entertained and informed.

Blogs are affecting the manner in which people communicate, and some experts predict they will one day become our primary method of sharing information.

FIGURE 9 The Cooeey Web site allows members to share their insights by posting to their personal blogs.

BLOGS WEB SITES

BLOG	Web Address
A List Apart	alistapart.com
Blog Top Sites — Internet Blogs	blogtopsites.com/internet
Blog.com	blog.com
Blogger	blogger.com
Bloglines	bloglines.com
Blogstream	blogstream.com
Boing Boing: A Directory of Wonderful Things	boingboing.net
Cooeey	www.cooeey.com
Davenetics * Politics + Media + Musings	davenetics.com
Geek News Central	geeknewscentral.com
GM FastLane Blog	fastlane.gmblogs.com
kottke.org: home of fine hypertext products	kottke.org
MetaFilter Community Weblog	metafilter.com
Scripting News	scripting.com
TypePad	typepad.com
For more information about blogs Web sites, visit scsite.com/dc2008/ch2/web.	

FIGURE 10 These blogs offer information about technology, news, politics, and entertainment.

BLOGS WEB EXERCISES

1. Visit three of the blog Web sites listed in Figure 10. Make a table listing the blog name, its purpose, the author, its audience, and advertisers, if any, who sponsor the blog. Then, write a paragraph that describes the information you found on each of these blogs.

2. Many Internet users read the technology blogs to keep abreast of the latest developments. Visit the Geek News Central and Scripting News blogs listed in Figure 10 and write a paragraph describing the top story in each blog. Read the posted comments, if any. Then, write another paragraph describing two other stories found on these blogs that cover material you have discussed in this course. Write a third paragraph discussing which one is more interesting to you. Would you add reading blogs to your list of Internet activities? Why or why not?

Government
STAMP OF APPROVAL

Making a Federal Case for Useful Information

When it is time to buy stamps to mail your correspondence, you no longer need to wait in long lines at your local post office. The U.S. Postal Service has authorized several corporations to sell stamps online.

You can recognize U.S. Government Web sites on the Internet by their .gov top-level domain abbreviation. For example, The Library of Congress Web site is loc.gov. Government and military Web sites offer a wide range of information, and some of the more popular sites are listed in Figure 12. The Time Service Department Web site will provide you with the correct time. If you are looking for a federal document, FedWorld (Figure 11) lists thousands of documents distributed by the government on its Web site. For access to the names of your congressional representatives, visit the extensive Hieros Gamos Web site.

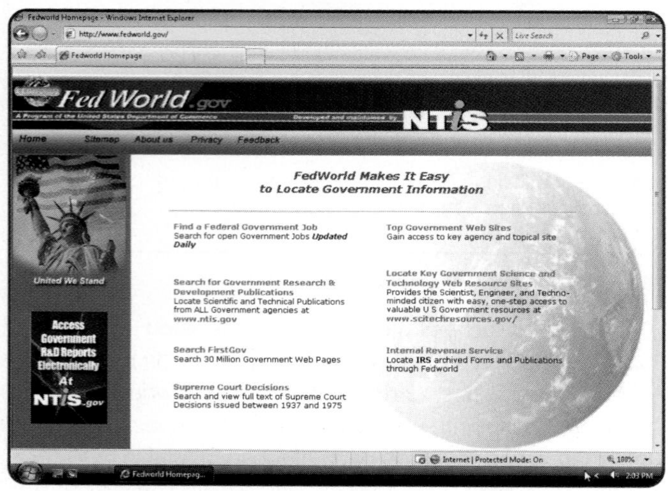

FIGURE 11 The FedWorld Web site contains a wealth of information disseminated by the federal government.

GOVERNMENT RESOURCES WEB SITES

Postage	Web Address
Endicia	endicia.com
Pitney Bowes	pb.com
Stamps.com	stamps.com
Government	**Web Address**
FedWorld	www.fedworld.gov
Hieros Gamos — Worldwide Legal Directories	hg.org
The Library of Congress	loc.gov
National Agricultural Library	nal.usda.gov
The National Archives	archives.gov
THOMAS Legislative Information	thomas.loc.gov
Time Service Department	tycho.usno.navy.mil
U.S. Department of Education	ed.gov
United States Department of the Treasury	treas.gov
U.S. Government Printing Office	www.access.gpo.gov
United States National Library of Medicine	www.nlm.nih.gov
United States Patent and Trademark Office	www.uspto.gov
USAJOBS	usajobs.opm.gov
The White House	whitehouse.gov

For more information about government Web sites, visit scsite.com/dc2008/ch2/web.

FIGURE 12 These Web sites offer information about buying U.S.-approved postage online and researching federal agencies.

GOVERNMENT WEB EXERCISES

1. View the three postage Web sites listed in Figure 12. Compare and contrast the available services on each one. Consider postage cost, necessary equipment, shipping services, security techniques, and tracking capability. Explain why you would or would not like to use this service.

2. Visit the Hieros Gamos Web site listed in Figure 12. What are the names, addresses, and telephone numbers of your two state senators and your local congressional representative? On what committees do they serve? Who is the chief justice of the Supreme Court, and what has been this justice's opinion on two recently decided cases? Who are the members of the president's cabinet? Then, visit two other Web sites listed in Figure 12. Write a paragraph about each Web site describing its content and features.

Shopping and Auctions
BARGAINS GALORE

Let Your Mouse Do Your Shopping

From groceries to clothing to computers, you can buy just about everything you need with just a few clicks of your mouse. Electronic retailers (e-tailers) are cashing in on cybershoppers' purchases. Books, computer software and hardware, and music are the hottest commodities.

The two categories of Internet shopping Web sites are those with physical counterparts, such as Wal-Mart and Best Buy, and those with only a Web presence, such as Amazon.com and Buy.com (Figure 13). Popular Web shopping sites are listed in Figure 14.

Another method of shopping for the items you need, and maybe some you really do not need, is to visit auction Web sites, including those listed in Figure 14. Categories include antiques and collectibles, automotive, computers, electronics, music, sports, sports cards and memorabilia, and toys. Online auction Web sites can offer unusual items, including *Star Wars* props and memorabilia and a round of golf with Tiger Woods. eBay is one of thousands of Internet auction Web sites and is the world's largest personal online trading community.

FIGURE 13 Buy.com is a popular electronic retailer that sells a variety of products.

SHOPPING AND AUCTIONS WEB SITES

Auctions	Web Address
craigslist	craigslist.org
eBay®	ebay.com
Sotheby's	sothebys.com
uBid.com	ubid.com
Yahoo! Auctions	auctions.yahoo.com
Books and Music	**Web Address**
Amazon.com	amazon.com
Barnes & Noble.com	bn.com
BookFinder.com	bookfinder.com
Computers and Electronics	**Web Address**
BestBuy	bestbuy.com
Buy.com	buy.com
Crutchfield	crutchfield.com
Miscellaneous	**Web Address**
drugstore.com	drugstore.com
Froogle	froogle.com
Sharper Image	sharperimage.com
Walmart.com	walmart.com
For more information about shopping and auctions Web sites, visit scsite.com/dc2008/ch2/web.	

FIGURE 14 Making online purchases can help ease the burden of driving to and fighting the crowds in local malls.

SHOPPING AND AUCTIONS WEB EXERCISES

1. Visit two of the computers and electronics and two of the miscellaneous Web sites listed in Figure 14. Write a paragraph describing the features these Web sites offer compared with the same offerings from stores. In another paragraph, describe any disadvantages of shopping at these Web sites instead of actually visiting a store. Then, describe their policies for returning unwanted merchandise and for handling complaints.

2. Using one of the auction Web sites listed in Figure 14, search for two objects pertaining to your hobbies. For example, if you are a sports fan, you can search for a complete set of Upper Deck cards. If you are a car buff, search for your dream car. Describe these two items. How many people have bid on these items? Who are the sellers? What are the opening and current bids?

Weather, Sports, and News
WHAT'S NEWS?

Weather, Sports, and News Web Sites Score Big Hits

Rain or sun? Hot or cold? Weather is the leading online news item, with at least 10,000 Web sites devoted to this field. Millions of people view the WX.com Web site (Figure 15) each month.

Baseball may be the national pastime, but sports aficionados yearn for everything from auto racing to cricket. The Internet has more than one million pages of multimedia sports news, entertainment, and merchandise.

The Internet has emerged as a major source for news, with one-third of Americans going online at least once a week and 15 percent going online daily for reports of major news events. Many of these viewers are using Really Simple Syndication (RSS) technology to be notified when new stories about their favorite topics are available on the Internet. Popular weather, sports, and news Web sites are listed in Figure 16.

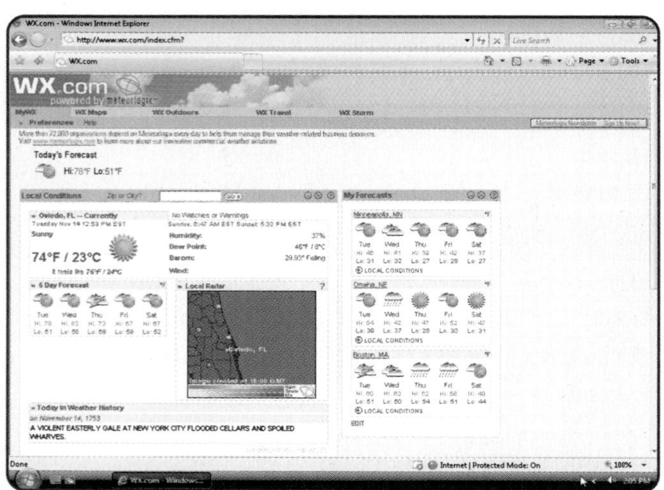

FIGURE 15 Local, national, and international weather conditions and details about breaking weather stories are available on WX.com.

WEATHER, SPORTS, AND NEWS WEB SITES

Weather	Web Address
Infoplease Weather	infoplease.com/weather.html
Intellicast.com	intellicast.com
National Weather Service	www.crh.noaa.gov
STORMFAX	stormfax.com
The Weather Channel	weather.com
WX.com	wx.com
Sports	**Web Address**
CBS SportsLine.com	cbs.sportsline.com
ESPN.com	espn.com
NCAAsports.com	ncaasports.com
OFFICIAL WEBSITE OF THE OLYMPIC MOVEMENT	olympic.org
SIRC — A World of Sport Information	sirc.ca
Sporting News Radio	radio.sportingnews.com
News	**Web Address**
Google News	news.google.com
MSNBC	msnbc.com
New York Post Online Edition	nypost.com
onlinenewspapers.com	onlinenewspapers.com
Privacy.org	privacy.org
SiliconValley.com	siliconvalley.com
Starting Page	startingpage.com/html/news.html
USATODAY.com	usatoday.com
washingtonpost.com	washingtonpost.com
For more information about weather, sports, and news Web sites, visit scsite.com/dc2008/ch2/web.	

FIGURE 16 Keep informed about the latest weather, sports, and news events with these Web sites.

WEATHER, SPORTS, AND NEWS EXERCISES

1 Visit two of the sports Web sites in Figure 16 and write a paragraph describing the content these Web sites provide concerning your favorite sport. Visit news.google.com and then search for stories about this sport team or athlete. Then, create a customized news page with stories about your sports interests. Include RSS feeds to get regularly updated summaries on this subject.

2 Visit the onlinenewspapers.com and Starting Page Web sites listed in Figure 16 and select two newspapers from each site. Write a paragraph describing the top national news story featured in each of these four Web pages. Then, write another paragraph describing the top international news story displayed at each Web site. In the third paragraph, discuss which of the four Web sites is the most interesting in terms of story selection, photographs, and Web page design.

Learning
YEARN TO LEARN

Discover New Worlds Online

While you may believe your education ends when you finally graduate from college, learning is a lifelong process. For example, enhancing your culinary skills can be a rewarding endeavor. No matter if you are a gourmet chef or a weekend cook, you will be cooking in style with the help of online resources, including those listed in Figure 17.

LEARNING WEB SITES

Cooking	Web Address
Betty Crocker	bettycrocker.com
recipecenter.com	www.recipecenter.com
Internet	**Web Address**
Learn the Net	learnthenet.com
Search Engine Watch	searchenginewatch.com
Wiredguide	wiredguide.com
Technology and Science	**Web Address**
CBT Nuggets	cbtnuggets.com
HowStuffWorks	howstuffworks.com
ScienceMaster	sciencemaster.com
General Learning	**Web Address**
Bartleby.com: Great Books Online	bartleby.com
Blue Web'n	www.kn.pacbell.com/ wired/bluewebn
MSN Encarta	encarta.msn.com
For more information about learning Web sites, visit scsite.com/ dc2008/ch2/web.	

FIGURE 17 The information gleaned from these Web sites can help you learn about many aspects of our existence.

If you would rather sit in front of the computer than stand in front of the stove, you can increase your technological knowledge by visiting several Web sites with tutorials on building your own Web sites, the latest news about the Internet, and resources for visually impaired users.

Have you ever wondered how to make a key lime pie? How about learning how to cook some easy, low-calorie dishes? Are you seeking advice from expert chefs? The recipecenter.com Web site (Figure 18) is filled with information related to recipes.

FIGURE 18 The recipecenter.com Web site provides access to over 100,000 recipes, as well as software to help manage your recipes.

LEARNING WEB EXERCISES

1. Visit one of the cooking Web sites listed in Figure 17 and find two recipes or cooking tips that you can use when preparing your next meal. Write a paragraph about each one, summarizing your discoveries. What are the advantages and disadvantages of accessing these Web sites on the new Web appliances that might someday be in your kitchen?

2. Using one of the technology and science Web sites and one of the other Web sites listed in Figure 17, search for information about communications and networks. Write a paragraph about your findings. Then, review the material in the general learning Web sites listed in Figure 17, and write a paragraph describing the content on each Web site that is pertinent to your major.

Science

$E = MC^2$

Rocket Science on the Web

For some people, space exploration is a hobby. Building and launching model rockets allow these scientists to participate in exploring the great frontier of space. For others, space exploration is their life. Numerous Web sites, including those in Figure 19, provide in-depth information about the universe.

SCIENCE WEB SITES

Periodicals	Web Address
Archaeology Magazine	archaeology.org
Astronomy.com	astronomy.com
NewScientist.com	newscientist.com
OceanLink	oceanlink.island.net
Science / AAAS	sciencemag.org
Scientific American.com	sciam.com
Resources	**Web Address**
Department of Education & Training, Victoria, Australia	www.education.vic.gov.au
National Science Foundation (NSF)	nsf.gov
Science.gov: FirstGov for Science	science.gov
Science Community	**Web Address**
American Scientist, The Magazine of Sigma Xi, The Scientific Research Society	amsci.org
Federation of American Scientists	fas.org
Librarians' Internet Index	lii.org
NASA	www.nasa.gov
Sigma Xi, The Scientific Research Society	sigmaxi.org
For more information about science Web sites, visit scsite.com/dc2008/ch2/web.	

FIGURE 19 Resources available on the Internet offer a wide range of subjects for enthusiasts who want to delve into familiar and unknown territories in the world of science.

NASA's Astronaut Flight Lounge Web site contains information about rockets, the space shuttle, the International Space Station, space transportation, and communications. Other science resources explore space-related questions about astronomy, physics, the earth sciences, microgravity, and robotics.

Rockets and space are not the only areas to explore in the world of science. Where can you find the latest pictures taken with the Hubble Space Telescope? Do you know which cities experienced an earthquake today? Have you ever wondered what a 3-D model of the amino acid glutamine looks like? You can find the answers to these questions and many others through the Science.gov Web site (science.gov) shown in Figure 20.

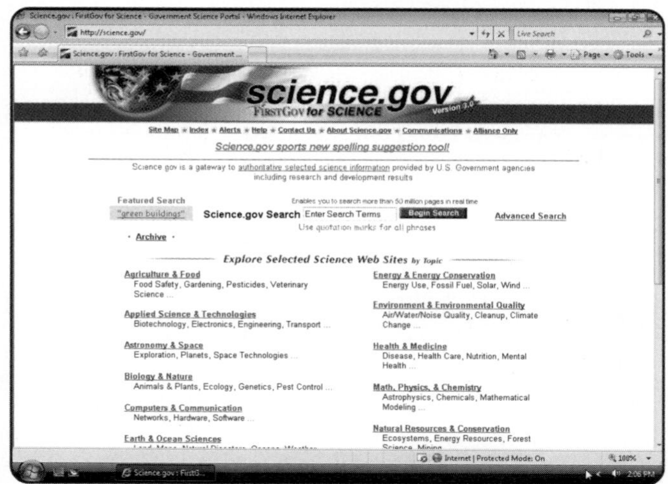

FIGURE 20 The Science.gov Web site provides easy access to the information in various federal science databases.

SCIENCE WEB EXERCISES

1. Visit the NASA Web site listed in the table in Figure 19. View the links about spacecraft, the universe, or tracking satellites and spacecraft, and then write a summary of your findings.

2. Visit the Librarians' Internet Index listed in the table in Figure 19. Click the Technology link and then click the Inventions & Inventors topic. View the Web site for the Greatest Engineering Achievements of the Twentieth Century. Pick two achievements, read their history, and write a paragraph summarizing each of these accomplishments. Then, view two of the science Web sites listed in Figure 19 and write a paragraph about each of these Web sites describing the information each contains.

Environment

THE FATE OF THE ENVIRONMENT

Protecting the Planet's Ecosystem

From the rain forests of Africa to the marine life in the Pacific Ocean, the fragile ecosystem is under extreme stress. Many environmental groups have developed Web sites, including those listed in Figure 21, in attempts to educate worldwide populations and to increase resource conservation. The GreenNet Web site (Figure 22) contains information for people who would like to help safeguard the environment.

On an international scale, the Environmental Sites on the Internet Web page developed by the Royal Institute of Technology in Stockholm, Sweden, has been rated as one of the better ecological Web sites. Its comprehensive listing of environmental concerns range from aquatic ecology to wetlands.

The U.S. federal government has a number of Web sites devoted to specific environmental concerns. For example, the U.S. Environmental Protection Agency (EPA) provides pollution data, including ozone levels and air pollutants, for specific areas. Its AirData Web site displays air pollution emissions and monitoring data from the entire United States and is the world's most extensive collection of air pollution data.

ENVIRONMENT WEB SITES

NAME	Web Address
Central African Regional Program for the Environment (CARPE)	carpe.umd.edu
Earthjustice	earthjustice.org
EarthTrends: The Environmental Information Portal	earthtrends.wri.org
Environmental Defense	edf.org
Environmental Sites on the Internet	www.ima.kth.se/im/envsite/envsite.htm
EPA AirData — Access to Air Pollution Data	epa.gov/air/data
Global Change and Environmental Education Resources	gcrio.org/educ.html
GreenNet	gn.apc.org
New American Dream	newdream.org
University of Wisconsin — Milwaukee Environmental Health and Safety Resources	www.uwm.edu/Dept/EHSRM/EHSLINKS
USGS Acid rain data and reports	bqs.usgs.gov/acidrain
World-Wide Web Virtual Library: Botany / Plant Biology	ou.edu/cas/botany-micro/www-vl/

For more information about environment Web sites, visit scsite.com/dc2008/ch2/web.

FIGURE 21 Environment Web sites provide vast resources for ecological data and action groups.

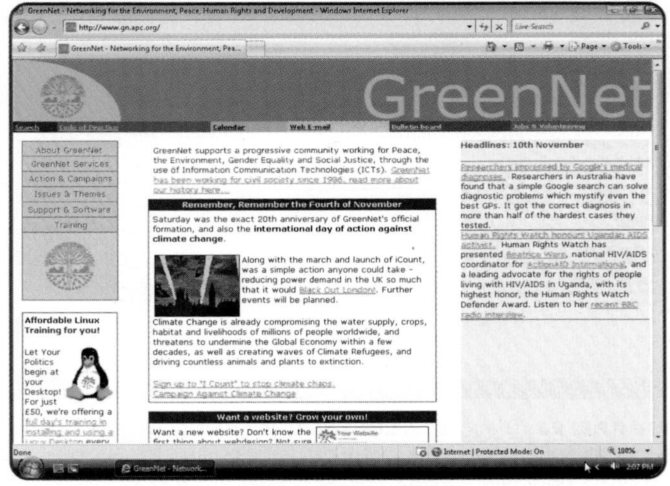

FIGURE 22 A visit to the GreenNet Web site provides information about people who work to support the environment.

ENVIRONMENT WEB EXERCISES

1. The New American Dream Web site encourages consumers to reduce the amount of junk mail sent to their homes. Using the table in Figure 21, visit the Web site and write a paragraph stating how many trees are leveled each year to provide paper for these mailings, how many garbage trucks are needed to haul this waste, and other statistics. Read the letters that you can use to eliminate your name from bulk mail lists. To whom would you mail these letters? How long does it take to stop these unsolicited letters?

2. Visit the EPA AirData Web site. What is the highest ozone level recorded in your state this past year? Where are the nearest air pollution monitoring Web sites, and what are their levels? Where are the nearest sources of air pollution? Read two reports about two different topics, such as acid rain and air quality, and summarize their findings. Include information about who sponsored the research, who conducted the studies, when the data was collected, and the impact of this pollution on the atmosphere, water, forests, and human health. Whom would you contact for further information regarding the data and studies?

Health
NO PAIN, ALL GAIN

Store Personal Health Records Online

More than 70 million consumers use the Internet yearly to search for health information, so using the Web to store personal medical data is a natural extension of the Internet's capabilities. Internet health services and portals are available online to store your personal health history, including prescriptions, lab test results, doctor visits, allergies, and immunizations. Web sites such as MedlinePlus (Figure 23) provide free health information to consumers.

In minutes, you can register with a health Web site by choosing a user name and password. Then, you create a record to enter your medical history. You also can store data for your emergency contacts, primary care physicians, specialists, blood type, cholesterol levels, blood pressure, and insurance plan. No matter where you are in the world, you and medical personnel can obtain records via the Internet or fax machine. Some popular online health database management systems are shown in Figure 24.

FIGURE 23 The MedLine Plus Web site provides health information from the U.S. Library of Medicine and the National Institutes of Health.

HEALTH WEB SITES

Medical History	Web Address
PersonalMD	personalmd.com
Practice Solutions	practicesolutions.ca
Records for Living, Inc — Personal Health and Living Management	recordsforliving.com
WebMD	webmd.com
General Health	**Web Address**
Centers for Disease Control and Prevention	www.cdc.gov
familydoctor.org	familydoctor.org
healthfinder	healthfinder.gov
HealthWeb	healthweb.org
Medical Library Association Consumer and Patient Health Information Section (CAPHIS)	caphis.mlanet.org/consumer
MedlinePlus	medlineplus.gov
PEC: Health and Nutrition Web Sites	pecentral.org/websites/healthsites.html
www.health.gov	health.gov
For more information about health Web sites, visit scsite.com/dc2008/ch2/web.	

FIGURE 24 These health Web sites allow you to organize your medical information and store it in an online database and also obtain information about a variety of medical conditions and treatments.

HEALTH WEB EXERCISES

1. Access one of the health Web sites listed in Figure 24. Register yourself or a family member, and then enter the full health history. Create an emergency medical card if the Web site provides the card option. Submit this record and emergency card to your instructor. If you feel uncomfortable disclosing medical information for yourself or a family member, you may enter fictitious information.

2. Visit three of the health Web sites listed in Figure 24. Describe the features of each. Which of the three is the most user-friendly? Why? Describe the privacy policies of these three Web sites. Submit your analysis of these Web sites to your instructor.

Research and Resources
SEARCH AND YE SHALL FIND

Info on the Web

A recent Web Usability survey conducted by the Nielsen Norman Group found that 88 percent of people log onto a computer and then use a search engine as their first action. Search engines require users to type words and phrases that characterize the information being sought. Yahoo! (Figure 25), Google, and AltaVista are some of the more popular search engines. The key to effective searching on the Web is composing search queries that narrow the search results and place the most relevant Web sites at the top of the results list.

Keep up with the latest developments by viewing online dictionaries and encyclopedias that add to their collections of computer and product terms on a regular basis. Shopping for a new computer can be a daunting experience, but many online guides can help you select the components that best fit your needs and budget. If you are not confident in your ability to solve a problem alone, turn to online technical support. Web sites often provide streaming how-to video lessons, tutorials, and real-time chats with experienced technicians. Hardware and software reviews, price comparisons, shareware, technical questions and answers, and breaking technology news are found on comprehensive portals. Figure 26 lists popular research and resources Web sites.

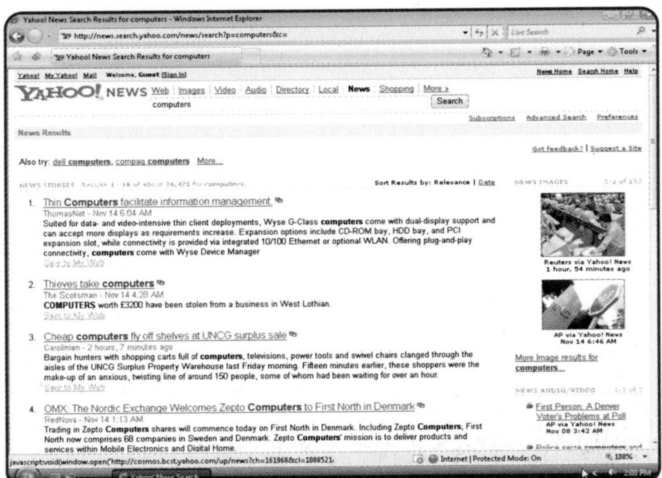

FIGURE 25 The Yahoo! News search results for the phrase, computer, lists more than 26,000 stories.

RESEARCH AND RESOURCES WEB SITES

Research	Web Address
A9.com	a9.com
AlltheWeb	alltheweb.com
AltaVista	altavista.com
Ask.com	ask.com
Google	google.com
HotBot	hotbot.com
Overture	overture.com
Windows Live	live.com
Yahoo!	yahoo.com
Resources	**Web Address**
CNET.com	cnet.com
eHow	ehow.com
PC911	pcnineoneone.com
TechBargains	techbargains.com
Webopedia	webopedia.com
ZDNet	zdnet.com

For more information about research and resources Web sites, visit scsite.com/dc2008/ch2/web.

FIGURE 26 Web users can find information by using research and resources Web sites.

RESEARCH AND RESOURCE WEB EXERCISES

1. Use two of the search engines listed in the Research category in Figure 26 to find three Web sites that review the latest digital cameras from Sony and Kodak. Make a table listing the search engines, Web site names, and the cameras' model numbers, suggested retail price, megapixels, memory, and features.

2. Visit the Webopedia Web site. Search this site for five terms. Create a table with two columns: one for the cyberterm and one for the Web definition. Then, create a second table listing five recently added or updated words and their definitions on this Web site. Next, visit the TechBargains Web site to choose the components you would buy if you were building a customized desktop computer and notebook computer. Create a table for both computers, listing the computer manufacturer, processor model name or number and manufacturer, clock speed, RAM, cache, number of expansion slots, and number of bays.

Careers
IN SEARCH OF THE PERFECT JOB

Web Helps Career Hunt

While your teachers give you valuable training to prepare you for a career, they rarely teach you how to begin that career. You can broaden your horizons by searching the Internet for career information and job openings.

First, examine some of the job search Web sites. These resources list thousands of openings in hundreds of fields, companies, and locations. For example, the U.S. Department of Labor Web site, shown in Figure 27, allows you to find information for different types of jobs. This information may include the training and education required, salary data, working conditions, job descriptions, and more.

When a company contacts you for an interview, learn as much about it and the industry as possible before the interview. Many of the Web sites listed in Figure 28 include detailed company profiles and links to their corporate Web sites.

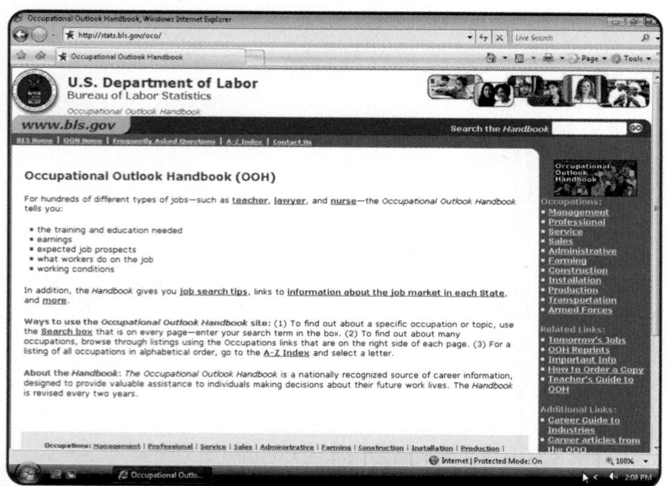

FIGURE 27 The Occupational Outlook Handbook provides career information to those searching for jobs.

CAREER WEB SITES

Job Search	Web Address
BestJobsUSA.com	bestjobsusa.com
CareerBuilder	careerbuilder.com
CareerNet	careernet.com
CAREERXCHANGE	careerexchange.com
College Grad Job Hunter	collegegrad.com
EmploymentGuide.com	employmentguide.com
Job.com	job.com
JobBank USA	jobbankusa.com
JobWeb.com	www.jobweb.com
Monster	monster.com
Spherion	spherion.com
USAJOBS	usajobs.opm.gov
VolunteerMatch	volunteermatch.org
Yahoo! HotJobs	hotjobs.yahoo.com
Company/Industry Information	**Web Address**
Career ResourceCenter.com	resourcecenter.com
Forbes.com	forbes.com/careers
FORTUNE	fortune.com
Hoover's	hoovers.com
Occupational Outlook Handbook	stats.bls.gov/oco
For more information about career Web sites, visit scsite.com/dc2008/ch2/web.	

FIGURE 28 Career Web sites provide a variety of job openings and information about major companies worldwide.

CAREERS WEB EXERCISES

1. Use two of the job search Web sites listed in Figure 28 to find three companies with job openings in your field. Make a table listing the Web site name, position available, description, salary, location, desired education, and desired experience.

2. It is a good idea to acquire information before graduation about the industry in which you would like to work. Are you interested in the automotive manufacturing industry, the restaurant service industry, or the financial industry? Use two of the company/industry information Web sites listed in Figure 28 to research a particular career related to your major. Write a paragraph naming the Web sites and the specific information you found, such as the nature of the work, recommended training and qualifications, employment outlook, and earnings. Then, use two other Web sites to profile three companies with positions available in this field. Write a paragraph about each of these companies, describing the headquarters' location, sales and earnings for the previous year, total number of employees, working conditions, perks, and competitors.

Arts and Literature

FIND SOME CULTURE

Get Ready to Read, Paint, and Dance

Brush up your knowledge of Shakespeare, grab a canvas, and put on your dancing shoes. Visual arts and literature Web sites, including those in Figure 29, are about to sweep you off your cyberfeet.

ARTS AND LITERATURE WEB SITES

Arts	Web Address
accessplace arts	accessplace.com/arts.htm
Art News — absolutearts.com	absolutearts.com
The Children's Museum of Indianapolis	childrensmuseum.org
GalleryGuide.com	galleryguide.com
The Getty	getty.edu
Louvre Museum	louvre.fr
Montreal Museum of Fine Arts	mmfa.qc.ca
The New York Times: Arts	nytimes.com/pages/arts/index.html
Virtual Library museums pages (VLmp)	vlmp.museophile.com
Literature	**Web Address**
Bartleby.com	bartleby.com
Bibliomania	bibliomania.com
Fantastic Fiction	fantasticfiction.co.uk
Literary History	literaryhistory.com
The Modern Library eBook List	randomhouse.com/modernlibrary/ebookslist.html
Project Gutenberg	gutenberg.org
William Shakespeare at eNotes	shakespeare.com

For more information about arts and literature Web sites, visit scsite.com/dc2008/ch2/web.

FIGURE 29 Discover culture throughout the world by visiting these arts and literature Web sites.

The full text of hundreds of books is available online from the Bibliomania and Project Gutenberg Web sites. Shakespeare.com provides in-depth reviews and news of the world's most famous playwright and his works. The Bartleby.com Web site features biographies, definitions, quotations, dictionaries, and indexes.

When you are ready to absorb more culture, you can turn to various art Web sites. Many museums have images of their collections online. Among them are the Getty Museum in Los Angeles (Figure 30), the Montreal Museum of Fine Arts, and the Louvre Museum in Paris.

The accessplace arts and The New York Times Web sites focus on the arts and humanities and provide fascinating glimpses into the worlds of dance, music, performance, cinema, and other topics pertaining to creative expression.

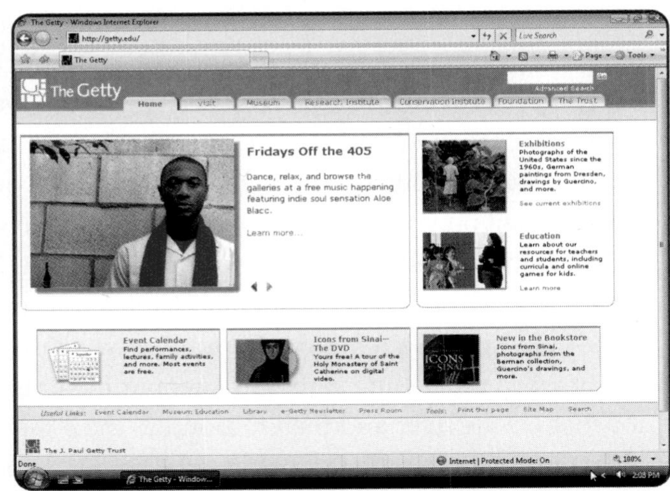

FIGURE 30 Permanent and temporary exhibitions, educational activities, and a bookstore are featured on the Getty Museum Web site.

ARTS AND LITERATURE WEB EXERCISES

1. Visit The Modern Library eBook List Web site listed in Figure 29 and view one book in the 20th CENTURY NOVELS, 19th CENTURY NOVELS, BRITISH LITERATURE, and HISTORY sections. Create a table with columns for the book name, author, cost, online store, local store, and description. Then, read the excerpt from each of the four books and write a paragraph describing which of these four books is the most interesting to you. What are the advantages and disadvantages of reading classic literature electronically?

2. Using the arts Web sites listed in Figure 29, search for three temporary exhibitions in galleries throughout the world. Describe the venues, the artists, and the works. What permanent collections are found in these museums? Some people shop for gifts in the museums' stores. View and describe three items for sale.

CHAPTER THREE

Application Software

Picture Yourself Using Software

This is a busy semester for you. Besides a full load of classes, you have joined your school's Hospitality Club. In addition, your brother has enlisted you to help plan your grandparents' fiftieth anniversary party, a job that entails retouching some of their old photographs and tracking the party's budget. You plan to use software on your notebook computer and PDA to assist with these tasks.

In the student lounge before geography class, you check e-mail on your notebook computer. You have a message from a fellow club member asking if you have finished the flyer for the Hospitality Club's upcoming dance, along with a reminder for tomorrow's meeting. Using word processing software, you put the finishing touches on the flyer and then respond to the e-mail message, including the flyer as an attachment. You enter the meeting date in your appointment calendar in your PDA and then return to your notebook computer. You then start your photo editing software and finish retouching your grandparents' wedding photograph. Next, you use personal finance software to enter the latest figures for your grandparents' party. Deciding you have worked enough today, you spend some time creating a blog about the party and designing a spectacular roller coaster.

Read Chapter 3 to learn more about word processing software, e-mail programs, photo editing software, desktop publishing software, PDA application software, personal finance software, and entertainment software, and discover many other types of application software.

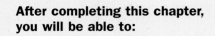

OBJECTIVES

After completing this chapter, you will be able to:

1. **Identify the categories of application software**
2. **Explain ways software is distributed**
3. **Explain how to work with application software**
4. **Identify the key features of widely used business programs**
5. **Identify the key features of widely used graphics and multimedia programs**
6. **Identify the key features of widely used home, personal, and educational programs**
7. **Identify the types of application software used in communications**
8. **Describe the function of several utility programs**
9. **Discuss the advantages of using Web-based software**
10. **Describe the learning aids available for application software**

CONTENTS

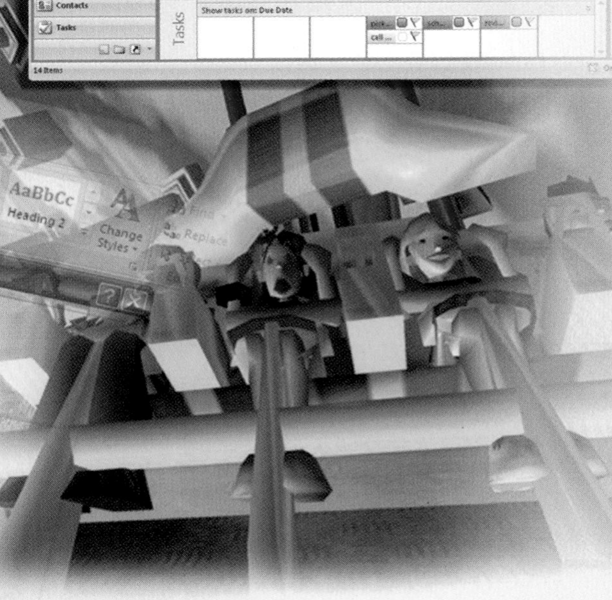

APPLICATION SOFTWARE

With the proper software, a computer is a valuable tool. Software allows users to create letters, memos, reports, and other documents; design Web pages and diagrams; draw and alter images; record and enhance audio and video clips; prepare and file taxes; play single player or multiplayer games; compose e-mail messages and instant messages; and much more. To accomplish these and many other tasks, users work with application software. **Application software** consists of programs designed to make users more productive and/or assist them with personal tasks. Application software has a variety of uses:

1. To make business activities more efficient
2. To assist with graphics and multimedia projects
3. To support home, personal, and educational tasks
4. To facilitate communications

The table in Figure 3-1 categorizes popular types of application software by their general use. Although many types of communications software exist, the ones listed in Figure 3-1 are application software oriented. Successful use of application software often requires the use of one or more of the utility programs identified in Figure 3-1.

The categories in Figure 3-1 are not mutually exclusive. Software listed in one category may be used in other categories. For example, desktop publishing programs, which are categorized as graphics and multimedia software, often are used for business or personal reasons.

Application software is available in a variety of forms: packaged, custom, Web-based, open source, shareware, freeware, and public domain.

- **Packaged software** is mass-produced, copyrighted retail software that meets the needs of a wide variety of users, not just a single user or company. Word processing and spreadsheet software are examples of packaged software. Packaged software is available in retail stores or on the Web.
- **Custom software** performs functions specific to a business or industry. Sometimes a company cannot find packaged software that meets its unique requirements. In this case, the company may use programmers to develop tailor-made custom software, which usually costs more than packaged software.

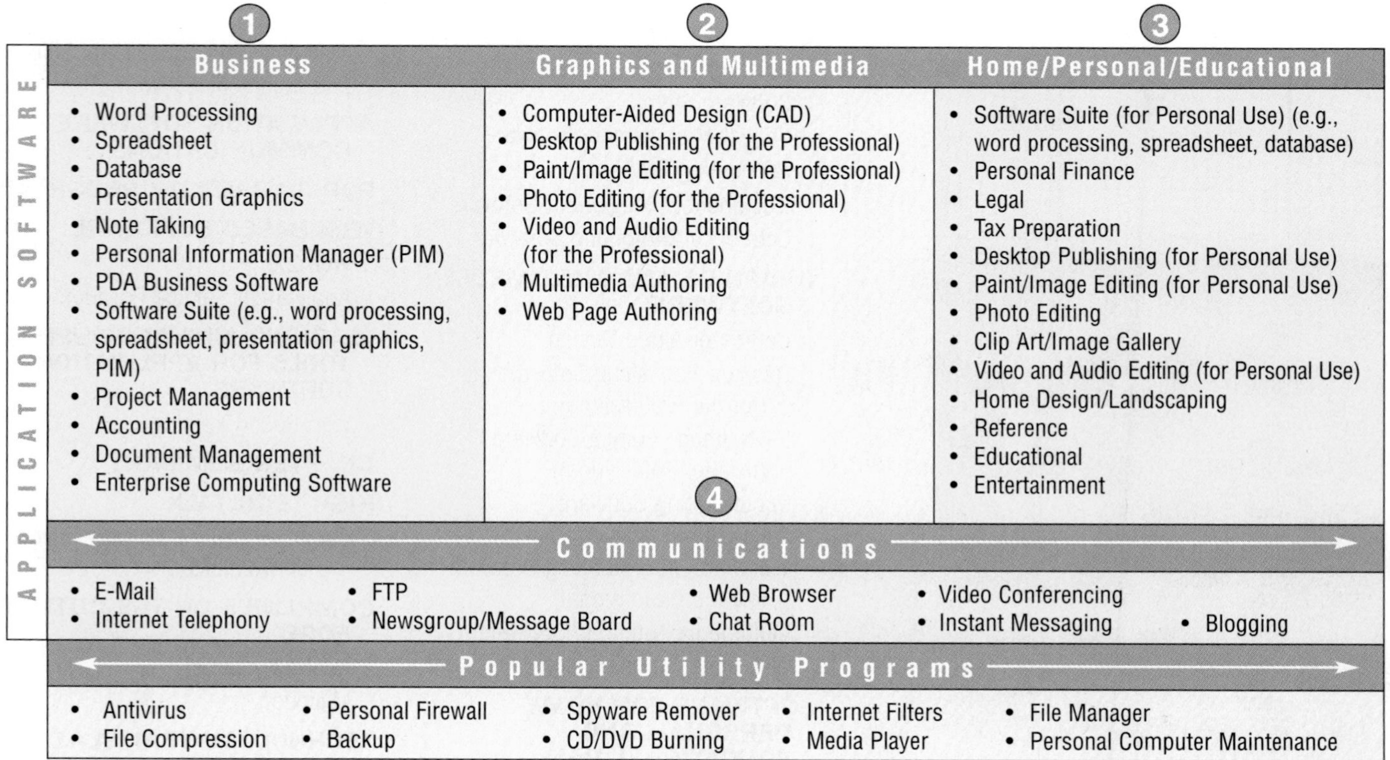

CATEGORIES OF APPLICATION SOFTWARE

APPLICATION SOFTWARE

1 Business	2 Graphics and Multimedia	3 Home/Personal/Educational
• Word Processing • Spreadsheet • Database • Presentation Graphics • Note Taking • Personal Information Manager (PIM) • PDA Business Software • Software Suite (e.g., word processing, spreadsheet, presentation graphics, PIM) • Project Management • Accounting • Document Management • Enterprise Computing Software	• Computer-Aided Design (CAD) • Desktop Publishing (for the Professional) • Paint/Image Editing (for the Professional) • Photo Editing (for the Professional) • Video and Audio Editing (for the Professional) • Multimedia Authoring • Web Page Authoring	• Software Suite (for Personal Use) (e.g., word processing, spreadsheet, database) • Personal Finance • Legal • Tax Preparation • Desktop Publishing (for Personal Use) • Paint/Image Editing (for Personal Use) • Photo Editing • Clip Art/Image Gallery • Video and Audio Editing (for Personal Use) • Home Design/Landscaping • Reference • Educational • Entertainment

4 Communications

- E-Mail
- Internet Telephony
- FTP
- Newsgroup/Message Board
- Web Browser
- Chat Room
- Video Conferencing
- Instant Messaging
- Blogging

Popular Utility Programs

- Antivirus
- File Compression
- Personal Firewall
- Backup
- Spyware Remover
- CD/DVD Burning
- Internet Filters
- Media Player
- File Manager
- Personal Computer Maintenance

FIGURE 3-1 The four major categories of popular application software are outlined in this table. Communications software often is bundled with other application or system software. Also identified in the table are widely used utility programs.

- **Web-based software** refers to programs hosted by a Web site. Users access and interact with Web-based software from any computer or device that is connected to the Internet. Many Web sites provide free access to their programs; some charge a fee. Examples of Web-based software include e-mail, word processing, tax preparation, and game programs. Web-based programs are discussed in more depth later in the chapter.
- **Open source software** is software provided for use, modification, and redistribution. This software has no restrictions from the copyright holder regarding modification of the software's internal instructions and redistribution of the software. Open source software usually can be downloaded from the Internet, sometimes at no cost.
- **Shareware** is copyrighted software that is distributed at no cost for a trial period. To use a shareware program beyond that period, you send payment to the program developer. Shareware developers trust users to send payment if software use extends beyond the stated trial period. In some cases, a scaled-down version of the software is distributed free, and payment entitles the user to the fully functional product.
- **Freeware** is copyrighted software provided at no cost by an individual or a company that retains all rights to the software. Thus, programmers typically cannot incorporate freeware in applications they intend to sell. The word, free, in freeware indicates the software has no charge.
- **Public-domain software** has been donated for public use and has no copyright restrictions. Anyone can copy or distribute public-domain software to others at no cost.

Thousands of shareware, freeware, and public-domain programs are available on the Internet for users to download. Examples include communications programs, graphics programs, and games. These programs usually have fewer capabilities than retail programs.

After you purchase or download software, you install it. During installation, the program may ask you to register and/or activate the software. Registering the software is optional and usually involves submitting your name and other personal information to the software manufacturer or developer. Registering the software often entitles you to product support. *Product activation* is a technique that some software manufacturers use to ensure the software is not installed on more computers than legally licensed. Usually, the software does not function or has limited functionality until you activate it via the Internet or telephone. Thus, activation is a required process for programs requesting it. Registering and/or activating the software also usually entitles you to free program updates for a specified time period, such as a year.

The Role of System Software

System software serves as the interface between the user, the application software, and the computer's hardware (Figure 3-2). To use application software, such as a word processing program, your computer must be running system software — specifically, an operating system. Four popular personal computer operating systems are Windows Vista, Windows XP, Linux, and Mac OS X.

Each time you start a computer, the operating system is *loaded* (copied) from the computer's hard disk into memory. Once the operating system is loaded, it coordinates all the activities of the computer. This includes starting application software and transferring data among input and output devices and memory. While the computer is running, the operating system remains in memory.

FIGURE 3-2 A user does not communicate directly with the computer hardware. Instead, system software is the interface between the user, the application software, and the hardware. For example, when a user instructs the application software to print, the application software sends the print instruction to the system software, which in turn sends the print instruction to the hardware.

Working with Application Software

To use application software, you must instruct the operating system to start the program. The steps in Figure 3-3 illustrate how to start and interact with the Paint program, which is included with the Windows Vista operating system. The following paragraphs explain the steps in Figure 3-3.

Personal computer operating systems often use the concept of a desktop to make the computer easier to use. The **desktop** is an on-screen work area that has a graphical user interface (read Looking Ahead 3-1 for a look at the next generation of user interfaces). Step 1 of Figure 3-3 shows icons, a button, a pointer, and a menu on the Windows Vista desktop. An **icon** is a small image displayed on the screen that represents a program, a document, or some other object. A **button** is a graphical element that you activate to cause a specific action to take place. One way to activate a button is to click it. To **click** a button on the screen requires moving the pointer to the button and then pressing and releasing a button on the mouse (usually the left mouse button). The **pointer** is a small symbol displayed on the screen that moves as you move the mouse. Common pointer shapes are an I-beam (I), a block arrow (↖), and a pointing hand (☝).

FIGURE 3-3 HOW TO START A PROGRAM FROM WINDOWS VISTA

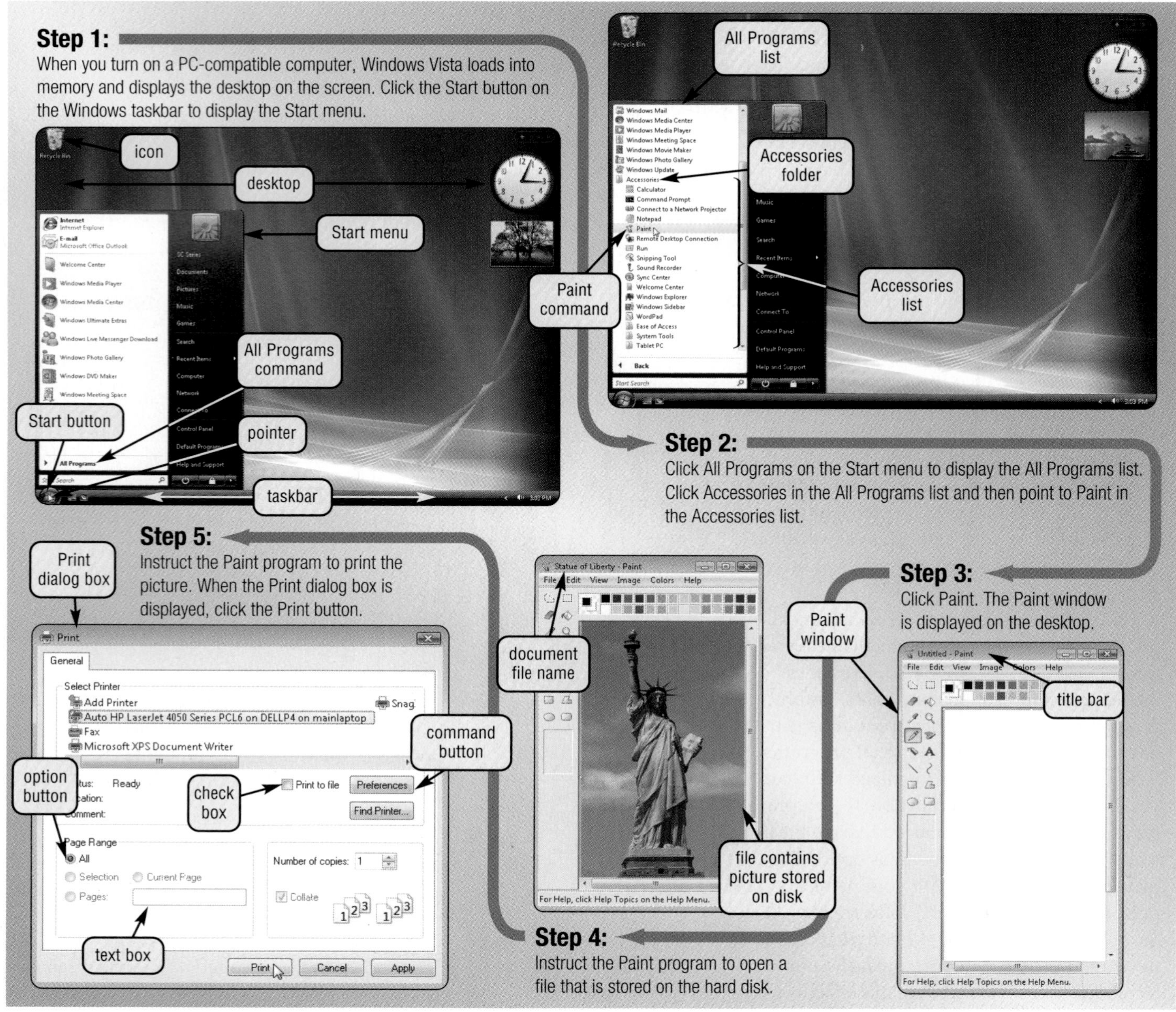
Step 1:
When you turn on a PC-compatible computer, Windows Vista loads into memory and displays the desktop on the screen. Click the Start button on the Windows taskbar to display the Start menu.
icon
desktop
Start menu
All Programs command
Start button
pointer
taskbar
All Programs list
Accessories folder
Paint command
Accessories list
Step 2:
Click All Programs on the Start menu to display the All Programs list. Click Accessories in the All Programs list and then point to Paint in the Accessories list.
Step 3:
Click Paint. The Paint window is displayed on the desktop.
Paint window
title bar
Step 4:
Instruct the Paint program to open a file that is stored on the hard disk.
document file name
file contains picture stored on disk
Step 5:
Instruct the Paint program to print the picture. When the Print dialog box is displayed, click the Print button.
Print dialog box
command button
option button
check box
text box

LOOKING AHEAD 3-1

Touch Drive Your Computer Screen

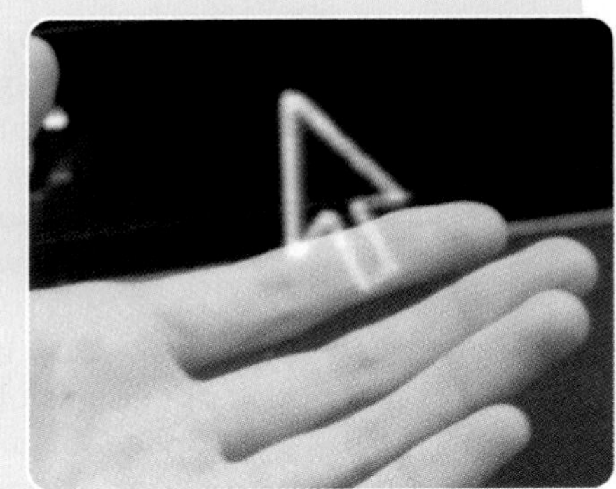

Computer users soon may discard the mouse and let their fingers do the work with an innovative user interface system that displays images in thin air.

The virtual touch screen uses a rear projector system to create images that look three dimensional and appear to float in midair. Users interact with projected objects with their hands, so there is no need for a mouse, monitor, physical surface, or special gloves or eyeglasses. In specialized environments, users also can use a scalpel, scissors, pen, or pencil to move objects.

The only hardware required to project these images is a standard video source, such as a computer, television, DVD player, or video game console. The projected images can be as large as 30 inches diagonally and are viewed best against a black background to emphasize the color contrast. For more information, visit scsite.com/dc2008/ch3/looking and then click Gesture Recognition.

The Windows Vista desktop contains a Start button on the lower-left corner of the taskbar. When you click the Start button, the Start menu is displayed on the desktop. A **menu** contains a list of commands from which you make selections. A **command** is an instruction that causes a program to perform a specific action.

As illustrated in Steps 1 and 2 of Figure 3-3, when you click the Start button and click the All Programs command on the Start menu, the All Programs list is displayed on the Start menu. Clicking the Accessories folder in the All Programs list displays the Accessories list.

To start a program, you can click its program name on a menu or in a list. This action instructs the operating system to start the program, which means the program's instructions load from a storage medium (such as a hard disk) into memory. For example, when you click Paint in the Accessories list, Windows Vista loads the Paint program instructions from the computer's hard disk into memory.

Once loaded into memory, the program is displayed in a window on the desktop (Step 3 of Figure 3-3). A **window** is a rectangular area of the screen that displays data and information. The top of a window has a **title bar**, which is a horizontal space that contains the window's name.

With the program loaded, you can create a new file or open an existing one. A *file* is a named collection of stored data, instructions, or information. A file can contain text, images, audio, and video. To distinguish among various files, each file has a file name. A *file name* is a unique combination of letters of the alphabet, numbers, and other characters that identifies a file. The title bar of the document window usually displays a document's file name. Step 4 of Figure 3-3 shows the contents of the file, Statue of Liberty, displaying in the Paint window. The file contains an image photographed with a digital camera.

In some cases, when you instruct a program to perform an activity such as printing, the program displays a dialog box. A *dialog box* is a window that provides information, presents available options, or requests a response. Dialog boxes, such as the one shown in Step 5 of Figure 3-3, often contain option buttons, text boxes, check boxes, and command buttons. Clicking the Print button in the dialog box instructs the computer to print the picture.

FAQ 3-1

What programs are included with Windows Vista?

Every version of Windows Vista includes Calculator, Notepad, WordPad, Internet Explorer, Windows Photo Gallery, Windows Mail, Windows Calendar, and a variety of games. For more information, visit scsite.com/dc2008/ch3/faq and then click Windows Vista Programs.

Test your knowledge of pages 134 through 137 in Quiz Yourself 3-1.

QUIZ YOURSELF 3-1

Instructions: Find the true statement below. Then, rewrite the remaining false statements so they are true.

1. Application software is used to make business activities more efficient; assist with graphics and multimedia projects; support home, personal, and educational tasks; and facilitate communications.
2. Public-domain software is mass-produced, copyrighted retail software that meets the needs of a wide variety of users, not just a single user or company.
3. To use system software, your computer must be running application software.
4. When a program is started, its instructions load from memory into a storage medium.

Quiz Yourself Online: To further check your knowledge of application software categories, ways software is distributed, and working with application software, visit scsite.com/dc2008/ch3/quiz and then click Objectives 1 – 3.

BUSINESS SOFTWARE

Business software is application software that assists people in becoming more effective and efficient while performing their daily business activities. Business software includes programs such as word processing, spreadsheet, database, presentation graphics, note taking, personal information manager software, PDA business software, software suites, project management, accounting, document management, and enterprise computing software. Figure 3-4 lists popular programs for each of these categories.

The following sections discuss the features and functions of business software. Word processing and spreadsheet software have a heavier emphasis because of their predominant use.

Word Processing Software

Word processing software is one of the more widely used types of application software. **Word processing software**, sometimes called a *word processor*, allows users to create and manipulate documents containing mostly text and sometimes graphics (Figure 3-5). Millions of people use word processing software every day to develop documents such as letters, memos, reports, fax cover sheets, mailing labels, newsletters, and Web pages.

Word processing software has many features to make documents look professional and visually appealing. Some of these features include the capability of changing the shape and size of characters, changing the color of characters, applying special effects such as three-dimensional shadows, and organizing text in newspaper-style columns. When using colors for characters, however, they will print as black or gray unless you have a color printer.

Most word processing software allows users to incorporate many types of graphical images, such as digital pictures and clip art, in documents. **Clip art** is a collection of drawings,

POPULAR BUSINESS PROGRAMS

Application Software	Manufacturer	Program Name
Word Processing	Microsoft	Word 2007
	Sun	StarOffice Writer
	Corel	WordPerfect
Spreadsheet	Microsoft	Excel 2007
	Sun	StarOffice Calc
	Corel	Quattro Pro
Database	Microsoft	Access 2007
	Sun	StarOffice Base
	Corel	Paradox
	Microsoft	Visual FoxPro SQL Server
	Oracle	Oracle Database
	MySQL AB	MySQL
Presentation Graphics	Microsoft	PowerPoint 2007
	Sun	StarOffice Impress
	Corel	Presentations
Note Taking	Microsoft	OneNote 2007
	Agilix	GoBinder
	Corel	Grafigo
Personal Information Manager (PIM)	Microsoft	Outlook 2007
	IBM	Organizer
	Palm	Desktop
PDA Business Software	CNetX	Pocket SlideShow
	Microsoft	Pocket Word Pocket Excel Pocket Outlook
	Mobile Systems	MobiSystems Office Suite Professional
	Mozilla	Thunderbird
	Ultrasoft	Money
Software Suite (for the Professional)	Microsoft	Office 2007 Office for Mac
	Sun	StarOffice Office Suite
	Corel	WordPerfect Office
	IBM	Lotus SmartSuite
Project Management	Microsoft	Project 2007
	Primavera	SureTrak Project Manager
Accounting	Intuit	QuickBooks
	Sage Software	Peachtree
Document Management	Adobe	Acrobat
	Enfocus	PitStop
	Nuance	PDF Converter PaperPort
Enterprise Computing Software	Oracle	PeopleSoft Enterprise Human Resources
	Sage Software	Sage MAS 500
	MSC Software	MSC.SimManager
	Oracle	Oracle Manufacturing
	SAP	mySAP Customer Relationship Management
	NetSuite	NetERP
	Apropos Technology	Apropos Interaction Management Suite

FIGURE 3-4 Popular business software.

photographs, and other images that you can insert in documents. In Figure 3-5, a user inserted an image of a lake in the document. Word processing software usually includes public-domain images. You can find additional public-domain and proprietary images on the Web or purchase them on CD or DVD.

All word processing software provides at least some basic capabilities to help users create and modify documents. Defining the size of the paper on which to print and specifying the *margins* — that is, the portion of the page outside the main body of text, including the top, the bottom, and both sides of the paper — are examples of some of these capabilities. If you type text that extends beyond the right page margin, the word processing software automatically positions text at the beginning of the next line. This feature, called *wordwrap*, allows users to type words in a paragraph continually without pressing the ENTER key at the end of each line. When you modify paper size or margins, the word processing software automatically rewraps text so it fits in the adjusted paper size and margins.

As you type more lines of text than can be displayed on the screen, the top portion of the document moves upward, or scrolls, off the screen. *Scrolling* is the process of moving different portions of the document on the screen into view.

A major advantage of using word processing software is that users easily can change what they have written. For example, a user can insert, delete, or rearrange words, sentences, paragraphs, or entire sections. The find, or *search*, feature allows you to locate all occurrences of a certain character, word, or phrase. This feature, in combination with the *replace* feature, allows you to substitute existing characters or words with new ones.

Word processing software includes a *spelling checker*, which reviews the spelling of individual words, sections of a document, or the entire document. The spelling checker compares the words in the document with an electronic dictionary that is part of the word processing software. You can customize the electronic dictionary by adding words such as

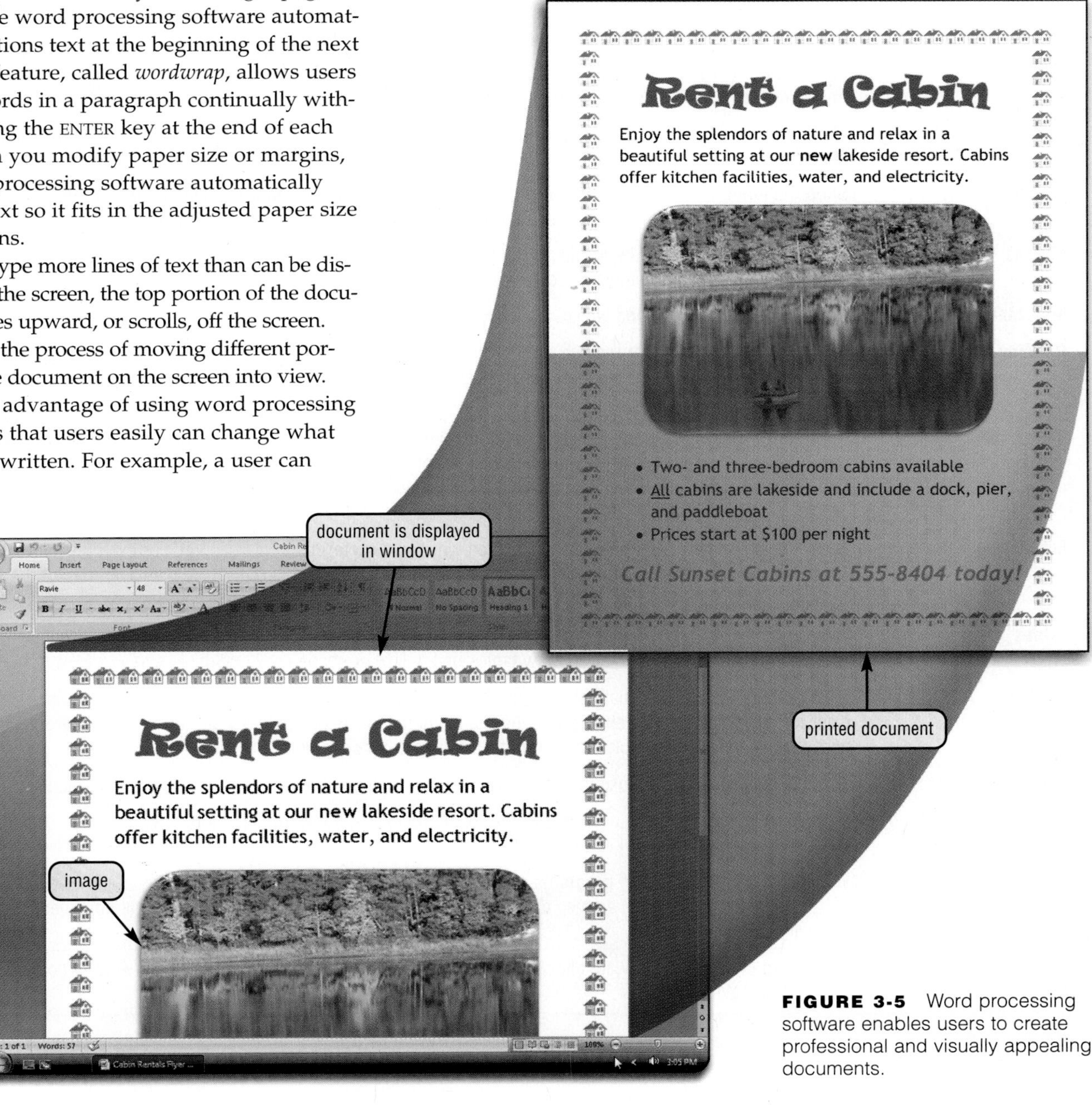

FIGURE 3-5 Word processing software enables users to create professional and visually appealing documents.

Word Processing Software

For more information, visit scsite.com/dc2008/ch3/weblink and then click Word Processing Software.

companies, streets, cities, and personal names, so the software can check the spelling of those words too.

Another benefit of word processing software is the capability to insert headers and footers in a document. A *header* is text that appears at the top of each page, and a *footer* is text that appears at the bottom of each page. Page numbers, company names, report titles, and dates are examples of items often included in headers and footers.

In addition to these basic capabilities, most current word processing programs provide numerous additional features, which are listed in the table in Figure 3-6.

ADDITIONAL WORD PROCESSING FEATURES

AutoCorrect	As you type words, the AutoCorrect feature corrects common spelling errors. AutoCorrect also corrects capitalization mistakes.
AutoFormat	As you type, the AutoFormat feature automatically applies formatting to the text. For example, it automatically numbers a list or converts a Web address to a hyperlink.
Collaboration	Collaboration includes discussions and online meetings. Discussions allow multiple users to enter comments in a document and read and reply to each other's comments. Through an online meeting, users share documents with others in real time and view changes as they are being made.
Columns	Most word processing software can arrange text in two or more columns to look like text in a newspaper or magazine. The text from the bottom of one column automatically flows to the top of the next column.
Grammar Checker	The grammar checker proofreads documents for grammar, writing style, sentence structure errors, and reading statistics.
Ink Input	Supports input from a digital pen. Word processing software that supports ink input incorporates user's handwritten text and drawings in a word processing document. Ink input is popular on Tablet PCs.
Macros	A *macro* is a sequence of keystrokes and instructions that a user records and saves. When you want to execute the same series of instructions, execute the macro instead.
Mail Merge	Creates form letters, mailing labels, and envelopes.
Reading Layout	For those users who prefer reading on the screen, reading layout increases the readability and legibility of an on-screen document by hiding unnecessary buttons, increasing the size of displayed characters, and providing navigation tools.
Research	Some word processing software allows you to search through various forms of online and Internet reference information — based on selected text in a document. Research services available include a thesaurus, English and bilingual dictionaries, encyclopedias, and Web sites that provide information such as stock quotes, news articles, and company profiles.
Smart Tags	*Smart tags* automatically appear on the screen when you perform a certain action. For example, typing an address causes a smart tag to appear. Clicking this smart tag provides options to display a map of the address or driving directions to or from the address.
Tables	Tables organize information into rows and columns. In addition to evenly spaced rows and columns, some word processing programs allow you to draw tables of any size or shape.
Templates	A *template* is a document that contains the formatting necessary for a specific document type. Templates usually exist for memos, fax cover sheets, and letters. In addition to templates provided with the software, users have access to many online templates through the manufacturer's Web site.
Thesaurus	With a thesaurus, a user looks up a synonym (word with the same meaning) for a word in a document.
Tracking Changes	If multiple users work with a document, the word processing software highlights or color-codes changes made by various users.
Voice Recognition	With some word processing programs, users can speak into the computer's microphone and watch the spoken words appear on the screen as they talk. With these programs, users edit and format the document by speaking or spelling an instruction.
Web Page Development	Most word processing software allows users to create, edit, format, and convert documents to be displayed on the World Wide Web.

FIGURE 3-6 Many additional features are included with word processing software.

Developing a Document

With application software, such as word processing, users create, edit, format, save, and print documents. During the process of developing a document, users likely will switch back and forth among all of these activities.

When you **create** a document, you enter text or numbers, insert images, and perform other tasks using an input device such as a keyboard, mouse, or digital pen. If you are using Microsoft Office Word 2007 to design a flyer, for example, you are creating a document.

To **edit** a document means to make changes to its existing content. Common editing tasks include inserting, deleting, cutting, copying, and pasting. Inserting text involves adding text to a document. Deleting text means that you are removing text or other content. Cutting is the process of removing a portion of the document and storing it in a temporary storage location, sometimes called a *clipboard*. A clipboard also contains items that you copy (duplicate) in a document. *Pasting* is the process of transferring an item from a clipboard to a specific location in a document. Read Ethics & Issues 3-1 for a related discussion.

When users **format** a document, they change its appearance. Formatting is important because the overall look of a document significantly can affect its ability to communicate clearly. Examples of formatting tasks are changing the font, font size, or font style of text.

A **font** is a name assigned to a specific design of characters. Two basic types of fonts are serif and sans serif. A *serif font* has short decorative lines at the upper and lower ends of the characters. Sans means without. Thus, a *sans serif font* does not have the short decorative lines at the upper and lower ends of the characters. Times New Roman is an example of a serif font. Arial is an example of a sans serif font.

Font size indicates the size of the characters in a particular font. Font size is gauged by a measurement system called points. A single *point* is about 1/72 of an inch in height. The text you are reading in this book is about 10 point. Thus, each character is about 5/36 (10/72) of an inch in height. A *font style* adds emphasis to a font. Bold, italic, and underline are examples of font styles. Figure 3-7 illustrates fonts, font sizes, and font styles.

ETHICS & ISSUES 3-1

How Should Schools Deal with Internet Plagiarism?

A high school teacher failed 28 students for plagiarizing, or copying, material from the Internet. When parents complained, the school board passed the students, and the teacher resigned. Word processing software and the Internet make plagiarism easier than ever. Students can use term paper Web sites, such as CheatHouse.com, to copy complete papers on a variety of topics. According to one survey, half of those who responded said that cheating does not or may not matter in the long run, and 60 percent had plagiarized in the past. Students who plagiarize blame peer pressure, classroom competition, the "busy work" nature of some assignments, and the permissive attitude that pervades the Internet. Teachers have several tools to catch plagiarists, including a variety of Internet-based services, such as Turnitin, that compare suspected papers to papers found on the Internet and produce an originality report highlighting text that may have been copied. Some instructors, however, are reluctant to investigate the integrity of a student's work and possibly ruin an academic career, but more and more schools require instructors to do such checking using paid services to check papers. How should educators deal with plagiarism? Should a school's response to plagiarism depend on such factors as the material copied, the assignment for which it was copied, or the reason it was copied? Why or why not?

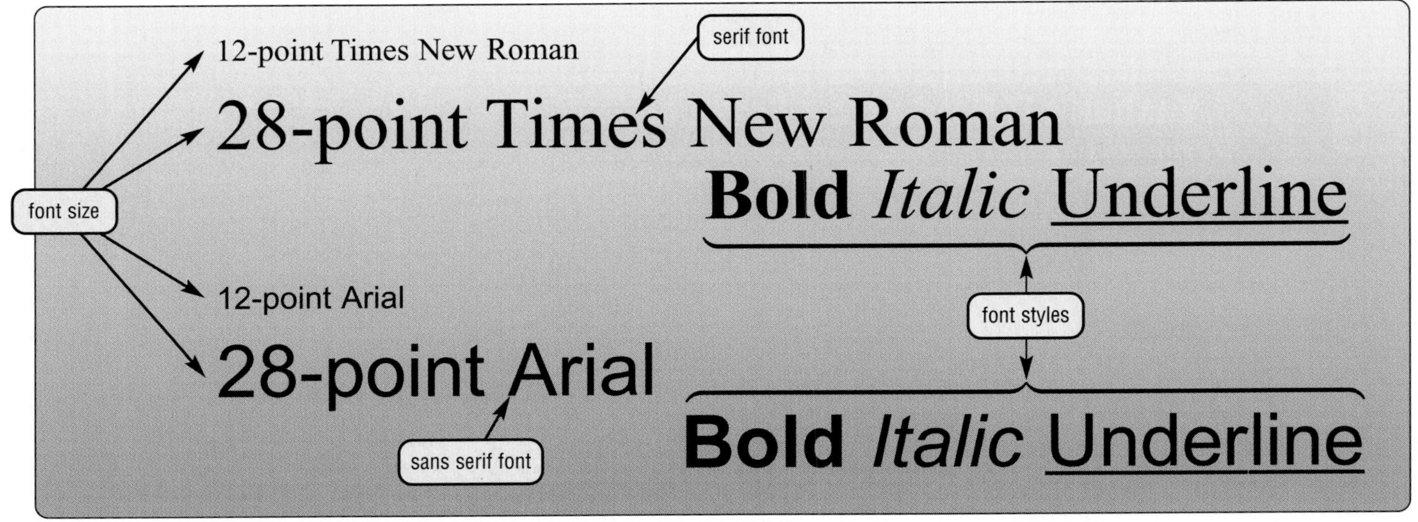

FIGURE 3-7 The Times New Roman and Arial fonts are shown in two font sizes and a variety of font styles.

During the process of creating, editing, and formatting a document, the computer holds it in memory. To keep the document for future use requires that you save it. When you **save** a document, the computer transfers the document from memory to a storage medium such as a USB flash drive, hard disk, or CD. Once saved, a document is stored permanently as a file on the storage medium.

When you **print** a document, the computer places the contents of the document on paper or some other medium. One of the benefits of word processing software is the ability to print the same document many times, with each copy looking just like the first. Instead of printing a document and physically distributing it, some users e-mail the document to others on a network such as the Internet.

FAQ 3-2

How often should I save a document?

Saving at regular intervals ensures that the majority of your work will not be lost in the event of a power loss or system failure. Many programs have an AutoSave feature that automatically saves open documents at specified time intervals, such as every 10 minutes. For more information, visit scsite.com/dc2008/ch3/faq and then click Saving Documents.

Spreadsheet Software

Spreadsheet software is another widely used type of application software. **Spreadsheet software** allows users to organize data in rows and columns and perform calculations on the data. These rows and columns collectively are called a *worksheet*. For years, people used paper to organize data and perform calculations by hand. In an electronic worksheet, you organize data in the same manner, and the computer performs the calculations more quickly and accurately (Figure 3-8). Because of spreadsheet software's logical approach to organizing data, many people use this software to organize and present nonfinancial data, as well as financial data.

As with word processing software, most spreadsheet software has basic features to help users create, edit, and format worksheets. Spreadsheet software also incorporates many of the features found in word processing software such as macros, checking spelling, changing fonts and font sizes, adding colors, tracking changes, inserting audio and video clips, providing research capabilities, recognizing handwritten text and drawings, and creating Web pages from existing spreadsheet documents.

The following sections describe the features of most spreadsheet programs.

handwritten spreadsheet

columns B, C, D, and E

function assigned to active cell

=SUM(B10:B15)

rows 3, 4, 5, and 6

cell B6

cell B16 is active

worksheet

Vashon's IT Hardware & Services
Projected Annual Revenue and Expenditures

	Qtr 1	Qtr 2	Qtr 3	Qtr 4	
Revenue					
Sales	$77,230,192	$82,822,010	$79,401,034	$73,010,3[illegible]	$31[illegible]
Consulting	67,023,910	62,912,013	80,771,819	62,010,498	272,718,240
Total Net Revenue	$144,254,102	$145,734,023	$160,172,853	$135,020,802	$585,181,780
Expenditures					
Marketing	$19,113,669	$19,309,758	$21,222,903	$17,890,256	$77,536,586
Payroll	34,116,095	34,466,096	37,880,880	31,932,420	138,395,491
Equipment	31,375,267	31,697,150	34,837,596	29,367,024	127,277,037
Bonus	-	-	300,000	-	300,000
Production	9,376,517	9,472,711	10,411,235	8,776,352	38,036,816
Administrative	19,474,304	19,674,093	21,623,335	18,227,808	78,999,540
Total Expenditures	$113,455,851	$114,619,809	$126,275,949	$106,193,861	$460,545,470
Operating Income	$30,798,251	[illegible]	$33,896,904	$28,826,941	$124,636,310

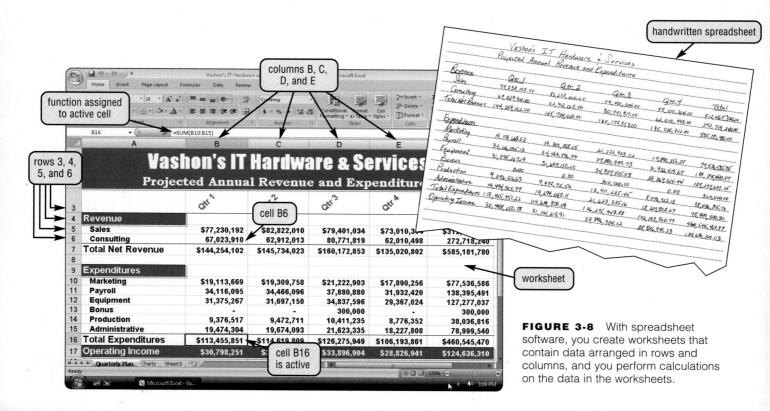

FIGURE 3-8 With spreadsheet software, you create worksheets that contain data arranged in rows and columns, and you perform calculations on the data in the worksheets.

Spreadsheet Organization A spreadsheet file is similar to a notebook that can contain more than 1,000 related individual worksheets. Data is organized vertically in columns and horizontally in rows on each worksheet (Figure 3-8). Each worksheet usually can have more than 16,000 columns and 1 million rows. One or more letters identify each column, and a number identifies each row. Only a small fraction of the columns and rows are displayed on the screen at one time. Scrolling through the worksheet displays different parts of it on the screen.

A *cell* is the intersection of a column and row. Each worksheet has more than 17 billion cells in which you can enter data. The spreadsheet software identifies cells by the column and row in which they are located. For example, the intersection of column B and row 6 is referred to as cell B6. As shown in Figure 3-8, cell B6 contains the number, 67,023,910, which represents the consulting revenue for the first quarter.

Cells may contain three types of data: labels, values, and formulas. The text, or *label*, entered in a cell identifies the worksheet data and helps organize the worksheet. Using descriptive labels, such as Total Net Revenue and Total Expenditures, helps make a worksheet more meaningful.

Calculations Many of the worksheet cells shown in Figure 3-8 contain a number, called a *value,* that can be used in a calculation. Other cells, however, contain formulas that generate values. A *formula* performs calculations on the data in the worksheet and displays the resulting value in a cell, usually the cell containing the formula. When creating a worksheet, you can enter your own formulas.

In many spreadsheet programs, you begin a formula with an equal sign, a plus sign, or a minus sign. Next, you enter the formula, separating cell references (e.g., B10) with operators. Common operators are + for addition, − for subtraction, * for multiplication, and / for division. In Figure 3-8, for example, cell B16 could contain the formula =B10+B11+B12+B13+B14+B15, which would add together (sum) the contents of cells B10, B11, B12, B13, B14, and B15. That is, this formula calculates the total expenditures for the first quarter. A more efficient way to sum the contents of cells, however, is to use a special type of formula, called a function.

A *function* is a predefined formula that performs common calculations such as adding the values in a group of cells or generating a value such as the time or date. For example, instead of using the formula =B10+B11+B12+B13+B14+B15 to calculate the total expenditures for the first quarter, you could use the SUM function. This function requires you to identify the starting cell and the ending cell in a group to be summed, separating these two cell references with a colon. For example, the function =SUM(B10:B15) instructs the spreadsheet program to add all of the numbers in cells B10 through B15. Figure 3-9 lists functions commonly included in spreadsheet programs.

SPREADSHEET FUNCTIONS

Function	Description
Financial	
FV (rate, number of periods, payment)	Calculates the future value of an investment
NPV (rate, range)	Calculates the net present value of an investment
PMT (rate, number of periods, present value)	Calculates the periodic payment for an annuity
PV (rate, number of periods, payment)	Calculates the present value of an investment
RATE (number of periods, payment, present value)	Calculates the periodic interest rate of an annuity
Date and Time	
DATE	Returns the current date
NOW	Returns the current date and time
TIME	Returns the current time
Mathematical	
ABS (number)	Returns the absolute value of a number
INT (number)	Rounds a number down to the nearest integer
LN (number)	Calculates the natural logarithm of a number
LOG (number, base)	Calculates the logarithm of a number to a specified base
ROUND (number, number of digits)	Rounds a number to a specified number of digits
SQRT (number)	Calculates the square root of a number
SUM (range)	Calculates the total of a range of numbers
Statistical	
AVERAGE (range)	Calculates the average value of a range of numbers
COUNT (range)	Counts how many cells in the range have numeric entries
MAX (range)	Returns the maximum value in a range
MIN (range)	Returns the minimum value in a range
STDEV (range)	Calculates the standard deviation of a range of numbers
Logical	
IF (logical test, value if true, value if false)	Performs a test and returns one value if the result of the test is true and another value if the result is false

FIGURE 3-9 Functions typically found in spreadsheet software.

Recalculation One of the more powerful features of spreadsheet software is its capability of recalculating the rest of the worksheet when data in a worksheet changes. When you enter a new value to change data in a cell, any value affected by the change is updated automatically and instantaneously. In Figure 3-8 on page 142, for example, if you change the consulting revenue for the first quarter from 67,023,910 to 67,523,910, the total net revenue in cell B7 automatically changes from $144,254,102 to $144,754,102.

Spreadsheet software's capability of recalculating data also makes it a valuable budgeting, forecasting, and decision making tool. Most spreadsheet software includes a *what-if analysis* feature, where you change certain values in a spreadsheet to reveal the effects of those changes.

WEB LINK 3-2

Spreadsheet Software

For more information, visit scsite.com/dc2008/ch3/weblink and then click Spreadsheet Software.

Charting Another standard feature of spreadsheet software is *charting*, which depicts the data in graphical form. A visual representation of data through charts often makes it easier for users to see at a glance the relationship among the numbers.

Three popular chart types are line charts, column charts, and pie charts. Figure 3-10 shows examples of these charts that were plotted from the data in Figure 3-8. A *line chart* shows a trend during a period of time, as indicated by a rising or falling line. For example, a line chart could show the total expenses for the four quarters. A *column chart*, also called a *bar chart*, displays bars of various lengths to show the relationship of data. The bars can be horizontal, vertical, or stacked on top of one another. For example, a column chart might show the total quarterly expenditures, with each bar representing a different category of expenditure. A *pie chart*, which has the shape of a round pie cut into slices, shows the relationship of parts to a whole. For example, you might use a pie chart to show the percentage each expenditure category contributed to the total expenditures.

When you modify data in a worksheet, any associated charts automatically update to reflect the worksheet changes. Charts, as well as any other part of a workbook, can be linked to or embedded in a word processing document.

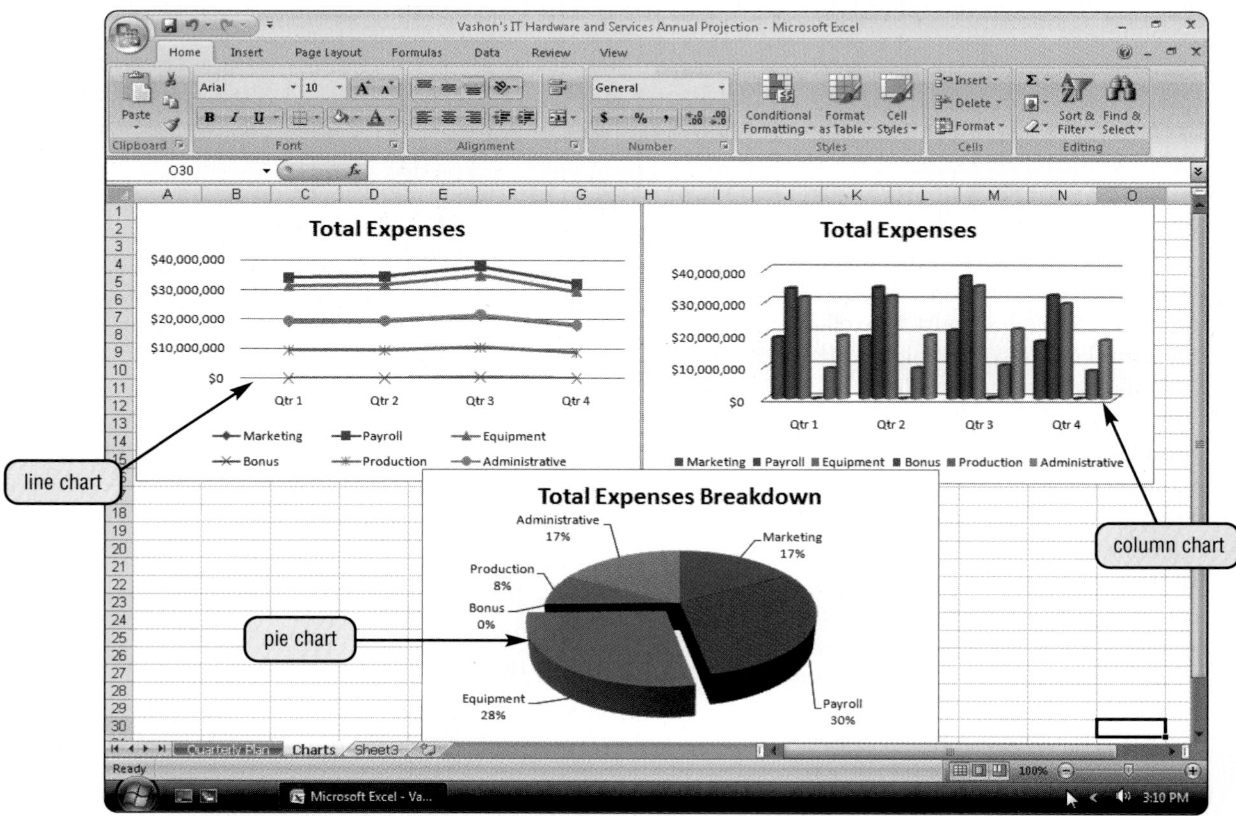

FIGURE 3-10 Three basic types of charts provided with spreadsheet software are line charts, column charts, and pie charts. The charts shown here were created from the data in the worksheet in Figure 3-8.

Database Software

A **database** is a collection of data organized in a manner that allows access, retrieval, and use of that data. In a manual database, you might record data on paper and store it in a filing cabinet. With a computerized database, such as the one shown in Figure 3-11, the computer stores the data in an electronic format on a storage medium such as a hard disk.

Database software is application software that allows users to create, access, and manage a database. Using database software, you can add, change, and delete data in a database; sort and retrieve data from the database; and create forms and reports using the data in the database.

With most popular personal computer database programs, a database consists of a collection of tables, organized in rows and columns. Each row, called a *record*, contains data about a given person, product, object, or event. Each column, called a *field*, contains a specific category of data within a record.

The Sports Store database shown in Figure 3-11 consists of two tables: an Item table and a Supplier table. The Item table contains nine records (rows), each storing data about one item. The item data is grouped into six fields (columns): Item Number, Description, On Hand, Cost, Selling Price, and Supplier Code. The On Hand field, for instance, contains the quantity on hand in inventory. The Item and Supplier tables relate to one another through a common field, Supplier Code.

Users run queries to retrieve data. A *query* is a request for specific data from the database. For example, a query might request items that are low on hand. Database software can take the results of a query and present it in a window on the screen or send it to the printer.

FAQ 3-3

How big is the largest database?

According to a recent survey, the world's largest database holds more than 100 trillion characters. In the next few years, the size of the largest database is expected to exceed 5 quadrillion characters. For more information, visit scsite.com/dc2008/ch3/faq and then click Enterprise Databases.

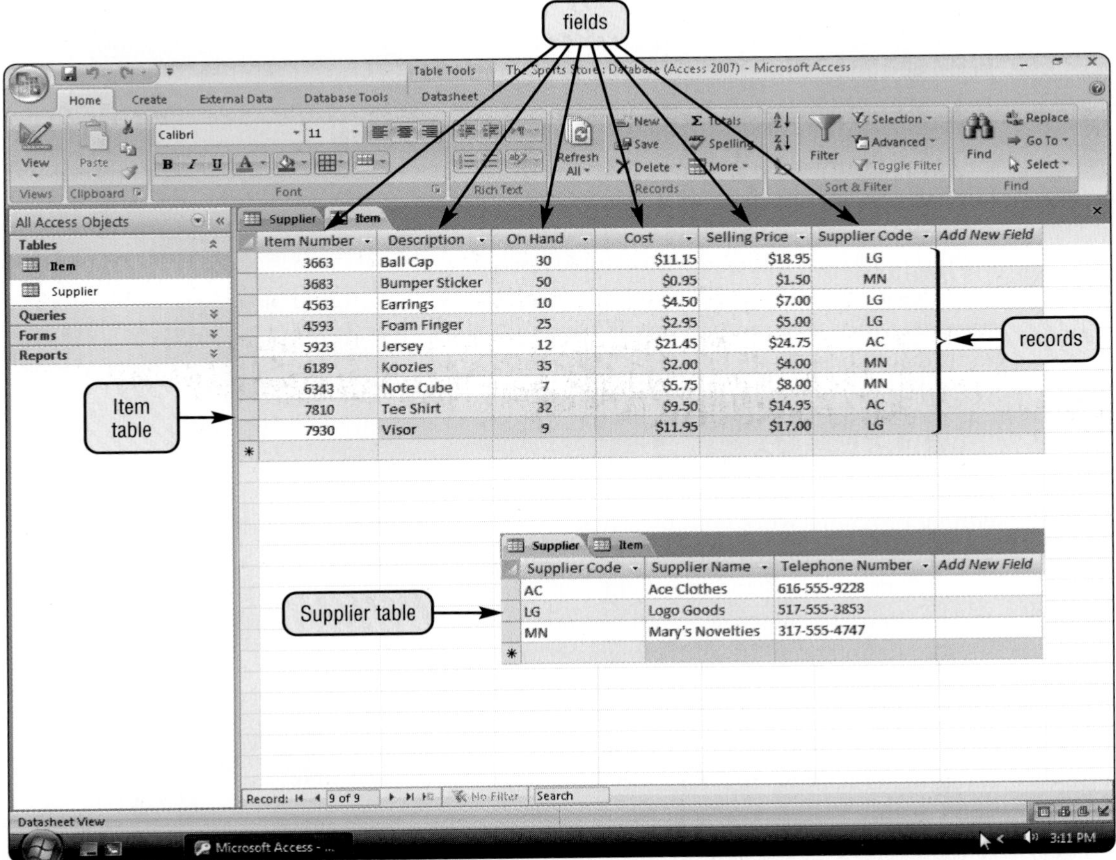

FIGURE 3-11 This database contains two tables: one for the items and one for the suppliers. The Item table has nine records and six fields; the Supplier table has three records and three fields.

Presentation Graphics Software

Presentation graphics software is application software that allows users to create visual aids for presentations to communicate ideas, messages, and other information to a group. The presentations can be viewed as slides, sometimes called a *slide show*, that are displayed on a large monitor or on a projection screen (Figure 3-12).

Presentation graphics software typically provides a variety of predefined presentation formats that define complementary colors for backgrounds, text, and graphical accents on the slides. This software also provides a variety of layouts for each individual slide such as a title slide, a two-column slide, and a slide with clip art, a picture, a chart, a table, a diagram (Figure 3-13), or animation. In addition, you can enhance any text, charts, and graphical images on a slide with 3-D and other special effects such as shading, shadows, and textures.

When building a presentation, users can set the slide timing so the presentation automatically displays the next slide after a preset delay. Presentation graphics software allows you to apply special effects to the transition between slides. One slide, for example, might fade away as the next slide is displayed.

To help organize the presentation, you can view thumbnail versions of all the slides similarly to how 35mm slides look on a photographer's light table.

Presentation graphics software typically includes a clip gallery that provides images, pictures, video clips, and audio clips to enhance multimedia presentations. Users with an artistic ability can create their own graphics using paint/image editing software (discussed later in the chapter) and then *import* (bring in) the graphics into the slide. Some audio and video editing programs work with presentation graphics software, providing users with an easy means to record and insert video, music, and audio commentary in a presentation.

Presentation graphics software incorporates some of the features found in word processing software such as checking spelling, formatting, providing research capabilities, recognizing handwritten text and drawings, and creating Web pages from existing slide shows.

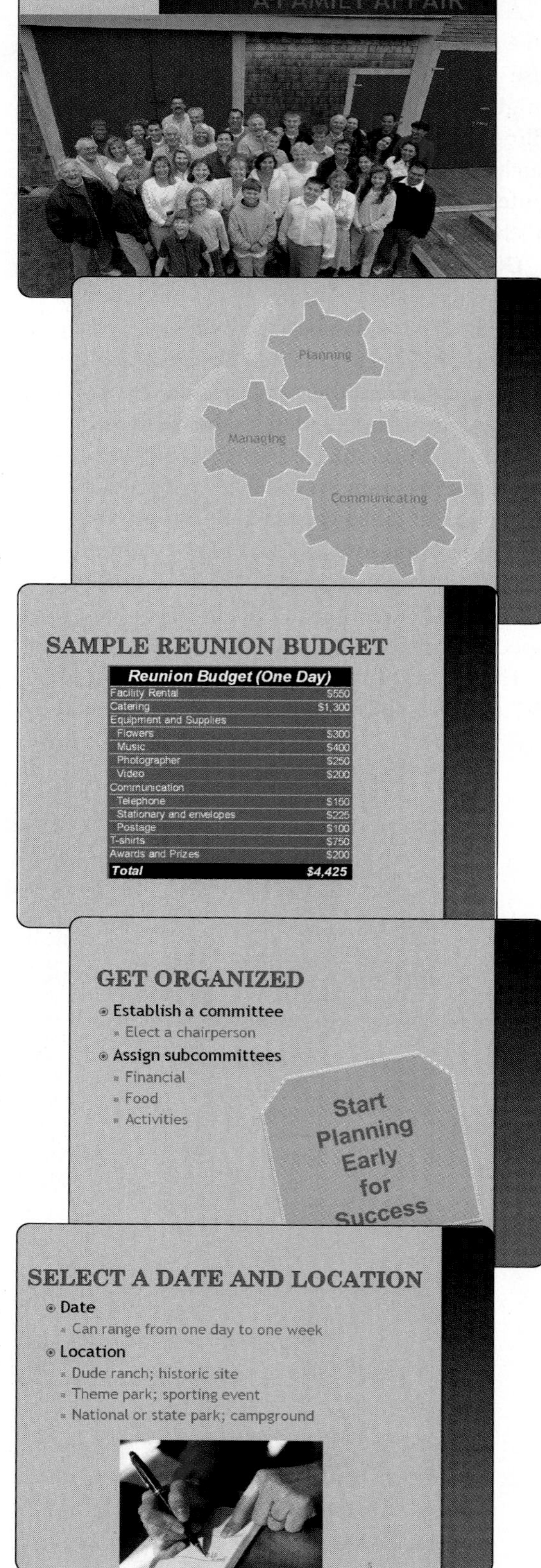

FIGURE 3-12 This presentation created with presentation graphics software consists of five slides.

Presentation Graphics Software

For more information, visit scsite.com/dc2008/ch3/weblink and then click Presentation Graphics Software.

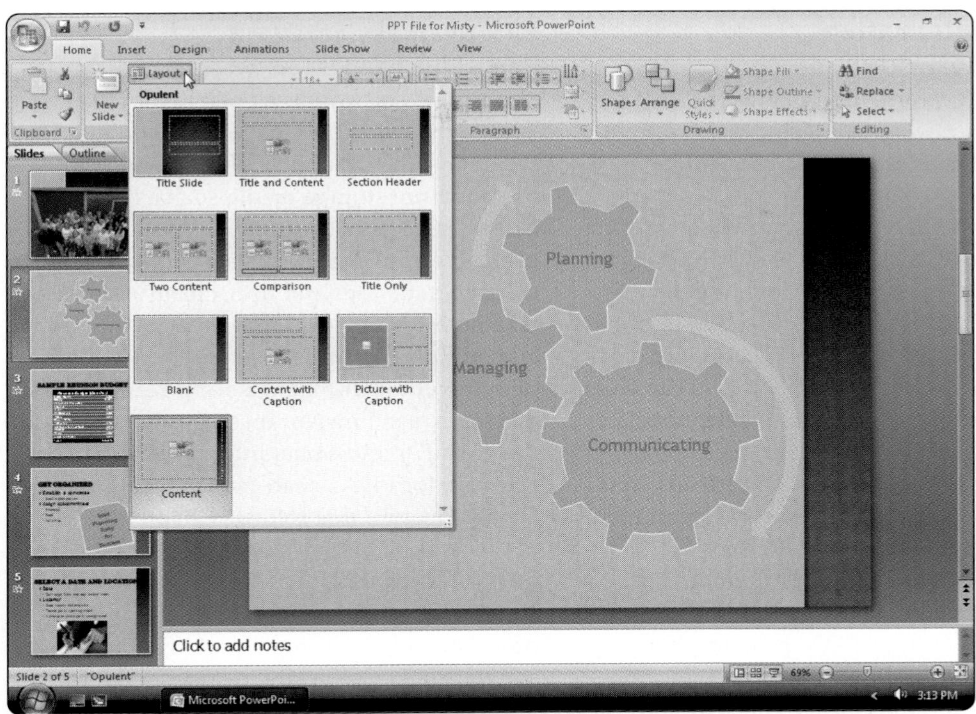

FIGURE 3-13 In presentation graphics software, users can change the design and layout of any slide in a presentation.

Note Taking Software

Note taking software is application software that enables users to enter typed text, handwritten comments, drawings, or sketches anywhere on a page and then save the page as part of a notebook (Figure 3-14). The software can convert handwritten comments to typed text or store the notes in handwritten form. Users also can include audio recordings as part of their notes.

Once the notes are captured (entered and saved), users easily can organize them, reuse them, and share them. This software allows users to search through saved notes for specific text. It even can search through an entire notebook. Users also can flag important notes with color, highlights, and shapes.

On a desktop or notebook computer, users enter notes primarily via the keyboard or microphone. On a Tablet PC, however, the primary input device is a digital pen. Users find note taking software convenient during meetings, class lectures, conferences, in libraries, and other settings that previously required a pencil and tablet of paper for recording thoughts and discussions.

Note taking software incorporates many of the features found in word processing software such as checking spelling, changing fonts and font sizes, adding colors, inserting audio and video clips, and providing research capabilities.

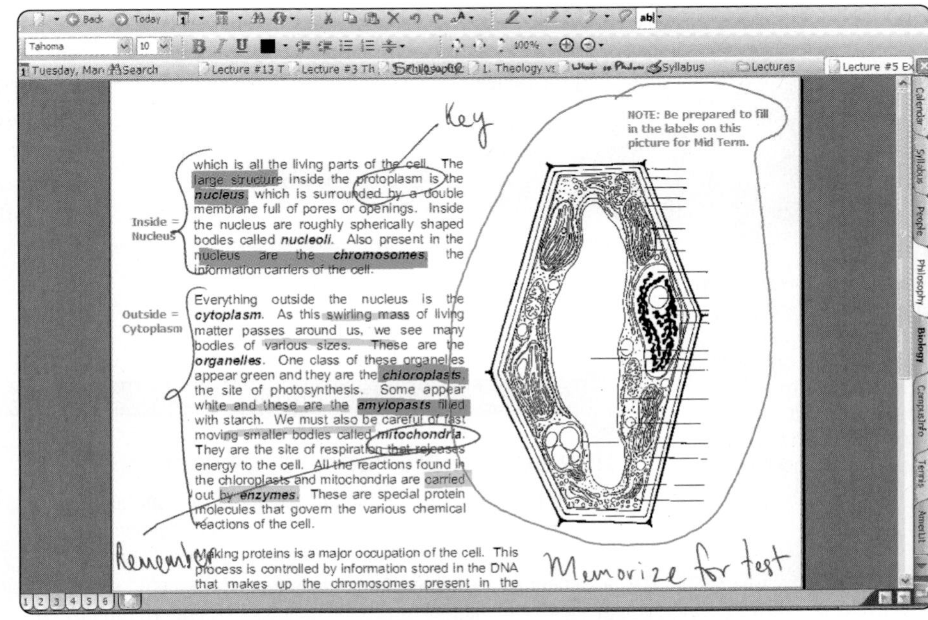

FIGURE 3-14 With note taking software, students and other mobile users can handwrite notes, draw sketches, and type text.

Personal Information Manager Software

A **personal information manager** (**PIM**) is application software that includes an appointment calendar, address book, notepad, and other features to help users organize personal information. With a PIM, you can take information previously tracked in a weekly or daily calendar, and organize and store it on your computer. The appointment calendar allows you to schedule activities for a particular day and time. With the address book, you can enter and maintain names, addresses, telephone numbers, and e-mail addresses of customers, coworkers, family members, and friends. You can use the notepad to record ideas, reminders, and other important information.

Most PDAs and many smart phones today include, among many other features, PIM functionality. Using a PDA or smart phone, you can synchronize, or coordinate, information so that both the PDA or smart phone and your personal computer and/or organization's server have the latest version of the information. Some PDAs and smart phones synchronize with the computer wirelessly. With others, you connect the PDA or smart phone to the computer with a cable, or you insert the device in a cradle, which has a cable that plugs in the computer (Figure 3-15).

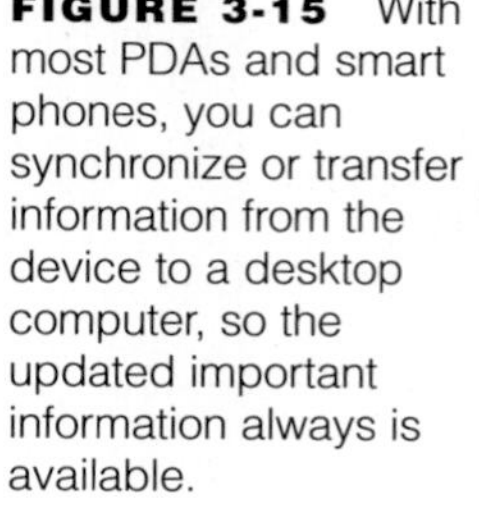

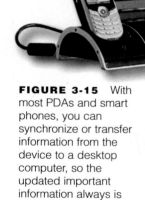

FIGURE 3-15 With most PDAs and smart phones, you can synchronize or transfer information from the device to a desktop computer, so the updated important information always is available.

PDA Business Software

In addition to PIM software, a huge variety of business software is available for PDAs. Although some PDAs have software built in, most have the capability of accessing software on miniature storage media such as memory cards. Business software for PDAs allows users to create documents and worksheets, manage databases and lists, create slide shows, take notes, manage budgets and finances, view and edit photographs, read electronic books, plan travel routes, compose and read e-mail messages, send instant messages, and browse the Web. For additional information about software for PDAs, read the Personal Mobile Devices feature that follows Chapter 5.

Software Suite

A **software suite** is a collection of individual programs sold as a single package. Business software suites typically include, at a minimum, the following programs: word processing, spreadsheet, e-mail, and presentation graphics. Two of the more widely used software suites are Microsoft Office 2007 and Sun StarOffice.

Software suites offer two major advantages: lower cost and ease of use. Buying a collection of programs in a software suite usually costs significantly less than purchasing them individually. Software suites provide ease of use because the programs in a software suite normally use a similar interface and share features such as clip art and spelling checker. For example, once you learn how to print using the software suite's word processing program, you can apply the same skill to the spreadsheet and presentation graphics programs in the software suite.

FAQ 3-4

How popular are handheld devices?

During the past year, the overall popularity of handheld devices, including smart phones and PDAs, has been increasing at an average rate of approximately 55 percent. Smart phones have experienced a growth of approximately 75 percent, while the use of PDAs declined by approximately 33 percent. The following table illustrates the market shares for the more popular companies in the handheld device market. For more information, visit scsite.com/dc2008/ch3/faq and then click Handheld Devices.

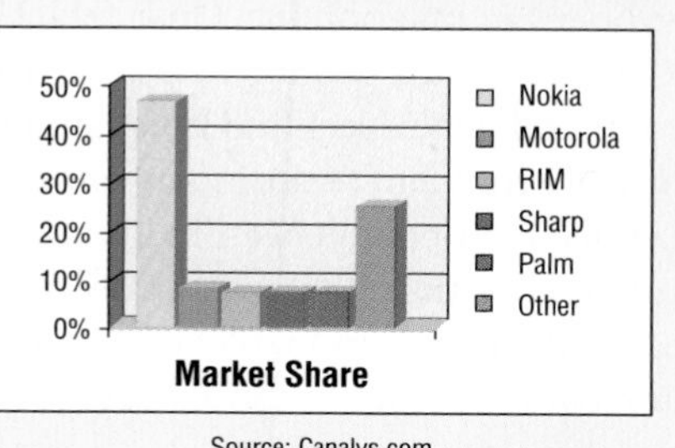

Source: Canalys.com

Project Management Software

Project management software allows a user to plan, schedule, track, and analyze the events, resources, and costs of a project (Figure 3-16). Project management software helps users manage project variables, allowing them to complete a project on time and within budget. An engineer, for example, might use project management software to manage new product development to schedule product screening, market evaluation, technical product evaluation, and manufacturing processes.

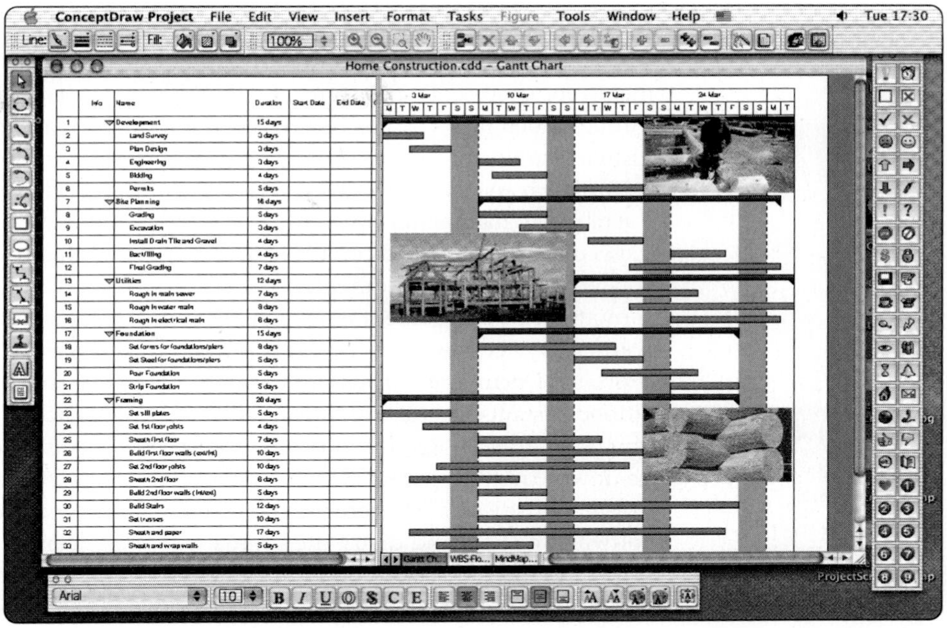

FIGURE 3-16 Shown here is project management software, which allows you to track, control, and manage the events, resources, and costs of a project.

Accounting Software

Accounting software helps companies record and report their financial transactions (Figure 3-17). With accounting software, business users perform accounting activities related to the general ledger, accounts receivable, accounts payable, purchasing, invoicing, and payroll functions. Accounting software also enables users to write and print checks, track checking account activity, and update and reconcile balances on demand.

Newer accounting software supports online credit checks, billing, direct deposit, and payroll services. Some accounting software offers more complex features such as job costing and estimating, time tracking, multiple company reporting, foreign currency reporting, and forecasting the amount of raw materials needed for products. The cost of accounting software for small businesses ranges from less than one hundred to several thousand dollars. Accounting software for large businesses can cost several hundred thousand dollars.

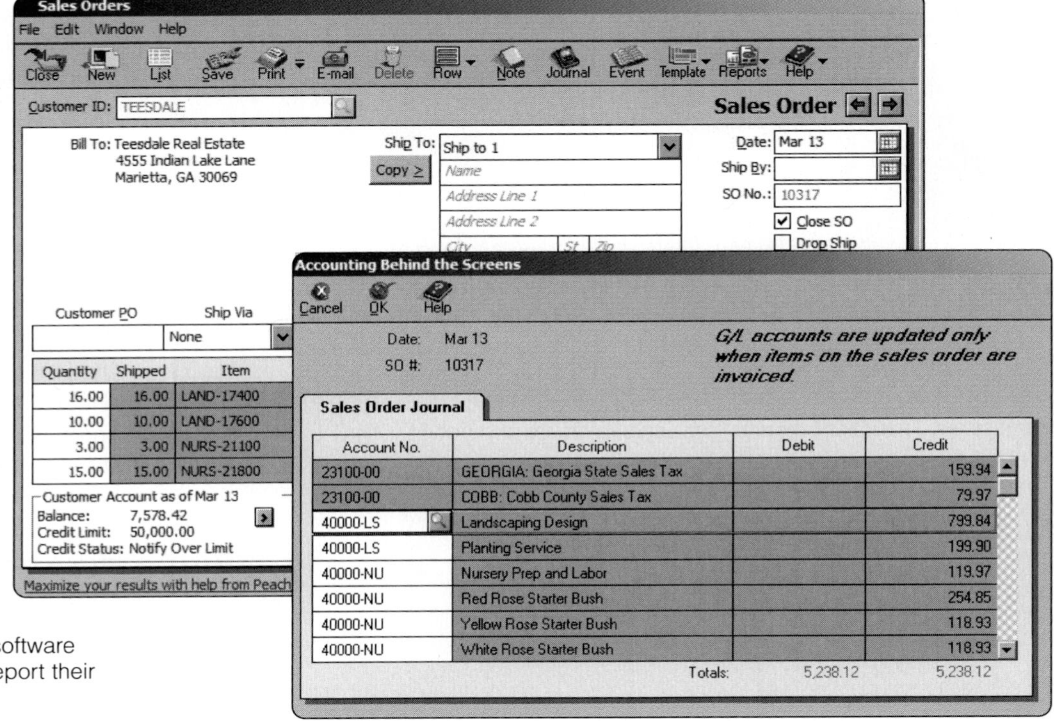

FIGURE 3-17 Accounting software helps companies record and report their financial transactions.

Document Management Software

Document management software provides a means for sharing, distributing, and searching through documents by converting them into a format that can be viewed by any user (Figure 3-18). The converted document, which mirrors the original document's appearance, can be viewed and printed without the software that created the original document. A popular file format used by document management software to save converted documents is *PDF* (Portable Document Format), developed by Adobe Systems. To view and print a PDF file, you need Acrobat Reader software, which can be downloaded free from Adobe's Web site.

Many businesses use document management software to share and distribute company brochures, literature, and other documents electronically. Home users distribute fliers, announcements, and graphics electronically. Some document management software allows users to edit and add comments to the converted document.

WEB LINK 3-4

Document Management Software

For more information, visit scsite.com/dc2008/ch3/weblink and then click Document Management Software.

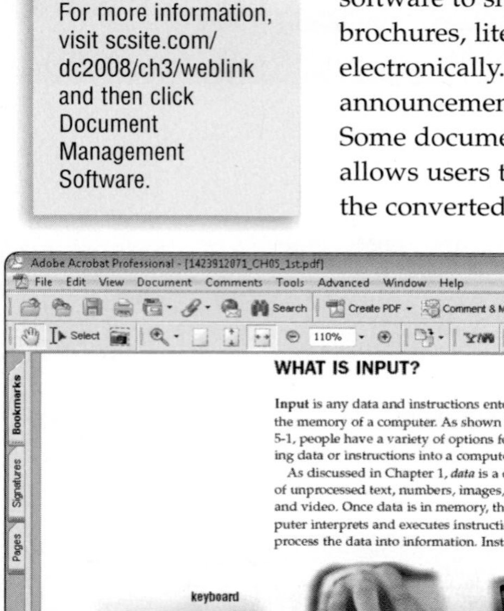

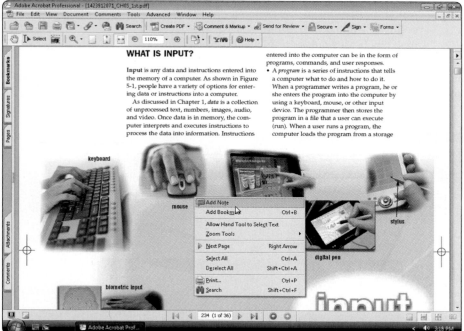

FIGURE 3-18 Adobe Acrobat allows users to create and edit PDF files.

Enterprise Computing Software

A large organization, commonly referred to as an enterprise, requires special computing solutions because of its size and large geographic distribution. A typical enterprise consists of a wide variety of departments, centers, and divisions — collectively known as functional units. Nearly every enterprise has the following functional units: human resources, accounting and finance, engineering or product development, manufacturing, marketing, sales, distribution, customer service, and information technology. Each of these functional units has specialized software requirements, as outlined below.

- Human resources software manages employee information such as benefits, personal information, performance evaluations, training, and vacation time.
- Accounting software manages everyday transactions, such as sales and payments to suppliers. Financial software helps managers budget, forecast, and analyze.
- Engineering or product development software allows engineers to develop plans for new products and test their product designs.
- Manufacturing software assists in the assembly process, as well as in scheduling and managing the inventory of parts and products.
- Marketing software allows marketing personnel to create marketing campaigns and track their effectiveness.
- Sales software enables the sales force to manage contacts, schedule meetings, log customer interactions, manage product information, and take customer orders.
- Distribution software analyzes and tracks inventory and manages product shipping status.
- Customer service software manages the day-to-day interactions with customers, such as telephone calls, e-mail messages, Web interactions, and instant messaging sessions.
- Information technology staff use a variety of software to maintain and secure the hardware and software in an enterprise.

GRAPHICS AND MULTIMEDIA SOFTWARE

In addition to business software, many people work with software designed specifically for their field of work. Power users such as engineers, architects, desktop publishers, and graphic artists often use sophisticated software that allows them to work with graphics and multimedia. This software includes computer-aided design, desktop publishing, paint/image editing, photo editing, video and audio editing, multimedia authoring, and Web page authoring. Figure 3-19 lists some popular programs in each of these categories, specifically designed for professional or more technically astute users. These programs often cost several hundred dollars or more. Many of these programs incorporate user-friendly interfaces and/or have scaled-down versions, making it possible for the home and small business users to create documents using these programs. The following sections discuss the features and functions of graphics and multimedia software.

POPULAR GRAPHICS AND MULTIMEDIA SOFTWARE

Application Software	Manufacturer	Program Name
Computer-Aided Design (CAD)	Autodesk	AutoCAD
	Chief Architect	Chief Architect
	Microsoft	Visio 2007
Desktop Publishing (for the Professional)	Adobe	InDesign
	Corel	Ventura
	Quark	QuarkXPress
Paint/Image Editing (for the Professional)	Adobe	Freehand Illustrator
	Corel	Painter
	Microsoft	Expression Graphic Designer
Photo Editing (for the Professional)	Adobe	Photoshop
	Nik Software	Nik Sharpener Pro
Video and Audio Editing (for the Professional)	Adobe	Audition Encore DVD Premiere Pro
	Avid Technology	Avid Xpress Pro
	Cakewalk	SONAR
	Sony	ACID Pro
	Ulead	MediaStudio Pro DVD Workshop
Multimedia Authoring	Adobe	Authorware Director
	SumTotal Systems	ToolBook Instructor
Web Page Authoring	Adobe	Dreamweaver Fireworks Flash GoLive
	Microsoft	SharePoint Designer 2007

FIGURE 3-19 Popular graphics and multimedia programs — for the professional.

Computer-Aided Design

Computer-aided design (CAD) software is a sophisticated type of application software that assists a professional user in creating engineering, architectural, and scientific designs. For example, engineers create design plans for vehicles (Figure 3-20) and security systems. Architects design building structures and floor plans. Scientists design drawings of molecular structures.

CAD software eliminates the laborious manual drafting that design processes can require. Three-dimensional CAD programs allow designers to rotate designs of 3-D objects to view them from any angle. Some CAD software even can generate material lists for building designs.

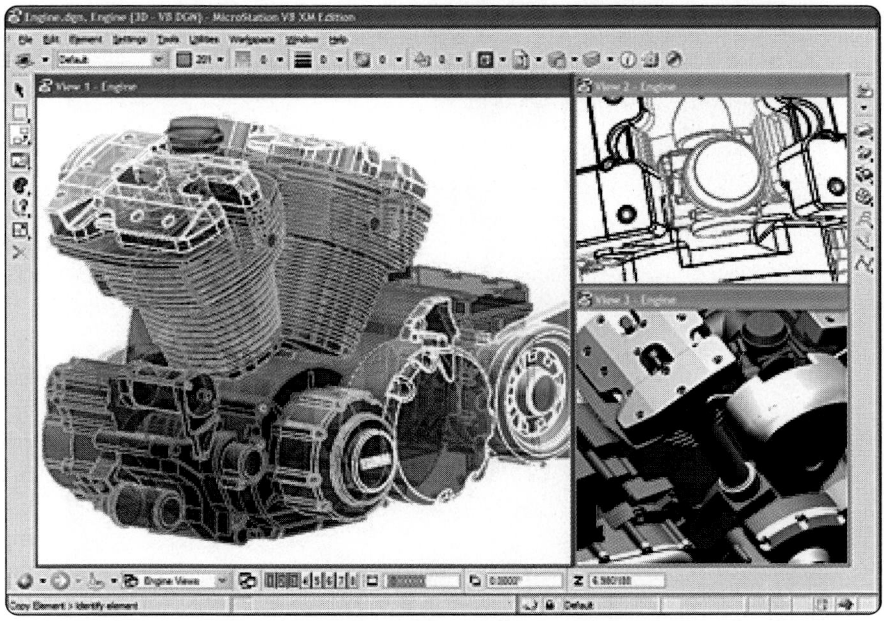

FIGURE 3-20 Architects use CAD software to create vehicle components.

Desktop Publishing Software (for the Professional)

Desktop publishing (**DTP**) **software** enables professional designers to create sophisticated documents that contain text, graphics, and many colors (Figure 3-21). Professional DTP software is ideal for the production of high-quality color documents such as textbooks, corporate newsletters, marketing literature, product catalogs, and annual reports. Today's DTP software allows designers to convert a color document into a format for use on the World Wide Web.

Although many word processing programs have some of the capabilities of DTP software, professional designers and graphic artists use DTP software because it supports page layout. *Page layout* is the process of arranging text and graphics in a document on a page-by-page basis. DTP software includes color libraries to assist in color selections for text and graphics. A *color library* is a standard set of colors used by designers and printers to ensure that colors will print exactly as specified. Designers and graphic artists can print finished publications on a color printer, take them to a professional printer, or post them on the Web.

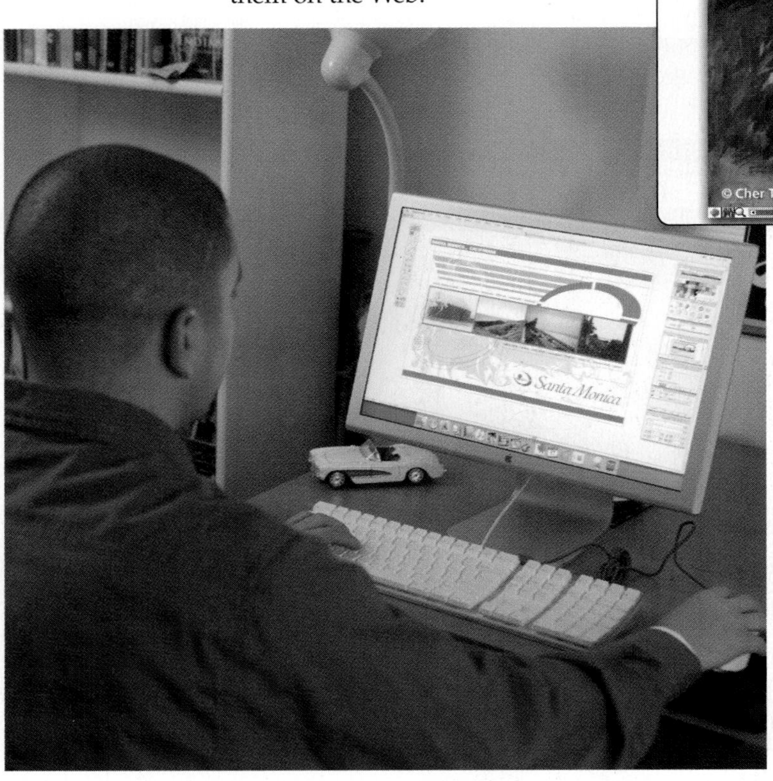

FIGURE 3-21 Professional designers and graphic artists use DTP software to produce sophisticated publications such as marketing literature.

Paint/Image Editing Software (for the Professional)

Graphic artists, multimedia professionals, technical illustrators, and desktop publishers use paint software and image editing software to create and modify graphical images such as those used in DTP documents and Web pages. **Paint software**, also called *illustration software*, allows users to draw pictures, shapes, and other graphical images with various on-screen tools such as a pen, brush, eyedropper, and paint bucket (Figure 3-22). **Image editing software** provides the capabilities of paint software and also includes the capability to enhance and modify existing images and pictures. Modifications can include adjusting or enhancing image colors, adding special effects such as shadows and glows, and creating animations.

FIGURE 3-22 With paint software, artists can create and modify any type of graphical image.

Photo Editing Software (for the Professional)

Professional photo editing software is a type of image editing software that allows photographers, videographers, engineers, scientists, and other high-volume digital photo users to edit and customize digital photographs (Figure 3-23). Professional photo editing software allows users to save images in a wide variety of file formats. With professional photo editing software, users can retouch photos, crop images, remove red-eye, change image shapes, color-correct images, straighten images, remove or rearrange objects in a photo, and apply filters. Read Ethics & Issues 3-2 for a related discussion.

FIGURE 3-23 With professional photo editing software, users can edit and customize digital photographs.

ETHICS & ISSUES 3-2

Altering Digital Photographs — Art or Fraud?

In several recent high-profile cases, major news sources have published purposefully altered photographs. The alterations were more than just touching up a bad-hair day; rather, they were attempts to alter the facts. Typically, those responsible for the deception are fired from their jobs. Many commercial artists, photojournalists, and creators of cartoons, book covers, and billboards use photo editing software to alter photographs. With this software, an artist can convert photographs to a digital form that can be colorized, stretched, squeezed, texturized, or otherwise altered. For example, tabloid newspapers or dubious online sources may alter a photograph by switching a head on a body in a photo with someone else's head. The National Press Photographers Association, however, has expressed reservations about digital altering and endorses the following: "As [photo] journalists we believe the guiding principle of our profession is accuracy; therefore, we believe it is wrong to alter the content of a photograph in any way … that deceives the public." Yet, some insist that the extent to which a photo "deceives the public" is in the eye of the beholder. Is it ethical to alter digital photographs? Why or why not? Does the answer depend on the reason for the alteration, the extent of the alteration, or some other factor? If some alteration is accepted, can photographic integrity still be guaranteed? Why or why not?

Video and Audio Editing Software (for the Professional)

Video editing software (Figure 3-24) allows professionals to modify a segment of a video, called a clip. For example, users can reduce the length of a video clip, reorder a series of clips, or add special effects such as words that move horizontally across the screen.

Video editing software typically includes audio editing capabilities. **Audio editing software** lets users modify audio clips, produce studio-quality soundtracks, and add audio to video clips. Audio editing software usually includes *filters*, which are designed to enhance audio quality. For example, a filter might remove a distracting background noise from the audio clip.

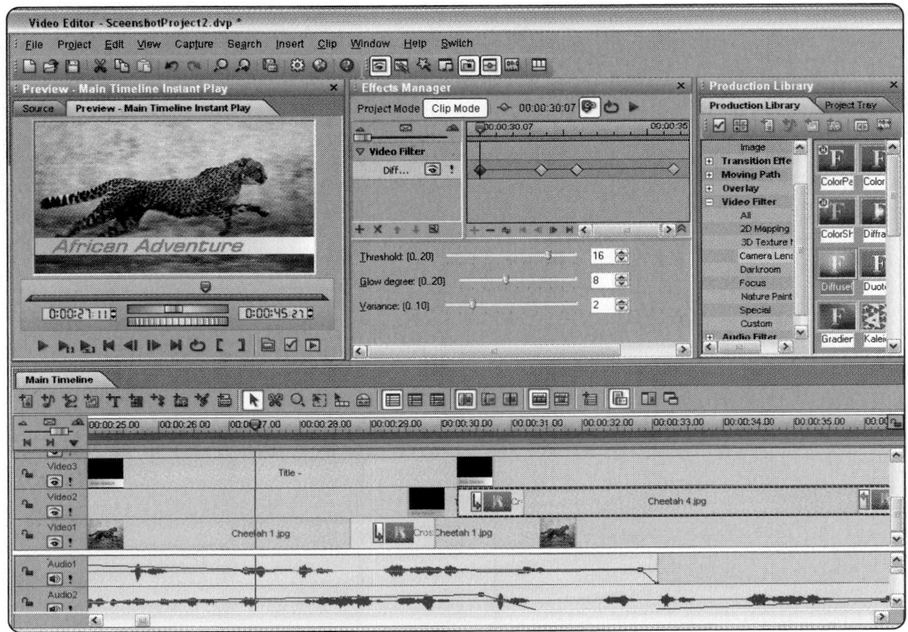

FIGURE 3-24 With video editing software, users modify video images.

Multimedia Authoring Software

Multimedia authoring software allows users to combine text, graphics, audio, video, and animation in an interactive application (Figure 3-25). With this software, users control the placement of text and images and the duration of sounds, video, and animation. Once created, multimedia presentations often take the form of interactive computer-based presentations or Web-based presentations designed to facilitate learning, demonstrate product functionality, and elicit direct-user participation. Training centers, educational institutions, and online magazine publishers all use multimedia authoring software to develop interactive applications. These applications may be available on a CD or DVD, over a local area network, or via the Internet.

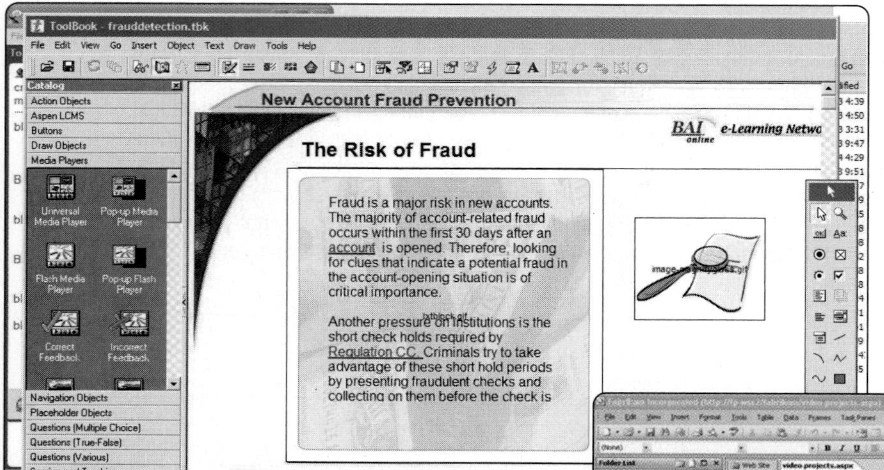

FIGURE 3-25 Multimedia authoring software allows you to create dynamic presentations that include text, graphics, video, sound, and animation.

> **FAQ 3-5**
>
> ### How do I know which program to buy?
>
> Many companies, such as Adobe Systems and Corel, offer downloadable *trial versions* of their software that allow you to use the software free for a limited time. Try a few. Read computer magazines and Web sites for reviews of various products. For more information, visit scsite.com/dc2008/ch3/faq and then click Trial Versions.

Web Page Authoring Software

Web page authoring software helps users of all skill levels create Web pages that include graphical images, video, audio, animation, and other special effects with interactive content (Figure 3-26). In addition, many Web page authoring programs allow users to organize, manage, and maintain Web sites.

Application software, such as Word and Excel, often includes Web page authoring features. This allows home users to create basic Web pages using application software they already own. For more sophisticated Web pages, users work with Web page authoring software. Many Web page developers also use multimedia authoring software along with, or instead of, Web page authoring software for Web page development.

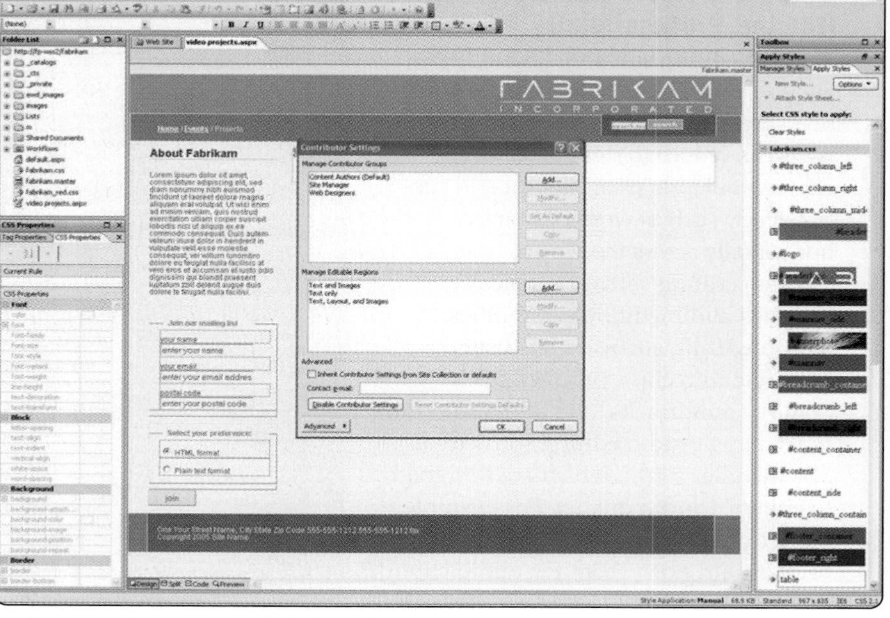

FIGURE 3-26 With Web page authoring software, users create sophisticated Web pages.

Test your knowledge of pages 138 through 154 in Quiz Yourself 3-2.

QUIZ YOURSELF 3-2

Instructions: Find the true statement below. Then, rewrite the remaining false statements so they are true.

1. Audio editing software typically includes video editing capabilities.
2. Enterprise computing software provides the capabilities of paint software and also includes the capability to modify existing images.
3. Millions of people use spreadsheet software every day to develop documents such as letters, memos, reports, fax cover sheets, mailing labels, newsletters, and Web pages.
4. Professional accounting software is ideal for the production of high-quality color documents such as textbooks, corporate newsletters, marketing literature, product catalogs, and annual reports.
5. Spreadsheet software is application software that allows users to create visual aids for presentations to communicate ideas, messages, and other information to a group.
6. Two of the more widely used CAD programs are Microsoft Office 2007 and Sun StarOffice.
7. Web page authoring software helps users of all skill levels create Web pages.

Quiz Yourself Online: To further check your knowledge of types and features of business programs and graphics/multimedia programs, visit scsite.com/dc2008/ch3/quiz and then click Objectives 4 – 5.

SOFTWARE FOR HOME, PERSONAL, AND EDUCATIONAL USE

A large amount of application software is designed specifically for home, personal, and educational use. Most of the programs in this category are relatively inexpensive, often priced less than $100 and sometimes free. Figure 3-27 lists popular programs for many of these categories. The following sections discuss the features and functions of this application software.

POPULAR PROGRAMS FOR HOME/PERSONAL/EDUCATIONAL USE

Application Software	Manufacturer	Program Name
Software Suite (for Personal Use)	Microsoft	Works
	Sun	OpenOffice.org
Personal Finance	Intuit	Quicken
	Microsoft	Money
Legal	Broderbund	Family Lawyer Home and Business Lawyer WillWriter
	Cosmi	Perfect Attorney
	Nolo	Quicken Legal Business Quicken WillMaker
Tax Preparation	2nd Story Software	TaxACT
	H&R Block	TaxCut
	Intuit	TurboTax
Desktop Publishing (for Personal Use)	Broderbund	The Print Shop PrintMaster
	Microsoft	Publisher 2007
Paint/Image Editing (for Personal Use)	Corel	CorelDRAW Paint Shop Pro
	Sun	StarOffice Draw
	The GIMP Team	The Gimp
Photo Editing (for Personal Use)	Adobe	Photoshop Elements
	Corel	Paint Shop Pro Photo
	Microsoft	Digital Image Photo Story
	Roxio	PhotoSuite
	Ulead	PhotoImpact Photo Express
Clip Art/Image Gallery	Broderbund	ClickArt
	Nova Development	Art Explosion
Video and Audio Editing (for Personal Use)	Microsoft	Movie Maker
	Pinnacle Systems	Studio MovieBox
	Roxio	VideoWave
	Ulead	VideoStudio
Home Design/ Landscaping	Broderbund	Instant Architect
	Quality Plans	3D Home Architect Better Homes & Gardens Home Designer
	ValuSoft	LandDesigner
Reference	DeLorme	Street Atlas
	Fogware Publishing	Merriam-Webster Collegiate Dictionary & Thesaurus
	Microsoft	Encarta Streets & Trips

FIGURE 3-27 Many popular programs are available for home, personal, and educational use.

Software Suite (for Personal Use)

A software suite (for personal use) combines application software such as word processing, spreadsheet, database, and other programs in a single, easy-to-use package. Many computer vendors install a software suite for personal use, such as Microsoft Works, on new computers sold to home users.

As mentioned earlier, the programs in a software suite use a similar interface and share some common features. The programs in software suites for personal use typically are available only through the software suite; that is, you cannot purchase them individually. These programs may not have all the capabilities of business application software. For many home users, however, the capabilities of software suites for personal use more than meet their needs.

Personal Finance Software

Personal finance software is a simplified accounting program that helps home users and small office/home office users balance their checkbooks, pay bills, track personal income and expenses, set up budgets, manage home inventory (Figure 3-28), track investments, and evaluate financial plans. Personal finance software helps determine where, and for what purpose, you are spending money so you can manage your finances. Reports can summarize transactions by category (such as dining), by payee (such as the electric company), or by time (such as the last two months). Financial planning features include analyzing home and personal loans, preparing income taxes, and managing retirement savings.

Most of these personal finance programs also offer a variety of online services, which require access to the Internet. For example, users can track investments online, compare insurance rates from leading insurance companies, and bank online. **Online banking** offers access to account balances, provides bill paying services, and allows you to download monthly transactions and statements from the Web directly to your computer.

FIGURE 3-28 Personal finance software assists home users with tracking personal income and expenses.

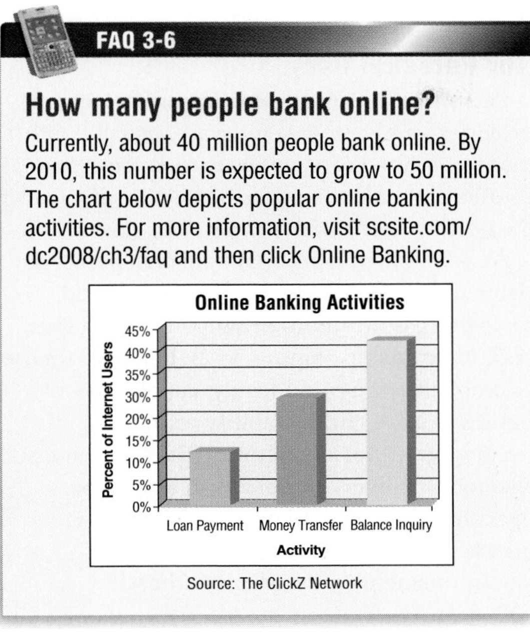

FAQ 3-6

How many people bank online?

Currently, about 40 million people bank online. By 2010, this number is expected to grow to 50 million. The chart below depicts popular online banking activities. For more information, visit scsite.com/dc2008/ch3/faq and then click Online Banking.

Source: The ClickZ Network

Legal Software

Legal software assists in the preparation of legal documents and provides legal information to individuals, families, and small businesses (Figure 3-29). Legal software provides standard contracts and documents associated with buying, selling, and renting property; estate planning; marriage and divorce; and preparing a will or living trust. By answering a series of questions or completing a form, the legal software tailors the legal document to specific needs.

FIGURE 3-29 Legal software provides legal information to individuals, families, and small businesses and assists in record keeping and the preparation of legal documents.

Once the legal document is created, you can file the paperwork with the appropriate agency, court, or office; or take the document to your attorney for his or her review and signature. Before using one of these software programs to create a document, you may want to check with your local bar association for its legality.

WEB LINK 3-5

Legal Software

For more information, visit scsite.com/dc2008/ch3/weblink and then click Legal Software.

Tax Preparation Software

Tax preparation software is used to guide individuals, families, or small businesses through the process of filing federal taxes (Figure 3-30). These programs forecast tax liability and offer money-saving tax tips, designed to lower your tax bill. After you answer a series of questions and complete basic forms, the software creates and analyzes your tax forms to search for potential errors and deduction opportunities. Once the forms are complete, you can print any necessary paperwork, and then they are ready for filing. Instead of mailing forms through the postal service, the IRS allows taxpayers to file their taxes online.

FAQ 3-7

What are the benefits of filing taxes online?

More than 72 million taxpayers *e-file*, or use tax software and/or tax preparation Web sites to file state and federal tax returns electronically. Filing your taxes online not only increases the accuracy of your return, but also decreases its processing time. If you are expecting a refund, online filing will ensure you receive your refund as quickly as possible. For more information, visit scsite.com/dc2008/ch3/faq and then click E-Filing Taxes.

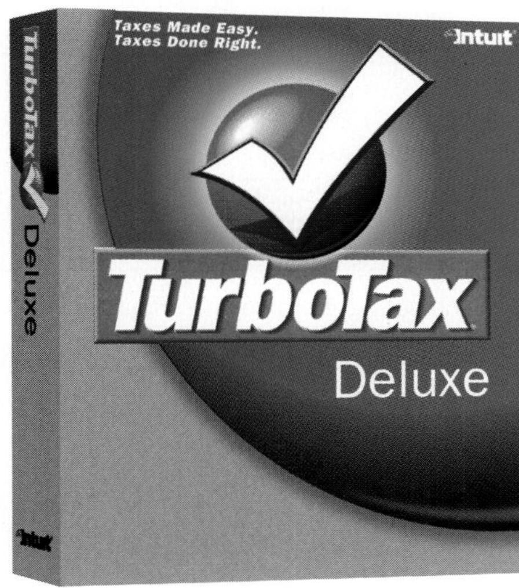

FIGURE 3-30 Tax preparation software guides individuals, families, or small businesses through the process of filing federal taxes.

Desktop Publishing Software (for Personal Use)

Instead of using professional DTP software (as discussed earlier in this chapter), many home and small business users work with simpler, easy-to-understand DTP software designed for smaller-scale desktop publishing projects (Figure 3-31). **Personal DTP software** helps home and small business users create newsletters, brochures, advertisements, post-cards, greeting cards, letterhead, business cards, banners, calendars, logos, and Web pages.

Personal DTP programs provide hundreds of thousands of graphical images. You also can import (bring in) your own digital photographs into the documents. These programs typically guide you through the development of a document by asking a series of questions, offering numerous predefined layouts, and providing standard text you can add to documents. Then, you can print a finished publication on a color printer or post it on the Web.

Many personal DTP programs also include paint/image editing software and photo editing software.

WEB LINK 3-6

Personal DTP Software

For more information, visit scsite.com/dc2008/ch3/weblink and then click Personal DTP Software.

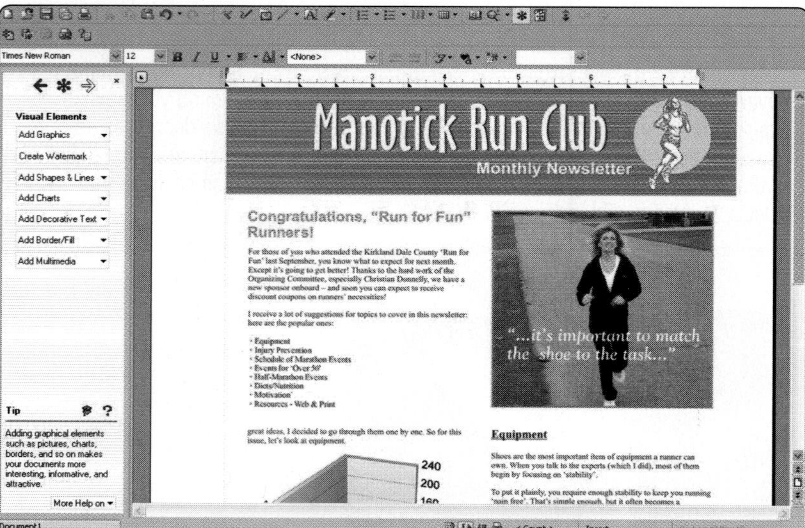

FIGURE 3-31 With desktop publishing software, home and small business users can create professional-looking newsletters.

Paint/Image Editing Software (for Personal Use)

Personal paint/image editing software provides an easy-to-use interface, usually with more simplified capabilities than its professional counterpart, including functions tailored to meet the needs of the home and small business user.

As with the professional versions, personal paint software includes various simplified tools that allow you to draw pictures, shapes, and other images (Figure 3-32). Personal image editing software provides the capabilities of paint software and the ability to modify existing graphics and photos. These products also include many templates to assist you in adding an image to documents such as greeting cards, banners, calendars, signs, labels, business cards, and letterhead.

FAQ 3-8

How do I print my pictures from my digital camera?

Your digital camera may connect with a cable directly to your computer or to a kiosk at a store. You also may be able to remove the media card from the digital camera and transfer pictures from the card to your computer and/or printer for printing. Online services also are available that allow you to transfer your pictures to them electronically, and they will mail you the prints. For more information, visit scsite.com/dc2008/ch3/faq and then click Printing Digital Pictures.

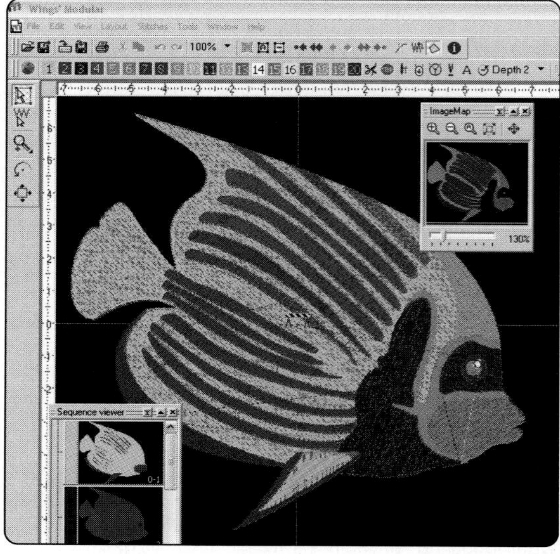

FIGURE 3-32 Home users can purchase affordable paint/image editing programs that enable them to draw images.

Photo Editing Software

Instead of professional photo editing software, many home and small business users work with easier-to-use personal photo editing software. **Personal photo editing software** allows users to edit digital photographs by removing red-eye, erasing blemishes, restoring aged photos, adding special effects (Figure 3-33), or creating electronic photo albums. When you purchase a digital camera, it usually includes photo editing software. You can print edited photographs on labels, calendars, business cards, and banners; or post them on a Web page. Some photo editing software allows users to send digital photographs to an online print service, which will deliver high-resolution printed images through the postal service. Many online print services have a photo community where users can post photographs on the Web for others to view.

FIGURE 3-33 Personal photo editing software enables home users to edit digital photographs.

Clip Art/Image Gallery

Application software often includes a **clip art/image gallery**, which is a collection of clip art and photographs. Some applications have links to additional clips available on the Web. You also can purchase clip art/image gallery software that contains hundreds of thousands of images (Figure 3-34).

In addition to clip art, many clip art/image galleries provide fonts, animations, sounds, video clips, and audio clips. You can use the images, fonts, and other items from the clip art/image gallery in all types of documents, including word processing, desktop publishing, spreadsheet, and presentation graphics.

FIGURE 3-34 Clip art/image gallery software contains hundreds of thousands of images.

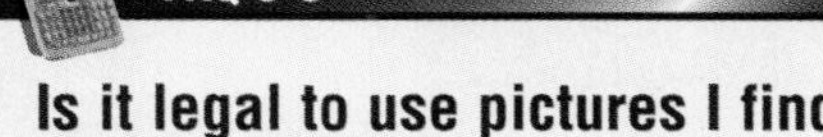

Is it legal to use pictures I find on the Internet?

Not always. Before deciding to use a picture you find on the Internet, you first should check whether the image is protected by a copyright. You may find a copyright symbol (©) or notice, either on the image itself or elsewhere. Contact the person or company hosting the Web site to obtain permission to use any pictures if you are unsure whether they are protected by a copyright. For more information, visit scsite.com/dc2008/ch3/faq and then click Online Pictures.

Video and Audio Editing Software (for Personal Use)

Many home users work with easy-to-use video and audio editing software, which is much simpler to use than its professional counterpart, for small-scale movie making projects (Figure 3-35). With these programs, home users can edit home movies, add music or other sounds to the video, and share their movies on the Web. Some operating systems include video editing and audio editing software.

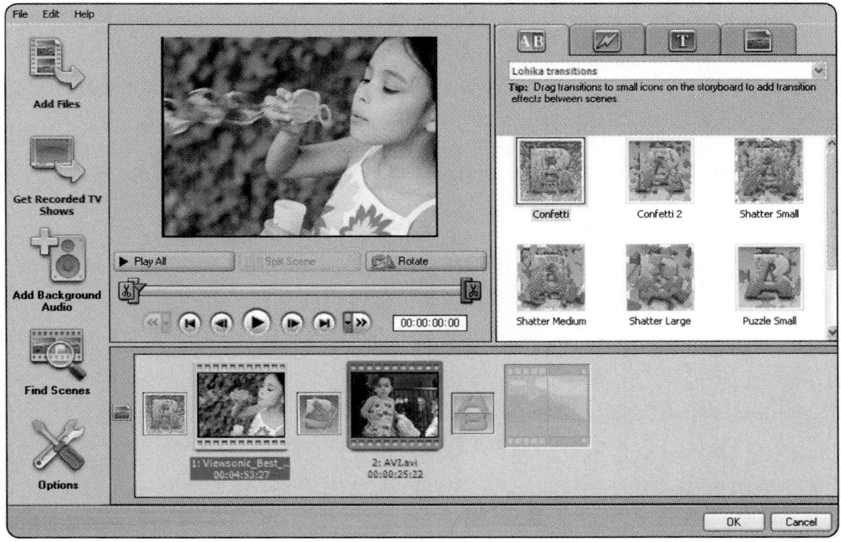

FIGURE 3-35 With personal video and audio editing software, home users can edit their home movies.

Home Design/Landscaping Software

Homeowners or potential homeowners can use **home design/landscaping software** to assist them with the design, remodeling, or improvement of a home, deck, or landscape (Figure 3-36). Home design/landscaping software includes hundreds of predrawn plans that you can customize to meet your needs. These programs show changes to home designs and landscapes, allowing homeowners to preview proposed modifications. Once designed, many home design/landscaping programs print a materials list outlining costs and quantities for the entire project.

FIGURE 3-36 Home design/landscaping software can help you design or remodel a home, deck, or landscape.

WEB LINK 3-7

Home Design/Landscaping Software

For more information, visit scsite.com/dc2008/ch3/weblink and then click Home Design/Landscaping Software.

Reference and Educational Software

Reference software provides valuable and thorough information for all individuals (Figure 3-37). Popular reference software includes encyclopedias, dictionaries, health/medical guides, maps, and travel directories.

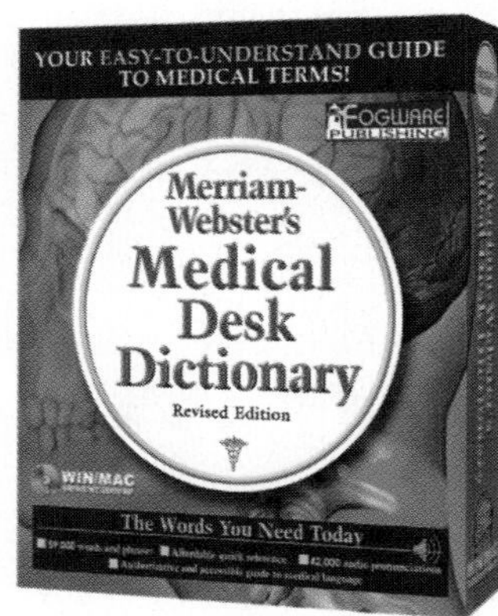

FIGURE 3-37 This reference dictionary gives text definitions and audio pronunciations of medical terms.

WEB LINK 3-8

Reference Software

For more information, visit scsite.com/dc2008/ch3/weblink and then click Reference Software.

Educational software is software that teaches a particular skill. Educational software exists for just about any subject, from learning how to type to learning how to cook. Preschool to high-school learners use educational software to assist them with subjects such as reading and math or to prepare them for class or college entry exams. Educational software often includes games and other content to make the learning experience more fun.

Many educational programs use a computer-based training approach. **Computer-based training (CBT)**, also called computer-aided instruction (CAI), is a type of education in which students learn by using and completing exercises with instructional software. CBT typically consists of self-directed, self-paced instruction about a topic. Beginning athletes, for example, use CBT programs to learn the intricacies of baseball, football, soccer, tennis, and golf. The military and airlines use CBT simulations to train pilots to fly in various conditions and environments. Schools use CBT to teach students math, language, and software skills.

Entertainment Software

Entertainment software for personal computers includes interactive games, videos, and other programs designed to support a hobby or provide amusement and enjoyment. For example, you might use entertainment software to play games (Figure 3-38) individually or with others online, make a family tree, listen to music, or fly an aircraft.

FIGURE 3-38 Entertainment software can provide hours of recreation.

APPLICATION SOFTWARE FOR COMMUNICATIONS

One of the main reasons people use computers is to communicate and share information with others. Some communications software is considered system software because it works with hardware and transmission media. Other communications software makes users more productive and/or assists them with personal tasks, and thus, is considered application software. Chapter 2 presented a variety of application software for communications, which is summarized in the table in Figure 3-39. Read Ethics & Issues 3-3 for a related discussion.

APPLICATION SOFTWARE FOR COMMUNICATIONS

E-Mail
- Messages and files sent via a network such as the Internet
- Requires an e-mail program
  - Integrated in many software suites and operating systems
  - Available free at portals on the Web
  - Included with paid Internet access service
  - Can be purchased separately from retailers

FTP
- Method of uploading and downloading files with other computers on the Internet
- May require an FTP program
  - Integrated in some operating systems
  - Available for download on the Web for a small fee

Web Browser
- Allows users to access and view Web pages on the Internet
- Requires a Web browser program
  - Integrated in some operating systems
  - Available for download on the Web free or for a fee

Video Conferencing
- Meeting between geographically separated people who use a network such as the Internet to transmit video/audio
- Requires video conferencing software, a microphone, speakers, and sometimes a video camera attached to your computer

Internet Telephony (VoIP)
- Allows users to speak to other users over the Internet
- Requires Internet connection, Internet telephone service, microphone or telephone, and Internet telephone software or telephone adapter

Newsgroup/Message Board
- Online area where users have written discussions
- Newsgroup may require a newsreader program
  - Integrated in some operating systems, e-mail programs, and Web browsers; built into some Web sites
  - Available for download on the Web, usually at no cost
  - Included with some paid Internet access services

Chat Room
- Real-time, online typed conversation
- Requires chat client software
  - Integrated in some operating systems, e-mail programs, and Web browsers
  - Available for download on the Web, usually at no cost
  - Included with some paid Internet access services
  - Built into some Web sites

Instant Messaging
- Real-time exchange of messages, files, audio, and/or video with another online user
- Requires instant messenger software
  - Integrated in some operating systems
  - Available for download on the Web, usually at no cost
  - Included with some paid Internet access services

Blogging
- Time-stamped articles, or posts, in a diary or journal format, usually listed in reverse chronological order
- Blogger needs *blog software*, or *blogware*, to create/maintain blog
  - Some Web sites do not require installation of blog software

FIGURE 3-39 A summary of application software for home and business communications.

ETHICS & ISSUES 3-3

Should Companies Monitor Employees' E-Mail and Internet Traffic?

According to one survey, more than 42 percent of all companies monitor (after transmission) or intercept (during transmission) employees' e-mail. Employers can use software to find automatically personal or offensive e-mail messages that have been sent or received, and intercept and filter messages while they are being sent or received. Companies also monitor other Internet traffic such as Web sites visited by employees and how much time employees spend instant messaging and visiting chat rooms. Companies perform this monitoring to improve productivity, increase security, reduce misconduct, and control liability risks. Few laws regulate employee monitoring, and courts have given employers a great deal of leeway in watching work on company-owned computers. In one case, an employee's termination for using her office e-mail system to complain about her boss was upheld, even though the company allowed e-mail use for personal communications. The court decreed that the employee's messages were inappropriate for workplace communications. Executives have not escaped scrutiny, either. Prominent leaders, such as Bill Gates, have had e-mail messages they sent used against them in court. Many employees believe that monitoring software violates their privacy rights. State laws usually favor the privacy of the employee, while federal laws tend to favor the employer's right to perform such monitoring. To reduce employee anxiety about monitoring and to follow some state laws, legal experts suggest that companies publish written policies and accept employee feedback, provide clear descriptions of acceptable and unacceptable behavior, respect employee needs and time, and establish a balance between security and privacy. Should companies monitor or intercept employees' Internet communications? Why or why not? How can a company balance workplace security and productivity with employee privacy? If a company monitors Internet use, what guidelines should be followed to maintain worker morale? Why? Is intercepting and filtering e-mail more offensive than monitoring e-mail? Why?

POPULAR UTILITY PROGRAMS

Utility programs are considered system software because they assist a user with controlling or maintaining the operation of a computer, its devices, or its software. Some utility programs are included with the operating system, and others are available as stand-alone programs.

Utility programs typically offer features that provide an environment conducive to successful use of application software. One of the more important utility programs protects a computer against viruses. A computer *virus* is a potentially damaging computer program that affects, or infects, a computer negatively by altering the way the computer works without the user's knowledge or permission. For a technical discussion about viruses, read the High-Tech Talk article on page 168.

Other features of utility programs include protecting a computer against unauthorized intrusions; removing spyware from a computer; filtering e-mail messages, Web content, and advertisements; managing files and disks; compressing files; backing up; playing media files; burning (recording on) a CD or DVD; and maintaining a personal computer. The table in Figure 3-40 briefly describes several utility programs. Chapter 8 discusses them in more depth.

FAQ 3-10

How much does a computer virus attack cost a company?

A recent survey found that it typically costs an enterprise about $10,000 to recover from a computer virus attack. When the virus attacks multiple servers, however, the costs can exceed $100,000. For more information, visit scsite.com/dc2008/ch3/faq and then click Computer Virus Attacks.

WEB LINK 3-9

Antivirus Programs

For more information, visit scsite.com/dc2008/ch3/weblink and then click Antivirus Programs.

WIDELY USED UTILITY PROGRAMS

Utility Program	Description
Antivirus Program	An *antivirus program* protects a computer against viruses by identifying and removing any computer viruses found in memory, on storage media, or in incoming files.
Personal Firewall	A *personal firewall* detects and protects a personal computer from unauthorized intrusions.
Spyware Remover	A *spyware remover* detects and deletes spyware, adware, and other similar programs on your computer.
Internet Filters	
• Anti-Spam Program	An *anti-spam program* attempts to remove spam (Internet junk mail) before it reaches your e-mail inbox.
• Web Filter	A *Web filter* restricts access to specified Web sites.
• Pop-Up Blocker	A *pop-up blocker* stops advertisements from displaying on Web pages and disables pop-up windows.
File Manager	A *file manager* provides functions related to file management.
File Compression	A *file compression utility* shrinks the size of a file(s), so the file takes up less storage space than the original file.
Backup	A *backup utility* allows users to copy selected files or an entire hard disk to another storage medium.
Media Player	A *media player* allows you to view images and animation, listen to audio, and watch video files.
CD/DVD Burning	A *CD/DVD burner* writes text, graphics, audio, and video files on a recordable or rewritable CD or DVD.
Personal Computer Maintenance	A *personal computer maintenance utility* identifies and fixes operating system problems, detects and repairs disk problems, and includes the capability of improving a computer's performance.

FIGURE 3-40 A summary of widely used utility programs.

WEB-BASED SOFTWARE

As discussed earlier in this chapter, users can purchase application software from a software vendor, retail store, or Web-based business. Users typically install purchased application software on a computer before they run it. Installed software has two disadvantages: (1) it requires disk space on your computer, and (2) it can be costly to upgrade as vendors release new versions. As an alternative, some users opt to access Web-based software.

As previously mentioned, Web-based software refers to programs hosted by a Web site. Users often interact with Web-based software, sometimes called a *Web application*, directly at the host's Web site. Some Web sites, however, require you download the software to your local computer or device. Web-based software sites often store users' data and information on their servers. Users concerned with data security may shy away from this type of Web-based software. For this reason, some Web-based software sites provide users with an option of storing data locally on their own personal computer or mobile device.

Many of the previously discussed types of application software have Web-based options. For example, word processing, e-mail, personal information manager, software suite, photo editing, Web page authoring, tax preparation, clip art/image gallery, reference, educational, and entertainment programs are available as Web-based software.

Some Web sites provide free access to their Web-based software. For example, one site creates a map and driving directions when a user enters a starting and destination point. Others offer part of their Web-based software free and charge for access to a more comprehensive program (Figure 3-41). Another type allows you to use the program free and pay a fee when a certain action occurs. For example, you can prepare your tax return free using TurboTax for the Web, but if you elect to print it or file it electronically, you pay a minimal fee.

Web 2.0

Experts often use the term Web 2.0 to describe Web sites that offer Web-based software. Recall that Web 2.0, or participatory Web, refers to Web sites that provide users with a means to share and/or store personal information through Web-based software and may allow users to modify Web site content. Several types of Web 2.0 sites have emerged:

- Web-based software that focuses on user communications — i.e., e-mail, instant messaging, and Internet telephony software
- Web-based software you download from the Web site — i.e., mapping software
- Web-based software you download from the Web site that also has a Web component that offers additional features — i.e., word processing software that allow others to access documents, media player programs that connect to an online store for downloading media
- Web-based software you interact with only through the Web site that provides users with an online community for user input and/or collaboration — i.e., social networks, photo sharing, wikis

FIGURE 3-41 This program displays three-dimensional maps, satellite images, and aerial photography of the entire earth.

Application Service Providers

Storing and maintaining programs can be a costly investment for businesses. Thus, some have elected to outsource one or more facets of their information technology (IT) needs to an application service provider. An *application service provider* (*ASP*) is a third-party organization that manages and distributes software and services on the Web.

The five categories of ASPs are:

1. *Enterprise ASP*: customizes and delivers high-end business applications, such as finance and database
2. *Local/Regional ASP*: offers a variety of software applications to a specific geographic region
3. *Specialist ASP*: delivers applications to meet a specific business need, such as human resources or project management
4. *Vertical Market ASP*: provides applications for a particular industry, such as construction, health care, or retail
5. *Volume Business ASP*: supplies prepackaged applications, such as accounting, to businesses

A variety of payment schemes are available. Some rent use of the application on a monthly basis or charge based on the number of user accesses. Others charge a one-time fee.

LEARNING AIDS AND SUPPORT TOOLS FOR APPLICATION SOFTWARE

Learning how to use application software effectively involves time and practice (read Looking Ahead 3-2 for a look at how effective use of software potentially can help the medical field). To assist in the learning process, many programs provide online Help, Web-based Help, and templates.

Online Help is the electronic equivalent of a user manual (Figure 3-42a). It usually is integrated in a program. In most programs, a function key or a button on the screen starts the Help feature. When using a program, you can use the Help feature to ask a question or access the Help topics in subject or alphabetical order.

Most online Help also links to Web sites that offer *Web-based Help*, which provides updates and more comprehensive resources to respond to technical issues about software (Figure 3-42b). Many can search for answers to questions you enter in complete sentences. Some Web sites contain chat rooms, in which a user can talk directly with a technical support person or join a conversation with other users who may be able to answer questions or solve problems.

A *template* is a document that contains the formatting necessary for a specific document type (Figure 3-42c). Many programs include templates. For example, word processing software contains templates for memorandums, meeting agendas, fax cover sheets, flyers, letters, and resumes. Spreadsheet software includes templates for invoices and purchase orders.

If you want to learn more about a particular program from a printed manual, many books are available to help you learn to use the features of personal computer programs. These books typically are available in bookstores and software stores (Figure 3-43).

Many colleges and schools provide training on several of the applications discussed in this chapter. For more information, contact your local school for a list of class offerings.

LOOKING AHEAD 3-2

3-D Scans May Reduce Surgeries

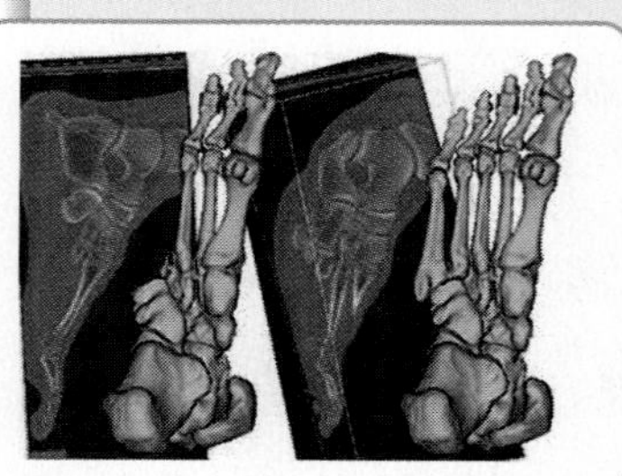

When commercial software developers collaborate with computer scientists, the results can benefit users as diverse as doctors and moviemakers.

Doctors using Live Surface software can turn data from MRI, CAT, or other medical scans into 3-D images of any part of a patient's body. Created by computer scientists at Brigham Young University, the software uses a paint-by-number approach to isolate specific areas, such as the heart, so doctors more closely can examine and better diagnose medical problems.

Using the software may eliminate the need for some exploratory surgeries and provide visual roadmaps to guide surgeries. The software tools also can be used by moviemakers to pull 3-D images of specific objects or a single actor from video clips. Adobe Systems funded the research for Live Surface and previously supported the development of a program manipulating two-dimensional objects that is now part of Adobe Photoshop. For more information, visit scsite.com/dc2008/ch3/looking and then click 3-D Scans.

FIGURE 3-42a (online Help)

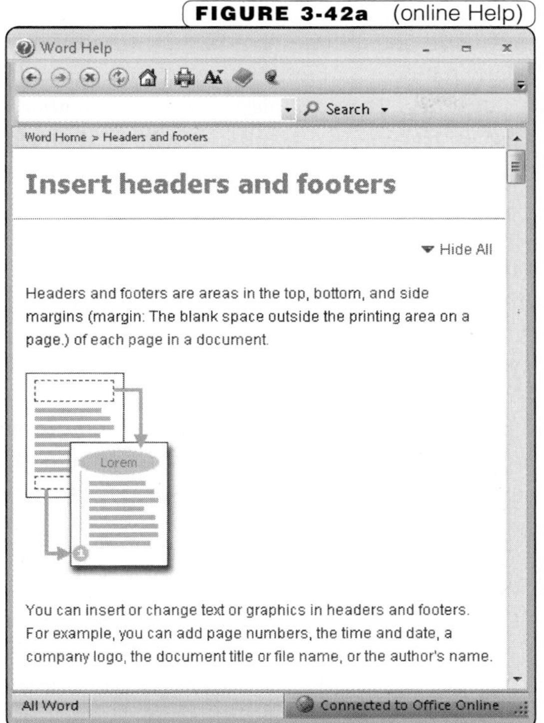

FIGURE 3-42b (Web-based Help)

FIGURE 3-42c (template)

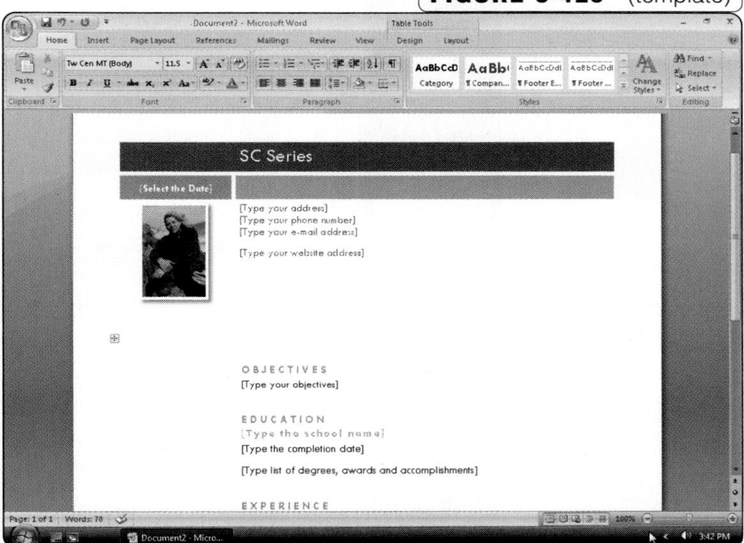

FIGURE 3-42 Many programs include online Help, Web-based Help, and templates.

FIGURE 3-43 Bookstores often sell trade books to help you learn to use the features of personal computer application software.

Web-Based Training

Web-based training (*WBT*) is a type of CBT (computer-based training) that uses Internet technology and consists of application software on the Web. Similar to CBT, WBT typically consists of self-directed, self-paced instruction about a topic. WBT is popular in business, industry, and schools for teaching new skills or enhancing existing skills of employees, teachers, or students. When using a WBT product, students actively become involved in the learning process instead of remaining passive recipients of information.

Many Web sites offer WBT to the general public. Such training covers a wide range of topics, from how to change a flat tire to creating documents in Word. Many of these Web sites are free. Others require registration and payment to take the complete Web-based course.

WBT often is combined with other materials for distance learning and e-learning. **Distance learning (DL)** is the delivery of education at one location while the learning takes place at other locations. DL courses provide time, distance, and place advantages for students who live far from a college campus or work full time. These courses enable students to attend class from anywhere in the world and at times that fit their schedules. Many national and international companies offer DL training. These training courses eliminate the costs of airfare, hotels, and meals for centralized training sessions.

WEB LINK 3-10

E-Learning

For more information, visit scsite.com/dc2008/ch3/weblink and then click E-Learning.

E-learning, short for electronic learning, is the delivery of education via some electronic method such as the Internet, networks, or CDs/DVDs. To enhance communications, e-learning systems also may include video conferencing, e-mail, blogs, wikis, newsgroups, chat rooms, and groupware. Read Ethics & Issues 3-4 for a related discussion.

E-learning providers often specialize in presenting instructors with the tools for preparation, distribution, and management of DL courses (Figure 3-44). These tools enable instructors to create rich, educational Web-based training sites and allow the students to interact with a powerful Web learning environment. Through the training site, students can check their progress, take practice tests, search for topics, send e-mail messages, and participate in discussions and chats.

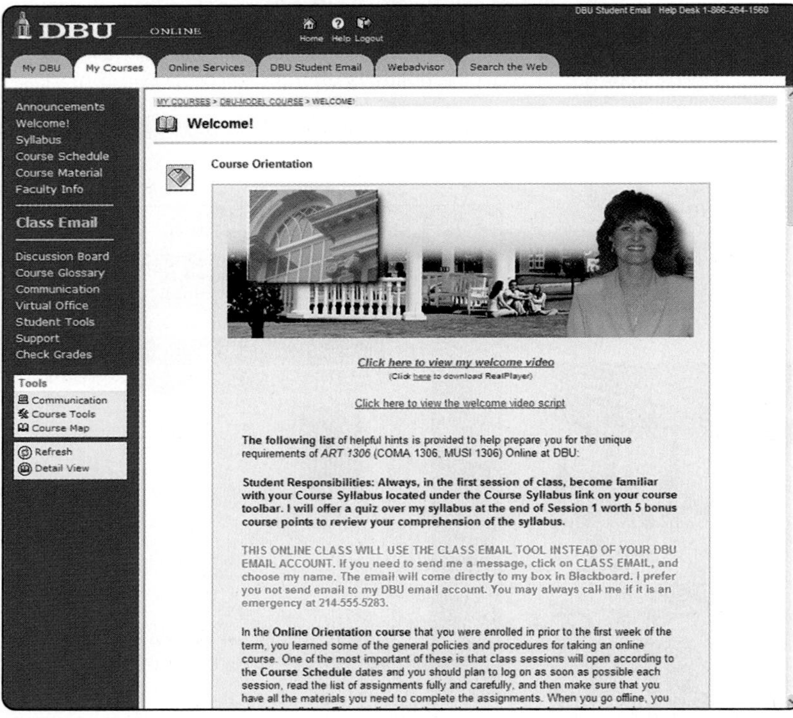

FIGURE 3-44 Using Blackboard Academic Suite, instructors can communicate online with their students.

ETHICS & ISSUES 3-4

Will Patents Endanger E-Learning?

Approximately 90 percent of colleges use e-learning systems. Recently, a provider of a popular e-learning system declared it had been awarded a patent on some of the most fundamental aspects of e-learning. The company immediately filed a lawsuit against one of its largest competitors for patent infringement, claiming they simply are protecting a great investment that they have made in developing the technology. They are not trying to stop any companies from selling similar software; they just expect a small royalty from the other companies for using the patents. Critics point out that the United States Patent and Trademark Office may have erred because it is not allowed to grant patents for obvious ideas, and e-learning systems are rather obvious. Critics also claim that due to its importance in education, this technology should be given special consideration. In fact, the technology was invented as part of a research project at a respected university. In Europe and the U.S., there are political movements against the patenting of any software. Should companies be able to patent software? Why or why not? Should a higher standard apply in granting patents for systems directly related to academia? Why or why not? In what ways do you think the e-learning provider should be able to protect the investments it has made in the technology? Are e-learning systems an obvious idea to you?

Test your knowledge of pages 155 through 166 in Quiz Yourself 3-3.

QUIZ YOURSELF 3-3

Instructions: Find the true statement below. Then, rewrite the remaining false statements so they are true.

1. An anti-spam program protects a computer against viruses by identifying and removing any computer viruses found in memory, on storage media, or in incoming files.
2. Computer-based training is a type of Web-based training that uses Internet technology and consists of application software on the Web.
3. E-mail and Web browsers are examples of communications software that are considered application software.
4. Legal software is a simplified accounting program that helps home users and small office/home office users balance their checkbooks, pay bills, track investments, and evaluate financial plans.
5. Personal DTP software is a popular type of image editing software that allows users to edit digital photographs.

Quiz Yourself Online: To further check your knowledge of types and features of home, personal, educational, and communications programs, utility programs, Web-based software, and software learning aids, visit scsite.com/dc2008/ch3/quiz and then click Objectives 6 – 10.

CHAPTER SUMMARY

This chapter illustrated how to start and use application software. It then presented an overview of a variety of business software, graphics and multimedia software, home/personal/educational software, and communications software (read Ethics & Issues 3-5 for a related discussion).

The chapter also described widely used utility programs and discussed Web-based software. Finally, learning aids and support tools for application software were presented.

ETHICS & ISSUES 3-5

Copying Software — A Computer Crime!

Usually, when you buy software, you legally can make one copy of the software for backup purposes. Despite the law, many people make multiple copies, either to share or to sell. Often, the sharing is done online. In a recent survey, more than 50 percent of students and 25 percent of instructors admitted that they had illegally copied, or would illegally copy, software. Microsoft, a leading software manufacturer, estimates that almost 25 percent of software in the United States has been copied illegally. Among small businesses, the rate may be even higher. The Business Software Alliance, an industry trade association, believes that 40 percent of small U.S. businesses use illegally copied software and that cutting the amount of illegal software by 10 percent would add $125 billion to the U.S. economy. Illegally copied software costs the software industry billions a year in lost revenues, and the law allows fines up to $150,000 for each illegal copy of software. People and companies copy software illegally for a variety of reasons, insisting that software prices are too high, software often is copied for educational or other altruistic purposes, copied software makes people more productive, no restrictions should be placed on the use of software after it is purchased, and everyone copies software. What should be the penalty for copying software? Why? Can you counter the reasons people give for copying software illegally? How? Would you copy software illegally? Why or why not?

CAREER CORNER

Help Desk Specialist

A Help Desk specialist position is an entryway into the information technology (IT) field. A *Help Desk specialist* deals with problems in hardware, software, or communications systems. Job requirements may include the following: solve procedural and software questions both in person and over the telephone, develop and maintain Help Desk operations manuals, and assist in training new Help Desk personnel.

Usually, a Help Desk specialist must be knowledgeable about the major programs in use. Entry-level positions primarily involve answering calls from people with questions. Other positions provide additional assistance and assume further responsibilities, often demanding greater knowledge and problem-solving skills that can lead to more advanced IT positions. This job is ideal for people who must work irregular hours, because many companies need support people to work evenings, weekends, or part-time.

Educational requirements are less stringent than they are for other jobs in the computer field. In some cases, a high school diploma is sufficient. Advancement requires a minimum of a two-year degree, while management generally requires a bachelor's degree in IT or a related field. Certification is another way Help Desk specialists can increase their attractiveness in the marketplace. Entry-level salaries range from $38,000 to $60,000 per year. Managers range from $55,000 to $95,000. For more information, visit scsite.com/dc2008/ch3/careers and then click Help Desk Specialist.

High-Tech Talk

COMPUTER VIRUSES: DELIVERY, INFECTION, AND AVOIDANCE

Klez. Melissa. Netsky. Nimda. Like the common cold, virtually countless variations of computer viruses exist. Unlike the biological viruses that cause the common cold, people create computer viruses. To create a virus, an unscrupulous programmer must code and then test the virus code to ensure the virus can replicate itself, conceal itself, monitor for certain events, and then deliver its *payload* — the destructive event or prank the virus was created to deliver. Despite the many variations of viruses, most have two phases to their execution: infection and delivery.

To start the infection phase, the virus must be activated. Today, the most common way viruses spread is by people running infected programs disguised as e-mail attachments. During the infection phase, viruses typically perform three actions:

1. First, a virus replicates by attaching itself to program files. A *macro virus* hides in the macro language of an application, such as Word. A *boot sector virus* targets the master boot record and executes when the computer boots up. A *file virus* attaches itself to program files. The file virus, Win32.Hatred, for example, replicates by first infecting Windows executable files for the Calculator, Notepad, Help, and other programs on the hard disk. The virus then scans the computer to locate .exe files on other drives and stores this information in the system registry. The next time an infected file is run, the virus reads the registry and continues infecting another drive.
2. Viruses also conceal themselves to avoid detection. A *stealth virus* disguises itself by hiding in fake code sections, which it inserts within working code in a file. A *polymorphic virus* actually changes its code as it infects computers. Win32.Hatred uses both concealment techniques. The virus writes itself to the last file section, while modifying the file header to hide the increased file size. It also scrambles and encrypts the virus code as it infects files.
3. Finally, viruses watch for a certain condition or event and activate when that condition or event occurs. The event might be booting up the computer or hitting a date on the system clock. A *logic bomb* activates when it detects a specific condition (say, a name deleted from the employee list). A *time bomb* is a logic bomb that activates on a particular date or time. Win32.Hatred, for instance, unleashes its destruction when the computer clock hits the seventh day of any month. If the triggering condition does not exist, the virus simply replicates.

During the delivery phase, the virus unleashes its payload, which might be a harmless prank that displays a meaningless message — or it might be destructive, corrupting or deleting data and files. When Win32.Hatred triggers, it displays the author's message and then covers the screen with black dots. The virus also deletes several antivirus files as it infects the system. The most dangerous viruses do not have an obvious payload, instead they quietly modify files. A virus, for example, could randomly change numbers in an inventory program or introduce delays to slow a computer.

Other kinds of electronic annoyances exist in addition to viruses. While often called viruses, worms and Trojan horse applications actually are part of a broader category called *malicious-logic programs.*

- A *worm*, such as the CodeRed or Sircam worm, resides in active memory and replicates itself over a network to infect machines, using up the system resources and possibly shutting the system down.
- A *Trojan horse* is a destructive program disguised as a real application, such as a screen saver. When a user runs a seemingly innocent program, a Trojan horse hiding inside can capture information, such as user names and passwords, from your system or open up a backdoor that allows a hacker remotely to control your computer. Unlike viruses, Trojan horses do not replicate themselves.

As with the common cold, every computer user is susceptible to a computer virus. In 1995, the chance that a virus would infect your computer was 1 in 1,000; by 2004, the odds were only 1 in 7. Even with better antivirus software, viruses are tough to avoid, as deceitful programmers craft new electronic maladies to infect your computer. Due to the increasing threat of viruses attacking your computer, it is more important than ever to protect your computer from viruses. Figure 3-45 lists steps you can follow to protect your computer from a virus infection. For more information, visit scsite.com/dc2008/ch3/tech and then click Computer Viruses.

STEPS TO VIRUS PROTECTION

1. Install the latest Microsoft updates.
2. Purchase a good antivirus program.
3. After installing an antivirus program, scan your entire computer to be sure your system is clean.
4. Update your antivirus definitions regularly.
5. Be suspicious of any and all unsolicited e-mail attachments.
6. Stay informed about viruses and virus hoaxes.
7. Install a personal firewall program.
8. Download software only if you are sure the Web site is legitimate.
9. Avoid as best you can visiting unscrupulous Web sites.

FIGURE 3-45 Guidelines to keep your computer virus free.

Companies on the Cutting Edge

ADOBE SYSTEMS
DIGITAL IMAGING LEADER

Practically every image seen on a computer and in print has been shaped by software developed by *Adobe Systems, Inc.* The company, based in San Jose, California, is one of the world's largest application software corporations and is committed to helping people communicate effectively.

Adobe's acquisition of Macromedia in 2005 expanded its product line. Print, Internet, and mobile publishers use the software included in Creative Suite, such as Photoshop, Illustrator, and InDesign. Web page designers also use the Studio programs, which include Dreamweaver, Flash, Fireworks, Contribute, and FlashPaper. Acrobat software is used to share documents electronically; the free Reader has been downloaded more than 600 million times in 26 different languages, and the full-featured version accounts for approximately 20 percent of sales.

Adobe was named the greenest corporate building in the United States in 2006 for reducing electricity consumption by 35 percent and natural gas consumption by 41 percent since 2001. For more information, visit scsite.com/dc2008/ch3/companies and then click Adobe Systems.

MICROSOFT
REALIZING POTENTIAL WITH BUSINESS SOFTWARE

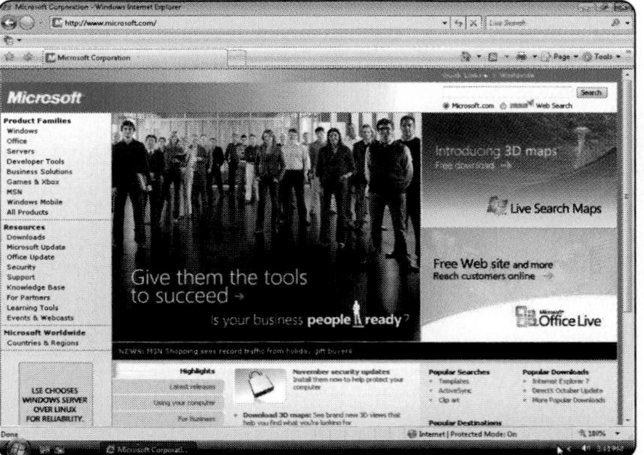

Microsoft's mission is "to enable people and businesses throughout the world to realize their potential." As the largest software company in the world, *Microsoft* has indeed helped computer users in every field reach their goals.

When Microsoft was incorporated in 1975, the company had three programmers, one product, and revenues of $16,000. Thirty years later, the company employs more than 71,000 people, produces scores of software titles with Office and Windows leading the industry, and has annual revenue of approximately $50 billion.

The Zune portable media player, Windows Vista operating system, and Office 2007 expand the corporation's offerings in the consumer and business marketplace. For more information, visit scsite.com/dc2008/ch3/companies and then click Microsoft.

Technology Trailblazers

DAN BRICKLIN
VISICALC DEVELOPER

When *Dan Bricklin* was enrolled at the Harvard Business School in the 1970s, he often used his calculator to determine the effect of changing one value on a balance sheet. He recognized the need to develop a program that would perform a series of calculations automatically when the first number was entered.

He named his creation VisiCalc, short for Visible Calculator. He and a friend formed a company called Software Arts and programmed the VisiCalc prototype using Apple Basic on an Apple II computer. The small program was the first piece of application software that provided a reason for businesses to buy Apple computers. It laid the foundation for the development of other spreadsheets and included many of the features found in today's spreadsheet software.

As president of Software Garden, Inc., a small consulting and software-development firm, one of his latest projects was producing a training video explaining copyright law basics to software developers. For more information, visit scsite.com/dc2008/ch3/people and then click Dan Bricklin.

MASAYOSHI SON
SOFTBANK PRESIDENT AND CEO

Many students carry photographs of family and friends in their wallets and book bags. As a 16-year-old student in the 1970s, *Masayoshi Son* carried a picture of a microchip. He predicted that the microchip was going to change people's lives, and he wanted to be part of that trend.

While majoring in economics at the University of California, Berkeley, he earned his first million dollars by importing arcade games from Japan to the campus, developing new computer games, and selling a patent for a multilingual pocket translator to Sharp Corporation.

At age 23 he founded Softbank, which is Japan's second-largest broadband Internet service and telephone provider. In 2006, he was named to Asiamoney's list of the most powerful and influential people in business and finance in the Asia Pacific region. For more information, visit scsite.com/dc2008/ch3/people and then click Masayoshi Son.

Quizzes and Learning Games
Computer Genius
Crossword Puzzle
DC Track and Field
Practice Test
Quiz Yourself
Wheel of Terms
You're Hired!

Exercises
Case Studies
Chapter Review
Checkpoint
Key Terms
Learn How To
Learn It Online
Web Research

Beyond the Book
Career Corner
Companies
FAQs
High-Tech Talk
Looking Ahead
Making Use of the Web
Trailblazers
Web Links

Features
Chapter Forum
Install Computer
Lab Exercises
Maintain Computer
Tech News
Timeline 2008

Chapter Review

The Chapter Review section summarizes the concepts presented in this chapter. To listen to the audio version of this Chapter Review, visit scsite.com/dc2008/ch3/review. To obtain help from other students regarding any subject in this chapter, visit scsite.com/dc2008/ch3/forum and post your thoughts or questions.

1 What Are the Categories of Application Software? **Application software** consists of programs designed to make users more productive and/or assist them with personal tasks. The major categories of application software are business software; graphics and multimedia software; home, personal, and educational software; and communications software.

2 How Is Software Distributed? Application software is available in a variety of forms. **Packaged software** is mass-produced, copyrighted retail software that meets the needs of a variety of users. **Custom software** performs functions specific to a business or industry. **Web-based software** refers to programs hosted by a Web site. **Open source software** is provided for use, modification, and redistribution. **Shareware** is copyrighted software that is distributed free for a trial period. **Freeware** is copyrighted software provided at no cost by an individual or a company that retains all rights to the software. **Public-domain software** is free software donated for public use and has no copyright restrictions.

3 How Do You Work with Application Software? Personal computer operating systems often use the concept of a **desktop**, which is an on-screen work area that has a graphical user interface. To start an application in Windows Vista, move the **pointer** to the Start **button** on the taskbar and **click** the Start button by pressing and releasing a button on the mouse. Then, click the program name on the **menu** or in a list. Once loaded into memory, the program is displayed in a **window** on the desktop.

connect

Visit scsite.com/dc2008/ch3/quiz or click the Quiz Yourself button. Click Objectives 1 – 3.

4 What Are the Key Features of Widely Used Business Programs? **Business software** assists people in becoming more effective and efficient while performing daily business activities. Business software includes the following programs. **Word processing software** allows users to **create** a document by entering text and inserting images, **edit** the document by making changes, and **format** the document by changing its appearance. **Spreadsheet software** allows users to organize data in rows and columns, perform calculations, recalculate when data changes, and chart the data. **Database software** allows users to create a **database**, which is a collection of data organized to allow access, retrieval, and use of that data. **Presentation graphics software** allows users to create a *slide show* that is displayed on a monitor or projection screen. **Note taking software** enables users to enter typed text, handwritten comments, drawings, or sketches on a page and then save the page as part of a notebook. A **personal information manager (PIM)** is software that includes features to help users organize personal information. A **software suite** is a collection of individual programs sold as a single package. **Project management software** allows users to plan, schedule, track, and analyze a project. **Accounting software** helps companies record and report their financial transactions. **Document management software** provides a means for sharing, distributing, and searching through documents by converting them into a format that can be viewed by any user.

5 What Are the Key Features of Widely Used Graphics and Multimedia Programs? Graphics and multimedia software includes the following programs. **Computer-aided design (CAD) software** assists in creating engineering, architectural, and scientific designs. **Desktop publishing (DTP) software** enables professional designers to create sophisticated documents that contain text, graphics, and colors. **Paint software** lets users draw graphical images with various on-screen tools. **Image editing software** provides the capabilities of paint software and includes the capability to modify existing images. **Professional photo editing software** is a type of image editing software that allows high-volume digital photo users to edit and customize digital photographs. **Video editing software** allows professionals to modify segments of a video. **Audio editing software** lets users modify audio clips, produce studio-quality soundtracks, and add audio to video clips.

Chapter Review

Multimedia authoring software allows users to combine text, graphics, audio, video, and animation in an interactive application. **Web page authoring software** helps users create Web pages that include graphical images, video, audio, animation, and other special effects.

connect Visit scsite.com/dc2008/ch3/quiz or click the Quiz Yourself button. Click Objectives 4 – 5.

6 **What Are the Key Features of Widely Used Home, Personal, and Educational Programs?** Software for home, personal, and educational use includes the following applications. A software suite (for personal use) combines application software such as word processing, spreadsheet, and database into a single package. **Personal finance software** is an accounting program that helps users balance their checkbooks, pay bills, track income and expenses, track investments, and evaluate financial plans. **Legal software** assists in the preparation of legal documents. **Tax preparation software** guides users through filing federal taxes. **Personal DTP software** helps users create newsletters, brochures, advertisements, greeting and business cards, logos, and Web pages. **Personal paint/image editing software** provides an easy-to-use interface with functions tailored to meet the needs of home and small business users. **Personal photo editing software** is a type of image editing software used to edit digital photographs. Application software often includes a **clip art/image gallery**, which is a collection of clip art and photographs. Video and audio editing software is used to edit home movies, add music or other sounds, and share movies on the Web. **Home design/landscaping software** assists with the design, remodeling, or improvement of a home or landscape. **Reference software** provides valuable and thorough information for all individuals. **Educational software** teaches a particular skill. **Entertainment software** includes interactive games, videos, and other programs to support hobbies or provide amusement.

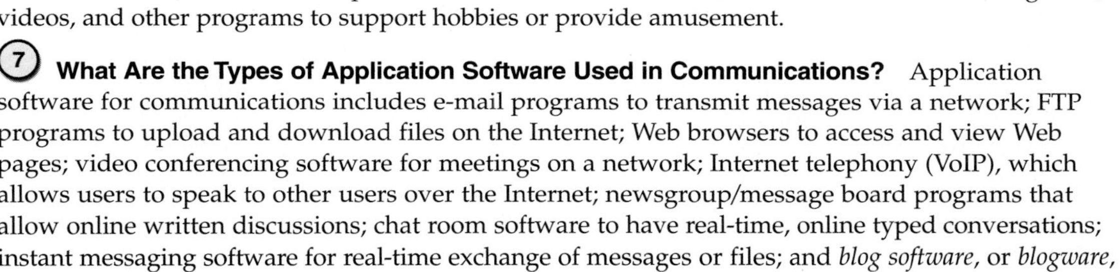

7 **What Are the Types of Application Software Used in Communications?** Application software for communications includes e-mail programs to transmit messages via a network; FTP programs to upload and download files on the Internet; Web browsers to access and view Web pages; video conferencing software for meetings on a network; Internet telephony (VoIP), which allows users to speak to other users over the Internet; newsgroup/message board programs that allow online written discussions; chat room software to have real-time, online typed conversations; instant messaging software for real-time exchange of messages or files; and *blog software*, or *blogware*, to create and maintain a blog.

8 **What Are the Functions of Utility Programs?** Utility programs support the successful use of application software. An *antivirus program* protects a computer against a computer *virus*, which is a potentially damaging computer program. A *personal firewall* detects and protects a personal computer from unauthorized intrusions. A *spyware remover* detects and deletes spyware, adware, and other similar programs. An *anti-spam program* removes spam (Internet junk mail). A *Web filter* restricts access to specified Web sites. A *pop-up blocker* disables pop-up windows. A *file manager* provides functions related to file and disk management. A *file compression utility* shrinks the size of a file. A *backup utility* allows users to copy selected files or an entire hard disk to another storage medium. A *media player* allows you to view images and animation, listen to audio, and watch video. A *CD/DVD burner* writes files on a CD or DVD. A *personal computer maintenance utility* fixes operating system and disk problems.

9 **What Are the Advantages of Using Web-Based Software?** A *Web application* requires less disk space on a computer than installed software and is less costly to upgrade. An *application service provider (ASP)* is a third-party organization that manages and distributes software and services on the Web.

10 **What Learning Aids Are Available for Application Software?** To assist in the learning process, many programs offer Help features. **Online Help** is the electronic equivalent of a user manual. Most online Help links to *Web-based help*, which provides updates and more comprehensive resources. A *template* is a document that contains the formatting necessary for a specific document type.

connect Visit scsite.com/dc2008/ch3/quiz or click the Quiz Yourself button. Click Objectives 6 – 10.

Quizzes and Learning Games
Computer Genius
Crossword Puzzle
DC Track and Field
Practice Test
Quiz Yourself
Wheel of Terms
You're Hired!

Exercises
Case Studies
Chapter Review
Checkpoint
Key Terms
Learn How To
Learn It Online
Web Research

Beyond the Book
Career Corner
Companies
FAQs
High-Tech Talk
Looking Ahead
Making Use of the Web
Trailblazers
Web Links

Features
Chapter Forum
Install Computer
Lab Exercises
Maintain Computer
Tech News
Timeline 2008

Key Terms

You should know the Primary Terms and be familiar with the Secondary Terms. Use the list below to help focus your study. To further enhance your understanding of the Key Terms in this chapter, visit scsite.com/dc2008/ch3/terms. See an example of and a definition for each term, and access current and additional information about the term from the Web.

Primary Terms

(shown in bold-black characters in the chapter)

accounting software (149)
application software (134)
audio editing software (153)
business software (138)
button (136)
click (136)
clip art (138)
clip art/image gallery (159)
command (137)
computer-aided design (CAD) software (151)
computer-based training (CBT) (160)
create (141)
custom software (134)
database (145)
database software (145)
desktop (136)
desktop publishing (DTP) software (152)
distance learning (DL) (166)
document management software (150)
edit (141)
educational software (160)
entertainment software (160)
font (141)
font size (141)
format (141)
freeware (135)
home design/ landscaping software (160)
icon (136)
image editing software (152)
legal software (157)
menu (137)
multimedia authoring software (154)
note taking software (147)
online banking (156)
online Help (164)
open source software (135)
packaged software (134)
paint software (152)
personal DTP software (158)
personal finance software (156)
personal information manager (PIM) (148)
personal paint/image editing software (158)
personal photo editing software (159)
pointer (136)
presentation graphics software (146)
print (142)
professional photo editing software (152)
project management software (149)
public-domain software (135)
reference software (160)
save (142)
shareware (135)
software suite (148)
spreadsheet software (142)
tax preparation software (157)
title bar (137)
video editing software (153)
Web page authoring software (154)
Web-based software (135)
Web-based training (165)
window (137)
word processing software (138)

Secondary Terms

(shown in italic characters in the chapter)

anti-spam program (162)
antivirus program (162)
application service provider (ASP) (164)
backup utility (162)
bar chart (144)
blog software (161)
blogware (161)
CD/DVD burner (162)
cell (143)
charting (144)
clipboard (141)
color library (152)
column chart (144)
dialog box (137)
e-learning (166)
enterprise ASP (164)
field (145)
file (137)
file compression utility (162)
file manager (162)
file name (137)
filters (153)
font style (141)
footer (140)
formula (143)
function (143)
header (140)
illustration software (152)
import (146)
label (143)
line chart (144)
loaded (135)
local/regional ASP (164)
macro (140)
margins (139)
media player (162)
page layout (152)
pasting (141)
PDF (150)
personal computer maintenance utility (162)
personal firewall (162)
pie chart (144)
point (141)
pop-up blocker (162)
product activation (135)
query (145)
record (145)
replace (139)
sans serif font (141)
scrolling (139)
search (139)
serif font (141)
slide show (146)
smart tags (140)
specialist ASP (164)
spelling checker (139)
spyware remover (162)
system software (135)
template (140, 164)
value (143)
vertical market ASP (164)
virus (162)
volume business ASP (164)
WBT (165)
Web-based Help (164)
Web application (163)
Web filter (162)
what-if analysis (144)
word processor (138)
wordwrap (139)
worksheet (142)

Checkpoint

Use the Checkpoint exercises to check your knowledge level of the chapter. The Beyond the Book exercises will help broaden your understanding of the concepts presented in this chapter. To complete the Checkpoint exercises interactively, visit scsite.com/dc2008/ch3/check.

Label the Figure

Identify these elements in the Windows Vista graphical user interface.

a. Accessories folder
b. Accessories list
c. Back command
d. All Programs list
e. Start button
f. Paint program

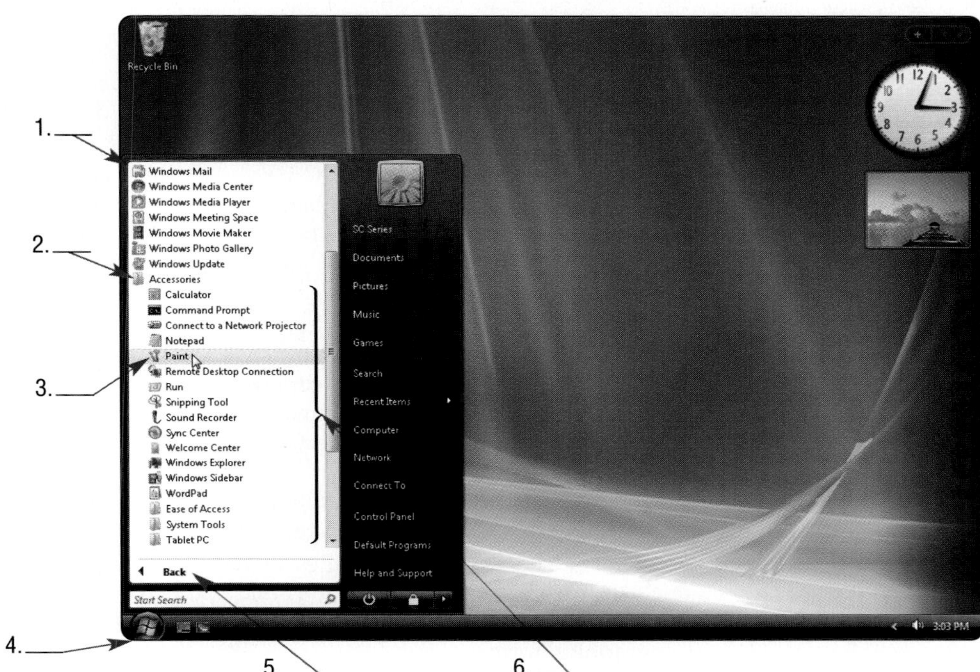

True/False

Mark T for True and F for False. (See page numbers in parentheses.)

_____ 1. The categories of application software are not mutually exclusive. (134)

_____ 2. Public-domain software is available to the public for a fee. (135)

_____ 3. To click a button on the screen requires moving the pointer away from the button and then pressing and holding down a button on the mouse (usually the right mouse button). (136)

_____ 4. A menu is an instruction that causes a program to perform a specific action. (137)

_____ 5. A font is a name assigned to a specific design of characters. (141)

_____ 6. In a spreadsheet program, a formula performs calculations and displays the resulting value in a cell. (143)

_____ 7. Professional photo editing software is a type of image editing software that allows photographers, videographers, engineers, scientists, and other high-volume digital photo users to edit and customize digital photographs. (152)

_____ 8. Legal software assists in the preparation of legal documents and provides legal information to individuals, families, and small businesses. (157)

_____ 9. Personal DTP programs never include paint/image editing software or photo editing software. (158)

_____ 10. Some communications software is considered system software because it works with hardware and transmission media. (161)

_____ 11. Antivirus programs, personal firewalls, and file managers are all examples of utility programs. (162)

_____ 12. Some Web sites require you to download software in order to run their Web applications. (163)

Checkpoint

Multiple Choice

Select the best answer. (See page numbers in parentheses.)

1. Examples of _____, which is hosted on a Web site, include e-mail, word processing, tax preparation, and game programs. (135)
   a. shareware
   b. Web-based software
   c. e-learning software
   d. public-domain software
2. In a document window, the _____ usually displays a document's file name. (137)
   a. title bar b. status bar
   c. menu d. dialog box
3. In word processing, pasting is the process of _____. (141)
   a. moving different portions of the document on the screen into view
   b. transferring an item from the clipboard to a specific location in a document
   c. locating all occurrences of a certain character, word, or phrase
   d. removing a portion of a document and storing it in a temporary storage location
4. Most spreadsheet software includes a what-if analysis feature, where you _____. (144)
   a. depict the data in a spreadsheet in graphical form
   b. enter labels to identify worksheet data and organize the worksheet
   c. change values in a spreadsheet to identify the effects of those changes
   d. review the spelling of individual words and sections of a worksheet
5. With database software, users can run a _____, which is a request for specific data from the database. (145)
   a. record b. function
   c. query d. field
6. _____ software provides a means for sharing, distributing, and searching through documents by converting them into a format that can be viewed by any user. (150)
   a. Database
   b. Document management
   c. Portable Document Format
   d. Word processing
7. _____ combines application software such as word processing, spreadsheet, database, and other programs in a single, easy-to-use package. (156)
   a. A software suite b. Shareware
   c. Packaged software d. Custom software
8. _____ helps home users determine where, and for what purpose, they are spending money. (156)
   a. Legal software
   b. Personal DTP software
   c. Personal finance software
   d. Tax preparation software
9. _____ helps home and small business users create newsletters, brochures, advertisements, postcards, greeting cards, letterhead, business cards, banners, calendars, logos, and Web pages. (158)
   a. Blogware
   b. Note taking software
   c. A personal information manager
   d. Personal DTP software
10. _____ is a collection of clip art and photographs. (159)
    a. Professional photo editing software
    b. Personal photo editing software
    c. Clip art/image gallery
    d. Entertainment software
11. A(n) _____ restricts access to specified Web sites. (162)
    a. anti-spam program
    b. antivirus program
    c. spyware remover
    d. Web filter
12. _____ allows you to view images and animation, listen to audio, and watch video files. (162)
    a. A software suite
    b. Video editing software
    c. A media player
    d. A CD/DVD burner
13. An enterprise ASP _____. (164)
    a. supplies packaged applications
    b. provides applications for a particular industry
    c. customizes and delivers high-end business applications
    d. offers a variety of software applications to specific regions
14. _____ is the delivery of education via some electronic method such as the Internet, networks, or CDs/DVDs. (166)
    a. A software wizard
    b. E-learning
    c. Online help
    d. Distance learning

Checkpoint

Matching

Match the terms with their definitions. (See page numbers in parentheses.)

_____ 1. icon (136)
_____ 2. button (136)
_____ 3. window (137)
_____ 4. clip art (138)
_____ 5. format (141)
_____ 6. cell (143)
_____ 7. database (145)
_____ 8. PDF (150)
_____ 9. virus (162)
_____ 10. volume business ASP (164)

a. popular file format used by document management software to save converted documents
b. provides prepackaged applications, such as accounting, to businesses
c. small symbol on the screen that moves as you move the mouse
d. potentially damaging computer program that affects, or infects, a computer negatively by altering the way the computer works without the user's knowledge or permission
e. collection of data organized in a manner that allows access, retrieval, and use of that data
f. collection of drawings, photographs, and other images that can be inserted
g. text that appears at the bottom of every page
h. rectangular area of the screen that displays data and information
i. graphical image activated to cause a specific action to take place
j. change the appearance of a document
k. intersection of a row and column in a spreadsheet
l. small image that represents a program, document, or some other object

Short Answer

Write a brief answer to each of the following questions.

1. What are the features of presentation graphics software? ____________ What types of media might a person use to enhance a presentation? ____________
2. What are the features of personal information manager software? ____________ Where might you find personal information manager software? ____________
3. What are disadvantages of installed software? ____________ How can you access Web-based software? ____________
4. What is Web 2.0? ____________ Describe four types of Web 2.0 sites. ____________
5. In most programs, how do you start the online Help feature? ____________ What are some of the templates included with word processing software? ____________

Beyond the Book

Read the following book elements, learn more about each using the Web, and then write a brief report.

1. Ethics & Issues — How Should Schools Deal with Internet Plagiarism? (141), Altering Digital Photographs — Art or Fraud? (153), Should Companies Monitor Employees' E-Mail and Internet Traffic? (161), Will Patents Endanger E-Learning? (166), or Copying Software — A Computer Crime! (167)
2. Career Corner — Help Desk Specialist (167)
3. Companies on the Cutting Edge — Adobe Systems or Microsoft (169)
4. FAQs (137, 142, 145, 148, 154, 157, 158, 159, 162)
5. High-Tech Talk — Computer Viruses: Delivery, Infection, and Avoidance (168)
6. Looking Ahead — Touch Drive Your Computer Screen (137) or 3-D Scans May Reduce Surgeries (164)
7. Making Use of the Web — Finance (119)
8. Picture Yourself Using Software (132)
9. Technology Trailblazers — Dan Bricklin or Masayoshi Son (169)
10. Web Links (140, 144, 146, 150, 157, 158, 160, 162, 166)

Quizzes and Learning Games
Computer Genius
Crossword Puzzle
DC Track and Field
Practice Test
Quiz Yourself
Wheel of Terms
You're Hired!

Exercises
Case Studies
Chapter Review
Checkpoint
Key Terms
Learn How To
Learn It Online
Web Research

Beyond the Book
Career Corner
Companies
FAQs
High-Tech Talk
Looking Ahead
Making Use of the Web
Trailblazers
Web Links

Features
Chapter Forum
Install Computer
Lab Exercises
Maintain Computer
Tech News
Timeline 2008

Learn It Online

Use the Learn It Online exercises to reinforce your understanding of the chapter concepts. To access the Learn It Online exercises, visit scsite.com/dc2008/ch3/learn.

1 At the Movies — Your Very Own Video Game Oracle

To view the Your Very Own Video Game Oracle movie, click the number 1 button. Locate your video and click the corresponding High-Speed or Dial-Up link, depending on your Internet connection. Watch the movie and then complete the exercise by answering the question that follows. Explore Microsoft Game Advisor, a Web site that offers free computer scans that let you know whether or not your computer can handle specific computer games. What are the basic functions of Microsoft's Game Advisor?

2 Video and Audio: You Review It — Video Editing Software

In this chapter you learned about video editing software. Click the number 2 button to view the suggested links and begin your search for videos, podcasts, or vodcasts related to video editing software. Choose a video, podcast, or vodcast that discusses video editing software and is of interest to you, and then write a description of its contents. Explain why you chose this piece, what you liked about it, what you disliked about it, and whether you would recommend it to a fellow student. Finish your review by giving the video, podcast, or vodcast a rating of 1-5 stars. Submit your review in the format requested by your instructor.

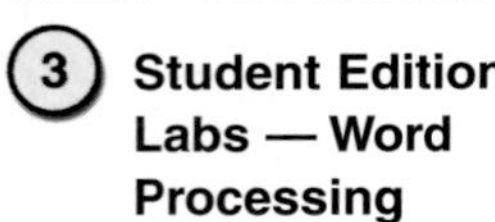

3 Student Edition Labs — Word Processing

Click the number 3 button. A new browser window will open, displaying the Student Edition Labs. Follow the on-screen instructions, and complete the Word Processing Lab. When finished, click the Exit button. If required, submit your results to your instructor.

4 Student Edition Labs — Spreadsheets

Click the number 4 button. A new browser window will open, displaying the Student Edition Labs. Follow the on-screen instructions, and complete the Spreadsheets Lab. When finished, click the Exit button. If required, submit your results to your instructor.

5 Student Edition Labs — Databases

Click the number 5 button. A new browser window will open, displaying the Student Edition Labs. Follow the on-screen instructions, and complete the Databases Lab. When finished, click the Exit button. If required, submit your results to your instructor.

6 Student Edition Labs — Presentation Software

Click the number 6 button. A new browser window will open, displaying the Student Edition Labs. Follow the on-screen instructions, and complete the Presentation Software Lab. When finished, click the Exit button. If required, submit your results to your instructor.

7 Practice Test

Click the number 7 button. Answer each question. When completed, enter your name and click the Grade Test button to submit the quiz for grading. Make a note of any missed questions. If required, submit your score to your instructor.

8 Who Wants To Be a Computer Genius^2?

Click the number 8 button to find out if you are a computer genius. Directions about how to play the game will be displayed. When you are ready to play, click the Play button. Submit your score to your instructor.

Learn It Online

9 Wheel of Terms

Click the number 9 button to reinforce important terms you learned in this chapter by playing the Shelly Cashman Series version of this popular game. Directions about how to play the game will be displayed. When you are ready to play, click the Play button. Submit your score to your instructor.

10 DC Track and Field

Click the number 10 button to use what you have learned in this chapter to compete against other students in three track and field events. Directions about how to play the game will be displayed. When you are ready to play, click the start first event button. If required, submit your score to your instructor.

11 You're Hired!

Click the number 11 button to use what you have learned in this chapter to embark on the path to a career in computers. Directions about how to play the game will be displayed. When you are ready to play, click the begin game button. If required, submit your score to your instructor.

12 Crossword Puzzle Challenge

Click the number 12 button, then click the Crossword Puzzle Challenge link. Directions about how to play the game will be displayed. Complete the puzzle to reinforce skills you learned in this chapter. When you are ready to play, click the Continue button. Submit the completed puzzle to your instructor.

13 Vista Exercises

Click the number 13 button. When the Vista Exercises menu appears, click the exercise assigned by your instructor. A new browser window will open. Follow the on-screen instructions to complete the exercise. When finished, click the Exit button. If required, submit your results to your instructor.

14 In the News

It is a computer user's worst fear — he or she opens an unfamiliar e-mail message or uses a disc of unknown origin and a computer virus is released that damages and/or deletes files. Fortunately, specialized software prevents such things from happening to your computer. Click the number 14 button and read a news article about antivirus programs. Which program does the article recommend? What does it do? Who will benefit from using this software? Why? Where can the software be obtained? Would you be interested in this software? Why or why not?

15 Chapter Discussion Forum

Select an objective from this chapter on page 133 about which you would like more information. Click the number 15 button and post a short message listing a meaningful message title accompanied by one or more questions concerning the selected objective. In two days, return to the threaded discussion by clicking the number 15 button. Submit to your instructor your original message and at least one response to your message.

16 Google Home Page

Click the number 16 button to learn how to make the Google home page your default home page. Explore the different sections of the Google home page (Images, Groups, News, Froogle, Local, and more). On the News page, use the Customize this page feature to rearrange the page and to add other sections. Print the Google News page and then step through the exercise. If required, submit your results to your instructor.

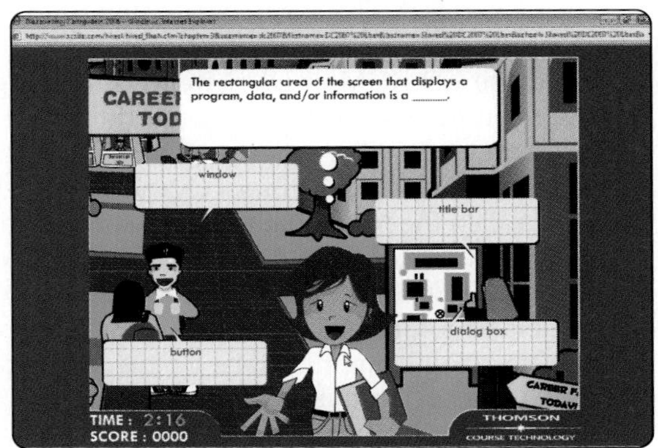

Learn How To

Use the Learn How To activities to learn fundamental skills when using a computer and accompanying technology. Complete the exercises and submit them to your instructor. To see a video of a Learn How To activity, visit scsite.com/dc2008/ch3/howto.

LEARN HOW TO 1: Save a File in Application Software

When you use application software, usually you either will create a new file or modify an existing file. If you turn off your computer or lose electrical power while working on the file, the file will not be retained. In order to retain the file, you must save it.

To save a new file, you must complete several tasks:

1. Initiate an action indicating you want to save the file, such as selecting Save from the File menu.
2. Designate where the file should be stored. This includes identifying both the device (such as drive C) and the folder (such as Documents).
3. Specify the name of the file.
4. Click the Save button to save the file.

Tasks 2 through 4 normally can be completed using a dialog box such as shown in Figure 3-46.

If you close a program prior to saving a new or modified file, the program may display a dialog box asking if you want to save the file. If you click the Yes button, a modified file will be saved using the same file name in the same location. Saving a new file requires that you complete tasks 2 through 4.

FIGURE 3-46

Exercise

1. Start the WordPad program from the Accessories list in the All Programs list.
2. Type `Saving a file is the best insurance against losing work.`
3. Click the Save button on the WordPad toolbar. What dialog box is displayed? Where will the file be saved? What is the default file name? If you wanted to save the file on the desktop, what would you do? Click the Cancel button in the dialog box. Submit your answers to your instructor.
4. Click the Close button in the WordPad window. What happened? Click the Yes button in the WordPad dialog box. What happened? Connect a USB flash drive to one of the computer's USB ports. Select the USB drive as the location for saving the file. Name the file, Chapter 3 How To 1. Save the file. What happened? Submit your answers to your instructor.

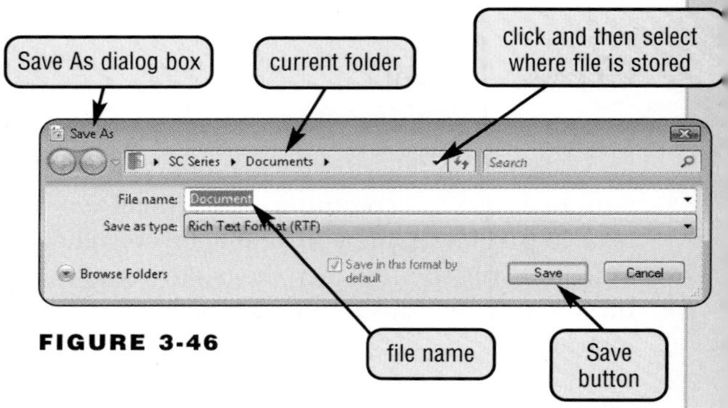

LEARN HOW TO 2: Install and Uninstall Application Software

When you purchase application software, you must install the software on the computer where you want to run it. The exact installation process varies with each program, but generally you must complete the following steps:

1. Insert the CD-ROM or DVD-ROM containing the application software into a drive.
2. The opening window will appear. If the CD-ROM or DVD-ROM contains more than one program, choose the program you want to install. Click the Continue or Next button.
3. Some file extractions will occur and then an Install Wizard will begin. You normally must accomplish the following steps by completing the directions within the wizard:
   a. Accept the terms of the license agreement.
   b. Identify where on your computer the software will be stored. The software usually selects a default location on drive C, and you normally will accept the default location.
   c. Select any default options for the software.
   d. Click a button to install the software.
4. A Welcome/Help screen often will be displayed. Click a button to finish the installation process.

Learn How To

At some point, you may want to remove software. Most software includes an uninstall program that will remove the program and all its software components. To uninstall a program, complete the following steps:

1. Click the Start button on the Windows taskbar.
2. Click Control Panel on the Start menu.
3. Click Uninstall a program to display the Uninstall or change a program window (Figure 3-47).
4. Select the program you wish to remove. In Figure 3-47, Corel Paint Shop Pro Photo XI is selected as the program to remove.
5. Click the Uninstall button.
6. A dialog box will be displayed informing you that the software is being prepared for uninstall. You then will be informed that the process you are following will remove the program. You will be asked if you want to continue. To uninstall the program, click the Yes button.

The program will be removed from the computer.

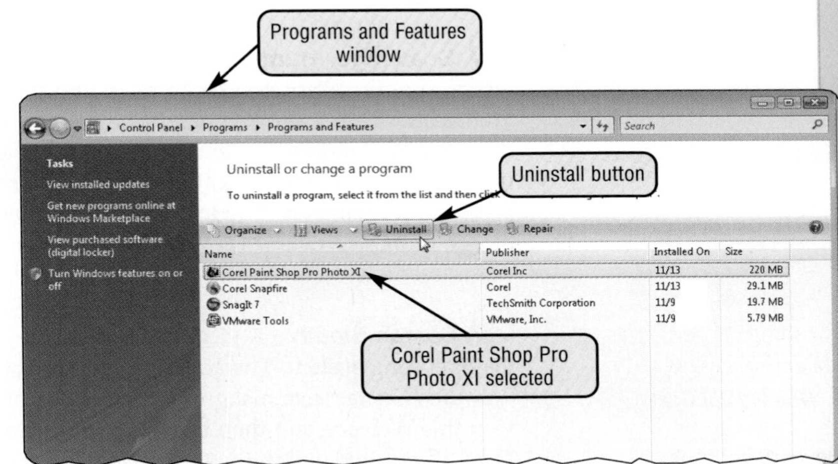

FIGURE 3-47

Exercise

1. Optional: Insert the CD-ROM or DVD-ROM containing the software you want to install into a drive and follow the instructions for installing the software. **Warning: If you are using a computer other than your own, particularly in a school laboratory, do not perform this exercise unless you have specific permission from your instructor.**
2. Optional: Follow the steps above to uninstall software you want to remove. Be aware that if you uninstall software, the software will not be available for use until you reinstall it. **Warning: If you are using a computer other than your own, particularly in a school laboratory, do not perform this exercise unless you have specific permission from your instructor.**

LEARN HOW TO 3: Check Application Software Version

Most application software will be modified from time to time by its developer. Each time the software is changed, it acquires a new version number and sometimes an entirely new name. To determine what version of software you have, perform the following steps:

1. Start the application program.
2. Click Help on the menu bar and then click About on the Help menu (the program name often follows the word, About) to open the About window (Figure 3-48).
3. To close the About window, click the OK button.

Depending on the software, in the About window you also might be able to determine further information.

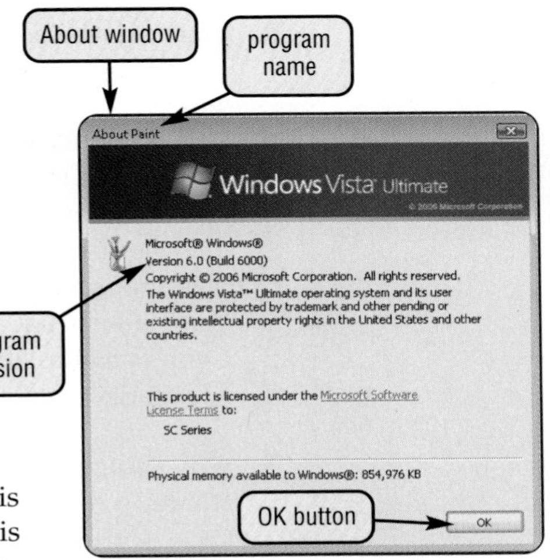

FIGURE 3-48

Exercise

1. Start your Web browser and open the About window for the browser. What is the name of the browser? What version of the browser are you using? What is the product ID? What does the copyright notice say? Submit your answers to your instructor.
2. Start any other application software. Open the About window. What is the name of the program? What is the version number? What information do you find that you did not see in Exercise 1? Which window do you find more useful? Why? Submit your answers to your instructor.

Quizzes and Learning Games
Computer Genius
Crossword Puzzle
DC Track and Field
Practice Test
Quiz Yourself
Wheel of Terms
You're Hired!

Exercises
Case Studies
Chapter Review
Checkpoint
Key Terms
Learn How To
Learn It Online
Web Research

Beyond the Book
Career Corner
Companies
FAQs
High-Tech Talk
Looking Ahead
Making Use of the Web
Trailblazers
Web Links

Features
Chapter Forum
Install Computer
Lab Exercises
Maintain Computer
Tech News
Timeline 2008

Web Research

Use the Internet-based Web Research exercises to broaden your understanding of the concepts presented in this chapter. Visit scsite.com/dc2008/ch3/research to obtain more information pertaining to each exercise. To discuss any of the Web Research exercises in this chapter with other students, post your thoughts or questions at scsite.com/dc2008/ch3/forum.

1 **Scavenger Hunt** Use one of the search engines listed in Figure 2-10 in Chapter 2 on page 78 or your own favorite search engine to find the answers to the questions below. Copy and paste the Web address from the Web page where you found the answer. Some questions may have more than one answer. If required, submit your answers to your instructor. (1) What are some new features in the latest edition of Microsoft Streets and Trips? (2) What was the inspiration for the Pac-Man computer game character? (3) How did Ivan Sutherland influence the development of computer-aided design (CAD) software? (4) What Web site features software that creates a game requiring a player to put numbers in nine rows of nine boxes?

2 **Search Sleuth** A virus is a potentially damaging computer program that can harm files and the operating system. The National Institute of Standards and Technology Computer Security Resource Center (csrc.nist.gov/virus/) is one of the more comprehensive Web sites discussing viruses. Visit this Web site and then use your word processing program to answer the following questions. Then, if required, submit your answers to your instructor. (1) The Virus Information page provides general information about viruses and links to various resources that provide more specific details. What two steps does the National Institute recommend to detect and prevent viruses from spreading? (2) Click the Computer Associates' Virus Information Center link in the Virus Resources & Other Areas of Interest section. What viruses are listed in the Top 5 Virus Threats section? (3) Click the link of a Top 5 threat and read the summary information. According to the Method of Distribution section, how does this virus spread? (4) Type `bots` as the keyword in the Search text box at the top of the page. Click the first results link that answers this question: What is a bot, and what does it do? Review the information you read and then write a 50-word summary.

3 **Journaling** Respond to your readings in this chapter by writing at least one page about your reactions, evaluations, and reflections about the first time you used home, personal, and educational software. For example, do you use software to balance your checkbook, share photos, or play computer games? Which programs do you use most? How do your favorite programs make it easier or more enjoyable for you to perform personal tasks? You also can write about the new terms you learned by reading this chapter. If required, submit your journal to your instructor.

4 **Expanding Your Understanding** Microsoft seeks to help customers use its products by maintaining the Microsoft Help and Support Web site (support.microsoft.com). This Web site has a link to the Knowledge Base, which contains more than 250,000 articles written by Microsoft employees who support the company's products. Also included are software downloads and updates, public newsgroups, methods of getting online or telephone assistance, and the Security Support Center. View this site and then search the Knowledge Base for information on Microsoft Word. Also view the common issues, updates, security issues, and visitors' top links listed on the Web site. Write a report summarizing your findings. If required, submit your report to your instructor.

5 **Ethics in Action** A hacker is someone who tries to access a computer or network illegally. Although the activity sometimes is a harmless prank, it sometimes causes extensive damage. Some hackers say their activities give them a sense of excitement and test their skills. Others say their activities are a form of civil disobedience that allows them to challenge authority and force companies to make their products more secure. View online sites such as Hackers: Outlaws & Angels (tlc.discovery.com/convergence/hackers/hackers.html) that provide information about whether hackers provide some benefit to the Internet society. Write a report summarizing your findings and include a table of links to Web sites that provide additional details. If required, submit your report to your instructor.

Case Studies

Use the Case Studies to apply the concepts presented in the chapter to real-world situations. Visit scsite.com/dc2008/ch3/cases to obtain more information pertaining to each exercise. To discuss the Case Studies in this chapter with other students, visit scsite.com/dc2008/ch3/forum and post your thoughts or questions.

CASE STUDY 1 – Class Discussion The owner of Mel's Hair Salon for Men and Women has decided to obtain a personal desktop computer for use in his business. In addition to using the computer for writing letters, developing advertising pieces, performing basic accounting, and maintaining lists of customers, the owner would like his employees to use a digital camera to take pictures of customers after they have had their hair done and create a file of printed full-color pictures of customers for marketing purposes. The owner has asked you to recommend the type of camera, software, and computer he should buy. Prepare a brief report detailing your findings and recommendations. Be prepared to discuss your recommendations in class.

CASE STUDY 2 – Class Discussion Your manager at Dave's Office Supply Outlet intends to choose a spreadsheet program that the entire company will use. He prefers to learn about software using trade books — written texts that explain the features of a program and how to use it — rather than using online Help or tutorials. He has asked you to evaluate the spreadsheet trade books available in bookstores on the Web. Visit a bookstore Web site and other Web sites that sell books to survey the spreadsheet trade books available for Microsoft Excel, Lotus, Quattro Pro, and StarOffice Calc. Which spreadsheet program has the most books available? How difficult would it be to learn each program using the trade books at hand? Which trade book do you think is the best? Why? If you were going to purchase software solely on the basis of the related trade books, which program would you buy? Why? Be prepared to discuss your recommendations in class.

CASE STUDY 3 – Research Karl's Game Den sells new and used computer and video games. Karl recently purchased a large quantity of children's games; however, they are not selling as he expected. You recently read that 62 percent of entertainment software purchases are made by males, and the average age of frequent purchasers is 40. You suggest that Karl may be selling to the wrong demographic. Karl has asked you to investigate what type of games and how many games he should stock. Use the Web and/or print media to determine the top five selling games in the United States. Prepare a brief report that includes your list and answers the following questions. Do males and females favor different types of software? If so, should software developers adapt their products? Why or why not? Is it important to modify educational/entertainment software to meet the interests of different groups? Why?

CASE STUDY 4 – Research Frank's Custom Design frequently enhances its work with scanned photographs or graphics obtained with illustration software. The owner recently read that the Internet is providing a new resource for desktop publishers. Companies such as Corbis, Picture Network International, Muse, and Liaison International are offering archives of artwork and photographs. You have been asked to investigate the feasibility of using this new resource. Information about all four companies can be found on the World Wide Web. Pick two companies that provide digital images and find out more about their product. Prepare a brief report that answers the following questions. What kinds of illustrations are available? How are pictures on a specific subject located? How are the illustrations provided? What fees are involved? Would the cost be different for a high school student creating one paper than for an organization newsletter with a statewide distribution? Which company do you prefer? Why?

CASE STUDY 5 – Team Challenge The new superintendent of Lisle Elementary School District 205 has recommended that educational software play a major role in the learning process at every grade level. In her presentation to the school board, she claimed that educational software is available for a wide variety of skills and subjects. She also indicated that educational software lets students learn at their own pace, shows infinite patience, and usually offers an entertaining approach. The president of the school board is not so sure. Unlike human instructors, educational software often does not recognize unique problems, fails to address individual goals, and provides limited feedback. Form a three-member team and investigate the use of educational software. Have each member of your team visit a software vendor's Web site, or an educational cooperative's Web site and list the advantages and disadvantages of using educational software. Select a program on the Web or from your school's education department library and use it. Note the subject being taught, the audience to which the software is directed, the approach used, and any special features. Then, meet with your team, discuss your findings, prepare a team report or PowerPoint presentation, and share it with your class.

CHAPTER FOUR

The Components of the System Unit

Picture Yourself Computer Shopping

In the months since paying off your car, you have been saving up for your next large purchase — a personal computer. Your school offers a student discount for computers purchased online, so you hope to realize some savings from that. You have talked to several knowledgeable friends and coworkers about what you need and want in a computer. Armed with this knowledge and your wish list, you are ready to shop.

After visiting several computer vendors' Web sites and comparing prices and features, you finally decide on a model. Because you enjoy computer gaming, you opt for a high-performance video card. You also are staff photographer for your school's newspaper, so you want to have the necessary storage to work with digital photographs. The model you have chosen has an Intel Core 2 Duo processor, 4 GB of dual-channel DDR2 SDRAM, and a 500 GB SATA hard drive. With a DVI port, eight USB 2.0 ports, two FireWire ports, built-in card readers, a headphone jack, speakers, a network card, and a CD/DVD drive, it should more than meet your needs. The computer's preloaded software includes the Microsoft Windows Vista operating system. You are delighted to see that the vendor is offering an online promotion of free shipping and a free upgrade to a flat-panel display. You submit your order and look forward to it being delivered right to your door.

By buying online, you have a computer customized to your needs, but you also know you have much to learn. Read Chapter 4 to learn about drives, adapter cards, processors, ports, RAM, and other components of the system unit.

OBJECTIVES

After completing this chapter, you will be able to:

1. Differentiate among various styles of system units
2. Identify chips, adapter cards, and other components of a motherboard
3. Describe the components of a processor and how they complete a machine cycle
4. Identify characteristics of various personal computer processors on the market today
5. Define a bit and describe how a series of bits represents data
6. Explain how programs transfer in and out of memory
7. Differentiate among the various types of memory
8. Describe the types of expansion slots and adapter cards
9. Explain the differences among a serial port, a parallel port, a USB port, a FireWire port, and other ports
10. Describe how buses contribute to a computer's processing speed
11. Identify components in mobile computers and mobile devices
12. Understand how to clean a system unit

CONTENTS

THE SYSTEM UNIT

Whether you are a home user or a business user, you most likely will make the decision to purchase a new computer or upgrade an existing computer within the next several years. Thus, you should understand the purpose of each component in a computer. As Chapter 1 discussed, a computer includes devices used for input, processing, output, storage, and communications. Many of these components are part of the system unit.

The **system unit** is a case that contains electronic components of the computer used to process data. System units are available in a variety of shapes and sizes. The case of the system unit, sometimes called the *chassis*, is made of metal or plastic and protects the internal electronic components from damage. All computers have a system unit (Figure 4-1).

On desktop personal computers, the electronic components and most storage devices are part of the system unit. Other devices, such as the keyboard, mouse, microphone, monitor, printer, USB flash drive, portable media player, scanner, PC video camera, and speakers, normally occupy space outside the system unit. The trend is toward a smaller *form factor*, or size and shape, of the desktop personal computer system unit.

FIGURE 4-1 All sizes of computers have a system unit.

On notebook computers, the keyboard and pointing device often occupy the area on the top of the system unit, and the display attaches to the system unit by hinges. The location of the system unit on a Tablet PC varies, depending on the design of the Tablet PC. Some models build the system unit behind the display (as shown in Figure 4-1), while others position the system unit below the keyboard (shown later in the chapter). The system unit on an ultra personal computer, a PDA, and a smart phone usually consumes the entire device. On these mobile computers and devices, the display often is built into the system unit.

With game consoles, the input and output devices, such as controllers and a television, reside outside the system unit. On handheld game consoles and portable media players, by contrast, the packaging around the system unit houses the input devices and display.

At some point, you might have to open the system unit on a desktop personal computer to replace or install a new electronic component. For this reason, you should be familiar with the electronic components of a system unit. Figure 4-2 identifies some of these components, which include the processor, memory, adapter cards, drive bays, and the power supply.

The processor interprets and carries out the basic instructions that operate a computer. Memory typically holds data waiting to be processed and instructions waiting to be executed. The electronic components and circuitry of the system unit, such as the processor and memory, usually are part of or are connected to a circuit board called the motherboard. Many current motherboards also integrate sound, video, modem, and networking capabilities.

FIGURE 4-2 The system unit on a typical personal computer consists of numerous electronic components, some of which are shown in this figure. The sound card and video card are two types of adapter cards.

Adapter cards are circuit boards that provide connections and functions not built into the motherboard or expand on the capability of features integrated into the motherboard. For example, a sound card and a video card are two types of adapter cards found in some desktop personal computers today. Devices outside the system unit often attach to ports on the system unit by a connector on a cable. These devices may include a keyboard, mouse, microphone, monitor, printer, scanner, portable media player, USB flash drive, card reader/writer, digital camera, PC video camera, and speakers. A drive bay holds one or more disk drives. The power supply converts electricity from a power cord plugged in a wall outlet into a form that can be used by the computer.

WEB LINK 4-1

Motherboards

For more information, visit scsite.com/dc2008/ch4/weblink and then click Motherboards.

The Motherboard

The **motherboard**, sometimes called a *system board*, is the main circuit board of the system unit. Many electronic components attach to the motherboard; others are built into it. Figure 4-3 shows a photograph of a current desktop personal computer motherboard and identifies its expansion slots, processor chip, and memory slots. Memory chips are installed on memory cards (modules) that fit in a slot on the motherboard.

A computer **chip** is a small piece of semiconducting material, usually silicon, on which integrated circuits are etched. An *integrated circuit* contains many microscopic pathways capable of carrying electrical current. Each integrated circuit can contain millions of elements such as resistors, capacitors, and transistors. A *transistor*, for example, can act as an electronic switch that opens or closes the circuit for electrical charges. Most chips are no bigger than one-half-inch square. Manufacturers package chips so the chips can be attached to a circuit board, such as a motherboard or an adapter card. Specific types of chips are discussed later in the chapter.

FIGURE 4-3 Many electronic components attach to the motherboard in a desktop personal computer, including a processor chip, memory modules, and adapter cards.

PROCESSOR

The **processor**, also called the **central processing unit** (**CPU**), interprets and carries out the basic instructions that operate a computer. The processor significantly impacts overall computing power and manages most of a computer's operations. On larger computers, such as mainframes and supercomputers, the various functions performed by the processor extend over many separate chips and often multiple circuit boards. On a personal computer, all functions of the processor usually are on a single chip. Some computer and chip manufacturers use the term *microprocessor* to refer to a personal computer processor chip.

Processors contain a control unit and an arithmetic logic unit (ALU). These two components work together to perform processing operations. Figure 4-4 illustrates how other devices connected to the computer communicate with the processor to carry out a task.

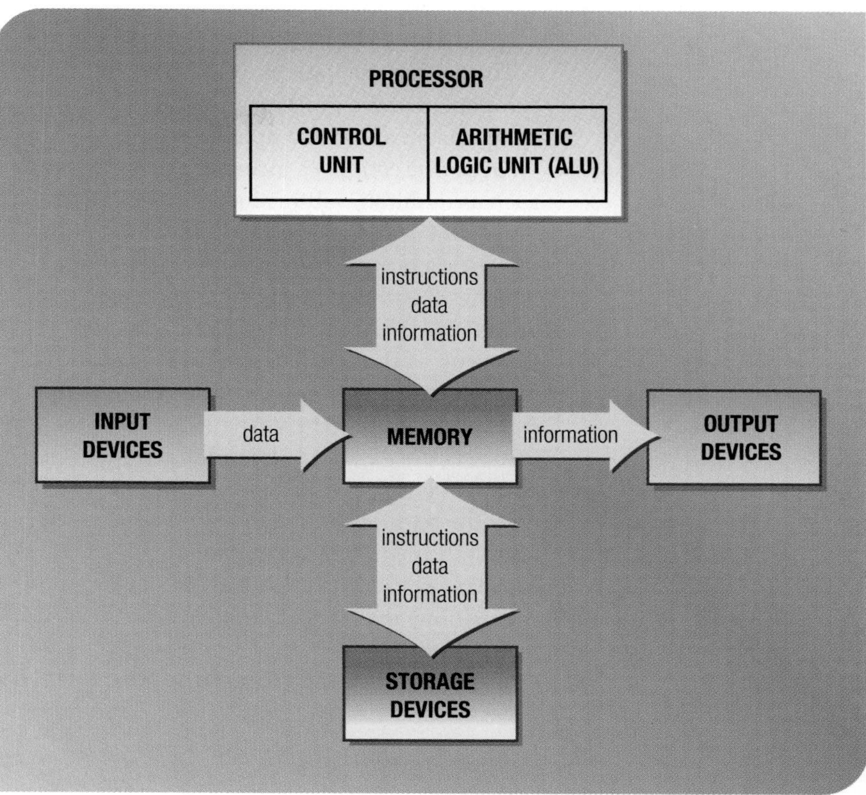

FIGURE 4-4 Most devices connected to the computer communicate with the processor to carry out a task. When a user starts a program, for example, its instructions transfer from a storage device to memory. Data needed by programs enters memory from either an input device or a storage device. The control unit interprets and executes instructions in memory, and the ALU performs calculations on the data in memory. Resulting information is stored in memory, from which it can be sent to an output device or a storage device for future access, as needed.

The Control Unit

The **control unit** is the component of the processor that directs and coordinates most of the operations in the computer. The control unit has a role much like a traffic cop: it interprets each instruction issued by a program and then initiates the appropriate action to carry out the instruction. Types of internal components that the control unit directs include the arithmetic/logic unit, registers, and buses, each discussed later in this chapter. Read Ethics & Issues 4-1 for a related discussion.

ETHICS & ISSUES 4-1

Can Computers Think?

Since the dawn of the computing age, people have wondered if a computer ever would be capable of thought. As computer processors and software become more powerful, the question is more hotly debated. People who believe computers can think argue that, if a person had a conversation with a computer and was convinced the computer was really human, then the computer is intelligent. This criteria is known as the Turing Test, named after British mathematician Alan Turing who proposed the test in 1950. If a computer can pass a modern version of the Turing Test, it is considered to be intelligent, and it may win the prestigious $100,000 Loebner Prize. Opponents counter this argument by saying that, if a question written in a foreign language was submitted to a person who can read and write the language and a person who cannot read or write the language but has a list of questions and appropriate answers, it might be impossible to tell the response of one person from the other. But, the person who cannot read or write the language really does not understand it, any more than a computer really can think. Besides, computers lack at least two essential components of human thinking — common sense and emotion. Computers can consider millions of chess moves a second, but humans have the common sense to recognize that some moves are not worthy of consideration. Can computers think? Why or why not? If computers cannot think now, might they be able to think in the future? Why? How important is emotion in the ability to think?

The Arithmetic Logic Unit

The **arithmetic logic unit** (*ALU*), another component of the processor, performs arithmetic, comparison, and other operations.

Arithmetic operations include basic calculations such as addition, subtraction, multiplication, and division. *Comparison operations* involve comparing one data item with another to determine whether the first item is greater than, equal to, or less than the other item. Depending on the result of the comparison, different actions may occur. For example, to determine if an employee should receive overtime pay, software instructs the ALU to compare the number of hours an employee worked during the week with the regular time hours allowed (e.g., 40 hours). If the hours worked are greater than 40, software instructs the ALU to perform calculations that compute the overtime wage.

Machine Cycle

For every instruction, a processor repeats a set of four basic operations, which comprise a *machine cycle* (Figure 4-5): (1) fetching, (2) decoding, (3) executing, and, if necessary, (4) storing. *Fetching* is the process of obtaining a program instruction or data item from memory. The term *decoding* refers to the process of translating the instruction into signals the computer can execute. *Executing* is the process of carrying out the commands. *Storing*, in this context, means writing the result to memory (not to a storage medium).

In some computers, the processor fetches, decodes, executes, and stores only one instruction at a time. In these computers, the processor waits until an instruction completes all four stages of the machine cycle (fetch, decode, execute, and store) before beginning work on the next instruction.

FIGURE 4-5 THE STEPS IN A MACHINE CYCLE

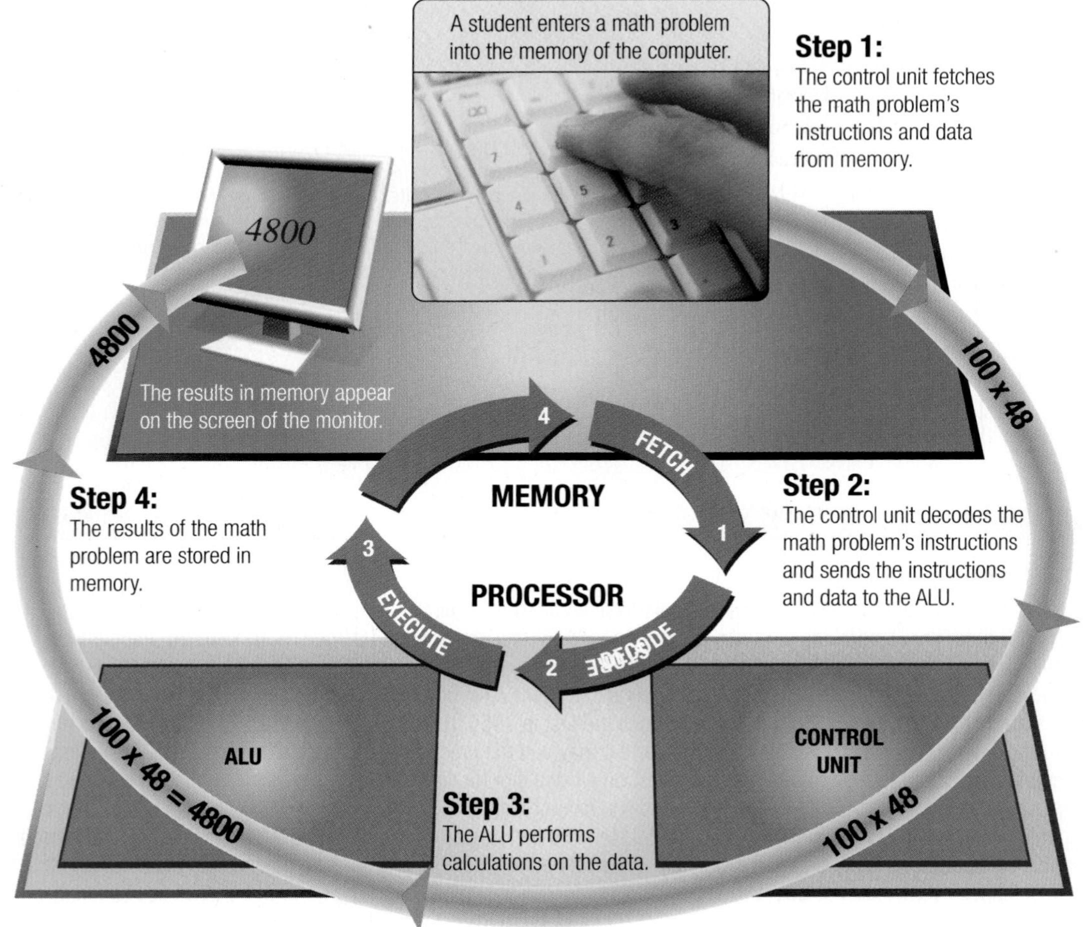

A student enters a math problem into the memory of the computer.
Step 1:
The control unit fetches the math problem's instructions and data from memory.
4800
4800
The results in memory appear on the screen of the monitor.
100 x 48
4
FETCH
1
MEMORY
PROCESSOR
3
EXECUTE
2
DECODE
STORE
Step 2:
The control unit decodes the math problem's instructions and sends the instructions and data to the ALU.
Step 4:
The results of the math problem are stored in memory.
ALU
CONTROL UNIT
100 x 48 = 4800
100 x 48
Step 3:
The ALU performs calculations on the data.

Most of today's personal computers support a concept called pipelining. With *pipelining*, the processor begins fetching a second instruction before it completes the machine cycle for the first instruction. Processors that use pipelining are faster because they do not have to wait for one instruction to complete the machine cycle before fetching the next. Think of a pipeline as an assembly line. By the time the first instruction is in the last stage of the machine cycle, three other instructions could have been fetched and started through the machine cycle (Figure 4-6).

MACHINE CYCLE (without pipelining):

MACHINE CYCLE (with pipelining):

FETCH DECODE EXECUTE STORE

INSTRUCTION 1

INSTRUCTION 2

INSTRUCTION 3

INSTRUCTION 4

FIGURE 4-6 Most modern personal computers support pipelining. With pipelining, the processor fetches a second instruction before the first instruction is completed. The result is faster processing.

Registers

A processor contains small, high-speed storage locations, called *registers*, that temporarily hold data and instructions. Registers are part of the processor, not part of memory or a permanent storage device. Processors have many different types of registers, each with a specific storage function. Register functions include storing the location from where an instruction was fetched, storing an instruction while the control unit decodes it, storing data while the ALU computes it, and storing the results of a calculation.

The System Clock

The processor relies on a small quartz crystal circuit called the **system clock** to control the timing of all computer operations. Just as your heart beats at a regular rate to keep your body functioning, the system clock generates regular electronic pulses, or ticks, that set the operating pace of components of the system unit.

Each tick equates to a *clock cycle*. In the past, processors used one or more clock cycles to execute each instruction. Processors today often are *superscalar*, which means they can execute more than one instruction per clock cycle.

The pace of the system clock, called the **clock speed**, is measured by the number of ticks per second. Current personal computer processors have clock speeds in the gigahertz range. Giga is a prefix that stands for billion, and a *hertz* is one cycle per second. Thus, one **gigahertz (GHz)** equals one billion ticks of the system clock per second. A computer that operates at 2.6 GHz has 2.6 billion (giga) clock cycles in one second (hertz).

The faster the clock speed, the more instructions the processor can execute per second. The speed of the system clock has no effect on devices such as a printer or disk drive. The speed of the system clock is just one factor that influences a computer's performance. Other factors, such as the type of processor chip, amount of cache, memory access time, bus width, and bus clock speed, are discussed later in this chapter.

FAQ 4-1

Does the system clock also keep track of the current date and time?

No, a separate battery-backed chip, called the *real-time clock*, keeps track of the date and time in a computer. The battery continues to run the real-time clock even when the computer is off. For more information, visit scsite.com/dc2008/ch4/faq and then click Computer Clock.

Some computer professionals measure a processor's speed according to the number of *MIPS* (*millions of instructions per second*) it can process. Current desktop personal computers can process more than 27,000 MIPS. No real standard for measuring MIPS exists, however, because different instructions require varying amounts of processing time. Read Looking Ahead 4-1 for a look at the next generation of processing speeds.

LOOKING AHEAD 4-1

Hybrid Technology to Power Supercomputer

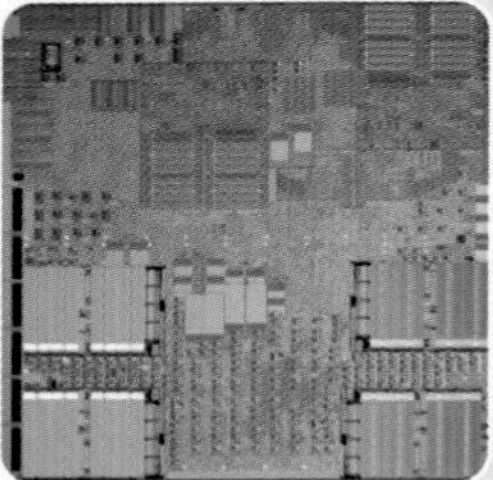

In the race to build the world's fastest, more powerful computers, IBM is using a combination of processors to power a supercomputer that can process 1 quadrillion calculations per second.

IBM's *Roadrunner* supercomputer features a hybrid design that pairs conventional supercomputer processors with processors designed for Sony's PlayStation 3 and uses commercially available IBM hardware. The supercomputer's more than 16,000 AMD Opteron processors and more than 16,000 processors communicate continuously with each other to handle complex calculations with large numbers of constantly changing, interacting variables, such as those required for weather simulations.

When completed in 2008, the supercomputer will occupy 12,000 square feet at the Los Alamos National Laboratory. Roadrunner was designed in 2006 to reach four times the computing speed of the U.S. government's then fastest machine, IBM's Blue Gene, housed at the Lawrence Livermore National Laboratory.

For more information, visit scsite.com/dc2008/ch4/looking and then click Hybrid Supercomputer.

Dual-Core and Multi-Core Processors

Several processor chip manufacturers now offer dual-core and multi-core processors. A **dual-core processor** is a single chip that contains two separate processors. Similarly, a **multi-core processor** is a chip with two or more separate processors. Each processor on a dual-core/multi-core chip generally runs at a slower clock speed than a single-core processor, but dual-core/multi-core chips typically increase overall performance. Although a dual-core processor does not double the processing speed of a single-core processor, it can approach those speeds. The performance increase is especially noticeable when users are running multiple programs simultaneously such as antivirus software, spyware remover, e-mail program, instant messaging, media player, CD burning software, and photo editing software. Dual-core and multi-core processors also are energy efficient, requiring lower levels of power consumption and emitting less heat in the system unit.

WEB LINK 4-2

Multi-Core Processors

For more information, visit scsite.com/dc2008/ch4/weblink and then click Multi-Core Processors.

Comparison of Personal Computer Processors

The leading processor chip manufacturers for personal computers are Intel, AMD (Advanced Micro Devices), Transmeta, IBM, and Motorola. These manufacturers often identify their processor chips by a model name or model number. Figure 4-7 categorizes the historical development of the personal computer processor and documents the increases in clock speed and number of transistors in chips since 1982. The greater the number of transistors, the more complex and powerful the chip.

With its earlier processors, Intel used a model number to identify the various chips. After learning that processor model numbers could not be trademarked and protected from use by competitors, Intel began identifying its processors with names. Most high-performance PCs today use a processor in the Intel **Core** family or the **Pentium** family. Less expensive, basic PCs use a brand of Intel processor in the **Celeron** family. The **Xeon** and **Itanium** families of processors are ideal for workstations and low-end servers.

Today, AMD is the leading manufacturer of *Intel-compatible processors*, which have an internal design similar to Intel processors, perform the same functions, and can be as powerful, but often are less expensive. Transmeta, also a manufacturer of Intel-compatible processors, specializes in processors for mobile computers and devices. Intel and Intel-compatible processors are used in PCs.

Until recently, Apple computers used only an *IBM processor* or a *Motorola processor*, which had a design different from the Intel-style processor. Today's Apple computers, however, use Intel processors.

In the past, chip manufacturers listed a processor's clock speed in marketing literature and advertisements. As previously mentioned, though, clock speed is only one factor that impacts processing speed in today's computers. To help consumers evaluate various processors, manufacturers such as Intel and AMD now use a numbering scheme that more accurately reflects the processing speed of their chips.

Processor chips include technologies to improve processing performance. For example, many processors today use dual-core or multi-core chips. Some of Intel's processor chips contain *Hyper-Threading* (*HT*) *Technology*, which improves

COMPARISON OF PERSONAL COMPUTER PROCESSORS

* Clock speed is not the only factor that determines processor performance.

	NAME	DATE INTRODUCED/ UPDATED	MANUFACTURER	CLOCK SPEED*	NUMBER OF TRANSISTORS
SERVER PROCESSORS	**Xeon**	2001/2006	Intel	1.4 – 3.73 GHz	42 – 169 million
	Itanium 2	2003/2006	Intel	1.3 – 1.66 GHz	220 – 410 million
	Itanium	2001	Intel	733 – 800 MHz	25.4 – 60 million
	Pentium III Xeon	1999/2000	Intel	500 – 900 MHz	9.5 – 28 million
	Pentium II Xeon	1998/1999	Intel	400 – 450 MHz	7.5 – 27 million
	Opteron	2003/2006	AMD	1.4 – 3 GHz	233 million
	Athlon MP	2002	AMD	1.53 – 2.25 GHz	54.3 million
DESKTOP PERSONAL COMPUTER PROCESSORS	**Core 2 Extreme**	2006	Intel	2.93 GHz	291 million
	Core 2 Duo	2006	Intel	1.86 – 2.66 GHz	291 million
	Pentium Extreme Edition	2005/2006	Intel	3.2 – 3.73 GHz	178 million
	Pentium D	2005/2006	Intel	2.66 – 3.6 GHz	376 million
	Pentium 4	2000/2005	Intel	1.3 – 3.8 GHz	42 – 178 million
	Pentium III	1999/2003	Intel	450 MHz – 1.4 GHz	9.5 – 44 million
	Celeron D	2004/2006	Intel	2.13 – 3.46 GHz	26.2 – 125 million
	Celeron	1998/2003	Intel	266 MHz – 2.8 GHz	7.5 – 55 million
	Pentium II	1997/1998	Intel	233 – 450 MHz	7.5 million
	Pentium Pro	1995/1999	Intel	150 – 200 MHz	5.5 million
	Pentium	1993/1997	Intel	75 – 233 MHz	3.3 – 4.5 million
	80486DX	1989/1994	Intel	25 – 100 MHz	1.6 million
	80386	1985/1990	Intel	16 – 33 MHz	275,000
	80286	1982	Intel	6 – 12 MHz	134,000
	Athlon 64 FX/X2	2005	AMD	2 – 2.8 GHz	114 – 233 million
	Sempron	2004	AMD	1.5 – 2 GHz	68.5 million
	Athlon 64	2003/2004	AMD	2 – 2.4 GHz	105.9 – 114 million
	Athlon	1999/2002	AMD	500 MHz – 1.4 GHz	22 – 38 million
	Duron	1999/2001	AMD	600 MHz – 1.3 GHz	25 million
	AMD–K6	1997/1999	AMD	300 – 450 MHz	8.8 – 21.3 million
	PowerPC (G1 to G5)	1994/2005	Motorola/IBM	60 MHz – 2.7 GHz	2.8 – 58 million
	68040	1989	Motorola	25 – 40 MHz	1.2 million
	68030	1987	Motorola	16 – 50 MHz	270,000
	68020	1984	Motorola	16 – 33 MHz	190,000
MOBILE PROCESSORS	**Core 2 Duo**	2006	Intel	1.66 – 2.33 GHz	291 million
	Core Duo	2006	Intel	1.20 – 2.33 GHz	151 million
	Core Solo	2006	Intel	1.06 – 1.83 GHz	151 million
	Celeron M	2004	Intel	900 MHz – 1.6 GHz	55 million
	Pentium M	2003/2004	Intel	1.10 – 2 GHz	77 – 140 million
	Mobile Celeron	1999/2003	Intel	266 MHz – 2.8 GHz	18.9 million
	Mobile Pentium 4	1997/2002	Intel	200 MHz – 3.46 GHz	55 million
	Turion 64	2005	AMD	1.6 – 2 GHz	114 million
	Mobile Sempron	2004	AMD	1.6 – 1.8 GHz	37.5 million
	Mobile Athlon	2001/2002	AMD	1.4 – 2.2 GHz	37.5 – 105.9 million
	Mobile Duron	2000/2001	AMD	1.3 GHz	25 million
	Efficeon	2003	Transmeta	1 – 1.7 GHz	79 million
	Crusoe	2000	Transmeta	500 MHz – 1 GHz	6.7 million

FIGURE 4-7 A comparison of some processors.

processing power and time by allowing a processor to mimic the power of two processors. Most processors have built-in instructions to improve the performance of multimedia and 3-D graphics.

Processors for notebook computers include technology to integrate wireless capabilities and optimize and extend battery life. For example, Intel's *Centrino* and *Centrino Duo* mobile technology integrates wireless capabilities in notebook computers and Tablet PCs. PDAs and other smaller mobile devices often use a processor that consumes less power yet offers high performance.

Another type of processor, called *system on a chip*, integrates the functions of a processor, memory, and a video card on a single chip. Lower-priced personal computers, Tablet PCs, networking devices, portable media players, and game consoles sometimes have a system-on-a-chip processor. The goal of system-on-a-chip manufacturers is to create processors that have faster clock speeds, consume less power, are small, and are cost effective.

Buying a Personal Computer

If you are ready to buy a new computer, the processor you select should depend on how you plan to use the computer. If you purchase an IBM-compatible PC or Apple computer, you will choose an Intel processor or, in some cases, an Intel-compatible processor (Figure 4-8).

Most users will realize greater processing performance with a dual-core/multi-core processor. Intel's dual-core and multi-core processors also include *vPro technology*, which provides the ability to track computer hardware and software, diagnose and resolve computer problems, and secure computers from outside threats. If you plan to purchase an entertainment desktop computer, you will want it to use Intel's *Viiv technology*, which is designed to enhance digital entertainment through a home computer.

Instead of buying an entirely new computer, you might be able to upgrade your processor to increase the computer's performance. Be certain the processor you buy is compatible with your computer's motherboard; otherwise, you will have to replace the motherboard, too. Replacing a processor is a fairly simple process, whereas replacing a motherboard is much more complicated.

For detailed computer purchasing guidelines, read the Buyer's Guide 2008 feature that follows Chapter 8. Read Ethics & Issues 4-2 for a related discussion.

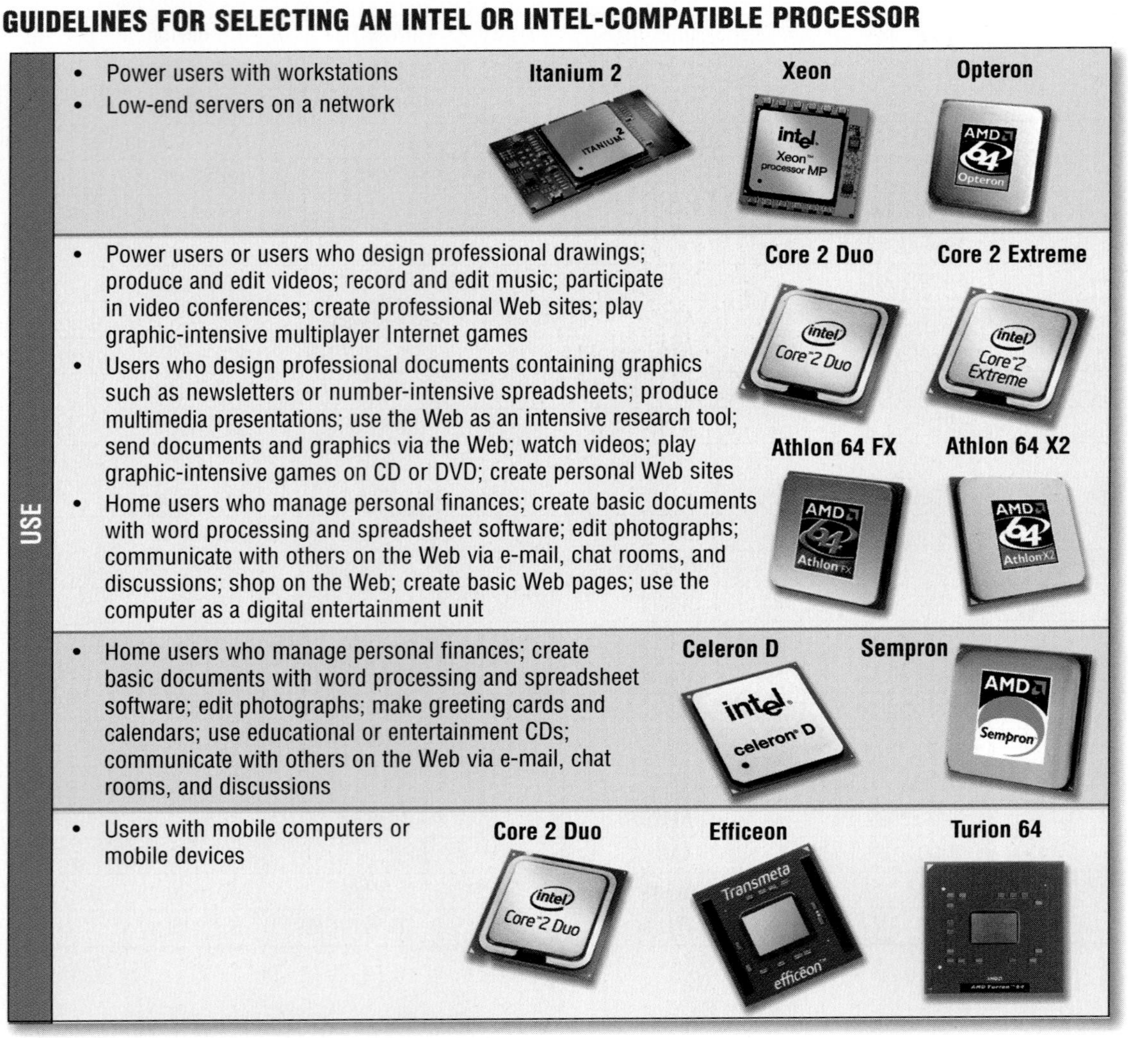

GUIDELINES FOR SELECTING AN INTEL OR INTEL-COMPATIBLE PROCESSOR

USE	Processors
• Power users with workstations • Low-end servers on a network	Itanium 2, Xeon, Opteron
• Power users or users who design professional drawings; produce and edit videos; record and edit music; participate in video conferences; create professional Web sites; play graphic-intensive multiplayer Internet games • Users who design professional documents containing graphics such as newsletters or number-intensive spreadsheets; produce multimedia presentations; use the Web as an intensive research tool; send documents and graphics via the Web; watch videos; play graphic-intensive games on CD or DVD; create personal Web sites • Home users who manage personal finances; create basic documents with word processing and spreadsheet software; edit photographs; communicate with others on the Web via e-mail, chat rooms, and discussions; shop on the Web; create basic Web pages; use the computer as a digital entertainment unit	Core 2 Duo, Core 2 Extreme, Athlon 64 FX, Athlon 64 X2
• Home users who manage personal finances; create basic documents with word processing and spreadsheet software; edit photographs; make greeting cards and calendars; use educational or entertainment CDs; communicate with others on the Web via e-mail, chat rooms, and discussions	Celeron D, Sempron
• Users with mobile computers or mobile devices	Core 2 Duo, Efficeon, Turion 64

FIGURE 4-8 Determining which processor to obtain when you purchase a computer depends on computer usage.

FAQ 4-2

What is Moore's Law?

Moore's Law is a prediction made by one of the founders of Intel, Gordon Moore, that the number of transistors and resistors placed on computer chips would double every year, with a proportional increase in computing power and decrease in cost. The chart below shows the growth of Intel processors. For more information, read the Technology Trailblazer article on page 219 and visit scsite.com/dc2008/ch4/faq and then click Moore's Law.

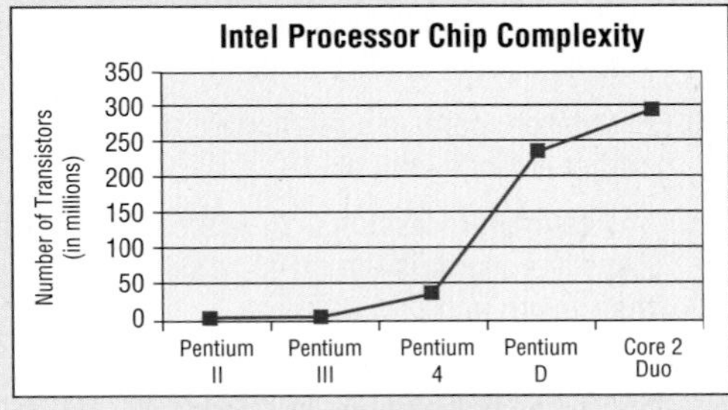

ETHICS & ISSUES 4-2

Discarded Computer Components: Whose Problem Is It?

Experts estimate that about 1 billion computers will be discarded by 2010. The discarded items often are known as *e-waste*. As technology advances and prices fall, many people think of computers as disposable items. Computers contain several toxic elements, including lead, mercury, and barium. Computers thrown into landfills or burned in incinerators can pollute the ground and the air. A vast amount of e-waste ends up polluting third world countries. One solution is to recycle old computers. Some lawmakers prefer a more aggressive approach, such as setting up a recycling program that would be paid for by adding a $10 fee to a computer's purchase price, or forcing computer makers to be responsible for collecting and recycling their products. California already requires a $6 to $10 recycling fee for any products sold that include a CRT monitor. Manufacturers have taken steps, such as offering to recycle old computers and using energy efficient and environmentally friendly manufacturing techniques, but some claim that consumers should bear the responsibility of disposing of their old computer parts. Several have reduced the amount of toxic material in their products, and manufacturers have set up their own recycling programs, for which users pay a fee. What can be done to ensure that computers are disposed of safely? Should government, manufacturers, or users be responsible for safe disposal? Why? How can computer users be motivated to recycle obsolete equipment?

Heat Sinks, Heat Pipes, and Liquid Cooling

Processor chips generate quite a bit of heat, which could cause the chip to burn up. Although the computer's main fan generates airflow, many of today's processors require additional cooling. A *heat sink* is a small ceramic or metal component with fins on its surface that absorbs and disperses heat produced by electrical components such as a processor (Figure 4-9). Some heat sinks are packaged as part of a processor chip. Others are installed on the top or the side of the chip. Because a heat sink consumes extra space, a smaller device called a *heat pipe* cools processors in notebook computers.

Some computers use liquid cooling technology to reduce the temperature of a processor. *Liquid cooling technology* uses a continuous flow of fluid(s), such as water and glycol, in a process that transfers the heated fluid away from the processor to a radiator-type grill, which cools the liquid, and then returns the cooled fluid to the processor.

Mobile computers and devices often have Low Voltage or Ultra Low Voltage (ULV) processors, which have such low power demands that they do not require additional cooling.

FIGURE 4-9 A heat sink, which is attached to the top of a processor, prevents the chip from overheating. The heat sink fan, which attaches to the top of the heat sink, helps distribute air dissipated by the heat sink.

Parallel Processing

Parallel processing is a method that uses multiple processors simultaneously to execute a single program or task (Figure 4-10). Parallel processing divides a single problem into portions so that multiple processors work on their assigned portion of the problem at the same time. Parallel processing requires special software that recognizes how to divide the problem and then bring the results back together again.

Some personal computers implement parallel processing with dual-core processors or multi-core processors. Others have two or more separate processor chips, respectively called dual processor or multiprocessor computers.

Massively parallel processing is large scale parallel processing that involves hundreds or thousands of processors. Supercomputers use massively parallel processing for applications such as artificial intelligence and weather forecasting. Some applications draw on the idle time of home users' personal computers to achieve parallel processing. For example, the *SETI@home* scientific project runs a program on home users' Internet-connected computers whose purpose is to detect possible intelligent life outside Earth.

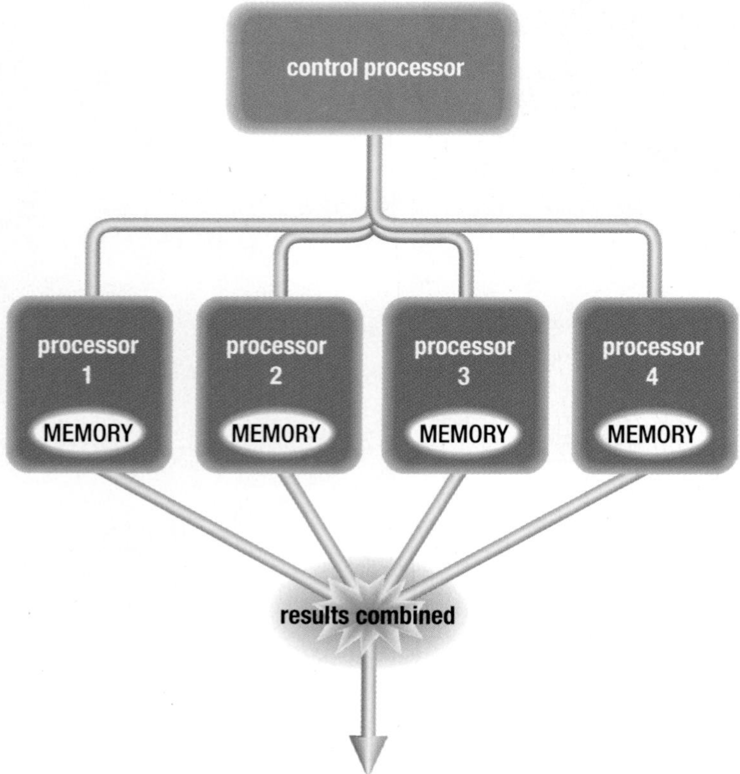

FIGURE 4-10 Parallel processing divides a problem into portions so that multiple processors work on their assigned portion of a problem at the same time. In this illustration, one processor, called the control processor, is managing the operations of four other processors.

Test your knowledge of pages 184 through 194 in Quiz Yourself 4-1.

QUIZ YOURSELF 4-1

Instructions: Find the true statement below. Then, rewrite the remaining false statements so they are true.

1. A computer chip is a small piece of semiconducting material, usually silicon, on which integrated circuits are etched.
2. Four basic operations in a machine cycle are: (1) comparing, (2) decoding, (3) executing, and, if necessary, (4) pipelining.
3. Processors contain a motherboard and an arithmetic logic unit (ALU).
4. The central processing unit, sometimes called a system board, is the main circuit board of the system unit.
5. The leading processor chip manufacturers for personal computers are Microsoft, AMD, IBM, Motorola, and Transmeta.
6. The pace of the system clock, called the clock speed, is measured by the number of ticks per minute.
7. The system unit is a case that contains mechanical components of the computer used to process data.

Quiz Yourself Online: To further check your knowledge of system unit styles, motherboards, processor components and machine cycles, and characteristics of personal computer processors, visit scsite.com/dc2008/ch4/quiz and then click Objectives 1 – 4.

DATA REPRESENTATION

To understand fully the way a computer processes data, you should know how a computer represents data. People communicate through speech by combining words into sentences. Human speech is **analog** because it uses continuous (wave form) signals that vary in strength and quality. Most computers are **digital**. They recognize only two discrete states: on and off. This is because computers are electronic devices powered by electricity, which also has only two states: on and off.

The two digits, 0 and 1, easily can represent these two states (Figure 4-11). The digit 0 represents the electronic state of off (absence of an electronic charge). The digit 1 represents the electronic state of on (presence of an electronic charge).

When people count, they use the digits in the decimal system (0 through 9). The computer, by contrast, uses a binary system because it recognizes only two states. The **binary system** is a number system that has just two unique digits, 0 and 1, called bits. A **bit** (short for *binary digit*) is the smallest unit of data the computer can process. By itself, a bit is not very informative.

When 8 bits are grouped together as a unit, they form a **byte**. A byte provides enough different combinations of 0s and 1s to represent 256 individual characters. These characters include numbers, uppercase and lowercase letters of the alphabet, punctuation marks, and others, such as the letters of the Greek alphabet.

The combinations of 0s and 1s that represent characters are defined by patterns called a coding scheme. In one coding scheme, the number 4 is represented as 00110100, the number 6 as 00110110, and the capital letter E as 01000101 (Figure 4-12). Two popular coding schemes are ASCII and EBCDIC (Figure 4-13). The American Standard Code for Information Interchange (*ASCII* pronounced ASK-ee) scheme is the most widely used coding system to represent data. Most personal computers and servers use the ASCII coding scheme. The Extended Binary Coded Decimal Interchange Code (*EBCDIC* pronounced EB-see-dik) scheme is used primarily on mainframe computers and high-end servers.

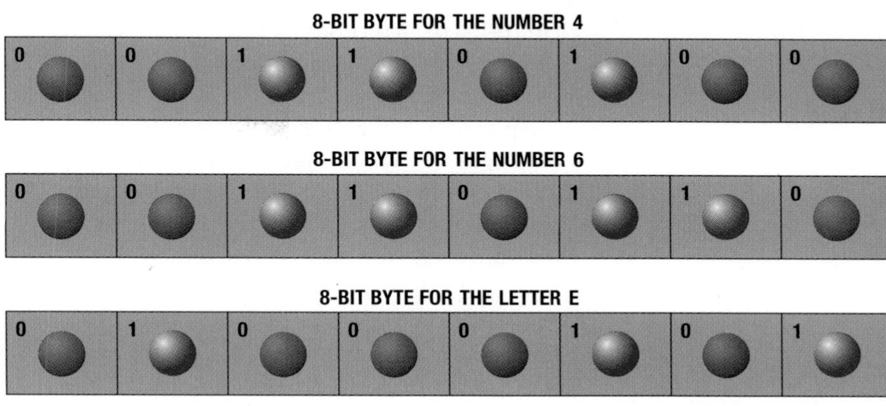

FIGURE 4-12 Eight bits grouped together as a unit are called a byte. A byte represents a single character in the computer.

The ASCII and EBCDIC coding schemes are sufficient for English and Western European languages but are not large enough for Asian and other languages that use different alphabets. *Unicode* is a 16-bit coding scheme that has the capacity of representing more than 65,000 characters and symbols. The Unicode coding scheme is capable of representing almost all the world's current written languages, as well as classic and historical languages. To allow for expansion, Unicode reserves 30,000 codes for future use and 6,000 codes for private use. Unicode is implemented in several operating systems, including Windows Vista, Windows XP, Mac OS X, and Linux.

BINARY DIGIT (BIT)	ELECTRONIC CHARGE	ELECTRONIC STATE
1		ON
0		OFF

FIGURE 4-11 A computer circuit represents the 0 or the 1 electronically by the presence or absence of an electronic charge.

ASCII	SYMBOL	EBCDIC
00110000	0	11110000
00110001	1	11110001
00110010	2	11110010
00110011	3	11110011
00110100	4	11110100
00110101	5	11110101
00110110	6	11110110
00110111	7	11110111
00111000	8	11111000
00111001	9	11111001
01000001	A	11000001
01000010	B	11000010
01000011	C	11000011
01000100	D	11000100
01000101	E	11000101
01000110	F	11000110
01000111	G	11000111
01001000	H	11001000
01001001	I	11001001
01001010	J	11010001
01001011	K	11010010
01001100	L	11010011
01001101	M	11010100
01001110	N	11010101
01001111	O	11010110
01010000	P	11010111
01010001	Q	11011000
01010010	R	11011001
01010011	S	11100010
01010100	T	11100011
01010101	U	11100100
01010110	V	11100101
01010111	W	11100110
01011000	X	11100111
01011001	Y	11101000
01011010	Z	11101001
00100001	!	01011010
00100010	"	01111111
00100011	#	01111011
00100100	$	01011011
00100101	%	01101100
00100110	&	01010000
00101000	(	01001101
00101001	)	01011101
00101010	*	01011100
00101011	+	01001110

FIGURE 4-13 Two popular coding schemes are ASCII and EBCDIC.

Unicode-enabled programming languages and software products include Java, XML, Microsoft Office, and Oracle.

Appendix A at the back of this book discusses the ASCII, EBCDIC, and Unicode schemes in more depth, along with the parity bit and number systems.

Coding schemes such as ASCII make it possible for humans to interact with a digital computer that processes only bits. When you press a key on a keyboard, a chip in the keyboard converts the key's electronic signal into a special code that is sent to the system unit. Then, the system unit converts the code into a binary form the computer can process and stores it in memory. Every character is converted to its corresponding byte. The computer then processes the data as bytes, which actually is a series of on/off electrical states. When processing is finished, software converts the byte into a human-recognizable number, letter of the alphabet, or special character that is displayed on a screen or is printed (Figure 4-14). All of these conversions take place so quickly that you do not realize they are occurring.

Standards, such as those defined by ASCII, EBCDIC, and Unicode, also make it possible for components in computers to communicate with each other successfully. By following these and other standards, manufacturers can produce a component and be assured that it will operate correctly in a computer.

FIGURE 4-14 HOW A LETTER IS CONVERTED TO BINARY FORM AND BACK

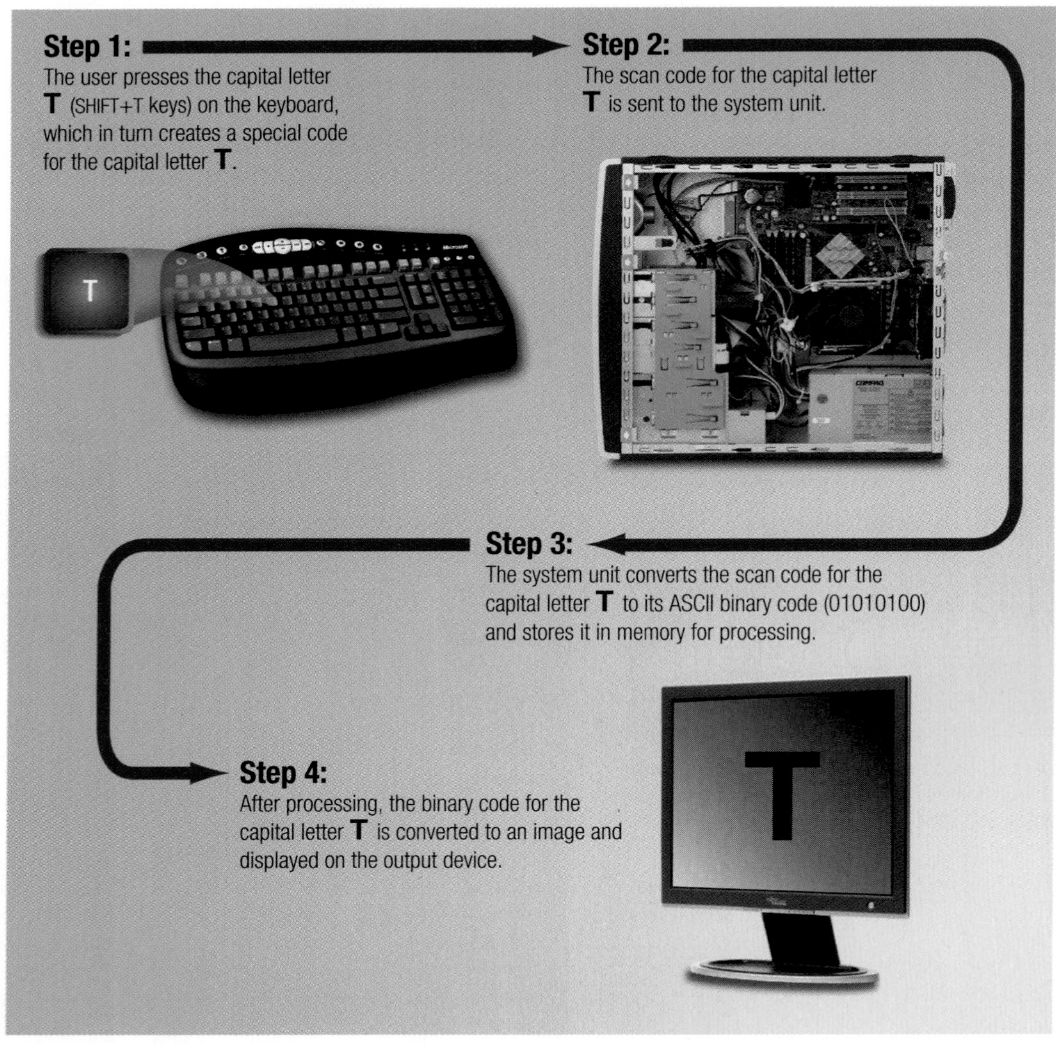

Step 1:
The user presses the capital letter T (SHIFT+T keys) on the keyboard, which in turn creates a special code for the capital letter T.
T
Step 2:
The scan code for the capital letter T is sent to the system unit.
Step 3:
The system unit converts the scan code for the capital letter T to its ASCII binary code (01010100) and stores it in memory for processing.
Step 4:
After processing, the binary code for the capital letter T is converted to an image and displayed on the output device.
T

MEMORY

Memory consists of electronic components that store instructions waiting to be executed by the processor, data needed by those instructions, and the results of processed data (information). Memory usually consists of one or more chips on the motherboard or some other circuit board in the computer.

Memory stores three basic categories of items: (1) the operating system and other system software that control or maintain the computer and its devices; (2) application programs that carry out a specific task such as word processing; and (3) the data being processed by the application programs and resulting information. This role of memory to store both data and programs is known as the *stored program concept*.

Bytes and Addressable Memory

A byte (character) is the basic storage unit in memory. When application program instructions and data are transferred to memory from storage devices, the instructions and data exist as bytes. Each byte resides temporarily in a location in memory that has an *address*. An address simply is a unique number that identifies the location of a byte in memory. The illustration in Figure 4-15 shows how seats in a concert hall are similar to addresses in memory: (1) a seat, which is identified by a unique seat number, holds one person at a time, and a location in memory, which is identified by a unique address, holds a single byte; and (2) both a seat, identified by a seat number, and a byte, identified by an address, can be empty. To access data or instructions in memory, the computer references the addresses that contain bytes of data.

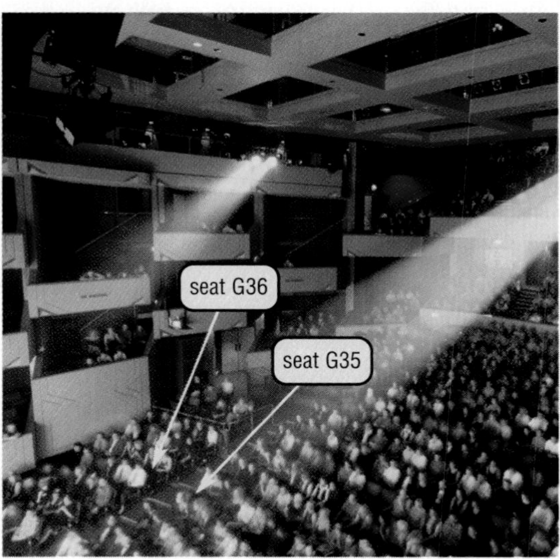

FIGURE 4-15 Seats in a concert hall are similar to addresses in memory: a seat holds one person at a time, and a location in memory holds a single byte; and both a seat and a byte can be empty.

Memory Sizes

Manufacturers state the size of memory chips and storage devices in terms of the number of bytes the chip or device has available for storage (Figure 4-16). Recall that storage devices hold data, instructions, and information for future use, while most memory holds these items temporarily. A **kilobyte** (**KB** or **K**) is equal to exactly 1,024 bytes. To simplify memory and storage definitions, computer users often round a kilobyte down to 1,000 bytes. For example, if a memory chip can store 100 KB, it can hold approximately 100,000 bytes (characters). A **megabyte** (**MB**) is equal to approximately 1 million bytes. A **gigabyte** (**GB**) equals approximately 1 billion bytes. A **terabyte** (**TB**) is equal to approximately 1 trillion bytes.

MEMORY AND STORAGE SIZES

Term	Abbreviation	Approximate Number of Bytes	Exact Amount of Bytes	Approximate Number of Pages of Text
Kilobyte	KB or K	1 thousand	1,024	1/2
Megabyte	MB	1 million	1,048,576	500
Gigabyte	GB	1 billion	1,073,741,824	500,000
Terabyte	TB	1 trillion	1,099,511,627,776	500,000,000

FIGURE 4-16 Terms commonly used to define memory and storage sizes.

Types of Memory

The system unit contains two types of memory: volatile and nonvolatile. When the computer's power is turned off, *volatile memory* loses its contents. *Nonvolatile memory*, by contrast, does not lose its contents when power is removed from the computer. Thus, volatile memory is temporary and nonvolatile memory is permanent. RAM is the most common type of volatile memory. Examples of nonvolatile memory include ROM, flash memory, and CMOS. The following pages discuss these types of memory.

RAM

Users typically are referring to RAM when discussing computer memory. **RAM** (*random access memory*), also called *main memory*, consists of memory chips that can be read from and written to by the processor and other devices. When you turn on power to a computer, certain operating system files (such as the files that determine how the Windows Vista desktop appears) load into RAM from a storage device such as a hard disk. These files remain in RAM as long as the computer has continuous power. As additional programs and data are requested, they also load into RAM from storage.

The processor interprets and executes a program's instructions while the program is in RAM. During this time, the contents of RAM may change (Figure 4-17). RAM can accommodate multiple programs simultaneously.

Most RAM is volatile, which means it loses its contents when the power is removed from the computer. For this reason, you must save any data, instructions, and information you

FIGURE 4-17 HOW PROGRAM INSTRUCTIONS TRANSFER IN AND OUT OF RAM

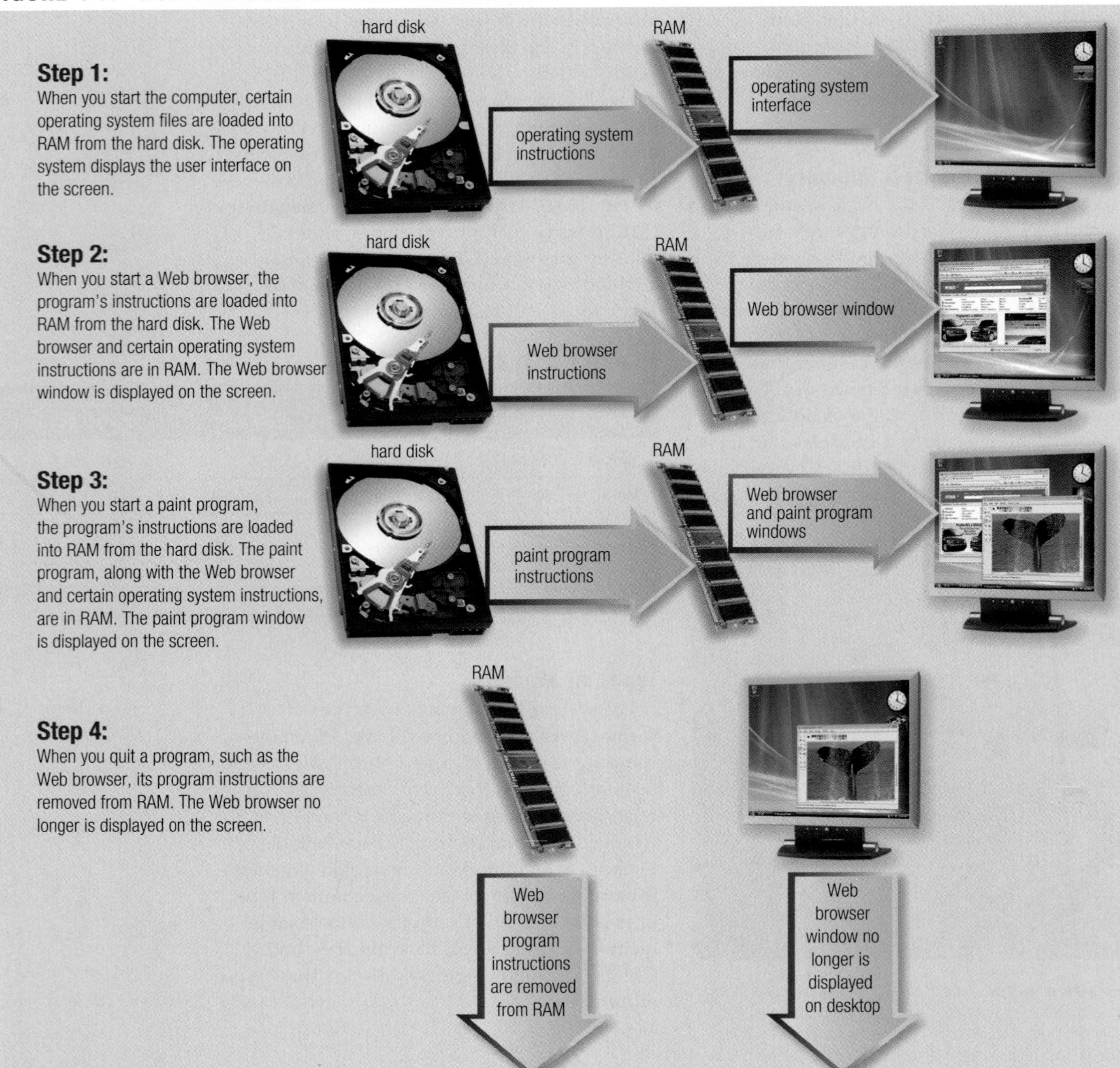
hard disk
RAM
Step 1:
When you start the computer, certain operating system files are loaded into RAM from the hard disk. The operating system displays the user interface on the screen.
operating system instructions
operating system interface
hard disk
RAM
Step 2:
When you start a Web browser, the program's instructions are loaded into RAM from the hard disk. The Web browser and certain operating system instructions are in RAM. The Web browser window is displayed on the screen.
Web browser instructions
Web browser window
hard disk
RAM
Step 3:
When you start a paint program, the program's instructions are loaded into RAM from the hard disk. The paint program, along with the Web browser and certain operating system instructions, are in RAM. The paint program window is displayed on the screen.
paint program instructions
Web browser and paint program windows
RAM
Step 4:
When you quit a program, such as the Web browser, its program instructions are removed from RAM. The Web browser no longer is displayed on the screen.
Web browser program instructions are removed from RAM
Web browser window no longer is displayed on desktop

may need in the future. Saving is the process of copying data, instructions, and information from RAM to a storage device such as a hard disk.

Three basic types of RAM chips exist: dynamic RAM, static RAM, and magnetoresistive RAM.

- *Dynamic RAM* (*DRAM* pronounced DEE-ram) chips must be re-energized constantly or they lose their contents. Many variations of DRAM chips exist, most of which are faster than the basic DRAM. *Synchronous DRAM* (*SDRAM*) chips are much faster than DRAM chips because they are synchronized to the system clock. Double Data Rate SDRAM (*DDR SDRAM*) chips are even faster than SDRAM chips because they transfer data twice for each clock cycle, instead of just once, and DDR2 is even faster than DDR. Dual channel SDRAM is faster than single channel SDRAM because it delivers twice the amount of data to the processor. *Rambus DRAM* (*RDRAM*) is yet another type of DRAM that is much faster than SDRAM because it uses pipelining techniques. Most personal computers today use some form of SDRAM chips or RDRAM chips.
- *Static RAM* (*SRAM* pronounced ESS-ram) chips are faster and more reliable than any variation of DRAM chips. These chips do not have to be re-energized as often as DRAM chips, thus, the term static. SRAM chips, however, are much more expensive than DRAM chips. Special applications such as cache use SRAM chips. A later section in this chapter discusses cache.
- A newer type of RAM, called *magnetoresistive RAM* (*MRAM* pronounced EM-ram), stores data using magnetic charges instead of electrical charges. Manufacturers claim that MRAM has greater storage capacity, consumes less power, and has faster access times than electronic RAM. Also, MRAM retains its contents after power is removed from the computer, which could prevent loss of data for users. As the cost of MRAM declines, experts predict MRAM could replace both DRAM and SRAM.

RAM chips usually reside on a **memory module**, which is a small circuit board. **Memory slots** on the motherboard hold memory modules (Figure 4-18). Three types of memory modules are SIMMs, DIMMs, and RIMMs. A *SIMM* (*single inline memory module*) has pins on opposite sides of the circuit board that connect together to form a single set of contacts. With a *DIMM* (*dual inline memory module*), by contrast, the pins on opposite sides of the circuit board do not connect and thus form two sets of contacts. SIMMs and DIMMs typically hold SDRAM chips. A *RIMM* (*Rambus inline memory module*) houses RDRAM chips. For a more technical discussion about RAM, read the High-Tech Talk article on page 218 at the end of this chapter.

RAM

For more information, visit scsite.com/dc2008/ch4/weblink and then click RAM.

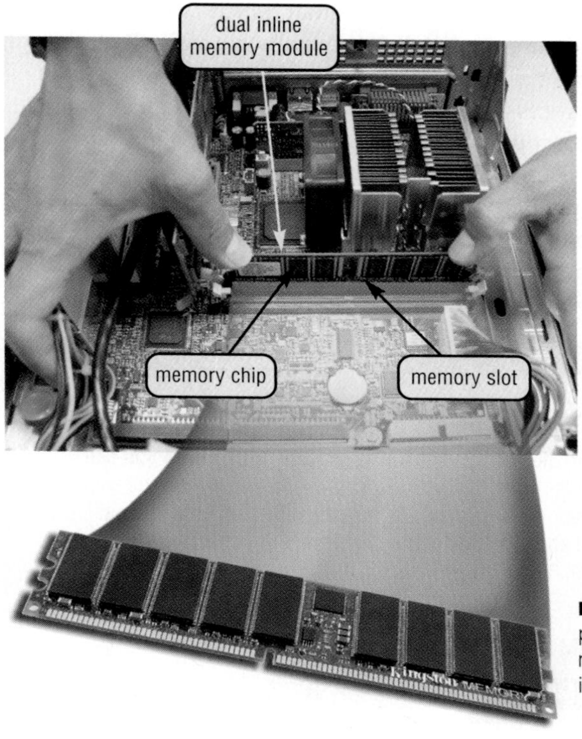

FIGURE 4-18 This photo shows a memory module being inserted in a motherboard.

RAM CONFIGURATIONS The amount of RAM necessary in a computer often depends on the types of software you plan to use. A computer executes programs that are in RAM. Think of RAM as the workspace on the top of your desk. Just as the top of your desk needs a certain amount of space to hold papers, a computer needs a certain amount of memory to store programs, data, and information. The more RAM a computer has, the faster the computer will respond.

A software package typically indicates the minimum amount of RAM it requires. If you want the application to perform optimally, usually you need more than the minimum specifications on the software package.

Generally, home users running Windows Vista and using basic application software such as word processing should have at least 512 MB of RAM. Most business users who work with accounting, financial, or spreadsheet programs, and programs requiring multimedia capabilities should have a minimum of 1 GB of RAM. Users creating professional Web sites or using graphics-intensive applications will want at least 2 GB of RAM.

Figure 4-19a lists guidelines for the amount of RAM for various types of users. Figure 4-19b shows advertisements that match to each user requirement. Advertisements normally list the type of processor, the clock speed of the processor, and the amount of RAM in the computer. The amount of RAM in computers purchased today ranges from 512 MB to 16 GB. In an advertisement, manufacturers specify the maximum amount of RAM a computer can hold, for example, 1 GB expandable to 2 GB. Read Ethics & Issues 4-3 for a related discussion.

FAQ 4-3

Can I add more RAM to my computer?

Check your computer documentation to see how much RAM you can add. RAM modules are relatively inexpensive and usually include easy-to-follow installation instructions. Be sure to purchase RAM compatible with your brand and model of computer. For more information, visit scsite.com/dc2008/ch4/faq and then click Upgrading RAM.

ETHICS & ISSUES 4-3

Should Schools Supply Computers to All Students?

Around the country and around the world, local and national governments have begun to supply schoolchildren with inexpensive notebook computers. Many school districts in the United States purchase a notebook computer priced at approximately $600 for each student when the student enters a particular grade level. The United Nations endorses a plan known as *One Laptop per Child* to supply $100 notebook computers to developing countries, some of which already pledged to purchase millions of the devices for schoolchildren. The device, which recharges with a hand crank, includes Wi-Fi networking and a simple, intuitive user interface. Supporters of these plans maintain that computer literacy and electronic communication are vital skills in today's world, and students should be introduced to computers as early in their school years as possible. Many people oppose plans to equip every student with a computer because they say that the technology detracts from traditional educational subjects, such as basic reading and math. They also point out the number of college instructors who ban the use of computers in the classroom. The computers require maintenance, support, and instructional time to teach students how to use the devices. Young children may lack the responsibility to care for and use the computers properly. Should schools supply computers to all students? Why or why not? What is the appropriate grade level at which to require computer literacy? Why? Who should bear the cost of purchasing required computers for students? Why?

FIGURE 4-19a (RAM guidelines)

RAM	512 MB to 1 GB	1 GB to 2 GB	2 GB and up
Use	Home and business users managing personal finances; using standard application software such as word processing; using educational or entertainment CD-ROMs; communicating with others on the Web	Users requiring more advanced multimedia capabilities; running number-intensive accounting, financial, or spreadsheet programs; using voice recognition; working with videos, music, and digital imaging; creating Web sites; participating in video conferences; playing Internet games	Power users creating professional Web sites; running sophisticated CAD, 3-D design, or other graphics-intensive software

FIGURE 4-19b (computers for sale)

Model	A200	I280	A220	I213	I293	A280
Processor	2.00 GHz Sempron processor	2.80 GHz Celeron D processor	2.20 GHz Athlon 64 X2 processor	2.13 GHz Core 2 Duo processor	2.93 GHz Core 2 Extreme processor	2.80 GHz Opteron processor
Memory	512 MB DDR SDRAM	1 GB DDR SDRAM	1 GB DDR2 SDRAM	2 GB DDR2 SDRAM	4 GB DDR2 SDRAM	4 GB DDR2 SDRAM

FIGURE 4-19 Determining how much RAM you need depends on the applications you intend to run on your computer. Advertisements for computers normally list the type of processor, the speed of the processor, and the amount of RAM installed.

Cache

Most of today's computers improve processing times with **cache** (pronounced cash). Two types of cache are memory cache and disk cache. This chapter discusses memory cache. Chapter 7 discusses disk cache.

Memory cache helps speed the processes of the computer because it stores frequently used instructions and data. Most personal computers today have two types of memory cache: L1 cache and L2 cache. Some also have L3 cache.

- *L1 cache* is built directly in the processor chip. L1 cache usually has a very small capacity, ranging from 8 KB to 128 KB. The more common sizes for personal computers are 32 KB or 64 KB.
- *L2 cache* is slightly slower than L1 cache but has a much larger capacity, ranging from 64 KB to 16 MB. When discussing cache, most users are referring to L2 cache. Current processors include *advanced transfer cache (ATC)*, a type of L2 cache built directly on the processor chip. Processors that use ATC perform at much faster rates than those that do not use it.

  Personal computers today typically have from 512 KB to 4 MB of advanced transfer cache. Servers and workstations have from 4 MB to 6 MB of advanced transfer cache.
- *L3 cache* is a cache on the motherboard that is separate from the processor chip. L3 cache exists only on computers that use L2 advanced transfer cache. Personal computers often have up to 2 MB of L3 cache; servers and workstations have from 8 MB to 24 MB of L3 cache.

Cache speeds up processing time because it stores frequently used instructions and data. When the processor needs an instruction or data, it searches memory in this order: L1 cache, then L2 cache, then L3 cache (if it exists), then RAM — with a greater delay in processing for each level of memory it must search (Figure 4-20). If the instruction or data is not found in memory, then it must search a slower speed storage medium such as a hard disk, CD, or DVD.

WEB LINK 4-4

Cache

For more information, visit scsite.com/dc2008/ch4/weblink and then click Cache.

ROM

Read-only memory (**ROM** pronounced rahm) refers to memory chips storing permanent data and instructions. The data on most ROM chips cannot be modified — hence, the name read-only. ROM is nonvolatile, which means its contents are not lost when power is removed from the computer. In addition to computers, many devices contain ROM chips. For example, ROM chips in printers contain data for fonts.

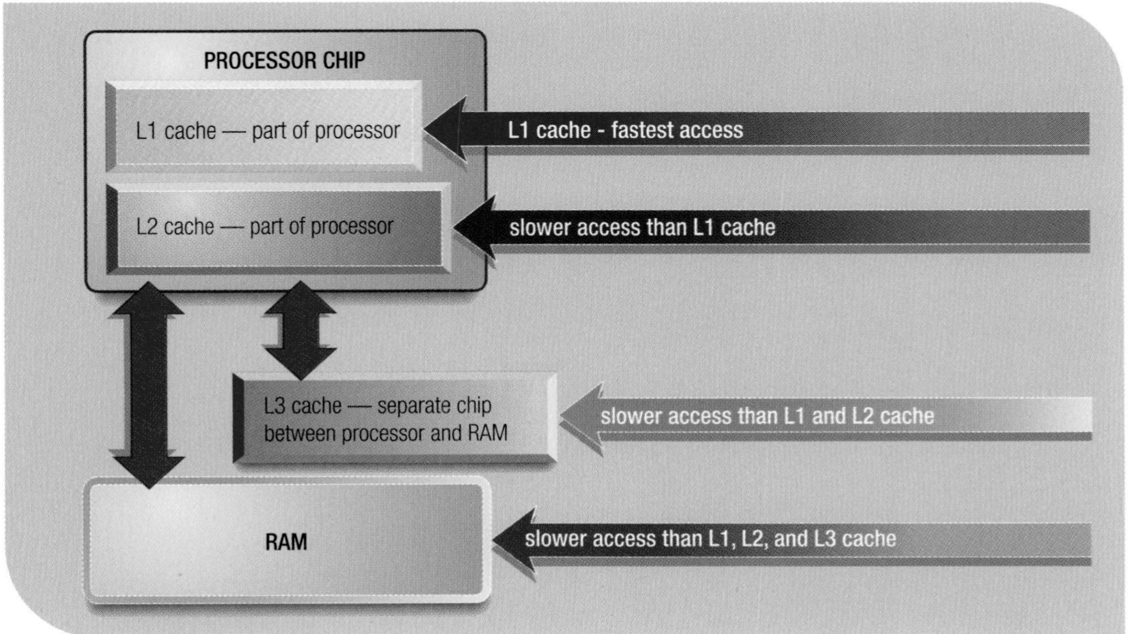

FIGURE 4-20 Cache helps speed processing times when the processor requests data, instructions, or information.

Manufacturers of ROM chips often record data, instructions, or information on the chips when they manufacture the chips. These ROM chips, called **firmware**, contain permanently written data, instructions, or information.

A *PROM* (*programmable read-only memory*) *chip* is a blank ROM chip on which a programmer can write permanently. Programmers use *microcode* instructions to program a PROM chip. Once a programmer writes the microcode on the PROM chip, it functions like a regular ROM chip and cannot be erased or changed.

A variation of the PROM chip, called an *EEPROM* (electrically erasable programmable read-only memory) *chip*, allows a programmer to erase the microcode with an electric signal.

Flash Memory

Flash memory is a type of nonvolatile memory that can be erased electronically and rewritten, similar to EEPROM. Most computers use flash memory to hold their startup instructions because it allows the computer easily to update its contents. For example, when the computer changes from standard time to daylight savings time, the contents of a flash memory chip (and the real-time clock chip) change to reflect the new time.

Flash Memory

For more information, visit scsite.com/dc2008/ch4/weblink and then click Flash Memory.

Flash memory chips also store data and programs on many mobile computers and devices, such as PDAs, smart phones, printers, digital cameras, automotive devices, portable media players, digital voice recorders, and pagers. When you enter names and addresses in a PDA or smart phone, a flash memory chip stores the data. Some portable media players store music on flash memory chips (Figure 4-21); others store music on tiny hard disks or flash memory cards. A later section in this chapter discusses flash memory cards, which contain flash memory on a removable device instead of a chip.

FAQ 4-4

How much music can I store on a portable media player?

Portable media players that store music on flash memory chips can hold up to 2,000 songs. Portable media players with tiny hard disks have a much greater storage capacity — from 1,000 to 20,000 songs. For more information, visit scsite.com/dc2008/ch4/faq and then click Portable Media Players.

FIGURE 4-21 HOW A PORTABLE MEDIA PLAYER MIGHT STORE MUSIC IN FLASH MEMORY

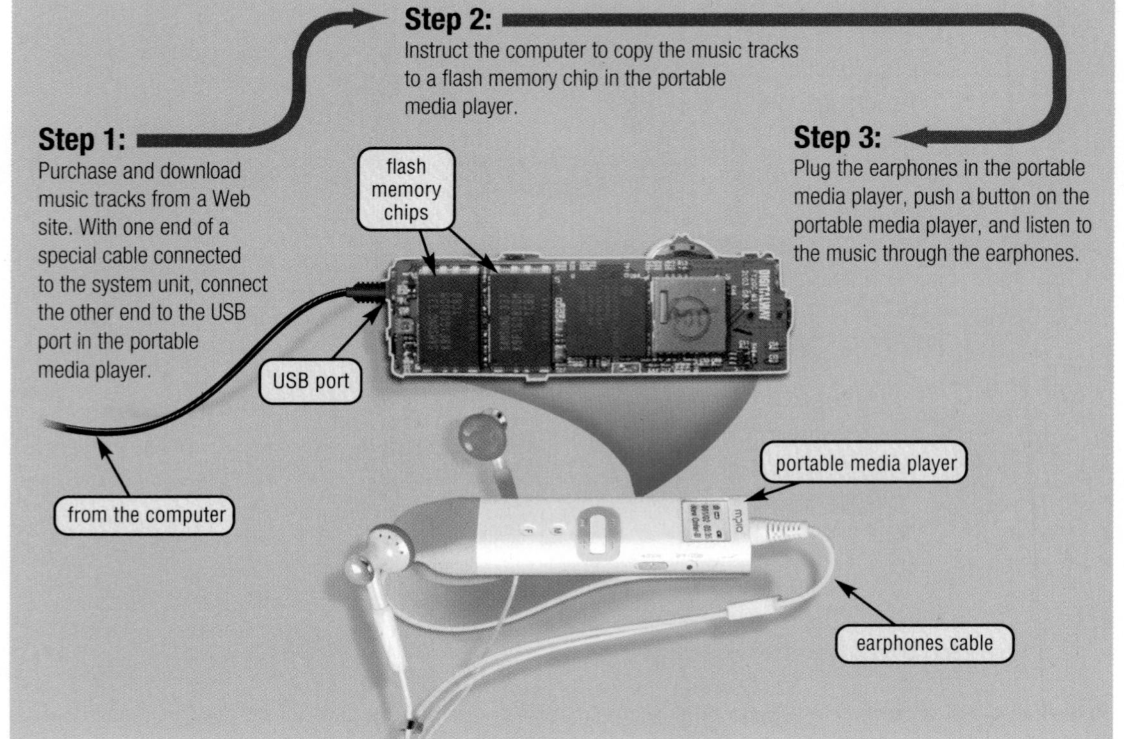

Step 1:
Purchase and download music tracks from a Web site. With one end of a special cable connected to the system unit, connect the other end to the USB port in the portable media player.
Step 2:
Instruct the computer to copy the music tracks to a flash memory chip in the portable media player.
Step 3:
Plug the earphones in the portable media player, push a button on the portable media player, and listen to the music through the earphones.
flash memory chips
USB port
from the computer
portable media player
earphones cable

CMOS

Some RAM chips, flash memory chips, and other types of memory chips use **complementary metal-oxide semiconductor** (**CMOS** pronounced SEE-moss) technology because it provides high speeds and consumes little power. CMOS technology uses battery power to retain information even when the power to the computer is off. Battery-backed CMOS memory chips, for example, can keep the calendar, date, and time current even when the computer is off. The flash memory chips that store a computer's startup information often use CMOS technology.

FAQ 4-5

What should I do if my computer's date and time are wrong?

First, try resetting the date and time. To do this in Windows Vista, double-click the time at the right edge of the taskbar. If the computer continues to lose time or display an incorrect date, you may need to replace the CMOS battery on the motherboard that powers the system clock. For more information, visit scsite.com/dc2008/ch4/faq and then click CMOS Battery.

Memory Access Times

Access time is the amount of time it takes the processor to read data, instructions, and information from memory. A computer's access time directly affects how fast the computer processes data. Accessing data in memory can be more than 200,000 times faster than accessing data on a hard disk because of the mechanical motion of the hard disk.

Today's manufacturers use a variety of terminology to state access times (Figure 4-22). Some use fractions of a second, which for memory occurs in nanoseconds. A **nanosecond** (abbreviated *ns*) is one billionth of a second. A nanosecond is extremely fast (Figure 4-23). In fact, electricity travels about one foot in a nanosecond.

Other manufacturers state access times in MHz; for example, 667 MHz DDR2 SDRAM. If a manufacturer states access time in megahertz, you can convert it to nanoseconds by dividing 1 billion ns by the megahertz number. For example, 667 MHz equals approximately 1.5 ns (1,000,000,000/667,000,000).

The access time (speed) of memory contributes to the overall performance of the computer. Standard SDRAM chips can have access times up to 133 MHz (about 7.5 ns), and access times of the DDR SDRAM chips reach 667 MHz. The higher the megahertz, the faster the access time; conversely, the lower the nanoseconds, the faster the access time. The faster RDRAM chips can have access times up to 1600 MHz (about 0.625 ns). ROM access times range from 25 to 250 ns.

While access times of memory greatly affect overall computer performance, manufacturers and retailers usually list a computer's memory in terms of its size, not its access time. Thus, an advertisement might describe a computer as having 512 MB of SDRAM upgradeable to 4 GB.

ACCESS TIME TERMINOLOGY

Term	Abbreviation	Speed
Millisecond	ms	One-thousandth of a second
Microsecond	μs	One-millionth of a second
Nanosecond	ns	One-billionth of a second
Picosecond	ps	One-trillionth of a second

FIGURE 4-22 Access times are measured in fractions of a second. This table lists the terms used to define access times.

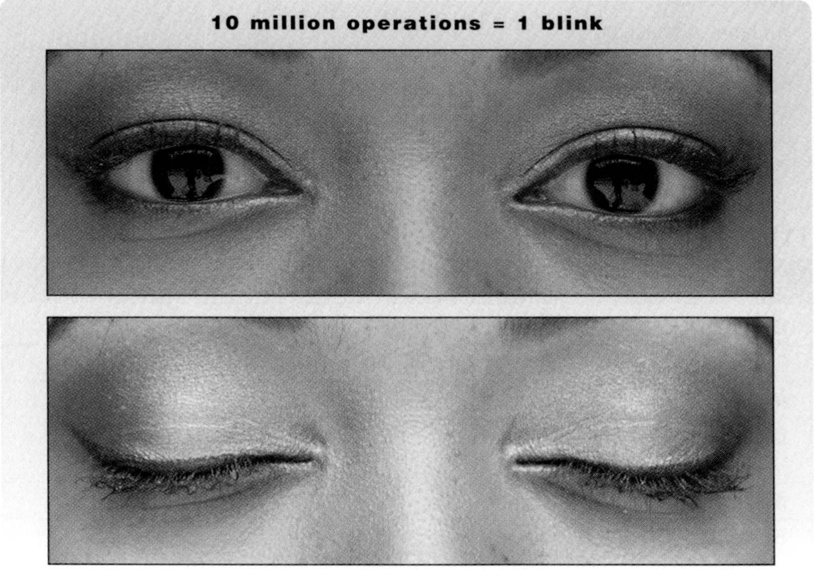

10 million operations = 1 blink

FIGURE 4-23 It takes about one-tenth of a second to blink your eye, which is the equivalent of 100 million nanoseconds. In the time it takes to blink your eye, a computer can perform some operations 10 million times.

Test your knowledge of pages 194 through 203 in Quiz Yourself 4-2.

QUIZ YOURSELF 4-2

Instructions: Find the true statement below. Then, rewrite the remaining false statements so they are true.

1. A computer's memory access time directly affects how fast the computer processes data.
2. A gigabyte (GB) equals approximately 1 trillion bytes.
3. Memory cache helps speed the processes of the computer because it stores seldom used instructions and data.
4. Most computers are analog, which means they recognize only two discrete states: on and off.
5. Most RAM retains its contents when the power is removed from the computer.
6. Read-only memory (ROM) refers to memory chips storing temporary data and instructions.

Quiz Yourself Online: To further check your knowledge of bits, bytes, data representation, and types of memory, visit scsite.com/dc2008/ch4/quiz and then click Objectives 5 – 7.

EXPANSION SLOTS AND ADAPTER CARDS

An **expansion slot** is a socket on the motherboard that can hold an adapter card. An **adapter card**, sometimes called an *expansion card*, is a circuit board that enhances functions of a component of the system unit and/or provides connections to peripherals. A **peripheral** is a device that connects to the system unit and is controlled by the processor in the computer. Examples of peripherals are modems, disk drives, printers, scanners, and keyboards.

Figure 4-24 lists currently used types of adapter cards. Sometimes, all functionality is built in the adapter card. With others, a cable connects the adapter card to a device, such as a digital video camera, outside the system unit. Figure 4-25 shows an adapter card being inserted in an expansion slot on a personal computer motherboard.

Some motherboards include all necessary capabilities and do not require adapter cards. Other motherboards may require adapter cards to provide capabilities such as sound and video. A **sound card** enhances the sound-generating capabilities of a personal computer by allowing sound to be input through a microphone and output through external speakers or headphones. A **video card**, also called a *graphics card*, converts computer output into a video signal that travels through a cable to the monitor, which displays an image on the screen.

Sound Cards

For more information, visit scsite.com/dc2008/ch4/weblink and then click Sound Cards.

TYPES OF ADAPTER CARDS

Adapter Card	Purpose
Disk controller	Connects disk drives
FireWire	Connects to FireWire devices
MIDI	Connects musical instruments
Modem	Connects other computers through telephone or cable television lines
Network	Connects other computers and peripherals
PC-to-TV converter	Connects a television
Sound	Connects speakers or a microphone
TV tuner	Allows viewing of television channels on the monitor
USB 2.0	Connects to USB 2.0 devices
Video	Connects a monitor
Video capture	Connects a camcorder

FIGURE 4-24 Currently used adapter cards and their functions.

FIGURE 4-25 An adapter card being inserted in an expansion slot on the motherboard of a personal computer.

In the past, installing a card was not easy and required you to set switches and other elements on the motherboard. Many of today's computers support **Plug and Play**, which means the computer automatically can configure adapter cards and other peripherals as you install them. Having Plug and Play support means you can plug in a device, turn on the computer, and then immediately begin using the device.

Flash Memory Cards, USB Flash Drives, PC Cards, and ExpressCard Modules

Four widely used types of removable flash memory devices include flash memory cards, USB flash drives, PC Cards, and ExpressCard modules. Unlike adapter cards that require you to open the system unit and install the card on the motherboard, you can change a removable flash memory device without having to open the system unit or restart the computer. This feature, called *hot plugging*, allows you to insert and remove the removable flash memory and other devices while the computer is running.

- A **flash memory card** is a removable flash memory device, usually no bigger than 1.5" in height or width, that you insert and remove from a slot in a computer, mobile device, or card reader/writer (Figure 4-26). Many mobile and consumer devices, such as PDAs, smart phones, digital cameras, and portable media players, use these memory cards. Some printers and computers have built-in card readers/writers or slots that read flash memory cards. In addition, you can purchase an external card reader/writer that attaches to any computer. Flash memory cards are available in a variety of shapes and sizes. The type of flash memory card you have will determine the type of card reader/writer you need. Storage capacities of flash memory cards range from 32 MB to 8 GB.
- A *USB flash drive* is a flash memory storage device that plugs in a USB port on a computer or portable device. (The next section discusses USB ports.) A special type of USB flash drive, called a *U3 smart drive*, includes preinstalled software accessed through a Windows-type interface. Storage capacities of USB flash drives range from 32 MB to 64 GB, with the latter being extremely expensive.
- Many computers have a **PC Card slot** or an **ExpressCard slot**, which is a special type of expansion slot that holds a PC Card or an ExpressCard module, respectively. A **PC Card** is a thin, credit card-sized removable flash memory device that primarily is used today to enable notebook computers to access the Internet wirelessly. ExpressCard modules, about one-half the size of PC Cards, are the next generation of PC Cards. An **ExpressCard module**, which can be used as a removable flash memory device, adds memory, communications, multimedia, and security capabilities to computers (Figure 4-27). Both PC Cards and ExpressCard modules conform to standards developed by the *Personal Computer Memory Card International Association* (PCMCIA). These standards help to ensure the interchangeability of PC Cards and ExpressCard modules among personal computers.

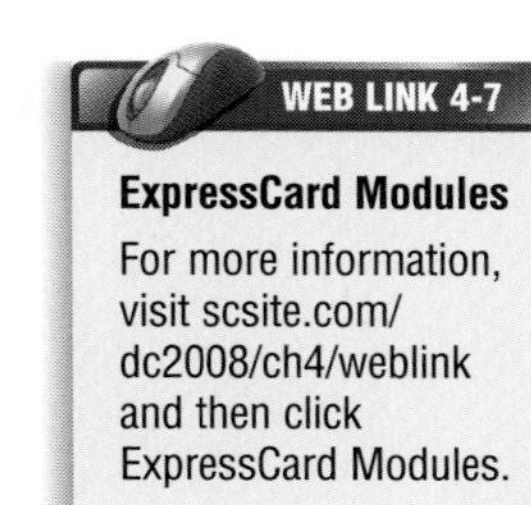

ExpressCard Modules

For more information, visit scsite.com/dc2008/ch4/weblink and then click ExpressCard Modules.

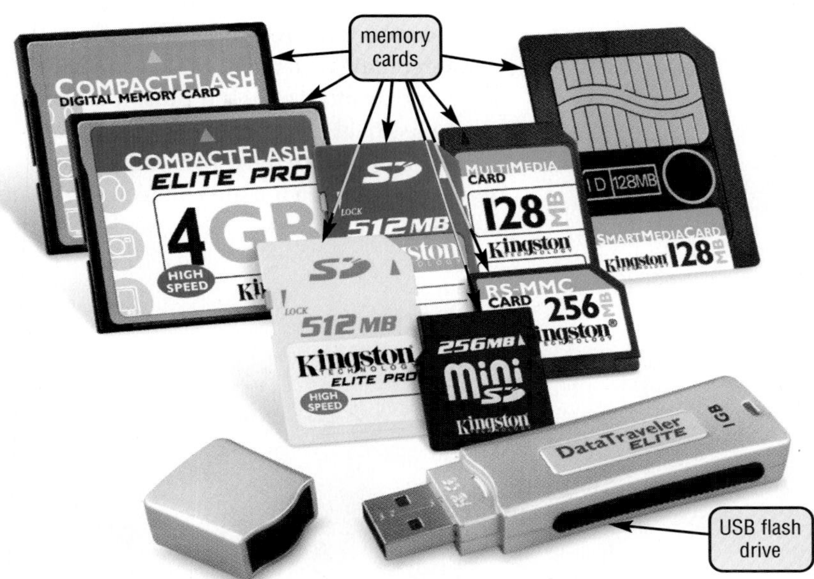

FIGURE 4-26 Removable flash memory devices are available in a range of sizes.

FIGURE 4-27 An ExpressCard module slides in an ExpressCard slot on a computer.

PORTS AND CONNECTORS

A **port** is the point at which a peripheral attaches to or communicates with a system unit so the peripheral can send data to or receive information from the computer. An external device, such as a keyboard, monitor, printer, mouse, and microphone, often attaches by a cable to a port on the system unit. Instead of port, the term **jack** sometimes is used to identify audio and video ports. The front and back of the system unit contain many ports (Figure 4-28).

Ports have different types of connectors. A **connector** joins a cable to a peripheral. One end of a cable attaches to the connector on the system unit, and the other end of the cable attaches to a connector on the peripheral. Most connectors are available in one of two genders: male or female. Male connectors have one or more exposed pins, like the end of an electrical cord you plug in the wall. Female connectors have matching holes to accept the pins on a male connector, like an electrical wall outlet.

Sometimes, you cannot attach a new peripheral to the computer because the connector on the system unit is the same gender as the connector on the cable. In this case, purchasing a gender changer solves this problem. A *gender changer* is a device that enables you to join two connectors that are both female or both male.

Manufacturers often identify the cables by their connector types to assist you with purchasing a cable to connect a computer to a peripheral. Figure 4-29 shows the different types of connectors you may find on a system unit. Notice that many are color-coded to help you match the connector to the correct port. Some system units include these connectors when you buy the computer. You add other connectors by inserting adapter cards on the motherboard. Certain adapter cards have ports that allow you to attach a peripheral to the adapter card.

Desktop personal computers may have a serial port, a parallel port, several USB ports, and a FireWire port. The next section discusses these and other ports.

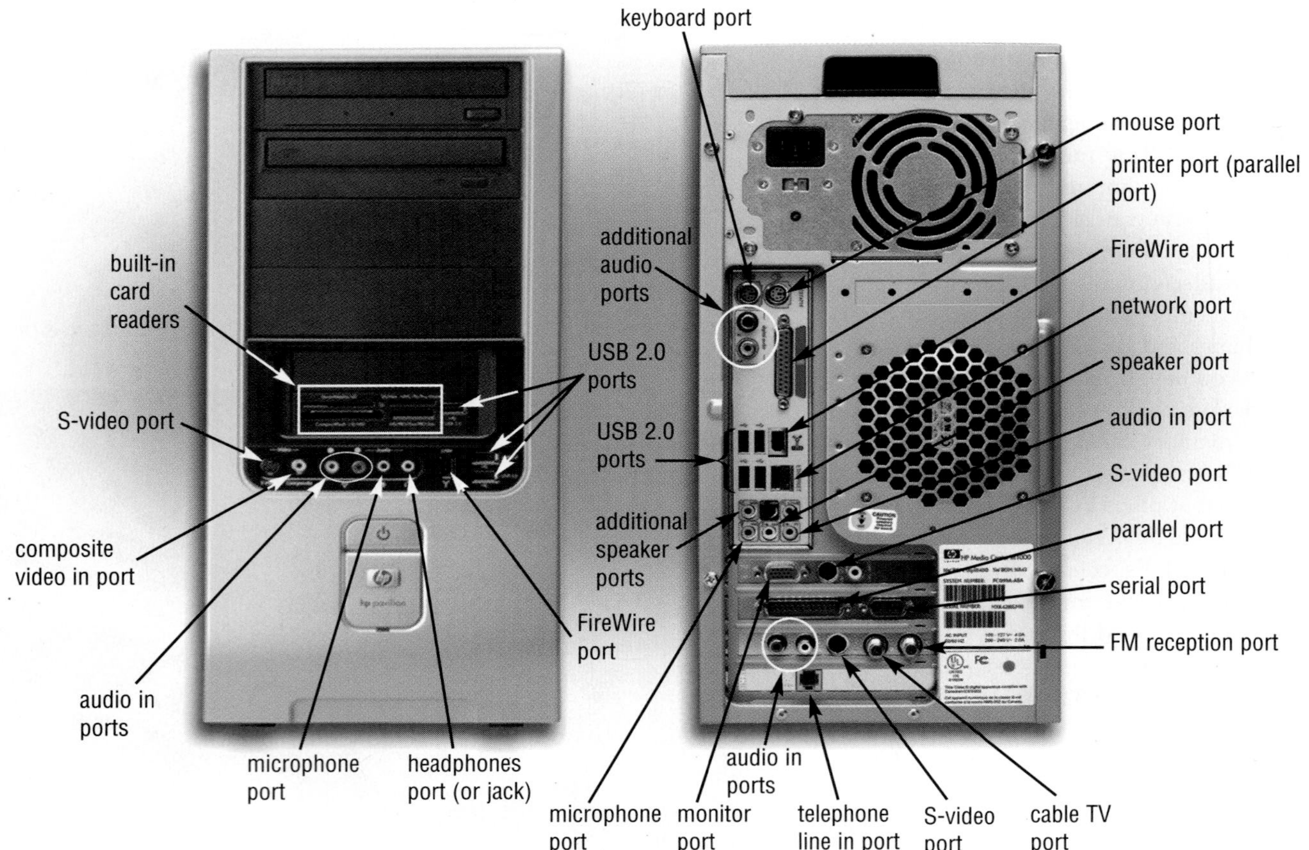

FIGURE 4-28 A system unit has many ports on its front and back.

CONNECTOR TYPES

Connector Type	Picture	Connector Type	Picture
Audio in		Monitor	
Cable TV		Mouse	
Center Surround Sound/Subwoofer		Network	
Composite video in		Printer	
Digital Video Interface (DVI)		Rear Surround Sound	
eSATA port		Serial	
FireWire		Side Surround Sound	
FM reception		S/PDIF	
HDMI port		Speaker	
Headphones		S-video	
Keyboard		Telephone line in	
Microphone		USB	

FIGURE 4-29 Examples of different types of connectors on a system unit.

Serial Ports

A **serial port** is a type of interface that connects a device to the system unit by transmitting data one bit at a time (Figure 4-30). Serial ports usually connect devices that do not require fast data transmission rates, such as a mouse, keyboard, or modem. The *COM port* (short for communications port) on the system unit is one type of serial port.

Some modems that connect the system unit to a telephone line use a serial port because the telephone line expects the data in a specific frequency. Serial ports conform to either the RS-232 or RS-422 standard, which specifies the number of pins used on the port's connector.

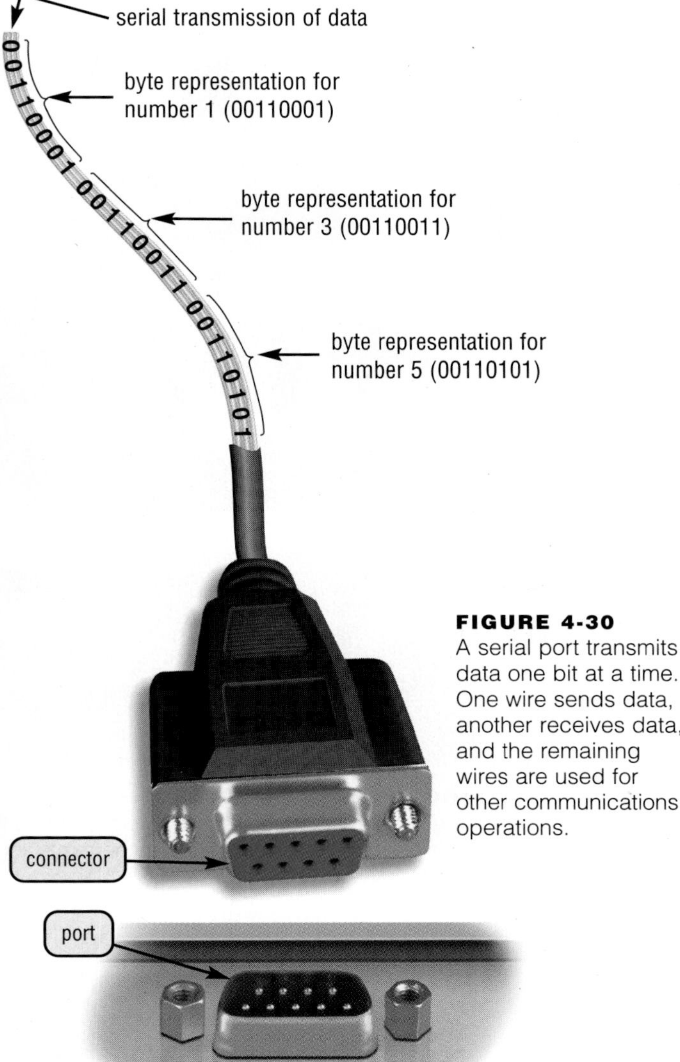

FIGURE 4-30 A serial port transmits data one bit at a time. One wire sends data, another receives data, and the remaining wires are used for other communications operations.

Parallel Ports

Unlike a serial port, a **parallel port** is an interface that connects devices by transferring more than one bit at a time (Figure 4-31). Originally, parallel ports were developed as an alternative to the slower speed serial ports.

Some printers can connect to the system unit using a parallel port. This parallel port can transfer eight bits of data (one byte) simultaneously through eight separate lines in a single cable.

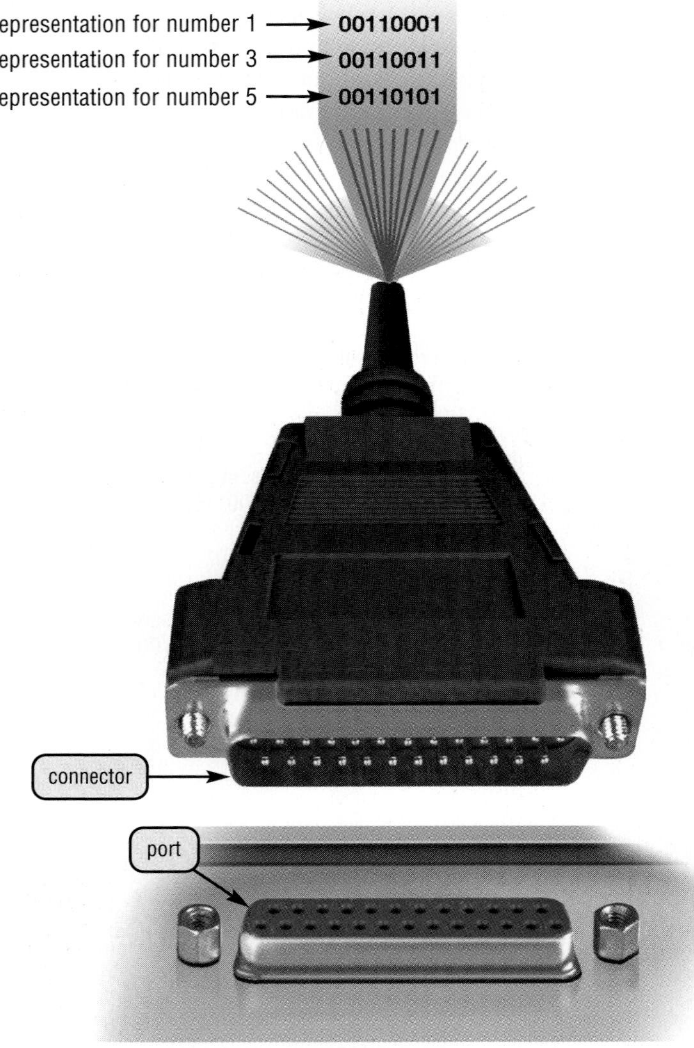

FIGURE 4-31 A parallel port is capable of transmitting more than one bit at a time. The port shown in this figure has eight wires that transmit data; the remaining wires are used for other communications operations.

USB Ports

A **USB port**, short for *universal serial bus port*, can connect up to 127 different peripherals together with a single connector. Devices that connect to a USB port include the following: mouse, printer, digital camera, scanner, speakers, portable media player, CD, DVD, smart phone, PDA, game console, and removable hard disk. Personal computers typically have six to eight USB ports on the front and/or back of the system unit (Figure 4-28 on page 206). The latest version of USB, called *USB 2.0*, is a more advanced and faster USB, with speeds 40 times higher than that of its predecessor.

To attach multiple peripherals using a single USB port, you can daisy chain the devices together outside the system unit. *Daisy chain* means the first USB device connects to the USB port on the computer, the second USB device connects to the first USB device, the third USB device connects to the second USB device, and so on. An alternative to daisy chaining is to use a USB hub. A **USB hub** is a device that plugs in a USB port on the system unit and contains multiple USB ports in which you plug cables from USB devices.

USB also supports hot plugging and Plug and Play, which means you can attach peripherals while the computer is running. With serial and parallel port connections, by contrast, you often must restart the computer after attaching the peripheral.

Some newer peripherals may attach only to a USB port. Others attach to either a serial or parallel port, as well as a USB port.

FAQ 4-6

Can older USB devices plug in a USB 2.0 port?

Yes. USB 2.0 is *backward compatible*, which means that it supports older USB devices as well as new USB 2.0 devices. Keep in mind, though, that older USB devices do not run any faster in a USB 2.0 port. For more information, visit scsite.com/dc2008/ch4/faq and then click USB 2.0.

FireWire Ports

Previously called an *IEEE 1394 port*, a **FireWire port** is similar to a USB port in that it can connect multiple types of devices that require faster data transmission speeds, such as digital video cameras, digital VCRs, color printers, scanners, digital cameras, and DVD drives, to a single connector. A FireWire port allows you to connect up to 63 devices together. The latest FireWire version, called *FireWire 800*, is much more advanced than its predecessor, FireWire 400.

You can use a FireWire hub to attach multiple devices to a single FireWire port. A **FireWire hub** is a device that plugs in a FireWire port on the system unit and contains multiple FireWire ports in which you plug cables from FireWire devices. The FireWire port supports Plug and Play.

Some newer peripherals may attach only to a FireWire port. Having standard ports and connectors, such as FireWire and USB, greatly simplify the process of attaching devices to a personal computer. For newer computers that do not have a serial or parallel port, users plug the device in a USB or FireWire port — as specified by the device's manufacturer. In general, FireWire has replaced audio, parallel, and SCSI ports, which are discussed in the next section. USB ports have replaced mouse, keyboard, serial, audio, parallel, and SCSI ports. Figure 4-32 shows how FireWire and USB ports are replacing other ports completely.

FAQ 4-7

Why are some of my USB and FireWire cables different?

Some smaller computers and devices, such as digital cameras and game consoles, have a mini-USB or mini-FireWire port that requires the USB or FireWire cable have a mini connector at one end and a standard connector at the other end to attach to the computer. Other devices, such as some smart phones, may require the USB or FireWire cable have a device-specific connector at one end for special uses such as wireless Internet connections. For more information, visit scsite.com/dc2008/ch4/faq and then click USB and FireWire Cables.

Special-Purpose Ports

Five special-purpose ports are MIDI, eSATA, SCSI, IrDA, and Bluetooth. These ports are not included in typical computers. For a computer to have these ports, you often must customize the computer purchase order. The following sections discuss these special-purpose ports.

MIDI PORT A special type of serial port that connects the system unit to a musical instrument, such as an electronic keyboard, is called a **MIDI port**. Short for *Musical Instrument Digital Interface*, MIDI (pronounced MID-dee) is the electronic music industry's standard that defines how devices, such as sound cards and synthesizers, represent sounds electronically. A *synthesizer*, which can be a peripheral or a chip, creates sound from digital instructions.

A system unit with a MIDI port has the capability of recording sounds that have been created by a synthesizer and then processing the sounds (the data) to create new sounds. Nearly every sound card supports the MIDI standard, so you can play and manipulate on one computer sounds that originally were created on another computer.

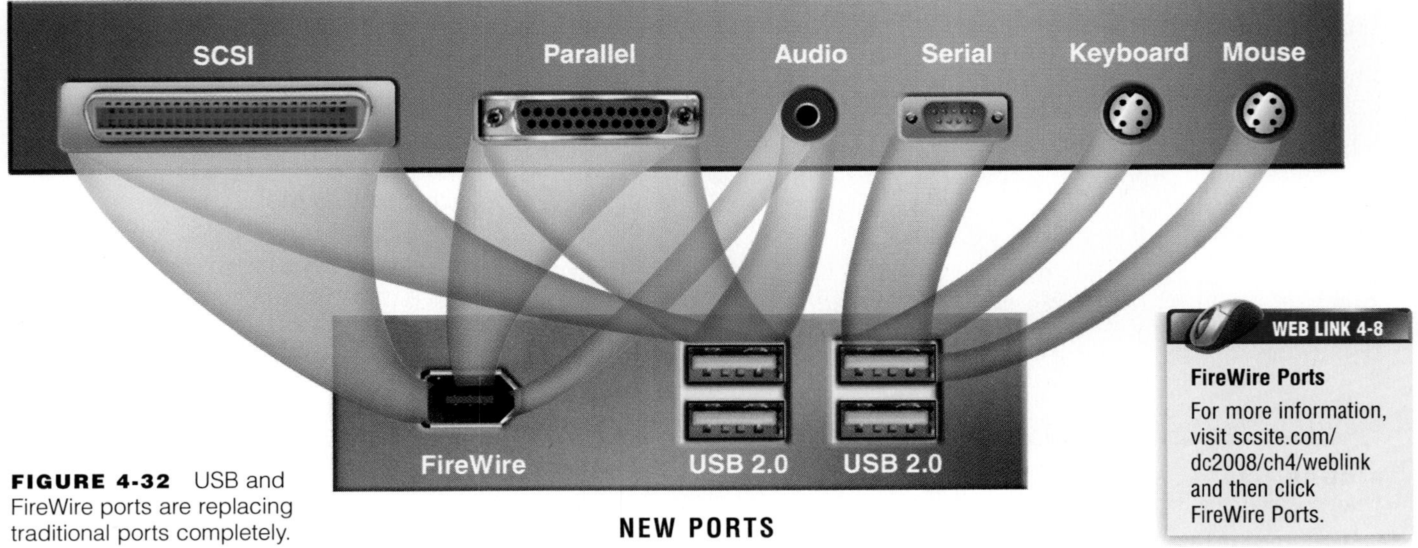

FIGURE 4-32 USB and FireWire ports are replacing traditional ports completely.

WEB LINK 4-8

FireWire Ports

For more information, visit scsite.com/dc2008/ch4/weblink and then click FireWire Ports.

WEB LINK 4-9

eSATA

For more information, visit scsite.com/dc2008/ch4/weblink and then click eSATA.

eSATA Port An **eSATA port**, or *external SATA port*, allows you to connect an external SATA (Serial Advanced Technology Attachment) hard disk to a computer. SATA hard disks are popular because of their fast data transmission speeds. eSATA connections provide up to six times faster data transmission speeds than external hard disks attached to a computer's USB or FireWire port.

SCSI Port A special high-speed parallel port, called a **SCSI port**, allows you to attach SCSI (pronounced skuzzy) peripherals such as disk drives and printers. Depending on the type of *SCSI*, which stands for small computer system interface, you can daisy chain up to either 7 or 15 devices together. Some computers include a SCSI port. Others have a slot that supports a SCSI card.

IrDA Port Some devices can transmit data via infrared light waves. For these wireless devices to transmit signals to a computer, both the computer and the device must have an **IrDA port** (Figure 4-33). These ports conform to standards developed by the *IrDA* (Infrared Data Association).

To ensure nothing obstructs the path of the infrared light wave, you must align the IrDA port on the device with the IrDA port on the computer, similarly to the way you operate a television remote control. Devices that use IrDA ports include a PDA, smart phone, keyboard, mouse, printer, and pager. Several of these devices use a high-speed IrDA port, sometimes called a *fast infrared port*.

Bluetooth Port An alternative to IrDA, **Bluetooth** technology uses radio waves to transmit data between two devices (Figure 4-34). Unlike IrDA, the Bluetooth devices do not have to be aligned with each other. Many computers, peripherals, PDAs, smart phones, cars, and other consumer electronics are Bluetooth-enabled, which means they contain a small chip that allows them to communicate with other Bluetooth-enabled computers and devices. Bluetooth headsets allow smart phone users to connect their phone to a headset wirelessly. The latest version of Bluetooth, called Bluetooth 2.0, supports higher connection speeds and is backward compatible with its predecessors.

If you have a computer that is not Bluetooth enabled, you can purchase a Bluetooth wireless port adapter that will convert an existing USB port or serial port into a Bluetooth port. Also available are Bluetooth PC Cards and ExpressCard modules for notebook computers and Bluetooth cards for PDAs and smart phones.

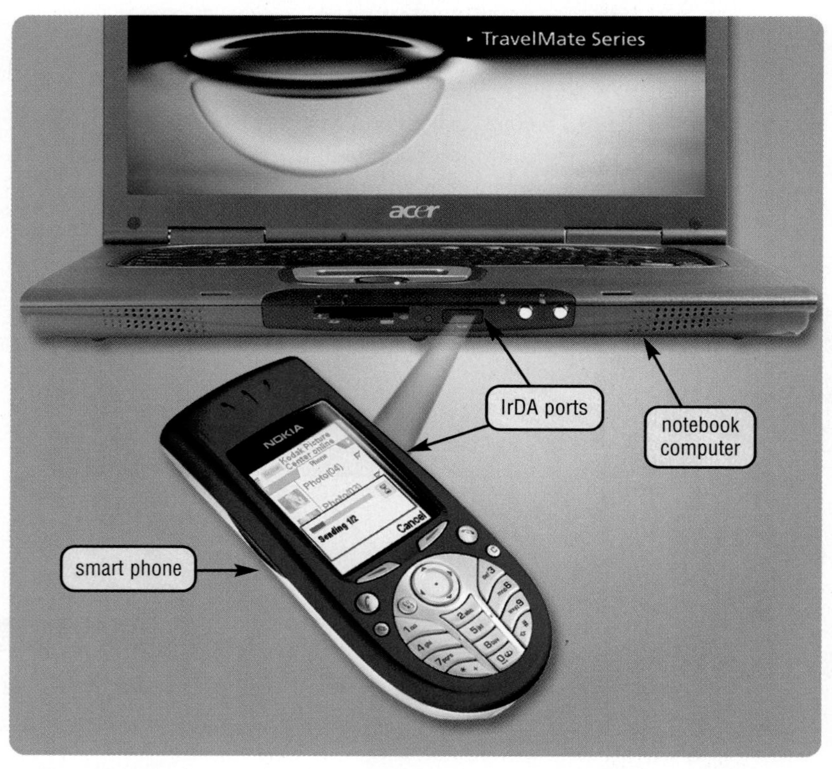

FIGURE 4-33 Many devices communicate wirelessly with desktop or notebook computers through IrDA ports.

FAQ 4-8

How popular is Bluetooth?

Experts predict Bluetooth chip sales will grow to 866 million units by 2009 with revenues of $3 billion, as shown in the chart below. For more information, visit scsite.com/dc2008/ch4/faq and then click Bluetooth Growth.

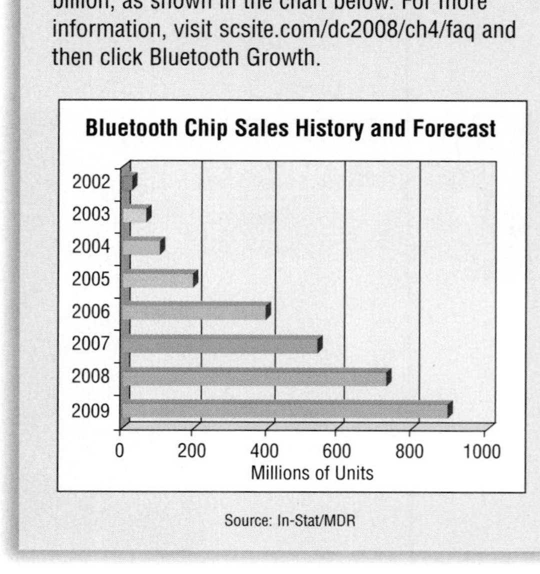

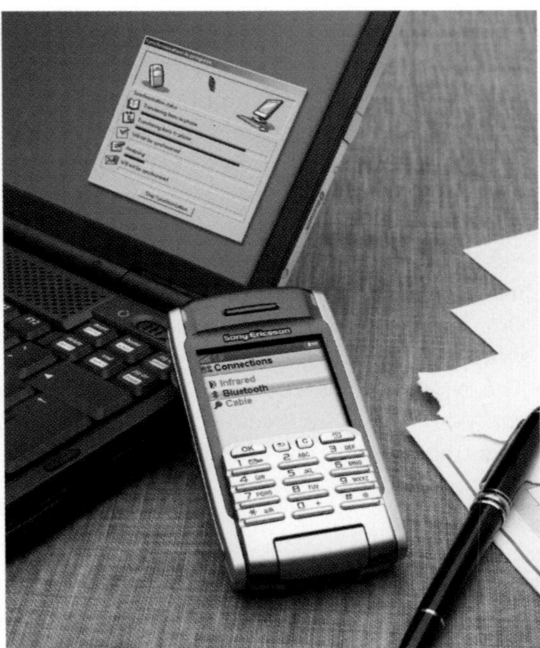

FIGURE 4-34 This smart phone wirelessly communicates with a Bluetooth-enabled notebook computer.

BUSES

As explained earlier in this chapter, a computer processes and stores data as a series of electronic bits. These bits transfer internally within the circuitry of the computer along electrical channels. Each channel, called a **bus**, allows the various devices both inside and attached to the system unit to communicate with each other. Just as vehicles travel on a highway to move from one destination to another, bits travel on a bus (Figure 4-35).

Buses transfer bits from input devices to memory, from memory to the processor, from the processor to memory, and from memory to output or storage devices. Buses consist of two parts: a data bus and an address bus. The *data bus* transfers actual data and the *address bus* transfers information about where the data should reside in memory.

The size of a bus, called the *bus width*, determines the number of bits that the computer can transmit at one time. For example, a 32-bit bus can transmit 32 bits (4 bytes) at a time. On a 64-bit bus, bits transmit from one location to another 64 bits (8 bytes) at a time. The larger the number of bits handled by the bus, the faster the computer transfers data. Using the highway analogy again, assume that one lane on a highway can carry one bit. A 32-bit bus is like a 32-lane highway. A 64-bit bus is like a 64-lane highway.

If a number in memory occupies 8 bytes, or 64 bits, the computer must transmit it in two separate steps when using a 32-bit bus: once for the first 32 bits and once for the second 32 bits. Using a 64-bit bus, the computer can transmit the number in a single step, transferring all 64 bits at once. The wider the bus, the fewer number of transfer steps required and the faster the transfer of data. Most personal computers today use a 64-bit bus.

In conjunction with the bus width, many computer professionals refer to a computer's word size. **Word size** is the number of bits the processor can interpret and execute at a given time. That is, a 64-bit processor can manipulate 64 bits at a time. Computers with a larger word size can process more data in the same amount of time than computers with a smaller word size. In most computers, the word size is the same as the bus width.

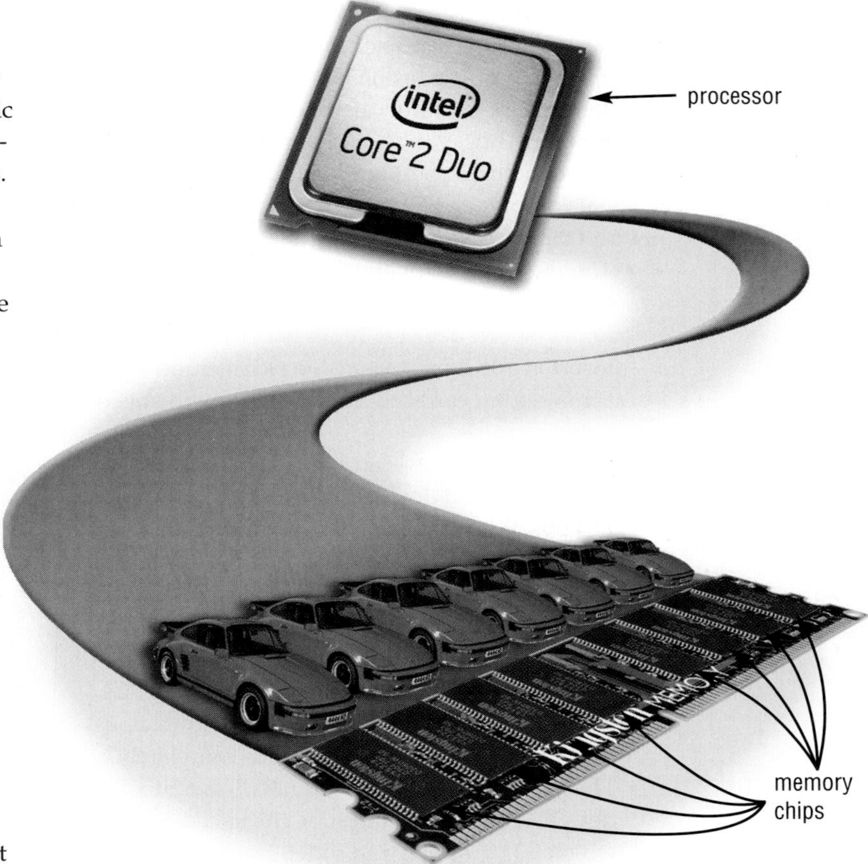

FIGURE 4-35 Just as vehicles travel on a highway, bits travel on a bus. Buses transfer bits from input devices to memory, from memory to the processor, from the processor to memory, and from memory to output or storage devices.

Every bus also has a clock speed. Just like the processor, manufacturers state the clock speed for a bus in hertz. Recall that one megahertz (MHz) is equal to one million ticks per second. Most of today's processors have a bus clock speed of 400, 533, 667, 800, or 1066 MHz. The higher the bus clock speed, the faster the transmission of data, which results in applications running faster.

A computer has two basic types of buses: a system bus and an expansion bus. A *system bus*, also called the *front side bus* (*FSB*), is part of the motherboard and connects the processor to main memory. An *expansion bus* allows the processor to communicate with peripherals. When computer professionals use the term bus by itself, they usually are referring to the system bus.

Expansion Bus

Some peripherals outside the system unit connect to a port on an adapter card, which is inserted in an expansion slot on the motherboard. This expansion slot connects to the expansion bus, which allows the processor to communicate with the peripheral attached to the adapter card. Data transmitted to memory or the processor travels from the expansion slot via the expansion bus and the system bus.

The types of expansion buses on a motherboard determine the types of cards you can add to the computer. Thus, you should understand these expansion buses commonly found in today's personal computers: PCI bus, PCI Express bus, AGP bus, USB, FireWire bus, and PC Card bus.

- The *PCI bus* (Peripheral Component Interconnect bus) is a high-speed expansion bus that connects higher speed devices. Types of cards you can insert in a PCI bus expansion slot include video cards, sound cards, SCSI cards, and high-speed network cards.
- The *PCI Express bus* is an expansion bus that expands on and doubles the speed of the original PCI bus. PCI Express is backward compatible with PCI; that is, it will work with devices that use the PCI bus. Nearly all video cards today use the PCI Express bus, as well as many hard disks and network cards. The ExpressCard technology used in notebook computers also works with the PCI Express bus. Experts predict the PCI Express bus eventually will replace the PCI bus completely.
- The *Accelerated Graphics Port* (*AGP*) is a bus designed by Intel to improve the speed with which 3-D graphics and video transmit. With an AGP video card in an AGP bus slot, the AGP bus provides a faster, dedicated interface between the video card and memory. Newer processors support AGP technology.
- The USB (universal serial bus) and *FireWire bus* are buses that eliminate the need to install cards in expansion slots. In a computer with a USB, for example, USB devices connect to each other outside the system unit, and then a single cable attaches to the USB port. The USB port then connects to the USB, which connects to the PCI bus on the motherboard. The FireWire bus works in a similar fashion. With these buses, expansion slots are available for devices not compatible with USB or FireWire.
- The expansion bus for a PC Card is the *PC Card bus*. With a PC Card inserted in a PC Card slot, data travels on the PC Card bus to the PCI bus.

BAYS

After you purchase a computer, you may want to install an additional storage device, such as a disk drive, in the system unit. A **bay** is an opening inside the system unit in which you can install additional equipment. A bay is different from a slot, which is used for the installation of adapter cards. Rectangular openings, called **drive bays**, typically hold disk drives.

Two types of drive bays exist: external and internal. An *external drive bay* allows a user to access the drive from outside the system unit (Figure 4-36). CD drives, DVD drives, and tape drives are examples of devices installed in external drive bays. An *internal drive bay* is concealed entirely within the system unit. Hard disk drives are installed in internal bays.

FIGURE 4-36 External drive bays usually are located beside or on top of one another.

POWER SUPPLY

Many personal computers plug in standard wall outlets, which supply an alternating current (AC) of 115 to 120 volts. This type of power is unsuitable for use with a computer, which requires a direct current (DC) ranging from 5 to 12 volts. The **power supply** is the component of the system unit that converts the wall outlet AC power into DC power. Different motherboards and computers require different wattages on the power supply. If a power supply is not providing the necessary power, the computer will not function properly.

Built into the power supply is a fan that keeps the power supply and other components of the system unit cool. This fan dissipates heat generated by the processor and other components of the system unit. Many newer computers have additional fans near certain components in the system unit such as the processor, hard disk, and ports.

Some external peripherals such as an external modem, speakers, or a tape drive have an **AC adapter**, which is an external power supply. One end of the AC adapter plugs in the wall outlet and the other end attaches to the peripheral. The AC adapter converts the AC power into DC power that the peripheral requires.

FAQ 4-9

How many fans are in a system unit?

Most system units have at least three fans: one in the power supply, one in the case, and one on the processor heat sink. In addition, you also may find a fan on the video card. While some computers contain fans that are designed to be quiet or operate in a quiet mode, others allow you to turn off noisy fans until they are needed. You also can purchase utility programs that slow or stop the fan until the temperature reaches a certain level. For more information, visit scsite.com/dc2008/ch4/faq and then click Computer Fans.

MOBILE COMPUTERS AND DEVICES

As businesses and schools expand to serve people across the country and around the world, increasingly more people need to use a computer while traveling to and from a main office or school to conduct business, communicate, or do homework. As Chapter 1 discussed, users with such mobile computing needs — known as mobile users — often have a mobile computer, such as a notebook computer or Tablet PC, or a mobile device such as a smart phone or PDA (Figure 4-37).

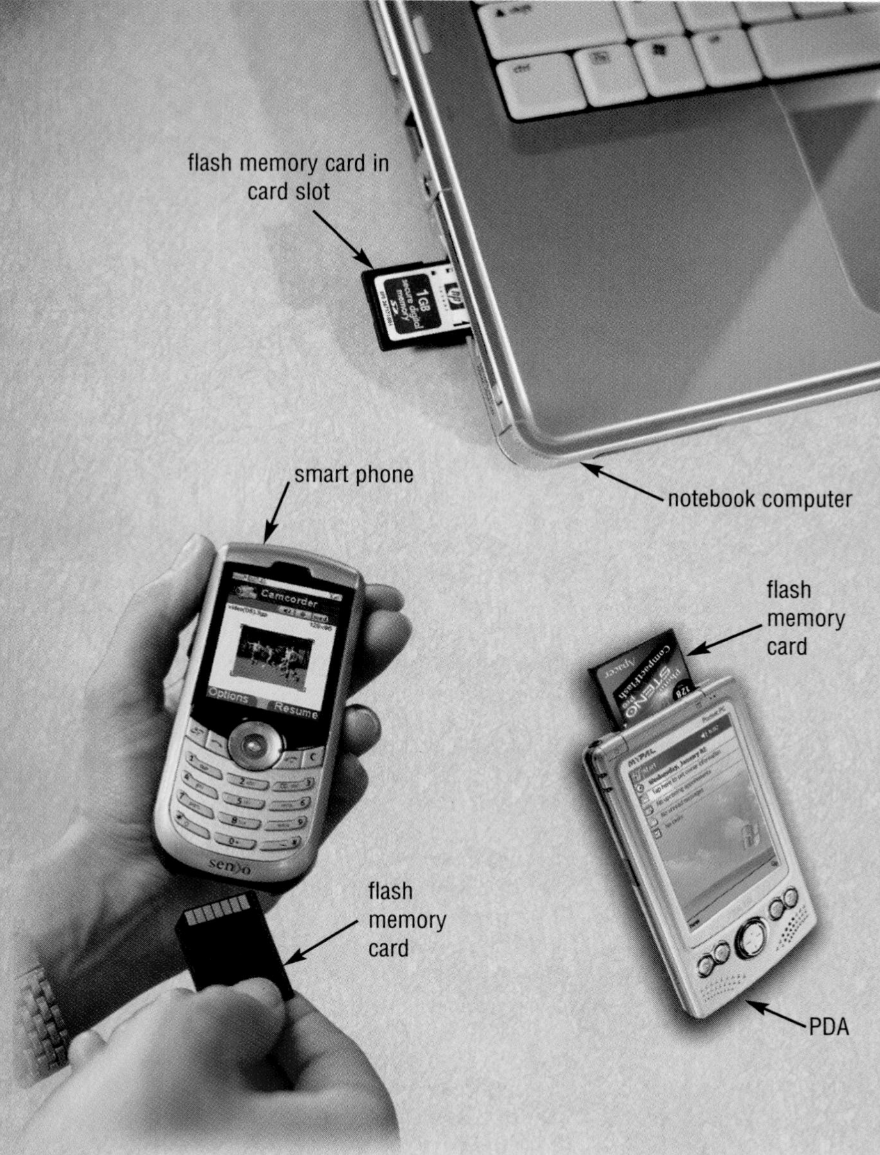

FIGURE 4-37 Users with mobile computing needs often have a notebook computer, PDA, and/or smart phone.

Weighing on average between 2.5 and 9 pounds, notebook computers can run either using batteries or using a standard power supply. Smaller PDAs and smart phones run strictly on batteries. Like their desktop counterparts, mobile computers and devices have a motherboard that contains electronic components that process data.

A notebook computer usually is more expensive than a desktop computer with the same capabilities because it is more costly to miniaturize the components. Notebook computers may have video, modem, network, FireWire, USB, headphones, and microphone ports (Figure 4-38). Read Ethics & Issues 4-4 for a related discussion.

Two basic designs of Tablet PC are available: slate and convertible. With the slate Tablet PC (shown in Figure 4-1 on page 184), all the hardware is behind the display — much like a PDA. Users can attach a removable keyboard to the slate Tablet PC. The display on the convertible Tablet PC, which is attached to a keyboard, can be rotated 180 degrees and folded down over the keyboard. Thus, the convertible Tablet PC can be repositioned to look like either a notebook computer or a slate Tablet PC. Tablet PCs usually include several slots and ports (Figure 4-39).

PDAs and smart phones are quite affordable, usually priced at a few hundred dollars or less.

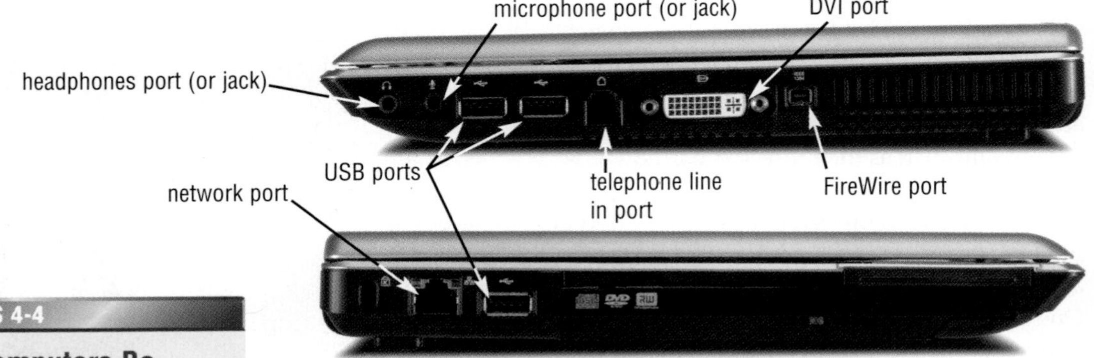

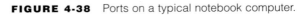

FIGURE 4-38 Ports on a typical notebook computer.

ETHICS & ISSUES 4-4

Should Notebook Computers Be Banned on Airplanes?

After a series of terrorist threats and other incidents, several international airlines banned the use or possession of notebook computers on their flights. Some worry about the threat of a terrorist smuggling a weapon inside the notebook computer. Others banned certain brands of computers after it was discovered the batteries, in rare circumstances, could cause a fire. Still other airlines are concerned about new wireless technology interfering with critical electronics in their airplanes. Those opposed to such measures argue that the risks associated with notebook computers are extremely minor and no higher than the risk from most other everyday items. No major accidents or incidents have been linked to the use or possession of notebook computers on airplanes. Also, the gain in productivity from the use of computers by passengers in airplanes must be taken into consideration as well, they argue. Many people rely on computers for their work; if good security measures were in place, an outright ban would be unnecessary, and people would be more productive on long flights. Should notebook computers be banned on airplanes? Why or why not? Who should evaluate the risks associated with notebook computers, and what standard, if any, should be set for an acceptable level of risk? Why? If notebook computers are banned on airplanes, what other devices should be banned or regulated? Why?

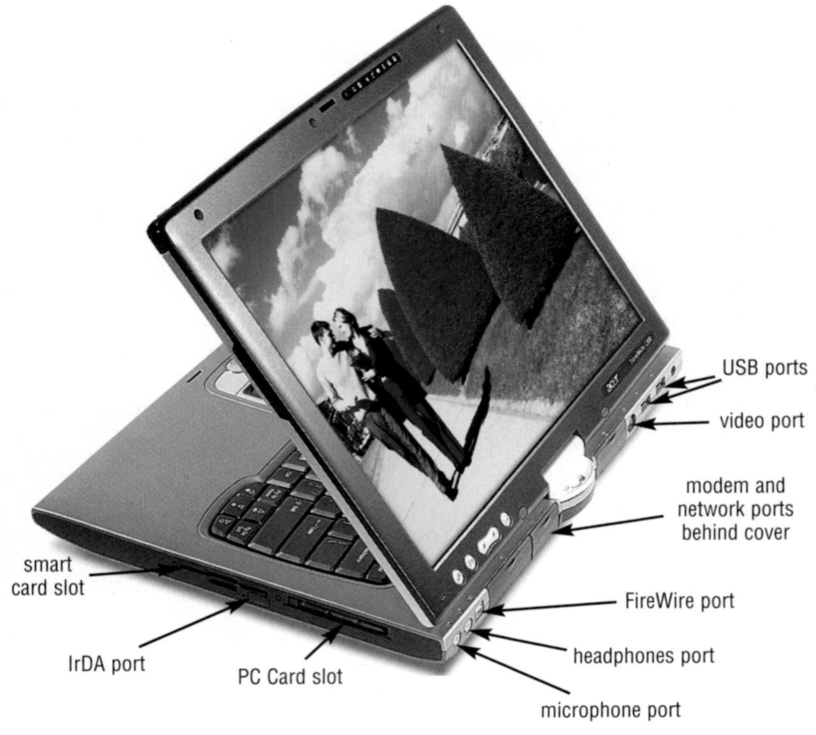

FIGURE 4-39 Ports and slots on a convertible Tablet PC.

These mobile devices often have an IrDA port or are Bluetooth enabled so users can communicate wirelessly with other computers or devices such as a printer.

PUTTING IT ALL TOGETHER

When you purchase a computer, it is important to understand how the components of the system unit work. Many components of the system unit influence the speed and power of a computer. These include the type of processor, the clock speed of the processor, the amount of RAM, bus width, and the clock speed of the bus. The configuration you require depends on your intended use.

The table in Figure 4-40 lists the suggested minimum processor and RAM requirements based on the needs of various types of computer users. Read Looking Ahead 4-2 for a look at a future use of chips.

LOOKING AHEAD 4-2

Healing Bodies with Nanotechnology

Human organs damaged or destroyed through disease, accidents, or the aging process may regain functionality through recent breakthroughs in *nanotechnology*, which involves the design and manufacture of molecule-sized chips. This engineering combines a patient's live cells and plastic covered with nanometer-size patterns to stimulate the growth of new tissue.

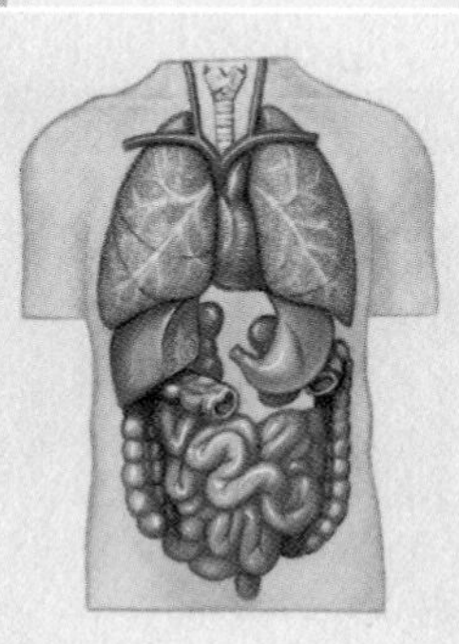

More than 1,700 companies in 34 countries are pushing the limits of science and engineering by manipulating single atoms, electrons, and lasers in the quest to improve health, protect the environment, provide national security, and speed up the telecommunication industry. For example, researchers are using nanotechnology to store data in record time, with one experiment saving the entire content of the *Encyclopedia Britannica* in approximately one minute. Other scientists are examining breaks in chromosomes in an attempt to identify people's cancer susceptibility.

New materials and more effective chip designs are expected to stimulate the nanotechnology field into becoming a $1 trillion market within the decade. For more information, visit scsite.com/dc2008/ch4/looking and then click Nanotechnology.

SUGGESTED MINIMUM CONFIGURATIONS BY USER

User	Processor and RAM
HOME	Intel Celeron D or AMD Sempron or Intel Core 2 Duo or AMD Athlon 64 FX Minimum RAM: 512 MB
SMALL OFFICE/ HOME OFFICE	Intel Core 2 Duo or AMD Athlon 64 FX Minimum RAM: 1 GB
MOBILE	Intel Core Solo or Intel Core 2 Duo or AMD Turion 64 Minimum RAM: 1 GB
POWER 	Intel Itanium 2 or AMD Opteron or Intel Core 2 Extreme or Intel Xeon Minimum RAM: 2 GB
LARGE BUSINESS 	Intel Core 2 Duo or AMD Athlon 64 FX Minimum RAM: 1 GB

FIGURE 4-40 Suggested processor and RAM configurations by user.

KEEPING YOUR COMPUTER CLEAN

Over time, the system unit collects dust — even in a clean environment. Built up dust can block airflow in the computer, which can cause it to overheat, corrode, or even stop working. By cleaning your computer once or twice a year, you can help extend its life. This preventive maintenance task requires a few basic products (Figure 4-41):

- can of compressed air — removes dust and lint from difficult-to-reach areas
- lint-free antistatic wipes and swabs
- bottle of rubbing alcohol
- small computer vacuum (or small attachments on your house vacuum)
- antistatic wristband — to avoid damaging internal components with static electricity
- small screwdriver (may be required to open the case or remove adapter cards)

Before cleaning the computer, turn it off, unplug it from the electrical outlet, and unplug all cables from the ports. Blow away any dust from all openings on the computer case, such as drives, slots, and ports. Vacuum the power supply fan on the back of the computer case to remove any dust that has accumulated on it. Next, release short blasts of compressed air on the power supply fan. Then, use an antistatic wipe to clean the exterior of the case.

If you need assistance opening the computer case, refer to the instructions that came with the computer. Once the case is open, put the antistatic wristband on your wrist and attach its clip to the case of the computer. Use the antistatic wipes to clean dust and grime inside the walls of the computer case. Vacuum as much dust as possible from the interior of the case, including the wires, chips, adapter cards, and fan blades. Next, release short blasts of compressed air in areas the vacuum cannot reach. If the motherboard and adapter cards still look dirty, gently clean them with lint-free wipes or swabs lightly dampened with alcohol.

When finished, be sure all adapter cards are set tightly in their expansion slots. Then close the case, plug in all cables, and attach the power cord. Write down the date you cleaned the computer so you have a record for your next cleaning.

If you do not feel comfortable cleaning the system unit yourself, have a local computer company clean it for you.

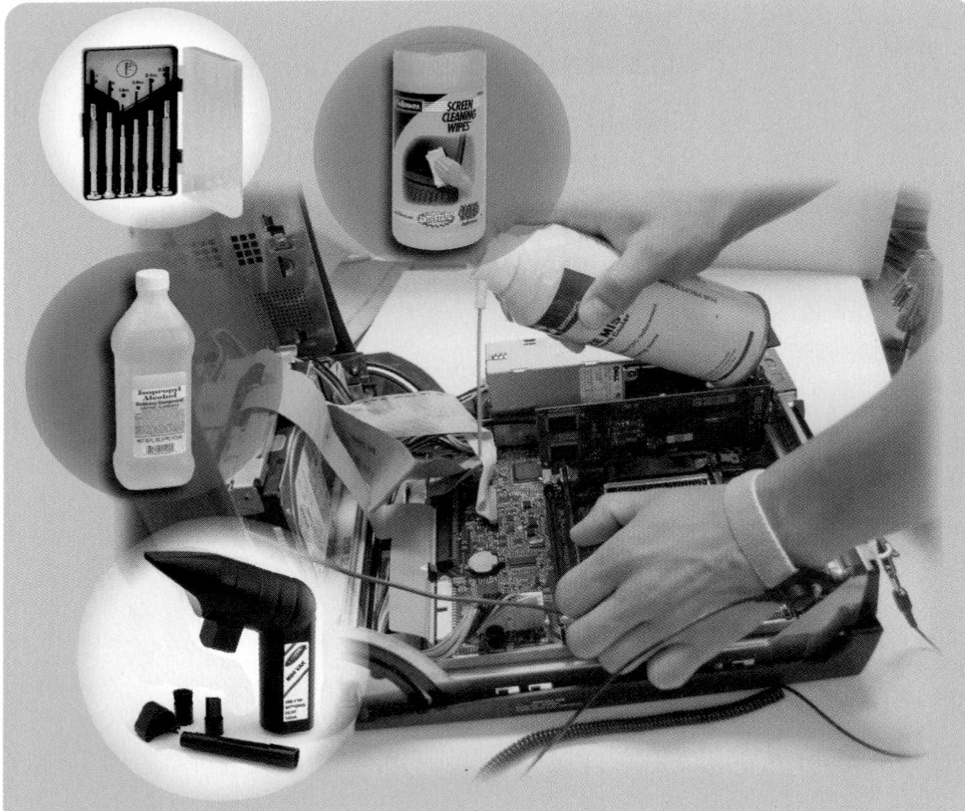

FIGURE 4-41 With a few products, this computer user keeps his computer clean.

FAQ 4-10

Is it safe to open my computer case?

Yes, as long as you are careful and wear an antistatic wristband. Before opening the case, though, check with the computer manufacturer to be sure you will not void a warranty if you clean the computer or install additional components. Also, do not handle any internal components unless you intend to repair or replace them, as unnecessary handling may decrease the life of the component(s). For more information, visit scsite.com/dc2008/ch4/faq and then click Computer Cases.

Test your knowledge of pages 204 through 216 in Quiz Yourself 4-3.

QUIZ YOURSELF 4-3

Instructions: Find the true statement below. Then, rewrite the remaining false statements so they are true.

1. A bus is the point at which a peripheral attaches to or communicates with a system unit so the peripheral can send data to or receive information from the computer.
2. An AC adapter is a socket on the motherboard that can hold an adapter card.
3. Built into the power supply is a heater that keeps components of the system unit warm.
4. Serial ports can connect up to 127 different peripherals together with a single connector.
5. The higher the bus clock speed, the slower the transmission of data.
6. When cleaning the inside of the system unit, wear an antistatic wristband to avoid damaging internal components with static electricity.

Quiz Yourself Online: To further check your knowledge of expansion slots, adapter cards, ports, buses, components of mobile computers and devices, and cleaning a computer, visit scsite.com/dc2008/ch4/quiz and then click Objectives 8 – 12.

CHAPTER SUMMARY

Chapter 4 presented the components of the system unit; described how memory stores data, instructions, and information; and discussed the sequence of operations that occur when a computer executes an instruction. The chapter included a comparison of various personal computer processors on the market today. It also discussed how to clean a system unit.

CAREER CORNER — Computer Engineer

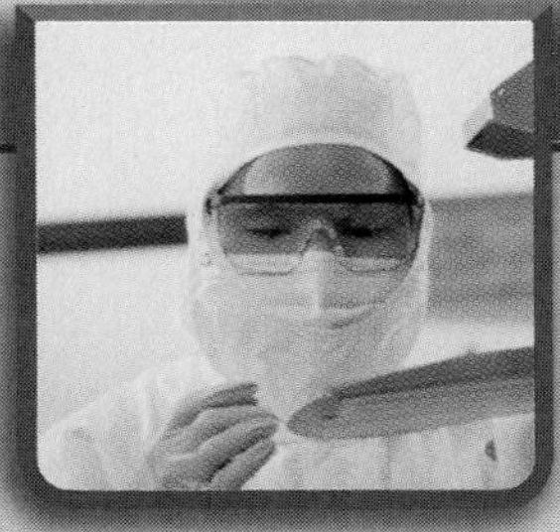

A *computer engineer* designs and develops the electronic components found in computers and peripheral devices. They also can work as researchers, theorists, and inventors. Companies may hire computer engineers for permanent positions or as consultants, with jobs that extend from a few months to a few years, depending on the project. Engineers in research and development often work on projects that will not be released to the general public for two years.

Responsibilities vary from company to company. All computer engineering work, however, demands problem-solving skills and the ability to create and use new technologies. The ability to handle multiple tasks and concentrate on detail is a key component. Assignments often are taken on as part of a team. Therefore, computer engineers must be able to communicate clearly with both computer personnel and computer users, who may have little technical knowledge.

Before taking in-depth computer engineering design and development classes, students usually take mathematics, physics, and basic engineering. Computer engineering degrees include B.S., M.S., and Ph.D. Because computer engineers employed in private industry often advance into managerial positions, many computer engineering graduates obtain a master's degree in business administration (M.B.A.). Most computer engineers earn between $70,000 and $115,000 annually, depending on their experience and employer, but salaries can exceed $150,000. For more information, visit scsite.com/dc2008/ch4/careers and then click Computer Engineer.

High-Tech Talk

RANDOM ACCESS MEMORY (RAM): THE GENIUS OF MEMORY

Inside your computer, RAM takes the form of separate microchip modules that plug in slots on the computer's motherboard. These slots connect through a line (bus) or set of electrical paths to the computer's processor. Before you turn on a computer, its RAM is a blank slate. As you start and use your computer, the operating system files, applications, and any data currently being used by the processor are written to and stored in RAM so the processor can access them quickly.

How is this data written to and stored in RAM? In the most common form of RAM, dynamic random access memory (DRAM), *transistors* (in this case, acting as switches) and a *capacitor* (as a data storage element) create a *memory cell*, which represents a single bit of data.

Memory cells are etched onto a silicon wafer in a series of columns (bitlines) and rows (wordlines), known as an *array*. The intersection of a column and row constitutes the *address* of the memory cell (Figure 4-42). Each memory cell has a unique address that can be found by counting across columns and then counting down by row. The address of a character consists of a series of memory cell addresses put together.

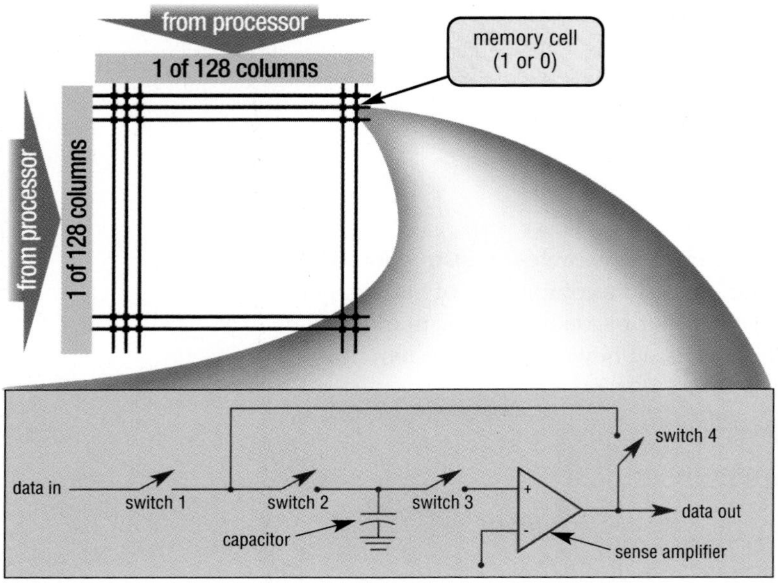

FIGURE 4-42 An illustration of one type of DRAM. When writing data, switches 1 and 2 in the circuit are closed and switches 3 and 4 are open. When reading data, switches 2, 3, and 4 in the circuit are closed and switch 1 is open. Most DRAM chips actually have arrays of memory cells (upper-left corner of figure) that are 16 rows deep.

To write data to RAM, the processor sends the memory controller the address of a memory cell in which to store data. The *memory controller* organizes the request and sends the column and row address in an electrical charge along the appropriate address lines, which are very thin electrical lines etched into the RAM chip. This causes the transistors along those address lines to close.

These transistors act as a switch to control the flow of electrical current in an either closed or open circuit. While the transistors are closed, the software sends bursts of electricity along selected data lines. When the electrical charge traveling down the data line reaches an address line where a transistor is closed, the charge flows through the closed transistor and charges the capacitor.

A capacitor works as electronic storage that holds an electrical charge. Each charged capacitor along the address line represents a 1 bit. An uncharged capacitor represents a 0 bit. The combination of 1s and 0s from eight data lines forms a single byte of data.

The capacitors used in dynamic RAM, however, lose their electrical charge. The processor or memory controller continuously has to recharge all of the capacitors holding a charge (a 1 bit) before the capacitor discharges. During this *refresh operation*, which happens automatically thousands of times per second, the memory controller reads memory and then immediately rewrites it. This refresh operation is what gives dynamic RAM its name. Dynamic RAM has to be refreshed continually, or it loses the charges that represent bits of data. A specialized circuit called a counter tracks the refresh sequence to ensure that all of the rows are refreshed.

The process of reading data from RAM uses a similar, but reverse, series of steps. When the processor gets the next instruction it is to perform, the instruction may contain the address of a memory cell from which to read data. This address is sent to the memory controller. To locate the memory cell, the memory controller sends the column and row address in an electrical charge down the appropriate address lines.

This electrical charge causes the transistors along the address line to close. At every point along the address line where a capacitor is holding a charge, the capacitor discharges through the circuit created by the closed transistors, sending electrical charges along the data lines.

A specialized circuit called a *sense amplifier* determines and amplifies the level of charge in the capacitor. A capacitor charge over a certain voltage level represents the binary value 1; a capacitor charge below that level represents a 0. The sensed and amplified value is sent back down the address line to the processor.

As long as a computer is running, data continuously is being written to and read from RAM. As soon as you shut down a computer, RAM loses its data. The next time you turn on a computer, operating system files and other data are again loaded into RAM and the read/write process starts all over. For more information, visit scsite.com/dc2008/ch4/tech and then click Memory.

Companies on the Cutting Edge

AMD

PC PROCESSOR SUPPLIER

Customer needs influence the integrated circuits *Advanced Micro Devices* (*AMD*) develops for the computing, communications, and consumer electronics industries. AMD calls this philosophy "customer-centric innovation."

As a global supplier of PC processors, AMD engineers its technologies at its Submicron Development Center (SDC) in Sunnyvale, California. The technologies are put into production at manufacturing facilities in the United States, Europe, Asia, and Japan.

Among the company's more successful line of processors is the AMD 64 family, which is composed of the AMD Athlon 64 processor for desktop and personal computers, the AMD Opteron processor for servers and workstations, and the AMD Turion mobile technology for notebook computers. The company's memory chips introduced in 2006 use less power and perform 10 percent faster than its older forms of memory. For more information, visit scsite.com/dc2008/ch4/companies and then click AMD.

INTEL

CHIP MAKER DOMINATES THE COMPUTER MARKET

When Gordon Moore and Robert Noyce started *Intel* in 1968, their goal was to replace magnetic core memory with semiconductor memory. Noyce and Moore, together with Andy Grove, refined the process of placing thousands of tiny electronic devices on a silicon chip. In 1971, the company introduced the Intel 4004, the first single-chip microprocessor.

When IBM chose the Intel 8008 chip for its new personal computer in 1980, Intel chips became standard for all IBM-compatible personal computers. Today, Intel's microprocessors are the building blocks in countless personal computers, servers, networks, and communications devices. The company achieved a breakthrough in 2006 by creating lasers on computer chips, which will increase connection speeds and distances dramatically and drop laser prices from $50 to $1. For more information, visit scsite.com/dc2008/ch4/companies and then click Intel.

Technology Trailblazers

JACK KILBY

INTEGRATED CIRCUIT INVENTOR

Jack Kilby was awarded more than 60 patents during his lifetime, but one has changed the world. His integrated circuit, or microchip, invention made microprocessors possible. He was awarded the Nobel Prize in physics in 2000 for his part in the invention of the integrated circuit.

Kilby started his work with miniature electrical components at Centralab, where he developed transistors for hearing aids. He then took a research position with Texas Instruments and developed a working model of the first integrated circuit, which was patented in 1959. Kilby applied this invention to various industrial, military, and commercial applications, including the first pocket calculator, called the Pocketronic.

Kilby is considered one of the more influential people in the world who has had the greatest impact on business computing in the past 50 years. Kilby died in 2005, but his legacy lives on. His first circuit has fostered a worldwide integrated circuit market with sales of nearly $200 billion annually. For more information, visit scsite.com/dc2008/ch4/people and then click Jack Kilby.

GORDON MOORE

INTEL COFOUNDER

More than 40 years ago, *Gordon Moore* predicted that the number of transistors and resistors placed on computer chips would double every year, with a proportional increase in computing power and decrease in cost. This bold forecast, now known as Moore's Law, proved amazingly accurate for 10 years. Then, Moore revised the estimate to doubling every two years.

Convinced of the future of silicon chips, Moore cofounded Intel in 1968. Moore's lifelong interest in technology was kindled at an early age when he experimented with a neighbor's chemistry set. Even then, he displayed the passion for practical outcomes that has typified his work as a scientist and engineer.

He recently starred in a documentary, *The Microprocessor Chronicles*, which traces the history of microprocessor innovations. For more information, visit scsite.com/dc2008/ch4/people and then click Gordon Moore.

Quizzes and Learning Games

- Computer Genius
- Crossword Puzzle
- DC Track and Field
- Practice Test
- Quiz Yourself
- Wheel of Terms
- You're Hired!

Exercises

- Case Studies
- Chapter Review
- Checkpoint
- Key Terms
- Learn How To
- Learn It Online
- Web Research

Beyond the Book

- Career Corner
- Companies
- FAQs
- High-Tech Talk
- Looking Ahead
- Making Use of the Web
- Trailblazers
- Web Links

Features

- Chapter Forum
- Install Computer
- Lab Exercises
- Maintain Computer
- Tech News
- Timeline 2008

Chapter Review

The Chapter Review section summarizes the concepts presented in this chapter. To listen to the audio version of this Chapter Review, visit scsite.com/dc2008/ch4/review. To obtain help from other students regarding any subject in this chapter, visit scsite.com/dc2008/ch4/forum and post your thoughts or questions.

① **How Are Various Styles of System Units Different?** The **system unit** is a case that contains electronic components of the computer used to process data. On desktop personal computers, most storage devices also are part of the system unit. On notebook computers, the keyboard and pointing device often occupy the area on top of the system unit, and the display attaches to the system unit by hinges. On mobile devices, the display often is built into the system unit. With game consoles, the input and output devices, such as controllers and a television, reside outside the system unit. On handheld game consoles and portable media players, by contrast, the packaging around the system unit houses the input devices and display.

② **What Are Chips, Adapter Cards, and Other Components of the Motherboard?** The **motherboard** is the main circuit board of the system unit. The motherboard contains many electronic components including a processor chip, memory chips, expansion slots, and adapter cards. A **chip** is a small piece of semiconducting material, usually silicon, on which integrated circuits are etched. Expansion slots hold adapter cards that provide connections and functions not built into the motherboard.

③ **What Are the Components of a Processor, and How Do They Complete a Machine Cycle?** The **processor** interprets and carries out the basic instructions that operate a computer. Processors contain a **control unit** that directs and coordinates most of the operations in the computer and an **arithmetic logic unit** (*ALU*) that performs arithmetic, comparison, and other operations. The *machine cycle* is a set of four basic operations — *fetching*, *decoding*, *executing*, and *storing* — that the processor repeats for every instruction. The control unit fetches program instructions and data from memory and decodes the instructions into commands the computer can execute.

④ **What Are the Characteristics of Various Personal Computer Processors?** A **dual-core processor** is a single chip that has two separate processors. A **multi-core processor** is a chip with two or more separate processors. Intel produces the **Core** and **Pentium** processor families for high-performance PCs, the **Celeron** processor family for basic PCs, and the **Xeon** and **Itanium** processor families for workstations and low-end servers. AMD manufactures *Intel-compatible processors*, which have an internal design similar to Intel processors. Some devices have a *system on a chip* processor that integrates the functions of a processor, memory, and a video card on a single chip.

connect
Visit scsite.com/dc2008/ch4/quiz or click the Quiz Yourself button. Click Objectives 1 – 4.

⑤ **What Is a Bit, and How Does a Series of Bits Represent Data?** Most computers are **digital** and recognize only two discrete states: off and on. To represent these states, computers use the **binary system**, which is a number system that has just two unique digits — 0 (for off) and 1 (for on) — called bits. A **bit** is the smallest unit of data a computer can process. Grouped together as a unit, 8 bits form a **byte**, which provides enough different combinations of 0s and 1s to represent 256 individual characters. The combinations are defined by patterns, called coding schemes, such as *ASCII*, *EBCDIC*, and *Unicode*.

⑥ **How Do Programs Transfer In and Out of Memory?** When an application program starts, the program's instructions load into **memory** from the hard disk. The program and operating system instructions are in memory, and the program's window is displayed on the screen. When you quit the program, the program instructions are removed from memory, and the program no longer is displayed on the screen.

Chapter Review

7 What Are the Various Types of Memory? The system unit contains volatile and nonvolatile memory. *Volatile memory* loses its contents when the computer's power is turned off. *Nonvolatile memory* does not lose its contents when the computer's power is turned off. RAM is the most common type of volatile memory. ROM, flash memory, and CMOS are examples of nonvolatile memory. **RAM** consists of memory chips that can be read from and written to by the processor and other devices. **ROM** refers to memory chips storing permanent data and instructions that usually cannot be modified. **Flash memory** can be erased electronically and rewritten. **CMOS** technology uses battery power to retain information even when the power to the computer is turned off.

connect Visit scsite.com/dc2008/ch4/quiz or click the Quiz Yourself button. Click Objectives 5 – 7.

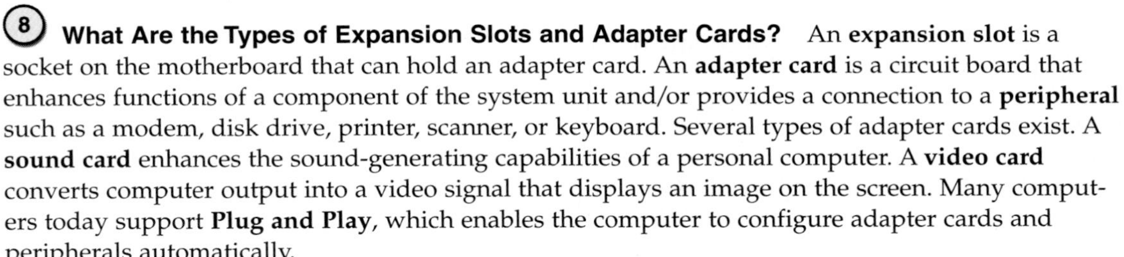

8 What Are the Types of Expansion Slots and Adapter Cards? An **expansion slot** is a socket on the motherboard that can hold an adapter card. An **adapter card** is a circuit board that enhances functions of a component of the system unit and/or provides a connection to a **peripheral** such as a modem, disk drive, printer, scanner, or keyboard. Several types of adapter cards exist. A **sound card** enhances the sound-generating capabilities of a personal computer. A **video card** converts computer output into a video signal that displays an image on the screen. Many computers today support **Plug and Play**, which enables the computer to configure adapter cards and peripherals automatically.

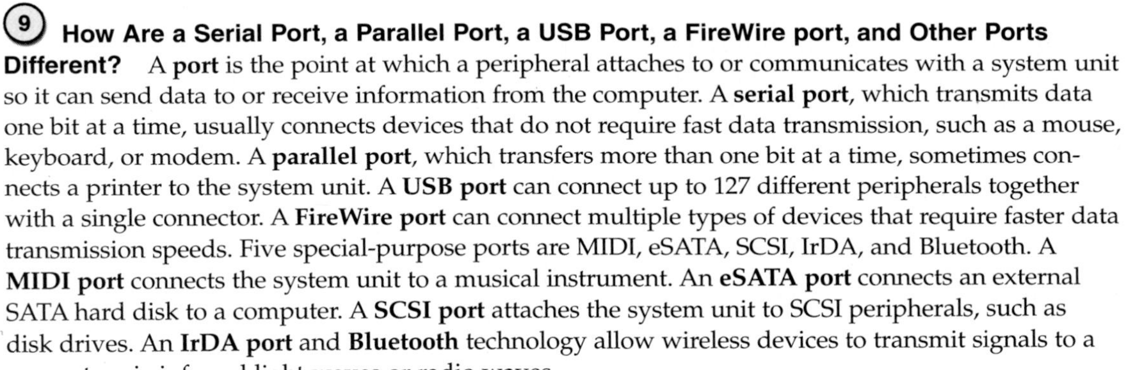

9 How Are a Serial Port, a Parallel Port, a USB Port, a FireWire port, and Other Ports Different? A **port** is the point at which a peripheral attaches to or communicates with a system unit so it can send data to or receive information from the computer. A **serial port**, which transmits data one bit at a time, usually connects devices that do not require fast data transmission, such as a mouse, keyboard, or modem. A **parallel port**, which transfers more than one bit at a time, sometimes connects a printer to the system unit. A **USB port** can connect up to 127 different peripherals together with a single connector. A **FireWire port** can connect multiple types of devices that require faster data transmission speeds. Five special-purpose ports are MIDI, eSATA, SCSI, IrDA, and Bluetooth. A **MIDI port** connects the system unit to a musical instrument. An **eSATA port** connects an external SATA hard disk to a computer. A **SCSI port** attaches the system unit to SCSI peripherals, such as disk drives. An **IrDA port** and **Bluetooth** technology allow wireless devices to transmit signals to a computer via infrared light waves or radio waves.

10 How Do Buses Contribute to a Computer's Processing Speed? A **bus** is an electrical channel along which bits transfer within the circuitry of a computer, allowing devices both inside and attached to the system unit to communicate. The size of a bus, called the *bus width*, determines the number of bits that the computer can transmit at one time. The larger the bus width, the faster the computer transfers data.

11 What Are the Components in Mobile Computers and Mobile Devices? In addition to the motherboard, processor, memory, sound card, PC Card slot, and **drive bay**, a mobile computer's system unit also houses devices such as the keyboard, pointing device, speakers, and display. The system unit for a typical notebook computer often has video, modem, network, FireWire, USB, headphone, and microphone ports. Tablet PCs usually include several slots and ports. PDAs and smart phones often have an IrDA port or are Bluetooth enabled so users can communicate wirelessly.

12 How Do You Clean a System Unit? Before cleaning a system unit, turn off the computer and unplug it from the wall. Use a small vacuum and a can of compressed air to remove external dust. After opening the case, wear an antistatic wristband and vacuum the interior. Wipe away dust and grime using lint-free antistatic wipes and rubbing alcohol.

connect Visit scsite.com/dc2008/ch4/quiz or click the Quiz Yourself button. Click Objectives 8 – 12.

Quizzes and Learning Games
Computer Genius
Crossword Puzzle
DC Track and Field
Practice Test
Quiz Yourself
Wheel of Terms
You're Hired!

Exercises
Case Studies
Chapter Review
Checkpoint
Key Terms
Learn How To
Learn It Online
Web Research

Beyond the Book
Career Corner
Companies
FAQs
High-Tech Talk
Looking Ahead
Making Use of the Web
Trailblazers
Web Links

Features
Chapter Forum
Install Computer
Lab Exercises
Maintain Computer
Tech News
Timeline 2008

Key Terms

You should know the Primary Terms and be familiar with the Secondary Terms. Use the list below to help focus your study. To further enhance your understanding of the Key Terms in this chapter, visit scsite.com/dc2008/ch4/terms. See an example of and a definition for each term, and access current and additional information about the term from the Web.

Primary Terms

(shown in bold-black characters in the chapter)

AC adapter (213)
access time (203)
adapter card (204)
analog (194)
arithmetic logic unit (188)
bay (212)
binary system (195)
bit (195)
Bluetooth (210)
bus (211)
byte (195)
cache (201)
Celeron (190)
central processing unit (CPU) (187)
chip (186)
clock speed (189)
complementary metal-oxide semiconductor (CMOS) (203)
connector (206)
control unit (187)
Core (190)
digital (194)
drive bays (212)
dual-core processor (190)
eSATA port (210)
expansion slot (204)
ExpressCard module (205)
ExpressCard slot (205)
FireWire hub (209)
FireWire port (209)
firmware (202)
flash memory (202)
flash memory card (205)
gigabyte (GB) (197)
gigahertz (GHz) (189)
IrDA port (210)
Itanium (190)
jack (206)
kilobyte (KB or K) (197)
megabyte (MB) (197)
memory (197)
memory cache (201)
memory module (199)
memory slots (199)
MIDI port (209)
motherboard (186)
multi-core processor (190)
nanosecond (203)
parallel port (208)
PC Card (205)
PC Card slot (205)
Pentium (190)
peripheral (204)
Plug and Play (205)
port (206)
power supply (213)
processor (187)
RAM (198)
read-only memory (ROM) (201)
SCSI port (210)
serial port (207)
sound card (204)
system clock (189)
system unit (184)
terabyte (TB) (197)
USB hub (208)
USB port (208)
video card (204)
word size (211)
Xeon (190)

Secondary Terms

(shown in italic characters in the chapter)

Accelerated Graphics Port (AGP) (212)
address (197)
address bus (211)
advanced transfer cache (ATC) (201)
ALU (188)
arithmetic operations (188)
ASCII (195)
binary digit (195)
bus width (211)
Centrino (192)
Centrino Duo (192)
chassis (184)
clock cycle (189)
COM port (207)
comparison operations (188)
daisy chain (208)
data bus (211)
decoding (188)
DDR SDRAM (199)
DIMM (dual inline memory module) (199)
dynamic RAM (DRAM) (199)
EBCDIC (195)
EEPROM chip (202)
executing (188)
expansion bus (212)
expansion card (204)
external drive bay (212)
external SATA port (210)
fast infrared port (210)
fetching (188)
FireWire 800 (209)
FireWire bus (212)
form factor (184)
front side bus (FSB) (212)
gender changer (206)
graphics card (204)
heat pipe (193)
heat sink (193)
hertz (189)
hot plugging (205)
Hyper-Threading (HT) Technology (190)
IBM processor (190)
IEEE 1394 port (209)
integrated circuit (186)
Intel-compatible processors (190)
internal drive bay (212)
IrDA (210)
L1 cache (201)
L2 cache (201)
L3 cache (201)
liquid cooling technology (193)
machine cycle (188)
magnetoresistive RAM (MRAM) (199)
main memory (198)
massively parallel processing (194)
microcode (202)
microprocessor (187)
MIPS (millions of instructions per second) (190)
Motorola processor (190)
Musical Instrument Digital Interface (209)
nonvolatile memory (197)
ns (203)
parallel processing (194)
PC Card bus (212)
PCI bus (212)
PCI Express bus (212)
Personal Computer Memory Card International Association (205)
pipelining (189)
PROM (programmable read-only memory) chip (202)
Rambus DRAM (RDRAM) (199)
random access memory (198)
registers (189)
RIMM (Rambus inline memory module) (199)
SCSI (210)
SETI@home (194)
SIMM (single inline memory module) (199)
static RAM (SRAM) (199)
stored program concept (197)
storing (188)
superscalar (189)
synchronous DRAM (SDRAM) (199)
synthesizer (209)
system board (186)
system bus (212)
system on a chip (192)
transistor (186)
U3 smart drive (205)
Unicode (195)
universal serial bus port (212)
USB 2.0 (208)
USB flash drive (205)
Viiv technology (192)
vPro technology (192)
volatile memory (197)

Checkpoint

Use the Checkpoint exercises to check your knowledge level of the chapter. The Beyond the Book exercises will help broaden your understanding of the concepts presented in this chapter. To complete the Checkpoint exercises interactively, visit scsite.com/dc2008/ch4/check.

Label the Figure

Identify these components.

a. expansion slots
b. memory slots
c. motherboard
d. processor chip in a processor slot

True/False

Mark T for True and F for False. (See page numbers in parentheses.)

_____ 1. The system unit is a case that contains electronic components of the computer used to process data. (184)

_____ 2. The processor interprets and carries out the basic instructions that operate a computer. (187)

_____ 3. The speed of the system clock is just one factor that influences a computer's performance. (189)

_____ 4. Most high-performance PCs use a processor in the Intel Core family or the Pentium family. (190)

_____ 5. Replacing a motherboard is a fairly simple process, whereas replacing a processor is much more complicated. (192)

_____ 6. The SETI@home scientific project runs a program on home users' Internet-connected computers whose purpose is to detect possible intelligent life outside Earth. (194)

_____ 7. A byte is the smallest unit of data the computer can process. (195)

_____ 8. Coding schemes make it possible for humans to interact with a digital computer that processes only bits. (196)

_____ 9. Two types of cache are keyboard cache and mouse cache. (201)

_____ 10. Read-only memory refers to memory chips storing permanent data and instructions. (201)

_____ 11. Serial ports usually connect devices that require fast data transmission rates. (207)

_____ 12. A hard disk connected via an eSATA port will operate much slower than one connected via a computer's USB or FireWire port. (210)

Checkpoint

Multiple Choice

Select the best answer. (See page numbers in parentheses.)

1. The _____ describes the size and shape of the desktop personal computer system unit. (184)
   a. bus width
   b. form factor
   c. processor
   d. chassis
2. On _____, the display often is built into the system unit. (185)
   a. mobile computers and devices
   b. notebook computers
   c. desktop personal computers
   d. all of the above
3. The processor also is called the _____. (187)
   a. central processing unit (CPU)
   b. adapter card
   c. motherboard
   d. chip
4. The _____ is the component of the processor that directs and coordinates most of the operations in the computer. (187)
   a. control unit
   b. arithmetic logic unit
   c. register
   d. machine cycle
5. A processor contains small, high-speed storage locations, called _____, that temporarily hold data and instructions. (189)
   a. flash drives
   b. registers
   c. jacks
   d. heat sinks
6. Processors that can execute more than one instruction per clock cycle are said to be _____. (189)
   a. flash drives
   b. dual-core processors
   c. system on a chip
   d. superscalar
7. Each processor on a dual-core/multi-core chip generally runs at _____ clock speed than a single-core processor. (190)
   a. a faster
   b. the same
   c. a slower
   d. twice the
8. If you plan to purchase an entertainment desktop computer, you will want it to use Intel's _____ technology, which is designed to enhance digital entertainment through a home computer. (192)
   a. vPro
   b. Centrino Duo
   c. Viiv
   d. Itanium
9. Supercomputers use _____ for applications such as artificial intelligence and weather forecasting. (194)
   a. system on a chip technology
   b. massively parallel processing
   c. SCSI
   d. Accelerated Graphics Ports
10. _____ is a 16-bit coding scheme that is capable of representing more than 65,000 characters and symbols, enough for almost all the world's current written languages. (195)
    a. ASCII
    b. Unicode
    c. Microcode
    d. EBCDIC
11. A(n) _____ is a unique number that identifies the location of a byte in memory. (197)
    a. register
    b. kilobyte
    c. address
    d. bit
12. Many of today's computers support _____, which means the computer automatically can configure adapter cards and other peripherals as you install them. (205)
    a. Pack and Go
    b. Pick and Choose
    c. Plug and Play
    d. Park and Ride
13. A _____ port is an interface that connects devices by transferring more than one bit at a time. (208)
    a. serial
    b. parallel
    c. USB
    d. mouse
14. The PCI Express bus is an expansion bus that _____. (212)
    a. expands on and doubles the speed of the original PCI bus
    b. is backward compatible with PCI
    c. is used by nearly all video cards today
    d. all of the above

Checkpoint

Matching

Match the terms with their definitions. (See page numbers in parentheses.)

_____ 1. motherboard (186)
_____ 2. processor (187)
_____ 3. ALU (188)
_____ 4. vPro technology (192)
_____ 5. memory (197)
_____ 6. firmware (202)
_____ 7. flash memory (202)
_____ 8. access time (203)
_____ 9. U3 smart drive (205)
_____ 10. Bluetooth (210)

a. technology that uses radio waves to transmit data between two devices
b. provides the ability to track computer hardware and software, diagnose and resolve computer problems, and secure computers from outside threats
c. main circuit board of the system unit
d. performs arithmetic, comparison, and other operations
e. ROM chips that contain permanently written data, instructions, or information
f. amount of time it takes the processor to read data, instructions, and information from memory
g. stores frequently used instructions and data
h. nonvolatile memory that can be erased electronically and rewritten
i. USB device that includes pre-installed software accessed through a Windows-type interface
j. number of bits the processor can interpret and execute at a given time
k. electronic components that store instructions, data, and results of processed data
l. interprets and carries out the basic instructions that operate a computer

Short Answer

Write a brief answer to each of the following questions.

1. What is the motherboard? ___________ What is a computer chip? ___________
2. What are the four basic operations in a machine cycle? ___________ What are some functions of registers? ___________
3. What is the system clock? ___________ What are some capabilities that processors for notebook computers may include? ___________
4. What is a system on a chip? ___________ What types of devices typically have them? ___________
5. Describe the two basic types of buses in a computer. ___________ Describe the different types of expansion buses. ___________

Beyond the Book

Read the following book elements, learn more about each using the Web, and then write a brief report.

1. Ethics & Issues — Can Computers Think? (187), Discarded Computer Components: Whose Problem Is It? (193), Should Schools Supply Computers to All Students? (200), or Should Notebook Computers Be Banned on Airplanes? (214)
2. Career Corner — Computer Engineer (217)
3. Companies on the Cutting Edge — AMD or Intel (219)
4. FAQs (189, 193, 200, 202, 203, 208, 209, 210, 213, 216)
5. High-Tech Talk — Random Access Memory (RAM): The Genius of Memory (218)
6. Looking Ahead — Hybrid Technology to Power Supercomputer (190) or Healing Bodies with Nanotechnology (215)
7. Making Use of the Web — Online Social Networks and Media Sharing (120)
8. Picture Yourself Computer Shopping (182)
9. Technology Trailblazers — Jack Kilby or Gordon Moore (219)
10. Web Links (186, 190, 199, 201, 202, 204, 205, 209, 210)

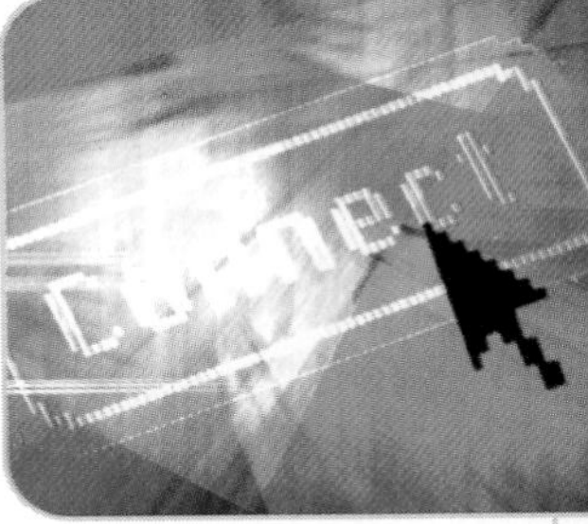

Learn It Online

Use the Learn It Online exercises to reinforce your understanding of the chapter concepts. To access the Learn It Online exercises, visit scsite.com/dc2008/ch4/learn.

1 At the Movies — The Leopard with a Time Machine

To view the The Leopard with a Time Machine movie, click the number 1 button. Locate your video and click the corresponding High-Speed or Dial-Up link, depending on your Internet connection. Watch the movie and then complete the exercise by answering the question that follows. Apple Computer's "Time Machine" software allows users to travel through time by scrolling through different windows that represent days, to help them find the files that they need. What does Time Machine do for your Mac?

2 Video and Audio: You Review It — Bluetooth Technology

In this chapter you learned about Bluetooth technology. Click the number 2 button to view the suggested links and begin your search for videos, podcasts, or vodcasts related to Bluetooth technology. Choose a video, podcast, or vodcast that discusses Bluetooth technology and is of interest to you, and then write a description of its contents. Explain why you chose this piece, what you liked about it, what you disliked about it, and whether you would recommend it to a fellow student. Finish your review by giving the video, podcast, or vodcast a rating of 1 – 5 stars. Submit your review in the format requested by your instructor.

3 Student Edition Labs — Understanding the Motherboard

Click the number 3 button. A new browser window will open, displaying the Student Edition Labs. Follow the on-screen instructions, and complete the Understanding the Motherboard Lab. When finished, click the Exit button. If required, submit your results to your instructor.

4 Student Edition Labs — Binary Numbers

Click the number 4 button. A new browser window will open, displaying the Student Edition Labs. Follow the on-screen instructions, and complete the Binary Numbers Lab. When finished, click the Exit button. If required, submit your results to your instructor.

5 Practice Test

Click the number 5 button. Answer each question. When completed, enter your name and click the Grade Test button to submit the quiz for grading. Make a note of any missed questions. If required, submit your score to your instructor.

6 Who Wants To Be a Computer Genius^2?

Click the number 6 button to find out if you are a computer genius. Directions about how to play the game will be displayed. When you are ready to play, click the Play button. Submit your score to your instructor.

7 Wheel of Terms

Click the number 7 button to reinforce important terms you learned in this chapter by playing the Shelly Cashman Series version of this popular game. Directions about how to play the game will be displayed. When you are ready to play, click the Play button. Submit your score to your instructor.

Learn It Online

8 DC Track and Field

Click the number 8 button to use what you have learned in this chapter to compete against other students in three track and field events. Directions about how to play the game will be displayed. When you are ready to play, click the start first event button. If required, submit your score to your instructor.

9 You're Hired!

Click the number 9 button to use what you have learned in this chapter to embark on the path to a career in computers. Directions about how to play the game will be displayed. When you are ready to play, click the begin game button. If required, submit your score to your instructor.

10 Crossword Puzzle Challenge

Click the number 10 button, then click the Crossword Puzzle Challenge link. Directions about how to play the game will be displayed. Complete the puzzle to reinforce skills you learned in this chapter. When you are ready to play, click the Continue button. Submit the completed puzzle to your instructor.

11 Vista Exercises

Click the number 11 button. When the Vista Exercises menu appears, click the exercise assigned by your instructor. A new browser window will open. Follow the on-screen instructions to complete the exercise. When finished, click the Exit button. If required, submit your results to your instructor.

12 In the News

In February 2006, the forerunner of the modern computer had its 60th anniversary. By today's standards for electronic computers, the ENIAC (Electronic Numerical Integrator And Computer) was a grotesque monster. With 30 separate units, plus a power supply and forced-air cooling, it weighed more than 30 tons. Its 19,000 vacuum tubes, 1,500 relays, and hundreds of thousands of resistors, capacitors, and inductors consumed almost 200 kilowatts of electrical power. The ENIAC performed fewer than 1,000 calculations per minute; today, personal computers can process more than 300 million instructions per second. The rapid development of computing power and capabilities is astonishing, and the rate of that development is accelerating. Click the number 12 button and read a news article about the introduction of a new or improved computer component. What is the component? Who is introducing it? Will the component change the way people use computers? If so, how?

13 Chapter Discussion Forum

Select an objective from this chapter on page 183 about which you would like more information. Click the number 13 button, and post a short message listing a meaningful message title accompanied by one or more questions concerning the selected objective. In two days, return to the threaded discussion by clicking the number 13 button. Submit to your instructor your original message and at least one response to your message.

14 Configuring and Pricing Computers

Click the number 14 button to learn how to configure and price a custom computer. Research at least two manufacturers' Web sites, and get a quote from each site you visit. Make sure you include any software you may require. Also, add any upgrade items that you would like to have on your system including peripheral items (printer, scanner, etc.). Print the quotes from each site and submit the results to your instructor.

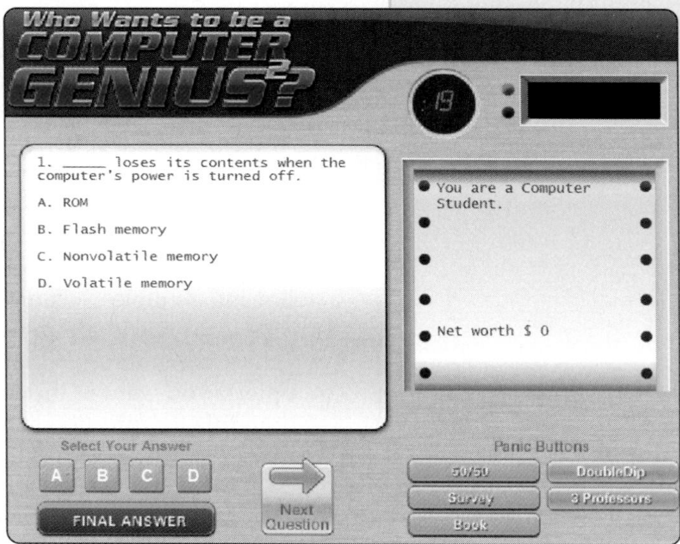

Quizzes and Learning Games
Computer Genius
Crossword Puzzle
DC Track and Field
Practice Test
Quiz Yourself
Wheel of Terms
You're Hired!

Exercises
Case Studies
Chapter Review
Checkpoint
Key Terms
Learn How To
Learn It Online
Web Research

Beyond the Book
Career Corner
Companies
FAQs
High-Tech Talk
Looking Ahead
Making Use of the Web
Trailblazers
Web Links

Features
Chapter Forum
Install Computer
Lab Exercises
Maintain Computer
Tech News
Timeline 2008

Learn How To

Use the Learn How To activities to learn fundamental skills when using a computer and accompanying technology. Complete the exercises and submit them to your instructor. Visit scsite.com/dc2008/ch4/howto to obtain more information pertaining to each activity.

LEARN HOW TO 1: Purchase and Install Memory in a Computer

One of the less expensive and more effective ways to speed up a computer, make it capable of processing more programs at the same time, and enable it to handle graphics, gaming, and other high-level programs is to increase the amount of memory. The process of increasing memory is accomplished in two phases — purchasing the memory and installing the memory. To purchase memory for a computer, complete the following steps:

1. Determine the amount of memory currently in the computer. For a method to do this, see Learn How To number 3 in Chapter 1.
2. Determine the maximum amount of memory your computer can contain. This value can change for different computers, based primarily on the number of slots on the motherboard available for memory and the size of the memory modules you can place in each slot. On most computers, different size memory modules can be inserted in slots. A computer, therefore, might allow a 128 MB, 256 MB, 512 MB, or 1 GB memory module to be inserted in each slot. To determine the maximum memory for a computer, in many cases you can multiply the number of memory slots on the computer by the maximum size memory module that can be inserted in each slot.

   For example, if a computer contains four memory slots and is able to accept memory modules of 128 MB, 256 MB, 512 MB, or 1 GB in each of its memory slots, the maximum amount of memory the computer can contain is 4 GB (4 x 1 GB).

   You can find the number of slots and the allowable sizes of each memory module by contacting the computer manufacturer, looking in the computer's documentation, or contacting sellers of memory such as Kingston (www.kingston.com) or Crucial (www.crucial.com) on the Web. These sellers have documentation for most computers, and even programs you can download to run on your computer that will specify how much memory your computer currently has and how much you can add.
3. Determine how much memory you want to add, which will be somewhere between the current memory and the maximum memory allowed on the computer.
4. Determine the current configuration of memory on the computer. For example, if a computer with four memory slots contains 512 MB of memory, it could be using one memory module of 512 MB in a single slot and the other three slots would be empty; two memory modules of 256 MB each in two slots with two slots empty; one memory module of 256 MB and two memory modules of 128 MB each in three slots with one slot empty; or four memory modules of 128 MB each in four slots with no slots empty. You may be required to look inside the system unit to make this determination. The current memory configuration on a computer will determine what new memory modules you should buy to increase the memory to the amount determined in Step 3.

   You also should be aware that a few computers require memory to be installed in matching pairs. This means a computer with four slots could obtain 512 MB of memory with two memory modules of 256 MB in two slots, or four memory modules of 128 MB in four slots.
5. Determine the number of available memory slots on your computer and the number and size memory modules you must buy to fulfill your requirement. Several scenarios can occur (in the following examples, assume you can install memory one module at a time).
   a. Scenario 1: The computer has one or more open slots. In this case, you might be able to purchase a memory module that matches the amount of memory increase you desire. For example, if you want to increase memory by 256 MB, you should purchase a 256 MB memory module for insertion in the open slot. Generally, you should buy the maximum size module you can for an open slot. So, if you find two empty slots and wish to increase memory by 256 MB, it is smarter to buy one 256 MB module and leave one empty slot rather than buy two 128 MB memory modules and use both slots. This allows you to increase memory again without removing currently used modules.

Learn How To

b. Scenario 2: The computer has no open slots. For example, a computer containing 512 MB of memory could have four slots each containing 128 MB memory modules. If you want to increase the memory on the computer to 1 GB, you will have to remove some of the 128 MB memory modules and replace them with the new memory modules you purchase. In this example, you want to increase the memory by 512 MB. You would have several options: (1) You could replace all four 128 MB memory modules with 256 MB memory modules; (2) You could replace all four 128 MB memory modules with two 512 MB memory modules; (3) You could replace one 128 MB memory module with a 512 MB memory module, and replace a second 128 MB module with a 256 MB memory module. Each of these options results in a total memory of 1 GB. The best option will depend on the price of memory and whether you anticipate increasing the memory size at a later time. The least expensive option probably would be number 3.

c. Scenario 3: Many combinations can occur. You may have to perform calculations to decide the combination of modules that will work for the number of slots on the computer and the desired additional memory.

6. Determine the type of memory to buy for the computer. Computer memory has many types and configurations, and it is critical that you buy the kind of memory for which the computer was designed. It is preferable to buy the same type of memory that currently is found in the computer. That is, if the memory is DDR2 SDRAM with a certain clock speed, then that is the type of additional memory you should place in the computer. The documentation for the computer should specify the memory type. In addition, the Web sites cited on the previous page, and others as well, will present a list of memory modules that will work with your computer. Enough emphasis cannot be placed on the fact that the memory you buy must be compatible with the type of memory usable on your computer. Because there are so many types and configurations, you must be especially diligent to ensure you purchase the proper memory for your computer.
7. Once you have determined the type and size of memory to purchase, buy it from a reputable dealer. Buying poor or mismatched memory is a major reason for a computer's erratic performance and is a difficult problem to troubleshoot.

After purchasing the memory, you must install it on your computer. Complete the following steps to install memory:

1. Unplug the computer, and remove all electrical cords and device cables from the ports on the computer. Open the case of the system unit. You may want to consult the computer's documentation to determine the exact procedure.
2. Ground yourself so you do not generate static electricity that can cause memory or other components within the system unit to be damaged. To do this, wear an antistatic wristband you can purchase inexpensively in a computer or electronics store; or, before you touch any component within the system unit, touch an unpainted metal surface. If you are not wearing an antistatic wristband, periodically touch an unpainted metal surface to dissipate any static electricity.
3. Within the system unit, find the memory slots on the motherboard. The easiest way to do this is look for memory modules that are similar to those you purchased. The memory slots often are located near the processor. If you cannot find the slots, consult the documentation. A diagram often is available to help you spot the memory slots.
4. Insert the memory module in the next empty slot. Orient the memory module in the slot to match the modules currently installed. A notch or notches on the memory module will ensure you do not install the module backwards. If your memory module is a DIMM, insert the module straight down into grooves on the clips and then apply gentle pressure (see Figure 4-18 on page 199). If your memory is SIMM, insert the module at a 45 degree angle and then rotate it to a vertical position until the module snaps into place.
5. If you must remove one or more memory modules before inserting the new memory, carefully release the clips before lifting the memory module out of the memory slot.
6. Plug in the machine and replace all the device cables without replacing the cover.
7. Start the computer. In most cases, the new memory will be recognized and the computer will run normally. If an error message appears, determine the cause of the error.
8. Replace the computer cover.

Exercise

1. Assume you have a computer that contains 512 MB of memory. It contains four memory slots. Each slot can contain 128 MB, 256 MB, or 512 MB memory modules. Two of the slots contain 256 MB memory modules. What memory chip(s) would you buy to increase the memory on the computer to 1 GB? What is the maximum memory on the computer? Submit your answers to your instructor.
2. Assume you have a computer that contains 1 GB of memory. It contains four memory slots. Each slot can contain 128 MB, 256 MB, 512 MB, or 1 GB memory modules. Currently, each slot contains a 256 MB memory module. What combinations of memory modules will satisfy your memory upgrade to 2 GB? Visit a Web site to determine which of these combinations is the least expensive. Submit your answers and recommendations to your instructor.

Quizzes and Learning Games
- Computer Genius
- Crossword Puzzle
- DC Track and Field
- Practice Test
- Quiz Yourself
- Wheel of Terms
- You're Hired!

Exercises
- Case Studies
- Chapter Review
- Checkpoint
- Key Terms
- Learn How To
- Learn It Online
- Web Research

Beyond the Book
- Career Corner
- Companies
- FAQs
- High-Tech Talk
- Looking Ahead
- Making Use of the Web
- Trailblazers
- Web Links

Features
- Chapter Forum
- Install Computer
- Lab Exercises
- Maintain Computer
- Tech News
- Timeline 2008

Web Research

Use the Internet-based Web Research exercises to broaden your understanding of the concepts presented in this chapter. Visit scsite.com/dc2008/ch4/research to obtain more information pertaining to each exercise. To discuss any of the Web Research exercises in this chapter with other students, post your thoughts or questions at scsite.com/dc2008/ch4/forum.

1 **Scavenger Hunt** Use one of the search engines listed in Figure 2-8 in Chapter 2 on page 78 or your own favorite search engine to find the answers to the questions below. Copy and paste the Web address from the Web page where you found the answer. Some questions may have more than one answer. If required, submit your answers to your instructor. (1) What is an ultracapacitator? (2) When was the Xerox Alto developed? Why is it an important step in computer development? (3) What is a daughterboard? (4) What is CAS Latency? (5) What are rune stones and their connection to Danish King Harald Blatand (Bluetooth)? (6) What is the name of the type of memory that retains its contents until it is exposed to ultraviolet light?

2 **Search Sleuth** Ask.com, a popular search engine, uses natural language, which allows researchers to type millions of questions each day using words a human would use rather than code a computer understands. Visit this Web site and then use your word processing program to answer the following questions. Then, if required, submit your answers to your instructor. (1) Click the Search text box, type `What is a memory stick?`, and then click the Search button. Review the Narrow Your Search links on the right side of the page. Click the How Does a Memory Stick Work link, and then scroll through the links and click one to find the answer to this question. (2) Click your browser's Back button or press the BACKSPACE key to return to the Ask.com home page. Review the list of Search Tools on the right side of the page. In addition to Web and News, what are the names of the other available tools? (3) Click the Weather search tool. What city is listed in the Example Weather Result? What is the current temperature there? (4) Click the News search tool on the right side of the page. Click the Top Stories link in the News Photos column. Click one of the Top Stories Photos links and review the material. If required, submit to your instructor a 50-word summary of the information.

3 **Journaling** Respond to your readings in this chapter by writing at least one page containing your reactions, evaluations, and reflections about buying a computer. For example, based on your needs, would you consider buying or have you bought an Apple? What are the pros and cons of buying a notebook versus a desktop computer? How much memory should your computer have? What type of processor? How many ports? Will you need adapter cards or other hardware? You also can write about the new terms you learned by reading this chapter. If required, submit your journal to your instructor.

4 **Expanding Your Understanding** A brick-and-click business allows customers to conduct transactions at a physical location as well as online. Many banks and retailers, such as Citibank and Best Buy, are brick-and-click businesses. Choose a brick-and-click business and then visit the physical location and its Web site. Compare the type, availability, and cost of products or services. Write a report summarizing your findings, focusing on the advantages and disadvantages of conducting business at a physical location and online. If required, submit your report to your instructor.

5 **Ethics in Action** More than 50 law enforcement agencies use handheld wireless devices to access commercial databases. For example, Massachusetts state police stationed at Logan International Airport use the LocatePLUS Holdings Corporation's database, which has information on 98 percent of Americans. The data is composed of motor vehicle records, credit bureau reports, property tax payments, and telephone directories. Police say accessing this information helps them perform their jobs more efficiently. Privacy experts, in contrast, say that information collected for one purpose should not be available in other contexts. View online sites that provide information about commercial databases for sale. Write a report summarizing your findings, and include a table of links to Web sites that provide additional details. If required, submit your report to your instructor.

Case Studies

Use the Case Studies to apply the concepts presented in the chapter to real-world situations. Visit scsite.com/dc2008/ch4/cases to obtain more information pertaining to each exercise. To discuss the Case Studies in this chapter with other students, visit scsite.com/dc2008/ch4/forum and post your thoughts or questions.

CASE STUDY 1 — Class Discussion You are the purchasing manager at TechnoInk, a company that specializes in designing and producing logos for local high school and college sports teams. The company has 35 nonnetworked computers that are used throughout the company for common business applications. The computers are four years old, and you would like to replace them. The director of information technology agrees, but he has reservations. He has asked you to complete a study on the cost of new computers, comparing the major features found on system units at three different price levels: less than $1,000; $1,000 to $1,750; and greater than $1,750. Prepare a brief summary report on the major features of system units at the various price levels. Include recommendations on which system units would meet the company's needs most economically. Be prepared to discuss your recommendations in class.

CASE STUDY 2 — Class Discussion Universal Computing, Inc. has decided to upgrade several hundred PCs used in their offices nationwide. The Information Technology Department has recommended that the company again purchase PCs for approximately $1,500 each. The system units would include Intel Core family processors with speeds of 2.60 GHz with 1 GB of RAM. From her days in college, the CFO has preferred Apple computers and currently uses an Apple iMac at home. She has hired you as a consultant to determine if the company would be better off purchasing iMacs in the same price range and with similar capabilities. Use the Web and/or print media to select a comparable iMac. Which one starts faster? Which one opens files faster? Which one loads Web pages faster? Is the iMac in the same price range as the PC? List any other advantages and disadvantages of each. Prepare a brief summary report and be prepared to discuss your findings in class.

CASE STUDY 3 — Research Your company wants to make the transition to Bluetooth technology. As manager of the IT department, you have been assigned the task of researching the most economical way to make the switch. None of the portable devices the company owns is Bluetooth enabled. Use the Internet and/or print media to research Bluetooth devices. Based on your findings, would it be more economical to purchase Bluetooth ExpressCard modules and port adapters, or would it be better to purchase all new portable devices that are Bluetooth enabled? Write a brief report and share your findings with your class.

CASE STUDY 4 — Research Many system unit manufacturers provide a toll-free telephone number that customers can call with technical problems or questions. If the service technician determines a difficulty is a hardware problem that the customer can fix, the technician might ask the customer to open the system unit and make some adjustments. For this reason, every computer user can benefit by being familiar with the inside of the system unit. If you own a personal computer or have access to a personal computer, unplug the power supply and take the cover off the system unit. Be careful not to touch any of the system unit components. Make a sketch of the system unit and try to identify each part. By referring to the computer's *User Guide*, list some of the computer's specifications (clock speed, memory size, and so on). Compare your sketch and list with a classmate who has done this exercise with a different computer. How are the computers similar? How are they different?

CASE STUDY 5 — Team Challenge Computers have become an integral part of military operations. Many military research projects are done with simulators that resemble civilian computer games. Your company has been contacted by the Department of Defense for a research project. Form a four-member team, and then form two two-member groups. Assign each group one of the following topics to research: 1) How have notebook computers changed the combat environment, and how have these military uses impacted the design of your personal computer? 2) How can the utilization of microchips worn by soldiers, or wearable computers, be integrated into civilian use? Write a summary report or use PowerPoint to create a group presentation and share your findings with the class.

CHAPTER FIVE

Input

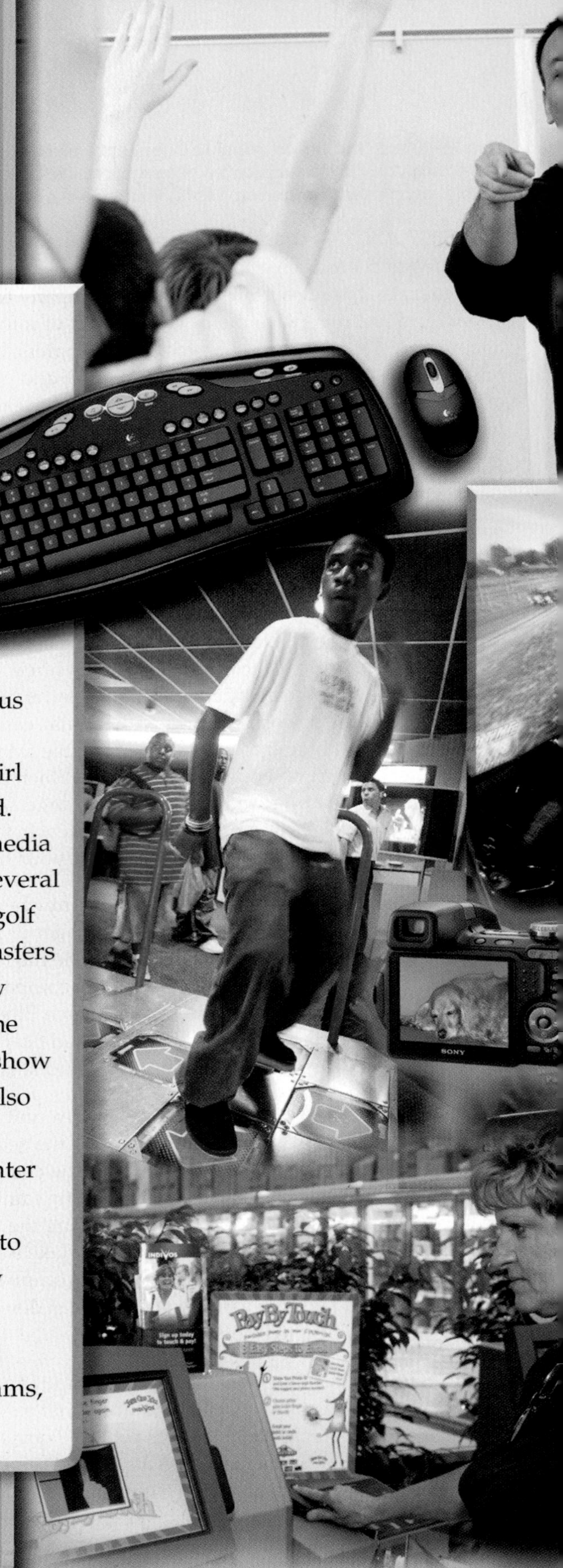

Picture Yourself Using Input Devices

As part of the community service requirements for your scholarship, you have volunteered to teach a brief computer literacy class to a group of middle-school students at your community center. This week, you are discussing input devices, and you have asked the children to compile a list of input devices they see being used each day. You are bringing your PDA and stylus as examples.

When class begins that evening, you are expecting rather obvious choices from their lists, such as keyboard and mouse. You are pleasantly surprised at how knowledgeable these kids are. One girl says her father uses RFID when he drives to work on the toll road. Another girl says that she uses the Click Wheel on her portable media player each day. Two boys had visited a video arcade and used several gaming input devices, including game controllers, baseball bats, golf putters, and dance pads while playing video games. Another transfers images from her parents' digital camera to the computer. One boy says his parents pay for groceries using a fingerprint scanner at the local supermarket, and another one's brother uses a Web cam to show Web site visitors his home construction business in action. They also mention handheld scanners used by delivery staff.

You had planned to use your Tablet PC and a digital pen to enter their answers so that you could illustrate another type of input device. After hearing their knowledgeable answers, you decide to connect your microphone to your notebook computer and show them voice input instead!

Read Chapter 5 to learn about the keyboard and mouse, RFID readers, game controllers, digital cameras, scanners, and Web cams, and discover many other types of input devices.

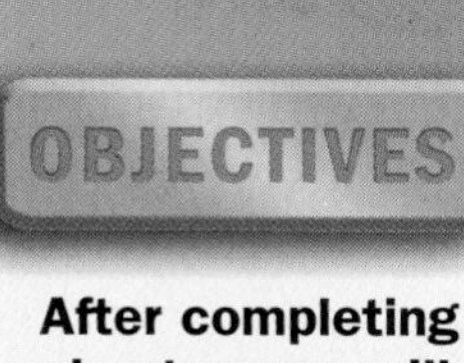

OBJECTIVES

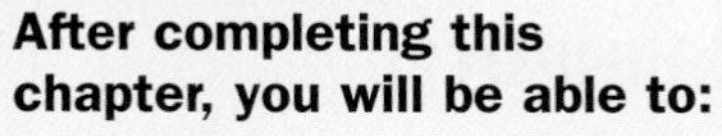

After completing this chapter, you will be able to:

1. Define input
2. List the characteristics of a keyboard
3. Describe different mouse types and how they work
4. Summarize how various pointing devices and controllers for gaming and media players work
5. Explain how voice recognition works
6. Describe various input devices for PDAs, smart phones, and Tablet PCs
7. Explain how a digital camera works
8. Describe the uses of PC video cameras, Web cams, and video conferencing
9. Discuss various scanners and reading devices and how they work
10. Explain the types of terminals
11. Summarize the various biometric devices
12. Identify alternative input devices for physically challenged users

CONTENTS

WHAT IS INPUT?

Input is any data and instructions entered into the memory of a computer. As shown in Figure 5-1, people have a variety of options for entering data or instructions into a computer.

As discussed in Chapter 1, *data* is a collection of unprocessed text, numbers, images, audio, and video. Once data is in memory, the computer interprets and executes instructions to process the data into information. Instructions entered into the computer can be in the form of programs, commands, and user responses.

- A *program* is a series of instructions that tells a computer what to do and how to do it. When a programmer writes a program, he or she enters the program into the computer by using a keyboard, mouse, or other input device. The programmer then stores the program in a file that a user can execute (run). When a user runs a program, the computer loads the program from a storage

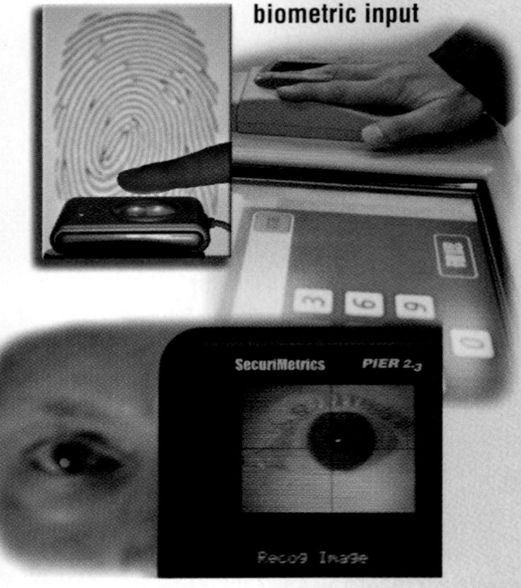

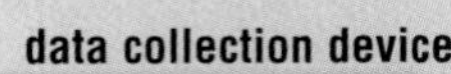

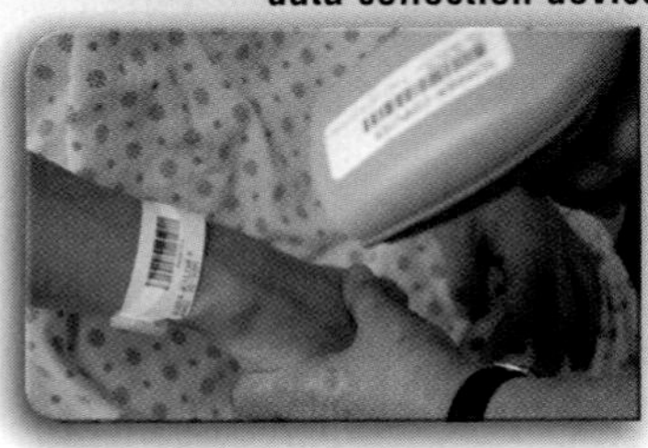

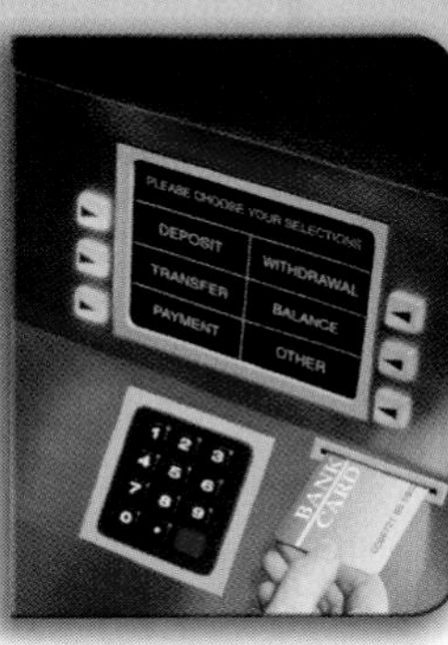

FIGURE 5-1 Users can enter data and instructions into a computer in a variety of ways.

medium into memory. Thus, a program is entered into a computer's memory.

- Programs respond to commands that a user issues. A *command* is an instruction that causes a program to perform a specific action. Users issue commands by typing or pressing keys on the keyboard, clicking a mouse button, speaking into a microphone, or touching an area on a screen.
- A *user response* is an instruction a user issues by replying to a question displayed by a program. A response to the question instructs the program to perform certain actions. Assume the program asks the question, Is the time card correct? If you answer Yes, the program processes the time card. If you answer No, the program gives you the opportunity to modify the time card entries.

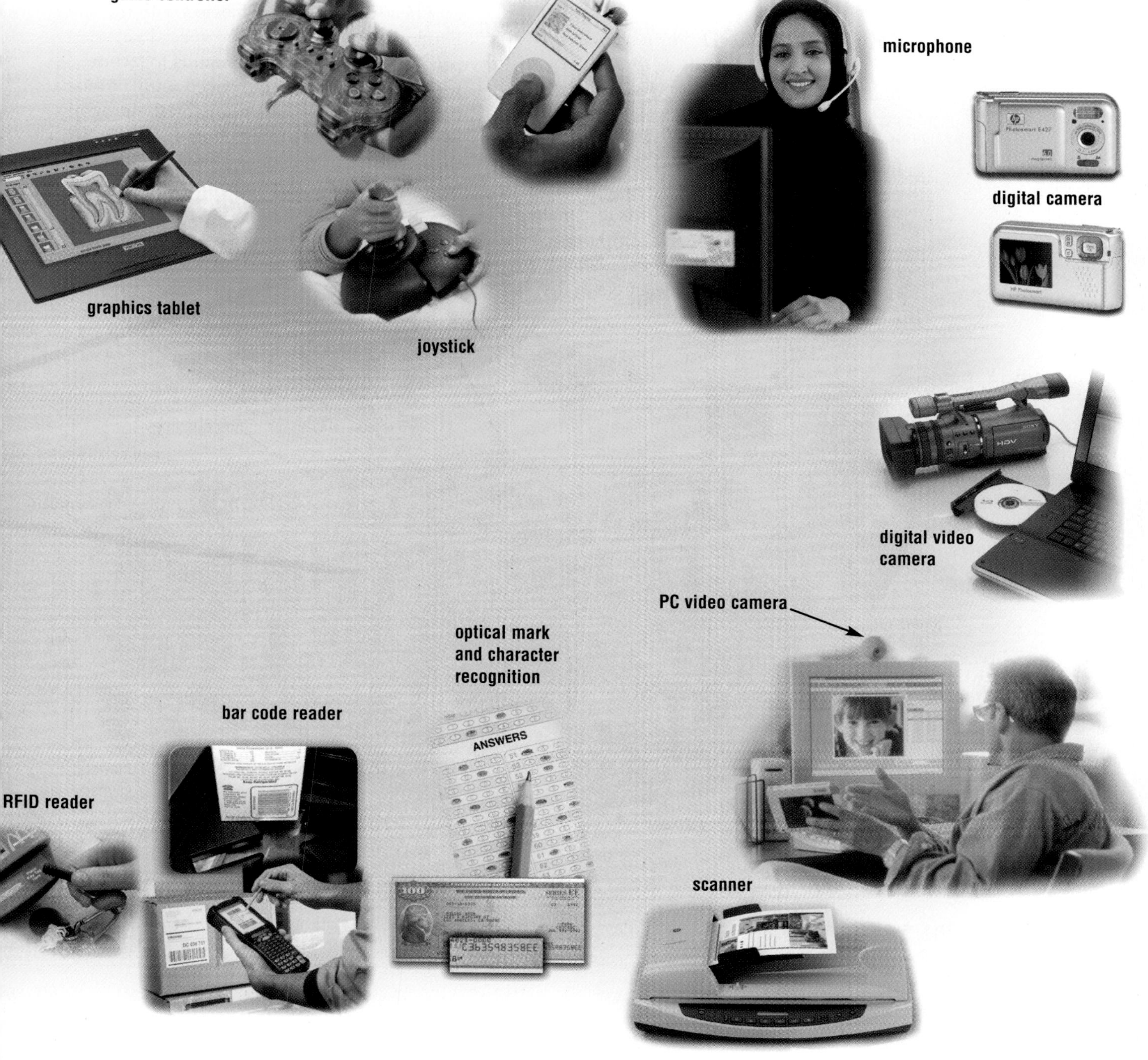

WHAT ARE INPUT DEVICES?

An **input device** is any hardware component that allows users to enter data and instructions (programs, commands, and user responses) into a computer. Depending on the application and your particular requirements, the input device selected may vary. The following pages discuss a variety of input devices.

Storage devices, such as disk drives, serve as both input and output devices. Chapter 7 discusses storage devices.

THE KEYBOARD

Many people use a keyboard as one of their input devices. A **keyboard** is an input device that contains keys users press to enter data and instructions into a computer (Figure 5-2).

Desktop computer keyboards typically have from 101 to 105 keys. Keyboards for smaller computers such as notebook computers contain fewer keys. All computer keyboards have a typing area that includes the letters of the alphabet, numbers, punctuation marks, and other basic keys. Many desktop computer keyboards also have a numeric keypad on the right side of the keyboard. A keyboard also contains other keys that allow users to enter data and instructions into the computer. Read Ethics & Issues 5-1 for a related discussion.

Most of today's desktop computer keyboards are enhanced keyboards. An *enhanced keyboard* has twelve or more function keys along the top; it also has two CTRL keys, two ALT keys, and a set of arrow and additional keys between the typing area and the numeric keypad (Figure 5-2). *Function keys,* which are labeled with the letter F followed by a number, are special keys programmed to issue commands to a computer. The command associated with a function key may vary, depending on the program with which you are interacting. For example, the F3 key may issue one command to an operating system and an entirely different command to a word processing program. To issue commands, users often can press a function key in combination with other special keys (SHIFT, CTRL, ALT, and others).

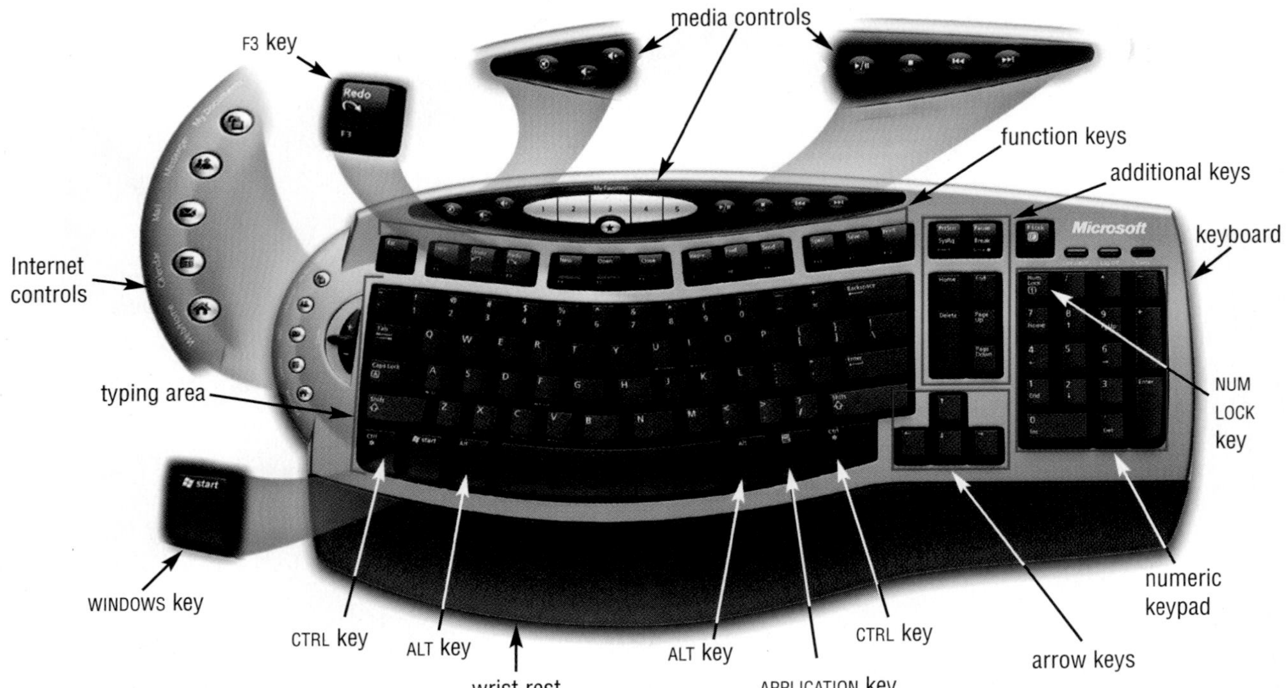

FIGURE 5-2 On a desktop computer keyboard, you type using keys in the typing area and on the numeric keypad.

ETHICS & ISSUES 5-1

Keyboard Monitoring — Privacy Risk?

Do you get the feeling that someone is watching everything you type on your computer at work? Are you concerned about your teenager's conversations in Internet chat rooms? Keyboard monitoring software can dispel your doubts. When installed on a computer, *keyboard monitoring software*, also called a *keylogger*, records every keystroke in a hidden file, which later can be accessed by supplying the correct password. With keyboard monitoring software, you can see everything that was typed on the computer keyboard. Some programs also store a record of software used, Web sites visited, user logons, and periodic screen shots. The software can run completely undetected. With keyboard monitoring software, you can discover that an employee is providing sensitive information to a competitor or recognize that your teenager has made a potentially dangerous contact in a chat room. Businesses sometimes use keyboard monitoring software to analyze the efficiency of data entry personnel. Recently, courts ruled that law-enforcement agencies secretly can install keyboard monitoring software on suspects' computers if a proper search warrant is obtained. Many maintain, however, that keyboard monitoring software is an invasion of privacy, even in the workplace, and some states have outlawed the secret installation of such software. Should keyboard monitoring software ever be used? If so, when? Some marketers of keyboard monitoring software recommend computer users be informed that the software is installed. Is this a good idea? Why or why not?

Nearly all keyboards have toggle keys. A *toggle key* is a key that switches between two states each time a user presses the key. When you press the NUM LOCK key, for example, it locks the numeric keypad so you can use the keypad to type numbers. When you press the NUM LOCK key again, the numeric keypad unlocks so the same keys can serve to move the insertion point. Many keyboards have status lights that light up when you activate a toggle key.

Keyboards also often have a WINDOWS key(s) and an APPLICATION key. When pressed, the WINDOWS key displays the Windows Start menu, and the APPLICATION key displays an item's shortcut menu.

Keyboards also contain keys that allow you to position the insertion point, also known as a *cursor* in some programs. The **insertion point** is a symbol on the screen, usually a blinking vertical bar, that indicates where the next character you type will be displayed (Figure 5-3). Users can move the insertion point left, right, up, or down by pressing the arrow keys and other keys on the keyboard.

Keyboards with media control buttons allow you to run and control your media player program, access the computer's CD/DVD drive, and adjust speaker volume. Internet control buttons allow you to open an e-mail program, start a Web browser, and search the Internet. Some keyboards have USB ports so you can plug a USB device directly in the keyboard instead of in the system unit. Some keyboards include a fingerprint scanner, which is discussed later in this chapter.

A *gaming keyboard* is a keyboard designed specifically for users that enjoy playing games on the computer. Gaming keyboards typically include programmable keys so gamers can customize the keyboard to the game being played. The keys on gaming keyboards light up so they are visible in all lighting conditions. Some even have small displays that show important game statistics, such as time or targets remaining.

FAQ 5-1

What is the rationale for the arrangement of keys in the typing area?

The keys originally were arranged to reduce the frequency of key jams on old mechanical typewriters. Called a *QWERTY keyboard*, the first letters on the top alphabetic line spell QWERTY. A *Dvorak keyboard*, by contrast, places frequently typed letters in the middle of the typing area. Despite the Dvorak keyboard's logical design, most people and computers use a QWERTY keyboard. For more information, visit scsite.com/dc2008/ch5/faq and then click Keyboards.

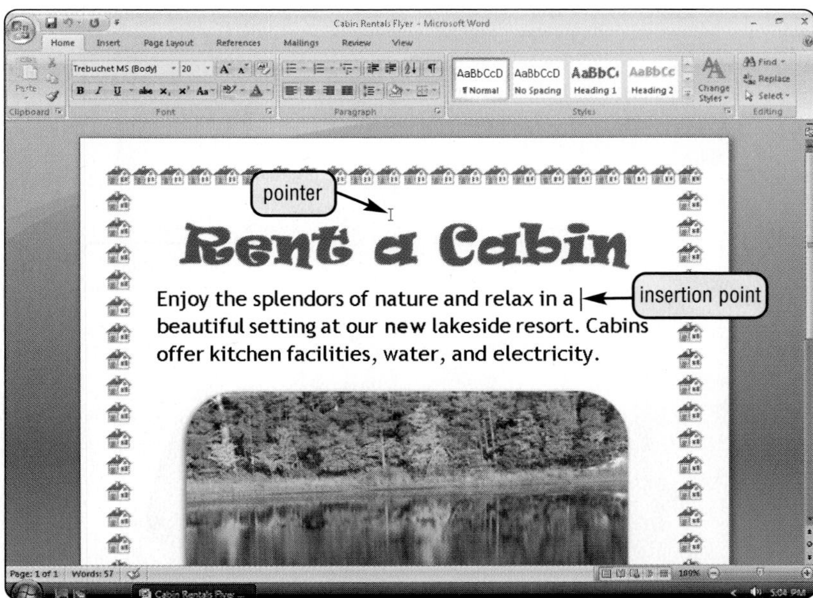

FIGURE 5-3 In most programs, such as Word, the insertion point is a blinking vertical bar. You use the keyboard or other input device to move the insertion point. The pointer, another symbol that is displayed on the screen, is controlled using a pointing device such as a mouse.

Keyboard Connections

Desktop computer keyboards often attach via a cable to a serial port, a keyboard port, or a USB port on the system unit. Some keyboards, however, do not have any wires connecting the keyboard to the system unit. A *wireless keyboard*, or *cordless keyboard*, is a battery-powered device that transmits data using wireless technology, such as radio waves or infrared light waves. Wireless keyboards often communicate with a receiver attached to a port on the system unit. The port type varies depending on the type of wireless technology. For example, a Bluetooth-enabled keyboard communicates via radio waves with a Bluetooth receiver that typically plugs in a USB port (Figure 5-4).

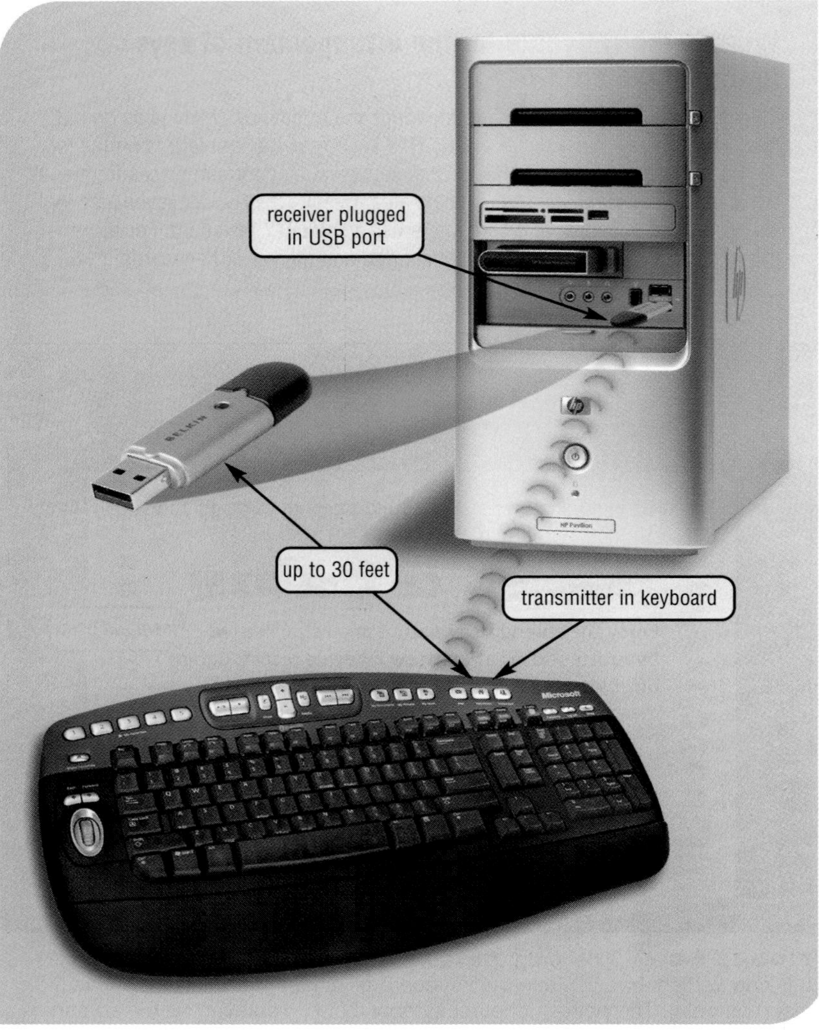

FIGURE 5-4 Some personal computers have built-in Bluetooth technology. On computers that are not Bluetooth-enabled, you plug a Bluetooth receiver in a USB port on the system unit. A transmitter inside the keyboard communicates with the receiver, which should be within 30 feet from each other.

On notebook computers and some handheld computers, PDAs, and smart phones, the keyboard is built in the top of the system unit. To fit in these mobile computers and devices, the keyboards usually are smaller and have fewer keys. A typical notebook computer keyboard usually has only about 85 keys. To provide all of the functionality of a desktop computer keyboard, manufacturers design many of the keys to serve two or three purposes.

Keyboard Ergonomics

Regardless of size, many keyboards have a rectangular shape with the keys aligned in straight, horizontal rows. Users who spend a lot of time typing on these keyboards sometimes experience repetitive strain injuries (RSI) of their wrists and hands. For this reason, some manufacturers offer ergonomic keyboards. An *ergonomic keyboard* has a design that reduces the chance of wrist and hand injuries. Even keyboards that are not ergonomically designed attempt to offer a user more comfort by including a wrist rest or palm rest (Figure 5-2 on page 236).

The goal of **ergonomics** is to incorporate comfort, efficiency, and safety in the design of the workplace. Employees can be injured or develop disorders of the muscles, nerves, tendons, ligaments, and joints from working in an area that is not ergonomically designed.

FAQ 5-2

What can I do to reduce chances of experiencing repetitive strain injuries?

Do not rest your wrist on the edge of a desk; use a wrist rest. Keep your forearm and wrist level so your wrist does not bend. Take a break and do hand exercises every 15 minutes. Keep your shoulders, arms, hands, and wrists relaxed while you work. Maintain good posture. Keep feet flat on the floor, with one foot slightly in front of the other. Immediately stop using the computer if you begin to experience pain or fatigue. For more information, visit scsite.com/dc2008/ch5/faq and then click Repetitive Strain Injuries.

POINTING DEVICES

A **pointing device** is an input device that allows a user to control a pointer on the screen. In a graphical user interface, a **pointer** is a small symbol on the screen (Figure 5-3 on page 237) whose location and shape change as a user moves a pointing device. A pointing device can be used to move the insertion point; select text, graphics, and other objects; and click buttons, icons, links, and menu commands. The following sections discuss the mouse and other pointing devices.

MOUSE

A **mouse** is a pointing device that fits under the palm of your hand comfortably. The mouse is the most widely used pointing device on desktop computers.

With a mouse, users control the movement of the pointer, often called a *mouse pointer* in this case. As you move a mouse, the pointer on the screen also moves. Generally, you use the mouse to move the pointer on the screen to an object such as a button, a menu, an icon, a link, or text. Then, you press a mouse button to perform a certain action associated with that object. The top and sides of a mouse have one to four buttons; some also have a small wheel. The bottom of a mouse is flat and contains a mechanism, such as a ball or a light, that detects movement of the mouse.

A *mechanical mouse,* which was the first type of mouse used with personal computers, has a rubber or metal ball on its underside. Electronic circuits in the mouse translate the movement of the mouse into signals the computer can process. A mechanical mouse is placed on a *mouse pad*, which is a rectangular rubber or foam pad that provides better traction than the top of a desk. The mouse pad also protects the ball in the mouse from a build-up of dust and dirt, which could cause it to malfunction.

Most computer users today have some type of optical mouse, which has no moving mechanical parts inside. Instead, an *optical mouse* uses devices that emit and sense light to detect the mouse's movement. Some use optical sensors, and others use a laser. The latter type often is referred to as a *laser mouse* (Figure 5-5), which is more expensive than the former. You can place an optical mouse on nearly all types of surfaces, eliminating the need for a mouse pad. An optical mouse is more precise than a mechanical mouse and does not require cleaning as does a mechanical mouse, but it also is more expensive.

The mobile user who makes presentations may prefer a mouse that has additional buttons on the bottom for running a slide show and controlling media, similar to a remote control (Figure 5-6). An *air mouse* is a newer type of motion-sensing mouse that, in addition to the typical buttons, allows you to control objects, media players, and slide shows by moving the mouse in predetermined directions through the air. For example, raising the mouse up would increase the volume on your media player.

A mouse connects to a computer in several ways. Many types connect with a cable that attaches to a serial port, mouse port, or USB port on the system unit. A *wireless mouse*, or *cordless mouse,* is a battery-powered device that transmits data using wireless technology, such as radio waves or infrared light waves. The technology used for a wireless mouse is similar to that of a wireless keyboard discussed earlier. Some users prefer a wireless mouse because it frees up desk space and eliminates the clutter of a cord.

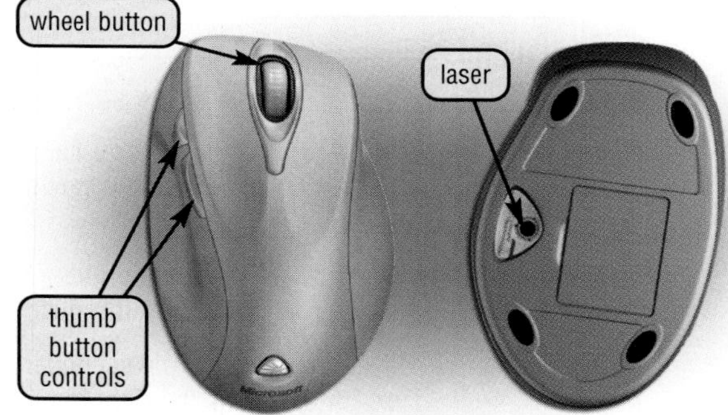

FIGURE 5-5 This mouse uses a laser to detect movement of the mouse. It also includes buttons you push with your thumb that enable forward and backward navigation through Web pages.

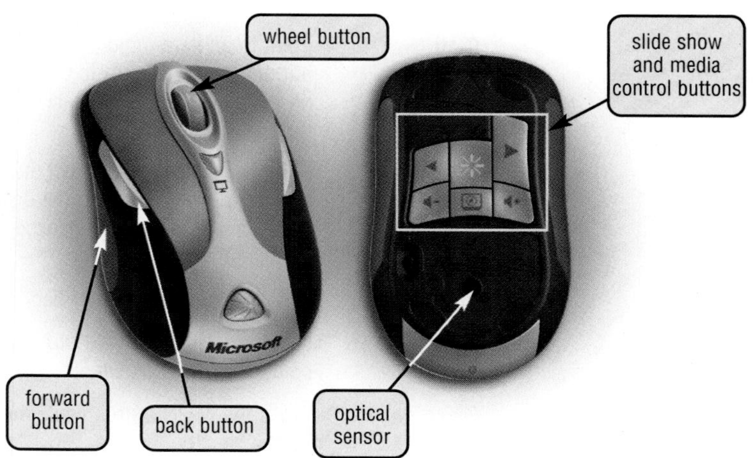

FIGURE 5-6 The bottom of this mouse has buttons that allow you to advance forward and backward through a slide show and also adjust media controls.

Using a Mouse

Windows users work with a mouse that has at least two buttons. For a right-handed user, the left button usually is the primary mouse button, and the right mouse button is the secondary mouse button. Left-handed people, however, can reverse the function of these buttons.

Operations you can perform with the mouse include point, click, right-click, double-click, triple-click, drag, right-drag, rotate wheel, free-spin wheel, press wheel button, and tilt wheel. The table in Figure 5-7 explains how to perform these mouse operations. Some programs also use keys in combination with the mouse to perform certain actions. The function of the mouse buttons and the wheel varies depending on the program. Read Ethics & Issues 5-2 for a related discussion.

Some programs support *mouse gestures*, where the user performs certain operations by holding a mouse button while moving the mouse in a particular pattern. For example, moving the mouse down and to the left may close all open windows. Mouse gestures minimize the amount of time users spend navigating through menus or toolbars because users can perform these tasks by simply moving (gesturing) the mouse.

WEB LINK 5-1

Mouse

For more information, visit scsite.com/dc2008/ch5/weblink and then click Mouse.

FAQ 5-3

How do I use a wheel on a mouse?

Roll it forward or backward to scroll up or down. Tilt it to the right or left to scroll horizontally. Hold down the CTRL key while rolling the wheel to make the text on the screen bigger or smaller. These scrolling and zooming functions work with most software and also on the Web. For more information, visit scsite.com/dc2008/ch5/faq and then click Using a Mouse.

MOUSE OPERATIONS

Operation	Mouse Action	Example
Point	Move the mouse across a flat surface until the pointer on the desktop is positioned on the item of choice.	Position the pointer on the screen.
Click	Press and release the primary mouse button, which usually is the left mouse button.	Select or deselect items on the screen or start a program or program feature.
Right-click	Press and release the secondary mouse button, which usually is the right mouse button.	Display a shortcut menu.
Double-click	Quickly press and release the left mouse button twice without moving the mouse.	Start a program or program feature.
Triple-click	Quickly press and release the left mouse button three times without moving the mouse.	Select a paragraph.
Drag	Point to an item, hold down the left mouse button, move the item to the desired location on the screen, and then release the left mouse button.	Move an object from one location to another or draw pictures.
Right-drag	Point to an item, hold down the right mouse button, move the item to the desired location on the screen, and then release the right mouse button.	Display a shortcut menu after moving an object from one location to another.
Rotate wheel	Roll the wheel forward or backward.	Scroll vertically.
Free-spin wheel	Whirl the wheel forward or backward so it spins freely on its own.	Scroll through hundreds of pages in seconds.
Press wheel button	Press the wheel button while moving the mouse on the desktop.	Scroll continuously.
Tilt wheel	Press the wheel toward the right or left.	Scroll horizontally.

FIGURE 5-7 The more common mouse operations.

ETHICS & ISSUES 5-2

Are Employers Responsible for Medical Problems Related to Computer Use?

When you consider the causes of workplace injuries, you might not put clicking a mouse in the same category with lifting a bag of concrete, but perhaps you should. According to the chairman of a National Academy of Sciences panel that investigated workplace injuries, every year one million Americans lose workdays because of repetitive strain injuries. Repetitive strain injuries are caused when muscle groups perform the same actions over and over again. Once, repetitive strain injuries were common among factory workers who performed the same tasks on an assembly line for hours a day. Today, these injuries, which often result from prolonged use of a computer mouse and keyboard, are the largest job-related injury and illness problem in the United States and are almost completely avoidable with proper computer use. OSHA proposed standards whereby employers would have to establish programs to prevent workplace injuries with respect to computer use. Yet, congress rejected the standards, accepting the argument that the cost to employers would be prohibitive and unfair. Some argue that it is each employee's responsibility to be aware of preventative measures against repetitive strain injuries. Should the government establish laws regarding computer use? Why or why not? Are employees, employers, or the government responsible for repetitive strain injuries? Why? Who should be responsible for the costs of prevention and medical care? Why?

WEB LINK 5-2

Repetitive Strain Injuries

For more information, visit scsite.com/dc2008/ch5/weblink and then click Repetitive Strain Injuries.

OTHER POINTING DEVICES

The mouse is the most widely used pointing device today. Some users, however, work with other pointing devices. These include the trackball, touchpad, pointing stick, light pen, touch screen, stylus, and pens. The following sections discuss each of these pointing devices.

Trackball

A **trackball** is a stationary pointing device with a ball on its top or side (Figure 5-8). The ball in most trackballs is about the size of a Ping-Pong ball.

To move the pointer using a trackball, you rotate the ball with your thumb, fingers, or the palm of your hand. In addition to the ball, a trackball usually has one or more buttons that work just like mouse buttons.

A trackball requires frequent cleaning because it picks up oils from fingers and dust from the environment. For users who have limited desk space, however, a trackball is a good alternative to a mouse because the device is stationary.

Touchpad

A **touchpad** is a small, flat, rectangular pointing device that is sensitive to pressure and motion (Figure 5-9). To move the pointer using a touchpad, slide your fingertip across the surface of the pad. Some touchpads have one or more buttons around the edge of the pad that work like mouse buttons. On most touchpads, you also can tap the pad's surface to imitate mouse operations such as clicking. Touchpads are found most often on notebook computers.

FIGURE 5-8 A trackball.

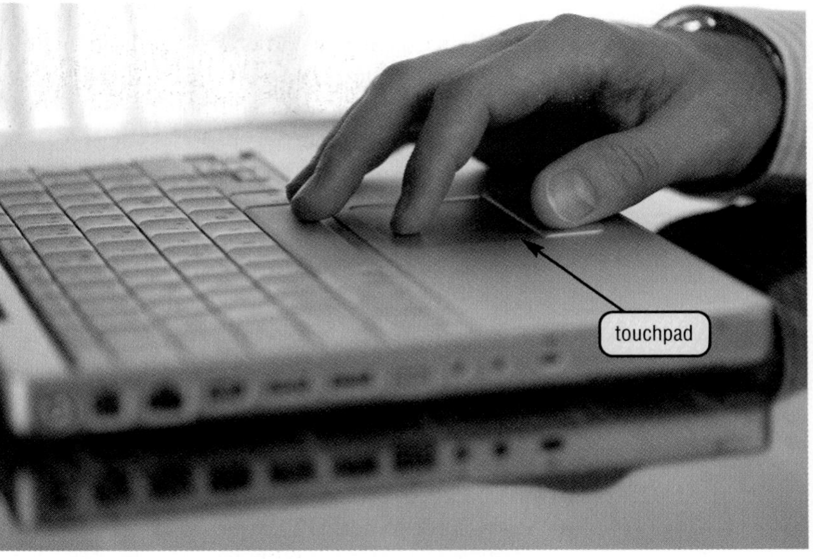

FIGURE 5-9 Most notebook computers have a touchpad that allows users to control the movement of the pointer.

Pointing Stick

A **pointing stick** is a pressure-sensitive pointing device shaped like a pencil eraser that is positioned between keys on a keyboard (Figure 5-10). To move the pointer using a pointing stick, you push the pointing stick with a finger. The pointer on the screen moves in the direction you push the pointing stick. By pressing buttons below the keyboard, users can click and perform other mouse-type operations with a pointing stick. A pointing stick does not require any additional desk space.

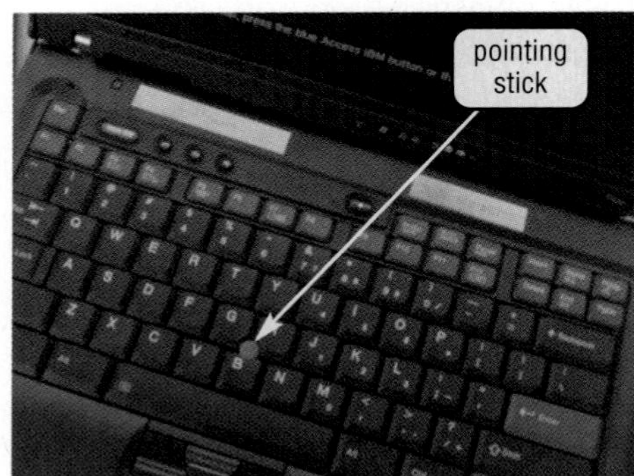

FIGURE 5-10 Some notebook computers include a pointing stick to allow a user to control the movement of the pointer.

Light Pen

A **light pen** is a handheld input device that can detect the presence of light. To select objects on the screen, a user presses the light pen against the surface of the screen or points the light pen at the screen and then presses a button on the pen. Light pens also are ideal for areas where employees' hands might contain food, dirt, grease, or other chemicals that could damage the computer.

Touch Screen

A **touch screen** is a touch-sensitive display device. Users can interact with these devices by touching areas of the screen. Because touch screens require a lot of arm movements, you do not enter large amounts of data using a touch screen. Instead, you touch words, pictures, numbers, letters, or locations identified on the screen.

Kiosks, which are freestanding computers, often have touch screens (Figure 5-11). For example, travelers use kiosks in airports to print tickets ordered online and in hotels for easy check in and check out. To allow easy access of your bank account from a car, many ATMs have touch screens. Many handheld game consoles also have touch screens.

WEB LINK 5-3

Touch Screen

For more information, visit scsite.com/dc2008/ch5/weblink and then click Touch Screen.

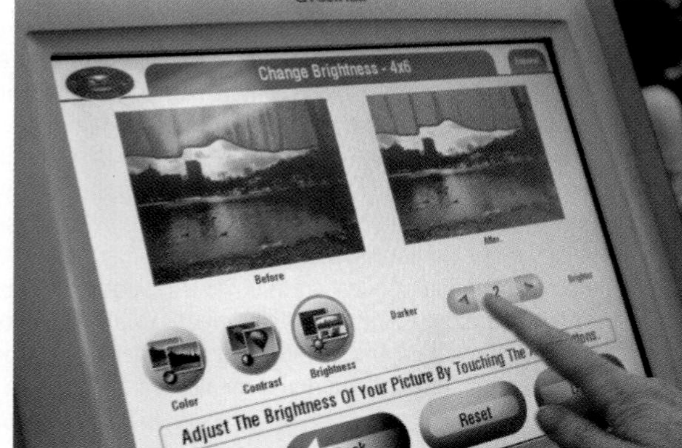

FIGURE 5-11 This user edits digital pictures using a photo kiosk.

Pen Input

Mobile users often enter data and instructions with a pen-type device. With **pen input**, users write, draw, and tap on a flat surface to enter input. The surface may be a monitor, a screen, a special type of paper, or a graphics tablet. Two devices used for pen input are the stylus and digital pen. A **stylus** is a small metal or plastic device that looks like a tiny ink pen but uses pressure instead of ink (Figure 5-12). A **digital pen**, which is slightly larger than a stylus, is available in two forms: some are pressure-sensitive; others have a tiny built-in digital camera.

FIGURE 5-12 PDAs and smart phones use a stylus.

Some mobile computers and nearly all mobile devices have touch screens. Instead of using a finger to enter data and instructions, most of these devices include a pressure-sensitive digital pen or stylus. You write, draw, or make selections on the computer screen by touching the screen with the pen or stylus. For example, Tablet PCs use a pressure-sensitive digital pen (Figure 5-13) and PDAs use a stylus. Pressure-sensitive digital pens, often simply called pens, typically provide more functionality than a stylus, featuring electronic erasers and programmable buttons.

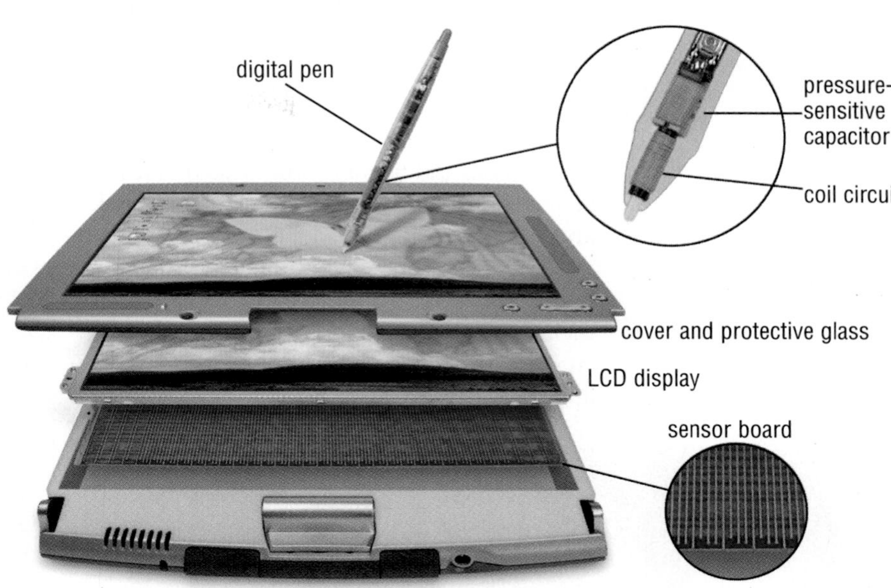

FIGURE 5-13 Tablet PCs use a pressure-sensitive digital pen.

Computers and mobile devices often use *handwriting recognition software* that translates the handwritten letters and symbols into characters that the computer or device can process.

If you want to use pen input on a computer that does not have a touch screen, you can attach a graphics tablet to the computer. A **graphics tablet** is a flat, rectangular, electronic, plastic board. Architects, mapmakers, designers, artists, and home users create drawings and sketches by using a pressure-sensitive pen or a cursor on a graphics tablet (Figure 5-14). A *cursor* looks similar to a mouse, except it has a window with cross hairs, so the user can see through to the tablet. Each location on the graphics tablet corresponds to a specific location on the screen. When drawing on the tablet with a pen or cursor, the tablet detects and converts the movements into digital signals that are sent in the computer. Large-scale applications sometimes refer to the graphics tablet as a *digitizer*.

Digital pens that have built-in digital cameras work differently from pressure-sensitive digital pens. These pens look much like a ballpoint pen and typically do not contain any additional buttons. In addition to the tiny digital camera, these pens contain a processor, memory, and an ink cartridge. As you write or draw on special digital paper with the pen, it captures every handwritten mark by taking more than 100 pictures per second and then stores the images in the pen's memory. You transfer the images from the pen to a computer or mobile device, such as a smart phone. Some pens have a cradle for transferring images; others communicate wirelessly using Bluetooth.

Pen Input

For more information, visit scsite.com/dc2008/ch5/weblink and then click Pen Input.

FIGURE 5-14a
(artist using a pen)

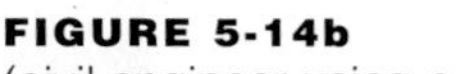

FIGURE 5-14b
(civil engineer using a cursor)

FIGURE 5-14 Graphics tablets use digital pens or cursors.

CONTROLLERS FOR GAMING AND MEDIA PLAYERS

Video games and computer games use a **game controller** as the input device that directs movements and actions of on-screen objects. Game controllers include gamepads, joysticks and wheels, light guns, dance pads, and a variety of motion-sensing controllers. Portable media players use a touch-sensitive pad as their input device. The following sections discuss a variety of game controllers (Figure 5-15) and the touch-sensitive scroll pad.

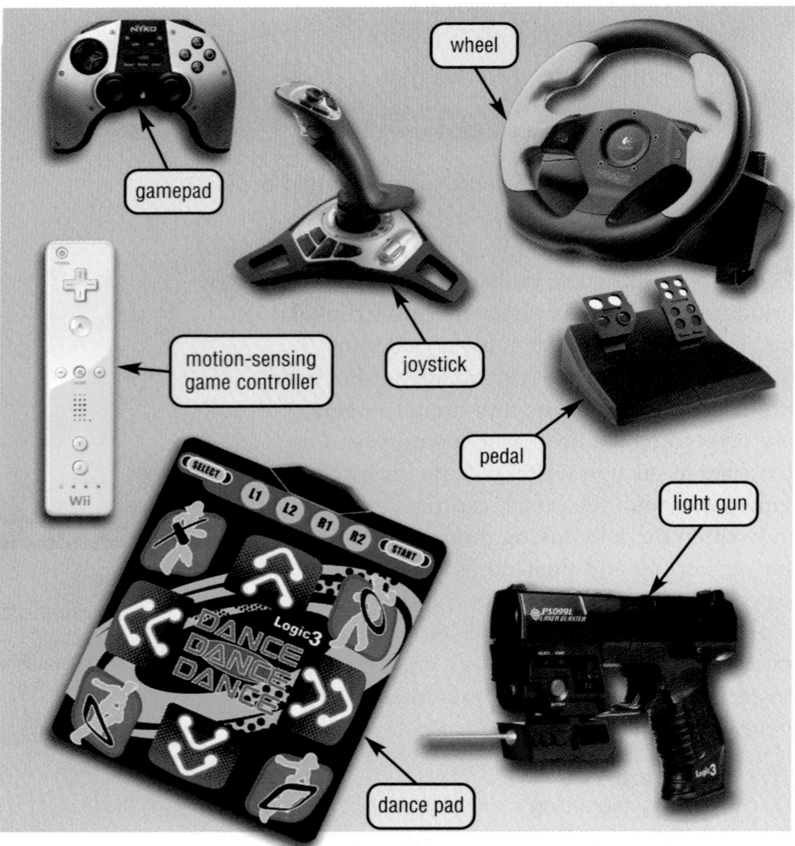

FIGURE 5-15 A variety of game controllers.

Gamepads

A **gamepad**, which is held with both hands, controls the movement and actions of players or objects in video games or computer games. On the gamepad, users press buttons with their thumbs or move sticks in various directions to trigger events. Gamepads communicate with a game console or a personal computer via wired or wireless technology.

WEB LINK 5-5

Wii Remote

For more information, visit scsite.com/dc2008/ch5/weblink and then click Wii Remote.

Joysticks and Wheels

Users running game software or flight and driving simulation software often use a joystick or wheel to control an airplane, vehicle, or player. A **joystick** is a handheld vertical lever mounted on a base. You move the lever in different directions to control the actions of the simulated vehicle or player. The lever usually includes buttons, called triggers, that you press to initiate certain events. Some joysticks also have additional buttons you press to perform other actions.

A **wheel** is a steering-wheel-type input device. Users turn the wheel to simulate driving a car, truck, or other vehicle. Most wheels also include foot pedals for acceleration and braking actions. Joysticks and wheels typically attach via a cable to a personal computer or game console.

Light Guns

A **light gun** is used to shoot targets and moving objects after you pull the trigger on the weapon. Instead of emitting light, most light guns work by detecting light. When the user pulls the trigger, the screen uses one of several techniques to send light, which is received by a receptor in the barrel of the gun. Light guns typically attach via a cable to a game console or personal computer.

Dance Pads

A **dance pad** is a flat electronic device divided into panels that users press with their feet in response to instructions from a music video game. These games test the user's ability to step on the correct panel at the correct time, following a pattern that is synchronized with the rhythm or beat of a song. Dance pads communicate with a game console or a personal computer via wired or wireless technology.

Motion-Sensing Game Controllers

Motion-sensing game controllers allow the user to guide on-screen elements by moving a handheld input device in predetermined directions through the air. Some are sold with a particular type of game; others are general purpose. Sports games, for example, use motion-sensing game controllers, such as baseball bats and golf clubs, as their input device. These types of controllers communicate with a game console or a personal computer via wired or wireless technology.

A popular general-purpose, motion-sensing game controller is Nintendo's Wii Remote. Shaped like a television remote control and operated with one hand, the *Wii Remote* is a motion-sensing input device that uses Bluetooth wireless technology to communicate with the Wii game console. Users point the Wii Remote in different directions and rotate it to control on-screen players, vehicles, and other objects.

Touch-Sensitive Pads

The *touch-sensitive pad* on a portable media player is an input device that enables users to scroll through and play music, view pictures, watch videos or movies, adjust volume, and customize settings. Touch-sensitive pads typically contain buttons and/or wheels that are operated with a thumb or finger. For example, users rotate a *Click Wheel* to browse through its song, picture, or movie lists and press the Click Wheel's buttons to play or pause media, display a menu, and other actions (Figure 5-16).

FIGURE 5-16 You use your thumb to rotate or press buttons on a Click Wheel.

Test your knowledge of pages 234 through 245 in Quiz Yourself 5-1.

QUIZ YOURSELF 5-1

Instructions: Find the true statement below. Then, rewrite the remaining false statements so they are true.

1. A keyboard is an output device that contains keys users press to enter data in a computer.
2. A light pen is a flat, rectangular, electronic, plastic board.
3. A trackball is a small, flat, rectangular pointing device commonly found on notebook computers.
4. Input is any data or instructions entered into the memory of a computer.
5. Operations you can perform with a wheel include point, click, right-click, double-click, triple-click, drag, right-drag, rotate wheel, free-spin wheel, press wheel button, and tilt wheel.
6. PDAs use a pressure-sensitive digital pen, and Tablet PCs use a stylus.

Quiz Yourself Online: To further check your knowledge of input techniques, the keyboard, the mouse and other pointing devices, and controllers for gaming and media players, visit scsite.com/dc2008/ch5/quiz and then click Objectives 1 – 4.

VOICE INPUT

As an alternative to using a keyboard to enter data and instructions, some users talk to their computers and watch the spoken words appear on the screen as they talk. **Voice input** is the process of entering input by speaking into a microphone. The microphone may be a stand-alone peripheral that sits on top of a desk, or built in the computer or device, or in headphones or earphones. Some external microphones have a cable that attaches to a port on the sound card on the computer. Others communicate using wireless technology such as Bluetooth.

Uses of voice input include instant messaging that supports voice conversations, chat rooms that support voice chats, Internet telephony, and voice recognition. Recall that Internet telephony, or Voice over IP, enables users to speak to other users over the Internet. **Voice recognition**, also called *speech recognition*, is the computer's capability of distinguishing spoken words. Popular voice recognition programs include IBM ViaVoice and Dragon NaturallySpeaking (Figure 5-17).

FIGURE 5-17 With voice recognition software, users can dictate text and enter instructions to the computer by speaking into a microphone.

Voice recognition programs recognize a vocabulary of preprogrammed words, which can range from two words to millions of words. The automated telephone system at your bank may ask you to answer questions by speaking the words Yes or No into the telephone. A voice recognition program on your computer, by contrast, may recognize up to two million words.

Most voice recognition programs are a combination of speaker dependent and speaker independent. With *speaker-dependent software*, the computer makes a profile of your voice, which means you have to train the computer to recognize your voice. To train the computer, you must speak words and phrases into the computer repeatedly. *Speaker-independent software* has a built-in set of word patterns so you do not have to train a computer to recognize your voice. Many products today include a built-in set of words that grows as the software learns your words. Most of today's programs allow you to speak in a flowing conversational tone, called *continuous speech*.

Keep in mind that the best voice recognition programs are 90 to 95 percent accurate, which means the software may interpret as many as one in ten words incorrectly.

WEB LINK 5-6

Voice Input

For more information, visit scsite.com/dc2008/ch5/weblink and then click Voice Input.

Audio Input

Voice input is part of a larger category of input called audio input. **Audio input** is the process of entering any sound into the computer such as speech, music, and sound effects. To enter high-quality sound into a personal computer, the computer must have a sound card. Users enter sound into a computer via devices such as microphones, tape players, CD/DVD players, or radios, each of which plugs in a port on the sound card.

Some users also enter music and other sound effects into a computer using external MIDI devices such as an electronic piano keyboard (Figure 5-18). As discussed in the previous chapter, in addition to being a port, *MIDI* (*musical instrument digital interface*) is the electronic music industry's standard that defines how digital musical devices represent sounds electronically. These devices connect to the sound card on a computer. Software that conforms to the MIDI standard allows users to compose and edit music and many other sounds. For example, you can change the speed, add notes, or rearrange the score to produce an entirely new sound.

FIGURE 5-18 An electronic piano keyboard is an external MIDI device that allows users to record music, which can be stored in the computer.

INPUT FOR PDAs, SMART PHONES, AND TABLET PCs

Mobile devices, such as the PDA and smart phone, and mobile computers, such as the Tablet PC, offer convenience for the mobile user. A variety of alternatives for entering data and instructions is available for these devices and computers.

PDAs

A user enters data and instructions into a PDA in many ways (Figure 5-19). PDAs ship with a basic stylus, which is the primary input device. Users often purchase a more elaborate stylus that has a ballpoint pen at one end and a stylus at the other. With the stylus, you enter data in two ways: using an on-screen keyboard or using handwriting recognition software that

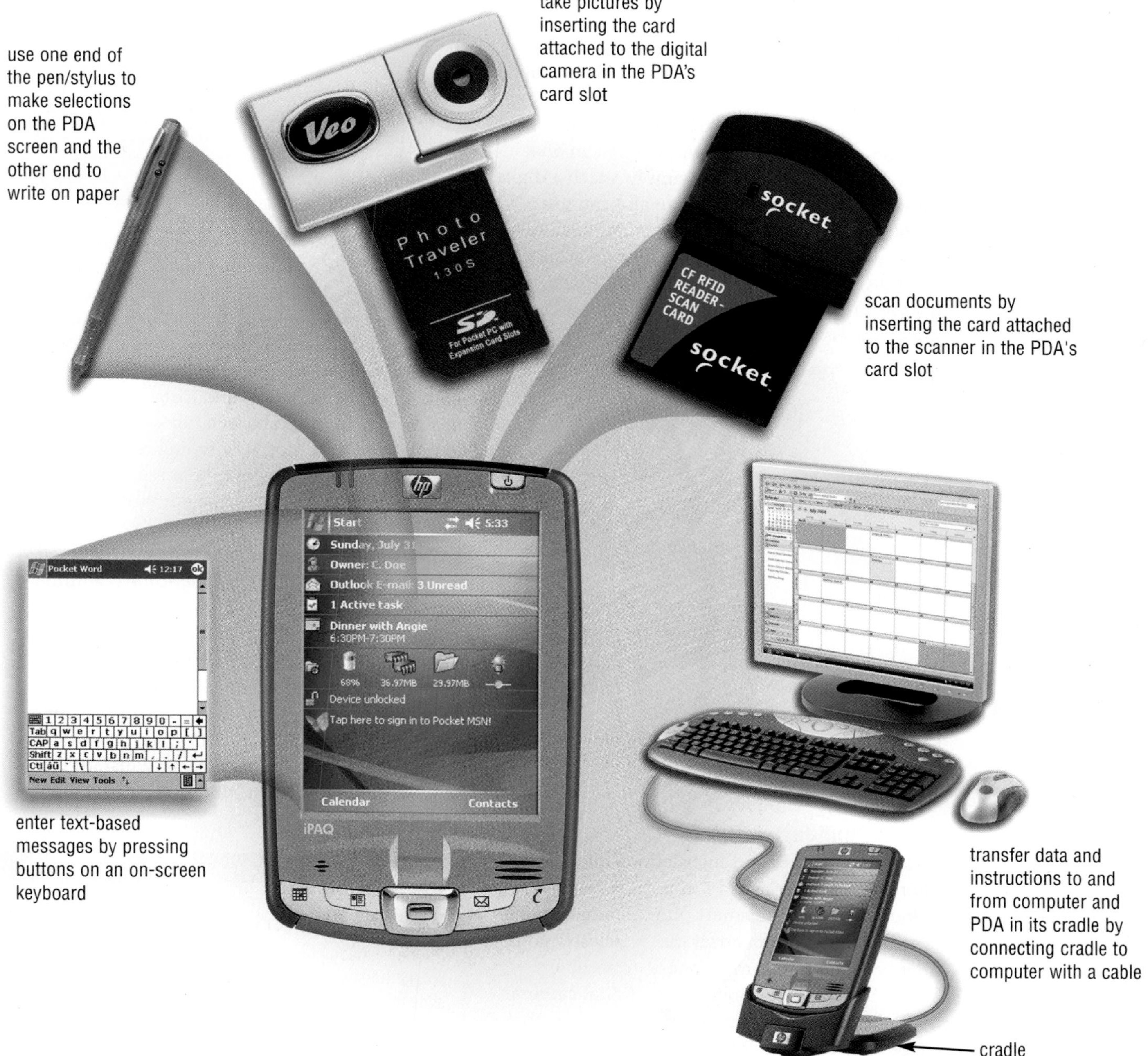
use one end of the pen/stylus to make selections on the PDA screen and the other end to write on paper
take pictures by inserting the card attached to the digital camera in the PDA's card slot
Veo
Photo Traveler 130S
socket
CF RFID READER-SCAN CARD
scan documents by inserting the card attached to the scanner in the PDA's card slot
enter text-based messages by pressing buttons on an on-screen keyboard
transfer data and instructions to and from computer and PDA in its cradle by connecting cradle to computer with a cable
cradle

FIGURE 5-19 Users enter data and instructions into a PDA using a variety of techniques.

is built in the PDA. For example, drawing a straight vertical line in a downward motion displays the number 1 on the PDA.

For users who prefer typing to handwriting, some PDAs have a built-in mini keyboard. Other users type on a desktop computer or notebook computer keyboard and transfer the data to the PDA. Some users prefer to enter data into a PDA using a portable keyboard. A *portable keyboard* is a full-sized keyboard you conveniently use with a PDA or other mobile device (Figure 5-20). Some portable keyboards physically attach to and remove from a PDA; others are wireless.

As an alternative to typing, some PDAs allow users to speak data and instructions into the device. Some PDAs also have cameras built in so you can take photographs and view them on a PDA. On other models, you simply attach a digital camera directly to the PDA. You also can use a PDA to scan small documents, such as business cards and product labels, by attaching a scanner to the PDA. For more information about PDAs, read the Personal Mobile Devices feature that follows this chapter.

FIGURE 5-20 This convenient portable wireless keyboard unfolds into a full-sized keyboard, to which you can attach a PDA.

Smart Phones

Users enter data and instructions into a smart phone using a variety of techniques. You can talk directly into the smart phone's microphone or into a Bluetooth headset that wirelessly communicates with the smart phone to receive audio. Some smart phones have digital cameras that take pictures and touch-sensitive pads that enable you to interact with media, such as music and pictures. Most smart phones include PDA capabilities. Thus, input devices used with PDAs typically also are available for smart phones. For example, some smart phones have a built-in mini keyboard. For those that do not, users enter data and messages into the smart phone using its keypad (Figure 5-21). Types of messages users send with smart phones include text messages, instant messages, and picture messages.

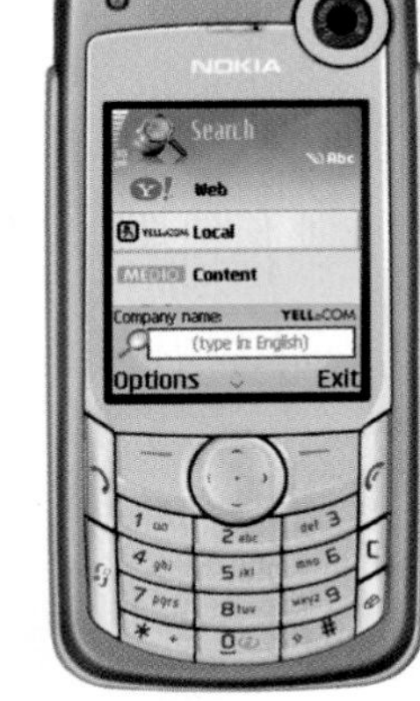

FIGURE 5-21 Users send text messages, instant messages, and picture messages with smart phones.

TEXT MESSAGING Instead of calling someone's smart phone or cellular telephone, users can enter and send typed messages using *text messaging*. To send a text message, you type a short message, typically less than 160 characters, to another smart phone by pressing buttons on the telephone's keypad. As with chat rooms and instant messaging, text messaging uses abbreviations and emoticons to minimize the amount of typing required. For example, instead of typing the message, I am surprised, a user can type the emoticon, :-O.

INSTANT MESSAGING As previously discussed, instant messaging (IM) is a real-time communications service that allows you to exchange messages with other online users. Some wireless Internet service providers (WISPs) partner with IM services so you can use your smart phone to communicate with computer users of the same IM service. For example, with Cingular Wireless service, users can send and receive instant messages with AOL Instant Messenger and Yahoo! Messenger.

FAQ 5-4

How do I type text using a phone keypad?

Phone keypads often contain fewer keys than there are letters in the alphabet. For this reason, each key is responsible for typing multiple characters, which are identified on the key. For example, the "2" key displays the letters A, B, and C on its face. Pressing a key multiple times on the phone's keypad will allow you to cycle through the number, letters, and any other symbols displayed on that key. For more information, visit scsite.com/dc2008/ch5/faq and then click Phone Keypads.

Picture Messaging With *picture messaging,* users can send graphics, pictures, video clips, and sound files, as well as short text messages to another smart phone with a compatible picture messaging service. Many smart phones today have a built-in camera so users easily can take pictures and videos and even incorporate short voice recordings in their picture messages (Figure 5-22). After taking the pictures, users can send them to another smart phone, e-mail them to any e-mail address, or post them on a Web site.

As an alternative to text messaging, some users write a message with a digital pen, transfer the message from the pen to the smart phone, and then use picture messaging to send the handwritten message. Read Ethics & Issues 5-3 for a related discussion.

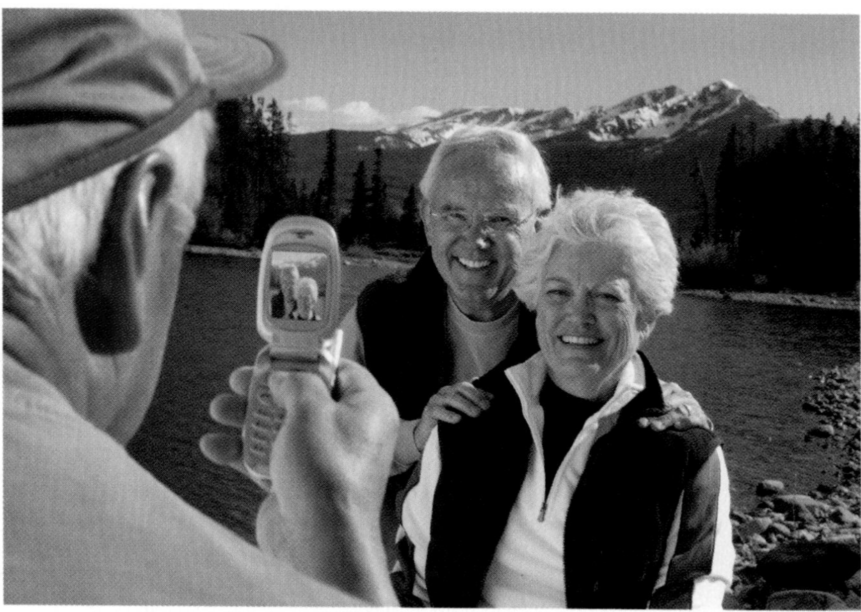

FIGURE 5-22 Many smart phones include a digital camera so users can send pictures and videos to others.

ETHICS & ISSUES 5-3

Should Talking on a Cellular Phone While Driving Be Illegal?

Cellular phone sales are soaring. In addition to talking on the phone, many drivers are using their phones to send and receive text messages, instant messages, picture messages, and e-mail, and to access and view Web pages. For drivers, however, cellular phones may be a liability. Estimates vary widely, but studies link between 800 and 8,000 fatalities on U.S. highways to phone use. Because of their additional capabilities, some experts believe cellular phones pose an even greater risk. Many countries have placed bans or restrictions on the use of phones while driving. In the United States, several states have considered or enacted similar legislation. New York and California, for example, permit vehicle operators to use only hands-free phones. Yet, some studies report that just talking on a phone can cause enough driver inattention to trigger an accident. Supporters of a cellular phone ban cite a British study that found drivers talking on phones had reaction times 50 percent slower than when not talking on a phone, and 30 percent slower than drivers who were intoxicated. Opponents of a ban note, however, that other driver activities, like tuning a radio or having a conversation, can be equally distracting and that phones are a factor in fewer than 1 percent of crashes. They also claim that the economic benefits of using a phone while driving may be greater than the costs associated with more accidents. Furthermore, drivers may have good reasons to use phones while driving, and laws may not take this into account. Should the use of phones be banned while driving? Why? What other measures, if any, could be taken to prevent drivers from endangering themselves and others while using phones?

Tablet PCs

The primary input device for a Tablet PC is a pressure-sensitive digital pen, which allows users to write on the device's screen. A Tablet PC's handwriting recognition software works similarly to that of a PDA. The computer converts the handwriting into characters it can process.

Both the slate and convertible designs of a Tablet PC provide a means for keyboard input for those users who prefer typing to handwriting. You can attach a removable keyboard to the slate Tablet PC. The convertible Tablet PC has an attached keyboard that can be rotated 180 degrees so the computer resembles a notebook computer.

To access peripherals at their home or office, users can slide their Tablet PC in a docking station. A *docking station,* which is an external device that attaches to a mobile computer or device, contains a power connection and provides connections to peripherals.

In the docking station, Tablet PC users can work with a full-sized keyboard, mouse, CD/DVD drives, and other desktop peripherals (Figure 5-23). The design of docking stations varies, depending on the type of mobile computer or the device to which they are attached.

FAQ 5-5

What security issues affect mobile computers or devices?

Mobile computers and mobile devices are susceptible to virus threats when you download infected Web pages or open infected e-mail messages. Another risk involves wireless networks, which provide a means for others to connect to your computer or device without your knowledge. Once users connect to your computer or device, they may be able to add to, change, or remove your data. For more information, visit scsite.com/dc2008/ch5/faq and then click Security Threats and Mobile Devices.

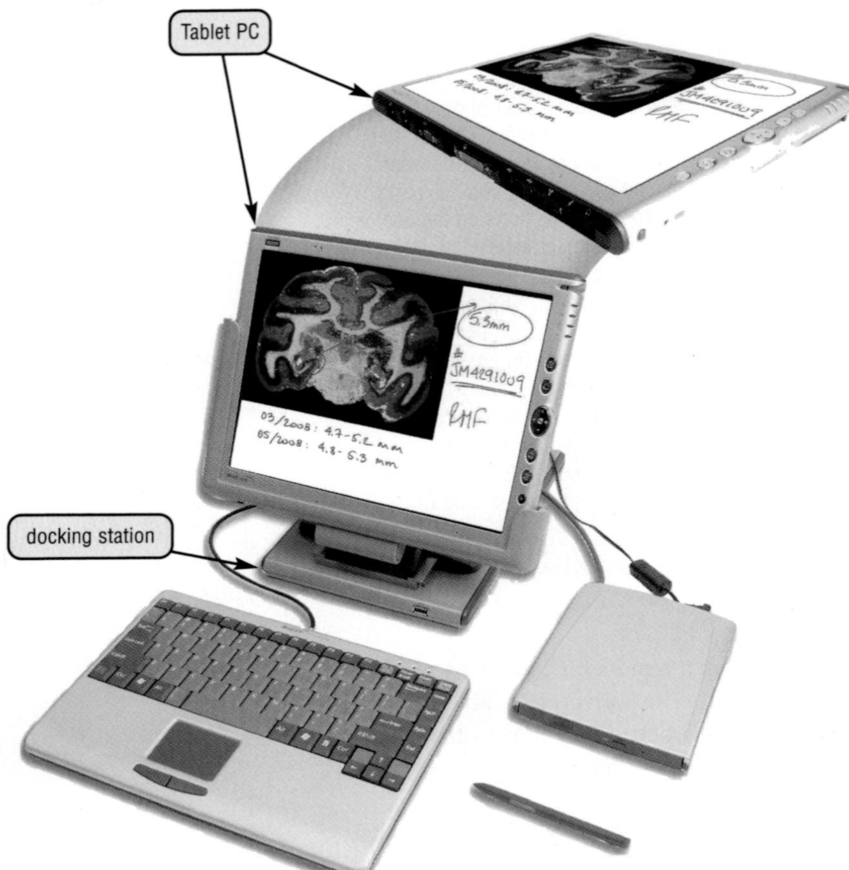

FIGURE 5-23 To use a slate Tablet PC while working at a desk, insert the Tablet PC in a docking station. Devices such as a keyboard and CD drive can be plugged in the docking station.

DIGITAL CAMERAS

A **digital camera** allows users to take pictures and store the photographed images digitally, instead of on traditional film (Figure 5-24). While many digital cameras look like a traditional camera, some models attach to PDAs or are built in PDAs and smart phones usually via a memory card. Mobile users such as real estate agents, insurance agents, general contractors, and photojournalists use digital cameras so they immediately can view photographed images on the camera. Home and business users have digital cameras to save the expense of film developing, duplication, and postage.

Most digital cameras have some amount of internal flash memory to store images. Many also can store additional images on mobile storage media, such as a flash memory card, memory stick, and mini-disc. Chapter 7 discusses these and other storage media in depth. Generally, higher-capacity storage devices can hold more pictures.

Digital cameras typically allow users to review, and sometimes edit, images while they are in the camera. Some digital cameras can connect to or communicate wirelessly with a printer, allowing users to print or view images directly from the camera. Most cameras can connect with a cable to a computer's USB port, so you can use the computer to access the media in the camera just like you access any other drive on the computer.

FIGURE 5-24 With a digital camera, users can view photographed images immediately through a small screen on the camera to see if the picture is worth keeping.

Often users prefer to *download*, or transfer a copy of, the images from the digital camera to the computer's hard disk. With some digital cameras, images download through a cable that connects between the digital camera (or the camera's docking station) and a USB port or a FireWire port on the system unit. For cameras that store images on miniature mobile storage media, simply insert the media in a reading/writing device that communicates wirelessly or attaches to a port on the system unit. Copying images from the miniature media to the computer's hard disk is just like copying files from any other disk drive. Some cameras store images on a mini CD/DVD. In this case, insert the disc in the computer's disc drive and then copy the pictures to the computer's hard disk (or you can view the contents of the disc by inserting it in a CD or DVD player).

When you copy images to the hard disk in a computer, the images are available for editing with photo editing software, printing, faxing, sending via e-mail, including in another document, or posting to a Web site or photo community for everyone to see. Many users add pictures to greeting cards, a computerized photo album, a family newsletter, certificates, and awards.

The three basic types of digital cameras are studio cameras, field cameras, and point-and-shoot cameras. The most expensive and highest quality of the three is a *studio camera*, which is a stationary camera used for professional studio work. Often used by photojournalists, a *field camera* is a portable camera that has many lenses and other attachments. As with the studio camera, a field camera can be quite expensive. A *point-and-shoot camera* is much more affordable and lightweight and provides acceptable quality photographic images for the home or small business user. Figure 5-25 illustrates how one make of point-and-shoot digital camera works.

A point-and-shoot camera often features flash, zoom, automatic focus, and special effects. Some allow users to record short audio narrations for photographed images. Others even record short video clips in addition to still images. Point-and-shoot digital cameras often have a built-in TV out port, allowing users to

FAQ 5-6

What should I look for when shopping for a digital camera?

First, determine your price range and search for cameras within that range. Consider factors such as the physical size and weight, the type of removable storage media, the size of the display, the built-in features, and the method of zooming. An *optical zoom* changes the position of the camera lens to zoom in and out, while a *digital zoom* digitally alters the pixels at the center of the CCD (see Figure 5-25), at the expense of the image quality, to give the appearance of a zoomed image. For more information, visit scsite.com/dc2008/ch5/faq and then click Digital Cameras.

FIGURE 5-25 HOW A DIGITAL CAMERA MIGHT WORK

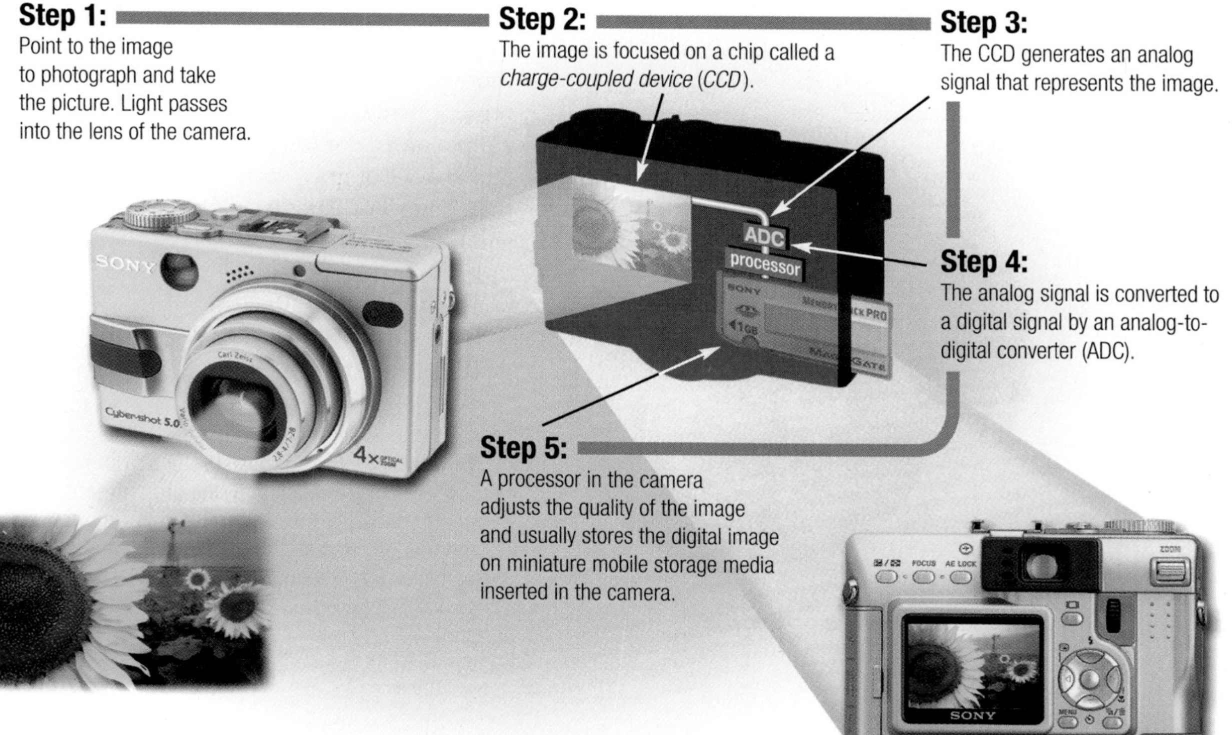
Step 1:
Point to the image to photograph and take the picture. Light passes into the lens of the camera.
Step 2:
The image is focused on a chip called a *charge-coupled device* (*CCD*).
Step 3:
The CCD generates an analog signal that represents the image.
ADC
processor
Step 4:
The analog signal is converted to a digital signal by an analog-to-digital converter (ADC).
Step 5:
A processor in the camera adjusts the quality of the image and usually stores the digital image on miniature mobile storage media inserted in the camera.
SONY

display photographed images or play recorded video clips directly on a television.

For additional information about digital cameras, read the Digital Imaging and Video Technology feature that follows Chapter 6.

Digital Camera Quality

One factor that affects the quality of a digital camera is its resolution. **Resolution** is the number of horizontal and vertical pixels in a display device. A *pixel* (short for picture element) is the smallest element in an electronic image (Figure 5-26). The greater the number of pixels the camera uses to capture an image, the better the quality of the image. Thus, the higher the resolution, the better the image quality, but the more expensive the camera.

Digital camera resolutions range from approximately 3 million to more than 16 million pixels (*MP*). A camera with a 5.1-megapixel (5,100,000 pixels) resolution will provide a better quality than one with a 3.2-megapixel resolution. As a general rule, a 3-megapixel camera is fine for pictures sent via e-mail or posted on the Web. For good quality printed photographs, users should have a 4-megapixel camera for 4 × 6 inch photographs, a 5-megapixel camera for 8 × 10 photographs, and 6-megapixel or greater camera for larger size prints or more professional results.

Manufacturers often use pixels per inch to represent a digital camera's resolution. *Pixels per inch* (*ppi*) is the number of pixels in one inch of screen display. For example, a 2304 × 1728 (pronounced 2304 by 1728) ppi camera has 2,304 pixels per vertical inch and 1,728 pixels per horizontal inch. Multiplying these two numbers together gives an approximate total number of pixels. For example, 2304 times 1728 equals approximately 4 million, or 4 megapixels. If just one number is stated, such as 1600 ppi, then both the vertical and horizontal numbers are the same.

Many digital cameras provide a means to adjust the ppi to the desired resolution. With a lower ppi, you can capture and store more images in the camera. For example, a camera set at 1280 × 960 ppi might capture and store 61 images, if it has sufficient storage capacity. The number of images may reduce to 24 on the same camera set at 2592 × 1944 ppi, because each image consumes more storage space.

The actual photographed resolution is known as the *optical resolution*. Some manufacturers state *enhanced resolution*, instead of, or in addition to, optical resolution. Optical resolution is different from enhanced resolution. The enhanced resolution usually is higher because it uses a special formula to add pixels between those generated by the optical resolution. Be aware that some manufacturers compute a digital camera's megapixels from the enhanced resolution, instead of optical resolution.

Another measure of a digital camera's quality is the number of bits it stores in a pixel. Each pixel consists of one or more bits of data. The more bits used to represent a pixel, the more colors and shades of gray that can be represented. One bit per pixel is enough for simple one-color images. For multiple colors and shades of gray, each pixel requires more than one bit of data. A point-and-shoot camera should be at least 24 bit.

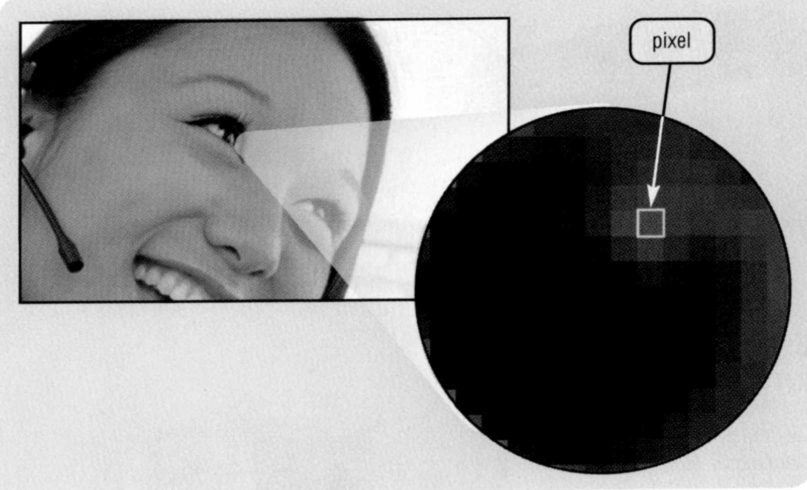

FIGURE 5-26 A pixel is a single point in an electronic image.

FAQ 5-7

What is dpi?

Some advertisements incorrectly use dpi to mean the same as ppi. The acronym *dpi*, which stands for *dots per inch*, is a measure of a print resolution. For screen resolution, the proper measurement term is ppi (pixels per inch). For more information, visit scsite.com/dc2008/ch5/faq and then click Resolution.

VIDEO INPUT

Video input is the process of capturing full-motion images and storing them on a computer's storage medium such as a hard disk or DVD.

Some video devices record video using analog signals. Computers, by contrast, use digital signals. To enter video from an analog device into a personal computer, the analog signal must be converted to a digital signal. To do this, plug a video camera, VCR, or other analog video device in a video capture port on the system unit. One type of adapter card that has a video capture port is a *video capture card*, which converts an analog video signal into a digital signal that a computer can process. Most new computers are not equipped with a video capture card because not all users have the need for this type of adapter card.

A **digital video (DV) camera**, by contrast, records video as digital signals instead of analog signals. Many DV cameras can capture still frames, as well as motion. To transfer recorded images to a hard disk or CD or DVD, users connect DV cameras directly to a USB port or a FireWire port on the system unit. Thus, the computer does not need a video capture card. Simply connect the video device to the computer and begin transferring images. After saving the video on a storage medium, such as a hard disk or DVD, you can play it or edit it using video editing software on a computer (Figure 5-27).

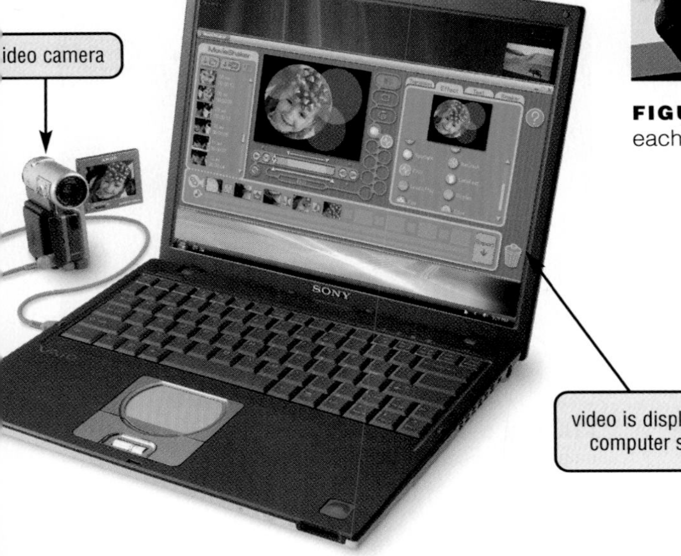

FIGURE 5-27 Home users can transfer videos to their computers and then use video editing software to edit the video.

PC Video Cameras

A **PC video camera**, or **PC camera**, is a type of digital video camera that enables a home or small business user to capture video and still images, send e-mail messages with video attachments, add live images to instant messages, broadcast live images over the Internet, and make video telephone calls. During a *video telephone call*, both parties see each other as they communicate over the Internet (Figure 5-28). The cost of PC video cameras usually is less than $100.

Attached to the computer's USB port or FireWire port, a PC video camera usually sits on top of the monitor. For more flexibility, some PC video cameras are portable. That is, you can detach them from the base and use them as a stand-alone digital camera. Some notebook computers have built-in PC video cameras.

FIGURE 5-28 Using a PC video camera, home users can see each other as they communicate over the Internet.

Web Cams

A **Web cam** is any video camera that displays its output on a Web page. A Web cam attracts Web site visitors by showing images that change regularly. Home or small business users might use Web cams to show a work in progress, weather and traffic information, employees at work, photographs of a vacation, and countless other images. Read Ethics & Issues 5-4 for a related discussion.

Some Web sites have live Web cams that display still pictures and update the displayed image at a specified time or time intervals, such as 15 seconds. Another type of Web cam, called a *streaming cam*, has the illusion of moving images because it sends a continual stream of still images.

WEB LINK 5-7

Web Cams

For more information, visit scsite.com/dc2008/ch5/weblink and then click Web Cams.

ETHICS & ISSUES 5-4

Should Cameras Be Able to Monitor Your Every Move?

In the world of George Orwell's classic novel *1984*, "Telescreens" constantly monitor each citizen's every word and movement. Since its publication more than 50 years ago, most people have viewed the novel as a warning against a future that should be avoided. Whether it is on a busy street corner, on a casino floor, in a subway station, in the neighborhood grocery store, in an elevator, or even in the workplace, the watchful eye continues to become more and more ubiquitous. In Chicago, cameras monitor high-crime areas and even listen for gunshots. The software used with such cameras continues to get more sophisticated, and the automatic recognition of a broad range of suspicious activities and crimes is just around the corner. Some software instantly scans images from a crowd in an attempt to match a face in the crowd to known or wanted criminals and then alerts authorities. Businesses and governments claim that advances in the technology and the low cost as compared to other options allow them to provide greater security and safety. Privacy advocates say that the cameras violate the Constitution's guarantee against unreasonable searches. Many cases of abuse of video monitoring have been noted, such as stores secretly listening in on spouses discussing a potential purchase. What are the differences between George Orwell's Telescreens and the current state of video monitoring? What are the similarities? Would you feel more secure or more paranoid living in a continuously monitored society? Why? What are the benefits of video monitoring? Should you have nothing to fear from security cameras if you have done nothing wrong?

Video Conferencing

A **video conference** is a meeting between two or more geographically separated people who use a network or the Internet to transmit audio and video data (Figure 5-29). To participate in a video conference, you need video conferencing software along with a microphone, speakers, and a video camera attached to a computer. Examples of video conferencing software include CUworld, Live Meeting, and WebEx.

As you speak, members of the meeting hear your voice on their speakers. Any image in front of the video camera, such as a person's face, appears in a window on each participant's screen. A *whiteboard* is another window on the screen that displays notes and drawings simultaneously on all participants' screens. This window provides multiple users with an area on which they can write or draw.

As the costs of video conferencing hardware and software decrease, increasingly more business meetings, corporate training, and educational classes will be conducted as video conferences.

FAQ 5-8

Do I need a fast Internet connection to participate in a video conference?

Yes. Video conferences transfer a large amount of audio and video in a short time frame. A fast Internet connection allows you to see the video and hear the audio with minimal delay. For more information, visit scsite.com/dc2008/ch5/faq and then click Video Conferencing.

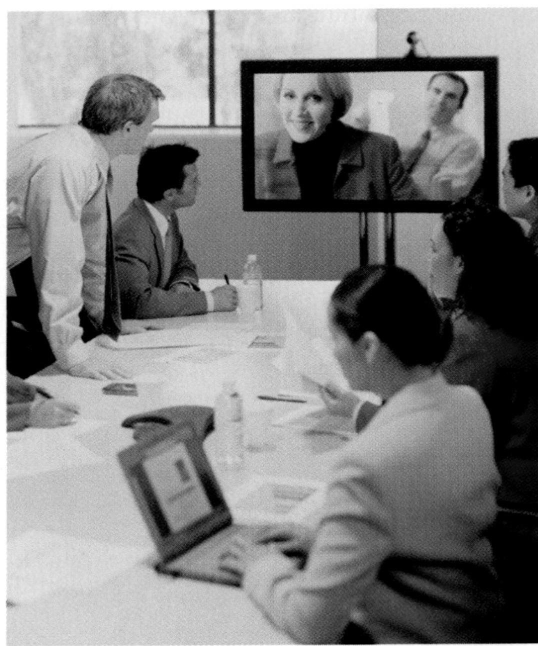

FIGURE 5-29 To save on travel expenses, many large businesses are turning to video conferencing.

Test your knowledge of pages 245 through 254 in Quiz Yourself 5-2.

QUIZ YOURSELF 5-2

Instructions: Find the true statement below. Then, rewrite the remaining false statements so they are true.

1. A digital camera allows users to take pictures and store the photographed images digitally, instead of on traditional film.
2. DV cameras record video as analog signals.
3. Instant messaging is the computer's capability of distinguishing spoken words.
4. Many smart phones today have a built-in camera so users easily can send text messages.
5. The lower the resolution of a digital camera, the better the image quality, but the more expensive the camera.

Quiz Yourself Online: To further check your knowledge of voice input; input for PDAs, smart phones, and Tablet PCs; digital cameras; and video input, visit scsite.com/dc2008/ch5/quiz and then click Objectives 5 – 8.

SCANNERS AND READING DEVICES

Some input devices save users time by eliminating manual data entry. With these devices, users do not type, speak, or write into the computer. Instead, these devices capture data from a *source document*, which is the original form of the data. Examples of source documents include time cards, order forms, invoices, paychecks, advertisements, brochures, photographs, inventory tags, or any other document that contains data to be processed.

Devices that can capture data directly from a source document include optical scanners, optical readers, bar code readers, RFID readers, magnetic stripe card readers, and magnetic-ink character recognition readers. The following pages discuss each of these devices.

Optical Scanners

An *optical scanner*, usually called a **scanner**, is a light-sensing input device that reads printed text and graphics and then translates the results into a form the computer can process. Four types of scanners are flatbed, pen, sheet-fed, and drum (Figure 5-30).

TYPES OF SCANNERS

Scanner	Method of Scanning and Use	Scannable Items
Flatbed 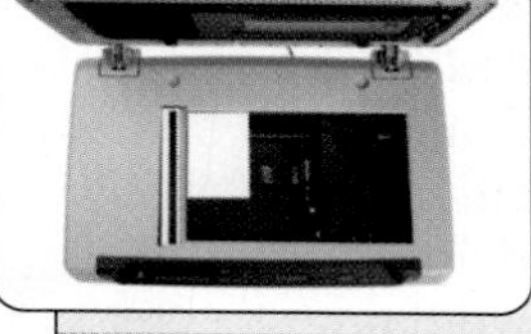	• Similar to a copy machine • Scanning mechanism passes under the item to be scanned, which is placed on a glass surface	• Single-sheet documents • Bound material • Photographs • Some models include trays for slides, transparencies, and negatives
Pen or Handheld	• Move pen over text to be scanned, then transfer data to computer • Ideal for mobile users, students, and researchers • Some connect to a PDA or smart phone	• Any printed text
Sheet-fed 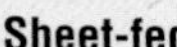 	• Item to be scanned is pulled into a stationary scanning mechanism • Smaller than a flatbed scanner • A model designed specifically for photographs is called a *photo scanner*	• Single-sheet documents • Photographs • Slides (with an adapter) • Negatives
Drum 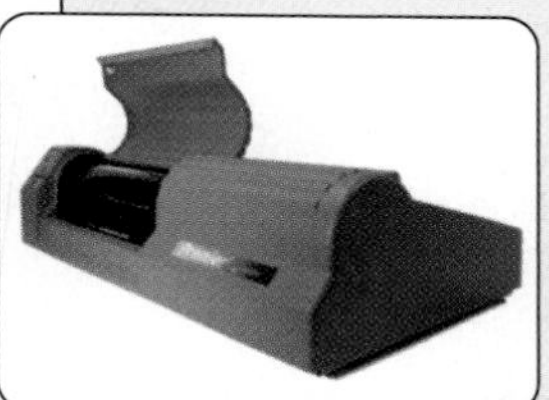	• Item to be scanned rotates around stationary scanning mechanism • Very expensive • Used in large businesses	• Single-sheet documents • Photographs • Slides • Negatives

FIGURE 5-30 This table describes the various types of scanners.

A **flatbed scanner** works in a manner similar to a copy machine except it creates a file of the document in memory instead of a paper copy (Figure 5-31). Once you scan a document or picture, you can display the scanned object on the screen, modify its appearance, store it on a storage medium, print it, fax it, attach it to an e-mail message, include it in another document, or post it to a Web site or photo community for everyone to see.

As with a digital camera, the quality of a scanner is measured by the number of bits it stores in a pixel and the number of pixels per inch, or resolution. The higher each number, the better the quality, but the more expensive the scanner. Most of today's affordable color desktop scanners for the home or small business range from 30 to 48 bits and have an optical resolution ranging from 600 to 9600 ppi. Commercial scanners designed for power users range from 9600 to 14,000 ppi.

Many scanners include *OCR (optical character recognition) software*, which can read and convert text documents into electronic files. OCR software is useful if you need to modify a document but do not have the original word processing file. For example, if you scan a business report with a flatbed scanner and do not use OCR software, you cannot edit the report because the scanner saves the report as an image. This is because the scanner does not differentiate between text and graphics. OCR software, however, would convert the scanned image into a text file that you could edit, for example, with a word processing program. Current OCR software has a high success rate and usually can identify more than 99 percent of scanned material.

Businesses often use scanners for *image processing*, which consists of capturing, storing, analyzing, displaying, printing, and manipulating images. Image processing allows users to convert paper documents such as reports, memos, and procedure manuals into electronic images. Users distribute and publish these electronic documents on networks and the Internet.

Business users typically store and index electronic documents with an image processing system. An *image processing system* is similar to an electronic filing cabinet that provides access to exact reproductions of the original documents. Local governments, for example, use image processing systems to store property deeds and titles to provide the public and professionals, such as lawyers and loan officers, quick access to electronic documents.

FAQ 5-9

How can I improve the quality of scanned documents?

Place a blank sheet of paper behind translucent papers, newspapers, and other see-through types of paper. If the original image is crooked, draw a line on the back at the bottom of the image. Use that mark to align the original on the scanner. Use photo editing software to fix imperfections in images. For more information, visit scsite.com/dc2008/ch5/faq and then click Scanning.

FIGURE 5-31 HOW A FLATBED SCANNER WORKS

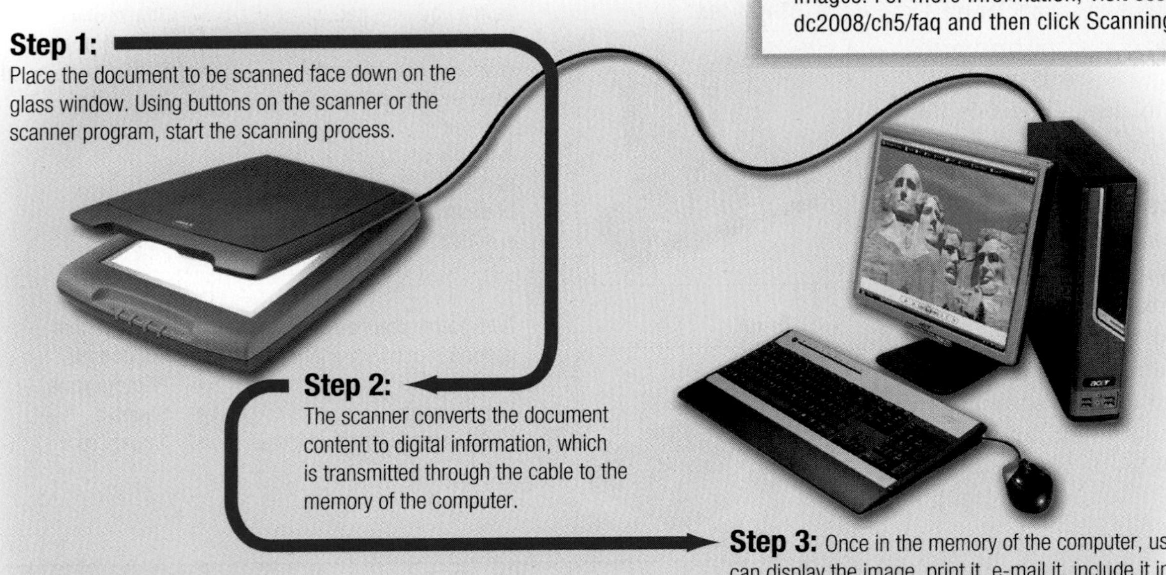

Step 1: Place the document to be scanned face down on the glass window. Using buttons on the scanner or the scanner program, start the scanning process.
Step 2: The scanner converts the document content to digital information, which is transmitted through the cable to the memory of the computer.
Step 3: Once in the memory of the computer, users can display the image, print it, e-mail it, include it in a document, or place it on a Web page.

Optical Readers

An *optical reader* is a device that uses a light source to read characters, marks, and codes and then converts them into digital data that a computer can process. Two technologies used by optical readers are optical character recognition and optical mark recognition.

OPTICAL CHARACTER RECOGNITION **Optical character recognition** (**OCR**) is a technology that involves reading typewritten, computer-printed, or hand-printed characters from ordinary documents and translating the images into a form that the computer can process. Most **OCR devices** include a small optical scanner for reading characters and sophisticated software to analyze what is read.

OCR devices range from large machines that can read thousands of documents per minute to handheld wands that read one document at a time. OCR devices read printed characters in an OCR font. A widely used OCR font is called OCR-A (Figure 5-32). During the scan of a document, an OCR device determines the shapes of characters by detecting patterns of light and dark. OCR software then compares these shapes with predefined shapes stored in memory and converts the shapes into characters the computer can process.

ABCDEFGHIJKLM
NOPQRSTUVWXYZ
1234567890
-=▮;',./

FIGURE 5-32 A portion of the characters in the OCR-A font. Notice how characters such as the number 0 and the letter O are shaped differently so the reading device easily can distinguish between them.

Many companies use OCR characters on turnaround documents. A **turnaround document** is a document that you return (turn around) to the company that creates and sends it. For example, when consumers receive a bill, they often tear off a portion of the bill and send it back to the company with their payment (Figure 5-33). The portion of the bill they return usually has their payment amount, account number, and other information printed in OCR characters.

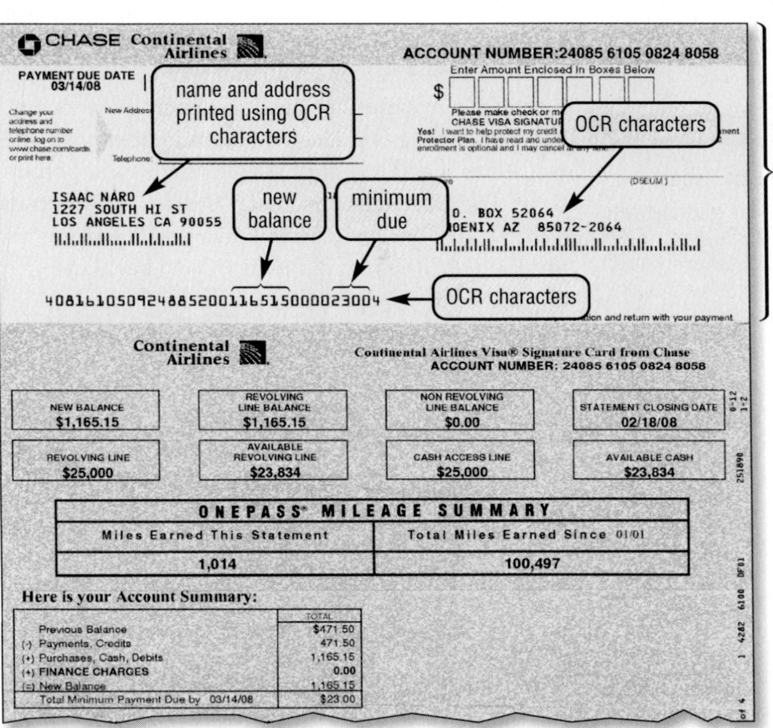

FIGURE 5-33 OCR characters frequently are used with turnaround documents. With this bill, you tear off the top portion and return it with a payment.

OPTICAL MARK RECOGNITION **Optical mark recognition** (**OMR**) is a technology that reads hand-drawn marks such as small circles or rectangles. A person places these marks on a form, such as a test, survey, or questionnaire answer sheet. With a test, the OMR device first scans the answer key sheet to record correct answers based on patterns of light. The OMR device then scans the remaining documents and matches their patterns of light against the answer key sheet.

Bar Code Readers

A **bar code reader**, also called a **bar code scanner**, is an optical reader that uses laser beams to read bar codes by using light patterns that pass through the bar code lines (Figure 5-34). A **bar code** is an identification code that consists either of a set of vertical lines and spaces of different widths or a two-dimensional pattern of dots, squares, and other images. A 2-D bar code can store much more data than the traditional linear bar code. The bar code represents data that identifies the manufacturer and the item.

Manufacturers print a bar code either on a product's package or on a label that is affixed to a product. A variety of products such as groceries, books, clothing, vehicles, mail, and packages have bar codes. Each industry uses its own type of bar code. The United States Postal Service (USPS) uses a POSTNET bar code. Retail and grocery stores use the *UPC (Universal Product Code)* bar code (Figure 5-35). Read Ethics & Issues 5-5 for a related discussion.

WEB LINK 5-8

Bar Code Readers

For more information, visit scsite.com/dc2008/ch5/weblink and then click Bar Code Readers.

ETHICS & ISSUES 5-5

Scanner Errors at the Checkout Counter?

Have you ever taken an item to a store's checkout and discovered that the price displayed when the item's bar code was scanned was different from the price shown on a shelf tag, sign, or advertisement? If you have, you are not alone. A government survey found that eight percent of the time, an item's scanned price is different from the price presented elsewhere. When an item is scanned at a store's checkout counter, a computer finds the item's price in the store's database. Store owners claim that discrepancies between the scanned price and a listed price are the result of human error — either failure to update the store's price database or incorrect shelf tags, signs, or advertisements. Yet, some consumer advocates claim that the discrepancy sometimes is intentional. They accuse stores of *scanner fraud*, insisting that some stores advertise one price and then charge another, hoping buyers will not recognize the difference. Most states have laws that protect consumers against scanner fraud. Some laws even require stores to pay consumers an immediate reward, sometimes $5 or more, if the consumer finds a scanner error. Who do you think is responsible for differences between scanned prices and posted costs? Why? Should stores be responsible for pricing errors? Why or why not? Do you think that the increased use of self-checkout registers will increase or decrease scanner fraud claims? Why or why not?

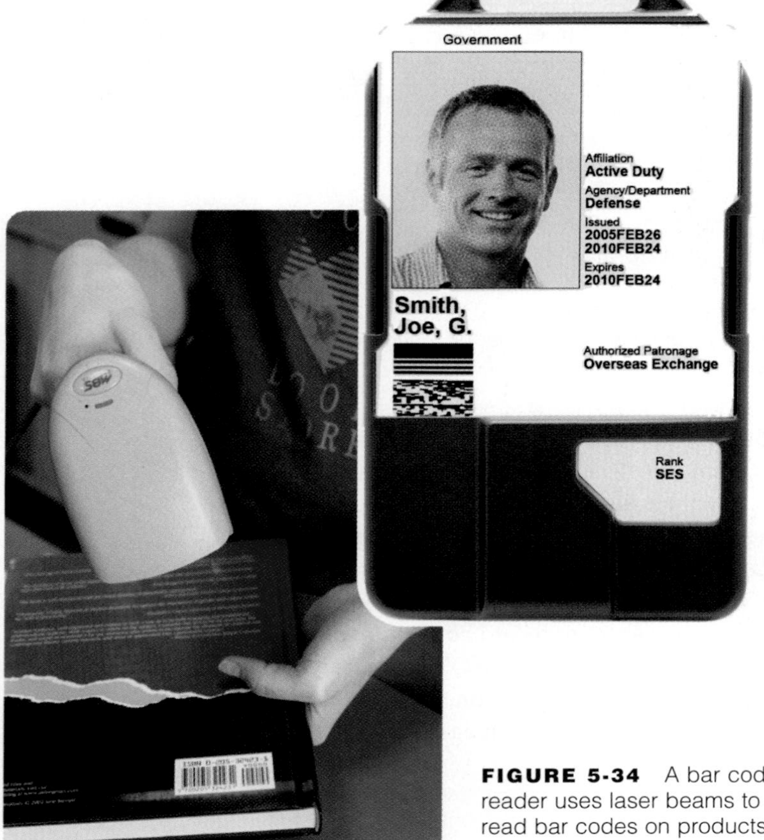

FIGURE 5-34 A bar code reader uses laser beams to read bar codes on products such as ID cards and books.

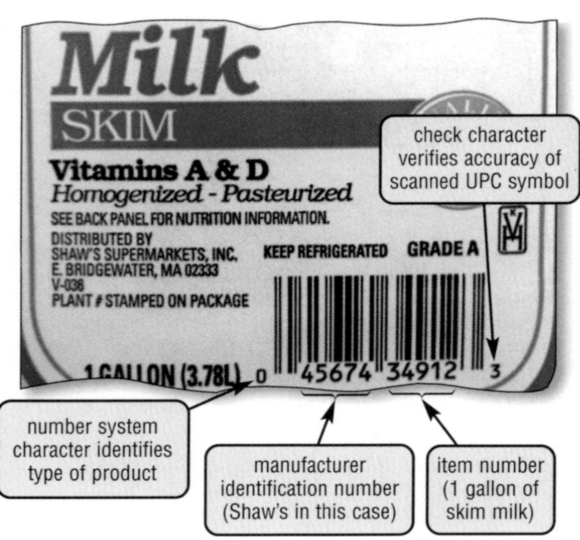

FIGURE 5-35 This UPC identifies a carton of skim milk.

RFID Readers

RFID (*radio frequency identification*) is a technology that uses radio signals to communicate with a tag placed in or attached to an object, an animal, or a person. RFID tags, which contain a memory chip and an antenna, are available in many shapes and sizes and sometimes are embedded in glass, labels, or cards. Some RFID tags are as small as a grain of sand; others are the size of a luggage tag. An **RFID reader** reads information on the tag via radio waves. RFID readers can be handheld devices or mounted in a stationary object such as a doorway.

Many retailers see RFID as an alternative to bar code identification because it does not require direct contact or line-of-site transmission. Each product in a store would contain a tag that identifies the product (Figure 5-36). As consumers remove products from the store shelves and walk through a checkout area, an RFID reader reads the tag(s) and communicates with a computer that calculates the amount due, eliminating the need for checking out each item.

Other uses of RFID include tracking times of runners in a marathon; tracking location of soldiers, employee wardrobes, and airline baggage; checking lift tickets of skiers; gauging pressure and temperature of tires on a vehicle; checking out library books; and tracking payment as vehicles pass through booths on tollway systems. Read Ethics & Issues 5-6 for a related discussion. Read Looking Ahead 5-1 for a look at the next generation of RFID.

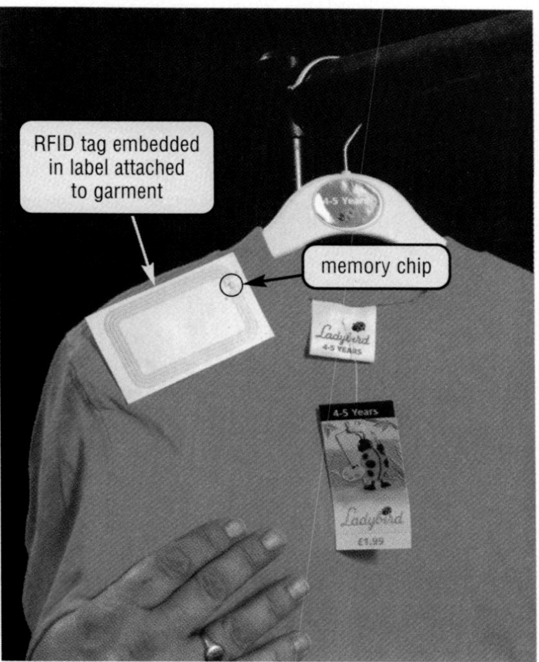

FIGURE 5-36 RFID readers read information stored on an RFID tag and then communicate this information to computers, which instantaneously compute payments and update inventory records. In this example, the RFID tag is embedded in a label attached to the garment.

ETHICS & ISSUES 5-6

Will RFID Track Your Every Move?

The rapid growth of RFID worries some privacy advocates. RFID (radio frequency identification) uses a tiny computer chip that can be mounted on a tag attached to a product, sewn into an article of clothing, or even attached to a document. For merchants, RFID can help to locate items in a warehouse and identify items that need to be replenished. For consumers, RFID can supply detailed product information, and someday let buyers bypass check-out lines and take purchases directly from the store, with the item's cost charged to their card. The federal government started a program to include RFID chips on all passports. Privacy advocates worry, however, that RFID could obliterate a person's anonymity. They fear that with an RFID reader, any individual or organization could track a person's movements and make that information available to marketers or government agencies. Some fear that the RFID chip in a passport could be copied by a hidden RFID reader and then used for nefarious purposes such as faking one's identity. To protect privacy, privacy advocates insist that merchants should be forced to disable RFID transmitters as soon as buyers leave a store. They also recommend that RFID-enabled documents, such as passports, be kept in special containers made of material that will not allow the chip to be read until it is removed from the container. Would you be comfortable purchasing a product that includes RFID? Why or why not? Should buyers be allowed to request that RFID transmitters be disabled after they make a purchase, or should merchants be required to render transmitters inoperative when the product leaves the store? Why? Would you feel comfortable carrying a form of identification that is RFID-enabled? Why or why not?

LOOKING AHEAD 5-1

Paying with Your Cellular Telephone

Your waiting time in the checkout lane may be shortened if merchants adopt new RFID technology. Cellular telephone manufacturers, including Nokia, are building the RFID chips into their products, so shoppers will be able to wave their phones one inch in front of a contactless reader to pay for merchandise. They also will need to enter a code number if the purchase is more than $25.

Similar RFID technology already is in place with 20 million Americans' credit or debit cards. Nokia says, however, shoppers can leave those cards at home and carry only their cellular phones.

Cellular telephone manufacturers currently are testing their RFID systems worldwide, and some merchants are hopeful the technology will provide faster service in line, fewer thefts, and increased profits. Some consumer advocates, however, predict some merchants will install RFID chip readers in their stores' doorways and then track customers' shopping patterns without their knowledge. For more information, visit scsite.com/dc2008/ch5/looking and then click RFID Chips.

Magnetic Stripe Card Readers

A **magnetic stripe card reader**, often called a *magstripe reader*, reads the magnetic stripe on the back of credit cards, entertainment cards, bank cards, and other similar cards. The stripe, which is divided in three horizontal tracks, contains information identifying you and the card issuer (Figure 5-37). Some information stored in the stripe includes your name, account number, the card's expiration date, and a country code.

When a consumer swipes a credit card through the magstripe reader, it reads the information stored on the magnetic stripe on the card. If the magstripe reader rejects your card, it is possible that the magnetic stripe on the card is scratched, dirty, or erased. Exposure to a magnet or magnetic field can erase the contents of a card's magnetic stripe.

In many cases, a magstripe reader is part of a point-of-sale terminal. The function of point-of-sale terminals is discussed later in this chapter.

FIGURE 5-37 A magnetic stripe card reader reads information encoded on the stripe on the back of your credit card.

MICR Readers

MICR (*magnetic-ink character recognition*) devices read text printed with magnetized ink. An **MICR reader** converts MICR characters into a form the computer can process. The banking industry almost exclusively uses MICR for check processing. Each check in your checkbook has precoded MICR characters beginning at the lower-left edge (Figure 5-38). The MICR characters represent the bank routing number, the customer account number, and the check number. These numbers may appear in a different order than the ones shown in the sample in Figure 5-38.

When a bank receives a check for payment, it uses an MICR inscriber to print the amount of the check in MICR characters in the lower-right corner. The check then is sorted or routed to the customer's bank, along with thousands of others. Each check is inserted in an MICR reader, which sends the check information — including the amount of the check — to a computer for processing. When you balance your checkbook, verify that the amount printed in the lower-right corner is the same as the amount written on the check; otherwise, your statement will not balance.

The banking industry has established an international standard not only for bank numbers, but also for the font of the MICR characters. This standardization makes it possible for people to write checks in other countries.

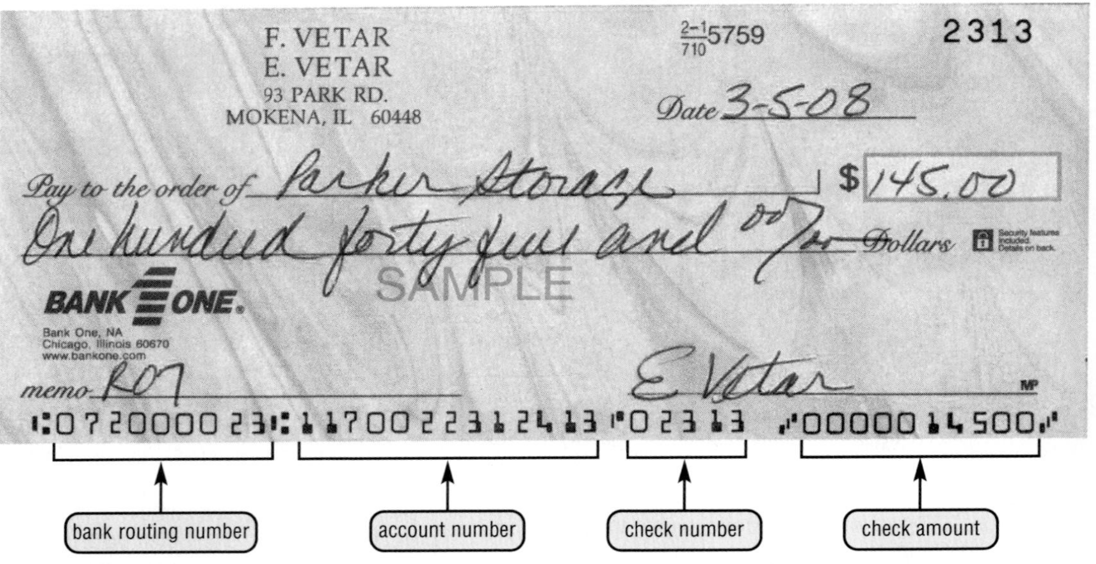

FIGURE 5-38 The MICR characters preprinted on the check represent the bank routing number, the customer account number, and the check number. The amount of the check in the lower-right corner is added after the check is cashed.

Data Collection Devices

Instead of reading or scanning data from a source document, a *data collection device* obtains data directly at the location where the transaction or event takes place. For example, employees use bar code readers, PDAs, handheld computers, or other mobile devices to collect data wirelessly (Figure 5-39). These types of data collection devices are used in restaurants, grocery stores, factories, warehouses, the outdoors, or other locations where heat, humidity, and cleanliness are not easy to control.

Data collection devices and many mobile computers and devices have the capability of wirelessly transmitting data over a network or the Internet. Increasingly more users today send data wirelessly to central office computers using these devices.

FIGURE 5-39 A grocery store employee uses this rugged handheld computer, which includes a bar code reader, that wirelessly transmits information about the scanned item to the store's inventory system.

TERMINALS

A *terminal* consists of a keyboard, a monitor, a video card, and memory. Often, these components are housed in a single unit.

Terminals fall into three basic categories: dumb terminals, smart terminals, and special-purpose terminals. A *dumb terminal* has no processing power; thus, it cannot function as an independent device. Users enter data and instructions in a dumb terminal and then transmit the data to a host computer over a network. The host computer processes the input and then, if necessary, sends information (output) back to the dumb terminal. The host computer usually is a server or mainframe. A *smart terminal* has a processor, giving it the capability of performing some functions independent of the host computer. In recent years, personal computers have replaced most smart terminals.

Special-purpose terminals perform specific tasks and contain features uniquely designed for use in a particular industry. Two widely used special-purpose terminals are point-of-sale (POS) terminals and automated teller machines.

Point-of-Sale Terminals

The location in a retail or grocery store where a consumer pays for goods or services is the *point of sale* (*POS*). Most retail stores use a **POS terminal** to record purchases, process credit or debit cards, and update inventory.

In a grocery store, the POS terminal is a combination of an electronic cash register, bar code reader, and printer. When the checkout clerk scans the bar code on the food product, the computer uses the manufacturer and item numbers to look up the price of the item and the complete product name in a database. Then, the price of the item in the database shows on the display device, the name of the item and its price print on a receipt, and the item being sold is recorded so the inventory can be updated. Thus, the output from a POS terminal serves as input to other computers to maintain sales records, update inventory, verify credit, and perform other activities associated with the sales transactions that are critical to running the business. Some POS terminals are Web-enabled, which allows updates to inventory at geographically separate locations.

Many POS terminals handle credit card or debit card payments and thus also include a magstripe reader. Some have fingerprint scanners (discussed in the next section) that read your fingerprint, which is linked to a payment method such as a checking account or credit card. After swiping your card through the reader or reading your fingerprint, the POS terminal connects to a system that authenticates the purchase. Once the transaction is approved, the terminal prints a receipt for the customer.

A self-service POS terminal allows consumers to perform all checkout-related activities (Figure 5-40). That is, they scan the items, bag the items, and pay for the items themselves. Consumers with small orders find the self-service POS terminals convenient because these terminals often eliminate the hassle of waiting in long lines.

FIGURE 5-40 Many grocery stores offer self-serve checkouts, where the consumers themselves use the POS terminals to scan purchases, scan their store saver card and coupons, and then pay for the goods.

Automated Teller Machines

An **automated teller machine** (**ATM**) is a self-service banking machine that connects to a host computer through a network (Figure 5-41). Banks place ATMs in convenient locations, including grocery stores, convenience stores, retail outlets, shopping malls, and gas stations, so customers conveniently can access their bank accounts.

Using an ATM, people withdraw cash, deposit money, transfer funds, or inquire about an account balance. Some ATMs have a touch screen; others have special buttons or keypads for entering input. To access a bank account, you insert a plastic bankcard in the ATM's magstripe reader. The ATM asks you to enter a password, called a *personal identification number* (*PIN*), which verifies that you are the holder of the bankcard. When your transaction is complete, the ATM prints a receipt for your records.

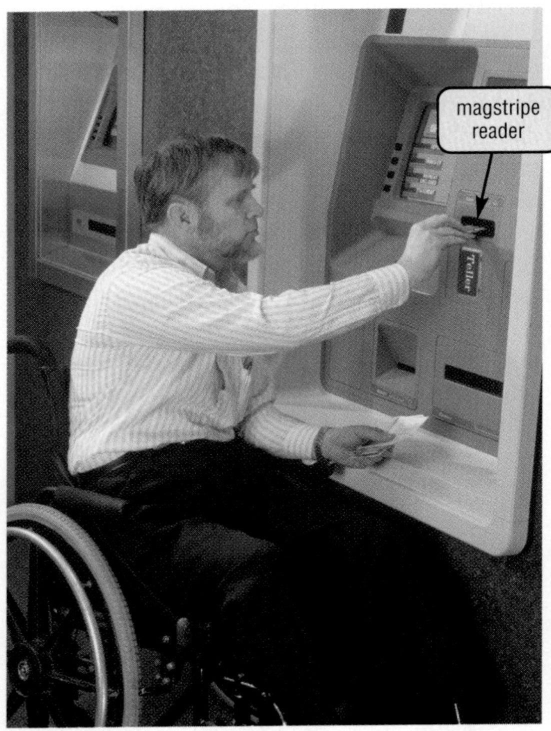

FIGURE 5-41 An ATM is a self-service banking terminal that allows customers to access their bank accounts.

BIOMETRIC INPUT

Biometrics is the technology of authenticating a person's identity by verifying a personal characteristic. Biometric devices grant users access to programs, systems, or rooms by analyzing some biometric identifier. A *biometric identifier* is a physiological (related to physical or chemical activities in the body) or behavioral characteristic. Examples include fingerprints, hand geometry, facial features, voice, signatures, and eye patterns.

A *biometric device* translates a personal characteristic (the input) into a digital code that is compared with a digital code stored in the computer. If the digital code in the computer does not match the personal characteristic's code, the computer denies access to the individual.

The most widely used biometric device today is a fingerprint scanner. A **fingerprint scanner** captures curves and indentations of a fingerprint. With the cost of fingerprint scanners less than $100, home and small business users install fingerprint scanners to authenticate users before they can access a personal computer. External fingerprint scanners usually plug into a parallel or USB port. To save on desk space, some newer keyboards and notebook computers have a fingerprint scanner built into them, which allows users to log on to programs and Web sites via their fingerprint instead of entering a user name and password (Figure 5-42). Grocery and retail stores now use fingerprint scanners as a means of payment, where the customer's fingerprint is linked to a payment method such as a checking account or credit card. For a technical discussion about fingerprint scanners, read the High-Tech Talk article on page 268.

A *face recognition system* captures a live face image and compares it with a stored image to determine if the person is a legitimate user. Some buildings use face recognition systems to secure access to rooms. Law enforcement, surveillance systems, and airports use face recognition to protect the public. Some notebook computers use this security technique to safeguard a computer. The computer will not start unless the user is legitimate. These programs are becoming more sophisticated and can recognize people with or without glasses, makeup, or jewelry, and with new hairstyles.

Biometric devices measure the shape and size of a person's hand using a *hand geometry system* (Figure 5-43). Because their cost is more than $1,000, larger companies use these systems as time and attendance devices or as security devices. Colleges use hand geometry systems to verify students' identities. Day-care centers and hospital nurseries use them to verify parents who pick up their children.

A *voice verification system* compares a person's live speech with their stored voice pattern. Larger organizations sometimes use voice verification systems as time and attendance devices. Many companies also use this technology for access to sensitive files and networks. Some financial services use voice verification systems to secure telephone banking transactions. These systems use speaker-dependent voice recognition software. That is, users train the computer to recognize their inflection patterns.

A *signature verification system* recognizes the shape of your handwritten signature, as well as measures the pressure exerted and the motion used to write the signature. Signature verification systems use a specialized pen and tablet.

FIGURE 5-42 Keyboard with built-in fingerprint scanner.

FIGURE 5-43 A hand geometry system verifies this student's identity before he is allowed access to the school recreation center.

High security areas use iris recognition systems. The camera in an *iris recognition system* uses iris recognition technology to read patterns in the iris of the eye (Figure 5-44). These patterns are as unique as a fingerprint. Iris recognition systems are quite expensive and are used by government security organizations, the military, and financial institutions that deal with highly sensitive data. Some organizations use *retinal scanners*, which work similarly but instead scan patterns of blood vessels in the back of the retina.

WEB LINK 5-9

Biometric Input

For more information, visit scsite.com/dc2008/ch5/weblink and then click Biometric Input.

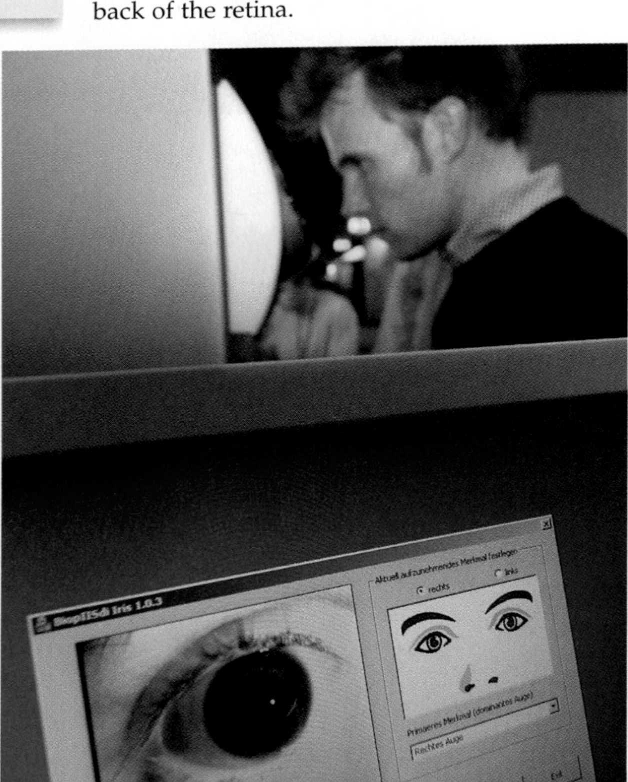

FIGURE 5-44 An iris recognition system.

Sometimes, fingerprint, iris, retina, and other biometric data are stored on a smart card. A **smart card**, which is comparable in size to a credit card or ATM card, stores the personal data on a thin microprocessor embedded in the card (Figure 5-45). Smart cards add an extra layer of protection. For example, when a user places a smart card through a smart card reader, the computer compares a fingerprint stored on the card with the one read by the fingerprint scanner. Some credit cards are smart cards; that is, the microprocessor contains the card holder's information instead of a magnetic stripe.

FAQ 5-10

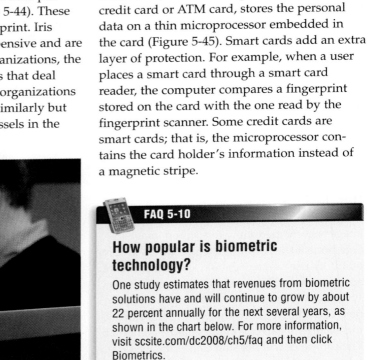

How popular is biometric technology?

One study estimates that revenues from biometric solutions have and will continue to grow by about 22 percent annually for the next several years, as shown in the chart below. For more information, visit scsite.com/dc2008/ch5/faq and then click Biometrics.

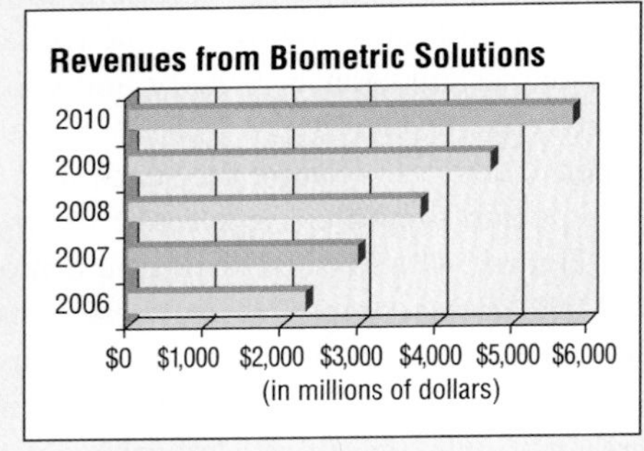

Source: International Biometric Group

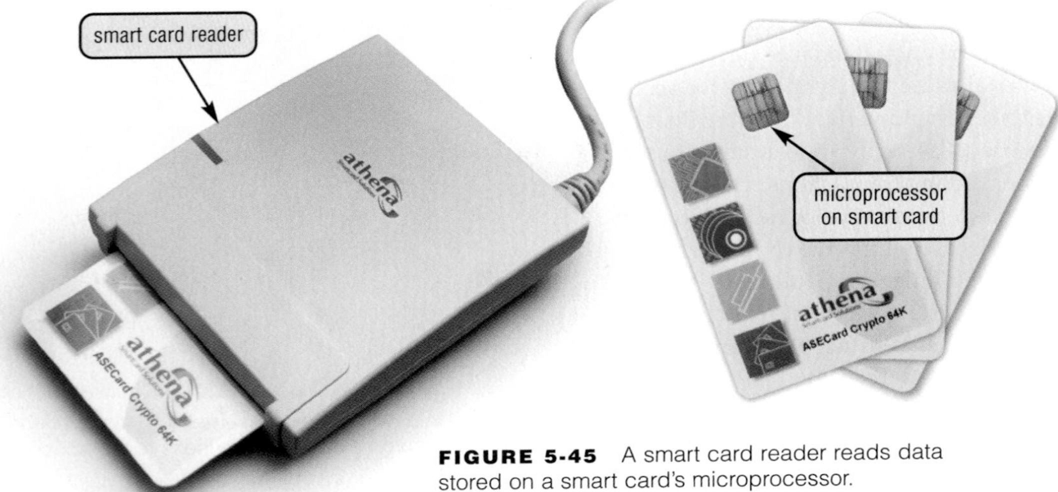

FIGURE 5-45 A smart card reader reads data stored on a smart card's microprocessor.

PUTTING IT ALL TOGETHER

When you purchase a computer, you should have an understanding of the input devices included with the computer, as well as those you may need that are not included. Many factors influence the type of input devices you may use: the type of input desired, the hardware and software in use, and the desired cost. The type of input devices you require depends on your intended use. Figure 5-46 outlines several suggested input devices for specific computer users.

SUGGESTED INPUT DEVICES BY USER

User	Input Device
HOME 	• Enhanced keyboard or ergonomic keyboard • Mouse • Stylus for PDA or smart phone • Game controller(s) • 30-bit 600 × 1200 ppi color scanner • 3-megapixel digital camera • Headphones that include a microphone (headset) • PC video camera
SMALL OFFICE/ HOME OFFICE 	• Enhanced keyboard or ergonomic keyboard • Mouse • Stylus and portable keyboard for PDA or smart phone, or digital pen for Tablet PC • 36-bit 600 × 1200 ppi color scanner • 4-megapixel digital camera • Headphones that include a microphone (headset) • PC video camera
MOBILE 	• Wireless mouse for notebook computer • Touchpad or pointing stick on notebook computer • Stylus and portable keyboard for PDA or smart phone, or digital pen for Tablet PC • 3- or 4-megapixel digital camera • Headphones that include a microphone (headset) • Fingerprint scanner for notebook computer
POWER 	• Enhanced keyboard or ergonomic keyboard • Mouse • Stylus and portable keyboard for PDA or smart phone • Pen for graphics tablet • 48-bit 1200 × 1200 ppi color scanner • 6- to 12-megapixel digital camera • Headphones that include a microphone (headset) • PC video camera
LARGE BUSINESS 	• Enhanced keyboard or ergonomic keyboard • Mouse • Stylus and portable keyboard for PDA or smart phone, or digital pen for Tablet PC • Touch screen • Light pen • 42-bit 1200 × 1200 ppi color scanner • 6- to 12-megapixel digital camera • OCR/OMR readers, bar code readers, MICR reader, or data collection devices • Microphone • Video camera for video conferences • Fingerprint scanner or other biometric device

FIGURE 5-46 This table recommends suggested input devices.

INPUT DEVICES FOR PHYSICALLY CHALLENGED USERS

The ever-increasing presence of computers in everyone's lives has generated an awareness of the need to address computing requirements for those who have or may develop physical limitations. The **Americans with Disabilities Act (ADA)** requires any company with 15 or more employees to make reasonable attempts to accommodate the needs of physically challenged workers.

Besides voice recognition, which is ideal for blind or visually impaired users, several other input devices are available. A *keyguard* is a metal or plastic plate placed over the keyboard that allows users to rest their hands on the keyboard without accidentally pressing any keys (Figure 5-47). A keyguard also guides a finger or pointing device so a user presses only one key at a time.

FIGURE 5-47 A keyguard.

Keyboards with larger keys also are available. Still another option is the *on-screen keyboard*, in which a graphic of a standard keyboard is displayed on the user's screen (Figure 5-48).

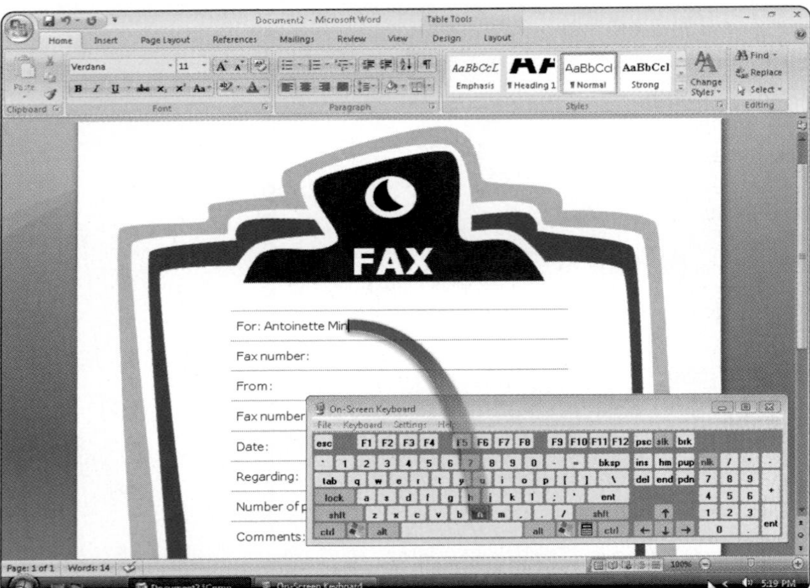

FIGURE 5-48 As you click letters on the on-screen keyboard, they appear in the document at the location of the insertion point.

Various pointing devices are available for users with motor disabilities. Small trackballs that the user controls with a thumb or one finger can be attached to a table, mounted to a wheelchair, or held in the user's hand. Another option for people with limited hand movement is a *head-mounted pointer* to control the pointer or insertion point (Figure 5-49). To simulate the functions of a mouse button, a user works with switches that control the pointer. The switch might be a hand pad, a foot pedal, a receptor that detects facial motions, or a pneumatic instrument controlled by puffs of air.

Two exciting developments in this area are gesture recognition and computerized implant devices. Both in the prototype stage, they attempt to provide users with a natural computer interface.

With *gesture recognition,* the computer will detect human motions. Computers with gesture recognition capability have the potential to recognize sign language, read lips, track facial movements, or follow eye gazes. For paralyzed or speech impaired individuals, a doctor will implant a computerized device into the brain. This device will contain a transmitter. As the user thinks thoughts, the transmitter will send signals to the computer.

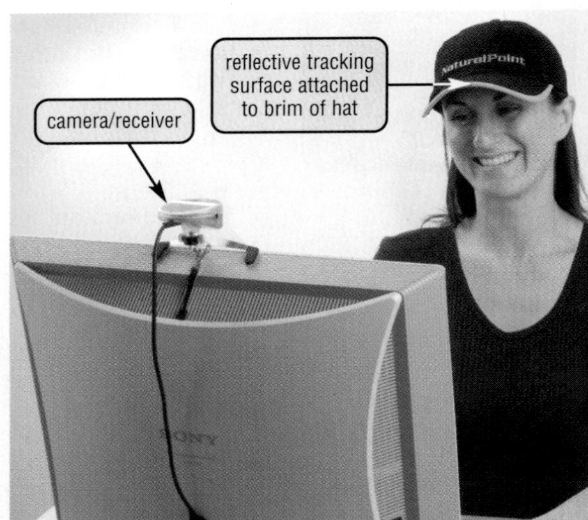

FIGURE 5-49 A camera/receiver mounted on the monitor tracks the position of the head-mounted pointer, which is reflective material that this user is wearing on the brim of her hat. As the user moves her head, the pointer on the screen also moves.

Test your knowledge of pages 255 through 266 in Quiz Yourself 5-3.

QUIZ YOURSELF 5-3

Instructions: Find the true statement below. Then, rewrite the remaining false statements so they are true.

1. A fingerprint scanner captures curves and indentations of a signature.
2. After swiping a credit card through an MICR reader, a POS terminal connects to a system that authenticates the purchase.
3. ATMs ask you to enter a password, called a biometric identifier, which verifies that you are the holder of the bankcard.
4. Four types of source documents are flatbed, pen, sheet-fed, and drum.
5. Retail and grocery stores use the POSTNET bar code.
6. RFID is a technology that uses laser signals to communicate with a tag placed in an object, an animal, or a person.
7. The Americans with Disabilities Act (ADA) requires any company with 15 or more employees to make reasonable attempts to accommodate the needs of physically challenged workers.

Quiz Yourself Online: To further check your knowledge of scanners and reading devices, terminals, biometric devices, and input for physically challenged users, visit scsite.com/dc2008/ch5/quiz and then click Objectives 9 – 12.

CHAPTER SUMMARY

Input is any data and instructions you enter into the memory of a computer. This chapter described the various techniques of entering input and several commonly used input devices (read Looking Ahead 5-2 for a look at the next generation of input devices). Topics presented included the keyboard, mouse, and other pointing devices; controllers for gaming and media players; voice input; input for PDAs, smart phones, and Tablet PCs; digital cameras; video input; scanners and reading devices; terminals; biometric input; and input devices for physically challenged users.

LOOKING AHEAD 5-2

Controlling Games by Thinking

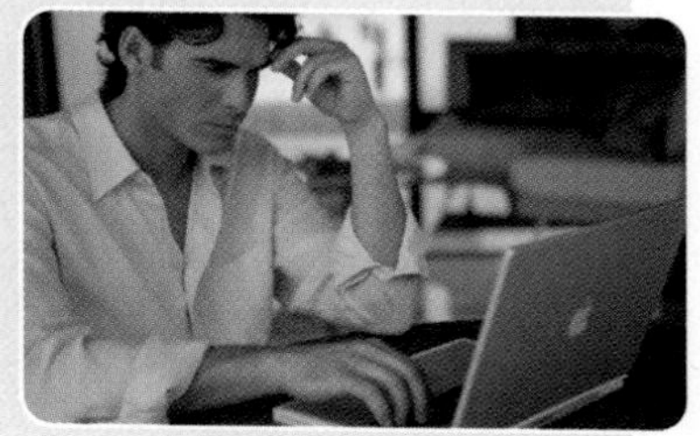

Putting on your thinking cap one day may take on a whole new meaning for gamers. A brain-machine interface being developed in Berlin could replace a joystick in traditional gaming. Scientists are envisioning a gamer wearing a baseball-cap device and then having a wireless connection with a computer. Tiny, metal sensors will detect brainwave activity without skin contact.

Using special software, the wearer must calibrate his individual brainwaves with the computer. During this five-minute process, the wearer will imagine moving his left or right hand or foot or rotating an object. Electrodes then pick up these thought signals. Once the person is in sync with the computer, he can imagine moving his hands or feet to trigger an action in the game.

The thought-controlled cap also could be used as a communication tool for people who cannot speak or sign by translating their brainwave electrical impulses into letters and words. For more information, visit scsite.com/dc2008/ch5/looking and then click Thought-Controlled Input.

CAREER CORNER

Data Entry Clerk

Data entry clerks have an essential role in today's information-producing industry. A *data entry clerk* enters data into documents, databases, and other applications using computer keyboards and visual display devices. Duties can include manipulating, editing, and maintaining data to ensure that it is accurate and up-to-date, and researching information.

Some data entry clerks telecommute. Although they generally use keyboards, they also work with other input from scanners or electronically transmitted files. Because of the nature of their job, data entry clerks often sit for hours typing in front of monitors. They can be susceptible to repetitive stress injuries and neck, back, and eye strain. To prevent these injuries, many offices use ergonomically designed input devices and incorporate regularly scheduled exercise breaks.

Data entry clerks usually are high school graduates with keyboarding skills. Some employers require an associate's degree or at least two years of post-high-school education plus two years of office experience. Data entry training, basic language skills, and familiarity with word processing, spreadsheet, and database programs are important. Data entry often serves as a stepping-stone to other administrative positions. The average annual salary for data entry clerks is around $24,000. Salaries start at about $21,500 and, with experience, can exceed $35,000. For more information, visit scsite.com/dc2008/ch5/careers and then click Data Entry Clerk.

High-Tech Talk

BIOMETRICS: PERSONALIZED SECURITY

Biometric authentication is based on the measurement of an individual's unique physiological and behavioral characteristics. The most common measurements, described earlier in this chapter, such as fingerprints, hand geometry, facial features, and eye patterns are physiological biometrics. Some of the more novel measurements, such as body odor, brain wave patterns, DNA, ear shape, sweat pores, and vein patterns also fall into the category of physiological biometrics. Voice scan and signature scan are examples of behavioral biometrics.

Any biometric technology process involves two basic steps — enrollment and matching. To illustrate these steps, this High-Tech Talk uses the most common biometric technology, finger-scan technology.

ENROLLMENT Enrollment is the process in which a user presents the fingerprint data to be stored in a template for future use, as shown in the top of Figure 5-50. This initial template is called the *enrollment template.* Creating the enrollment template involves four basic steps: (1) acquire fingerprint, (2) extract fingerprint feature, (3) create enrollment template, and (4) store enrollment template. The enrollment template usually is created only after the user has submitted several samples of the same fingerprint. Most fingerprint images will have false details, usually caused by cuts, scars, or even dirt, which must be filtered out.

The first step, acquire fingerprint, presents a major challenge to finger-scan technology. The quality of a fingerprint may vary substantially from person to person and even finger to finger. The two main methods of acquiring images are optical and silicon. With optical technology, a camera is used to register the fingerprint image against a plastic or glass platen (scanner). Silicon technology uses a silicon chip as a platen, which usually produces a higher quality fingerprint image than optical devices.

The second step, extract fingerprint feature, involves thinning the ridges of the raw image to a minuscule size and then converting the characteristics to binary format. Fingerprints are comprised of ridges and valleys that have unique patterns, such as arches, loops, and swirls. Irregularities and discontinuities in these ridges and valleys are known as *minutiae.* Minutiae are the distinctive characteristics upon which most finger-scan technology is based. The fingerprint-feature extraction process used is highly sophisticated, patented, and a closely-held vendor secret.

In the third step, the binary format is used to create the enrollment template. The fourth and final step involves storing the template on a storage device, such as a hard disk or smart card for future use when the same person attempts to be authenticated.

MATCHING Matching is the process of comparing a match template to an enrollment template. A *match template* is created when the user attempts to gain access through a fingerprint scanner. Most computer and network systems are set up so that the person also must claim an identity, such as a user name, along with the fingerprint. In this case, the match template is compared directly to the enrollment template for that user name. Other systems, such as those used for criminal investigations, will search the entire enrollment template database for a match.

The match template is created in the same fashion as the enrollment template described earlier. Rather than storing the match template on disk, however, it is compared to the user's stored enrollment template, as shown in the bottom of Figure 5-50. The result of the matching process is a score. The score is compared against a threshold. The threshold is a predefined number that can be adjusted depending on the desired level of security.

The scoring process leads to the decision process. The decision process will produce one of three actions: (1) the threshold has been exceeded, thereby resulting in a match; (2) the threshold has not been met, thereby resulting in a nonmatch; or (3) the data may have been insufficient, resulting in the system requesting a new sample from the user to begin a new comparison.

Finger-scan technology is likely to continue to grow as the centerpiece of the biometric industry. For more information, visit scsite.com/dc2008/ch5/tech and then click Biometrics.

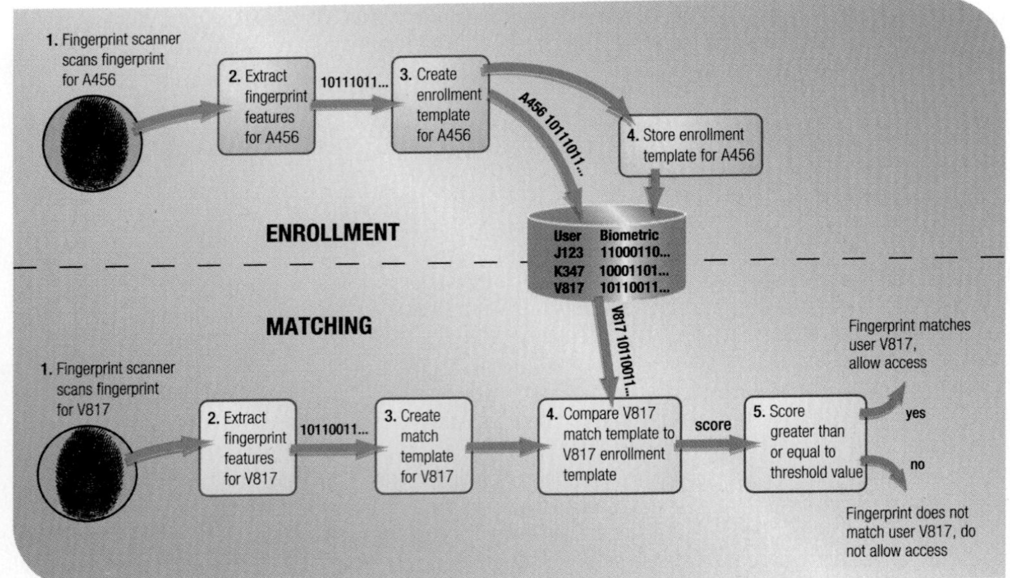

FIGURE 5-50 The two steps in biometric technology.

Companies on the Cutting Edge

LOGITECH

PERSONAL INTERFACE PRODUCTS LEADER

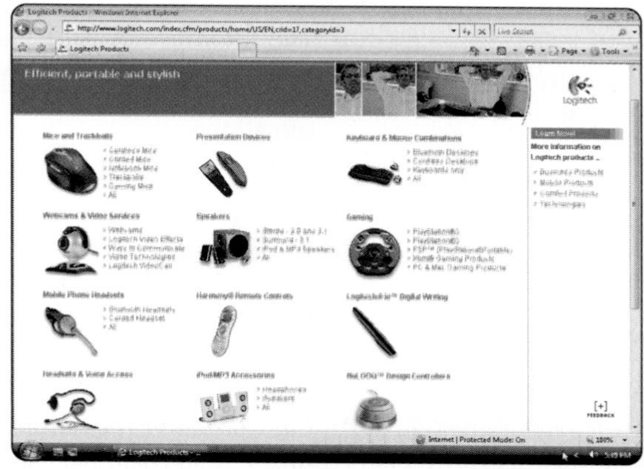

The average Internet user has more than 40 inches of cords on his desktop, according to a *Logitech* survey. This company is working to reduce desktop clutter with a variety of cordless peripherals, including mouse devices, keyboards, mobile headphones and earphones, and game controllers.

A market leader, Logitech has sold more than 50 million wireless devices. It also designs, manufactures, and markets corded devices. The company's retail sales account for more than 85 percent of its revenue.

Two engineering students from Stanford University, Italian-born Pierluigi Zappacosta and Swiss-born Daniel Borel, launched Logitech in 1981. Today, the corporation is the world's largest manufacturer of the mouse and reached a milestone in 2006 when it sold its 700 millionth mouse. For more information, visit scsite.com/dc2008/ch5/companies and then click Logitech.

Palm

HANDHELD COMPUTING DEVICES MANUFACTURER

Palm's original Pilot organizer holds the distinction of being the most rapidly adopted new computing product ever manufactured. More than two million units of this PDA were sold since Palm Computing introduced the product in 1996.

Palm Computing was founded in 1992 and became a subsidiary of 3Com Corp. in 1997. In 2000, the Palm subsidiary became an independent, publicly traded company. In 2003, shareholders voted to spin off PalmSource, Inc., maker of the Palm operating system, as an independent company called palmOne, Inc., and acquire Handspring, Inc. In 2005, the company changed its name to *Palm*, Inc., after it acquired full rights to the brand name, Palm.

In the ten-year history of Palm products, the devices have collected data in space, been on a Mount Everest climb, and helped doctors provide care at patients' bedsides. For more information, visit scsite.com/dc2008/ch5/companies and then click Palm.

Technology Trailblazers

CHARLES WALTON

RFID DEVELOPER

The next time you use a key card to unlock a door, you can thank *Charles Walton* for simplifying your life. He holds the first patent in RFID technology, issued in 1973, which he called "an automatic identification system."

He believed his invention would interest General Motors executives, but they thought his automatic door lock reader was too futuristic. He then went to lock manufacturer Schlage, where management licensed his technology. Walton also created an automatic toll collection system more than 20 years ago. He has been awarded more than 50 patents, 10 of which are for his RFID-related products.

In recent years, he has been working in his California electronics laboratory and applying creative problem solving in the political and social fields. For more information, visit scsite.com/dc2008/ch5/people and then click Charles Walton.

DOUGLAS ENGELBART

CREATOR OF THE MOUSE

The phrase "point and click" might not be part of every computer user's vocabulary if *Douglas Engelbart* had not pursued his engineering dreams. In 1964, he developed the first prototype computer mouse with the goal of making it easier to move a cursor around a computer screen.

Ten years later, engineers at Xerox refined Engelbart's prototype and showed the redesigned product to Apple's Steve Jobs, who applied the concept to his graphical Macintosh computer. The mouse was mass produced in the mid-1980s, and today it is the most widely used pointing device.

Engelbart currently is refining his Collective IQ philosophy at his Bootstrap Institute; this concept optimizes collaboration, creativity, and competition to solve problems. For more information, visit scsite.com/dc2008/ch5/people and then click Douglas Engelbart.

Chapter Review

The Chapter Review section summarizes the concepts presented in this chapter. To listen to the audio version of this Chapter Review, visit scsite.com/dc2008/ch5/review. To obtain help from other students regarding any subject in this chapter, visit scsite.com/dc2008/ch5/forum and post your thoughts or questions.

① **What Is Input?** **Input** is any *data* or instructions entered into the memory of a computer. An **input device** is any hardware component that allows users to enter data and instructions.

② **What Are the Characteristics of a Keyboard?** A **keyboard** is an input device that contains keys users press to enter data into a computer. Computer keyboards have a typing area that includes letters of the alphabet, numbers, punctuation marks, and other basic keys. Most keyboards also have *function keys* programmed to issue commands; keys used to move the **insertion point**, usually a blinking vertical bar, on the screen; and *toggle keys* that switch between two states when pressed. A *gaming keyboard* is a keyboard designed specifically for users that enjoy playing games on the computer.

③ **What Are Different Mouse Types, and How Do They Work?** A **pointing device** is an input device that allows users to control a small graphical symbol, called a **pointer**, on the screen. A **mouse** is a pointing device that fits under the palm of your hand. As you move a mouse, the pointer on the screen also moves. A *mechanical mouse* translates the movement of a ball on its underside into signals the computer can process. An *optical mouse* uses devices that emit and sense light to detect the mouse's movement. A *laser mouse* uses a laser to detect movement. A *wireless mouse* transmits data using wireless technology.

④ **How Do Pointing Devices and Controllers for Gaming and Media Players Work?** A **trackball** is a stationary pointing device with a ball that you rotate to move the pointer. A **touchpad** is a flat, pressure-sensitive device that you slide your finger across to move the pointer. A **pointing stick** is a device positioned on the keyboard that you push to move the pointer. A **light pen** is a light-sensitive device that you press against or point at the screen to select objects. A **touch screen** is a touch-sensitive display device that you interact with by touching areas of the screen. A **stylus** and a **digital pen** use pressure to write or draw. A **gamepad** controls the movement and actions of players or objects in video games or computer games. A **joystick** is a vertical lever that you move to control a simulated vehicle or player. A **wheel** is a steering-wheel-type device that you turn to simulate driving a vehicle. A **light gun** is used to shoot targets as you pull the trigger on the weapon. A **dance pad** is an electronic device, divided into panels, that users press with their feet. A *motion-sensing game controller*, such as the *Wii Remote*, guides on-screen elements by moving a handheld input device through the air. A *Click Wheel* is used to browse through songs, pictures, or movie lists on a portable media player.

connect
Visit scsite.com/dc2008/ch5/quiz or click the Quiz Yourself button. Click Objectives 1 – 4.

⑤ **How Does Voice Recognition Work?** **Voice recognition** is the computer's capability of distinguishing spoken words. Voice recognition programs recognize a vocabulary of preprogrammed words. Most voice recognition programs are a combination of *speaker-dependent software*, which makes a profile of your voice, and *speaker-independent software*, which has a built-in set of word patterns.

⑥ **What Are Input Devices for PDAs, Smart Phones, and Tablet PCs?** A primary input device for a PDA is a basic stylus. Some PDAs have a built-in keyboard or support voice input. You can attach a full-sized *portable keyboard* to a PDA. Because most smart phones include PDA capabilities, input devices used with PDAs usually are available for smart phones. You can send typed messages using *text messaging*. Some smart phones can use IM to communicate over the Internet, and many have a camera so that users can use *picture messaging*. The primary input device for a Tablet PC is a digital pen, with which you can write on the device's screen. If you slide a Tablet PC into a *docking station*, you can use a full-sized keyboard, mouse, and other peripherals.

Chapter Review

7 How Does a Digital Camera Work? A **digital camera** allows users to take pictures and store the photographed images digitally. When you take a picture, light passes into the camera lens, which focuses the image on a *charge-coupled device (CCD)*. The CCD generates an analog signal that represents the image. An analog-to-digital converter (ADC) converts the analog signal to a digital signal. A processor in the camera stores the digital image on the camera's storage media. The image is downloaded to a computer's hard disk via cable or copied from the camera's storage media.

8 How Are PC Video Cameras, Web Cams, and Video Conferencing Used? A **PC video camera** is a digital video camera that enables users to capture video and still images and then send or broadcast the images over the Internet. A **Web cam** is any video camera that displays its output on a Web page. A **video conference** is a meeting between geographically separated people who use a network or the Internet to transmit audio and video data.

connect
Visit scsite.com/dc2008/ch5/quiz or click the Quiz Yourself button. Click Objectives 5 – 8.

9 What Are Various Types of Scanners and Reading Devices, and How Do They Work? A **scanner** is a light-sensing input device that reads printed text and graphics and translates the results into a form the computer can process. A **flatbed scanner** works in a manner similar to a copy machine except it creates a file of the document. An *optical reader* uses a light source to read characters, marks, and codes and converts them into digital data. **Optical character recognition** (**OCR**) reads characters from ordinary documents. **Optical mark recognition** (**OMR**) reads hand-drawn marks such as small circles. A **bar code reader** is an optical reader that uses laser beams to read a **bar code**, or identification code. **RFID** (*radio frequency identification*) uses radio signals to communicate with an embedded tag. A *magstripe reader* reads the magnetic stripe on the back of credit cards and other similar cards. **MICR** (*magnetic-ink character recognition*) reads text printed with magnetized ink.

10 What Are Types of Terminals? A *terminal* consists of a keyboard, a monitor, a video card, and memory. A *dumb terminal* has no processing power and relies on a host computer for processing. A *smart terminal* has a processor and can perform some functions independent of the host computer. POS terminals and ATMs are special-purpose terminals. A **POS** *(point-of-sale)* **terminal** records purchases, processes credit or debit cards, and updates inventory. An **automated teller machine** (**ATM**) is a self-service banking machine that connects to a host computer. To access a bank account, you insert a bankcard into the ATM's card reader and enter a *personal identification number (PIN)*.

11 What Are Various Biometric Devices? A *biometric device* translates a personal characteristic into digital code that is compared with a digital code stored in the computer to identify an individual. A **fingerprint scanner** captures curves and indentations of a fingerprint. A *face recognition system* captures a live face image. A *hand geometry system* measures the shape and size of a hand. A *voice verification system* compares live speech with a stored voice pattern. A *signature verification system* recognizes the shape of a signature. An *iris recognition system* reads patterns in the iris of the eye. *Retinal scanners* scan patterns of blood vessels in the back of the retina.

12 What Are Alternative Input Devices for Physically Challenged Users? Voice recognition is ideal for visually impaired users. A *keyguard* is a plate placed over the keyboard that allows users with limited hand mobility to rest their hands and press only one key at a time. Keyboards with larger keys or an *on-screen keyboard* displayed on a user's screen also are available. A small trackball or a *head-mounted pointer* helps users with limited hand movement to control the pointer. Two developments in the prototype stage are *gesture recognition* and computerized implant devices.

connect
Visit scsite.com/dc2008/ch5/quiz or click the Quiz Yourself button. Click Objectives 9 – 12.

Quizzes and Learning Games
Computer Genius
Crossword Puzzle
DC Track and Field
Practice Test
Quiz Yourself
Wheel of Terms
You're Hired!

Exercises
Case Studies
Chapter Review
Checkpoint
Key Terms
Learn How To
Learn It Online
Web Research

Beyond the Book
Career Corner
Companies
FAQs
High-Tech Talk
Looking Ahead
Making Use of the Web
Trailblazers
Web Links

Features
Chapter Forum
Install Computer
Lab Exercises
Maintain Computer
Tech News
Timeline 2008

Key Terms

You should know the Primary Terms and be familiar with the Secondary Terms. Use the list below to help focus your study. To further enhance your understanding of the Key Terms in this chapter, visit scsite.com/dc2008/ch5/terms. See an example of and a definition for each term, and access current and additional information about the term from the Web.

Primary Terms

(shown in bold-black characters in the chapter)

Americans with Disabilities Act (ADA) (266)
audio input (246)
automated teller machine (ATM) (262)
bar code (258)
bar code reader (258)
bar code scanner (258)
dance pad (244)
digital camera (250)
digital pen (242)
digital video (DV) camera (253)
ergonomics (238)
fingerprint scanner (262)
flatbed scanner (256)
game controller (244)
gamepad (244)
graphics tablet (243)
input (234)
input device (236)
insertion point (237)
joystick (244)
keyboard (236)
light gun (244)
light pen (242)
magnetic stripe card reader (260)
MICR (260)
MICR reader (260)
mouse (239)
OCR devices (257)
optical character recognition (OCR) (257)
optical mark recognition (OMR) (257)
PC camera (253)
PC video camera (253)
pen input (242)
pointer (239)
pointing device (239)
pointing stick (242)
POS terminal (261)
resolution (252)
RFID (259)
RFID reader (259)
scanner (255)
smart card (264)
stylus (242)
touch screen (242)
touchpad (241)
trackball (241)
turnaround document (257)
video conference (254)
video input (253)
voice input (245)
voice recognition (245)
Web cam (254)
wheel (244)

Secondary Terms

(shown in italic characters in the chapter)

air mouse (239)
biometric device (262)
biometric identifier (262)
biometrics (262)
charge-coupled device (CCD) (251)
Click Wheel (245)
command (235)
continuous speech (246)
cordless keyboard (238)
cordless mouse (239)
cursor (application program) (237)
cursor (graphics tablet) (243)
data (234)
data collection device (261)
digitizer (243)
docking station (249)
download (251)
dumb terminal (261)
enhanced keyboard (236)
enhanced resolution (252)
ergonomic keyboard (238)
face recognition system (263)
field camera (251)
function keys (236)
gaming keyboard (237)
gesture recognition (266)
hand geometry system (263)
handwriting recognition software (243)
head-mounted pointer (266)
image processing (256)
image processing system (256)
iris recognition system (264)
keyguard (266)
laser mouse (239)
magnetic-ink character recognition (260)
magstripe reader (260)
mechanical mouse (239)
MIDI (musical instrument digital interface) (246)
motion-sensing game controllers (244)
mouse gestures (240)
mouse pad (239)
mouse pointer (239)
MP (252)
OCR (optical character recognition) software (256)
on-screen keyboard (266)
optical mouse (239)
optical reader (257)
optical resolution (252)
optical scanner (255)
personal identification number (PIN) (262)
photo scanner (255)
picture messaging (249)
pixel (252)
pixels per inch (ppi) (252)
point-and-shoot camera (251)
point of sale (POS) (261)
portable keyboard (248)
program (234)
radio frequency identification (259)
retinal scanners (264)
signature verification system (263)
smart terminal (261)
source document (255)
speaker-dependent software (246)
speaker-independent software (246)
speech recognition (245)
streaming cam (254)
studio camera (251)
terminal (261)
text messaging (248)
toggle key (237)
touch-sensitive pad (245)
UPC (Universal Product Code) (258)
user response (235)
video capture card (253)
video telephone call (253)
voice verification system (263)
whiteboard (254)
Wii Remote (245)
wireless keyboard (238)
wireless mouse (239)

Checkpoint

Use the Checkpoint exercises to check your knowledge level of the chapter. The Beyond the Book exercises will help broaden your understanding of the concepts presented in this chapter. To complete the Checkpoint exercises interactively, visit scsite.com/dc2008/ch5/check.

Label the Figure

Identify these areas and keys on a desktop computer keyboard.

a. arrow keys
b. function keys
c. Internet controls
d. media controls
e. numeric keypad
f. typing area
g. WINDOWS key
h. wrist rest

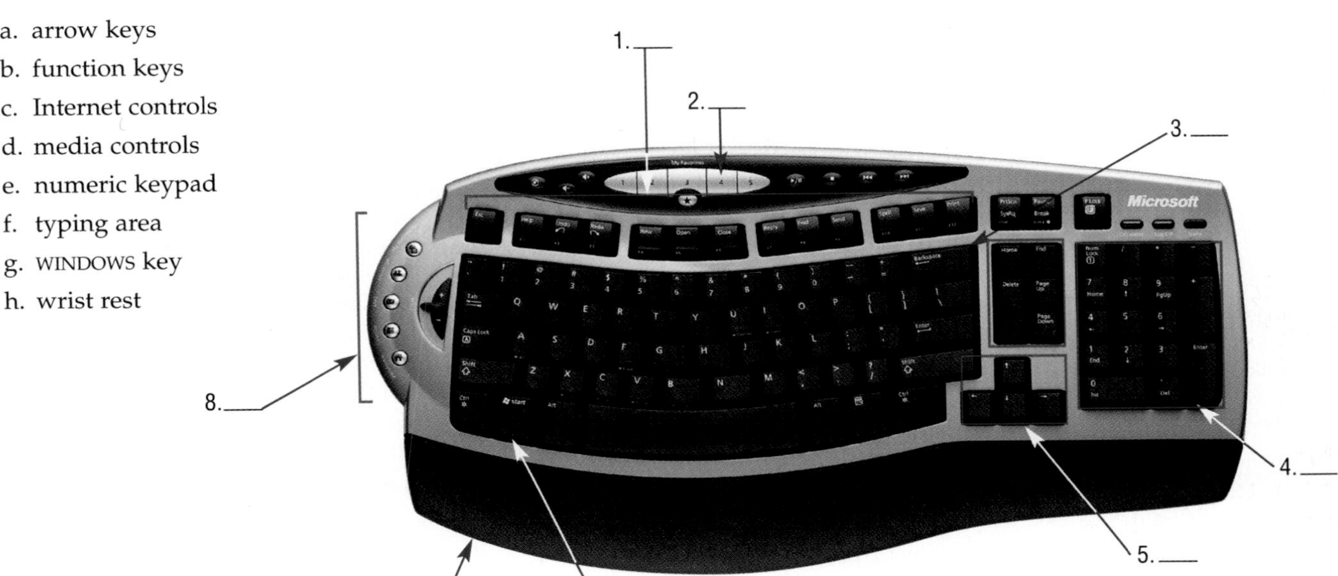

True/False

Mark T for True and F for False. (See page numbers in parentheses.)

_____ 1. Once data is in memory, the computer interprets and executes instructions to process the data into information. (234)

_____ 2. An input device is any hardware component that allows users to enter data and instructions into a computer. (236)

_____ 3. The command associated with a function key will remain the same from program to program. (236)

_____ 4. An air mouse allows you to control objects, media players, and slide shows by moving the mouse in predetermined directions through the air. (239)

_____ 5. A touchpad is a small, flat, rectangular pointing device that is sensitive to pressure and motion. (241)

_____ 6. A light pen is a handheld input device that can detect the presence of light. (242)

_____ 7. Pressure-sensitive digital pens typically provide less functionality than a stylus. (243)

_____ 8. Speaker-dependent software has a built-in set of word patterns so you do not have to train a computer to recognize your voice. (246)

_____ 9. The primary input device for a Tablet PC is a mouse. (249)

_____ 10. Resolution is the smallest element in an electronic image. (252)

_____ 11. A whiteboard is a meeting between two or more geographically separated people who use a network or the Internet to transmit audio and video data. (254)

_____ 12. A scanner is a light-sensing input device that reads printed text and graphics and then translates the results into a form the computer can process. (255)

Checkpoint

Multiple Choice

Select the best answer. (See page numbers in parentheses.)

1. _____ is a series of instructions that tells a computer what to do and how to do it. (234)
   a. Data
   b. A program
   c. A command
   d. A user response
2. A(n) _____ has twelve function keys along the top; it also has two CTRL keys, two ALT keys, and a set of arrow and additional keys between the typing area and the numeric keypad. (236)
   a. portable keyboard
   b. enhanced keyboard
   c. keyguard
   d. touchpad
3. A(n) _____ has a design that reduces the chance of wrist and hand injuries. (238)
   a. ergonomic keyboard
   b. cordless keyboard
   c. gaming keyboard
   d. function key
4. A(n) _____ has a rubber or metal ball on its underside. (239)
   a. air mouse
   b. laser mouse
   c. optical mouse
   d. mechanical mouse
5. Architects, mapmakers, designers, artists, and home users create drawings and sketches on a _____. (243)
   a. trackball
   b. smart terminal
   c. graphics tablet
   d. touchpad
6. A _____ controls the movement and actions of players or objects in video games or computer games. (244)
   a. control pad
   b. gamepad
   c. dance pad
   d. touchpad
7. _____ is the process of entering any sound into the computer such as speech, music, and sound effects. (246)
   a. MIDI
   b. Voice input
   c. Voice recognition
   d. Audio input
8. The most expensive and highest quality digital camera is a _____, which is a stationary camera used for professional work. (251)
   a. PC camera
   b. point-and-shoot camera
   c. studio camera
   d. field camera
9. A(n) _____ is a type of digital video camera that enables a home or small business user to capture video and still images, send e-mail messages with video attachments, add live images to instant messages, broadcast live images over the Internet, and make video telephone calls. (253)
   a. PC camera
   b. digital video camera
   c. Web cam
   d. optical scanner
10. Scanners capture data from a _____, which is the original form of the data. (255)
    a. duplicate document
    b. secondary document
    c. derivative document
    d. source document
11. RFID is a technology that uses _____ to communicate with a tag placed in or attached to an object, an animal, or a person. (259)
    a. a thin wire
    b. pixels
    c. radio signals
    d. light waves
12. The most widely used biometric device is the _____. (262)
    a. fingerprint scanner
    b. iris recognition system
    c. retinal scanner
    d. face recognition system
13. A smart card stores the personal data on a _____ embedded in the card. (264)
    a. biometric device
    b. thin microprocessor
    c. magnetic strip
    d. optical mark
14. With _____, the computer will detect human motion. (266)
    a. an on-screen keyboard
    b. a head-mounted pointer
    c. gesture recognition
    d. a computerized implant

Checkpoint

Matching

Match the terms with their definitions. (See page numbers in parentheses.)

_____ 1. insertion point (237)
_____ 2. gaming keyboard (237)
_____ 3. pointer (239)
_____ 4. gamepad (244)
_____ 5. game controller (244)
_____ 6. light gun (244)
_____ 7. dance pad (244)
_____ 8. video capture card (253)
_____ 9. bar code (258)
_____ 10. retinal scanner (264)

a. projects an infrared image of a keyboard on any flat surface
b. identification code that consists either of vertical lines and spaces of different widths or a two-dimensional pattern of dots, squares, and other images
c. scans patterns of blood vessels in the back of the retina
d. controls the movement and actions of players or objects in video games or computer games
e. graphical symbol whose location and shape change with the movement of a pointing device
f. symbol on the screen that indicates where the next character typed will be displayed
g. keyboard designed specifically for users that enjoy playing games on the computer
h. a flat electronic device divided into panels that users press with their feet in response to instructions from a music video game
i. used to shoot targets and moving objects after you pull the trigger on the weapon
j. converts an analog video signal to a digital signal that a computer can process
k. self-service banking machine that connects to a host computer
l. used by video games and computer games as the input device that directs movements and actions of on-screen objects

Short Answer

Write a brief answer to each of the following questions.

1. What are three different types of mouse devices? __________ What makes them different from each other? __________
2. How do motion-sensing game controllers work? __________ What is the Wii Remote and how is it used? __________
3. What is OCR (optical character recognition)? __________ What is OMR (optical mark recognition)? __________
4. What is a biometric identifier and what are some examples? __________ How does a biometric device work? __________
5. What is the Americans with Disabilities Act (ADA)? __________ How might gesture recognition and computerized implant devices help physically challenged users in the future? __________

Beyond the Book

Read the following book elements, learn more about each using the Web, and then write a brief report.

1. Ethics & Issues — Keyboard Monitoring — Privacy Risk? (237), Are Employers Responsible for Medical Problems Related to Computer Use? (241), Should Talking on a Cellular Phone While Driving Be Illegal? (249), Should Cameras Be Able to Monitor Your Every Move? (254), Scanner Errors at the Checkout Counter? (258), or Will RFID Track Your Every Move? (259)
2. Career Corner — Data Entry Clerk (267)
3. Companies on the Cutting Edge — Logitech or Palm (269)
4. FAQs (237, 238, 240, 248, 250, 251, 252, 254, 256, 264)
5. High-Tech Talk — Biometrics: Personalized Security (268)
6. Looking Ahead — Paying with Your Cellular Telephone (259) or Controlling Games by Thinking (267)
7. Making Use of the Web — Blogs (121)
8. Picture Yourself Using Input Devices (232)
9. Technology Trailblazers — Charles Walton and Douglas Engelbart (269)
10. Web Links (240, 241, 242, 243, 244, 246, 254, 258, 264)

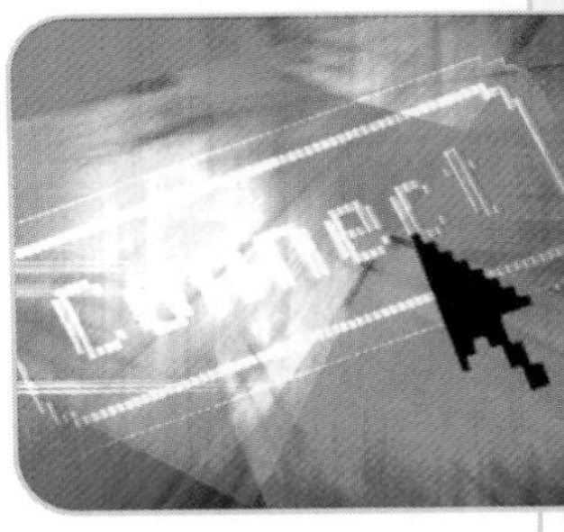

Learn It Online

Use the Learn It Online exercises to reinforce your understanding of the chapter concepts. To access the Learn It Online exercises, visit scsite.com/dc2008/ch5/learn.

1 At the Movies — A Digital Whiteboard to Make Presentations Roar

To view the A Digital Whiteboard to Make Presentations Roar movie, click the number 1 button. Locate your video and click the corresponding High-Speed or Dial-Up link, depending on your Internet connection. Watch the movie and then complete the exercise by answering the question that follows. Polyvision CEO Michael Dunn shares his vision of the whiteboards and meetings of the future. Why is using the digital whiteboard more effective than using a regular wipe board and markers?

2 Video and Audio: You Review It — Voice Recognition

In this chapter you learned about voice recognition. Click the number 2 button to view the suggested links and begin your search for videos, podcasts, or vodcasts related to voice recognition. Choose a video, podcast, or vodcast that discusses voice recognition and is of interest to you, and then write a description of its contents. Explain why you chose this piece, what you liked about it, what you disliked about it, and whether you would recommend it to a fellow student. Finish your review by giving the video, podcast, or vodcast a rating of 1 – 5 stars. Submit your review in the format requested by your instructor.

3 Student Edition Labs — Working with Audio

Click the number 3 button. A new browser window will open, displaying the Student Edition Labs. Follow the on-screen instructions to complete the Working with Audio Lab. When finished, click the Exit button. If required, submit your results to your instructor.

4 Student Edition Labs — Working with Video

Click the number 4 button. A new browser window will open, displaying the Student Edition Labs. Follow the on-screen instructions to complete the Working with Video Lab. When finished, click the Exit button. If required, submit your results to your instructor.

5 Practice Test

Click the number 5 button. Answer each question. When completed, enter your name and click the Grade Test button to submit the quiz for grading. Make a note of any missed questions. If required, submit your results to your instructor.

6 Who Wants To Be a Computer Genius^2?

Click the number 6 button to find out if you are a computer genius. Directions about how to play the game will be displayed. When you are ready to play, click the Play button. Submit your score to your instructor.

7 Wheel of Terms

Click the number 7 button to reinforce important terms you learned in this chapter by playing the Shelly Cashman Series version of this popular game. Directions about how to play the game will be displayed. When you are ready to play, click the Play button. Submit your score to your instructor.

Learn It Online

8 DC Track and Field

Click the number 8 button to use what you have learned in this chapter to compete against other students in three track and field events. Directions about how to play the game will be displayed. When you are ready to play, click the start first event button. If required, submit your score to your instructor.

9 You're Hired!

Click the number 9 button to use what you have learned in this chapter to embark on the path to a career in computers. Directions about how to play the game will be displayed. When you are ready to play, click the begin game button. If required, submit your score to your instructor.

10 Crossword Puzzle Challenge

Click the number 10 button, then click the Crossword Puzzle Challenge link. Directions about how to play the game will be displayed. Complete the puzzle to reinforce skills you learned in this chapter. When you are ready to play, click the Continue button. Submit the completed puzzle to your instructor.

11 Vista Exercises

Click the number 11 button. When the Vista Exercises menu appears, click the exercise assigned by your instructor. A new browser window will open. Follow the on-screen instructions to complete the exercise. When finished, click the Exit button. If required, submit your results to your instructor.

12 In the News

Many people spend a great deal of time jotting notes on scratch pads, napkins, or self-stick notes. This may be fine for the occasional thought; however, in a situation where you would rather concentrate on the substance of the ideas being expressed, you may need a more sophisticated method for taking notes. Tape recorders have long been the mainstay for recording lectures, interviews, or one's thoughts, but they are restricted by the fact that the tapes last only so long before they have to be flipped over or switched altogether. One new development is the voice pen, which is a flash-memory-based recording device. It records digitally, which offers higher quality over standard tapes, easy indexing, and instant erasure. It is approximately the size of a small cellular telephone or remote control unit and can record up to 500 minutes on long play settings. Click the number 12 button and read a news article about a new or improved input device, an input device being used in a new way, or an input device being made more available. What is the device? Who is promoting it? How will it be used? Will the input device change the number, or effectiveness, of potential users? If so, why?

13 Chapter Discussion Forum

Select an objective from this chapter on page 233 about which you would like more information. Click the number 13 button and post a short message listing a meaningful message title accompanied by one or more questions concerning the selected objective. In two days, return to the threaded discussion by clicking the number 13 button. Submit to your instructor your original message and at least one response to your message.

14 eHow.com

Click the number 14 button to learn how to use eHow.com to locate information about a project you want to learn how to complete. Read other users contributions' and then complete the project. Write a brief report about your experience and then post your report to the topic you chose so that others can learn from your experience. Print your report and submit to your instructor.

Learn How To

Use the Learn How To activities to learn fundamental skills when using a computer and accompanying technology. Complete the exercises and submit them to your instructor. To see a video of a Learn How To activity, visit scsite.com/dc2008/ch5/howto.

LEARN HOW TO 1: Install and Use a PC Video Camera

A PC video camera, sometimes called a Web cam, is a digital video camera that allows you to capture video and still images. The videos can be used in live instant messages or for live images over the Internet. Recordings of the videos can be included on Web pages or in e-mail messages as attachments. In addition, some cameras include software that enables you to establish a visual security environment where the camera can be used to detect and record movement in its general vicinity.

Using a PC video camera requires two phases: 1) purchasing and installing the PC video camera, and 2) using the video camera to transmit live video or to record video or digital images.

To purchase and install a PC video camera, complete the following steps:

1. Determine how you want to use the video camera in order to decide the quality of camera you require and the camera software you need. PC video cameras range in price from about $25 to more than $125, and vary in picture quality, features, and accompanying software. If you are not sure of all features and prices, search the Web to determine the best camera for your use.
2. After making your purchase, you will find that most cameras are accompanied by a CD-ROM containing the software that enables the camera to communicate and work with the computer. Often, the instructions with the device will specify that you should place the CD-ROM in a CD or DVD drive and follow the on-screen instructions to install the software on the computer.
3. After the software is installed, you likely will be told to connect the camera to the computer. You do so by connecting the USB cable first to the camera and then to a USB port on your computer. When the camera is connected, you will be able to start the camera software from either the All Programs list or the desktop.

Once you have started the camera software, you will be able to use the camera for any of the tasks you require. Each camera and its accompanying software will allow you to create a video, use instant messaging to send live video to your IM contacts, and other uses as well. In addition, you often will be able to control the quality of your video output by modifying brightness, contrast, and clarity. With many cameras, you will be able to zoom in and out, and, from your keyboard, enter commands to move the camera lens left, right, up, and down.

On some cameras, you even can use a feature called face tracking, where the camera will remain focused on your face even when you move. This feature allows you to be more natural and not be concerned with always making sure you are placed exactly right for the camera.

As you can see, once you have purchased and installed a PC video camera, you will open an entirely new world of communication right from your computer.

Exercise

1. Assume you have decided to purchase a PC video camera to use for instant messaging. Search the Web to find the highest rated cameras available for purchase that can be used for your purposes. What is the most expensive camera you found? The least expensive? What features distinguish the two? Based on your use of the camera for instant messaging, what camera would you choose to buy? Why? Submit your answers to your instructor.
2. Optional: Purchase a PC video camera or borrow one from a friend. Install the camera software on a computer. Warning: If you are using a computer that is not your own, complete this exercise only with the owner's permission. Connect the camera to the computer. Practice with the camera and the accompanying software. What features does the software provide? Which feature do you find the most compelling? What features could you do without? Record a video of yourself answering these questions. Submit the video to your instructor.

LEARN HOW TO 2: Use the On-Screen Keyboard for Physically Challenged Users

Everyone who uses a computer must enter data and instructions into the computer. For people with limited hand and arm mobility, this can prove a daunting task. Windows Vista and a variety of other applications provide a number of aids that can be useful. One of these is the on-screen keyboard.

The on-screen keyboard allows a user to view the keyboard on the screen and select characters to enter by using several different methods. To display and use the on-screen keyboard, complete the following steps:

1. Click the Start button on the Windows taskbar, click All Programs on the Start menu, click Accessories in the All Programs list, click Ease of Access in the Accessories list, and then click On-Screen Keyboard in the Ease of Access list to display the On-Screen Keyboard window.
2. In the On-Screen Keyboard window, click Settings on the menu bar. Ensure a checkmark is next to Always on Top.
3. If necessary, click Settings on the menu bar again. Click Typing Mode on the Settings menu to display the Typing Mode dialog box (Figure 5-51).
4. Ensure the Click to select option button is selected and then click the OK button in the Typing Mode dialog box.
5. Start your Web browser and click the Address bar.
6. Using the on-screen keyboard, enter the characters `www.cnn.com` and then click the ENT key.
7. When the cnn.com Web page appears, click the Enter Symbol box in the Market Update section of the page. Using the on-screen keyboard, enter `ibm` and then click the ENT key.
8. After finding the stock price for IBM, close the browser window.
9. Start the WordPad program (see Learn How To number 1 on page 48).
10. In the On-Screen Keyboard window, click Settings on the menu bar and then click Typing Mode on the Settings menu.
11. Click the Hover to select option button to select it. If necessary, click the Minimum time to hover box arrow and select 1.00 seconds in the list. Click the OK button.
12. Click in the WordPad window to position the insertion point.
13. You can cause a character to be entered in the WordPad window by placing the mouse pointer over the desired key (hovering) for one second. Type the following using the on-screen keyboard: `Ease of Access tools are vital for computer users.`
14. Close the WordPad window without saving changes, and then close the On-Screen Keyboard window.

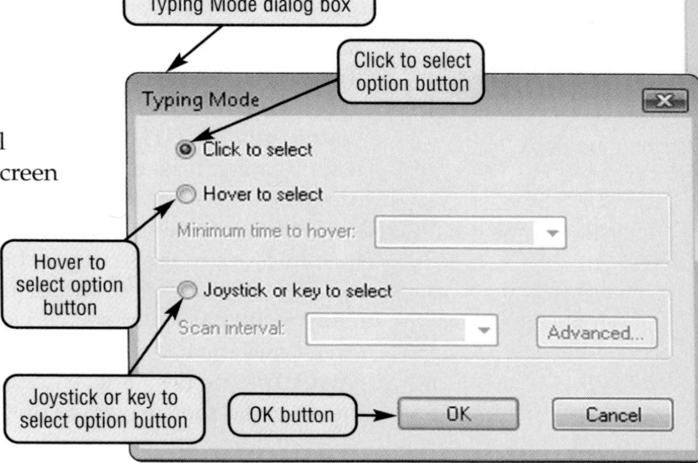

FIGURE 5-51

You have seen how one of the Ease of Access tools within Windows Vista functions. You are encouraged to explore all of the tools and discover how these tools can be useful to those people for whom they were designed.

Exercise

1. Start WordPad and then display the on-screen keyboard. In the On-Screen Keyboard window, click Settings on the menu bar and then click Typing Mode. In the Typing Mode dialog box, select Joystick or key to select. Click the Advanced button. Ensure the Keyboard key box contains a checkmark and then click Space in the list. Click the OK buttons to close the dialog boxes. Then, on the Keyboard menu, select Block Layout. Click in the WordPad window and then press the SPACEBAR. What happened? Keep pressing the SPACEBAR until you cause a character to be entered in the WordPad window. Use the BKSP key on the on-screen keyboard to backspace and erase the character, and then use the on-screen keyboard to type `On-Screen Keyboard usage` in the WordPad window. When you are done, close the WordPad window and the On-Screen Keyboard window. Which means of using the on-screen keyboard (click a key, hover, or the SPACEBAR) did you find easiest to use? Why? Why would a physically challenged person prefer one method over another? Prepare your answers using the on-screen keyboard and then submit your answers to your instructor.

Quizzes and Learning Games
- Computer Genius
- Crossword Puzzle
- DC Track and Field
- Practice Test
- Quiz Yourself
- Wheel of Terms
- You're Hired!

Exercises
- Case Studies
- Chapter Review
- Checkpoint
- Key Terms
- Learn How To
- Learn It Online
- Web Research

Beyond the Book
- Career Corner
- Companies
- FAQs
- High-Tech Talk
- Looking Ahead
- Making Use of the Web
- Trailblazers
- Web Links

Features
- Chapter Forum
- Install Computer
- Lab Exercises
- Maintain Computer
- Tech News
- Timeline 2008

Web Research

Use the Internet-based Web Research exercises to broaden your understanding of the concepts presented in this chapter. Visit scsite.com/dc2008/ch5/research to obtain more information pertaining to each exercise. To discuss any of the Web Research exercises in this chapter with other students, post your thoughts or questions at scsite.com/dc2008/ch5/forum.

1 **Scavenger Hunt** Use one of the search engines listed in Figure 2-10 in Chapter 2 on page 78 or your own favorite search engine to find the answers to the questions below. Copy and paste the Web address from the Web page where you found the answer. Some questions may have more than one answer. If required, submit your answers to your instructor. (1) Consumers use touch screens at bank ATMs, airport check-ins, and mall kiosks. What did Dr. Samuel C. Hurst invent in 1971 that led to the development of touch screen technology? (2) What are some of the services available from providers, such as Yahoo! Photo, to help consumers store and share digital photos online? What are the costs of some of these services? (3) Who holds patents awarded in the 1950s for automatic video scanning and inspection methods, which led to bar code technology?

2 **Search Sleuth** MetaCrawler (metacrawler.com) is a different type of search Web site because it returns combined results from leading search engines. Visit this Web site and then use your word processing program to answer the following questions. Then, if required, submit your answers to your instructor. (1) Click the About MetaCrawler link at the bottom of the page. Which search engines are you searching when you use MetaCrawler? (2) Click your browser's Back button or press the BACKSPACE key to return to the MetaCrawler home page. Locate the Popular Searches section. What are the six most popular searches today? (3) Click the Images link on the home page, type `sunset` in the search text box, and then click the Search button. How many results did your search yield? Click the Audio link above the search text box to search for audio files of sunsets. How many results did your search yield? (4) Click your browser's Back button or press the BACKSPACE key three times to return to the MetaCrawler home page. Click the Tools & Tips link at the bottom of the page. Click the FAQ link. Click several question links concerning conducting searches on this Web site and read the answers to these questions. Summarize the information you read and then write a 50-word summary that may be submitted to your instructor.

3 **Journaling** Respond to your readings in this chapter by writing at least one page about your reactions, evaluations, and reflections about using input devices. For example, which pointing devices, such as a trackball, touchpad, stylus, digital pen, joystick, or gamepad, do you use? Are they wireless? Do you use text messaging or picture messaging on your cellular telephone? You also can write about the new terms you learned by reading this chapter. If required, submit your journal to your instructor.

4 **Expanding Your Understanding** Journalists, attorneys, law enforcement officials, and students consider tape recorders and notepads essential components of their daily activities. An alternate means of capturing information is a voice pen, which is a flash-memory-based recording device approximately the size of a small smart phone. Visit a local electronics store or view electronics Web sites to learn more about voice pens. Compare their features, cost, recording time, and warranty. Write a report summarizing your findings, focusing on comparing and contrasting the voice pens. If required, submit your report to your instructor.

5 **Ethics in Action** Some reports suggest that a global surveillance system is monitoring e-mail messages, telephone calls, and faxes. This organization known as Echelon attempts to intercept more than three billion satellite, microwave, cellular, and fiber-optic messages per day, according to the reports. The National Security Agency is forbidden to monitor U.S. citizens, but privacy experts contend that at least 90 percent of U.S. communication is gathered and reviewed. View online sites that provide information about Echelon, including Echelon Watch (www.echelonwatch.org). Write a report summarizing your findings, and include a table of links to Web sites that provide additional details. If required, submit your report to your instructor.

Case Studies

Use the Case Studies to apply the concepts presented in the chapter to real-world situations. Visit scsite.com/dc2008/ch5/cases to obtain more information pertaining to each exercise. To discuss the Case Studies in this chapter with other students, visit scsite.com/dc2008/ch5/forum and post your thoughts or questions.

CASE STUDY 1 — Class Discussion You work in the Efficiency Analysis department of one of the largest retail companies in the world, with multiple stores in every state and many other countries. For the past 25 years, the company has used optical scanners at checkout counters that read the UPC bar code on products to determine from a database the price to charge customers. The company is considering replacing the optical scanners with radio frequency identification, or RFID. The reader receives the code identifying the product via a chip with an antenna that is part of the box or label on the outside of the product. Your manager has asked you to draft a memo outlining the impact such a change would have on the company, its suppliers, and its customers. Be prepared to discuss your findings in class.

CASE STUDY 2 — Class Discussion Your company recently purchased several notebook computers. While the recipients of the notebook computers enjoy having the ability to work outside the office, they have found that working with the notebook computer's touchpad functioning as a mouse has affected their productivity. You have been asked to research purchasing mouse devices that are compatible with the new notebook computers. Your boss has recommended the MoGo Wireless Bluetooth Mouse based on an article she recently read. Research at least three other wireless mouse devices and compare with the MoGo mouse. Write a brief report summarizing your findings. Include your recommendation in the report and the reasons for that recommendation. Be prepared to share your findings with your class.

CASE STUDY 3 — Research While attending college part-time for the past two years, you have worked as a data entry clerk for Salmon Mirror. Recently, you began to feel an unusual pain in your right wrist. Your doctor diagnosed the problem as carpal tunnel syndrome, which is the most well-known of a series of musculoskeletal disorders that fall under the umbrella of repetitive strain injuries (RSIs). Your doctor made several recommendations to relieve the pain, one of which was to find a new job. Before you begin job hunting, however, you want to learn more about this debilitating injury. Use the Web and/or print media to investigate carpal tunnel syndrome. Prepare a report and/or PowerPoint presentation on your findings. Include information about carpal tunnel syndrome warning signs, risk factors, suggestions about proper workstation ergonomics, and procedures for healing the injury. Share your report or presentation with your class.

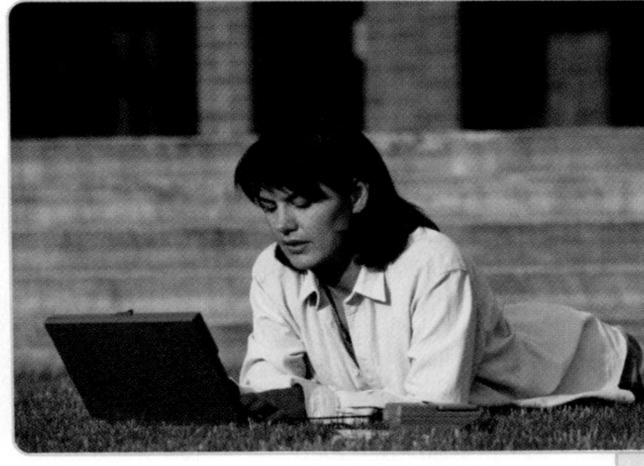

CASE STUDY 4 — Research An electronics company where you are employed as an analyst spends hundreds of thousands of dollars each year on travel to the multiple locations where they operate around the country. In an effort to curb the ever-increasing costs of travel, the CFO has asked you to look into the feasibility of adopting video conferencing at all of its major locations. Use the Web and/or print media to determine the advantages and disadvantages of video conferencing. Can the technology replace all or most face-to-face meetings? What are the costs of common video conferencing systems and the recurring costs their use incurs? Compare those costs to the cost of travel for a team of three people making six trips per year between New York and Los Angeles, including hotel, airline, and food expenses. Write a brief report or use PowerPoint to create a presentation and share your findings with your class.

CASE STUDY 5 — Team Challenge The Transportation Security Administration (TSA) is looking into ways to expedite the airport screening experience of frequent flyers without compromising security. The TSA has hired your team as consultants to investigate biometric technology. In particular, they want your team to review three biometric devices for screening frequent flyers — fingerprint scanner, face recognition system, and iris recognition system. Form a three-member team and have each team member choose a different biometric device. Using the Web and/or print media, have each team member determine the advantages and disadvantages of their chosen biometric device. Include in each report how frequent flyer applicants would apply, accuracy rates of the device, and whether the device would indeed enhance security or open a loophole for terrorists. As a team, merge your findings into a team report and/or PowerPoint presentation and share your recommendations with your class.

Special Feature

Personal Mobile Devices

Personal mobile devices usually can fit in your pocket, and include such devices as PDAs, smart phones, portable media players, ultra personal computers, handheld navigation devices, and handheld game consoles (Figure 1). Page 22 in Chapter 1 discusses PDAs and smart phones. A **PDA** provides personal organizer functions, such as calendar, appointment book, address book, calculator, and notepad. A **smart phone** is an Internet-enabled telephone that usually provides PDA functionality. Both smart phones and PDAs usually allow you to send and receive e-mail, access the Web, download and play media files, and take photos and make short video clips. A **portable media player** is a handheld device capable of video playback, audio playback, or photo display. Portable media players sometimes provide PDA functionality. An **ultra personal computer (uPC)** is a personal computer small enough to fit in one hand and allows you to run a desktop operating system. Page 21 discusses ultra personal computers. A **handheld navigation device** includes a GPS receiver and application software that assist in guiding you from one location to another. A **handheld game console** is a mobile computing device, small enough to fit in one hand, that is designed for single-player or multiplayer video games.

Because the various types of personal mobile devices usually offer similar capabilities, they often are categorized by their form factor. A device's **form factor** refers to its size, shape, and configuration. For example, Figure 1 shows a smart phone that has a PDA form factor and a smart phone that has a phone form factor. While the device with the phone form factor may include PDA functionality, its main purpose is to be used as a phone. Its smaller size may make using it as a PDA more cumbersome than the smart phone with a PDA form factor. The PDA form factor, while larger, provides a better interface for accessing the PDA functionality. An ultra personal computer includes most of the functionality of a typical personal computer or notebook computer, but its form factor is what differentiates it from those types of computers.

This special feature provides an overview of accessories and software available for personal mobile devices. The final section of the feature lists the criteria you should consider when deciding which personal mobile device is right for you.

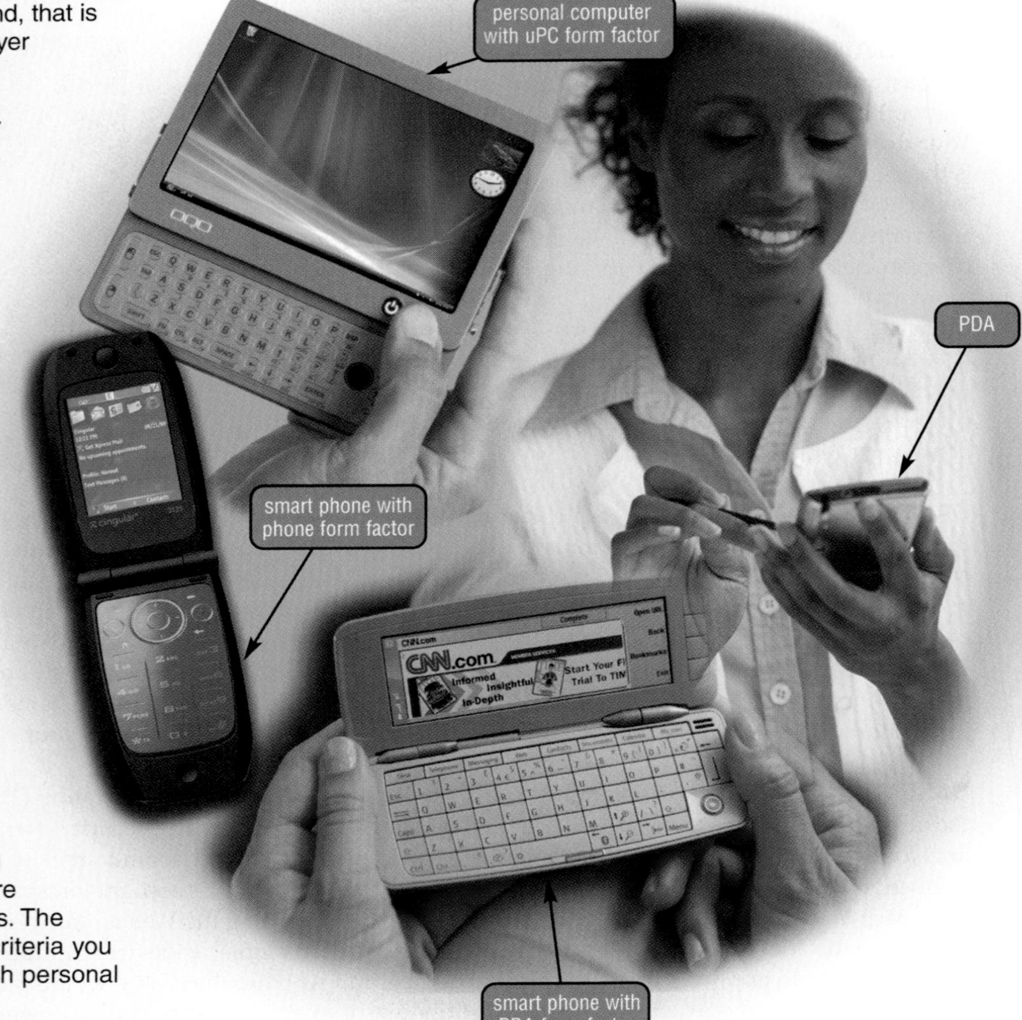

FIGURE 1 Your choice of a personal mobile device depends on the features you require, the desired form factor, the available accessories, and the available software for the device.

EXAMPLES OF PERSONAL MOBILE DEVICES

Personal mobile devices are available in many shapes and sizes and run a variety of operating systems. Figure 2 shows examples of some popular personal mobile devices. The device you choose depends on several factors. Some of the decisions you must make before you purchase a device are listed on pages 296 and 297.

PDA running Palm OS		PDAs that run the Palm OS are popular due to the tens of thousands of programs that have been written for them. The devices also run longer on a battery recharge than most other devices and are among the smallest PDAs. The device shown includes Wi-Fi and Bluetooth wireless technology and is capable of playing music and short video clips.
PDA running Windows Mobile for Pocket PC		Smart phones that run a Windows-based mobile operating system give users the same look and feel of the Windows operating system that they use on their desktop or notebook computers. The devices often run mobile versions of some Microsoft Office programs. The user interacts with the device using a stylus to touch the screen. This device includes both Wi-Fi and Bluetooth wireless technology.
smart phone running Palm OS		A smart phone that runs the Palm OS includes all the advantages of the Palm OS along with the capability to make and receive phone calls. The smart phone shown includes a QWERTY keyboard, high-speed Internet access, a camera, and Bluetooth wireless technology.
smart phone running Symbian operating system		This Nokia smart phone does not include a keyboard. Instead, the user interacts with the phone using a stylus and controls on either side of the device. This smart phone includes a camera to take pictures and video, a radio receiver, and high-speed wireless Internet connectivity. The large screen allows the user to view word processing documents and spreadsheets.
smart phone running Windows Mobile Pocket PC Phone Edition		Smart phones that run a Windows-based mobile operating system give users the same look and feel of the Windows operating system that they use on their desktop or notebook computers. This device includes a slide-out keyboard on which the user types. The device also includes high-speed Internet access.
BlackBerry		BlackBerry devices from Research in Motion (RIM) are popular with business people who are on the move. The devices handle corporate e-mail and messaging especially well, but also include the capability to make and receive phone calls.
portable media player		The iPod is the most popular portable media player. With an iPod, you listen to music, watch videos, view photos, and play games. Most portable media players synchronize media with the user's desktop or notebook computer. Some devices also can serve as secondary storage for the user's computer. Portable media players typically include only a few controls that are simple and intuitive to use.
ultra personal computer running Windows Vista		Ultra personal computers are popular with physicians, realtors, and other professionals who need a great deal of computing power wherever they go. An ultra personal computer serves as a mobile device, but is powerful enough to double as a desktop computer.
handheld navigation device		Handheld navigation devices include a GPS receiver, which receives signals from GPS satellites to determine a location and/or speed. The devices typically include programs and maps to guide you from location to location. Some devices, such as the one shown, show you a 3-D representation of any area so that you easily can navigate to your destination.
handheld game console		Handheld game consoles allow you to take your favorite games on the road. This device includes two screens — one of which is touch-sensitive, wireless Internet access, virtual surround sound, and a microphone. The wireless connectivity also can be used to play games against your friends.

FIGURE 2 Personal mobile devices are available in many shapes and sizes and run a variety of operating systems.

ACCESSORIES FOR PERSONAL MOBILE DEVICE SOFTWARE

Most personal mobile devices have the capability to take advantage of add-on accessories. For example, using an external keyboard with a device greatly enhances the ability to enter data or notes quickly. Figure 3 lists the more common accessories available for a personal mobile device.

ACCESSORIES FOR PERSONAL MOBILE DEVICES

Accessory	Description
Keyboard	External keyboards provide much faster input when taking notes as opposed to using a small, built-in keyboard on a device or relying on handwriting recognition. Keyboards may be wireless or attached to the device using a special cable.
Memory card	Memory cards provide additional storage space for a device. Some memory cards may include hardware enhancements such as wireless capability, a camera, or Bluetooth capability. Some cards contain preinstalled software or a vast amount of data, such as a dictionary.
Car kit	Car kits allow you to integrate a device with your car by providing mounting and/or hands-free operation of a device.
Camera	Add-on cameras provide picture and video taking capability to devices with no such built-in functionality.
Case	Most mobile devices can be placed in a case or holster for protection while the device is not in use. Some devices include built-in flip screens to protect the device. You may want a case that fits comfortably in your pocket, or one that includes a belt clip. A good case protects the device when it is dropped from a height of 3 or 4 feet.
Headset/earphones/ microphone	Headsets allow you to wear a combined earpiece and microphone while keeping the device in your hand, pocket, or next to you. Some headsets use Bluetooth to communicate wirelessly with the device. Earphones are used when you want to listen to sound on your device, such as when listening to music or an e-book, or when watching a video. Some portable media players allow you to add a microphone with which you record voice memos or other audio.
GPS receiver	A GPS receiver contains an antenna, radio receiver, and processor and receives signals from GPS satellites to determine a location and/or speed. GPS receivers turn a personal mobile device into a complete GPS unit. The receivers typically include software that you must install on the device.
Media transmission	Some portable media players allow you to add accessories to broadcast or transmit media to other devices, such as a television or radio. For example, you can add an FM transmitter which broadcasts audio output from the player to a nearby FM radio.

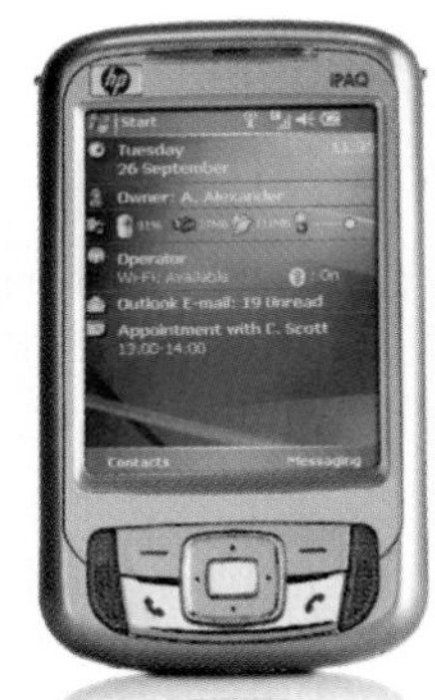

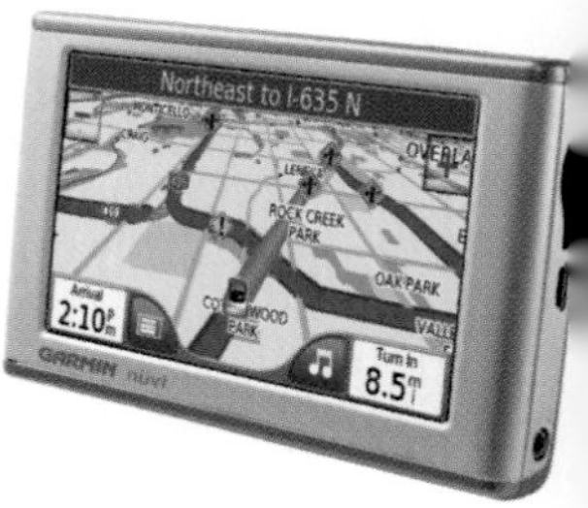

FIGURE 3 Some accessories for personal mobile devices are common to most devices, while others are specialized.

BUILT-IN PERSONAL MOBILE DEVICE SOFTWARE

Most personal mobile devices include several programs that provide basic functionality, such as an **address book** and **date book**. Figure 4 lists the types of software that usually are preinstalled on a personal mobile device.

BUILT-IN PERSONAL MOBILE DEVICE SOFTWARE

Application	Description
Address book and contacts	Maintains a list of acquaintances, including names, addresses, telephone numbers, e-mail addresses, and notes.
To-do list	Maintains a list of tasks. Tasks can be categorized and assigned a priority.
Calculator	Offers functionality of standard desktop calculators.
Datebook and calendar	Maintains appointments and important dates, such as birthdays and holidays. You also set audio or visual alarms to trigger when an appointment time arrives.
Media player	Allows you to play audio and video or display photos. A media player on a phone may pause a song automatically when a phone call is received. Some devices may allow you to watch streaming video in real-time over a wireless Internet connection.
Memos and notepad	Keeps track of notes.
Launcher	The interface that allows you to execute, or launch, programs.
Dialer	Smart phones typically include dialer software that assists you in using the telephone capabilities of a device. Some dialer software is integrated into the operating system so that you use dialing capabilities in other programs. For example, you can select a telephone number in the word processing program and request that the number be dialed.

FIGURE 4 Personal mobile devices typically contain this preinstalled software.

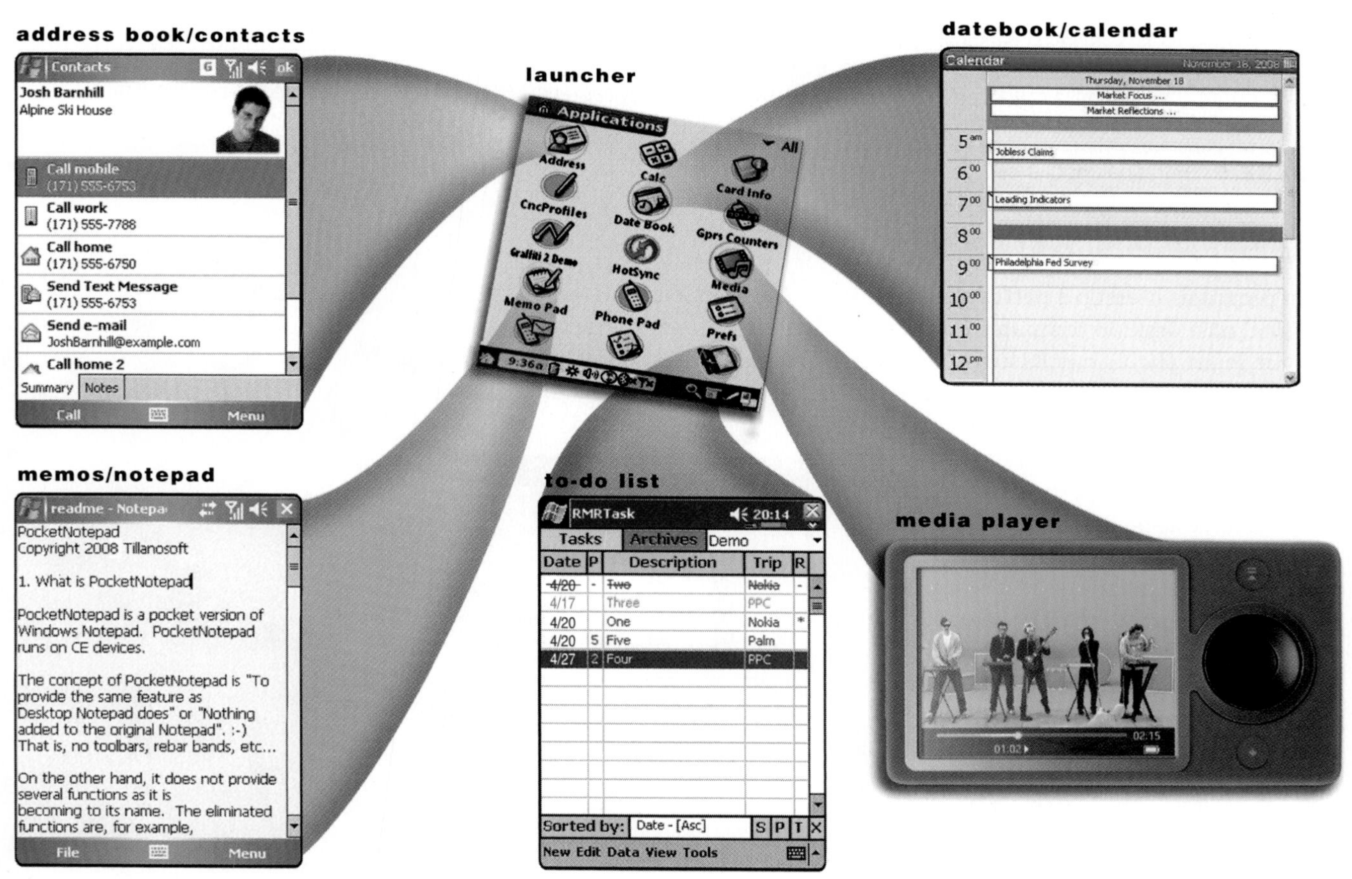

SYNCHRONIZATION SOFTWARE

Most personal mobile devices allow you to share data and information between a personal computer and your device. The software that enables the sharing is called **synchronization software**. A personal mobile device may synchronize, or sync (pronounced sink), with a personal computer or a server on a network. Corporations often standardize their synchronization software so that employees share data across the corporate network, and so the data is backed up properly on a server. Figure 5 lists popular synchronization software for personal mobile devices.

SYNCHRONIZATION SOFTWARE FOR PERSONAL MOBILE DEVICES

Application	Description	Samples
Built-in	Most devices include software that the user loads on a personal computer that allows the computer to communicate with the device and share data and information.	• The Palm OS includes HotSync software • Pocket PC PDAs include ActiveSync software • Blackberry devices use the Blackberry Desktop Software
iSync	Apple's iSync software allows a user to keep a calendar and contact information synchronized up to the minute between a smart phone, an Apple iPod, a Palm OS device, or multiple Macs.	• Apple iSync
Portable media player	Most portable media players sync with a personal computer through a media player on a personal computer. Some portable media players also will synchronize to a personal computer's calendar or contact list.	• Apple iTunes • Microsoft Media Player
Synching many sources	Some device users have data and information stored in many places. For example, users may want to have their address books on the Web, on their personal computers, on their cellular phones, and on their PDAs. Special synchronization software allows users to keep all of the address books up-to-date.	• Intellisync Handheld Edition • PocketMirror • Susteen DataPilot
SyncML	**SyncML** is a standard that is being adopted by many companies that create personal mobile devices. SyncML allows for common information stored on a device to be shared among many devices, such as cellular telephones, other personal mobile devices, and personal computers.	• IBM WebSphere Everyplace Access • Intellisync Handheld Edition • fusionOne MightyPhone • Symbian based devices use SyncML

FIGURE 5 Personal mobile devices use synchronization software to share data and information with a personal computer or server.

BUSINESS SOFTWARE

Most programs used on a personal mobile device have some counterpart program on a desktop computer. For example, both a personal computer and a PDA or smart phone may include a word processing program. Many business programs have counterparts on personal mobile devices. The personal mobile device versions of these programs generally have fewer features and options. For example, a word processing program on a PDA may not have a spelling checker, and a spreadsheet program may not include all of the built-in calculations of its desktop computer counterpart. A smart phone with a phone form factor may allow you only to view documents, rather than edit documents. Figure 6 lists business software for personal mobile devices. The software for an ultra personal computer usually is the same software that is used on a desktop computer and is, therefore, not listed in the figure.

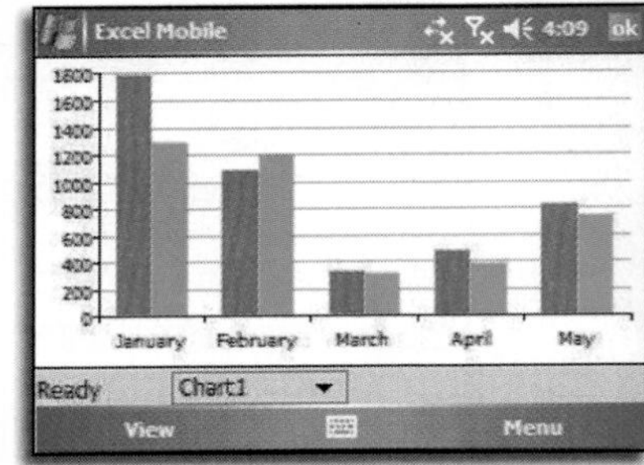

BUSINESS SOFTWARE FOR PERSONAL MOBILE DEVICES

Application	Description	Samples
Word processing	Allows for simple creation, editing, and viewing of documents.	• Documents To Go • WordSmith • Pocket Word
Spreadsheet	Allows you to create, edit, and view worksheets.	• Pocket Excel • TinySheet • MiniCalc • SmartSheet
Readers	Allows read-only (view only) access to word processing documents, spreadsheets, or databases that you download to a personal mobile device from a personal computer. Readers are useful for taking large documents on the road to read them without the ability to modify them. Some readers allow you to view all of these types of documents, while others are targeted to specific desktop program counterparts, such as presentation viewers or word processing document viewers.	• Pocket SlideShow • TealDoc • iSilo • Microsoft Reader for Pocket PC • Mobipocket Reader
Database and list management	Allows creation, editing, and viewing of databases or lists. List management is a popular use of personal mobile devices. Some examples of lists that are handy to store on a device include shopping lists, to-do lists, exercise logs, and automobile maintenance logs.	• HanDBase • thinkDB • SmartList To Go • JFile • ListPro • Mobile Data Viewer
Financial	Financial software includes programs to manage a bank account, track expenses during a trip, manage a budget, or track an investment portfolio. Many personal computer financial programs include personal mobile device companion software that keeps the information on a device synchronized with the financial information on a personal computer or the Web.	• Microsoft Money for Windows Mobile-based Pocket PC • Pocket Quicken • BankBook • Ultrasoft Money • Handy Expense

FIGURE 6 Business software provides scaled-down versions of common desktop programs.

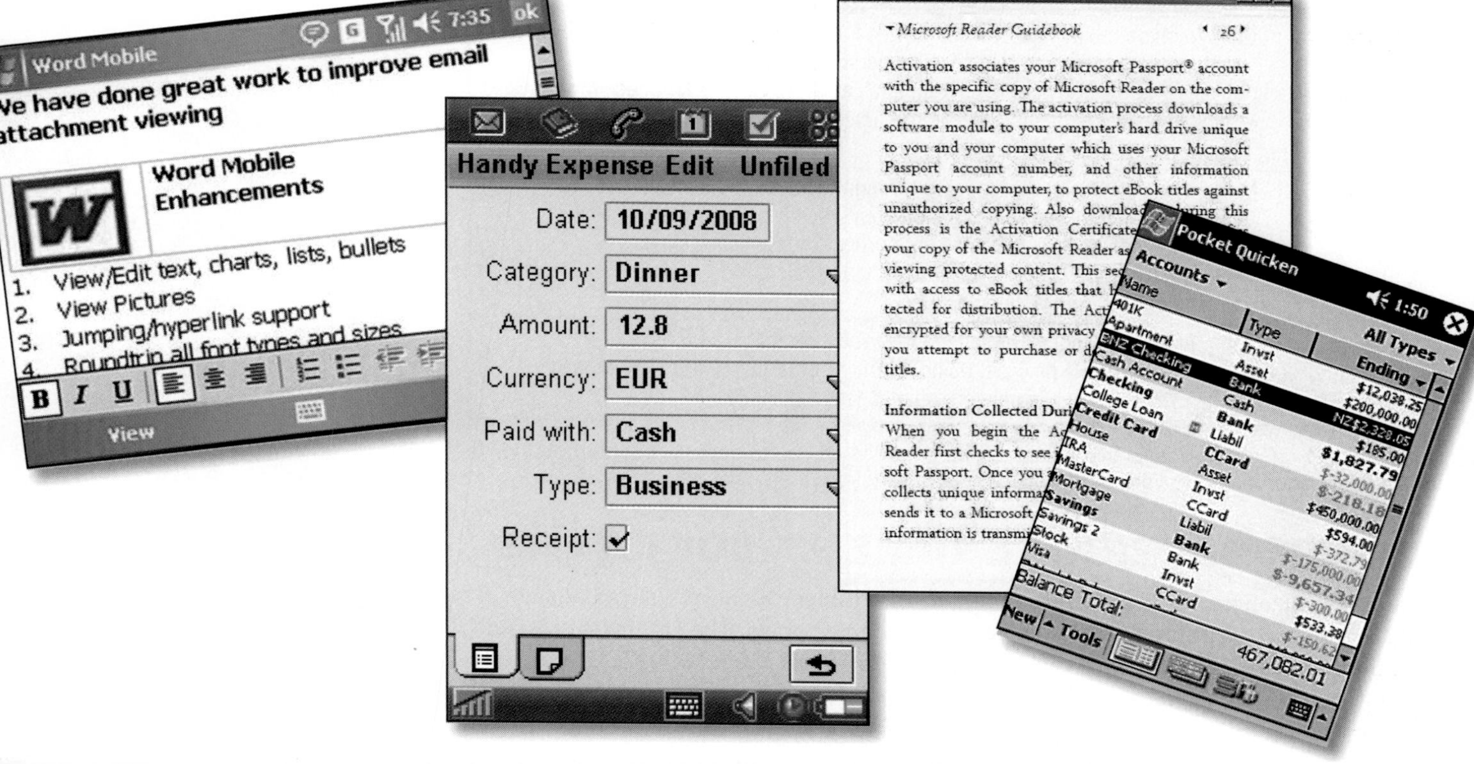

SOFTWARE AND SERVICES FOR WIRELESS DEVICES

Most of the software used to interact with the Internet using a personal computer has a counterpart on wireless mobile devices. Some devices come equipped with e-mail software or a Web browser. Often, special servers allow the device to communicate securely with corporate databases or Web sites. Many Web sites include enhanced services for mobile devices, such as the ability to make payment or purchases through the use of text messaging. For personal mobile devices that do not include wireless Internet connectivity, a special modem connects the device to the Internet. Often, a device without built-in wireless capability can be connected to a mobile phone that can connect the device to the Internet. Web content and e-mail also synchronize to the device from a personal computer, and the information may be browsed offline while using the device. Figure 7 provides a list of popular communications software for personal mobile devices.

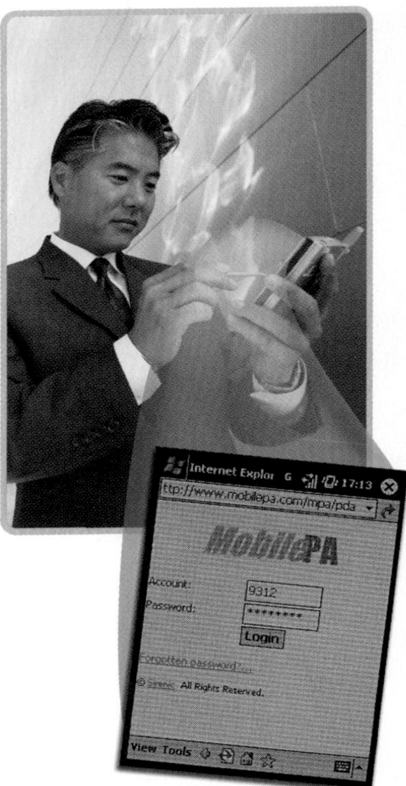

COMMUNICATIONS SOFTWARE FOR PERSONAL MOBILE DEVICES

Application	Description	Samples
E-mail	Used for composing and reading e-mail. Many personal mobile devices include a preinstalled e-mail program.	• Pocket Outlook • riteMail • Mail+ • SnapperMail
Web browsers	Allows Web browsing. Some browsers use an **intermediate server** to make the pages smaller by removing images or making images smaller. Others attempt to display the full Web page on the personal mobile device. Many personal mobile devices include a preinstalled Web browser.	• Pocket Internet Explorer • ThunderHawk • AvantGo • Opera browser
Instant messaging	Instant messaging programs usually allow you to use the same instant messaging ID as that used on a personal computer.	• Windows Live Messenger • AIM for Palm OS • Agile Messenger
Clipping	**Web clippings** are programs that gather and display only the critical elements, or clips, of a Web page.	• Travelocity.com • The Weather Channel • Moviefone.com
Media sharing software	Used to share media, such as audio, video, and photos with other computers, Web sites, or personal mobile devices. Some software is built-in, such as software that allows users to share music or games with other users with a similar device.	• YouTube Mobile Upload • MySpace Mobile
Blogging	Many smart phones allow blogging through the use of text messaging. A **moblog** is a blog created with a personal mobile device. Some blogs provide software for personal mobile devices that allow you to blog and upload photos, podcasts, and video.	• Nokia Lifeblog • Blogger Mobile
Internet telephony	Some Internet telephony providers offer software that works with mobile devices. Using Internet telephony rather than the mobile network often is less expensive.	• Skype • Vonage Mobile

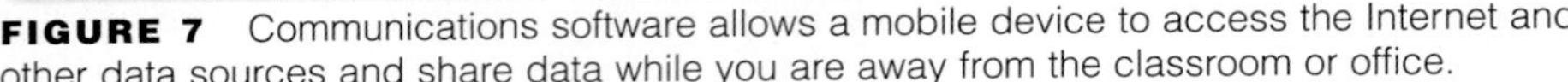

FIGURE 7 Communications software allows a mobile device to access the Internet and other data sources and share data while you are away from the classroom or office.

CORPORATE/GOVERNMENT SOFTWARE

Large organizations, such as corporations and government agencies, take advantage of some personal mobile devices' capability of keeping current information in the hands of their personnel. The organization's central employee telephone book is kept up-to-date and synchronized to each employee's device on a regular basis. Executives synchronize key corporate information. Traveling sales personnel and field technicians synchronize appointments, e-mail, notes about contact with customers, product lists, corporate podcasts, and sales information. Corporate/government software for personal mobile devices is listed in Figure 8.

CORPORATE/GOVERNMENT SOFTWARE FOR PERSONAL MOBILE DEVICES

Application	Description	Samples
Executive	Executives keep up-to-date corporate information on their personal mobile devices. Executives may keep current sales information, financial information, and inventory information available to make informed decisions.	• mySAP.com • Siebel 7 Mobile Solutions
Sales	Sales people working away from the office are perhaps the largest group of personal mobile device users. The devices are useful for keeping product information handy, keeping scheduled appointments, and maintaining customer information.	• Siebel 7 Mobile Sales • Salesforce.com • ActionNames
Field technicians and mobile workers	Field technicians visit customer locations to troubleshoot problems. Personal mobile devices help technicians keep track of customer information, maintain up-to-date information on replacement parts, and log troubleshooting information.	• UPS and FedEx use specialized devices and software for their drivers to track package pickups and drop-offs.
Military and law enforcement	The military and law enforcement agencies deploy personal mobile devices to manage the special needs of the military and law enforcement.	• Most software of this nature is custom made for the needs of particular agencies. Such programs help track cases or serve as legal references.
Connecting and synchronizing with corporate data sources	Several solutions exist for synchronizing corporate data with personal mobile devices. Special software keeps track of user permissions and makes certain that the right people get the data they require on a day-to-day basis.	• Intellisync Gold • MessageWireless
Large organization management issues	In organizations with thousands of personal mobile device users, the support of those devices becomes tedious, especially when users install unsupported software on the devices that may interfere with the corporate software and data for which the device was intended. Server software may detect these conflicts when the user synchronizes with the corporate server and deletes or reports the offending software.	• Much of the software of this nature is custom built for each enterprise, as needs and infrastructure of each organization are different.

FIGURE 8 Large organizations utilize special software to keep their employees synchronized.

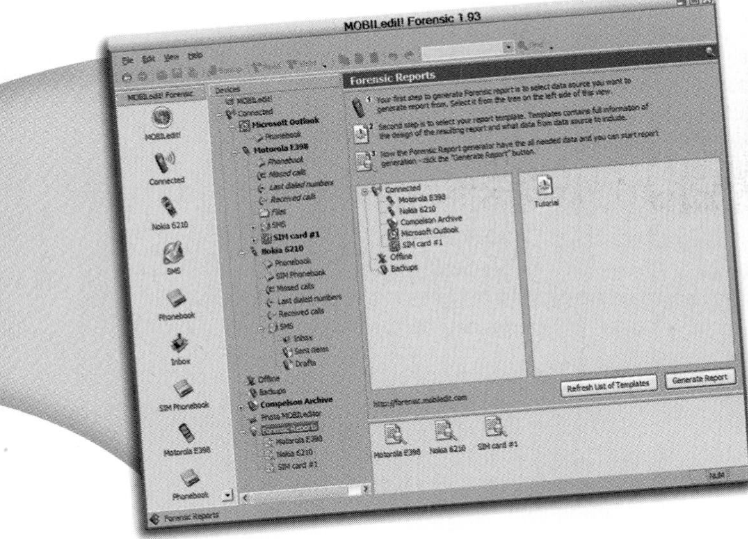

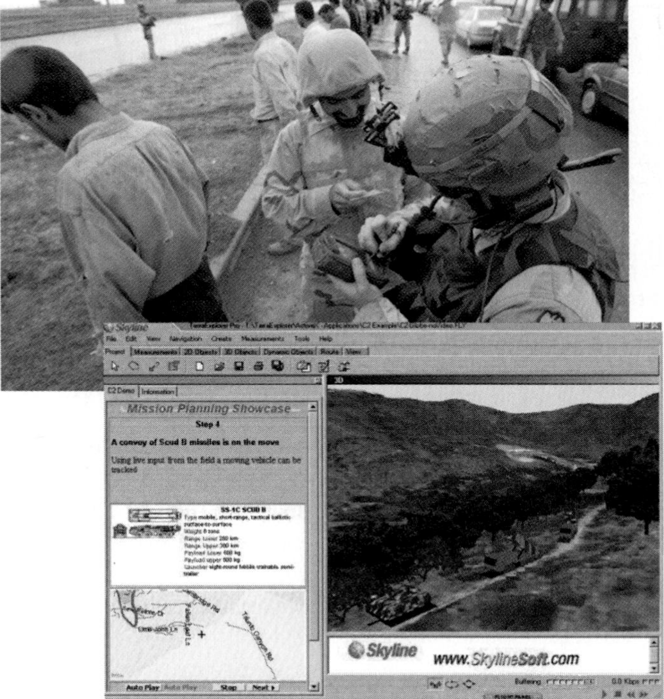

MEDICAL SOFTWARE

One of the largest communities to adopt personal mobile device software in significant numbers is the medical community. Physicians and other medical workers routinely use specialized software to track patient charts, check information on drugs, and browse electronic versions of large reference books. The end result is a savings in time and money, and an increase in the level of care for the patient. Physicians have become one of the main groups of professionals to use ultra personal computers because of the devices' power and portability. Figure 9 lists some popular medical software for personal mobile devices.

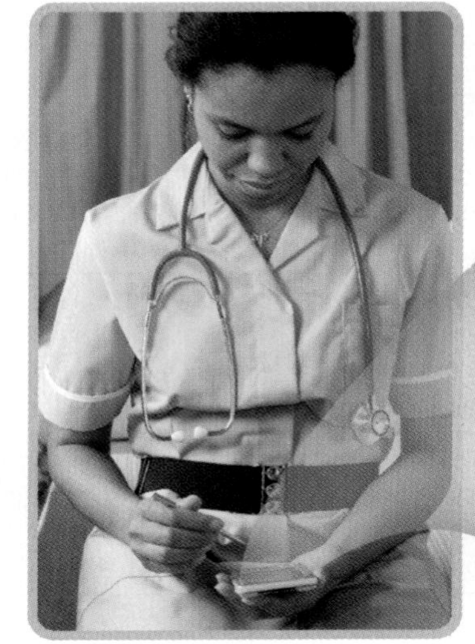

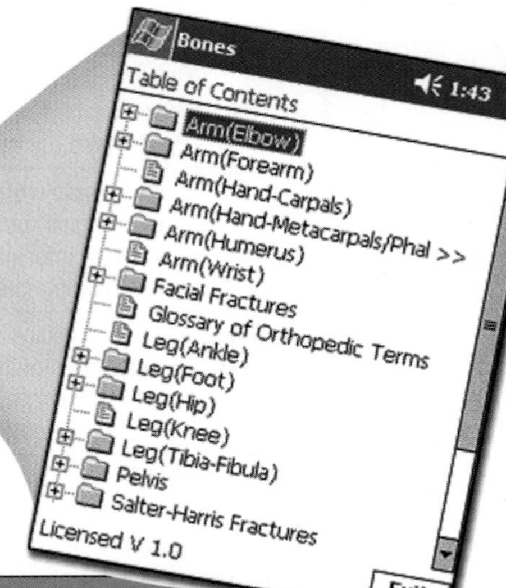

MEDICAL SOFTWARE FOR PERSONAL MOBILE DEVICES

Application	Description	Samples
Patient and case management	Patient and case management programs allow medical workers to enter data as they interact with the patient. This eliminates transcription errors or the need for the worker to find a computer to do his or her work.	• MedLogs • PatientKeeper Personal • Handy Patients • MD Coder PocketPC Edition
Drug information and drug interactions	Allows for fast access to critical drug information, such as dosages and drug interactions.	• Epocrates Rx • eDrugsDatabase • Dr. Drugs
Reference books	Medical workers often rely on a large collection of references to do their jobs. Electronic versions of many popular references, such as the *Physicians' Desk Reference*, are available in electronic format and are kept up-to-date easily through regular downloads.	• PDRDrugs • eDrugs Database • DiagnosisPro for Pocket PC • MedRules
Prescriptions	With electronic prescribing, physicians write prescriptions electronically. Physicians print legible prescriptions and hand the prescriptions to the patient. If the personal mobile device is connected to the Internet or hospital network, the physician checks the patient's medication or medical history.	• iScribe • PocketRx • Medicalis
Medical calculations	Medical workers often make quick calculations for medication dosages or patient status. Programs assist many of these calculations and target the worker's specialty.	• MedMath • MedCalc • Medical MathPad

FIGURE 9 The medical community quickly has become one of the larger users of specialized PDA software.

SCIENTIFIC SOFTWARE

The mobility of personal mobile devices makes them valuable tools for scientific use. Researchers use these devices to gather and record data in the field and later download the data to a personal computer or server. Scientists also use specialized software targeted to their specific field, such as astronomy or meteorology, as a replacement for bulky reference manuals or observation notes (Figure 10).

SCIENTIFIC SOFTWARE FOR PERSONAL MOBILE DEVICES

Application	Description	Samples
Data gathering	Scientists can enter observations quickly into a personal mobile device. These programs often are used in the field for gathering research statistics.	• iCollect
Calculations and conversions	Users can perform specialized calculations or data conversions. Many fields of science, such as astronomy, require special calculations that are useful to have available on a personal mobile device.	• ME Tools • CoolCalc for the Pocket PC • Convert It! • APCalc Converter
Reference	Scientists can look up information quickly, rather than using cumbersome manuals or textbooks.	• ChemRef Basic • Packed Periodic Table • Gene • ABC's of Science
Astronomy	Observers can follow the stars. With the large number of amateur astronomers in the world, programs specific to astronomy are some of the more popular scientific titles.	• Pocket Universe • Planetarium • Astronomist • Pocket Stars
Weather	Meteorologists' specific needs are addressed because these programs allow quick calculations or data gathering in a changing environment. Some programs are linked to add-on hardware that measure temperature, humidity, and other meteorological data.	• Weather Manager • WorldMate • Weather Calculator for Palm OS • Weather.com

FIGURE 10 Scientific programs help scientists manage complex information.

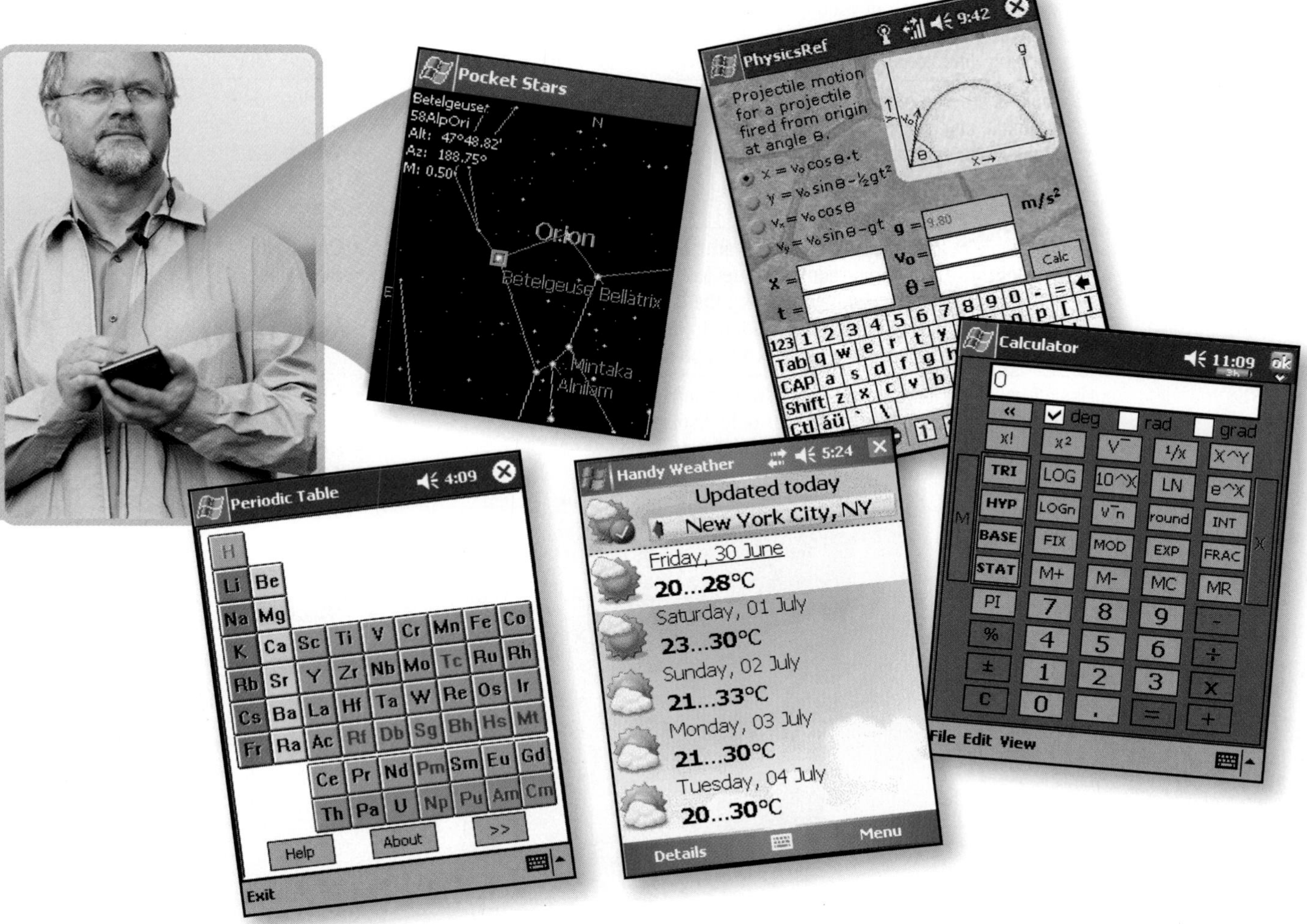

TRAVEL SOFTWARE AND SERVICES

The portable nature of personal mobile devices makes them ideal for the business or leisure traveler. Even a night on the town can be enhanced by a list of popular attractions. The user keeps his or her itinerary handy along with maps and directions while traveling to new places. A GPS-enabled mobile device tracks a user's route and keeps the user on course. Wireless connectivity allows the user to book flights and hotels from the back of a taxi cab. Figure 11 lists travel software for personal mobile devices.

TRAVEL SOFTWARE AND SERVICES FOR PERSONAL MOBILE DEVICES

Application	Description	Samples
Itinerary consolidation	Manages travel itineraries, including flights, hotels, and car rentals. The software may keep track of travel preferences and make suggestions about travel and accommodations when planning a new trip.	• Traveler (Pocket PC edition) • Time Traveler • WorldMate
Mapping	Mapping software may download maps from the Web or a personal computer. Or, the software may include maps. The software may suggest travel routes or driving directions from point to point, or simply serve as a reference.	• Yahoo! Mobile Driving Directions • Pocket Streets • Google Maps for Mobile
City guides	City guides are one of the more popular personal mobile device programs. You install city guides for specific cities or an entire country. Guides include restaurant listings and ratings, hotels, directions, popular attractions, and local customs.	• Intelliguide Professional • Vindigo for Palm OS or Pocket PC • WorldMate • Frommer's Port@ble Guide • iFodor's
Hotel and flight	You can view current hotel and flight information while planning a trip. Some of these programs require the device to connect to the Internet. Others occasionally allow downloading the information to a device from a personal computer. Some programs link to booking systems on the Internet, so you make reservations directly from a personal mobile device.	• OAG Club • SkyGuide
GPS	Usually requires additional GPS hardware connected to the device. Some software includes mapping data or only displays and saves GPS information, such as location and speed.	• GPS Port@ble Navigator — Travelers Edition • GPS Wireless Navigation System • GPS Atlas

FIGURE 11 Travel software and services act as a personal concierge for the business or leisure traveler.

EDUCATIONAL SOFTWARE

With so much to organize, students and instructors greatly benefit from mobile software geared for educational uses (Figure 12). Students load textbook chapters or entire textbooks onto media cards and use special software to read the books and highlight key material. Instructors distribute electronic versions of the class syllabus, automatically updating each student's calendar on the students' devices. Some schools even acquire PDAs for the entire student body and require their use in the classroom.

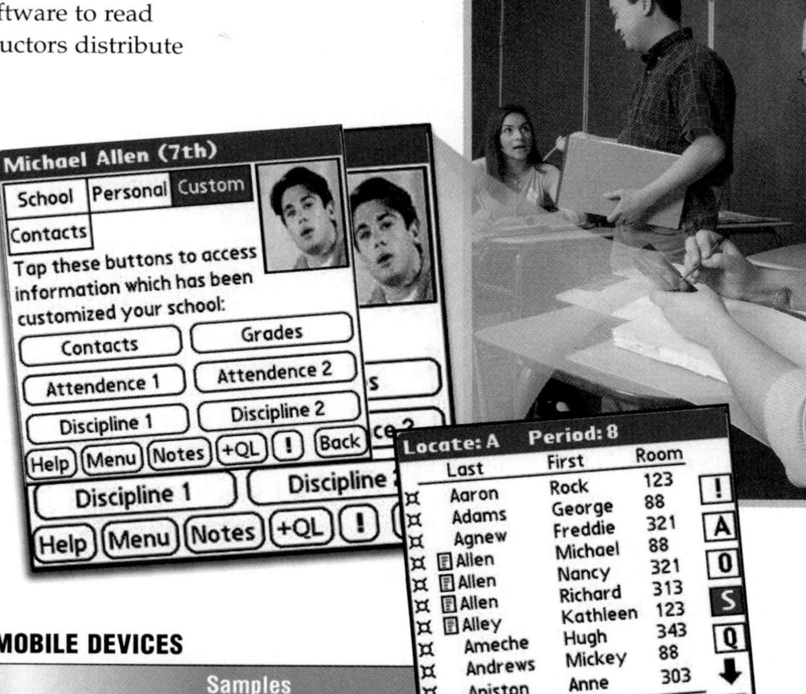

EDUCATIONAL SOFTWARE FOR PERSONAL MOBILE DEVICES

Application	Description	Samples
E-books and references	E-books are electronic versions of books. E-books are specially formatted files that may be viewed using Reader software, as noted in Figure 6 on page 287. Many e-books are available at no cost, and many authors and publishing companies make e-books available to those who have purchased a hard copy of a particular book.	• TomeRaider • PocketLingo Pro • Formulas for Palm OS • Speed Reader Plus • The collected works of William Shakespeare for Microsoft Reader • eWord for Blackberry • Mobipocket Reader Pro for Symbian OS
Class schedules and course management	Helps instructors and students manage their respective schedules. The information may include syllabus details distributed in electronic format by an instructor. The software also may link to a central data repository of a school. The software helps track grading, assignments, to-do lists, instructor office hours, and notes.	• 4.0Student by Handmark course management • Pocket ClassPro for Pocket PC • MyClasses • Hi-CE handheld software • MxWeb eTeacher
Roster	Manages grading, rosters, attendance, and contact information for students.	• Teachers PET • Teach File
Review	Includes programs for quizzing students and reviewing coursework. Students often train the application to help them review troublesome material.	• Herbert's Math Time • Mental Arithmetic • Quizzler

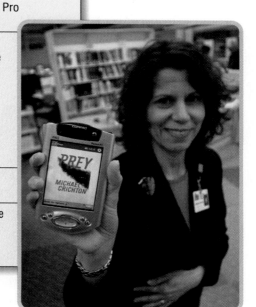

FIGURE 12 Educational software benefits both students and instructors.

MULTIMEDIA SOFTWARE

Most personal mobile devices include the capability of viewing images and video and listening to audio. Devices often contain, or allow you to attach, a camera or recording device to capture video or audio and then download the captured images and sounds to a personal computer or send them directly to an e-mail address, blog, or Web site. Some image viewers allow you to use a personal mobile device as an electronic picture frame while the device rests in its cradle on your desk. Many devices include built-in media players, and some devices allow you to install additional multimedia software. Popular multimedia software for personal mobile devices is listed in Figure 13.

MULTIMEDIA SOFTWARE FOR PERSONAL MOBILE DEVICES

Application	Description	Samples
Picture viewer	Allows you to view images uploaded to a personal mobile device using software on a personal computer or camera. Some viewers have a slide show mode that rotates through a list of images automatically.	• SplashPhoto • PocketPhoto • Palbum Picture Viewer • Resco Photo Viewer for Smartphone • Pictures
Media player	Allows you to watch video clips and listen to audio, such as music or podcasts, on a personal mobile device. Some devices are equipped with additional hardware, such as microphones, headphones, or media controls to enhance the multimedia experience.	• Windows Media Player Mobile • PocketTV for Pocket PC • ActiveSky Media Player

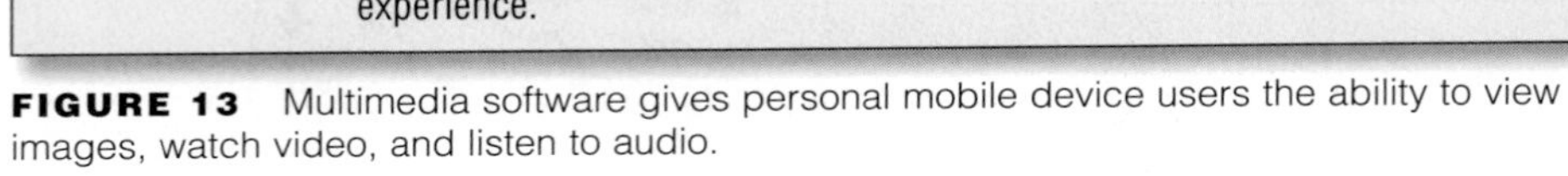

FIGURE 13 Multimedia software gives personal mobile device users the ability to view images, watch video, and listen to audio.

ENTERTAINMENT SOFTWARE

While on the train ride to work or waiting at the airport, a personal mobile device user can enjoy his or her favorite games. The infrared port or wireless connectivity of a device allows a user to play some games against other players. Most devices include buttons to control games. Figure 14 lists popular entertainment software for personal mobile devices.

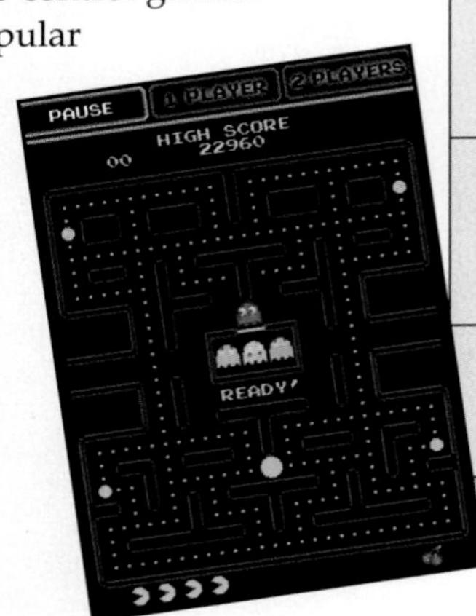

ENTERTAINMENT SOFTWARE FOR PERSONAL MOBILE DEVICES

Application	Description	Samples
Strategy	Includes classic board games such as chess, backgammon, and Monopoly.	• PocketChess • ChessGenius • Handmark Monopoly • SimCity
Card	Includes casino games, solitaire games, and other card games.	• AcidSolitaire • BlackJack++ • Pocket Cribbage
Action	Games that require quick reflexes, including many arcade-style games.	• Tomb Raider • Breakfast • Vexed for Symbian
Puzzle	Thought-provoking puzzles to pass time and sharpen the mind, such as crossword puzzles, mazes, and word games.	• Handmark SCRABBLE • Crossword • Advanced Brain Trainer
Sports	Games that mimic real-life sports.	• Pocket Mini Golf • Smart Tennis • Bowling Master

FIGURE 14 Entertainment software allows you to relax with a personal mobile device and enjoy your favorite games.

OBTAINING AND INSTALLING PERSONAL MOBILE DEVICE SOFTWARE

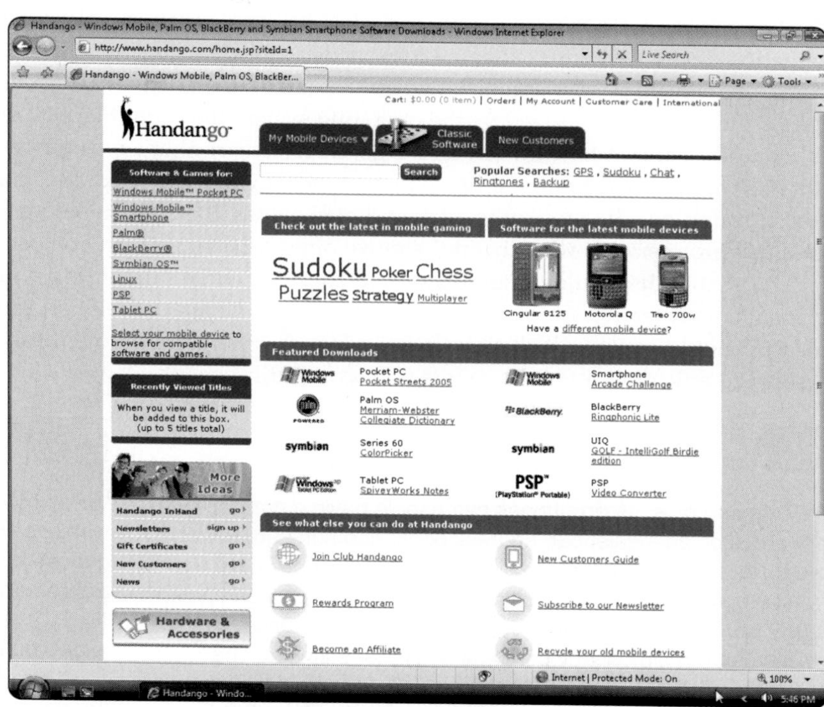

Software often is available at computer or electronics stores. Ultra personal computers can run any software made for personal computers. A significant number of programs are available as shareware, freeware, or trial editions at various Web sites. Most of the software listed in the previous figures is accessible on the Web sites listed in Figure 15. Because software for personal mobile devices usually is smaller than the personal computer counterparts, downloading the software from the Web to your personal computer and then uploading it to your device often is the best alternative when you want to try something new. Software downloaded from the Web to a personal computer requires that the software be installed using the device's synchronization software. Additionally, some personal computer application software includes accompanying mobile device software that corresponds with the personal computer software. Wireless-enabled devices may allow you to download new software over the wireless connection.

Software for personal mobile devices sold in a retail location often is supplied on a CD-ROM. The CD-ROM first installs the software on a personal computer. The device's synchronization software then is used to load the software onto the device while the device is connected to the personal computer. Depending on the type of software installed, this process may be automatic. Some software is packaged as an add-on card that you insert into the device's expansion slot. Some Web sites allow you to browse a software catalog from a wireless device's Web browser and download the software directly to the device. When synchronizing a personal mobile device on a corporate network, some companies automatically install software on the employees' devices with no interaction required from the employee.

WHERE TO OBTAIN PERSONAL MOBILE DEVICE SOFTWARE

Application	Description	Samples
Web sites	Software publishers make their products available at their Web sites. Several Web sites also exist specifically to distribute mobile device software. Tens of thousands of titles are available, and most can be downloaded on a trial basis.	palmgear.com handandgo.com pdamd.com tucows.com itunes.com
Retail	Many popular software titles can be purchased at electronics and computer stores. The most popular titles at these locations include productivity and entertainment software.	bestbuy.com compusa.com
Develop in-house	Many corporations develop their own personal mobile device software to use internally to meet specific needs. These programs usually tap into existing corporate databases of product and customer information. The companies that produce mobile device operating systems often make the development tools for such software available at no cost or a minimal cost.	palmsource.com/developers microsoft.com/windowsmobile/developers blackberry.net/developers symbian.com/developer

For an updated list of where to obtain PDA software, visit scsite.com/dc2008/ch5/pda.

FIGURE 15 Personal mobile device software is available from a number of sources.

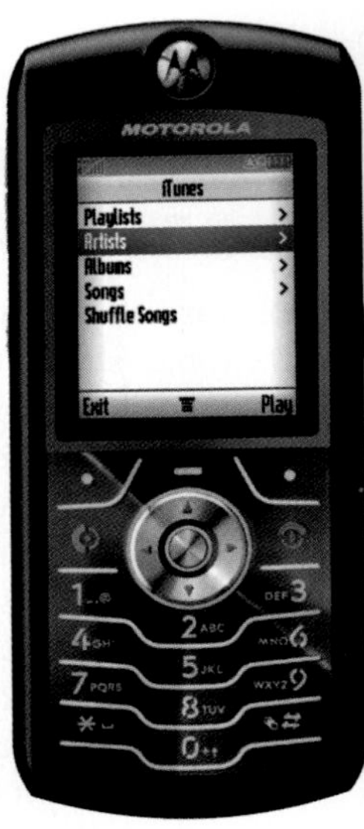

HOW TO PURCHASE A PERSONAL MOBILE DEVICE

Whether you choose a PDA, smart phone, ultra personal computer, or portable media player, handheld navigation device, or handheld game console depends on where, when, and how you will use the device. If you need to stay organized when you are on the go, then a PDA may be the right choice. PDAs typically are categorized by the operating system they run (Figure 2 on page 283). If you need to stay organized and in touch when on the go, then a smart phone or ultra personal computer may be the right choice. Choose a handheld navigation device if you often need directions or information about your surroundings. If you plan to relax and play games, then a handheld game console may be right for you. Busy professionals who are on the move often carry more than one personal mobile device.

This section lists guidelines you should consider when purchasing a PDA, smart phone, ultra personal computer, portable media player, handheld navigation device, or handheld game console. You also should visit the Web sites listed in Figure 16 to gather more information about the type of personal mobile device that best suits your computing needs.

1 DETERMINE THE PROGRAMS YOU PLAN TO RUN ON YOUR DEVICE.

All PDAs and most smart phones can handle basic organizer-type software such as a calendar, address book, and notepad. Portable media players and handheld navigation devices usually have the fewest programs available to run on them. Ultra personal computers usually have the most number of programs available because the devices can run almost any personal computer software. The availability of other software depends on the operating system you choose. The depth and breadth of software for the Palm OS is significant, with more than 20,000 basic programs and more than 600 wireless programs. Devices that run Windows-based operating systems, such as Windows Mobile may have fewer programs available, but the operating system and application software are similar to those with which you are familiar, such as Word and Excel. When choosing a handheld game console, consider whether your favorite games are available for the device. Consider if you want extras on the device, such as the capability of playing media files.

2 CONSIDER HOW MUCH YOU WANT TO PAY.

The price of a personal mobile device can range from $100 to more than $2,000, depending on its capabilities. Some Palm OS devices are at the lower end of the cost spectrum, and ultra personal computers often are at the higher end. A PDA will be less expensive than a smart phone with a similar configuration. For the latest prices, capabilities, and accessories, visit the Web sites listed in Figure 16.

3 DETERMINE WHETHER YOU NEED WIRELESS ACCESS TO THE INTERNET AND E-MAIL OR MOBILE TELEPHONE CAPABILITIES WITH YOUR DEVICE.

Smart phones often give you access to e-mail and other data and Internet services. Some PDAs, smart phones, ultra personal computers, and handheld game consoles include wireless networking capability to allow you to connect to the Internet wirelessly. These wireless features and services allow users to access real-time information from anywhere to help make decisions while on the go. Most portable media players do not include the capability to access Internet services.

4 FOR WIRELESS DEVICES, DETERMINE HOW AND WHERE YOU WILL USE THE SERVICE.

When purchasing a wireless device, you must subscribe to a wireless service. Determine if the wireless network (carrier) you choose has service in the area where you plan to use the device. Some networks have high-speed data networks only in certain areas, such as large cities or business districts. Also, a few carriers allow you to use your device in other countries.

When purchasing a smart phone, determine if you plan to use the device more as a phone, PDA, or wireless data device. Some smart phones, such as those based on the Pocket PC Phone edition or the Palm OS, are geared more for use as a PDA and have a PDA form factor. Other smart phones, such as those based on Microsoft Smartphone or Symbian operating systems, mainly are phone devices that include robust PDA functionality. Research in Motion Blackberry-based smart phones include robust data features that are oriented to accessing e-mail and wireless data services.

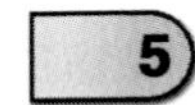

5 MAKE SURE YOUR DEVICE HAS ENOUGH MEMORY AND STORAGE.

Memory (RAM) is not a major issue with low-end devices with monochrome displays and basic organizer functions. Memory is a major issue, however, for high-end devices that have color displays and wireless features. Without enough memory, the performance level of your device will drop dramatically. If you plan to purchase a high-end device running the Palm OS operating system, the device should have at least 32 MB of RAM. If you plan to purchase a high-end device running the Windows Mobile operating system, the PDA should have at least 64 MB of RAM. An ultra personal computer can have 512 MB of RAM or more while a handheld navigation device may have over 2 GB of flash memory.

An ultra personal computer can have 512 MB of RAM or more while a handheld navigation device may have over 2 GB of flash memory.

Many personal mobile devices include a hard disk for storage. Portable media players, ultra personal computers, and some smart phones include hard disks to store media and other data. Consider how much media and other data you need to store on your device. The hard disk size may range from 4 GB to more than 80 GB.

PRACTICE WITH THE TOUCH SCREEN, HANDWRITING RECOGNITION, AND BUILT-IN KEYBOARD BEFORE DECIDING ON A MODEL.

To enter data into a PDA, smart phone, and some ultra personal computers and handheld game consoles, you use a pen-like stylus to handwrite on the screen or a keyboard. The keyboard either slides out or is mounted on the front of the device. With handwriting recognition, the device translates the handwriting into a computerized font. You also can use the stylus as a pointing device to select items on the screen and enter data by tapping on an on-screen keyboard. By practicing data entry before buying a device, you can learn if one device may be easier for you to use than another. You also can buy third-party software to improve a device's handwriting recognition.

DECIDE WHETHER YOU WANT A COLOR DISPLAY.

PDAs, ultra personal computers, some handheld navigation devices, and some handheld game consoles usually come with a color display that supports as many as 65,536 colors. Smart phones also have the option for color displays. Having a color display does result in greater on-screen detail, but it also requires more memory and uses more power. Resolution also influences the quality of the display.

COMPARE BATTERY LIFE.

Any mobile device is good only if it has the power required to run. For example, smart phones with monochrome screens typically have a much longer battery life than Pocket PC devices with color screens. The use of wireless networking will shorten battery time considerably. To help alleviate this problem, most devices have incorporated rechargeable batteries that can be recharged by placing the device in a cradle or connecting it to a charger.

SERIOUSLY CONSIDER THE IMPORTANCE OF ERGONOMICS.

Will you put the device in your pocket, a carrying case, or wear it on your belt? How does it feel in your hand? Will you use it indoors or outdoors? Many screens are unreadable outdoors. Do you need extra ruggedness, such as would be required in construction, in a plant, or in a warehouse? A smart phone with a PDA form factor may be larger than a typical PDA. A smart phone with a phone form factor may be smaller, but have fewer capabilities.

CHECK OUT THE ACCESSORIES.

Determine which accessories you want for your personal mobile device. Accessories include carrying cases, portable mini- and full-sized keyboards, removable storage, modems, synchronization cradles and cables, car chargers, wireless communications, global positioning system modules, digital camera modules, expansion cards, dashboard mounts, replacement styli, headsets, microphones, and more.

DECIDE WHETHER YOU WANT ADDITIONAL FUNCTIONALITY.

In general, off-the-shelf Microsoft operating system-based devices have broader functionality than devices with other operating systems. For example, voice-recording capability, e-book players, and media players are standard on most Windows Mobile devices. If you are leaning towards a Palm OS device and want these additional functions, you may need to purchase additional software or expansion modules to add them later. Determine whether your employer permits devices with cameras on the premises, and if not, do not consider devices with cameras. Some handheld game consoles include the capability to access the Web. High-end handheld navigation devices may include destination information, such as information about restaurants and points of interest, an e-book reader, a media player, and currency converter.

DETERMINE WHETHER SYNCHRONIZATION OF DATA WITH OTHER DEVICES OR PERSONAL COMPUTERS IS IMPORTANT.

Most devices include a cradle that connects to the USB or serial port on your computer so you can synchronize data on your device with your desktop or notebook computer. Increasingly more devices are Bluetooth and/or wireless networking enabled, which gives them the capability of synchronizing wirelessly. Many devices today also have an infrared port that allows you to synchronize data with any device that has a similar infrared port, including desktop and notebook computers or other personal mobile devices.

Web Site	Web Address
CNET Shopper	shopper.cnet.com
iPod	ipod.com
Palm	palm.com
Microsoft	windowsmobile.com pocketpc.com microsoft.com/smartphone
Oqo	oqo.com
MobileTechReview	pdabuyersguide.com
Nintendo	nintendo.com/channel/ds
Research in Motion	rim.com
Garmin	garmin.com
Symbian	symbian.com
Wireless Developer Network	wirelessdevnet.com
Sharp	www.myzaurus.com

For an updated list of reviews and information about personal mobile devices and their Web addresses, visit scsite.com/dc2008/ch5/pda.

FIGURE 16 Web site reviews and information about personal mobile devices.

CHAPTER SIX

Output

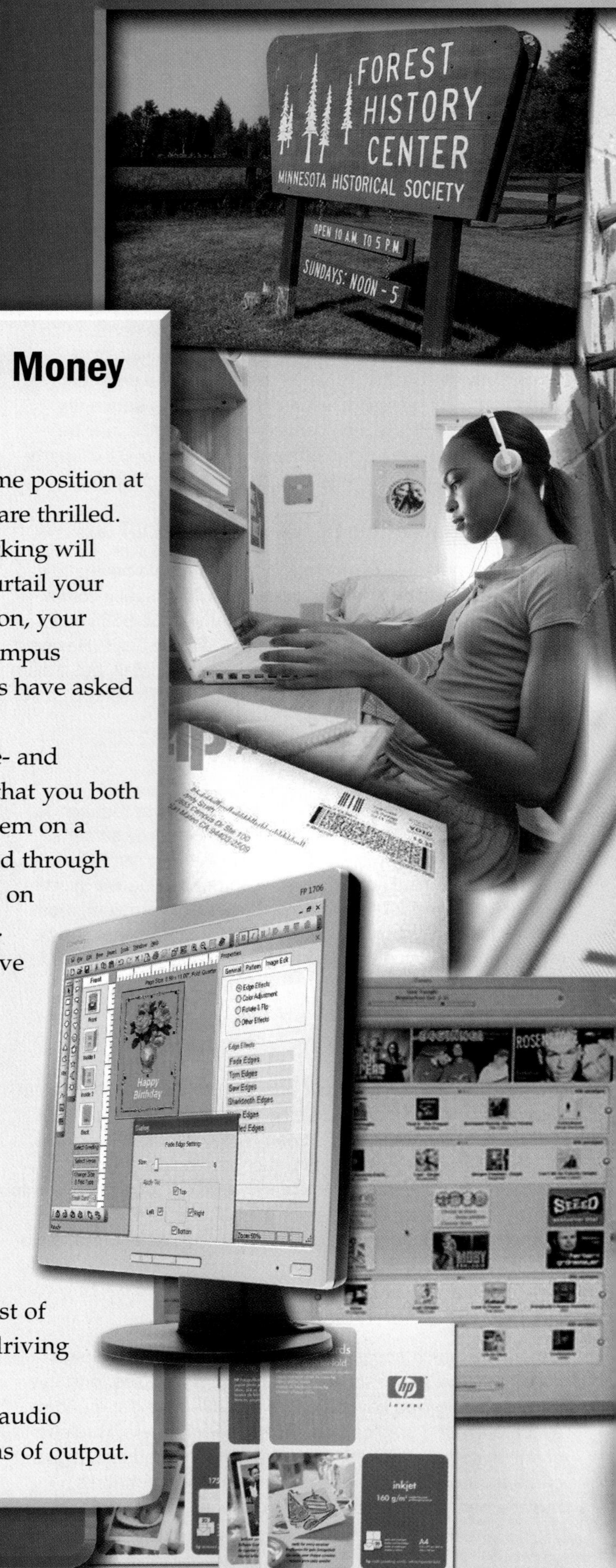

Picture Yourself Saving Time and Money Using a Computer

At last, you have landed your dream job — a part-time position at the county historical society. As a history major, you are thrilled. As a full-time student, however, you realize that working will limit your free time. You fear that you will have to curtail your volunteer work with the local youth group. In addition, your sister now is a freshman and has moved into your campus apartment. With two children in college, your parents have asked you to economize.

Your sister, a computer major, has some great time- and money-saving ideas. She sets up online banking so that you both can pay bills and balance accounts while viewing them on a computer monitor. For items that still must be mailed through the postal service, you will print the postage stamps on your printer, along with envelopes or mailing labels. Besides saving an enormous amount of time, you save money by not driving to the bank or post office.

With your sister's guidance, you use software to create and print flyers and announcements for the youth group. The time savings enable you to continue volunteering. For special occasions, your sister and you will use greeting card software to design cards on the computer screen, personalizing them with digital pictures, and then print them in color on card paper. You both plan to download music to your portable media players to save the cost of purchasing an entire CD, as well as the time spent driving to the store.

Read Chapter 6 to learn about monitors, printers, audio output, and paper, and to discover many other forms of output.

OBJECTIVES

After completing this chapter, you will be able to:

1. Describe the four categories of output
2. Summarize the characteristics of LCD monitors, LCD screens, and plasma monitors
3. Describe the characteristics of a CRT monitor and factors that affect its quality
4. Explain the relationship between graphics chips and monitors
5. Describe various ways to print
6. Differentiate between a nonimpact printer and an impact printer
7. Summarize the characteristics of ink-jet printers, photo printers, laser printers, thermal printers, mobile printers, label and postage printers, and plotters and large-format printers
8. Describe the uses of speakers, headphones, and earphones
9. Identify the output characteristics of fax machines and fax modems, multifunction peripherals, data projectors, joysticks, wheels, and gamepads
10. Identify output options for physically challenged users

CONTENTS

WHAT IS OUTPUT?

Output is data that has been processed into a useful form. That is, computers process data (input) into information (output). A computer generates several types of output, depending on the hardware and software being used and the requirements of the user.

Users view or watch output on a screen, print it, or hear it through speakers, headphones, or earphones. Monitors, notebook computers, Tablet PCs, portable media players, PDAs, and smart phones have screens that allow users to view documents, Web sites, e-mail messages, pictures, videos, movies, and other types of output. Some printers produce black-and-white documents, and others produce brilliant colors, enabling users to print color documents, photographs, and transparencies. Through the computer's speakers, headphones, or earphones, users listen to sounds, music, and voice messages.

While working with a computer, a user encounters four basic categories of output: text, graphics, audio, and video (Figure 6-1). Very often, a single form of output, such as a Web page, includes more than one of these categories.

- Text — Examples of text-based output are memos, letters, press releases, reports, advertisements, newsletters, envelopes, mailing labels, and e-mail messages. On the Web, users view and print many other types of text-based output. These include blogs, newspapers, magazines, books, play or television show transcripts, stock quotes, famous speeches, and historical lectures.
- Graphics — Output often includes graphics to enhance its visual appeal and convey information. Business letters have logos. Reports include charts. Newsletters use drawings, clip art, and photographs. Users print high-quality photographs taken with a digital camera. Many Web sites use animated

FIGURE 6-1 Four categories of output are text, graphics, audio, and video.

graphics, such as blinking icons, scrolling messages, or simulations.

- Audio — Users insert their favorite music CD in a CD or DVD drive and listen to the music while working on the computer. Software such as games, encyclopedias, and simulations often have musical accompaniments for entertainment and audio clips, such as narrations and speeches, to enhance understanding. On the Web, users tune into radio and television stations and listen to audio clips, podcasts, or live broadcasts of interviews, talk shows, sporting events, news, music, and concerts. They also use the Internet to conduct real-time conversations with friends, coworkers, or family members, just as if they were speaking on the telephone.
- Video — As with audio, software and Web sites often include video clips to enhance understanding. Vodcasts and video blogs, for example, add a video component to the traditional podcast and blog. Users watch a live or prerecorded news report, view a replay while attending a live sporting event, observe weather conditions, or enjoy a live performance of their favorite musician or musical group on the computer. Instead of renting a movie, users can download movie content from a Web site for a fee and then watch the entire movie on a computer or mobile device. Attaching a video camera to the computer allows users to watch home movies on the computer. They also can attach a television's antenna or cable to the computer and watch a television program on the computer screen.

An **output device** is any type of hardware component that conveys information to one or more people. Commonly used output devices include display devices; printers; speakers, headphones, and earphones; fax machines and fax modems; multifunction peripherals; data projectors; and force-feedback joysticks, wheels, and gamepads. This chapter discusses each of these output devices.

DISPLAY DEVICES

A **display device**, or simply *display*, is an output device that visually conveys text, graphics, and video information. Information on a display device, sometimes called *soft copy*, exists electronically and appears for a temporary period.

Display devices consist of a screen and the components that produce the information on the screen. Desktop computers typically use a monitor as their display device. A **monitor** is a display device that is packaged as a separate peripheral. Most monitors have a tilt-and-swivel base that allows users to adjust the angle of the screen to minimize neck strain and reduce glare from overhead lighting. Monitor controls permit users to adjust the brightness, contrast, positioning, height, and width of images. Some have integrated speakers.

Most mobile computers and devices integrate the display and other components into the same physical case. For example, the display on a notebook computer attaches with hinges. Notebook computers also are available that have two displays: one that attaches with a hinge and one built into the top of the case. Some smart phone displays also attach with a hinge to the device. On other smart phones and most PDAs, portable media players, and ultra personal computers, the display is built into the case.

Most display devices show text, graphics, and video information in color. Some, however, are monochrome. *Monochrome* means the information appears in one color (such as white, amber, green, black, blue, or gray) on a different color background (such as black or grayish-white). Some mobile devices use monochrome displays because they require less battery power.

Two types of display devices are flat-panel displays and CRT monitors. The following sections discuss each of these display devices.

FAQ 6-1

What can I do to ease eyestrain while using my computer?

Position the computer screen about 20 degrees below eye level. Clean the screen regularly. Blink your eyes every five seconds. Adjust the room lighting. Face into an open space beyond the computer screen. Use larger fonts or zoom a display. Take an eye break every 30 minutes: look into the distance and focus on an object for 20 to 30 seconds, roll your eyes in a complete circle, and then close your eyes for at least 30 seconds. If you wear glasses, ask your doctor about computer glasses. For more information, visit scsite.com/dc2008/ch6/faq and then click Eye Strain.

FLAT-PANEL DISPLAYS

A *flat-panel display* is a lightweight display device with a shallow depth and flat screen that typically uses LCD (liquid crystal display) or gas plasma technology. Types of flat-panel displays include LCD monitors, LCD screens, and plasma monitors.

LCD Monitors and Screens

An **LCD monitor**, also called a *flat panel monitor*, is a desktop monitor that uses a liquid crystal display to produce images (Figure 6-2). These monitors produce sharp, flicker-free images.

LCD monitors have a small *footprint*; that is, they do not take up much desk space. For additional space savings, some LCD monitors are wall mountable. LCD monitors are available in a variety of sizes, with the more common being 15, 17, 18, 19, 20, 21, 22, and 23 inches — some are 30 or 40 inches. You measure a monitor the same way you measure a television, that is, diagonally from one corner to the other.

Determining what size monitor to purchase depends on your intended use. A large monitor allows you to view more information on the screen at once, but usually is more expensive. You may want to invest in a 21-inch monitor if you use multiple programs at one time or do a lot of research on the Web. Users working with intense graphics applications, such as desktop publishing and engineering, typically have larger monitors.

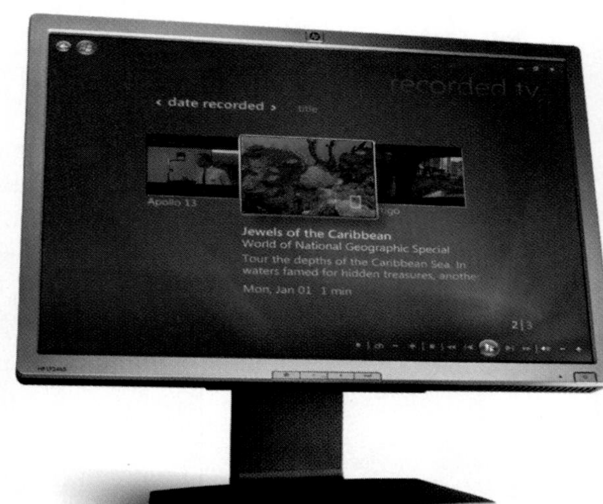

FIGURE 6-2 An LCD monitor is thin and lightweight.

For an even wider screen area, some users position two or more monitors side by side or stacked (Figure 6-3). For example, one monitor can show the left side of a document, game, graphic design, or other item, with the other monitor showing the right side. This arrangement also is convenient if you want to run multiple programs simultaneously. Users of side-by-side or stacked monitors include music editors, video editors, network administrators, gamers, researchers, Web developers, graphic designers, and engineers.

Mobile computers, such as notebook computers and Tablet PCs, and mobile devices, such as ultra personal computers, portable media players, smart phones, and PDAs often have built-in LCD screens (Figure 6-4). Notebook computer screens are available in a variety of sizes, with the more common being 14.1, 15.4, 17, and 20.1 inches. Tablet PC screens range from 8.4 inches to 14.1 inches. Typical screen sizes of ultra personal computers are 5 inches to 7 inches. Portable media players usually have screen sizes from 1.5 inches to 3 inches. PDA screens average 3.5 inches. On smart phones, screen sizes range from 2.5 to 3.5 inches.

FIGURE 6-3 Users sometimes have multiple monitors stacked or side by side to increase their viewing area.

FAQ 6-2

Can I watch a movie on a PDA, smart phone, portable media player, or handheld game console screen?

Yes, some mobile devices have built-in capabilities to play movies. Other mobile devices may require special software to be installed to play movies. A computer program usually is necessary to convert a movie from its original form to a format that can play on a mobile device. For more information, visit scsite.com/dc2008/ch6/faq and then click Mobile Device Movies.

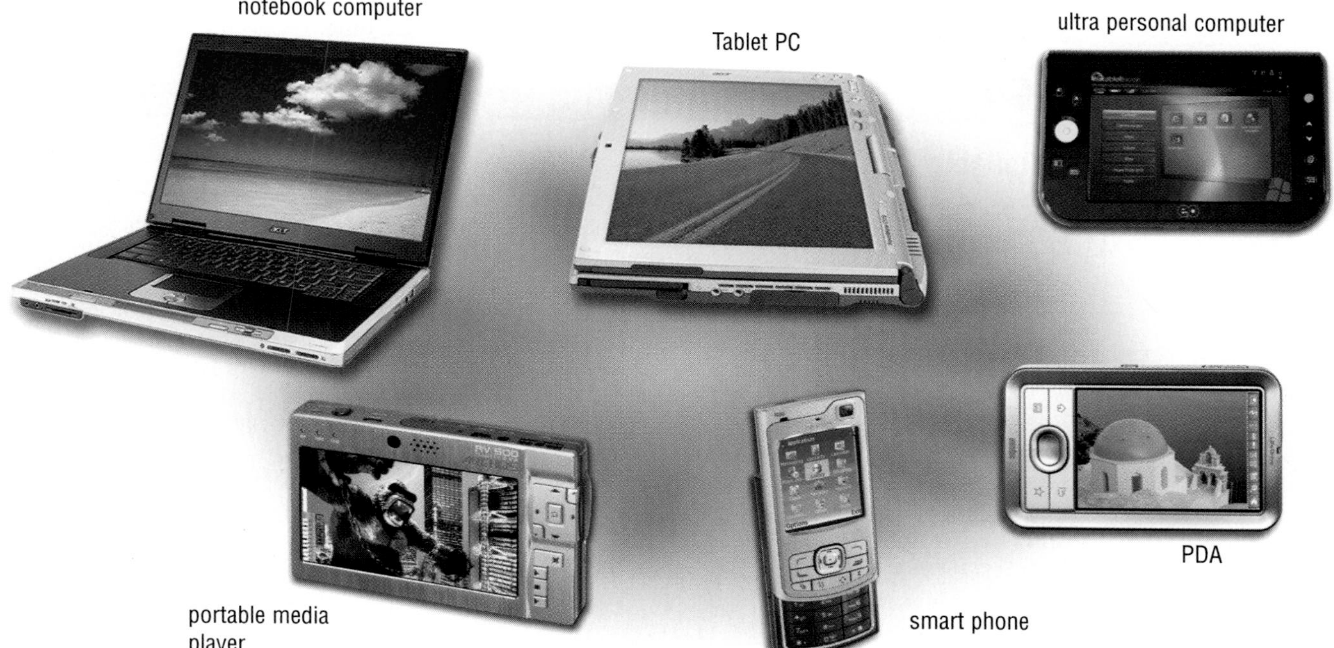

FIGURE 6-4 Many people use their notebook computers, Tablet PCs, ultra personal computers, portable media players, smart phones, and PDAs to view pictures or watch videos and movies.

LCD Technology

A **liquid crystal display** (**LCD**) uses a liquid compound to present information on a display device. Computer LCDs typically contain fluorescent tubes that emit light waves toward the liquid-crystal cells, which are sandwiched between two sheets of material. When an electrical charge passes through the cells, the cells twist. This twisting causes some light waves to be blocked and allows others to pass through, creating images on the display.

LCD monitors and LCD screens produce color using either passive-matrix or active-matrix technology. An *active-matrix display*, also known as a *TFT (thin-film transistor) display*, uses a separate transistor to apply charges to each liquid crystal cell and thus displays high-quality color that is viewable from all angles. A newer type of TFT technology, called *organic LED (OLED)*, uses organic molecules that produce an even brighter, easier-to-read display than standard TFT displays. OLEDs are less expensive to produce, consume less power, and can be fabricated on flexible surfaces. Read Looking Ahead 6-1 for a look at the next generation of OLEDs.

WEB LINK 6-1

LCD Technology

For more information, visit scsite.com/dc2008/ch6/weblink and then click LCD Technology.

A *passive-matrix display* uses fewer transistors, requires less power, and is less expensive than an active-matrix display. The color on a passive-matrix display often is not as bright as an active-matrix display. Users view images on a passive-matrix display best when working directly in front of it.

LCD Quality

The quality of an LCD monitor or LCD screen depends primarily on its resolution, response time, brightness, dot pitch, and contrast ratio.

- **Resolution** is the number of horizontal and vertical pixels in a display device. For example, a monitor that has a 1600 × 1200 resolution displays up to 1600 pixels per horizontal row and 1200 pixels per vertical row, for a total of 1,920,000 pixels to create a screen image. Recall that a *pixel* (short for picture element) is a single point in an electronic image. A higher resolution uses a greater number of pixels and thus provides a smoother, sharper, and clearer image. As you increase the resolution, however, some items on the screen appear smaller (Figure 6-5).

  With LCD monitors and screens, resolution generally is proportional to the size of the device. For example, a 17-inch LCD monitor typically has a resolution of 1280 × 1024, while a 20-inch LCD monitor has a resolution of 1600 × 1200. LCDs are geared for a specific resolution, called the *native resolution*. Check the monitor's documentation for its native resolution, and for optimal results, be sure the computer uses the native resolution setting.
- *Response time* of an LCD monitor or screen is the time in milliseconds (ms) that it takes to turn a pixel on or off. LCD monitors' and screens' response times range from 5 to 16 ms. The lower the number, the faster the response time.

LOOKING AHEAD 6-1

Rollable Displays Lock and Roll

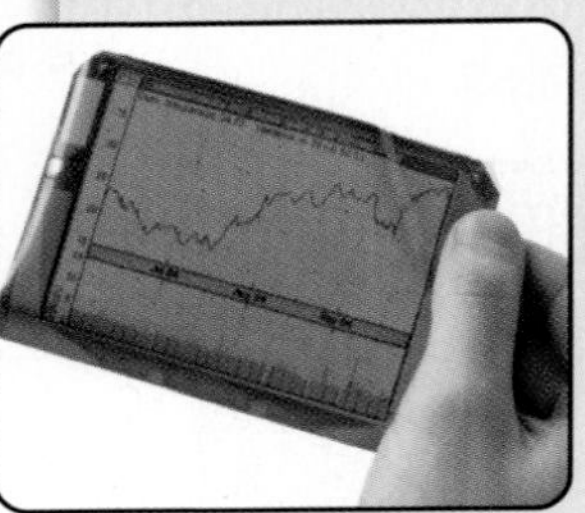

Your newspaper arrives each morning at your front door rolled up and secured with a rubber band or in a plastic bag. Your computer monitor soon may arrive rolled up so you can transport it easily in your book bag or luggage.

Lightweight, flexible screens can be stored in pen-sized cases and then unrolled when needed. They can be connected wirelessly with various electronic devices, such as cellular telephones and CD and DVD players, so gamers could play on a moment's notice and movie buffs could watch the latest releases easily while sitting on airplanes and buses. GPS programs would allow hikers and bikers to view their locations, then slip the rugged screen back inside the case and then into their backpacks or pockets.

Engineers are developing stand-alone products with touch screens and keypads. For more information, visit scsite.com/dc2008/ch6/looking and then click Rollable Displays.

FIGURE 6-5a (screen resolution at 800 × 600)

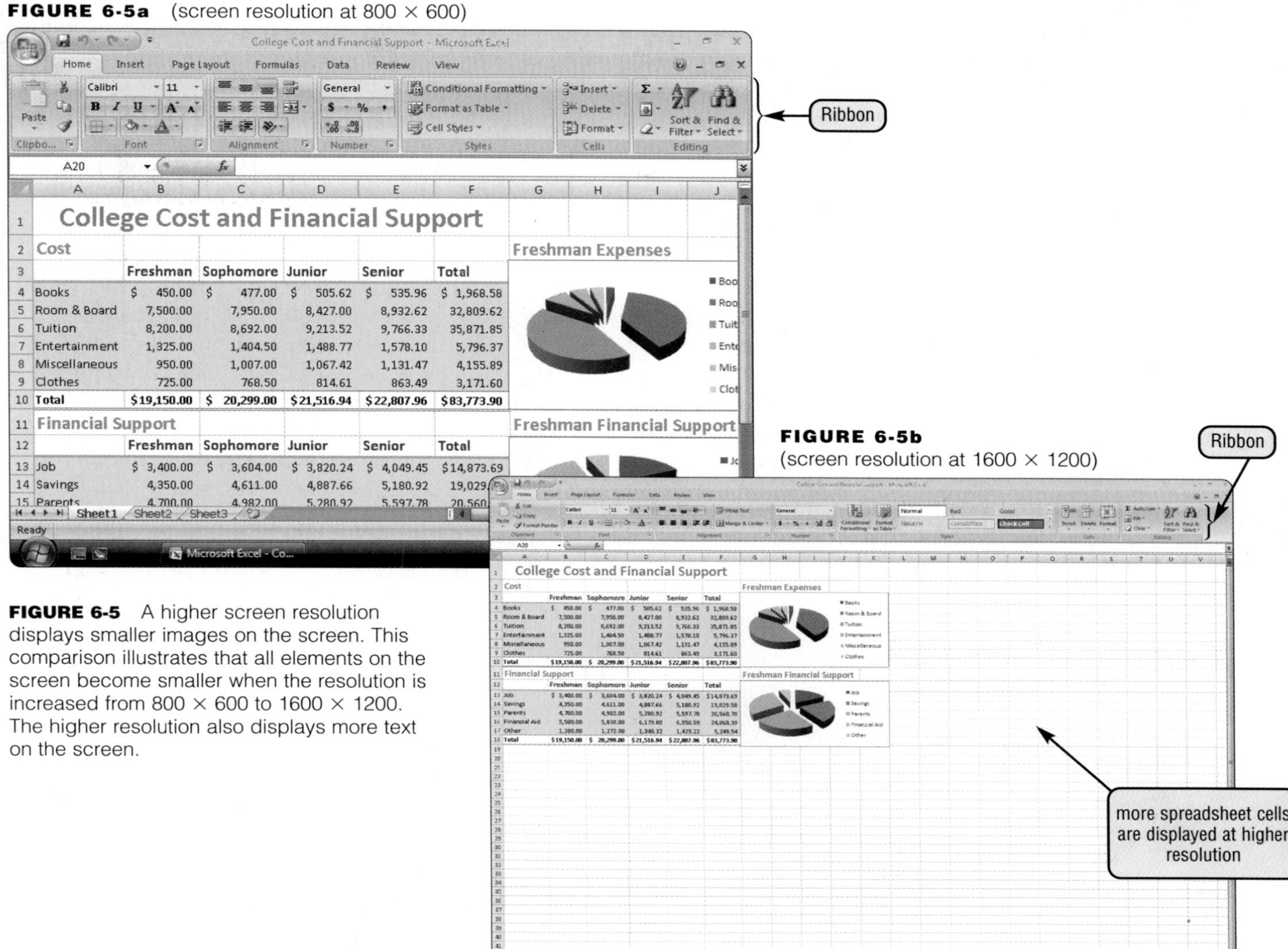

FIGURE 6-5 A higher screen resolution displays smaller images on the screen. This comparison illustrates that all elements on the screen become smaller when the resolution is increased from 800 × 600 to 1600 × 1200. The higher resolution also displays more text on the screen.

- Brightness of an LCD monitor or LCD screen is measured in nits. A *nit* is a unit of visible light intensity equal to one candela (formerly called candlepower) per square meter. The *candela* is the standard unit of luminous intensity. LCD monitors and screens today range from 250 to 550 nits. The higher the nits, the brighter the images.
- *Dot pitch,* sometimes called *pixel pitch,* is the distance in millimeters between pixels on a display device. Text created with a smaller dot pitch is easier to read. Advertisements normally specify a monitor's dot pitch or pixel pitch. Average dot pitch on LCD monitors and screens should be .28 mm or lower. The lower the number, the sharper the image.
- *Contrast ratio* describes the difference in light intensity between the brightest white and darkest black that can be displayed on an LCD monitor. Contrast ratios today range from 400:1 to 800:1. Higher contrast ratios represent colors better.

Graphics Chips, Ports, and LCD Monitors

A cable on a monitor plugs in a port on the system unit, which enables communications from a graphics chip. This chip, called the *graphics processing unit (GPU),* controls the manipulation and display of graphics on a display device. The graphics processing unit either is integrated on the motherboard or resides on a video card (graphics card) in a slot in the motherboard. Video cards usually contain a fan or heat sink to keep this and other chips from overheating.

LCD monitors use a digital signal to produce a picture. To display the highest quality images, an LCD monitor should plug in a *DVI (Digital Video Interface) port*, which enables digital signals to transmit directly to the LCD monitor. Current models of system units either have an integrated DVI chip or contain a video card that has a DVI port. They usually also have a standard monitor port and an *S-video port*, allowing users to connect external devices such as a television, DVD player, or video recorder, to the computer (Figure 6-6).

WEB LINK 6-2

Video Cards

For more information, visit scsite.com/dc2008/ch6/weblink and then click Video Cards.

Over the years, several video standards have been developed to define the resolution, number of colors, and other display properties. The table in Figure 6-7 identifies the more common video standards available today, along with their typical resolution and aspect ratio. The *aspect ratio* defines a display's width relative to its height. A 2:1 aspect ratio, for example, means the display is twice as wide as it is tall. Some display devices support multiple video standards. For a display device to show images as defined by a video standard, both the display device and graphics processing unit must support the same video standard.

The number of colors a graphics processing unit displays is determined by bit depth. The *bit depth*, also called *color depth*, is the number of bits used to store information about each pixel. For example, a video card with a 24-bit depth uses 24 bits to store information about each pixel. Thus, this video card can display 2^{24} or 16.7 million colors. The greater the number of bits, the better the resulting image. Today's video cards typically have a 24-bit depth or a 32-bit depth.

A video card or motherboard, in the case of integrated video, must have enough video memory to generate the resolution and number of colors you want to display. This memory, which often is 256 MB or 512 MB on current video cards, stores information about each pixel.

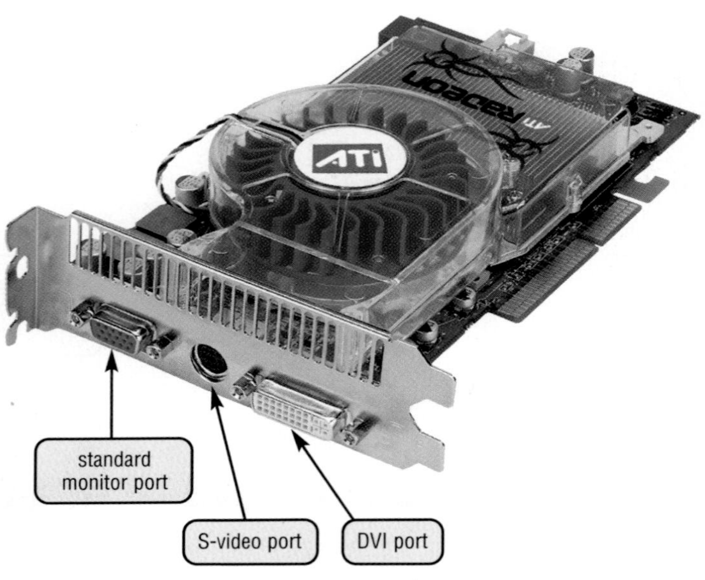

FIGURE 6-6 Ports on current video cards.

FAQ 6-3

How do I change my screen resolution?

You can change your monitor's screen resolution through your operating system's display properties. Before changing your screen resolution, you first should make sure your monitor and video card support your desired resolution. For more information, visit scsite.com/dc2008/ch6/faq and then click Screen Resolution.

Video Standard		Typical Resolution	Aspect Ratio
SVGA	Super Video Graphics Array	800 × 600	4:3
XGA	Extended Graphics Array	1024 × 768	4:3
SXGA	Super XGA	1280 × 1024	5:4
WXGA	Wide XGA	1280 × 1024 or 1366 × 768	16:10 or 16:9
UXGA	Ultra XGA	1600 × 1200	4:3
WSXGA	Wide Super XGA	1680 × 1050	16:10
WUXGA	Wide Ultra XGA	1920 × 1200	16:10
WQXGA	Wide Quad XGA	2560 × 1600	16:10

FIGURE 6-7 Wide video standard formats are preferable for users who watch movies and play video games on the computer.

Plasma Monitors

Large business or power users sometimes have plasma monitors, which often measure more than 60 inches wide (Figure 6-8). A **plasma monitor** is a display device that uses gas plasma technology, which sandwiches a layer of gas between two glass plates. When voltage is applied, the gas releases ultraviolet (UV) light. This UV light causes the pixels on the screen to glow and form an image.

Plasma monitors offer larger screen sizes and richer colors than LCD monitors but are more expensive. Like LCD monitors, plasma monitors can hang directly on a wall.

FIGURE 6-8 Large plasma monitors can measure more than 60 inches wide.

Televisions

Home users sometimes use their television as a display device. Connecting a computer to an analog television requires a converter that translates the digital signal from the computer into an analog signal that the television can display. The best analog televisions have a resolution of only 520 × 400 pixels. Thus, users are turning to *digital television (DTV)* for crisper, higher-quality output on their LCD or plasma televisions.

Digital television signals provide two major advantages over analog signals. First, digital signals produce a higher-quality picture. Second, many programs can be broadcast on a single digital channel, whereas only one program can be broadcast on an analog channel. Today, all broadcast stations must transmit digital signals, as mandated by the FCC.

HDTV (*high-definition television*) is the most advanced form of digital television, working with digital broadcast signals, transmitting digital sound, supporting wide screens, and providing resolutions up to 1920 × 1080 pixels. With HDTV, the broadcast signals are digitized when they are sent via over-the-air (OTA) broadcasts from local television networks, satellite, or cable. To receive the HDTV signals via OTA broadcasts, you need a VHF/UHF antenna; via satellite, you need an HDTV-compatible satellite receiver/tuner; and via cable, you need an HDTV-compatible cable box.

With game consoles, such as Microsoft's Xbox 360, Nintendo's Wii, and Sony's PlayStation 3, the output device often is a television (Figure 6-9). Users plug one end of a cable in the game console and the other end in the video port on the television. Although some game consoles include a small LCD screen (usually 5 inches or smaller), home users often prefer the larger television displays for game playing, watching movies, and browsing the Internet on a television connected to a game console.

FIGURE 6-9 Video game players often use a television as their game console's output device.

FAQ 6-4

What is the largest high-definition display to date?

Dolphin Stadium in Miami, Florida has a 1,750-inch display, measuring about 37 feet wide and 50 feet tall. For more information, visit scsite.com/dc2008/ch6/faq and then click Largest High-Definition Display.

CRT MONITORS

A **CRT monitor** is a desktop monitor that contains a cathode-ray tube (Figure 6-10). A *cathode-ray tube* (*CRT*) is a large, sealed glass tube. The front of the tube is the screen. Tiny dots of phosphor material coat the screen on a CRT. Each dot consists of a red, a green, and a blue phosphor. The three dots combine to make up each pixel. Inside the CRT, an electron beam moves back and forth across the back of the screen. This causes the dots on the front of the screen to glow, which produces an image on the screen.

CRT monitors have a much larger footprint than do LCD monitors; that is, they take up more desk space. CRT monitors for desktop computers are available in various sizes, with the more common being 15, 17, 19, 21, and 22 inches. In addition to monitor size, advertisements also list a CRT monitor's viewable size. The *viewable size* is the diagonal measurement of the actual viewing area provided by the screen in the CRT monitor. A 21-inch monitor, for example, may have a viewable size of 20 inches.

A CRT monitor usually costs less than an LCD monitor, but it also generates more heat and uses more power than an LCD monitor. To help reduce the amount of electricity used by monitors and other computer components, the United States Department of Energy (DOE) and the United States Environmental Protection Agency (EPA) developed the **ENERGY STAR program**. This program encourages manufacturers to create energy-efficient devices that require little power when they are not in use. Monitors and devices that meet ENERGY STAR guidelines display an ENERGY STAR label.

CRT monitors produce a small amount of electromagnetic radiation. *Electromagnetic radiation* (*EMR*) is a magnetic field that travels at the speed of light. Excessive amounts of EMR can pose a health risk. To be safe, all high-quality CRT monitors comply with MPR II standards. *MPR II* is a set of standards that defines acceptable levels of EMR for a monitor. To protect yourself even further, sit at arm's length from the CRT monitor because EMR travels only a short distance.

FAQ 6-5

Are CRT monitor sales decreasing?

Yes. Decreasing flat-panel display prices are enabling consumers to purchase these more attractive alternatives to CRT monitors. In addition, consumers now are able to purchase larger flat-panel displays than they previously were able to afford. For more information, visit scsite.com/dc2008/ch6/faq and then click Monitor Sales.

FIGURE 6-10 The core of a CRT monitor is a cathode-ray tube.

Quality of a CRT Monitor

The quality of a CRT monitor depends largely on its resolution, dot pitch, and refresh rate.

- Most CRT monitors support a variety of screen resolutions. Standard CRT monitors today usually display up to a maximum of 1800 × 1440 pixels, with 1280 × 1024 often the norm. High-end CRT monitors (for the power user) can display 2048 × 1536 pixels or more.
- As with LCD monitors, text created with a smaller dot pitch, or pixel pitch, is easier to read. To minimize eye fatigue, use a CRT monitor with a dot pitch of .27 millimeters or lower.
- Electron beams inside a CRT monitor "draw" an image on the entire screen many times per second so the phosphor dots, and therefore the image, do not fade. The number of times the image is drawn per second is called the *refresh rate*, or *scan rate*. A CRT monitor's refresh rate, which is expressed in hertz (Hz), should be fast enough to maintain a constant, flicker-free image. A slower refresh rate causes the image to fade and then flicker as it is redrawn. This flicker can lead to eye fatigue and cause headaches for some users.

  A high-quality CRT monitor will provide a vertical refresh rate of at least 68 Hz. This means the image on the screen redraws itself vertically 68 times in a second.

Graphics Chips and CRT Monitors

Many CRT monitors use an analog signal to produce an image. As with an LCD monitor, a cable on the CRT monitor plugs in a port on the system unit, which enables communications from a graphics chip. If the graphics chip resides on a video card, for example, the video card converts digital output from the computer into an analog video signal and sends the signal through the cable to the monitor, which displays output on the screen.

As with LCD monitors, the greater the video card's bit depth, the better the resulting image. Both the video card and the monitor must support the video standard to generate the desired resolution and number of colors, and the video card must have enough memory to generate the resolution and number of colors you want to display. Some users place additional video cards in their system unit, allowing multiple monitors to display output from a single computer simultaneously.

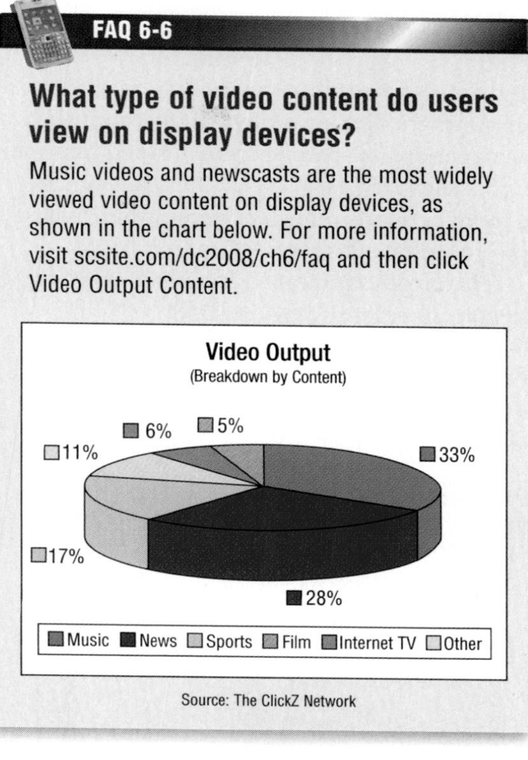

FAQ 6-6

What type of video content do users view on display devices?

Music videos and newscasts are the most widely viewed video content on display devices, as shown in the chart below. For more information, visit scsite.com/dc2008/ch6/faq and then click Video Output Content.

Source: The ClickZ Network

Test your knowledge of pages 300 through 309 in Quiz Yourself 6-1.

QUIZ YOURSELF 6-1

Instructions: Find the true statement below. Then, rewrite the remaining false statements so they are true.

1. A lower resolution uses a greater number of pixels and thus provides a smoother image.
2. An output device is any type of software component that conveys information to one or more people.
3. Documents often include text to enhance their visual appeal and convey information.
4. LCD monitors have a larger footprint than CRT monitors.
5. Types of CRTs include LCD monitors, LCD screens, and plasma monitors.
6. You measure a monitor diagonally from one corner to the other.

Quiz Yourself Online: To further check your knowledge of output, flat-panel displays, and CRT monitors, visit scsite.com/dc2008/ch6/quiz and then click Objectives 1 – 4.

PRINTERS

A **printer** is an output device that produces text and graphics on a physical medium such as paper or transparency film. Printed information, called *hard copy*, exists physically and is a more permanent form of output than that presented on a display device (soft copy).

A hard copy, also called a *printout*, is either in portrait or landscape orientation (Figure 6-11). A printout in *portrait orientation* is taller than it is wide, with information printed across the shorter width of the paper. A printout in *landscape orientation* is wider than it is tall, with information printed across the widest part of the paper. Letters, reports, and books typically use portrait orientation. Spreadsheets, slide shows, and graphics often use landscape orientation.

FIGURE 6-11a (portrait orientation)

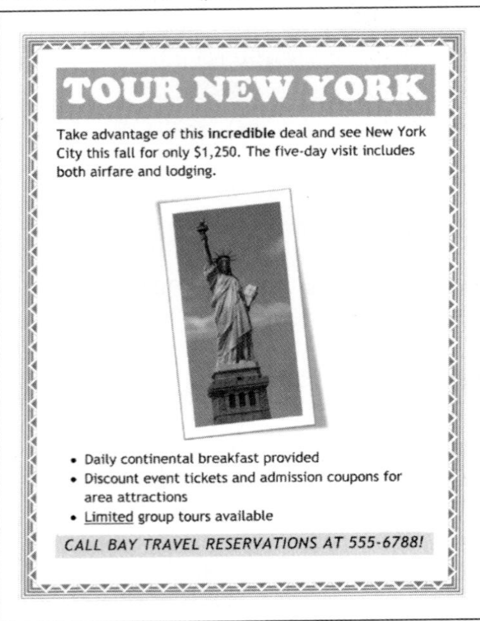

FIGURE 6-11b (landscape orientation)

DRINK PLENTY OF WATER
At least eight 8-ounce servings
Drink throughout the day
Start and end your day with water
Do not wait until you are thirsty
Do not substitute with caffeinated beverages
Cool water is best for keeping hydrated
KEEP YOUR COOL ON HOT DAYS

FIGURE 6-11 Portrait orientation is taller than it is wide. Landscape orientation is wider than it is tall.

Home computer users might print less than a hundred pages a week. Small business computer users might print several hundred pages a day. Users of mainframe computers, such as large utility companies that send printed statements to hundreds of thousands of customers each month, require printers that are capable of printing thousands of pages per hour.

To meet this range of printing needs, many different printers exist with varying speeds, capabilities, and printing methods. Figure 6-12 presents a list of questions to help you decide on the printer best suited to your needs.

The following pages discuss various ways of producing printed output, as well as many different types of printers.

1. What is my budget?
2. How fast must my printer print?
3. Do I need a color printer?
4. What is the cost per page for printing?
5. Do I need multiple copies of documents?
6. Will I print graphics?
7. Do I want to print photographs?
8. Do I want to print directly from a memory card or other type of miniature storage media?
9. What types of paper does the printer use?
10. What sizes of paper does the printer accept?
11. Do I want to print on both sides of the paper?
12. How much paper can the printer tray hold?
13. Will the printer work with my computer and software?
14. How much do supplies such as ink and paper cost?
15. Can the printer print on envelopes and transparencies?
16. How many envelopes can the printer print at a time?
17. How much do I print now, and how much will I be printing in a year or two?
18. Will the printer be connected to a network?
19. Do I want wireless printing capability?

FIGURE 6-12 Questions to ask when purchasing a printer.

Producing Printed Output

Until a few years ago, printing a document required connecting a computer to a printer with a cable via the USB or parallel port on the computer. Although many users today continue to print using this method, a variety of printing options are available, as shown in Figure 6-13.

Today, wireless printing technology makes the task of printing from a notebook computer, Tablet PC, PDA, smart phone, or digital camera much easier. As discussed in Chapter 4, two wireless technologies for printing are Bluetooth and infrared. With *Bluetooth printing*, a computer or other device transmits output to a printer via radio waves. The computer or other device and the printer do not have to be aligned with each other; rather, they need to be within an approximate 30-foot range. With *infrared printing*, a printer communicates with a computer or other device using infrared light waves. To print from a smart phone, for example, a user lines up the IrDA port on the smart phone with the IrDA port on the printer.

Printing Digital Camera Images

For more information, visit scsite.com/dc2008/ch6/weblink and then click Printing Digital Camera Images.

Various Ways Users Print Documents and Pictures

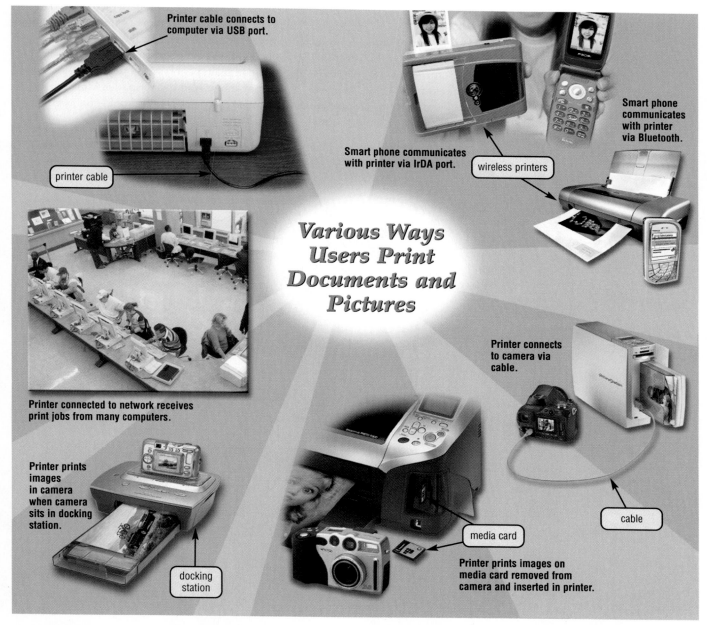

Printer cable connects to computer via USB port.

printer cable

Smart phone communicates with printer via IrDA port.

wireless printers

Smart phone communicates with printer via Bluetooth.

Printer connected to network receives print jobs from many computers.

Printer connects to camera via cable.

cable

Printer prints images in camera when camera sits in docking station.

docking station

media card

Printer prints images on media card removed from camera and inserted in printer.

FIGURE 6-13 Users print documents and pictures using a variety of printing methods.

Users can print images taken with a digital camera without downloading the images to the computer using a variety of techniques. Some cameras connect directly to a printer via a cable. Others store images on media cards that can be removed and inserted in the printer. Some printers have a docking station, into which the user inserts the camera to print pictures stored in the camera.

Finally, many home and business users print to a central printer on a network. Their computer may communicate with the network printer via cables or wirelessly.

Nonimpact Printers

A **nonimpact printer** forms characters and graphics on a piece of paper without actually striking the paper. Some spray ink, while others use heat or pressure to create images.

Commonly used nonimpact printers are ink-jet printers, photo printers, laser printers, thermal printers, mobile printers, label and postage printers, plotters, and large-format printers.

Ink-Jet Printers

An **ink-jet printer** is a type of nonimpact printer that forms characters and graphics by spraying tiny drops of liquid ink onto a piece of paper. Ink-jet printers have become a popular type of color printer for use in the home. A reasonable quality ink-jet printer costs less than $100.

Ink-jet printers produce text and graphics in both black-and-white and color on a variety of paper types (Figure 6-14). These printers normally use individual sheets of paper stored in one or two removable or stationary trays. Ink-jet printers accept papers in many sizes, ranging from 3×5 inches to $8\frac{1}{2} \times 14$ inches. Available paper types include plain paper, ink-jet paper, photo paper, glossy paper, and banner paper. Most ink-jet printers can print photographic-quality images on any of these types of paper.

FIGURE 6-14 Ink-jet printers are a popular type of color printer used in the home.

Ink-jet printers also print on other materials such as envelopes, labels, index cards, greeting card paper (card stock), transparencies, and iron-on T-shirt transfers. Many ink-jet printers include software for creating greeting cards, banners, business cards, letterheads, and transparencies.

As with many other input and output devices, one factor that determines the quality of an ink-jet printer is its resolution. Printer resolution is measured by the number of *dots per inch* (*dpi*) a printer can print. With an ink-jet printer, a dot is a drop of ink. A higher dpi means the drops of ink are smaller. Most ink-jet printers can print from 1200 to 4800 dpi.

As shown in Figure 6-15, the higher the dpi, the better the print quality. The difference in quality becomes noticeable when the size of the printed image increases. That is, a wallet-sized image printed at 1200 dpi may look similar in quality to one printed at 2400 dpi. When you increase the size of the image, to 8 × 10 for example, the printout of the 1200 dpi resolution may look grainier than the one printed using a 2400 dpi resolution.

The speed of an ink-jet printer is measured by the number of pages per minute (ppm) it can print. Most ink-jet printers print from 6 to 33 ppm. Graphics and colors print at a slower rate. For example, an ink-jet printer may print 20 ppm for black text and only 15 ppm for color and/or graphics.

300 dpi
600 dpi
1200 dpi

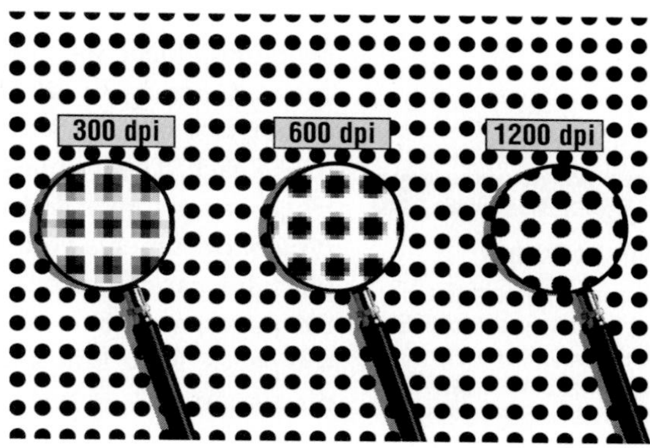

FIGURE 6-15 You will notice a higher quality output with printers that can print at a higher dpi.

The print head mechanism in an ink-jet printer contains ink-filled print cartridges. Each cartridge has fifty to several hundred small ink holes, or nozzles. The steps in Figure 6-16 illustrate how a drop of ink appears on a page. The ink propels through any combination of the nozzles to form a character or image on the paper.

When the print cartridge runs out of ink, you simply replace the cartridge. Most ink-jet printers have at least two print cartridges: one

FIGURE 6-16 HOW AN INK-JET PRINTER WORKS

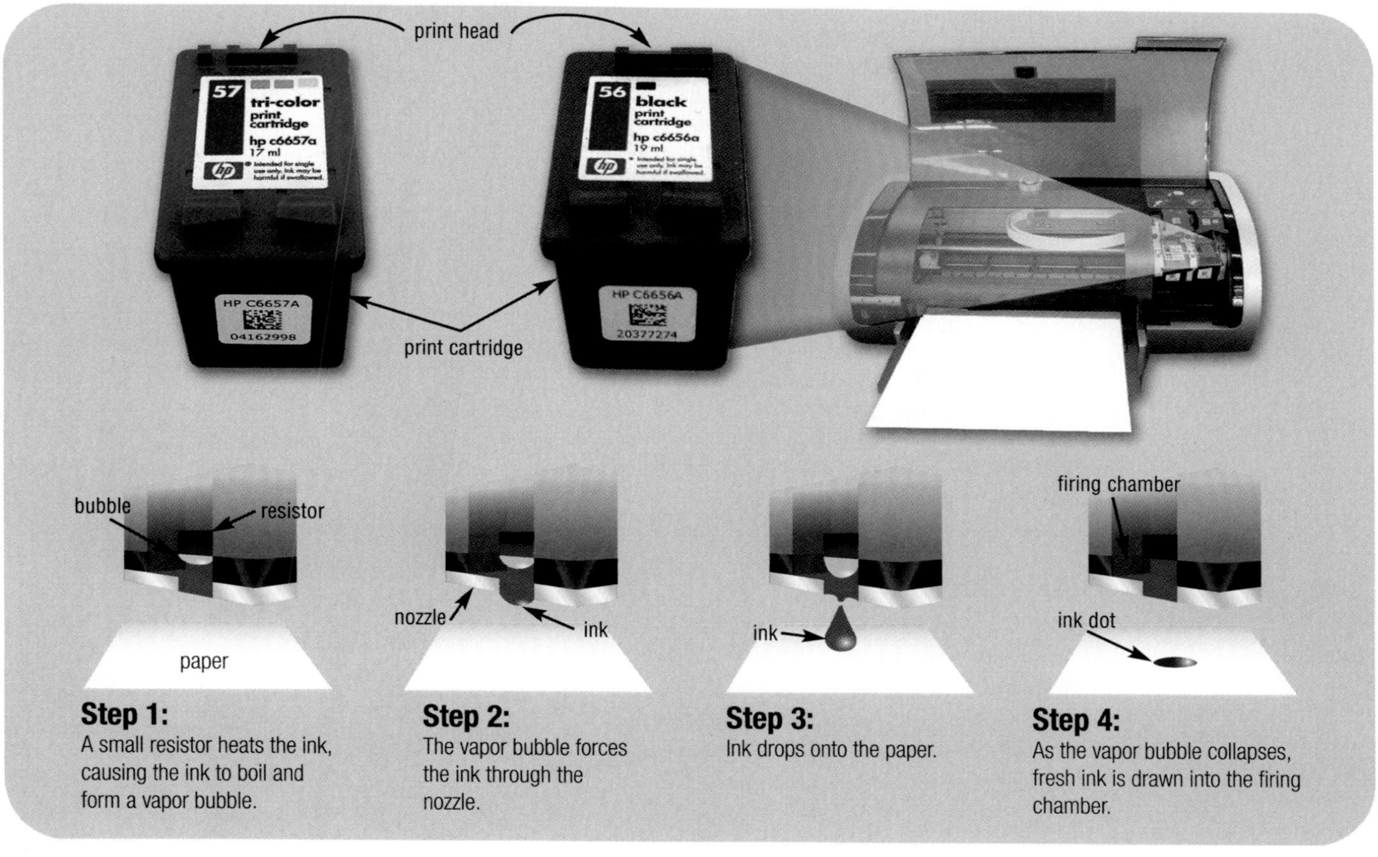

print head
57
tri-color
print cartridge
hp c6657a
17 ml
56
black
print cartridge
hp c6656a
19 ml
HP C6657A
04162998
HP C6656A
20377274
print cartridge
bubble
resistor
paper
nozzle
ink
ink
firing chamber
ink dot
Step 1:
A small resistor heats the ink, causing the ink to boil and form a vapor bubble.
Step 2:
The vapor bubble forces the ink through the nozzle.
Step 3:
Ink drops onto the paper.
Step 4:
As the vapor bubble collapses, fresh ink is drawn into the firing chamber.

containing black ink and the other(s) containing colors. Cartridges with black ink cost $15 to $30 each. Color ink cartridge prices range from $20 to $35 each. The number of pages a single cartridge can print varies by manufacturer and the type of documents you print. For example, black ink cartridges typically print from 200 to 800 pages, and color ink cartridges from 125 to 450 pages. Read Ethics & Issues 6-1 for a related discussion.

WEB LINK 6-4

Ink-Jet Printers

For more information, visit scsite.com/dc2008/ch6/weblink and then click Ink-Jet Printers.

ETHICS & ISSUES 6-1

Should Companies Prohibit Consumers from Refilling Ink Cartridges?

In 1903, King Camp Gillette introduced an innovative product — a safety razor with disposable blades. Gillette accompanied his product with an even more innovative idea — sell the razor, which was purchased once, at or below cost, and rely on sales of the razor blades, which were purchased repeatedly, for profit. The idea made Gillette a millionaire. Manufacturers of ink-jet printers use a similar approach. The printers are inexpensive, often less than $100. The ink cartridges the printers use, however, can cost from $30 to $50 each time they are replaced. To avoid the high cost of cartridges, some people get cartridges refilled cheaply by a third party vendor. At least one printer company, which holds approximately 4,000 patents related to ink and cartridges, legally prohibits the practice, and violators may be breaking patent and contract law if they refill a cartridge. Additionally, some printer manufacturers have inserted special chips that keep a cartridge from being refilled and, some claim, shut down a cartridge before it really is out of ink. This charge led to consumers winning a class-action lawsuit against one manufacturer. Opponents of these practices say that the printer companies are gouging customers and that no legitimate reason exists why someone should not be able to refill an ink-jet cartridge in the same way a soap dispenser can be refilled. Should manufacturers be allowed to prohibit people from refilling ink cartridges? Why? Would you use an ink refill kit? Why or why not?

Photo Printers

A **photo printer** is a color printer that produces photo-lab-quality pictures (Figure 6-17). Some photo printers print just one or two sizes of images, for example, 3 × 5 inches and 4 × 6 inches. Others print up to letter size, legal size, or even larger. Some even print panoramic photographs. Generally, the more sizes the printer prints, the more expensive the printer.

WEB LINK 6-5

PictBridge

For more information, visit scsite.com/dc2008/ch6/weblink and then click PictBridge.

Many photo printers use ink-jet technology. With models that can print letter-sized documents, users connect the photo printer to their computer and use it for all their printing needs. For a few hundred dollars, this type of photo printer is ideal for the home or small business user. Other photo printer technologies are discussed later in the chapter. Read Ethics & Issues 6-2 for a related discussion.

Most photo printers are PictBridge enabled, so you can print pictures without a computer. *PictBridge* is a standard technology that allows you to print pictures directly from a digital camera by connecting a cable from the digital camera to a USB port on the printer.

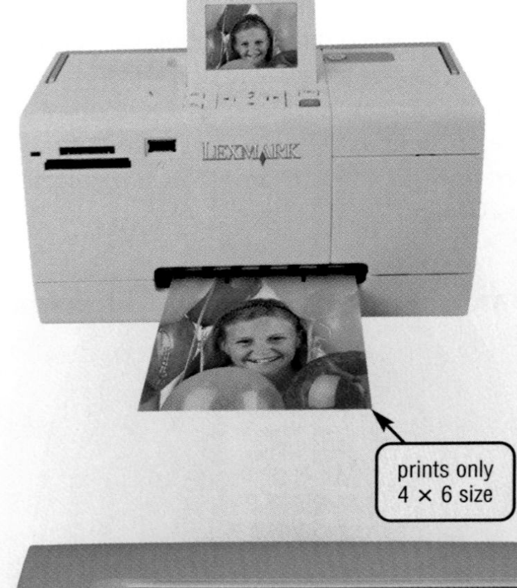

FIGURE 6-17 Photo printers print in a range of sizes.

ETHICS & ISSUES 6-2

Who Is Responsible for Stopping Counterfeiting?

Some college students found a solution to their money problems: they made their own. With a scanner, personal computer, and color printer, they produced bogus bills and passed more than $1,000 in counterfeit currency before they were caught. As printer and scanner quality continues to improve, it is estimated that more than $1 million in fraudulent funds is produced every week. As one federal agent points out, counterfeiting has gone from a high-skill, low-tech job to a high-tech, low-skill job. While counterfeiters previously specialized in higher-domination bills ($20, $50, and $100), today phony $10, $5, and even $1 bills are circulated. Spotting fake money is not that difficult, but most people never look that closely. Manufacturers of printers have introduced technology to produce lines or streaks when a printed image contains too much bank-note green color. Many color laser printers and copiers print nearly undetectable information on every page that includes the machine's serial number and/or the current date and time. The information can be used to track counterfeit currency. Producers of scanners and scanning software often include technology that prevents the scanner from scanning currency. Should the manufacturers of high-quality printers and scanners take responsibility for this problem? Why or why not? It is illegal to pass counterfeit currency knowingly. Should it be illegal to offer templates knowingly online that could be used to produce counterfeit documents? Can you offer any other possible solutions?

Photo printers also usually have a built-in card slot(s) so the printer can print digital photographs directly from a media card. Simply remove the media card from the digital camera and insert it in the printer's card slot. Then, push buttons on the printer to select the desired photo, specify the number of copies, and indicate the size of the printed image. Some photo printers have built-in LCD color screens, allowing users to view and enhance the pictures before printing them.

FAQ 6-7

What type of paper is available for a photo printer?

Many photo papers are available in various surface finishes, brightness, and weights. Surface finishes include high gloss, soft gloss, satin, or matte. The higher the brightness rating, the more brilliant the whiteness. The greater the paper weight, which is measured in pounds, the thicker the paper. In the United States, the weight of paper is stated in pounds per 500 sheets of 17 × 22-inch paper, each sheet of which equals four letter-sized sheets. For more information, visit scsite.com/dc2008/ch6/faq and then click Photo Paper.

Laser Printers

A **laser printer** is a high-speed, high-quality nonimpact printer (Figure 6-18). Laser printers are available in both black-and-white and color models. A laser printer for personal computers ordinarily uses individual 8½ × 11-inch sheets of paper stored in one or more removable trays that slide in the printer case. Some laser printers have built-in trays that accommodate different sizes of paper, while others require separate trays for letter- and legal-sized paper. Most laser printers have a manual feed slot where you can insert individual sheets and envelopes. You also can print transparencies on a laser printer.

Laser printers print text and graphics in high-quality resolutions, usually 1200 dpi for black-and-white printers and up to 2400 dpi for color printers. While laser printers usually cost more than ink-jet printers, they also are much faster. A laser printer for the home and small office user typically prints black-and-white text at speeds of 12 to 35 ppm. Color laser printers print 8 to 30 ppm. Laser printers for large business users print more than 150 ppm.

Depending on the quality, speed, and type of laser printer, the cost ranges from a few hundred to a few thousand dollars for the home and small

FIGURE 6-18 Laser printers are available in both black-and-white and color models.

office user, and several hundred thousand dollars for the large business user. Color laser printers are slightly higher priced than otherwise equivalent black-and-white laser printers.

When printing a document, laser printers process and store the entire page before they actually print it. For this reason, laser printers sometimes are called page printers. Storing a page before printing requires that the laser printer has a certain amount of memory in the device.

Depending on the amount of graphics you intend to print, a laser printer for the small business user can have up to 544 MB of memory and a 20 GB hard disk. To print a full-page 1200-dpi picture, for instance, you might need 32 MB of memory in the printer. If the printer does not have enough memory to print the picture, either it will print as much of the picture as its memory will allow, or it will display an error message and not print any of the picture.

Laser printers use software that enables them to interpret a *page description language* (*PDL*), which tells the printer how to lay out the contents of a printed page. When you purchase a laser printer, it comes with at least one of two common page description languages: PCL or PostScript. Developed by Hewlett-Packard, a leading printer manufacturer, *PCL* (*Printer Control Language*) is a standard printer language that supports the fonts and layout used in standard office documents. Professionals in the desktop publishing and graphic art fields commonly use *PostScript* because it is designed for complex documents with intense graphics and colors.

WEB LINK 6-6

Laser Printers

For more information, visit scsite.com/dc2008/ch6/weblink and then click Laser Printers.

Operating in a manner similar to a copy machine, a laser printer creates images using a laser beam and powdered ink, called *toner*. The laser beam produces an image on a special drum inside the printer. The light of the laser alters the electrical charge on the drum wherever it hits. When this occurs, the toner sticks to the drum and then transfers to the paper through a combination of pressure and heat (Figure 6-19).

When the toner runs out, you replace the toner cartridge. Toner cartridge prices range from $50 to $100 for about 5,000 printed pages.

FAQ 6-8

How do I dispose of toner cartridges?

Do not throw them in the garbage. The housing contains iron, metal, and aluminum that is not biodegradable. The ink toner inside the cartridges contains toxic chemicals that pollute water and soil if discarded in dumps. Instead, recycle empty toner cartridges. Recycling programs in which some schools and organizations participate offer discounts or cash to customers who bring in depleted cartridges. If you are unable to find a recycling program in your area, contact your printer manufacturer to see if it has a recycling program. For more information, visit scsite.com/dc2008/ch6/faq and then click Recycling Toner Cartridges.

FIGURE 6-19 HOW A BLACK-AND-WHITE LASER PRINTER WORKS

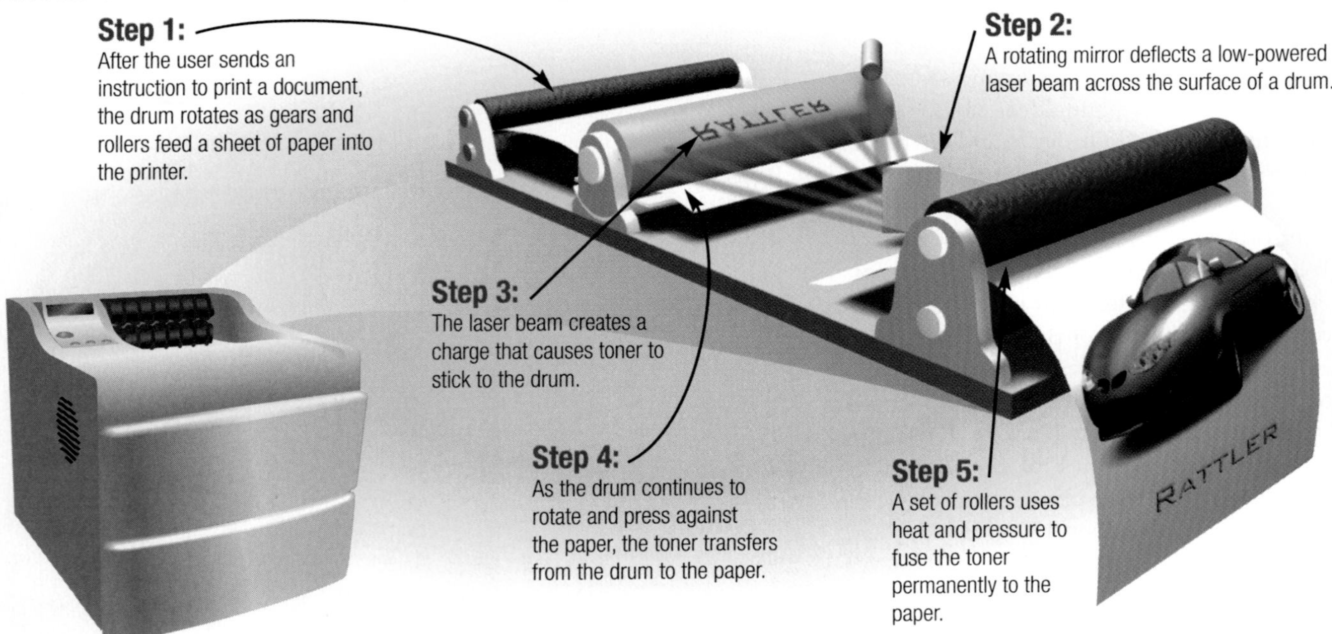

Step 1:
After the user sends an instruction to print a document, the drum rotates as gears and rollers feed a sheet of paper into the printer.
Step 2:
A rotating mirror deflects a low-powered laser beam across the surface of a drum.
Step 3:
The laser beam creates a charge that causes toner to stick to the drum.
Step 4:
As the drum continues to rotate and press against the paper, the toner transfers from the drum to the paper.
Step 5:
A set of rollers uses heat and pressure to fuse the toner permanently to the paper.
RATTLER

Thermal Printers

A **thermal printer** generates images by pushing electrically heated pins against heat-sensitive paper. Basic thermal printers are inexpensive, but the print quality is low and the images tend to fade over time. Self-service gas pumps often print gas receipts using a built-in lower-quality thermal printer.

Two special types of thermal printers have high print quality. A *thermal wax-transfer printer* generates rich, nonsmearing images by using heat to melt colored wax onto heat-sensitive paper. Thermal wax-transfer printers are more expensive than ink-jet printers, but less expensive than many color laser printers.

A *dye-sublimation printer*, sometimes called a *digital photo printer*, uses heat to transfer colored dye to specially coated paper. Most dye-sublimation printers create images that are of photographic quality (Figure 6-20). Professional applications requiring high image quality, such as photography studios, medical labs, and security identification systems, use dye-sublimation printers. These high-end printers cost thousands of dollars and print images in a wide range of sizes. Most dye-sublimation printers for the home or small business user, by contrast, typically print images in only one or two sizes and are much slower than their professional counterparts. These lower-end dye-sublimation printers are comparable in cost to a photo printer based on ink-jet technology. Some are small enough for the mobile user to carry the printer in a briefcase.

FIGURE 6-20a (dye-sublimation printer for the professional)

FIGURE 6-20b (dye-sublimation printer for the home or small office user)

FIGURE 6-20 The printers shown in this figure use dye-sublimation technology to create photographic-quality output.

Mobile Printers

A **mobile printer** is a small, lightweight, battery-powered printer that allows a mobile user to print from a notebook computer, Tablet PC, PDA, or smart phone while traveling (Figure 6-21). Barely wider than the paper on which they print, mobile printers fit easily in a briefcase alongside a notebook computer.

Mobile printers mainly use ink-jet, thermal, thermal wax-transfer, or dye-sublimation technology. Many of these printers connect to a USB port. Others have a built-in wireless port through which they communicate with the computer wirelessly.

FIGURE 6-21 A mobile printer is a compact printer that allows the mobile user to print from a notebook computer or mobile device.

Label and Postage Printers

A **label printer** is a small printer that prints on an adhesive-type material (Figure 6-22) that can be placed on a variety of items such as envelopes, packages, CDs, DVDs, audiocassettes, photographs, file folders, and toys. Most label printers also print bar codes. Label printers typically use thermal technology.

A *postage printer* is a special type of label printer that has a built-in digital scale and prints postage stamps. Postage printers allow users to buy and print digital postage, called *Internet postage*, right from their computer. That is, you purchase an amount of postage from an authorized postal service Web site. As you need a stamp, you print it on the postage printer. Each time a postage stamp prints, your postage account is updated.

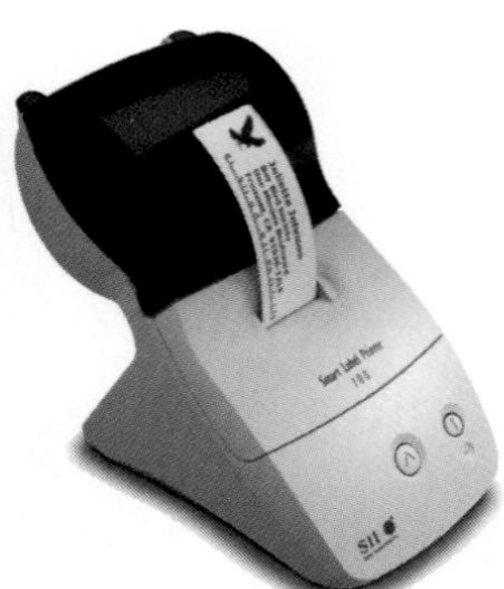

FIGURE 6-22
A label printer.

Plotters and Large-Format Printers

Plotters are sophisticated printers used to produce high-quality drawings such as blueprints, maps, and circuit diagrams. These printers are used in specialized fields such as engineering and drafting and usually are very costly. Current plotters use a row of charged wires (called styli) to draw an electrostatic pattern on specially coated paper and then fuse toner to the pattern. The printed image consists of a series of very small dots, which provides high-quality output.

Using ink-jet printer technology, but on a much larger scale, a **large-format printer** creates photo-realistic-quality color prints. Graphic artists use these high-cost, high-performance printers for signs, posters, and other professional quality displays (Figure 6-23).

Plotters and large-format printers can accommodate paper with widths up to 60 inches because blueprints, maps, signs, posters and other such drawings and displays can be quite large. Some plotters and large-format printers use individual sheets of paper, while others take large rolls.

Impact Printers

An **impact printer** forms characters and graphics on a piece of paper by striking a mechanism against an inked ribbon that physically contacts the paper. Impact printers characteristically are noisy because of this striking activity. These printers commonly produce *near letter quality* (*NLQ*) output, which is print quality slightly less clear than what is acceptable for business letters. Companies may use impact printers for routine jobs such as printing mailing labels, envelopes, and invoices. Impact printers also are ideal for printing multipart forms because they easily print through many layers of paper. Factories and retail counters use impact printers because these printers withstand dusty environments, vibrations, and extreme temperatures.

Two commonly used types of impact printers are dot-matrix printers and line printers.

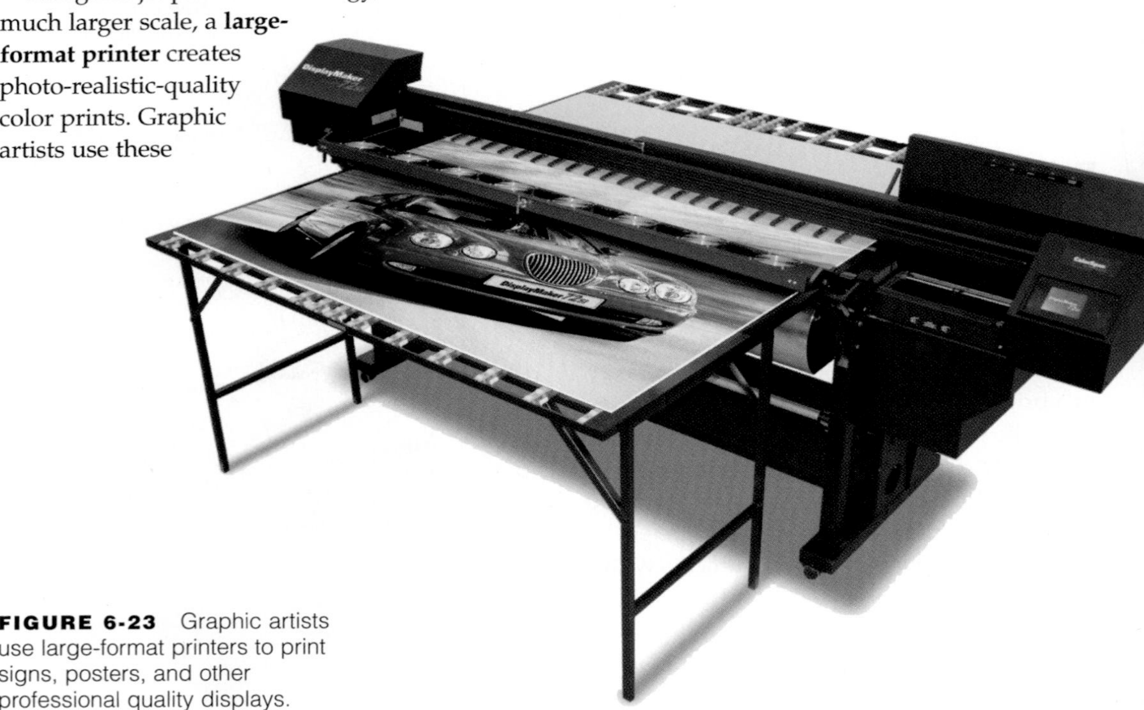

FIGURE 6-23 Graphic artists use large-format printers to print signs, posters, and other professional quality displays.

DOT-MATRIX PRINTERS A **dot-matrix printer** is an impact printer that produces printed images when tiny wire pins on a print head mechanism strike an inked ribbon (Figure 6-24). When the ribbon presses against the paper, it creates dots that form characters and graphics.

Most dot-matrix printers use *continuous-form paper*, in which thousands of sheets of paper are connected together end to end. The pages have holes along the sides to help feed the paper through the printer.

The print head mechanism on a dot-matrix printer contains 9 to 24 pins, depending on the manufacturer and the printer model. A higher number of pins means the printer prints more dots per character, which results in higher print quality.

The speed of a dot-matrix printer is measured by the number of characters per second (cps) it can print. The speed of most dot-matrix printers ranges from 300 to 1100 characters per second (cps), depending on the desired print quality.

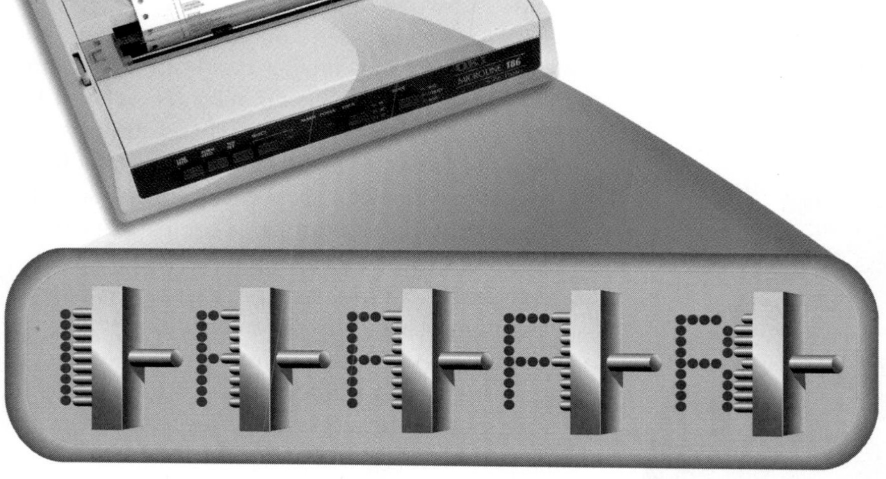

FIGURE 6-24 A dot-matrix printer produces printed images when tiny pins strike an inked ribbon.

LINE PRINTERS A **line printer** is a high-speed impact printer that prints an entire line at a time (Figure 6-25). The speed of a line printer is measured by the number of lines per minute (lpm) it can print. Some line printers print as many as 3,000 lpm. Mainframes, servers, or networked applications, such as manufacturing, distribution, or shipping, often use line printers. These printers typically use 11 × 17-inch continuous-form paper.

Two popular types of line printers used for high-volume output are band and shuttle-matrix. A *band printer* prints fully formed characters when hammers strike a horizontal, rotating band that contains shapes of numbers, letters of the alphabet, and other characters. A *shuttle-matrix printer* functions more like a dot-matrix printer. The difference is the shuttle-matrix printer moves a series of print hammers back and forth horizontally at incredibly high speeds, as compared with standard line printers. Unlike a band printer, a shuttle-matrix printer prints characters in various fonts and font sizes.

FIGURE 6-25 A line printer is a high-speed printer often connected to a mainframe, server, or network.

Test your knowledge of pages 310 through 319 in Quiz Yourself 6-2.

QUIZ YOURSELF 6-2

Instructions: Find the true statement below. Then, rewrite the remaining false statements so they are true.

1. A laser printer generates images by pushing electrically heated pins against heat-sensitive paper.
2. A photo printer creates images using a laser beam and powdered ink, called toner.
3. An ink-jet printer is a type of impact printer that forms characters and graphics by spraying tiny drops of liquid nitrogen onto a piece of paper.
4. Printed information is called soft copy.
5. Two commonly used types of impact printers are ink-jet printers and line printers.
6. With Bluetooth printing, a computer or other device transmits output to a printer via radio waves.

Quiz Yourself Online: To further check your knowledge of ways to print and various types of printers, visit scsite.com/dc2008/ch6/quiz and then click Objectives 5 – 7.

SPEAKERS, HEADPHONES, AND EARPHONES

An **audio output device** is a component of a computer that produces music, speech, or other sounds, such as beeps. Three commonly used audio output devices are speakers, headphones, and earphones.

Most personal computers have a small internal speaker that usually emits only low-quality sound. Thus, many personal computer users add surround sound **speakers** to their computers to generate a higher-quality sound for playing games, interacting with multimedia presentations, listening to music CDs, and viewing DVDs (Figure 6-26).

FIGURE 6-26 Most personal computer users add high-quality surround sound speaker systems to their computers.

Most surround sound computer speaker systems include one or two center speakers and two or more *satellite speakers* that are positioned so sound emits from all directions. Speakers typically have tone and volume controls, allowing users to adjust settings. To boost the low bass sounds, surround sound speaker systems also include a *subwoofer*.

Surround sound systems are available in a variety of configurations. For example, a 2.1 speaker system contains two speakers and a subwoofer. A 5.1 speaker system has four satellite speakers, a center speaker, and a subwoofer. A 6.1 speaker system has four satellite speakers, a front center speaker, a rear center speaker, and a subwoofer. A 7.1 speaker system has four satellite speakers, two side speakers, a center speaker, and a subwoofer.

In many cases, users connect the speakers and subwoofer to ports on the sound card. With wireless speakers, however, a transmitter connects to the sound card, which wirelessly communicates with the speakers. To take full advantage of high-end surround sound speaker systems, be sure the sound card in the computer is compatible with the speaker system. For a more technical discussion about how sound cards produce sound, read the High-Tech Talk article on page 328.

Many users opt for a wireless music system, which includes a USB transmitter that plugs into a computer, a receiver that connects to a television or stereo system, and a remote control.

With this system, you can play any CD, DVD, or media file on your computer and transmit the audio to a home or office stereo or television at a distance of up to 330 feet. You also can plug a portable media player, such as an iPod, into the computer to hear its songs on the stereo or television speakers.

When using speakers, anyone in listening distance can hear the output. In a computer laboratory or other crowded environment, speakers might not be practical. Instead, users can plug headphones or earphones in a port on the sound card, in a speaker, or on the front of the system unit. With headphones or earphones, only the individual wearing the headphones or earphones hears the sound from the computer. The difference is that **headphones** cover or are placed outside of the ear (Figure 6-27), whereas **earphones**, or *earbuds* (shown in Figure 6-1 on page 300), rest inside the ear canal.

Electronically produced voice output is growing in popularity. **Voice output** occurs when you hear a person's voice or when the computer talks to you through the speakers on the computer. In some programs, the computer can speak the contents of a document through voice output. On the Web, you can listen to (or download and then listen to) interviews, talk shows, sporting events, news, recorded music, and live concerts from many radio and television stations. Some Web sites dedicate themselves to providing voice output, where you can hear songs, quotes, historical lectures, speeches, and books (Figure 6-28). Read Ethics & Issues 6-3 for a related discussion.

WEB LINK 6-7

Wireless Music System

For more information, visit scsite.com/dc2008/ch6/weblink and then click Wireless Music System.

FIGURE 6-27 In a crowded environment where speakers are not practical, users wear headphones or earphones to hear audio output.

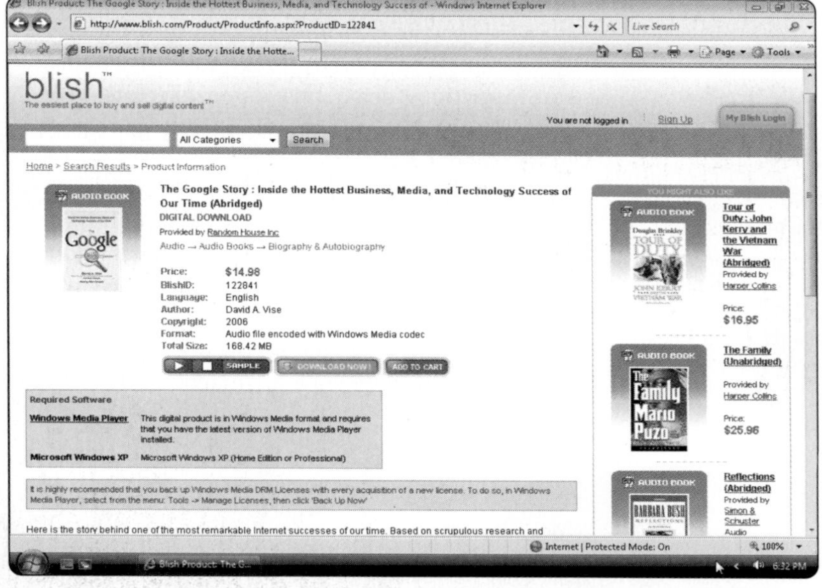

FIGURE 6-28 Through this Web site, users can purchase and then download a book in digital audio format and then listen to the book's contents via their computer's speakers or a portable media player such as an iPod.

ETHICS & ISSUES 6-3

Should Colleges Provide Free Access to Music for Students?

In recent years, many college administrators discovered that their computer networks had become completely saturated with the illegal sharing of copyrighted music files. At peak usage times during the day, the networks quickly were becoming unusable for legitimate purposes as students shared large music files. At the same time, the music industry began threatening colleges with legal action, claiming that the colleges are responsible for the illegal file sharing done by students on the school's network. College administrators and some music companies decided that a good solution is to allow a school to purchase licenses for music and then set up a shared music service for all students to access. While the university pays a fee for the service, the music is made available for free to students. The music files include, however, some restrictions. For example, in some agreements students are not allowed to use the files after they leave the school. In other arrangements, the files cannot be shared with others or burned on a CD. Some services include technology that helps the school identify illegal file sharing. Students have had a mixed reaction to the services due to the number of restrictions placed on the music. Some college administrators feel that the services amount to legalized blackmail because of the threat of legal action if the schools do not stop illegal file sharing. Should colleges provide free access to music for students? Why or why not? How could colleges make their free music services more attractive to students? What restrictions would you be comfortable with if you were able to obtain free music files at your school? Why?

Very often, voice output works with voice input. For example, when you call an airline to check the status of gates, terminals, and arrival times, your voice interacts with a computer-generated voice output. Another example is *Internet telephony*, which allows users to speak to other users over the Internet using their desktop computer, mobile computer, or mobile device.

Sophisticated programs enable the computer to converse with you. Talk into the microphone and say, "I'd like today's weather report." The computer replies, "For which city?" You reply, "Chicago." The computer says, "Sunny and 80 degrees."

OTHER OUTPUT DEVICES

In addition to display devices, printers, and speakers, many other output devices are available for specific uses and applications. These devices include fax machines and fax modems, multifunction peripherals, data projectors, and force-feedback joysticks, wheels, and gamepads.

WEB LINK 6-8

Fax Modems

For more information, visit scsite.com/dc2008/ch6/weblink and then click Fax Modems.

Fax Machines and Fax Modems

A **fax machine** is a device that codes and encodes documents so they can be transmitted over telephone lines. The documents can contain text, drawings, or photographs, or can be handwritten. The term *fax* refers to a document that you send or receive via a fax machine.

A stand-alone fax machine scans an original document, converts the image into digitized data, and transmits the digitized image (Figure 6-29). A fax machine at the receiving end reads the incoming data, converts the digitized data back into an image, and prints or stores a copy of the original image.

Many computers include fax capability by using a fax modem. A *fax modem* is a modem that also allows you to send (and sometimes receive) electronic documents as faxes (Figure 6-30). A fax modem transmits computer-prepared documents, such as a word processing letter, or documents that have been digitized with a scanner or digital camera. A fax modem transmits these faxes to a fax machine or to another fax modem.

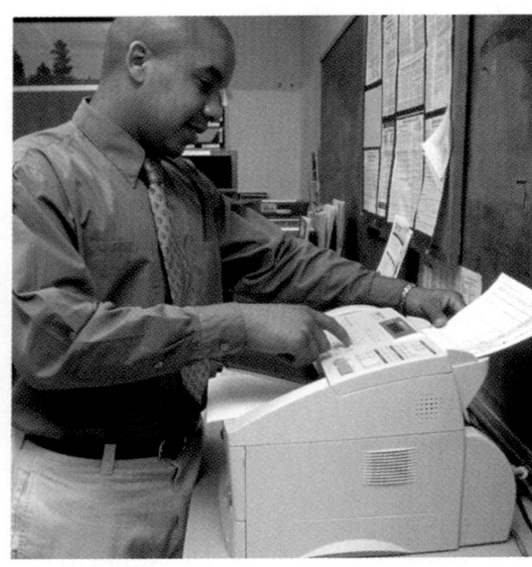

FIGURE 6-29 A stand-alone fax machine.

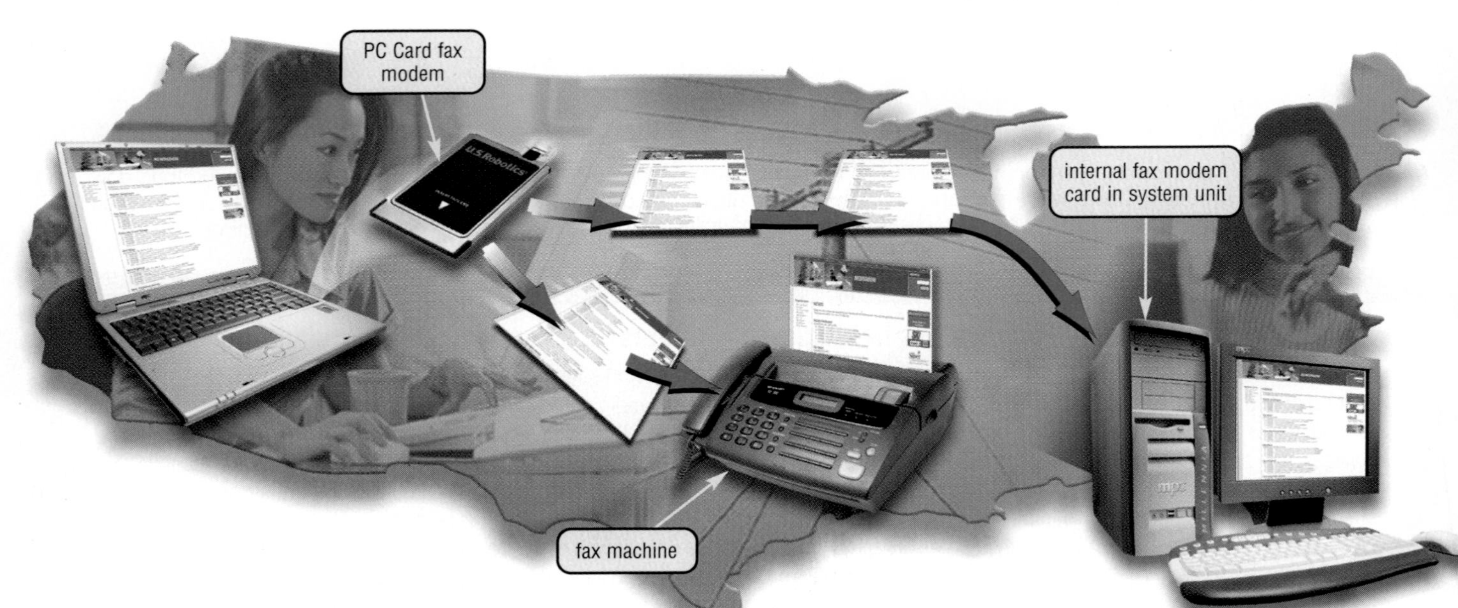

FIGURE 6-30 A fax modem allows users to send (and sometimes receive) electronic documents as faxes to a fax machine or another computer.

When a computer (instead of a fax machine) receives a fax, users can view the fax on the screen, saving the time and expense of printing it. If necessary, you also can print the fax. The quality of a viewed or printed fax is less than that of a word processing document because the fax actually is an image. Optical character recognition (OCR) software, which was discussed in Chapter 5, enables you to convert the image to text and then edit it.

A fax modem can be an external device that plugs in a port on the system unit, an internal adapter card inserted in an expansion slot on the motherboard, a chip integrated on the motherboard, or a PC Card that inserts in a PC Card slot.

Multifunction Peripherals

A **multifunction peripheral** is a single device that looks like a copy machine but provides the functionality of a printer, scanner, copy machine, and perhaps a fax machine (Figure 6-31). The features of these devices, which sometimes are called *all-in-one devices*, vary. For example, some use color ink-jet printer technology, while others include a black-and-white laser printer.

Small offices and home office (SOHO) users have multifunction peripherals because these devices require less space than having a separate printer, scanner, copy machine, and fax machine. Another advantage of these devices is they are significantly less expensive than if you purchase each device separately. If the device breaks down, however, you lose all four functions, which is the primary disadvantage.

Multifunction Peripherals

For more information, visit scsite.com/dc2008/ch6/weblink and then click Multifunction Peripherals.

Data Projectors

A **data projector** is a device that takes the text and images displaying on a computer screen and projects them on a larger screen so an audience can see the image clearly (Figure 6-32). For example, many classrooms use data projectors so all students easily can see an instructor's presentation on the screen.

Some data projectors are large devices that attach to a ceiling or wall in an auditorium. Others, designed for the mobile user, are small portable devices that can be transported easily. Two types of smaller, lower-cost units are LCD projectors and DLP projectors.

An *LCD projector*, which uses liquid crystal display technology, attaches directly to a computer, and uses its own light source to display the information shown on the computer screen. Because LCD projectors tend to produce lower-quality images, users often prefer DLP projectors for their sharper, brighter images.

FIGURE 6-31 This multifunction peripheral is a color printer, scanner, copy machine, and fax machine all-in-one device.

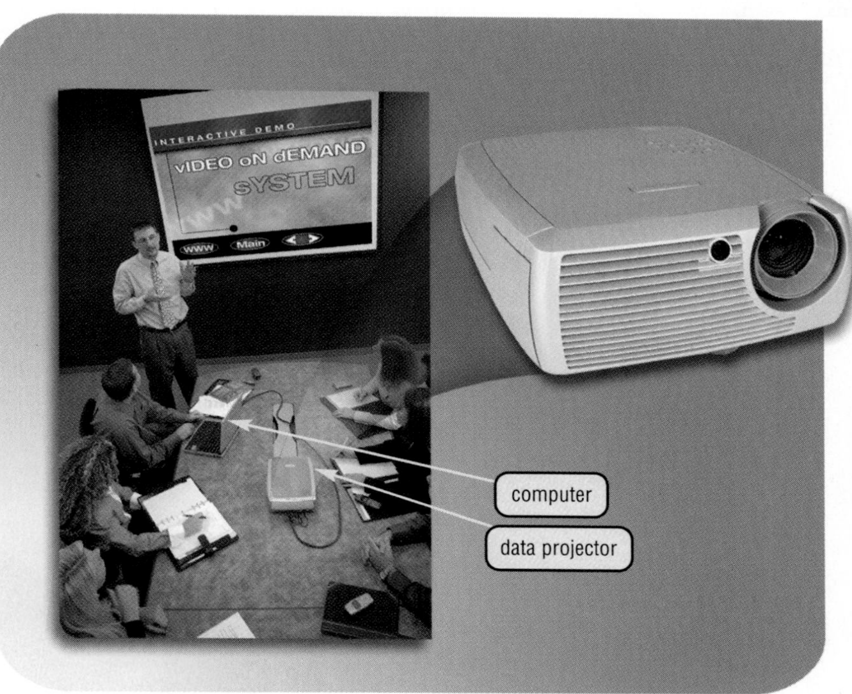

FIGURE 6-32 A data projector projects an image from a computer screen on a larger screen so an audience easily can see the image.

A *digital light processing* (*DLP*) *projector* uses tiny mirrors to reflect light, which produces crisp, bright, colorful images that remain in focus and can be seen clearly even in a well-lit room. Some newer televisions use DLP instead of LCD or plasma technology. Read Looking Ahead 6-2 for a look at the next generation of picture technology.

LOOKING AHEAD 6-2

Ultra HDTV Puts Viewers in the Picture

Vibrant colors and pictures so detailed television viewers feel like they actually are courtside at a basketball game or squishing wet sand between their toes at the beach are the promise of *Ultra High Definition TV (U-HDTV)*.

Using dramatically enhanced picture quality and sound, U-HDTV moves television viewers from merely watching real objects to feeling like they are part of the scenes they are viewing. U-HDTV, demonstrated by researchers from Japanese state broadcaster NHK at the 2006 International Broadcasting Convention, featured 16 times the resolution of current HDTV and incorporated advanced surround sound utilizing 24 speakers.

With no currently available LCD or plasma screens with resolution high enough to display U-HDTV pictures, commercial development is still years away; however, the technology may have more immediate applications for movie studios or museum archives. For more information, visit scsite.com/dc2008/ch6/looking and then click U-HDTV.

Force-Feedback Joysticks, Wheels, and Gamepads

As discussed in Chapter 5, joysticks, wheels, and gamepads are input devices used to control movement and actions of a player or object in computer games, simulations, and video games. Today's joysticks, wheels, and gamepads also include *force feedback*, which is a technology that sends resistance to the device in response to actions of the user (Figure 6-33). For example, as you use the simulation software to drive from a smooth road onto a gravel alley, the steering wheel trembles or vibrates, making the driving experience as realistic as possible. In addition to games, these devices are used in practical training applications such as in the military and aviation.

FAQ 6-9

Who plays video games?

Studies have shown that people between 18 and 34 years of age spend the most time playing video games. This age group spends more money on video games than in movie theaters. For more information, visit scsite.com/dc2008/ch6/faq and then click Video Gaming.

FIGURE 6-33 Gaming devices often provide force feedback, giving the user a realistic experience.

WEB LINK 6-10

Force Feedback Devices

For more information, visit scsite.com/dc2008/ch6/weblink and then click Force Feedback Devices.

PUTTING IT ALL TOGETHER

Many factors influence the type of output devices you should use: the type of output desired, the hardware and software in use, and the anticipated cost. Figure 6-34 outlines several suggested monitors, printers, and other output devices for various types of computer users.

SUGGESTED OUTPUT DEVICES BY USER

User	Monitor	Printer	Other
HOME 	• 17- or 19-inch LCD monitor	• Ink-jet color printer; or • Photo printer	• Speakers • Headphones or earphones • Force-feedback joystick, wheel, and/or gamepad
SMALL OFFICE/ HOME OFFICE 	• 19- or 21-inch LCD monitor • LCD screen on Tablet PC, PDA, or smart phone	• Multifunction peripheral; or • Ink-jet color printer; or • Laser printer (black-and-white or color) • Label printer • Postage printer	• Fax machine • Speakers
MOBILE 	• 17-inch LCD screen on notebook computer • LCD screen on Tablet PC, PDA, or smart phone	• Mobile color printer • Ink-jet color printer; or • Laser printer for in-office use (black-and-white or color) • Photo printer	• Fax modem • Headphones or earphones • DLP data projector
POWER 	• 23-inch LCD monitor	• Laser printer (black-and-white or color) • Plotter or large-format printer; or • Photo printer; or • Dye-sublimation printer	• Fax machine or fax modem • Speakers • Headphones or earphones
LARGE BUSINESS 	• 19- or 21-inch LCD monitor • LCD screen on Tablet PC, PDA, or smart phone	• High-speed laser printer • Laser printer, color • Line printer (for large reports from a mainframe) • Label printer	• Fax machine or fax modem • Speakers • Headphones or earphones • DLP data projector

FIGURE 6-34 This table recommends suggested output devices for various types of users.

OUTPUT DEVICES FOR PHYSICALLY CHALLENGED USERS

As Chapter 5 discussed, the growing presence of computers has generated an awareness of the need to address computing requirements for those with physical limitations. Read Ethics & Issues 6-4 for a related discussion.

For users with mobility, hearing, or vision disabilities, many different types of output devices are available. Hearing-impaired users, for example, can instruct programs to display words instead of sounds. With the Windows Vista operating system, users also can set options to make programs easier to use. The Magnifier, for example, enlarges text and other items in a window on the screen (Figure 6-35).

Visually impaired users can change Windows Vista settings, such as increasing the size or changing the color of the text to make the words easier to read. Instead of using a monitor, blind users can work with voice output via Windows Vista's Narrator. That is, the computer reads the information that is displayed on the screen. Another alternative is a *Braille printer*, which prints information on paper in Braille (Figure 6-36).

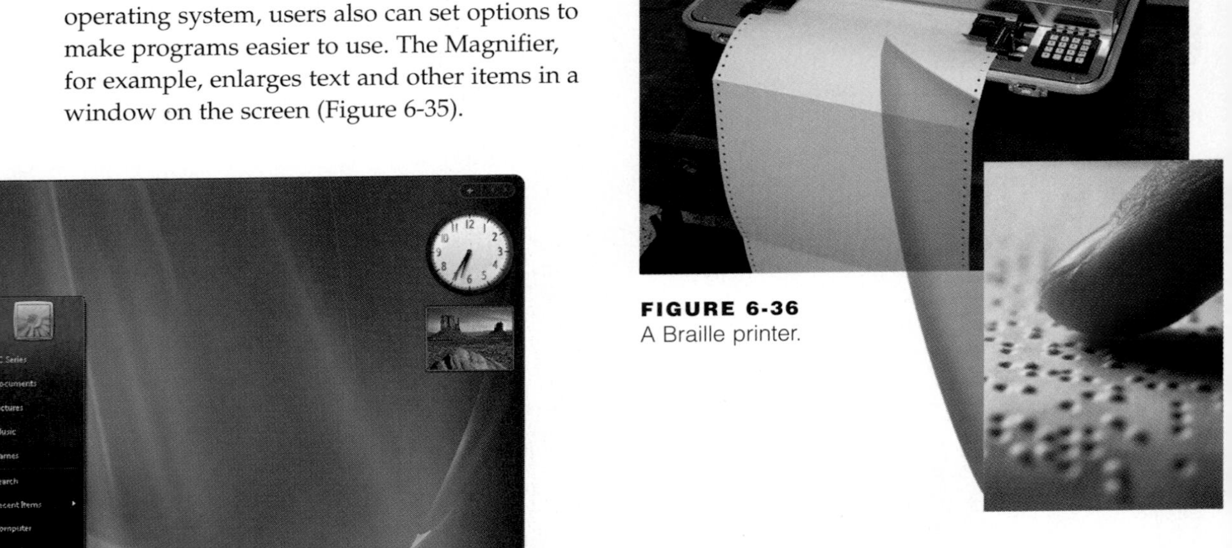

FIGURE 6-36 A Braille printer.

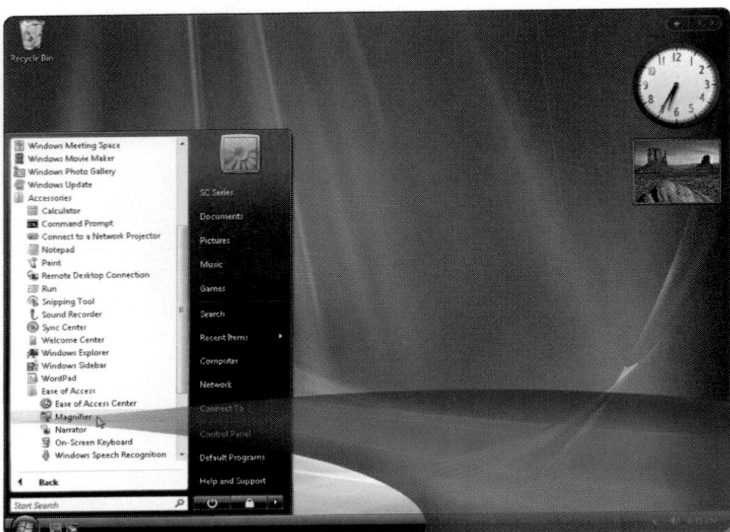

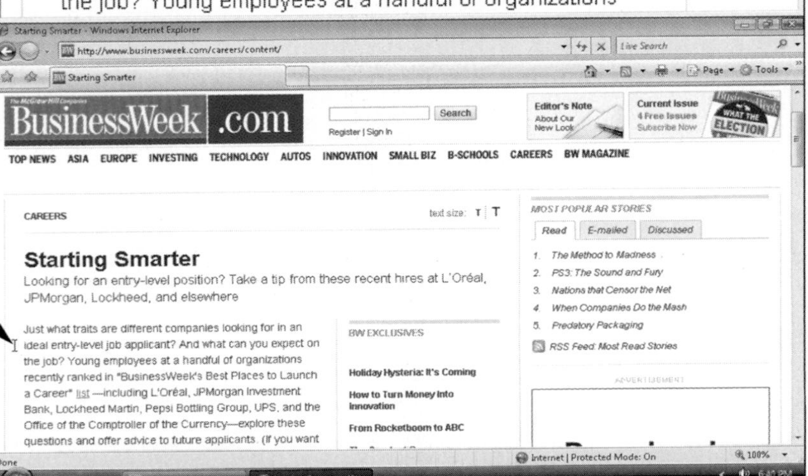

FIGURE 6-35 The Magnifier in Windows Vista enlarges text and other on-screen items for visually impaired users.

ETHICS & ISSUES 6-4

Should Web Sites Be Held Accountable for Accessibility Levels for Physically Challenged People?

The World Wide Web Consortium (W3C) has published accessibility guidelines for Web sites. The guidelines specify measures that Web site designers can take to increase accessibility for physically challenged users. Among its guidelines, the W3C urges Web site designers to provide equivalent text for audio or visual content, include features that allow elements to be activated and understood using a variety of input and output devices, and make the user interface follow principles of accessible design. A recent report found that most Web sites do not meet all of the W3C guidelines. This failure is disappointing, because many physically challenged users could benefit from the Web's capability to bring products and services into the home. Ironically, a survey discovered that more than 50 percent of the Web sites run by disability organizations also fail to meet the W3C guidelines. Critics contend that these Web sites neglect the needs of their users and fail to lead by example. The Web site supporters contend, however, that many sponsoring organizations lack the funding necessary to comply with the guidelines. Should the government require that all Web sites meet the W3C accessibility guidelines? Why or why not? Do Web sites run by disability organizations have a moral obligation to meet the guidelines? Why? What can be done to encourage people and organizations to make their Web sites more accessible?

Test your knowledge of pages 320 through 327 in Quiz Yourself 6-3.

QUIZ YOURSELF 6-3

Instructions: Find the true statement below. Then, rewrite the remaining false statements so they are true.

1. A digital light processing (DLP) projector uses tiny lightbulbs to reflect light.
2. A stand-alone fax machine scans an original document, converts the image into digitized data, and transmits the digitized image.
3. Many personal computer users add surround sound printer systems to their computers to generate a higher-quality sound.
4. Multifunction peripherals require more space than having a separate printer, scanner, copy machine, and fax machine.
5. Some joysticks, wheels, and gamepads include real-time action, which is a technology that sends resistance to the device in response to actions of the user.

Quiz Yourself Online: To further check your knowledge of speakers, headphones, and earphones; other output devices; and output for physically challenged users, visit scsite.com/dc2008/ch6/quiz and then click Objectives 8 – 10.

CHAPTER SUMMARY

Computers process and organize data (input) into information (output). This chapter described the various methods of output and several commonly used output devices. Output devices presented were flat-panel displays; CRT monitors; printers; speakers, headphones, and earphones; fax machines and fax modems; multifunction peripherals; data projectors; and force-feedback joysticks, wheels, and gamepads.

CAREER CORNER

Graphic Designer/Illustrator

Graphic designers and *graphic illustrators* are artists, but many do not create original works. Instead, they portray visually the ideas of their clients. Illustrators create pictures for books and other publications and sometimes for commercial products, such as greeting cards. They work in fields such as fashion, technology, medicine, animation, or even cartoons. Illustrators often prepare their images on a computer. Designers combine practical skills with artistic talent to convert abstract concepts into designs for products and advertisements. Many use computer-aided design (CAD) tools to create, visualize, and modify designs. Designer careers usually are specialized in particular areas, such as:

- Graphic designers — book covers, stationery, and CD covers
- Commercial and industrial designers — products and equipment
- Costume and theater designers — costumes and settings for theater and television
- Interior designers — layout, decor, and furnishings of homes and buildings
- Merchandise displayers — commercial displays
- Fashion designers — clothing, shoes, and other fashion accessories

Certificate, two-year, four-year, and masters-level educational programs are available within design areas. About 30 percent of graphic designers/illustrators choose to freelance, while others work with advertising agencies, publishing companies, design studios, or specialized departments within large companies. Salaries range from $35,000 to $100,000-plus, based on experience and educational background. For more information, visit scsite.com/dc2008/ch6/careers and then click Graphic Designer/Illustrator.

High-Tech Talk

SOUND CARDS: BRINGING YOUR COMPUTER TO LIFE

Speakers, headphones, earphones, and other audio output devices rely on sound cards or integrated sound card functionality to produce sounds such as music, voice, beeps, and chimes. Sound cards contain the chips and circuitry to record and play back a wide range of sounds using analog-to-digital conversion and digital-to-analog conversion, as described in the Chapter 1 High-Tech Talk on page 38.

To record a sound, the sound card must be connected to an input device, such as a microphone or audio CD player. The input device sends the sound to the sound card as an analog signal. The analog signal flows to the sound card's analog-to-digital-converter (ADC). The ADC converts the signal into digital (binary) data of 1s and 0s by sampling the signal at set intervals.

The analog sound is a continuous waveform, with a range of frequencies and volumes. To represent the waveform in a recording, the computer would have to store the waveform's value at every instant in time. Because this is not possible, the sound is recorded using a sampling process. *Sampling* involves breaking up the waveform into set intervals and representing all values during that interval with a single value.

Several factors in the sampling process — sampling rate, audio resolution, and mono or stereo recording — affect the quality of the recorded sound during playback.

- *Sampling rate*, also called sampling frequency, refers to the number of times per second the sound is recorded. The more frequently a sound is recorded, the smaller the intervals and the better the quality. The sampling frequency used for audio CDs, for example, is 44,100 times per second, which is expressed in hertz (Hz) as 44,100 Hz. Cassette-tape-quality multimedia files use a sampling rate of 22,050 Hz; and basic Windows sounds use a sampling rate of 11,025 Hz.
- *Audio resolution* — defined as a bit rate such as 8-bit, 16-bit, or 24-bit — refers to the number of bytes used to represent the sound at any one interval. A sound card using 8-bit resolution, for example, represents a sound with any 1 of 256 values (2^8). A 16-bit sound card uses any 1 of 65,536 values (2^{16}) for each interval. Using a higher resolution provides a finer measurement scale, which results in a more accurate representation of the value of each sample and better sound quality. With 8-bit resolution, the sound quality is like that of an AM radio; 16-bit resolution gives CD-quality sound, and a 24-bit resolution is used for high-quality digital audio editing.
- Mono or stereo recording refers to the number of channels used during recording. *Mono* means that the same sound emits from both the left and right speaker during playback; *stereo* means that two separate channels exist in the recording: one each for the left and right speakers. Most sound cards support stereo recording for better playback.

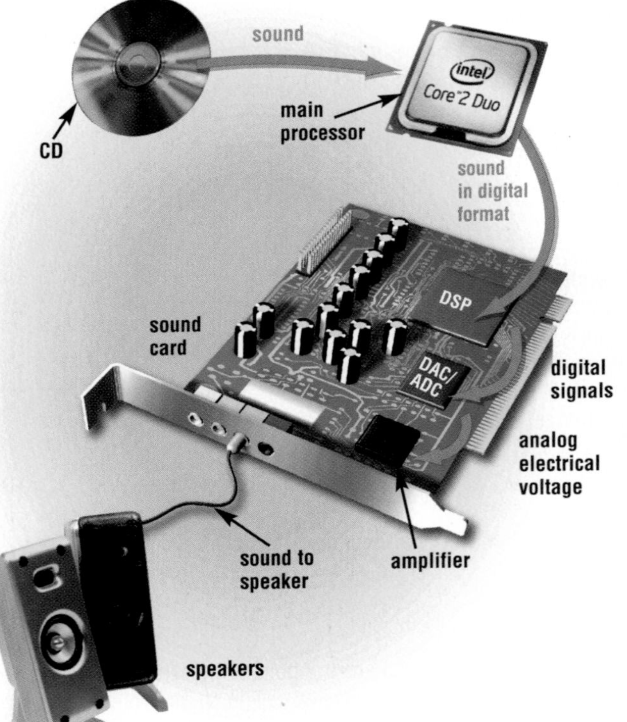

FIGURE 6-37
The path of sound from media to speakers.

After the ADC converts the analog sound through sampling, the digital data flows to the digital signal processor (DSP) on the sound card. The DSP then requests instructions from the sound card's memory chip on how to process the digital data. Typically, the DSP then compresses the digital data to save space. Finally, the DSP sends the compressed data to the computer's main processor, which stores the data in .WAV, .MP3, or other audio file format.

To play a recorded sound, such as a WAV, an MP3, or a CD track, the main processor retrieves the sound file from a hard disk, CD, or other storage device (Figure 6-37). The processor then sends the digital data to the DSP, which decompresses the data and looks to the memory chip to determine how to recreate the sound.

The DSP then sends the digital signals to the sound card's digital-to-analog converter (DAC), which converts the sound in digital format back to an analog electrical voltage. An output device, such as a speaker, uses an amplifier to strengthen the electrical voltage. This causes the speaker's cone to vibrate, recreating the sound.

All of this happens in an instant. The next time your computer beeps or chirps, consider the complex process required to make that simple sound. Then, insert your favorite CD and hear your computer come to life with the sweet music provided courtesy of the sound card. For more information, visit scsite.com/dc2008/ch6/tech and then click Sound Cards.

Companies on the Cutting Edge

HEWLETT-PACKARD
TECHNOLOGY FOR BUSINESS AND LIFE

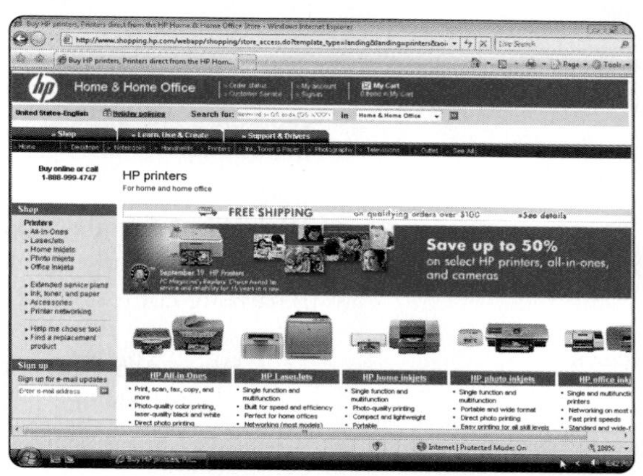

If you have printed a document recently, chances are the printer manufacturer was *Hewlett-Packard (HP)*. Market analysts estimate that 60 percent of printers sold today bear the HP logo, and HP says it ships one million printers each week.

HP is noted for a range of high-quality printers, disk storage systems, UNIX and Windows servers, and notebook, desktop, and handheld computers. The company grew to become the world's number one personal computer vendor in 2006.

William Hewlett and David Packard started the company in a one-car garage in 1939 with the goal of manufacturing test and measurement equipment. HP has been developing personal information devices, including calculators and computers, for more than 30 years. For more information, visit scsite.com/dc2008/ch6/companies and then click Hewlett-Packard.

VIEWSONIC
VISUAL TECHNOLOGY LEADER

We live in a "display-centric world" according to industry leaders at *ViewSonic*. ViewSonic's products focus on visual technology, including CRT and LCD monitors, data projectors, plasma screens, and high-definition television. The company also designs mobile products, such as Tablet PCs and wireless monitors. The company's logo consisting of three colorful Gouldian finches represent outstanding quality and value, radiant color, and crisp resolution.

President and CEO James Chu founded ViewSonic in 1987 with the goal of increasing workers' productivity while creating an ergonomically comfortable workspace. A 2006 study, commissioned by ViewSonic, found that at least 40 percent of European office workers are suffering from health, productivity, and motivation ailments from using old and poor computer equipment. For more information, visit scsite.com/dc2008/ch6/companies and then click ViewSonic.

Technology Trailblazers

STEVE JOBS
APPLE COMPUTER AND PIXAR COFOUNDER

Steve Jobs has an uncompromising drive for perfection. He helped build the first desktop personal computer, cofounded Apple Computer Corporation, marketed a revolutionary operating system, and became a millionaire all before his 35th birthday. He is a brilliant motivator and charismatic corporate leader.

Under his direction, Apple took advantage of advances in both memory and battery technology to develop the iPod, the world's most popular portable media player.

Jobs has led Pixar's award-winning animators to create some of the most beloved animated films, such as *Toy Story, Cars, A Bug's Life, Monsters, Inc.*, and *Finding Nemo*. Pixar merged with The Walt Disney Company in 2006, and Jobs now serves on Disney's board of directors. For more information, visit scsite.com/dc2008/ch6/people and then click Steve Jobs.

DONNA DUBINSKY
Palm Cofounder

PDAs are ubiquitous, partly due to the efforts of *Donna Dubinsky*. In the mid-1990s, she sensed that people wanted to own an electronic version of their paper appointment books. She and Jeff Hawkins introduced the original Palm Pilot at Palm Computing in 1996. Sales of more than two million units made the Palm Pilot the most rapidly adopted new computing product ever manufactured.

Dubinsky and Hawkins left Palm in 1998 to cofound Handspring, where they introduced several successful products, including the Treo smart phone. In 2003, Handspring merged with the Palm hardware group to create palmOne, now called Palm.

Dubinsky currently serves as CEO and chairman of Numenta, Inc., which develops computer memory. She was appointed trustee of her alma mater, Yale University, in 2006. For more information, visit scsite.com/dc2008/ch6/people and then click Donna Dubinsky.

Chapter Review

The Chapter Review section summarizes the concepts presented in this chapter. To listen to the audio version of this Chapter Review, visit scsite.com/dc2008/ch6/review. To obtain help from other students regarding any subject in this chapter, visit scsite.com/dc2008/ch6/forum and post your thoughts or questions.

1 **What Are the Four Categories of Output?** **Output** is data that has been processed into a useful form. Four categories of output are text, graphics, audio, and video. An **output device** is any hardware component that conveys information to one or more people.

2 **What Are LCD Monitors, LCD Screens, and Plasma Monitors?** LCD monitors, LCD screens, and plasma monitors are types of flat-panel displays. A *flat-panel display* is a display with a shallow depth that typically uses LCD or gas plasma technology. An **LCD** monitor is a desktop monitor that uses a liquid crystal display to produce images. A **liquid crystal display** (**LCD**) uses a liquid compound to present information on a display. A **plasma monitor** is a display device that uses gas plasma technology, which substitutes a layer of gas for the liquid crystal material in an LCD monitor. Although some game consoles include a small LCD screen (usually 5 inches or smaller), home users often prefer the larger television displays for game playing, watching movies, and browsing the Internet on a television connected to a game console.

3 **What Is a CRT Monitor, and What Factors Affect Its Quality?** A **CRT monitor** is a desktop monitor that contains a *cathode-ray tube (CRT)*. The screen on the front of the CRT is coated with tiny dots of red, green, and blue phosphor that combine to make up each *pixel*, which is a single element in an electronic image. As an electron beam inside the CRT moves back and forth across the back of the screen, the dots glow, which produces an image. The quality of a CRT monitor depends largely on its resolution, dot pitch, and refresh rate. **Resolution** is the number of horizontal and vertical pixels in a display device. *Dot pitch*, sometimes called *pixel pitch*, is the distance in millimeters between pixels on a display device. *Refresh rate* is the speed that a monitor redraws the images on the screen.

4 **How Are Graphics Chips and CRT Monitors Related?** Many CRT monitors use an analog signal to produce an image. A cable on the CRT monitor plugs in a port on the system unit, which enables communications from a graphics chip. If the graphics chip is on a video card, the card converts digital output from the computer into an analog video signal and sends the signal through a cable to the CRT monitor, which displays output on the screen.

connect
Visit scsite.com/dc2008/ch6/quiz or click the Quiz Yourself button. Click Objectives 1 – 4.

5 **What Are the Various Ways to Print?** Users can print by connecting a computer to a printer with a cable that plugs in a port on the computer. *Bluetooth printing* uses radio waves to transmit output to a printer. With *infrared* printing, a computer or other device communicates with the printer via infrared light waves. Some digital cameras connect directly to a printer via a cable; others store images on media cards that can be removed and inserted in the printer. Networked computers can communicate with the network printer via cables or wirelessly.

6 **How Is a Nonimpact Printer Different from an Impact Printer?** A **printer** is an output device that produces text and graphics on a physical medium, such as paper or transparency film. A **nonimpact printer** forms characters and graphics on a piece of paper without actually striking the paper. Commonly used nonimpact printers are ink-jet printers, photo printers, laser printers, thermal printers, mobile printers, label and postage printers, plotters, and large-format printers. An **impact printer** forms characters and graphics on a piece of paper by striking a mechanism against an inked ribbon that physically contacts the paper. Two commonly used types of impact printers are a **dot-matrix printer** and a **line printer**.

Chapter Review

(7) What Are Ink-Jet Printers, Photo Printers, Laser Printers, Thermal Printers, Mobile Printers, Label and Postage Printers, and Plotters and Large-Format Printers? An **ink-jet printer** is a type of nonimpact printer that forms characters and graphics by spraying tiny drops of liquid ink onto a piece of paper. A **photo printer** is a color printer that produces photo-lab-quality pictures. A **laser printer** is a high-speed, high-quality nonimpact printer that operates in a manner similar to a copy machine, creating images using a laser beam and powdered ink, called *toner*. A **thermal printer** generates images by pushing electrically heated pins against heat-sensitive paper. A **mobile printer** is a small, lightweight, battery-powered printer that allows a mobile user to print from a notebook computer. A **label printer** is a small printer that prints on an adhesive-type material that can be placed on a variety of items. A *postage printer* is a special type of label printer that has a built-in scale and prints postage stamps. **Plotters** are sophisticated printers used to produce high-quality drawings. A **large-format printer** uses ink-jet technology on a large scale to create photo-realistic-quality color prints.

connect
Visit scsite.com/dc2008/ch6/quiz or click the Quiz Yourself button. Click Objectives 5 – 7.

(8) How Are Speakers, Headphones, and Earphones Used? Speakers, headphones, and earphones are three commonly used audio output devices. An **audio output device** is a component of a computer that produces sound. Many personal computer users add stereo **speakers** to their computers to generate a higher-quality sound. With headphones or earphones, only the individual wearing the headphones or earphones hears the sound from the computer. The difference is that **headphones** cover or are placed outside of the ear, whereas **earphones**, or *earbuds*, rest inside the ear canal.

(9) What Are Fax Machines and Fax Modems, Multifunction Peripherals, Data Projectors, Joysticks, Wheels, and Gamepads? A **fax machine** is a device that codes and encodes documents so they can be transmitted over telephone lines. A document sent or received via a fax machine is a *fax*. Many computers include fax capability using a *fax modem*, which is a modem that allows you to send (and sometimes receive) electronic documents as faxes. A **multifunction peripheral** is a single device that looks like a copy machine but provides the functionality of a printer, scanner, copy machine, and perhaps a fax machine. A **data projector** is a device that takes the text and images displaying on a computer screen and projects them onto a larger screen so an audience of people can see the image clearly. Joysticks, wheels, and gamepads are input devices used to control actions of a player or vehicle. Today's joysticks, wheels, and gamepads also include *force feedback*, which is a technology that sends resistance to the device in response to actions of the user.

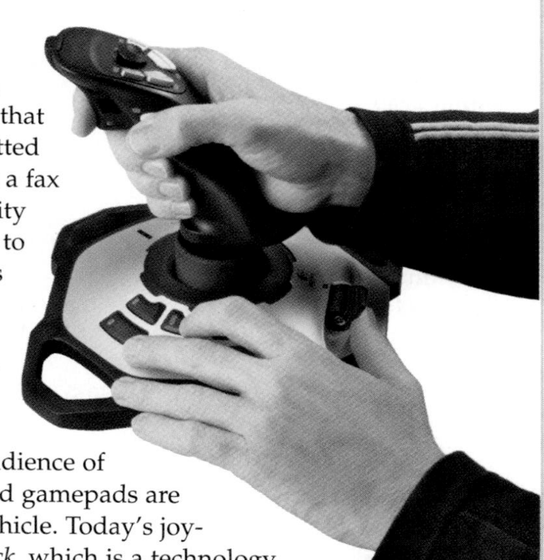

(10) What Output Options Are Available for Physically Challenged Users? Hearing-impaired users can instruct programs to display words instead of sound. With Windows Vista, visually impaired users can enlarge items on the screen and change other settings, such as increasing the size or changing the color of text to make words easier to read. Blind users can work with voice output instead of a monitor. Another alternative is a *Braille printer*, which prints information in Braille on paper.

connect
Visit scsite.com/dc2008/ch6/quiz or click the Quiz Yourself button. Click Objectives 8 – 10.

Key Terms

You should know the Primary Terms and be familiar with the Secondary Terms. Use the list below to help focus your study. To further enhance your understanding of the Key Terms in this chapter, visit scsite.com/dc2008/ch6/terms. See an example of and a definition for each term, and access current and additional information about the term from the Web.

Primary Terms

(shown in bold-black characters in the chapter)

audio output device (320)
CRT monitor (308)
data projector (323)
display device (302)
dot-matrix printer (319)
earphones (321)
ENERGY STAR program (308)
fax machine (322)
HDTV (307)
headphones (321)
impact printer (318)
ink-jet printer (312)
label printer (318)
large-format printer (318)
laser printer (315)
LCD monitor (302)
line printer (319)
liquid crystal display (LCD) (304)
mobile printer (317)
monitor (302)
multifunction peripheral (323)
nonimpact printer (312)
output (300)
output device (301)
photo printer (314)
plasma monitor (307)
plotters (318)
printer (310)
resolution (304)
speakers (320)
thermal printer (317)
voice output (321)

Secondary Terms

(shown in italic characters in the chapter)

active-matrix display (304)
all-in-one devices (323)
aspect ratio (306)
band printer (319)
bit depth (306)
Bluetooth printing (311)
Braille printer (326)
candela (305)
cathode-ray tube (CRT) (308)
color depth (306)
continuous-form paper (319)
contrast ratio (305)
digital light processing (DLP) projector (324)
digital photo printer (317)
digital television (DTV) (307)
display (302)
dot pitch (305)
dots per inch (dpi) (313)
DVI (Digital Video Interface) port (306)
dye-sublimation printer (317)
earbuds (321)
electromagnetic radiation (EMR) (308)
fax (322)
fax modem (322)
flat-panel monitor (302)
flat-panel display (302)
footprint (302)
force feedback (324)
graphics processing unit (GPU) (305)
hard copy (310)
high-definition television (307)
infrared printing (311)
Internet postage (318)
Internet telephony (322)
landscape orientation (310)
LCD projector (323)
monochrome (302)
MPR II (308)
native resolution (304)
near letter quality (NLQ) (318)
nit (305)
organic LED (OLED) (304)
page description language (PDL) (316)
passive-matrix display (304)
PCL (Printer Control Language) (316)
PictBridge (314)
pixel (304)
pixel pitch (305)
portrait orientation (310)
postage printer (318)
PostScript (316)
printout (310)
refresh rate (309)
response time (304)
satellite speakers (320)
scan rate (309)
shuttle-matrix printer (319)
soft copy (302)
subwoofer (320)
S-video port (306)
SVGA (306)
SXGA (306)
TFT (thin-film transistor) display (304)
thermal wax-transfer printer (317)
toner (316)
UXGA (306)
viewable size (308)
WQXGA (306)
WSXGA (306)
WUXGA (306)
WXGA (306)
XGA (306)

Checkpoint

Use the Checkpoint exercises to check your knowledge level of the chapter. The Beyond the Book exercises will help broaden your understanding of the concepts presented in this chapter. To complete the Checkpoint exercises interactively, visit scsite.com/dc2008/ch6/check.

Label the Figure

Identify the ports on this video card.

a. DVI port
b. standard monitor port
c. S-video port

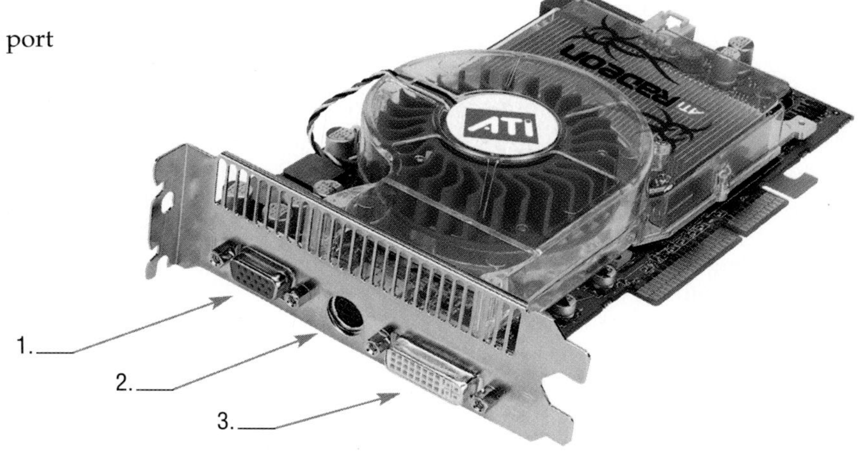

True/False

Mark T for True and F for False. (See page numbers in parentheses.)

_____ 1. A computer generates several types of output, depending on the hardware and software being used and the requirements of the user. (300)

_____ 2. Information on a display device sometimes is called soft copy. (302)

_____ 3. Most mobile computers and devices do not integrate the display and other components into the same physical case. (302)

_____ 4. The color on an active-matrix display often is not as bright as a passive-matrix display. (304)

_____ 5. LCD monitors use an analog signal to produce a picture. (306)

_____ 6. The WUXGA video standard has a higher typical resolution than the WXGA video standard. (306)

_____ 7. With game consoles, the output device often is a television. (307)

_____ 8. A printout in portrait orientation is taller than it is wide. (310)

_____ 9. With Bluetooth printing, a computer or other device transmits output to a printer via infrared light waves. (311)

_____ 10. Most photo printers are PictBridge enabled, which requires the use of a computer to print pictures. (314)

_____ 11. A laser printer is a high-speed, low-quality nonimpact printer. (315)

_____ 12. Mobile printers mainly use ink-jet, thermal, thermal wax-transfer, or dye-sublimation technology. (317)

Checkpoint

Multiple Choice

Select the best answer. (See page numbers in parentheses.)

1. Examples of text-based documents are _____. (300)
   a. drawings, clip art, and photographs
   b. home movies and live performances
   c. letters, reports, and e-mail messages
   d. music, narrations, and speeches
2. _____ uses organic molecules that produce an even brighter, easier-to-read display than standard TFT displays. (304)
   a. HDTV
   b. OLED
   c. LCD
   d. LED
3. The _____ defines a display's width relative to its height. (306)
   a. bit depth
   b. nit
   c. aspect ratio
   d. resolution
4. For a display device to show images as defined by a video standard, both the display device and the graphics processing unit must _____. (306)
   a. be the same size
   b. contain a heat sink or fan
   c. use an analog signal
   d. support the same video standard
5. Plasma monitors offer larger screens _____. (307)
   a. but poorer color than LCD monitors and are less expensive
   b. but poorer color than LCD monitors and are more expensive
   c. and richer colors than LCD monitors but are less expensive
   d. and richer colors than LCD monitors but are more expensive
6. The viewable size of a monitor is the _____ measurement of the actual viewing area provided by the screen in the monitor. (308)
   a. horizontal
   b. vertical
   c. three-dimensional
   d. diagonal
7. On a CRT monitor, the number of times the image is drawn per second is called the _____. (309)
   a. contrast ratio
   b. refresh rate
   c. bit rate
   d. response time
8. Printer resolution is measured by the number of _____ a printer can print. (313)
   a. pages per minute (ppm)
   b. pixels per inch (ppi)
   c. lines per minute (lpm)
   d. dots per inch (dpi)
9. Laser printers usually cost _____. (315)
   a. more than ink-jet printers and are faster
   b. less than ink-jet printers and are faster
   c. more than ink-jet printers and are slower
   d. less than ink-jet printers and are slower
10. The speed of a(n) _____ is measured by the number of characters per second (cps) it can print. (319)
    a. dot-matrix printer
    b. laser printer
    c. ink-jet printer
    d. thermal printer
11. Most surround sound computer speaker systems include one or two center speakers and two or more _____ that are positioned so sound emits from all directions. (320)
    a. satellite speakers
    b. subwoofers
    c. headphones
    d. none of the above
12. A(n) _____ is a device that takes the text and images displaying on a computer screen and projects them on a larger screen so an audience can see the image clearly. (323)
    a. DLP projector
    b. LCD projector
    c. data projector
    d. all of the above
13. The disadvantage of multifunction peripherals is that _____. (323)
    a. if the multifunction peripheral breaks down, all functions are lost
    b. they require more space than having separate devices
    c. they are significantly more expensive than purchasing each device separately
    d. all of the above
14. A(n) _____ uses tiny mirrors to reflect light, which produces crisp, bright, colorful images that remain in focus and can be seen clearly even in a well-lit room. (324)
    a. plasma monitor
    b. LCD projector
    c. CRT
    d. digital light processing projector

Checkpoint

Matching

Match the terms with their definitions. (See page numbers in parentheses.)

_____ 1. soft copy (302)
_____ 2. LCD monitor (302)
_____ 3. nit (305)
_____ 4. candela (305)
_____ 5. dot pitch (305)
_____ 6. ENERGY STAR program (308)
_____ 7. hard copy (310)
_____ 8. nonimpact printer (312)
_____ 9. LCD projector (323)
_____ 10. force feedback (324)

a. information on a display device that exists electronically and appears for a temporary period
b. technology that sends resistance to a device in response to actions of the user
c. distance in millimeters between pixels on a display device
d. unit of visible light intensity equal to one candela per square meter
e. forms characters and graphics on a piece of paper without actually striking the paper
f. standard unit of luminous intensity
g. attaches directly to a computer and uses its own light source to display information
h. changes the brightness and contrast of pixels surrounding each letter
i. encourages manufacturers to create energy-efficient devices that require little power when they are not in use
j. a desktop monitor that uses a liquid crystal display to produce images
k. uses many shades of gray from white to black to enhance the quality of graphics
l. printed information that exists physically and is a more permanent form of output

Short Answer

Write a brief answer to each of the following questions.

1. What determines the quality of an LCD monitor or LCD screen? ____________ What are the differences between active-matrix and passive-matrix displays? ____________
2. What type of monitor emits electromagnetic radiation? ____________ What can you do to protect yourself from electromagnetic radiation from a monitor? ____________
3. How is portrait orientation different from landscape orientation? ____________ What is continuous-form paper? ____________
4. What are two types of wireless printing technology? ____________ How do they differ in how they communicate with a computer or other device? ____________
5. How does an ink-jet printer work? ____________ What are the differences between dye-sublimation printers used by professionals as compared to home or small business users? ____________

Beyond the Book

Read the following book elements, learn more about each using the Web, and then write a brief report.

1. Ethics & Issues — Should Companies Prohibit Consumers from Refilling Ink Cartridges? (314), Who Is Responsible for Stopping Counterfeiting? (315), Should Colleges Provide Free Access to Music for Students? (321), or Should Web Sites Be Held Accountable for Accessibility Levels for Physically Challenged People? (327)
2. Career Corner — Graphic Designer/Illustrator (327)
3. Companies on the Cutting Edge — Hewlett-Packard or ViewSonic (329)
4. FAQs (302, 303, 306, 308, 309, 315, 316, 324)
5. High-Tech Talk — Sound Cards: Bringing Your Computer to Life (328)
6. Looking Ahead — Rollable Displays Lock and Roll (304), or Ultra HDTV Puts Viewers in the Picture (324)
7. Making Use of the Web — Government (122)
8. Picture Yourself Saving Time and Money Using a Computer (298)
9. Technology Trailblazers — Steve Jobs and Donna Dubinsky (329)
10. Web Links (304, 306, 311, 314, 316, 321, 322, 323, 324)

Learn It Online

Use the Learn It Online exercises to reinforce your understanding of the chapter concepts. To access the Learn It Online exercises, visit scsite.com/dc2008/ch6/learn.

1 At the Movies — Plasma vs. LCD

To view the SID: Size Matters movie, click the number 1 button. Locate your video and click the corresponding High-Speed or Dial-Up link, depending on your Internet connection. Watch the movie and then complete the exercise by answering the question that follows. A 100-inch HD screen and a dual-image screen are displayed at a technology trade show exhibit showing the use of two-way viewing. What is two-way viewing? List one possible application and one drawback to this new technology.

2 Video and Audio: You Review It — HDTV

In this chapter you learned about HDTV. Click the number 2 button to view the suggested links and begin your search for videos, podcasts, or vodcasts related to HDTV. Choose a video, podcast, or vodcast that discusses HDTV and is of interest to you, and then write a description of its contents. Explain why you chose this piece, what you liked about it, what you disliked about it, and whether you would recommend it to a fellow student. Finish your review by giving the video, podcast, or vodcast a rating of 1 – 5 stars. Submit your review in the format requested by your instructor.

3 Student Edition Labs — Peripheral Devices

Click the number 3 button. A new browser window will open, displaying the Student Edition Labs. Follow the on-screen instructions to complete the Peripheral Devices Lab. When finished, click the Exit button. If required, submit your results to your instructor.

4 Student Edition Labs — Working with Graphics

Click the number 4 button. A new browser window will open, displaying the Student Edition Labs. Follow the on-screen instructions to complete the Working with Graphics Lab. When finished, click the Exit button. If required, submit your results to your instructor.

5 Practice Test

Click the number 5 button. Answer each question. When completed, enter your name and click the Grade Test button to submit the quiz for grading. Make a note of any missed questions. If required, submit your results to your instructor.

6 Who Wants To Be a Computer Genius^2?

Click the number 6 button to find out if you are a computer genius. Directions about how to play the game will be displayed. When you are ready to play, click the Play button. Submit your score to your instructor.

7 Wheel of Terms

Click the number 7 button to reinforce important terms you learned in this chapter by playing the Shelly Cashman Series version of this popular game. Directions about how to play the game will be displayed. When you are ready to play, click the Play button. Submit your score to your instructor.

Learn It Online

(8) DC Track and Field

Click the number 8 button to use what you have learned in this chapter to compete against other students in three track and field events. Directions about how to play the game will be displayed. When you are ready to play, click the start first event button. If required, submit your score to your instructor.

(9) You're Hired!

Click the number 9 button to use what you have learned in this chapter to embark on the path to a career in computers. Directions about how to play the game will be displayed. When you are ready to play, click the begin game button. If required, submit your score to your instructor.

(10) Crossword Puzzle Challenge

Click the number 10 button, then click the Crossword Puzzle Challenge link. Directions about how to play the game will be displayed. Complete the puzzle to reinforce skills you learned in this chapter. When you are ready to play, click the Continue button. Submit the completed puzzle to your instructor.

(11) Vista Exercises

Click the number 11 button. When the Vista Exercises menu appears, click the exercise assigned by your instructor. A new browser window will open. Follow the on-screen instructions to complete the exercise. When finished, click the Exit button. If required, submit your results to your instructor.

(12) Choosing a Printer

The printer is a key component of any new personal computer that you purchase. Whether you are printing black-and-white reports or producing photo-lab-quality pictures, determining which printer is best for your individual needs requires some research. Printers are available in a range of speeds and capabilities. Click the number 12 button for a tutorial about how to select the printer that is best for your particular requirements.

(13) In the News

Display device technology continues to advance. Not long ago, computer users would have considered connecting their $1,000 computers to a color television instead of paying outrageous prices for a color monitor. Today, you can purchase a 20-inch monitor that is faster and sharper than that color television for less than $300. Yet, as prices fall, consumers surely will purchase the display devices for HDTV and crystal-clear Internet access. Click the number 13 button and then read a news article about a new or improved output device. What is the device? Who manufactures it? How is the output device better than, or different from, earlier devices? Who do you think is most likely to use the device? Why?

(14) Chapter Discussion Forum

Select an objective from this chapter on page 299 about which you would like more information. Click the number 14 button and post a short message listing a meaningful message title accompanied by one or more questions concerning the selected objective. In two days, return to the threaded discussion by clicking the number 14 button. Submit to your instructor your original message and at least one response to your message.

(15) Howstuffworks.com

Click the number 15 button to learn how to use Howstuffworks.com to discover how a laser printer works in comparison to an ink-jet printer. Follow the instructions to display the computer peripherals page. Read the articles about how both types of printers work. Write a report listing the major differences between the printers. Which type of printer would you recommend to your fellow students? Why? Print your report and submit it to your instructor.

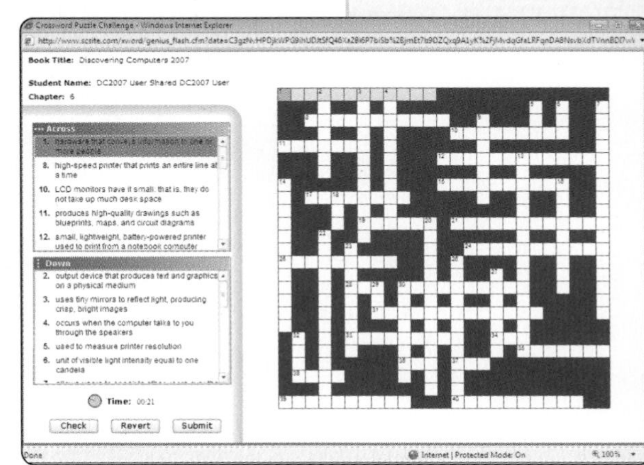

Quizzes and Learning Games
Computer Genius
Crossword Puzzle
DC Track and Field
Practice Test
Quiz Yourself
Wheel of Terms
You're Hired!

Exercises
Case Studies
Chapter Review
Checkpoint
Key Terms
Learn How To
Learn It Online
Web Research

Beyond the Book
Career Corner
Companies
FAQs
High-Tech Talk
Looking Ahead
Making Use of the Web
Trailblazers
Web Links

Features
Chapter Forum
Install Computer
Lab Exercises
Maintain Computer
Tech News
Timeline 2008

Learn How To

Use the Learn How To activities to learn fundamental skills when using a computer and accompanying technology. Complete the exercises and submit them to your instructor. To see a video of a Learn How To activity, visit scsite.com/dc2008/ch6/howto.

LEARN HOW TO 1: Adjust the Sound on a Computer

Every computer today contains a sound card and associated hardware and software that allow you to play and record sound. You can adjust the sound by completing the following steps:

1. Click the Start button on the Windows taskbar and then click Control Panel on the Start menu to display the Control Panel window.
2. Click Hardware and Sound and then click Adjust the system volume to display the Volume Mixer dialog box (Figure 6-38).
3. To adjust the volume for all devices connected to the sound card, drag the Device Volume slider down or up to decrease or increase the volume.
4. If you want to mute the sound on the computer, click the Mute button so it contains a red x, and then click the Close button on the title bar.
5. If you want to remove the volume icon from the notification area on the Windows taskbar, right-click an empty area on the Windows taskbar and then click Properties to display the Taskbar and Start Menu Properties dialog box. Click the Notification Area tab, click the Volume check box to remove the checkmark, and then click the OK button or the Apply button. You can click the icon on the taskbar to set the volume level or mute the sound.
6. To make sound and other adjustments for each device on the computer, click the Manage audio devices link on the Hardware and Sound page of the Control Panel to display the Sound dialog box, and then click the Properties button to display the Speakers Properties dialog box.
7. Click the Levels tab to display the volume controls (Figure 6-39).
8. To adjust volumes, drag the Volume Control slider left or right for each device. To adjust the speaker balance, click the Balance button to display the Balance dialog box (Figure 6-40), drag the Balance sliders, and then click the OK button.

FIGURE 6-38

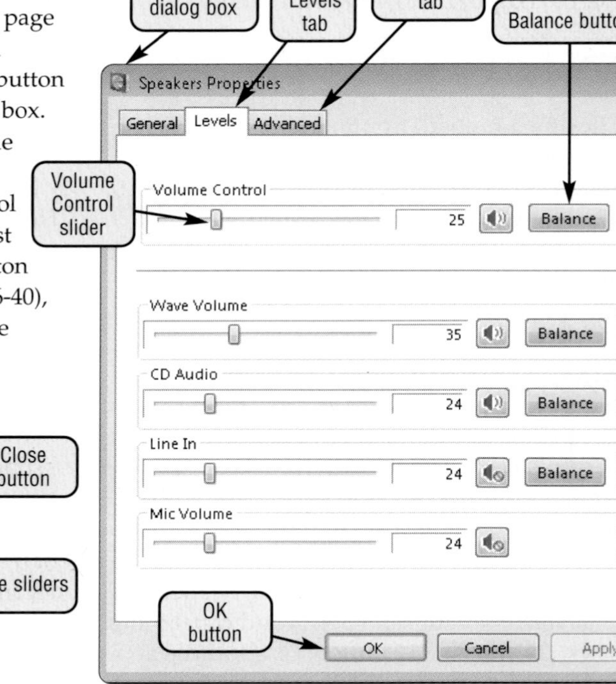

FIGURE 6-39

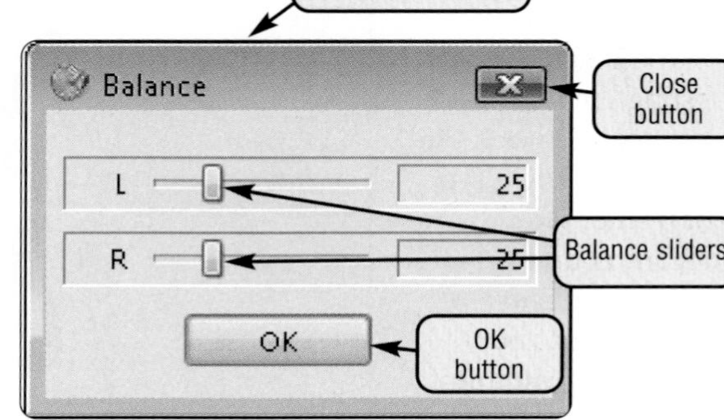

FIGURE 6-40

9. If you click the Advanced tab in the Speakers Properties dialog box, you can control the sample rate and bit depth by using the drop-down list in the Default Format area of the Speakers Properties dialog box.

Exercise

1. Open the Control Panel window, click Hardware and Sound, and then click the Manage audio devices link to display the Sound dialog box. What kind of sound card is on the computer? Click the Place volume icon in the taskbar check box and then click the Apply button. What change did you notice on the Windows taskbar? Do the same thing again. What change occurred on the Windows taskbar? Click Speakers, click the Properties button, and then click the Levels tab. What volumes are you able to control? How would you change the balance? How do you hide the Volume icon from the Notification Area on the Windows taskbar? Submit your answers to your instructor.

LEARN HOW TO 2: Control Printing on Your Computer

When you print using a computer, you control printing at two different points: first, before the printing actually begins, and second, after the document has been sent to the printer and either is physically printing or is waiting to be printed. To set the parameters for printing and then print the document, complete the following steps:

1. Click File on the menu bar of the program that will be used for printing and then click Print on the File menu to display the Print dialog box (Figure 6-41). The Print dialog box will vary somewhat depending on the program used.
2. In the Print dialog box, make the selections for what printer will be used, what pages will be printed, the number of copies to be printed, and any other choices available. For further options, click the Preferences button (or, sometimes, the Properties button) or click the Options button.
3. Click the OK button or the Print button. The document being printed is sent to a print queue, which is an area on disk storage from which documents actually are printed.

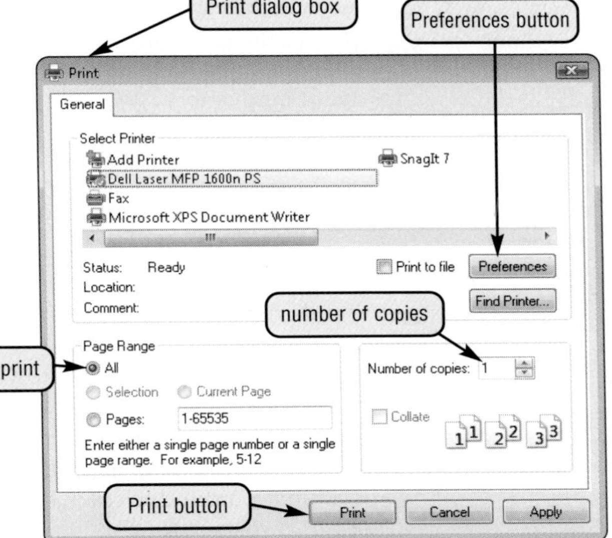

FIGURE 6-41

When you click the Print button to send the document to the print queue, a printer icon may appear on the Windows taskbar. To see the print queue and control the actual printing of documents on the printer, complete the following steps:

1. If the printer icon appears on the Windows taskbar, double-click it; otherwise, click the Start button on the Windows taskbar, click Control Panel on the Start menu, click the Printers link, and then double-click the printer icon with the checkmark. The checkmark indicates the default printer. A window opens with the name of the printer on the title bar. All documents either printing or waiting to be printed are listed in the window. The Status column indicates whether the document is printing or waiting. In addition, the owner of the file, number of pages, size, date and time submitted, and printer port are listed.
2. If you click Printer on the menu bar in the printer window, you can set printing preferences from the Printer menu. In addition, you can pause all printing and cancel all printing jobs from the Printer menu.
3. If you select a document in the document list and then click Document on the menu bar, you can cancel the selected document for printing, or you can pause the printing for the selected document. To continue printing for the selected document, click Document on the menu bar and then click Resume on the Document menu.

Exercise

1. Start WordPad from the Accessories list. Type `Click Print on the File menu to display the Print dialog box.`
2. Display the Print dialog box and then click the Preferences button. What choices do you have in the Layout sheet? Close the Printing Preferences dialog box. How do you select the number of copies you want to print? How would you print pages 25–35 of a document? Submit your answers to your instructor.

Web Research

Use the Internet-based Web Research exercises to broaden your understanding of the concepts presented in this chapter. Visit scsite.com/dc2008/ch6/research to obtain more information pertaining to each exercise. To discuss any of the Web Research exercises in this chapter with other students, post your thoughts or questions at scsite.com/dc2008/ch6/forum.

1 Scavenger Hunt Use one of the search engines listed in Figure 2-10 in Chapter 2 on page 78 or your own favorite search engine to find the answers to the questions below. Copy and paste the Web address from the Web page where you found the answer. Some questions may have more than one answer. If required, submit your answers to your instructor. (1) Who invented the liquid crystal display? (2) What company introduced acoustic waveguide technology? What problem did it solve? (3) What is the current cost of a surround sound computer speaker system? (4) What is an ambient light sensor on a monitor? (5) What company introduced the first laser printer?

2 Search Sleuth Some search engines use computers to index the World Wide Web automatically, so they generally find more Web sites than human indexers can catalog. One of the most aggressive automatic, or robot, search engines is AltaVista (altavista.com), which attempts to catalog the entire World Wide Web. AltaVista also developed Babel Fish, the Web's first Internet machine translation service. Visit this Web site and then use your word processing program to answer the following questions. Then, if required, submit your answers to your instructor. (1) Click the About AltaVista link and then click the Search link. Scroll down and then read the information about innovations. What languages are translated by Babel Fish? (2) Click your browser's Back button or press the BACKSPACE key twice to return to the AltaVista home page. Click the Babel Fish Translation link. In addition to a block of text, what else can Babel Fish translate? (3) Click the Tools link at the top of the page. Click the Converter link. Read the information about AltaVista shortcuts. Click the Temperature link. Click the example. How many degrees Celsius does 32 degrees Fahrenheit equal? (4) Click the Advanced Search link. Click the Help link and read the information on using the Query Builder and the Free-form Boolean query. Summarize the information you read and then write a 50-word summary that may be submitted to your instructor.

3 Journaling Respond to your readings in this chapter by writing at least one page about your reactions, evaluations, and reflections about using output devices. For example, what is most important to you when buying a printer? Do you use more than one printer for different purposes, such as printing photos taken with a digital camera, or do you use a multifunction peripheral that combines output devices in one unit? Do you use headphones or earphones for listening to music or other voice output? Where would you dispose of old monitors? You also can write about the new terms you learned by reading this chapter. If required, submit your journal to your instructor.

4 Expanding Your Understanding If you are using a Tablet PC and your coworker is using a PDA, it is cumbersome to transfer files from one device to the other. Engineers are developing digital pens that might ease the file exchange process. Using this special pen, one user can select a file on his computer and then place the pen on the other user's computer to transfer the file. Other digital pens allow users to write or draw and then retrieve all the handwritten information on a computer. Visit a local electronics store or Web site to learn more about digital pens. Compare their features, cost, file transfer process, and warranty. Write a report summarizing your findings, focusing on comparing and contrasting the digital pens. If required, submit your report to your instructor.

5 Ethics in Action Internet addiction disorder (IAD) may be affecting some Internet users. People claim to be addicted when they spend up to 10 hours a day online, they occasionally binge for extended Internet sessions, and they suffer withdrawal symptoms when they have not been online for some time. "Netomania" is not a recognized disorder, however, and some researchers believe the Internet problem is just a symptom of other psychiatric disorders, such as manic-depression. View online sites that provide information about IAD, including the Center for Online and Internet Addiction (netaddiction.com). Write a report summarizing your findings and include a table of links to Web sites that provide additional details. If required, submit your report to your instructor.

Case Studies

Use the Case Studies to apply the concepts presented in the chapter to real-world situations. Visit scsite.com/dc2008/ch6/cases to obtain more information pertaining to each exercise. To discuss the Case Studies in this chapter with other students, visit scsite.com/dc2008/ch6/forum and post your thoughts or questions.

Case Study 1 — Class Discussion Several of the administrative assistants in your company say they need larger monitors. They claim the small monitors they use now are hard on their eyes and that larger, clearer monitors would help with their efficiency. Your boss wants you to explore the use of **widescreen monitors** versus side-by-side monitors. Use the Web and/or print media to compare the costs associated with each setup. What would be the advantages of having side-by-side monitors? Write a brief report to your boss summarizing your recommendations. Be prepared to discuss your recommendations in class.

Case Study 2 — Class Discussion Your company currently uses ink-jet printers for printing color documents and photos. Your manager is tired of frequently ordering replacement ink cartridges and thinks that it may be time to upgrade to **color laser printers**. He knows the initial costs of the laser printers will be high, but he thinks the quality of the printout and the longevity of the printer cartridges will offset that initial cost. He wants you to submit a report summarizing the long-term costs associated with both types of printers. Be sure to include the average number of copies each printer can produce before changing cartridges. Be prepared to discuss your findings in class.

Case Study 3 — Research Printing requirements vary greatly among users. The local insurance agency where you are employed part time is shopping for a **printer**. The owner is aware that you are taking a computer class and has asked you to assist her in making a decision on what printer to buy. Figure 6-12 on page 310 lists several questions that should be considered when choosing a printer. Use what you learned in class to answer the questions posed in Figure 6-12. Answer each question according to what you believe to be your employer's needs. Then, use the Web and/or print media to find at least two printers that fit the requirements. List the name of each printer and note their advantages and disadvantages. Which of the two printers would you buy? Why? Prepare a report and/or PowerPoint presentation and share your findings with your class.

Case Study 4 — Research While printers produce an image on a page from top to bottom, **plotters** can draw on any part of a page at random, and then move on to any other part. This capability, coupled with their capacity to use large sheets of paper, makes plotters particularly valuable to people who produce maps or blueprints. A local engineering firm that has used hand drawings for the past 50 years has hired you to assist them in purchasing three 42-inch plotters with a maximum print length of 300 feet and at least 1200 × 600 dpi. What is the advantage or disadvantage of using a plotter compared to simply creating a drawing by hand? Use the Web and/or print media to research both the initial and recurring costs of plotters that meet the stated requirements from three different manufacturers. Include in your research how long each plotter takes to produce an image and other noteworthy information. Prepare a report and/or PowerPoint presentation summarizing your findings.

Case Study 5 — Team Challenge Three accountants at the company you work for want to go off on their own and set up a small accounting office with approximately 20 to 25 employees. They have hired your group as consultants to help with the setup. The goal is to determine the type of output devices you think they will need within the office. Consider the types and number of printers, types and number of display devices, **audio devices**, microphones, LCD projectors, considerations for the physically challenged, and whether fax machines, fax modems, and/or multifunction peripherals are needed. Form a three-member team and assign each team member one or more categories of output devices. Have the team members use the Web and/or print media to research their assignments. Combine your findings in a table listing the advantages and disadvantages of the various devices, your team's recommendations, and a short explanation of why the team selected each device. Share your findings with your class.

Digital Imaging and Video Technology

Everywhere you look, people are capturing moments they want to remember. They take pictures or make movies of their vacations, birthday parties, activities, accomplishments, sporting events, weddings, and more. Because of the popularity of digital cameras and digital video cameras, increasingly more people desire to capture their memories digitally, instead of on film. With digital technology, photographers have the ability to modify and share the digital images and videos they create. When you use special hardware and/or software, you can copy, manipulate, print, and distribute digital images and videos using your personal computer and the Internet. Amateurs can achieve professional quality results by using more sophisticated hardware and software.

digital camera (input)

FireWire or USB 2.0

digital video camera (input)

television (output)

FIGURE 1 The top portion of the figure shows a typical home digital imaging setup, and the lower portion of the figure shows a typical home setup for editing personal video.

Digital photography and recordings deliver significant benefits over film-based photography and movie making. With digital cameras, no developing is needed. Instead, the images reside on storage media such as a hard disk, DVD, or flash memory card. Unlike film, storage media can be reused, which reduces costs, saves time, and provides immediate results. Digital technology allows greater control over the creative process, both while taking pictures and video and in the editing process. You can check results immediately after capturing a picture or video to determine whether it meets your expectations. If you are dissatisfied with a picture or video, you can erase it and recapture it, again and again.

As shown in the top portion of Figure 1, a digital camera functions as an input device when it transmits pictures through a cable to a personal computer via a USB port or FireWire port. Using a digital camera in this way allows you to edit the pictures, save them on storage media, and print them on a photographic-quality printer via a USB port or FireWire port.

The lower portion of Figure 1 illustrates how you might use a digital video camera with a personal computer. The process typically is the same for most digital video cameras. You capture the images or video with the video camera. Next, you connect the video camera to your personal computer using a FireWire or USB 2.0 port, or you place the storage media used on the camera in the computer. The video then is copied or downloaded to the computer's hard disk. Then, you can edit the video using video editing software. If desired, you can preview the video during the editing process on a television. Finally, you save the finished result to the desired media, such as a DVD+RW or, perhaps, e-mail the edited video or post it to a media sharing Web site. In this example, a DVD player also can be used to input video from a DVD.

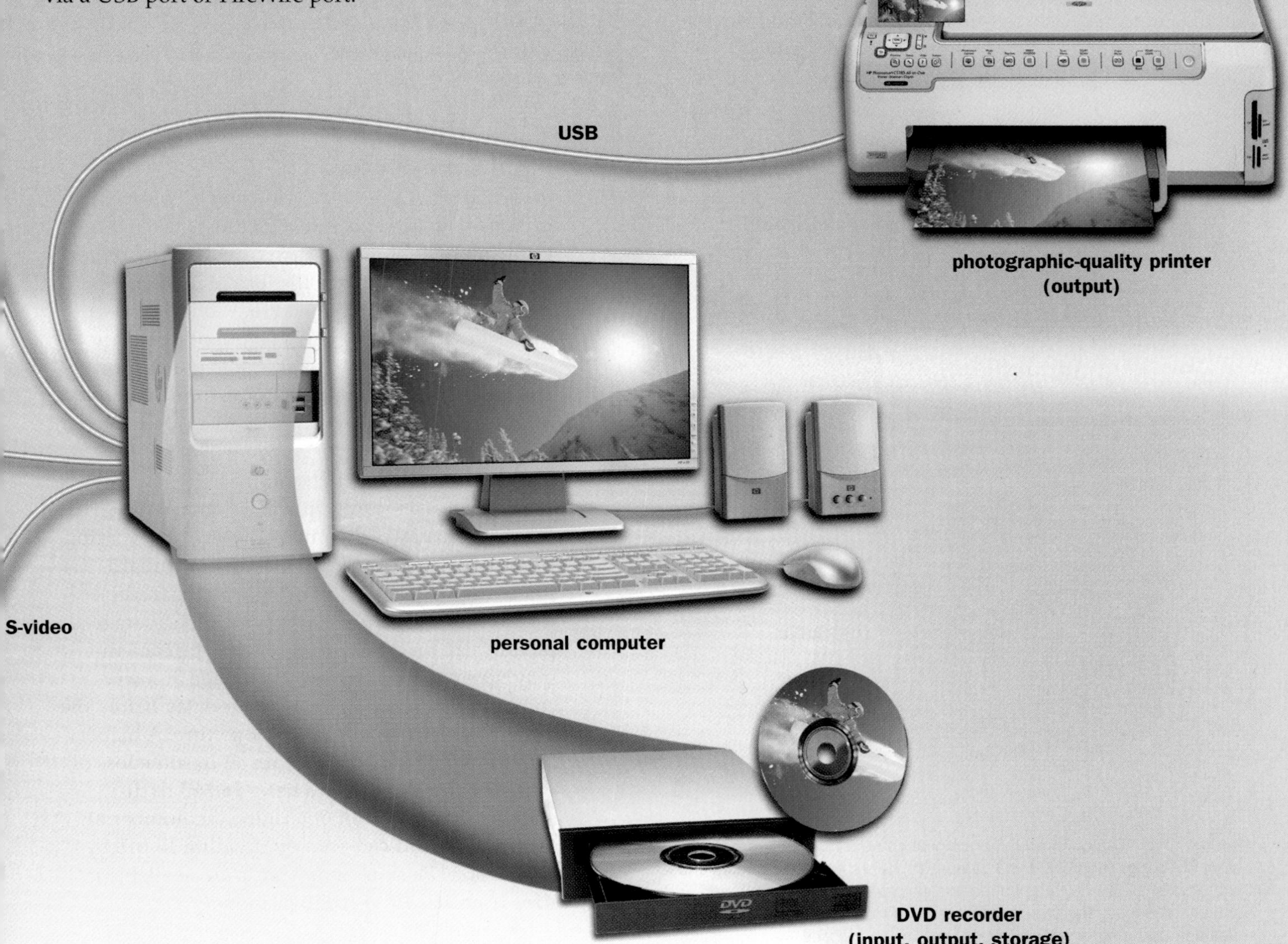

DIGITAL IMAGING TECHNOLOGY

Digital imaging technology involves capturing and manipulating still photographic images in an electronic format. The following sections outline the steps involved in the process of using digital imaging technology.

1 Select a Digital Camera

A **digital camera** is a type of camera that stores photographed images electronically instead of on traditional film. Digital cameras are divided into three categories (Figure 2) based mainly on image resolution, features, and of course, price. The image resolution is measured in pixels (short for picture element). The image quality increases with the number of pixels. The image resolution usually is measured in **megapixels** (million of pixels), often abbreviated as **MP**. Features of digital cameras include red-eye reduction, zoom, autofocus, flash, self-timer, and manual mode for fine-tuning settings. Figure 3 summarizes the three categories of digital cameras.

(a) point-and-shoot

(b) field

(c) studio

FIGURE 2 The point-and-shoot digital camera (a) requires no adjustments before shooting. The field digital camera (b) offers improved quality and features that allow you to make manual adjustments before shooting and use a variety of lenses. The studio digital camera (c) offers better color and resolution and greater control over exposure and lenses.

TYPES OF DIGITAL CAMERAS

Type	Resolution Range	Features	Price
Point-and-shoot cameras	Less than 6 MP	Fully automatic; fits in your pocket; easy to use; ideal for average consumer usage.	Less than $450
Field cameras	Greater than 7 MP	Used by photojournalists; portable but flexible; provides ability to change lenses and use other attachments; great deal of control over exposure and other photo settings.	$450 to $2,000
Studio cameras	Greater than 8 MP	Stationary camera used for professional studio work; flexible; widest range of lenses and settings.	$1,500 and up

FIGURE 3 Digital cameras often are categorized by image resolution, features, and price.

2 Take Pictures

Digital cameras provide you with several options that are set before a picture is taken. Three of the more important options are the resolution, compression, and image file format in which the camera should save the picture. While a camera may allow for a very high resolution for a large print, you may choose to take a picture at a lower resolution if the image does not require great detail or must be a small size. For example, you may want to use the image on a Web page where smaller image file sizes are beneficial.

Compression results in smaller image file sizes. Figure 4 illustrates the image file sizes for varying resolutions and compressions under standard photographic conditions using a 6-megapixel digital camera. Figure 4 also shows the average picture size for a given resolution. The camera may take more time to save an image at lower compression, resulting in a longer delay before the camera is ready to take another picture. A higher compression, however, may result in some loss of image quality. If a camera has a 16 MB flash memory card, you can determine the number of pictures the card can hold by dividing 16 MB by the file size. Flash memory cards are available in sizes from 16 MB to 16 GB or more.

Most digital cameras also allow you to choose an image file format. Two popular file formats are TIFF and JPEG. The **TIFF** file format saves the image uncompressed. All of the image detail is captured and stored, but the file sizes can be large. The **JPEG** file format is compressed. The resolution of the image may be the same as a TIFF file, but some detail may be lost in the image.

Finally, before you take the photograph, you should choose the type of media on which to store the resulting image file. Some cameras allow for a choice of media to which you can store the image, such as a CompactFlash card or Memory Stick, while others allow for only one type of storage media. One major advantage of a digital camera is that you easily can erase pictures from its media, freeing up space for new pictures.

IMAGE FILE SIZE WITH A SIX MEGAPIXEL DIGITAL CAMERA

Resolution in Pixels	COMPRESSION Low	COMPRESSION Medium	COMPRESSION High	Picture Size in Inches
	Resulting Image File Size			
3000 × 2000	8.9 MB	3.3 MB	780 KB	16 × 20
2272 × 1704	2 MB	1.1 MB	556 KB	11 × 17
1600 × 1200	1 MB	558 KB	278 KB	8 × 10
1024 × 768	570 KB	320 KB	170 KB	4 × 6

FIGURE 4 Image file sizes for varying resolutions and compressions under standard photographic conditions using a 6-megapixel digital camera.

3 Transfer and Manage Image Files

The method of transferring images from the camera to the personal computer differs greatly depending on the capabilities of both. Digital cameras use a variety of storage media (Figure 5). If your camera uses a flash memory card such as CompactFlash, Memory Stick, SmartMedia, xD Picture card, or Secure Digital (SD), you can remove the media from the camera and place it in a slot on the personal computer or in a device, such as a card reader, connected to the personal computer. Your camera or card reader also may connect to the personal computer using a USB, USB 2.0, or FireWire (Figure 6) port. Some personal computers include an internal card reader. When you insert the memory card or connect the camera, software on the personal computer guides you through the process of transferring the images to the hard disk. Some operating systems and software recognize a memory card or camera as though it is another hard disk on the computer. This feature allows you to access the files, navigate them, and then copy, delete, or rename the files while the media still is in the camera.

After you transfer the files to the hard disk on your personal computer, you should organize the files by sorting them or renaming them so that information, such as the subject, date, time, and purpose, is saved along with the image. Finally, before altering the images digitally or using the images for other purposes, you should back up the images to another location, such as a CD or DVD, so the original image is recoverable.

FIGURE 5 SD Cards, CompactFlash Cards, and xD Picture Cards are popular storage devices for digital cameras.

FIGURE 6 Using a USB or FireWire connection, you can add a card reader to your personal computer.

4 Edit Images

Image editing software allows you to edit digital images. You should edit a copy, not the original image file, so that you always have the original file to use as a backup or for other editing projects. The following list summarizes the more common image enhancements or alterations:

- Adjust the contrast and brightness; correct lighting problems; or help give the photograph a particular feeling, such as warm or stark.
- Remove red-eye.
- Crop an image to remove unnecessary elements and resize it.
- Rotate the image to change its orientation.
- Add elements to the image, such as descriptive text, a date, a logo, or decorative items; create collages or add missing elements.
- Replace individual colors with a new color.
- Add special effects, such as texture, motion blurring or reflections to enhance the image.
- Add aging to make the image appear as it was taken a long time ago.

Some popular image editing programs are Adobe Photoshop, Microsoft Digital Image Suite, and Corel Paint Shop Pro Photo. Figure 7 shows some of the effects available in Corel Paint Shop Pro X on the Artistic Effects submenu.

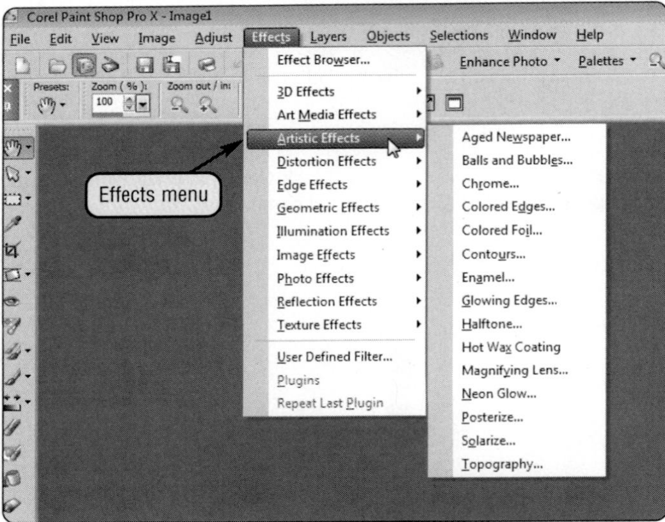

FIGURE 7 The capability of applying effects separates digital photography from film photography.

5 Print Images

Once an image is altered digitally, it is ready to be printed. You can print images on a personal color printer or send them to a professional service that specializes in digital photo printing.

When printing the images yourself, make sure that the resolution used to create the image was high enough for the size of the print you want to create. For example, if the camera used a resolution of 640 × 480 pixels, then the ideal print size is a wallet size. If you print such an image at a size of 8 × 10 inches, then the image will appear **pixilated**, or blurry. Use high-quality photo paper for the best results. A photo printer gives the best results when printing digital photography.

Many services print digital images, either over the Internet or through traditional photo developing locations and kiosks (Figure 8), such as those found in drug stores or shopping marts. Some services allow you to e-mail or upload the files to the service, specify the size, quality, and quantity of print; and then receive the finished prints via the postal service. Other services allow you to drop off flash memory cards or CD-ROMs at a photo shop and later pick up the prints, just as you do with traditional photo developing shops.

FIGURE 8 A kiosk allows you to print digital images in high resolution on photo paper.

6 Distribute Images Electronically

Rather than printing images, you often need to use the images electronically. Depending on the electronic use of the image, the image may require additional processing. If you use the images on a Web site or want to e-mail a photo, you probably want to send a lower-resolution image. Image editing software allows you to lower the resolution of the image, resulting in a smaller file size. Some photo sharing Web sites automatically will change the resolution of your photos for you. You also should use standard file formats when distributing an electronic photo. The JPEG format is viewable using most personal computers or Web browsers. Some online services allow you to upload and share your photos free of charge and will automatically change your photos to a lower resolution and JPEG format.

You can store very high resolution photos on a DVD or a CD. **DVD and CD mastering software** allows you to create slide show presentations on a recordable DVD or CD that can play in many home DVD players or personal computer DVD drives. Photo sharing Web sites, such as Fotki and Flickr (Figure 9), allow you to share your photos with acquaintances or with the whole world. You also can search for and view photos of others.

Finally, you should back up and store images that you distribute electronically with the same care as you store your traditional film negatives.

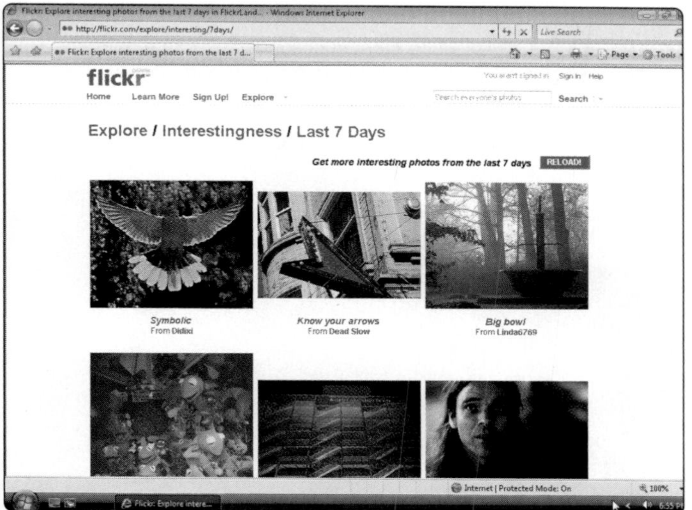

FIGURE 9 The Flickr photo sharing Web site allows you to share your photos, organize your photos, and search for photos.

DIGITAL VIDEO TECHNOLOGY

Digital video technology allows you to input, edit, manage, publish, and share your videos using a personal computer. With digital video technology, you can transform home videos into Hollywood-style movies by enhancing the videos with scrolling titles and transitions, cutting out or adding scenes, and adding background music and voice-over narration. The following sections outline the steps involved in the process of using digital video technology.

1 Select a Video Camera

Video cameras record in either analog or digital format. **Analog formats** include 8mm, Hi8, VHS-C, and Super VHS-C. **Digital formats** include Mini-DV, MICROMV, Digital8, DVD, and HDV (high-definition video format). Digital video cameras fall into three general categories: high-end consumer, consumer, and webcasting and monitoring (Figure 10). Consumer digital video cameras are by far the most popular type among consumers. High-end consumer models may support the HDV high-definition standard. Others may allow you to record directly on a DVD disc. A video recorded in high-definition can be played back on a high-definition display. Digital video cameras provide more features than analog video cameras, such as a higher level of zoom, better sound, or greater control over color and lighting.

FIGURE 10 The high-end consumer digital video camera (a) can produce professional-grade results. The consumer digital video camera (b) produces amateur-grade results. The webcasting and monitoring digital video camera (c) is appropriate for webcasting and security monitoring.

2 Record a Video

Most video cameras provide you with a choice of recording programs, which sometimes are called automatic settings. Each recording program includes a different combination of camera settings, so you can adjust the exposure and other functions to match the recording environment. Usually, several different programs are available, such as point-and-shoot, point-and-shoot with manual adjustment, sports, portrait, spotlit scenes, and low light. You also have the ability to select special digital effects, such as fade, wipe, and black and white. If you are recording outside on a windy day, then you can enable the wind screen to prevent wind noise. If you are recording home videos or video meant for a Web site, then the point-and-shoot recording program is sufficient.

3 Transfer and Manage Videos

After recording the video, the next step is to transfer the video to your personal computer. Most video cameras connect directly to a USB 2.0 or FireWire port on your personal computer (Figure 11). Transferring video with a digital camera is easy, because the video already is in a digital format that the computer can recognize.

An analog camcorder or VCR requires additional hardware to convert the analog signals to a digital format before the video can be manipulated on a personal computer. The additional hardware includes a special video capture card using a standard RCA video cable or an S-video cable (Figure 12). *S-video* cables provide sharper images and greater overall quality. When you use video capture hardware with an analog video, be sure to close all open programs on your computer because capturing video requires a great deal of processing power.

FIGURE 11 A digital video camera is connected to the personal computer via a FireWire or USB 2.0 port. No additional hardware is needed.

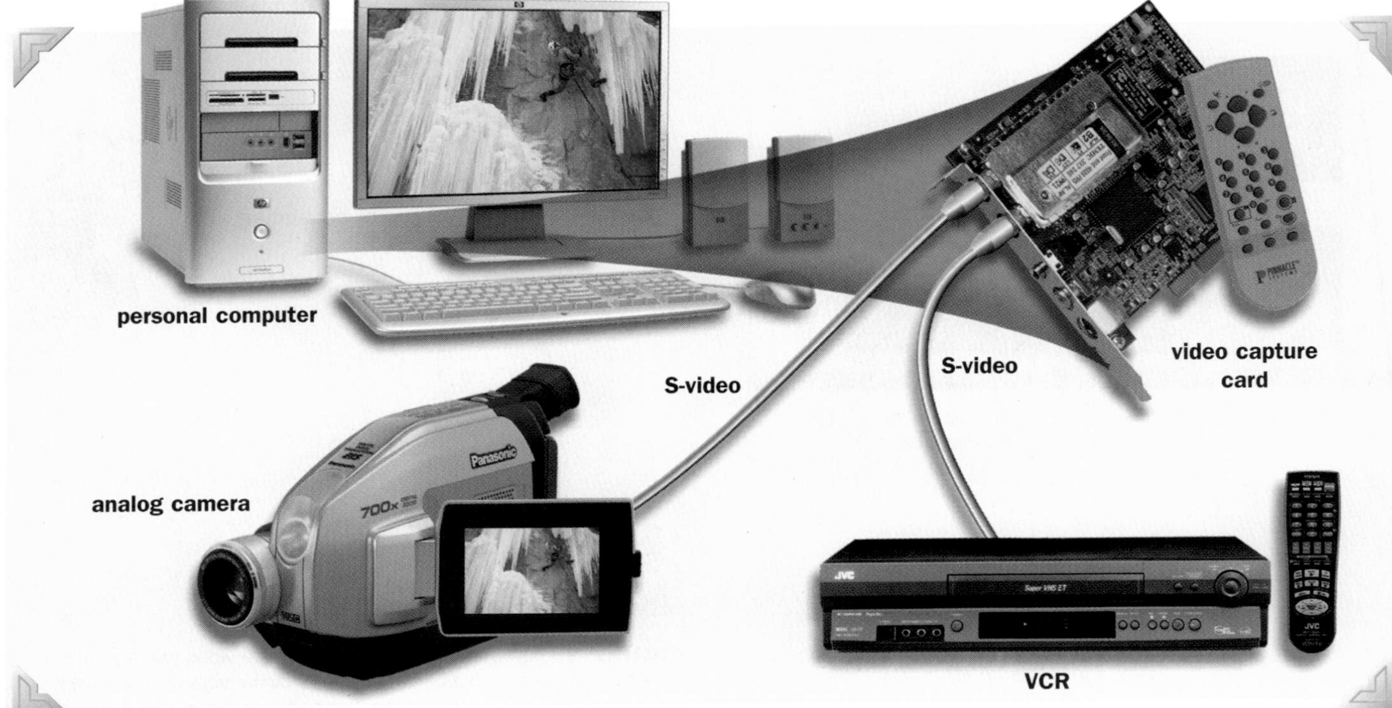

FIGURE 12 An analog camcorder or VCR is connected to the personal computer via an S-video port on a video capture card.

When transferring video, plan to use approximately 15 to 30 gigabytes of hard disk storage space per hour of digital video. A typical video project requires about four times the amount of raw footage as the final product. Therefore, at the high end, a video that lasts an hour may require up to 120 gigabytes of storage for the raw footage, editing process, and final video. This storage requirement can vary depending on the software you use to copy the video from the video camera to the hard disk and the format you select to save the video. For example, Microsoft's Windows Movie Maker can save 15 hours of video in 10 gigabytes when creating video for playback on a computer, but saves only 1 hour of video in 10 gigabytes when creating video for playback on a DVD. A high-definition video file may require over 10 gigabytes per hour.

The video transfer requires application software on the personal computer (Figure 13). Windows Vista includes the Windows Movie Maker software that allows you to transfer the video from your video camera. Depending on the length of video and the type of connection used, the video may take a long time to download. Make certain that no other programs are running on your personal computer while transferring the video.

The frame rate of a video refers to the number of frames per second (fps) that are captured in the video. The most widely used frame rate is 30 fps. A smaller frame rate results in a smaller file size for the video, but playback of the video will not be as smooth as one recorded with a higher frame rate.

When transferring video, the software may allow you to choose a file format and a codec to store the video. A video **file format** holds the video information in a manner specified by a vendor, such as Apple or Microsoft. Four of the more popular file formats are listed in Figure 14.

File formats support codecs to encode the audio and video into the file formats. A particular file format may be able to store audio and video in a number of different codecs. A **codec** specifies how the audio and video is compressed and stored within the file. Figure 15 shows some options available for specifying a file format and codec in a video capture program. The dialog box in Figure 15 allows the user to determine whether the video is smoother in playback or if the video is more crisp, meaning that it includes more detail. The file format and codec you choose often is based on what you plan to do with the movie. For example, if you plan to upload your video to the YouTube video sharing Web site, the best choices are DivX and Xvid MPEG-4 file formats.

After transferring the video to a personal computer, and before manipulating the video, you should store the video files in appropriate folders, named correctly, and backed up. Most video transfer application software helps manage these tasks.

FIGURE 13 Some video editing software allows you to transfer your video from any video source to a hard disk.

POPULAR VIDEO FILE FORMATS

File Format	File Extensions
Apple QuickTime	.MOV or .QT
DivX	.DIVX
Microsoft Windows Media Video	.WMV or .ASF
Real RealMedia	.RM or .RAM

FIGURE 14 Apple, DivX, Microsoft, and Real offer the more popular video file formats.

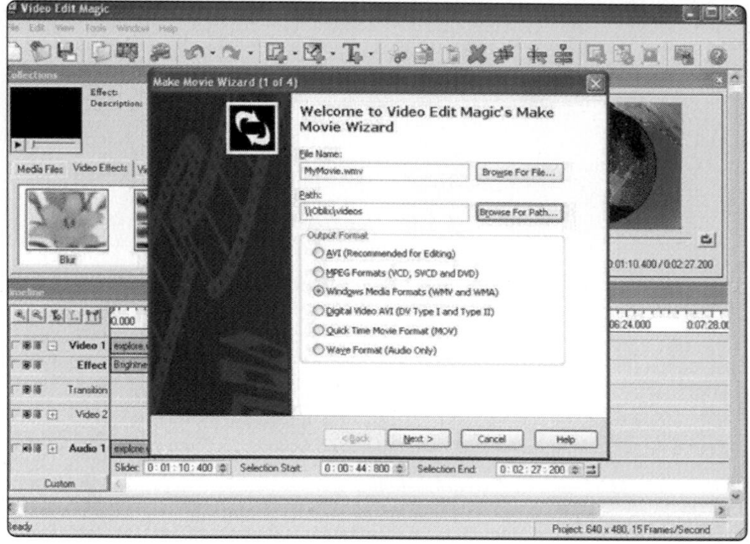

FIGURE 15 Video editing software allows you to specify a combination of file format and codec when saving a video.

4 Edit a Video

Once the video is stored on your hard disk, the next step is to edit, or manipulate, the video. If you used a video capture card to transfer analog video to your computer (Figure 12 on page 348), the files may require extra initial processing. When you use a video capture card, some of the video frames may be lost in the transfer process. Some video editing programs allow you to fix this problem with **frame rate correction** tools.

The first step in the editing process is to split the video into smaller pieces, or *scenes*, that you can manipulate more easily. This process is called *splitting*. Most video software automatically splits the video into scenes, thus sparing you the task. After splitting, you should cut out unwanted scenes or portions of scenes. This process is called *pruning*.

After you create the scenes you want to use in your final production, you edit each individual scene. You can *crop*, or change the size of, scenes. That is, you may want to cut out the top or a side of a scene that is irrelevant. You also can resize the scene. For example, you may be creating a video that will be displayed in a Web browser. Making a smaller video, such as 320 × 200 pixels instead of 640 × 480 pixels, results in a smaller file that transmits faster over the Internet. Some video sharing Web sites recommend smaller video resolutions, such as 320 × 200 pixels.

If video has been recorded over a long period, using different cameras or under different lighting conditions, the video may need color correction. *Color correction tools* (Figure 16) analyze your video and match brightness, colors, and other attributes of video clips to ensure a smooth look to the video.

You can add logos, special effects, or titles to scenes. You can place a company logo or personal logo in a video to identify yourself or the company producing the video. Logos often are added on the lower-right corner of a video and remain for the duration of the video. Special effects include warping, changing from color to black and white, morphing, or zoom motion. *Morphing* is a special effect in which one video image is transformed into another image over the course of several frames of video, creating the illusion of metamorphosis. You usually add titles at the beginning and end of a video to give the video context. A training video may have titles throughout the video to label a particular scene, or each scene may begin with a title.

FIGURE 16 Color correction tools in video editing software allow a great deal of control over the mood of your video creation.

The next step in editing a video is to add audio effects, including voice-over narration and background music. Many video editing programs allow you to add additional tracks, or *layers*, of sound to a video in addition to the sound that was recorded on the video camera. You also can add special audio effects.

The final step in editing a video is to combine the scenes into a complete video (Figure 17). This process involves ordering scenes and adding transition effects between scenes (Figure 18). Video editing software allows you to combine scenes and separate each scene with a transition. *Transitions* include fading, wiping, blurry, bursts, ruptures, erosions, and more.

FIGURE 17 In Ulead VideoStudio, scenes, shown on the top, are combined into a sequence on the bottom of the screen.

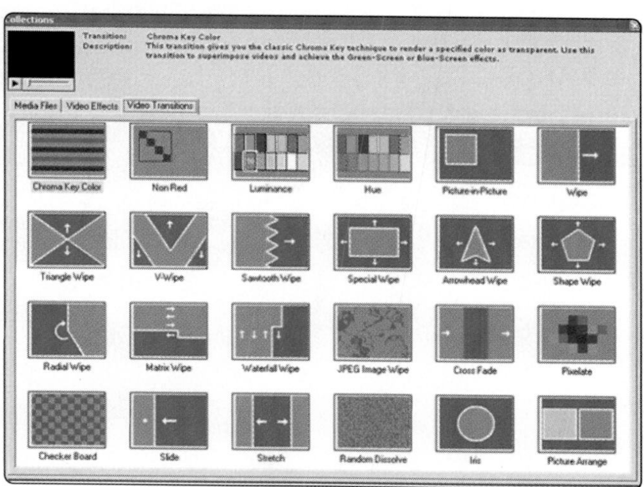

FIGURE 18 Smooth and dynamic transitions eliminate the hard cuts between scenes typically found in raw footage.

5 Distribute the Video

After editing the video, the final step is to distribute it or save it on an appropriate medium. You can save video in a variety of formats. Using special hardware, you can save the video on standard video tape. *A digital-to-analog converter* is necessary to allow your personal computer to transmit video to a VCR. A digital-to-analog converter may be an external device that connects to both the computer and input device, or may be a video capture card inside the computer.

Video also can be stored in digital formats in any of several DVD formats, on CD-R, on a video sharing Web site, or on video CD (VCD). *DVD* or *CD creation software*, which often is packaged with video editing software, allows you to create, or *master*, DVDs and CDs. You can add interactivity to your DVDs. For example, you can allow viewers to jump to certain scenes using a menu. A *video CD* (*VCD*) is a CD format that stores video on a CD-R that can be played in many DVD players.

You also can save your video creation in electronic format for distribution over the Web or via e-mail. Popular video sharing Web sites, such as YouTube (Figure 19), have recommendations for the best file format and codecs to use for video that you upload to them. Your video editing software must support the file format and codec you want to use. For example, Apple's iMovie software typically saves files in the QuickTime file format.

Professionals use hardware and software that allow them to create a film version of digital video that can be played in movie theaters. This technology is becoming increasingly popular. The cost of professional video editing software ranges from thousands to hundreds of thousands of dollars. Video editing software for the home user is available for a few hundred dollars or less. Some Hollywood directors believe that eventually, all movies will be recorded and edited digitally.

After creating your final video for distribution or your personal video collection, you should back up the final video file. You can save your scenes for inclusion in other video creations or create new masters using different effects, transitions, and ordering of scenes.

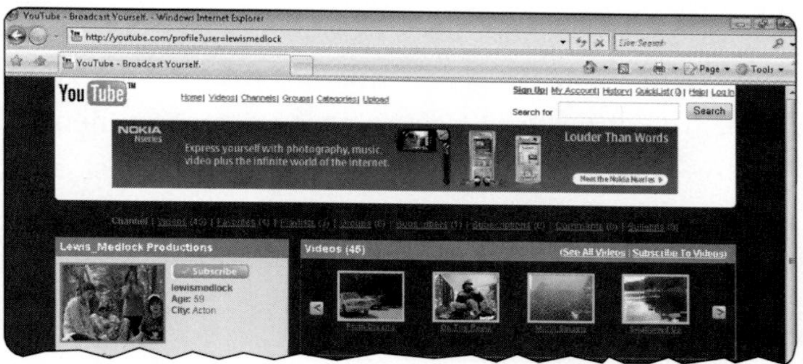

FIGURE 19 Video sharing Web sites allow you to share your videos with acquaintances or the entire world.

CHAPTER SEVEN

Storage

Picture Yourself Working with Mobile Storage Media

Your friend, Kara, announces excitedly, "I did it! I'm going to Spain! But I need a favor." She explains that she is going to study abroad for a semester and needs you to fill in for her at the student newspaper, where she is photo editor. You are a journalism major, so this is a good opportunity for you, but you are not sure what her job entails. You decide to meet at the newspaper office on campus, where she will walk you through the process.

Kara explains that you will be working with the student photographers — more precisely, with their mobile media. The photographers take many pictures while on various assignments. All of them use digital cameras. Part of your job is to print pictures taken by the student photographers. Because each student uses a different make and model of camera, the digital pictures are stored on a variety of mobile media. Some of the cameras use flash memory cards such as CompactFlash cards, xD Picture cards, and Memory Sticks. One student transfers his pictures to a pocket hard drive. Some copy their pictures on a CD, and another submits a USB flash drive containing all her pictures.

After you receive the media, you will insert it in the appropriate card reader, card slot, drive, or port. You then will begin the process of storing the images on a hard disk and finally printing the images.

To learn about these various types of mobile media, read Chapter 7 and discover many other types of storage devices.

OBJECTIVES

After completing this chapter, you will be able to:

1. Differentiate between storage devices and storage media
2. Describe the characteristics of magnetic disks
3. Describe the characteristics of a hard disk
4. Discuss various types of miniature, external, and removable hard disks
5. Describe the characteristics of optical discs
6. Differentiate among CD-ROMs, recordable CDs, rewritable CDs, DVD-ROMs, BD-ROMs, HD DVD-ROMs, recordable DVDs, and rewritable DVDs
7. Identify the uses of tape
8. Discuss PC Cards, ExpressCard modules, and the various types of miniature mobile storage media
9. Identify uses of microfilm and microfiche

CONTENTS

STORAGE

Storage holds data, instructions, and information for future use. Every computer stores system software and application software. To start up, a computer locates an operating system (system software) in storage, usually a hard disk, and loads it into memory (RAM). When a user issues a command to start application software, such as a word processing program or a Web browser, the operating system locates the program in storage, such as on a hard disk, CD, or DVD, and loads it into memory (RAM).

In addition to programs, users store a variety of data and information on mainframe computers, servers, desktop computers, notebook computers, Tablet PCs, handheld computers, PDAs, and smart phones. For example, all types of users store digital photographs; appointments, schedules, and contact/address information; and correspondence, such as letters and e-mail messages. Other items stored by specific types of users include the following:

- The home user might also store budgets, bank statements, a household inventory, records of stock purchases, tax data, homework assignments, recipes, music, and videos.
- The small office/home office user also often stores faxes, business reports, financial records, tax data, travel records, customer orders, payroll records, inventory records, and Web pages.
- The mobile user usually also stores faxes, presentations, travel records, homework assignments, and quotations.

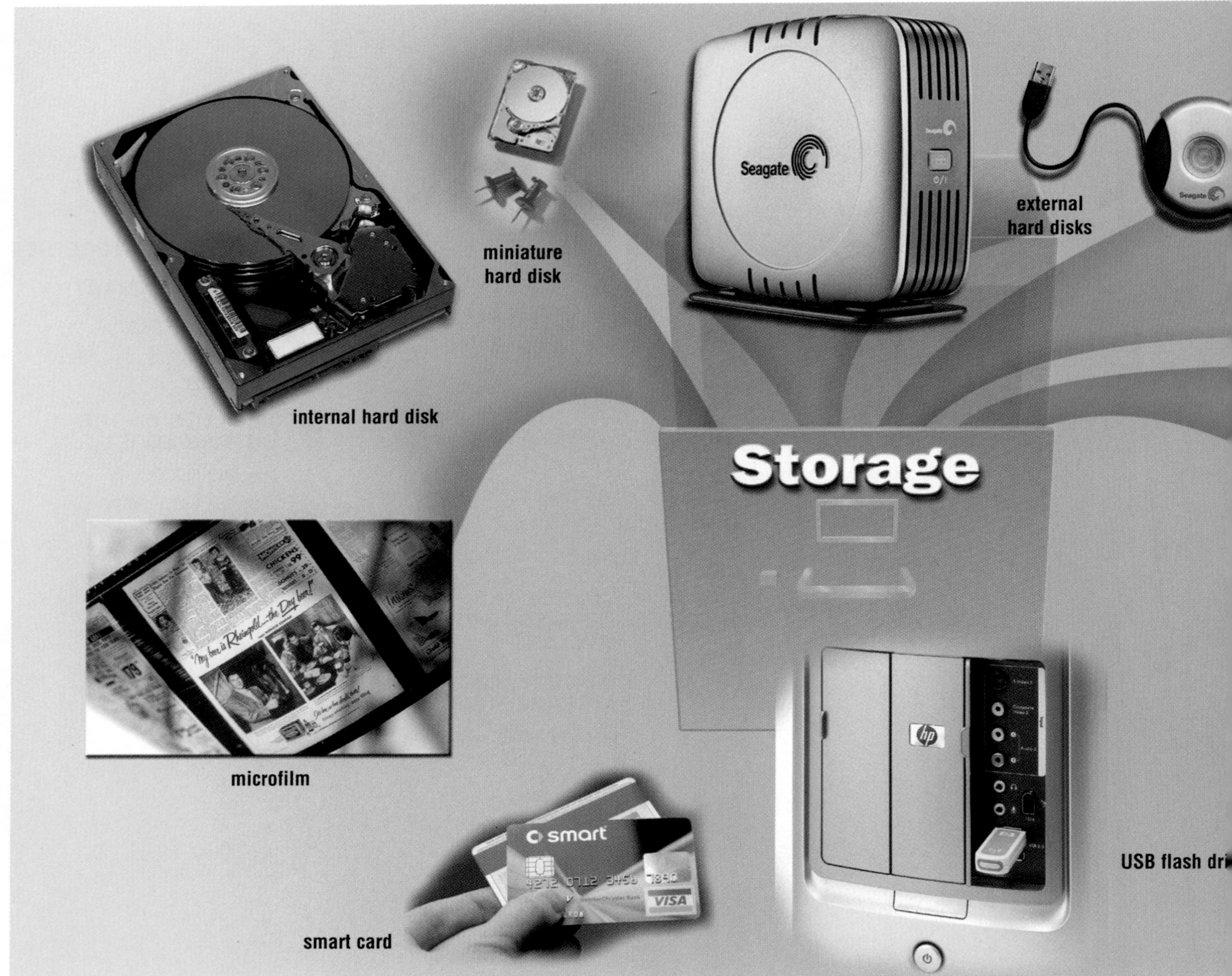

FIGURE 7-1 A variety of storage media.

- The power user also stores diagrams, drawings, blueprints, designs, marketing literature, corporate newsletters, product catalogs, audio recordings, multimedia presentations, videos, and Web pages.
- The large business user also accesses many stored items such as tax data, inventory records, presentations, contracts, marketing literature, and Web pages. The large business user accesses hundreds or thousands of employee, customer, and vendor records, including data and information about orders, invoices, payments, and payroll.

Storage requirements among these users vary greatly. Home users, small office/home office users, and mobile users typically have much smaller storage requirements than the large business user or power user. For example, a home user may need 160 billion bytes of storage, while large businesses may require 50 quadrillion bytes of storage.

A **storage medium** (media is the plural), also called *secondary storage*, is the physical material on which a computer keeps data, instructions, and information. Examples of storage media are hard disks, floppy disks, CDs and DVDs, tape, PC Cards and ExpressCard modules, flash memory cards, USB flash drives, smart cards, and microfilm (Figure 7-1). Memory (RAM), by contrast, typically consists of one or more chips on the motherboard or some other circuit board in the computer.

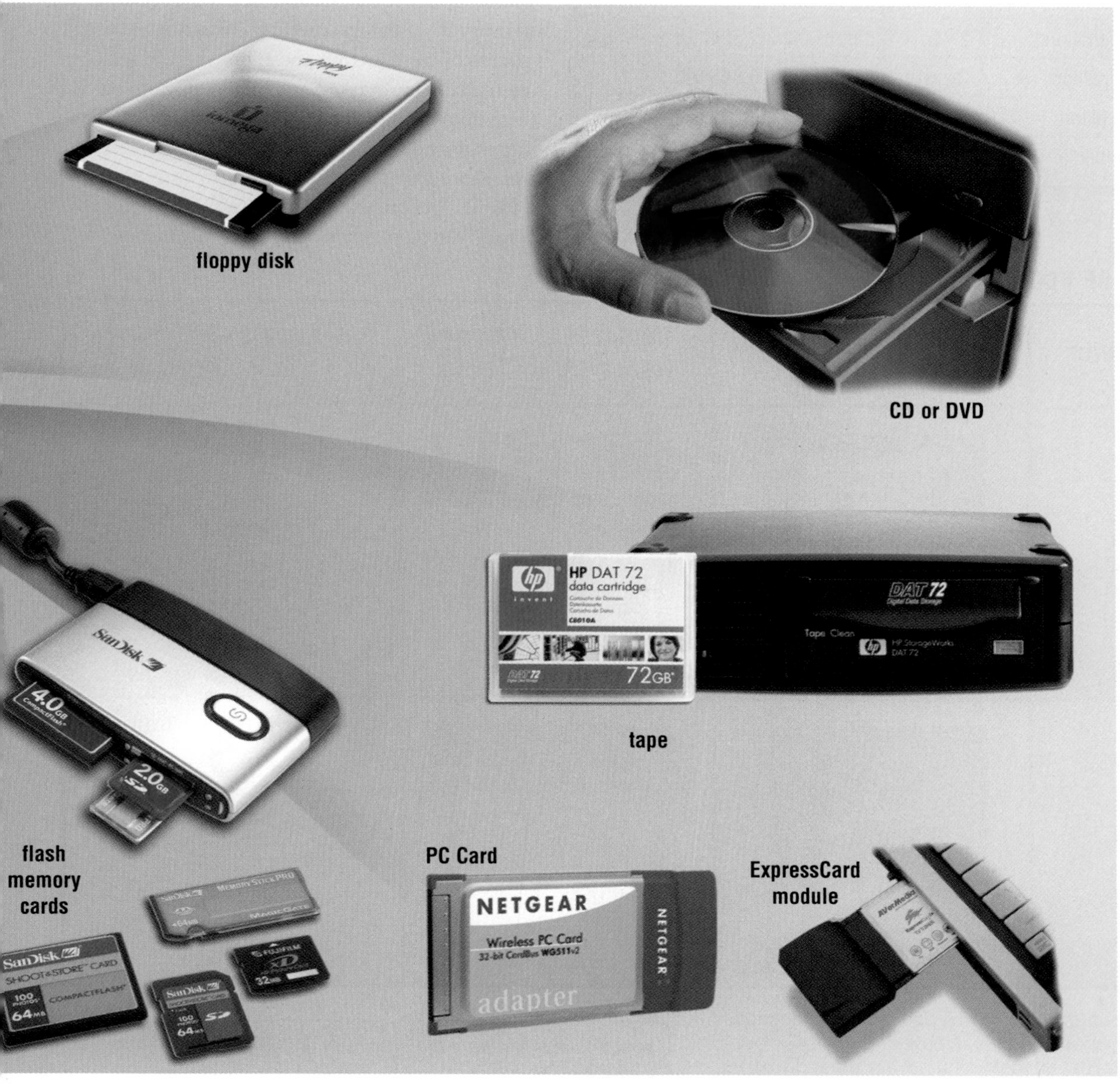

Capacity is the number of bytes (characters) a storage medium can hold. Figure 7-2 identifies the terms manufacturers use to define the capacity of storage media. For example, a reasonably priced USB flash drive can store up to 512 MB of data (approximately 512 million bytes) and a typical hard disk has 250 GB (approximately 250 billion bytes) of storage capacity.

STORAGE TERMS

Storage Term	Approximate Number of Bytes	Exact Number of Bytes
Kilobyte (KB)	1 thousand	2^{10} or 1,024
Megabyte (MB)	1 million	2^{20} or 1,048,576
Gigabyte (GB)	1 billion	2^{30} or 1,073,741,824
Terabyte (TB)	1 trillion	2^{40} or 1,099,511,627,776
Petabyte (PB)	1 quadrillion	2^{50} or 1,125,899,906,842,624
Exabyte (EB)	1 quintillion	2^{60} or 1,152,921,504,606,846,976
Zettabyte (ZB)	1 sextillion	2^{70} or 1,180,591,620,717,411,303,424
Yottabyte (YB)	1 septillion	2^{80} or 1,208,925,819,614,629,174,706,176

FIGURE 7-2 The capacity of a storage medium is measured by the number of bytes it can hold.

Items on a storage medium remain intact even when power is removed from the computer. Thus, a storage medium is nonvolatile. Most memory (i.e., RAM), by contrast, holds data and instructions temporarily and thus is volatile. Figure 7-3 illustrates the concept of volatility. For an analogy, think of a filing cabinet that holds file folders as a storage medium, and the top of your desk as memory. When you want to work with a file, you remove it from the filing cabinet (storage medium) and place it on your desk (memory). When you are finished with the file, you remove it from your desk (memory) and return it to the filing cabinet (storage medium).

A **storage device** is the computer hardware that records and/or retrieves items to and from storage media. **Writing** is the process of transferring data, instructions, and information from memory to a storage medium. **Reading** is the process of transferring these items from a storage medium into memory. When storage devices write data on storage media, they are creating output. Similarly, when storage devices read from storage media, they function as a source of input. Nevertheless, they are categorized as storage devices, not as input or output devices.

AN ILLUSTRATION OF VOLATILITY

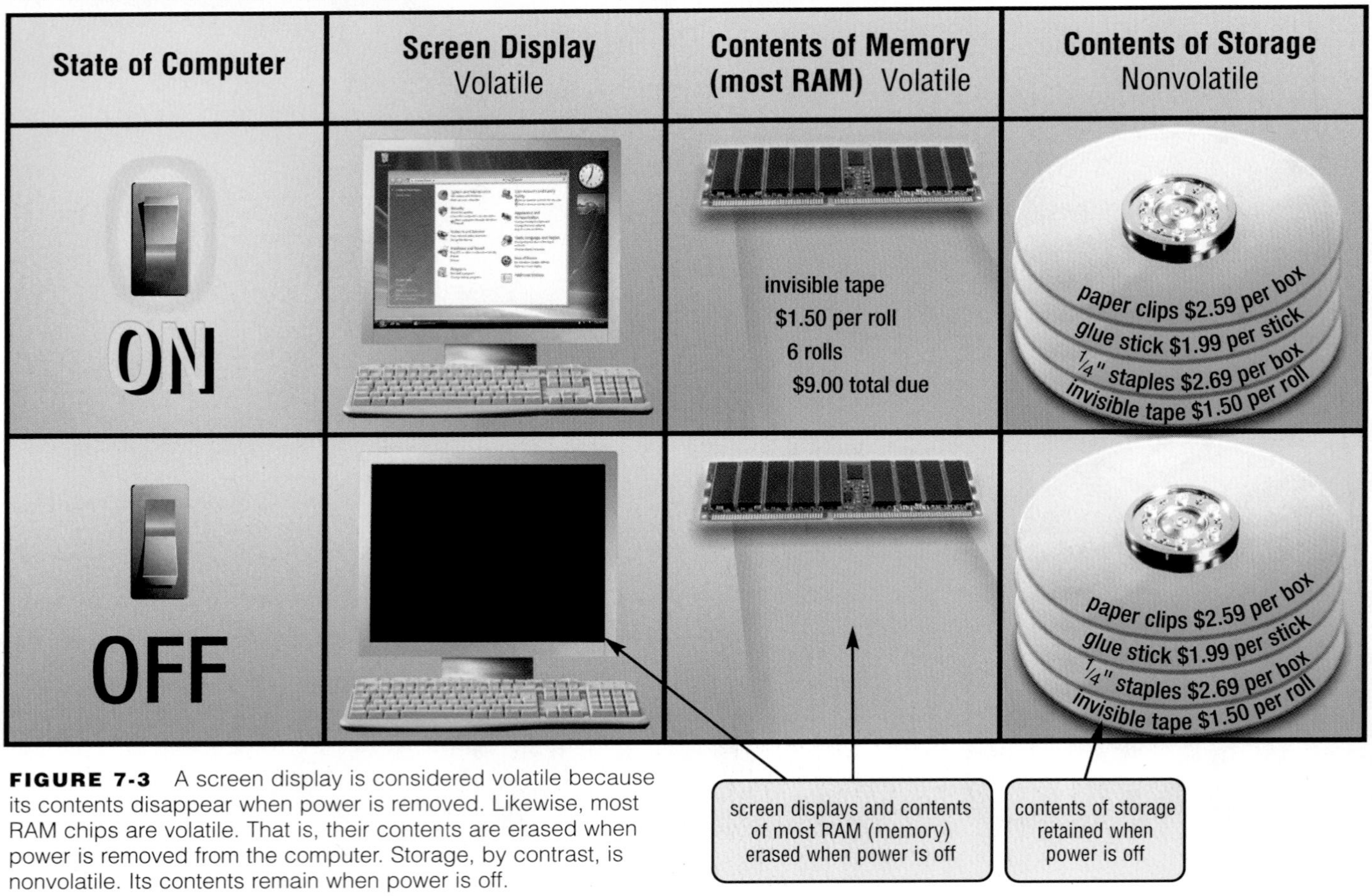

FIGURE 7-3 A screen display is considered volatile because its contents disappear when power is removed. Likewise, most RAM chips are volatile. That is, their contents are erased when power is removed from the computer. Storage, by contrast, is nonvolatile. Its contents remain when power is off.

The speed of storage devices and memory is defined by access time. **Access time** measures (1) the amount of time it takes a storage device to locate an item on a storage medium or (2) the time required to deliver an item from memory to the processor. The access time of storage devices is slow, compared with the access time of memory. Memory (chips) accesses items in billionths of a second (nanoseconds). Storage devices, by contrast, access items in thousandths of a second (milliseconds) or millionths of a second (microseconds).

Instead of, or in addition to access time, some manufacturers state a storage device's transfer rate because it affects access time. *Transfer rate* is the speed with which data, instructions, and information transfer to and from a device. Transfer rates for storage are stated in *KBps* (kilobytes per second) and *MBps* (megabytes per second).

Numerous types of storage media and storage devices exist to meet a variety of users' needs. Figure 7-4 shows how different types of storage media and memory compare in terms of transfer rates and uses. This chapter discusses these and other storage media.

faster transfer rates

		Stores...
Memory	Memory (most RAM)	Items waiting to be interpreted and executed by the processor
Storage	Hard Disk	Operating system, application software, user data and information, including pictures, music, and videos
	Flash Memory Cards and USB Flash Drives	Digital pictures or files to be transported
	CDs and DVDs	Software, backups, movies, music
	Tape	Backups
	Floppy Disk	Small files to be transported

slower transfer rates

FIGURE 7-4 A comparison of different types of storage media and memory in terms of relative speed and uses. Memory is faster than storage but is expensive and not practical for all storage requirements. Storage is less expensive but is slower than memory.

MAGNETIC DISKS

Magnetic disks use magnetic particles to store items such as data, instructions, and information on a disk's surface. Depending on how the magnetic particles are aligned, they represent either a 0 bit or a 1 bit. Recall from Chapter 4 that a bit (binary digit) is the smallest unit of data a computer can process. Thus, the alignment of the magnetic particles represents the data.

Before any data can be read from or written on a magnetic disk, the disk must be formatted. **Formatting** is the process of dividing the disk into tracks and sectors (Figure 7-5), so the operating system can store and locate data and information on the disk. A *track* is a narrow recording band that forms a full circle on the surface of the disk. The disk's storage locations consist of pie-shaped sections, which break the tracks into small arcs called *sectors*. On a magnetic disk, a sector typically stores up to 512 bytes of data.

For reading and writing purposes, sectors are grouped into clusters. A *cluster* is the smallest unit of disk space that stores data and information. Each cluster, also called an *allocation unit*, consists of two to eight sectors (the number varies depending on the operating system). Even if a file consists of only a few bytes, it uses an entire cluster. Each cluster holds data from only one file. One file, however, can span many clusters.

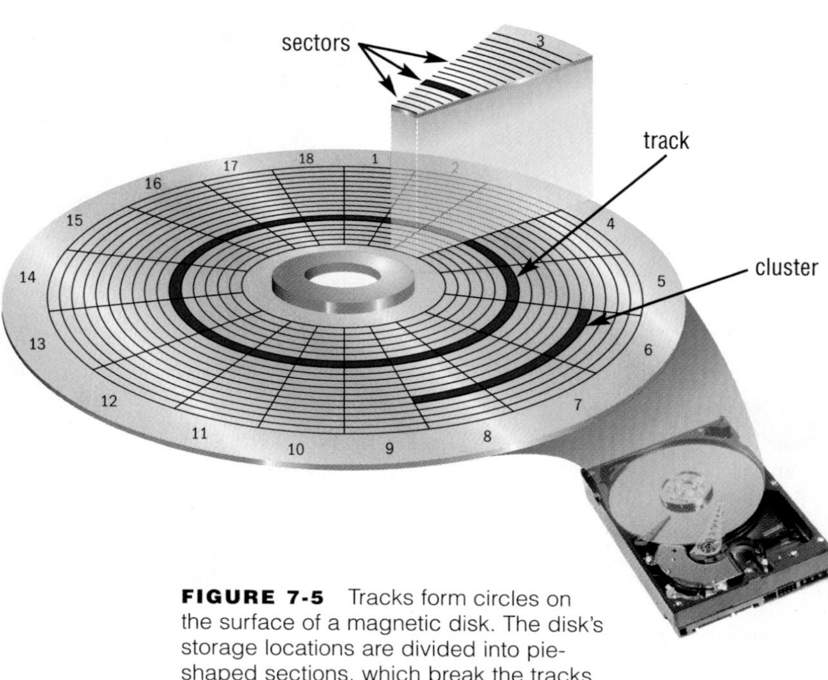

FIGURE 7-5 Tracks form circles on the surface of a magnetic disk. The disk's storage locations are divided into pie-shaped sections, which break the tracks into small arcs called sectors.

Sometimes, a sector has a flaw and cannot store data. When you format a disk, the operating system marks these bad sectors as unusable. For a technical discussion about formatting, read the High-Tech Talk article on page 382.

Two types of magnetic disks are hard disks and floppy disks. Some disks are portable; others are not. With respect to a storage medium, the term *portable* means you can remove the medium from one computer and carry it to another computer.

Hard Disks

A **hard disk**, also called a *hard disk drive* or hard drive, is a storage device that contains one or more inflexible, circular platters that magnetically store data, instructions, and information. Home users store documents, spreadsheets, presentations, databases, e-mail messages, Web pages, digital photographs, music, videos, and software on hard disks. Businesses use hard disks to store correspondence, reports, financial records, e-mail messages, customer orders and invoices, payroll records, inventory records, presentations, contracts, marketing literature, schedules, and Web sites.

The system unit on most desktop and notebook computers contains at least one hard disk. The entire device is enclosed in an airtight, sealed case to protect it from contamination. A hard disk that is mounted inside the system unit sometimes is called a *fixed disk* because it is not portable (Figure 7-6). Portable hard disks are discussed later in this chapter.

Current personal computer hard disks have storage capacities from 80 to 750 GB and more. Traditionally, hard disks stored data using *longitudinal recording*, which aligned the magnetic particles horizontally around the surface of the disk. With *perpendicular recording*, by contrast, hard disks align the magnetic particles vertically, or perpendicular to the disk's surface, making much greater storage capacities possible. Experts estimate that hard disks using perpendicular recording will provide storage capacities about 10 times greater than disks that use longitudinal recording. Read Looking Ahead 7-1 for a look at the next generation of hard disk storage capacities.

Hard disks are read/write storage media. That is, you can read from and write on a hard disk any number of times. If the computer contains only one hard disk, the operating system designates it as drive C. Additional hard disks are assigned the next available drive letter.

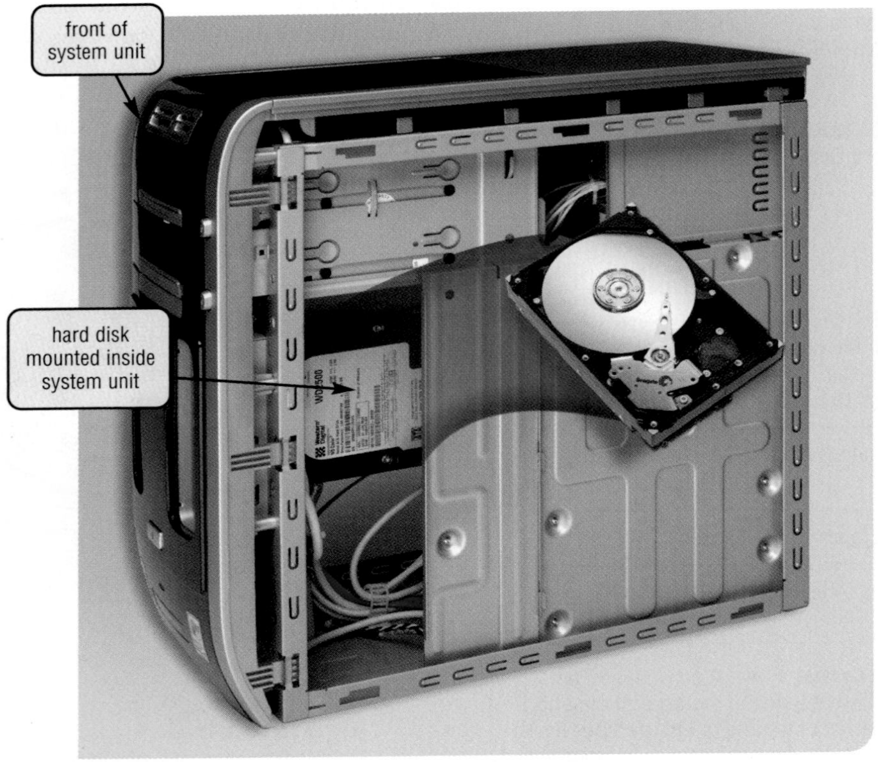

FIGURE 7-6 The hard disk in a desktop personal computer is enclosed inside an airtight, sealed case inside the system unit.

WEB LINK 7-1

Perpendicular Recording

For more information, visit scsite.com/dc2008/ch7/weblink and then click Perpendicular Recording.

FAQ 7-1

Have personal computer hard disk capacities grown much since their inception?

Yes, hard disk capacities have grown phenomenally over the past several years, as shown in the chart to the right. This trend is expected to continue at a rate of 60 percent annually. For more information, visit scsite.com/dc2008/ch7/faq and then click Hard Disk Capacities.

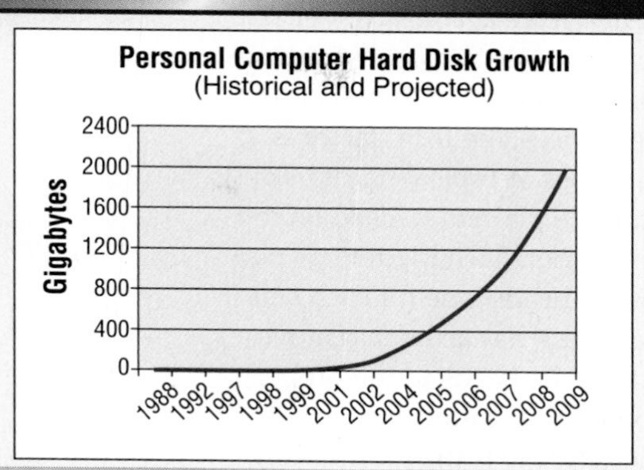

LOOKING AHEAD 7-1

Heat Increases Disk Capacity

Things are heating up in the data storage industry. Engineers at IBM Research are testing the use of heat to record data inexpensively on magnetic media, such as hard disks.

Within the next ten years, the researchers predict that this new technique will allow storage of more than one terabit per square inch, which is the equivalent of 25 DVDs on an area the size of a postage stamp. With this capacity, a hard disk that can store seven terabits will be commonplace.

IBM calls this new storage system *Millipede.* It uses heated tips mounted on the ends of cantilevers, in a fashion similar to the way the stylus on an old phonograph sat on the grooves of vinyl records. For more information, visit scsite.com/dc2008/ch7/looking and then click Heated Storage.

CHARACTERISTICS OF A HARD DISK Characteristics of a hard disk include its capacity, platters, read/write heads, cylinders, sectors and tracks, revolutions per minute, transfer rate, and access time. Figure 7-7 shows characteristics of a sample 500 GB hard disk. The following paragraphs discuss each of these characteristics.

The capacity of a hard disk is determined from the number of platters it contains, together with composition of the magnetic coating on the platters. A *platter* is made of aluminum, glass, or ceramic and is coated with an alloy material that allows items to be recorded magnetically on its surface. The coating usually is three millionths of an inch thick.

SAMPLE HARD DISK CHARACTERISTICS

Advertised capacity	500 GB
Platters	4
Read/write heads	8
Cylinders	16,383
Bytes per sector	512
Sectors per track	63
Sectors per drive	976,773,168
Revolutions per minute	7,200
Transfer rate	300 MB per second
Access time	8.5 ms

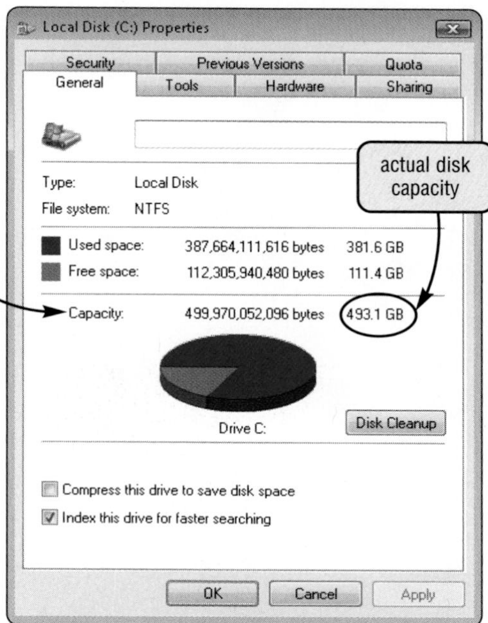

FIGURE 7-7 Characteristics of a sample 500 GB hard disk. The actual disk's capacity sometimes is different from the advertised capacity because of bad sectors on the disk.

On desktop computers, platters most often have a *form factor*, or size, of approximately 3.5 inches in diameter; on notebook computers and mobile devices, the form factor is 2.5 inches or less. A typical hard disk has multiple platters stacked on top of one another. Each platter has two read/write heads, one for each side. The hard disk has arms that move the read/write heads to the proper location on the platter (Figure 7-8). A *read/write head* is the mechanism that reads items and writes items in the drive as it barely touches the disk's recording surface.

The location of the read/write heads often is referred to by its cylinder. A *cylinder* is the vertical section of a track that passes through all platters (Figure 7-9). A single movement of the read/write head arms accesses all the platters in a cylinder. If a hard disk has two platters (four sides), each with 1,000 tracks, then it will have 1,000 cylinders with each cylinder consisting of 4 tracks (2 tracks for each platter).

FIGURE 7-9 A cylinder is the vertical section of track through all platters on a hard disk.

FIGURE 7-8 HOW A HARD DISK WORKS

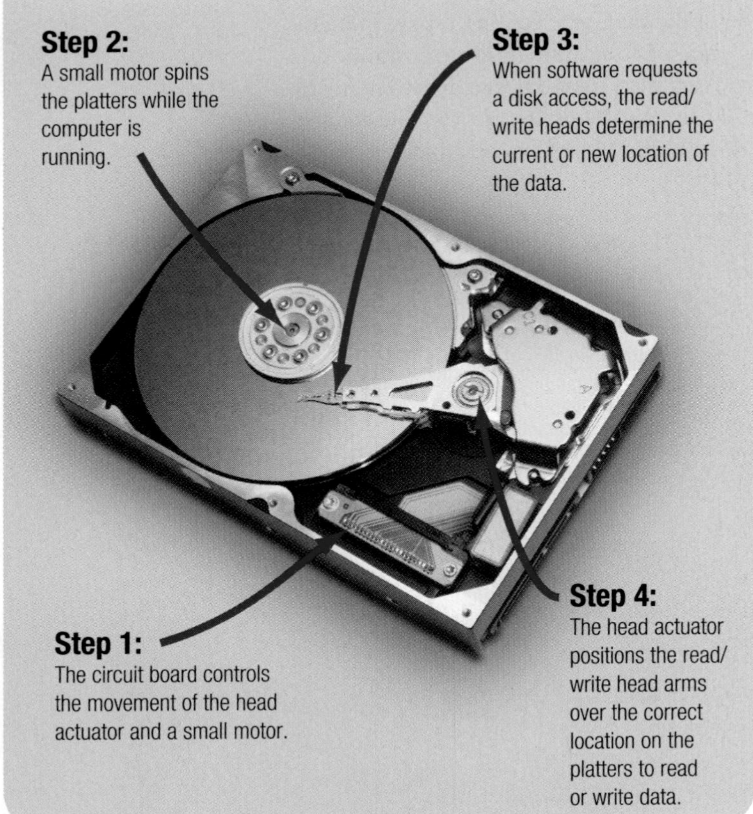

Step 2:
A small motor spins the platters while the computer is running.
Step 3:
When software requests a disk access, the read/write heads determine the current or new location of the data.
Step 4:
The head actuator positions the read/write head arms over the correct location on the platters to read or write data.
Step 1:
The circuit board controls the movement of the head actuator and a small motor.

While the computer is running, the platters in the hard disk rotate at a high rate of speed. This spinning, which usually is 5,400 to 15,000 *revolutions per minute* (*rpm*), allows nearly instant access to all tracks and sectors on the platters. The platters typically continue to spin until power is removed from the computer. (On many computers, the hard disk stops spinning or slows down after a specified time to save power.) The spinning motion creates a cushion of air between the platter and its read/write head. This cushion ensures that the read/write head floats above the platter instead of making direct contact with the platter surface. The distance between the read/write head and the platter is about two millionths of one inch.

As shown in Figure 7-10, this close clearance leaves no room for any type of contamination. Dirt, hair, dust, smoke, and other particles could cause the hard disk to have a head crash. A *head crash* occurs when a read/write head touches the surface of a platter, usually resulting in a loss of data or sometimes loss of the entire drive.

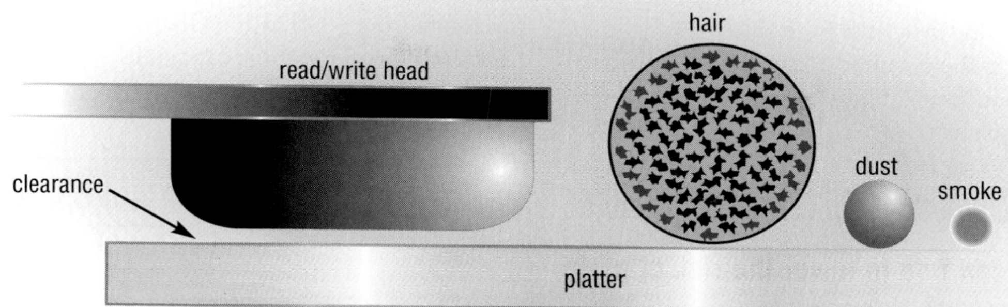

FIGURE 7-10 The clearance between a disk read/write head and the platter is about two millionths of an inch. A smoke particle, dust particle, human hair, or other contaminant could render the drive unusable.

Although current internal hard disks are built to withstand shocks and are sealed tightly to keep out contaminants, head crashes do occasionally still occur. Thus, it is crucial that you back up your hard disk regularly. A **backup** is a duplicate of a file, program, or disk placed on a separate storage medium that you can use in case the original is lost, damaged, or destroyed. Chapter 8 discusses backup techniques.

Depending on the type of hard disk, transfer rates range from 15 MBps to 320 MBps. Access time for today's hard disks ranges from about 3 to 12 ms (milliseconds).

Hard disks improve their access time by using disk caching. *Disk cache* (pronounced cash), sometimes called a buffer, consists of a memory chip(s) on a hard disk that stores frequently accessed items such as data, instructions, and information (Figure 7-11). Disk cache and memory cache work in a similar fashion. When a processor requests data, instructions, or information from the hard disk, the hard disk first checks its disk cache — before moving any mechanical parts to access the platters. If the requested item is in disk cache, the hard disk sends it to the processor. If the hard disk does not find the requested item in the disk cache, then the processor must wait for the hard disk to locate and transfer the item from the disk to the processor. Hard disks today contain between

FIGURE 7-11 HOW DISK CACHE WORKS

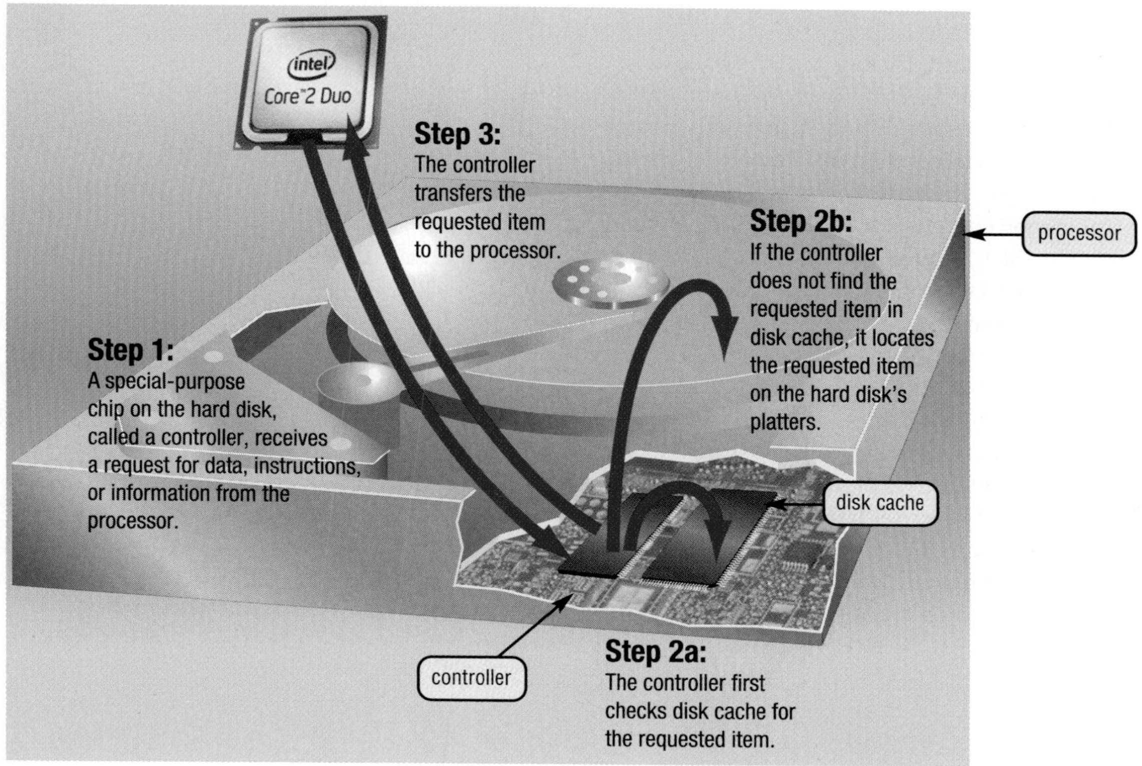

intel
Core 2 Duo
Step 3:
The controller transfers the requested item to the processor.
Step 2b:
If the controller does not find the requested item in disk cache, it locates the requested item on the hard disk's platters.
processor
Step 1:
A special-purpose chip on the hard disk, called a controller, receives a request for data, instructions, or information from the processor.
disk cache
controller
Step 2a:
The controller first checks disk cache for the requested item.

2 MB and 16 MB of disk cache. The greater the disk cache, the faster the hard disk.

Density is the number of bits in an area on a storage medium. A higher density means more storage capacity.

FAQ 7-2

What can I do to lower the risk of a head crash?

To prevent a head crash, you first should take precautionary measures to prevent any small particles from entering or remaining inside your computer case. Do not smoke around your computer. Regularly blow the dust out of your computer case. If you must move your computer, move it slowly and carefully. Do not place your computer in a location where other objects, such as your feet or your chair, may frequently hit your computer. For more information, visit scsite.com/dc2008/ch7/faq and then click Head Crash.

RAID Some personal computer manufacturers now provide a hard disk configuration that connects multiple smaller disks into a single unit that acts like a single large hard disk. A group of two or more integrated hard disks is called a **RAID** (redundant array of independent disks). RAID is an ideal storage solution for users who must have the data available when they attempt to access it.

WEB LINK 7-2

RAID

For more information, visit scsite.com/dc2008/ch7/weblink and then click RAID.

MINIATURE HARD DISKS Many mobile devices and consumer electronics include miniature hard disks, which provide users with greater storage capacities than flash memory. These tiny hard disks, which are smaller than the notebook computer hard disks, often have form factors of 1.8 inch, 1 inch, and 0.85 inch (Figure 7-12). Devices such as portable media players, digital cameras, smart phones, and PDAs often have built-in miniature hard disks. When the device containing the miniature hard disk is connected to the computer, the user can read from and write on the device as a separate drive. Another type of miniature hard disk, often called a **pocket hard drive**, is a self-contained unit that you insert in and remove from a slot in a device or a computer or plug in a USB port on a computer (Figure 7-13).

WEB LINK 7-3

Pocket Hard Drives

For more information, visit scsite.com/dc2008/ch7/weblink and then click Pocket Hard Drives.

Miniature hard disks have storage capacities that range from 4 GB to 160 GB. Miniature hard disks with greater storage capacities typically use perpendicular recording.

FIGURE 7-12 This miniature hard disk is used in portable media players and other small devices.

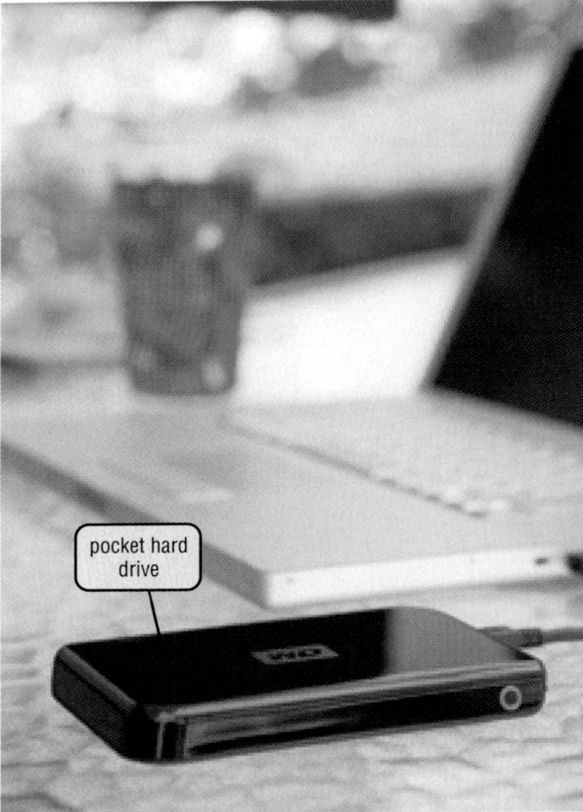

FIGURE 7-13 Users easily can transport data from one computer to another with a pocket hard drive.

External and Removable Hard Disks An **external hard disk**, shown in the left picture in Figure 7-14, is a separate free-standing hard disk that connects with a cable to a USB port or FireWire port on the system unit. As with the internal hard disk, the entire hard disk is enclosed in an airtight, sealed case. External hard disks have storage capacities of up to 750 GB. Some external hard disk units include multiple hard disks that act as one in order to increase total capacity in excess of 1 TB.

A **removable hard disk** is a hard disk that you insert and remove from a drive. Sometimes the drive is built in the system unit. Others are external devices that connect with a cable to a USB port or FireWire port on the system unit. A removable hard disk drive, shown in the right picture in Figure 7-14, reads from and writes on the removable hard disk. Removable hard disks have storage capacities up to 500 GB.

External and removable hard disks offer the following advantages over internal hard disks (fixed disks):

- Transport a large number of files
- Back up important files or an entire internal hard disk (several external hard disk models allow you to back up simply by pushing a button on the disk)
- Easily store large audio and video files
- Secure your data; for example, at the end of a work session, remove the hard disk and lock it up, leaving no data in the computer
- Add storage space to a notebook computer or Tablet PC
- Add storage space to a desktop computer without having to open the system unit
- Share a drive with multiple computers

As the prices of external and removable hard disks drop, increasingly more users will purchase one to supplement a home or office internal hard disk. Keep in mind, though, that external or removable hard disks transfer data at slower rates than internal hard disks.

Hard Disk Controllers A *disk controller* consists of a special-purpose chip and electronic circuits that control the transfer of data, instructions, and information from a disk to and from the system bus and other components in the computer. That is, it controls the interface between the hard disk and the system bus. A disk controller for a hard disk, called the hard disk controller, may be part of a hard disk or the motherboard, or it may be a separate adapter card inside the system unit.

In their personal computer advertisements, vendors usually state the type of hard disk interface supported by the hard disk controller. Thus, you should understand the types of available hard disk interfaces. In addition to USB and FireWire (external hard disk interfaces), three other types of hard disk interfaces for internal use in personal computers are SATA, EIDE, and SCSI.

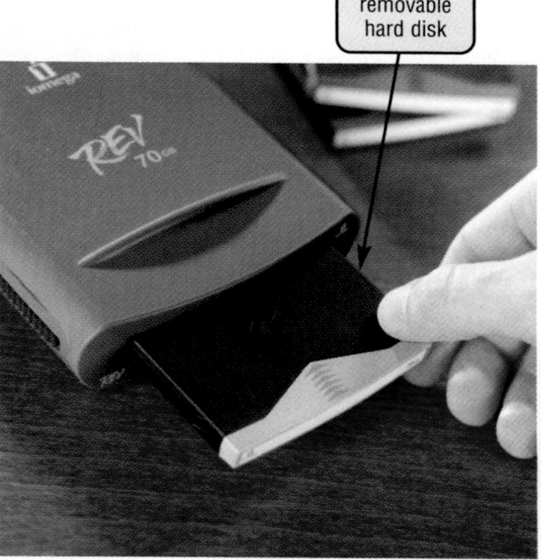

FIGURE 7-14 Examples of external and removable hard disks.

- *SATA* (*Serial Advanced Technology Attachment*), the newest type of hard disk interface, uses serial signals to transfer data, instructions, and information. The primary advantage of SATA interfaces is their cables are thinner, longer, more flexible, and less susceptible to interference than cables used by hard disks that use parallel signals. SATA interfaces have data transfer rates of up to 300 MBps. In addition to hard disks, SATA interfaces support connections to CD and DVD drives.
- *EIDE* (*Enhanced Integrated Drive Electronics*) is a hard disk interface that uses parallel signals to transfer data, instructions, and information. EIDE interfaces can support up to four hard disks at 137 GB per disk. These interfaces have data transfer rates up to 100 MBps. EIDE interfaces also provide connections for CD and DVD drives and tape drives. Some manufacturers market their EIDE interfaces as Fast ATA or Ultra ATA.
- *SCSI* interfaces, which also use parallel signals, can support up to eight or fifteen peripheral devices. Supported devices include hard disks, CD and DVD drives, tape drives, printers, scanners, network cards, and much more. Recall from Chapter 4 that SCSI is an acronym for Small Computer System Interface. Some computers have a built-in SCSI interface, while others use an adapter card to add a SCSI interface. SCSI interfaces provide up to 320 MBps data transfer rates.

FAQ 7-3

What are the transfer rates of USB 2.0 and FireWire 800?

USB 2.0, also called *Hi-Speed USB*, has transfer rates up to 480 *Mbps* (megabits per second). FireWire 800 has transfer rates up to 800 Mbps. For more information, visit scsite.com/dc2008/ch7/faq and then click USB 2.0 and FireWire 800.

MAINTAINING DATA STORED ON A HARD DISK Most manufacturers guarantee their hard disks to last approximately three to five years. Many last much longer with proper care. To prevent the loss of items stored on a hard disk, you regularly should perform preventive maintenance such as defragmenting or scanning the disk for errors. Chapter 8 discusses these and other utilities in depth.

ONLINE STORAGE Some users choose online storage instead of storing data locally on a hard disk. **Online storage** is a service on the Web that provides hard disk storage to computer users, for free or for a minimal monthly fee (Figure 7-15). Fee arrangements for use of these Internet hard disks vary. For example, one online storage service provides 5 GB of storage free to registered users; another charges $10 per month for 5 GB of storage.

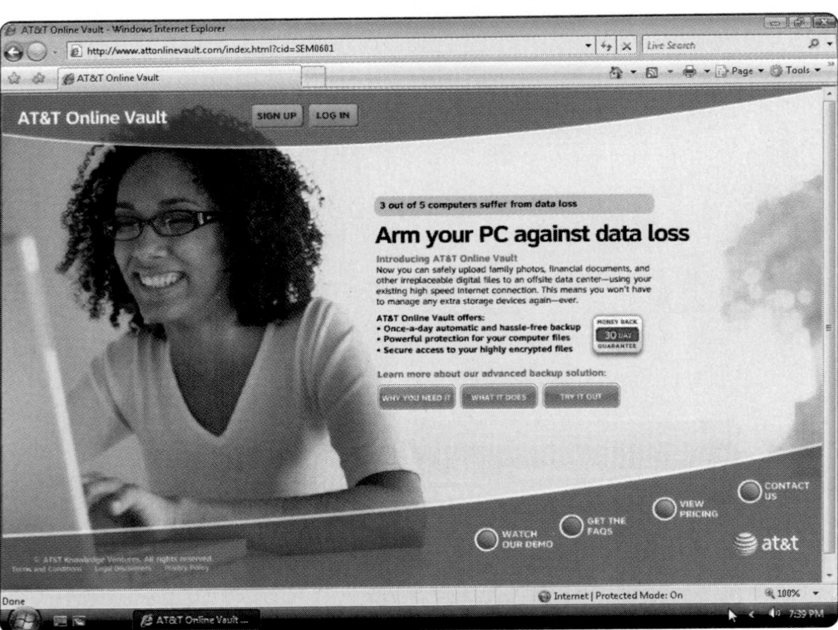

FIGURE 7-15 An example of one Web site advertising its online storage service.

WEB LINK 7-4

Online Storage

For more information, visit scsite.com/dc2008/ch7/weblink and then click Online Storage.

Users subscribe to an online storage service for a variety of reasons:

- To access files on the Internet hard disk from any computer or device that has Internet access
- To store large audio, video, and graphics files on an Internet hard disk instantaneously, instead of spending time downloading to a local hard disk
- To allow others to access files on their Internet hard disk so others can listen to an audio file, watch a video clip, or view a picture — instead of e-mailing the file to them
- To view time-critical data and images immediately while away from the main office or location; for example, doctors can view x-ray images from another hospital, home, or office, or while on vacation
- To store offsite backups of data (Chapter 8 presents this and other backup strategies)

Once users subscribe to the online storage service, they can save on the Internet hard disk in the same manner they save on their local hard disk or any other drive.

Floppy Disks

A **floppy disk**, also called a *diskette*, is a portable, inexpensive storage medium that consists of a thin, circular, flexible plastic Mylar film with a magnetic coating enclosed in a square-shaped plastic shell. Although the exterior of current floppy disks is not bendable, users refer to this storage medium as a floppy disk because of the flexible film inside the rigid plastic 3.5-inch outer cover.

A standard floppy disk has storage capacities up to 1.44 MB. Floppy disks are not as widely used as they were 15 years ago because of their low storage capacity.

A **floppy disk drive** is a device that reads from and writes on a floppy disk. A user inserts a floppy disk in and removes it from a floppy disk drive. In the past, desktop personal computers and notebook computers had a floppy disk drive installed inside the system unit. Most computers today do not include a floppy disk drive as standard equipment. On these computers, you can use an *external floppy disk drive*, in which the drive is a separate device with a cable that plugs in a port on the system unit (Figure 7-16). These external drives are attached to the computer only when the user needs to access items on a floppy disk. If a personal computer has one floppy disk drive, it is named drive A.

Floppy disk drive access times are about 84 milliseconds, or approximately 1/12 of a second. The transfer rates range from 250 to 500 KBps.

You can read from and write on a floppy disk any number of times. A typical floppy disk stores data on both sides of the disk, has 80 tracks on each side of the recording surface, and has 18 sectors per track.

FIGURE 7-16 An external floppy disk drive attached to a computer with a cable.

Test your knowledge of pages 354 through 365 in Quiz Yourself 7-1.

QUIZ YOURSELF 7-1

Instructions: Find the true statement below. Then, rewrite the remaining false statements so they are true.

1. Miniature hard disks are a type of optical disc.
2. Hard disks contain one or more inflexible, circular platters that magnetically store data, instructions, and information.
3. SATA is a hard disk interface that uses parallel signals to transfer data, instructions, and information.
4. Storage media is the computer hardware that records and/or retrieves items to and from a storage device.
5. Two types of manual disks are hard disks and floppy disks.
6. Users can move an internal hard disk from computer to computer as needed by connecting the disk to a USB port or FireWire port on the system unit.

Quiz Yourself Online: To further check your knowledge of storage devices and storage media, hard disks, and floppy disks, visit scsite.com/dc2008/ch7/quiz and then click Objectives 1 – 4.

OPTICAL DISCS

An *optical disc* is a type of storage media that consists of a flat, round, portable disc made of metal, plastic, and lacquer that is written and read by a laser. (The spelling, disk, is used for magnetic media, and disc is used for optical media.) Optical discs used in personal computers are 4.75 inches in diameter and less than one-twentieth of an inch thick. Smaller computers and devices, however, use *mini discs* that have a diameter of 3 inches or less.

Optical discs primarily store software, data, digital photographs, movies, and music. Some optical disc formats are read only, meaning users cannot write (save) on the media. Others are read/write, which allows users to save on the disc just as they save on a hard disk.

Nearly every personal computer today has some type of optical disc drive installed in a drive bay. On these drives, you push a button to slide out a tray, insert the disc, and then push the same button to close the tray (Figure 7-17). Other convenient features on most of these drives include a volume control button and a headphone port (or jack) so you can use headphones to listen to audio without disturbing others nearby.

With some discs, you can read and/or write on one side only. Manufacturers usually place a silk-screened label on the top layer of these single-sided discs. You insert a single-sided disc in the drive with the label side up. Other discs are double-sided. Simply remove the disc from the drive, flip it over, and reinsert it in the drive to use the other side of the disc. Double-sided discs often have no label; instead each side of the disc is identified with small writing

Push the button to slide out the tray.
Insert the disc, label side up.
Push the same button to close the tray.

FIGURE 7-17 On optical disc drives, you push a button to slide out a tray, insert the disc, and then push the same button to close the tray.

around the center of the disc. Some drives use *LightScribe technology,* which works with specially coated optical discs, to etch labels directly on the disc (as opposed to placing an adhesive label on the disc).

The drive designation of an optical disc drive usually follows alphabetically after that of all the hard disks and portable disks. For example, if the computer has one internal hard disk (drive C) and an external hard disk (drive D), then the first optical disc drive is drive E. A second optical disc drive would be drive F.

Optical discs store items by using microscopic pits (indentations) and lands (flat areas) that are in the middle layer of the disc (Figure 7-18). A high-powered laser light creates the pits. A lower-powered laser light reads items from the disc by reflecting light through the bottom of the disc, which usually is either solid gold or silver in color. The reflected light is converted into a series of bits the computer can process. A land causes light to reflect, which is read as binary digit 1. Pits absorb the light; this absence of light is read as binary digit 0.

Optical discs commonly store items in a single track that spirals from the center of the disc to the edge of the disc. As with a hard disk, this single track is divided into evenly sized sectors on which items are stored (Figure 7-19).

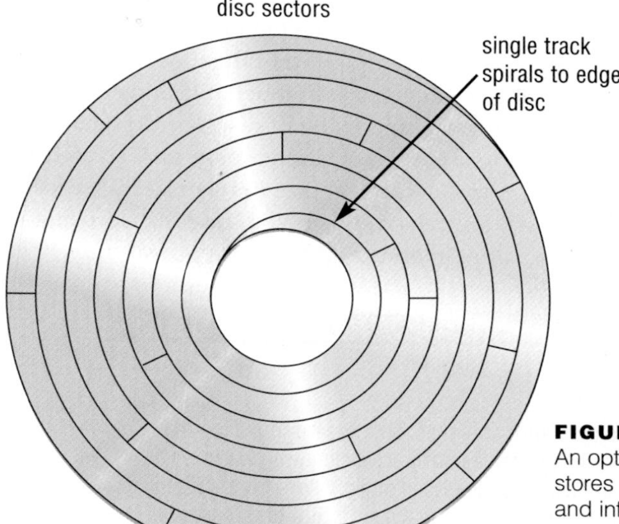

FIGURE 7-19
An optical disc typically stores data, instructions, and information in a single track that spirals from the center of the disc to the edge of a disc.

FIGURE 7-18 HOW A LASER READS DATA ON AN OPTICAL DISC

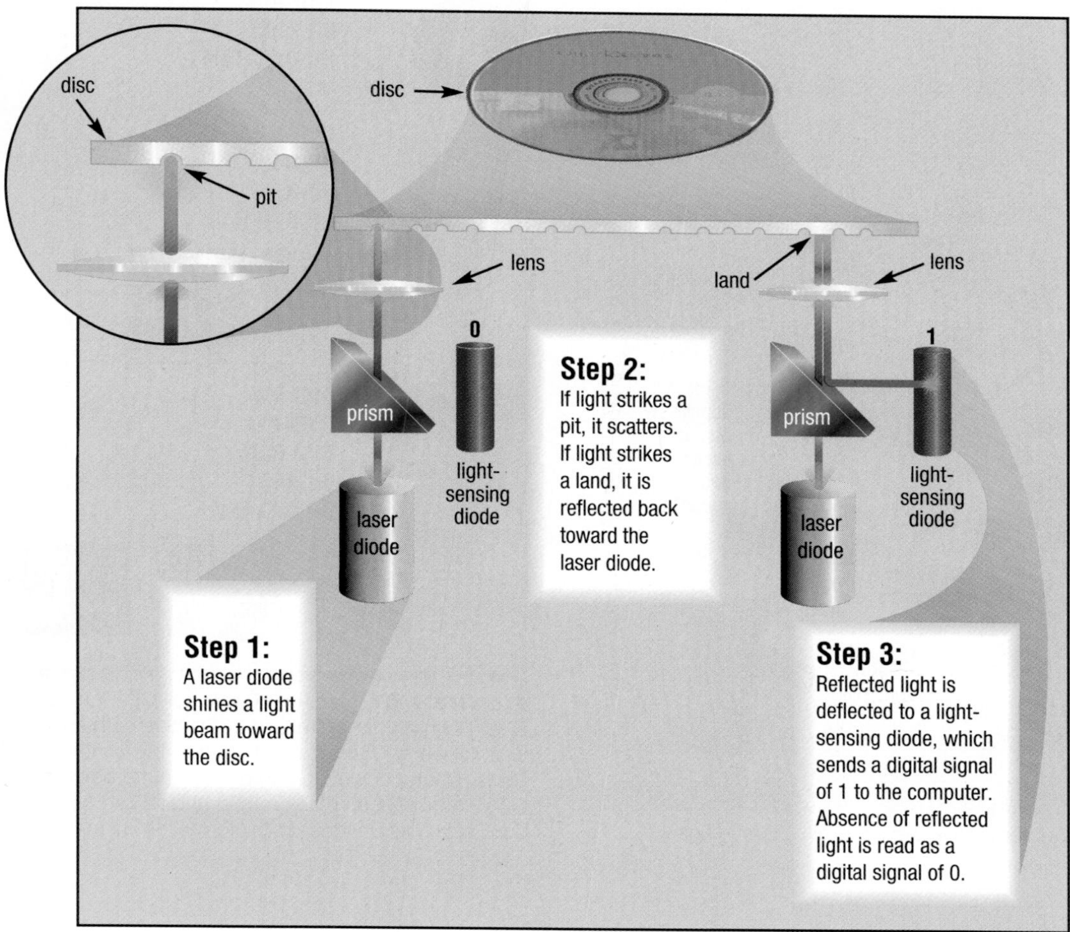

disc
pit
disc
lens
land
lens
0
1
prism
light-sensing diode
laser diode
prism
light-sensing diode
laser diode
Step 1:
A laser diode shines a light beam toward the disc.
Step 2:
If light strikes a pit, it scatters. If light strikes a land, it is reflected back toward the laser diode.
Step 3:
Reflected light is deflected to a light-sensing diode, which sends a digital signal of 1 to the computer. Absence of reflected light is read as a digital signal of 0.

Care of Optical Discs

Manufacturers claim that a properly cared for high-quality optical disc will last 5 years but could last up to 100 years. Figure 7-20 offers some guidelines for the proper care of optical discs. Never bend a disc; it may break. Do not expose discs to extreme temperatures or humidity. The ideal temperature range for disc storage is 50 to 70 degrees Fahrenheit. Stacking discs, touching the underside of discs, or exposing them to any type of contaminant may scratch a disc. Place an optical disc in its protective case, called a *jewel box,* when you are finished using it and store in an upright (vertical) position.

FAQ 7-4

Can I clean a disc?

Yes, you can remove dust, dirt, smudges, and fingerprints from the surface of an optical disc. Moisten a nonabrasive cloth with warm water or rubbing alcohol and then wipe the disc in straight lines from the center outward. You also can repair scratches on the surface with a specialized disc repair kit. For more information, visit scsite.com/dc2008/ch7/faq and then click Cleaning and Repairing Discs.

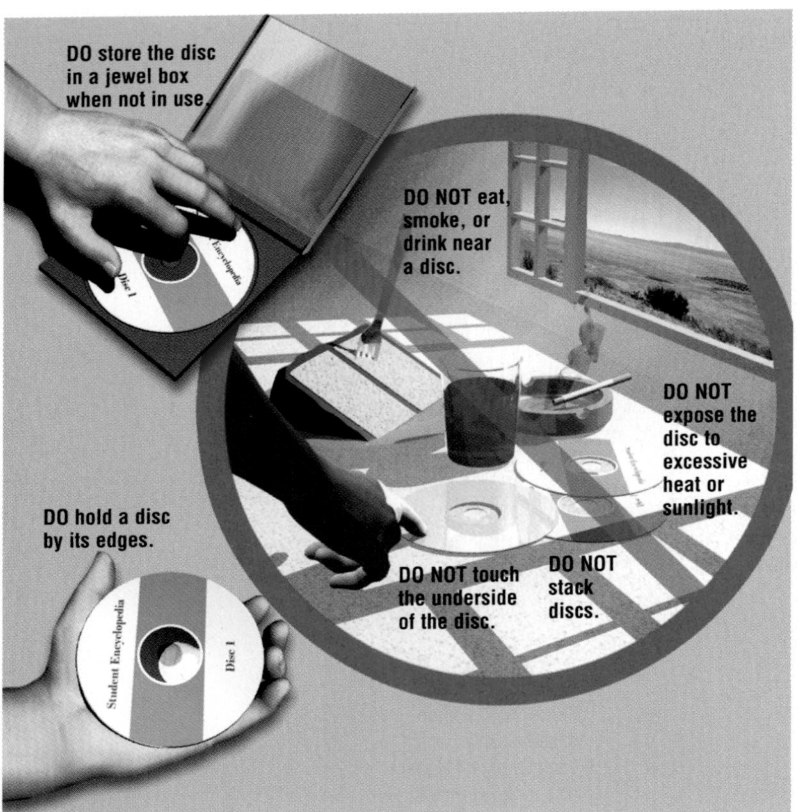
DO store the disc in a jewel box when not in use.
DO NOT eat, smoke, or drink near a disc.
DO NOT expose the disc to excessive heat or sunlight.
DO hold a disc by its edges.
DO NOT touch the underside of the disc.
DO NOT stack discs.
Student Encyclopedia
Disc 1

FIGURE 7-20 Some guidelines for the proper care of optical discs.

Types of Optical Discs

Many different formats of optical discs exist today. Figure 7-21 identifies a variety of optical disc formats and specifies whether a user can read from the disc, write to the disc, and/or erase the disc. The following sections describe characteristics unique to each of these disc formats.

OPTICAL DISC FORMATS

Optical Disc	Read	Write	Erase
CD-ROM	Y	N	N
CD-R	Y	Y	N
CD-RW	Y	Y	Y
DVD-ROM BD-ROM HD DVD-ROM	Y	N	N
DVD-R DVD+R BD-R HD DVD-R	Y	Y	N
DVD-RW DVD+RW DVD-RAM BD-RE HD DVD-RW	Y	Y	Y

FIGURE 7-21 Manufacturers sell CD-ROM and DVD-ROM media prerecorded (written) with audio, video, and software. Users cannot change the contents of these discs. Users, however, can purchase the other formats of CDs and DVDs as blank media and record (write) their own data, instructions, and information on these discs.

CD-ROMs

A **CD-ROM** (pronounced SEE-DEE-rom), or *compact disc read-only memory*, is a type of optical disc that users can read but not write (record) or erase — hence, the name read-only. Manufacturers write the contents of standard CD-ROMs. A standard CD-ROM is called a *single-session disc* because manufacturers write all items on the disc at one time. Software manufacturers often distribute their programs using CD-ROMs (Figure 7-22).

A typical CD-ROM holds from 650 MB to 1 GB of data, instructions, and information. To read a CD-ROM, insert the disc in a **CD-ROM drive** or a CD-ROM player. Because audio CDs and CD-ROMs use the same laser technology, you may be able to use a CD-ROM drive to listen to an audio CD while working on the computer. Some music companies, however, configure their CDs so the music will not play on a computer. They do this to protect themselves from customers illegally copying and sharing the music.

The speed of a CD-ROM drive determines how fast it installs programs and accesses the disc. Original CD-ROM drives were single-speed drives with transfer rates of 150 KBps (kilobytes per second). Manufacturers measure all optical disc drives relative to this original CD-ROM drive. They use an X to denote the original transfer rate of 150 KBps. For example, a 48X CD-ROM drive has a data transfer rate of 7,200 (48 × 150) KBps, or 7.2 MBps.

Current CD-ROM drives have transfer rates, or speeds, ranging from 48X to 75X or faster. The higher the number, the faster the CD-ROM drive. Faster CD-ROM drives are more expensive than slower drives. Read Looking Ahead 7-2 for a look at the future of storage.

CD-ROMs

For more information, visit scsite.com/dc2008/ch7/weblink and then click CD-ROMs.

LOOKING AHEAD 7-2

Bookshelf Design Streamlines Entertainment Storage

Imagine tossing bulky collections of CDs, movies, and video games and replacing them with a streamlined storage system that turns a personal computer into a digital bookshelf.

Two Purdue University industrial designers created *Bookshelf*, a personal computer design featuring a 7-inch cube-shaped central processing unit with add-on hard disk attachments arranged on a shelf and held in place with latched bookends. By adding hardware attachments containing multiple movies, magazines, or games, users easily can create their own custom-designed multimedia libraries at their computers. The attachments, supplied by digital service providers through subscription payments, feature a universal design, so they can be arranged side by side on the computer shelf.

Content categories are viewed much like looking at book titles. The design protects entertainment copyrights while also increasing convenience and portability for users. For more information, visit scsite.com/dc2008/ch7/looking and then click Bookshelf.

FIGURE 7-22 Encyclopedias, games, simulations, and many other programs are distributed on CD-ROM.

PICTURE CDs A Kodak **Picture CD** is a single-session CD-ROM that stores digital versions of film using a jpg file format. Many film developers offer Picture CD service for consumers when they drop off film to be developed. The resolution of images stored on a Picture CD usually is 1024 × 1536 pixels. The average cost for a Picture CD is about $3 per roll of film.

Most optical disc drives can read a Picture CD. Using photo editing software and photographs on the Picture CD, you can remove red eye, crop the photograph, enhance colors, trim away edges, adjust the lighting, and edit just about any aspect of a photograph. In addition, a Picture CD allows you to print copies of the photographs on glossy paper with an ink-jet printer. If you do not have a printer to print the images, many stores have kiosks at which you can print pictures from a Picture CD or other media (Figure 7-23).

> **WEB LINK 7-6**
> **Picture CDs**
> For more information, visit scsite.com/dc2008/ch7/weblink and then click Picture CDs.

CD-Rs and CD-RWs

A **CD-R** (*compact disc-recordable*) is a multisession optical disc on which users can write, but not erase, their own items such as text, graphics, and audio. *Multisession* means you can write on part of the disc at one time and another part at a later time. Each part of a CD-R, however, can be written on only one time, and the disc's contents cannot be erased.

Writing on the CD-R requires a *CD recorder* or a **CD-R drive**. A CD-R drive usually can read both audio CDs and standard CD-ROMs. These

FIGURE 7-23 HOW A PICTURE CD WORKS

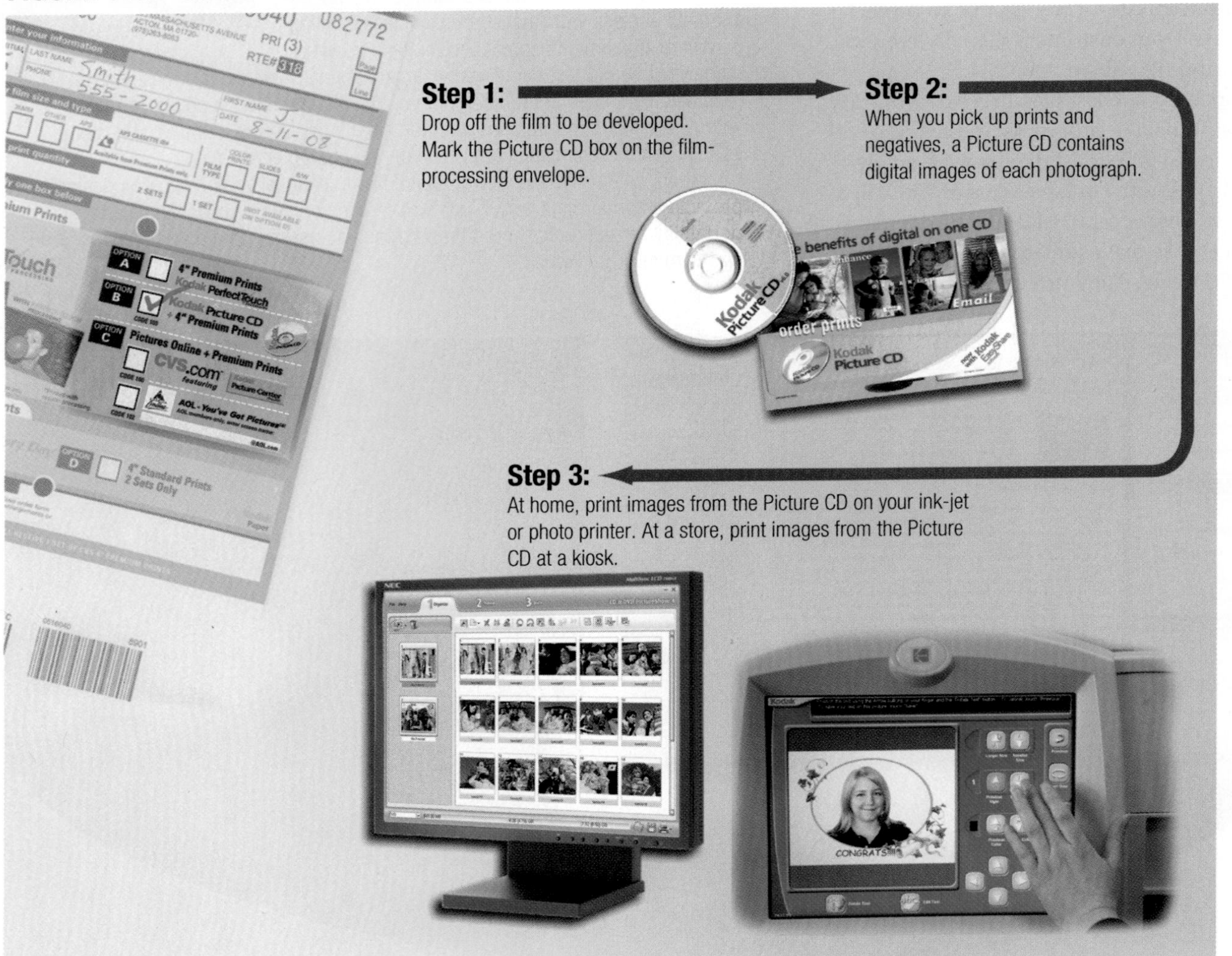

Step 1:
Drop off the film to be developed. Mark the Picture CD box on the film-processing envelope.
Step 2:
When you pick up prints and negatives, a Picture CD contains digital images of each photograph.
Step 3:
At home, print images from the Picture CD on your ink-jet or photo printer. At a store, print images from the Picture CD at a kiosk.
Kodak Picture CD
order prints
CONGRATS

drives read at speeds of 48X or more and write at speeds of 40X or more. Manufacturers often list the write speed first, for example, as 40/48.

A **CD-RW** (*compact disc-rewritable*) is an erasable multisession disc you can write on multiple times. CD-RW overcomes the major disadvantage of CD-R because it allows users to write and rewrite data, instructions, and information on the CD-RW disc multiple times — instead of just once. Reliability of the disc tends to drop, however, with each successive rewrite.

To write on a CD-RW disc, you must have CD-RW software and a **CD-RW drive**. These drives have write speeds of 52X or more, rewrite speeds of 24X or more, and read speeds of 52X or more. Manufacturers state the speeds in this order; that is, write speed, rewrite speed, and read speed is stated as 52/24/52. Most CD-RW drives can read audio CDs, CD-ROMs, CD-Rs, and CD-RWs.

Many personal computers today include a CD-RW drive as a standard feature so users can burn their own discs. The process of writing on an optical disc is called *burning*. Some operating systems, such as Windows Vista, include the capability of burning discs.

Using a CD-RW disc, users easily back up large files from a hard disk. Another popular use of CD-RW and CD-R discs is to create audio CDs. For example, users can record their own music and save it on a CD, purchase and download MP3 songs from the Web, or rearrange tracks on a purchased music CD. The process of copying audio and/or video data from a purchased disc and saving it on digital media is called *ripping*. Read Ethics & Issues 7-1 for a related discussion.

FAQ 7-5

Is it legal to copy songs or movies to a disc or other media?

It is legal to copy songs or movies from a disc that you obtained legally, if you use the copied music or movie for your own personal use. If you share the copy with a friend, however, you are violating copyright law. It is legal to download copyrighted material if the copyright holder has granted permission to do so. In most cases, you pay a fee. For more information, visit scsite.com/dc2008/ch7/faq and then click Copying Songs and Movies.

VIDEO CDs A *video CD (VCD)* is a CD format that stores video on a CD-R that can be played in CD or DVD drives, many DVD players, and some game consoles. Standard VCDs can hold from 74 to 80 minutes of video. Although the quality is not as high as DVD, some users opt to burn video CDs with their existing CD-R drive because it saves the expense of purchasing a DVD burner.

FAQ 7-6

How do I share my digital videos online?

Web sites such as Yahoo! Video and YouTube allow you to share videos online. Before sharing a video, you must first create an account on the site and agree to the terms of service. Once your account is created, you may upload your video and specify characteristics such as its title, description, and category. Do not post any videos that are protected by copyright laws. For more information, visit scsite.com/dc2008/ch7/faq and then click Video Sharing.

ETHICS & ISSUES 7-1

Does Music and Movie Downloading Harm CD and DVD Sales?

With millions of songs and movies both legally and illegally available on the Internet, the entertainment industry claims that sharing music is harming CD and DVD sales, which results in less money in the artists' and studios' pockets. When Apple Computer announced that the company would sell movies through its iTunes online service, large retailer chains complained that their DVD movie sales would suffer. Both retailers and the entertainment companies make far more money when someone purchases a CD or DVD instead of buying the media online. A study by researchers showed that the availability and sharing of recent CD releases did not have an effect on the sales of the CDs. While music publishing companies have seen a modest decline in sales since the advent of illegal music sharing, they have released significantly fewer titles, and some claim that the quality of music has declined. Also, CD and DVD sales may have been exceptionally high in the 1990s as people replaced older media, such as cassette tapes and VHS tapes, with the newer CD and DVD formats. Do readily available online music and movies harm CD and DVD sales? Why? Are there any situations in which the availability can increase sales? How? Are the entertainment industry and retail chain complaints justified? Why?

WEB LINK 7-7

CD-Rs and CD-RWs

For more information, visit scsite.com/dc2008/ch7/weblink and then click CD-Rs and CD-RWs.

DVD-ROMs, BD-ROMs, and HD DVD-ROMs

A **DVD-ROM** (*digital versatile disc-read-only memory* or *digital video disc-read-only memory*) is a high-capacity optical disc on which users can read but not write or erase. Manufacturers write the contents of DVD-ROMs and distribute them to consumers. DVD-ROMs store movies, music, music videos, huge databases, and complex software (Figure 7-24).

The storage capacity of a DVD-ROM is more than enough to hold a telephone book containing every resident in the United States. Not only is the storage capacity of a DVD-ROM greater than that of a CD, a DVD-ROM's quality also far surpasses that of CDs because images are stored at higher resolution.

To read a DVD-ROM, you must have a **DVD-ROM drive** or DVD player. Most DVD-ROM drives also can read audio CDs, CD-ROMs, CD-Rs, and CD-RWs. DVD-ROM drives can read DVDs at speeds of 16X or more and CDs at speeds of 52X or more.

Although the size and shape of a CD-ROM and DVD-ROM are similar, a DVD-ROM stores data, instructions, and information in a slightly different manner and thus achieves a higher storage capacity. Widely used DVD-ROMs are capable of storing 4.7 GB to 17 GB, depending on the storage techniques used. The first storage technique involves making the disc denser by packing the pits closer together. The second involves using two layers of pits. For this technique to work, the lower layer of pits is semitransparent so the laser can read through it to the upper layer. This technique doubles the capacity of the disc. Finally, some DVD-ROMs are double-sided.

FIGURE 7-24 A DVD-ROM is a high-capacity optical disc.

Two newer, more expensive competing DVD formats are Blu-ray and HD DVD, both of which are higher capacity and better quality than standard DVDs. A *Blu-ray Disc-ROM (BD-ROM)* has storage capacities of 100 GB, with expectations of exceeding 200 GB in the future. Blu-ray drives and players are backward compatible with DVD and CD formats. Some game consoles include a Blu-ray drive. The *HD DVD-ROM disc*, which stands for high-density DVD-ROM, has storage capacities up to 60 GB with future projections of 90 GB capacities. HD DVD drives and players are backward compatible with DVD formats. Some game consoles work with an HD DVD drive. Figure 7-25 compares the current storage capacities of DVD-ROM, BD-ROM, and HD DVD-ROM media. Read Ethics & Issues 7-2 for a related discussion.

A mini-DVD that has grown in popularity is the UMD, which works specifically with the PlayStation Portable handheld game console. The *UMD* (Universal Media Disc), which has a diameter of about 2.4 inches, can store up to 1.8 GB of games, movies, or music (Figure 7-26).

FAQ 7-7

What is a DVD/CD-RW drive?

It is a combination drive that reads DVD and CD media; it also writes on CD-RW media. This drive allows you to watch a DVD or burn a CD. For more information, visit scsite.com/dc2008/ch7/faq and then click DVD/CD-RW Drives.

DVD, BD, AND HD DVD STORAGE CAPACITIES

Sides	Layers	DVD-ROM	BD-ROM	HD DVD-ROM
1	1	4.7 GB	25 GB	15 GB
1	2	8.5 GB	50 GB	30 GB
2	1	9.4 GB	50 GB	30 GB
2	2	17 GB	100 GB	60 GB

FIGURE 7-25 Storage capacities of DVDs, BDs, and HD DVDs.

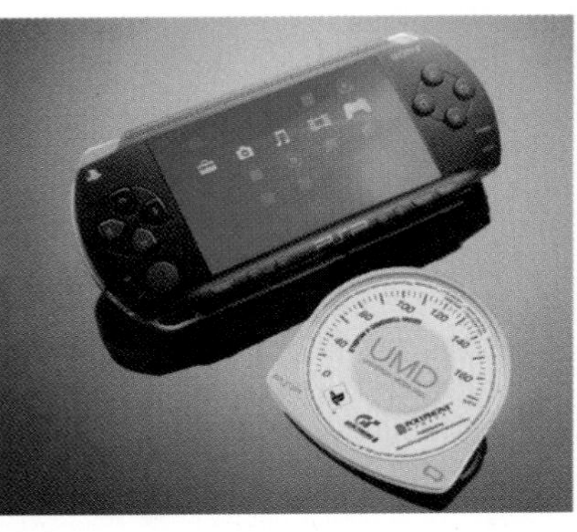

FIGURE 7-26 This UMD contains the game, Gran Turismo.

ETHICS & ISSUES 7-2

Is the Blu-ray and HD DVD Competition Good for Consumers?

In the early 1980s, a battle raged over the VHS and Betamax video tape formats. Eventually, the VHS format won over the hearts and dollars of consumers despite experts' claims of the superiority of the Betamax format, and the Betamax format remains a footnote in the history of consumer electronics. Today, a similar rivalry exists between the Blu-ray and HD DVD formats as two competing groups of consumer electronic corporate giants vie to get their players and discs in your home.

Some differences exist between the standards. While a Blu-ray Disc (BD) can hold more data than an HD DVD disc, the HD DVD players are much less expensive and still include enough capacity to hold a high-definition movie. HD DVD discs are less expensive to make, though more movie studios have announced support for Blu-ray. Some consumer advocates claim that the competition between the standards will benefit consumers as each side tries to win through lower prices and more features. Others claim that two standards hurt consumers because some movie studios, computer companies, and software providers will choose to support only one format. If this happens, consumers may choose to purchase both types of devices or, in frustration, not purchase a player at all. Some predict that high-definition DVD players eventually will support both formats. Is the availability of two high-definition DVD formats good for consumers? Why or why not? Do you think that prices will go up if one format eventually wins over the other? Why or why not? With limited shelf space, how should video rental and retail stores cope with keeping both formats for a movie in stock?

Recordable and Rewritable DVDs

Many types of recordable and rewritable DVD formats are available. *DVD-R* and *DVD+R* are competing DVD-recordable formats, each with up to 4.7 GB storage capacity. Similarly, *BD-R* and *HD DVD-R* are competing high-capacity DVD-recordable formats. Each of these formats allows users to write on the disc once and read (play) it many times. In concept, DVD-R, DVD+R, BD-R, and HD DVD-R are similar to CD-R.

Instead of recordable DVDs, however, most users work with rewritable DVDs because these discs can be written on multiple times and also erased. Three competing rewritable DVD formats, each with storage capacities up to 4.7 GB per side are **DVD-RW**, **DVD+RW**, and **DVD+RAM**. Likewise, *BD-RE* and *HD DVD-RW* are competing high-capacity rewritable DVD formats. These rewritable DVDs are similar in concept to CD-RW. To write on these discs, you must have a compatible drive or recorder. Rewritable drives usually can read a variety of DVD and CD media. Before investing in equipment, check to be sure it is compatible with the media on which you intend to record.

As the cost of DVD technologies becomes more reasonable, many industry professionals expect that DVD eventually will replace all CD media.

FAQ 7-8

Are DVD drives and recorders compatible with both the + and – DVD formats?

When you purchase recordable or rewritable DVDs, you will notice that they are available in either the + (plus) or – (minus) format. You first should check your DVD drive or recorder to identify the DVD formats it will accept. Many new DVD drives and recorders accept both + and – formats, while some still accept only one or the other. For more information, visit scsite.com/dc2008/ch7/faq and then click DVD Formats.

WEB LINK 7-8

Blu-ray and HD DVD

For more information, visit scsite.com/dc2008/ch7/weblink and then click Blu-ray and HD DVD.

Test your knowledge of pages 366 through 373 in Quiz Yourself 7-2.

QUIZ YOURSELF 7-2

Instructions: Find the true statement below. Then, rewrite the remaining false statements so they are true.

1. A CD-RW is a type of optical disc on which users can read but not write (record) or erase.
2. A DVD-RAM is a single-session disc that stores digital versions of film using a jpg file format.
3. DVDs have the same storage capacities as CDs.
4. Optical discs are written and read by mirrors.
5. Single session means you can write on part of the disc at one time and another part at a later time.
6. Three competing rewritable DVD formats are DVD-RW, DVD+RW, and DVD+RAM.

Quiz Yourself Online: To further check your knowledge of optical discs and various optical disc formats, visit scsite.com/dc2008/ch7/quiz and then click Objectives 5 – 6.

TAPE

One of the first storage media used with mainframe computers was tape. **Tape** is a magnetically coated ribbon of plastic capable of storing large amounts of data and information at a low cost. Tape no longer is used as a primary method of storage. Instead, business users utilize tape most often for long-term storage and backup.

Comparable to a tape recorder, a **tape drive** reads and writes data and information on a tape. Although older computers used reel-to-reel tape drives, today's tape drives use tape cartridges. A *tape cartridge* is a small, rectangular, plastic housing for tape (Figure 7-27). Tape cartridges that contain quarter-inch-wide tape are slightly larger than audiocassette tapes. Business users sometimes back up personal computer hard disks to tape, often using an external tape drive. On larger computers, tape cartridges are mounted in a separate cabinet called a *tape library*. Transfer rates of tape drives range from 1.25 MBps to 6 MBps.

Tape storage requires *sequential access*, which refers to reading or writing data consecutively. As with a music tape, you must forward or rewind the tape to a specific point to access a specific piece of data. For example, to access item W requires passing through points A through V sequentially.

Hard disks, CDs, and DVDs all use direct access. *Direct access*, also called *random access*, means that the device can locate a particular data item or file immediately, without having to move consecutively through items stored in front of the desired data item or file. When writing or reading specific data, direct access is much faster than sequential access.

FIGURE 7-27 A tape drive and a tape cartridge.

PC CARDS AND EXPRESSCARD MODULES

As discussed in Chapter 4, a **PC Card** is a thin, credit-card-sized removable flash memory device that fits into a PC Card slot. An **ExpressCard module** is a removable device, smaller than a PC Card, that fits in an ExpressCard slot. PC Cards and ExpressCard modules can be used to add memory, storage, communications, multimedia, and security capabilities to a computer. Both developed by the PCMCIA (Personal Computer Memory Card International Association), PC Cards and ExpressCard modules commonly are used in notebook computers.

PC Cards are about 86 mm long and 54 mm wide. ExpressCard modules, by contrast, are either rectangular at 75 mm long and 34 mm wide or L-shaped with a width of 54 mm (Figure 7-28).

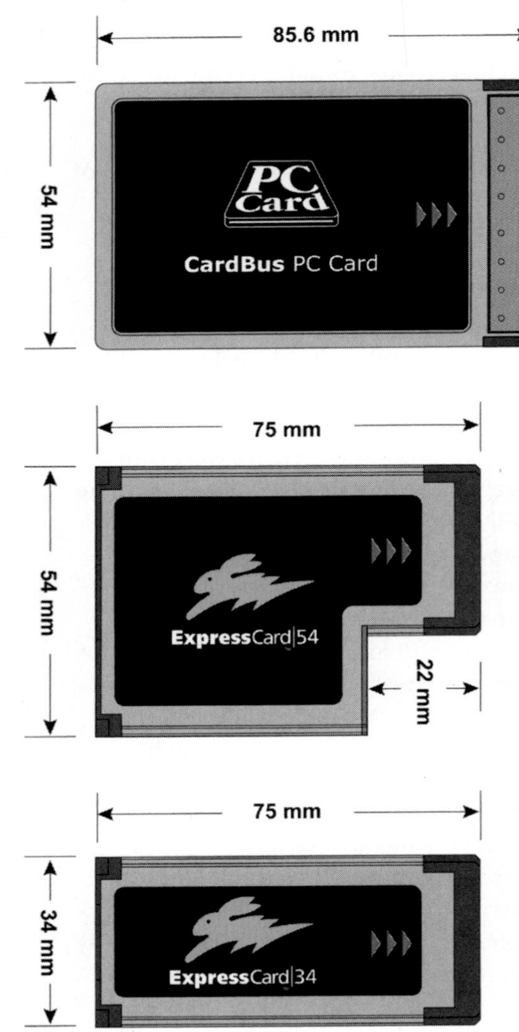

FIGURE 7-28 Comparison of PC Card and ExpressCard module form factors.

MINIATURE MOBILE STORAGE MEDIA

Miniature mobile storage media allow mobile users easily to transport digital images, music, or documents to and from computers and other devices (Figure 7-29). Many desktop computers, notebook computers, Tablet PCs, PDAs, smart phones, digital cameras, and portable media players have built-in slots or ports to read from and write on miniature mobile storage media. For computers or devices without built-in slots, users insert the media in separate peripherals such as a card reader/writer, which typically plugs in a USB port. The following sections discuss the widely used miniature storage media: flash memory cards, USB flash drives, and smart cards.

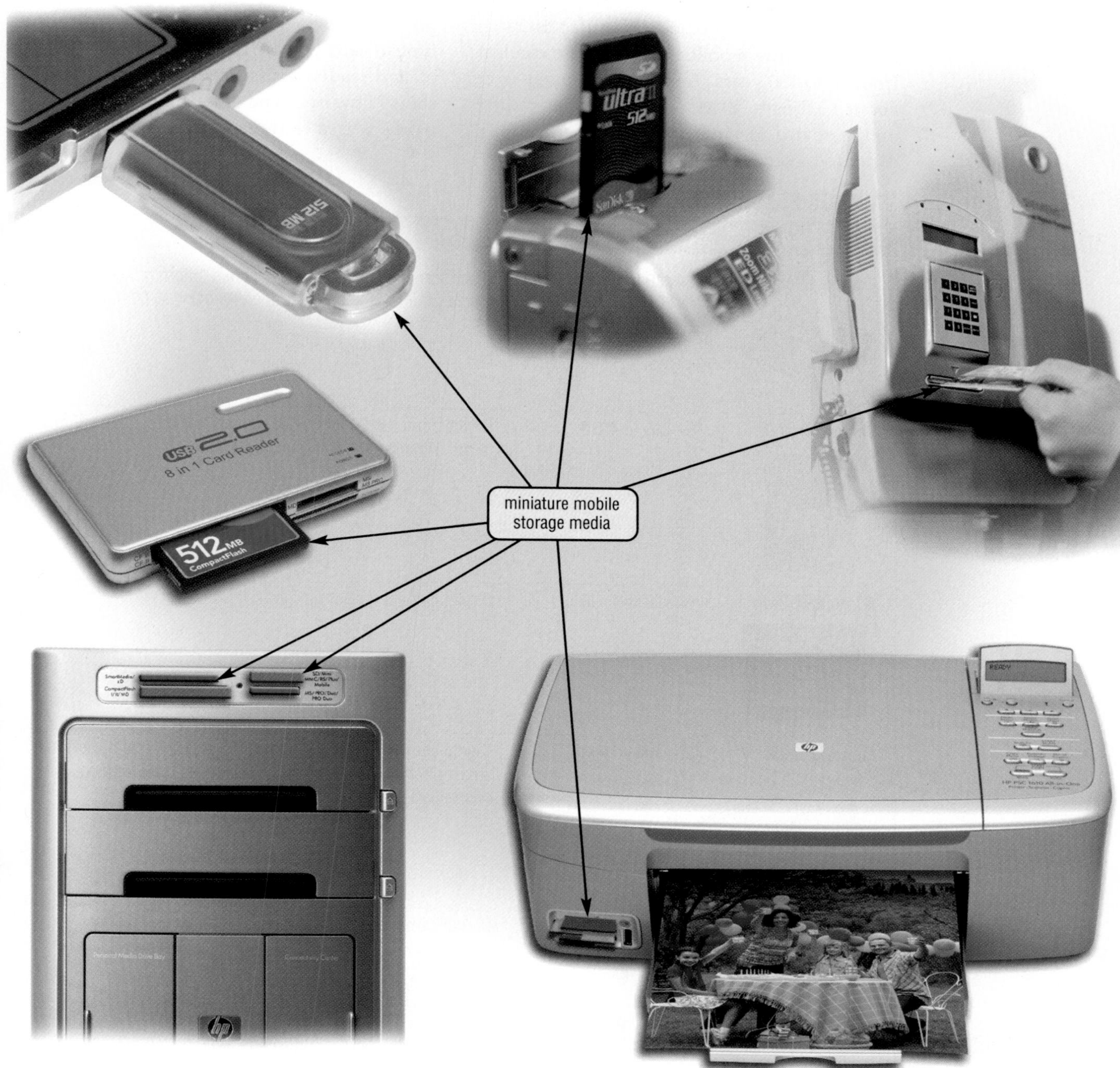

FIGURE 7-29 Many types of computers and devices use miniature mobile storage media.

Flash Memory Cards

Previously, this chapter discussed miniature hard disks (magnetic media) and mini discs such as the UMD (optical media). Flash memory cards, by contrast, are a type of *solid-state media*, which means they consist entirely of electronic components and contain no moving parts. Common types of flash memory cards include *CompactFlash* (*CF*), *Secure Digital* (*SD*), *xD Picture Card*, and *Memory Stick*. The table in Figure 7-30 compares storage capacities and uses of these media.

Depending on the device, manufacturers claim miniature mobile storage media can last from 10 to 100 years. Transfer rates range from about 1 MBps to 10 MBps or more, depending on the device. Flash memory cards are quite expensive compared to other storage media. For example, the cost of a 4 GB CompactFlash card is the same as a 500 GB SATA hard disk.

To view, edit, or print images and information stored on miniature mobile storage media, you transfer the contents to your desktop computer or other device. Some printers have slots to read flash memory cards. If your computer or printer does not have a built-in slot, you can purchase a *card reader/writer*, which is a device that reads and writes data, instructions, and information stored on flash memory cards. Card reader/writers usually connect to the USB port or FireWire port on the system unit. The type of card you have will determine the type of card reader/writer needed. Figure 7-31 shows how one type of flash memory card works with a card reader/writer.

VARIOUS FLASH MEMORY CARDS

Media Name	Storage Capacity	Use
CompactFlash	64 MB to 16 GB	Digital cameras, PDAs, smart phones, photo printers, portable media players, notebook computers, desktop computers
Secure Digital	64 MB to 4 GB	Digital cameras, digital video cameras, PDAs, smart phones, photo printers, portable media players
xD Picture Card	64 MB to 2 GB	Digital cameras, photo printers
Memory Stick	256 MB to 4 GB	Digital cameras, digital video cameras, PDAs, photo printers, smart phones, handheld game consoles, notebook computers
Memory Stick PRO Duo	128 MB to 4 GB	Digital cameras, smart phones, handheld game consoles

FIGURE 7-30 A variety of flash memory cards.

FIGURE 7-31 HOW ONE TYPE OF FLASH MEMORY CARD WORKS

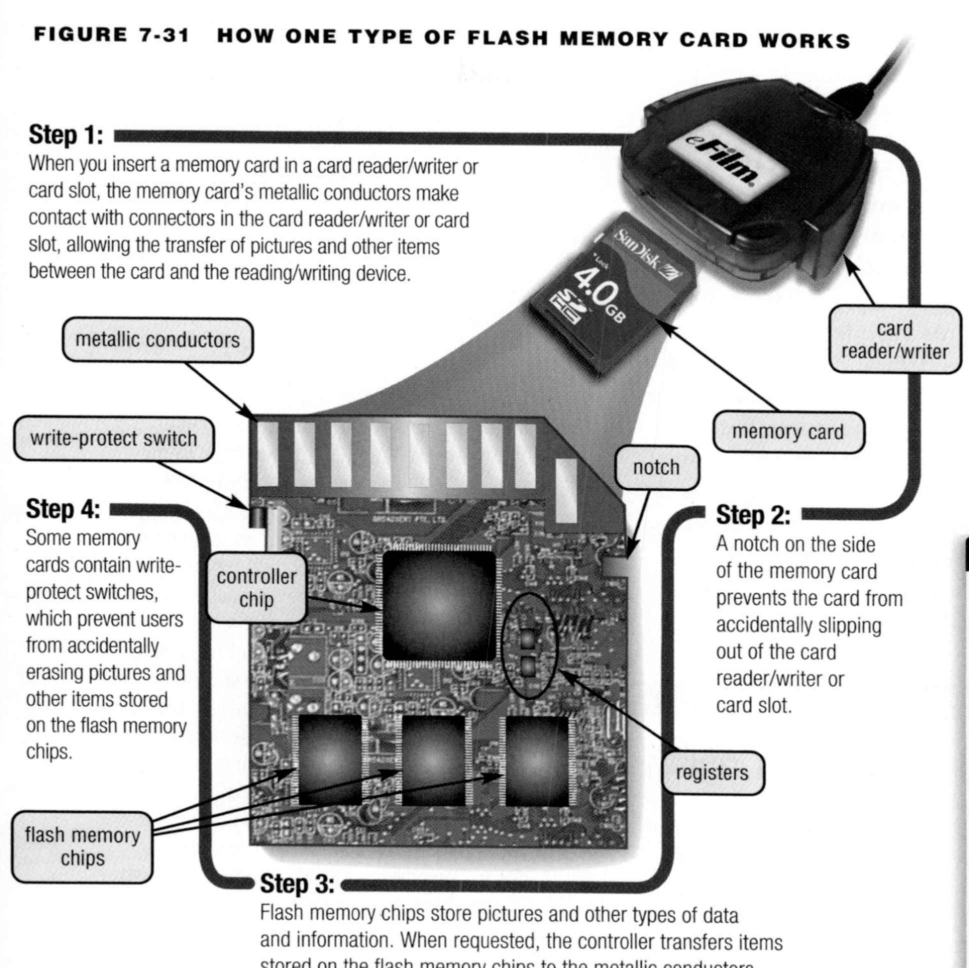

Step 1:
When you insert a memory card in a card reader/writer or card slot, the memory card's metallic conductors make contact with connectors in the card reader/writer or card slot, allowing the transfer of pictures and other items between the card and the reading/writing device.
metallic conductors
card reader/writer
memory card
write-protect switch
notch
Step 4:
Some memory cards contain write-protect switches, which prevent users from accidentally erasing pictures and other items stored on the flash memory chips.
controller chip
Step 2:
A notch on the side of the memory card prevents the card from accidentally slipping out of the card reader/writer or card slot.
registers
flash memory chips
Step 3:
Flash memory chips store pictures and other types of data and information. When requested, the controller transfers items stored on the flash memory chips to the metallic conductors, using registers for temporary storage, as needed.

WEB LINK 7-9

Flash Memory Cards

For more information, visit scsite.com/dc2008/ch7/weblink and then click Flash Memory Cards.

FAQ 7-7

Why do drive letters for removable media sometimes change?

When you connect a removable storage device, such as a USB flash drive or pocket hard drive, to your computer, Windows assigns the device the next available drive letter. If the last drive letter used on your computer is D, your removable storage device will be assigned the letter E. Because the number of drives in a computer will vary from computer to computer, the next available drive letter also will vary. For more information, visit scsite.com/dc2008/ch7/faq and then click Drive Letters.

USB Flash Drives

A **USB flash drive**, sometimes called a *pen drive* or *thumb drive*, is a flash memory storage device that plugs in a USB port on a computer or mobile device (Figure 7-32). USB flash drives are convenient for mobile users because they are small and lightweight enough to be transported on a keychain or in a pocket. With a USB flash drive, users easily transfer documents, pictures, music, and videos from one computer to another. Current USB flash drives have data transfer rates of about 12 MBps and storage capacities ranging from 32 MB to 64 GB, with the latter being extremely expensive.

USB flash drives have become the mobile user's primary portable storage device, making the floppy disk nearly obsolete because they have much greater storage capacities and are much more convenient to carry. A special type of USB flash drive, called a *U3 smart drive*, offers even more convenience because it includes preinstalled software accessed through a Windows-type interface.

The drive designation of a USB flash drive usually follows alphabetically after all other disks. For example, if the computer has one internal hard disk (drive C) and a DVD drive (drive D) and no other disk drives, then the USB flash drive probably will be drive E.

WEB LINK 7-10

USB Flash Drives

For more information, visit scsite.com/dc2008/ch7/weblink and then click USB Flash Drives.

FIGURE 7-32 A USB flash drive.

Smart Cards

A **smart card**, which is similar in size to a credit card or ATM card, stores data on a thin microprocessor embedded in the card. Smart cards contain a processor and have input, process, output, and storage capabilities. When you insert the smart card in a specialized card reader, the information on the smart card is read and, if necessary, updated (Figure 7-33).

Uses of smart cards include storing medical records, vaccination data, and other health-care and identification information; tracking information such as employee attendance or customer purchases; storing a prepaid amount of money, such as for student purchases on campus; and authenticating users such as for Internet purchases or building access. In addition, smart cards can double as an ID card. Read Ethics & Issues 7-3 for a related discussion.

FAQ 7-10

Are some credit cards smart cards?

Yes. More than 200 million smart Visa cards, which contain a microchip filled with their personal information, currently are in use around the world. Credit card smart cards offer the consumer the convenience of using the card to make purchases in stores and online. For more information, visit scsite.com/dc2008/ch7/faq and then click Credit Card Smart Cards.

ETHICS & ISSUES 7-3

Should the World Become a Cashless Society?

Do you toss your loose change in a jar with the hopes of making a special purchase with the savings someday? This habit may become futile if the world goes cashless. Some forecasters say that the world is moving toward a cashless society. One form of payment that could end the need for cash is the smart card, which can store a dollar amount on a thin microprocessor and update the amount whenever a transaction is made. Advocates claim that smart cards would eliminate muggings and robberies, make it difficult to purchase illegal goods, and reduce taxes by identifying tax cheats. Also, payment using biometrics, such as fingerprints, is becoming more common. Several high-profile security breaches at credit reporting and credit card companies, however, have heightened concerns over privacy. In a recent survey, most Americans said that they would not use a smart card even if privacy was guaranteed. Another survey shows that most Americans believe that fingerprints are a trustworthy form of identification. A cash purchase usually is anonymous. Yet, a smart card purchase preserves a record of the transaction that could become available to other merchants, advertisers, government agencies, or hackers. Considering the advantages and disadvantages, should the world become a cashless society? Why or why not? Would you be comfortable using a smart card or fingerprint instead of cash for all transactions? Why?

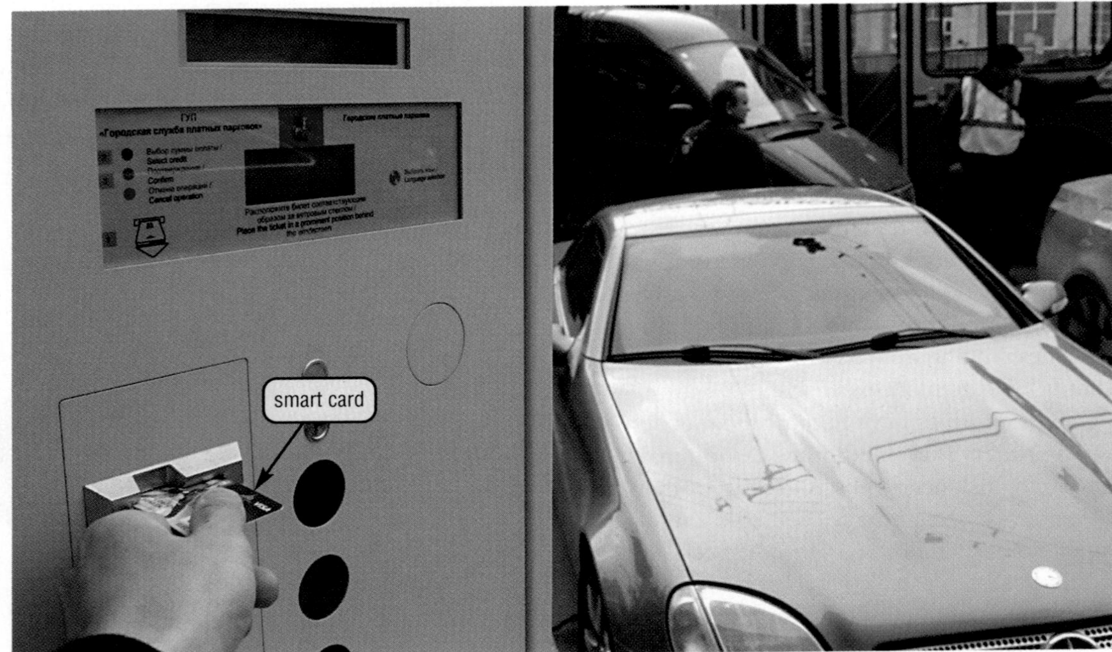

FIGURE 7-33 Motorists use their smart cards to pay parking fees.

WEB LINK 7-11

Smart Cards

For more information, visit scsite.com/dc2008/ch7/weblink and then click Smart Cards.

MICROFILM AND MICROFICHE

Microfilm and microfiche store microscopic images of documents on roll or sheet film. **Microfilm** is a 100- to 215-foot roll of film. **Microfiche** is a small sheet of film, usually about 4 × 6 inches. A *computer output microfilm recorder* is the device that records the images on the film. The stored images are so small that you can read them only with a microfilm or microfiche reader (Figure 7-34).

Applications of microfilm and microfiche are widespread. Libraries use these media to store back issues of newspapers, magazines, and genealogy records. Some large organizations use microfilm and microfiche to archive inactive files. Some banks use them to store transactions and canceled checks. The U.S. Army uses them to store personnel records.

The use of microfilm and microfiche provides a number of advantages. They greatly reduce the amount of paper firms must handle. They are inexpensive and have the longest life of any storage media (Figure 7-35).

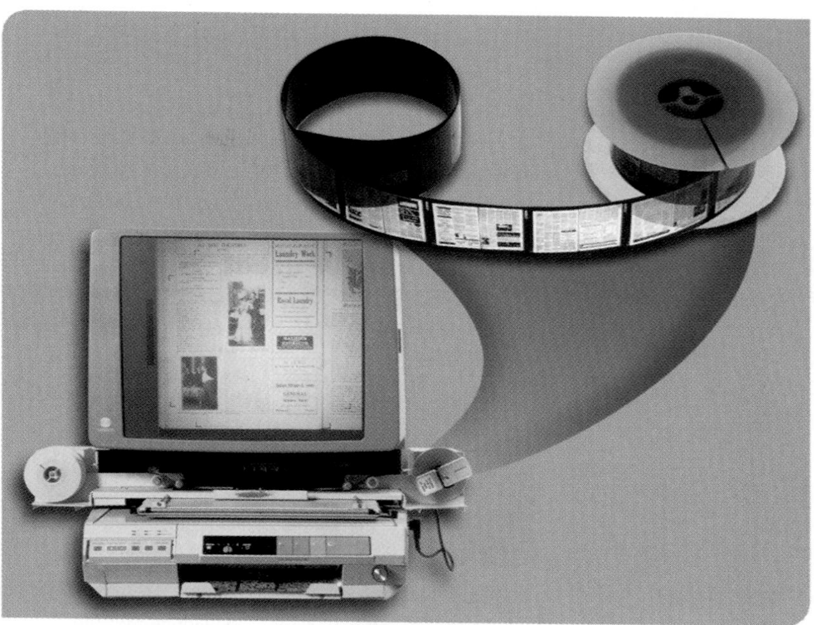

FIGURE 7-34 Images on microfilm can be read only with a microfilm reader.

MEDIA LIFE EXPECTANCIES* **(when using high-quality media)**

Media Type	Guaranteed Life Expectancy	Potential Life Expectancy
Magnetic disks	3 to 5 years	20 to 30 years
Optical discs	5 to 10 years	50 to 100 years
Microfilm	100 years	500 years

* according to manufacturers of the media

FIGURE 7-35 Microfilm is the medium with the longest life.

ENTERPRISE STORAGE

A large business, commonly referred to as an enterprise, has hundreds or thousands of employees in offices across the country or around the world. Enterprises use computers and computer networks to manage and store huge volumes of data and information about customers, suppliers, and employees (Figure 7-36).

To meet their large-scale needs, enterprises use special hardware geared for heavy use, maximum availability, and maximum efficiency. One or more servers on the network have the sole purpose of providing storage to connected users. For high-speed storage access, entire networks are dedicated exclusively to connecting devices that provide storage to other servers. In an enterprise, some storage systems can provide more than 185 terabytes (trillion bytes) of storage capacity. CD-ROM servers and DVD-ROM servers hold hundreds of CD-ROMs or DVD-ROMs.

An enterprise's storage needs usually grow daily. Thus, the storage solutions an enterprise chooses must be able to store its data and information requirements today and tomorrow.

FIGURE 7-36 An enterprise uses computers and high-capacity storage devices.

PUTTING IT ALL TOGETHER

Many factors influence the type of storage devices you should use: the amount of data, instructions, and information to be stored; the hardware and software in use; and the desired cost. The table in Figure 7-37 outlines several suggested storage devices for various types of computer users.

CATEGORIES OF USERS

User	Typical Storage Devices
HOME 	• 250 GB hard disk • Online storage • CD or DVD drive • Card reader/writer • USB flash drive
SMALL OFFICE/ HOME OFFICE 	• 500 GB hard disk • Online storage • CD or DVD drive • External hard disk for backup • USB flash drive
MOBILE 	• 100 GB hard disk • Online storage • CD or DVD drive • Card reader/writer • Portable hard disk for backup • USB flash drive
POWER	• 1.5 TB hard disk • Online storage • CD or DVD drive • Portable hard disk for backup • USB flash drive
LARGE BUSINESS 	• Desktop Computer - 500 GB hard disk - CD or DVD drive - Smart card reader - Tape drive - USB flash drive • Server or Mainframe - Network storage server - 40 TB hard disk system - CD-ROM or DVD-ROM server - Microfilm or microfiche

FIGURE 7-37 Recommended storage devices for various users.

Test your knowledge of pages 374 through 380 in Quiz Yourself 7-3.

QUIZ YOURSELF 7-3

Instructions: Find the true statement below. Then, rewrite the remaining false statements so they are true.

1. A smart card stores data on a thin magnetic stripe embedded in the card.
2. A USB flash drive is a flash memory storage device that plugs in a parallel port on a computer or mobile device.
3. Flash memory cards are a type of magnetic media, which means they consist entirely of electronic components and contain no moving parts.
4. Microfilm and microfiche have the shortest life of any storage media.
5. Tape storage requires direct access, which refers to reading or writing data consecutively.
6. An ExpressCard module is a removable smart card device that fits in an ExpressCard slot.

Quiz Yourself Online: To further check your knowledge of tape, PC Cards and ExpressCard modules, miniature mobile storage media, and microfilm and microfiche, visit scsite.com/dc2008/ch7/quiz and then click Objectives 7 – 9.

CHAPTER SUMMARY

Storage holds data, instructions, and information, which includes pictures, music, and videos, for future use. Users depend on storage devices to provide access to their storage media for years and decades to come. Read Ethics & Issues 7-4 for a discussion about the future of storage.

This chapter identified and discussed various storage media and storage devices. Storage media covered included internal hard disks, external and removable hard disks, floppy disks, CD-ROMs, recordable CDs, rewritable CDs, DVD-ROMs, Blu-ray Discs (BDs), HD DVD discs, recordable DVDs, rewritable DVDs, tape, PC Cards and ExpressCard modules, flash memory cards, USB flash drives, smart cards, and microfilm and microfiche.

ETHICS & ISSUES 7-4

Who Should Be Looking at Your Medical Records?

A medical transcriber based in a foreign country and hired by a U.S. medical center threatened to post private medical records to the Internet if she was not paid more. With the widespread use of computers and an explosion in data storage capacity around the world, private information, such as medical records, requires increased diligence by companies, governments, and individuals to maintain this privacy. The government would like most Americans' health care records available in privacy-protected electronic format by 2014. Although these records will be stored by a corporation or the government, individuals will have complete control, or ownership, of these electronic records. Updates to the Health Insurance Portability and Accountability Act (HIPAA) effective in 2003 set rigorous standards for medical record privacy. The law, however, still leaves much of your medical information at risk. The law does not cover financial records, education records, or employment records — each of which may contain medical information about you. Your medical information also may be examined by insurance companies, government agencies, the Medical Information Bureau (MIB), employers, and the courts. You also inadvertently may pass on medical information to direct marketers when you participate in informal health screenings or surveys. Some people have found that discussing medical conditions via Internet chat rooms or newsgroups has resulted in unwanted attention, and they later regret the disclosures. Proponents of greater electronic access to medical records claim that more access means that physicians can be better prepared when they see patients, physicians will make fewer errors, and insurance companies can better root out fraud. Should more limits be placed on what other people can do with your medical information? Why or why not? What are the advantages of increased access to medical records? What are the disadvantages?

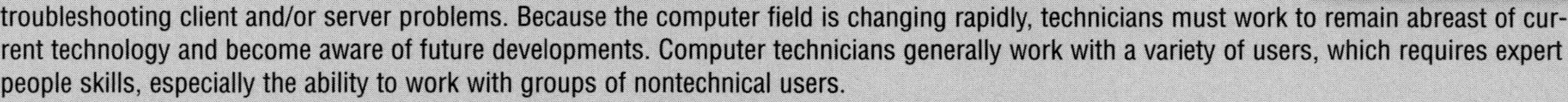

CAREER CORNER

Computer Technician

The demand for computer technicians is growing in every organization and industry. For many, this is the entry point for a career in the computer/information technology field. The responsibilities of a *computer technician*, also called a computer service technician, include a variety of duties. Most companies that employ someone with this title expect the technician to have basic across-the-board knowledge of concepts in the computer electronics field. Some of the tasks are hardware repair and installation; software installation, upgrade, and configuration; and troubleshooting client and/or server problems. Because the computer field is changing rapidly, technicians must work to remain abreast of current technology and become aware of future developments. Computer technicians generally work with a variety of users, which requires expert people skills, especially the ability to work with groups of nontechnical users.

Most entry-level computer technicians possess the *A+ certification*. This certification attests that a computer technician has demonstrated knowledge of core hardware and operating system technology including installation, configuration, diagnosing, preventive maintenance and basic networking that meets industry standards and has at least six months of experience in the field. The Electronics Technicians Association also provides a Computer Service Technician (CST) certification program.

Because this is an entry-level position, the pay scale is not as high as other more demanding and skilled positions. Individuals can expect an average annual starting salary of around $36,000 to $45,000. Companies pay more for computer technicians with experience and certification. For more information, visit scsite.com/dc2008/ch7/careers and then click Computer Technician.

High-Tech Talk

DISK FORMATTING AND FILE SYSTEMS

Formatting a disk can be compared to starting a library. Before any books can be put in place, you must install the bookshelves and a catalog system. Similarly, a disk must have a file system set up to make it ready to receive data. This is true of many different storage media — including hard disks, removable hard disks, and CDs and DVDs — all of which must be formatted, to allow a way to organize and find files saved on the disk.

This discussion focuses on the formatting process required to take a hard disk from its newly manufactured state to a fully functional storage medium. Three main steps are involved in the process of formatting a hard disk: (1) low-level (physical) formatting, (2) partitioning, and (3) high-level (logical) formatting.

A hard disk must be formatted physically before it can be formatted logically. The hard disk manufacturer usually performs a hard disk's physical formatting, or *low-level formatting*. The hard disk manufacturer physically formats a hard disk by writing a pattern of 1s and 0s on the surface of the disk. The 1s and 0s act as small electronic markers, which divide the hard disk platter into its basic physical elements: tracks, sectors, and cylinders.

These elements define the way data is written on and read from the disk physically. As the read/write head moves over the spinning disks, it reads the electronic markers that define the tracks, sectors, and cylinders to determine where it is in relation to the data on the disk's surface.

Once a hard disk has been formatted physically, it can be partitioned. *Partitioning* is the process of dividing the hard disk into regions called partitions. Each partition occupies a group of adjacent cylinders. Partitioning allows you to organize a hard disk into segments and lets you run multiple operating systems on a single computer. You also can keep the entire hard disk as one partition. After a disk partition has been formatted, it is referred to as a *volume*.

After a hard disk has been formatted physically and partitioned, it must be formatted logically. Logical formatting, known as *high-level formatting*, places a file system on the disk. A *file system* allows an operating system to use the space available on a hard disk to store and retrieve files. The operating system uses the file system to store information about the disk's directory, or folder, structure.

The file system also defines the size of the clusters used to store data on the hard disk. A cluster, or *block*, is made up of two or more sectors on a single track on a hard disk. Even if a file has a size of 1 byte, a cluster as large as 64 KB might be used to store the file on large drives. The number of sectors and tracks and, therefore, the number of clusters that a drive can create on a disk's surface determine the capacity of the disk.

While creating the file system during logical formatting, the drive creates a special table in the disk's first sector, sector 0. This table stores entries that the operating system uses to locate files on a disk. Each entry in the table takes up a certain number of bits, which is why file systems often are referred to as 12-bit, 16-bit, or 32-bit. The content of each entry consists of a whole number, which identifies one or more clusters where the file is stored.

Depending on the operating system used to format the disk, the file system can be one of several types, as shown in the table in Figure 7-38. Whatever file system is used, the file system is the interface between the operating system and drives. For more information, visit scsite.com/dc2008/ch7/tech and then click Disk Formatting.

File System	Description	Key Features
FAT (also called FAT12 and FAT16)	The standard file system for DOS and Windows. Because of its widespread use, FAT also is accessible by most other operating systems.	• FAT12 is used for floppy disk drives and very small hard disks (up to 16 MB) • FAT16 is used for small to medium-sized hard disk volumes (up to 2 GB)
VFAT (Virtual FAT)	A newer protected-mode version of the FAT file system, introduced with Windows 95.	• Supports long file names up to 255 characters • Faster than FAT because the computer can read files at least 32 bits at a time
FAT32	A 32-bit version of FAT, introduced with Windows 95.	• Same key features as VFAT • Used for medium-sized to large hard disk volumes (up to 2 terabytes)
NTFS (NT File System)	The 32-bit file system currently used for Windows NT, Windows 2000, Windows XP, and Windows Vista.	• 32- or 64-bit entries in file system table • Fully recoverable file system, designed to restore consistency after a system crash • Used for medium-sized to very large hard disk volumes (up to 256 terabytes)
WinFS (Windows Future Storage)	Originally planned as a file storage subsystem meant to be used with Windows XP and Windows Vista, technologies from this file storage subsystem instead will be used in future versions of other Microsoft products, such as ADO.NET and Microsoft SQL Server.	• Uses database technology; allows users to query for data items • Works in conjunction with the NTFS file system

FIGURE 7-38 Comparison of various file systems.

Companies on the Cutting Edge

SEAGATE TECHNOLOGY
INFORMATION STORAGE SUPPLIER

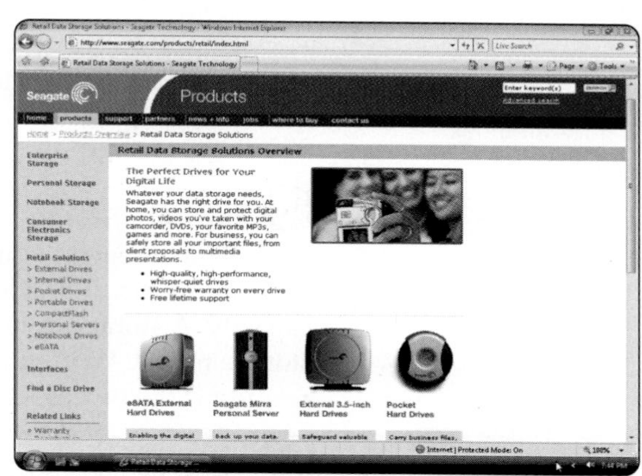

Consumers understand the need to back up their data, but fewer than 25 percent of computer users back up their data on a weekly basis. Hard-disk manufacturer *Seagate* has been persuading people to save copies of their important documents so they will suffer less data loss in the event of a fire or natural disaster.

Seagate is a leading manufacturer of hard disks and storage solutions for desktop computers, high-performance servers, and consumer electronics, including digital video recorders and game consoles. *Forbes Magazine* named Seagate the "2006 Company of the Year" for operational excellence, market leadership, innovation, and efficiency.

Seagate completed its acquisition of rival Maxtor Corporation in 2006. For more information, visit scsite.com/dc2008/ch7/companies and then click Seagate.

SANDISK CORPORATION
WORLD'S LARGEST FLASH MEMORY CARD SUPPLIER

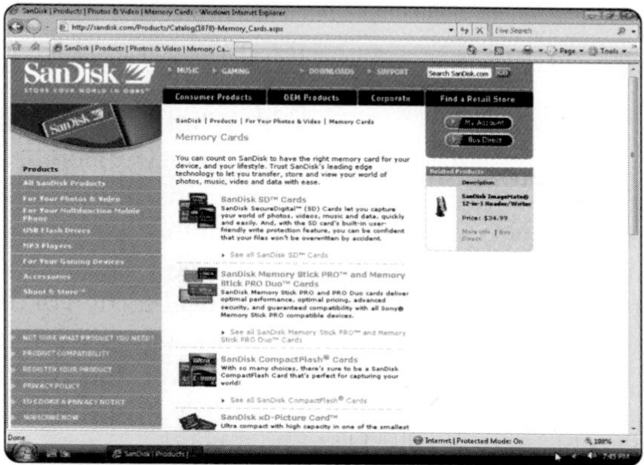

The next time you buy milk at the grocery store or shampoo at the drug store, you might want to purchase a flash memory card for your digital camera, too. *SanDisk Corporation* products can be found in more than 100,000 retail stores across the United States. Best Buy teamed with SanDisk and RealNetworks' Rhapsody in 2006 to launch the Best Buy Digital Music Store.

With retail sales of flash memory cards soaring, SanDisk executives believe consumers buy multiple flash memory cards to store their digital photographs in much the same manner as they formerly stored film negatives in shoe boxes. They also prefer to take a separate flash memory card to digital photo processing centers, which produce high-quality prints.

SanDisk is the only company with the rights to manufacture and sell every flash card format. For more information, visit scsite.com/dc2008/ch7/companies and then click SanDisk.

Technology Trailblazers

AL SHUGART
STORAGE EXPERT

Al Shugart enjoyed fixing broken items and developing new technology. The day after receiving his bachelor's degree in 1951, he went to work at IBM to repair broken machines. IBM then promoted him to supervisor of the product development team that developed the first removable rigid read/write disk drive.

He left IBM in 1969 and went to work as vice president of product development for Memorex. In 1973, he started Shugart Associates, a pioneer in the manufacture of floppy disks. Six years later, he and some associates founded Seagate Technology, Inc., which is a leader in designing and manufacturing storage products.

He served as president and CEO of Al Shugart International, a venture capital firm in California, until his death in 2006. For more information, visit scsite.com/dc2008/ch7/people and then click Al Shugart.

MARK DEAN
IBM INVENTOR

The next generation of IBM's hardware and software might be the work of *Mark Dean*. As vice president of IBM's Almaden Research Center lab in California, Dean is responsible for developing innovative products.

His designs are used in more than 40 million personal computers manufactured each year. He has more than 40 patents or patents pending, including four of the original seven for the architecture of the original personal computer.

Dean joined IBM in 1979 after graduating at the top of his class at the University of Tennessee. Dean earned his Ph.D. degree at Stanford, and he headed a team at IBM that invented the first CMOS microprocessor to operate at 1 gigahertz (1,000 MHz). For more information, visit scsite.com/dc2008/ch7/people and then click Mark Dean.

Quizzes and Learning Games
Computer Genius
Crossword Puzzle
DC Track and Field
Practice Test
Quiz Yourself
Wheel of Terms
You're Hired!

Exercises
Case Studies
Chapter Review
Checkpoint
Key Terms
Learn How To
Learn It Online
Web Research

Beyond the Book
Career Corner
Companies
FAQs
High-Tech Talk
Looking Ahead
Making Use of the Web
Trailblazers
Web Links

Features
Chapter Forum
Install Computer
Lab Exercises
Maintain Computer
Tech News
Timeline 2008

Chapter Review

The Chapter Review section summarizes the concepts presented in this chapter. To listen to the audio version of this Chapter Review, visit scsite.com/dc2008/ch7/review. To obtain help from other students regarding any subject in this chapter, visit scsite.com/dc2008/ch7/forum and post your thoughts or questions.

1 **How Are Storage Devices Different from Storage Medium?** A **storage medium** is the physical material on which a computer keeps data, instructions, and information, which includes pictures, music, and videos. The number of bytes (characters) a storage medium can hold is its **capacity**. A **storage device** is the computer hardware that records and/or retrieves items to and from storage media. **Writing** is the process of transferring items from memory to a storage medium, and **reading** is the process of transferring these items from a storage medium into memory.

2 **What Are the Characteristics of Magnetic Disks?** *Magnetic disks* use magnetic particles to store data, instructions, and information on a disk's surface. Before any data can be read from or written on a magnetic disk, the disk must be formatted. **Formatting** is the process of dividing the disk into *tracks* and *sectors*. Two types of magnetic disks are hard disks and floppy disks.

3 **What Are the Characteristics of a Hard Disk?** A **hard disk**, also called a *hard disk drive* or hard drive, is a storage device that contains one or more inflexible, circular platters that store data, instructions, and information. A *platter* is made of aluminum, glass, or ceramic and is coated with a material that allows items to be recorded magnetically on its surface. Each platter has two read/write heads, one for each side. The location of a *read/write head* often is referred to by its *cylinder*, which is the vertical section of a track that passes through all platters. While the computer is running, the platters rotate at 5,400 to 15,000 *revolutions per minute* (*rpm*), which allows nearly instant access to all tracks and sectors on the platters. The spinning creates a cushion of air between the platters and the read/write heads. A *head crash* occurs when a read/write head touches the surface of a platter, usually resulting in a loss of data. A **backup** is a duplicate of a file, program, or disk placed on a separate storage medium that you can use in case the original is lost, damaged, or destroyed.

4 **What Are the Various Types of Miniature, External, and Removable Hard Disks?** Many mobile devices include miniature hard disks. A type of miniature hard disk called a **pocket hard drive** is a self-contained unit that you insert in or remove from a slot in a device or computer or plug in a USB port on a computer. Miniature hard disks have storage capacities that range from 4 GB to 160 GB. An **external hard disk** is a separate free-standing hard disk that connects with a cable to a USB or FireWire port. External hard disks have storage capacities up to 750 GB. A **removable hard disk** can be inserted or removed from a built-in or external drive. Removable hard disks have storage capacities up to 500 GB.

connect
Visit scsite.com/dc2008/ch7/quiz or click the Quiz Yourself button. Click Objectives 1 – 4.

5 **What Are the Characteristics of Optical Discs?** An *optical disc* is a type of storage media that consists of a flat, round, portable disc made of metal, plastic, and lacquer that is written and read by a laser. Optical discs, which primarily store software, data, digital photographs, movies, and music, contain microscopic pits (indentations) and lands (flat areas) in their middle layer. Optical discs commonly store items in a single track that spirals from the center of the disc to its edge. Like a hard disk, the single track is divided into evenly sized sectors. Common optical discs used today are CD-ROM, CD-R, CD-RW, DVD-ROM, BD-ROM, HD DVD-ROM, UMD, DVD-R, DVD+R, BD-R, HD DVD-R, DVD-RW, DVD+RW, DVD+RAM, BD-RE, and HD DVD-RW.

Chapter Review

6 How Are CD-ROMs, Recordable CDs, Rewritable CDs, DVD-ROMs, Recordable DVDs, and Rewritable DVDs Different? A **CD-ROM**, or *compact disc read-only memory*, is a type of optical disc that uses laser technology to store items. A typical CD-ROM holds from 650 MB to 1 GB of data, instructions, and information. Users can read the contents of standard CD-ROMs but cannot erase or modify their contents. A **CD-R** (*compact disc-recordable*) is a *multisession* disc on which users can record their own items. Each part of a CD-R can be written on only one time, and the disc's contents cannot be erased. A **CD-RW** (*compact disc-rewritable*) is an erasable disc that can be written on multiple times. A **DVD-ROM** (*digital versatile disc-ROM* or *digital video disc-ROM*) is a high capacity optical disc that you can read but not write on or erase. Not only is the storage capacity of a DVD-ROM greater than that of a CD-ROM, a DVD-ROM's quality also far surpasses that of a CD-ROM. Two newer, competing DVD formats are *Blu-ray Disc* and *HD DVD*, both with higher capacity and better quality than standard DVDs. **DVD-RW**, **DVD+RW**, and **DVD+RAM** discs are a recordable version of DVD that allows users to erase and record multiple times.

connect Visit scsite.com/dc2008/ch7/quiz or click the Quiz Yourself button. Click Objectives 5 – 6.

7 How Is Tape Used? **Tape** is a magnetically coated ribbon of plastic capable of storing large amounts of data and information at a low cost. A **tape drive** reads and writes data and information on tape. Businesses sometimes back up personal computer hard disks on tape.

8 What Are PC Cards, ExpressCard Modules, and Other Types of Miniature Mobile Storage Media? A **PC Card** is a thin, credit-card-sized removable flash memory device that fits into a PC Card slot. An **ExpressCard module** is a removable device, smaller than a PC Card, that fits in an ExpressCard slot. Both PC Cards and ExpressCard modules can add memory, storage, communications, or other capabilities to a computer. Many desktop and notebook computers, Tablet PCs, PDAs, smart phones, digital cameras, and portable media players have built-in slots or ports for miniature mobile storage media. Common types of miniature mobile storage media include flash memory cards, USB flash drives, and smart cards. Common flash memory cards include *CompactFlash* (*CF*), *Secure Digital* (*SD*), *xD Picture Card*, and *Memory Stick*. A **USB flash drive** is a flash memory storage device that plugs in a port on a computer or mobile device. A **smart card**, which is similar in size to a credit or ATM card, stores data on a thin microprocessor embedded in the card.

9 How Are Microfilm and Microfiche Used? **Microfilm** is a 100- to 215-foot roll of film. **Microfiche** is a small sheet of film, usually about 4 × 6 inches. Libraries use microfilm and microfiche to store back issues of newspapers, magazines, and records; some large organizations use them to archive inactive files; some banks use them to store transactions and canceled checks; and the U.S. Army uses them to store personnel records.

connect Visit scsite.com/dc2008/ch7/quiz or click the Quiz Yourself button. Click Objectives 7 – 9.

Quizzes and Learning Games
Computer Genius
Crossword Puzzle
DC Track and Field
Practice Test
Quiz Yourself
Wheel of Terms
You're Hired!

Exercises
Case Studies
Chapter Review
Checkpoint
Key Terms
Learn How To
Learn It Online
Web Research

Beyond the Book
Career Corner
Companies
FAQs
High-Tech Talk
Looking Ahead
Making Use of the Web
Trailblazers
Web Links

Features
Chapter Forum
Install Computer
Lab Exercises
Maintain Computer
Tech News
Timeline 2008

Key Terms

You should know the Primary Terms and be familiar with the Secondary Terms. Use the list below to help focus your study. To further enhance your understanding of the Key Terms in this chapter, visit scsite.com/dc2008/ch7/terms. See an example of and a definition for each term, and access current and additional information about the term from the Web.

Primary Terms

(shown in bold-black characters in the chapter)

access time (357)
backup (361)
capacity (356)
CD-R (370)
CD-R drive (370)
CD-ROM (369)
CD-ROM drive (369)
CD-RW (371)
CD-RW drive (371)
DVD+RAM (373)
DVD+RW (373)
DVD-ROM (372)
DVD-ROM drive (372)
DVD-RW (373)
ExpressCard module (374)
external hard disk (363)
floppy disk (365)
floppy disk drive (365)
formatting (357)
hard disk (358)
microfiche (379)
microfilm (379)
online storage (364)
PC Card (374)
Picture CD (370)
pocket hard drive (362)
RAID (362)
reading (356)
removable hard disk (363)
smart card (378)
storage device (356)
storage medium (355)
tape (374)
tape drive (374)
USB flash drive (377)
writing (356)

Secondary Terms

(shown in italic characters in the chapter)

allocation unit (357)
BD-R (373)
BD-RE (373)
Blu-ray Disc-ROM (BD-ROM) (372)
burning (371)
card reader/writer (376)
CD recorder (370)
cluster (357)
compact disc read-only memory (369)
compact disc-recordable (370)
compact disc-rewritable (371)
CompactFlash (CF) (376)
computer output microfilm recorder (379)
cylinder (360)
density (362)
digital versatile disc-read-only memory (372)
digital video disc-read-only memory (372)
direct access (374)
disk cache (361)
disk controller (363)
diskette (365)
DVD+R (373)
DVD-R (373)
EIDE (Enhanced Integrated Drive Electronics) (364)
external floppy disk drive (365)
fixed disk (358)
form factor (360)
hard disk drive (358)
head crash (360)
HD DVD-R (373)
HD DVD-RW (373)
HD DVD-ROM disc (372)
jewel box (368)
KBps (357)
LightScribe technology (367)
longitudinal recording (358)
magnetic disks (357)
MBps (357)
Memory Stick (376)
mini discs (366)
multisession (370)
optical disc (366)
pen drive (377)
perpendicular recording (358)
platter (359)
portable (358)
random access (374)
read/write head (360)
revolutions per minute (rpm) (360)
ripping (371)
SATA (Serial Advanced Technology Attachment) (364)
SCSI (364)
secondary storage (355)
sectors (357)
Secure Digital (SD) (376)
sequential access (374)
single-session disc (369)
solid-state media (376)
storage (354)
tape cartridge (374)
tape library (374)
thumb drive (377)
track (357)
transfer rate (357)
U3 smart drive (377)
UMD (372)
video CD (VCD) (371)
xD Picture Card (376)

Checkpoint

Use the Checkpoint exercises to check your knowledge level of the chapter. The Beyond the Book exercises will help broaden your understanding of the concepts presented in this chapter. To complete the Checkpoint exercises interactively, visit scsite.com/dc2008/ch7/check.

Label the Figure

Identify the storage media.

a. flash memory card
b. internal hard disk
c. tape
d. CD or DVD
e. external hard disk
f. miniature hard disk
g. floppy disk
h. USB flash drive

1. ___

2. ___

3. ___

5. ___

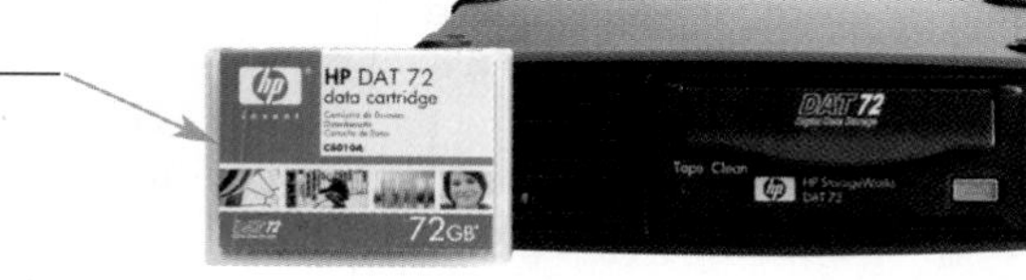

7. ___

6. ___

4. ___

True/False

Mark T for True and F for False. (See page numbers in parentheses.)

_____ 1. Every computer stores system software and application software. (354)

_____ 2. A storage medium is the physical material on which a computer keeps data, instructions, and information. (355)

_____ 3. Reading is the process of transferring data, instructions, and information from memory to a storage medium. (356)

_____ 4. Formatting is the process of dividing the disk into clusters and cylinders. (357)

_____ 5. A cluster can hold data from only one file. (357)

_____ 6. A typical hard disk contains multiple platters. (360)

_____ 7. A removable hard disk is a separate, free-standing hard disk that connects with a cable to a port on the system unit. (363)

_____ 8. SCSI interfaces can support up to eight or fifteen peripheral devices. (364)

_____ 9. BD-R is an older low-capacity DVD-recordable format. (373)

_____ 10. BD-RE and HD DVD-RW are competing high-capacity rewritable DVD formats. (373)

_____ 11. Unlike PC Cards, ExpressCard modules can be used to add memory, storage, communications, multimedia, and security capabilities to a computer. (374)

_____ 12. A U3 smart drive includes preinstalled software accessed through a Windows-type interface. (377)

Checkpoint

Multiple Choice

Select the best answer. (See page numbers in parentheses.)

1. Examples of storage media include all of the following, except _____. (355)
   a. CDs and DVDs
   b. monitors and printers
   c. floppy disks and hard disks
   d. tape and PC Cards
2. _____ is the speed with which data, instructions, and information transfer to and from a device. (357)
   a. Formatting
   b. Access time
   c. Transfer rate
   d. Reading
3. A group of two or more integrated hard disks is called a _____. (362)
   a. backup
   b. disk cache
   c. RAID
   d. portable hard disk
4. A(n) _____ is a self-contained unit that you insert in and remove from a slot or USB port in a device or a computer. (362)
   a. RAID
   b. pocket hard drive
   c. online storage unit
   d. hard disk controller
5. Users store data and information on online storage to _____. (365)
   a. save time by storing large files instantaneously
   b. allow others to access files
   c. store offsite backups of data
   d. all of the above
6. Floppy disks are not as widely used as they were 15 years ago because _____. (365)
   a. they are expensive
   b. they are not portable
   c. of their low storage capacity
   d. they would bend too easily
7. A(n) _____ is a type of storage media that consists of a flat, round, portable disc made of metal, plastic, and lacquer that is written and read by a laser. (366)
   a. optical disc
   b. hard disk
   c. floppy disk
   d. pen drive
8. _____ technology works with specially coated optical discs to etch labels directly on the disc. (367)
   a. SCSI
   b. SATA
   c. LightSaber
   d. LightScribe
9. All of the following are guidelines for the proper care of optical discs except _____. (368)
   a. do not expose the disc to extreme temperatures
   b. do not stack discs
   c. do not hold a disc by its edges
   d. do not eat, smoke, or drink near a disc
10. The process of copying audio and/or video data from a purchased disc and saving it on digital media is called _____. (371)
    a. formatting
    b. ripping
    c. burning
    d. reading
11. _____ are competing high-capacity DVD-recordable formats. (373)
    a. DVD-R and DVD+R
    b. BD-R and HD DVD-R
    c. DVD-RAM and DVD-ROM
    d. BD-RE and BM-W
12. _____ storage requires sequential access. (374)
    a. Hard disk
    b. Tape
    c. UMD
    d. CD
13. A thumb drive is a(n) _____ storage device that plugs in a USB port on a computer or mobile device. (377)
    a. flash memory
    b. optical
    c. magnetic
    d. tape
14. Microfilm and microfiche _____. (379)
    a. greatly increase the amount of paper firms must handle
    b. are expensive
    c. have the longest life of any storage media
    d. all of the above

Checkpoint

Matching

Match the terms with their definitions. (See page numbers in parentheses.)

_____ 1. capacity (356)
_____ 2. cluster (357)
_____ 3. form factor (360)
_____ 4. head crash (360)
_____ 5. disk cache (361)
_____ 6. disk controller (363)
_____ 7. Picture CD (370)
_____ 8. burning (371)
_____ 9. tape drive (374)
_____ 10. pen drive (377)

a. special-purpose chip and electronic circuits that control the transfer of items to and from the system bus
b. the number of bytes (characters) a storage medium can hold
c. size of hard disk platters on computers
d. flash memory storage device that plugs in a USB port
e. memory chips that the processor uses to store frequently accessed items
f. smallest unit of disk space that stores data and information
g. occurs when a read/write head touches the surface of a platter on a hard disk
h. the process of writing on an optical disc
i. piece of metal on a floppy disk that slides to expose the surface of the disk
j. single-session CD-ROM that stores digital versions of film using a jpg file format
k. reads and writes data and information on a tape

Short Answer

Write a brief answer to each of the following questions.

1. What is access time? _____________ What is the difference between a sector and a track? _____________
2. Why is a hard disk inside the system unit sometimes called a fixed disk? _____________ What are some advantages of external and removable hard disks over internal hard disks? _____________
3. How is a single-session disc different from a multisession disc? _____________ What is a VCD? _____________
4. Why might you use miniature mobile storage? _____________ What types of devices might include miniature mobile storage? _____________
5. What are the common types of flash memory cards? _____________ How might you transfer the contents of a miniature mobile storage device to your computer or printer? _____________

Beyond the Book

Read the following book elements, learn more about each using the Web, and then write a brief report.

1. Ethics & Issues — Does Music and Movie Downloading Harm CD and DVD Sales? (371), Is the Blu-ray and HD DVD Competition Good for Consumers? (373), Should the World Become a Cashless Society? (378), or Who Should Be Looking at Your Medical Records? (381)
2. Career Corner — Computer Technician (381)
3. Companies on the Cutting Edge — Seagate Technology or SanDisk Corporation (383)
4. FAQs (359, 362, 364, 368, 371, 372, 373, 377, 378)
5. High-Tech Talk — Disk Formatting and File Systems (382)
6. Looking Ahead — Heat Increases Disk Capacity (359) or Bookshelf Design Streamlines Entertainment Storage (369)
7. Making Use of the Web — Shopping and Auctions (123)
8. Picture Yourself Working with Mobile Storage Media (352)
9. Technology Trailblazers — Al Shugart or Mark Dean (383)
10. Web Links (358, 362, 364, 369, 370, 371, 373, 377, 378)

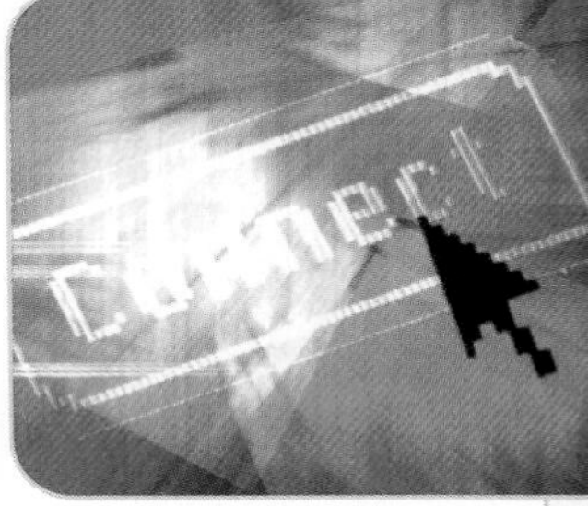

Learn It Online

Use the Learn It Online exercises to reinforce your understanding of the chapter concepts. To access the Learn It Online exercises, visit scsite.com/dc2008/ch7/learn.

1 At the Movies — Got Your Video Right Here

To view the Got Your Video Right Here movie, click the number 1 button. Locate your video and click the corresponding High-Speed or Dial-Up link, depending on your Internet connection. Watch the movie and then complete the exercise by answering the questions that follow. The Sling Media Slingbox is the best way to beam your favorite shows to any broadband-connected computer or Windows Mobile device in the world. How does the Slingbox work? What is one function that it currently is not able to support?

2 At the Movies — Blu-ray Disc

In this chapter, you learned about BD-ROM. Click the number 2 button to view the suggested links and begin your search for videos, podcasts, or vodcasts related to BD-ROM. Choose a video, podcast, or vodcast that discusses BD-ROM and is of interest to you, and then write a description of its contents. Explain why you chose this piece, what you liked about it, what you disliked about it, and whether you would recommend it to a fellow student. Finish your review by giving the video, podcast, or vodcast a rating of 1 – 5 stars. Submit your review in the format requested by your instructor.

3 Student Edition Labs — Maintaining a Hard Drive

Click the number 3 button. A new browser window will open, displaying the Student Edition Labs. Follow the on-screen instructions to complete the Maintaining a Hard Drive Lab. When finished, click the Exit button. If required, submit your results to your instructor.

4 Student Edition Labs — Managing Files and Folders

Click the number 4 button. A new browser window will open, displaying the Student Edition Labs. Follow the on-screen instructions to complete the Managing Files and Folders Lab. When finished, click the Exit button. If required, submit your results to your instructor.

5 Practice Test

Click the number 5 button. Answer each question. When completed, enter your name and click the Grade Test button to submit the quiz for grading. Make a note of any missed questions. If required, submit your results to your instructor.

6 Who Wants To Be a Computer Genius^2?

Click the number 6 button to find out if you are a computer genius. Directions about how to play the game will be displayed. When you are ready to play, click the Play button. Submit your score to your instructor.

7 Wheel of Terms

Click the number 7 button to reinforce important terms you learned in this chapter by playing the Shelly Cashman Series version of this popular game. Directions about how to play the game will be displayed. When you are ready to play, click the Play button. Submit your score to your instructor.

Learn It Online

8 DC Track and Field

Click the number 8 button to use what you have learned in this chapter to compete against other students in three track and field events. Directions about how to play the game will be displayed. When you are ready to play, click the start first event button. If required, submit your score to your instructor.

9 You're Hired!

Click the number 9 button to use what you have learned in this chapter to embark on the path to a career in computers. Directions about how to play the game will be displayed. When you are ready to play, click the begin game button. If required, submit your score to your instructor.

10 Crossword Puzzle Challenge

Click the number 10 button, then click the Crossword Puzzle Challenge link. Directions about how to play the game will be displayed. Complete the puzzle to reinforce skills you learned in this chapter. When you are ready to play, click the Continue button. Submit the completed puzzle to your instructor.

11 Vista Exercises

Click the number 11 button. When the Vista Exercises menu appears, click the exercise assigned by your instructor. A new browser window will open. Follow the on-screen instructions to complete the exercise. When finished, click the Exit button. If required, submit your results to your instructor.

12 In the News

Hitachi sells a small disk drive, about the size of a quarter, which is capable of storing up to 4 GB of information, as much as 50 CDs. The drive is used in devices such as PDAs or digital cameras. What other storage devices are on the horizon? Click the number 12 button and read a news article about a new or improved storage device. What is the device? Who manufactures it? How is the storage device better than, or different from, earlier devices? How will the device be used? Why?

13 Chapter Discussion Forum

Select an objective from this chapter on page 353 about which you would like more information. Click the number 13 button and post a short message listing a meaningful message title accompanied by one or more questions concerning the selected objective. In two days, return to the threaded discussion by clicking the number 13 button. Submit to your instructor your original message and at least one response to your message.

14 Blogs

Click the number 14 button to learn how to use blogs to find information about a topic. Follow the instructions to use MSNBC.com's Blogs Etc. to find a blog about a popular topic, such as the hottest national news story or another topic of national interest. Write a report comparing opinions of two different people about the selected topic. Print your report and submit to your instructor.

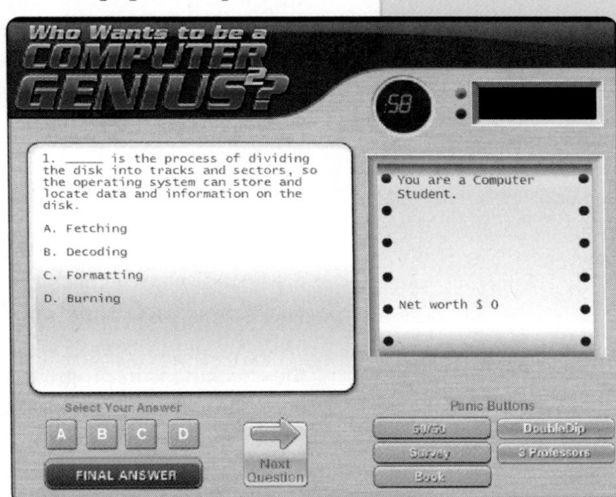

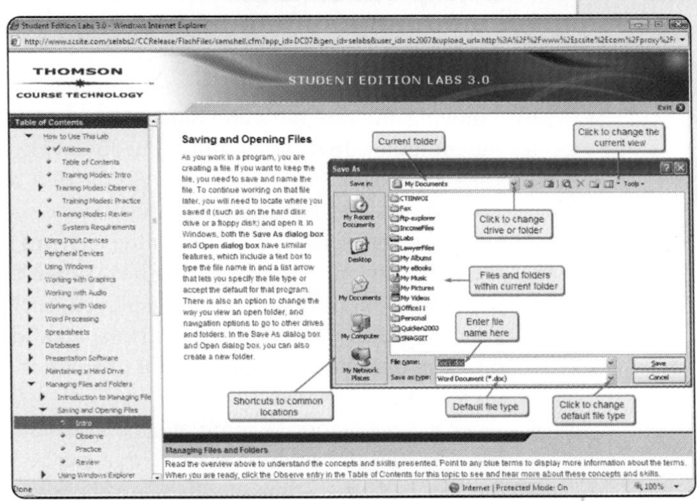

Quizzes and Learning Games
- Computer Genius
- Crossword Puzzle
- DC Track and Field
- Practice Test
- Quiz Yourself
- Wheel of Terms
- You're Hired!

Exercises
- Case Studies
- Chapter Review
- Checkpoint
- Key Terms
- Learn How To
- Learn It Online
- Web Research

Beyond the Book
- Career Corner
- Companies
- FAQs
- High-Tech Talk
- Looking Ahead
- Making Use of the Web
- Trailblazers
- Web Links

Features
- Chapter Forum
- Install Computer
- Lab Exercises
- Maintain Computer
- Tech News
- Timeline 2008

Learn How To

Use the Learn How To activities to learn fundamental skills when using a computer and accompanying technology. Complete the exercises and submit them to your instructor. To see a video of a Learn How To activity, visit scsite.com/dc2008/ch7/howto.

LEARN HOW TO 1: Maintain a Hard Disk

A computer's hard disk is used for the majority of storage requirements. It is important, therefore, to ensure that each hard disk on a computer is operating at peak efficiency.

Three tasks that maximize disk operations are detecting and repairing disk errors by using the Check Disk utility program; removing unused or unnecessary files and folders by using the Disk Cleanup utility program; and, consolidating files and folders into contiguous storage areas using the Disk Defragmenter utility program.

A. Check Disk

To detect and repair disk errors using the Check Disk utility program, complete the following steps:

1. Click the Start button on the Windows taskbar and then click Computer on the Start menu.
2. When the Computer window opens, right-click the hard disk icon for drive C (or any other hard disk you want to select), and then click Properties on the shortcut menu.
3. In the Properties dialog box, if necessary click the Tools tab to display the Tools sheet. The Tools sheet contains buttons to start the Check Disk program, the Defragment program, and the Backup program (Figure 7-39).
4. Click the Check Now button to display the Check Disk dialog box.
5. To do a complete scan of the disk and correct any errors that are found, place a checkmark in the Scan for and attempt recovery of bad sectors check box, and then click the Start button. Four phases of checking the disk will occur. While the checking is in progress, the disk being checked cannot be used for any purpose whatsoever; furthermore, once it has started, the process cannot be stopped.
6. When the four phases are complete (this may take more than one-half hour, depending on the size of the hard disk and how many corrections must occur), a dialog box is displayed with the message, Disk Check Complete. Click the OK button in the dialog box.

FIGURE 7-39

B. Cleanup Disk

After checking the disk, your next step can be to clean up the disk by removing any programs and data that are not required for the computer. To do so, complete the following steps:

1. Click the General tab (Figure 7-39) in the disk drive Properties dialog box to display the General sheet.
2. Click the Disk Cleanup button in the General sheet to display the Disk Cleanup Options dialog box. When the Disk Cleanup Options dialog box is displayed, click My files only.
3. The Disk Cleanup dialog box is displayed and contains a message that indicates the amount of space that can be freed up is being calculated.
4. After the calculation is complete, the Disk Cleanup dialog box specifies the amount of space that can be freed up and the files to delete, some of which are checked automatically (Figure 7-40). Select those items from which you wish to delete files.

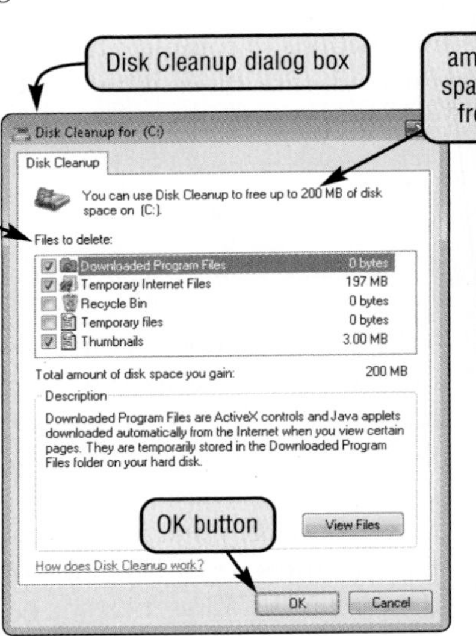

FIGURE 7-40

Learn How To

5. Click the OK button in the Disk Cleanup dialog box.
6. A dialog box asks if you are sure you want to perform these actions. Click the Delete Files button. The Disk Cleanup dialog box illustrates the progress of the cleanup. When the cleanup is complete, the dialog box closes.

C. Defragment Disk

The next step in disk maintenance is to defragment all the files on the disk. When a file is stored on disk, the data in the file sometimes is stored contiguously, and other times is stored in a noncontiguous manner. When a file is stored in a noncontiguous manner, it can take significantly longer to find and retrieve data from the file. Therefore, one of the more useful utilities to speed up disk operations is the defragmentation program, which combines all files so that no files are stored in a noncontiguous manner. To use the defragmentation program, complete the following steps:

1. If necessary, click the Tools tab in the Properties dialog box for the hard disk to be defragmented.
2. Click the Defragment Now button in the Tools sheet to display the Disk Defragmenter dialog box (Figure 7-41). This window displays the Disk Defragmenter schedule, when Disk Defragmenter was last run, and when Disk Defragmenter is next scheduled to run.
3. Click the Defragment now button. The defragmentation process begins. During the defragmentation process, the Cancel defragmentation button replaces the Defragment now button. The defragmentation process can consume more than one hour in some cases. You can cancel the operation at any time by clicking the Cancel defragmentation button in the Disk Defragmenter window.
4. When the process is complete, the Defragment now button will replace the Cancel defragmentation button.
5. Click the Close button to close the Disk Defragmenter dialog box.

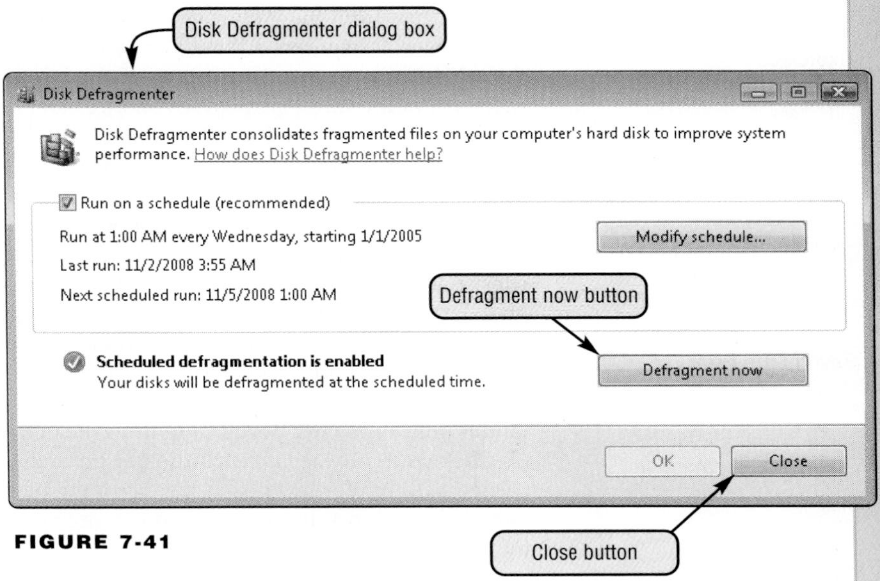

FIGURE 7-41

Exercise

Caution: The exercises for this chapter that require the actual disk maintenance are optional. If you are performing these exercises on a computer that is not your own, obtain explicit permission to complete these exercises. Keep in mind that these exercises can require significant computer time and the computer may be unusable during this time.

1. Display the Properties dialog box for a hard disk found on the computer. Display the Tools sheet. Click the Check Now button and then place a checkmark in the Scan for and attempt recovery of bad sectors check box. Click the Start button. How long did it take to complete the check of the hard disk? Were any errors discovered and corrected? Submit your answers to your instructor.
2. Display the Properties dialog box for a hard disk found on the computer. Display the General sheet. What is the capacity of the hard disk? How much space is used? How much free space is available? Click the Disk Cleanup button. How much space can be freed up if you use the Disk Cleanup program? Click the OK button to clean up the disk. How long did it take to perform the disk cleanup? Submit your answers to your instructor.
3. Display the Properties dialog box for a hard disk found on the computer. Display the Tools sheet. Click the Defragment Now button. In the Disk Defragmenter window, click the Defragment now button. How could you tell when the defragmentation process completes? How long did defragmentation require? Submit your answers to your instructor.

Web Research

Use the Internet-based Web Research exercises to broaden your understanding of the concepts presented in this chapter. Visit scsite.com/dc2008/ch7/research to obtain more information pertaining to each exercise. To discuss any of the Web Research exercises in this chapter with other students, post your thoughts or questions at scsite.com/dc2008/ch7/forum.

1 Scavenger Hunt Use one of the search engines listed in Figure 2-10 in Chapter 2 on page 78 or your own favorite search engine to find the answers to the questions that follow. Copy and paste the Web address from the Web page where you found the answer. Some questions may have more than one answer. If required, submit your answers to your instructor. (1) Who invented and patented smart cards? How many smart cards are expected to be produced this year? (2) What companies are sponsor members of the USB Flash Drive Alliance? (3) What is the Red Book standard? (4) During which decade were optical discs introduced? (5) What is areal density? What unit of measurement is used to describe this density? (6) What is IBM's Millipede project?

2 Search Sleuth Many computer users search the World Wide Web by typing words in the search text box, and often they are overwhelmed when the search engine returns thousands of possible Web sites. You can narrow your search by typing quotation marks around phrases and by adding words that give details about the phrase. Go.com is a Web portal developed by the Walt Disney Internet Group. It features a search engine, the latest news and entertainment information, stock market quotes, weather forecasts, maps, and games. Visit this Web site and then use your word processing program to answer the following questions. Then, if required, submit your answers to your instructor. (1) Locate the Movie Finder link. Type your postal code in the Search text box. What movies are playing in your area today? (2) Click your browser's Back button or press the BACKSPACE key to return to the Go.com home page. (3) Click the Search for text box at the top of the page. Type `"USB flash drive"` in the box. How many pages of search results are returned that are not Sponsored links? What are Sponsored results? (4) Click the Search for text box after the words, "USB flash drive". Add `+"8 GB"` and `+"data reliability"` as the search terms. How many pages of search results are returned that are not Sponsored links? (5) Review your search results and then write a 50-word summary of your findings.

3 Journaling Respond to your readings in this chapter by writing at least one page about your reactions, evaluations, and reflections about using storage devices. For example, which of these storage devices do you currently use: CDs, DVDs, USB flash drives? How do you care for your mobile storage media? Do you use a Picture CD or a credit card smart card? What is the storage capacity of your school, office, or home computer's hard disk? Have you attempted to repair a scratched CD or DVD? You also can write about the new terms you learned by reading this chapter. If required, submit your journal to your instructor.

4 Expanding Your Understanding Bill Gates, Microsoft's founder, considers holographic storage an impressive new storage system. The holographic process can store more than 100 movie, photo, and music files on one disc holding one terabyte of data. View Web sites to learn more about holographic storage. What factors are driving the rush to develop this system? How are images stored? What companies are researching and developing this technology? Write a report summarizing your findings, focusing on the possible uses of this storage medium and current engineering efforts to commercialize the technology. If required, submit your report to your instructor.

5 Ethics in Action The United States Federal Bureau of Investigation used a controversial program until January 2005 to monitor and store the e-mail and Internet activity of suspected criminals. Originally called Carnivore, the surveillance program was renamed DCS1000. The program was designed to track the activities of potential terrorists, spies, drug traffickers, and organized crime ring members. FBI agents needed to obtain a court order to monitor an individual, but privacy advocates claim the software tracked people not covered under the court order. View online sites that provide information about DCS1000 or Carnivore, including HowStuffWorks (computer.howstuffworks.com/carnivore.htm). Write a report summarizing your findings, and include a table of links to Web sites that provide additional details. If required, submit your report to your instructor.

Case Studies

Use the Case Studies to apply the concepts presented in the chapter to real-world situations. Visit scsite.com/dc2008/ch7/cases to obtain more information pertaining to each exercise. To discuss the Case Studies in this chapter with other students, visit scsite.com/dc2008/ch7/forum and post your thoughts or questions.

CASE STUDY 1 — Class Discussion The owner of the motorcycle repair shop where you are employed as a part-time office manager is tired of continually upgrading the company's computer system. After attending a seminar on how small businesses can make use of the Internet, she asked you to look into the feasibility of using **online storage** (also called an Internet hard disk), rather than purchasing additional storage for the company's computer. Write a brief report outlining the advantages and disadvantages of using online storage. Compare Yahoo! Briefcase and Google's Gmail online storage offerings. Which company offers the best arrangement? Why? Be prepared to discuss your recommendations in class.

CASE STUDY 2 — Class Discussion Paul's Trucking Company has hired you as an IT consultant. The company plans to purchase 15 computers for use in the accounting department. The first task assigned to you by the president of the company is to recommend the number and types of **CD and DVD drives** to include with the computers they plan to purchase. They want to use CDs and/or DVDs to share data and information among employees and to back up critical files. Create a brief memo that includes a table summarizing the advantages and disadvantages of using CD-ROM, recordable CD, rewritable CD, DVD-ROM, recordable DVD, and rewritable DVD. Include in the table both the approximate cost of the drive and the media. Be prepared to discuss your findings in class.

CASE STUDY 3 — Research An old aphorism claims, "You never can have too much money." Many computer users support a similar maxim, "You never can have too much storage." Your manager at MJ National Bank where you are employed as an analyst, however, is tired of buying more hardware to meet the bank's storage needs. She wants you to investigate alternative ways to improve **storage capacity**. Use the Web and/or print media to find out more about hard disk partitions and data compression as a means of increasing storage capacity. How do partitions increase the capacity of hard disks? What kind of data compression is most suitable for communications devices? What are the most well known data compression algorithms? How can compression ratios of different algorithms be compared? What are some formats for data compression archives? Prepare a report and/or PowerPoint presentation and share your findings with your class.

CASE STUDY 4 — Research Data and information backup is as important for people with personal computers as it is for companies. If data is not backed up regularly, a company could suffer a setback of weeks or months trying to get current after a crash. Having had a recent data loss scare, a local health club has hired your firm to recommend a **backup system**. The club uses ten computers through a server. They store all member information, such as name, address, membership type, and payment information. They constantly are updating their database, but have never backed up the data. Using the Web and/or print media, prepare a report or PowerPoint presentation detailing what you would consider the ideal system for the club. Include in your report the devices you would require and information that supports your choices.

CASE STUDY 5 — Team Challenge Your team has been assigned to do IT research for a new local magazine-subscription telemarketing company that is about to open for business. The company's business plan calls for 150 telemarketers to make a minimum of 100 calls a day. If a telemarketer does not meet the minimum number of calls, then he or she is required to finish the calls from home. The company plans to buy used computers for each telemarketer to use at home. The company also has to decide on the type of **storage device** to provide the telemarketers so that when they have to make calls from home, they have a way to take the necessary data home with them. Senior management has narrowed down their choice to three storage devices — rewritable CDs, rewritable DVDs, or USB flash drives. Form a three-member team and have each team member choose a different storage device. Using the Web and/or print media, have each team member determine the advantages and disadvantages of their chosen device. Include such features as capacity, access time, durability of media, and cost. As a team, merge your findings into a team report and/or PowerPoint presentation and share your recommendations with your class.

CHAPTER EIGHT

Operating Systems and Utility Programs

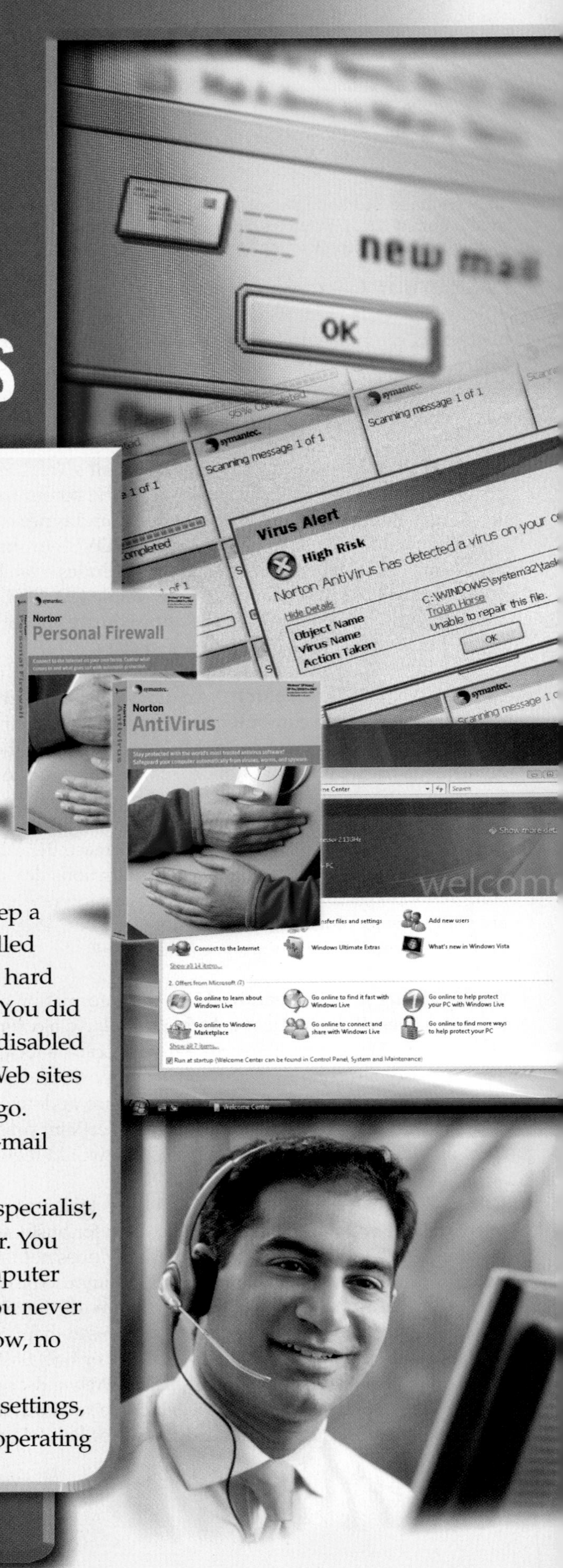

Picture Yourself Getting a Virus through E-Mail

Arriving home after class, you eagerly check your e-mail. You have been looking for a new job and have submitted your resume online to several places. You are delighted when you see an e-mail with "Your job search" as the subject line. You open the e-mail and realize too late that you have made an enormous mistake. Your computer freezes. The mouse and keyboard are unresponsive. You restart the computer, but the Windows Vista desktop never appears. You know that you unwittingly caused your computer to get a virus by opening the e-mail.

In your computer literacy course, you learned how to keep a computer safe from viruses and other infections. You installed antivirus software, enabled a firewall, and backed up your hard disk. Unfortunately, many weeks have elapsed since then. You did not keep the antivirus software updated. You temporarily disabled the firewall so that you could access one of your favorite Web sites more easily. Your last hard disk backup was two months ago. Furthermore, you broke the cardinal rule: never open an e-mail from someone you do not know.

After an hour on the telephone with a technical support specialist, your computer is functional again, and you are much wiser. You mentally resolve to be scrupulous about keeping your computer safe with regular updates and backups. Needless to say, you never will open an e-mail message from someone you do not know, no matter how enticing the subject line.

Read Chapter 8 to learn about antivirus software, firewall settings, backups, and recovery discs, and discover features of most operating systems and utility programs.

OBJECTIVES

After completing this chapter, you will be able to:

1. **Identify the types of system software**
2. **Summarize the startup process on a personal computer**
3. **Describe the functions of an operating system**
4. **Discuss ways that some operating systems help administrators control a network and administer security**
5. **Explain the purpose of the utilities included with most operating systems**
6. **Summarize the features of several stand-alone operating systems**
7. **Identify various network operating systems**
8. **Identify devices that use several embedded operating systems**
9. **Explain the purpose of several stand-alone utility programs**

CONTENTS

SYSTEM SOFTWARE

When you purchase a personal computer, it usually has system software installed on its hard disk. **System software** consists of the programs that control or maintain the operations of the computer and its devices. System software serves as the interface between the user, the application software, and the computer's hardware.

Two types of system software are operating systems and utility programs. Several types of utility programs are provided with an operating system. Other utility programs are available stand-alone, that is, as programs separate from the operating system. This chapter discusses the operating system and its functions, as well as several types of utility programs for personal computers.

OPERATING SYSTEMS

An **operating system** (**OS**) is a set of programs containing instructions that coordinate all the activities among computer hardware resources. Most operating systems perform similar functions that include starting a computer, providing a user interface, managing programs, managing memory, scheduling jobs, configuring devices,

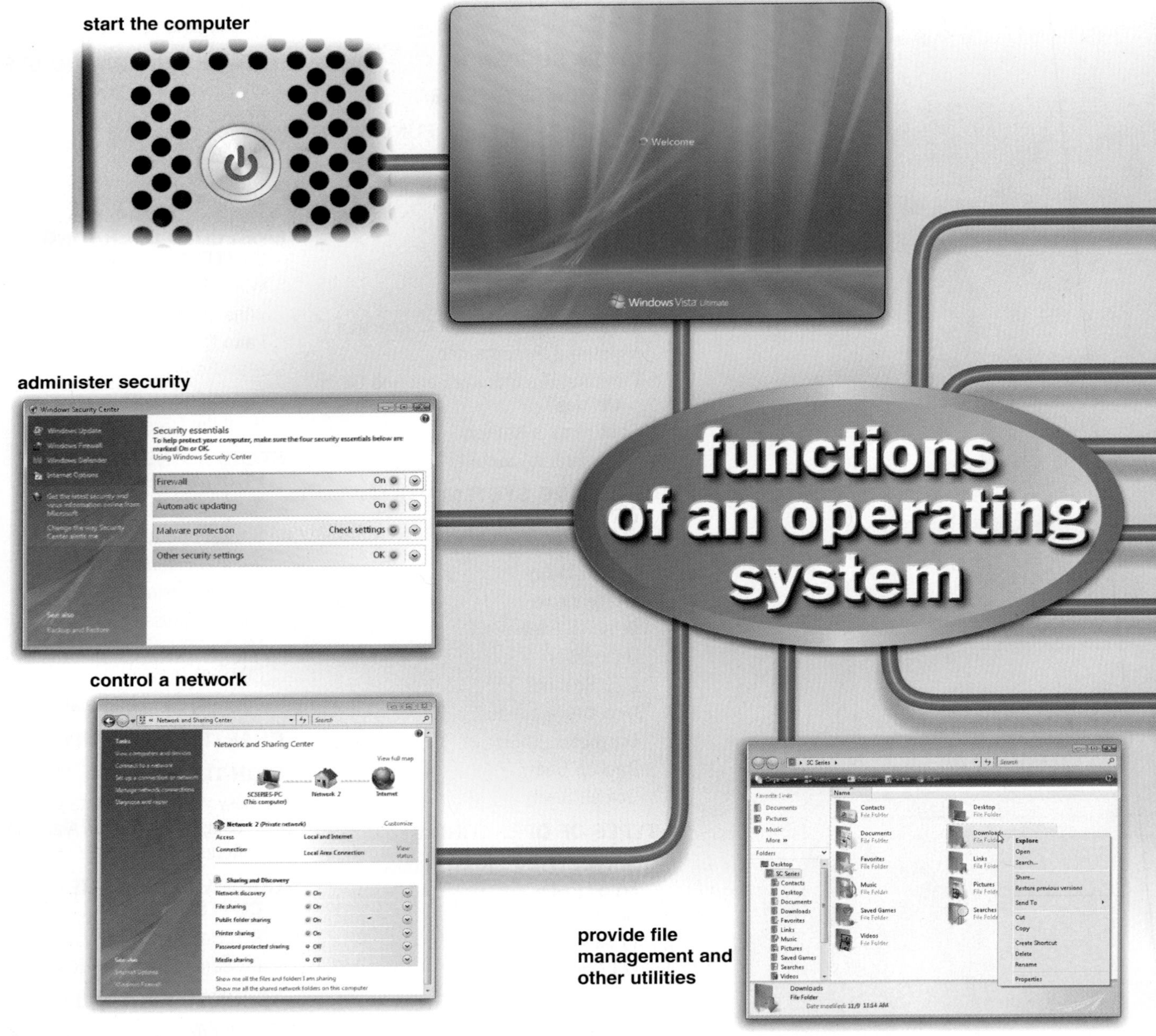

FIGURE 8-1 Most operating systems perform similar functions, which are illustrated with Windows Vista in this figure.

establishing an Internet connection, monitoring performance, and providing file management utilities. Some operating systems also allow users to control a network and administer security (Figure 8-1).

In most cases, the operating system is installed and resides on the computer's hard disk. On handheld computers and many mobile devices such as PDAs and smart phones, however, the operating system may reside on a ROM chip.

Different sizes of computers typically use different operating systems. For example, a mainframe computer does not use the same operating system as a personal computer. Even the same types of computers, such as desktop computers, may not use the same operating system. Some, however, can run multiple operating systems. When purchasing application software, you must ensure that it works with the operating system installed on your computer.

The operating system that a computer uses sometimes is called the *platform*. On purchased application software, the package identifies the required platform (operating system). A *cross-platform* program is one that runs the same on multiple operating systems.

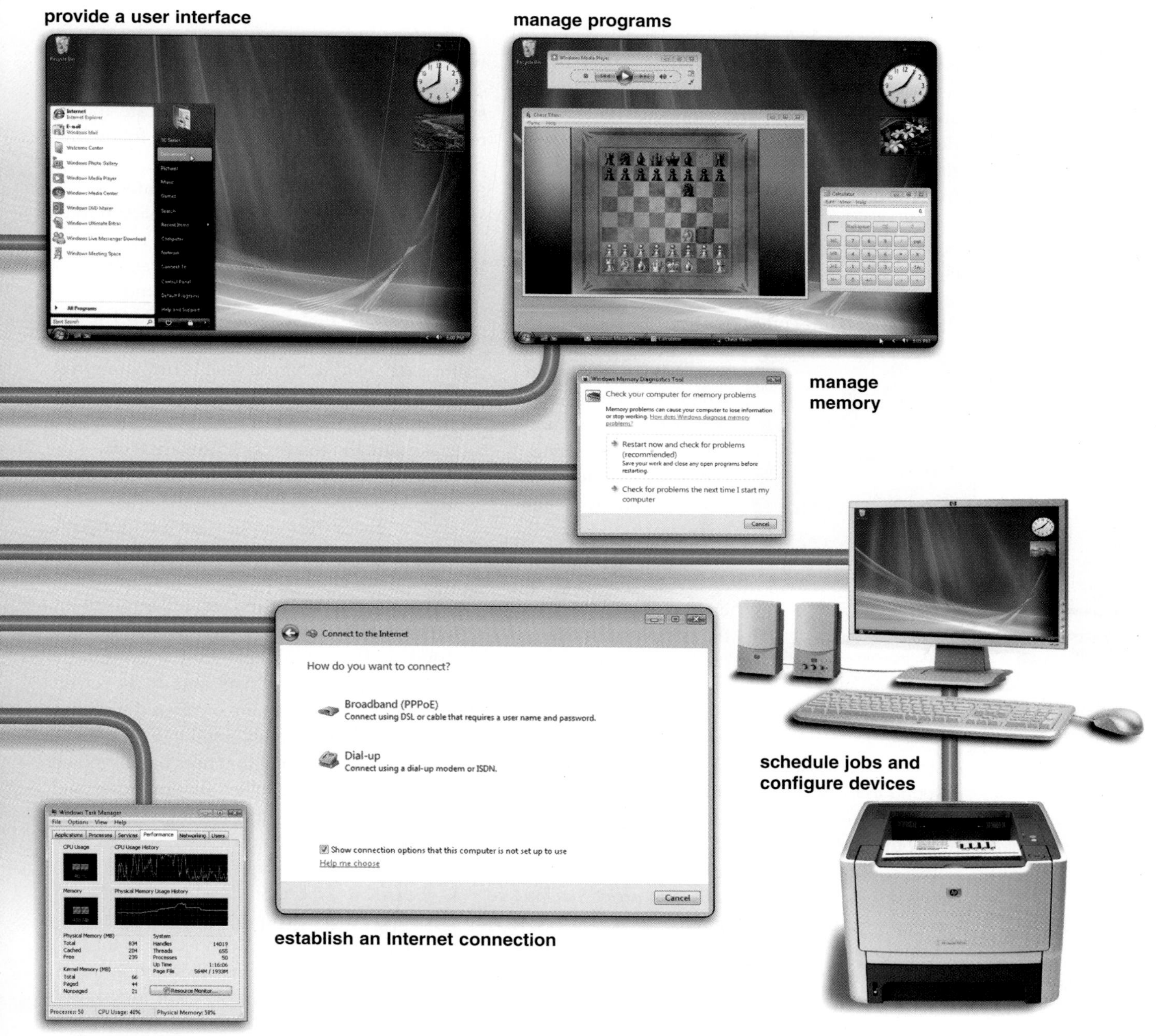

OPERATING SYSTEM FUNCTIONS

Many different operating systems exist, designed for all types of computers. Regardless of the size of the computer, however, most operating systems provide similar functions. The following sections discuss functions common to most operating systems. The operating system handles many of these functions automatically, without requiring any instructions from a user.

Starting a Computer

The process of starting or restarting a computer is called **booting**. When turning on a computer that has been powered off completely, you are performing a **cold boot**. A **warm boot**, by contrast, is the process of using the operating system to restart a computer. A warm boot properly closes any running processes and programs; however, it does not save any unsaved work. Thus, always remember to save your work before rebooting (restarting) a computer.

With Windows Vista, you can perform a warm boot by clicking the Start button on the taskbar, clicking the Lock button arrow on the Start menu, and then clicking Restart on the Lock button menu (Figure 8-2). Some computers have a reset button that when pressed restarts a computer as if it had been powered off. A reset button does not properly close running processes and programs.

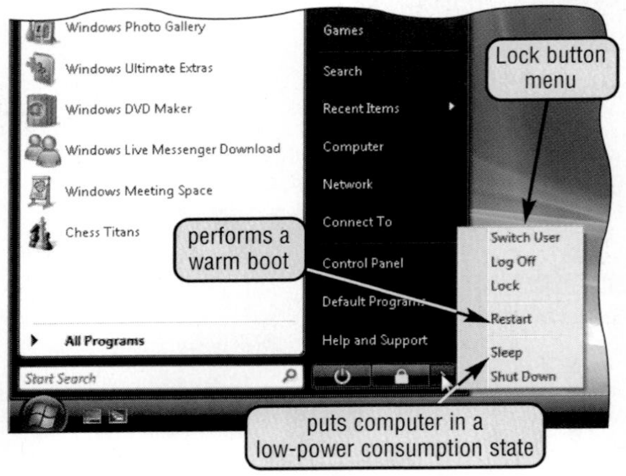

FIGURE 8-2 To reboot a running computer, click Restart on the Lock button menu.

When you install new software or update existing software, often an on-screen prompt instructs you to restart the computer. In this case, a warm boot is appropriate. If your computer stops responding, try to restart it with a warm boot first. If it does not respond to the warm boot, then try pushing the reset button on the computer, if the computer has a reset button. As a last resort, restart the computer with a cold boot; that is, push the power button. Pushing the power button does not properly close running processes and programs.

Each time you boot a computer, the kernel and other frequently used operating system instructions are loaded, or copied, from the hard disk (storage) into the computer's memory (RAM). The *kernel* is the core of an operating system that manages memory and devices, maintains the computer's clock, starts applications, and assigns the computer's resources, such as devices, programs, data, and information. The kernel is *memory resident*, which means it remains in memory while the computer is running. Other parts of the operating system are *nonresident*, that is, these instructions remain on the hard disk until they are needed.

When you boot a computer, a series of messages may be displayed on the screen. The actual information displayed varies depending on the make and type of the computer and the equipment installed. The boot process, however, is similar for large and small computers.

The steps in the following paragraphs explain what occurs during a cold boot on a personal computer using the Windows Vista operating system. The steps in Figure 8-3 illustrate and correspond to the steps discussed in the following paragraphs.

Step 1: When you turn on the computer, the power supply sends an electrical signal to the components in the system unit.

Step 2: The charge of electricity causes the processor chip to reset itself and find the ROM chip(s) that contains the BIOS. The **BIOS** (pronounced BYE-ose), which stands for *basic input/output system*, is firmware that contains the computer's startup instructions.

Step 3: The BIOS executes a series of tests to make sure the computer hardware is connected properly and operating correctly. The tests, collectively called the *power-on self test* (*POST*), check the various system components including the buses, system clock, adapter cards, RAM chips, mouse, keyboard, and drives. As the POST executes, LEDs (tiny lights) flicker on devices such as the disk drives and keyboard. Beeps also may sound, and messages may be displayed on the screen.

Step 4: The POST results are compared with data in a CMOS chip. As discussed in Chapter 4, CMOS is a technology that uses battery power to retain information when the computer is off. The CMOS chip stores configuration information about the computer, such as the amount of memory; type of disk drives, keyboard, and monitor; the current date and time; and other startup information. It also detects any new devices connected to the computer. If any problems are identified, the computer may beep, display error messages, or cease operating — depending on the severity of the problem.

Step 5: If the POST completes successfully, the BIOS searches for specific operating system files called *system files*. The BIOS may look first to see if a USB flash drive plugged in a USB port or a disc in a CD or DVD drive contains the system files. If these ports or drives do not contain media or if the system files are not on media in the port or drive, the BIOS looks in drive C (the designation usually given to the first hard disk) for the system files.

Step 6: Once located, the system files load into memory (RAM) from storage (usually the hard disk) and execute. Next, the kernel of the operating system loads into memory. Then, the operating system in memory takes control of the computer.

Step 7: The operating system loads system configuration information. In Windows Vista, the *registry* consists of several files that contain the system configuration information. Windows Vista constantly accesses the registry during the computer's operation for information such as installed hardware and software devices and individual user preferences for mouse speed, passwords, and other information. The Windows Vista registry also constantly checks user credentials to verify they have the necessary privileges to run programs.

Necessary operating system files are loaded into memory. On some computers, the operating system verifies that the person attempting to use the computer is a legitimate user. Finally, the Windows Vista desktop and icons are displayed on the screen. The operating system executes programs in the *Startup folder*, which contains a list of programs that open automatically when you boot the computer.

Windows Registry

For more information, visit scsite.com/dc2008/ch8/weblink and then click Windows Registry.

FIGURE 8-3 HOW A PC BOOTS UP

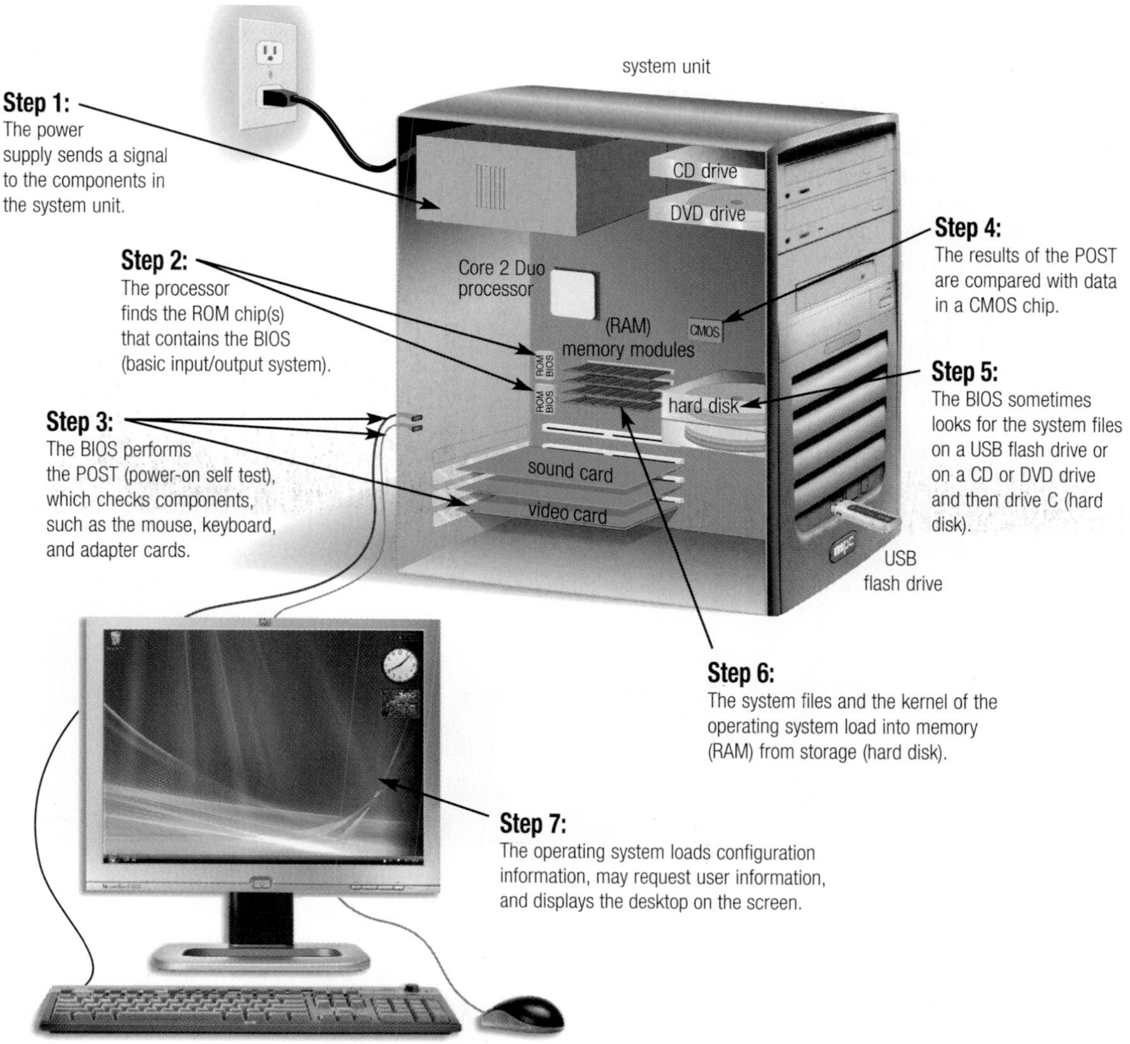

system unit

Step 1: The power supply sends a signal to the components in the system unit.

Step 2: The processor finds the ROM chip(s) that contains the BIOS (basic input/output system).

Step 3: The BIOS performs the POST (power-on self test), which checks components, such as the mouse, keyboard, and adapter cards.

Step 4: The results of the POST are compared with data in a CMOS chip.

Step 5: The BIOS sometimes looks for the system files on a USB flash drive or on a CD or DVD drive and then drive C (hard disk).

Step 6: The system files and the kernel of the operating system load into memory (RAM) from storage (hard disk).

Step 7: The operating system loads configuration information, may request user information, and displays the desktop on the screen.

CD drive

DVD drive

Core 2 Duo processor

CMOS

(RAM) memory modules

ROM BIOS

ROM BIOS

hard disk

sound card

video card

USB flash drive

BOOT DISK A **boot drive** is the drive from which your personal computer boots (starts). In most cases, drive C (the hard disk) is the boot drive. Sometimes a hard disk becomes damaged and the computer cannot boot from the hard disk. In this case, you can boot from a special disk, called a **boot disk** or a **recovery disk**, that contains a few system files that will start the computer. When you purchase a computer, it usually includes a boot disk in the form of a CD. If you do not have a boot disk, the operating system may provide a means to create one. The Windows Vista installation disc is itself a boot disk, which you can use to start Windows Vista in the event you cannot boot from the hard disk.

FAQ 8-1

How do I shut down a computer that uses Windows Vista?

The Start menu in Windows Vista provides many options from which to choose when you are finished using your computer. Clicking the Power button on the Start menu will place your computer in *sleep mode*, which is a low-power state that allows you to resume your work quickly when you return to your computer. If you click the Lock button arrow, you can select commands that allow you to switch users, log off, lock the computer, restart the computer, put the computer to sleep, and shut down (power off) the computer. For more information, visit scsite.com/dc2008/ch8/faq and then click Shut-Down Options.

Providing a User Interface

You interact with software through its user interface. That is, a **user interface** controls how you enter data and instructions and how information is displayed on the screen. Two types of user interfaces are command-line and graphical. Operating systems often use a combination of these interfaces to define how a user interacts with a computer.

COMMAND-LINE INTERFACE To configure devices, manage system resources, and troubleshoot network connections, network administrators and other advanced users work with a command-line interface. In a *command-line interface*, a user types commands or presses special keys on the keyboard (such as function keys or key combinations) to enter data and instructions (Figure 8-4). Command-line interfaces often are difficult to use because they require exact spelling, grammar, and punctuation. Minor errors, such as a missing period, generate an error message. Command-line interfaces, however, give a user more control to manage detailed settings. When working with a command-line interface, the set of commands entered into the computer is called the *command language*.

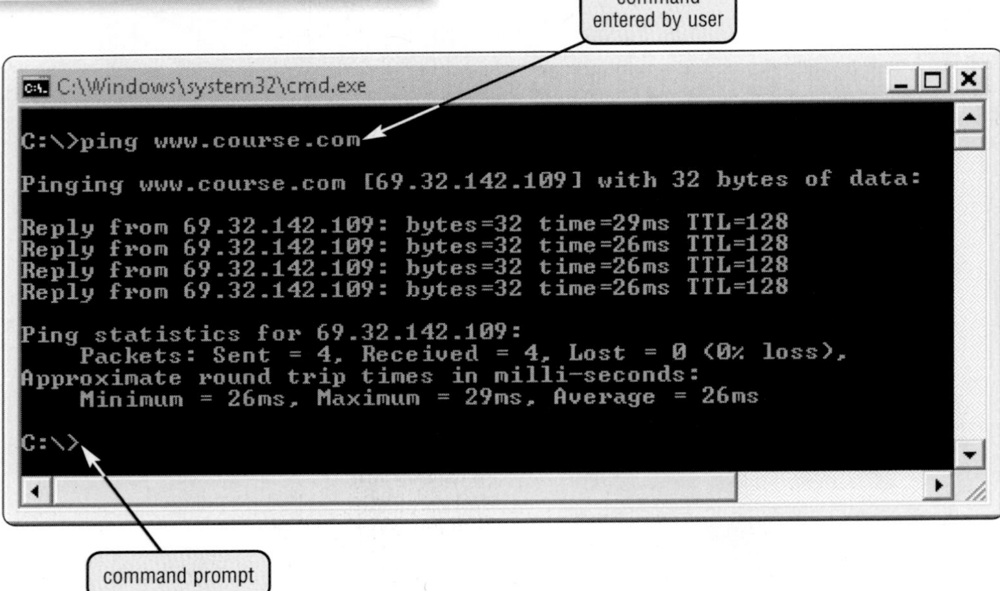

FIGURE 8-4 A command-line interface is difficult to use because it requires you enter exact spelling, grammar, and punctuation.

GRAPHICAL USER INTERFACE Most users today work with a graphical user interface. With a *graphical user interface (GUI)*, you interact with menus and visual images such as buttons and other graphical objects to issue commands. Many current GUI operating systems incorporate features similar to those of a Web browser, such as links and navigation buttons (i.e., Back button and Forward button). Windows Vista offers two different GUIs, depending on your hardware configuration. Computers with less than 1 GB of RAM work with the *Windows Vista Basic* interface (Figure 8-5a). Computers with more than 1 GB of RAM work with the *Windows Aero* interface (Figure 8-5b), which provides an enhanced visual look, additional navigation options, and animation.

Managing Programs

Some operating systems support a single user and only one running program at a time. Others support thousands of users running multiple programs. How an operating system handles programs directly affects your productivity.

A *single user/single tasking* operating system allows only one user to run one program at a time. For example, if you are working in a graphics program and want to check e-mail messages, you must quit the graphics program before you can run the e-mail program. Early systems were single user/single tasking. Most of today's operating systems are multitasking. PDAs, smart phones, and other small computing devices, however, often use a single user/single tasking operating system.

A *single user/multitasking* operating system allows a single user to work on two or more programs that reside in memory at the same time. Using the example just cited, if you are

FIGURE 8-5a (Windows Vista Basic interface)

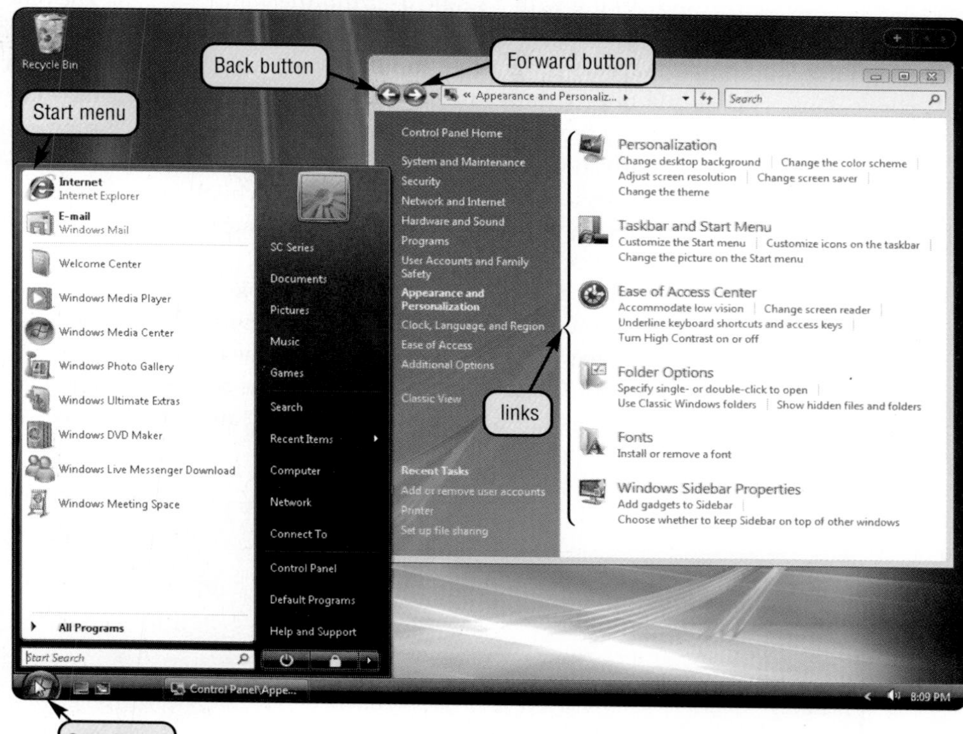

FIGURE 8-5b (Windows Aero interface)

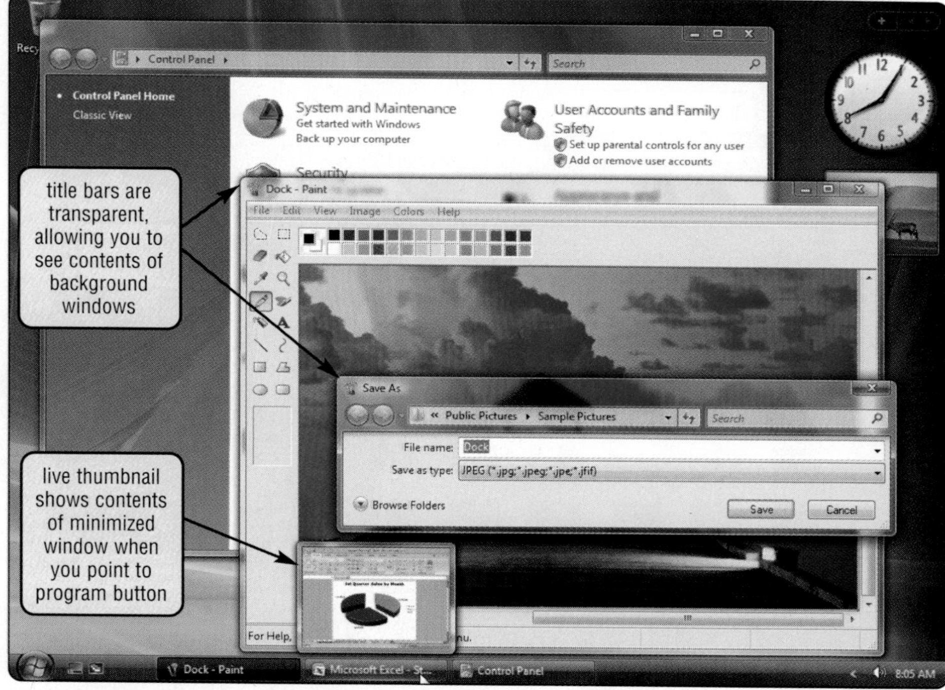

FIGURE 8-5 Windows Vista offers two different graphical user interfaces, depending on your hardware configuration.

working with a single user/multitasking operating system, you do not have to quit the graphics program to run the e-mail program. Both programs can run concurrently. Users today typically run multiple programs concurrently. It is common to have an e-mail program and Web browser open at all times, while working with application programs such as word processing or graphics.

When a computer is running multiple programs concurrently, one program is in the foreground and the others are in the background. The one in the *foreground* is the active program, that is, the one you currently are using. The other programs running but not in use are in the *background*. In Figure 8-6, the PowerPoint program, which is showing a slide show, is in the foreground, and three other programs are running in the background (Windows Media Player, Microsoft Excel, and Chess Titans). For example, Windows Media Player can be playing music while you are modifying the slide show.

The foreground program typically displays on the desktop, and the background programs are partially or completely hidden behind the foreground program. You easily can switch between foreground and background programs. To make a program active (in the foreground) in

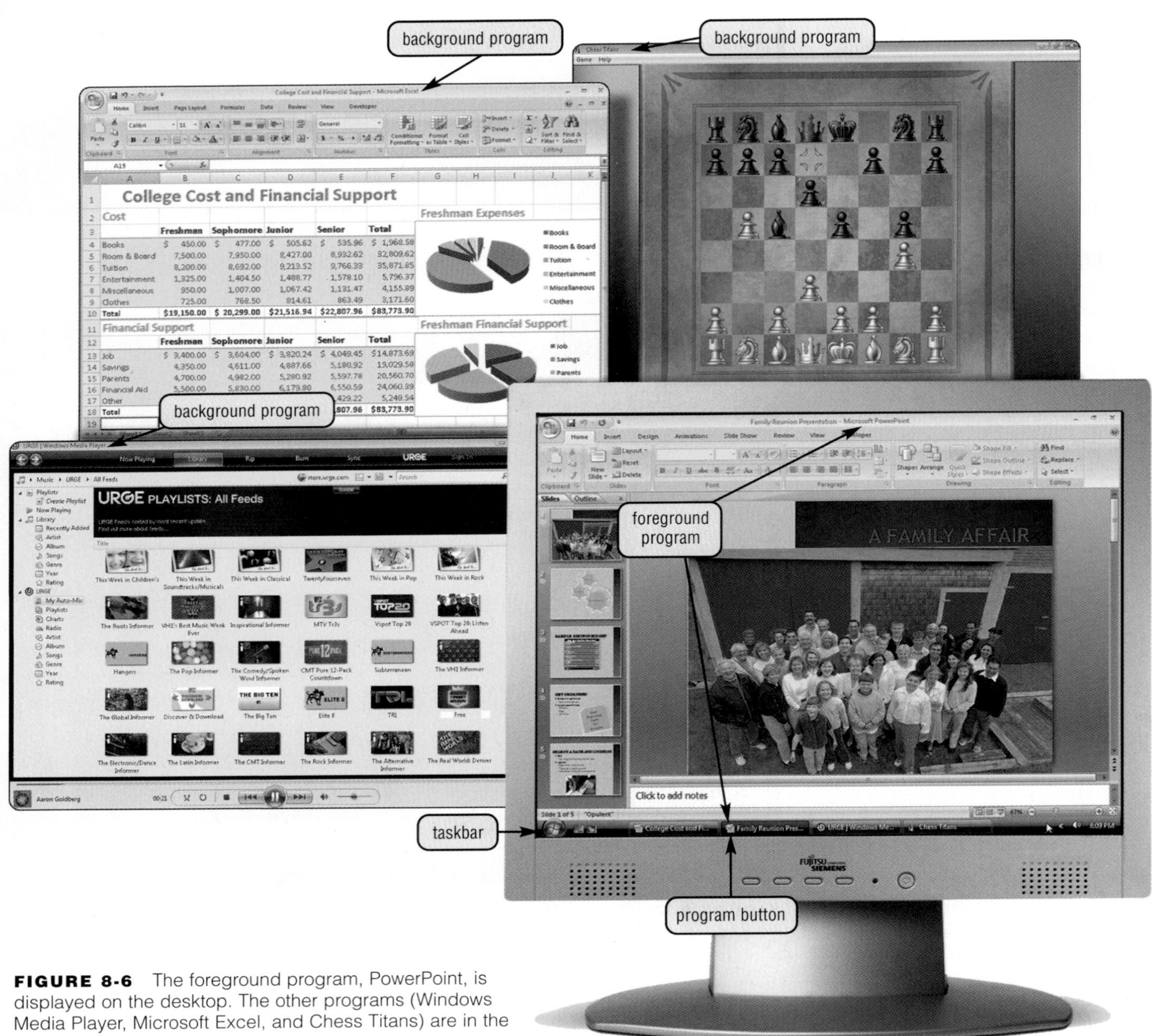

FIGURE 8-6 The foreground program, PowerPoint, is displayed on the desktop. The other programs (Windows Media Player, Microsoft Excel, and Chess Titans) are in the background.

Windows Vista, click its program button on the taskbar. This causes the operating system to place all other programs in the background.

In addition to application programs, an operating system manages other processes. These processes include utilities or routines that provide support to other programs or hardware. Some are memory resident. Others run as they are required. Figure 8-7 shows a list of all processes running on a Windows Vista computer. The list contains the applications programs running, as well as other programs and processes.

Some operating systems use preemptive multitasking to prevent any one process from monopolizing the computer's resources. With *preemptive multitasking*, the operating system interrupts a program that is executing and passes control to another program waiting to be executed. An advantage of preemptive multitasking is the operating system regains control if one program stops operating properly.

A *multiuser* operating system enables two or more users to run programs simultaneously. Networks, servers, mainframes, and supercomputers allow hundreds to thousands of users to connect at the same time, and thus are multiuser.

A *multiprocessing* operating system supports two or more processors running programs at the same time. Multiprocessing involves the coordinated processing of programs by more than one processor. Multiprocessing increases a computer's processing speed.

A computer with separate processors also can serve as a fault-tolerant computer. A *fault-tolerant computer* continues to operate when one of its components fails, ensuring that no data is lost. Fault-tolerant computers have duplicate components such as processors, memory, and disk drives. If any one of these components fails, the computer switches to the duplicate component and continues to operate. Airline reservation systems, communications networks, automated teller machines, and other systems that must be operational at all times use fault-tolerant computers.

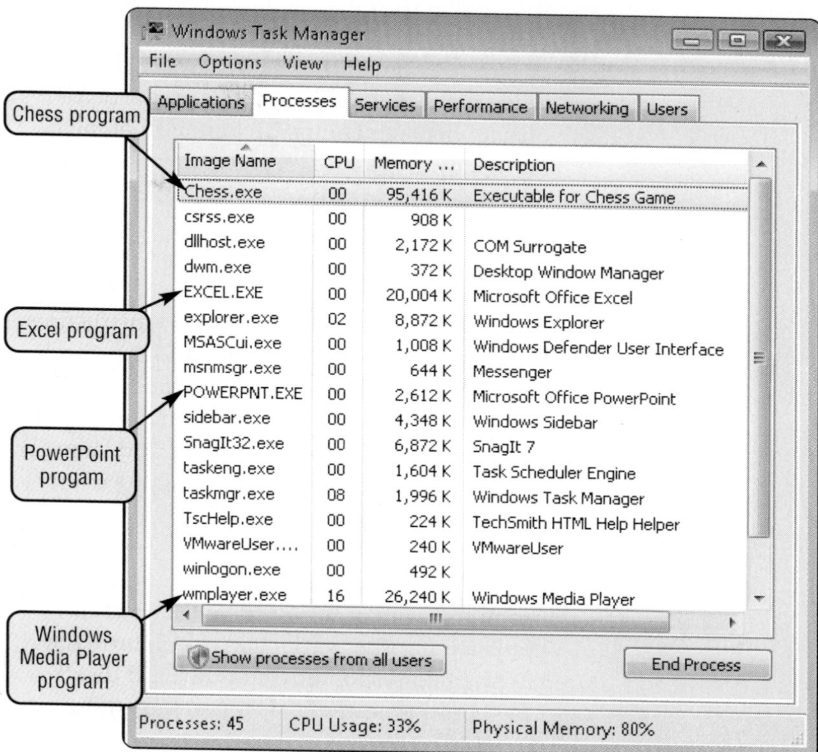

FIGURE 8-7 An operating system manages multiple programs and processes while you use the computer.

Managing Memory

The purpose of **memory management** is to optimize the use of random access memory (RAM). As Chapter 4 discussed, RAM consists of one or more chips on the motherboard that hold items such as data and instructions while the processor interprets and executes them. The operating system allocates, or assigns, data and instructions to an area of memory while they are being processed. Then, it carefully monitors the contents of memory. Finally, the operating system releases these items from being monitored in memory when the processor no longer requires them.

If you have multiple programs running simultaneously, it is possible to run out of RAM. For example, assume an operating system requires 512 MB of RAM, an antivirus program — 256 MB of RAM, a Web browser — 128 MB of RAM, a business software suite — 512 MB of RAM, and a photo editing program — 256 MB of RAM. With all these programs running simultaneously, the total RAM required would be 1664 MB of RAM (512 + 256 + 128 + 512 + 256). If the computer has only 512 MB of RAM, the operating system may have to use virtual memory to solve the problem.

With **virtual memory**, the operating system allocates a portion of a storage medium, usually the hard disk, to function as additional RAM (Figure 8-8). As you interact with a program, part of it may be in physical RAM, while the rest of the program is on the hard disk as virtual memory. Because virtual memory is slower than RAM, users may notice the computer slowing down while it uses virtual memory.

The area of the hard disk used for virtual memory is called a *swap file* because it swaps (exchanges) data, information, and instructions between memory and storage. A *page* is the amount of data and program instructions that can swap at a given time. The technique of swapping items between memory and storage, called *paging*, is a time-consuming process for the computer.

When an operating system spends much of its time paging, instead of executing application software, it is said to be *thrashing*. If application software, such as a Web browser, has stopped responding and the hard disk's LED blinks repeatedly, the operating system probably is thrashing.

FAQ 8-2

How can I stop a computer from thrashing?

Try to quit the program that stopped responding. If the computer does not respond and continues to thrash, do a warm boot. When the computer reboots, check whether the available hard disk space is less than 200 MB. If it is, remove unnecessary files from the hard disk and if possible uninstall seldom used programs. Defragment the hard disk (discussed later in this chapter). If thrashing continues to occur, you may need to install more RAM in the computer. For more information, visit scsite.com/dc2008/ch8/faq and then click Optimizing Memory.

Scheduling Jobs

The operating system determines the order in which jobs are processed. A **job** is an operation the processor manages. Jobs include receiving data from an input device, processing instructions, sending information to an output device, and transferring items from storage to memory and from memory to storage.

FIGURE 8-8 HOW A COMPUTER MIGHT USE VIRTUAL MEMORY

page swapped out
RAM (physical memory)
disk (virtual memory)
swap file
Step 1:
The operating system transfers the least recently used data and program instructions from RAM to the hard disk because RAM is needed for other functions.
Step 2:
The operating system transfers data and program instructions from the hard disk to RAM when they are needed.
page swapped in

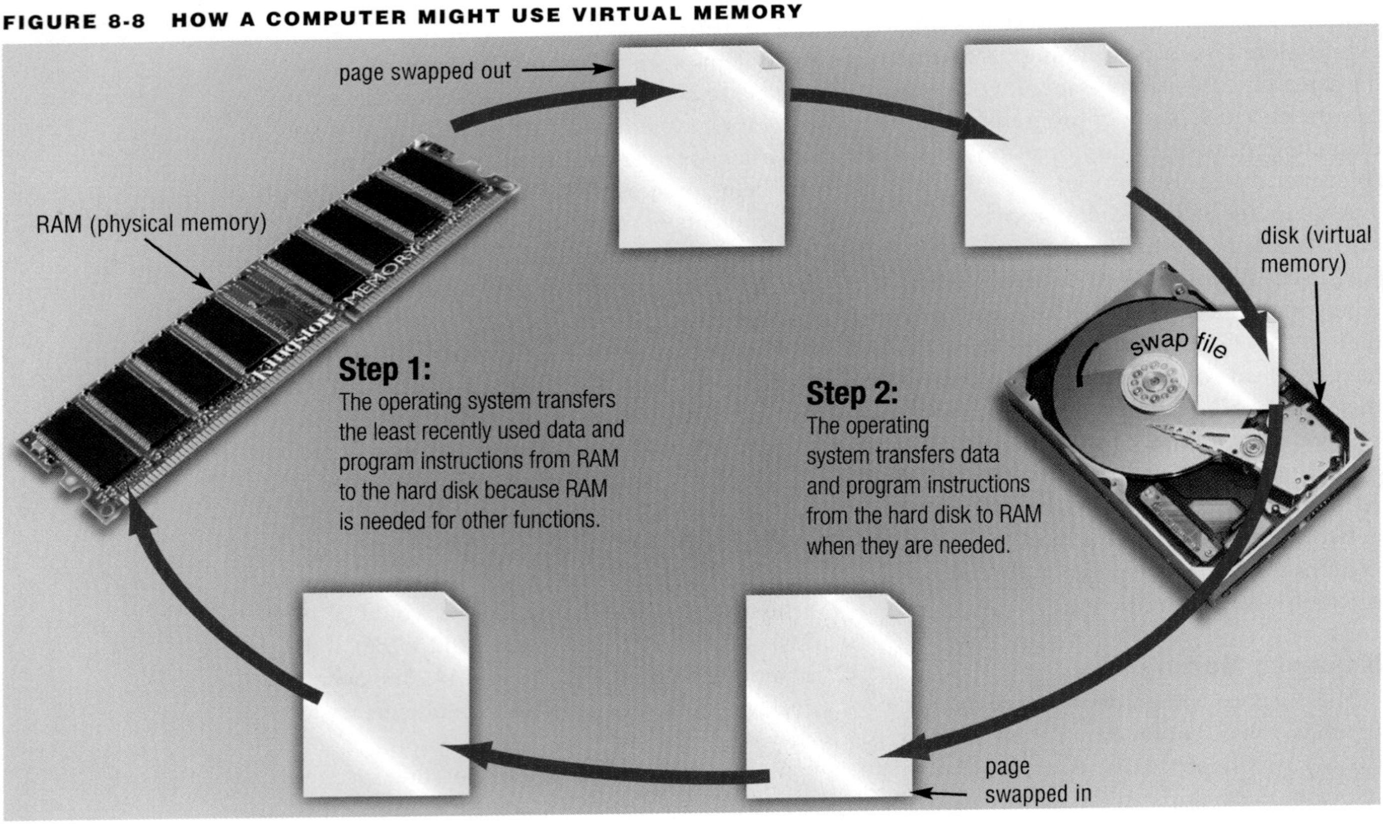

A mulituser operating system does not always process jobs on a first-come, first-served basis. Sometimes, one user may have a higher priority than other users. In this case, the operating system adjusts the schedule of jobs.

Sometimes, a device already may be busy processing one job when it receives a second job. This occurs because the processor operates at a much faster rate of speed than peripheral devices. For example, if the processor sends five print jobs to a printer, the printer can print only one document at a time and store as many documents as its memory can handle.

While waiting for devices to become idle, the operating system places items in buffers. A **buffer** is a segment of memory or storage in which items are placed while waiting to be transferred from an input device or to an output device.

The operating system commonly uses buffers with print jobs. This process, called **spooling**, sends print jobs to a buffer instead of sending them immediately to the printer. The buffer holds the information waiting to print while the printer prints from the buffer at its own rate of speed. By spooling print jobs to a buffer, the processor can continue interpreting and executing instructions while the printer prints. This allows users to work on the computer for other tasks while a printer is printing. Multiple print jobs line up in a **queue** (pronounced Q) in the buffer. A program, called a *print spooler*, intercepts print jobs from the operating system and places them in the queue (Figure 8-9).

Configuring Devices

A **driver**, short for *device driver*, is a small program that tells the operating system how to communicate with a specific device. Each device on a computer, such as the mouse, keyboard, monitor, printer, card reader/writer, and scanner, has its own specialized set of commands and thus requires its own specific driver. When you boot a computer, the operating system loads each device's driver. These devices will not function without their correct drivers.

If you attach a new device to a computer, such as a printer or scanner, its driver must be installed before you can use the device. Today, many devices and operating systems support Plug and Play. As discussed in Chapter 4, **Plug and Play** means the operating system automatically configures new devices as you install them. Specifically, it assists you in the device's installation by loading the necessary drivers automatically and checking for conflicts with other devices. With Plug and Play, a user plugs in a device, turns on the computer, and then uses the device without having to configure the system manually. Devices that connect to a USB port on the system unit typically are Plug and Play.

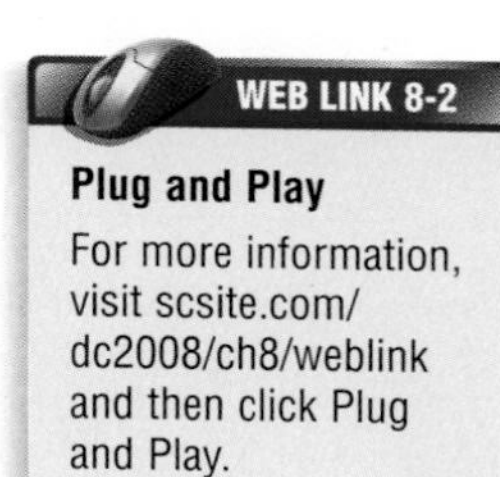

WEB LINK 8-2

Plug and Play

For more information, visit scsite.com/dc2008/ch8/weblink and then click Plug and Play.

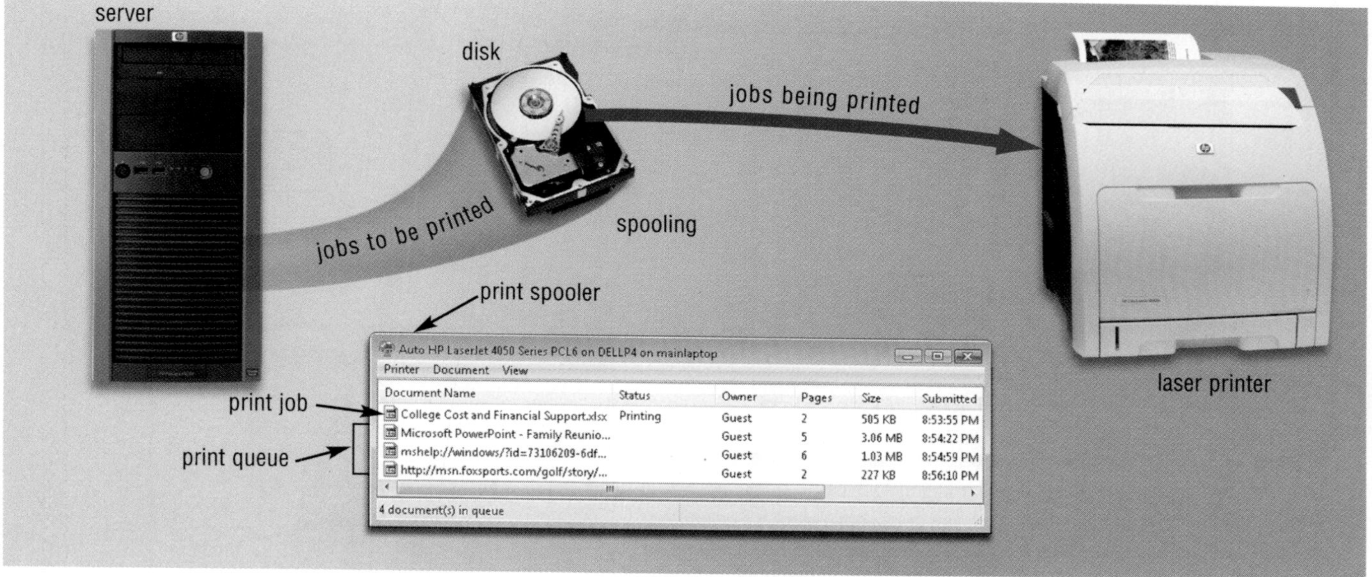

FIGURE 8-9 Spooling increases both processor and printer efficiency by placing print jobs in a buffer on disk before they are printed. This figure illustrates three jobs in the queue with one job printing.

If you have a device that is not Plug and Play, you can install the driver manually. Figure 8-10 shows how to use Windows Vista to install a driver for a scanner or camera. For many devices, the computer's operating system includes the necessary drivers. Windows Vista, for example, automatically updates drivers on your computer regularly. If, however, the required drivers are not on your computer, you can install them from the CD provided with the purchased device.

When you attach a Plug and Play device to a computer, the operating system determines an

FIGURE 8-10 HOW TO USE WINDOWS VISTA TO INSTALL DRIVERS FOR AN UNRECOGNIZED SCANNER OR CAMERA

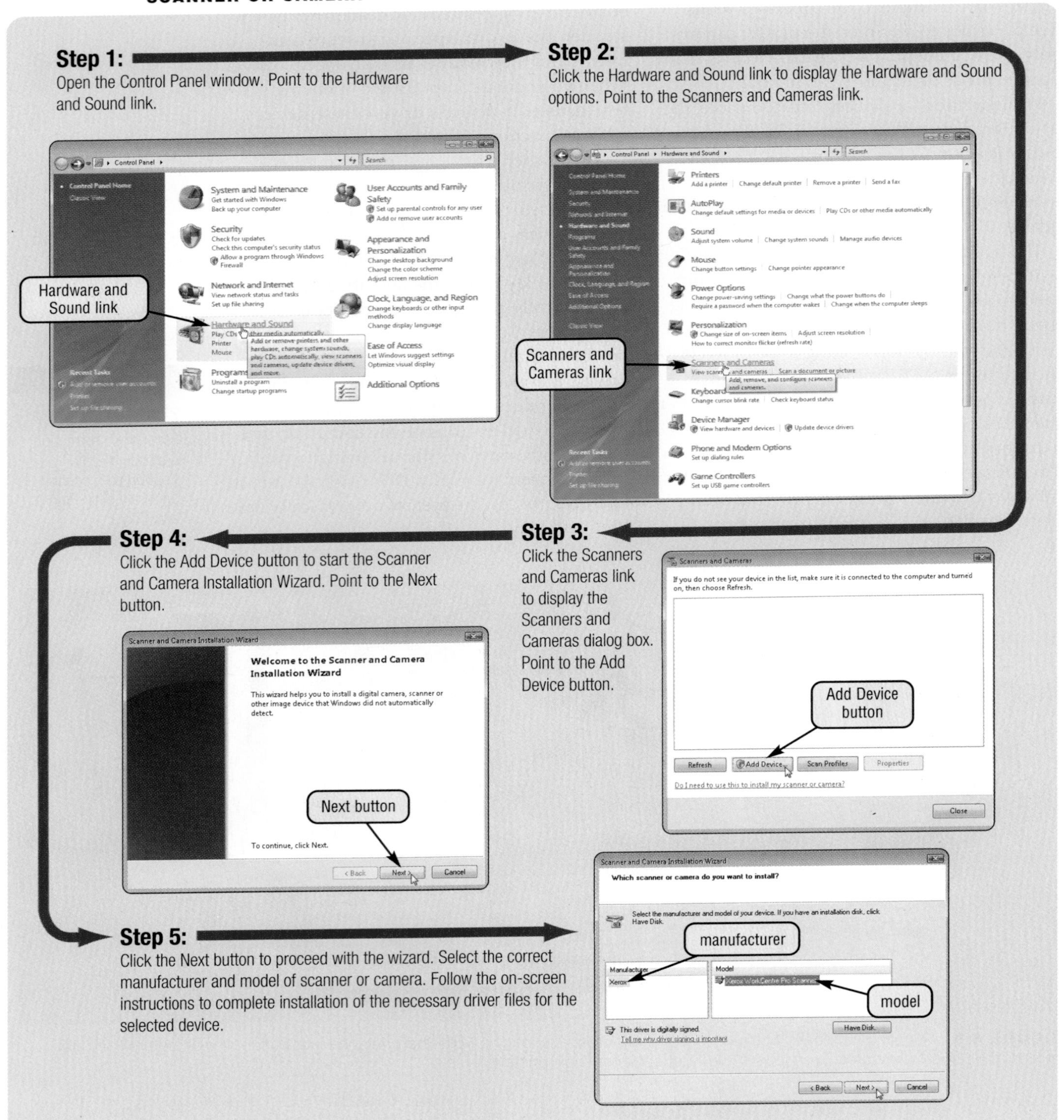
Step 1:
Open the Control Panel window. Point to the Hardware and Sound link.
Hardware and Sound link
Step 2:
Click the Hardware and Sound link to display the Hardware and Sound options. Point to the Scanners and Cameras link.
Scanners and Cameras link
Step 3:
Click the Scanners and Cameras link to display the Scanners and Cameras dialog box. Point to the Add Device button.
Add Device button
Step 4:
Click the Add Device button to start the Scanner and Camera Installation Wizard. Point to the Next button.
Welcome to the Scanner and Camera Installation Wizard
This wizard helps you to install a digital camera, scanner or other image device that Windows did not automatically detect.
Next button
Step 5:
Click the Next button to proceed with the wizard. Select the correct manufacturer and model of scanner or camera. Follow the on-screen instructions to complete installation of the necessary driver files for the selected device.
Which scanner or camera do you want to install?
manufacturer
model

appropriate IRQ to use. An *IRQ* (*interrupt request line*) is a communications line between a device and the processor.

FAQ 8-3

What if I do not have the driver for a device?

When reinstalling an operating system, you may have to supply a device's driver. If you do not have the original driver disc, visit the manufacturer's Web site. Most post drivers for download at no cost, or they may suggest a similar driver that will work. If you do not have Internet access, call the manufacturer and request a new disc via the postal service. For more information, visit scsite.com/dc2008/ch8/faq and then click Drivers.

Establishing an Internet Connection

Operating systems typically provide a means to establish Internet connections. For example, Windows Vista includes a Connect to a network wizard that guides users through the process of setting up a connection between a computer and an Internet service provider (Figure 8-11).

Some operating systems also include a Web browser and an e-mail program, enabling you to begin using the Web and communicate with others as soon as you set up the Internet connection. Some also include utilities to protect computers from unauthorized intrusions and unwanted software such as viruses and spyware. Read Ethics & Issues 8-1 for a related discussion.

Monitoring Performance

Operating systems typically contain a performance monitor. A **performance monitor** is a program that assesses and reports information about various computer resources and devices (Figure 8-12). For example, users can monitor the processor, disks, network, and memory usage.

The information in performance reports helps users and administrators identify a problem with resources so they can try to resolve any problems. If a computer is running extremely slow, for example, the performance monitor may determine that the computer's memory is being used to its maximum. Thus, you might consider installing additional memory in the computer.

ETHICS & ISSUES 8-1

What Should Be in an Operating System?

Microsoft includes a Web browser, movie making software, a word processing program, plug-ins, a personal firewall, spyware remover, and other programs, utilities, and features with its Windows operating systems. Apple bundles QuickTime, CD burning software, and other programs, utilities, and features into Mac OS X. Manufacturers say that combining additional features and programs with their operating systems is a convenience for consumers and sometimes integral to the operating systems' performance. Microsoft's bundling of its Web browser with its Windows operating system was the proximate cause of an antitrust action against the software giant. Microsoft no longer includes its media player and other software in its Windows Vista operating system that it sells in the European Union and other countries as a result of antitrust action. Critics also insist that bundling applications with an operating system forces consumers to pay for programs that may be inferior to those available elsewhere. Is bundling applications with an operating system fair, or is it a monopolistic practice? Why? Who should decide what an operating system should include? Why? Should computer manufacturers be allowed to choose which bundled applications are installed on computers that they ship to customers? Why or why not?

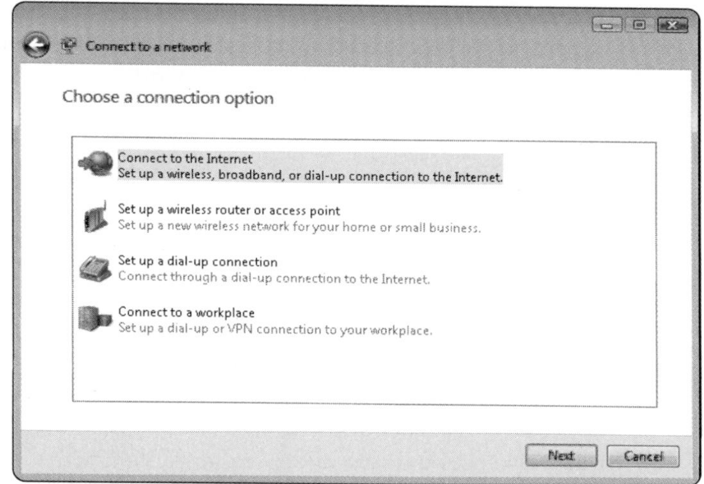

FIGURE 8-11 To connect to a network using Windows Vista, click the Start button, click Connect To, and then click Set up a connection or network.

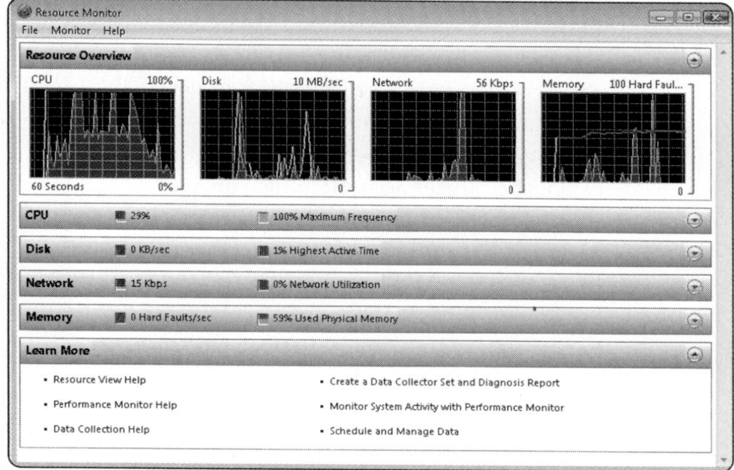

FIGURE 8-12 The Windows Vista Resource Monitor above is tracking CPU (processor), disk, network, and memory usage.

Providing File Management and Other Utilities

Operating systems often provide users with the capability of managing files, searching for files, viewing images, securing a computer from unauthorized access, uninstalling programs, scanning disks, defragmenting disks, diagnosing problems, backing up files and disks, and setting up screen savers. A later section in the chapter discusses these utilities in depth.

Controlling a Network

Some operating systems are network operating systems. A **network operating system**, or *network OS*, is an operating system that organizes and coordinates how multiple users access and share resources on a network. Resources include hardware, software, data, and information. For example, a network OS allows multiple users to share a printer, Internet access, files, and programs.

Some operating systems have network features built into them. In other cases, the network OS is a set of programs separate from the operating system on the client computers that access the network. When not connected to the network, the client computers use their own operating system. When connected to the network, the network OS may assume some of the operating system functions.

The *network administrator*, the person overseeing network operations, uses the network OS to add and remove users, computers, and other devices to and from the network. The network administrator also uses the network operating system to install software and administer network security.

Administering Security

The network administrator uses the network OS to establish permissions to resources. These permissions define who can access certain resources and when they can access those resources.

For each user, the network administrator establishes a user account, which enables a user to access, or **log on** to, a computer or a network. Each user account typically consists of a user name and password (Figure 8-13). A **user name**, or **user ID**, is a unique combination of characters, such as letters of the alphabet or numbers, that identifies one specific user. Many users select a combination of their first and last names as their user name. A user named Henry Baker might choose H Baker as his user name.

A **password** is a private combination of characters associated with the user name that allows access to certain computer resources. Some operating systems allow the network administrator to assign passwords to files and commands, restricting access to only authorized users.

To prevent unauthorized users from accessing computer resources, keep your password confidential. While entering your password, most computers hide the actual password characters by displaying some other characters, such as asterisks (*) or dots. After entering a user name and password, the operating system compares the user's entry with a list of authorized user names and passwords. If the entry matches the user name and password kept on file, the operating system grants the user access. If the entry does not match, the operating system denies access to the user.

The operating system records successful and unsuccessful logon attempts in a file. This allows the network administrator to review who is using or attempting to use the computer. Network administrators also use these files to monitor computer usage.

To protect sensitive data and information further as it travels over the network, a network operating system may encrypt it. *Encryption* is the process of encoding data and information into an unreadable form. Network administrators can set up a network to encrypt data as it travels over the network to prevent unauthorized users from reading the data. When an authorized user attempts to read the data, it automatically is decrypted, or converted back into a readable form. Read Ethics & Issues 8-2 for a related discussion.

FIGURE 8-13 Most multiuser operating systems allow each user to log on, which is the process of entering a user name and a password into the computer.

ETHICS & ISSUES 8-2

Who Should Be Responsible for Notebook Computer Security?

As notebook computers now outsell desktop computers, they increasingly have become the focus of security breaches. A notebook computer's greatest asset, portability, also may be its greatest weakness. Recently, the theft of a notebook computer from an employee's home resulted in information regarding more than 25 million veterans to fall into the wrong hands. The information included Social Security numbers, and the resulting fallout cost the organization millions of dollars. Security experts claim that organizations have become lax about allowing employees to store sensitive information on notebook computers. Too often, they argue, organizations allow employees to take computers home on a daily basis when no such need exists. Employers, on the other hand, feel that workers are more productive when allowed to work during the evenings and weekends using notebook computers. One possible solution is the use of *full-disk encryption*, which scrambles all of the notebook computer's data on its hard disk and requires a password to unlock. If the computer is stolen, the thief cannot access the data on the hard disk. Those who opposed the widespread use of full-disk encryption say that its use results in slower system performance, is still vulnerable when users are lax with securing their passwords, and may result in lost data when an employee leaves the organization without disclosing the password. Who should be responsible for notebook computer security? Why? Should employees be allowed to take their notebook computers home every night or should the computers be taken offsite only for legitimate, preapproved business purposes? Why or why not? Should more organizations use full-disk encryption? Why or why not?

FAQ 8-4

What are the guidelines for selecting a good password?

Choose a password that is easy to remember, and that no one could guess. Do not use any part of your first or last name, your spouse's or child's name, telephone number, street address, license plate number, Social Security number, birthday, and so on. Be sure your password is at least six characters long, mixed with uppercase and lowercase letters, numbers, and special characters. You also should avoid using single-word passwords that are found in the dictionary. For more information, visit scsite.com/dc2008/ch8/faq and then click Passwords.

Test your knowledge of pages 398 through 410 in Quiz Yourself 8-1.

QUIZ YOURSELF 8-1

Instructions: Find the true statement below. Then, rewrite the remaining false statements so they are true.

1. A buffer is a small program that tells the operating system how to communicate with a specific device.
2. A cold boot is the process of using the operating system to restart a computer.
3. A password is a public combination of characters associated with the user name that allows access to certain computer resources.
4. Firmware that contains the computer's startup instructions is called the kernel.
5. The program you currently are using is in the background, and the other programs running but not in use are in the foreground.
6. Two types of system software are operating systems and application programs.
7. With virtual memory, the operating system allocates a portion of a storage medium, usually the hard disk, to function as additional RAM.

Quiz Yourself Online: To further check your knowledge of system software and features common to most operating systems, visit scsite.com/dc2008/ch8/quiz and then click Objectives 1 – 4.

OPERATING SYSTEM UTILITY PROGRAMS

A **utility program**, also called a **utility**, is a type of system software that allows a user to perform maintenance-type tasks, usually related to managing a computer, its devices, or its programs. Most operating systems include several built-in utility programs (Figure 8-14). Users often buy stand-alone utilities, however, because they offer improvements over those included with the operating system.

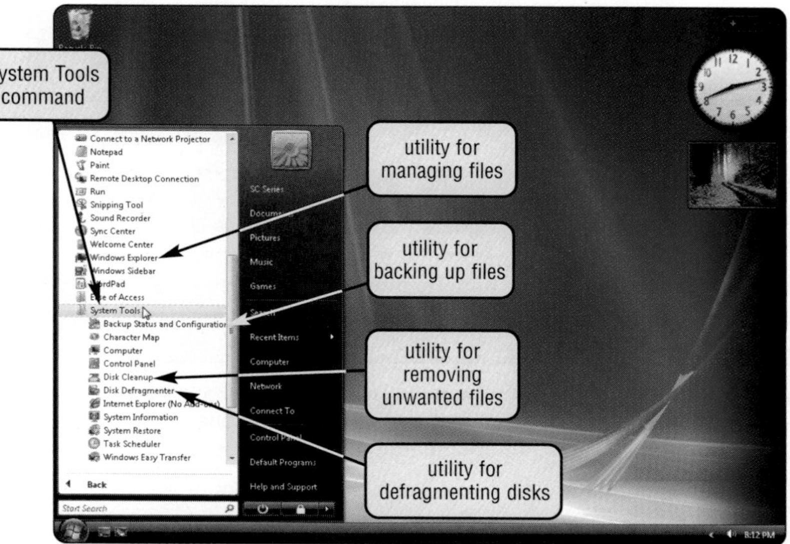

FIGURE 8-14 To display the utilities available in the Windows Vista System Tools list, click the Start button, click All Programs, click Accessories, and then click System Tools.

Utility programs included with most operating systems provide the following functions: managing files, searching for files, viewing images, securing a computer from unauthorized access, uninstalling programs, scanning disks, defragmenting disks, diagnosing problems, backing up files and disks, and setting up screen savers. The following sections briefly discuss each of these utilities.

File Manager

A **file manager** is a utility that performs functions related to file management. Windows Vista includes file managers called *Explorers:* the Document Explorer, Picture Explorer, and Music Explorer. Some of the file management functions that a file manager performs are displaying a list of files on a storage medium (Figure 8-15); organizing files in folders; copying, renaming, deleting, moving, and sorting files and folders; and creating shortcuts. A **folder** is a specific named location on a storage medium that contains related documents. A **shortcut** is an icon on the desktop that provides a user with immediate access to a program or file.

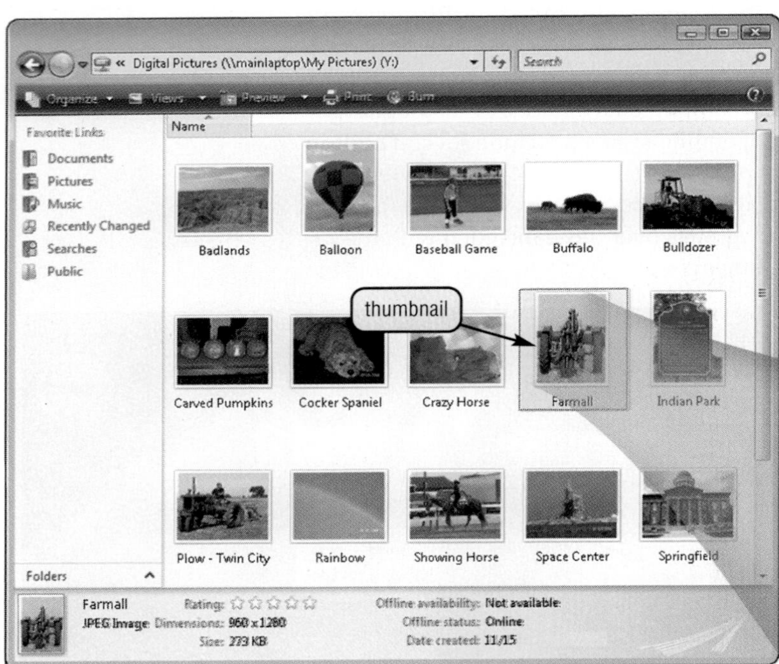

FIGURE 8-15 Windows Vista includes file managers that allow you to view documents, pictures, and music. In this case, thumbnails of pictures are displayed.

Search Utility

A **search utility** is a program that attempts to locate a file on your computer based on criteria you specify. The criteria could be a word or words contained in a file, date the file was created or modified, size of the file, location of the file, file name, author/artist, and other similar properties. Search utilities can look through documents, pictures, music, and other files.

Search utilities typically use an index to assist with locating files quickly. An *index* stores a variety of information about a file, including its name, date created, date modified, author name, and so on. When you enter search criteria, instead of looking through every file and folder on the storage medium, the search utility looks through the index first to find a match. Each entry in the index contains a link to the actual file on the disk for easy retrieval. Windows Vista has a built-in search utility. All the Explorer windows, as well as the Start menu, contain a Search box where you enter the search criteria.

Image Viewer

An **image viewer** is a utility that allows users to display, copy, and print the contents of a graphics file, such as a picture. With an image viewer, users can see images without having to open them in a paint or image editing program. Windows Vista includes an image viewer called *Windows Photo Gallery,* which also allows you to manage and edit pictures (Figure 8-16). To display a file in this image viewer, simply double-click the thumbnail of the image in the file manager. For example, double-clicking a thumbnail in the Picture Explorer (Figure 8-15) displays the image in a Windows Photo Gallery window.

FIGURE 8-16 Windows Photo Gallery allows users to see the contents of a picture file.

Personal Firewall

A **personal firewall** is a utility that detects and protects a personal computer from unauthorized intrusions. Personal firewalls constantly monitor all transmissions to and from a computer.

When connected to the Internet, your computer is vulnerable to attacks from a hacker. A *hacker* is someone who tries to access a computer or network illegally. Users with broadband Internet connections, such as through DSL and Internet cable television service, are even more susceptible than those with dial-up access because the Internet connection is always on.

Windows Vista automatically enables its built-in personal firewall upon installation. This firewall, called Windows Firewall, is easy to access and configure (Figure 8-17). If your operating system does not include a personal firewall or you want additional protection, you can purchase a stand-alone personal firewall utility or a hardware firewall, which is a device such as a router that has a built-in firewall.

Uninstaller

An **uninstaller** is a utility that removes a program, as well as any associated entries in the system files. In Windows Vista, the uninstaller is available through the Uninstall a program command in the Control Panel.

When you install a program, the operating system records the information it uses to run the software in the system files. The uninstaller deletes files and folders from the hard disk, as well as removes program entries from the system files.

Personal Firewalls

For more information, visit scsite.com/dc2008/ch8/weblink and then click Personal Firewalls.

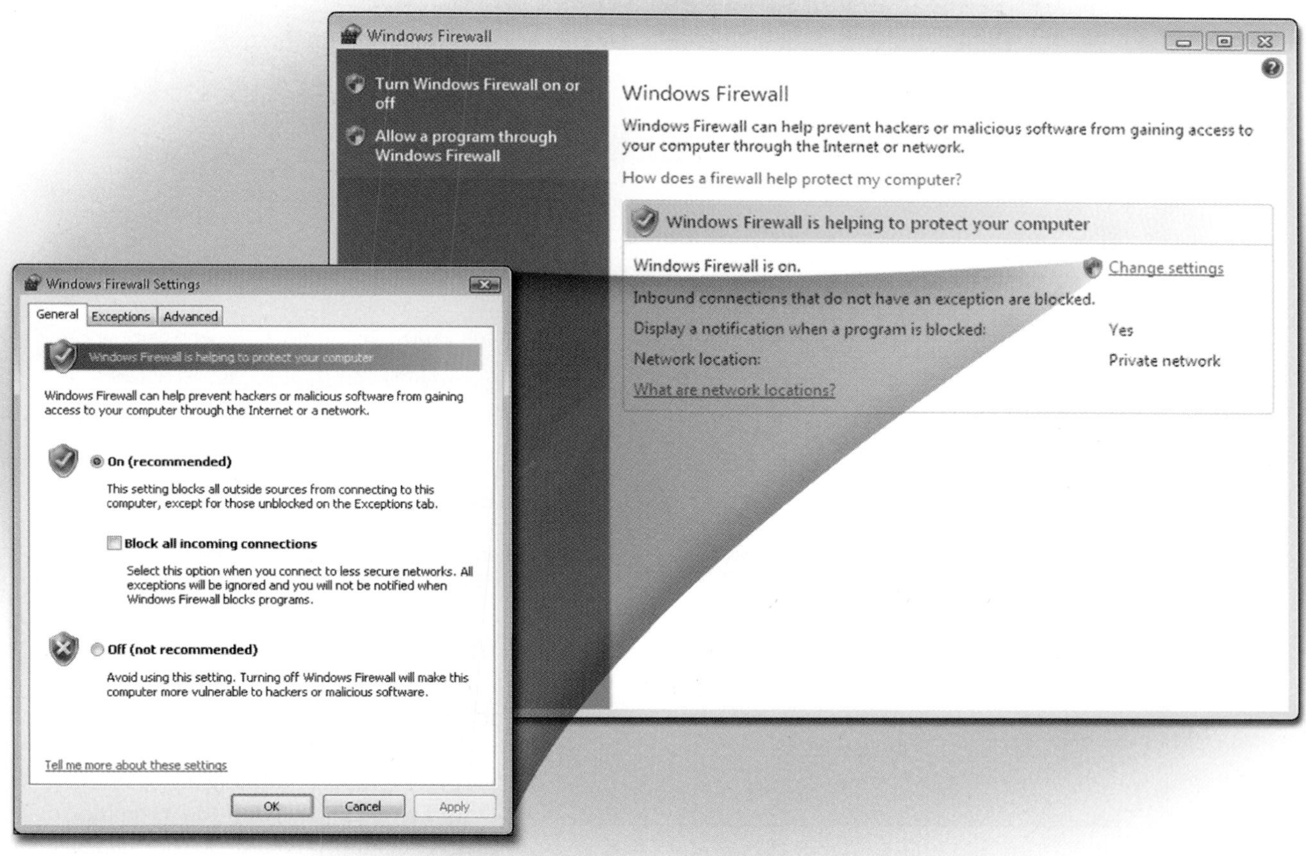

FIGURE 8-17 Through the Security Center in the Control Panel of Windows Vista, users can configure Windows Firewall, which is a personal firewall utility built into Windows Vista.

Should I use Document Explorer to delete a program?

No! If you remove software from a computer by deleting the files and folders associated with the program without running the uninstaller, the system file entries are not updated. This may cause the operating system to display error messages when you start the computer. If the program has an uninstaller, always use it to remove software. For more information, visit scsite.com/dc2008/ch8/faq and then click Uninstalling Programs.

Disk Scanner

A **disk scanner** is a utility that searches for and removes unnecessary files. Windows Vista includes a disk scanner utility, called *Disk Cleanup*, which searches for and removes unnecessary files such as temporary files (Figure 8-18).

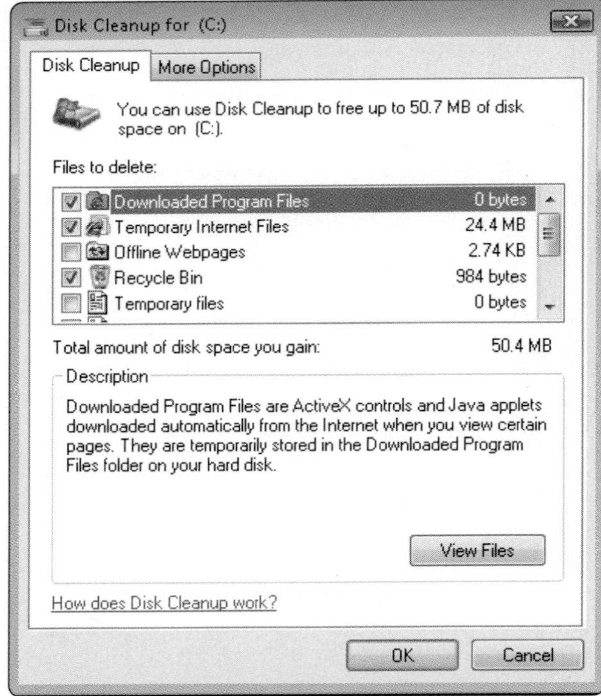

FIGURE 8-18 Disk Cleanup searches for and removes unnecessary files.

Disk Defragmenter

A **disk defragmenter** is a utility that reorganizes the files and unused space on a computer's hard disk so the operating system accesses data more quickly and programs run faster. When an operating system stores data on a disk, it places the data in the first available sector on the disk. It attempts to place data in sectors that are contiguous (next to each other), but this is not always possible. When the contents of a file are scattered across two or more noncontiguous sectors, the file is *fragmented*.

Fragmentation slows down disk access and thus the performance of the entire computer. **Defragmenting** the disk, or reorganizing it so the files are stored in contiguous sectors, solves this problem (Figure 8-19). Windows Vista includes a disk defragmenter available in the System Tools list.

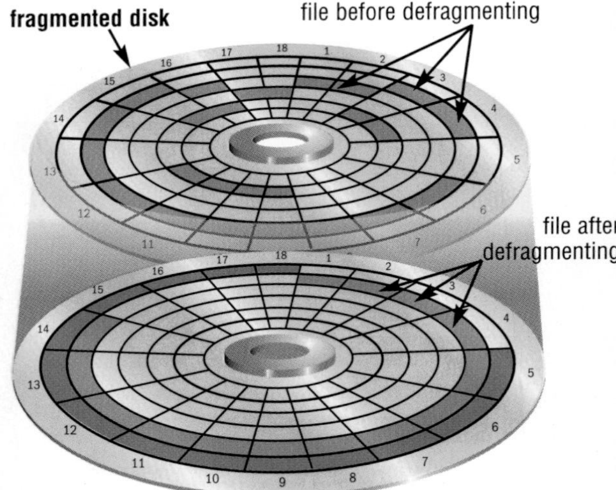

FIGURE 8-19 A fragmented disk has many files stored in noncontiguous sectors. Defragmenting reorganizes the files so they are located in contiguous sectors, which speeds access time.

Diagnostic Utility

A **diagnostic utility** compiles technical information about your computer's hardware and certain system software programs and then prepares a report outlining any identified problems. For example, Windows Vista includes the diagnostic utility, *Problem Reports and Solutions*, which diagnoses problems as well as suggests courses of action. Information in the report assists technical support staff in remedying any problems.

Backup Utility

A **backup utility** allows users to copy, or *back up*, selected files or an entire hard disk to another storage medium such as CD, DVD, external hard disk, tape, or USB flash drive. During the backup process, the backup utility monitors progress and alerts you if it needs additional discs or tapes. Many backup programs *compress*, or shrink the size of, files during the backup process. By compressing the files, the backup program requires less storage space for the backup files than for the original files.

Because they are compressed, you usually cannot use backup files in their backed up form. In the event you need to use a backup file, a **restore program** reverses the process and returns backed up files to their original form. Backup utilities include restore programs.

You should back up files and disks regularly in the event your originals are lost, damaged, or destroyed. Windows Vista includes a backup utility (Figure 8-20). Instead of backing up to a local disk storage device, some users opt to use online storage to back up their files. As described in Chapter 7, online storage is a service on the Web that provides hard disk storage to computer users, usually for free or for a minimal monthly fee.

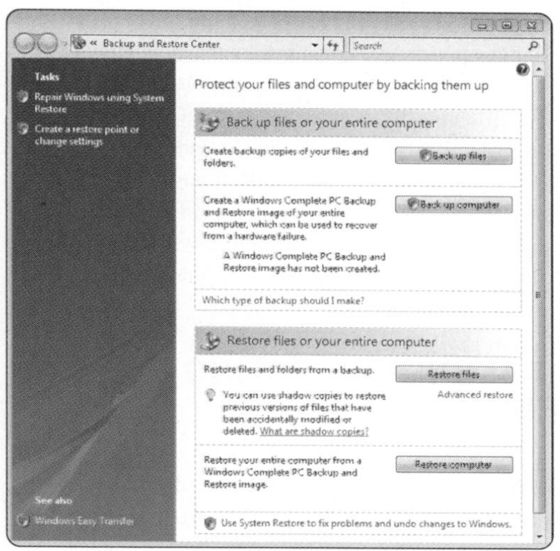

FIGURE 8-20 A backup utility allows users to copy files or an entire hard disk to another storage medium.

Screen Saver

A **screen saver** is a utility that causes a display device's screen to show a moving image or blank screen if no keyboard or mouse activity occurs for a specified time (Figure 8-21). When you press a key on the keyboard or move the mouse, the screen saver disappears and the screen returns to the previous state.

Screen savers originally were developed to prevent a problem called *ghosting*, in which images could be permanently etched on a monitor's screen. Although ghosting is not as severe of a problem with today's displays, manufacturers continue to recommend that users install screen savers for this reason. Screen savers also are popular for security, business, and entertainment purposes. To secure a computer, users configure their screen saver to require a password to deactivate. Many of the Windows Vista screen savers require the Windows Aero interface. In addition to those included with the operating system, many screen savers are available in stores and on the Web for free or a minimal fee.

Screen Savers

For more information, visit scsite.com/dc2008/ch8/weblink and then click Screen Savers.

FIGURE 8-21 Windows Vista has built-in screen savers.

TYPES OF OPERATING SYSTEMS

Many of the first operating systems were device dependent and proprietary. A *device-dependent* program is one that runs only on a specific type or make of computer. *Proprietary software* is privately owned and limited to a specific vendor or computer model. Some operating systems still are device dependent. The trend today, however, is toward *device-independent* operating systems that run on computers provided by a variety of manufacturers. The advantage of device-independent operating systems is you can retain existing application software and data files even if you change computer models or vendors.

When you purchase a new computer, it typically has an operating system preinstalled. As new versions of the operating system are released, users upgrade their existing computers to incorporate features of the new version. An upgrade usually costs less than purchasing the entire operating system.

Some software manufacturers, such as Microsoft and IBM, release free downloadable updates to their software, often called a *service pack*. Users also can order service packs on CD for a minimal shipping fee. Service packs provide enhancements to the original software and fix bugs (errors) in the software. Read Ethics & Issues 8-3 for a related discussion.

New versions of an operating system usually are downward compatible. That is, they recognize and work with application software written for an earlier version of the operating system (or platform). The application software, by contrast, is said to be upward compatible, meaning it will run on new versions of the operating system.

The three basic categories of operating systems that exist today are stand-alone, network, and embedded. The table in Figure 8-22 lists specific names of operating systems in each category. The following pages discuss the operating systems listed in the table.

WEB LINK 8-5

Windows Vista

For more information, visit scsite.com/dc2008/ch8/weblink and then click Windows Vista.

CATEGORIES OF OPERATING SYSTEMS

Category	Operating System Name
Stand-alone	• DOS • Early Windows versions (Windows 3.x, Windows 95, Windows NT Workstation, Windows 98, Windows 2000 Professional, Windows Millennium Edition) • Windows XP • Windows Vista • Mac OS X • UNIX • Linux
Network	• Early Windows Server versions (Windows NT Server, Windows 2000 Server) • Windows Server 2003 • UNIX • Linux • Solaris • NetWare
Embedded	• Windows CE • Windows Mobile • Palm OS • Embedded Linux • Symbian OS

FIGURE 8-22 Examples of stand-alone, network, and embedded operating systems. Some stand-alone operating systems include the capability of configuring small home or office networks.

ETHICS & ISSUES 8-3

Does Windows Genuine Advantage Give an Advantage to Hackers?

When Microsoft releases new software updates for a Windows operating system, the *Windows Genuine Advantage* program that is built into the operating system determines whether the operating system is a fully licensed, legitimate copy and is not a pirated copy. If the computer does not pass the test, then the updates are not installed and the computer user is notified of the potential infraction. Microsoft claims that users are being protected from potentially dangerous pirated versions of the operating system. The company also has no obligation to provide security updates or software patches to those who obtain the operating system illegally, and Microsoft has the right to protect its operating system from being pirated. Critics of the Windows Genuine Advantage program, however, want the updates available to all. Even if a user owns a pirated version of the operating system, a computer that does not receive the updates may be more susceptible to viruses and other malware. For example, the computer may become a zombie for a hacker, which means that a hacker secretly can use the computer over the Internet to spread more malware or to send spam e-mail. Furthermore, in some cases a computer owner is not aware that an unscrupulous computer seller has sold them a pirated copy of the operating system. In such cases, experts claim that the user should not suffer the consequences of the computer seller's actions. Do you think that Microsoft has legitimate reasons for the Windows Genuine Advantage program? Why or why not? Should users of pirated copies of an operating system be allowed to receive security updates and software patches? Why or why not? If a computer user is unaware that they have purchased a pirated copy of the operating system, should Microsoft have the ability to remotely disable the computer? Why?

STAND-ALONE OPERATING SYSTEMS

A **stand-alone operating system** is a complete operating system that works on a desktop computer, notebook computer, or mobile computing device. Some stand-alone operating systems are called *client operating systems* because they also work in conjunction with a network operating system. Client operating systems can operate with or without a network. Other stand-alone operating systems include networking capabilities, allowing the home and small business user to set up a small network.

Examples of currently used stand-alone operating systems are Windows XP, Windows Vista, Mac OS X, UNIX, and Linux. The following paragraphs briefly discuss these operating systems.

FAQ 8-6

What was Microsoft's first operating system?

In the early 1980s, Microsoft introduced *DOS* (Disk Operating System) as its first operating system. The two more widely used versions of DOS were PC-DOS and MS-DOS. At first, DOS used a command-line interface, but later versions introduced a menu-driven interface. DOS once was used on an estimated 70 million computers, but hardly is used today because it lacks a graphical user interface and does not take full advantage of modern personal computer processors. For more information, visit scsite.com/dc2008/ch8/faq and then click DOS.

Windows XP

In the mid-1980s, Microsoft developed its first version of Windows, which provided a graphical user interface (GUI). Since then, Microsoft continually has updated its Windows operating system, incorporating innovative features and functions with each subsequent version (Figure 8-23). **Windows XP** is a fast, reliable Windows operating system, providing quicker startup, better performance, increased security, and a simpler visual look than previous Windows versions. Using Windows XP, home and small office users easily can set up a network and secure it from hackers with Windows Firewall. Windows Messenger, included with Windows XP, enables users to send instant messages. Windows XP

HIGHLIGHTS OF STAND-ALONE WINDOWS VERSIONS

Windows Version	Year Released	Highlights
Windows 3.x	1990	• Provided a GUI • An operating environment only — worked in combination with DOS
Windows NT 3.1	1993	• Client OS that connected to a Windows NT Advanced Server • Interface similar to Windows 3.x
Windows 95	1995	• True multitasking operating system • Improved GUI • Included support for networking, Plug and Play technology, longer file names, and e-mail
Windows NT Workstation 4.0	1996	• Client OS that connected to a Windows NT Server • Interface similar to Windows 95 • Network integration
Windows 98	1998	• Upgrade to Windows 95 • More integrated with the Internet; included *Internet Explorer* (a Web browser) • Faster system startup and shutdown, better file management, support for multimedia technologies (e.g., DVDs), and USB connectivity
Windows Millennium Edition	2000	• Upgrade to Windows 98 • Designed for the home user who wanted music playing, video editing, and networking capabilities
Windows 2000 Professional	2000	• Upgrade to Windows NT Workstation 4.0 • Complete multitasking client OS designed for business personal computers • Certified device drivers, faster performance, adaptive Start menu, image viewer, enhanced for mobile users
Windows XP	2001	• Upgrade to Windows Millennium Edition called Windows XP Home Edition • Upgrade to Windows 2000 Professional called Windows XP Professional • Windows XP Tablet PC Edition designed for Tablet PC users • Windows XP Media Center Edition designed for PCs used for home entertainment • Windows XP Professional x64 Edition designed for workstations that use 64-bit processors • Improved interface and increased performance in all editions
Windows XP SP2 (Service Pack 2)	2004	• Enhancement to Windows XP that offers more built-in security technologies • Improved firewall utility • Automatic blocking of Internet pop-up advertisements
Windows Vista	2006	• Upgrade to Windows XP • Easier to navigate user interface • Enhanced administration of user accounts • Improved firewall • Simplified customization techniques • New Instant Search improves searching capabilities • New Document Explorer, Picture Explorer, and Music Explorer improve organizing capabilities • Improved performance and reliability

FIGURE 8-23 Microsoft has released many versions of Windows.

also includes Windows Media Player, which allows users to listen to Internet radio stations, play MP3 and other music formats, copy music and data to CDs, and watch DVD movies.

Windows XP is available in five editions: Home Edition, Professional (Figure 8-24), Media Center Edition, Tablet PC Edition, and Professional x64 Edition. With Windows XP Home Edition, users easily can organize and share digital pictures, download and listen to music, create and edit videos, network home computers, send and receive instant messages, and recover from problems with easy-to-use tools. Windows XP Professional includes all the capabilities of Windows XP Home Edition and also offers greater data security, remote access to a computer, simpler administration of groups of users, multiple language user interface, and support for a wireless network.

Windows XP Media Center Edition includes all features of Windows XP Professional and is designed for Media Center PCs. A *Media Center PC* is a home entertainment personal computer that includes a mid- to high-end processor, large-capacity hard disk, CD and DVD drives, a remote control, and advanced graphics and audio capabilities.

Windows XP Tablet PC Edition includes all features of Windows XP Professional and provides additional features designed to make users more productive while working on their Tablet PC. Windows XP Professional x64 Edition is designed for power users with workstations that use 64-bit processors.

Windows Vista

Windows Vista, the successor to Windows XP, is Microsoft's fastest, most reliable and efficient operating system to date, offering quicker application start up, built-in diagnostics, automatic recovery, improved security, and enhanced searching and organizing capabilities (Figure 8-25).

Windows Vista is available in five editions: Windows Vista Home Basic, Windows Vista Home Premium, Windows Vista Ultimate, Windows Vista Business, and Windows Vista Enterprise.

- *Windows Vista Home Basic*, designed for the basic home user, includes the Windows Vista Basic interface and allows users easily to search for files, protect their computer from unauthorized intruders and unwanted programs, and set parental controls to monitor the use of games, the Internet, instant messaging, and other communications programs.
- *Windows Vista Home Premium* includes all the capabilities of Windows Vista Home Basic and also offers the Windows Aero interface with its Flip 3D feature (Figure 8-26). It also provides tools to create DVDs and edit movies, record and watch television shows, connect to a game console, securely connect to Wi-Fi networks, work with a Tablet PC, and quickly view messages on a powered-off, specially equipped notebook computer.
- *Windows Vista Ultimate* includes all features of Windows Vista Home Premium and provides additional features designed to make mobile users' computers more secure and easier to network. Windows Vista features are summarized in Figure 8-27.

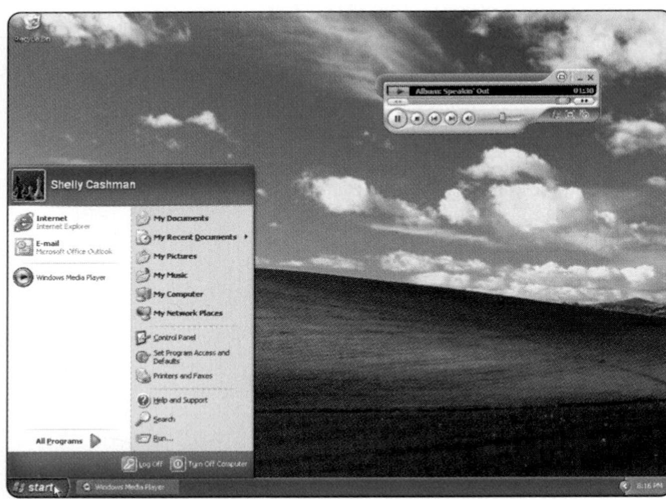

FIGURE 8-24 Windows XP, with its simplified look, is a fast, reliable Windows operating system.

FIGURE 8-25 Windows Vista has a new interface, easier navigation and searching techniques, and improved security.

- With *Windows Vista Business*, users in all sizes of businesses are provided a secure operating environment that uses the Windows Aero interface where they easily can search for files, protect their computers from unauthorized intruders and unwanted programs, use improved backup technologies, securely connect to Wi-Fi networks, quickly view messages on a powered-off, specially equipped notebook computer, and easily share documents and collaborate with other users.
- *Windows Vista Enterprise* includes all the features of Windows Vista Business and also offers greater levels of data protection and a multi-language interface.

To run Windows Vista Basic, your computer must have at least 512 MB of RAM. For all other editions, your computer must have at least 1 GB of RAM and at least 128 MB of video (graphics) memory. Windows Vista adapts to the hardware configuration on which it is installed. Thus, two users with the same edition of Windows Vista may experience different functionality and interfaces.

FIGURE 8-26 With Windows Vista Flip 3D, users flip through open windows by rolling the wheel on their mouse.

FAQ 8-7

How do I know that my hardware and software will work with Windows Vista?

Hardware and software compatible with Windows Vista may display either the Certified for Windows Vista or Works with Windows Vista logo on the packaging. If neither of these logos appears, check the manufacturer's Web site for compatibility information. For more information, visit scsite.com/dc2008/ch8/faq and then click Windows Vista Compatibility.

WINDOWS VISTA FEATURES

Reliability and Performance	• New Sleep state combines the resume to your work speed of Windows XP Standby mode and low power consumption of Hibernate mode • Programs start faster with Windows SuperFetch technology • Automatically detects and fine tunes performance problems • Built-in hardware diagnostics detect and repair problems automatically • Automatically recovers from failures, including restoring an unbootable computer to a usable state
Security	• User Account Control allows administrators to restrict permissions • Improved firewall • Protects users from dangerous Web sites • *Windows Defender* protects your computer from spyware
Information Management	• *Document Explorer*, *Picture Explorer*, and *Music Explorer* help users locate documents by showing thumbnails that preview documents' content and allowing users to adjust thumbnail size to view a document without opening it • Use Instant Search to locate files based on file name or any other property saved with the file • Easily share files with other users
Appearance and Navigation	• Easy-to-navigate user interface with translucent windows to minimize distraction, customizes itself based on the hardware capabilities of the computer on which it is installed • *Flip 3D* works with the mouse to flip through open windows arranged in a stack • *Windows Sidebar* connects to personalized mini-applications, called gadgets, such as weather, photos, or headline news • Display a preview of the current window when you point to a program button on the taskbar • *Windows SideShow* allows viewing of messages on a powered-off notebook computer equipped with a secondary display • Common dialog boxes shared by all applications
Communications and the Internet	• Enhanced Internet Explorer • Improved e-mail program with built-in spam filter • Consistent and secure wireless network connections • Speech recognition allows you to interact with the computer by voice

FIGURE 8-27 Some features of Windows Vista.

Mac OS X

Since it was released in 1984 with Macintosh computers, Apple's **Macintosh operating system** has set the standard for operating system ease of use and has been the model for most of the new GUIs developed for non-Macintosh systems. The latest version, **Mac OS X**, is a multitasking operating system available only for computers manufactured by Apple (Figure 8-28). Read Looking Ahead 8-1 for a look at the future of Apple and Mac OS X.

Mac OS X includes features from previous versions of the Macintosh operating system such as large photo-quality icons, built-in networking support, e-mail, online shopping, enhanced speech recognition, CD burning, and enhanced multimedia capabilities. In addition, Mac OS X includes these features:

- New desktop search technology
- Dashboard, a desktop area for mini-applications
- Built-in, fast Web browser
- Parental controls
- Accessibility interface reads e-mail messages
- 3-D personal video and audio conferencing
- Filter to eliminate junk e-mail messages
- Contact lists synchronized with PDA or Bluetooth-enabled smart phone
- Latest version of QuickTime to listen to music and view videos on the Internet
- Easy networking of computers and devices
- Windows network connection and shared Windows documents

WEB LINK 8-6

Mac OS X

For more information, visit scsite.com/dc2008/ch8/weblink and then click Mac OS X.

FIGURE 8-28 Mac OS X is the operating system used with Apple Macintosh computers.

LOOKING AHEAD 8-1

Apple Marching to Its Own Tune

When the iPod hit the marketplace in 2001, few people expected that it would become one of the most successful products of the young century. More than 60 million people, including England's Queen Elizabeth and Pope Benedict, own one of these units. Five years later, Apple CEO Steve Jobs acknowledged that although the iPod and iTunes account for more than 40 percent of the company's revenues, the entire line will be entirely overhauled and become a significant part of wearable technology.

At Apple's annual Worldwide Developers Conference in 2006, Jobs and other company executives announced key future updates. Among them are improvements to Mac OS X, including effortless backups, the capability for Intel-based Macs to run more Windows applications, and an expanded search engine.

Photographs, music, movies, and downloaded videos will be accessed from a single interface, and users with physical disabilities will have improved universal access. For more information, visit scsite.com/dc2008/ch8/looking and then click Apple Future.

UNIX

UNIX (pronounced YOU-nix) is a multitasking operating system developed in the early 1970s by scientists at Bell Laboratories. Bell Labs (a subsidiary of AT&T) was prohibited from actively promoting UNIX in the commercial marketplace because of federal regulations. Bell Labs instead licensed UNIX for a low fee to numerous colleges and universities, where UNIX obtained a wide following. UNIX was implemented on many different types of computers. After deregulation of the telephone companies in the 1980s, UNIX was licensed to many hardware and software companies.

Several versions of this operating system exist, each slightly different. When programmers move application software from one UNIX version to another, they sometimes have to rewrite some of the programs. Although some versions of UNIX have a command-line interface, most versions of UNIX offer a graphical user interface (Figure 8-29).

Today, a version of UNIX is available for most computers of all sizes.

WEB LINK 8-7

UNIX

For more information, visit scsite.com/dc2008/ch8/weblink and then click UNIX.

Power users often work with UNIX because of its flexibility and power. Manufacturers such as Sun and IBM sell personal computers and workstations with a UNIX operating system.

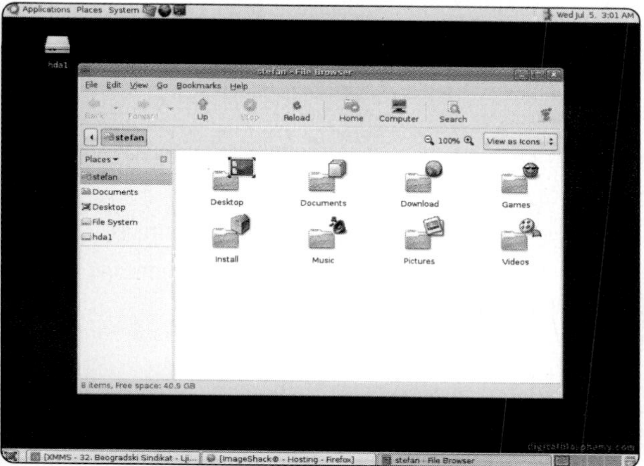

FIGURE 8-29 Some versions of UNIX have a graphical user interface.

Linux

Linux is one of the faster growing operating systems. **Linux** (pronounced LINN-uks) is a popular, multitasking UNIX-type operating system. In addition to the basic operating system, Linux also includes many free programming languages and utility programs.

Linux is not proprietary software like the operating systems discussed thus far. Instead, Linux is *open source software*, which means its code is provided for use, modification, and redistribution. It has no restrictions from the copyright holder regarding modification of the software's internal instructions and redistribution of the software. Many programmers have donated time to modify and redistribute Linux to make it the best possible version of UNIX. Promoters of open source software state two main advantages: users who modify the software share their improvements with others, and customers can personalize the software to meet their needs. Read Ethics & Issues 8-4 for a related discussion.

Some versions of Linux are command-line. Others are GUI. The two most popular GUIs available for Linux are GNOME and KDE. Some companies such as Red Hat market software applications that run on their own version of Linux (Figure 8-30). Many application programs, utilities, and plug-ins have Linux versions, including OpenOffice.org, StarOffice, Mozilla, Netscape, Yahoo! Messenger, RealPlayer, QuickTime, and Acrobat Reader.

Users obtain Linux in a variety of ways. Some download it free from the Web. Others purchase it from vendors such as Red Hat or IBM, who bundle their own software with the operating system. Linux CD-ROMs are included in many Linux books and also are available for purchase from vendors. Another option is *Live CD* or *Live USB*, where the CD or USB flash drive is bootable. In this case, the CD or USB drive contains files necessary to boot and work with the Linux operating system, which allows users to preview the operating system without installing it. Some retailers such as Dell will preinstall Linux on a new computer's hard disk on request.

ETHICS & ISSUES 8-4

Closed Source vs. Open Source Operating Systems

Linux is a fast-growing, innovative operating system. One of the features that make it different from other operating systems is that Linux is open source and its source code, along with any changes, remains public. Since its introduction in 1991, Linux has been altered, adapted, and improved by thousands of programmers. Unlike Linux, most operating systems are proprietary, and their program code often is a zealously guarded secret. At one large software developer, an employee reported that application programmers had little opportunity to contribute to operating system programs because they had no access to the operating system program source code. Supporters of open source maintain that source code should be open to the public so that it can be scrutinized, corrected, and enhanced. In light of concerns about security and fears of possible virus problems, however, some people are not sure open source software is a good idea. Besides, they argue, companies and programmers should be able to control, and profit from, the operating systems they create. On the other hand, open source software can be scrutinized for errors by a much larger group of people and changes can be made immediately. Are open source operating systems a good idea? Why or why not? How can the concerns about open source operating systems be addressed? What are the advantages and disadvantages of open versus closed source operating systems? Does the open source model lead to better software?

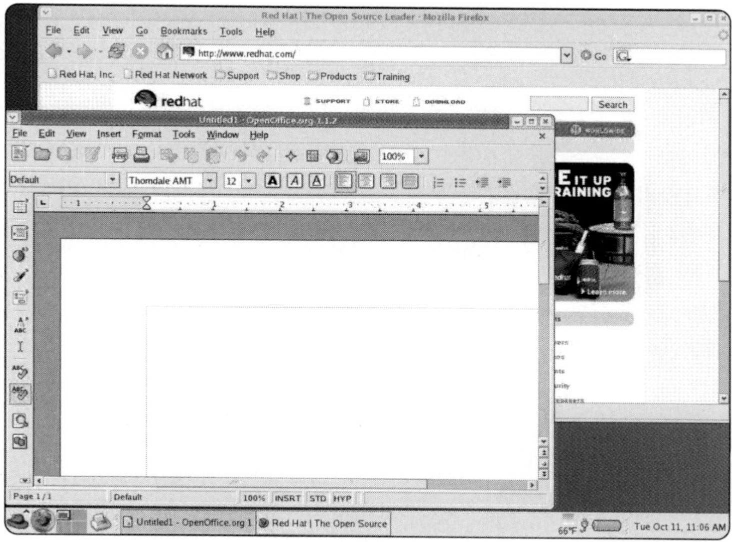

FIGURE 8-30 Red Hat provides a version of Linux called Red Hat Enterprise Linux.

Test your knowledge of pages 410 through 421 in Quiz Yourself 8-2.

QUIZ YOURSELF 8-2

Instructions: Find the true statement below. Then, rewrite the remaining false statements so they are true.

1. A file manager is a utility that detects and protects a personal computer from unauthorized intrusions.
2. Fragmenting a disk is the process of reorganizing it so the files are stored in contiguous sectors.
3. Windows Vista Home Basic uses the Windows Aero interface.
4. Mac OS X is a multitasking operating system available only for computers manufactured by Apple.
5. Flip 3D is a UNIX-type operating system that is open source software.
6. You should uninstall files and disks regularly in the event your originals are lost, damaged, or destroyed.

Quiz Yourself Online: To further check your knowledge of utilities included with most operating systems and stand-alone operating systems, visit scsite.com/dc2008/ch8/quiz and then click Objectives 5 – 6.

NETWORK OPERATING SYSTEMS

As discussed earlier in this chapter, a network operating system is an operating system that is designed specifically to support a network. A network operating system typically resides on a server. The client computers on the network rely on the server(s) for resources. Many of the client operating systems discussed in the previous section work in conjunction with a network operating system.

Some of the stand-alone operating systems discussed in the previous section include networking capability; however, network operating systems are designed specifically to support all sizes of networks, including medium to large-sized businesses and Web servers. Examples of network operating systems include Windows Server 2003, UNIX, Linux, Solaris, and NetWare.

Windows Server 2003

Windows Server 2003 is an upgrade to Windows 2000 Server, which was an upgrade to Windows NT Server. Windows Server 2003, which includes features of previous server versions, offers the following capabilities:

- Web site management and hosting
- Delivery and management of multimedia across intranets and the Internet
- Document storage in Web folders
- Central information repository about network users and resources with *Active Directory*
- Client support using Windows, Mac OS X, UNIX, and Linux

To meet the needs of all sizes of businesses, the **Windows Server 2003 family** includes five products:

- *Windows Small Business Server 2003* designed for businesses with fewer than 75 users and limited networking expertise
- *Windows Server 2003, Standard Edition* for the typical small- to medium-sized business network
- *Windows Server 2003, Enterprise Edition* for medium- to large-sized businesses, including those with e-commerce operations; available in 64-bit version
- *Windows Server 2003, Datacenter Edition* for businesses with huge volumes of transactions and large-scale databases; available in 64-bit version
- *Windows Server 2003, Web Edition* for Web server and Web hosting businesses

Windows Server 2003 is part of Windows Server System. In addition to Windows Server 2003, *Windows Server System* provides developers with dynamic development tools that allow businesses and customers to connect and communicate easily via the Internet. Through Windows Server System, programmers have the ability to use *Web services*, which are Web applications created with any programming language or any operating system to communicate and share data seamlessly.

UNIX

In addition to being a stand-alone operating system, UNIX also is a network operating system. That is, UNIX is capable of handling a high volume of transactions in a multiuser environment and working with multiple processors using multiprocessing. For this reason, some computer professionals call UNIX a *multipurpose operating system* because it is both a stand-alone and network operating system. Many Web servers use UNIX as their operating system.

Linux

Some network servers use Linux as their operating system. Thus, Linux also is a multipurpose operating system. With Linux, a network administrator can configure the network, administer security, run a Web server, and process e-mail. Clients on the network can run Linux, UNIX, or Windows. Versions of Linux include both the Netscape and Mozilla Web browsers.

FAQ 8-8

How widespread is Linux usage?

Forecasters predict that Linux will command more than one-third of the server market by 2009. Desktop personal computers, however, have a much lower Linux usage — only six percent worldwide. For more information, visit scsite.com/dc2008/ch8/faq and then click Linux Users.

Solaris

Solaris, a version of UNIX developed by Sun Microsystems, is a network operating system designed specifically for e-commerce applications. Solaris manages high-traffic accounts and incorporates security necessary for Web transactions. Client computers often use a desktop program, such as GNOME desktop, that communicates with the Solaris operating system.

NetWare

Novell's *NetWare* is a network operating system designed for client/server networks. NetWare has a server portion that resides on the network server and a client portion that resides on each client computer connected to the network. NetWare supports open source software and runs on all types of computers from mainframes to personal computers.

The server portion of NetWare allows users to share hardware devices attached to the server (such as a printer), as well as e-mail, databases, or any other files and software stored on the server. The client portion of NetWare communicates with the server. Client computers also can have their own stand-alone operating system such as Windows Vista, Windows XP, Mac OS X, or a Linux-based client.

WEB LINK 8-8

Solaris

For more information, visit scsite.com/dc2008/ch8/weblink and then click Solaris.

EMBEDDED OPERATING SYSTEMS

The operating system on most PDAs and small devices, called an **embedded operating system**, resides on a ROM chip. Popular embedded operating systems today include Windows CE, Windows Mobile, Palm OS, Blackberry, embedded Linux, and Symbian OS. The following sections discuss these operating systems.

Windows CE

Windows CE is a scaled-down Windows operating system designed for use on communications, entertainment, and computing devices with limited functionality. Examples of devices that use Windows CE include Voice over IP devices, industrial control devices, point-of-sale terminals, security robots, navigation systems, media players, ticket machines, and computerized sewing machines (Figure 8-31).

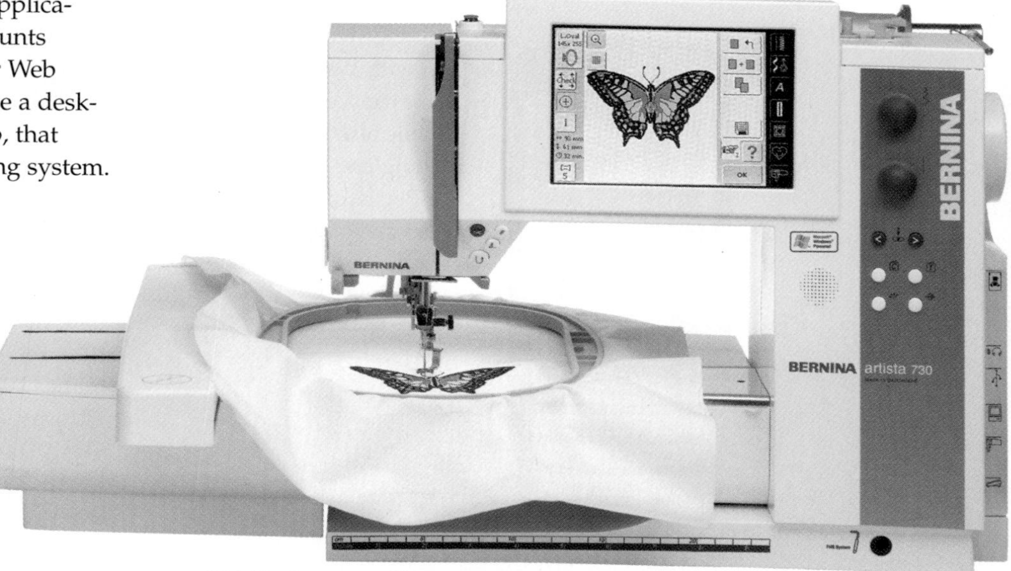

FIGURE 8-31 This sewing machine uses Windows CE to assist with stitching quilts, garments, crafts, decorations, and embroidery.

Windows CE is a GUI that supports color, sound, multitasking, multimedia, e-mail, Internet access, and Web browsing. A built-in file viewer allows users to view files created in popular applications such as Word, Excel, and PowerPoint.

Devices equipped with Windows CE can communicate wirelessly with computers and other devices using Bluetooth or other wireless technologies, as long as the device is equipped with the necessary communications hardware.

Windows Mobile

Windows Mobile, an operating system based on Windows CE, includes functionality, applications, and a user interface designed for specific types of devices. Windows Mobile-based devices include PDAs, called the **Pocket PC**, and smart phones (Figure 8-32). With the Windows Mobile operating system and a Pocket PC or smart phone, users have access to all the basic PIM (personal information manager) functions such as contact lists, schedules, tasks, calendars, and notes. Information on the PDA or smart phone easily synchronizes with a personal computer or prints on a printer using a cable or a wireless technology.

Windows Mobile

For more information, visit scsite.com/dc2008/ch8/weblink and then click Windows Mobile.

Windows Mobile also provides numerous additional features that allow users to check e-mail, browse the Web, listen to music, take pictures or record video, watch a video, send and receive instant messages, record a voice message, manage finances, or read an e-book. Many applications, such as Word, Excel, Outlook, and Internet Explorer, have scaled-down versions that run with Windows Mobile. Some devices with Windows Mobile also support handwriting and voice input. With the Pocket PC Phone devices, users can make telephone calls and send text messages using the PDA.

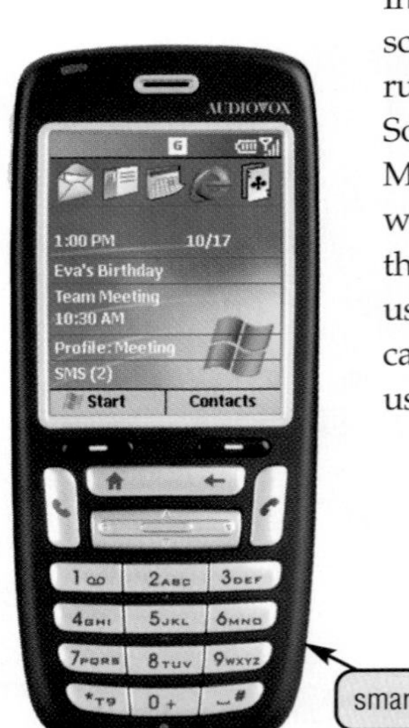

FIGURE 8-32 Windows Mobile runs on Pocket PCs and many smart phones.

Palm OS

A competing operating system to Windows Mobile is *Palm OS*, which runs on PDAs and smart phones (Figure 8-33). With Palm OS devices, users manage schedules and contacts, telephone messages, project notes, reminders, task and address lists, and important dates and appointments. Information on the PDA or smart phone easily synchronizes with a personal computer or prints on a printer using a cable or a wireless technology. Palm users also can exchange information with other Palm users wirelessly through IrDA technology.

Palm OS includes handwriting recognition software, called Graffiti. Many Palm OS devices allow users to connect wirelessly to the Internet, browse the Web, send and receive e-mail messages and instant messages, listen to music, record voice messages, and view digital photos. The latest version of Palm OS includes improved security for data transmission, allows for biometric identification, and supports the use of smart cards.

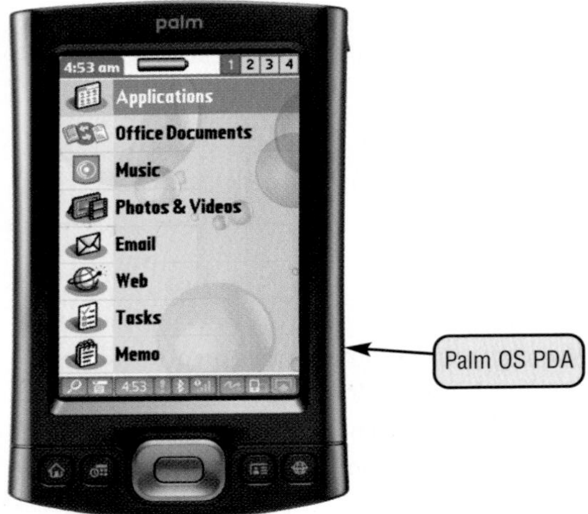

FIGURE 8-33 Palm OS runs on PDAs and smart phones.

BlackBerry

The *BlackBerry* operating system runs on handheld devices supplied by RIM (Research in Motion). BlackBerry devices provide PDA capabilities such as managing schedules and contacts, as well as telephone capabilities (Figure 8-34). They also provide wireless functionality that includes sending e-mail messages, text messages, and instant messages; connecting to the Internet; and accessing Bluetooth devices. Some BlackBerry devices allow users to take pictures, play music, and access maps and directions.

FIGURE 8-34 A handheld device that uses the BlackBerry operating system.

Embedded Linux

Embedded Linux is a scaled-down Linux operating system designed for PDAs, smart phones, smart watches, set-top boxes, Internet telephones, and many other types of devices and computers requiring an embedded operating system. PDAs and smart phones with embedded Linux offer calendar and address book and other PIM functions, touch screens, and handwriting recognition. Many also allow you to connect to the Internet, take pictures, play videos, listen to music, and send e-mail and instant messages. Devices that use embedded Linux synchronize with desktop computers using a variety of technologies including Bluetooth.

Symbian OS

Symbian OS is an open source multitasking operating system designed for smart phones (Figure 8-35). In addition to making telephone calls, users of Symbian OS can maintain contact lists; save appointments; browse the Web; and send and receive text and picture messages, e-mail messages, and faxes using a smart phone. Users enter data by pressing keys on the keypad or keyboard, touching the screen, writing on the screen with a stylus, or speaking into the smart phone. Symbian OS allows users to communicate wirelessly using a variety of technologies including Bluetooth and IrDA.

FIGURE 8-35 This smart phone uses the Symbian OS.

WEB LINK 8-10

BlackBerry

For more information, visit scsite.com/dc2008/ch8/weblink and then click BlackBerry.

STAND-ALONE UTILITY PROGRAMS

Although operating systems typically include some built-in utilities, many stand-alone utility programs are available for purchase. For example, you can purchase personal firewall, backup utilities, and screen savers. These stand-alone utilities typically offer improvements over those features built into the operating system or provide features not included in an operating system.

Other functions provided by stand-alone utilities include protecting against viruses, removing spyware and adware, filtering Internet content, converting files, compressing files, playing media files, burning CDs and DVDs, and maintaining a personal computer. The following sections discuss each of these utilities.

Antivirus Programs

The term, computer **virus**, describes a potentially damaging computer program that affects, or infects, a computer negatively by altering the way the computer works without the user's knowledge or permission. More specifically, a computer virus is a segment of program code from some outside source that implants itself in a computer. Once the virus is in a computer, it can spread throughout and may damage your files and operating system.

Computer viruses do not generate by chance. The programmer of a virus, known as a *virus author*, intentionally writes a virus program. Some virus authors find writing viruses a challenge. Others write virus programs to cause destruction. Writing a virus program usually requires significant programming skills.

Some viruses are harmless pranks that simply freeze a computer temporarily or display sounds or messages. The Music Bug virus, for example, instructs the computer to play a few chords of music. Other viruses destroy or corrupt data stored on the hard disk of the infected computer. If you notice any unusual changes in your computer's performance, it may be infected with a virus. Figure 8-36 outlines some common symptoms of virus infection.

Viruses are just one type of malicious software. *Malware* (short for malicious software) is software that acts without a user's knowledge and deliberately alters the computer's operations. In addition to viruses, worms and Trojan horses are malware.

A **worm**, such as Sasser or Klez, copies itself repeatedly, for example, in memory or over a network, using up system resources and possibly shutting the system down. A **Trojan horse** (named after the Greek myth) hides within or looks like a legitimate program such as a screen saver. A certain condition or action usually triggers the Trojan horse. Unlike a virus or worm, a Trojan horse does not replicate itself to other computers. Currently, more than 180,000 known viruses, worms, Trojan horses, and other malware exist. For a more technical discussion about computer viruses, read the High-Tech Talk article in Chapter 3 on page 168.

To protect a computer from virus attacks, users should install an antivirus program and update it frequently. An **antivirus program** protects a computer against viruses by identifying and removing any computer viruses found in memory, on storage media, or on incoming files (Figure 8-37). Most antivirus programs also protect against worms and Trojan horses. When you purchase a new computer, it often includes antivirus software.

Three more popular antivirus programs are McAfee VirusScan, Norton AntiVirus, and Windows Live OneCare, the latter of which also contains spyware removers, Internet filters, PC maintenance, and backup utilities. As an alternative to purchasing these products on CD, both McAfee and Norton offer Web-based antivirus programs.

FAQ 8-9

What steps should I take to prevent virus infections on my computer?

Set up the antivirus software to scan on a regular basis. Update your virus definitions regularly. Never open an e-mail attachment unless you are expecting the attachment and it is from a trusted source. If you use Windows, install the latest Microsoft updates. Set macro security in programs such as word processing and spreadsheet so you can enable or disable macros. Back up files regularly. For more information, visit scsite.com/dc2008/ch8/faq and then click Preventing Virus Infections.

SIGNS OF VIRUS INFECTION

- An unusual message or image is displayed on the computer screen
- An unusual sound or music plays randomly
- The available memory is less than what should be available
- A program or file suddenly is missing
- An unknown program or file mysteriously appears
- The size of a file changes without explanation
- A file becomes corrupted
- A program or file does not work properly
- System properties change

FIGURE 8-36 Viruses attack computers in a variety of ways. This list indicates some of the more common signs of virus infection.

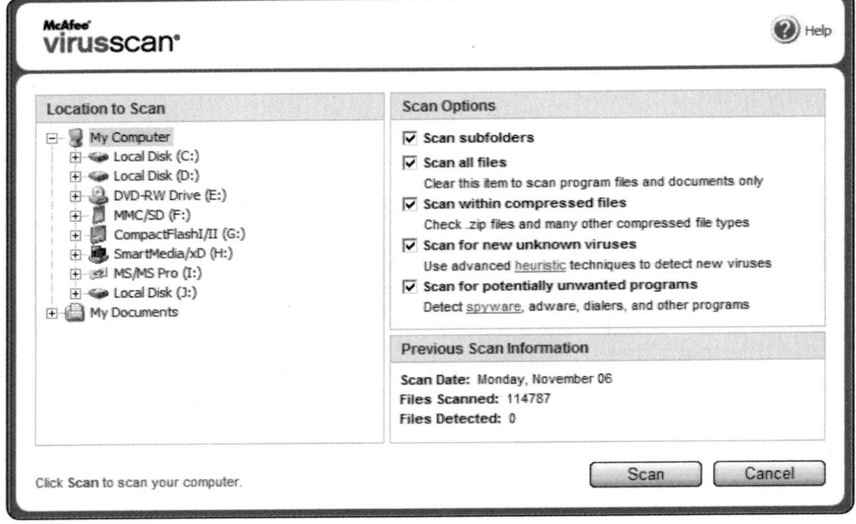

FIGURE 8-37 An antivirus program scans memory, disks, and incoming e-mail messages and attachments for viruses and attempts to remove any viruses it finds.

Spyware Removers

Spyware is a program placed on a computer without the user's knowledge that secretly collects information about the user, often related to Web browsing habits. Spyware often enters a computer when a user installs a new program. The spyware program communicates information it collects to an outside source while you are online.

Adware is a program that displays an online advertisement in a banner or pop-up window on Web pages, e-mail, or other Internet services. Sometimes, spyware is hidden in adware. A **spyware remover** is a program that detects and deletes spyware, adware, and other similar programs. Most spyware removers cost less than $50; some are available on the Web at no cost. Some operating systems include spyware removers and adware blockers. Popular spyware and adware removers include Ad-Aware, Spy Sweeper, Spybot - Search and Destroy, and Windows Defender.

Internet Filters

Filters are programs that remove or block certain items from being displayed. Three widely used Internet filters are anti-spam programs, Web filters, and pop-up blockers.

ANTI-SPAM PROGRAMS *Spam* is an unsolicited e-mail message or newsgroup posting sent to many recipients or newsgroups at once. Spam is Internet junk mail. The content of spam ranges from selling a product or service, to promoting a business opportunity, to advertising offensive material. An **anti-spam program** is a filtering program that attempts to remove spam before it reaches your inbox. If your e-mail program does not filter spam, many anti-spam programs are available at no cost on the Web. Internet access providers often filter spam as a service for their subscribers.

WEB FILTERS **Web filtering software** is a program that restricts access to certain material on the Web. Some restrict access to specific Web sites; others filter sites that use certain words or phrases. Many businesses use Web filtering software to limit employee's Web access. Some schools, libraries, and parents use this software to restrict access to minors.

POP-UP BLOCKERS A *pop-up ad* is an Internet advertisement that appears in a new window in the foreground of a Web page displayed in your browser. A **pop-up blocker** is a filtering program that stops pop-up ads from displaying on Web pages. If your Web browser does not block pop-up ads, many pop-up blockers can be downloaded from the Web at no cost.

FAQ 8-10

Should anti-spam programs be installed on home computers?

Yes. Reports indicate that spam originated as early as 1978, when an e-mail was sent to several ARPANET addresses. As shown in the chart below, spam now accounts for approximately 90 percent of e-mail traffic, with that number increasing daily. Fortunately, anti-spam programs installed on your computer, combined with your Internet access provider's anti-spam measures, greatly reduce the amount of spam you receive. For more information, visit scsite.com/dc2008/ch8/faq and then click Spam.

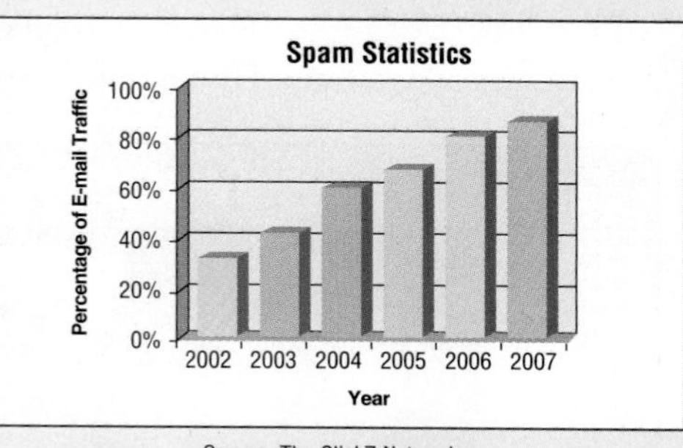

Source: The ClickZ Network

File Conversion

A *file conversion utility* transforms the contents of a file or data from one format to another. When a business develops a new information system, often the data in the current system is not in the correct format for the new system. Thus, part of the system development process is to convert data — instead of having users reenter all the existing data in the new system. On a smaller scale, when home users purchase new software, they may need to convert files so the files will be displayed properly in the new software.

File Compression

A **file compression utility** shrinks the size of a file(s). A compressed file takes up less storage space than the original file. Compressing files frees up room on the storage media and improves system performance. Attaching a compressed file to an e-mail message, for example, reduces the time needed for file transmission. Uploading and downloading compressed files to and from the Internet reduces the file transmission time.

Compressed files, sometimes called **zipped files**, usually have a .zip extension. When you receive or download a compressed file, you must uncompress it. To **uncompress**, or *unzip*, a file, you restore it to its original form. Some operating systems such as Windows Vista include file compression and uncompression capabilities. Two popular stand-alone file compression utilities are PKZIP and WinZip.

Media Player

A **media player** is a program that allows you to view images and animation, listen to audio, and watch video files on your computer (Figure 8-38). Media players may also include the capability to organize media files, convert them to different formats, connect to and purchase media from an online media store, download podcasts and vodcasts, burn audio CDs, and transfer media to portable media players such as an iPod. Windows Vista includes Windows Media Player. Two other popular media players are iTunes and RealPlayer.

Media Players

For more information, visit scsite.com/dc2008/ch8/weblink and then click Media Players.

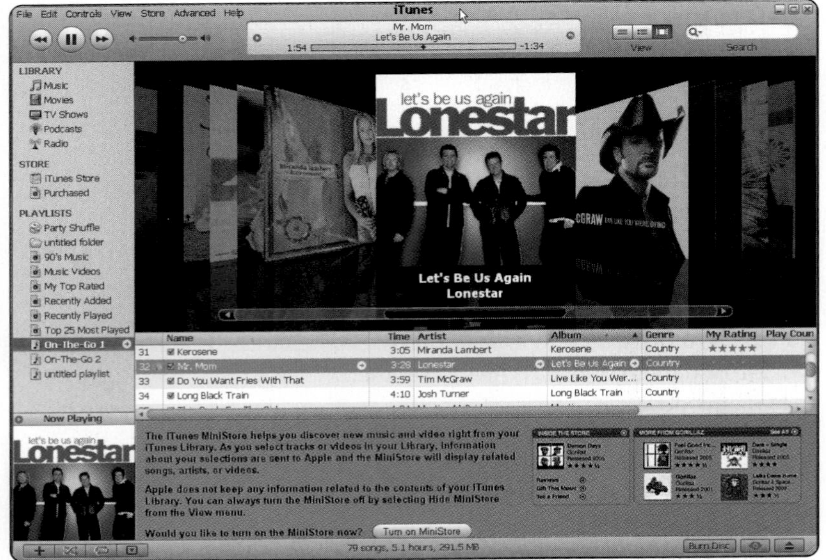

FIGURE 8-38 iTunes is a popular media player.

CD/DVD Burning

CD/DVD burning software writes text, graphics, audio, and video files on a recordable or rewritable CD or DVD, including Blu-ray and HD DVD. This software enables the home user easily to back up contents of their hard disk on a CD/DVD and make duplicates of uncopyrighted music or movies. CD/DVD burning software usually also includes photo editing, audio editing, and video editing capabilities (Figure 8-39).

When you buy a recordable or rewritable CD or DVD, it typically includes CD/DVD burning software. You also can buy CD/DVD burning software for a cost of less than $100.

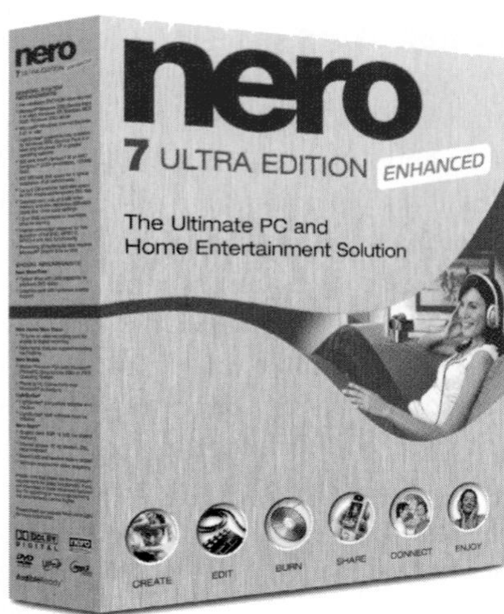

FIGURE 8-39 Using CD/DVD burning software, you can copy text, graphics, audio, and video files on CD or DVD, provided you have the correct type of CD/DVD drive and media.

Personal Computer Maintenance

Operating systems typically include a diagnostic utility that diagnoses computer problems but does not repair them. A **personal computer maintenance utility** identifies and fixes operating system problems, detects and repairs disk problems, and includes the capability of improving a computer's performance. Additionally, some personal computer maintenance utilities continuously monitor a computer while you use it to identify and repair problems before they occur. Norton SystemWorks is a popular personal computer maintenance utility designed for Windows operating systems (Figure 8-40).

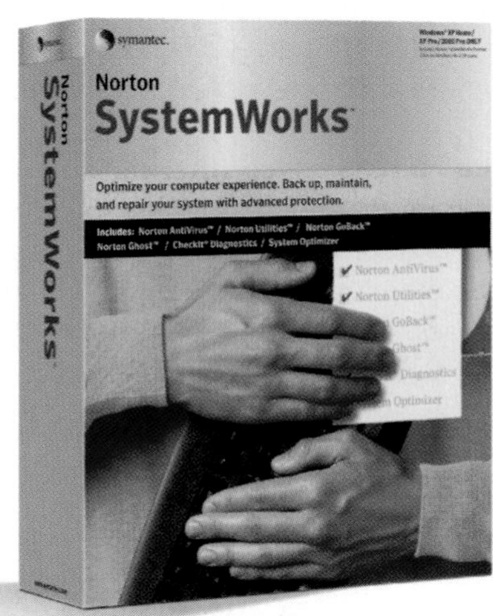

FIGURE 8-40 A popular maintenance program for Windows users.

Test your knowledge of pages 422 through 428 in Quiz Yourself 8-3.

QUIZ YOURSELF 8-3

Instructions: Find the true statement below. Then, rewrite the remaining false statements so they are true.

1. A pop-up blocker shrinks the size of a file(s).
2. An anti-spam program protects a computer against viruses by identifying and removing any computer viruses found in memory, on storage media, or on incoming files.
3. Examples of network operating systems include Windows Server 2003, UNIX, Linux, Solaris, and Netware.
4. Pocket PCs use Palm OS as their operating system.
5. Web filtering software writes text, graphics, audio, and video files to a recordable or rewritable CD or DVD.

Quiz Yourself Online: To further check your knowledge of network operating systems, embedded operating systems, and stand-alone utility programs, visit scsite.com/dc2008/ch8/quiz and then click Objectives 7 – 9.

LOOKING AHEAD 8-2

Online Operating Systems Proposed

Microsoft Windows' dominance in the operating system world is being challenged by proposed Web operating systems. Experts predict that within a few years computer users will see Google, Yahoo!, and Mozilla release Internet-enabled products. Independent programmers are developing their own online operating systems, such as YouOS and XIN.

If these operating systems come to fruition, computer users will access content and manage data using a Web browser. Applications will be written for this Web browser and will not be dependent upon a specific machine or cellular phone.

Proposed applications include reading e-mail, blogs, and news offline; backing up files to an online service; and managing audio and video files. For more information, visit scsite.com/dc2008/ch8/looking and then click Operating Systems.

CHAPTER SUMMARY

This chapter defined an operating system and then discussed the functions common to most operating systems. Next, it introduced several utility programs commonly found in operating systems. The chapter discussed a variety of stand-alone operating systems, network operating systems, and embedded operating systems (read Looking Ahead 8-2 for a look at the next generation of operating systems). Finally, the chapter described several stand-alone utility programs.

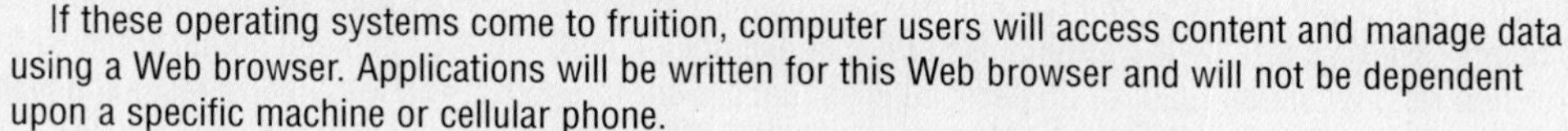

CAREER CORNER

Systems Programmer

System software is a key component in any computer. A *systems programmer* evaluates, installs, and maintains system software and provides technical support to the programming staff.

Systems programmers work with the programs that control computers, such as operating systems, network operating systems, and database systems. They identify current and future processing needs and then recommend the software and hardware necessary to meet those needs. In addition to selecting and installing system software, systems programmers must be able to adapt system software to the requirements of an organization, provide regular maintenance, measure system performance, determine the impact of new or updated software on the system, design and implement special software, and provide documentation. Because they are familiar with the entire system, systems programmers often help application programmers to diagnose technical problems.

Systems programmers must be acquainted thoroughly with a variety of operating systems. They must be able to think logically, pay attention to detail, work with abstract concepts, and devise solutions to complex problems. Systems programmers often work in teams and interact with programmers and nontechnical users, so communications skills are important.

Most systems programmers have a four-year B.S. degree in Computer Science or Information Technology. Depending on responsibilities and experience, salaries range from $60,000 to more than $115,000. For more information, visit scsite.com/dc2008/ch8/careers and then click Systems Programmer.

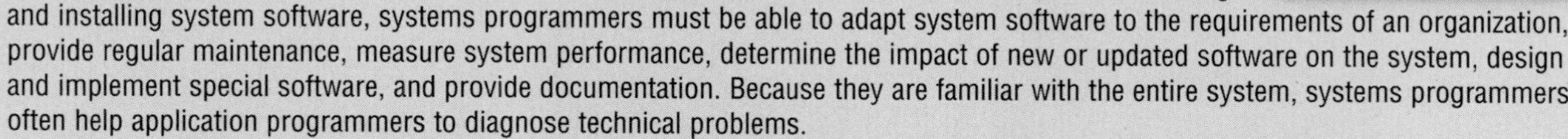

High-Tech Talk

LOSSY VS. LOSSLESS DATA COMPRESSION: USING COMPRESSION ALGORITHMS TO REDUCE FILE SIZE

As discussed earlier in this chapter, compression is the process of shrinking the size of a file. Text, graphics, audio, and video are the four types of files that can be compressed. Whether you are backing up data, transferring media to or from a portable media player, recording video with a digital video camera, or taking pictures with a digital camera, you usually will need to choose a file compression type. Take, for example, a digital video camera. If you want to share the videos electronically, you first must transfer it from the camera to your computer. Before or after the transfer process completes, you will choose how to save the video. At this point, you can choose a compression type. A digital video camera also may allow you to specify what type of compression to use while it records the video. Each option for saving or recording the video corresponds with a different type, or level, of compression. Depending on the type of compression you apply, you may or may not be able to view or modify the file before it is uncompressed, or restored to its original form.

Before you can make an informed decision about a compression type, you first should understand the differences between lossy and lossless compression. When *lossy* data compression is applied to a file, the quality of the file will decrease slightly each time you compress the file, and you will be unable to restore the file to its exact original state. Degradations in quality resulting from lossy compression sometimes are unrecognizable; however, these degradations, also known as the *compression artifacts*, will become more apparent if a higher rate of compression is applied to a file, or if the file has been compressed and uncompressed multiple times. The extent to which a file is compressed is known as the *data compression ratio*. Figure 8-41 displays three versions of the same image, each saved with a different compression ratio. Audio files can be compressed up to one-tenth of their original size before you may notice a decrease in quality. Video files can retain the same noticeable visible quality with a much higher data compression ratio, but graphics often can afford only a small compression ratio before sacrificing quality. You can calculate the compression ratio by dividing the compressed file size by the original file size. For example, if a 20 MB file has been compressed to 5 MB, the data compression ratio would be 5/20, or 25 percent. Files that are compressed using lossy compression usually are smaller files than those compressed using lossless compression.

Lossless data compression is used when you must compress a file, but also must be able to return that file to its exact original state. For example, if you want to compress a series of word processing files before e-mailing them to a colleague, your colleague must be able to return those files to their original state without a reduction in quality. If a word processing file is affected by a reduction in quality, letters, words, or entire paragraphs may be lost or otherwise unreadable when the file is uncompressed. For this reason, lossless compression is more appropriate for text files.

Programs use a *compression algorithm*, which is a set of steps that are used to compress a file. Multiple compression algorithms currently exist and determine the extent to which you can compress a file. Backup programs, such as Windows Vista's Backup and Restore Center, often use a lossless compression algorithm so that backed up files can be restored to their original state. Programs, such as iTunes, that are used to play media, as well as transfer media to and from portable media players can apply lossy or lossless compression. If you prefer high-quality audio, you should use lossless compression. For low-quality audio, lossy compression is sufficient. Similarly, digital cameras and digital video cameras also allow you select from lossy and lossless compression. Once again, lossless compression algorithms should be used to maintain high-quality files, and lossy compression algorithms should be used when lower quality is acceptable. For more information, visit scsite.com/dc2008/ch8/tech and then click Compression.

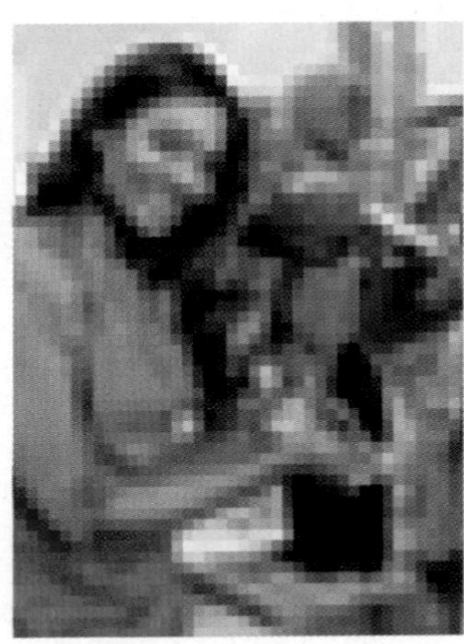

FIGURE 8-41 Each of these three photos was saved with a different compression ratio. Notice that the photo on the left, which was compressed the most, has the lowest quality, and the photo on the right, which was compressed the least, has the highest quality.

Companies on the Cutting Edge

RED HAT
OPEN SOURCE SOFTWARE DISTRIBUTOR

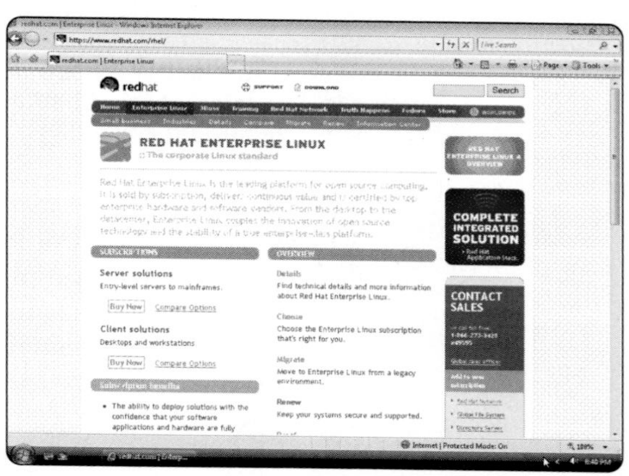

When you were young, you were taught to share. University professors share their research with colleagues throughout the world; and *Red Hat* shares software code, or instructions, with computer users.

Red Hat is the largest supplier of open source software, which allows buyers to view, modify, and perhaps improve, the software. The company delivers the software improvements to customers through the Red Hat Network, the company's Internet service.

Bob Young and Marc Ewing founded Red Hat in 1994 and started distributing a version of the Red Hat Linux operating system complete with documentation and support. Today, Linux is Red Hat's most well-known product. Subscriptions to the company's premium Linux software have helped boost the company to profitability. The company expanded its global presence in 2006 when it announced its participation in the next-generation telecommunication service used across the European Union. For more information, visit scsite.com/dc2008/ch8/companies and then click Red Hat.

RESEARCH IN MOTION (RIM)
WIRELESS MOBILE COMMUNICATIONS DEVICES MANUFACTURER

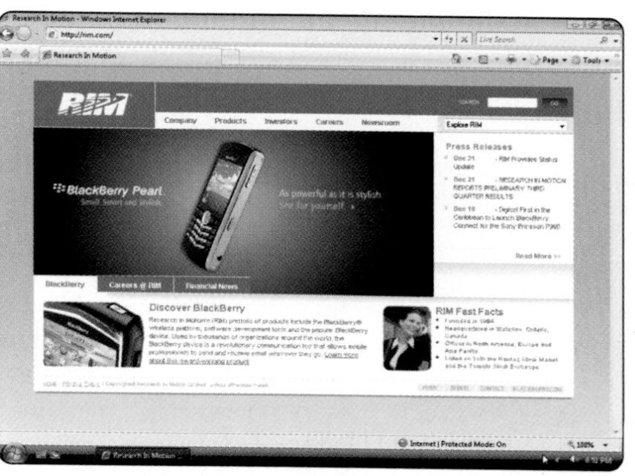

In today's mobile world, people often need to access their e-mail wirelessly. Chances are they find *Research in Motion (RIM)*'s products valuable. More than 4 million people are using RIM's popular BlackBerry models, which combine e-mail, telephone, Internet browsing, and organizer features. The built-in keyboards allow users to send and receive text messages.

Mike Lazaridis, the current co-CEO, founded RIM in 1984 in Waterloo, Ontario. His passion for wireless technology emerged in high school as a member of the local amateur radio and television club. He developed RIM's first major product, the Inter@ctive Pager, in 1996. Two years later, the same hardware was used in the first BlackBerry; this product's success was due to its capability to combine a wireless mailbox with a corporate mailbox so that users could access e-mail continuously.

In 2006, RIM settled a long-time patent dispute, which allowed its wireless service to continue to its more than 3 million customers. For more information, visit scsite.com/dc2008/ch8/companies and then click RIM.

Technology Trailblazers

ALAN KAY
COMPUTER PIONEER

Chances are that every time you use your computer you use one of *Alan Kay*'s ideas. More than 35 years ago — long before the personal computer became ubiquitous — he was developing a notebook computer complete with a flat screen, wireless network, and storage. More than 20 years ago, he engineered a graphical user interface, object-oriented languages, and personal computer networks.

Kay did much of his early work at the U.S. Defense Department's Advance Research Project Agency (DARPA) and Xerox's Palo Alto Research Center (PARC). Today he is a computer science professor at UCLA and president of the Viewpoints Research Institute, a nonprofit organization dedicated to helping children develop fluency in critical thinking, math, and science. For more information, visit scsite.com/dc2008/ch8/people and then click Alan Kay.

LINUS TORVALDS
LINUX CREATOR

When *Linus Torvalds* developed a new operating system in 1991, he announced his project in an Internet newsgroup, made the source code available, and asked for suggestions. Computer users responded by reviewing the system and offering enhancements. Three years later, Torvalds released a much-enhanced version of an open source operating system he called Linux.

Torvalds developed the innovative operating system when he was a 21-year-old computer science student in Finland. Today, Linux is estimated to be running on at least 10 percent of computers and is Microsoft's main competitor. Torvalds leads the development of Linux as a fellow at OSDL (Open Source Development Labs), a not-for-profit consortium of companies dedicated to developing and promoting the operating system. In 2006, he took fifth place in *Computer Weekly*'s list of the Top 10 greatest IT people. For more information, visit scsite.com/dc2008/ch8/people and then click Linus Torvalds.

Quizzes and Learning Games
- Computer Genius
- Crossword Puzzle
- DC Track and Field
- Practice Test
- Quiz Yourself
- Wheel of Terms
- You're Hired!

Exercises
- Case Studies
- Chapter Review
- Checkpoint
- Key Terms
- Learn How To
- Learn It Online
- Web Research

Beyond the Book
- Career Corner
- Companies
- FAQs
- High-Tech Talk
- Looking Ahead
- Making Use of the Web
- Trailblazers
- Web Links

Features
- Chapter Forum
- Install Computer
- Lab Exercises
- Maintain Computer
- Tech News
- Timeline 2008

Chapter Review

The Chapter Review section summarizes the concepts presented in this chapter. To listen to the audio version of this Chapter Review, visit scsite.com/dc2008/ch8/review. To obtain help from other students regarding any subject in this chapter, visit scsite.com/dc2008/ch8/forum and post your thoughts or questions.

(1) **What Are the Types of System Software?** **System software** consists of the programs that control or maintain the operations of a computer and its devices. Two types of system software are operating systems and utility programs. An **operating system** (**OS**) contains instructions that coordinate all the activities among computer hardware resources. A **utility program** performs maintenance-type tasks, usually related to managing a computer, its devices, or its programs.

(2) **What Is the Startup Process on a Personal Computer?** **Booting** is the process of starting or restarting a computer. When a user turns on a computer, the power supply sends a signal to the system unit. The processor chip finds the ROM chip(s) that contains the **BIOS**, which is firmware with the computer's startup instructions. The BIOS performs the *power-on self test* (*POST*) to check system components and compares the results with data in a CMOS chip. If the POST completes successfully, the BIOS searches for the *system files* and the *kernel* of the operating system, which manages memory and devices, and loads them into memory from storage. Finally, the operating system loads configuration information, requests any necessary user information, and displays the desktop on the screen.

(3) **What Are the Functions of an Operating System?** The operating system provides a user interface, manages programs, manages memory, schedules jobs, configures devices, establishes an Internet connection, and monitors performance. The **user interface** controls how data and instructions are entered and how information is displayed. Two types of user interfaces are a *command-line interface* and a *graphical user interface* (*GUI*). Managing programs refers to how many users, and how many programs, an operating system can support at one time. An operating system can be *single user/single tasking*, *single user/multitasking*, *multiuser*, or *multiprocessing*. **Memory management** optimizes the use of random access memory (RAM). If memory is insufficient, the operating system may use **virtual memory**, which allocates a portion of a storage medium to function as additional RAM. Scheduling jobs determines the order in which jobs are processed. A **job** is an operation the processor manages. Configuring devices involves loading each device's driver when a user boots the computer. A **driver** is a program that tells the operating system how to communicate with a specific device. Establishing an Internet connection sets up a connection between a computer and an Internet service provider. A **performance monitor** is an operating system program that assesses and reports information about computer resources and devices.

(4) **How Can Operating Systems Help Administrators Control a Network and Manage Security?** A **network operating system**, or *network OS*, is an operating system that organizes and coordinates how multiple users access and share network resources. A *network administrator* uses the network OS to add and remove users, computers, and other devices to and from the network. A network administrator also uses the network OS to administer network security. For each user, the network administrator establishes a user account that enables the user to **log on**, or access, the network by supplying the correct **user name** and **password**.

connect Visit scsite.com/dc2008/ch8/quiz or click the Quiz Yourself button. Click Objectives 1 – 4.

(5) **What Is the Purpose of the Utilities Included with Most Operating Systems?** Most operating systems include several built-in utility programs. A **file manager** performs functions related to file management. A **search utility** attempts to locate a file on your computer based on criteria you specify. An **image viewer** displays, copies, and prints the contents of a graphics file, such as a picture. A **personal firewall** detects and protects a computer from unauthorized intrusions. An **uninstaller** removes a program and any associated entries in the system files. A **disk scanner** searches for and removes unnecessary files. A **disk defragmenter** reorganizes the

Chapter Review

files and unused space on a computer's hard disk. A **diagnostic utility** compiles and reports technical information about a computer's hardware and certain system software programs. A **backup utility** is used to copy, or *back up*, selected files or an entire hard disk. A **screen saver** displays a moving image or blank screen if no keyboard or mouse activity occurs for a specified time.

6 What Are Features of Several Stand-Alone Operating Systems? A **stand-alone operating system** is a complete operating system that works on a desktop computer, notebook computer, or mobile computing device. Stand-alone operating systems include DOS, Windows XP, Windows Vista, Mac OS X, UNIX, and Linux. **Windows XP** is a fast, reliable Windows operating system, providing better performance, increased security, and a simpler look. **Windows Vista**, successor to Windows XP, is Microsoft's fastest, most reliable and efficient operating system to date, offering quicker application start up, built-in diagnostics, automatic recovery, improved security, and enhanced searching and organizing capabilities. **Mac OS X** is a multitasking operating system available only for Apple computers. **UNIX** is a multitasking operating system developed at Bell Laboratories. **Linux** is a popular, multitasking UNIX-type operating system that is *open source software*, which means its code is available to the public.

connect Visit scsite.com/dc2008/ch8/quiz or click the Quiz Yourself button. Click Objectives 5 – 6.

7 What Are Various Network Operating Systems? Network operating systems include Windows Server 2003, UNIX, Linux, and Netware. **Windows Server 2003** is an upgrade to Windows 2000 Server and includes features of previous server versions. Linux, like UNIX, is a *multipurpose operating system* because it is both a stand-alone and network operating system. *Solaris*, a version of UNIX developed by Sun Microsystems, is a network OS designed for e-commerce applications. Novell's *NetWare* is a network OS designed for client/server networks.

8 What Devices Use Embedded Operating Systems? Most PDAs and small devices have an **embedded operating system** that resides on a ROM chip. Popular embedded operating systems include Windows CE, Windows Mobile, Palm OS, BlackBerry, embedded Linux, and Symbian OS. **Windows CE** is a scaled-down Windows operating system designed for use on communications, entertainment, and computing devices with limited functionality. **Windows Mobile**, an operating system based on Windows CE, provides a user interface designed for a specific type of devices, such as PDAs, called the **Pocket PC**. *Palm OS* is an operating system used on PDAs and smart phones. The *BlackBerry* operating system runs on handheld devices supplied by RIM. *Embedded Linux* is a scaled-down Linux operating system for PDAs, smart phones, and other devices. *Symbian OS* is an open source multitasking operating system designed for smart phones.

9 What Is the Purpose of Several Stand-Alone Utility Programs? Stand-alone utility programs offer improvements over features built into the operating system or provide features not included in the operating system. An **antivirus program** protects computers against a **virus**, or potentially damaging computer program, by identifying and removing any computer viruses. A **spyware remover** detects and deletes *spyware*, *adware*, and other similar programs. Internet filter programs can include an **anti-spam** program, **Web filtering software**, and a **pop-up blocker**. A *file conversion utility* transforms the contents of a file from one format to another. A **file compression utility** shrinks the size of a file so that it takes up less storage space. A **media player** allows you to view images and animation, listen to audio, and watch video files on a computer. **CD/DVD burning software** writes on a recordable or rewritable CD or DVD. A **personal computer maintenance utility** identifies and fixes operating system problems and improves a computer's performance.

connect Visit scsite.com/dc2008/ch8/quiz or click the Quiz Yourself button. Click Objectives 7 – 9.

Quizzes and Learning Games
Computer Genius
Crossword Puzzle
DC Track and Field
Practice Test
Quiz Yourself
Wheel of Terms
You're Hired!

Exercises
Case Studies
Chapter Review
Checkpoint
Key Terms
Learn How To
Learn It Online
Web Research

Beyond the Book
Career Corner
Companies
FAQs
High-Tech Talk
Looking Ahead
Making Use of the Web
Trailblazers
Web Links

Features
Chapter Forum
Install Computer
Lab Exercises
Maintain Computer
Tech News
Timeline 2008

Key Terms

You should know the Primary Terms and be familiar with the Secondary Terms. Use the list below to help focus your study. To further enhance your understanding of the Key Terms in this chapter, visit scsite.com/dc2008/ch8/terms. See an example of and a definition for each term, and access current and additional information about the term from the Web.

Primary Terms

(shown in bold-black characters in the chapter)

Secondary Terms

(shown in italic characters in the chapter)

Checkpoint

Use the Checkpoint exercises to check your knowledge level of the chapter. The Beyond the Book exercises will help broaden your understanding of the concepts presented in this chapter. To complete the Checkpoint exercises interactively, visit scsite.com/dc2008/ch8/check.

Label the Figure

Identify the various elements of these user interfaces.

a. Forward button
b. links
c. Back button
d. Start menu
e. command prompt
f. command entered by user

1. ____
2. ____
3. ____
4. ____
5. ____
6. ____

True/False

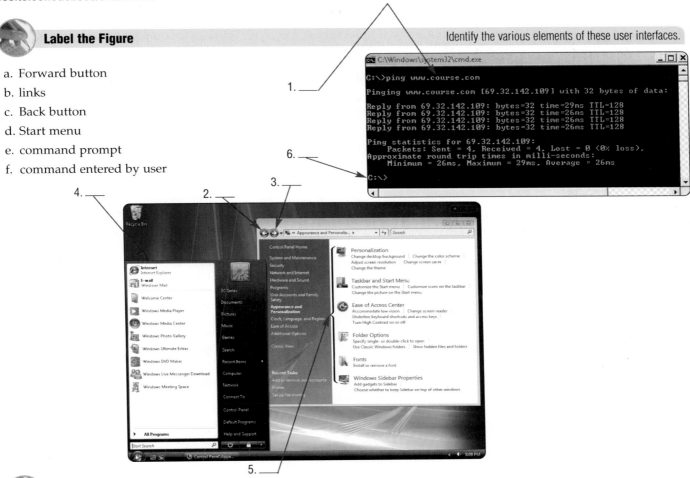

Mark T for True and F for False. (See page numbers in parentheses.)

_____ 1. All sizes of computers typically use the same operating system. (399)

_____ 2. Booting is the process of permanently removing a computer from operation. (400)

_____ 3. A user interface controls how you enter data and instructions and how information is displayed on the screen. (402)

_____ 4. When spooling print jobs to a buffer, multiple print jobs line up in a queue in the buffer. (407)

_____ 5. Encryption is the process of encoding data and information into an unreadable form. (410)

_____ 6. A disk scanner is a utility that reorganizes the files and unused space on a computer's hard disk so the operating system accesses data more quickly and programs run faster. (414)

_____ 7. Windows Defender protects your computer from theft. (419)

_____ 8. Linux is open source software, which means its code cannot be modified or redistributed. (421)

_____ 9. BlackBerry devices provide PDA capabilities such as managing schedules and contacts, as well as telephone capabilities. (424)

_____ 10. A pop-up blocker is a filtering program that stops pop-up ads from displaying on Web pages. (427)

Checkpoint

Multiple Choice

Select the best answer. (See page numbers in parentheses.)

1. The _____ chip, which uses battery power, stores configuration information about the computer. (400)
   a. CMOS b. BIOS
   c. POST d. RAM
2. _____ often are difficult to use because they require exact spelling, grammar, and punctuation. (402)
   a. Graphical user interfaces
   b. Command-line interfaces
   c. Menu-driven interfaces
   d. All of the above
3. In the Windows Vista operating system, the _____ interface provides an enhanced visual look, additional navigation options, and animation. (403)
   a. Plug and Play
   b. Windows Vista Basic
   c. Mac OS X
   d. Windows Aero
4. When an operating system spends much of its time paging, instead of executing application software, it is said to be _____. (406)
   a. booting
   b. thrashing
   c. spooling
   d. formatting
5. A _____ is a small program that tells the operating system how to communicate with a specific device. (407)
   a. buffer
   b. driver
   c. performance monitor
   d. device
6. When you enter search criteria, instead of looking through every file and folder on the storage medium, a search utility looks through the _____ first to find a match. (412)
   a. file manager
   b. buffer
   c. index
   d. driver
7. A _____ is a program that attempts to locate a file on your computer based on criteria you specify. (412)
   a. file manager
   b. search utility
   c. Startup folder
   d. kernel
8. Defragmenting reorganizes the files on a disk so they are located in _____ access time. (414)
   a. noncontiguous sectors, which slows
   b. noncontiguous sectors, which speeds
   c. contiguous sectors, which speeds
   d. contiguous sectors, which slows
9. A _____ contains files necessary to boot and work with the Linux operating system, which allows users to preview the operating system without installing it. (421)
   a. UNIX
   b. Web service
   c. Live CD
   d. BIOS
10. _____, developed by Sun Microsystems, manages high-traffic accounts and incorporates security necessary for Web transactions. (423)
    a. Solaris
    b. Linux
    c. Windows Server 2003
    d. Netware
11. _____ is an open source multitasking operating system designed for smart phones. (425)
    a. Symbian OS
    b. Linux
    c. Palm OS
    d. Solaris
12. A _____ is malware that does not replicate itself to other computers. (426)
    a. virus b. Trojan horse
    c. worm d. all of the above
13. _____ is a program that displays an online advertisement in a banner or pop-up window on Web pages, e-mail, or other Internet services. (427)
    a. Spyware
    b. A Trojan horse
    c. Adware
    d. A pop-up ad
14. A _____ is a program that allows you to view images and animation, listen to audio, and watch video files on your computer. (428)
    a. file manager
    b. media player
    c. service pack
    d. Media Center PC

Checkpoint

Matching

Match the terms with their definitions. (See page numbers in parentheses.)

_____ 1. boot disk (402)
_____ 2. fault-tolerant computer (405)
_____ 3. page (406)
_____ 4. spooling (407)
_____ 5. IRQ (409)
_____ 6. user name (410)
_____ 7. image viewer (412)
_____ 8. Flip 3D (419)
_____ 9. Live USB (421)
_____ 10. spam (427)

a. a utility that allows users to display, copy, and print the contents of a graphics file
b. communications line between a device and the processor
c. continues to operate when one of its components fails
d. a bootable USB flash drive
e. works with the mouse to flip through open windows arranged in a stack in Windows Vista
f. program that tells the operating system how to communicate with a device
g. unsolicited e-mail message or newsgroup posting sent to many recipients or newsgroups at once
h. disk that contains a few system files that will start the computer
i. with virtual memory, the amount of data and program instructions that can be swapped at a given time
j. hides within or looks like a legitimate program such as a screen saver
k. process that sends print jobs to a buffer instead of sending them immediately to the printer
l. unique combination of characters that identifies one specific user

Short Answer

Write a brief answer to each of the following questions.

1. How is a cold boot different from a warm boot? ____________ How is a memory-resident part of an operating system different from a nonresident part of an operating system? ____________
2. What is a user interface? ____________ How are a command-line interface and a graphical user interface different? ____________
3. What is the purpose of memory management? ____________ What is the purpose of virtual memory, and where is virtual memory stored? ____________
4. What Explorers are included in the Windows Vista operating system? ____________ What is the purpose of each Explorer? ____________
5. What is the difference between Windows Vista Home Basic and Windows Vista Home Premium? ____________ What is the difference between Windows Vista Business and Windows Vista Enterprise? ____________

Beyond the Book

Read the following book elements, learn more about each using the Web, and then write a brief report.

1. Ethics & Issues — What Should Be in an Operating System? (409), Who Should Be Responsible for Notebook Computer Security? (411), Does Windows Genuine Advantage Give an Advantage to Hackers? (416), or Closed Source vs. Open Source Operating Systems (421)
2. Career Corner — Systems Programmer (429)
3. Companies on the Cutting Edge – Red Hat or Research in Motion (RIM) (431)
4. FAQs (402, 406, 409, 411, 414, 417, 419, 423, 426, 427)
5. High-Tech Talk — Lossy vs. Lossless Data Compression: Using Compression Algorithms to Reduce File Size (430)
6. Looking Ahead — Apple Marching to Its Own Tune (420) or Online Operating Systems Proposed (429)
7. Making Use of the Web — Weather, Sports, and News (124)
8. Picture Yourself Getting a Virus through E-Mail (396)
9. Technology Trailblazers — Alan Kay or Linus Torvalds (431)
10. Web Links (401, 407, 413, 415, 416, 420, 423, 424, 425, 428)

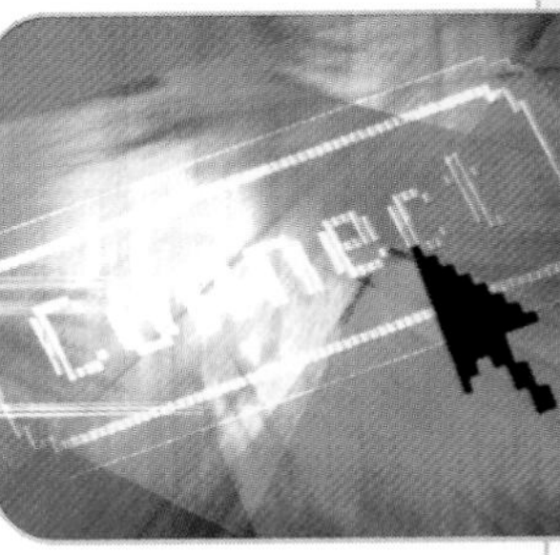

Quizzes and Learning Games
Computer Genius
Crossword Puzzle
DC Track and Field
Practice Test
Quiz Yourself
Wheel of Terms
You're Hired!

Exercises
Case Studies
Chapter Review
Checkpoint
Key Terms
Learn How To
Learn It Online
Web Research

Beyond the Book
Career Corner
Companies
FAQs
High-Tech Talk
Looking Ahead
Making Use of the Web
Trailblazers
Web Links

Features
Chapter Forum
Install Computer
Lab Exercises
Maintain Computer
Tech News
Timeline 2008

Learn It Online

Use the Learn It Online exercises to reinforce your understanding of the chapter concepts. To access the Learn It Online exercises, visit scsite.com/dc2008/ch8/learn.

1 At the Movies — New View of Vista

To view the New View of Vista movie, click the number 1 button. Locate your video and click the corresponding High-Speed or Dial-Up link, depending on your Internet connection. Watch the movie and then complete the exercise by answering the questions that follow. Take a look at some of the key features in Microsoft's new Windows Vista operating system. What are some of the new features Microsoft has made available in their new Windows Vista operating system?

2 Video and Audio: You Review It — Spyware

In this chapter you learned about spyware. Click the number 2 button to view the suggested links and begin your search for videos, podcasts, or vodcasts related to spyware. Choose a video, podcast, or vodcast that discusses spyware and is of interest to you, and then write a description of its contents. Explain why you chose this piece, what you liked about it, what you disliked about it, and whether you would recommend it to a fellow student. Finish your review by giving the video, podcast, or vodcast a rating of 1 – 5 stars. Submit your review in the format requested by your instructor.

3 Student Edition Labs — Installing and Uninstalling Software

Click the number 3 button. A new browser window will open, displaying the Student Edition Labs. Follow the on-screen instructions to complete the Installing and Uninstalling Software Lab. When finished, click the Exit button. If required, submit your results to your instructor.

4 Student Edition Labs — Keeping Your Computer Virus Free

Click the number 4 button. A new browser window will open, displaying the Student Edition Labs. Follow the on-screen instructions to complete the Keeping Your Computer Virus Free Lab. When finished, click the Exit button. If required, submit your results to your instructor.

5 Practice Test

Click the number 5 button. Answer each question. When completed, enter your name and click the Grade Test button to submit the quiz for grading. Make a note of any missed questions. If required, submit your results to your instructor.

6 Who Wants To Be a Computer Genius^2?

Click the number 6 button to find out if you are a computer genius. Directions about how to play the game will be displayed. When you are ready to play, click the Play button. Submit your score to your instructor.

7 Wheel of Terms

Click the number 7 button to reinforce important terms you learned in this chapter by playing the Shelly Cashman Series version of this popular game. Directions about how to play the game will be displayed. When you are ready to play, click the Play button. Submit your score to your instructor.

Learn It Online

8 DC Track and Field

Click the number 8 button to use what you have learned in this chapter to compete against other students in three track and field events. Directions about how to play the game will be displayed. When you are ready to play, click the start first event button. If required, submit your score to your instructor.

9 You're Hired!

Click the number 9 button to use what you have learned in this chapter to embark on the path to a career in computers. Directions about how to play the game will be displayed. When you are ready to play, click the begin game button. If required, submit your score to your instructor.

10 Crossword Puzzle Challenge

Click the number 10 button, then click the Crossword Puzzle Challenge link. Directions about how to play the game will be displayed. Complete the puzzle to reinforce skills you learned in this chapter. When you are ready to play, click the Continue button. Submit the completed puzzle to your instructor.

11 Vista Exercises

Click the number 11 button. When the Vista Exercises menu appears, click the exercise assigned by your instructor. A new browser window will open. Follow the on-screen instructions to complete the exercise. When finished, click the Exit button. If required, submit your results to your instructor.

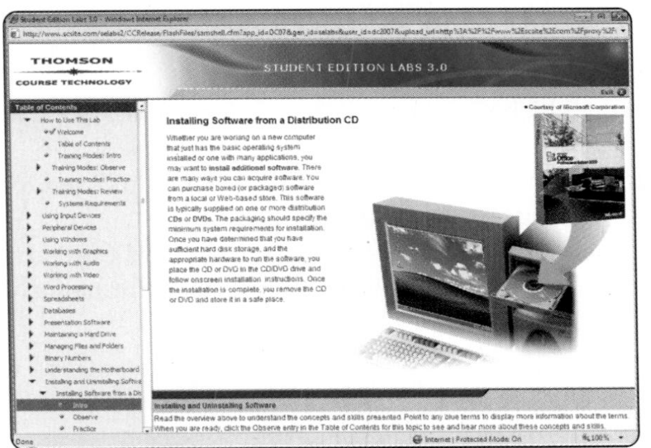

12 In the News

When Windows XP was introduced in October 2001, hundreds queued up at computer outlets. It is unclear, however, whether the anticipation was caused by the new operating system or by the promotions many dealers offered. Click the number 12 button and read a news article about the impact, quality, or promotion of an operating system. What operating system was it? What was done to sell the operating system? Is the operating system recommended? Why or why not?

13 Chapter Discussion Forum

Select an objective from this chapter on page 397 about which you would like more information. Click the number 13 button and post a short message listing a meaningful message title accompanied by one or more questions concerning the selected objective. In two days, return to the threaded discussion by clicking the number 13 button. Submit to your instructor your original message and at least one response to your message.

14 Airline Schedules

Click the number 14 button to learn how to use the Internet to price, reserve, and track airline flights. Follow the instructions to use Southwest Airlines' Web site to price a flight from Chicago to Las Vegas. Using the Schedules link, check for available flights for the dates you select. Once you have selected a flight, use the Reservations link to price the flight. Print a copy of the pricing for your selected flight. Check the status of a current flight comparable to the flight you priced. Write a report comparing the different fares available and summarizing what information is available when you check the status of a flight. Include in your report what the circumstances would have to be for you to choose a more expensive flight. Print your report and submit it to your instructor.

Learn How To

Use the Learn How To activities to learn fundamental skills when using a computer and accompanying technology. Complete the exercises and submit them to your instructor. To see a video of a Learn How To activity, visit scsite.com/dc2008/ch8/howto.

LEARN HOW TO 1: Install a Computer

Once you have purchased a computer, you must install it for use. Based on years of experience, a set of guidelines for installing and using your computer has been developed. To examine these guidelines, complete the following steps:

1. Start the browser on your computer.
2. Type the Web address `scsite.com/dc2008` in the Address box and then press the ENTER key.
3. Click the Chapter 8 link in the top navigation bar.
4. Click Install Computer in the left sidebar below the heading, Beyond the Book.
5. Read the material presented about how to install a computer.

Exercise

1. Using your Web search skills, research the latest recommendations with respect to proper ergonomics for using a computer. What information did you find that you did not know before? What changes would you make to your current computer setup that might make you more productive? Submit your answers to your instructor.
2. Many people report illnesses or injuries from using computers. Perform research in a library or on the Web to discover the five most common ailments associated with using a computer. Determine the actions people can take to minimize or eliminate these ailments. Submit a report to your instructor describing your findings.
3. Your computer lab at school contains multiple computers for student use. Using the knowledge you have obtained from this Learn How To activity, evaluate the computer installation in your school lab. In a report to your instructor, specify those items you think can be improved in the lab.

LEARN HOW TO 2: Maintain a Computer

While computers are amazingly resilient and reliable, you still should perform certain activities to ensure they maintain peak performance. To learn about these activities, complete the following steps:

1. Start the browser on your computer.
2. Type the Web address `scsite.com/dc2008` in the Address box and then press the ENTER key.
3. Click the Chapter 8 link in the top navigation bar.
4. Click Maintain Computer in the left sidebar below the heading, Beyond the Book.
5. Read the material presented about how to maintain a computer.

Exercise

1. On either your computer or the computer on which you are working, perform a hardware and software inventory of at least five hardware devices and five application programs on the computer. List the vendor, product, vendor Web address, vendor e-mail address, and vendor support telephone number. Submit your inventory to your instructor.
2. Record the serial number of the computer on which you are working. Then, record the serial number for seven different application programs on the computer. Submit this information to your instructor.

Learn How To 

LEARN HOW TO 3: Keep Windows Vista Up-to-Date

Keeping Windows Vista up-to-date is a critical part of keeping your computer in good working order. The updates made available by Microsoft for no charge over the Internet will keep errors from occurring on your computer and will ensure that all security safeguards are in place. To update Windows, complete the following steps:

1. Click the Start button on the Windows taskbar, click All Programs, and then click Windows Update in the All Programs list (Figure 8-42) to display the Windows Update window.
2. Click the Check for updates link to list the updates that are available for your computer.
3. If necessary, select those updates you wish to install and then click the Install button. Be aware that some updates might take 20 minutes or more to download and install, based primarily on your Internet access speed.
4. Often, after installation of updates, you must restart your computer to allow those updates to take effect. Be sure to save any open files before restarting your computer.

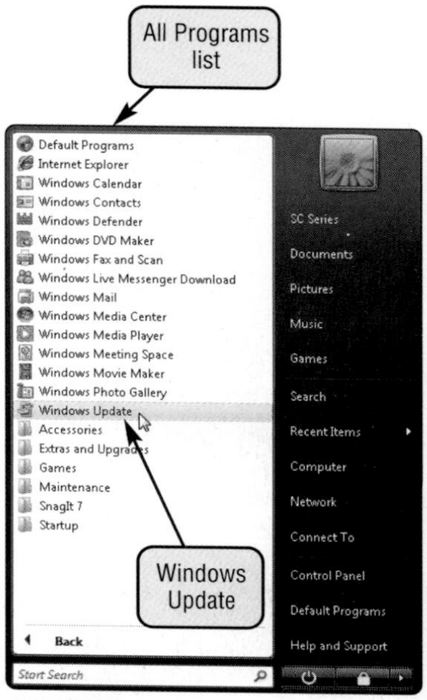

FIGURE 8-42

You also can schedule automatic updates for your computer. To do so, complete the following steps:

1. Click the Start button on the Windows taskbar and then click Control Panel on the Start menu.
2. In the Control Panel window, click System and Maintenance to display the System and Maintenance window.
3. In the System and Maintenance window, click Turn automatic updating on or off to display the Change settings window (Figure 8-43).
4. Select the option you want to use for Windows updates. Microsoft, together with all security and operating system experts, strongly recommends you select Install updates automatically so updates will be installed on your computer automatically. Notice that if you select Install updates automatically, you also should select a time when your computer will be on and be connected to the Internet. A secondary choice is to download the suggested updates and then choose when you want to install them, and a third choice allows you to check for updates and then choose when you want to download and install them.
5. When you have made your selection, click the OK button in the Change settings window.

Updating Windows on your computer is vital to maintain security and operational integrity.

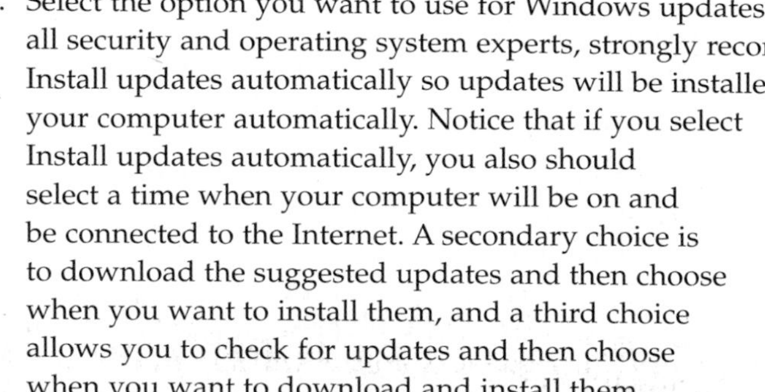

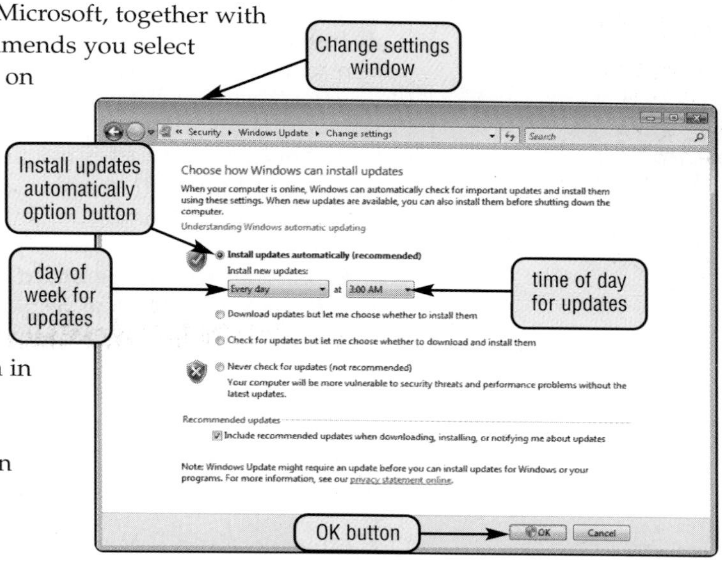

FIGURE 8-43

Exercise

1. Open the Windows Update window. Make a list of the important updates to Windows Vista on the computer you are using. Add to the list the optional updates that are available. If you are using your own computer, install the updates of your choice on your computer. Submit the list of updates to your instructor.
2. Optional: If you are not using your own computer, do not complete this exercise. Open the Control Panel, click System and Maintenance, and then click Turn automatic updating on or off. Select the level of automatic updates you want to use. Write a report justifying your choice of automatic updates and then submit the report to your instructor.

Web Research

Use the Internet-based Web Research exercises to broaden your understanding of the concepts presented in this chapter. Visit scsite.com/dc2008/ch8/research to obtain more information pertaining to each exercise. To discuss any of the Web Research exercises in this chapter with other students, post your thoughts or questions at scsite.com/dc2008/ch8/forum.

1 Scavenger Hunt Use one of the search engines listed in Figure 2-10 in Chapter 2 on page 78 or your own favorite search engine to find the answers to the questions that follow. Copy and paste the Web address from the Web page where you found the answer. Some questions may have more than one answer. If required, submit your answers to your instructor. (1) What is the UNIX billennium? (2) The term, spool, is an acronym for what words? What company invented the term? (3) What is the origin of the term, booting? (4) What are three applications that use a real-time operating system (RTOS)? (5) What is Larry the cow's relationship to Linux?

2 Search Sleuth A search engine using a concept-based search system seeks Web sites containing a search term along with related concepts. Google Book Search (books.google.com) has been created to help individuals locate books on a broad range of topics. Links to book previews, book reviews, and book purchasing information are available at this site, and visitors also can obtain information from the site's library partners to borrow books. Visit this Web site and then use your word processing program to answer the following questions. Then, if required, submit your answers to your instructor. (1) Type `Linux` in the search text box. How many search results are returned that are not sponsored links? (2) Click one of these book titles and review the information. Click the Find this book in a library link on the right side of the page. Type your postal code in the Enter Location Information text box and then click the Go button. How many libraries within a 25-mile radius carry this book? (3) Click your browser's Back button or press the BACKSPACE key several times to return to the Google Book Search home page. Click the Google Book Search Help link. Read the information and then write a 50-word summary of your findings.

3 Journaling Respond to your readings in this chapter by writing at least one page about your reactions, evaluations, and reflections about using stand-alone utility programs. For example, do you back up your hard disk? If not, why not? Do you use a spyware remover, anti-spam program, or pop-up blocker? Do you use a disk defragmenter or file compression utility? What CD/DVD burning software is installed on your computer? Do you have a recovery disk? Do you have a personal firewall? You also can write about the new terms you learned by reading this chapter. If required, submit your journal to your instructor.

4 Expanding Your Understanding Instant messaging (IM) is moving into the workplace. According to America Online, 59 percent of Internet users use IM, and 27 percent of these people use IM at work. Computer industry analysts predict this method of electronic communication will overtake e-mail during the next few years. With IM's popularity comes spim, a junk message. Yahoo! reports that 2 percent of the instant messages sent over its network are spim. View Web sites to learn more about IM's popularity and spim. What programs allow you to filter instant messages? Write a report summarizing your findings, focusing on the possible uses of this method of communication in the workplace. If required, submit your report to your instructor.

5 Ethics in Action Several automobile insurers, including Progressive Casualty Insurance Company, are promising drivers insurance premium discounts if they install a data recorder in their cars to track their driving and then exercise good driving behavior. Progressive customers voluntarily taking part in this TripSense program upload the data from their monitors monthly and hope to decrease their insurance bills by a maximum of 25 percent. Privacy experts predict more insurance companies will offer this monitoring system and that it eventually will become mandatory. These critics fear that negative data will be used against poor drivers and possibly be subpoenaed in litigation. View online sites that provide information about vehicle monitoring devices. Write a report summarizing your findings and include a table of links to Web sites that provide additional details. If required, submit your report to your instructor.

Case Studies

Use the Case Studies to apply the concepts presented in the chapter to real-world situations. Visit scsite.com/dc2008/ch8/cases to obtain more information pertaining to each exercise. To discuss the Case Studies in this chapter with other students, visit scsite.com/dc2008/ch8/forum and post your thoughts or questions.

CASE STUDY 1 — Class Discussion Many students at the local college have been using the college's computers to download music from the Internet. You have been asked to serve on a student committee to draft a policy addressing this questionable use of the college's computers. Is it the college's responsibility to block music downloads? Why or why not? How would the college prevent students from downloading music? What is the difference between taping a song heard on the radio and downloading music from the Internet? Should violators be expelled, fined, required to attend a seminar on the ethical use of computers, or given a verbal warning? What recommendations would you give to the committee regarding the downloading of music? Draft a memo addressed to all students regarding this matter. Be prepared to discuss your recommendations in class.

CASE STUDY 2 — Class Discussion Many application programs are designed to be used with specific operating systems. To determine if software is compatible with your operating system, you should read the packaging or research the software's Web site prior to purchasing the software. Select four application programs that interest you. Use the Web and/or print media to answer the following questions: What operating system is required for each application? What is the earliest version of the operating system that can be used? What operating system would you choose? Write a brief report, and be prepared to discuss your recommendations in class.

CASE STUDY 3 — Research Your cousin is buying a new computer both for personal use and to operate his consulting business, which he runs out of his home. He is undecided on the Windows operating system to purchase with his new computer. Windows Vista Business is intended for business users. Windows Vista Home Premium is designed for home computing. He has asked you to help him decide if he should buy one or the other. Use the Web and/or print media to develop a report that lists the differences. Which Windows Vista Business features are not available in Windows Vista Home Premium? Submit your report or use PowerPoint to create a presentation and share your findings with your class.

CASE STUDY 4 — Research Many programs are available for users of personal computers. The owner of the party supply store, Crazy Pete's Party Palace, where you work part time is interested in purchasing an antivirus program. Because you are taking a computer class, he has asked you to help him choose the best program. Choose at least two competing manufacturers of antivirus programs. Use the Web and/or print media and compare the programs. For each program, answer the following questions: What is the program's function? What are the system requirements? How easy is the program to use? Does it include a firewall? Does it protect against spam, spyware, and adware? How do you obtain updates to the program? How much does the program cost? In your opinion, is the program worth the price? Why or why not? Which one would you buy? Why? Write a brief report or use PowerPoint to create a presentation and share your findings with your class.

CASE STUDY 5 — Team Challenge Your team members are employed as analysts at Soap-n-Suds, an international manufacturer of laundry soaps. The company currently uses an early version of the Windows operating system on its 5,000 desktop computers. Next year, the company plans to upgrade the operating system and, if necessary, its desktop computers. The vice-president of information technology has asked your team to compare the latest desktop versions of the Windows operating system, the Mac operating system, and the Linux operating system. Assign each member of your team an operating system. Have each member use the Web and/or print media to develop a feature/benefit report. What is the initial cost of the operating system per computer? What are the memory and storage requirements? Will the operating system require the company to purchase new computers? Are training costs involved? Which one is best at avoiding viruses, spam, and spyware? Which operating system is easier to use? Why? Can Microsoft Office 2007 run under the operating system? As a team, merge your findings into a team report and/or PowerPoint presentation and share your findings with your class.

Buyer's Guide 2008:
How to Purchase a Personal Computer

(a) desktop computer

(b) mobile computer (notebook computer or Tablet PC)

Should I buy a desktop or mobile computer?

For what purposes will I use the computer?

Should the computer I buy be compatible with the computers at school or work?

FIGURE 1

At some point, perhaps while you are taking this course, you may decide to buy a personal computer. The decision is an important one and will require an investment of both time and money. Like many buyers, you may have little computer experience and find yourself unsure of how to proceed. You can get started by talking to your friends, coworkers, and instructors about their computers. What type of computers did they buy? Why? For what purposes do they use their computers? You also should answer the following three questions to help narrow your choices to a specific computer type, before reading this Buyer's Guide.

1 Do you want a desktop computer or mobile computer? A desktop computer (Figure 1a) is designed as a stationary device that sits on or below a desk or table in a location such as a home, office, or dormitory room. A desktop computer must be plugged in an electrical outlet to operate. A mobile computer, such as a notebook computer or Tablet PC (Figure 1b), is smaller than a desktop computer, more portable, and has a battery that allows you to operate it for a period without an electrical outlet.

Desktop computers are a good option if you work mostly in one place and have plenty of space in your work area. Desktop computers generally give you more performance for your money.

Increasingly, more corporations are buying mobile computers to take advantage of their portability to work while traveling and at home. The past disadvantages of mobile computers, such as lower processor speeds, poor-quality monitors, weight, short battery life, and significantly higher prices, have all but disappeared. Today, hard drive speed, capacity, processor speed, and graphics capability in notebook computers are equal to, if not better than, desktop computers.

If you are thinking of using a mobile computer to take notes in class or in business meetings, then consider a Tablet PC with handwriting and drawing capabilities. Typically, note-taking involves writing text notes and drawing charts, schematics, and other illustrations. By allowing you to write and draw directly on the screen with a digital pen, a Tablet PC eliminates the distracting sound of the notebook keyboard tapping and allows you to capture drawings. Some notebook computers can convert to Tablet PCs.

Mobile computers used to have several drawbacks, including the lack of high-end capabilities. Today's high-end notebook computers include most of the capabilities of a good desktop computer. Manufacturers have made great strides in improving durability and battery life. Most notebook computers are 1.5 to 2 inches thick and weigh less than 10 pounds, making them very portable and easy to carry.

2 For what purposes will you use the computer? Having a general idea of the purposes for which you want to use your computer will help you decide on the type of computer to buy. At this point in your research, it is not necessary to know the exact application software titles or version numbers you might want to use. Knowing that you plan to use the computer primarily to create word processing, spreadsheet, database, and presentation documents, however, will point you in the direction of a desktop or notebook computer. If you want the portability of a smart phone or PDA, but you need more computing power, then a Tablet PC may be the best alternative. You also must consider that some application software runs only on a Mac, while others run only on a PC with the Windows operating system. Still other software may run only on a PC running the UNIX or Linux operating system.

3 Should the computer be compatible with the computers at school or work? If you plan to bring work home, telecommute, or take distance education courses, then you should purchase a computer that is compatible with those at school or work.

Compatibility is primarily a software issue. If your computer runs the same operating system version, such as Microsoft Windows Vista, and the same application software, such as Microsoft Office, then your computer will be able to read documents created at school or work and vice versa. Incompatible hardware can become an issue if you plan to connect directly to a school or office network using a cable or wireless technology. You usually can obtain the minimum system requirements from the Information Technology department at your school or workplace.

After evaluating the answers to these three questions, you should have a general idea of how you plan to use your computer and the type of computer you want to buy. Once you have decided on the type of computer you want, you can follow the guidelines presented in this Buyer's Guide to help you purchase a specific computer, along with software, peripherals, and other accessories.

Many of the desktop computer guidelines presented also apply to the purchase of a notebook computer and a Tablet PC. Later in this Buyer's Guide, sections on purchasing a notebook computer or Tablet PC address additional considerations specific to those computer types.

This Buyer's Guide concentrates on recommendations for purchasing a desktop computer or mobile computer.

HOW TO PURCHASE A DESKTOP COMPUTER

Once you have decided that a desktop computer is most suited to your computing needs, the next step is to determine specific software, hardware, peripheral devices, and services to purchase, as well as where to buy the computer.

1 Determine the specific software you want to use on your computer. Before deciding to purchase software, be sure it contains the features necessary for the tasks you want to perform. Rely on the computer users in whom you have confidence to help you decide on the software to use. The minimum requirements of the software you select may determine the operating system (Microsoft Windows Vista, Linux, UNIX, Mac OS X) you need. If you have decided to use a particular operating system that does not support software you want to use, you may be able to purchase similar software from other manufacturers.

Many Web sites and trade magazines, such as those listed in Figure 2, provide reviews of software products. These Web sites frequently have articles that rate computers and software on cost, performance, and support.

Your hardware requirements depend on the minimum requirements of the software you will run on your computer.

Type of Computer	Web Site	Web Address
PC	CNET Shopper	shopper.cnet.com
	PC World Magazine	pcworld.com
	BYTE Magazine	byte.com
	PC Magazine	pcmag.com
	Yahoo! Computers	computers.yahoo.com
	MSN Shopping	shopping.msn.com
	Dave's Guide to Buying a Home Computer	css.msu.edu/PC-Guide
Mac	Macworld Magazine	macworld.com
	Apple	apple.com
	Switch to Mac Campaign	apple.com/switch

For an updated list of hardware and software reviews and their Web site addresses, visit scsite.com/dc2008/ch8/buyers.

FIGURE 2 Hardware and software reviews.

Some software requires more memory and disk space than others, as well as additional input, output, and storage devices. For example, suppose you want to run software that can copy one CD's or DVD's contents directly to another CD or DVD, without first copying the data to your hard disk. To support that, you should consider a desktop computer or a high-end notebook computer, because the computer will need two CD or DVD drives: one that reads from a CD or DVD, and one that reads from and writes on a CD or DVD. If you plan to run software that allows your computer to work as an entertainment system, then you will need a CD or DVD drive, quality speakers, and an upgraded sound card.

2 **Know the System Requirements of the Operating System.** After deciding the software you want to run on your new computer, you need to determine the operating system you want to use. If, however, you purchase a new computer, chances are it will have the latest version of your preferred operating system (Windows Vista, Linux, UNIX, Mac OS X). Figure 3 lists the minimum computer requirements of Windows Vista versions.

Windows Vista Versions	Minimum Computer Requirements
Windows Vista Home Basic	• 800 MHz processor • 512 MB of RAM • DirectX 9 capable graphics processor
Windows Vista Home Premium **Windows Vista Ultimate** **Windows Vista Business** **Windows Vista Enterprise**	• 1 GHz processor • 1 GB of RAM • DirectX 9 capable graphics processor with WDDM driver and 128 MB of graphics memory • 40 GB of hard disk capacity (15 GB free space) • DVD-ROM drive • Audio output capability • Internet access capability

FIGURE 3 Hardware requirements for Windows Vista.

3 **Look for bundled software.** When you purchase a computer, it may come bundled with software. Some sellers even let you choose which software you want. Remember, however, that bundled software has value only if you would have purchased the software even if it had not come with the computer. At the very least, you probably will want word processing software and a browser to access the Internet. If you need additional applications, such as a spreadsheet, a database, or presentation graphics, consider purchasing Microsoft Works, Microsoft Office, OpenOffice.org, or Sun StarOffice, which include several programs at a reduced price.

4 **Avoid buying the least powerful computer available.** Once you know the application software you want to use, you then can consider the following important criteria about the computer's components: (1) processor speed, (2) size and types of memory (RAM) and storage, (3) types of input/output devices, (4) types of ports and adapter cards, and (5) types of communications devices. You also need to consider if the computer is upgradeable and to what extent you are able to upgrade. For example, all manufacturers limit the amount of memory you can add. The information in Figures 4 and 5 can help you determine what system components are best for you. Figure 4 outlines considerations for specific hardware components. Figure 5 (on page 449) provides a Base Components worksheet that lists PC recommendations for each category of user discussed in this book: Home User, Small Office/Home Office User, Mobile User, Power User, and Large Business User. In the worksheet, the Home User category is divided into two groups: Application Home User and Game Home User. The Mobile User recommendations list criteria for a notebook computer, but do not include the PDA or Tablet PC options.

Computer technology changes rapidly, meaning a computer that seems powerful enough today may not serve your computing needs in a few years. In fact, studies show that many users regret not buying a more powerful computer. To avoid this, plan to buy a computer that will last you for two to three years. You can help delay obsolescence by purchasing the fastest processor, the most memory, and the largest hard disk you can afford. If you must buy a less powerful computer, be sure you can upgrade it with additional memory, components, and peripheral devices as your computer requirements grow.

5 **Consider upgrades to the mouse, keyboard, monitor, printer, microphone, and speakers.** You use these peripheral devices to interact with your computer, so you should make sure they are up to your standards. Review the peripheral devices listed in Figure 4 on pages 447 and 448 and then visit both local computer dealers and large retail stores to test the computers on display. Ask the salesperson what input and output devices would be best for you and whether you should upgrade beyond what comes standard. Consider purchasing a wireless keyboard and wireless mouse to eliminate bothersome wires on your desktop. A few extra dollars spent on these components when you initially purchase a computer can extend its usefulness by years.

CD/DVD Drives: Most computers come with a CD-RW drive. A CD-RW drive allows you to create your own custom data CDs for data backup or data transfer purposes. It also will allow you to store and share video files, digital photos, and other large files with other people who have access to a CD-ROM drive. An even better alternative is to upgrade to a DVD±RW combination drive. It allows you to read DVDs and CDs and to write data on (burn) a DVD or CD. A DVD has a capacity of at least 4.7 GB versus the 650 MB capacity of a CD. An HD DVD has a minimum capacity of 45 GB.

Card Reader/Writer: A card reader/writer is useful for transferring data directly to and from a removable flash memory card, such as the ones used in your camera or audio player. Make sure the card reader/writer can read from and write on the flash memory cards that you use.

Digital Camera: Consider an inexpensive point-and-shoot digital camera. They are small enough to carry around, usually operate automatically in terms of lighting and focus, and contain storage cards for storing photographs. A 5-megapixel camera with a 512 MB storage card is fine for creating images for use on the Web or to send via e-mail.

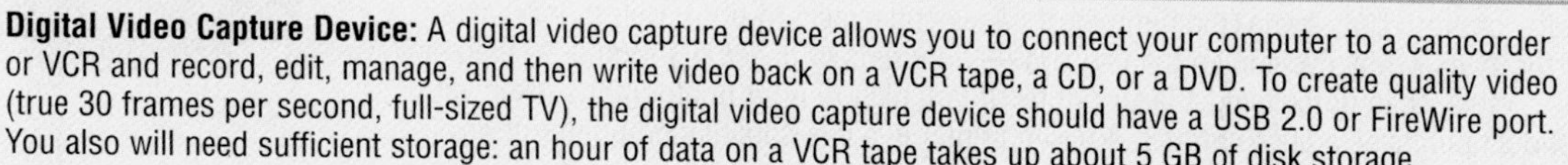

Digital Video Capture Device: A digital video capture device allows you to connect your computer to a camcorder or VCR and record, edit, manage, and then write video back on a VCR tape, a CD, or a DVD. To create quality video (true 30 frames per second, full-sized TV), the digital video capture device should have a USB 2.0 or FireWire port. You also will need sufficient storage: an hour of data on a VCR tape takes up about 5 GB of disk storage.

External Hard Disk: An external hard disk can serve many purposes: it can serve as extra storage for your computer, provide a way to store and transport large files or large quantities of files, and provide security by allowing you to keep all of your data on the external disk without leaving any data on the computer. External hard disks can be purchased with the same amount of capacity as any internal disk. If you are going to use it as a backup to your internal hard disk, you should purchase an external hard drive with at least as much capacity as your internal hard disk.

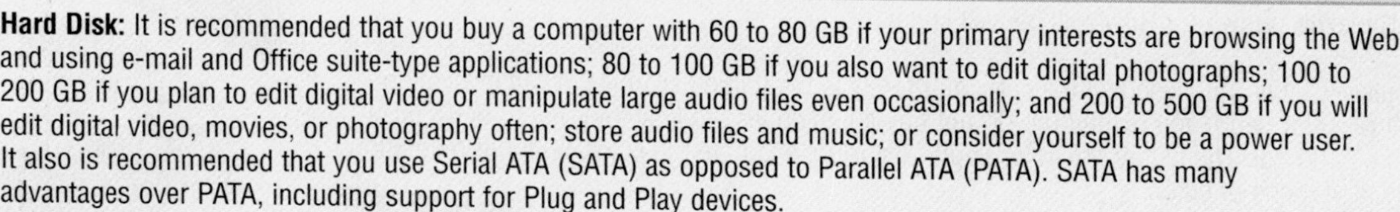

Hard Disk: It is recommended that you buy a computer with 60 to 80 GB if your primary interests are browsing the Web and using e-mail and Office suite-type applications; 80 to 100 GB if you also want to edit digital photographs; 100 to 200 GB if you plan to edit digital video or manipulate large audio files even occasionally; and 200 to 500 GB if you will edit digital video, movies, or photography often; store audio files and music; or consider yourself to be a power user. It also is recommended that you use Serial ATA (SATA) as opposed to Parallel ATA (PATA). SATA has many advantages over PATA, including support for Plug and Play devices.

Joystick/Wheel: If you use your computer to play games, then you will want to purchase a joystick or a wheel. These devices, especially the more expensive ones, provide for realistic game play with force feedback, programmable buttons, and specialized levers and wheels.

Keyboard: The keyboard is one of the more important devices used to communicate with the computer. For this reason, make sure the keyboard you purchase has 101 to 105 keys, is comfortable and easy to use, and has a USB connection. A wireless keyboard should be considered, especially if you have a small desk area.

Microphone: If you plan to record audio or use speech recognition to enter text and commands, then purchase a close-talk headset with gain adjustment support.

Modem: Most computers come with a modem so that you can use your telephone line to access the Internet. Some modems also have fax capabilities. Your modem should be rated at 56 Kbps.

Monitor: The monitor is where you will view documents, read e-mail messages, and view pictures. A minimum of a 17" screen is recommended, but if you are planning to use your computer for graphic design or game playing, then you may want to purchase a 19" or 21" monitor. The LCD flat panel monitor should be considered, especially if space is an issue.

Mouse: As you work with your computer, you use the mouse constantly. For this reason, spend a few extra dollars, if necessary, and purchase a mouse with an optical sensor and USB connection. The optical sensor replaces the need for a mouse ball, which means you do not need a mouse pad. For a PC, make sure your mouse has a wheel, which acts as a third button in addition to the top two buttons on the left and right. An ergonomic design is also important because your hand is on the mouse most of the time when you are using your computer. A wireless mouse should be considered to eliminate the cord and allow you to work at short distances from your computer.

FIGURE 4 Hardware guidelines.

Ports: Depending on how you are using your computer, you may need anywhere from 4 to 10 USB 2.0 ports. USB 2.0 ports have become the connection of choice in the computer industry. They offer an easy way to connect peripheral devices such as printers, digital cameras, portable media players, etc. Many computers intended for home or professional audio/video use have built-in FireWire ports. Most personal computers come with a minimum of six USB 2.0 ports and two FireWire ports.

Port Hub Expander: If you plan to connect several peripheral devices to your computer at the same time, then you need to be concerned with the number of ports available on your computer. If your computer does not have enough ports, then you should purchase a port hub expander. A port hub expander plugs into a single FireWire port or USB port and gives several additional ports.

Printer: Your two basic printer choices are ink-jet and laser. Color ink-jet printers cost on average between $50 and $300. Laser printers cost from $200 to $2,000. In general, the cheaper the printer, the lower the resolution and speed, and the more often you are required to change the ink cartridge or toner. Laser printers print faster and with a higher quality than an ink-jet, and their toner on average costs less. If you want color, then go with a high-end ink-jet printer to ensure quality of print. Duty cycle (the number of pages you expect to print each month) also should be a determining factor. If your duty cycle is on the low end — hundreds of pages per month — then stay with a high-end ink-jet printer, rather than purchasing a laser printer. If you plan to print photographs taken with a digital camera, then you should purchase a photo printer. A photo printer is a dye-sublimation printer or an ink-jet printer with higher resolution and features that allow you to print quality photographs.

Processor: For a PC, an Intel Core 2 Duo processor at 2.66 GHz is more than enough processor power for application home and small office/home office users. Game home, large business, and power users should upgrade to faster processors.

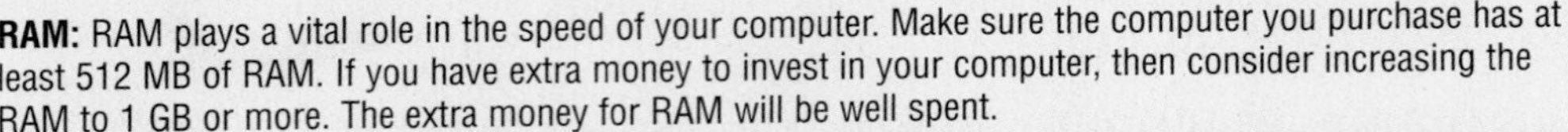

RAM: RAM plays a vital role in the speed of your computer. Make sure the computer you purchase has at least 512 MB of RAM. If you have extra money to invest in your computer, then consider increasing the RAM to 1 GB or more. The extra money for RAM will be well spent.

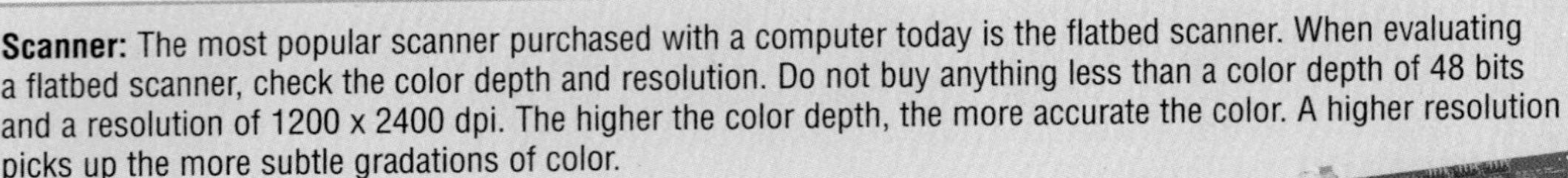

Scanner: The most popular scanner purchased with a computer today is the flatbed scanner. When evaluating a flatbed scanner, check the color depth and resolution. Do not buy anything less than a color depth of 48 bits and a resolution of 1200 x 2400 dpi. The higher the color depth, the more accurate the color. A higher resolution picks up the more subtle gradations of color.

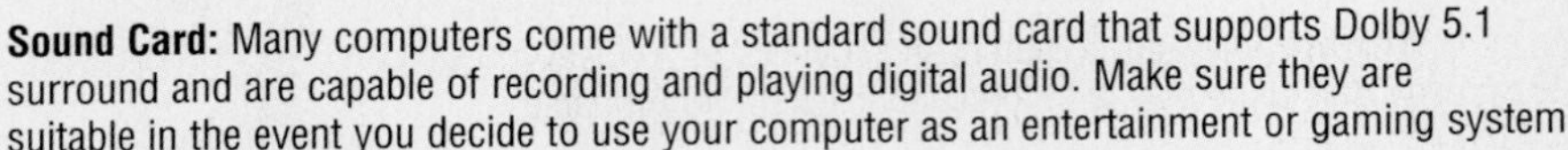

Sound Card: Many computers come with a standard sound card that supports Dolby 5.1 surround and are capable of recording and playing digital audio. Make sure they are suitable in the event you decide to use your computer as an entertainment or gaming system.

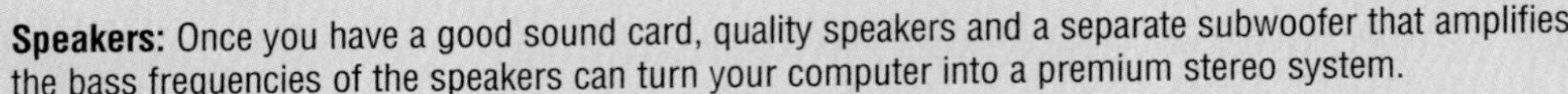

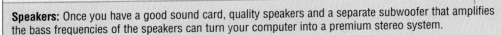

Speakers: Once you have a good sound card, quality speakers and a separate subwoofer that amplifies the bass frequencies of the speakers can turn your computer into a premium stereo system.

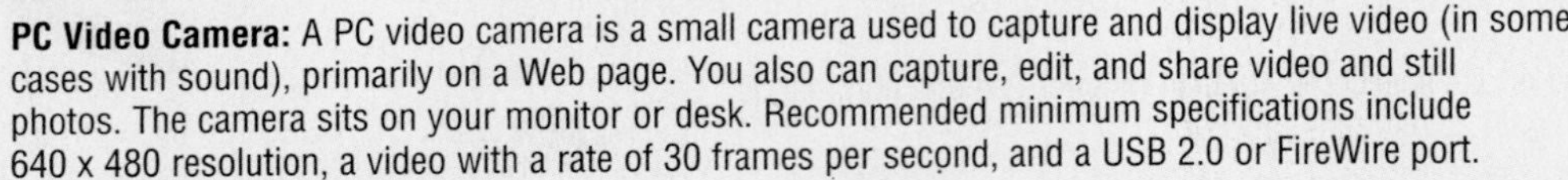

PC Video Camera: A PC video camera is a small camera used to capture and display live video (in some cases with sound), primarily on a Web page. You also can capture, edit, and share video and still photos. The camera sits on your monitor or desk. Recommended minimum specifications include 640 x 480 resolution, a video with a rate of 30 frames per second, and a USB 2.0 or FireWire port.

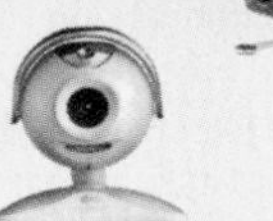

USB Flash Drive: If you work on different computers and need access to the same data and information, then this portable miniature mobile storage device is ideal. USB flash drive capacity varies from 16 MB to 4 GB.

Video Card: Most standard video cards satisfy the monitor display needs of application home and small office users. If you are a game home user or a graphic designer, you will want to upgrade to a higher quality video card. The higher refresh rates will further enhance the display of games, graphics, and movies.

Wireless LAN Access Point: A wireless LAN access point allows you to network several computers, so they can share files and access the Internet through a single cable modem or DSL connection. Each device that you connect requires a wireless card. A wireless LAN access point can offer a range of operations up to several hundred feet, so be sure the device has a high-powered antenna.

BASE COMPONENTS

	Application Home User	Game Home User	Small Office/Home Office User	Mobile User	Large Business User	Power User
HARDWARE						
Processor	Intel Core 2 Duo at 2.66 GHz	Intel Core 2 Duo at 2.93 GHz	Intel Core 2 Duo at 2.93 GHz	Intel Core 2 Duo at 2.33 GHz	Intel Core 2 Duo at 2.66 GHz	Intel Core 2 Extreme
RAM	512 MB	4 GB	1 GB	1 GB	1 GB	2 GB
Cache	512 KB L2	512 KB L2	512 KB L2	512 KB L2	512 KB L2	2 MB L3
Hard Disk	250 GB	300 GB	500 GB	100 GB	500 GB	1.5 TB
LCD Flat Panel	17" or 19"	21"	19" or 21"	17" Wide Display	19" of 21"	23"
Video Card	256 MB	512 MB	256 MB	256 MB	256 MB	256 MB
CD/DVD Bay 1	CD-RW	Blue-ray or HD DVD reader/writer	CD-RW	CD-RW/DVD	CD-RW	Blue-ray or HD DVD reader/writer
CD/DVD Bay 2	DVD±RW	DVD±RW	DVD±RW	DVD±RW	DVD±RW	DVD±RW
Printer	Color Ink-Jet	Color Ink-Jet	18 ppm Laser	Portable Ink-Jet	50 ppm Laser	10 ppm Color Laser
PC Video Camera	Yes	Yes	Yes	Yes	Yes	Yes
Fax/Modem	Yes	Yes	Yes	Yes	Yes	Yes
Microphone	Close-Talk Headset With Gain Adjustment	Close-Talk Headset With Gain Adjustment	Close-Talk Headset With Gain Adjustment	Close-Talk Headset With Gain Adjustment	Close-Talk Headset With Gain Adjustment	Close-Talk Headset With Gain Adjustment
Speakers	5.1 Dolby Surround	5.1 Dolby Surround	5.1 Dolby Surround	Stereo	5.1 Dolby Surround	5.1 Dolby Surround
Pointing Device	IntelliMouse or Optical Mouse	Laser Mouse and Joystick	IntelliMouse or Optical Mouse	Touchpad or Pointing Stick and Laser Mouse	IntelliMouse or Optical Mouse	IntelliMouse or Laser Mouse and Joystick
Keyboard	Yes	Yes	Yes	Built-In	Yes	Yes
Backup Disk/Tape Drive	External or Removable Hard Disk	External or Removable Hard Disk	External or Removable Hard Disk	External or Removable Hard Disk	Tape Drive	External or Removable Hard Disk
USB Flash Drive	256 MB	512 MB	512 MB	512 MB	4 GB	2 GB
Sound Card	Sound Blaster Compatible	Sound Blaster Audigy 2	Sound Blaster Compatible	Built-In	Sound Blaster Compatible	Sound Blaster Audigy 2
Network Card	Yes	Yes	Yes	Yes	Yes	Yes
TV-Out Connector	Yes	Yes	Yes	Yes	Yes	Yes
USB 2.0 Port	6	8	6	4	9	10
FireWire Port	2	2	2	1	2	2
SOFTWARE						
Operating System	Windows Vista Home Basic	Windows Vista Home Premium	Windows Vista Business	Windows Vista Business	Windows Vista Enterprise	Windows Vista Ultimate
Application Suite	Office Standard 2007	Office Standard 2007	Office Small Business 2007	Office Small Business 2007	Office Professional 2007	Office Professional 2007
Antivirus	Yes, 12-Mo. Subscription	Yes, 12-Mo. Subscription	Yes, 12-Mo. Subscription	Yes, 12-Mo. Subscription	Yes, 12-Mo. Subscription	Yes, 12-Mo. Subscription
Internet Access	Cable, DSL, or Dial-up	Cable or DSL	Cable or DSL	Wireless or Dial-up	LAN/WAN (T1/T3)	Cable or DSL
OTHER						
Surge Protector	Yes	Yes	Yes	Portable	Yes	Yes
Warranty	3-Year Limited, 1-Year Next Business Day On-Site Service	3-Year Limited, 1-Year Next Business Day On-Site Service	3-year On-Site Service	3-Year Limited, 1-Year Next Business Day On-Site Service	3-year On-Site Service	3-year On-Site Service
Other		Wheel	Postage Printer	Docking Station Carrying Case Fingerprint Scanner Portable Data Projector		Graphics Tablet Plotter or Large-Format Printer

Optional Components for all Categories	
802.11g Wireless Card	Graphics Tablet
Bluetooth Enabled	Portable Media Player
Biometric Input Device	IrDA Port
Card Reader/Writer	Multifunction Peripheral
Digital Camera	Photo Printer
Digital Video Capture Device	Port Hub Expander
Digital Video Camera	Portable Data Projector
Dual-Monitor Support with Second Monitor	Scanner
Ergonomic Keyboard	TV/FM Tuner
External Hard Disk	Uninterruptible Power Supply

URE 5 Base desktop and mobile computer components and optional components. A copy of the Base Components worksheet is part of Data Files for Students. To obtain a copy of the Data Files for Students, see the inside back cover of this book for instructions.

6 **Determine whether you want to use telephone lines or broadband (cable or DSL) to access the Internet.** If your computer has a modem, then you can access the Internet using a standard telephone line. Ordinarily, you call a local or toll-free 800 number to connect to an ISP (see Guideline 7 on the next page). Using a dial-up Internet connection is relatively inexpensive but slow.

DSL and cable connections provide much faster Internet connections, which are ideal if you want faster file download speeds for software, digital photos, and music. As you would expect, they also are more expensive. DSL, which is available through local telephone companies, also may require that you subscribe to an ISP. Cable is available through your local cable television provider and some online service providers (OSPs). If you get cable, then you would not use a separate Internet service provider or online service provider.

7 If you are using a dial-up or wireless connection to connect to the Internet, then select an ISP or OSP.

You can access the Internet via telephone lines in one of two ways: an ISP or an OSP. Both provide Internet access for a monthly fee that ranges from $6 to $25. Local ISPs offer Internet access to users in a limited geographic region, through local telephone numbers. National ISPs provide access for users nationwide (including mobile users), through local and toll-free telephone numbers and cable. Because of their size, national ISPs generally offer more services and have a larger technical support staff than local ISPs. OSPs furnish Internet access as well as members-only features for users nationwide. Figure 6 lists several national ISPs and OSPs. Before you choose an ISP or OSP, compare such features as the number of access hours, monthly fees, available services (e-mail, Web page hosting, chat), and reliability.

Company	Service	Web Address
America Online	OSP	aol.com
AT&T Worldnet	ISP	www.att.net
Comcast	OSP	comcast.net
CompuServe	OSP	compuserve.com
EarthLink	ISP	earthlink.net
Juno	OSP	juno.com
NetZero	OSP	netzero.com
MSN	OSP	msn.com
Prodigy	ISP/OSP	myhome.prodigy.net

For an updated list of national ISPs and OSPs and their Web site addresses, visit scsite.com/dc2008/ch8/buyers.

FIGURE 6 National ISPs and OSPs.

8 Use a worksheet to compare computers, services, and other considerations.

You can use a separate sheet of paper to take notes on each vendor's computer and then summarize the information on a worksheet, such as the one shown in Figure 7. You can use Figure 7 to compare prices for either a PC or a Mac. Most companies advertise a price for a base computer that includes components housed in the system unit (processor, RAM, sound card, video card), disk drives (hard disk, CD-ROM, CD-RW, DVD-ROM, and DVD±RW), a keyboard, mouse, monitor, printer, speakers, and modem. Be aware, however, that some advertisements list prices for computers with only some of these components. Monitors and printers, for example, often are not included in a base computer's price. Depending on how you plan to use the computer, you may want to invest in additional or more powerful components. When you are comparing the prices of computers, make sure you are comparing identical or similar configurations.

PC or MAC Cost Comparison Worksheet

Dealers list prices for computers with most of these components (instead of listing individual component costs). Some dealers do not supply a monitor. Some dealers offer significant discounts, but you must subscribe to an Internet service for a specified period to receive the dicounted price. To compare computers, enter overall system price at top and enter a 0 (zero) for components included in the system cost. For any additional components not covered in the system price, enter the cost in the appropriate cells.

Items to Purchase	Desired System (PC)	Desired System (Mac)	Local Dealer #1	Local Dealer #2	Online Dealer #1	Online Dealer #2	Comments
OVERALL SYSTEM							
Overall System Price	< $2,000	< $2,000					
HARDWARE							
Processor	Intel Core 2 Duo	Intel Core 2 Duo					
RAM	1 GB	1 GB					
Cache	256 KB L2	256 KB L2					
Hard Disk	250 GB	250 GB					
Monitor/LCD Flat Panel	20 Inch	20 Inch					
Video Card	256 MB	256 MB					
USB Flash Drive	1 GB	1 GB					
CD/DVD Bay 1	CD-RW	DVD±RW					
CD/DVD Bay 2	DVD±RW	NA					
Speakers	Dolby 5.1 Surround	Dolby 5.1 Surround					
Sound Card	Sound Blaster Compatible	Sound Blaster Compatible					
USB 2.0 Port	6	6					
FireWire Port	2	2					
Network Card	Yes	Yes					
Fax/Modem	56 Kbps	56 Kbps					
Keyboard	Standard	Apple Pro Keyboard					
Pointing Device	IntelliMouse	Intellimouse or Apple Pro Mouse					
Microphone	Close-Talk Headset with Gain Adjustment	Close-Talk Headset with Gain Adjustment					
Printer	Color Ink-Jet	Color Ink-Jet					
SOFTWARE							
Operating System	Windows Vista Ultimate	Mac OS X					
Application Software	Office 2007 Small Business	Office 2007 for Mac					
Antivirus	Yes - 12 Mo. Subscription	Yes - 12 Mo. Subscription					
OTHER							
Card Reader							
Digital Camera	5-Megapixel	5-Megapixel					
Internet Connection	1-Year Subscription	1-Year Subscription					
Joystick	Yes	Yes					
PC Video Camera	With Microphone	With Microphone					
Port Hub Expander							
Scanner							
Surge Protector							
Warranty	3-Year On-Site Service	3-Year On-Site Service					
Wireless Card	Internal	Internal					
Wireless LAN Access Point	LinkSys	Apple AirPort					
Total Cost			$ -	$ -	$ -	$ -	

FIGURE 7 A worksheet is an effective tool for summarizing and comparing components and prices of different computer vendors. A copy of the Computer Cost Comparison Worksheet is part of the Data Files for Students. To obtain a copy of the Data Files for Students, see the inside back cover of this book for instructions.

9 If you are buying a new computer, you have several purchasing options: buying from your school bookstore, a local computer dealer, a local large retail store, or ordering by mail via telephone or the Web. Each purchasing option has certain advantages. Many college bookstores, for example, sign exclusive pricing agreements with computer manufacturers and, thus, can offer student discounts. Local dealers and local large retail stores, however, more easily can provide hands-on support. Mail-order companies that sell computers by telephone or online via the Web (Figure 8) often provide the lowest prices, but extend less personal service. Some major mail-order companies, however, have started to provide next-business-day, on-site services. A credit card usually is required to buy from a mail-order company. Figure 9 lists some of the more popular mail-order companies and their Web site addresses.

10 If you are buying a used computer, stay with name brands such as Dell, Gateway, Hewlett-Packard, and Apple. Although brand-name equipment can cost more, most brand-name computers have longer, more comprehensive warranties, are better supported, and have more authorized centers for repair services. As with new computers, you can purchase a used computer from local computer dealers, local large retail stores, or mail order via the telephone or the Web. Classified ads and used computer sellers offer additional outlets for purchasing used computers. Figure 10 lists several major used computer brokers and their Web site addresses.

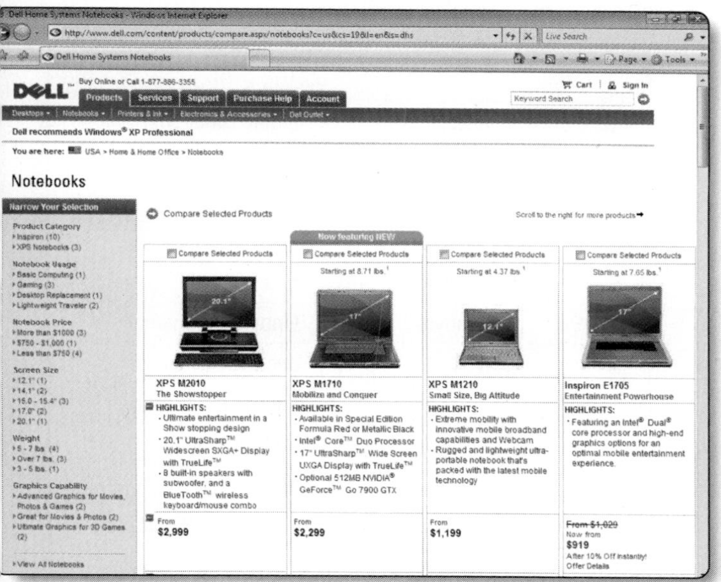

FIGURE 8 Mail-order companies, such as Dell, sell computers online.

11 If you have a computer and are upgrading to a new one, then consider selling or trading in the old one. If you are a replacement buyer, your older computer still may have value. If you cannot sell the computer through the classified ads, via a Web site, or to a friend, then ask if the computer dealer will buy your old computer. An increasing number of companies are taking trade-ins, but do not expect too much money for your old computer. Other companies offer free disposal of your old PC.

12 Be aware of hidden costs. Before purchasing, be sure to consider any additional costs associated with buying a computer, such as an additional telephone line, a cable or DSL modem, an uninterruptible power supply (UPS), computer furniture, a USB flash drive, paper, and computer training classes you may want to take. Depending on where you buy your computer, the seller may be willing to include some or all of these in the computer purchase price.

Type of Computer	Company	Web Address
PC	CNET Shopper	shopper.cnet.com
	Hewlett-Packard	hp.com
	CompUSA	compusa.com
	TigerDirect	tigerdirect.com
	Dell	dell.com
	Gateway	gateway.com
Macintosh	Apple Computer	store.apple.com
	ClubMac	clubmac.com
	MacConnection	macconnection.com
	PC & MacExchange	macx.com

For an updated list of mail-order computer companies and their Web site addresses, visit scsite.com/dc2008/ch8/buyers.

FIGURE 9 Computer mail-order companies.

Company	Web Address
Amazon.com	amazon.com
TigerDirect.com	tigerdirect.com
American Computer Express	americancomputerex.com
U.S. Computer Exchange	usce.org
eBay	ebay.com

For an updated list of used computer mail-order companies and their Web site addresses, visit scsite.com/dc2008/ch8/buyers.

FIGURE 10 Used computer mail-order companies.

13 Consider more than just price. The lowest-cost computer may not be the best long-term buy. Consider such intangibles as the vendor's time in business, the vendor's regard for quality, and the vendor's reputation for support. If you need to upgrade your computer often, you may want to consider a leasing arrangement, in which you pay monthly lease fees, but can upgrade or add on to your computer as your equipment needs change. No matter what type of buyer you are, insist on a 30-day, no-questions-asked return policy on your computer.

14 Avoid restocking fees. Some companies charge a restocking fee of 10 to 20 percent as part of their money-back return policy. In some cases, no restocking fee for hardware is applied, but it is applied for software. Ask about the existence and terms of any restocking policies before you buy.

15 Use a credit card to purchase your new computer. Many credit cards offer purchase protection and extended warranty benefits that cover you in case of loss of or damage to purchased goods. Paying by credit card also gives you time to install and use the computer before you have to pay for it. Finally, if you are dissatisfied with the computer and are unable to reach an agreement with the seller, paying by credit card gives you certain rights regarding withholding payment until the dispute is resolved. Check your credit card terms for specific details.

16 Consider purchasing an extended warranty or service plan. If you use your computer for business or require fast resolution to major computer problems, consider purchasing an extended warranty or a service plan through a local dealer or third-party company. Most extended warranties cover the repair and replacement of computer components beyond the standard warranty. Most service plans ensure that your technical support calls receive priority response from technicians. You also can purchase an on-site service plan that states that a technician will come to your home, work, or school within 24 hours. If your computer includes a warranty and service agreement for a year or less, think about extending the service for two or three years when you buy the computer.

CENTURY COMPUTERS
Performance Guarantee
(See reverse for terms & conditions of this contract)

Invoice #: 1984409
Invoice Date: 10/12/08
Effective Date: 10/12/08
Expiration Date: 10/12/11

Customer Name: Leon, Richard
Date: 10/12/08
Address: 1123 Roxbury
Sycamore, IL 60178
Day phone: (815) 555-0303
Evening Phone: (728) 555-0203

System & Serial Numbers
IMB computer
S/N: US759290C

John Smith
Print Name of Century's Authorized Signature

10/12/08
Date

HOW TO PURCHASE A NOTEBOOK COMPUTER

If you need computing capability when you travel or to use in lecture or meetings, you may find a notebook computer to be an appropriate choice. The guidelines mentioned in the previous section also apply to the purchase of a notebook computer. The following are additional considerations unique to notebook computers.

1 Purchase a notebook computer with a sufficiently large active-matrix screen. Active-matrix screens display high-quality color that is viewable from all angles. Less expensive, passive-matrix screens sometimes are difficult to see in low-light conditions and cannot be viewed from an angle. Notebook computers typically come with a 12.1-inch, 13.3-inch, 14.1-inch, 15.4-inch, or 17-inch display. For most users, a 14.1-inch display is satisfactory. If you intend to use your notebook computer as a desktop computer replacement, however, you may opt for a 15.7-inch or 17-inch display. Dell offers a notebook computer with a 20.1-inch display that looks like a briefcase when closed. Notebook computers with these larger displays weigh seven to ten pounds, however, so if you travel a lot and portability is essential, you might want a lighter computer with a smaller display. The lightest notebook computers, which weigh less than 3 pounds, are equipped with a 12.1-inch display. Regardless of size, the resolution of the display should be at least 1024 × 768 pixels. To compare the monitor size on various notebook computers, visit the company Web sites in Figure 11.

Type of Notebook	Company	Web Address
PC	Acer	global.acer.com
	Dell	dell.com
	Fujitsu	fujitsu.com
	Gateway	gateway.com
	Hewlett-Packard	hp.com
	Lenovo	lenovo.com/us/en/
	NEC	nec.com
	Sony	sony.com
	Toshiba	toshiba.com
Mac	Apple	apple.com

For an updated list of companies and their Web site addresses, visit scsite.com/dc2008/ch8/buyers.

FIGURE 11 Companies that sell notebook computers.

2 Experiment with different keyboards and pointing devices. Notebook computer keyboards are far less standardized than those for desktop computers. Some notebook computers, for example, have wide wrist rests, while others have none, and keyboard layouts on notebook computers often vary. Notebook computers also use a range of pointing devices, including pointing sticks, touchpads, and trackballs. Before you purchase a notebook computer, try various types of keyboard and pointing devices to determine which is easiest for you to use. Regardless of the pointing device you select, you also may want to purchase a regular mouse to use when you are working at a desk or other large surface.

3 Make sure the notebook computer you purchase has a CD and/or DVD drive. Most notebook computers come with a CD and/or a DVD drive. Although DVD drives are slightly more expensive, they allow you to play CDs and DVD movies using your notebook computer and a headset.

4 If necessary, upgrade the processor, memory, and disk storage at the time of purchase. As with a desktop computer, upgrading your notebook computer's memory and disk storage usually is less expensive at the time of initial purchase. Some disk storage is custom designed for notebook computer manufacturers, meaning an upgrade might not be available in the future. If you are purchasing a lightweight notebook computer, then it should include at least an Intel Core Duo processor, 512 MB RAM, and 80 GB of storage.

5 The availability of built-in ports and a port extender on a notebook computer is important. A notebook computer does not have a lot of room to add adapter cards. If you know the purpose for which you plan to use your notebook computer, then you can determine the ports you will need. Most notebooks come with common ports, such as a mouse port, IrDA port, serial port, parallel port, video port, a FireWire port, and multiple USB ports. If you plan to connect your notebook computer to a TV, however, then you will need a PCtoTV port. If you want to connect to networks at school or in various offices via a network cable, make sure the notebook computer you purchase has a network port. If your notebook computer does not come with a network port, then you will have to purchase an external network card that slides into an expansion slot in your notebook computer, as well as a network cable. While newer portable media players connect to a USB port, older ones require a FireWire port.

6 If you plan to use your notebook computer for note-taking at school or in meetings, consider a notebook computer that converts to a Tablet PC. Some computer manufacturers have developed convertible notebook computers that allow the screen to rotate 180 degrees on a central hinge and then fold down to cover the keyboard and become a Tablet PC (Figure 12). You then can use a stylus to enter text or drawings into the computer by writing on the screen. Some notebook computers have wide screens for better viewing and editing, and some even have a screen on top of the unit in addition to the regular screen.

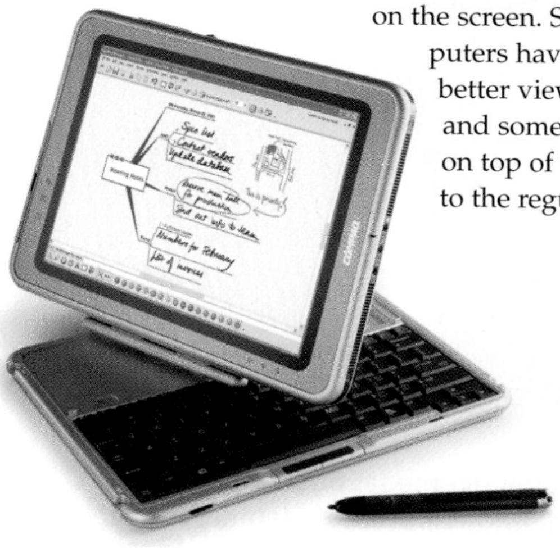

FIGURE 12
The HP Compaq tc4200 Tablet PC converts to a notebook computer.

7 Purchase a notebook computer with a built-in wireless network connection. A wireless network connection (Bluetooth, Wi-Fi a/b/g, WiMAX, etc.) can be useful when you travel or as part of a home network. Increasingly more airports, hotels, and cafes have wireless networks that allow you to connect to the Internet. Many users today are setting up wireless home networks. With a wireless home network, the desktop computer functions as the server, and your notebook computer can access the desktop computer from any location in the house to share files and hardware, such as a printer, and browse the Web. Most home wireless networks allow connections from distances of 150 to 800 feet.

8 If you are going to use your notebook computer for long periods without access to an electrical outlet, purchase a second battery. The trend among notebook computer users today is power and size over battery life, and notebook computer manufacturers have picked up on this. Many notebook computer users today are willing to give up longer battery life for a larger screen, faster processor, and more storage. In addition, some manufacturers typically sell the notebook with the lowest capacity battery. For this reason, you need to be careful in choosing a notebook computer if you plan to use it without access to electrical outlets for long periods, such as an airplane flight. You also might want to purchase a second battery as a backup. If you anticipate running your notebook computer on batteries frequently, choose a computer that uses lithium-ion batteries, which last longer than nickel cadmium or nickel hydride batteries.

9 Purchase a well-padded and well-designed carrying case. An amply padded carrying case will protect your notebook computer from the bumps it will receive while traveling. A well-designed carrying case will have room for accessories such as spare CDs and DVDs, a user manual, pens, and paperwork (Figure 13).

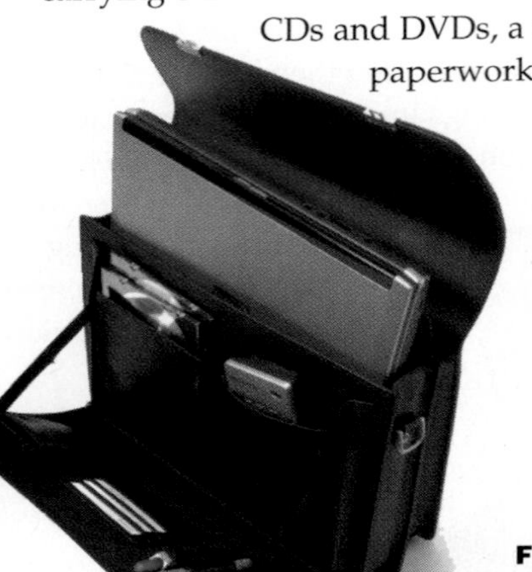

FIGURE 13 A well-designed notebook computer carrying case.

10 If you travel overseas, obtain a set of electrical and telephone adapters. Different countries use different outlets for electrical and telephone connections. Several manufacturers sell sets of adapters that will work in most countries.

11 If you plan to connect your notebook computer to a video projector, make sure the notebook computer is compatible with the video projector. You should check, for example, to be sure that your notebook computer will allow you to display an image on the computer screen and projection device at the same time (Figure 14). Also, ensure that your notebook computer has the ports required to connect to the video projector. You also may consider purchasing a notebook computer with a built-in video camera for videoconferencing purposes.

FIGURE 14 A notebook computer connected to a video projector projects the image displayed on the screen.

12 For improved security, consider a fingerprint scanner. More than half a million notebook computers are stolen or lost each year. If you have critical information stored on your notebook computer, then consider purchasing one with a fingerprint scanner (Figure 15) to protect the data if your computer is stolen or lost. Fingerprint security offers a level of protection that extends well beyond the standard password protection. If your notebook computer is stolen, the odds of recovering it improve dramatically with anti-theft tracking software. Manufacturers claim recovery rates of 90 percent or more for notebook computers using their product.

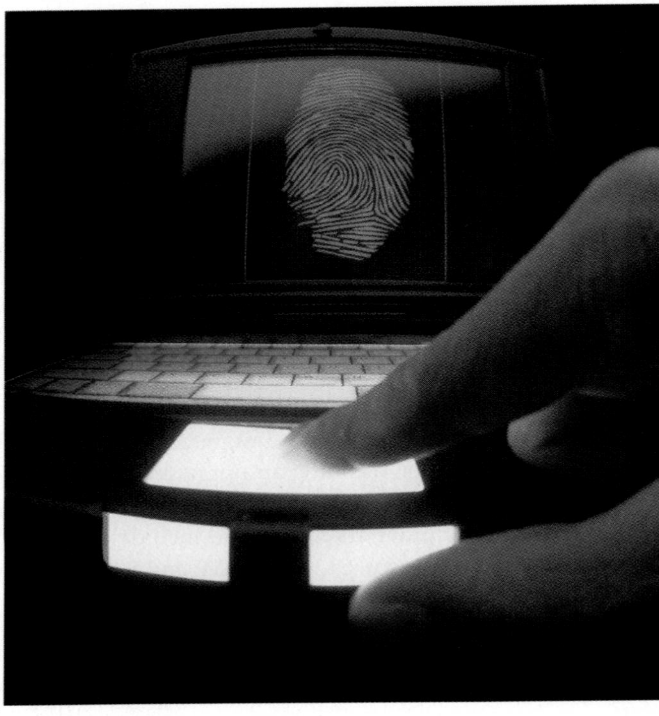

FIGURE 15 Fingerprint scanner technology offers greater security than passwords.

HOW TO PURCHASE A TABLET PC

The Tablet PC (Figure 16) combines the mobility features of a traditional notebook computer with the simplicity of pencil and paper, because you can create and save Office-type documents by writing and drawing directly on the screen with a digital pen. Tablet PCs use the Windows Tablet Technology in Windows Vista operating system. A notebook computer and a Tablet PC have many similarities. For this reason, if you are considering purchasing a Tablet PC, review the guidelines for purchasing a notebook computer, as well as the guidelines below.

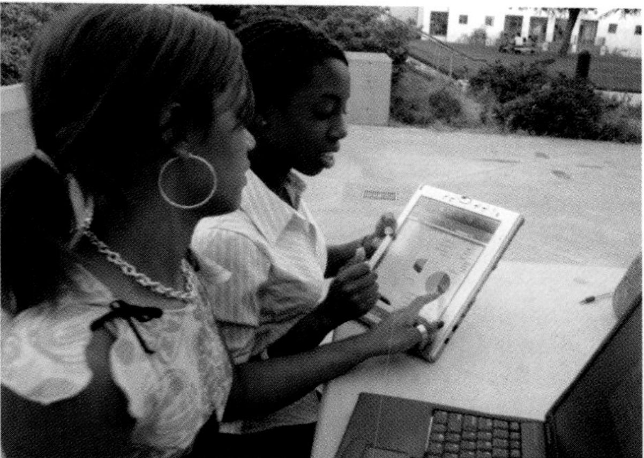

FIGURE 16 The lightweight Tablet PC, with its handwriting capabilities, is the latest addition to the family of mobile computers.

1 Make sure the Tablet PC fits your mobile computing needs. The Tablet PC is not for every mobile user. If you find yourself in need of a computer in class or you are spending more time in meetings than in your office, then the Tablet PC may be the answer. Before you invest money in a Tablet PC, however, determine the programs you plan to use on it. You should not buy a Tablet PC simply because it is an interesting type of computer. For additional information on the Tablet PC, visit the Web sites listed in Figure 17. You may have to use the search capabilities on the home page of the companies listed to locate information about the Tablet PC.

Company	Web Address
Fujitsu	fujitsu.com
Hewlett-Packard	hp.com
Microsoft	microsoft.com/windowsxp/tabletpc
ViewSonic	viewsonic.com

For an updated list of companies and their Web site addresses, visit scsite.com/dc2008/ch8/buyers.

FIGURE 17 Companies involved with Tablet PCs and their Web sites.

2 Decide whether you want a convertible or pure Tablet PC. Convertible Tablet PCs have an attached keyboard and look like a notebook computer. You rotate the screen and lay it flat against the computer for note-taking. The pure Tablet PCs are slim and lightweight, weighing less than four pounds. They have the capability of easily docking at a desktop to gain access to a large monitor, keyboard, and mouse. If you spend a lot of time attending lectures or meetings, then the pure Tablet PC is ideal. Acceptable specifications for a Tablet PC are shown in Figure 18.

TABLET PC SPECIFICATIONS

Dimensions	12" × 9" × 1.2"
Weight	Less than 5 Pounds
Processor	Pentium M Processor at 2 GHz
RAM	1 GB
Hard Disk	60 GB
Display	12.1" TFT
Digitizer	Electromagnetic Digitizer
Battery	6-Cell High Capacity Lithium-Ion
USB	3
FireWire	1
Docking Station	Grab and Go with CD-ROM, Keyboard, and Mouse
Bluetooth Port	Yes
Wireless	802.11a/b/g Card
Network Card	10/100 Ethernet
Modem	56 Kbps
Speakers	Internal
Microphone	Internal
Operating System	Windows Vista
Application Software	Office Small Business Edition
Antivirus Software	Yes – 12 Month Subscription
Warranty	1-Year Limited Warranty Parts and Labor

FIGURE 18 Tablet PC specifications.

3 Be sure the weight and dimensions are conducive to portability. The weight and dimensions of the Tablet PC are important because you carry it around like a notepad. The Tablet PC you buy should weigh four pounds or less. Its dimensions should be approximately 12 inches by 9 inches by 1.2 inches.

4 Port availability, battery life, and durability are even more important with a Tablet PC than they are with a notebook computer.

Make sure the Tablet PC you purchase has the ports required for the applications you plan to run. As with any mobile computer, battery life is important especially if you plan to use your Tablet PC for long periods without access to an electrical outlet. A Tablet PC must be durable because if you use it the way it was designed to be used, then you will be handling it much like you handle a pad of paper.

5 Experiment with different models of the Tablet PC to find the digital pen that works best for you.

The key to making use of the Tablet PC is to be comfortable with its handwriting capabilities and on-screen keyboard. Not only is the digital pen used to write on the screen (Figure 19), you also use it to make gestures to complete tasks, in a manner similar to the way you use a mouse. Figure 20 compares the standard point-and-click of a mouse with the gestures made with a digital pen. Other gestures with the digital pen replicate some of the commonly used keys on a keyboard.

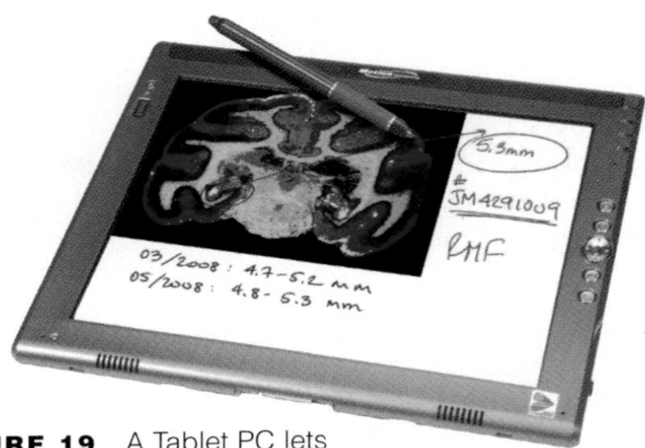

FIGURE 19 A Tablet PC lets you handwrite notes and draw on the screen using a digital pen.

Mouse	Digital Pen
Point	Point
Click	Tap
Double-click	Double-tap
Right-click	Tap and hold
Click and drag	Drag

FIGURE 20 Standard point-and-click of a mouse compared with the gestures made with a digital pen.

6 Check out the comfort level of handwriting in different positions.

You should be able to handwrite on a Tablet PC with your hand resting on the screen. You also should be able to handwrite holding the Tablet PC in one hand, as well as with it sitting in your lap.

7 Make sure the LCD display device has a resolution high enough to take advantage of Microsoft's ClearType technologies.

Tablet PCs use a digitizer under a standard 10.4-inch motion-sensitive LCD display to make the digital ink on the screen look like real ink on paper. To ensure you get the maximum benefits from the new ClearType technology, make sure the LCD display has a resolution of 800 × 600 in landscape mode and a 600 × 800 in portrait mode.

8 Test the built-in Tablet PC microphone and speakers.

Although most application software, including Microsoft Office, recognizes human speech, it is important that the Tablet PC's built-in microphone operates at an acceptable level. If the microphone is not to your liking, you may want to purchase a close-talk headset with your Tablet PC. Increasingly more users are sending information as audio files, rather than relying solely on text. For this reason, you also should check the speakers on the Tablet PC to make sure they meet your standards.

9 Consider a Tablet PC with a built-in PC video camera.

A PC video camera adds streaming video and still photography capabilities to your Tablet PC, while still allowing you to take notes in lectures or meetings.

10 Review the docking capabilities of the Tablet PC.

The Tablet Technology in Windows Vista operating system supports a grab-and-go form of docking, so you can pick up and take a docked Tablet PC with you, just as you would pick up a notepad on your way to a meeting (Figure 21).

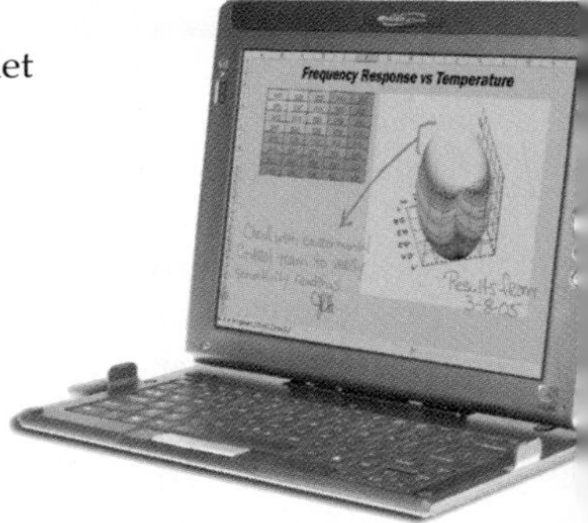

FIGURE 21 A Tablet PC docked to create a desktop computer with the Tablet as the monitor.

11 Wireless access to the Internet and your e-mail is essential with a Tablet PC.

Make sure the Tablet PC has wireless networking (Bluetooth, Wi-Fi a/b/g, WiMAX, etc.), so you can access the Internet and your e-mail anytime and anywhere. Your Tablet PC also should include standard network connections, such as dial-up and Ethernet connections.

12 Review available accessories to purchase with your Tablet PC.

Tablet PC accessories include docking stations, mouse units, keyboards, security cables, additional memory and storage, protective handgrips, screen protectors, and various types of digital pens.

APPENDIX A

Coding Schemes and Number Systems

CODING SCHEMES

As discussed in Chapter 4, a computer uses a coding scheme to represent characters. This section of the appendix presents the ASCII, EBCDIC, and Unicode coding schemes and discusses parity.

ASCII and EBCDIC

Two popular coding schemes that represent characters in a computer are ASCII and EBCDIC. The **American Standard Code for Information Interchange**, or ASCII (pronounced ASK-ee), coding scheme is the most widely used coding scheme to represent data. Many personal computers and midrange servers use ASCII. The **Extended Binary Coded Decimal Interchange Code**, or EBCDIC (pronounced EB-see-dik), coding scheme is used primarily on mainframe computers and high-end servers. As shown in Figure A-1, the combination of bits (0s and 1s) is unique for each character in the ASCII and EBCDIC coding schemes.

When a computer uses the ASCII or EBCDIC coding scheme, it stores each represented character in one byte of memory. Other binary formats exist, however, that the computer sometimes uses to represent numeric data. For example, a computer may store, or pack, two numeric characters in one byte of memory. The computer uses these binary formats to increase storage and processing efficiency.

Unicode

The 256 characters and symbols that are represented by ASCII and EBCDIC codes are sufficient for English and western European languages but are not large enough for Asian and other languages that use different alphabets. Further compounding the problem is that many of these languages use symbols, called **ideograms**, to represent multiple words and ideas. One solution to this situation is Unicode. **Unicode** is a 16-bit coding scheme that has the capacity of representing all the world's current languages, as well as classic and historical languages, in more than 65,000 characters and symbols.

ASCII	SYMBOL	EBCDIC
00110000	0	11110000
00110001	1	11110001
00110010	2	11110010
00110011	3	11110011
00110100	4	11110100
00110101	5	11110101
00110110	6	11110110
00110111	7	11110111
00111000	8	11111000
00111001	9	11111001
01000001	A	11000001
01000010	B	11000010
01000011	C	11000011
01000100	D	11000100
01000101	E	11000101
01000110	F	11000110
01000111	G	11000111
01001000	H	11001000
01001001	I	11001001
01001010	J	11010001
01001011	K	11010010
01001100	L	11010011
01001101	M	11010100
01001110	N	11010101
01001111	O	11010110
01010000	P	11010111
01010001	Q	11011000
01010010	R	11011001
01010011	S	11100010
01010100	T	11100011
01010101	U	11100100
01010110	V	11100101
01010111	W	11100110
01011000	X	11100111
01011001	Y	11101000
01011010	Z	11101001
00100001	!	01011010
00100010	"	01111111
00100011	#	01111011
00100100	$	01011011
00100101	%	01101100
00100110	&	01010000
00101000	(	01001101
00101001	)	01011101
00101010	*	01011100
00101011	+	01001110

FIGURE A-1

A Unicode code for a symbol, as shown in Figure A-2, is obtained by appending the symbol's corresponding digit in the left-most column to the end of the symbol's corresponding three-digit code in the column heading. For example, the Unicode for the capital letter C is 0043. In Unicode, 30,000 codes are reserved for future use, such as ancient languages, and 6,000 codes are reserved for private use. Existing ASCII coded data is fully compatible with Unicode because the first 256 codes are the same. Unicode is implemented in several operating systems, including Windows XP, Windows Vista, Mac OS X, and Linux. Unicode-enabled programming languages and software include Java, XML, Microsoft Office, and Oracle. Some experts believe that Unicode eventually will replace all other coding schemes.

	003	004	005	006	007
0	0 0030	@ 0040	P 0050	` 0060	p 0070
1	1 0031	A 0041	Q 0051	a 0061	q 0071
2	2 0032	B 0042	R 0052	b 0062	r 0072
3	3 0033	C 0043	S 0053	c 0063	s 0073
4	4 0034	D 0044	T 0054	d 0064	t 0074
5	5 0035	E 0045	U 0055	e 0065	u 0075
6	6 0036	F 0046	V 0056	f 0066	v 0076
7	7 0037	G 0047	W 0057	g 0067	w 0077
8	8 0038	H 0048	X 0058	h 0068	x 0078
9	9 0039	I 0049	Y 0059	i 0069	y 0079
A	: 003A	J 004A	Z 005A	j 006A	z 007A
B	; 003B	K 004B	[005B	k 006B	{ 007B
C	< 003C	L 004C	\ 005C	l 006C	| 007C
D	= 003D	M 004D	] 005D	m 006D	} 007D
E	> 003E	N 004E	^ 005E	n 006E	~ 007E
F	? 003F	O 004F	_ 005F	o 006F	DEL 007F

FIGURE A-2

Parity

Regardless of the coding scheme used to represent characters in memory, it is important that the computer store characters accurately. For each byte of memory, most computers have at least one extra bit, called a **parity bit**, that the computer uses for error checking. A parity bit can detect if one of the bits in a byte has been changed inadvertently. While such errors are extremely rare (most computers never have a parity error during their lifetime), they can occur because of voltage fluctuations, static electricity, or a memory failure.

Computers are either odd- or even-parity machines. In computers with odd-parity, the total number of on bits in the byte (including the parity bit) must be an odd number (Figure A-3). In computers with even parity, the total number of on bits must be an even number. The computer checks parity each time it uses a memory location. When the computer moves data from one location to another in memory, it compares the parity bits of both the sending and receiving locations to see if they are the same. If the computer detects a difference or if the wrong number of bits is on (e.g., an odd number in a computer with even parity), an error message is displayed. Many computers use multiple parity bits that enable them to detect and correct a single-bit error and detect multiple-bit errors.

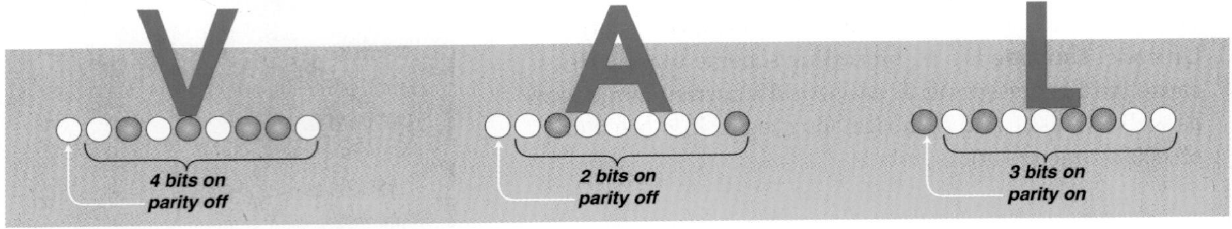

FIGURE A-3

NUMBER SYSTEMS

This section of the appendix describes the number systems used with computers. Technical computer personnel require a thorough knowledge of this subject, but most users need only a general understanding of number systems and how they relate to computers.

The binary (base 2) number system is used to represent the electronic status of the bits in memory. It also is used for other purposes such as addressing the memory locations. Another number system commonly used with computers is **hexadecimal** (base 16). The computer uses the hexadecimal number system to communicate with a programmer when a problem with a program exists, because it would be difficult for the programmer to understand the 0s and 1s of binary code. Figure A-4 shows how the decimal values 0 through 15 are represented in binary and hexadecimal number systems.

DECIMAL	BINARY	HEXADECIMAL
0	0000	0
1	0001	1
2	0010	2
3	0011	3
4	0100	4
5	0101	5
6	0110	6
7	0111	7
8	1000	8
9	1001	9
10	1010	A
11	1011	B
12	1100	C
13	1101	D
14	1110	E
15	1111	F

FIGURE A-4

The mathematical principles that apply to the binary and hexadecimal number systems are the same as those that apply to the decimal number system. To help you better understand these principles, this section starts with the familiar decimal system, then progresses to the binary and hexadecimal number systems.

The Decimal Number System

The decimal number system is a base 10 number system (deci means ten). The base of a number system indicates how many symbols it uses. The decimal number system uses 10 symbols: 0 through 9. Each of the symbols in the number system has a value associated with it. For example, 3 represents a quantity of three and 5 represents a quantity of five.

The decimal number system also is a positional number system. This means that in a number such as 143, each position in the number has a value associated with it. When you look at the decimal number 143, the 3 is in the ones, or units, position and represents three ones (3×1); the 4 is in the tens position and represents four tens (4×10); and the 1 is in the hundreds position and represents one hundred (1×100). The number 143 is the sum of the values in each position of the number ($100 + 40 + 3 = 143$). The chart in Figure A-5 shows how you can calculate the positional values (hundreds, tens, and units) for a number system. Starting on the right and working to the left, the base of the number system, in this case 10, is raised to consecutive powers (10^0, 10^1, 10^2). These calculations are a mathematical way of determining the place values in a number system.

When you use number systems other than decimal, the same principles apply. The base of the number system indicates the number of symbols that it uses, and each position in a number system has a value associated with it. By raising the base of the number system to consecutive powers beginning with zero, you can calculate the positional value.

power of 10	10^2	10^1	10^0
positional value	100	10	1
number	1	4	3

$$1 \quad 4 \quad 3 =$$
$$(1 \times 10^2) + (4 \times 10^1) + (3 \times 10^0) =$$
$$(1 \times 100) + (4 \times 10) + (3 \times 1) =$$
$$100 + 40 + 3 = 143$$

FIGURE A-5

The Binary Number System

As previously discussed, binary is a base 2 number system (bi means two), and the symbols it uses are 0 and 1. Just as each position in a decimal number has a place value associated with it, so does each position in a binary number. In binary, the place values, moving from right to left, are successive powers of two (2^0, 2^1, 2^2, 2^3 or 1, 2, 4, 8). To construct a binary number, place ones in the positions where the corresponding values add up to the quantity you want to represent and place zeros in the other positions. For example, in a four-digit binary number, the binary place values are (from right to left) 1, 2, 4, and 8. The binary number 1001 has ones in the positions for the values 1 and 8 and zeros in the positions for 2 and 4. Therefore, as shown in Figure A-6, the quantity represented by binary 1001 is 9 (8 + 0 + 0 + 1).

The Hexadecimal Number System

The hexadecimal number system uses 16 symbols to represent values (hex means six). These include the symbols 0 through 9 and A through F (Figure A-4 on the previous page). The mathematical principles previously discussed also apply to hexadecimal (Figure A-7).

The primary reasons the hexadecimal number system is used with computers are (1) it can represent binary values in a more compact and readable form, and (2) the conversion between the binary and the hexadecimal number systems is very efficient.

An eight-digit binary number (a byte) can be represented by a two-digit hexadecimal number. For example, in the ASCII code, the character M is represented as 01001101. This value can be represented in the hexadecimal number system as 4D. One way to convert this binary number (4D) to a hexadecimal number is to divide the binary number (from right to left) into groups of four digits, calculate the value of each group, and then change any two-digit values (10 through 15) to the symbols A through F that are used in the hexadecimal number system (Figure A-8).

power of 2	2^3	2^2	2^1	2^0
positional value	8	4	2	1
binary	1	0	0	1

$$1 \quad 0 \quad 0 \quad 1 =$$
$$(1 \times 2^3) + (0 \times 2^2) + (0 \times 2^1) + (1 \times 2^0) =$$
$$(1 \times 8) + (0 \times 4) + (0 \times 2) + (1 \times 1) =$$
$$8 + 0 + 0 + 1 = 9$$

FIGURE A-6

power of 16	16^1	16^0
positional value	16	1
hexadecimal	A	5

$$A \quad 5 =$$
$$(10 \times 16^1) + (5 \times 16^0) =$$
$$(10 \times 16) + (5 \times 1) =$$
$$160 + 5 = 165$$

FIGURE A-7

positional value	8421	8421
binary	0100	1101
decimal	4	13
hexadecimal	4	D

FIGURE A-8

APPENDIX B

Quiz Yourself Answers

Following are possible answers to the Quiz Yourself boxes throughout the book.

Quiz Yourself 1-1

1. A computer is ~~a motorized~~an electronic device that processes ~~output~~ input into ~~input~~output.
2. A storage device records (~~reads~~writes) and/or retrieves (~~writes~~reads) items to and from storage media.
3. An ~~output~~ input device is any hardware component that allows you to enter data and instructions into a computer.
4. True Statement
5. Computers have the ~~dis~~advantages of fast speeds, ~~high~~ low failure rates, producing consistent results, storing ~~small~~ enormous amounts of data, and communicating with others.
6. Four commonly used ~~input~~ output devices are a printer, a monitor, speakers, and a portable media player.

Quiz Yourself 1-2

1. A ~~resource~~ network is a collection of computers and devices connected together via communications devices and transmission media.
2. True Statement
3. Popular ~~system~~ application software includes Web browsers, word processing software, spreadsheet software, database software, and presentation graphics software.
4. The ~~Internet~~ Web is one of the more popular services on the ~~Web~~Internet.
5. Two types of ~~application~~ system software are the operating system and utility programs.

Quiz Yourself 1-3

1. A ~~desktop computer~~ notebook computer (or laptop computer) is a portable, personal computer designed to fit on your lap.
2. True Statement
3. Each ~~large business~~home user spends time on the computer for different reasons that include budgeting and personal financial management, Web access, communications, and entertainment.
4. A ~~home~~ power user requires the capabilities of a workstation or other powerful computer.
5. ~~Mainframes~~ Supercomputers are the fastest, most powerful computers — and the most expensive.
6. The elements of an information system are hardware, ~~e-mail~~software, data, people, and ~~the Internet~~ procedures.
7. With ~~embedded computers~~online banking, users access account balances, pay bills, and copy monthly transactions from the bank's computer right into their personal computers.

Quiz Yourself 2-1

1. True Statement
2. ~~A WISP~~An IP address (or Internet Protocol address) is a number that uniquely identifies each computer or device connected to the Internet.
3. ~~An IP address~~A domain name, such as www.google.com, is the text version of ~~a domain name~~an IP address.
4. Dial-up access takes place when the modem in your computer uses ~~the cable television network~~a standard telephone line to connect to the Internet.
5. The World Wide Web Consortium (W3C) oversees research and ~~owns~~ sets standards and guidelines for many areas of the Internet.

Quiz Yourself 2-2

1. True Statement
2. A ~~Web browser~~subject directory classifies Web pages in an organized set of categories, such as sports or shopping, and related subcategories.
3. Audio and video files are ~~downloaded~~ compressed to reduce their file sizes.
4. Popular ~~portals~~ players include iTunes, RealPlayer, and Windows Media Player.
5. The more widely used ~~search engines~~Web browsers for personal computers are Internet Explorer, Netscape, Firefox, Opera, and Safari.
6. To develop a Web page, you do not have to be a computer programmer.
7. To improve your Web searches, use ~~general~~ specific nouns and put the ~~least~~ most important terms first in the search text.

Quiz Yourself 2-3

1. True Statement
2. An e-mail address is a combination of a user name and ~~an e-mail program~~a domain name that identifies a user so he or she can receive Internet e-mail.
3. ~~Business~~Consumer-to-consumer e-commerce occurs when one consumer sells directly to another, such as in an online auction.
4. FTP is an Internet standard that permits file ~~reading~~ uploading and ~~writing~~ downloading with other computers on the Internet.
5. ~~Spam~~Internet telephony uses the Internet (instead of the public switched telephone network) to connect a calling party to one or more called parties.
6. Netiquette is the code of ~~un~~acceptable behaviors while on the Internet.
7. On a newsgroup, a ~~subscription~~ thread (or threaded discussion) consists of the original article and all subsequent related replies.

Quiz Yourself 3-1

1. True Statement
2. ~~Public domain~~Packaged software is mass produced, copyrighted retail software that meets the needs of a wide variety of users, not just a single user or company.
3. To use ~~system~~ application software, your computer must be running ~~application~~ system software.
4. When a program is started, its instructions load from ~~memory~~ a storage medium into ~~a storage medium~~memory.

Quiz Yourself 3-2

1. ~~Audio~~ Video editing software typically includes ~~video~~ audio editing capabilities.
2. ~~Enterprise computing~~Image editing software provides the capabilities of paint software and also includes the ability to modify existing images.
3. Millions of people use ~~spreadsheet~~ word processing software every day to develop documents such as letters, memos, reports, fax cover sheets, mailing labels, newsletters, and Web pages.
4. Professional ~~accounting~~ DTP (or desktop publishing) software is ideal for the production of high-quality color documents such as textbooks, corporate newsletters, marketing literature, product catalogs, and annual reports.
5. ~~Spreadsheet~~ Presentation graphics software is application software that allows users to create visual aids for presentations to communicate ideas, messages, and other information to a group.
6. Two of the more widely used ~~CAD programs~~software suites are Microsoft Office 2007 and Sun StarOffice.
7. True Statement

Quiz Yourself 3-3

1. An ~~anti-spam~~antivirus program protects a computer against viruses by identifying and removing any computer viruses found in memory, on storage media, or in incoming files.
2. ~~Computer~~Web-based training is a type of ~~Web~~computer-based training that uses Internet technology and consists of application software on the Web.
3. True Statement
4. ~~Legal~~ Personal finance software is a simplified accounting program that helps home users and small office/home office users balance their checkbooks, pay bills, track investments, and evaluate financial plans.
5. ~~Personal DTP~~Photo editing software is a popular type of image editing software that allows users to edit digital photographs.

Quiz Yourself 4-1

1. True Statement
2. Four basic operations in a machine cycle are: (1) ~~comparing~~fetching, (2) decoding, (3) executing, and, if necessary, (4) ~~pipelining~~storing.
3. Processors contain a ~~motherboard~~ control unit and an arithmetic logic unit (ALU).
4. The ~~central processing unit~~motherboard, sometimes called a system board, is the main circuit board of the system unit.
5. The leading processor chip manufacturers for personal computers are ~~Microsoft~~Intel, AMD, IBM, Motorola, and Transmeta.
6. The pace of the system clock, called the clock speed, is measured by the number of ticks per ~~minute~~second.
7. The system unit is a case that contains ~~mechanical~~ electronic components of the computer used to process data.

Quiz Yourself 4-2

1. True Statement
2. A gigabyte (GB) equals approximately 1 ~~trillion~~ billion bytes.
3. Memory cache helps speed the processes of the computer because it stores ~~seldom~~ frequently used instructions and data.
4. Most computers are ~~analog~~digital, which means they recognize only two discrete states: on and off.
5. Most RAM ~~retains~~ loses its contents when the power is removed from the computer.
6. Read-only memory (ROM) refers to memory chips storing ~~temporary~~ permanent data and instructions.

Quiz Yourself 4-3

1. A ~~bus~~ port is the point at which a peripheral attaches to or communicates with a system unit so the peripheral can send data to or receive information from the computer.
2. An ~~AC adapter~~expansion slot is a socket on the motherboard that can hold an adapter card.
3. Built into the power supply is a ~~heater~~ fan that keeps components of the system unit ~~warm~~cool.
4. ~~Serial~~ USB ports can connect up to 127 different peripherals together with a single connector type.
5. The higher the bus clock speed, the ~~slower~~ faster the transmission of data.
6. True Statement

Quiz Yourself 5-1

1. A keyboard is an ~~output~~ input device that contains keys users press to enter data in a computer.
2. A ~~light pen~~graphics tablet is a flat, rectangular, electronic plastic board.

3. A ~~trackball~~ touch pad is a small, flat, rectangular pointing device commonly found on notebook computers.
4. True Statement
5. Operations you can perform with a ~~wheel~~ mouse include point, click, right-click, double-click, triple-click, drag, right-drag, rotate wheel, free-spin wheel, press wheel button, and tilt wheel.
6. ~~PDAs~~ Tablet PCs use a pressure-sensitive digital pen, and ~~Tablet PCs~~PDAs use a stylus.

Quiz Yourself 5-2

1. True Statement
2. DV cameras record video as ~~analog~~ digital signals.
3. ~~Instant messaging~~Voice recognition (or speech recognition) is the computer's capability of distinguishing spoken words.
4. Many smart phones today have a built-in camera so users easily can send ~~text~~ picture messages.
5. The ~~lower~~ higher the resolution of a digital camera, the better the image quality, but the more expensive the camera.

Quiz Yourself 5-3

1. A fingerprint scanner captures curves and indentations of a ~~signature~~fingerprint.
2. After swiping a credit card through ~~an MICR~~ a magstripe (or magnetic stripe card) reader, a POS terminal connects to a system that authenticates the purchase.
3. ATMs ask you to enter a password, called a ~~biometric identifier~~PIN (or personal identification number), which verifies that you are the holder of the bankcard.
4. Four types of ~~source documents~~scanners are flatbed, pen, sheet-fed, and drum.
5. Retail and grocery stores use the ~~POSTNET~~ UPC (Universal Product Code) bar code.
6. RFID is a technology that uses ~~laser~~ radio signals to communicate with a tag placed in an object, an animal, or a person.
7. True Statement

Quiz Yourself 6-1

1. A ~~lower~~ higher resolution uses a greater number of pixels and thus provides a smoother image.
2. An output device is any type of ~~software~~ hardware component that conveys information to one or more people.
3. Documents often include ~~text~~ graphics to enhance their visual appeal and convey information.
4. ~~LCD~~ CRT monitors have a larger footprint than ~~CRT~~ LCD monitors.
5. Types of ~~CRTs~~ flat-panel displays include LCD monitors, LCD screens, and plasma monitors.
6. True Statement

Quiz Yourself 6-2

1. A ~~laser~~ thermal printer generates images by pushing electrically heated pins against heat-sensitive paper.
2. A ~~photo~~ laser printer creates images using a laser beam and powdered ink, called toner.
3. An ink-jet printer is a type of impact printer that forms characters and graphics by spraying tiny drops of liquid ~~nitrogen~~ ink onto a piece of paper.
4. Printed information is called ~~soft~~ hard copy.
5. Two commonly used types of impact printers are ~~ink-jet~~dot-matrix printers and line printers.
6. True Statement

Quiz Yourself 6-3

1. A digital light processing (DLP) projector uses tiny ~~lightbulbs~~ mirrors to reflect light.
2. True Statement
3. Many personal computer users add surround sound ~~printer systems~~speakers to their computers to generate a higher-quality sound.
4. Multifunction peripherals require ~~more~~ less space than having a separate printer, scanner, copy machine, and fax machine.
5. Some joysticks, wheels, and gamepads include ~~real-time action~~force feedback, which is a technology that sends resistance to the device in response to actions of the user.

Quiz Yourself 7-1

1. Miniature hard disks are a type of ~~optical disc~~magnetic disk.
2. True Statement
3. SATA is a hard disk interface that uses ~~parallel~~ serial signals to transfer data, instructions, and information.
4. ~~Storage media~~A storage device is the computer hardware that records and/or retrieves items to and from ~~a~~ storage ~~device~~media.
5. Two types of ~~manual~~ magnetic disks are hard disks and floppy disks.
6. Users can move an ~~internal~~ external hard disk from computer to computer as needed by connecting the disk to a USB port or FireWire port on the system unit.

Quiz Yourself 7-2

1. A ~~CD-RW~~CD-ROM is a type of optical disc on which users can read but not write (record) or erase.
2. A ~~DVD-RAM~~Picture CD is a single-session disc that stores digital versions of film using a jpg file format.
3. DVDs have ~~the same~~much greater storage capacities ~~as~~ than CDs.
4. Optical discs are written and read by ~~mirrors~~a laser.

5. ~~Single session~~Multisession means you can write on part of the disc at one time and another part at a later time.
6. True Statement

Quiz Yourself 7-3

1. A smart card stores data on a thin ~~magnetic stripe~~microprocessor embedded in the card.
2. A USB flash drive is a flash memory storage device that plugs in a ~~parallel~~ USB port on a computer or mobile device.
3. Flash memory cards are a type of ~~magnetic~~ solid-state media, which means they consist entirely of electronic components and contain no moving parts.
4. Microfilm and microfiche have the ~~shortest~~ longest life of any storage media.
5. Tape storage requires ~~direct~~ sequential access, which refers to reading or writing data consecutively.
6. True Statement

Quiz Yourself 8-1

1. A ~~buffer~~ driver is a small program that tells the operating system how to communicate with a specific device.
2. A ~~cold~~ warm boot is the process of using the operating system to restart a computer.
3. A password is a ~~public~~ private combination of characters associated with the user name that allows access to certain computer resources.
4. Firmware that contains the computer's startup instructions is called the ~~kernel~~BIOS.
5. The program you currently are using is in the ~~background~~foreground, and the other programs running but not in use are in the ~~foreground~~ background.
6. Two types of system software are operating systems and ~~application~~ utility programs.
7. True Statement

Quiz Yourself 8-2

1. A ~~file manager~~firewall is a utility that detects and protects a personal computer from unauthorized intrusions.
2. ~~Fragmenting~~ Defragmenting a disk is the process of reorganizing it so the files are stored in contiguous sectors.
3. Windows Vista Home Basic uses the Windows ~~Aero~~ Vista Basic interface.
4. True Statement
5. ~~Flip 3D~~Linux is a UNIX-type operating system that is open source software.
6. You should ~~uninstall~~ back up files and disks regularly in the event your originals are lost, damaged, or destroyed.

Quiz Yourself 8-3

1. A ~~pop-up blocker~~file compression utility shrinks the size of a file(s).
2. An ~~anti-spam~~antivirus program protects a computer against viruses by identifying and removing any computer viruses found in memory, on storage media, or on incoming files.
3. True Statement
4. Pocket PCs use ~~Palm OS~~Windows Mobile as their operating system.
5. ~~Web filtering~~CD/DVD burning software writes text, graphics, audio, and video files to a recordable or rewritable CD or DVD.

APPENDIX C
Computer Acronyms

Acronym	Description	Page
AA	Audible Audio	87
AAC	Advanced Audio Coding	87
AC	alternating current	213
ADA	Americans with Disabilities Act	266
ADC	analog-to-digital converter	38
AGP	Accelerated Graphics Port	212
AIFF	Audio Interchange File Format	87
ALU	arithmetic logic unit	188
AMD	Advanced Micro Devices	219
AOL	America Online	72, 82
ARPA	Advanced Research Projects Agency	69
ARPANET	Advanced Research Projects Agency network	69
ASCII	American Standard Code for Information Interchange	195
ASF	Advanced Streaming (or Systems) Format	87
ASP	application service provider	164
ATC	advanced transfer cache	201
ATM	automated teller machine	262
B2B	business-to-business	92
B2C	business-to-consumer	92
BD-R	Blu-ray Disc recordable	373
BD-RE	Blu-ray Disc rewritable	373
BD-ROM	Blu-ray Disc read-only memory	372
BIOS	basic input/output system	400
Bit	binary digit	195
BMP	bit map	85
BTW	by the way	100
C2C	consumer-to-consumer	92
CAD	computer-aided design	151, 327
CAI	computer-aided instruction	160
CAM	computer-aided manufacturing	36
CBT	computer-based training	160
CCD	charge-coupled device	251
ccTLD	country code top-level domain	74
CD	compact disc	8, 9, 17, 27, 89, 357
CD-R	compact disc-recordable	370
CD-ROM	compact disc read-only memory	369–70
CD-RW	compact disc-rewritable	371
CF	CompactFlash	376
CMOS	complementary metal-oxide semiconductor	203
COBOL	COmmon Business-Oriented Language	53
COM port	communications port	207
CPU	central processing unit	8, 187
CRT	cathode-ray tube	308
CST	Computer Service Technician	381
DAC	digital-to-analog converter	38
DDR SDRAM	double data rate synchronous dynamic random access memory	199
DHCP	Dynamic Host Configuration Protocol	102
DIMM	dual inline memory module	199
DL	distance learning	166
DLP projector	digital light processing projector	324

Acronym	Description	Page
DMCA	Digital Millennium Copyright Act	87
DNS	domain name system	74
DOS	Disk Operating System	417
Dpi	dots per inch	252, 313
DRAM	dynamic random access memory	199
DRM	digital rights management	86
DSL	Digital Subscriber Line	70, 449
DSP	digital signal processor	38
DTP	desktop publishing	152
DTV	digital television	307
DV camera	digital video camera	253
DVD	digital versatile disc or digital video disc	8, 17, 59, 89, 357
DVD+R	digital versatile disc or digital video disc recordable	373
DVD-R	digital versatile disc or digital video disc recordable	373
DVD+RAM	digital versatile disc or digital video disc + random access memory	373
DVD-ROM	digital versatile disc or digital video disc read-only memory	9, 372
DVD+RW	digital versatile disc or digital video disc + rewritable	373
DVD-RW	digital versatile disc or digital video disc + rewritable	373
DVI	Digital Video Interface	305
EB	exabyte	356
EBCDIC	Extended Binary Coded Decimal Interchange Code	195
E-book	electronic book	61, 303
E-commerce	electronic commerce	28, 30, 60, 61, 91–92
EEPROM	electrically erasable programmable read-only memory	202
E-file	electronic filing	157
EIDE	Enhanced Integrated Drive Electronics	364
E-mail	electronic mail	12, 31, 69, 92–95, 101, 161
EMR	electromagnetic radiation	308
ENIAC	Electronic Numerical Integrator and Computer	52
eSATA	external Serial Advanced Technology Attachment	210
FAQ	frequently asked questions	6, 100
Fax	facsimile	322–23
Fortran	FORmula TRANslator	53
FSB	front side bus	212
FTP	File Transfer Protocol	68, 96, 134, 161
FWIW	for what it's worth	100
FYI	for your information	100
GB	gigabyte	197, 356
GHz	gigahertz	189
GIF	Graphics Interchange Format	85
GIGO	garbage in, garbage out	10
GPU	graphics processing unit	305
gTLD	generic top-level domain	73
GUI	graphical user interface	15, 137, 403, 420, 421

Appendix C Computer Acronyms

Acronym	Description	Page
HD	high density	364
HD DVD-R	high-density DVD recordable	373
HD DVD-ROM	high-density DVD read-only memory	372
HD DVD-RW	high-density DVD rewritable	373
HDTV	high-definition television	307
HIPAA	Health Insurance Portability and Accountability Act	381
HP	Hewlett-Packard	329
HT	Hyper Threading	190
http	Hypertext Transfer Protocol	76
Hz	hertz	189
IBM	International Business Machines	53, 54, 55, 138
IC	integrated circuit	186
ICANN	Internet Corporation for Assigned Names and Numbers	74
IM	instant messaging	98
IMHO	in my humble opinion	100
Interactive TV	interactive television	307
IP address	Internet Protocol address	73, 102
IPng	Internet Protocol Next Generation	102
IPv6	Internet Protocol version 6	102
IrDA	Infrared Data Association	210
IRQ	interrupt request	409
IS	information system	25
ISP	Internet service provider	72
IT	information technology	25
JPEG	Joint Photographic Experts Group	85, 345
K	kilobyte	197
KB	kilobyte	197, 356
KBps	kilobytes per second	357, 369
L1 cache	Level 1 cache	201
L2 cache	Level 2 cache	201
L3 cache	Level 3 cache	201
LAN	local area network	55
LCD	liquid crystal display	304
Mac OS	Macintosh Operating System	19
Mac OS X	Macintosh Operating System X	39, 135, 195, 420
MB	megabyte	197, 356
MBps	megabytes per second	357, 364
Mbps	megabits per second	365
M-commerce	mobile commerce	91
MHz	megahertz	203
MIB	Medical Information Bureau	381
MICR	magnetic-ink character recognition	260
MIDI	Musical Instrument Digital Interface	209, 246
MIPS	millions of instructions per second	190
Modem	modulate/demodulate	9
MP	million pixels	252
MP3	Moving Pictures Experts Group Audio Layer 3 (MPEG-3)	86, 87, 89, 202
MPEG	Moving Pictures Experts Group	88
MRAM	magnetoresistive random access memory	199
μs	microsecond	203
ms	millisecond	203
MS-DOS	Microsoft Disk Operating System	417, 430
MSN	Microsoft Network, The	72, 82
MT/ST	Magnetic Tape/Selectric Typewriter	54

Acronym	Description	Page
Netiquette	Internet etiquette	100
NLQ	near letter quality	318
ns	nanosecond	203
NSF	National Science Foundation	70
OCR	optical character recognition	257
OLE	object linking and embedding	57
OLED	organic light emitting diode	304
OMR	optical mark recognition	257
OS	operating system	15–16, 398–425
OSP	online service provider	72
PATA	Parallel Serial Advanced Technology Attachment	447
PB	petabyte	356
PC	personal computer	19–20, 445
PC-DOS	personal computer Disk Operating System	417
PCI bus	Peripheral Component Interconnect bus	212
PCL	Printer Control Language	316
PCMCIA	Personal Computer Memory Card International Association	205
PC-to-TV port	personal computer-to-television port	453
PDA	personal digital assistant	21, 31, 265, 282, 325
PDF	Portable Document Format	150
PDL	page description language	316
PIM	personal information manager	148
PIN	personal identification number	262
Pixel	picture element	252, 304
PNG format	Portable Network Graphics format	85
POP	point of presence	72
POP	Post Office Protocol	95
POP3	Post Office Protocol 3	95
POS	point of sale	261
POST	power-on self test	400
ppi	pixels (picture elements) per inch	252
PROM chip	programmable read-only memory chip	202
ps	picosecond	203
QT	QuickTime	87
RA	RealAudio	87
RAID	redundant array of independent disks	362
RAM	random access memory	197, 198–200
RDRAM	Rambus dynamic random access memory	199
RFID	radio frequency identification	259
RIAA	Recording Industry Association of America	63
RIMM	Rambus inline memory module	199
ROM	read-only memory	201–202
Rpm	revolutions per minute	360
RSS 2.0	Really Simple Syndication	84
SATA	Serial Advanced Technology Attachment	210, 364
SCSI	small computer system interface	210, 364
SD	Secure Digital	376
SDRAM	synchronous dynamic random access memory	199, 203
SIMM	single inline memory module	199
SMTP	simple mail transfer protocol	94
SOHO	small office/home office	28
SRAM	static random access memory	199
SVGA	super video graphics array	306
SXGA	Super Extended Graphics Array	306
TB	terabyte	197, 356

Acronym	Description	Page
TFT display	thin-film transistor display	304
TIFF	Tagged Image File Format	85, 345
TLD	top-level domain	73
TRACERT	traceroute	430
TTFN	ta ta for now	100
TYVM	thank you very much	100
u-HDTV	Ultra High Definition TV	324
ULV	Ultra Low Voltage	193
UMD	Universal Media Disc	372
UMPC	Ultra-Mobile PC	21
UNIVAC I	UNIVersal Automatic Computer	52
uPC	ultra personal computer	21
UPC	Universal Product Code	258
UPS	uninterruptible power supply	451
URL	Uniform Resource Locator	76
USB	universal serial bus	208, 212
User ID	user identification	410
UXGA	Ultra Extended Graphics Array	305
VCD	video CD	371
VoIP	voice over Internet Protocol	99, 160
VR	virtual reality	88
W3C	World Wide Web Consortium	70, 327
WAV	Windows waveform	87
WBT	Web-based training	166
WinFS	Windows Future Storage	382
WISP	wireless Internet service provider	72
WMA	Windows Media Audio	87, 89, 202
WQXGA	Wide Quad Extended Graphics Array	306
WSXGA	Wide Super Extended Graphics Array	306
WUXGA	Wide Ultra Extended Graphics Array	306
WWW	World Wide Web	75, 103
WXGA	Wide Super Extended Graphics Array	306
XGA	Extended Graphics Array	306
YB	yottabyte	356
ZB	zettabyte	356

INDEX

PHOTO CREDITS

Chapter 1: 1a Courtesy of Hewlett-Packard Company; 1b Courtesy of Hewlett-Packard Company; 1c Courtesy of Apple; 1d Darrin Klimek/Getty Images; 4a Courtesy of Hewlett-Packard Company; 4b Courtesy of SanDisk Corporation; 4c Courtesy of Hewlett-Packard Company; 4d Courtesy of Avid Technology; 4e Courtesy of Seagate Technology; 4f Courtesy of Hewlett-Packard Company; 4g Courtesy of Logitech; 4h Courtesy of Microsoft Corporation; 4j Courtesy of Zoom Technologies Inc; 4k Courtesy of ViewSonic Corporation; 4l Courtesy of Microsoft Corporation; 4m Courtesy of Hewlett-Packard Company; 4n Courtesy of Hewlett-Packard Company; 4o Courtesy of Intel Corporation; 4p Courtesy of Kingston Technology; 4q Courtesy of UMAX; 4s Courtesy of Logitech; 4t Courtesy of Logitech; 4u Courtesy of SanDisk Corporation; 4v Courtesy of 3Com Corporation; 4w Courtesy of D-Link Corporation/D-Link Systems, Inc; 12 PRNewsFoto/Mindjet LLC; 13 Courtesy of Fujitsu-Siemens Computers; 14 Courtesy of InFocus Corporation; 15 © Digital Archive Japan/Alamy; 16 © Patrick Olear/PhotoEdit; 19 Courtesy of Motion Computing; 21 Courtesy of Motion Computing; **Special Feature 1:** 1937 Courtesy of Iowa State University; 1937 Courtesy of Iowa State University; 1937 Courtesy of Iowa State University; 1943 Photo courtesy of The Computer History Museum; 1943 Photo courtesy of The Computer History Museum; 1945 Courtesy of the Archives of the Institute for Advanced Study; 1946 From the Collections of the University of Pennsylvania Archives; 1947 © IBM Corporate Archives; 1947 © IBM Corporate Archives; 1951 Courtesy Unisys Corporation; 1952 Courtesy of Hagley Museum and Library; 1953 © IBM Corporate Archives; 1957 © IBM Corporate Archives; 1957 © IBM Corporate Archives; 1957 Courtesy of the Department of the Navy; 1958 Courtesy of Texas Instruments; 1958 Courtesy of Texas Instruments; 1958 Courtesy of Texas Instruments; 1959 © IBM Corporate Archives; 1960 Courtesy of Hagley Museum and Library; 1964 © IBM Corporate Archives; 1964 © IBM Corporate Archives; 1964 © IBM Corporate Archives; 1965 Courtesy of Dartmouth College; 1965 Courtesy of Digital Equipment Corporation; 1969 Courtesy of IBM Corporation; 1970 © IBM Corporate Archives; 1971 Courtesy of Intel Corporation; 1971 Courtesy of Intel Corporation; 1975 Photo courtesy of Computer History Museum; 1975 Courtesy of InfoWorld; 1976 Courtesy of Apple; 1976 © Bettmann/CORBIS; 1979 Photo courtesy of Computer History Museum; 1980 Courtesy of Microsoft Corporation; 1981 © IBM Corporate Archives; 1982 Courtesy of Zoom Telephonics, Inc; 1983 © Time Life Pictures/Getty Images; 1983 © IBM Corporate Archives; 1984 Courtesy of Apple; 1984 Courtesy of Hewlett-Packard Company; 1989 © 1997-1998W3C (MIT, INRIA, Keio); 1989 Courtesy of Intel Corporation; 1992 Courtesy of Microsoft Corporation; 1993 Courtesy of Intel Corporation; 1993 Courtesy of Microsoft Corporation; 1993 © Costa Cruise Lines/Getty Images; 1994 Courtesy of Netscape Communications Corporation; 1994 Courtesy of Larry Ewing and The Gimp; 1995 Courtesy of Sun Microsystems, Inc; 1995 Box shot reprinted with permission from Microsoft Corporation; 1996 Box shot reprinted with permission from Microsoft Corporation; 1996 Courtesy of palm, Inc. Palm, Treo, Tungsten, Zire, LifeDrive, VersaMail, Blazer, Addit, Handspring, "T" stylized, "Z" stylized, stylizations and design marks associated with all the preceding, and trade dress associated with Palm, Inc.'s products, are among the trademarks or registered trademarks owned by or licensed to Palm, Inc; 1997 Motion Picture & Television Archives; 1997 Courtesy of Denon Electronics; 1997 Courtesy of Intel Corporation; 1998 © Andersen Ross/Getty Images; 1998 Courtesy of Apple; 1998 Courtesy of Microsoft Corporation; 1999 Courtesy of Microsoft Corporation; 2000 Courtesy of Microsoft Corporation; 2000 Courtesy of Microsoft Corporation; 2000 © B Busco/Getty Images; 2000 Courtesy of Intel Corporation; 2001 Courtesy of Microsoft Corporation; 2001 Courtesy of Microsoft Corporation; 2002 Courtesy of RCA/Thomson Consumer Electronics; 2002 Courtesy of Sharp Electronics; 2002 Courtesy of Intel Corporation; 2003 Courtesy of ViewSonic Corporation; 2002 Courtesy of Intel Corporation; 2002 © Scott Goodwin Photography; 2002 Courtesy of Handspring, Inc; 2003 ©LWA- JDC/CORBIS; 2003 © Royalty- Free/CORBIS; 2003 © Jim Cummins/CORBIS; 2003 © Ed Bock/CORBIS; 2003 © Koichi Kamoshida/Getty Images; 2003 Courtesy of Microsoft Corporation; 2003 © Getty Images; 2003 © REUTERS/Mannie Garcia; 2004 Courtesy of Sony Electronics Inc; 2004 Courtesy of SanDisk Corporation; 2004 Courtesy of Apple; 2004 Courtesy of Palm, Inc. 2005 Courtesy of Apple; 2005 Courtesy of Microsoft Corporation; 2005 © PRNewsFoto/Microsoft Corporation; 2006 AP Images; 2006 AP Topic Gallery Photo; 2006 Mitchell Funk/Getty Images; 2006 Courtesy of Facebook; 2006 Courtesy of Intel Corporation; 2006 Courtesy of Intel Corporation; 2006 Courtesy of Microsoft Corporation; 2007 Courtesy of Belkin International; 2007 Courtesy of Intel Corporation; 2007 Courtesy of CinemaNow; 2007 Courtesy of Acer America; 2007 Courtesy of Microsoft Corporation; 2007 Courtesy of Microsoft Corporation; 2007 Courtesy of Memorex; **Chapter 2:** PY-2 © Erik Freeland/Corbis PY-2 © WireImageStock/Masterfile; PY-2 © image100/Alamy; PY-2 © Donna Day/Imagestate; PY-2 Stephen Roberts/Alamy; PY-2 © AP Wide World Photos; PY-2 © Martin Rogers/Workbook Stock/Getty Images; PY-2 © PM Images/Getty Images; PY-2 Courtesy of Nokia; 2-1f © David Young-Wolff/Photo Edit; 2-1g Courtesy of Skype; Looking Ahead 2-1 Courtesy of Internet2; 2-2a © Rob Lewine/CORBIS; 2-2b © Royalty-Free/Corbis; 2-2c ©LWA-Dann Tardif/CORBIS; 2-2d ©LWA-Dann Tardif/CORBIS; 2-2e © Paul C. Chauncey/CORBIS; 2-2f © Jiri Rezac/Alamy; 2-2g Courtesy of Motorola, Inc; 2-3, Step 2 Courtesy of Motorola, Inc; 2-3, Step 3 Courtesy of Terayon Communication Systems, Inc; 2-3, Step 4 © Stephen Chernin/Getty Images; 2-3, Step 6 Courtesy of Fujitsu Siemens Computers; 2-7a Courtesy of Hewlett-Packard Company; 2-7b Courtesy of Nokia; Looking Ahead 2-2 Courtesy of Identix Incorporated; 2-20, Step 2 © Stephen Chernin/Getty Images; Courtesy of Fujitsu Siemens Computers; 2-20, Step 3a Courtesy of Fujitsu Siemens Computers; 2-20, Step 3b © Swerve/Alamy; 2-24a © MedioImages; 2-24b © MedioImages; 2-24c © Inmagine/Alamy; 2-25 © Noel Hendrickson/Getty Images; Looking Ahead 2-3 © Darren McCollester/Getty Images; 2-27 ©Royalty-Free Corbis; 2-28 Step 1 and 4 Courtesy of Acer America Corp; 2-28, Step 2 Copyright 2005 Sun Microsystems, Inc. All Rights Reserved. Used by permission; 2-28 Step 3 Courtesy of Juniper Networks, Inc; 2-32 center © Blend Images/Alamy; 2-32a Courtesy of Acer America Corp; 2-32b Courtesy of Sony Electronics Inc; 2-32c © Gateway, Inc; 2-33 Step 2 Courtesy of Acer America Corp; 2-33 Step 4 and 5 Courtesy of Hewlett-Packard Company; 2-34a Courtesy of D-Link Systems; 2-34b Courtesy of Vonage; 2- 34c Courtesy of Hewlett-Packard Company; Career Corner © Manchan/Getty Images; Technology Trailblazer 1 © EPA /Landov; Technology Trailblazer 2 © LAURENT FIEVET/AFP/Getty Images; **Special Feature 2:** Opener1 © Justin Sullivan/Getty Images; Opener2 © DAVID HECKER/AFP/Getty Images; Opener3 © Muntz/Getty Images; Opener4 Courtesy of Siemens AG, Munich/Berlin; Opener 5 © Stockbyte/Getty Images; Opener 6 © Dominic DiSaia/Getty Images; Opener 7 © Purestock/Getty Images;

Chapter 3: PY-3 Lambert/Getty Images; PY-3 Courtesy of Adobe Systems Incorporated; PY-3 Courtesy of Microsoft Corporation; PY-3 David Young-Wolff/PhotoEdit; PY-3 Courtesy of Hewlett- Packard Company; PY-3 © Mary Kate Denny/ PhotoEdit; PY-3 Courtesy of Intuit; PY-3 Courtesy of Microsoft Corporation; 3-2a © John Feingersh/Masterfile; 3-2b Courtesy of Xerox Corporation; 3-2c Courtesy of Intel Corporation; Looking Ahead 3-1 Courtesy of IO2Technology; 3-14 Courtesy of Agilix; 3-15 Courtesy of Sendo; 3-16 Courtesy of Computer Systems Odessa Corp; 3-17 Courtesy of Sage Software; 3-20 Courtesy of Bentley Systems; 3-21 David Young- Wolff/PhotoEdit; 3-22 Screen shots are Copyright 2003 Corel Corporation and Corel Corporation Limited, reprinted by permission. Artwork © 2004 Cher Threinen-Pendarvis. 3-23 Courtesy of Adobe Systems Incorporated; 3-24 Courtesy of Ulead Systems, Inc; 3-25 Courtesy of SumTotal Systems, Inc; 3-26 Courtesy of Microsoft Corporation; 3-28a Courtesy of Intuit Inc; 3-28b © Digital Vision; 3-29 © 2003 Riverdeep Interactive Learning Limited, and its licensors; 3-30 Courtesy of Intuit Inc; 3-31, 32, 33 Screen shot(s) are © Copyright 2006 Corel Corporation and Corel Corporation Limited, reprinted by permission; 3-34 Used with permission. All TM and © 2006 Riverdeep Interactive Learning Limited, and its licensors. All rights reserved. www. riverdeep.net; 3-36 Courtesy of Punch! Software; 3-37 Courtesy of Merriam-Webster Inc; 3-38 Courtesy of Ubisoft; Looking Ahead 3-2 Photo © Chris Armstrong/Courtesy of Brigham Young University; 3-43 © Gary Herrington Photography; Career Corner © Royalty-Free/CORBIS; Technology Trailblazer 1 © Louis Fabian Bachrach/Daniel Bricklin; Technology Trailblazer 2 © Tom Wagner/Corbis; **Chapter 4:** PY-4 © Marc Rochon/Getty Images; PY-4 Courtesy of Seagate Technology; PY-4 Courtesy of Intel Corporation; PY-4 Courtesy of ATI Technologies Inc; PY-4 Courtesy of Hewlett-Packard Company; PY-4 Courtesy of Kingston Technology; PY-4 Courtesy of Hewlett-Packard Company; PY-4 Artifacts Images/Getty Images; 4-1a Courtesy of Hewlett-Packard Company; 4-1b Courtesy of Apple; 4-1c Courtesy of Microsoft Corporation; 4-1d © 2006 Sony Computer Entertainment Inc. All Rights Reserved; 4-1e Courtesy of Sony Ericsson Mobile Communications AB. All Rights Reserved; 4-1f Courtesy of Motion Computing; 4-1g Courtesy of Hewlett-Packard Company; 4-1h Courtesy of Acer America Corp; 4-1i Courtesy of Sony Electronics Inc; 4-2a Courtesy of Intel Corporation; 4-2b Courtesy of Hewlett-:Packard Company; 4-2c Courtesy of SMART Modular Technologies, Inc. © 2002; 4-2d Courtesy of Creative Labs, Inc. © 2003 Creative Technology Ltd. (SOUND BLASTER AUDIGY 2S). All rights reserved; 4-2e Courtesy of Matrox Graphics Inc; 4-03 © Kirsty Pargeter/istockphoto. com; 4-5, Step 1 © imagebroker/Alamy; Looking Ahead 4-1 Courtesy of IBM Corporation; 4-8a1 Courtesy of Intel Corporation; 4-8a2 Courtesy of Intel Corporation; 4-8a3 Courtesy of Advanced Micro Devices, Inc; 4-8b1 Courtesy of Intel Corporation; Figure 4-8b2 Courtesy of Intel Corporation; 4-8b3 Courtesy of Advanced Micro Devices, Inc; 4-8b4 Courtesy of Advanced Micro Devices, Inc; 4-8c1 Courtesy of Intel Corporation; Figure 4-8c2 Courtesy of Advanced Micro Devices, Inc; 4-8d1 Courtesy of Intel Corporation; 4-8d2 Courtesy of Transmeta Corporation; 4-8d3 Courtesy of Advanced Micro Devices, Inc; 4-9 © Gary Herrington Photography; 4-14 Step 1 Courtesy of Micosoft® Corporation; 4-14 Step 2 Courtesy of Hewlett-Packard Company; 4-14 Step 4 Courtesy of Fujitsu- Siemens; 4-15 © Jeremy Walker/Getty Images; 4-17a Courtesy of Seagate Technology; 4-17b Courtesy of Kingston Technology Company, Inc; 4-17c Courtesy of ViewSonic Corporation; 4-18a © Gary Herrington Photography; 4-18b Courtesy of Kingston Technology Company, Inc.; 4-21 Courtesy of MPIO America; 4-23 © WireImageStock/Masterfile; 4-23 © WireImageStock/Masterfile; 4-25 © Gary Herrington Photography; 4-26 Courtesy of Kingston Technology Company, Inc; 4-27 © 2006 Personal Computer Memory Card International Association; 4-28 Courtesy of Hewlett-Packard Company; 4-28 © Tim Gilman Photography; 4-33a Courtesy of Acer America Corp; 4-33b Courtesy of Nokia; 4-33c Courtesy of Nokia; 4-34 Courtesy of Sony Ericsson Mobile Communications AB. All Rights Reserved; 4-35b Courtesy of Intel Corporation; 4-35b Courtesy of Kingston Technology Company, Inc; 4-36 Courtesy of Fujitsu Siemens Computers; 4-37 Courtesy of Hewlett-Packard Company; 4-37b Courtesy of ASUSTeK Computer Inc; 4-37c Courtesy of Sendo; 4-38 Courtesy of Fujitsu Siemens Computers; 4-39 Courtesy of Acer America Corp; Looking Ahead 4-2 © Dorling Kindersley; 4-40a © Comstock Images; 4-40b © Paul Barton/CORBIS; 4-40c © C. Görling/zefa/Corbis; 4-40d © Mark Harmel/Alamy; 4-40e © Dynamic Graphics Group/IT Stock Free/Alamy; 4-41a Courtesy of Fellowes, Inc; 4-41b Courtesy of First-Aid-Product.com, a division of American CPR; Figure 4-41c Courtesy of Belkin International; 4-41d Courtesy of Fellowes, Inc; 4-41e © Gary Herrington Photography; Career Corner © Stephen Derr/Getty Images; Technology Trailblazer 1 © CORBIS SYGMA; Technology Trailblazer 2 © Andy Rain/Bloomberg News /Landov; **Chapter 5:** PY-5 © AP Photo; PY-5 © Jeff Greenberg/Alamy; PY-5 Courtesy of Sony Electronics Inc; PY-5 © Mario Tama/Getty Images; PY-5 © REUTERS/Jeff Zelevansky /Landov; PY-5 © David Young-Wolff/Photo Edit; PY-5 Courtesy of Logitech; PY-5 © Royalty-Free/Corbis; PY-5 © Raquel Ramirez/PhotoEdit; PY-5 Courtesy of Logitech; PY-5 Courtesy of Sony Electronics Inc; 5-1a © Stockbyte/Getty Images; 5-1b © Ciaran Griffin/Stockbyte Platinum; 5-1c © Royalty-Free/Corbis; 5-1d AP Images; 5-1e © Rebecca McAlpin/Bloomberg News /Landov; 5-1f © Thinkstock/Alamy; 5- 1g © Scott Olson/Getty Images; 5-1h1 © DAVID HECKER/AFP/Getty Images; 5-1h2 © Medioimages/Alamy; 5-1i Courtesy of Wacom Technology; 5-1j © Insy Shah/Getty Images; 5-1l1 Courtesy of Hewlett-Packard Company; 5-1l2 Courtesy of Hewlett-Packard Company; 5-1l3 Courtesy of Hewlett-Packard Company; 5-1m © Jose Luis Pelaez, Inc./CORBIS; 5-1n Courtesy of Sony Electronics Inc; 5-1o Courtesy of Hewlett-Packard Company; 5-1p1 © D. Hurst/Alamy; 5-1q1 © Susan Van Etten/Photo Edit; 5-1q2 © AP Photo; 5-1r © Tim Boyle/ Newsmakers/Getty Images; 5-1s © James Nazz/CORBIS 5-1t © David Young-Wolff/ Alamy 5-1u © Bill Aron/Photo Edit; 5-1v © Ingram Publishing/SuperStock; 5-1w © Blend Images/Alamy; 5-1x1 © Peter Macdiarmid/Getty Images; 5-1x2 © MICHAEL CARONNA/BLOOMBERG NEWS /Landov; 5-1x3 © Peter Macdiarmid/Getty Images; 5-2 Courtesy of Microsoft Corporation; | 5-4 Courtesy of Hewlett-Packard Company; 5-4 Courtesy of Belkin International; 5-6 Courtesy of Microsoft Corporation; 5-8 Courtesy of Logitech; 5-9 © Yo/Getty Images; 5-10 Courtesy of IBM Corporation; 5-11 © Frances M. Roberts/Alamy; 5-12 Courtesy of Sony Ericsson Mobile Communications AB. All rights reserved; 5-13 Courtesy of Wacom Technology Corp; 5-14a Courtesy of Wacom Technology Corp; 5-14b © Comstock Images; 5-15 Courtesy of Nyko; 5-15 Courtesy of Logic3 plc; 5-15 Courtesy of Logic3 plc; 5-15 Courtesy of Nintendo; 5-15 Courtesy of Logitech; 5-15 Courtesy of Logitech; 5-15 Courtesy of Logitech; 5-16 AP Image; 5-17 Courtesy of Nuance; 5-18 © ICP/Alamy; 5-19 Courtesy of Veo Intl; 5-19 Courtesy of Socket Communications Inc; 5-19 © Gustaf Brundin/istockphoto.com; 5-19 Courtesy of Hewlett-Packard Company; 5-20 Courtesy of Think Outside, Inc; 5-21 Courtesy of Nokia; 5-22 © Kaluzny-Thatcher/Getty Images; 5-23 Courtesy of Motion Computing, Inc; 5-24 © John Lawrence/Getty Images; 5-26 © Andersen RossGetty Images; 5-27 Courtesy of Sony Electronics Inc; 5-28a © Noel Hendrickson/Masterfile; 5-29a © Steve Chenn/CORBIS; 5-30 Courtesy of Hewlett-Packard Company; 5-30b Courtesy of

C Technologies AB; 5-30c Courtesy of Visioneer, Inc; 5-30d Howtek HiResolve 8000 Drum Scanner, image courtesy of Howtek, Inc; 5-31 Step 1 Courtesy of Umax Systems GmbH; 5-31 Courtesy of Acer America Inc; 5-34a © Colin Young-Wolff/Photo Edit; 5-34b Courtesy of Research In Motion; 5-34c © Susan Van Etten/Photo Edit; 5-36 Courtesy of Tibbett & Britten Group; Looking Ahead 5-1 © Silvia Otte/Getty Images; 5-37 © Spencer Grant/Photo Edit; 5-39 Courtesy of Symbol Technology; 5-40 © KARLHEINZ SCHINDLER/dpa /Landov; 5-41 © Steve Dunwell/Index Stock Imagery; 5-42a © AP/WIDE WORLD PHOTOS; 5-42b Courtesy of Microsoft Corporation; 15827 Courtesy of Recognition Systems, Inc; 5-44 © BORIS ROESSLER/ dpa /Landov; 5-45 Courtesy of Athena Smartcard Solutions — www.athena-scs.com; 5-47 Courtesy of www. keytools.com; 5-49 Courtesy of NaturalPoint, Inc. Looking Ahead 5-2 © Caroline von Tuempling/Getty Images; Career Corner © Romilly Lockyer/Getty Images; Technology Trailblazer 1 © 2002 Gary Reyes/San Jose Mercury News. All rights reserved; Technology Trailblazer 2 © AP Images; **Special Feature 5:** 1a Courtesy of OQO, Inc; 1b © Purestock/Getty Images; 1c Courtesy of Nokia; 1d Courtesy of Cingular; 2a Courtesy of Palm, Inc; 2b Courtesy of Hewlett-Packard Company; 2c Courtesy of Microsoft Corporation; 2d Courtesy of Nokia; 2e Courtesy of HTC; 2f Courtesy of Research In Motion; 2g Courtesy of Apple; 2h Courtesy of Sony Electronics; 2i Courtesy of Garmin Ltd; 2j Courtesy of Nintendo; 3b Courtesy Hewlett-Packard Company; 3c Courtesy of Garmin Ltd; 3d Courtesy of Think Outside Inc; 3e Courtesy of Griffin Technology; Fig 4 Courtesy of Microsoft Corporation; Fig 4 Courtesy of PocketGear; Fig 4c Courtesy of PocketGear; Fig 4d Courtesy of PocketGear; Fig 4e Courtesy of Microsoft Corporation; page 287 left Courtesy of Microsoft Corporation; page 287 right © Art Vandalay/Getty Images; 6a Courtesy of Microsoft Corporation; 6b Courtesy of Microsoft Corporation; 6c Courtesy of Handango; 6d Courtesy of PocketGear; 6e Courtesy of LandWare Inc; page 288 © Peter Griffith/Masterfile; page 288 © Hugh Threlfall/Alamy; page 288 Courtesy of Symbol Technologies; page 289 Courtesy of COMPELSON Laboratories; page 289 © CRIS BOURONCLE/AFP/Getty Images; page 289 Courtesy of Skyline Software Systems, Inc; page 290 © Dynamic Graphics Group/Creatas/Alamy; page 290 Courtesy of PocketGear; page 290 Courtesy of Symbol Technologies; page 291 © Orbit/Masterfile; page 291 Courtesy of Handango; page 291 Courtesy of PocketGear; page 291 Courtesy of PocketGear; page 291 Courtesy of PocketGear; page 291 Courtesy of PocketGear; page 291 Courtesy of PocketGear; page 292 top © Erik Dreyer/Getty Images; page 292 top Courtesy of PocketGear; page 292 Courtesy of PocketGear; page 292 Courtesy of PocketGear; page 292 Courtesy of Handango; page 293 top © Michael Newman/ Photo Edit; page 293 top Courtesy of Trusmart Technologies Corp; page 293 top page 293 bottom © AP Images; page 294 top Courtesy of Microsoft Corporation; page 294 top Courtesy of Nokia; page 294 bottom Courtesy of Namco Networks; page 296 Courtesy of Motorola; **Chapter 6:** PY6 © LWA/Getty Images; PY6 James Woodson/Getty Images; PY6 © imagebroker/ Alamy; PY6 Steve Cole/Getty Images PY6 AP Images; PY6 © David Young-Wolff/Alamy; PY6 © Jim West/Alamy; PY6 © Jack Sullivan/Alamy; PY6 ©Andre Jenny/The Image Works; PY6 Courtesy of Hewlett- Packard Company; PY6 Courtesy of Hewlett-Packard Company; PY6 Courtesy of Belltech Systems, LLC; 6-1a1 Courtesy of T-Mobile SDA; 6-1a2 Courtesy of Microsoft Corporation; 6-1b Courtesy of Xerox Corporation; 6-1c Courtesy of Fujitsu-Siemens Computers; 6-1d Courtesy of Logitech; 6-1e Courtesy of SanDisk Corporation; 6-1f Courtesy of Tatung Science and Technology, Inc; 6-1g Courtesy of Creative Technology Ltd; 6-1h Courtesy of Hewlett-Packard Company; 6-1i Courtesy of Hewlett-Packard Company; 6-1j Courtesy of Nokia; 6-2 Courtesy of Hewlett-Packard Company; 6-3 Courtesy of ViewSonic Corporation; 6-4a Courtesy of Acer America Corp; 6-4b Courtesy of Acer America Corp; 6-4c Image courtesy of TabletKiosk; 6-4d Courtesy of Archos; 6-4e Courtesy of Nokia; 6-4f Courtesy of Palm, Inc; Looking Ahead 6-1 Courtesy of Philips Polymer Vision; 6-6 Courteys of AMD; 6-8 Courtesy of Panasonic; 6-9 © BananaStock/Alamy; 6-10 Courtesy of NEC-Mitsubishi Electronics Display of America Inc; 6-13a Raimund Koch/Getty Images; 6-13b Courtesy of Hewlett-Packard Company; 6-13c © OSHIKAZU TSUNO/AFP/Getty Images; 6-13d Courtesy of Nokia; 6-13e Courtesy of Sony Electronics Inc; 6-13g Courtesy of Epson America, Inc; 6-13h QV3000EX camera photo courtesy of Casio Inc; 6-13i Courtesy of Eastman Kodak Company; 6-13j © Najlah Feanny/Corbis; 6-14 Courtesy of Hewlett-Packard Company; 6-14 Courtesy of Xerox Corporation; 6-14 Courtesy of Epson America, Inc; Figure 6-16 © Gary Herrington Photography; 6-17a Courtesy of Lexmark International, Inc; 6-17b Courtesy of Hewlett- Packard Company; 6-18a Courtesy of Xerox Corporation; 6-18b Courtesy of Xerox Corporation; 6-20a Courtesy of Mitsubishi Digital Electronics America, Inc; 6-21 Courtesy of Canon U.S.A, Inc; 6-22 Courtesy of Seiko Instruments USA Inc; 6-23 Courtesy of MacDermid ColorSpan Inc; 6-24 Courtesy of Oki Data Amercas, Inc; 6-25 Courtesy of IBM Corporation; 6-26 Courtesy of Logitech; 6-27 © Bill Aron/PhotoEdit; 6-29 © Tony Freeman/PhotoEdit; 6-30c Courtesy of MPC Computers, LLC; 6-30b Courtesy of U.S. Robotics Corporation; 6-30a ©Spencer Grant/PhotoEdit; 6-30d Courtesy of MPC Computers, LLC; 6-31 Courtesy of Lexmark International; 6-32a Courtesy of InFocus Corporation; 6-32b Courtesy of InFocus Corporation; Looking Ahead 6-2 AP Images; 6-33a & b © 2005 Guillemot Corporation S.A. All rights reserved. Thrustmaster® is a registered trademark of Guillemot Corporation S.A. Ferrari® is a registered trademark of Ferrari S.p.A. All other trademarks and brand names are hereby acknowledged and are property of their respective owners; 6-36a Courtesy of Enabling Technologies; 6-36b © Don Farrall/ Getty Images; Career Corner © David Young-Wolff/PhotoEdit; 6-37a Courtesy of Intel Corporation; 6-37b Gustaf Brundin/ istockphoto.com; Technology Trailblazer 1 ©Fujifotos/The Image Works; Technology Trailblazer 2 © AP Images; **Special Feature 6:** Opener © Photo Resource Hawaii/Alamy; Opener ©Masterfile (Royalty-Free Div.); Opener © Design Pics Inc./Alamy; 1a © Antonio Mo/Getty Images; 1b Courtesy of Sony Electronics. Inc; 1c © Larry Gatz/Getty Images; 1d Courtesy of Sony Electronics. Inc; 1e © Digital Vision/Getty Images; 1f Courtesy of Pioneer Electronics; 1g Courtesy of Hewlett-Packard Company; 1i Courtesy of Hewlett-Packard Company; 2a Courtesy of Hewlett-Packard Company; 2 Courtesy of FujiFilm USA Inc; 2 Courtesy of Nikon Inc; 5b Courtesy of SanDisk Corporation; 5a Courtesy of SanDisk Corporation; 5c Courtesy of SanDisk Corporation; 6 Courtesy of Iogear Inc; 8 Courtesy of Hewlett-Packard Company; 10a Courtesy of Sony Electronics. Inc; 10b Courtesy of JVC; 10c © Royalty-Free/CORBIS; 11 © John Giustina/Getty Images; 12 © Peter Moynes/Getty Images; 13 Courtesy of Apple; 15 Courtesy of DeskShare; 16 Courtesy of Ulead Systems Inc; 17 Courtesy of Ulead Systems Inc; 18 Courtesy of DeskShare; **Chapter 7:** PY7 © Richard Levine/Alamy; PY7 © Jeff Greenberg/Alamy; PY7 Courtesy of SanDisk Corporation; PY7 Courtesy of Seagate Technology; PY7 © Mark Boulton/Alamy; PY7 © walik/istockphoto.com; PY7 ©David Joel/Getty Images; PY7 © Keith Dannemiller/Alamy; PY7 Courtesy of Western Digital; PY7 © David McGlynn/Alamy; 7-1a Courtesy of Hewlett-Packard Company; 7-1b Courtesy of Hitachi Global Storage; 7-1c Courtesy of Seagate Technology; 7-1d Courtesy of Seagate Technology;

7-1e Courtesy of Iomega; 7-1f © Tetra Images/Alamy; 7-1g Courtesy of Hewlett-Packard Company; 7-1i Courtesy of PCMCIA; 7-1h Courtesy of Netgear; 7-1j Courtesy of SanDisk Corporation; 7-1k Courtesy of Hewlett-Packard Company; 7-1l © vario images GmbH & Co.KG/Alamy; 7-1m ©Aaron Flaum/Alamy; 7-6 Courtesy of Seagate Technology; 7-6 ©Tim Gilman Photography; Looking Ahead 7-1 Courtesy of IBM Zurich Research Laboratory. Unauthorized use not permitted; 7-8 Courtesy of Maxtor Corporation; 7-11 Courtesy of Intel Corporation; 7-12 Courtesy of Hitachi Global Storage; 7-13 Courtesy of Western Digital; 7-14 Courtesy of Iomega; 7-14 Courtesy of Western Digital; 7-16 Photo Courtesy of Iomega Corporation. © 2005 Iomega Corporation. All Rights Reserved. Zip is a registered trademark in the United States and/or other countries. Iomega, the sylized "i" logo and product images are property of Iomega Corporation in the United States and/or other countries; 7-17 © Gary Herrington Photography; 7-21a Courtesy of Merriam-Webster Inc; 7- 21b Courtesy of Memorex Products, Inc; 7-21c Courtesy of Memorex Products, Inc; 7-21d1 Coutesy of DeLorme; 7-21d2 Coutesy of DeLorme; 7-21e1 Courtesy of Memorex Products, Inc; 7-21e2 Courtesy of Memorex Products, Inc; 7-21f1 Courtesy of Memorex Products, Inc; 7-21f2 Courtesy of Memorex Products, Inc; 7-21f3 Courtesy of Memorex Products, Inc; 7-21 Courtesy of Memorex Products, Inc; 7-21 Courtesy of Memorex Products, Inc; LA 7-2 Courtesy of Purdue News Service; 7-22 Courtesy of Encyclopaedia Britannica; 7-22 Courtesy of Microsoft Corporation; 7-22 © Gary Herrington Photography; 7-23c Courtesy of NEC Solutions (America), Inc; 7-23c AP Images; 7-24 © 2005 Dell Inc. All Rights Reserved; 7-24 Courtesy of DeLorme; 7-26 GamesareFun.com; 7-27 Courtesy of Sony Electronics Inc; 7-28 Courtesy of PCMCIA; 7-29 © Sam Lee/istockphoto.com; 7-29 © Marianna Day Massey/ZUMA/Corbis; 7-29 Courtesy of Hewlett-Packard Company; 7-29 Courtesy of Hewlett-Packard Company; 7-29 Scrambled/istockphoto.com; 7-30 Courtesy of SanDisk Corporation; 7-30 Courtesy of SanDisk Corporation; 7-30 Courtesy of SanDisk Corporation; 7-30 Courtesy of SanDisk Corporation; 7-31 Courtesy of Delkin Devices, Inc; 7-31 Courtesy of Kingston Technology; 7-32 Toshiba America Information Systems, Inc; 7-32 Toshiba America Information Systems, Inc; 7-33 ITAR-TASS/Alexander Bundin /Landov; 7-34 ©Bill Aron/PhotoEdit; 7-34 © Bill Aron/Photo Edit 7-36 © Wes Thompson/CORBIS; Career Corner © Noel Hendrickson/Masterfile; Technology Trailblazer 1 Courtesy of Al Shugart International; Technology Trailblazer 2 Courtesy of IBM Research; page 386 Courtesy of SanDisk Corporation; **Chapter 8:** PY8 © imagebroker/Alamy; PY8 © Jupiter Media/Alamy; PY8 Daisuke Morita/Getty Images; PY8 © M. Timothy O'Keefe/Alamy; PY8 © Mark Sykes/Alamy; PY8 Flying Colours Ltd/Getty Images; PY8 Courtesy of Symantec; PY8 Courtesy of Symantec; PY8 Colin Young- Wolff/PhotoEdit; 8-1a Alex Nikada/istockphoto; 8-1c Courtesy of Hewlett-Packard Company; 8-1d Courtesy of Hewlett-Packard Company; 8-9a Courtesy of Hewlett-Packard Company; 8-9b Courtesy of Hewlett-Packard Company; 8-26 Courtesy of Microsoft Corporation; 8-28 Courtesy of Apple; Looking Ahead 8-1 AP Images; 8-31 Courtesy of BERNINA® of America, Inc.; 8-32b Courtesy of Audiovox; 8-33 Courtesy of Palm Inc; 8-34 Courtesy of Research in Motion; 8-35 Courtesy of Sony Ericsson; 8-39 "Nero" is a trademark of Nero AG. Image courtesy of Nero Inc; 8-40 Courtesy of Symantec; Career Corner © MTPA Stock/Masterfile; 8-41 Tanya Constantine/Getty Images; Technology Trailblazer 1 © AP Images; Technology Trailblazer 2 © Kim Kulish/CORBIS; **Special Feature 8:** 1a Courtesy of Hewlett-Packard Company; 1b Courtesy of Hewlett-Packard Company; 1c Courtesy of Apple; 1d Darrin Klimek/Getty Images; 4a Courtesy of Hewlett-Packard Company; 4b Courtesy of SanDisk Corporation; 4c Courtesy of Hewlett-Packard Company; 4d Courtesy of Avid Technology; 4e Courtesy of Seagate Technology; 4f Courtesy of Hewlett-Packard Company; 4g Courtesy of Logitech; 4h Courtesy of Microsoft Corporation; 4j Courtesy of Zoom Technologies Inc; 4k Courtesy of ViewSonic Corporation; 4l Courtesy of Microsoft Corporation; 4m Courtesy of Hewlett-Packard Company; 4n Courtesy of Hewlett-Packard Company; 4o Courtesy of Intel Corporation; 4p Courtesy of Kingston Technology; 4q Courtesy of UMAX; 4s Courtesy of Logitech; 4t Courtesy of Logitech; 4u Courtesy of SanDisk; 4v Courtesy of 3Com Corporation; 4w Courtesy of D-Link Corporation/D-Link Systems, Inc; 12 PRNewsFoto/Mindjet LLC; 13 Courtesy of Fujitsu-Siemens Computers; 14 Courtesy of InFocus Corporation; 15 © Digital Archive Japan/Alamy; 16 © Patrick Olear/PhotoEdit ; 19 Courtesy of Motion Computing; 21 Courtesy of Motion Computing